COMPLETE COVERAGE OF ALL FOUR EXAM SECTIONS

First Materials Updated to the New Closed Exam Content Specifications

FINANCIAL ACCOUNTING & REPORTING

Textbooks or "Textbooks on disk" for Windows or CD-ROM. 986 pages of text; complete, current, and comprehensive. 2,115 recent CPA exam questions, problems, essays, and answers; including analysis of recent exam coverage.

Software for Windows or MS-DOS. 2,115 recent CPA exam questions, problems, essays, and answers; including analysis of recent exam coverage.

Audiotapes. 14 hours of instruction cross-referenced to the textbooks.

Video Hot•Spot Lectures. Including: *Consolidations; FASBs 95 & 109; Leases & Pensions; Bonds & Other Liabilities; Assets; Revenue Recognition/Income Statement Presentation; Inventory.*

ACCOUNTING & REPORTING

Textbooks or "Textbooks on disk" for Windows or CD-ROM. 598 pages of text; complete, current, and comprehensive. 961 recent CPA exam questions and answers; including analysis of recent exam coverage.

Software for Windows or MS-DOS. 961 recent CPA exam questions and answers; including analysis of recent exam coverage.

Audiotapes. 12 hours of instruction cross-referenced to the textbooks.

Video Hot•Spot Lectures. Including: *Governmental & Nonprofit Accounting; Capital Gains & Losses; Corporate Taxation; Cost Accounting; Managerial Accounting; Estates, Trusts & Partnerships; Individual Taxation: Filing Status, Exemptions & Gross Income; Individual Taxation: Adjustments & Itemized Deductions; Tax Liabilities & Credits.*

AUDITING

Textbooks or "Textbooks on disk" for Windows or CD-ROM. 702 pages of text; complete, current, and comprehensive. 908 recent CPA exam questions, essays, and answers; including analysis of recent exam coverage.

Software for Windows or MS-DOS. 908 recent CPA exam questions, essays, and answers; including analysis of recent exam coverage.

Audiotapes. 12 hours of instruction cross-referenced to the textbooks.

Video Hot•Spot Lectures. Including: *Standard Audit Reports; Audit: Internal Control; Audit Evidence; Other Reports, Reviews & Compilations; EDP Auditing & Stat Sampling.*

BUSINESS LAW & PROFESSIONAL RESPONSIBILITIES

Textbooks or "Textbooks on disk" for Windows or CD-ROM. 696 pages of text; complete, current, and comprehensive. 832 recent CPA exam questions, essays, and answers; including analysis of recent exam coverage.

Software for Windows or MS-DOS. 832 recent CPA exam questions, essays, and answers; including analysis of recent exam coverage.

Audiotapes. 12 hours of instruction cross-referenced to the textbooks.

Video Hot•Spot Lectures. Including: *Contracts & Commercial Paper; Sales & Agency; Bankruptcy; Property & Secured Transactions.*

Call Now for Your Free CPA Review Demos or to Place Your Order 1-800-874-7599

The Only CPA Review Officially Licensed as Microsoft® Windows™ Compatible

MICROSOFT®
WINDOWS™
COMPATIBLE

YOUR PERSONAL CHOICE OF FORMATS

Totaltape's Flexible Learning Formats Let You Create a Personalized Study System That's Convenient For You

EXAMINATION HOT•SPOT VIDEO SERIES

Used in the Country's Largest Regional Live Reviews

These entertaining and fast paced, 2- to 3-hour video tutorial courses, feature Ivan Fox, Tim Gearty, and Bob Monette; three of the most popular CPA Review instructors in the country. They organize, prioritize, and summarize key concepts vital to your exam success, and demonstrate helpful memory aids, problem-solving tips, and short-cuts learned from more than 50 years combined exam preparation experience.

Watch, Listen, and Learn from the Country's Top-Rated CPA Review Instructors

IVAN FOX, J.D., LL.M., is a Professor of Law at Pace University, where he formerly served as Chairperson of the Law Department. He is a recipient of the Outstanding Teacher Award, and author of the country's best-selling business law text entitled, *Business Law & the Legal Environment.* With more than 20 years of CPA exam preparation experience, Mr. Fox is known as the "Dean" of CPA Law Review.

TIMOTHY F. GEARTY, M.B.A., J.D., C.P.A., is a former Professor of Accounting and currently manages and directs his own tax consulting and CPA practice. He is a frequent lecturer on tax and accounting topics. Mr. Gearty is the lead tax and accounting instructor for the Fox Gearty CPA Review, one of America's largest regional programs. He has over 12 years of experience teaching CPA Review, and is recognized nationally as an expert on the CPA exam.

ROBERT L. MONETTE, J.D., C.P.A., is nationally recognized as an expert on the CPA exam, and currently serves as the owner and instructor of the Gross-Monette CPA Review, the largest CPA Review seminar in Philadelphia. Mr. Monette's background also includes teaching CPA Review in Boston, New York, and New Jersey, where he has helped tens-of-thousands of candidates become CPAs.

Publisher and Editor-in-Chief

NATHAN M. BISK, J.D., C.P.A. (FL) is the Publisher and Editor-in-Chief of the Totaltape CPA Review System. He is both an attorney and a CPA in the State of Florida, and has written and taught CPA Review accounting, auditing, taxation, and business law programs since 1970. Mr. Bisk is also a pioneer in the development of video, audio, software, and CD-ROM Continuing Education programs for accountants and attorneys. He is recognized as the leading expert in the nation on the CPA exam.

Select from 25 New & Current Video Titles:

Capital Gains & Losses. Corporate Taxation. FASBs 95 & 109. Contracts & Commercial Paper. Governmental & Nonprofit Accounting. Standard Audit Reports. Consolidations. Leases & Pensions. Bonds & Other Liabilities. Audit: Internal Control. Audit Evidence. Individual Taxation: Filing Status, Exemptions & Gross Income. Individual Taxation: Adjustments & Itemized Deductions. Cost Accounting. Managerial Accounting. Sales & Agency. Assets. Revenue Recognition/Income Statement Presentation. Other Reports, Reviews & Compilations. Bankruptcy. Estates, Trusts & Partnerships. Tax Liabilities & Credits. Property and Secured Transactions. EDP Auditing & Stat Sampling. Inventory.

Totaltape's Examination Hot•Spot Videos are the perfect supplement to our other review materials.

Call Now for Your Free Video Demo
1-800-874-7599

INTERACTIVE SOFTWARE FOR WINDOWS & MS-DOS

The Only CPA Review Officially Licensed as Microsoft® Windows™ Compatible

Smart, fast and user-friendly, our latest software *for Windows* includes exclusive features and expanded coverage making it even easier to customize exam preparation to your specific needs. In fact, our software has more features than any other program on the market. Used in the country's largest regional live reviews!

From over 4,000 multiple choice, objective format, and essay questions, you select the actual questions you want to study; questions you've never seen, those you've missed; or the most recent from Uniform CPA Exams. Plus, if you need a fast answer to a specific question, you can pinpoint areas beyond topics and subtopics to microtopics; you can even make on-line notes for future reference.

An Interactive Progress Report keeps you right on track by monitoring your exam preparation from start to finish, with diagnostic analysis pinpointing weak areas that need additional study emphasis. Totaltape CPA Review is the only software that provides instant on-line grades. Just to make certain you are totally prepared, Totaltape's software allows you to take an unlimited number of final exams, covering the complete spectrum of exam questions. Each exam is made up from scratch every time. No two are exactly alike.

Look for us on the INTERNET!

In addition, we are the first publisher to offer our CPA Review "textbooks on disk" *for Windows*. Our entire 4-volume review textbooks are on-line, including the complete question and answer section. With a single click of a button, you can instantly move from question to relevant text coverage, and back again. Or you can use the synchronized text feature which automatically brings up the relevant text every time you answer a question.

At the end of your study session or when you need a break, a handy "bookmark" lets you tag the program and pick up later right where you left off. And remember, every software program is supported by unlimited toll-free technical assistance.

MICROSOFT® WINDOWS™ COMPATIBLE

The Only CPA Review Officially Licensed as Microsoft® Windows™ Compatible

Windows is a trademark of Microsoft Corporation.

Call Now for Your Free Software Demo
1-800-874-7599

INNOVATIVE MULTIMEDIA CD-ROM
The First and Only CPA Review Materials Available on CD-ROM

State-of-the-art, full-motion video, stereo-sound audio, and animated graphics combined with Totaltape's comprehensive textbook coverage virtually take you from behind your computer and transport you into a classroom setting with America's leading CPA Review Instructors. Totaltape's new CD-ROM CPA Review features our entire software *for Windows* program, including our 4-volume set of textbooks on disk, full search capabilities, and more than 4,000 recent multiple choice, objective format, and essay questions. Plus, you get our exciting new multimedia audiovisual coverage designed exclusively for the upcoming exam. A couple of minutes is all it takes to be up and running with Totaltape's CD-ROM. Hard drive space limited? No problem, you can run the entire program straight off the CD. A dramatic and dynamic way to learn.

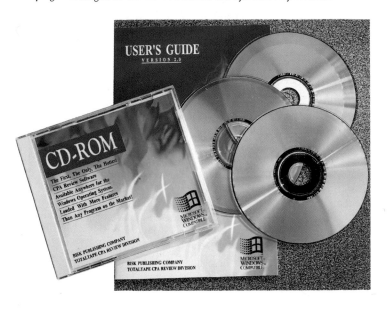

FLEXIBLE AUDIOTAPES
Quadruple Your Study Time

More than 50 hours of digitally-recorded audio lectures add insight and analysis to Totaltape's textbook coverage. The flexibility of audiotapes gives you complete control of your study program. Gain as much as two extra days study time per week simply by using our audio lectures in your car while commuting. Move ahead, repeat, review, and re-review as often as necessary until you understand the subject matter. Study on your own time. At your own pace. Whenever and wherever it's convenient for you. Plus, each audio lecture is indexed to help you locate specific topics of interest quickly.

COMPLETE AND AUTHORITATIVE TEXTBOOKS
Available in a 4-Volume Set & Individual Exam Sections Feature an Extensive Section on the Grading of Writing Skills, Now Worth 5% of Your Grade

Developed and written by the nation's foremost tax, accounting, auditing, and law experts, Totaltape's CPA Review textbooks feature complete and current coverage of every exam section and ALL official CPA exam changes. Available by individual exam section, our textbooks contain more than 3,000 pages of text and over 4,000 recent CPA exam questions, problems, and essays with solutions, including correct and incorrect answer explanations not available from the AICPA. We teach you the most important "how-to's" and exam topics; you get the kind of time-effective training you need to pass the exam. Plus, we show you how to set up a study plan, how to build exam confidence, and how to answer exam questions the way the graders are looking to see them for maximum points.

Call Now for Your Free Audio Demo
1-800-874-7599

Look for us on the INTERNET!

Here's how to access Totaltape's home page on the World Wide Web:
http://www.bisk.com
email: bisk@bisk.com

Totaltape CPA Review Order Form

	FINANCIAL ACCOUNTING & REPORTING	QTY	ACCOUNTING & REPORTING	QTY	AUDITING	QTY	BUSINESS LAW & PROFESSIONAL RESPONSIBILITIES	QTY	FULL SET	QTY	TOTAL $
Software *for Windows* **with Q&A and Text on Disk**	**$128.90** CPA2543		**$116.90** CPA2513		**$116.90** CPA2533		**$116.90** CPA2523		**$479.60** CPA2503		
Software *for Windows* **with Q&A**	**$89.95** CPA2855		**$84.95** CPA2856		**$84.95** CPA2857		**$84.95** CPA2858		**$344.80** CPA2859		
Software for DOS with Q&A*	**$89.95** CPA2851		**$84.95** CPA2850		**$84.95** CPA2853		**$84.95** CPA2852		**$344.80** CPA2854		
CD-ROM *for Windows* **with Q&A, Text on Disk & Multimedia**	**$138.90** CPA2700		**$126.90** CPA2701		**$126.90** CPA2702		**$126.90** CPA2703		**$519.60** CPA2704		
CPA Review Audiotape Lectures	**$99.95** CPA2542		**$99.95** CPA2512		**$99.95** CPA2532		**$99.95** CPA2522		**$399.80** CPA2502		
CPA Review Examination Hot•Spot Videos **ALL VIDEOS $99.00 each**	Bonds & Other Liabilities CPA2090		Governmental & Nonprofit Accounting CPA2040		Audit Evidence CPA2110		Contracts & Commercial Paper CPA2050		Examination Hot•Spot Video Series CPA2160		
	Consolidations CPA2020		Capital Gains & Losses CPA2015		Audit: Internal Control CPA2100		Sales & Agency CPA2150		**Money-Saving Discount Available with Purchase of Full Video Set! Call Now for Special Pricing and to Place Your Order.**		
	FASBs 95 & 109 CPA2030		Corporate Taxation CPA2016		Standard Audit Reports CPA2000		Bankruptcy CPA3190				
	Leases & Pensions CPA2080		Individual Taxation: Filing Status, Exemptions & Gross Income CPA2410		Other Reports, Reviews & Compilations CPA3230		Property and Secured Transactions CPA3200				
	Revenue Recognition/ Income Statement Presentation CPA3220		Individual Taxation: Adjustments & Itemized Deductions CPA2310		EDP Auditing & Stat Sampling CPA2548				**CALL FOR NEW TITLES!**		
	Assets CPA3210		Cost Accounting CPA2130								
	Inventory CPA3250		Managerial Accounting CPA2140								
			Estates, Trusts & Partnerships CPA3245								
			Tax Liabilities & Credits CPA2510								
CPA Review Textbooks 4-Volume	**$39.95** CPA2551		**$32.95** CPA2552		**$32.95** CPA2553		**$32.95** CPA2554		**$138.80** CPA2550		

*5¼ disks available upon request.

HOW TO PASS THE CPA EXAM VIDEO... $60.00 (CPA2560)

TERMS
We ship on account to qualified individuals, firms, bookstores, libraries, institutions, and government agencies with purchase order. Prices subject to change without notice. 10-day refund policy on resaleable textbooks. Rapid delivery via UPS with Air Service to the West Coast. *We ship within 48 hours.*

CALL TOLL-FREE
1-800-874-7599

METHOD OF PAYMENT

❏ Check enclosed, *made payable to Bisk Publishing Company*

Visa ❏ MC ❏ Amex ❏ Discover ❏ Exp Date _____

Card No _____

Signature _____

Name _____

Address _____

City _____ State ____ Zip _____

Day Phone _____ Eve Phone _____

DISCOUNTS
Orders Totaling $1,000 or More...**SAVE 10%**
Orders Totaling $1,400 or More...**SAVE 15%**
Orders Totaling $1,800 or More...**SAVE 25%**

GENERAL SHIPPING CHARGES
Orders up to $499.00   +7% of total
Orders over $500.00   +6% of total

TEXT ONLY SHIPPING CHARGES
Financial Accounting & Reporting, $6.95
All Others, $5.95 each

Additional shipping required for delivery outside the U.S. Call 813-621-6200 for details.

SUBTOTAL	
LESS APPLICABLE DISCOUNT	
IN FL ADD 6½% SALES TAX	
PLUS SHIPPING	
TOTAL DUE	

When ordering please use code #94043

Complete & Mail to: Bisk Publishing Company, TOTALTAPE CPA REVIEW
9417 Princess Palm Avenue, Tampa, FL 33619-8317 Fax Toll-Free 1-800-345-8273 Internet http://www.bisk.com Email bisk@bisk.com

May 1996

CPA
Comprehensive Exam Review

Business Law & Professional Responsibilities

Nathan M. Bisk, J.D., C.P.A.
Paul Munter, Ph.D., C.P.A.
Ivan Fox, J.D., LL.M.

ACKNOWLEDGEMENTS

We wish to thank the **American Institute of Certified Public Accountants** and the **Financial Accounting Standards Board** for permission to reprint the following copyright © materials:

1. Uniform CPA Examination Questions and Unofficial Answers Copyright© 1985 through 1996. Reprinted (or adapted) with permission.

2. Accounting Research Bulletins, APB Opinions, APB Statements, and Code of Professional Conduct.

3. FASB Statements, Interpretations, and Statements of Financial Accounting Concepts (SFAC), Copyright © Financial Accounting Standards Board, 401 Merrit 7, P.O. Box 5116, Norwalk, CT 06856, U.S.A. Reprinted with permission. Copies of the complete documents are available from the FASB.

4. Statements on Auditing Standards (SAS), Statements on Standards for Accounting and Review Services (SSARS), Statements on Standards for Management Advisory Services (SSMAS), Statements on Standards for Accountants' Services on Prospective Financial Information, and Statements on Standards for Attestation Engagements.

PREFACE

Our texts provide comprehensive, complete coverage of all the topics tested on all four sections of the CPA Examination, including **Business Law & Professional Responsibilities, Financial Accounting & Reporting, Accounting & Reporting,** and **Auditing**. Used effectively, our materials will enable you to achieve maximum preparedness for the Uniform CPA Examination. Here is a brief summary of the **features** and **benefits** that our texts will provide for you:

1. **New Edition For Closed Exam** . . . Beginning with the May 1996 Exam, the Uniform CPA Examination will be non-disclosed. See page F-5 for a full discussion of this issue. This edition contains up-to-date coverage, including complete coverage of all exam changes. This edition also includes all the latest pronouncements of the AICPA and FASB, the current tax rates, governmental and nonprofit accounting, and other topics that are tested on the CPA exam. Our coverage is based on the new **AICPA Content Specification Outlines for the Uniform CPA Exam,** effective May 1996.

2. **Separate and Complete Volumes** . . . Each text includes multiple choice and other objective questions with solutions, plus essays and problems where appropriate. There is no need to refer to any other volume.

3. **More than 3,000 Pages of Text** . . . As well as a selection of more than 4,000 recent CPA Examination questions, problems, and essays with Unofficial Answers. Solving these questions and problems under test conditions with immediate verification of results instills confidence and reinforces our **SOLUTIONS APPROACH™** to solving exam questions.

4. **Complete Coverage** . . . No extra materials required. We discuss and explain all important AICPA and FASB pronouncements, including all significant ARBs, APBs, SASs, SSARs, SFACs, and FASB materials. We also cite and identify all authoritative sources including the dates of all AICPA Questions and Unofficial Answers covered in our materials.

5. **Detailed Summaries** . . . We set forth the significant testable concepts in each CPA exam topic. These highly readable summaries are written in complete sentences using an outline format to facilitate rapid and complete comprehension. The summaries isolate and emphasize topics historically tested by the CPA examiners.

6. **Emphasis on "How to Answer Questions" and "How to Take the Exam"** . . . We teach you to solve problem, essay, and objective questions using our unique and famous **SOLUTIONS APPROACH.™**

7. **Discussion and Development of** . . . AICPA grading procedures, grader orientation strategies, examination confidence, and examination success.

8. **Unique Objective Question Coverage and Unofficial Answers Updated** . . . We explain *why* the multiple choice alternatives are either right or wrong. Plus, we clearly indicate the changes that need to be made in the Unofficial Answers to correctly reflect current business and tax laws and AICPA and FASB pronouncements.

9. **Writing Skills** . . . Financial Accounting and Reporting, Auditing, and Business Law and Professional Responsibilities contain a section to help you brush up on your writing skills, which are now tested on the CPA exam.

10. **Indexes** . . . We have included a comprehensively compiled index for easy topic reference in all four sections.

11. **Trend Analysis of Recent Exams** . . . We include short summaries of all essays and problems given on the most recent exams, to assist you in accurately pinpointing topics tested most frequently.

12. **Diagnostic Exam to Test Your Present Level of Knowledge** . . . And we include a **Final Exam** to test your exam preparedness under actual exam conditions. These testing materials are designed to help you single out for concentrated study the exam topic areas in which you are dangerously deficient.

Our materials are designed for the candidate who has previously studied accounting. Therefore, the rate at which a candidate studies and learns (not merely reads) our material will depend on a candidate's background and aptitude. Candidates who have been out of school for a period of years will need more time to study than recent graduates. The point to remember is that all the material you will need to know to pass the exam is here. All you need to do is apply yourself and learn this material at a rate that is appropriate to your situation. **As a final thought**, keep in mind that test confidence gained through disciplined preparation equals success.

OUR EDITORIAL BOARD INCLUDES THE NATION'S LEADING CPAs, ATTORNEYS AND EDUCATORS!

The Only CPA Review Texts Developed By Full-Time Experts.

YOU WILL LEARN FROM OUR OUTSTANDING EXPERTS . . . WITHOUT LEAVING YOUR HOME OR OFFICE.

Consulting Editor

MORTIMER M. CAPLIN, LL.B., J.S.D., LL.D., is a Senior Partner with the Washington D.C. law firm of Caplin and Drysdale. He has served as Commissioner of the Internal Revenue Service, and serves as a member of the President's Task Force on Taxation. He is a recipient of the Alexander Hamilton Award (the highest award conferred by the Secretary of the Treasury) "for outstanding and unusual leadership during service as a U.S. Commissioner of Internal Revenue." For more than 23 years, Mr. Caplin has been in private practice with his present law firm, and has served as Adjunct Professor for the University of Virginia Law School. He is a nationally acclaimed author of numerous articles on tax and corporate matters.

Consulting Editor

RICHARD M. FELDHEIM, M.B.A., J.D., LL.M., C.P.A. (NY), is a New York CPA as well as an Attorney in New York and Arizona. He holds a Masters in Tax Law from New York University Law School. Mr. Feldheim is a member of the New York State Society of CPAs, AICPA, New York State Bar Association, Association of the Bar of the City of New York, Arizona Bar, and American Bar Association. His background includes practice as both a CPA with Price Waterhouse & Co. and as a Senior Partner with the Arizona law firm of Wentworth & Lundin. He has lectured for the AICPA, the Practising Law Institute, Seton Hall University, and the University of Arizona.

Consulting Editor

MARILYN F. HUNT, M.A., C.P.A. (FL), currently serves as an Accounting instructor at the University of Central Florida, where she has been CPA Review Program Coordinator for more than 15 years. Ms. Hunt is a contributing editor for *The Internal Auditor* magazine and is an author and reviewer for various accounting and CPA Review texts. In addition, she regularly writes questions for the Certified Internal Auditor Examination. Ms. Hunt has conducted CPE programs for the AICPA, the Associated Regional Accounting Firms, the IMA, the Florida Institute of Certified Public Accountants, DisneyWorld, Blue Cross/ Blue Shield, and many local and national CPA firms. Her background includes public accounting experience with Price Waterhouse.

Consulting Editor

THOMAS A. RATCLIFFE, Ph.D., C.P.A. (TX), is Professor of Accounting and Chairman of the Department of Accounting and Finance at Troy State University. Dr. Ratcliffe teaches financial accounting courses and has published more than 100 technical works in accounting and auditing. He received the 1991 Alabama Society of CPAs Outstanding Accounting Educator award and has been named Alabama's Outstanding Discussion Leader and CPE instructor for the past four years. Dr. Ratcliffe serves as a consultant to several CPA firms and was past President of the Southeast Alabama Chapter of the Alabama Society of CPAs. He currently serves as a Council Representative for the Alabama Society of CPAs.

Consulting Editor

C. WILLIAM THOMAS, M.B.A., Ph.D., C.P.A. (TX), currently serves as a Professor and Chairman of the Department of Accounting and Business Law at Baylor University. He is a member of the AICPA, the Texas Society of CPAs, the Central Texas Chapter of CPAs, and the American Accounting Association, where he is past Chairperson for the Southwestern Regional Audit Section. Professor Thomas is a nationally known author and has extensive experience in Auditing CPA Review. In addition, he has received recognition for special audit education and curriculum projects he developed for Coopers & Lybrand. His background includes public accounting experience with KPMG Peat Marwick.

888- 264-2121

BUSINESS LAW & PROFESSIONAL RESPONSIBILITIES

VOLUME IV of IV

TABLE OF CONTENTS

		PAGE
Foreword:	Getting Started	E-1
Foreword:	Practical Advice for CPA Exam Preparation	F-1
Foreword:	Accounting for 5%	G-1
Chapter 43:	Contracts	43-1
Chapter 44:	Sales	44-1
Chapter 45:	Commercial Paper	45-1
Chapter 46:	Documents of Title and Investment Securities	46-1
Chapter 47:	Secured Transactions	47-1
Chapter 48:	Bankruptcy	48-1
Chapter 49:	Suretyship	49-1
Chapter 50:	Agency	50-1
Chapter 51:	Partnerships	51-1
Chapter 52:	Corporations	52-1
Chapter 53:	Estates and Trusts	53-1
Chapter 54:	Regulation of Employment	54-1
Chapter 55:	Federal Securities Regulations	55-1
Chapter 56:	Real and Personal Property	56-1
Chapter 57:	Fire and Casualty Insurance	57-1
Chapter 58:	Ethics and Professional Responsibilities	58-1
Chapter 59:	Accountant's Professional Liability	59-1
Appendix A:	Business Law & Professional Responsibilities Final Exam	A-1
Index		I-1
Appendix B:	November 1995 Examination	B-1

4 each day

1) Notes
2) Essays
3) Multiple Ch
4) Quick Rev.
5) Test Exam

NOTES

GETTING STARTED

STEP ONE: **READ PART ONE OF THE PRACTICAL ADVICE SECTION AT THE FRONT OF THE BOOK**

Part One of the Practical Advice section is designed to familiarize you with the CPA Examination. Included in this section are general comments about the exam, a schedule of future exam dates, the addresses and phone numbers of the state boards of accountancy, and attributes required for exam success.

STEP TWO: **TAKE THE DIAGNOSTIC EXAMS**

The diagnostic exams are designed to help you determine your strong and weak areas. This in turn will help you design your personalized training plan so that you spend more time in your weak areas and do not waste precious study time in areas where you are already strong. You can take the exams using either the books or CPA Review Software for Windows. CPA Review Software for Windows will automatically score your exams for you and give you a personalized analysis of your strong and weak areas. The books provide you with a worksheet which makes self diagnosis fast and easy.

NOTE: If you took a previous CPA Exam and did not pass one or more sections, we recommend that you analyze these exam sections to help you determine where you need to concentrate your efforts this time around.

STEP THREE: **DEVELOP A PERSONALIZED TRAINING PLAN**

Now, based on the results from your diagnostic exams, we will show you how to develop your personalized training plan. If you are taking the exam for the first time, and you are the "average" CPA candidate, we recommend that you train for 20 weeks at a minimum of 20 hours per week. This level of intensity should increase during the final four weeks of your training and peak at a minimum of 40 hours the final week before the exam. If you took the exam last time and did not condition (you still have to take all four sections), and you are the "average" CPA candidate, we recommend that you train for 12 weeks at a minimum of 20 hours per week. Again, this level of intensity should increase during the final four weeks of your training and peak at a minimum of 40 hours the final week before the exam. If you have conditioned (you have to take three or less sections), you can adjust these guidelines accordingly.

You are probably wondering what we mean by an "average" candidate. We are referring to the candidate who is just finishing or has just finished his or her academic training, attended a school which has a solid accounting curriculum, and received above average grades in his or her accounting and business law courses. Remember, "average" is a benchmark, many candidates are not "average", so adjust your training plan accordingly.

HOW TO FIND 20 HOURS A WEEK TO STUDY

The typical CPA candidate is a very busy individual. He or she goes to school and/or works full or part time. Some candidates have additional responsibilities such as a spouse, children, a house to take care of--the list can go on and on. Consequently, your first reaction may be, " I don't have 20 hours a week to devote to training for the CPA Exam." Using the chart on the following page, we will show you how to "find" the time that you need to develop your training schedule.

1. Keeping in mind what you would consider to be a typical week; first mark out in black the time that you know you won't be able to study. For example, mark an "X" in each block which represents time that you normally sleep, have a class, work, or have some other type of commitment.

2. Next, in a different color, put a "C" in each block which represents commute time, an "M" in each block which represents when you normally eat your meals, and an "E" in each block which represents when you normally exercise.

3. Now pick one hour each day to relax and give your mind a break. In black, write "BREAK" in one block each day. Do not skip this step. By taking a break, you will study more efficiently and effectively.

4. Count how many blocks are left. Are there 20? If so, in a different color write "STUDY" in 20 blocks. If not, write "STUDY" in the remaining blocks. Now count your "C", "M", and "E" blocks; if needed, these can be used to gain additional study time by using tapes and/or flashcards.

5. If you still do not have 20 blocks, and you scored 70% or more on your diagnostic exams, you may still be able to pass the exam even with your limited study time. If, however, you scored less than 70% on your diagnostic exams, you have 2 options: (1) re-prioritize and make a block which has an "X" in it, available study time; or (2) concentrate on conditioning (passing some but not all of the sections) instead of on passing the entire exam.

TIME AVAILABILITY

	MON	TUES	WED	THURS	FRI	SAT	SUN
1:00 AM							
2:00 AM							
3:00 AM							
4:00 AM							
5:00 AM							
6:00 AM							
7:00 AM							
8:00 AM							
9:00 AM							
10:00 AM							
11:00 AM							
12:00 PM							
1:00 PM							
2:00 PM							
3:00 PM							
4:00 PM							
5:00 PM							
6:00 PM							
7:00 PM							
8:00 PM							
9:00 PM							
10:00 PM							
11:00 PM							
12:00 AM							

HOW TO ALLOCATE YOUR 20 WEEKS

This is where we will develop your overall training plan. We will outline a recommended training plan based on 20 hours per week and 20 weeks of study. The suggested hours of study are based on 20 hours of study time per week. The time allocated to each topic was based on the length of the chapter, the difficulty of the material, and how heavily the topic is tested on the exam (refer to the exam specifications and our frequency analysis found in the Practical Advice section of your book). Keep in mind that this plan is for the "average" CPA candidate. Consequently, you should customize this plan based on the results of your diagnostic exams and level of knowledge in each area tested. For example, if you have not had a course in governmental accounting, you will need to adjust your training plan to allow for more time in this area. Conversely, do not fall into the trap of spending too much time covering an area which is rarely tested on the exam.

RECOMMENDED TRAINING PLAN

		Hours
WEEK 1:	READ PRACTICAL ADVICE SECTION	
	TAKE DIAGNOSTIC EXAMS	
	GET ORGANIZED	
WEEK 2:	CHAPTER 1-- OVERVIEW OF FINANCIAL ACCOUNTING	5
	CHAPTER 2-- CASH, SHORT-TERM INVESTMENTS, AND RECEIVABLES	8
	CHAPTER 3-- INVENTORIES	7
WEEK 3:	WEEKLY REVIEW OF WEEK 2	1
	CHAPTER 4-- PROPERTY, PLANT, AND EQUIPMENT	5
	CHAPTER 5-- INTANGIBLES, R & D, & OTHER ASSETS	4
	CHAPTER 6-- BONDS	4
	CHAPTER 7-- LIABILITIES	6
WEEK 4:	WEEKLY REVIEW OF WEEKS 2 - 3	2
	CHAPTER 34-- STANDARDS AND RELATED TOPICS	2
	CHAPTER 35-- PLANNING THE AUDIT	2
	CHAPTER 8-- LEASES	7
	CHAPTER 9-- PENSIONS	7
WEEK 5:	WEEKLY REVIEW OF WEEKS 2 - 4	2
	CHAPTER 36-- INTERNAL CONTROL	8
	CHAPTER 37-- AUDIT EVIDENCE, PROGRAMS, AND PROCEDURES	7
	CHAPTER 38-- AUDIT SAMPLING PROCEDURES	3
WEEK 6:	WEEKLY REVIEW OF WEEKS 2 - 5	2
	CHAPTER 10-- OWNERS' EQUITY	6
	CHAPTER 11-- REPORTING THE RESULTS OF OPERATIONS	8
	CHAPTER 39-- AUDITING EDP SYSTEMS	4
WEEK 7:	WEEKLY REVIEW OF WEEKS 2 - 6	2
	CHAPTER 12-- REVENUE & EXPENSE RECOGNITION: SPECIAL AREAS	7
	CHAPTER 40-- REPORTS ON AUDITED FINANCIAL STMTS	8
	CHAPTER 41-- OTHER TYPES OF REPORTS	3

Hours

WEEK 8:	WEEKLY REVIEW OF WEEKS 2 - 7	2
	CHAPTER 13-- ACCOUNTING FOR INCOME TAXES	9
	CHAPTER 14-- STATEMENT OF CASH FLOWS	6
	CHAPTER 15-- FINANCIAL STMT & RATIO ANALYSIS	3
WEEK 9:	WEEKLY REVIEW OF WEEKS 2 - 8	3
	CHAPTER 16-- FINANCIAL REPORTING AND CHANGING PRICES	3
	CHAPTER 17-- FOREIGN OPERATIONS	3
	CHAPTER 18-- EARNINGS PER SHARE	3
	CHAPTER 19-- PARTNERSHIPS & PERSONAL FS	5
	CHAPTER 42-- OTHER PROFESSIONAL SERVICES	3
WEEK 10:	WEEKLY REVIEW OF WEEKS 2 - 9	2
	OVERALL REVIEW OF AUDIT	2
	CHAPTER 20-- BUSINESS COMBINATIONS & CONSOLIDATED FS	10
	CHAPTER 43-- CONTRACTS	6
WEEK 11:	WEEKLY REVIEW OF WEEKS 2 - 10	4
	OVERALL REVIEW OF FINANCIAL ACCOUNTING & REPORTING	6
	CHAPTER 21-- GOVERNMENTAL ACCOUNTING	10
WEEK 12:	WEEKLY REVIEW OF WEEKS 2-11	4
	CHAPTER 44-- SALES	6
	CHAPTER 22-- NON-PROFIT ACCOUNTING	10
WEEK 13:	WEEKLY REVIEW OF WEEKS 2 - 12	4
	CHAPTER 45-- COMMERCIAL PAPER	4
	CHAPTER 46-- DOCUMENTS OF TITLE	2
	CHAPTER 47-- SECURED TRANSACTIONS	4
	CHAPTER 23-- MANUFACTURING COST ELEMENTS & CGMS	3
	CHAPTER 24-- PRODUCT COSTING	3
WEEK 14:	WEEKLY REVIEW OF WEEKS 2 - 13	4
	CHAPTER 25-- STANDARD COSTING	3
	CHAPTER 26-- COST-VOLUME-PROFIT ANALYSIS	3
	CHAPTER 48-- BANKRUPTCY	3
	CHAPTER 49-- SURETYSHIP	3
	CHAPTER 27-- DIRECT (VARIABLE COSTING)	2
	CHAPTER 28-- BUDGETING	2
WEEK 15:	WEEKLY REVIEW OF WEEKS 2 - 14	5
	CHAPTER 29-- QUANTITATIVE METHODS	5
	CHAPTER 30-- FEDERAL TAXATION: INDIVIDUALS	10
WEEK 16:	WEEKLY REVIEW OF WEEKS 2 - 15	5
	CHAPTER 50-- AGENCY	4
	CHAPTER 51-- PARTNERSHIPS	3
	CHAPTER 52-- CORPORATIONS	3
	CHAPTER 53-- ESTATES AND TRUSTS	3
	CHAPTER 54-- REGULATION OF EMPLOYMENT	2
	CHAPTER 31-- FEDERAL TAXATION: PROPERTY	5

Hours

WEEK 17:	WEEKLY REVIEW OF WEEKS 2 - 16	11
	CHAPTER 32-- FEDERAL TAXATION: CORPORATIONS	10
	CHAPTER 55-- FEDERAL SECURITIES REGULATIONS	3
	CHAPTER 56-- REAL & PERSONAL PROPERTY	4
	CHAPTER 57-- FIRE AND CASUALTY INSURANCE	2
WEEK 18:	WEEKLY REVIEW OF WEEKS 2 - 17	17
	CHAPTER 33-- FEDERAL TAXATION: P'SHIPS., ESTATES, & TRUSTS	4
	CHAPTER 58-- ETHICS & PROFESSIONAL RESPONSIBILITIES	2
	CHAPTER 59-- ACCOUNTANTS' PROFESSIONAL LIABILITIES	3
	OVERALL REVIEW OF ACCOUNTING & REPORTING	5
	OVERALL REVIEW OF BUSINESS LAW & PROFESSIONAL RESPONS.	4
WEEK 19:	REVIEW AREAS YOU STILL FEEL WEAK IN	40+
WEEK 20:	TAKE FINAL EXAMS UNDER EXAM CONDITIONS	8
	DO FINAL REVIEWS	32+

YOUR PERSONALIZED TRAINING PLAN:

WEEK	TASK	DIAGNOSTIC SCORE	ESTIMATED HOURS	DATE COMPLETE	POST-TEST SCORES
1					
2					
3					
4					
5					
6					
7					
8					

WEEK	TASK	DIAGNOSTIC SCORE	ESTIMATED HOURS	DATE COMPLETE	POST-TEST SCORES
9					
10					
11					
12					
13					
14					
15					
16					

WEEK	TASK	DIAGNOSTIC SCORE	ESTIMATED HOURS	DATE COMPLETE	POST-TEST SCORES
17					
18					
19					
20					

NOTES:

STEP FOUR: READ PART TWO OF THE PRACTICAL ADVICE SECTION AT THE FRONT OF YOUR BOOK

Part Two of the Practical Advice section of the book will familiarize you with how the CPA Examination is graded and tell you how you can earn extra points on the exam simply by knowing what the grader is going to look for. In addition, we explain our Solutions Approach, which is an efficient, systematic method of organizing and solving questions found on the CPA Exam. Using this approach will help you maximize your grade on the exam. In Part Two, we also outline the AICPA content specifications for each section of the exam.

STEP FIVE: HOW TO INTEGRATE YOUR REVIEW MATERIALS

In this section we will show you how to integrate the Totaltape CPA review products that you purchased to optimize the effectiveness of your training plan. Find the section that corresponds to the package that you purchased. Then read the material that follows to maximize your training.

BOOKS, AUDIOTAPES, and CPA REVIEW SOFTWARE FOR WINDOWS

This is our most comprehensive review package available. This combination is reserved expressly for the serious CPA candidate. It is intended for those candidates who want to make sure that they pass the exam the first time (or this time, if you have already taken the exam). In addition, by using this package, you are eligible to qualify for Totaltape's money-back guarantee.

How to Use This Package:

1. First take the diagnostic exams using CPA Review Software for Windows. CPA Review Software for Windows automatically scores your exams and tells you what your strong and weak areas are.

In chapters where you are strong (i.e. you scored 65% or better on the diagnostic exam):

2. Begin your study of that chapter by answering the multiple choice questions using CPA Review Software for Windows. Once again, CPA Computer Software for Windows will point out the subtopics where you are strong and where you are weak so that you can focus on your weak subtopics.

3. Read the subsections of the chapter which correspond to your weak areas.

4. At this point, listen to the tape for this chapter to reinforce your weak areas and review your strong areas.

5. Now, using CPA Review Software for Windows, answer the multiple choice questions that you previously answered incorrectly. If you answer 70% or more of the questions correctly, you are ready to move on to the next chapter. If you answer less than 70% of the questions correctly, go back and review the subtopics which are still giving you trouble. Then using CPA Review Software for Windows, answer the questions which you previously answered incorrectly. If you still do not get at least 70% of the questions correct, check the exam specification and frequency charts in the Practical Advice section of your book to find out how heavily this area is tested. If this is an area which is heavily tested, continue reviewing the material and answering questions until you can answer at least 70% of them correctly. Allocate more time than you originally budgeted, if necessary. If this area is not heavily tested, move on, but make a note to come back to this topic later as time allows.

In chapters where you are weak (i.e. you scored less than 65% on the diagnostic exam):

2. Read the chapter in the book.

3. Listen to the taped lecture on this chapter.

4. Re-read the subsections of the chapter which correspond to your weak subtopics.

5. Using CPA Review Software for Windows, answer the multiple choice questions for this chapter. If you answer 70% or more of the questions correctly, you are ready to move on to the next chapter. If you get less than 70% of the questions correct, use your book to review the subtopics where you are weak. Then answer the questions that you previously answered incorrectly. If you still do not get at least 70% correct, check the exam specification and frequency charts in the Practical Advice section of your book to find out how heavily the area is tested. If this is an area which is heavily tested, continue reviewing the material and answering multiple choice questions until you can answer at least 70% correctly. Allocate more time than you originally budgeted, if necessary. If this is not a heavily tested area, move on, but make a note to come back to this area later as time allows.

BOOKS AND CPA REVIEW SOFTWARE FOR WINDOWS

This combination allows you to use the books to review the material and CPA Review Software for Windows to practice exam questions. You can also use the books to practice exam questions when you do not have access to a computer. In addition, by using this package, you are eligible to qualify for Totaltape's money-back guarantee.

How to Use This Package:

1. Take the diagnostic exams using CPA Review Software for Windows. CPA Review Software for Windows automatically scores your exams and tells you what your strong and weak areas are.

In chapters where you are strong (i.e. you scored 65% or better on the diagnostic exam):

2. Begin your study of that chapter by first answering the multiple choice questions using CPA Review Software for Windows. Once again, CPA Review Software for Windows will point out the subtopics where you are strong and where you are weak so that you can focus on your weak subtopics.

3. Read the subsections of the chapter which correspond to your weak areas.

4. Now using CPA Review Software for Windows, answer the multiple choice questions that you previously answered incorrectly. If you answer 70% or more of the questions correctly, you are ready to move on to the next chapter. If you answer less than 70% of the questions correctly, go back and review the subtopics which are still giving you trouble. Then using CPA Review Software for Windows, answer the questions which you previously answered incorrectly. If you still do not get at least 70% of the questions correct, check the exam specification and frequency charts in the Practical Advice section of your book to find out how heavily this area is tested. If this is an area which is heavily tested, continue reviewing the material and answering questions until you can answer at least 70% of them correctly. Allocate more time than you originally budgeted, if necessary. If this area is not heavily tested, move on, but make a note to come back to this topic later as time allows.

In chapters where you are weak (i.e. you scored less than 65% on the diagnostic exam):

2. Read the chapter in the book.

3. Using CPA Review Software for Windows, answer the multiple choice questions for this chapter. If you answer 70% or more of the questions correctly, you are ready to move on to the next chapter. If

you get less than 70% of the questions correct, use your book to review the subtopics where you are weak. Then answer the questions that you previously answered incorrectly. If you still do not get at least 70% correct, check the exam specification and frequency charts in the Practical Advice section of your book to find out how heavily the area is tested. If this is an area which is heavily tested, continue reviewing the material and answering multiple choice questions until you can answer at least 70% correctly. Allocate more time than you originally budgeted, if necessary. If this is not a heavily tested area, move on, but make a note to come back to this area later as time allows.

BOOKS AND AUDIOTAPES

This combination is designed for the candidate who does not have access to a computer to study, who spends time commuting or doing other activities which could take valuable time away from studying, and for those who like to reinforce what they read by listening to a lecture on tape.

How to Use This Package:

1. Take the diagnostic exams found in the Practical Advice section of your book. Using the worksheets provided, score your exams to determine your strong and weak areas.

In chapters where you are strong (i.e. you scored 65% or better on the diagnostic exam):

2. Do the multiple choice questions for that chapter. Using the worksheet provided, analyze your strong and weak areas.

3. Read the subsections of the chapter which correspond to your weak subtopics.

4. At this point, listen to the audiotape on this chapter to reinforce your weak areas and review your strong areas.

5. Answer the multiple choice questions that you previously answered incorrectly. If you answer 70% or more of the questions correctly, you are ready to move on to the next chapter. If you answer less than 70% of the questions correctly, go back and review the subtopics which are still giving you trouble. Then answer the questions that you previously answered incorrectly. If you still do not get at least 70% of the questions correct, check the exam specification and frequency charts in the Practical Advice section of your book to find out how heavily this area is tested. If this is an area which is heavily tested, continue reviewing the material and answering questions until you can answer at least 70% of them correctly. Allocate more time than you originally budgeted, if necessary. If this area is not heavily tested, move on, but make a note to come back to this topic later as time allows.

In chapters where you are weak (i.e. you scored less than 65% on the diagnostic exam):

2. First read the chapter in the book.

3. Now listen to the lecture of this chapter on tape.

4. Re-read the subsections of the chapter which correspond to your weak subtopics.

5. Do the multiple choice questions and score yourself using the worksheet provided. If you answer 70% or more of the questions correctly, you are ready to move on to the next chapter. If you answer less than 70% of the questions correctly, go back and review the subtopics which are still giving you trouble. Then answer the questions which you have previously answered incorrectly. If you still do not get at least 70% of the questions correct, check the exam specification and frequency charts in the Practical Advice section of your book to find out how heavily this area is tested. If this is an area which is heavily tested, continue reviewing the material and answering questions until you can answer

at least 70% of them correctly. Allocate more time than you originally budgeted for if necessary. If this area is not heavily tested, move on, but make a note to come back to this topic later as time allows.

VIDEOTAPES

The videotapes are designed to supplement all of the study packages. Use them to help you study the areas which are most troubling for you. They contain concise, informative lectures, as well as CPA Exam tips, tricks, and techniques which will help you to learn the material and to pass the exam.

STEP SIX: HELPFUL HINTS

♦ HOW TO SPEND YOUR WEEKLY REVIEW TIME

Answer the multiple choice questions and objective format questions that you previously answered incorrectly or merely guessed correctly.

Read through your notes.

Pick one essay question or problem to work.

Read the other essay and problem questions and solutions.

Go through your flashcards.

♦ USE A SEPARATE SHEET OF PAPER TO ANSWER THE MULTIPLE CHOICE QUESTIONS

Do not circle the answer to the multiple choice questions in the book. You should work every multiple choice question at least twice and you do not want to influence your answer by knowing how you previously answered the question.

♦ CIRCLE THE NUMBER OF THE MULTIPLE CHOICE QUESTIONS THAT YOU ANSWER INCORRECTLY OR MERELY GUESS CORRECTLY.

This way you know to answer this question again at a later time.

♦ MAKE NOTES AS YOU STUDY

Make notes and/or highlight when you read the chapters in the book. When possible, make notes when you listen to the tapes. You will find these very useful for your weekly reviews and for your final review.

♦ MAKE FLASHCARDS

Make flashcards for topics which are heavily tested on the exam and/or are giving you trouble.   You will find these very useful for your weekly reviews and for your final review. Keep these handy and review them when you are waiting in line or on hold. This will turn nonproductive time into valuable study time.

◆ HOW TO MOST EFFECTIVELY USE THE AUDIO TAPES

Use the tapes to turn nonproductive time into valuable study time. For example, play the tapes when you are commuting, exercising, getting ready for school or work, doing laundry, etc. The tapes will help you to memorize and retain key concepts. They will also reinforce what you have read in the books. Get in the habit of listening to the tapes whenever you have a chance.   The more times that you listen to each tape, the more familiar you will become with the material and the easier it will be for you to recall it on the exam.

STEP SEVEN: IMPLEMENT YOUR TRAINING PLAN

This is it! You are primed and ready. You have decided which training tools will work best for you and you know how to use them. As you implement your personalized training plan, keep yourself focused. Your goal is to obtain a grade of 75 or better on each section and, thus, pass the CPA Exam. Therefore, you should concentrate on learning new material and reviewing old material only to the extent that it helps you reach this goal. Also, keep in mind that now is not the time to hone your procrastination skills. Utilize the personalized training plan that you developed in step three so that you do not fall behind schedule. Adjust it when necessary if you need more time in one chapter or less time in another. However, make sure to refer to the AICPA content specification and the frequency analysis to make sure that the adjustment is warranted.   Above all else, remember that passing the exam is an attainable goal. If, after reading forewords E, F, and G, you do not feel ready to implement your training plan, or if at any point you have problems, call and talk to one of our editors. Our editors have all passed the exam and stand ready to help you do the same. Good luck!

PRACTICAL ADVICE
FOR CPA EXAM PREPARATION

Your first step toward an effective CPA Review program is to <u>study</u> the material in this Foreword. It has been carefully developed to provide you with essential information which will help you succeed on the CPA Exam. This material will assist you in organizing an efficient study plan and will demonstrate effective techniques and strategies for taking the CPA Exam.

PART	CONTENTS	PAGE
1	General Comments on the CPA Exam	F-2
	The Nondisclosed Exam	F-5
	State Boards of Accountancy	F-7
	Ten Attributes of Examination Success	F-8
2	Examination Grading and Grader Orientation Skills	F-10
	The Solutions Approach	F-15
	Examination Strategies	F-21
	AICPA Content Specification Outlines for CPA Exams Beginning May 1996:	F-26
3	Business Law & Professional Responsibilities Diagnostic Examination	F-27
	Frequently Tested Areas	F-36

PART ONE

GENERAL COMMENTS ON THE CPA EXAM

The difficulty and comprehensiveness of the CPA Exam is a well-known fact to all candidates. However, success on the CPA Exam is a reasonable, attainable goal. You should keep this point in mind as you study this Foreword and develop your study plan. A positive attitude toward the examination, combined with determination and discipline, will enhance your opportunity to pass.

Purpose of the CPA Exam

The CPA Exam is designed as a licensing requirement to measure the technical competence of CPA candidates. Although licensing occurs at the State Board level, it is a uniform exam with national acceptance. Generally, passing the CPA Exam in one jurisdiction allows a candidate to obtain a reciprocal certificate or license if they meet all the requirements imposed by the jurisdiction from which reciprocity is being sought.

State Boards also rely upon other means to ensure that candidates possess the necessary technical and character attributes, including interviews, letters of reference, affidavits of employment, ethics examinations, and educational requirements.

Generally speaking, the CPA Exam is essentially an academic examination which tests the breadth of material covered by good accounting curricula; it also appears to emphasize the body of knowledge required for the practice of public accounting. It is to your advantage to take the exam as soon as possible after completing the formal education requirements. We also recommend that you study for the entire examination the first time you take it, since there is a synergistic learning effect to be derived through preparing for all four parts. That is, all sections of the exam share some common subjects (particularly Financial Accounting & Reporting, Accounting & Reporting, and Auditing); so as you study for one section, you are also studying for the others.

State Boards of Accountancy

Certified Public Accountants are licensed to practice by individual State Boards of Accountancy. Application forms and requirements to sit for the CPA Exam should be requested from your individual State Board. IT IS EXTREMELY IMPORTANT THAT YOU COMPLETE THE APPLICATION FORM CORRECTLY AND RETURN IT TO YOUR STATE BOARD BEFORE THE SPECIFIED DEADLINE. Errors and/or delays may result in the rejection of your application. Be extremely careful in filling out the application and be sure to enclose all required materials. In many states, applications must be received by the State Board at least ninety days before the examination date. Requirements as to education, experience, internship, and other matters vary. If you have not already done so, take a moment to call the appropriate State Board for specific and current requirements. Complete the application in a timely manner.

It may be possible to sit for the exam in another state as an out-of-state candidate. Candidates wishing to do so should contact the State Board of Accountancy in their home state. Addresses of State Boards of Accountancy are provided on page F-7 of this section.

Approximately one month before the exam, check to see that your application to sit for the exam has been processed. DON'T ASSUME THAT YOU ARE PROPERLY REGISTERED UNLESS YOU HAVE RECEIVED YOUR CANDIDATE ID NUMBER.

The AICPA publishes a booklet entitled Information for CPA Candidates, usually distributed by State Boards of Accountancy to candidates upon receipt of their applications. To request a complimentary copy, write your State Board or the AICPA, Examination Division, 1211 Avenue of the Americas, New York, NY 10036. The addresses of State Boards are on page F-7.

CPA Exam Schedule

The CPA Exam is given twice a year, on Wednesday and Thursday of the first week of May and November. The projected exam dates for May 1996 through November 1998 are as follows:

1996:	May 8, 9	1997:	May 7, 8	1998:	May 6, 7
	November 6, 7		November 5, 6		November 4, 5

The day and time for each section of the exam is also standardized as follows:

Business Law & Professional Responsibilities	Wed.	9:00 -	12:00	3 hours
Auditing	Wed.	2:00 -	6:30	4 1/2 hours
Financial Accounting & Reporting--Business Enterprises	Thur.	8:00 -	12:30	4 1/2 hours
Accounting & Reporting--Taxation, Managerial, and Governmental and Not-for-Profit Organizations	Thur.	2:30 -	6:00	3 1/2 hours
				15 1/2 hours

Conditional Status

You will receive four scores. A passing score for each section is 75. Conditional status is granted by the individual State Boards of Accountancy and may vary from state to state. **Conditional status** may be granted to those candidates who receive a passing grade in some, but not all, sections. Some Boards of Accountancy grant conditional status to candidates who pass only one section, while other Boards require that at least two sections be passed before conditional status is awarded. Many Boards require a minimum grade in the sections failed to receive conditional credit for the sections passed.

If you received credit for passing some sections of the CPA Exam before May 1994 and plan to sit for re-examination in May 1994 and thereafter, you will be required to pass new sections of the exam. Candidates that have obtained conditional status by passing some sections of the Examination before May 1994 should check with their Board of Accountancy to determine the new Examination sections they must pass to complete the Examination process. The AICPA's recommendation for transitional conditional status is shown below. Keep in mind that this is only a recommendation. The final determination is up to each State Board of Accountancy.

Examination Sections Before May 1994	Examination Sections May 1994 and After
Accounting Theory	Financial Accounting & Reporting--Business Enterprises
Accounting Practice	Accounting & Reporting--Taxation, Managerial, and Governmental and Not-for-Profit Organizations
Auditing	Auditing
Business Law	Business Law & Professional Responsibilities

The AICPA has recommended that Boards of Accountancy which currently waive the Business Law section for members of the state bar should consider deleting this waiver because the new exam section, Business Law & Professional Responsibilities, also tests candidates' knowledge of the CPA's professional responsibilities to the public and the profession. This subject matter was previously tested in the Auditing section. Once again, candidates should check with their State Board of Accountancy concerning this matter.

Writing Skills Content

Answers to selected essay responses from Business Law & Professional Responsibilities, Auditing, and Financial Accounting & Reporting sections will be used to assess candidates' writing skills. Five percent of the points available on each of these sections will be allocated to writing skills. Effective writing skills include the following six characteristics:

1. Coherent organization.
2. Conciseness.
3. Clarity.
4. Use of standard English.
5. Responsiveness to the requirements of the question.
6. Appropriateness for the reader.

Calculators

Candidates will be provided with calculators at the examination sites for use on the Accounting & Reporting and Financial Accounting & Reporting sections. The purpose of providing calculators is to save the time candidates spend on performing and rechecking manual calculations; it is not intended to allow for more difficult and complex calculations and problems.

Examination Format

The examination will consist of the following sections and formats:

| | Format | | |
Section	4-Option Multiple Choice	Other Objective Answer Formats	Essays or Problems
Financial Accounting & Reporting--Business Enterprises	50-60%	20-30%	20-30%
Accounting & Reporting--Taxation, Managerial, and Governmental and Not-for-Profit Organizations	50-60%	40-50%	---
Auditing	50-60%	20-30%	20-30%
Business Law & Professional Responsibilities	50-60%	20-30%	20-30%

The four sections of the exam cover the following:

1. **Business Law & Professional Responsibilities**--This section covers the legal implications of business transactions generally confronted by CPAs, and the CPA's professional responsibility to the public and the profession (formerly covered in the Auditing section). It comprises 3 hours of the exam, and five percent of the candidate's score on this section is based on writing skills.

2. **Auditing**--This section covers the generally accepted auditing standards, procedures, and related topics. The CPA's professional responsibility is no longer tested in this area. It comprises 4½ hours of the exam, and five percent of the candidate's score on this section is based on writing skills.

3. **Accounting & Reporting**--This section covers federal taxation, managerial accounting, and accounting for governmental and not-for-profit organizations. This section consists of multiple choice and other objective format questions only. It comprises 3½ hours of the exam.

4. **Financial Accounting & Reporting**--This section covers generally accepted accounting principles for business enterprises. It comprises 4½ hours of the exam, and five percent of the candidate's score on this section is based on writing skills.

Reference Materials

All the material you need to know to pass the CPA Exam is in your BISK <u>CPA Comprehensive Review</u> texts! However, should you desire more detailed coverage in any area, you should consult the actual promulgations. Individual copies of recent pronouncements are available from the FASB or AICPA.

To order materials from the <u>FASB</u> or <u>AICPA</u> contact:

FASB Order Department
P.O. Box 5116
Norwalk, CT 06856-5116
Telephone (203) 847-0700

AICPA Order Department
P.O. Box 1003
New York, NY 10108-1003
Telephone (800) 334-6961

The FASB offers a student discount, which varies depending on the publication. The AICPA offers a 30% educational discount, which students may claim by submitting proof of their eligibility (e.g., copy of ID card or teacher's letter). AICPA members get a 20% discount and delivery time will be speedier because members may order by phone.

THE NONDISCLOSED EXAM

Beginning with the May 1996 exam, the Uniform CPA Examination will be nondisclosed. This means that candidates will no longer be allowed to keep (or receive) their examination booklets after the test. Candidates will also be required to sign a statement of confidentiality in which they promise not to reveal questions or answers. The AICPA will continue to distribute *Selected Questions and Unofficial Answers,* but this publication will no longer contain actual questions from previous tests; instead, a sampling of questions which have been chosen as being similar to future test questions will be provided. After the exam, only the Institute will have access to the tests themselves. Totaltape's Editorial Board will continue to update our diagnostic tests for your convenience, with questions based upon the representative items which will be provided, items from previously disclosed tests, and the teaching expertise of our editors.

Background

The AICPA made this change, which was authorized in June 1991 by the Board of Examiners, in order to increase consistency, facilitate possible future computer administration of the test, and improve examination quality by pretesting questions. Because the examination will no longer be completely changed every year, statistical equating methods will be more relevant, and the usefulness of specific questions as indicators of candidates' knowledge can be tested.

Effects on Time Management

Approximately 10% of the multiple choice questions in every section of the May 1996 exam, and every exam thereafter, will be questions which are being pretested. These questions will <u>not</u> be included in candidates' final grades; they are presented only so that the Board of Examiners may evaluate them for effectiveness and possible ambiguity. The Scholastic Achievement Test and the Graduate Record Exam both employ similar but not identical strategies: those tests include an extra section, which is being pretested, and test-takers do not know which section is the one which will not be graded. On the Uniform CPA Examination, however, the extra questions will be mixed in among the graded questions. This will make time management even more crucial. Candidates who are deciding how much time to spend on a difficult multiple choice question must keep in mind that there is a 10% chance that the answer to the question will not affect them either way. Also, candidates should not allow a question that seems particularly difficult or confusing to shake their confidence or affect their attitude towards the rest of the test; it may not even count. However, this experimental 10% will work against candidates who are not sure whether or not they have answered enough questions to earn 75%. Candidates should try for a safety margin, so that they will have accumulated enough correct answers to pass, even though some of their correctly answered questions will not be scored.

Post-Exam Diagnostics

The AICPA Board of Examiners' Advisory Grading Service will provide boards of accountancy with individual diagnostic reports for all candidates along with the candidates' grades. The diagnostic reports will show the candidate's level of proficiency on each examination section. The boards of accountancy <u>may</u> mail the diagnostic reports to candidates along with their grades: candidates should contact the state board in their jurisdiction to find out its policy on this. As before, grades will be mailed approximately 90 days after the examination.

Question Re-evaluation

Candidates who believe that an examination question contains errors which will affect the grading should turn in the Question Comment Form to the proctor before leaving the examination room. Candidates may also fax their complaint to the AICPA Examinations Division, at (201) 938-3443, within 48 hours after taking the examination. Only these two methods of communication will satisfy the requirements of the AICPA. The Advisory Grading Service asks candidates to be as precise as possible about the question and their reason for believing that it should be re-evaluated, and, if possible, to supply references to support their position. Since candidates are no longer able to keep or discuss the examination questions, it is important to remember as much detail as possible about a disputed question.

Discussing the Exam

Remember that candidates will be required to sign a statement of confidentiality in which they promise not to reveal questions or answers. Due to the nondisclosure requirements, Totaltape's editors will no longer be able to address questions about specific examination questions, although we will continue to supply help with similar study problems and questions in our texts.

STATE BOARDS OF ACCOUNTANCY

STATE	ADDRESS	PHONE NUMBER
AL	770 Washington Ave., RSA Plaza, Suite 236, Montgomery 36130	205/242-5700
AK	P.O. Box 110806, Juneau 99811-0806	907/465-2580
AZ	3110 N. 19th Ave., Ste. 140, Phoenix 85015	602/255-3648
AR	101 E. Capitol Avenue, Ste. 430, Little Rock 72201	501/682-1520
CA	2000 Evergreen St., Ste. 250, Sacramento 95815	916/263-3680
CO	1560 Broadway, Ste. 1370, Denver 80202	303/894-7800
CT	30 Trinity St., Hartford 06106	203/566-7835
DE	P.O. Box 1401, Margaret O'Neill Bldg., Dover 19903	302/739-4522
DC	614 H Street, N.W., Room 923, Washington, DC 20001	202/727-7454
FL	2610 N.W. 43rd St., Ste. 1A, Gainesville 32606	904/955-2165
GA	166 Pryor St., S.W., Atlanta 30303	404/656-3941
GU	P.O. Box P, Bank of Guan Building, Ste. 800, Agana, GU 96910	671/472-2910
HI	P.O. Box 3469, Honolulu 96801 or 1010 Richard St., Honolulu 96813	808/586-2694
ID	1109 Main St., Owyhee Plaza #470, Boise 83720	208/334-2490
IL	Univ. of Illinois, 10 Henry Admin. Bldg., 506 S. Wright St., Urbana 61801	217/333-1566
IN	Indiana Gov. Center S. E034, 302 W. Washington St., Indianapolis 46204-2246	317/232-2980
IA	1918 S.E. Hulsizer, Ankeny 50021	515/281-4126
KS	900 S.W. Jackson St., Ste. 556, Topeka 66612-1239	913/296-2162
KY	332 W. Broadway, Ste. 310, Louisville 40202	502/595-3037
LA	1515 World Trade Center, 2 Canal St., New Orleans 70130	504/566-1244
ME	State House Station 35, Augusta 04333	207/582-8700
MD	501 St. Paul Place, Room 902, Baltimore 21202-2272	410/333-6322
MA	100 Cambridge Street, Room 1315, Boston 02202	617/727-1806
MI	Dept. of Commerce, P.O. Box 30018, Lansing 48909	814/238-3066
MN	113 E. 7th St., St. Paul 55101	612/296-7937
MS	961 Highway 80E, Ste. A., Clinton 39056-5246	601/354-7320
MO	3605 Missouri Blvd., P.O. Box 613, Jefferson City 65102	314/751-0012
MT	111 N. Jackson, P.O. Box 200513, Helena 59620-0513	406/444-3739
NE	P.O. Box 94725, Lincoln 68509	402/471-3595
NV	200 S. Virginia, Ste. 670, Reno 89501	702/786-0231
NH	57 Regional Dr., Concord 03301	603/271-3286
NJ	P.O. Box 45000, Newark 07101	201/504-6380
NM	1650 University Blvd., N.E., Ste. 400-A, Albuquerque 87102	505/841-9108
NY	The State Education Dept., Cultural Education Center, Room 3013, Albany 12230	518/474-3836
NC	P.O. Box 12827, Raleigh 27605-2827	919/733-4222
ND	U.N.D., P.O. Box 9037, Grand Forks 58202-9037	701/775-7100
OH	77 S. High St., 18th Floor, Columbus 43266-0301	614/466-4135
OK	4545 N. Lincoln Blvd., Ste. 165, Oklahoma City 73105-3413	405/521-2397
OR	3218 Pringle Rd. S.E., Ste. 110, Salem 97302	503/378-4181
PA	P.O. Box 2649, Harrisburg 17105-2649	717/783-1404
PR	Box 3671, San Juan 00904	809/722-2121
RI	233 Richmond St., Ste. 236, Providence 02903	401/277-3185
SC	P.O. Box 11329, Columbia 29211	803/734-4228
SD	301 E. 14th St., Ste. 200, Sioux Falls 57104	605/367-5770
TN	500 James Robertson Pkwy., 2nd Floor, Nashville 37243-1141	615/741-2550
TX	1033 La Posada, Ste. 340, Austin 78752-3892	512/505-5570
UT	P.O. Box 45805, Salt Lake City 84145	801/530-6628
VT	109 State Street, Montpelier 05609-1106	802/828-2837
VI	P.O. Box Y, Christiansted, St. Croix VI, 00822	809/773-4305
VA	3600 W. Broad Street, 5th Floor, Richmond 23230-4917	804/367-8505
WA	P.O. Box 9131, Olympia 98507-9131	360/664-9192
WV	201 L&S Bldg., 812 Quarrier Street, Charleston 25301	304/558-3557
WI	P.O. Box 8935, Madison 53708-8935	608/266-2112
WY	Barrett Bldg., 2nd Floor, Room 217-218, Cheyenne 82002	307/777-7551

TEN ATTRIBUTES OF EXAMINATION SUCCESS

1.	Positive Mental Attitude	6.	Examination Grading
2.	Development of a Plan	7.	Solutions Approach
3.	Adherence to the Plan	8.	Examination Strategies
4.	Time Management	9.	Focus on Ultimate Objective--Passing!
5.	Knowledge	10.	Examination Confidence

We believe that successful CPA candidates possess these ten characteristics that contribute to their ability to pass the exam. Because of their importance, we will consider each attribute individually.

1. Positive Mental Attitude

Preparation for the CPA Exam is a long, intense process. A positive mental attitude, above all else, can be the difference between passing and failing.

2. Development of a Plan

The significant commitment involved in preparing for the exam requires a plan. We have prepared a Study Plan in the preceding "Getting Started" section. Take time to read this plan. Whether you use our "Study Plan" or create your own, the importance of this attribute can't be overlooked.

3. Adherence to the Plan

You cannot expect to accomplish a successful and comprehensive review without adherence to your study plan.

4. Time Management

We all lead busy lives, and the ability to budget study time is a key to success. We have outlined steps to budgeting time in the <u>Personalized Training Plan</u> found in the "Getting Started" section.

5. Knowledge

There is a distinct difference between understanding the material and knowledge of the material. A superficial understanding of accounting, auditing, and business law is not enough. You must <u>know</u> the material likely to be tested on the exam. Your BISK text is designed to help you acquire the working knowledge which is essential to exam success.

6. Examination Grading

An understanding of the CPA Exam grading procedure will help you to <u>maximize</u> grading points on the exam. Remember that your objective is to score 75 points on each section. Points are assigned to individual questions by the grader who reads your exam. In essence, your job is to <u>satisfy the grader</u> by writing answers which closely conform to the grading guide. In Part Two, Section 1, we explain AICPA grading procedures and show you how to <u>tailor your answer</u> to the grading guide and thus earn more points on the exam.

7.   **Solutions Approach**

The Solutions Approach is an efficient, systematic method of organizing and solving questions found on the CPA Exam. This Approach will permit you to organize your thinking and your written answers in a logical manner that will maximize your exam score. Candidates who do not use a systematic answering method often neglect to show all their work on difficult problems or essays--work which could earn partial credit if it were presented to the grader in an orderly fashion. The Solutions Approach will help you avoid drawing "blanks" on the exam; with it, you always know where to begin.

Many candidates have never developed an effective problem-solving methodology in their undergraduate studies. The "cookbook" approach, in which students work problems by following examples, is widespread among accounting schools. Unfortunately, it is not an effective problem-solving method for the CPA Exam or for problems you will encounter in your professional career. Our Solutions Approach teaches you to derive solutions independently, without an example to guide you.

We feel that our **Solutions Approach** and grader orientation skills, when properly developed, can be worth at least 10 to 15 points for most candidates. As you can probably imagine, these 10 to 15 points can often make the difference between passing and failing.

The Solutions Approach for objective questions, problems, and essays is outlined in Part Two, Section 2. Examples are worked and explained.

8.   **Examination Strategies**

You should be familiar with the format of the CPA Exam and know exactly what you will do when you enter the examination room. In Part Two, Section 3, we discuss the steps you should take from the time you receive the test booklet, until you hand in your answer sheet. Planning in advance how you will spend your examination time will save you time and confusion on exam day.

9.   **Focus on Ultimate Objective--Passing!**

Your primary goal in preparing for the CPA Exam is to attain a grade of 75 or better on all sections and, thus, pass the examination. Your review should be focused on this goal. Other objectives, such as learning new material or reviewing old material, are important only insofar as they assist you in passing the exam.

10.   **Examination Confidence**

Examination confidence is actually a function of the other nine attributes. If you have acquired a good working knowledge of the material, an understanding of the grading system, a tactic for answering the problems or essays, and a plan for taking the exam, you can go into the examination room confident that you are in control.

PART TWO: SECTION 1

EXAMINATION GRADING AND GRADER ORIENTATION SKILLS

- Security   F-10

- Objective Questions   F-10

- Essay Questions   F-10

- Essay Question Example--Grading Guide   F-11

- Grading Implications for CPA Candidates   F-13

The CPA Exam is prepared and graded by the AICPA Examinations Division. It is administered by the various State Boards of Accountancy.

An understanding of the grading procedure will help you maximize grading points on the CPA Exam. Remember that your objective is to pass the exam. You cannot afford to spend time on activities that will not affect your grade, or to ignore opportunities to increase your points. The following material abstracted from the Information for CPA Candidates booklet summarizes the important substantive aspects of the Uniform CPA Examination itself and the grading procedures used by the AICPA.

Security

The examination is prepared and administered under tight security measures. The candidates' anonymity is preserved throughout the examination and grading process. Unusual similarities in answers among candidates are reported to the appropriate State Boards.

Objective Questions

Objective questions consist of four-option, multiple-choice questions and other objective answer formats, which include: yes-no, true-false, matching, and questions requiring a numerical response. Objective questions are machine graded. Thus, you will accomplish nothing (and only waste time) by writing explanations beside your answers--only the blackened response is considered by the optical scanner. It is also important to understand that there is no grade reduction for incorrect responses to objective questions--your total objective question grade is determined solely by the number of correct answers. Thus, you should answer every question. If you do not know the answer, make an intelligent guess.

There are two or three formats for questions on each section of the CPA Exam. In the past, difficulty points were assigned to these parts as a means of curving the entire section. Beginning with the May 1994 Exam, this will no longer occur. Instead, difficulty points will be assigned to the exam as a whole, not to each individual question. The point to remember is to avoid getting "bogged down" on one answer. Move along and answer all the questions. Finally, leaving questions unanswered or panic-answering questions due to poor budgeting of test time can mean disaster.

Essay Questions

Essay questions are graded by CPAs and AICPA staff members, using the following procedures as described in the Information for CPA Candidates booklet:

First grading

The first grading is done by graders assigned to individual questions. For example, each essay in the Business Law & Professional Responsibilities section will be graded by a different grader. A grader assigned to a single question, which will be graded during the full grading session of six or seven weeks, becomes an expert in the subject matter of the question and in the evaluation of the candidates' answers. Thus, grading is objective and uniform.

The purpose of the first grading is to separate the candidates' papers into three groups: obvious passes, marginal, and obvious failures.

Second grading

Upon completion of the first grading, a second grading is made by reviewers. Obvious passes and failures are subjected to cursory reviews as part of the grading controls. Marginal papers (papers with grades of 70 to 74), however, receive an extensive review. These papers are regraded to grades of 69 or 75.

The graders who make the extensive reviews have had years of experience grading the CPA Examination. They have also participated in the development of the grading bases and have access to item analysis for objective questions, identifying concepts as discriminating (those included by most candidates passing the exam) or as rudimentary (those included by candidates both passing and failing the exam). An important indicator of the competence of the candidate is whether grade points were earned chiefly from discriminating concepts or from rudimentary concepts.

Third grading

After the papers have been through the second grading for all parts of the examination, the resultant grades are listed by candidate number and compared for consistency among subjects. For example, if a candidate passes two subjects and receives a 69 in a third, the 69 paper will receive a third grading in the hope that the candidate, now identified as possessing considerable competence, can have the paper raised to a grade of 75 by finding additional points for which to grant positive credit. This third grading is done by the section head or a reviewer who did not do the second grading of the paper.

Fourth grading

The Director of Examinations applies a fourth grading to papers that have received the third grading but have grades that are inconsistent. The Director knows that the papers have already been subjected to three gradings, and that it would be difficult to find additional points for which the candidates should be given credit. Obviously, very few candidates are passed in this manner, but this fourth grading assures that marginal candidates receive every possible consideration.

Essay Question Example--Grading Guide

Points are assigned to essay questions on the basis of <u>key concepts</u>. A key concept is an idea, thought, or option that can be clearly defined and identified. Through a grading of sample papers, a list of key concepts related to each question is accumulated. These key concepts become the <u>grading bases</u> for the question. That is, your answer will be scored according to the number of key concepts it contains. Note that you need not include <u>all</u> possible key concepts to receive full credit on a question. The total number of grading bases exceeds the point value of the question. For example, a 10-point question may have 15 or more grading bases. Thus, a candidate would not have to provide all the key concepts to get the maximum available points. Conversely, a candidate cannot receive more points even if he or she provides more than 10 key concepts.

To illustrate the grading procedure and the importance of using key concepts in your answers, we will develop a hypothetical grading guide for a question adapted from a past Business Law exam. We will assume that the entire question is worth 10 points.

Example 1 (15 to 20 minutes)

Hardaway Lending, Inc., had a 4-year $800,000 callable loan to Superior Metals, Inc., outstanding. The loan was callable at the end of each year upon Hardaway's giving 60 days written notice. Two and one-half years remained of the four years. Hardaway reviewed the loan and decided that Superior Metals was no longer a prime lending risk and it therefore decided to call the loan. The required written notice was sent to and received by Superior 60 days prior to the expiration of the second year. Merriweather, Superior's chief executive officer and principal shareholder, requested Hardaway to continue the loan at least for another year. Hardaway agreed, provided that an acceptable commercial surety would guarantee $400,000 of the loan and Merriweather would personally guarantee repayment in full. These conditions were satisfied and the loan was permitted to continue.

The following year the loan was called and Superior defaulted. Hardaway released the commercial surety but retained its rights against Merriweather and demanded that Merriweather pay the full amount of the loan. Merriweather refused, asserting the following:

- There was no consideration for his promise. The loan was already outstanding and he personally received nothing.
- Hardaway must first proceed against Superior before it can collect from Merriweather.
- Hardaway had released the commercial surety, thereby releasing Merriweather.

Required: Answer the following, setting forth reasons for any conclusions stated.

Discuss the validity of each of Merriweather's assertions.   (11/80, Law, #3a)

Now let's look at the unofficial answer. Notice that we have underlined the key concepts in the answer. Later, as we develop a grading guide for the answer, you will see the importance of using key concepts to tailor your answer to parallel the grading guide.

Solution: Consideration/Liability of Debtor and Surety

The first two defenses asserted by Merriweather are invalid. The third defense is partially valid.

Consideration on Hardaway's part consisted of foregoing the right to call the Superior Metals loan. The fact that the loan was already outstanding is irrelevant. By permitting the loan to remain outstanding for an additional year instead of calling it, Hardaway relinquished a legal right, which is adequate consideration for Merriweather's surety promise. Consideration need not pass to the surety; in fact, it usually primarily benefits the principal debtor.

There is no requirement that the creditor first proceed against the debtor before it can proceed against the surety, unless the surety undertaking expressly provides such a condition. Basic to the usual surety undertaking is the right of the creditor to proceed immediately against the surety. Essentially, that is the reason for the surety.

Hardaway's release of the commercial surety from its $400,000 surety undertaking partially released Merriweather. The release had the legal effect of impairing Merriweather's right of contribution against its co-surety (the commercial surety). Thus, Merriweather is released to the extent of 1/3 [$400,000 (commercial surety's guarantee) ÷ $1,200,000 (the aggregate of the co-sureties' guarantees)] of the principal amount ($800,000), or $266,667.

A grading guide similar to the one in Example 2 is attached to every candidate's paper, with the grading bases for each question. Each key concept in the answer increases the candidate's grade. The candidate's total grade for the question is easily determined by converting raw points, using a conversion chart. For example, a candidate who provides 8 of the 10 key concepts for the questions would earn a grade of 5 for his/her answer to part **a**.

Example 2--Grading Guide for Sample Problem

STATE _____
CANDIDATE NO. _____

POINTS	KEY WORD CONCEPTS
2	Consideration was foregoing the right to call the loan
1	Irrelevant that the loan was outstanding
2	Consideration need not pass to the surety
1	No requirement to proceed against the creditor first
2	Hardaway's release of the commercial surety partly releases Merriweather
2	Ratio of partial release is 1/3 of $800,000
10	

GRADE	1	2	3	4	5
POINTS	1	2 3	4 5	6 7	8 9 10

Importance of Key Concepts

A grading guide similar to the one in Example 2 is attached to every candidate's paper, with the key concepts or grading bases for each question. On the first grading, answers may be scanned first for key words, then read carefully to ascertain that no key concepts were overlooked. Each key concept in the answer increases the candidate's grade. The candidate's total grade for the question is easily determined by converting raw points, using a conversion chart. For example, a candidate who provides 7 of the 10 key concepts for this question would earn a grade of 4 for the answer. The process is repeated by the second grader and subsequent graders if necessary (i.e., borderline papers).

The point you should notice is that key concepts earn points. The unofficial answer closely conforms to the grading guide, making the grader's task simple. In turn, the unofficial answer also conforms to the format of the question. That is, each answer is numbered and lettered to correspond to the requirements. This should be your standard format.

There are two more points you should observe as you study the unofficial answer for our example. First, the answer is written in standard English, with clear, concise sentences and short paragraphs. A simple listing of key words is unacceptable; the concepts and their interrelationships must be logically presented. Secondly, remember that the unofficial answer represents the most acceptable solution to a question. This is not to say, however, that alternative answers are not considered. During the accumulation of grading bases, many concepts are added to the original "correct answer." Additionally, a paper that is near the passing mark receives a third (and perhaps fourth) grading, at which time individual consideration is given to the merits of each answer.

Parenthetically, we should mention that all the BISK CPA Review essays and problems are solved using the unofficial AICPA answers. Thus, you have ample opportunity to accustom yourself to the favored answer format.

Importance of Writing Skills

At least two essay responses will be graded for writing skills. A response is defined as a part of an essay. Therefore, if an essay question has a **Part a** and a **Part b,** it has two responses. The two responses graded for writing skills may be from the same question or from different questions. Either way, they will be totally independent topics requiring different technical knowledge. Five percent of the candidate's grade for the essay portion of the exam will be allocated to writing skills. For more coverage of this area, refer to the section of your book entitled **Accounting for 5%.**

Grading Implications for CPA Candidates

To summarize this review of the AICPA's grading procedure, we can offer the following conclusions which will help you to satisfy the grader and maximize your score:

1. Attempt an answer on every question.

2. Do not explain answers to multiple choice questions or other objective answer formats.

3. Respond directly to the requirements of the questions.

4. Use of a well-chosen example is an easy way of expressing an understanding of the subject or supporting a conclusion.

5. Use formats favored by the AICPA examiners.

6. Answer all requirements.

7. Develop a **Solutions Approach** to each question type.

8. Essay questions:

    Label your solutions parallel to the requirements.

    Offer reasons for your conclusions.

    Emphasize key words by underlining them.

    Separate grading concepts into individual sentences or paragraphs.

    Do not present your answer in outline format.

9. Allocate your examination time based on AICPA minimum suggested time.

10. Write neatly and legibly to avoid demerits.

PART TWO: SECTION 2

THE SOLUTIONS APPROACH

- Solutions Approach for Essays   F-15

- Solutions Approach for Objective Questions   F-18

- Benefits of the Solutions Approach   F-20

The **BISK Solutions Approach** is an efficient, systematic method of organizing and solving questions found on the CPA Exam. Remember that all the knowledge in the world is worthless unless you can get it down on paper. Conversely, a little knowledge can go a long way if you use a proper approach. The Solutions Approach was developed by our Editorial Board in 1971; all subsequently developed stereotypes trace their roots from the original "Approach" which we formulated. We feel that our Solutions Approach and grader orientation skills, when properly developed, can be worth at least 10 to 15 points for most candidates. As you can probably imagine, these 10 to 15 points often make the difference between passing and failing.

We will suggest a number of steps for deriving a solution that will help maximize your grade on the exam. Although you should remember the important steps in our suggested approach, don't be afraid to adapt these steps to your own taste and requirements. When you work the questions at the conclusion of each chapter, make sure you use your variation of the Solutions Approach. It is also important for you to attempt to pattern the organization and format of your written solution to the unofficial answer reprinted after the text of the questions. However, DO NOT CONSULT THE UNOFFICIAL ANSWER UNTIL YOU FINISH THE QUESTION. The worst thing you can do is look at old questions and then turn to the answer without working the problem. This will build false confidence and provide no skills in developing a Solutions Approach. Therefore, in order to derive the maximum number of points from an essay solution, you should first apply the Solutions Approach to reading and answering the question, and secondly, write an essay answer using an organization and format identical to that which would be used by the AICPA in writing the unofficial answer to that essay question.

Solutions Approach for Essay Questions

Our **six steps** are as follows:

1. Scan the text of the question for an overview of the subject area and content of the question.
2. Study the question requirements slowly and thoroughly; underline portions of the requirements as needed.
3. Visualize the unofficial answer format based on the requirements of the question.
4. Carefully study the text of the question. Underline important data.
5. Outline the solution in key words and phrases. Be sure to respond to the requirements, telling the grader only what he or she needs to know. You must explain the reasons for your conclusions.
6. Write the solution in the proper format based upon your key word outline. Write legibly in concise, complete sentences. Do not forget to proofread and edit your solution.

Essay Question Example

To illustrate the Solutions Approach for essay questions, we have adapted a question from a past Business Law examination. Key words in the solution are underlined.

Example 1

Debco Electronics, Inc. sells various brands of computer equipment to retail and business customers. An audit of Debco's 1991 financial statements has revealed the following transactions:

- On September 1, 1991, a Debco salesperson orally agreed to sell Rapid Computers, Inc. eight TMI computers for $11,000, to be delivered on October 15, 1991. Rapid sells computers to the general public. The Debco salesperson sent Rapid a signed confirmation of the sales agreement. Rapid received the confirmation on September 3, but did not respond to it. On October 15, 1991, Debco tendered delivery of the computers to Rapid. Rapid refused to accept delivery, claiming it had no obligation to buy the computers because it had not signed a contract with Debco.

- On October 12, 1991, Debco mailed TMI Computers, Inc. a signed purchase order for certain specified computers for delivery by November 30, 1991. The purchase order also stated the following:

  This purchase order will not be withdrawn on or before October 31, 1991. You must accept by that date or we will assume you cannot meet our terms. Ship F.O.B.--our loading dock.

TMI received the purchase order on October 15, 1991.

- On October 25, Debco mailed the following signed correspondence to TMI, which TMI received on October 29:

  Cancel our October 12, 1991, purchase order. We have found a better price on the computers.

- On October 31, 1991, TMI mailed the following signed correspondence to Debco, which Debco received on November 3:

  We have set aside the computers you ordered and turned down other offers for them. Therefore, we will ship the computers to you for delivery by November 30, 1991, F.O.B.--your loading dock with payment terms 2/10; net 30.

There were no further communications between TMI and Debco.

TMI shipped the computers on November 15, and Debco received them on November 29. Debco refused to accept delivery. In justifying its refusal to accept delivery, Debco claimed the following:

- Its October 25 correspondence prevented the formation of a contract between Debco and TMI;

- TMI's October 31 correspondence was not an effective acceptance because it was not received by Debco until November 3;

- TMI's October 31 correspondence was not an effective acceptance because it added payment terms to Debco's purchase order.

Debco, Rapid, and TMI are located in a jurisdiction that has adopted the UCC.

Required:

    a.   State whether Rapid's claim is correct and give the reasons for your conclusions.

    b.   State whether Debco's claims are correct with regard to the transaction involving TMI and give the reasons for your conclusions.

Let's look at the steps you go through to arrive at your solution:

In **Step 1,** you scan the question. Do not read thoroughly, simply get an overview of the subject area and content of the question. You notice the question addresses a UCC sale of goods consisting of several transactions.

In **Step 2,** you study the question requirements thoroughly. **Part a** addresses Rapid's claim, while **Part b** refers to the various claims made by Debco. Underline key phrases and words.

In **Step 3,** you visualize the format of your solution. The solution will be in paragraph form. **Part a** will discuss Rapid's claim, whether it is correct, and why. **Part b** will discuss Debco's claims (note that there are several), whether they are correct, and why. It will be important to identify each of these claims in the text of the question to aid in organizing your thoughts.

In **Step 4,** you carefully study the text of the question, given the requirements you want to satisfy, i.e., read the question carefully, noting Rapid's claim and each of Debco's three claims. You should mark important information.

In **Step 5**, you outline your answer in keyword form. This will include an answer of "correct" or "incorrect" for the claim in **Part a** and each of the claims in **Part b** plus additional key concepts you want to include in your final answer. In your exam preparation, as you work Business Law essays, notice that sometimes you are not asked to render a decision in the case but rather you are asked to discuss <u>both sides</u> of the case.

Outline Answer

a. Rapid's claim--incorrect
  UCC Statute of Frauds is satisfied for oral contract between two merchants if
    Confirmed in writing
    Within reasonable period of time
    Signed by the party sending it
    Received by the other party
  Both parties are bound unless receive written objection within 10 days

b. Debco's first claim--incorrect
  Purchase order is firm offer
    Debco is merchant
    Purchase order is in writing and signed
    States will not be withdrawn for time specified

  Debco's second claim--incorrect
    Acceptance effective when dispatched (mailed)

  Debco's third claim--incorrect
    UCC provides acceptance will form a contract
      If definite and timely expression
      Even if terms are different
      Unless acceptance is made conditional on accepting the different terms

In **Step 6**, you write your solution in a format similar to the unofficial answer. Notice how clear and concise the AICPA unofficial answers are. There is no doubt as to their decision or the reasoning supporting the decision. Notice also how they answer each requirement separately and in the same order as in the question. Be sure to proofread and edit your solution.

In general, each requirement in Business Law is designed to elicit from you at least one rule of law which is different from any other rule of law covered by any other part of the question. Finally, if you discuss two sides of an issue, be sure to indicate that this is what you are doing so that it does not appear that you have inconsistencies in you answer.

Example 2: Solution

a. <u>Rapid's claim</u> is <u>incorrect</u>. Both <u>Debco and Rapid</u> are <u>merchants under</u> the <u>UCC</u> because they both deal in the type of goods involved in the transaction (computers).
  The UCC provides that a <u>confirmation satisfies</u> the <u>UCC Statute of Frauds</u>, if an <u>oral contract between merchants</u> is:

* <u>Confirmed in writing</u> within a <u>reasonable period of time</u>, and

* The confirmation is <u>signed by the party sending it</u> and <u>received by the other party</u>.

  <u>Both parties are bound</u> even though the party receiving the confirmation fails to sign it. This is correct <u>unless</u> the party receiving the confirmation submits a <u>written objection within 10 days of receipt</u>. Rapid will be bound even though it did not sign the confirmation because no written objection was made.

b.   Debco's first claim, that its October 25 correspondence prevented the formation of a contract, is incorrect. Debco's October 12 purchase order will be regarded as a firm offer under the UCC because:

- Debco is a merchant.

- The purchase order is in writing and signed.

- The purchase order states that it will not be withdrawn for the time specified.

Because Debco's October 12 purchase order is considered a firm offer, Debco cannot revoke it, and its October 25 attempt to do so is ineffective.

Debco's second claim, that TMI's October 31 correspondence is not an effective acceptance because it was not received until November 3, is incorrect. An acceptance of an offer is effective when dispatched (in this case, when mailed), provided that an appropriate mode of communication is used. The UCC provides that an offer shall be construed as inviting acceptance in any manner and by any medium reasonable in the circumstances. In this case, Debco made its offer by mail, which, if adequately addressed with proper postage affixed, would be considered a reasonable manner and medium for acceptance. As a result, TMI's acceptance was effective when mailed on October 31.

Debco's third claim, that TMI's acceptance is not effective because it added payment terms to Debco's offer, is also incorrect. The UCC provides that a definite and timely expression of acceptance of an offer will form a contract, even if the terms of the acceptance are different from those in the offer, unless acceptance is expressly made conditional on accepting the different terms. Therefore, TMI's October 31 correspondence, which expressly stated that TMI would ship the computers ordered by Debco, was an effective acceptance, and a contract was formed despite the fact that TMI added payment terms.

Solutions Approach for Objective Questions

The **Solutions Approach** is also adaptable to objective questions. We recommend the following framework:

1.   Read the "Instructions to Candidates" section on your particular exam to determine if the AICPA's standard is the same. Generally, your objective portion will be determined by the number of correct answers with no penalty for incorrect answers.

2.   Read the question carefully, noting exactly what the question is asking. Negative requirements are easily missed. Underline key words and note when the requirement is an exception (e.g., "except for...," or "which of the following does not..."). Perform any intermediate calculations necessary to the determination of the correct answer.

3.   Anticipate the answer by covering the possible answers and seeing if you know the correct answer.

4.   Read the answers given.

5.   Select the best alternative. Very often, one or two possible answers will be clearly incorrect. Of the other alternatives, be sure to select the alternative that **best** answers the question asked.

6.   Mark the correct answer on the examination booklet itself. After completing all of the individual questions in an overall question, transfer the answers to the machine readable answer sheet with extreme care. Before you hand in your answer sheet, go back and double check your answers--make sure the answer is correct and make sure the sequence is correct. The AICPA uses answer sheets with varying formats; it is extremely important to follow the correct sequence (across the sheet vs. down or vice versa). READ THE INSTRUCTIONS CAREFULLY.

7.   Answer the questions in order. This is a proven, systematic approach to objective test taking. You will generally be limited to a maximum of 2 minutes per question. Under no circumstances should you allow yourself to fall behind schedule. If a question is too difficult, too long, or is a multiple question fact situation, be sure you remain cognizant of the time you are using. If after a minute or so you feel that it is too costly to continue on with a particular question, select the letter answer you tentatively feel is the best answer and go on. Return to these questions at a later time and attempt to finally answer them when you have time for more consideration. If you cannot find a better answer when you return to the question, use your preliminary answer because your first

impressions are often correct. However, as you read other question(s), if something about these subsequent questions or answers jogs your memory, return to the previous tentatively answered question(s) and make a note of the idea for later consideration (time permitting).

A particularly challenging format is the group of three to five multiple choice questions based on one hypothetical situation. In this case, you should skim all the related questions (but not answer possibilities) before you begin your calculations, since an overall view of the problem will guide you in the work you do. Note also that many incorrect answer choices on the practice section are based on the erroneous application of one or more items in the text of the question. Thus, it is extremely important to <u>anticipate</u> the answer before you read the alternatives. Otherwise, you may be easily persuaded by an answer choice that is formulated through the incorrect use of the given data.

Objective Question Example

Let's consider a multiple choice question adapted from a past Business Law examination:

Example 3

Migrane Financial does a wide variety of lending. It provides funds to manufacturers, middlemen, retailers, consumers, and homeowners. In all instances, it intends to create a security interest in the loan transaction it enters into. To which of the following will Article 9 (Secured Transactions) of the Uniform Commercial Code <u>not</u> apply?

a.   A second mortgage on the borrower's home.
b.   An equipment lease.
c.   The sale of accounts.
d.   Field warehousing.

APPLYING THE SOLUTIONS APPROACH

Let's look at the steps you should go through to arrive at your objective question solution.

In **Step 1**, you must carefully read the "<u>Instructions</u>" which precede your particular objective CPA Exam portion.

In **Step 2**, you must read the question and its requirements carefully. Notice that the goods are on consignment.

In **Step 3**, you must anticipate the correct answer <u>after</u> reading the question <u>but before</u> reading the possible answers.

In **Step 4**, you must read the answer carefully and select the alternative which best answers the question asked. Ideally, the best alternative will immediately present itself because it roughly or exactly corresponds with the answer you anticipated before looking at the other possible choices.

In **Step 5**, you select the best alternative. If there are two close possibilities, make sure you select the **best** one in light of the <u>facts</u> and <u>requirements</u> of the question.

In **Step 6**, you must make sure you accurately mark the <u>correct answer</u> in the proper sequence. If <u>anything</u> seems wrong, stop, go back and double-check your answer sheet. As a fail-safe mechanism, circle the correct letter on the exam sheet first, before you move it to the answer sheet.

In **Step 7**, you must make sure you answer the questions on the answer sheet in order, with due regard to time constraints.

The answer is "a." Uniform Commercial Code (UCC) 9-102 states that the UCC applies to any transaction intended to create a security interest in <u>personal property</u> or <u>fixtures</u>. Expressly excluded from Article 9 UCC coverage are liens (mortgages) on real property. Answers "b," "c," and "d" are all forms of personal property, whereas answer "a" is clearly a real property interest.

Benefits of the Solutions Approach

The **Solutions Approach** may seem cumbersome the first time you attempt it; candidates frequently have a tendency to write as they think. It should be obvious to you that such a haphazard approach will result in a disorganized answer. The Solutions Approach will help you write a solution that parallels the question requirements. It will also help you recall information under the pressure of the exam. The technique assists you in directing your thoughts toward the information required for the answer. Without a Solutions Approach, you are apt to become distracted or confused by details which are irrelevant to the answer. Finally, the Solutions Approach is a <u>faster</u> way to answer exam questions. You will not waste time on false starts or rewrites. The approach may seem time-consuming at first, but as you become comfortable using it, you will see that it actually saves time and results in a better answer.

We urge you to give the **Solutions Approach** a good try by using it throughout your CPA review. As you practice, you may adapt or modify it to your own preferences and requirements. The important thing is to develop a system so that you do not approach exam questions with a storehouse of knowledge that you can not put down on paper.

PART TWO: SECTION 3

EXAMINATION STRATEGIES

- Overall Preparation   F-21

- CPA Exam Strategies   F-21

- Inventory of the Examination   F-22

- Order of Answering Questions   F-22

- Examination Time Budgeting   F-23

- Page Numbering   F-23

- Psychology of Examination Success   F-23

- AICPA General Rules Governing Examination   F-24

- CPA Exam Week Checklist   F-25

The CPA Exam is more than a test of your knowledge and technical competence. It is also a test of your ability to function under psychological pressure. You could easily be thrown off balance by an unexpected turn of events during the days of the exam. Your objective is to avoid surprises and eliminate hassles and distractions which might shake your confidence. You want to be in complete control so that you can concentrate on the exam material, rather than the exam situation. By taking charge of the exam, you will be able to handle pressure in a constructive manner.

The keys to control are adequate preparation and an effective examination strategy.

Overall Preparation

Advance preparation will arm you with the confidence you need to overcome the psychological pressure of the exam. As you complete your comprehensive review, you will cover most of the material that will be tested on the exam; it is unlikely that an essay, problem, or series of objective questions will deal with a topic you have not studied. But if an unfamiliar topic is tested, you will not be dismayed because you have learned to use the Solutions Approach to derive the best possible answer from the knowledge you possess. Similarly, you will not feel pressured to write "perfect" answers, because you understand the grading process. You recognize that there is a limit to the points you can earn for each answer, no matter how much you write.

The components of your advance preparation program have previously been discussed in this Foreword. Briefly summarizing, they include:

1. Comprehensive review materials such as your BISK CPA Review Program.

2. A method for pre-review and ongoing self-evaluation of your level of proficiency.

3. A study plan which enables you to review each subject area methodically and thoroughly.

4. A Solutions Approach for each type of examination question.

5. An understanding of the grading process and grader orientation skills.

CPA Exam Strategies

The second key to controlling the exam is to develop effective strategies for the days during which the exam is given. Your objective is to avoid surprises and frustrations so that you can focus your full concentration on the questions and your answers.

You should be familiar with the format of the CPA Exam and know exactly what you will do when you enter the examination room. Remember to carefully read the instructions on the cover page of the Exam booklet AND for each problem. Disregarding the instructions may mean loss of points.

On the following pages, we discuss the steps you should take from the time you receive the test booklet until the time you hand in your booklet. Planning in advance how you will spend your examination time will save you time and confusion on exam day.

Four topics are very important in a discussion of overall examination strategies. They are:

- Inventory of the examination
- Order of answering questions
- Time budgeting
- Page numbering

Inventory of the Examination

You should spend the first few minutes of the exam surveying the exam booklet and planning your work. Do not plunge head-first into answering the questions without a plan of action. You do not want to risk running out of time, becoming frustrated by a difficult question, or losing the opportunity to answer a question that you could have answered well.

1. Carefully read the "Instructions to Candidates" on the cover page.

2. Note the number of questions/problems and the time allocated to each on the cover page.

3. Once permission is given, go through the booklet and see what topics each question covers. Jot down the topics on the time schedule on the front cover, forming a table of contents.

Your inventory should take no longer than five minutes. The time you spend will help you "settle in" to the examination and develop a feel for your ability to answer the questions.

Order of Answering Questions

Once you have completed your inventory of the exam, the next step is to develop an order for answering the objective questions and problems/essays. We recommend that you begin with the objective questions and then proceed to the problems/essays, beginning with the problem/essay that you feel is the least difficult.

Objective questions comprise a majority of the point value of each section. Because of their objective nature, the correct solution is listed as one of the answer choices. By solving these questions, not only do you gain confidence, but they often involve the same or a related topic to that covered in one of the problems/essays.

A very effective and efficient manner of answering the objective questions is to make two passes through the questions. On the first pass, you should answer those questions that you find the easiest. If you come across a question that you find difficult to solve, mark it and proceed to the next one. This will allow you to avoid wasting precious time and will enable your mind to clear and start anew on your second pass. On the second pass, you should go back and solve those questions you left unanswered on the first pass. Some of these questions you may have skipped over without an attempt, while in others you may have been able to eliminate one or two of the answer choices. Either way, you should come up with an answer on the second pass, even if you have to guess!! After completing all of the individual questions in an overall question, transfer the answers to the machine readable answer sheet with extreme care. Simply make note of those questions that gave you difficulty and then proceed to the problems/essays.

Each **problem** should be worked through to the end using the **Solutions Approach**. All schedules and calculations should be labeled before leaving the problem. However, leave a problem if you get stuck and return to it later with a fresh perspective.

Essay questions should be worked only through the key word outlines on the first pass. Then return to write your essay solution with a fresh look at the question.

Examination Time Budgeting

You __must plan__ how you will use your examination time and adhere faithfully to your schedule. If you budget your time carefully, you should be able to answer all parts of all questions. To demonstrate a realistic time budget, refer again to the time parameters in the examination booklet.

The time limitation on the exam is 3 hours for Business Law & Professional Responsibilities. You should subtract five minutes for your initial inventory. Assuming you will use the Solutions Approach and there will be two problem/essay type questions, your time budget may be similar to the one below. The actual exam may differ from this scenario so be sure to adjust your time budget to accommodate the number and type of questions asked.

	Minutes
Inventory examination	5
Answer objective questions	120
Key word outline essays (10 min. for each)	20
Write essay solutions (10 min. for each)	20
Review answers	15
	180

Your objective in time budgeting is to avoid running out of time to answer a question. Work quickly but efficiently (i.e., use the Solutions Approach). If you see that you will not have time to finish a problem you are working on, state clearly how you would finish the problem. Remember that when you are answering an essay question, a partial answer is better than no answer at all.

Page Numbering

Follow all instructions on the front of each exam section. Remember to arrange your answers in numerical order and number pages consecutively. The multiple choice answer sheet should be numbered page 1 and the numbering of your other pages should start with page 2. Start every essay question on a new sheet of paper and write on one side. For problem type questions, identify and include scratch pages. Write "continued" on the bottom of sheets when another answer sheet for the same problem or essay follows.

Psychology of Examination Success

As stated previously, the CPA Exam is in itself a physical and mental strain. You can minimize this strain by avoiding all unnecessary distractions and inconveniences during exam week. For example:

- **Make reservations for lodging well in advance.** It's best to reserve a room for Tuesday night so that you can check in, get a good night's sleep, and locate the exam site early the next morning.

- **Stick to your normal eating, sleeping, and exercise habits**. Eat lightly before the exam, and take small candies with you for quick energy. Watch your caffeine and alcohol intake. If you are accustomed to regular exercise, continue a regular routine during exam week.

- **Visit the examination facilities before the examination** and familiarize yourself with the surroundings.

- **Arrive early for the exam.** Allow plenty of time for unexpected delays. Nothing is more demoralizing than getting caught in a traffic jam ten minutes before the exam is scheduled to begin.

- **Avoid possible distractions**, such as friends and pre-exam conversation, immediately before the exam.

- In general, **you should not attempt to study on the nights before exam sessions**. It's better to relax--go to a movie, read a novel, or watch television. If you feel you must study, spend half an hour or so going over the chapter outlines in the text.

- **Don't discuss exam answers with other candidates**. Someone is sure to disagree with your answer, and if you are easily influenced by his or her reasoning, you can become doubtful of your own ability. Wait and analyze the entire exam yourself after it's all over.

AICPA General Rules Governing Examination

1. Read carefully the identification card assigned to you; sign it; make note of your number for future reference; when it is requested, return the card to the examiner. Only the examination number on your card shall be used on your papers for the purpose of identification. The importance of remembering this number and recording it on your examination paper correctly cannot be over-emphasized. If a question calls for an answer involving a signature, <u>do not</u> sign your own name or initials.

2. Seating during the exam is assigned according to your ID number in most states.

3. Answers must be submitted on paper furnished by the Board and must be completed in the total time allotted for each subject stated on the printed examinations. Begin your answer to each question on a separate page.

4. Answers should be written in pencil using No. 2 lead. <u>Neatness and orderly presentation of work are important</u>. Credit cannot be given for answers that are illegible.

5. Use a soft No. 2 lead pencil to blacken the spaces on the answer sheets for the objective-type questions.

6. Supplies furnished by the Board shall remain its property and must be returned whether used or not. You must hand in your printed examination booklet before leaving the examination room or your examination will not be graded.

7. Any reference during the examination to books or other matters or the exchange of information with other persons shall be considered misconduct sufficient to bar you from further participation in the examination.

8. The only aids candidates are permitted to have in the examination room are pens, pencils, and erasers. Calculators will be provided. Handbags and purses must be placed on the floor at candidates' locations during the entire time they are taking the exam. Briefcases, files, books, and other material brought to the examination site by candidates must be placed in a designated area before the start of the examination.

9. The fixed time for each session must be observed by all candidates. Each period will start and end promptly. It is the candidate's responsibility to be present and ready at the start of the period and to stop writing when told to do so.

10. Candidates arriving late should not be permitted any extension of time, but may be allowed to take the examination with proctor approval.

11. Smoking is allowed only in designated areas away from the general examination area.

12. No telephone calls are permitted during the examination session.

13. Only two time warnings are given: (1) thirty minutes prior to the end of session, and (2) five minutes prior to the end of session. (Additional warnings are not considered necessary.)

CPA Exam Week Checklist

What to pack for exam week:

1. CPA Exam registration material.

2. Hotel confirmation.

3. Cash and/or a major credit card.

4. Alarm clock--Don't rely on a hotel wake-up call.

5. Comfortable clothing that can be layered to suit varying temperatures.

6. A watch.

7. Appropriate review materials, pencils, erasers, and pencil sharpener.

8. Healthy snack foods.

Evenings before exam sections:

1. Read through your BISK chapter outlines for the next day's section(s).

2. Eat lightly and monitor your intake of alcohol and caffeine. Get a good night's rest.

3. Do not try to cram. A brief review of your notes will help to focus your attention on important points and remind you that you are well prepared, but too much cramming can shatter your self-confidence. If you have reviewed conscientiously, you are already well-prepared for the CPA Exam.

The morning of each exam section:

1. Eat a satisfying breakfast. It will be several hours before your next meal. Eat enough to ward off hunger, but not so much that you feel uncomfortable.

2. Dress appropriately. Wear layers you can take off to suit varying temperatures in the room.

3. Take ample supplies.

4. Arrive at the exam center thirty minutes early. Check in as soon as you are allowed to do so.

What to bring to the exam:

1. ID card--This is your official entrance permit to the exam.

2. Several sharpened No. 2 pencils, erasers, and a small pencil sharpener.

3. A watch.

4. Tissues, small candies, gum, and aspirin.

5. Do not take articles that will not be allowed in the exam room.

During the exam:

1. Always read all instructions and follow the directions of the exam administrator. If you don't understand any written or verbal instructions, or if something doesn't seem right, ASK QUESTIONS. Remember that an error in following directions could invalidate your entire exam.

2. Budget your time. Always keep track of the time and avoid getting too involved with one question.

3. **Satisfy the grader.** Remember that the grader cannot read your mind. You must explain every point. Focus on key words and concepts. Tell the grader what you know, don't worry about any points you don't know.

4. Answer every question, even if you must guess.

5. Use all the allotted time. If you finish a section early, go back and reconsider the more difficult questions.

6. Check the answer sheet frequently to see that the number of each answer corresponds to the number of the question you intended. Many examinees get out of sequence on the answer sheet.

7. Stop working immediately when time is called. You do not want to risk being disqualified just to get one last answer recorded.

8. Get up and stretch if you feel sluggish. Walk around if you are allowed. Breathe deeply; focus your eyes on distant objects to avoid eye strain. Do some exercises to relax muscles in the face, neck, fingers, and back.

9. Take enough time to write neatly and organize your answer. Legible, well-organized answers will impress the grader.

10. Remember that you are well-prepared for the CPA Exam, and that you can expect to pass! A confident attitude will help you overcome examination anxiety.

PART TWO: SECTION 4

AICPA CONTENT SPECIFICATION OUTLINES FOR CPA EXAMS
BEGINNING MAY 1996

The AICPA Board of Examiners has developed a revised **Content Specification Outline** of each section of the exam to be tested, effective **May 1996**. These outlines list the areas, groups, and topics to be tested and indicate the approximate percentage of the total test score devoted to each area. The content of the examination is based primarily on the results of two national studies of public accounting practice and the evaluation of CPA practitioners and educators.

Business Law & Professional Responsibilities Section

I. **Professional and Legal Responsibilities (15%)**

    A. Code of Professional Conduct
    B. Proficiency, Independence, and Due Care
    C. Responsibilities in Other Professional Services
    D. Disciplinary Systems Within the Profession
    E. Common Law Liability to Clients and Third Parties
    F. Federal Statutory Liability
    G. Privileged Communications and Confidentiality

II. **Business Organizations (20%)**

    A. Agency

        1. Formation and Termination
        2. Duties of Agents and Principals
        3. Liabilities and Authority of Agents and Principals

    B. Partnership and Joint Ventures

        1. Formation, Operation, and Termination
        2. Liabilities and Authority of Partners and Joint Owners

    C. Corporations

        1. Formation and Operation
        2. Stockholders, Directors, and Officers
        3. Financial Structure, Capital, and Distributions
        4. Reorganization and Dissolution

    D. Estates and Trusts

        1. Formation, Operation, and Termination
        2. Allocation Between Principal and Income
        3. Fiduciary Responsibilities
        4. Distributions

III. **Contracts (10%)**

    A. Formation
    B. Performance
    C. Third-Party Assignments
    D. Discharge, Breach, and Remedies

IV. **Debtor-Creditor Relationships (10%)**

    A. Rights, Duties, and Liabilities of Debtors and Creditors
    B. Rights, Duties, and Liabilities of Guarantors
    C. Bankruptcy

V. **Government Regulation of Business (15%)**

    A. Federal Securities Acts
    B. Employment Regulation
    C. Environmental Regulation

VI. **Uniform Commercial Code (20%)**

    A. Commercial Paper
    B. Sales
    C. Secured Transactions
    D. Bailments and Documents of Title

VII. **Property (10%)**

    A. Real Property
    B. Personal Property
    C. Fire Insurance

PART THREE

BUSINESS LAW & PROFESSIONAL RESPONSIBILITIES
DIAGNOSTIC EXAMINATION

Time Allowance: 120 minutes

1.   A CPA in public practice must be independent in fact and appearance when providing which of the following services?

	Preparation of a tax return	Compilation of of a financial forecast	Compilation of of personal financial statements
a.	Yes	No	No
b.	No	Yes	No
c.	No	No	Yes
d.	No	No	No

(5/90, Aud., #60)

2.   The concept of materiality would be **least** important to an auditor when considering the
a.   Adequacy of disclosure of a client's illegal act.
b.   Discovery of weaknesses in a client's internal control structure.
c.   Effects of a direct financial interest in the client on the CPA's independence.
d.   Decision whether to use positive or negative confirmations of accounts receivable.

(5/91, Aud., #52)

3.   According to the profession's ethical standards, an auditor would be considered independent in which of the following instances?
a.   The auditor's checking account, which is fully insured by a federal agency, is held at a client financial institution.
b.   The auditor is also an attorney who advises the client as its general counsel.
c.   The auditor is an official stock transfer agent for the client.
d.   The client owes the auditor fees for two consecutive annual audits.

(5/89, Aud., #3, amended)

4.   Which of the following statements is correct concerning a CPA's responsibility when the CPA uses taxpayer estimates in preparing a tax return?

a.   Tax preparation requires the CPA to exercise judgment, but prohibits the CPA's use of estimates and approximations.
b.   Use of taxpayer estimates in a tax return is prohibited unless they are specifically disclosed by the CPA.
c.   When all facts relating to a transaction are **not** accurately known because records are missing, reasonable estimates made by the taxpayer of the missing data may be used by the CPA.
d.   The CPA may prepare tax returns involving the use of taxpayer estimates even if it is practical to obtain exact data. (11/91, Aud., #15)

5.   Which of the following general standards apply to consulting services?

	Due professional care	Independence in mental attitude	Planning and supervision
a.	No	Yes	No
b.	No	Yes	Yes
c.	Yes	No	Yes
d.	Yes	No	No

(11/91, Aud., #14, amended)

6.   When performing an audit, a CPA
a.   Must exercise the level of care, skill, and judgment expected of a reasonably prudent CPA under the circumstances.
b.   Must strictly adhere to generally accepted accounting principles.
c.   Is strictly liable for failing to discover client fraud.
d.   Is **not** liable unless the CPA commits gross negligence or intentionally disregards generally accepted auditing standards.

(11/91, Law, #2)

7.   West & Co., CPAs, was engaged by Sand Corp. to audit its financial statements. West issued an unqualified opinion on Sand's financial statements. Sand has been accused of making negligent misrepresentations in the financial statements, which

Reed relied upon when purchasing Sand stock. West was not aware of the misrepresentations nor was it negligent in performing the audit. If Reed sues West for damages based upon Section 10(b) and rule 10b-5 of the Securities Exchange Act of 1934, West will

a. Lose, because Reed relied upon the financial statements.
b. Lose, because the statements contained negligent misrepresentations.
c. Prevail, because some element of scienter must be proved.
d. Prevail, because Reed was **not** in privity of contract with West. (5/88, Law, #8)

8. In a jurisdiction having an accountant-client privilege statute, to whom may a CPA turn over workpapers without a client's permission?

a. Purchaser of the CPA's practice.
b. State tax authorities.
c. State court.
d. State CPA society quality control panel. (5/92, Law, #1)

9. A CPA who prepares clients' federal income tax returns for a fee must

a. File certain required notices and powers of attorney with the IRS before preparing any returns.
b. Keep a completed copy of each return for a specified period of time.
c. Receive client documentation supporting all travel and entertainment expenses deducted on the return.
d. Indicate the CPA's federal identification number on a tax return only if the return reflects tax due from the taxpayer. (11/91, Law, #9)

10. Carson Corp., a retail chain, asked Alto Construction to fix a broken window at one of Carson's stores. Alto offered to make the repairs within three days at a price to be agreed on after the work was completed. A contract based on Alto's offer would fail because of indefiniteness as to the

a. Price involved.
b. Nature of the subject matter.
c. Parties to the contract.
d. Time for performance. (5/91, Law, #12)

11. Dye sent Hill a written offer to sell a tract of land located in Newtown for $60,000. The parties were engaged in a separate dispute. The offer stated that it would be irrevocable for 60 days if Hill would promise to refrain from suing Dye during this time. Hill promptly delivered a promise not to sue during the term of the offer and to forego suit if Hill accepted the offer. Dye subsequently decided that the possible suit by Hill was groundless and therefore phoned Hill and revoked the offer 15 days after making it. Hill mailed an acceptance on the 20th day. Dye did not reply. Under the circumstances,

a. Dye's offer was supported by consideration and was **not** revocable when accepted.
b. Dye's written offer would be irrevocable even without consideration.
c. Dye's silence was an acceptance of Hill's promise.
d. Dye's revocation, **not** being in writing, was invalid. (5/89, Law, #24)

12. Nolan agreed orally with Train to sell Train a house for $100,000. Train sent Nolan a signed agreement and a downpayment of $10,000. Nolan did not sign the agreement, but allowed Train to move into the house. Before closing, Nolan refused to go through with the sale. Train sued Nolan to compel specific performance. Under the provisions of the Statute of Frauds,

a. Train will win because Train signed the agreement and Nolan did **not** object.
b. Train will win because Train made a downpayment and took possession.
c. Nolan will win because Nolan did **not** sign the agreement.
d. Nolan will win because the house was worth more than $500. (5/91, Law, #14)

13. Graham contracted with the city of Harris to train and employ high school dropouts residing in Harris. Graham breached the contract. Long, a resident of Harris and a high school dropout, sued Graham for damages. Under the circumstances, Long will

a. Win, because Long is a third-party beneficiary entitled to enforce the contract.
b. Win, because the intent of the contract was to confer a benefit on all high school dropouts residing in Harris.
c. Lose, because Long is merely an incidental beneficiary of the contract.
d. Lose, because Harris did **not** assign its contract rights to Long. (5/91, Law, #22)

14. Baxter, Inc. and Globe entered into a contract. After receiving valuable consideration from Clay, Baxter assigned its rights under the contract to Clay.

In which of the following circumstances would Baxter **not** be liable to Clay?
a. Clay released Globe.
b. Globe paid Baxter.
c. Baxter released Globe.
d. Baxter breached the contract. (5/92, Law, #31)

15. Jones, CPA, entered into a signed contract with Foster Corp. to perform accounting and review services. If Jones repudiates the contract prior to the date performance is due to begin, which of the following is **not** correct?
a. Foster could successfully maintain an action for breach of contract after the date performance was due to begin.
b. Foster can obtain a judgment ordering Jones to perform.
c. Foster could successfully maintain an action for breach of contract prior to the date performance is due to begin.
d. Foster can obtain a judgment for the monetary damages it incurred as a result of the repudiation. (5/89, Law, #35)

16. Under the UCC Sales Article, which of the following statements is correct concerning a contract involving a merchant seller and a nonmerchant buyer?
a. Only the seller is obligated to perform the contract in good faith.
b. The contract will be either a sale or return or sale on approval contract.
c. The contract may **not** involve the sale of personal property with a price of more than $500.
d. Whether the UCC Sales Article is applicable does **not** depend on the price of the goods involved. (5/91, Law, #43)

17. Which of the following conditions must be met for an implied warranty of fitness for a particular purpose to arise in connection with a sale of goods?

I. The warranty must be in writing.
II. The seller must know that the buyer was relying on the seller in selecting the goods.

a. I only.
b. II only.
c. Both I and II.
d. Neither I nor II. (5/92, Law, #55)

18. Under a contract governed by the UCC Sales Article, which of the following statements is correct?

a. Unless both the seller and the buyer are merchants, neither party is obligated to perform the contract in good faith.
b. The contract will **not** be enforceable if it fails to expressly specify a time and a place for delivery of the goods.
c. The seller may be excused from performance if the goods are accidentally destroyed before the risk of loss passes to the buyer.
d. If the price of the goods is less than $500, the goods need **not** be identified to the contract for title to pass to the buyer. (5/91, Law, #49)

19. Under the UCC Sales Article, a plaintiff who proves fraud in the formation of a contract may
a. Elect to rescind the contract and need **not** return the consideration received from the other party.
b. Be entitled to rescind the contract and sue for damages resulting from the fraud.
c. Be entitled to punitive damages provided physical injuries resulted from the fraud.
d. Rescind the contract even if there was **no** reliance on the fraudulent statement.
(11/91, Law, #22)

20. A bank issues a negotiable instrument that acknowledges receipt of $50,000. The instrument also provides that the bank will repay the $50,000 plus 8% interest per annum to the bearer 90 days from the date of the instrument. The instrument is a
a. Certificate of deposit.
b. Time draft.
c. Trade or banker's acceptance.
d. Cashier's check. (11/88, Law, #36)

21. Hand executed and delivered to Rex a $1,000 negotiable note payable to Rex or bearer. Rex then negotiated it to Ford and endorsed it on the back by merely signing his name. Which of the following is a correct statement?
a. Rex's endorsement was a special endorsement.
b. Rex's endorsement was necessary to Ford's qualification as a holder.
c. The instrument initially being bearer paper **cannot** be converted to order paper.
d. The instrument is bearer paper and Ford can convert it to order paper by writing "pay to the order of Ford" above Rex's signature.
(11/86, Law, #41)

22. For a person to be a holder in due course of a promissory note
a. The note must be payable in U.S. currency to the holder.
b. The holder must be the payee of the note.
c. The note must be negotiable.
d. All prior holders must have been holders in due course. (11/91, Law, #48)

23. Under the UCC, a warehouse receipt
a. Is negotiable if, by its terms, the goods are to be delivered to bearer or to the order of a named person.
b. Will **not** be negotiable if it contains a contractual limitation on the warehouser's liability.
c. May qualify as both a negotiable warehouse receipt and negotiable commercial paper if the instrument is payable either in cash or by the delivery of goods.
d. May be issued only by a bonded and licensed warehouser. (5/92, Law, #49)

24. The procedure necessary to negotiate a document of title depends principally on whether the document is
a. An order document or a bearer document.
b. Issued by a bailee or a consignee.
c. A receipt for goods stored or goods already shipped.
d. A bill of lading or a warehouse receipt.
(5/88, Law, #49)

25. Pix Co., which is engaged in the business of selling appliances, borrowed $18,000 from Lux Bank. Pix executed a promissory note for that amount and pledged all of its customer installment receivables as collateral for the loan. Pix executed a security agreement that described the collateral, but Lux did not file a financing statement. With respect to this transaction
a. Attachment of the security interest did **not** occur because Pix failed to file a financing statement.
b. Perfection of the security interest occurred despite Lux's failure to file a financing statement.
c. Attachment of the security interest took place when the loan was made and Pix executed the security agreement.
d. Perfection of the security interest did **not** occur because accounts receivable are intangibles. (5/91, Law, #57)

26. Carr Corp. sells VCRs and video tapes to the public. Carr sold and delivered a VCR to Sutter on credit. Sutter executed and delivered to Carr a promissory note for the purchase price and a security agreement covering the VCR. Sutter purchased the VCR for personal use. Carr did not file a financing statement. Is Carr's security interest perfected?
a. No, because the VCR was a consumer good.
b. No, because Carr failed to file a financing statement.
c. Yes, because Carr retained ownership of the VCR.
d. Yes, because it was perfected at the time of attachment. (5/91, Law, #58)

27. With regard to a prior perfected security interest in goods for which a financing statement has been filed, which of the following parties is most likely to have a superior interest in the same collateral?
a. A buyer in the ordinary course of business who purchased the goods from a merchant.
b. A subsequent buyer of consumer goods who purchased the goods from another consumer.
c. The trustee in bankruptcy of the debtor.
d. Lien creditors of the debtor. (11/88, Law, #54)

28. To file for bankruptcy under Chapter 7 of the Federal Bankruptcy Code, an individual must
a. Have debts of any amount.
b. Be insolvent.
c. Be indebted to more than three creditors.
d. Have debts in excess of $10,000.
(11/91, Law, #29, amended)

29. Which of the following claims would have the highest priority in the distribution of a bankruptcy estate under the liquidation provisions of Chapter 7 of the Federal Bankruptcy Code if the petition was filed June 1, 1995?
a. Federal tax lien filed May 15, 1995.
b. A secured debt properly perfected on February 10, 1995.
c. Trustee's administration costs filed September 30, 1995.
d. Employee wages due March 30, 1995.
(11/91, Law, #30, amended)

30. Decal Corp. incurred substantial operating losses for the past three years. Unable to meet its current obligations, Decal filed a petition for reorganization under Chapter 11 of the Federal

Bankruptcy Code. Which of the following statements is correct?

a. A creditors' committee, if appointed, will consist of unsecured creditors.

b. The court must appoint a trustee to manage Decal's affairs.

c. Decal may continue in business only with the approval of a trustee.

d. The creditors' committee must select a trustee to manage Decal's affairs. (5/91, Law, #35)

31. Brown was unable to repay a loan from Safe Bank when due. Safe refused to renew the loan unless Brown provided an acceptable surety. Brown asked King, a friend, to act as surety on the loan. To induce King to agree to become a surety, Brown fraudulently represented Brown's financial condition and promised King discounts on merchandise sold at Brown's store. King agree to act as surety and the loan was renewed. Later, Brown's obligation to Safe was discharged in Brown's bankruptcy. Safe wants to hold King liable. King may avoid liability

a. Because the discharge in bankruptcy will prevent King from having a right of reimbursement.

b. Because the arrangement was void at the inception.

c. If King was an uncompensated surety.

d. If King can show that Safe was aware of the fraudulent representations. (11/91, Law, #38)

32. Edwards Corp. lent Lark $200,000. At Edwards' request, Lark entered into an agreement with Owen and Ward for them to act as compensated co-sureties on the loan in the amount of $200,000 each. If Edwards releases Ward without Owen's or Lark's consent, and Lark later defaults, which of the following statements is correct?

a. Lark will be released for 50% of the loan balance.

b. Owen will be liable for the entire loan balance.

c. Owen will be liable for 50% of the loan balance.

d. Edwards' release of Ward will have **no** effect on Lark's and Owen's liability to Edwards. (5/91, Law, #26)

33. If a debtor defaults and the debtor's surety satisfies the obligation, the surety acquires the right of

a. Subrogation.

b. Primary lien.

c. Indemnification.

d. Satisfaction. (11/89, Law, #21)

34. Young was a purchasing agent for Wilson, a sole proprietor. Young had the express authority to place purchase orders with Wilson's suppliers. Young conducted business through the mail and had little contact with Wilson. Young placed an order with Vanguard, Inc. on Wilson's behalf after Wilson was declared incompetent in a judicial proceeding. Young was aware of Wilson's incapacity. With regard to the contract with Vanguard, Wilson (or Wilson's legal representative) will

a. Not be liable because Vanguard dealt only with Young.

b. Not be liable because Young did **not** have authority to enter into the contract.

c. Be liable because Vanguard was unaware of Wilson's incapacity.

d. Be liable because Young acted with express authority. (5/92, Law, #7)

35. When an agent acts for an undisclosed principal, the principal will **not** be liable to third parties if the

a. Principal ratifies a contract entered into by the agent.

b. Agent acts within an implied grant of authority.

c. Agent acts outside the grant of actual authority.

d. Principal seeks to conceal the agency relationship. (11/91, Law, #12)

36. Frost's accountant and business manager has the authority to

a. Mortgage Frost's business property.

b. Obtain bank loans for Frost.

c. Insure Frost's property against fire loss.

d. Sell Frost's business. (5/91, Law, #3)

37. Which of the following statements is correct with respect to the differences and similarities between a corporation and a limited partnership?

a. Directors owe fiduciary duties to the corporation and limited partners owe such duties to the partnership.

b. A corporation and a limited partnership may be created only pursuant to a state statute, and a copy of its organizational document must be filed with the proper state agency.

c. Shareholders may be entitled to vote on corporate matters, whereas limited partners are prohibited from voting on any partnership matters.

d. Stock of a corporation may be subject to the federal securities laws registration requirements, whereas limited partnership interests are automatically exempt from such requirements. (11/88, Law, #5)

38. On dissolution of a general partnership, distributions will be made on account of:

I. Partners' capital accounts
II. Amounts owed partners with respect to profits
III. Amounts owed partners for loans to the partnership

In the following order:
a. III, I, II.
b. I, II, III.
c. II, III, I.
d. III, II, I. (11/91, Law, #17)

39. Gillie, Taft, and Dall are partners in an architectural firm. The partnership agreement is silent about the payment of salaries and the division of profits and losses. Gillie works full-time in the firm, and Taft and Dall each work half-time. Taft invested $120,000 in the firm, and Gillie and Dall invested $60,000 each. Dall is responsible for bringing in 50% of the business, and Gillie and Taft 25% each. How should profits of $120,000 for the year be divided?
a. Gillie $60,000, Taft $30,000, Dall $30,000.
b. Gillie $40,000, Taft $40,000, Dall $40,000.
c. Gillie $30,000, Taft $60,000, Dall $30,000.
d. Gillie $30,000, Taft $30,000, Dall $60,000.
(11/89, Law, #6)

40. Generally, a corporation's articles of incorporation must include all of the following **except** the
a. Name of the corporation's registered agent.
b. Name of each incorporator.
c. Number of authorized shares.
d. Quorum requirements. (5/92, Law, #16)

41. Unless prohibited by the organization documents, a stockholder in a publicly held corporation and the owner of a limited partnership interest both have the right to
a. Ownership of the business' assets.
b. Control management of the business.

c. Assign their interest in the business.
d. An investment that has perpetual life.
(5/92, Law, #17)

42. Opal Corp. declared a 9% stock dividend on its common stock. The dividend
a. Requires a vote of Opal's stockholders.
b. Has **no** effect on Opal's earnings and profits for federal income tax purposes.
c. Is includable in the gross income of the recipient taxpayers in the year of receipt.
d. Must be registered with the SEC pursuant to the Securities Act of 1933. (11/90, Law, #18)

43. Under the Federal Insurance Contributions Act (FICA) and the Social Security Act (SSA),
a. Persons who are self-employed are **not** required to make FICA contributions.
b. Employees who participate in private retirement plans are **not** required to make FICA contributions.
c. Death benefits are payable to an employee's survivors only if the employee dies before reaching the age of retirement.
d. The receipt of earned income by a person who is also receiving social security retirement benefits may result in a reduction of such benefits. (5/89, Law, #37)

44. Unemployment tax payable under the Federal Unemployment Tax Act (FUTA), is
a. Payable by all employers.
b. Deducted from employee wages.
c. Paid to the Social Security Administration.
d. A tax deductible employer's expense.
(5/92, Law, #37)

45. The primary purpose for enacting workers' compensation statutes was to
a. Eliminate all employer-employee negligence lawsuits.
b. Enable employees to recover for injuries regardless of negligence.
c. Prevent employee negligence suits against third parties.
d. Allow employees to recover additional compensation for employer negligence.
(5/91, Law, #38)

46. Under the Securities Act of 1933, an initial offering of securities must be registered with the SEC, unless

a. The offering is made through a broker-dealer licensed in the states in which the securities are to be sold.

b. The offering prospectus makes a fair and full disclosure of all risks associated with purchasing the securities.

c. The issuer's financial condition meets certain standards established by the SEC.

d. The type of security or the offering involved is exempt from registration. (11/91, Law, #37)

47. Hamilton Corp. is making a $4,500,000 securities offering under Rule 505 of Regulation D of the Securities Act of 1933. Under this regulation, Hamilton is

a. Required to provide full financial information to accredited investors only.

b. Allowed to make the offering through a general solicitation.

c. Limited to selling to **no** more than 35 nonaccredited investors.

d. Allowed to sell to an unlimited number of investors both accredited and nonaccredited.
(11/90, Law, #44)

48. Pace Corp. previously issued 300,000 shares of its common stock. The shares are now actively traded on a national securities exchange. The original offering was exempt from registration under the Securities Act of 1933. Pace has $2,500,000 in assets and 425 shareholders. With regard to the Securities Exchange Act of 1934, Pace is

a. Required to file a registration statement because its assets exceed $2,000,000 in value.

b. Required to file a registration statement even though it has fewer than 500 shareholders.

c. Not required to file a registration statement because the original offering of its stock was exempt from registration.

d. Not required to file a registration statement unless insiders own at least 5% of its outstanding shares of stock. (5/89, Law, #41)

49. The registration provisions of the Securities Exchange Act of 1934 require disclosure of all of the following information **except** the

a. Names of owners of at least five (5) percent of any class of nonexempt equity security.

b. Bonus and profit-sharing arrangements.

c. Financial structure and nature of the business.

d. Names of officers and directors.
(11/90, Law, #40)

50. Corporations that are exempt from registration under the Securities Exchange Act of 1934 are subject to the Act's

a. Provisions dealing with the filing of annual reports.

b. Provisions imposing periodic audits.

c. Antifraud provisions.

d. Proxy solicitation provisions. (11/90, Law, #41)

51. For an offering to be exempt under Regulation D of the Securities Act of 1933, Rules 505 and 506 both require that

a. There be a maximum of 35 unaccredited investors.

b. All purchasers receive the issuer's financial information.

c. The SEC be notified within 10 days of the first sale.

d. The offering be made without general advertising. (5/92, Law, #45)

52. A tenant's personal property will become a fixture and belong to the landlord if its removal would

a. Increase the value of the personal property.

b. Cause a material change to the personal property.

c. Result in substantial harm to the landlord's property.

d. Change the use of the landlord's property back to its prior use. (11/91, Law, #51)

53. Konrad, Van, and Star own a parcel of land as joint tenants with right of survivorship. Konrad's interest was sold to Dawson. As a result of the sale from Konrad to Dawson,

a. Van and Star each own one-third of the land as tenants in common.

b. Van, Star, and Dawson each own one-third of the land as joint tenants.

c. Dawson owns one-third of the land as a joint tenant.

d. Dawson owns one-third of the land as a tenant in common. (11/91, Law, #52)

54. On February 2, Mazo deeded a warehouse to Parko for $450,000. Parko did not record the deed. On February 12, Mazo deeded the same warehouse to Nexis for $430,000. Nexis was aware of the prior conveyance to Parko. Nexis recorded its deed before Parko recorded. Who would prevail under the following recording status?

	Notice statute	Race statute	Race-Notice statute
a.	Nexis	Parko	Parko
b.	Parko	Nexis	Parko
c.	Parko	Nexis	Nexis
d.	Parko	Parko	Nexis

(5/90, Law, #55)

55. A mortgage on real property must
a. Be acknowledged by the mortgagee.
b. State the exact amount of the debt.
c. State the consideration given for the mortgage.
d. Be delivered to the mortgagee.

(11/91, Law, #55)

56. Mason Co. maintained two standard fire insurance policies on one of its warehouses. Both policies included an 80% coinsurance clause and a typical "other insurance" clause. One policy was with Ace Fire Insurance, Inc., for $24,000, and the other was with Thrifty Casualty Insurance Co., for $16,000. At a time when the warehouse was worth $100,000, a fire in the warehouse caused a $40,000 loss. What amounts can Mason recover from Ace and Thrifty, respectively?
a. $0 and $0.
b. $10,000 and $10,000.
c. $12,000 and $8,000.
d. $24,000 and $16,000.

(11/91, Law, #60)

57. On February 1, Papco Corp. entered into a contract to purchase an office building from Merit Company for $500,000 with closing scheduled for March 20. On February 2, Papco obtained a $400,000 standard fire insurance policy from Abex Insurance Company. On March 15, the office building sustained a $90,000 fire loss. On March 15, which of the following is correct?

I. Papco has an insurable interest in the building.
II. Merit has an insurable interest in the building.

a. I only.
b. II only.
c. Both I and II.
d. Neither I nor II.

(11/90, Law, #60)

58. Which of the following is **not** necessary to create an express trust?
a. A trust corpus.
b. A successor trustee.
c. A valid trust purpose.
d. A beneficiary.

(11/91, Law, #18)

59. On January 1, 1988, Dix transferred certain assets into a trust. The assets consisted of Lux Corp. bonds with a face amount of $500,000 and an interest rate of 12%. The trust instrument named Dix as trustee, Dix's child as life beneficiary, and Dix's grandchild as remainderman. Interest on the bonds is payable semiannually on May 1 and November 1. Dix had purchased the bonds at their face amount. As of January 1, 1988, the bonds had a fair market value of $600,000. The accounting period selected for the trust is a calendar year. The trust instrument is silent as to whether Dix may revoke the trust. Assuming the trust is valid, how should the amount of interest received in 1988 be allocated between principal and income if the trust instrument is otherwise silent?

	Principal	Income
a.	$0	$60,000
b.	$0	$72,000
c.	$10,000	$50,000
d.	$12,000	$60,000

(11/89, Law, #9)

60. A personal representative of an estate would breach fiduciary duties if the personal representative
a. Combined personal funds with funds of the estate so that both could purchase treasury bills.
b. Represented the estate in a lawsuit brought against it by a disgruntled relative of the decedent.
c. Distributed property in satisfaction of the decedent's debts.
d. Engaged a non-CPA to prepare the records for the estate's final accounting. (5/89, Law, #19)

ANSWERS TO BUSINESS LAW DIAGNOSTIC EXAM

1. d	6. a	11. a	16. d	21. d	26. d	31. d	36. c	41. c	46. d	51. d	56. c
2. c	7. c	12. b	17. b	22. c	27. a	32. c	37. b	42. b	47. c	52. c	57. c
3. a	8. d	13. c	18. c	23. a	28. a	33. a	38. a	43. d	48. b	53. d	58. b
4. c	9. b	14. a	19. b	24. a	29. b	34. b	39. b	44. d	49. a	54. b	59. c
5. c	10. a	15. b	20. a	25. c	30. a	35. c	40. d	45. b	50. c	55. d	60. a

---

PERFORMANCE BY TOPICS

Diagnostic exam question numbers corresponding to each chapter of your Business Law & Professional Responsibilities text are listed below. To assess your preparedness for the CPA Exam, record the number and percentage of questions you correctly answered in each topic area.

Chapter 58: Ethics and Professional Responsibilities

Question #	Correct √
1	✓
2	
3	
4	
5	
# Questions	5

Correct _____
% Correct _____

Chapter 59: Accountant's Professional Liability

Question #	Correct √
6	
7	✓
8	
9	
# Questions	4

Correct _____
% Correct _____

Chapter 43: Contracts

Question #	Correct √
10	
11	
12	
13	
14	
15	✓
# Questions	6

Correct _____
% Correct _____

Chapter 44: Sales

Question #	Correct √
16	
17	
18	
19	
# Questions	4

Correct _____
% Correct _____

Chapter 45: Commercial Paper

Question #	Correct √
20	
21	
22	✓
# Questions	3

Correct _____
% Correct _____

Chapter 46: Documents of Title and Investment Securities

Question #	Correct √
23	✓
24	
# Questions	2

Correct _____
% Correct _____

Chapter 47: Secured Transactions

Question #	Correct √
25	
26	
27	
# Questions	3

Correct _____
% Correct _____

Chapter 48: Bankruptcy

Question #	Correct √
28	
29	
30	
# Questions	3

Correct _____
% Correct _____

Chapter 49: Suretyship

Question #	Correct √
31	
32	
33	
# Questions	3

Correct _____
% Correct _____

Chapter 50: Agency

Question #	Correct √
34	✓
35	
36	
# Questions	3

Correct _____
% Correct _____

Chapter 51: Partnerships

Question #	Correct √
37	
38	
39	
# Questions	3

Correct _____
% Correct _____

Chapter 52: Corporations

Question #	Correct √
40	
41	
42	
# Questions	3

Correct _____
% Correct _____

Chapter 54: Regulation of Employment

Question #	Correct √
43	
44	
45	
# Questions	3

Correct _____
% Correct _____

Chapter 55: Federal Securities Regulations

Question #	Correct √
46	
47	
48	✓
49	
50	
51	
# Questions	6

Correct _____
% Correct _____

Chapter 56: Real and Personal Property

Question #	Correct √
52	
53	
54	
55	
# Questions	4
# Correct	_____
% Correct	_____

Chapter 57: Fire and Casualty Insurance

Question #	Correct √
56	
57	
# Questions	2
# Correct	_____
% Correct	_____

Chapter 53: Estates and Trusts

Question #	Correct √
58	
59	
60	
# Questions	3
# Correct	_____
% Correct	_____

Frequently Tested Areas

Although the new format of the exam and the many changes in content coverage make it difficult to know with certainty what the AICPA will now ask, we can use exam history to highlight those areas which have been emphasized. Based on analysis of past exams, we have identified the following areas as those most heavily tested in the past. We have also identified those tested the least. Keep in mind, however, that there is the potential for **any area to be tested**.

Heavy		Light	
Ch. 43	Contracts	Ch. 46	Documents of Title & Investment Securities
Ch. 44	Sales	Ch. 49	Suretyship
Ch. 45	Commercial Paper	Ch. 52	Corporations
Ch. 47	Secured Transactions	Ch. 57	Fire & Casualty Insurance
Ch. 48	Bankruptcy		
Ch. 51	Partnerships		
Ch. 53	Estates & Trusts		
Ch. 55	Federal Securities Regulations		
Ch. 56	Real & Personal Property		
Ch. 58	Ethics & Professional Responsibilities		
Ch. 59	Accountant's Professional Liability		

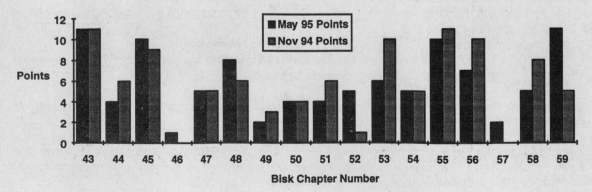

Business Law & Professional Responsibilities Coverage by Bisk Chapter

ACCOUNTING FOR 5%

CONTENTS

- Introduction   G-1
- Writing Skills Samples   G-2
- Paragraphs   G-3
- Writing an Answer to an Exam Question   G-6
- Diagnostic Quiz   G-8
- Sentence Structure   G-11
- Numbers   G-17
- Capitalization   G-18
- Punctuation   G-18
- Spelling   G-21
- Grammar   G-24

INTRODUCTION

Writing skills are utilized extensively in interactions with clients, colleagues, and other professionals. In response to the increasing need for good communication skills within the accounting profession, the AICPA began testing candidates on their writing skills with the May 1994 CPA Exam.

To assess candidates' writing skills, answers to selected essay responses from Business Law & Professional Responsibilities, Auditing, and Financial Accounting & Reporting sections will be used. Five percent of the points available on each of these sections will be allocated to writing skills.

If an essay question is divided into parts a, b, and c, for example, each of these parts is considered a separate response. It is possible that only one of these three parts will be graded for writing skills. However, at least two responses from each section will be used for this assessment. These responses may or may not be from the same question, but they will cover different technical areas. Therefore, if a question is graded differently for writing skills, then the number of points allocated to the technical concepts of the essay is reduced so that the total number of points per question does not change.

The AICPA considers the following six characteristics to constitute effective writing and will make its evaluations of candidates' writing skills based on these criteria:

1. **Coherent organization.** Does each paragraph begin with a topic sentence? Are ideas arranged logically, and do they flow smoothly?

2. **Conciseness.** Are complete thoughts presented in the fewest possible words?

3. **Clarity.** Are sentences constructed properly? Are meanings and reasons clear? Are proper technical terminology and key words and phrases used?

4. **Standard English.** Is your work free from nonstandard usage; that is, does it demonstrate proper spelling, punctuation, capitalization, diction, and knowledgeable usage choices?

5. **Responsiveness to the requirements of the question.** Make sure your answers respond directly to the question and are not broad discourses on the general subject.

6. **Appropriateness for the reader.** If not otherwise mentioned in the question, you should assume that the reader is a CPA. Questions asking that you write something for a client or anyone else with less technical knowledge should be answered with that particular audience in mind.

If you are not convinced that the five points in a section will make a significant difference, consider this: of the passing grades in each section, the vast majority are scored at 75, the minimum. For many candidates, therefore, writing skills may determine whether or not they pass a section.

> **TOTALTIP:** When writing your exam answers, write on **every other line only**. This will give you space for editing.

Accounting for 5% has been designed primarily to help CPA candidates polish their writing skills. Beyond this purpose, we hope that it will continue to serve as a useful reference in the future.

Before skipping this Foreword, review at least the following writing samples and the "Writing an Answer to an Exam Question" starting on page G-6. Be sure to take the Diagnostic Quiz beginning on G-8.

WRITING SKILLS SAMPLES

The following problems taken from past exams are answered in various ways to illustrate good, fair, and poor writing skills.

Business Law & Professional Responsibilities Problem

One of your firm's clients, Fancy Fashions, Inc., is a highly successful, rapidly expanding company. The company is owned predominately by the Munn family and key corporate officers. Although additional funds would be available on a short-term basis from its bankers, this would represent only a short-term solution to the company's need for capital to fund its expansion plans. In addition, the interest rates being charged are not appealing. Therefore, John Munn, Fancy's chairman of the board, in consultation with the other shareholders, has decided to explore raising additional equity capital of approximately $5.5 to $6 million which will provide the funds necessary to continue the growth and expansion of the company. This will be Fancy's first offering to persons other than the Munn family and key management personnel.

At a meeting of Fancy's major shareholders, its attorneys, and a CPA from your firm, the advantages and disadvantages of "going public" and registering an offering of its stock were discussed. One of the participants suggested that Regulation D under the Securities Act of 1933 might be a preferable alternative.

Assume there is a public offering for $5.5 million and, as a result, more than 500 persons own shares of Fancy. What implications, if any, will these facts have in respect to the Securities Exchange Act of 1934?

Good: Since the sale of equity securities results in more than 500 persons owning stock, coupled with the fact that Fancy will have more than $5 million of assets, the corporation will be subjected to the full application of the Securities Exchange Act of 1934. As such, it will be required to register pursuant to the Act and thereby become subject to the Act's reporting, insider trading, proxy, and other requirements.

Explanation: This is a good example of a tightly constructed, well-developed paragraph even though it contains only two sentences. The first sentence explains how the sale of securities makes the company subject to the Act, and the second sentence explains what the company will need to do and the result. There are no extraneous words, and the language is appropriate for the reader.

Fair: Fancy Fashions will have to register with the Securities and Exchange Comission because it will have more than 500 persons who own stock. Also because the company will have more than $5 million dollars in assets.

Explanation: Although this answer is essentially correct and addresses the question, it does not give enough detail nor is it as tightly or well constructed as the previous answer. The second sentence is not a complete sentence.

Poor: The Securities and Exchange Act of 1934 effects corporations with stock on the stock market. If this company has alot of stock it will have to register under this act with the SEC. To register with the SEC, you must file form 10-K and some other things.

Explanation: This paragraph is rather vague in attempting to address the question and fails to provide any details regarding implications. The mention of Form 10-K is inconsequential to the answer. The language is too informal, and the second sentence ignores the rules of parallel construction.

PARAGRAPHS

The kind of writing you do for the CPA Exam is called **expository writing** (writing in which something is explained in straightforward terms). Expository writing uses the basic techniques we will be discussing here. Other kinds of writing (i.e., narration, description, argument, and persuasion) will sometimes require different techniques.

Consider a paragraph as a division of an essay that consists of one or more sentences, deals with one point, and begins on a new, indented line. Paragraphs provide a way to write about a subject one point or one thought at a time.

Usually, a paragraph begins with a **topic sentence**. The topic sentence communicates the main idea of the paragraph, and the remainder of the paragraph explains or illuminates that central idea. The paragraph sometimes finishes with a restatement of the topic sentence. This format is easily read by the exam graders.

Often the topic sentence of the first paragraph is the central idea of the entire composition. Each succeeding paragraph then breaks down this idea into subtopics with each of the new topic sentences being the central thought of that subtopic.

Let's take a look at a simple paragraph to see how it's put together.

> The deductibility of home mortgage interest has been under recent review by Congress as a way to raise revenue. There have been two major reasons for this scrutiny. First, with consumer interest soon to be totally nondeductible and with investment interest being limited to net investment income, taxpayers would be motivated to rearrange their finances to maximize their tax deductions. Second, most voters do not own homes costing more than $500,000 and, therefore, putting a cap on mortgage loans does not affect the mass of voters. Given the pressure to raise revenue, two major changes have occurred in this area.

The first sentence of the example is the **topic sentence**. The second sentence introduces the supporting examples which appear in the next two sentences beginning with *first* and *second*. The final sentence of the paragraph acts as a preview to the contents of the next paragraph.

Now, let's examine the makeup of a single paragraph answer to a Business Law Exam essay question.

> Question: Dunhill fraudulently obtained a negotiable promissory note from Beeler by misrepresentation of a material fact. Dunhill subsequently negotiated the note to Gordon, a holder in due course. Pine, a business associate of Dunhill, was aware of the fraud perpetrated by Dunhill. Pine purchased the note for value from Gordon. Upon presentment, Beeler has defaulted on the note.
>
> Required: Answer the following, setting forth reasons for any conclusions stated.
>
> 1. What are the rights of Pine against Beeler?
> 2. What are the rights of Pine against Dunhill?

Examples of possible answers:

> 1.   The rights of Pine against Beeler arise from Pine's having acquired the note from Gordon, who was a holder in due course. Pine himself is not a holder in due course because he had knowledge of a defense against the note. The rule wherein a transferee, not a holder in due course, acquires the rights of one by taking from a holder in due course is known as the "shelter rule." Through these rights, Pine is entitled to recover the proceeds of the note from Beeler. The defense of fraud in the inducement is a personal defense and not valid against a holder in due course.

The first sentence of the paragraph is the topic sentence in which the basic answer to the question is given. The third and fourth sentence explains the rule governing Pine's rights. (The *shelter rule* would be considered a *key phrase* in this answer.) The final sentence of the paragraph is not really necessary to answer the question but was added as an explanation of what some might mistakenly believe to be the key to the answer.

> 2.   As one with the rights of a holder in due course, Pine is entitled to proceed against any person whose signature appears on the note, provided he gives notice of dishonor. When Dunhill negotiated the note to Gordon, Dunhill's signature on the note made him secondarily liable. As a result, if Pine brings suit against Dunhill, Pine will prevail because of Dunhill's secondary liability.

The first sentence of this paragraph restates the fact that Pine has the rights of a holder in due course and what these rights mean. The second sentence explains what happened when Dunhill negotiated the note, and the third sentence states the probable outcome of these results.

Note that in both answers 1. and 2., the sentences hang together in a logical fashion and lead the reader easily from one thought to the next. This is called *coherence*, a primary factor in considerations of conciseness and clarity.

Transitions

To demonstrate how to use **transitions** in a paragraph to carry the reader easily from one thought or example to another, let's consider a slightly longer and more detailed paragraph. The transitions are indicated in italics.

> A concerted effort to reduce book income in response to AMT could have a significant impact on corporations. *For example,* the auditor-client relationship may change. *Currently,* it isn't unusual for corporate management to argue for higher rather than lower book earnings, *while* the auditor would argue for conservative reported numbers. Such a corporate reporting posture may change as a consequence of the BURP adjustment. *Furthermore,* stock market analysts often rely on a price/earnings ratio. Lower earnings for essentially the same level of activity may have a significant effect on security prices.

The first sentence of the paragraph is the topic sentence. The next sentence, beginning with the transition *for example,* introduces the example with a broad statement. The following sentence, beginning with *currently,* gives a specific example to support the basic premise. The sentence beginning *furthermore* leads us into a final example. Without these transitions, the paragraph would be choppy and lack coherence.

What follows is a list of some transitions divided by usage. We suggest you commit some of these to memory so that you will never be at a loss as to how to tie your ideas together.

Transitional Words and Phrases

One idea plus one idea:

again	equally important	in addition	likewise	similarly
also	finally	in the same fashion	moreover	third
and	first	in the same respect	next	thirdly
and then	further	last	second	too
besides	furthermore	lastly	secondly	

To show time or place:

after a time	before	lately	soon
after a while	earlier	later	temporarily
afterwards	eventually	meanwhile	then
as long as	finally	next	thereafter
as soon as	first	of late	thereupon
at last	further	presently	to the left
at length	immediately	second	until
at that time	in due time	shortly	when
at the same time	in the meantime	since	while

To contrast or qualify:

after all	but	in contrast	on the contrary
although true	despite this fact	in spite of	on the other hand
and yet	for all that	nevertheless	otherwise
anyway	however	nonetheless	still
at the same time	in any case	notwithstanding	yet

To introduce an illustration:

for example	in other words	namely	to illustrate
for instance	in summary	specifically	
in fact	incidentally	that is	
in particular	indeed	thus	

To indicate concession:

after all
although this may be true
at the same time
even though
I admit
naturally
of course

To indicate comparison:

in a like manner
likewise
similarly

WRITING AN ANSWER TO AN EXAM QUESTION

Now that we have examined the makeup of an answer to an exam question, let's take an actual question from a past Business Law Exam and see how to go about writing a clear, comprehensive answer, step by step, sentence by sentence. A question similar to the one that follows would very likely be one for which the examiners would choose to grade writing skills.

Question:

Bar Manufacturing and Cole Enterprises were arch rivals in the high technology industry, and both were feverishly working on a new product which would give the first to develop it a significant competitive advantage. Bar engaged Abel Consultants on April 1, 1983, for one year, commencing immediately, at $7,500 a month to aid the company in the development of the new product. The contract was oral and was consummated by a handshake. Cole approached Abel and offered them a $10,000 bonus for signing, $10,000 a month for nine months, and a $40,000 bonus if Cole was the first to successfully market the new product. In this connection, Cole stated that the oral contract Abel made with Bar was unenforceable and that Abel could walk away from it without liability. In addition, Cole made certain misrepresentations regarding the dollar amount of its commitment to the project, the state of its development, and the expertise of its research staff. Abel accepted the offer.

Four months later, Bar successfully introduced the new product. Cole immediately dismissed Abel and has paid nothing beyond the first four $10,000 payments plus the initial bonus. Three lawsuits ensued: Bar sued Cole, Bar sued Abel, and Abel sued Cole.

Required: Answer the following, setting forth reasons for any conclusions stated.

Discuss the various theories on which each of the three lawsuits is based, the defenses which will be asserted, the measure of possible recovery, and the probable outcome of the litigation.

Composing an Answer:

Analyze requirements.

Plan on one paragraph for each lawsuit. Each paragraph will contain four elements: theory, defenses, recovery, and outcome.

Paragraph one:

Step 1: Begin with the first lawsuit mentioned, Bar vs. Cole. Write a topic sentence which will sum up the theory of the suit.

> **Topic sentence containing basic theory of the suit:** Bar's lawsuit against Cole will be based upon the intentional tort of wrongful interference with a contractual relationship.

Step 2: Back up this statement with law and facts from the question scenario.

> The primary requirement for this cause of action is a valid contractual relationship with which the defendant knowingly interferes. This requirement is met in the case of Cole.

Step 3: State defenses.

> The contract is not required to be in writing since it is for exactly one year from the time of its making. It is, therefore, valid even though oral.

Step 4: Introduce subject of recovery (damages).

> Cole's knowledge of the contract is obvious.

Step 5: Explain possible problems to recovery.

The principal problem, however, is damages. Since Bar was the first to market the product successfully, it would seem that damages are not present. It is possible there were actual damages incurred by Bar (for example, it hired another consulting firm at an increased price).

Step 6: Discuss possible outcome.

It also might be possible that some courts would permit the recovery of punitive damages since this is an intentional tort.

Thus, the complete paragraph reads as follows:

Bar's lawsuit against Cole will be based upon the intentional tort of wrongful interference with a contractual relationship. The primary requirement for this cause of action is a valid contractual relationship with which the defendant knowingly interferes. The requirement is met in the case of Cole. The contract is not required to be in writing since it is for exactly one year from the time of its making. It is, therefore, valid even though oral. Cole's knowledge of the contract is obvious. The principal problem, however, is damages. Since Bar was the first to market the product successfully, it would seem that damages are not present. It is possible there were actual damages incurred by Bar (for example, it hired another consulting firm at an increased price). It also might be possible that some courts would permit the recovery of punitive damages since this is an intentional tort.

Paragraph two:

Step 1: Discuss second lawsuit mentioned, Bar vs. Abel. Write a topic sentence which will sum up the theory of the suit.

Topic sentence containing basic theory of the suit: Bar's cause of action against Abel would be for breach of contract.

Step 2: State defenses. [*Same as for first paragraph; this could be left out.*]

The contract is not required to be in writing since it is for exactly one year from the time of its making. It is, therefore, valid even though oral.

Step 3: Introduce subject of recovery (damages).

Once again, [*indicating similarity and tying second paragraph to first*] damages would seem to be a serious problem.

Step 4: Explain possible problems to recovery.

Furthermore, punitive damages would rarely be available in a contract action. Finally, Bar cannot recover the same damages twice.

Step 5: Discuss possible outcome.

Hence, if it proceeds against Cole and recovers damages caused by Abel's breach of contract, it will not be able to recover a second time.

Thus, the complete paragraph reads as follows:

Bar's cause of action against Abel would be for breach of contract. [The contract is not required to be in writing since it is for exactly one year from the time of its making. It is, therefore, valid even though oral.] Once again, damages would seem to be a serious problem. Furthermore, punitive damages would rarely be available in a contract action. Finally, Bar cannot recover the same damages twice. Hence, if it proceeds against Cole and recovers damages caused by Abel's breach of contract, it will not be able to recover a second time.

Paragraph three:

Step 1: Discuss third lawsuit mentioned, Abel vs. Cole. Write a topic sentence which will sum up the theory of the suit.

Topic sentence containing basic theory of the suit: Abel's lawsuit against Cole will be based upon fraud and breach of contract.

Step 2: State defenses.

There were fraudulent statements made by Cole with the requisite intent and that were possibly to Abel's detriment. The breach of contract by Cole is obvious.

Step 3: Back up these statements with law and facts from the question scenario.

However, the contract that Cole induced Abel to enter into and which it subsequently breached was an illegal contract, that is, one calling for the commission of a tort.

Step 4: Explain possible problems to recovery and possible outcome.

Therefore, both parties are likely to be treated as wrongdoers, and Abel will be denied recovery.

Thus, the complete paragraph reads as follows:

Abel's lawsuit against Cole will be based upon fraud and breach of contract. There were fraudulent statements made by Cole with the requisite intent and that were possibly to Abel's detriment. The breach of contract by Cole is obvious. However, the contract that Cole induced Abel to enter into and which it subsequently breached was an illegal contract, that is, one calling for the commission of a tort. Therefore, both parties are likely to be treated as wrongdoers, and Abel will be denied recovery.

Paragraph Editing:

After you have written your essay, go back over your work to check for the six characteristics that the AICPA will be looking for; coherent organization, conciseness, clarity, use of standard English, responsiveness to the requirements of the question, and appropriateness to the reader.

DIAGNOSTIC QUIZ

The following quiz is designed to test your knowledge of standard English, and grammar in particular. The correct answers follow the quiz, along with references to the sections which cover that particular area. By identifying the sections that are troublesome for you, you will be able to assess your weaknesses and concentrate on reviewing these areas. Consequently, only a brief review of the areas associated with the items you answered correctly will be necessary. If you simply made a lucky guess, you'd better do a quick review anyway.

Circle the correct choice in the brackets for the following:

1.   The company can assert any defenses against third party beneficiaries that [they have/it has] against the promisee.

2. Among those securities [which/that] are exempt from registration under the 1933 Act [are/is] a class of stock given in exchange for another class by the issuer to its existing stockholders without the [issuer's/issuer] paying a commission.

3. This type of promise will not bind the promisor [as/because/since] there is no mutuality of obligation.

4. Under the cost method, treasury stock is presented on the balance sheet as an unallocated reduction of total [stockholders'/stockholders/stockholder's] equity.

5. Jones wished that he [was/were] not bound by the offer he made Smith, while Smith celebrated [his/him] having accepted the offer.

6. [Non-cash/Noncash] investing and financing transactions are not reported in the statement of cash flows because the statement reports only the [affects/effects] of operating, investing, and financing activities that directly [affect/effect] cash flows.

7. Since [its/it's] impossible to predict the future and because prospective financial statements can be [effected/affected] by numerous factors, the accountant must use [judgment/judgement] to estimate when and how conditions are [likely/liable] to change.

8. A common format of bank reconciliation statements [is/are] to reconcile both book and bank balances to a common amount known as the "true balance."

9. Corporations, clubs, churches, and other entities may be beneficiaries so long as they are sufficiently identifiable to permit a determination of [who/whom] is empowered to enforce the terms of the trust.

10. None of the beneficiaries [was/were] specifically referred to in the will.

11. Either Dr. Kline or Dr. Monroe [have/has] been elected to the board of directors.

12. The letter should be signed by Bill and [me/myself].

13. Any trust [which/that] is created for an illegal purpose is invalid.

14. When the nature of relevant information is such that it cannot appear in the accounts, this [principal/principle] dictates that such relevant information be included in the accompanying notes to the financial statements. Financial reporting is the [principal/principle] means of communicating financial information to those outside an entity.

15. The inheritance was divided [between/among] several beneficiaries.

16. Termination of an offer ends the offeree's power to [accept/except] it.

17. The consideration given by the participating creditors is [their/there] mutual promises to [accept/except] less than the full amount of [their/there] claims. Because [their/there] must be such mutual promises [between/among] all the participating creditors, a composition or extension agreement requires the participation of at least two or more creditors.

Follow instructions for each of the following items:

18. The duties assigned to the interns were to accompany the seniors on field work assignments and the organization and filing of the work papers.

    Fix this sentence so that it will read more smoothly. _____

    _____

    _____

19. Circle the correct spelling of the following pairs of words.

liaison laison   privilege priviledge   supersede supercede

achieve acheive   occasion occassion   accommodate accomodate

20. Each set of brackets in the following example represents a possible location for punctuation. If you believe a location needs no punctuation, leave it blank; if you think a location needs punctuation, enter a comma, a colon, or a semicolon.

If the promises supply the consideration [ ] there must be a mutuality of obligation [ ] in other words [ ] both parties must be bound.

ANSWERS TO DIAGNOSTIC QUIZ

Each answer includes a reference to the section that covers what you need to review.

1.	it has	Pronouns—Antecedents, p. G-31.
2.	that; is; issuer's	Subordinating Conjunctions, p. G-35; Verbs —Agreement, p. G-27; Nouns—Gerunds, p. G-29.
3.	because	Subordinating Conjunctions, p. G-35.
4.	stockholders'	Possessive Nouns, p. G-29.
5.	were; his	Verbs, p. G-24; Subjunctive Mood, p. G-25; Nouns—Gerunds, p. G-29.
6.	Noncash; effects; affect	Hyphens, p. G-21; Troublesome Words: Misused or Confused Terminology, p. G-14.
7.	it's; affected; judgment, likely	Troublesome Words: Misused or Confused Terminology, p. G-14; Troublesome Words: Spelling, p. G-21; Diction, List of Words p. G-11.
8.	is	Verbs—Agreement, p. G-27.
9.	who	Pronouns, Who/Whom, p. G-30.
10.	were	Verbs—Agreement with Each/None, p. G-28.
11.	has	Verbs—Agreement, p. G-27.
12.	me	Pronouns, that follow prepositions, p. G-31.
13.	that	Subordinating Conjunctions, p. G-35.
14.	principle; principal	Troublesome Words: Misused or Confused Terminology, p. G-14.
15.	among	Diction, List of Words, p. G-11.
16.	accept	Troublesome Words: Misused or Confused Terminology, p. G-14.

17.   their; accept; their; there; among;   Troublesome Words: Misused or Confused Terminology, p. G-14, G-16; Diction, List of Words, p. G-11.

18.   Two possible answers: Refer to Parallelism, p. G-17.

The duties assigned to the interns were *accompanying* the seniors on field work assignments and *organizing* and filing the work papers.
or
The duties assigned to the interns were to accompany the seniors on field work assignments and *to organize* and *file* the work papers.

19.   In every case, the **first choice** is the correct spelling.
Refer to Troublesome Words: Spelling, p. G-21.

20.   If the promises supply the consideration [,] there must be a mutuality of obligation [;] in other words [,] both parties must be bound.   Refer to Punctuation, p. G-18.

SCORING

Count one point for each item (some numbers contain more than one item) and one point for question number 18 if your sentence came close to the parallelism demonstrated by the answer choices. There are a total of 40 points.

If you scored 37-40, you did very well. A brief review of the items you missed should be sufficient to make you feel fairly confident about your grammar skills.

If you scored 33-36, you did fairly well—better than average—but you should do a thorough review of the items you missed.

If you scored 29-32, your score was average. Since "average" will probably not make it on the CPA Exam, you might want to consider a thorough grammar review, in addition to the items you missed.

If you scored below average (28 or less), you **definitely** should make grammar review a high priority when budgeting your exam study time.

SENTENCE STRUCTURE

A sentence is a statement or question, consisting of a subject and a predicate. A subject, at a minimum is a noun, usually accompanied by one or more modifiers (for example, "The Trial Balance"). A predicate consists, at a minimum, of a verb. Cultivate the habit of a quick verification for a subject, predicate, capitalized first word, and ending punctuation in each sentence of an essay.

A study of sentence structure is essentially a study of grammar but also moves just beyond grammar to diction, syntax, and parallelism. **Diction** is appropriate word choice. **Syntax** is the order of words in a sentence. In **parallelism,** parts of a sentence (or a paragraph) that are parallel in meaning are also parallel in structure. As we discuss how sentences are structured, there will naturally be some overlapping with grammar.

Diction

There is no substitute for a diversified vocabulary. If you have a diversified vocabulary or "a way with words," you are already a step ahead. A good general vocabulary, as well as a good accounting vocabulary, is a prerequisite of the exam. Develop your vocabulary as you review for the exam.

An important aspect of choosing the right words is knowing the audience for whom you are choosing those "perfect words." A perfect word for accountants is not necessarily the perfect word for mechanics or even lawyers or English professors. If a CPA Exam essay question asks you to write a specific document for a reader other than another accountant or CPA, you would need to be very specific but less technical than you would be otherwise.

Anyone who has waded through the statements of the FASB, and other legal and accounting literature knows that the language and sentence structure can be difficult. Nevertheless, accounting, auditing, and related areas do have a certain diction and syntax peculiar unto themselves. Complain as we may about the complexity of the sentence structure, we would be hard-pressed to construct the sentences much differently to convey the same meaning. Promulgations, for instance, are written very carefully so as to avoid possible misinterpretations or misunderstandings. Of course, you are not expected to write like this—for the CPA Exam or in other situations. Find the best word possible to explain clearly and concisely what it is you are trying to say. Often the "right word" is simply just not the "wrong word," so be certain you know the exact meaning of a word before you use it. As an accountant writing for accountants, what is most important is knowing the technical terms and the "key words" and placing them in your sentences properly and effectively. Defining or explaining key words demonstrates to graders that you understand the words you are using and not merely parroting the jargon.

As we work through the rest of this section on structure and organization, we will be giving some examples that will demonstrate how important diction can be.

The following is a list of words that frequently either are mistaken for one another or incorrectly assumed to be more or less synonymous.

Among—preposition, refers to more than two
Between—preposition, refers to two
(Between is used for three or more if the items are considered severally and individually.)

If only part of the seller's capacity to perform is affected, the seller must allocate deliveries *among* the customers, and he or she must give each one reasonable notice of the quota available to him or her.

Between merchants, the additional terms become part of the contract unless one of the following applies ...(This sentence is correct whether there are two merchants or many merchants.)

Amount—noun, an aggregate; total number or quantity
Number—noun, a sum of units; a countable number
Quantity—noun, an indefinite amount or number
The checks must be charged to the account in the order of lowest *amount* to highest *amount* to minimize the *number* of dishonored checks.
The contract is not enforceable under this paragraph beyond the *quantity* of goods shown in such writing.

Allude—verb, to state indirectly
Refer—verb, to state clearly and directly

She *alluded* to the fact that the company's management was unscrupulous.
She *referred* to his poor management in her report.

Bimonthly—adjective or adverb; every two months
Semimonthly—adjective or adverb; twice a month

Our company has *bimonthly* meetings.
We get paid *semimonthly*.

Can—verb (auxiliary), to be able
May—verb (auxiliary), to be permitted

Treasury shares *may* be sold for whatever the corporation *can* garner.

The distinction between **can** and **may** has virtually disappeared in speech and in informal writing. In formal writing, however, they are not synonymous.

Continual—adjective, that which is repeatedly renewed after each interruption or intermission
Continuous—adjective, that which is uninterrupted in time, space, or sequence

> The *continuous* ramblings of the managing partner caused the other partners to *continually* check the time.

Cost—noun, the amount paid for an item
Price—noun, the amount set for an item
Value—noun, the relative worth, utility, or importance of an item
Worth—noun, value of an item measured by its qualities or by the esteem in which it is held

> The *cost* of that stock is too much.
> The *price* of that stock is $100 a share.
> I place no *value* on that stock.
> That stock's *worth* is overestimated.

Decide—verb, to arrive at a solution
Conclude—verb, to reach a final determination; to exercise judgment

> Barbara *decided* to listen to what the accountant was saying; she then *concluded* that what he was saying was true.

Fewer—adjective, not as many; consisting of or amounting to a smaller number
(used of numbers; comparative of few)
Less—adjective, lower rank, degree, or importance; a more limited amount
(used of quantity— for the most part)

> My clients require *fewer* consultations than yours do.
> My clients are *less* demanding than yours are.

Good—adjective, of a favorable character or tendency;
   noun, something that is good
Well—adverb, good or proper manner; satisfactorily with respect to conduct or action;
   adjective, being in satisfactory condition or circumstances

> It was *good* [adjective] of you to help me study for the CPA exam.
> The decision was for the *good* [noun] of the firm.
> He performed that task *well* [adverb].
> His work was *well* [adjective] respected by the other accountants.

Imply—verb, to suggest
Infer—verb, to assume; deduce

> Her report seems to *imply* that my work was not up to par.
> From reading her report, the manager *inferred* that my work was not up to par.

Last—adjective, the end in a series or the next before the present; following all the rest
Latest—adjective, coming or remaining after the usual or proper time; last in time

> The bankrupt corporation issued its *last* prospectus.
> The *latest* quarterly report was issued yesterday.

Liable—adjective, a legal obligation; being exposed or subject to some adverse contingency
Likely—adjective, inclination or probability

    If the corporation continues to loose revenue, it is *liable* to fail.
    It is *likely* to fail by the first of the year.

Oral—adjective, by the mouth, spoken; not written
Verbal—adjective, relating to or consisting of words
Vocal—adjective, uttered by the voice, spoken; persistence and volume of speech

    Hawkins, Inc. made an *oral* agreement to the contract.
    One partner gave his *verbal* consent while the other partner was very *vocal* with his objections.

State—verb, to set forth in detail; completely
Assert—verb, to claim positively, sometimes aggressively or controversially
Affirm—verb, to validate, confirm, state positively

    The attorney *stated* the facts of the case.
    The plaintiff *asserted* that his rights had been violated.
    The judge *affirmed* the jury's decision.

Syntax

Errors in syntax occur in a number of ways; the number one way is through hasty composition. The only way to catch errors in word order is to read each of your sentences carefully to make sure that the words you meant to write or type are the words that actually appear on the page and that those words are in the best possible order. The following list should help you avoid errors in both diction and syntax and gives examples where necessary.

Troublesome Words: Misused or Confused Terminology

Accept—verb, to receive or to agree to willingly
Except—verb, to take out or leave out from a number or a whole;
        conjunction, on any other condition but that condition

    Except for the items we have mentioned, we will *accept* the conditions of the contract.

Advice—noun, information or recommendation
Advise—verb, to recommend, give advice

    The accountant *advised* us to take his *advice*.

Affect—verb, to influence or change
        (**Note:** affect is occasionally used as a noun in technical writing only.)
Effect—noun, result or cause;
        verb, to cause

    The *effect* [noun] of Ward, Inc.'s decision to cease operations *affected* many people.
    He quickly *effected* [verb] policy changes for office procedures.

All Ready—adjectival phrase, completely prepared
Already—adverb, before now; previously

    Although the tax return was *all ready* to be filed, the deadline had *already* passed.

All Right; Alright—adjective or adverb, beyond doubt; very well; satisfactory; agreeable, pleasing
(Although many grammarians insist that **alright** is not a proper form, it is widely accepted.)

Appraise—verb, set a value on
Apprise—verb, inform

      Dane Corp. *apprised* him of the equipment's age, so that he could *appraise* it more accurately.

Assure—verb, to give confidence to positively
Ensure—verb, to make sure, certain, or safe
Insure—verb, to obtain or provide insurance on or for; to make certain by taking necessary measures and precautions

      The accountant *assured* his client that he would file his return in a timely manner.
      He added the figures more than once to *ensure* their accuracy.
      She was advised to *insure* her diamond property.

Decedent—noun, a deceased person
Descendant—noun, proceeding from an ancestor or source

      The *decedent* left her vast fortune to her *descendants*.

Eminent—adjective, to stand out; important
Imminent—adjective, impending

      Although he was an *eminent* businessman, foreclosure on his house was *imminent*.

Its—possessive
It's—contraction, **it is**

      The company held *its* board of directors meeting on Saturday. *It's* the second meeting this month.

Percent—used with numbers only
Percentage—used with words or phrases

      Each employee received two *percent* of the profits.
      They all agreed this was a small *percentage*.

Precedence—noun, the fact of preceding in time, priority of importance
Precedent—noun, established authority;
            adjective, prior in time, order, or significance

      The board of directors meeting took *precedence* over his going away.
      The president set a *precedent* when making that decision.

Principal—noun, a capital sum placed at interest; a leading figure; the corpus of an estate;
            adjective, first, most important
Principle—noun, a basic truth or rule

      Paying interest on the *principal* [noun] of the loan was explained to the company's *principals* [noun].
      The *principal* [adjective] part of ...
      She refused to compromise her *principles*.

Than—conjunction, function word to indicate difference in kind, manner, or identity; preposition, in comparison with (indicates comparison)

Then—adverb, at that time; soon after that (indicates time)

BFE Corp. has more shareholders *than* Hills Corp.
First, we must write the report, and *then* we will meet with the clients.

Their—adjective, of or relating to them or themselves
There—adverb, in or at that place

There were fifty shareholders at the meeting to cast *their* votes.

Placement of Modifiers

Pay close attention to where modifiers are placed, especially adverbs such as **only** and **even**. In speech, inflection aids meaning but, in writing, placing modifiers improperly can be confusing and often changes the meaning of the sentence. The modifier should usually be placed before the word or words it modifies. Consider the following:

She *almost* finished the whole report.
She finished *almost* the whole report.

Only she finished the report.
She *only* finished the report.
She finished *only* the report.

Phrases also must be placed properly, usually, but not always, following the word or phrase they modify. Often, **reading the sentence aloud** will help you decide where the modifier belongs.

(1)　　Fleming introduced a client to John with a counter-offer.

Analysis:　*With a counter-offer* modifies *client*, not *John*, and should be placed after *client*.

(2)　　The accountant recommended a bankruptcy petition to the client under Chapter 7.

Analysis:　*Under Chapter 7* modifies *bankruptcy petition*, not *the client*, and should be placed after *bankruptcy petition*.

Splitting Infinitives

Infinitives are the root verb form (e.g., to be, to consider, to walk). Generally speaking, infinitives should not be split except when to do so makes the meaning clearer.

Awkward:　　Management's responsibility is to clearly represent its financial position.
Better:　　　Management's responsibility is to represent its financial position clearly.

Exception:　　Management's responsibility in the future is to better represent its financial position.

Sentence Fragments

To avoid sentence fragments, read over your work carefully. Each sentence needs at least (1) a subject and (2) a predicate.

Unlike the case of a forged endorsement, a drawee bank charged with the recognition of its drawer-customer's signature. (The verb *is*, before the word *charged*, has been left out.)

Parallelism

Parallelism refers to a similarity in structure and meaning of all parts of a sentence or a paragraph. Sentences that violate rules of parallelism will be difficult to read and may obscure meaning. The following are some examples of different **violations** of parallelism.

(1) A security interest can be effected through a financing statement or the creditor's taking possession of it.

Analysis: The two prepositional phrases separated by **or** should be parallel. The sentence may be corrected as follows:

A security interest can be effected through a financing statement or through possession by the creditor.

(2) The independent auditor should consider whether the scope is appropriate, adequate audit programs and working papers, appropriate conclusions, and reports prepared are consistent with results of the work performed.

Analysis: The clause beginning with **whether** (which acts as the direct object of the verb **should consider**) is faulty. The items mentioned must be similarly constructed to each other. The sentence may be corrected as follows:

The independent auditor should consider whether the scope is appropriate, audit programs and working papers are adequate, conclusions are appropriate, and reports prepared are consistent with results of the work performed.

(3) The CPA was responsible for performing the inquiry and analytical procedures and that the review report was completed in a timely manner.

Analysis: The prepositional phrase beginning with **for** is faulty. The sentence may be corrected as follows:

The CPA was responsible for performing the inquiry and analytical procedures and ensuring that the review report was completed in a timely manner.

(4) Procedures that should be applied in examining the stock accounts are as follows:
(1) Review the corporate charter ...
(2) Obtain or preparing an analysis of ...
(3) Determination of authorization for ...

Analysis: All items in a list must be in parallel structure. An example of how the list may be corrected follows:
1. Review the corporate charter ...
2. Obtain or prepare an analysis of ...
3. Determine the authorization for ...

There are many other types of faulty constructions that can creep into sentences—too many to detail here. Furthermore, if any of the above is not clear, syntax may be a problem for you and you might want to consider a more thorough review of this subject.

NUMBERS

The basic rule for writing numbers is to write out the numbers ten and under and use numerals for all the others. More formal writing may dictate writing out all round numbers and numbers under 101. Let style, context of the sentence and of the work, and common sense be your guide.

> The partnership was formed 18 years ago.
> Jim Bryant joined the firm four years ago.
> Baker purchased 200 shares of stock.

When there are two numbers next to each other, alternate the styles.

> three 4-year certificates of deposit   5 two-party instruments

Never begin a sentence with numerals, such as:

> 1989 was the last year that Zinc Co. filed a tax return.

This example can be corrected as follows:

> Nineteen hundred and eighty-nine was the last year that Zinc Co. filed a tax return. (For use only in very formal writing)
> **or**
> Zinc Co. has not filed a tax return since 1989.

CAPITALIZATION

Under the assumption that most of us know the basic rules for normal capitalization, this section mentions only two special but common areas that seem to cause difficulties.

(1)   The first word **after a colon** is capped only when it is the beginning of a complete sentence.

> We discussed several possibilities at the meeting: Among them were liquidation, reorganization, and rehabilitation.
> We discussed several possibilities at the meeting: liquidation, reorganization, and rehabilitation.

(2)   The capitalization of titles and headings is especially tricky. In general, the first word and all other important words, no matter what length they are, should be capped. Beyond this general rule, there are several variations relating to the capitalization of pronouns. The important thing here is to pick a style and use it consistently within a single document, article, etc.

For example, the following pair of headings would both be acceptable depending on the style and consistency of style:

> Securities to which SFAS 115 Applies   **or**   Securities to Which SFAS 115 Applies
> Issues for Property other than Cash   **or**   Issues For Property Other Than Cash

PUNCTUATION

Period

Probably the two most common errors involving periods occur when incorporating quotation marks and/or parentheses with periods.

(1)   When a period is used with closing quotation marks, the period is always placed **inside**, regardless of whether the entire sentence is a quote or only the end of the sentence.

(2)   When a period is used with parentheses, the period goes **inside** the closing parenthesis if the entire sentence is enclosed in parentheses. When only the last word or words is enclosed in parentheses, the period goes **outside** the closing parenthesis.

(See Chapter 38, Contracts.)
The answer to that question is in the section on contracts (Chapter 38).

Exclamation Point

An **exclamation point** is used for emphasis and when issuing a command. In many cases, this is determined by the author when he or she wants to convey urgency, irony, or stronger emotion than ordinarily would be inferred.

Colons

A **colon** is used to introduce something in the sentence—a list of related words, phrases, or items directly related to the first part of the sentence; a quotation; a **direct** question; or an example of what was stated in the first part of the sentence. The colon takes the place of **that is** or **such as** and should never be used **with** such phrases.

> The accountant discussed two possibilities with the clients: first, a joint voluntary bankruptcy petition under Chapter 7, and second, ...

> The following will be discussed: life insurance proceeds; inheritance; and property.

> My CPA accounting review book states the following: "All leases that do not meet any of the four criteria for capital leases are operating leases."

Colons are used in formal correspondence after the salutation.

> Dear Mr. Bennett:
> To Whom it May Concern:

Note: When **that is** or **such as** is followed by a numeric list, it may be followed by a colon.

TOTALTIP: When writing a sentence, if you're not sure whether or not a colon is appropriate, it probably isn't. When in doubt, change the sentence so that you're sure it doesn't need a colon.

Semicolons

A **semicolon** is used in a number of ways:

(1)　　Use a **semicolon in place of a conjunction** when there are two or more closely related thoughts and each is expressed in a coordinate clause (a clause that could stand as a complete sentence).

> A marketable title is one that is free from plausible or reasonable objections; it need not be perfect.

(2)　　Use a **semicolon** as in the above example **with a conjunction** when the sentence is very long and complex. This promotes **clarity** by making the sentence easier to read.

> Should the lease be prematurely terminated, the deposit may be retained only to cover the landlord's actual expenses or damages; *and* any excess must be returned to the tenant.

> An assignment establishes privity of estate between the lessor and assignee; *[and]* therefore, the assignee becomes personally liable for the rent.

(3)   When there are commas in a series of items, use a **semicolon** to separate the main items.

Addison, Inc. has distribution centers in Camden, Maine; Portsmouth, New Hampshire; and Rock Island, Rhode Island.

Commas

Informal English, in general, allows much freedom in the placement or the omission of commas, and the overall trend is away from commas. However, standard, formal English provides rules for its usage. Accounting "language" can be so complex that using commas and using them correctly and appropriately is a necessity to avoid obscurity and promote clarity. Accordingly, we encourage you to learn the basics about comma placement.

What follows is not a complete set of rules for commas but should be everything you need to know about commas to make your sentences clear and concise. Because the primary purpose of the comma is to clarify meaning, it is the opinion of the authors that in the case of a complex subject such as accounting, it is better to overpunctuate than to underpunctuate. If you are concerned about overpunctuation, try to reduce an unwieldly sentence to two or more sentences.

(1)   Use a **comma** to **separate a compound sentence** (one with two or more independent coordinate clauses joined by a conjunction).

Gil Corp. has current assets of $90,000, but the corporation has current liabilities of $180,000. Jim borrowed $60,000, and he used the proceeds to purchase outstanding common shares of stock.

Note: In these examples, a comma would **not** be necessary if the **and** or the **but** were not followed by a noun or pronoun (the subject of the second clause). In other words, if by removing the conjunction, the sentence could be separated into two complete sentences, it needs a comma.

(2)   Use a **comma** after an **introductory word or phrase**.

During 1992, Rand Co. purchased $960,000 of inventory.
On April 1, 1993, Wall's inventory had a fair value of $150,000.

Note: Writers often choose to omit this comma when the introductory phrase is very short. Again, we recommend using the comma. It will never be incorrect in this position.

(3)   Use a **comma** after an **introductory adverbial clause**.

Although insurance contracts are not required by the Statute of Frauds to be in writing, most states have enacted statutes which now require such.

(4)   Use **commas** to separate **items, phrases, or clauses in a series**.

To be negotiable, an instrument must be in writing, signed by the maker or drawer, contain an unconditional promise or order to pay a sum certain in money on demand or at a specific time, and be payable to order or to bearer.

Note: Modern practice often omits the last comma in the series (in the above example, the one before **and**). Again, for the sake of clarity, we recommend using this comma.

(5)   In most cases, use a **comma or commas** to separate **a series of adjectives**.

Silt Co. kept their inventory in an old, decrepit, brick building .
He purchased several outstanding shares of common stock. (*No* commas are needed.)

TOTALTIP: When in doubt as to whether or not to use a comma after a particular adjective, try inserting the word **and** between the adjectives. If it makes sense, use a comma. (In the second example, above, **several and outstanding**, or **outstanding and several** don't make sense.

---

(6) Use a **comma or commas** to set off any **word or words, phrase, or clause that interrupts the sentence** but does not change its essential meaning.

SLD Industries, as drawer of the instrument, is only secondarily liable.

(7) Use **commas** to set off **geographical names** and **dates**.

Feeney Co. moved its headquarters to Miami, Florida, on August 16, 1992.

Quotation Marks

Quotation marks are used with **direct quotations; direct discourse and direct questions;** and **definitions or explanations of words**. There are other uses of quotation marks that would be used rarely in the accounting profession and, therefore, are not discussed in this review.

Hyphens

Use a **hyphen** to separate words into syllables. It is always best to check a dictionary, because some words do not split where you would imagine.

Modern practice does not normally hyphenate prefixes and their root words, even when both the prefix and the root word begin with vowels. A common exception is when the root word begins with a capital letter or a date or number.

prenuptial   nonexempt   semiannual
pre-1987   nonnegotiable   non-American

Although modern practice is moving away from using hyphens for **compound adjectives** (a noun and an adjective in combination to make a single adjective), clarity dictates that hyphens still be used in many cases.

long-term investments   two-party instrument
a noninterest-bearing note   short-term capital losses

Use a hyphen **only** when the compound adjective or compound adjective-adverb **precedes the noun**.

The well-known company is going bankrupt.
The company is well known for its quality products.

Note: There are certain word combinations that are always hyphenated, always one word, or always two words. Use the dictionary.

The final item we want to mention regarding hyphenation is the **suspended hyphen**. Suspended hyphens are used to avoid repetition in compound adjectives. For example, instead of having to write **himself or herself**, especially when these forms are being used repeatedly as they often must be in our new nongender-biased world, use **him- or herself**.

10-, 15-, and 18-year depreciation   first-, second-, and third-class

SPELLING

Just as many of us believe that arithmetic can always be done by our calculators, we also believe that spelling will be done by our word processors and, therefore, we needn't worry too much about it. There is no doubt that these devices are tremendous boons to writers and others. However, although you soon will be able to use a calculator during the CPA Exam, you will not be able to use a word processor. And like it or not, you will encounter many other situations where a spell-checker will not be available to you, so you'd better be able to **spell!** Also, a spell-checker cannot tell the difference between words that you have misspelled which are nonetheless real words, such as **there** and **their**. (See the list in this section of words often confused.)

Let's hit some highlights here of troublesome spellings with some brief tips that should help you become a better speller.

(1) **IE or EI?** If you are still confused by words containing the **ie** or **ei** combinations, you'd better relearn those old rhymes we ridiculed in grade school.

"i before e except after c." (This works only for words where the ie-ei combination sounds like **ee**.)

ach**ie**ve	bel**ie**ve	ch**ie**f
c**ei**ling	rec**ei**ve	rec**ei**pt

Of course there are always **exceptions** such as:

either	neither	seize	financier

When **ie** or **ei** have a different sound than **ee**, the above rule does not apply. For example:

fr**ie**nd	s**ie**ve	effic**ie**nt
for**ei**gn	sover**ei**gn	surf**ei**t

(2) **Doubling final consonants.** When an ending (**suffix**) beginning with a vowel is added to a root word that ends in a single consonant, that final consonant is **usually doubled**.

lag—lagging	bid—bidding	top—topped

The exceptions generally fall under three rules.

First, double only after a short vowel and **not** after a double vowel.

big—bigger	tug—tugging	get—getting
need—needing	keep—keeping	pool—pooled

Second, a **long** vowel (one that "says its own name"), which is almost always followed by a silent **e** that must be dropped to add the suffix, is **not** doubled.

hope—hoping	tape—taped	rule—ruled

Note: Sometimes, as in the first two examples above, doubling the consonants would create entirely new words.

Third, with root words of two or more syllables ending in a single consonant, double the consonant **only** when the last syllable is the **stressed syllable**.

Double:	be**gin**—beginning, beginner	pre**fer**—preferred, preferring
	re**gret**—regretted, regrettable	ad**mit**—admitted, admittance
Don't Double:	pro**hib**it—prohibited, prohibitive	**ben**efit—benefited, benefiting
	de**vel**op—developing	**pref**erence—preferable

(3)   **Drop** the silent **e** before adding a suffix **beginning with a vowel**.

     store—storing   take—taking   value—valuing

Keep the **e** before adding a suffix **beginning with a consonant**, such as:

        move—movement   achieve—achievement

Again, there are **exceptions**.

     e: mile—mileage   dye—dyeing

     No e: argue—argument   due—duly   true—truly
               judge—judgment   acknowledge—acknowledgment

(4)   Change **y** to **ie** before adding **s** when it is the single final vowel.

     country—countries   study—studies   quantity—quantities

Change **y** to **i** before adding other endings **except s**.

     busy—business   dry—drier   copy—copier

     Exceptions: Keep **y** for the following:

     copying   studying   trying

Y is also usually preserved when it follows another vowel.

     delays   joys   played

     Exceptions:

     day—daily   lay—laid   pay—paid   say—said

(5)   **Forming Plurals.** The formation of some plurals does not follow the general rule of adding **s** or **es** to the singular. What follows are some of the more troublesome forms.

Some singular nouns that end in **o** form their plurals by adding **s**; some by adding **es**.

ratio**s**   zero**s**   hero**es**   potato**es**

Many nouns taken directly from **foreign languages** retain their original plural. Below are a few of the more common ones.

     alumnus—alumni   basis—bases   crisis—crises
     criterion—criteria   datum—data   matrix—matrices

Other nouns taken directly from foreign languages have **two acceptable plural forms**: the foreign language plural and the anglicized plural. Here are some of the more common:

     medium—media, mediums   appendix—appendices, appendixes
     formula—formulae, formulas   memorandum—memoranda, memorandums

Finally, in this foreign language category are some commonly used Latin nouns that form their plurals by adding **es**.

census—censuses	consensus—consensuses
hiatus—hiatuses	prospectus—prospectuses

Troublesome Words: Spelling

Spelling errors occur for different reasons; probably the two most common reasons are confusion with the spelling of similar words or mistaking the British spelling of certain words for the American spelling. The following is a list of commonly misspelled words. You will find those you may have misspelled in taking the Diagnostic Quiz, and you may recognize others you have problems with. Memorize them. And, whenever and wherever possible, have a dictionary handy so that you won't be tempted to guess at spelling.

accommodate	existence	liaison	resistance
achieve	fulfill	occasion	skillful
acknowledgment	irrelevant	paralleled	supersede
bankruptcy	judgment	privilege	surety

GRAMMAR

This section on grammar is intended to be a brief overview only. Consequently, the authors have chosen to focus on items that, in their experience, seem to cause the most problems. If you did not do well on the Diagnostic Quiz at the beginning of "Accounting for 5%," you would be well advised to go over all the material in this section and, if there are areas you still do not feel confident about, you should consider a more thorough grammar study than the review provided here.

VERBS

The verb is the driving force of the sentence: it is the word or words to which all other parts of the sentence relate. When trying to analyze a sentence to identify its grammatical parts or its meaning, or when attempting to amend a sentence, you should always identify the verb or verbs first. A verb expresses action or being.

Action: The accountant *visits* his clients regularly.
Being: Kyle *is* an accountant.

Voice

The **active voice** indicates that the subject of the sentence (the person or thing) does something. The **passive voice** indicates that the subject is acted upon.

Active: *The accountant worked* on the client's financial statements.
Passive: The client's financial statements *were worked on by the accountant*.

For most kinds of writing, the passive voice is considered "weak" and generally should be avoided. For expository writing (properly used for the exam), however, the passive voice is legitimate and is used frequently.

Once the computations *are tested*, mathematical accuracy will be assured.

The most important thing to understand about voice is that it should be consistent; that is, you should avoid shifts from one voice to another, especially within the same sentence as below.

Taylor Corporation *hired* an independent computer programmer to develop a simplified payroll application for its new computer, and an on-line, data-based microcomputer system *was developed*.

Use the active voice for the entire sentence:

Taylor Corporation *hired* an independent computer programmer to develop a simplified payroll application for its new computer, and he *developed* an on-line, data-based microcomputer system.

Mood

Common errors in syntax are made when **more than one mood** is used in a single sentence. The first example that follows begins with the **imperative** and shifts to the **indicative**. The second example corrects the sentence by using the imperative in both clauses, and the third example corrects the sentence by using the indicative in both clauses. The fourth example avoids the problem by forming two sentences.

Pick up (imperative) that work program for me at the printer, and then we will go (indicative) to the client.
Pick up that work program for me at the printer, and then go to the client with me.
After you pick up that work program for me at the printer, we will go to the client.
Pick up that work program for me at the printer. Then we will go to the client.

There are three moods: the indicative, the imperative, and the subjunctive. Most sentences are **indicative**:

The percentage-of-completion method is justified. Declarative indicative.
Is the percentage-of-completion method justified? Interrogative indicative.

Sentences that give a command are called **imperative** sentences:

Pick up your books!
Be sure to use the correct method of accounting for income taxes.

The **subjunctive** mood is headed toward extinction. Today's grammar books often disagree on the use of the subjunctive in clauses that express **conditions** or **contingencies**. In other words, in a sentence containing an "if" clause that expresses a **condition, contingency, or a condition clearly contrary to fact**, some books will tell you to use the **subjunctive**. Others will say the **indicative** is the proper form in all cases **except** when expressing a condition clearly contrary to fact. Thus, in standard English today, you will often see the indicative used where previously the subjunctive had been used.

That having been said, let's go over the rules for using the subjunctive that, for the most part, are alive and well.

The subjunctive is usually used to express conditions contrary to fact, contingencies, and wishes, demands, recommendations, requests, and speculations, as in the following examples:

(1)   In **if** clauses and some **unless** clauses for **conditions contrary to fact** or **speculations**.

If the internal control *were* (the indicative is *was*) strong, the auditor would rely on it more.

(2)   In clauses beginning with **as if** or **as though** to indicate **conditions or contingencies**.

The client acted as though he *were* (indicative is *was*) uncomfortable with the statement.

(3)   In clauses introduced by **that** for **wishes, demands, indirect requests, and recommendations**.

Martha wished that no one *were* (indicative is *was*) around to see the client yell at her.
The manager demanded that the workpapers *be* (indicative is *are*) turned in for review before the return is prepared.
The instructor recommends that she *retake* (indicative is *retakes*) the exam.
It is important that the manager *review* (indicative is *reviews*) the workpapers immediately.

(4)   In subordinate clauses beginning with **if** followed by the subjunctive verb form, the auxiliary verbs **would, could,** and **should** are usually used to indicate speculations or conditions contrary to fact.

If Harry *were* not over budget, he *would have* checked his work before giving it to the partner.

Warning: Beware of sentences in which the independent clause uses **would have**. The subordinate clause (the **if** clause) **does not also use would have**. The following is an example of a faulty construction which has crept comfortably into the language in recent years:

If I *would have* studied harder, I *would have* passed the exam.

Be sure to use **had** in the **if clause**.

If I *had* studied harder, I *would have* passed the exam.

(5)   In certain traditional words and phrases, the subjunctive remains with us, even if modern practice tends not to use it in similar constructions.

Let me *be*.   Be that as it *may* ...
Far *be* it from me ..   If I *were* you ...

TOTALTIP: Use the subjunctive form in clauses beginning with **if**, since it is still viable according to many grammar texts, and still commonly used in formal writing.

Tense

Tense is all about *time*. The **present tense** is used to express action or a state of being that is taking place in the present. The present tense is also used to express an action or a state of being that is habitual and when a definite time in the future is stated.

Dan *is taking* his CPA Exam.
Robin *goes* to the printer once a week.
The new computer *arrives* on Monday.

The **present perfect tense** is used to indicate action that began in the past and has continued to the present.

From the time of its founder, the CPA firm *has celebrated* April 16 with a fabulous dinner party.

The **future tense** is used to indicate action that takes place in the indefinite future.

A plan of reorganization *will determine* the amount and the manner in which the creditors *will be paid*, in what form the business *will continue*, and any other necessary details.

The **future perfect tense** is used to indicate action that has not taken place yet but will take place before a specific future time.

Before Susan arrives at the client's office, the client *will have prepared* the documents she needs.

The **past tense** is used to indicate an action that took place in the past. The **past tense** is also used to indicate a condition or state occurring at a specific time in the past.

The predecessor auditor *resigned* last week.
The company *contacted* its auditor the first of every new year.

The **past perfect tense** is used to indicate an action that is completed before another action that also took place in the past.

The work load *had been* so heavy that she was required to work overtime. (Not *was*)

As you can see by what we have just reviewed, the importance of using the proper tense is to properly indicate **time**. If the proper sequence of tenses is not used, confusion can arise as to what happened when. Consider:

> *Not getting* the raise he was expecting, John was unhappy about the additional work load. [???]
> *Having not gotten* the raise he was expecting, John was unhappy about the additional work load. [Much clearer]

Agreement

We cover **agreement** under the heading of verbs because the verb is the driving force of the sentence and, thus, it is the component with which everything else in the sentence should agree. The first element of agreement to examine is **verb** and **subject**. These two components must agree **in number**. We will see as we move along that **number** is just one of several things to consider when examining the agreement of the components of a sentence.

The subject of the sentence is the noun or pronoun (person, place, or thing) doing the action stated by the verb (in the case of the active voice) or being acted upon by the verb (in the case of the passive voice). Although the subject normally precedes the verb, this is not always the case. Thus, you must be able to identify sentence elements no matter where they happen to fall. This is not a difficult matter, at least most of the time. Consider:

(1)   Lewis, Bradford, Johnson & Co. [is or are] the client with the best pay record.

(2)   For me, one of the most difficult questions on the exam [was or were] concerned with correcting weaknesses in internal controls.

In both examples, the first choice, the singular verb form, is correct.

In sentence (1), Lewis, Bradford, Johnson & Co. is considered singular in number because we are talking about the company, not Lewis, Bradford, and Johnson per se.

In sentence (2), the verb is also singular because **one** is the subject of the sentence, not **questions**. **Questions** is the object of the preposition **of**. If this seems confusing, rearrange the sentence so that the prepositional phrase appears first, and the agreement of subject and verb will be clearer. Thus:

> Of the most difficult questions, one *was concerned* with correcting weaknesses in internal controls.

We will address special problems associated with prepositional phrases in other sections.

Beware of the word **number**. When it is preceded by the word **the**, it is always singular, and when it is preceded by the word **a**, it is always plural.

> *The number* of listings generated by the new EDP system *was* astounding.
> *A number* of listings *were generated* by the new EDP system.

A **compound subject**, even when made up of nouns singular in number, always takes a plural verb.

> The balance sheet, the independent auditor's report, and the quarterly report *are lying* on the desk. (Not *is lying*)

Having used a form of the verb **lie** in the above example, let's mention the difference between **lie** and **lay**.

There are two separate verbs: **to lie**, meaning **to recline**, and **to lay**, meaning **to place or set**.

> He *lies* down to rest.
> He *lays* down the book.

Continuing now with **compound subjects**, let's address the problem of when there are two or more subjects—one (or more) singular and one (or more) plural.

When the sentence contains subjects connected by **or** or **nor**, or **not only ... but also**, the verb should agree with the subject nearer to the verb.

> Either the auditors or the partner *is going* to the client.
> Not only the partner but also the auditors *are going* to the client.

In the case of the first example above, which sounds awkward, simply switch the order of the subjects **(the partner; the auditors)** and use the verb **are going** to make it read better.

When one subject is **positive** and one is **negative**, the verb always agrees with the positive.

> The partner, and not the auditors, *is going* to the client.
> Not the partner but the auditors frequently go to the client.

You should use **singular verbs** with the following: **each, every, everyone, everybody, anyone, anybody, either, neither, someone, somebody, no one, nobody,** and **one**.

> Anybody who wants to go *is* welcome.
> Neither the accountant nor the bookkeeper ever *arrives* on time.
> One never *knows* what to expect.

TOTALTIP: Watch out for the words **each** and **none**. They can trip up even the most careful writer.

Improper placement of **each** in the sentence will confuse the verb agreement.

> The balance sheet, the income statement, and the statement of cash flows each [*has/have*] several errors.

In this example, we know that the verb must be **has** (to agree with **each**), but then again, maybe it should be **have** to agree with the subjects. The problem is that we have a sentence with a compound subject that must take a plural verb, but here it is connected with a singular pronoun (each).

This is a very common error. This particular example may be fixed in one of two ways. First, if the word **each** is not really necessary in the sentence, simply drop it. Second, simply place the word **each** in a better position in the sentence. In the example below, placing the word **each** at the end of the sentence properly connects it to **errors**; also it no longer confuses verb agreement.

> The balance sheet, the income statement, and the statement of cash flows *have* several errors *each*.

The word **none** has special problems all its own. Not too many years ago, it was the accepted rule that every time **none** was the subject of the sentence, it should take a **singular verb**. Most modern grammarians now agree that the plural may be used when followed by a prepositional phrase with a plural object (noun) or with an object whose meaning in the sentence is plural.

> None of the statements *were* correct.

When **none** stands alone, some purists believe it should take the singular and others believe that the plural is the proper form when the meaning conveys plurality. Consequently, in the following example, either the singular or plural is generally acceptable.

> All the financial statements had been compiled, but none *was or were* correct.

> **TOTALTIP**: When in doubt or when the sentence sounds awkward, use **not one** in place of **none** (with a singular verb, of course).

NOUNS

Nouns are people, places, and things and can occur anywhere in the sentence. Make sure that, when necessary, the nouns are the same in number.

> Do the exercises at the end of each chapter by answering the *questions* true or false. (Not singular *question*)
> At the end of the engagement, everyone must turn in their *time sheets*. (Not singular *time sheet*)

Possessive Nouns

The basic rule for making a **singular noun** possessive is to add an **apostrophe and an s**. If a singular noun ends in s, **add apostrophe and an s**. To make a **plural noun** possessive, add an **apostrophe alone** when the plural ends in **s** or an **apostrophe and an s** when the plural does not end in an **s**.

| **Singular:** | client*'s* | system*'s* | beneficiary*'s* | *Chris'* |
| **Plural:** | clients*'* | systems*'* | beneficiaries*'* | |

A common area of difficulty has to do with **ownership**, that is, when two or more individuals or groups are mentioned as owning something. If the ownership is **not common** to all, apostrophes appear after each individual or group. If the ownership **is common** to all, only the last individual or group in the series takes an apostrophe.

> **Not common to all:**   The accountant's and the attorney's offices ...
> **Common to all:**   Robert, his brother, and their sons' company ...

> **TOTALTIP**: Most of the confusion associated with possessives seems to be with the plural possessive. Remember to make the noun **plural** first and **possessive** second.

Modern usage tends to make possessive forms into adjectives where appropriate. Thus:

> *Company's* (possessive) management becomes *company* (adjective) management.
> A *two weeks'* (possessive) vacation becomes a *two weeks* or *two-week* (both adjectives) vacation.

> **TOTALTIP**: In most instances, either the possessive form or the adjectival form is acceptable. Go with the form that seems most appropriate for that particular sentence.

Gerunds

A gerund is a verb changed to a noun by adding **ing**. A noun preceding a gerund must be possessive so that it may be construed as **modifying the noun**.

> *Caroline's auditing* the financial statements was approved by the partner.

In this example, the subject of the sentence is **auditing**, not Caroline or Caroline's. Since we know that nouns cannot modify nouns, Caroline must become **Caroline's** to create a possessive form which can modify the noun **auditing**.

The same holds true for **gerunds** used as **objects of prepositions**:

> The partner objected to *Caroline's auditing* the financial statements.

In this example, **auditing** is the object of the preposition **to**. Caroline's is an appositive (or possessive) form modifying **auditing**.

PRONOUNS

Like Latin where most words have "cases" according to their function in the sentence, English **pronouns** also have cases. Sometimes you may be aware that you are using a case when determining the proper form of the pronoun and sometimes you may not.

> *He* met *his* partner at *their* office.

Let's begin by tackling everybody's favorite: **who** and **whom**. We're going to take some time reviewing this one since it seems to be a major area of confusion.
There is little or no confusion when **who** is clearly the **subject** of the sentence:

> *Who* is going with us?

And little or no confusion when **whom** is clearly (1) the **object** of the sentence or (2) the **object** of the preposition.

> (1)   Jenny audited *whom*? *Whom* did Jenny audit?

> (2)   Jenny is working for *whom*? For *whom* is Jenny working?

TOTALTIP: If you are having difficulty with **questions**, try changing them into declarative sentences (statements) and substituting another pronoun. Thus: Jenny audits **them** (objective), obviously not **they** (subjective), or Jenny is working for **her**, obviously not **she**.

Who or **whoever** is the subjective case, and **whom** or **whomever** is the objective case. Common errors occur frequently in two instances: (1) when **who or whoever** is interrupted by a parenthetical phrase and (2) when an entire clause is the subject of a preposition.

> (1)   *Whoever* she decides is working with her should meet her at six o'clock.

In this example, **she decides** is a parenthetical phrase (one that could be left out of the sentence and the sentence would still be a complete thought). When you disregard **she decides**, you can see that **whoever** is the subject of the sentence, not **she**. The error occurs when **she** is believed to be the subject and **whomever**, the object of **decides**.

> (2)   Jenny will work with *whoever* shows up first.

This example represents what seems the most problematic of all the areas relating to who or whom. We have been taught to use the objective case after the preposition (in this case **with**). So why isn't **whomever** the correct form in this example? The answer is that it would be the correct form if the sentence ended with the word **whomever**. (**Whomever** would be the object of the preposition **with**.) In this case, it is not the last word but, rather, it is the **subject** of the clause **whoever shows up first**.

TOTALTIP: Again, make the substitution of another pronoun as a test of whether to use the subjective or objective case.

Let's look at a few more examples. See if you are better able to recognize the correct form using the **TOTALTIPS**.

> (1)   I'm sure I will be comfortable with [*whoever/whomever*] the manager decides to assign.

(2)   To [*who/whom*] should she speak regarding that matter?

(3)   He always chooses [*whoever/whomever*] in his opinion is the best auditor.

(4)   She usually enjoys working with [*whoever/whomever*] the partner assigns.

(5)   [*Who/Whom*] should I ask to accompany me?

Let's see how well you did.

(1)   **Whomever** is correct. The whole clause after the preposition **with** is the object of the preposition, and **whomever** is the object of the verb **to assign**. Turn the clause around and substitute another pronoun. Thus, **the manager decides to assign** *him* .

(2)   **Whom** is correct. **Whom** is the object of the preposition **to**. Make the question into a declarative sentence and substitute another pronoun. Thus, **She should speak to** *him* **regarding that matter**.

(3)   **Whoever** is correct. The entire clause **whoever is the best auditor** is the object of the main verb **chooses**. **Whoever** is the subject of that clause. **In his opinion** is a parenthetical phrase and doesn't affect the rest of the sentence.

(4)   **Whomever** is correct. The entire clause **whomever the partner assigns** is the object of the preposition **with**, and **whomever** is the object of the verb **assigns**. Again, turn the clause around and substitute another pronoun. Thus, **the partner assigns** *him*.

(5)   **Whom** is correct. **Whom** is the object of the main verb **ask**. Turn the question into a regular declarative sentence and substitute another pronoun. Thus, **I should ask** *her* **to accompany me**.

Pronouns that follow prepositions are always in the **objective case**, except when serving as the subject of a clause, as discussed above. The most popular misuse occurs when using a pronoun after the preposition **between**. (**I, he, she, they,** are never used after **between**, no matter where the prepositional phrase falls in the sentence.)

Between you and me, I don't believe our client will be able to continue as a going concern.
That matter is strictly between her and them.

Antecedents

An antecedent is the word or words for which a pronoun stands. Any time a pronoun is used, its antecedent must be clear and agree with the word or words for which it stands.

The accountant placed *his* work in the file.

In this example, **his** is the pronoun with **the accountant** as its antecedent. **His** agrees with **the accountant** in person and number. **His** is used so as not to repeat **the accountant**.

Confusion most often occurs when using indefinite pronouns such as **it**, **that**, **this**, and **which**.

The company for *which* he works always mails *its* paychecks on Friday.

In this example, the pronouns **which** and **its** both clearly refer to **the company**. But, what about this sentence?:

The company always mails my paycheck on Friday and *it* is a small one.

Since it is not clear what the antecedent for **it** is, we can't tell for sure whether the company or the paycheck is small.

The following examples demonstrate unclear antecedents and how they may be clarified.

> (1) When Claudia visited the client, *she* was ill. (Who was ill?)
>
> When she visited the client, Claudia was ill.
> Claudia was ill when she visited the client.
> The client was ill when Claudia visited her.

> (2) When a forecast contains a range, *it* is not selected in a biased or misleading manner. (The forecast or the range?)
>
> When a forecast contains a range, *the range* is not ...

> (3) Wanting to show all his workpapers to the auditors, Tom decided to get *them* all together right away. (To get what or whom together?)
>
> Tom decided to get all his workpapers together right away so he could show them to the auditors.
> Tom decided to get the auditors together right away so he could show them all his workpapers.

So far in our discussion of antecedents, we have talked about agreement in person. We have not addressed agreement in **number**. The following examples demonstrate pronouns that **do not agree** in number with their antecedents.

> The company issued quarterly financial reports to *their* shareholders. (*Its* is the correct antecedent to agree in number with *company*.)
>
> Each of the methods is introduced on a separate page, so that the student is made aware of *their* importance. (*Its* is the correct antecedent to agree in number with *each*.) **Note: Importance** refers to **each**, the subject of the sentence, not to **methods**, which is the object of the preposition **of**.

When a pronoun refers to singular antecedents that are connected by **or** or **nor**, the pronoun should be **singular**.

> Joe or Buddy has misplaced *his* workpapers.
> Neither Joe nor Buddy has misplaced *his* workpapers.

When a pronoun refers to a singular and a plural antecedent connected by **or** or **nor**, the pronoun should be **plural**.

> Neither Joe nor his associates can locate *their* workpapers.

Pronouns must also agree with their antecedents in **gender**.

The English language has no way of expressing gender-neutral in pronoun agreement and, therefore, it has long been the custom to use **his** as a convenience when referring to both sexes. Originally, it was the feminist movement that focused attention on this "gender bias" in writing and, consequently, there is a growing use of a more cumbersome construction in order not to be offensive to some readers. Thus, when pronouns must agree in gender with noun antecedents, you will be more "politically correct" when you communicate accordingly.

> **Old:** When a new partner's identifiable asset contribution is less than the ownership interest *he* is to receive, the excess capital allowed *him* is considered as goodwill attributable to *him*.

> **New:** When a new partner's identifiable asset contribution is less than the ownership interest *he or she* is to receive, the excess capital allowed *the new partner* is considered as goodwill attributable to *him or her*.

You will note in the above example that **he or she (he/she)** and **him or her (him/her)** have been used only once each and the antecedent **new partner** has been repeated once.

TOTALTIP: The idea is to not overload a single sentence with too many repetitions of each construction. When it seems that **he/she** constructions are overwhelming the sentence, repeat the noun antecedent where possible, even if it sounds a bit labored.

Reflexive pronouns are pronouns that are used for **emphasizing their antecedents** and should **not be used as substitutes** for regular pronouns. The reflexive pronouns are **myself, yourself, himself, herself, itself, ourselves, yourselves, and themselves.**

> The financing is being handled by the principals *themselves.* (Demonstrates emphasis)
> The partner *himself* will take care of that matter. (Demonstrates emphasis)
> My associate and *I* accept the engagement. (Not my associate and *myself*...)
> I am fine; how about *you*? (Not how about *yourself?*)

ADJECTIVES AND ADVERBS

Most of us understand that adjectives and adverbs are **modifiers**, but many of us can't tell them apart. And, it is not true that all adverbs end in **ly**. In fact, there are many words that can be used as either depending on their use in the sentence. Consequently, differentiating adjectives from adverbs is really not very important as long as you know how to use them. Understanding, however, that **adjectives modify nouns or pronouns**, and **adverbs modify verbs** and adjectives will help you choose the correct form.

> Falcone Co. purchased *two* computers from Wizard Corp., a very *small* manufacturer. (*two* is an adjective describing the noun *computers, very* is an adverb modifying the adjective *small*, and *small* is an adjective describing the noun *manufacturer.*)

> Acme advised Mason that it would deliver the appliances on July 2 as *originally* agreed. (*originally* is an adverb describing the verb *agreed.*)

In writing for the CPA Exam, avoid colloquial uses of the adjectives **real** and **sure**. In the following examples, adverbs are called for.

> I am *very* (not *real*) sorry that you didn't pass the exam.
> He will *surely* (not *sure*) be glad if he passes the exam.

Comparisons using adjectives frequently present problems.

Remember that when comparing two things, the **comparative** (often **er**) form is used, and when comparing more than two, the **superlative** (often **est**) form is used.

> This report is *larger* than the other one.
> This report is the *largest* of them all.

Other types of comparisons indicate **degree**:

> This report is *more* detailed than the others.
> This report is the *most* detailed of them all.

Articles are adjectives and are either **definite—the,** or **indefinite—a** and **an**, and need little discussion for our purposes here. A difficulty does seem to exist, however, in deciding when to use **a** and when to use **an** before certain constructions. We know that **an** precedes most vowels, but when the vowel begins with a **consonant sound**, we should use **a**.

a usual adjustment ...
a one in a million deal ...

Similarly, when **a** or **an** precedes abbreviations or initials, it is the next **sound** that we should consider, not the next letter. In other words, if the next sound is a vowel sound, **an** should be used.

An S.A. will be used to head up the field work on this engagement.
An F.O.B. contract is a contract indicating that the seller will bear that degree of risk and expense which is appropriate to the F.O.B. terms.

TOTALTIP: Be reasonably sure that your reader will be reading the abbreviations or initials, and not the whole term, title, etc. If that should be the case, stick with **a.**

CONJUNCTIONS

There are three types of conjunctions: coordinating, subordinating, and correlative.

Coordinating conjunctions

Coordinating conjunctions are conjunctions that connect equal elements in a sentence. These conjunctions include **and, but, for, yet, so, or,** and **nor.**

The partner *and* the manager ...
The manager wrote the engagement letter *and* the partner signed it.

Examples of common problems involving coordinating conjunctions:

(1)   Leaving out the **and,** leading to difficulties with comprehension and clarity.

The accountant studied some of management's representations, marked what she wanted to discuss in the meeting. (The word *and* should be in the place of the comma.)

Mike's summer job entails opening the mail, stamps it with a dater, routing it to the proper person. (Should be: ... opening the mail from other offices, *stamping* it with a dater, *and* routing it to the proper person. **This example also demonstrates a lack of parallelism,** which will be addressed in detail in a later section.)

Omission of **and** is correct when the sentence is a compound sentence (meaning that it contains two independent clauses), in which case a semicolon takes the place of **and.** When the semicolon is used, the ideas of each independent clause should be closely related.

The security is genuine; it has not been materially altered.

(2)   Although the rules for **or** and **nor** have become less strict over time, you should understand proper usage for the sake of comprehension and clarity. Most of us are familiar with **either ... or** and **neither ... nor:**

Either the creditor must take possession *or* the debtor must sign a security agreement that describes the collateral.

The company would neither accept delivery of the water coolers, nor pay for them, because Peterson did not have the authority to enter into the contract.

(3)   The only mention we want to make concerning the use of the conjunction **so** is simply to discourage using it very often. In many cases, there will be a more appropriate or explicit word or phrase. In other cases, the thought may be better expressed in another way.

She was not able to attend the meeting, *so* quorum was not met.

This example is acceptable; however, the following two examples are better.

She was not able to attend the meeting, *therefore*, quorum was not met.
Since she was unable to attend the meeting, quorum was not met.

Subordinating conjunctions

Subordinating conjunctions are conjunctions that introduce subordinate elements of the sentence. The most common and the ones we want to concentrate on here are **as, since, because, that, which, when, where,** and **while.**

As; Since; Because

Because is the only word of the three that **always** indicates cause. **Since** usually indicates **time** and, when introducing adverbial clauses, may mean either **when** or **because**. **As** should be avoided altogether in these constructions and used only for comparisons. We strongly recommend using the **exact** word to avoid any confusion, especially when **clarity** is essential.

Attachment of the security interest did not occur because Pix failed to file a financing statement. (Specifically indicates *cause*.)
Green has not paid any creditor since January 1, 1992. (Specifically indicates *time*.)

The following example is a typical misuse of the conjunction **as** and demonstrates why **as** should not be used as a substitute for **because:**

As the partners are contributing more capital to the company, the stock prices are going up.

The meaning of this sentence is ambiguous. Are the stock prices going up **while** the partners are contributing capital or are the stock prices going up **because** the partners are contributing more capital?

That; Which

Many people complain about not understanding when to use **that** and when to use **which** than just about anything else. The rule to follow requires that you know the difference between a restrictive and a nonrestrictive clause. A **restrictive clause** is one that must remain in the sentence for the sentence to make sense. A **nonrestrictive** clause is one that may be removed from a sentence and the sentence will still make sense.

That is used with restrictive clauses; *which* is used with nonrestrictive clauses.

(1)   An accountant who breaches his or her contract with a client may be subject to liability for damages and losses *which* the client suffers as a direct result of the breach.

(2)   As a result, the accountant is responsible for errors resulting from changes *that* occurred between the time he or she prepared the statement and its effective date.

(3)   A reply *that* purports to accept an offer but which adds material qualifications or conditions is not an acceptance; rather, it is a rejection and a counter-offer.

In example (1) above, the clause beginning with **which** is nonrestrictive (sentence would make sense without it). In examples (2) and (3), the clauses that follow **that** are restrictive (necessary for the meaning of the sentence).

> **TOTALTIP:** If you can put commas around the clause in question, it is usually nonrestrictive and thus takes **which**. Occasionally, there will be a fine line between what one might consider restrictive or nonrestrictive. In these cases, make your choice based on which sounds better and, if there is another **which** or **that** nearby, let that help your decision. (Unless truly necessary, don't have two or three uses of **which** or two or three uses of **that** in the same sentence.)

When; Where

Most uses of **when** and **where** are obvious. The most common incorrect usage associated with these words occurs when they are used to define something.

(1)   Exoneration is *where* the surety takes action against the debtor, which seeks to force the debtor to pay his or her debts.

(2)   A fiduciary relationship is *where* the agent acts for the benefit of the principal.

(3)   Joint liability is *when* all partners in a partnership are jointly liable for any contract actions against the partnership.

The above three examples are **faulty constructions**. The verb **to be** (**is**, in this case) must be followed by a predicate adjective (an adjective modifying the subject) or a predicate nominative (a noun meaning the same as the subject), **not** an adverbial phrase or clause. These sentences should be rewritten as follows:

(1)   Exoneration is *an action* by the surety against the debtor, which seeks to force the debtor to pay his or her debts.

(2)   A fiduciary relationship is *the association* of the agent and the principal whereby the agent acts for the benefit of the principal.

(3)   Joint liability is *the liability* of all partners in a partnership for any contract actions against the partnership.

While

Formerly, **while** was acceptable only to denote time. Modern practice accepts **while** and **although** as nearly synonymous.

> *While/Although* Acme contends that its agreement with Mason was not binding, it is willing to deliver the goods to Mason.

In the following example, however, **while** is **not** a proper substitution for **although**.

> Under a sale or return contract, the sale is considered as completed *although* it is voidable at the buyer's election.

> **TOTALTIP:** Don't be seduced by what some falsely consider the more "literary" or more "formal" conjunctions such as **as, which,** and **while**. Clarity is important!

Correlative Conjunction

The third type of conjunction is the **correlative conjunction**. We have briefly mentioned and presented examples of **either ... or** and **neither ... nor** earlier in connection with nouns, verbs, and agreement. Now we want to discuss these correlatives in connection with **parallelism**.

Not only should be followed by **but (also)**.

In determining whether a mere invitation or an offer exists, the courts generally will look *not only* to the specific language *but also* to the surrounding circumstances, the custom within the industry, and the prior practice between the parties.

Watch out for **placement of correlatives**. Faulty placement leads to faulty construction and obstructs clarity.

The lawyer *either* is asked to furnish specific information *or* comment as to where the lawyer's views differ from those of management.

Below is the same sentence in much clearer form. Note that the phrases introduced by *either* and *or* are now in parallel construction: *either to furnish ... or to comment.*

The lawyer is asked *either* to furnish specific information *or to* comment as to where the lawyer's views differ from those of management.

———————————

NOTES

CHAPTER 43

CONTRACTS

I.   **Definitions**..43-3
   A.   Bilateral Contract 43-3
   B.   Consideration 43-3
   C.   Contract 43-3
   D.   Executed Contract 43-3
   E.   Executory Contract 43-3
   F.   Express Contract 43-3
   G.   Implied Contract 43-3
   H.   Promise 43-3
   I.   Promisee 43-3
   J.   Promisor 43-3
   K.   Quasi-Contract 43-3
   L.   Unenforceable Contract 43-3
   M.   Unilateral Contract 43-3
   N.   Void Contract 43-3
   O.   Voidable Contract 43-4

II.   **Elements of a Contract**..43-4
   A.   Agreement 43-4
   B.   Consideration 43-4
   C.   Compliance With the Statute of Frauds 43-7
   D.   Capacity of the Parties to Contract 43-10
   E.   Offer 43-10
   F.   Legal Subject Matter 43-13
   G.   Acceptance 43-14

III.   **Interpreting the Written Contract**..43-16
   A.   General Rules 43-16
   B.   Parol Evidence Rule 43-16

IV.   **Actual Assent**..43-17
   A.   Mistake 43-17
   B.   Innocent Misrepresentation 43-17
   C.   Fraud 43-17
   D.   Duress 43-19
   E.   Undue Influence 43-19
   F.   Unconscionability 43-19

V.   **Assignment of Rights and Delegations of Duties**..43-19
   A.   Assignment 43-19
   B.   Delegation 43-20

VI.   **Third Party Beneficiary Contracts** 43-21
   A.   Definition 43-21
   B.   Types of Beneficiaries 43-21
   C.   Vesting Rights in Third Party Beneficiaries 43-22
   D.   Defenses to the Contract 43-22

VII. Joint and Several Obligations 43-22
    A.   Joint Obligors 43-22
    B.   Joint Obligees 43-22
    C.   Several Obligors 43-22
    D.   Several Obligees 43-23

VIII. Discharge of Contracts 43-23
    A.   By Performance 43-23
    B.   By Agreement 43-24
    C.   By Operation of Law 43-25
    D.   By Breach 43-26

IX. Remedies for Breach 43-27
    A.   Election of Remedies 43-27
    B.   Damages 43-27
    C.   Specific Performance 43-28
    D.   Injunction 43-28

CHAPTER 43

CONTRACTS

I. Definitions

A.   Bilateral Contract--A contract in which both the contracting parties are bound by their mutual promises to fulfill reciprocal obligations towards each other. For example, a contract in which an accountant promises to prepare a tax return and the accountant's client promises to pay an agreed fee would be a bilateral contract.

B.   Consideration--An act or forbearance, or the promise thereof, which is offered by one party to an agreement (contract) and accepted by the other party as an inducement for his or her act or promise.

C.   Contract--An express or implied legally binding agreement between two or more persons to perform or not to perform some specific act or undertaking. The law views the performance of a valid contract as a duty and provides a suitable remedy for its breach.

D.   Executed Contract--A contract that has been fully performed.

E.   Executory Contract--A contract that has not been fully performed. Note that a contract may be *executory* as to a party who has not rendered performance and *executed* as to a party who has completed performance.

F.   Express Contract--A contract created by the verbal or written expression of its terms by the parties involved.

G.   Implied Contract--A contract that does not exist in form but which is implied in fact from the acts and circumstances of the parties.

H.   Promise--A promise is a declaration or assurance, however expressed, to do or refrain from doing a specified act. A promise that is legally enforceable is a contract.

I.   Promisee--The person to whom the promise is made.

J.   Promisor--The person who makes the promise.

K.   Quasi-Contract--A concept or principle of law having its foundation in equity and good conscience. As implied by its name, a quasi-contract is not properly a contract. Rather, it is a legal obligation created by the law in cases in which there is no contract, but the law ought to imply a contract as a matter of equity and justice.

L.   Unenforceable Contract--A contract that cannot be enforced by legal proceedings. For example, an oral contract is unenforceable if required to be in writing by the Statute of Frauds.

M.   Unilateral Contract--A contract in which one party promises a performance in return for an act or forbearance, and a second party, without promising to do so, acts or forbears. The contract is completed upon the act or forbearance of the second party; only then is the first party obligated to render his or her performance. For example, if A promises to pay a $100 reward to whoever finds her missing cat, and B finds the cat, the result is a completed unilateral contract. Note, however, that B is not obligated to look for the cat. Distinguish this from a bilateral contract, wherein A hires B to look for the missing cat, and B agrees to do so.

N.   Void Contract--An agreement that lacks one or more of the essential elements of a contract and, therefore, does not create any legal obligations.

O.   Voidable Contract--A contract that may be avoided by rescission but which remains binding if not rescinded. For example, contracts of infants, incompetents, and contracts obtained by fraud are voidable contracts.

II. Elements of a Contract

A.   **Agreement**--Mutual assent by the parties. Both parties must agree to the same bargain through the medium of offer and acceptance. At common law, the acceptance must contain all the terms and conditions included in the offer. Doctrinally, this is known as the Mirror Acceptance Rule.

```
┌─────────────────────────┐
│  TotalRecall            │
└─────────────────────────┘
```

ELEMENTS OF A CONTRACT

Nuemonic is "A Cold Sip of COLA"

A   Agreement

C   Consideration
S   Statue of Limitations

C   Capacity
O   Offer
L   Legal subject matter
A   Acceptance

1.   Assent may be "expressed" or may be inferred from a party's conduct.

2.   The "Objective Rule of Contracts"-- There is assent if a party's outward conduct would lead a reasonable person to believe that a party is assenting.   An actual subjective "meeting of the minds" is not required. Instead, the courts use an objective test in which each party is bound by the intention which they manifest to the other party. For example, picking up a package of candy in a drugstore is an objective act which manifests conduct indicating an intent to purchase the candy. This is an implied contract to purchase goods as distinguished from an express contract.

3.   The normal manner in which parties arrive at a mutual manifestation of assent is for one to make an offer and the other to accept it.

B.   **Consideration**--An act or a forbearance to act, or a promise to do either, given by one party to a contract in exchange for another party's act or promise; the consideration must be understood by both parties to be the "quid pro quo," or purchase price. Contracts, to be enforceable, must be supported by consideration.

1.   Test--The party to a contract must suffer a "legal detriment." This means the party must do something or bind him- or herself to do something the party is not legally or otherwise bound to do, or the party must surrender a legal right to which he or she is otherwise entitled. To constitute consideration, it is not necessary that the other party receive a legal benefit. For example, assume A and B enter into a contract wherein A promises to pay B $25.00 if B quits smoking for 6 months. B's surrender of the right to smoke is a legal detriment and, therefore, constitutes consideration even though A gains no legal benefit through B's performance. On the other hand, A's payment of $25.00 to B is both a legal detriment to A and a legal benefit to B.

2.   Types of Consideration

a.   An act or forbearance given in exchange for a promise in a unilateral contract.

b.   A promise to do something, if the action promised would itself suffice as consideration that is given in exchange for another promise in a bilateral contract. If the promises supply the consideration, there must be mutuality of obligation; in other words, both parties must be bound.

(1)   An Illusory Promise--The promisor is free to perform or not perform the promise. This type of promise will not bind the promisor because there is no mutuality of obligation.

(2)   A conditional promise is valid consideration if the promisor is bound to perform upon the occurrence of a condition beyond the promisor's control. For example, an insurance company promises to pay B $100 a day if B is hospitalized.

(3)   If the promisor promises to do one of two or more acts but reserves the right to choose which one, there is no mutuality of obligation, unless each act is a legal detriment. However, if the promisee has the right to choose which act the promisor will perform, there is mutuality of obligation if at least one act would be a legal detriment to the promisor.

3.   Adequacy of Consideration

a.   General Rule--The law will not inquire into the adequacy of consideration, i.e., a contract need not be absolutely fair to both sides.

b.   Exceptions

(1)   An exceedingly disadvantageous bargain may be evidence of fraud, duress, or unconscionability, which furnishes a court with reason to refuse enforcement.

(2)   A contract to exchange unequal amounts of money or fungible goods at the same time is inadequate for lack of consideration. However, unequal amounts may be exchanged at different times.

(3)   Nominal consideration, e.g., $1, for an act or promise of some value may raise the question of whether it was actually the quid pro quo. However, nominal consideration is usually adequate for an option contract.

4.   Common Situations Which Fail to Supply the Requisite Consideration

a.   Performance of a Preexisting Duty or Promise to Perform a Preexisting Duty--There is no legal detriment if one does or promises to do that which one is already bound to do. Therefore, the following acts are not sufficient consideration:

(1)   Refraining from criminal or tortious conduct.

(2)   Performing acts which one is required to perform by law (for example, a promise to pay a policeman a sum of money for solving a crime is unenforceable for lack of consideration since the policeman has a preexisting duty to perform that act).

(3)   Performing acts that the promisee is already under contract to the promisor to perform (for example, a promise to pay a contractor more than originally agreed upon in exchange for the completion of a building by the time set forth in the contract is not enforceable because the contractor assumed no additional legal detriment in return for the additional payment).

(4)   Payment of a liquidated debt at or after the time it is due (for example, a promise to take $400 as full payment for a debt of $500 is not enforceable since the debtor was already obligated to pay the money).

NOTE: Any change in the preexisting duty may supply sufficient consideration to support the amended contract. For example, a promise to accept $400 as full payment for a $500 debt--provided the $400 is tendered one week before the $500 is due--would be enforceable.

b.   Past Consideration--A promise in exchange for an act completed prior to the making of the promise (past consideration) will not be enforced because the act was not done in exchange for the promise, but independent of it.

c.   A moral obligation is insufficient consideration to support a contract under the past consideration rationale, except in certain cases in which a former promise (for which good consideration was once given) is renewed or slightly qualified. <u>For example</u>, a new promise to pay a debt barred by the statute of limitations is enforceable without additional consideration because the debt barred by the statute has been renewed.

5.   Exceptions to the Rule Requiring Consideration

a.   Commercial Paper--If executed and delivered, consideration for commercial paper is rebuttably presumed between the parties. When commercial paper is negotiated, consideration is conclusively presumed.

b.   Contracts Under Seal--At common law, a contract under seal required no consideration to be enforceable; consideration was conclusively presumed. However, today most states have abolished this rule. Article 2 of the UCC has abolished the effect of a seal with regard to the sale of goods.

c.   There are other specific exceptions under the UCC.

d.   <u>Promissory Estoppel</u>--The promisor is "estopped" (prevented) from asserting the lack of consideration for the promise if the following elements are present:

(1)   The promisor makes an express promise.

(2)   The promisor expects or should expect the promise to induce and it does induce the promisee to act or forbear to act in a substantial way.

(3)   The promisee in fact relied on the promise and this reliance was justifiable.

(4)   An injustice will result (not merely a legal detriment) to the promisee, unless the promise is enforced.

6.   Requirement (Supply), Output, and Exclusive Dealing Contracts--As stated earlier, consideration must exist on both sides in order to have a valid contract. However, in certain situations, the courts have recognized mutual consideration when one party has substantial discretion while the other party is essentially bound.

a.   <u>A requirement contract</u> is an agreement by one party to buy his or her "requirements" of a certain product from a certain supplier. The supplier is bound to meet these requirements while the other party is bound to purchase only what he or she needs. The law generally recognizes, however, that the purchasing party is under a "good faith" requirement to stay in business and continue to use the product which is the subject of the contract. Consideration is also recognized on the part of the purchaser in that, generally, the purchaser has given up the right to purchase his or her requirements from other suppliers.

b.   <u>An output contract</u> is an agreement by a supplier to sell all or a specified part of the products that he or she manufactures to the purchasing party. Here, the roles are reversed. The purchaser is bound to purchase a specified portion or all that is produced, while the producer is not required to produce any fixed amount. The law places a "good faith" requirement on the producer, however, to stay in the business of making his or her product and to continue production at a steady rate. Again, the producer's consideration is recognized to be the surrender of his or her freedom to sell to others.

c.   Article 2 of the UCC has the following provisions concerning output, requirement, and exclusive dealing contracts. Recall that Article 2 governs only contracts for the sale of goods:

    (1)   A term which measures the quantity by the output of the seller or the requirements of the buyer means such actual output or requirements as may occur in "good faith," except that no quantity unreasonably disproportionate to any stated estimate, or in the absence of a stated estimate to any normal or prior output or requirements, may be tendered or demanded.

    (2)   A lawful agreement by the seller or the buyer for exclusive dealing in the kind of goods concerned imposes an obligation by the seller to use best efforts to supply the goods and by the buyer to use best efforts to promote their sale unless there is an express agreement to the contrary.

C.   Compliance With the Statute of Frauds

1.   The Statute of Frauds provides that certain kinds of contracts cannot be enforced unless they are: (1) evidenced by a writing or writings, and (2) signed by the party to be charged.

2.   The Writing Requirement

a.   No formal writing is required, and the contract itself need not be written.

b.   However, there must be at least a note or memorandum of the contract that contains all of the following:

    (1)   Identity of the parties.

    (2)   Subject matter.

    (3)   Essential terms and conditions.

    (4)   Consideration.

    (5)   Signature of the party against whom enforcement is sought.

c.   The writing may appear in a written contract or in letters, telegrams, receipts, memoranda, etc.

d.   The writing need not appear in a single document, so long as the several documents refer to the same transaction.

e.   The writing may be prepared at any time before suit is brought.

f.   If the writing is lost or destroyed before suit is brought, the requirement may be satisfied by oral proof that it existed.

3.   The Signature Requirement

a.   Any mark can be a signature as long as the party so signing authenticates it as his or her own (e.g., initials, nickname, "X").

b.   An agent can generally sign for his or her principal.

c.   If one party signs the memo and the other does not, the contract can be enforced only against the one who signed.

4.   Effect of Failure to Comply With the Statute--Failure to comply makes a contract <u>unenforceable</u>, but <u>not</u> void or voidable.

    a.   If one party performs, the party cannot sue on the contract for the other's breach, but the party can recover in quasi-contract for the value of benefits given.

    b.   An executed contract cannot be rescinded.

    c.   If suit is brought on a contract which fails to comply, and the defendant fails to plead the statute as a defense, the defendant waives the statute and the contract is enforceable.

    d.   If the contract is bilateral and one promise comes within the statute (requires a writing) while the other promise does not, and the promise that comes within the statute is executed, then the promise that does not come within the statute can be enforced.

5.   Contracts That Fall Within the Statute

    a.   Contracts for the sale of goods if the price is $500 or more.

    b.   Contracts for the transfer of an interest in real property including buildings, easements, mortgages, and leases longer than 1 year.

        •   An oral real estate contract will typically satisfy the statute if there is:

            (a)   Possession of the land.

            (b)   Either partial payment made or improvements that have been made.

    c.   Contracts that cannot be performed within one-year from the date of the agreement.

        (1)   Timing--The one-year period begins to run on the day after the date the contract is <u>entered into</u>, not from the date upon which performance under the contract begins.

        (2)   If performance <u>could</u> occur within the one-year period, the contract is not within the statute and need not be written.

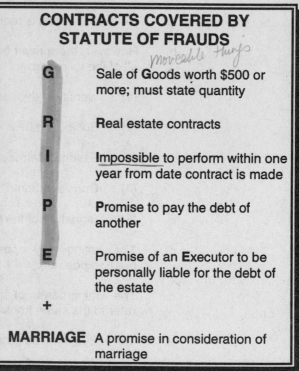

Total Recall

CONTRACTS COVERED BY STATUTE OF FRAUDS

moveable things

G   Sale of **G**oods worth $500 or more; must state quantity

R   **R**eal estate contracts

I   **I**mpossible to perform within one year from date contract is made

P   **P**romise to pay the debt of another

E   Promise of an **E**xecutor to be personally liable for the debt of the estate

+

MARRIAGE   A promise in consideration of marriage

(a)   A contract of employment for life need not be written because performance could be completely performed within a year, i.e., if the employee dies.

(b)   But a contract of employment for two years is within the statute because it cannot be performed within a year; the employee's death prior to one year merely excuses performance.

(3)   If one party can and does perform within a year, most courts will enforce the other party's promise even if it cannot be performed within a year.

d.   A promise to answer for the debt of another.

(1)   The promise must be collateral (for the benefit of another), and not primary (for the promisor's benefit). Thus, in order to fall within the statute the promise must

(a)   Be made for the primary purpose of paying the debt of a third person (debtor) with payment possibly coming out of the promisor's assets, and

(b)   Be directed to and relied on by the creditor. However, if the primary purpose of the promisor is to serve his or her own monetary ends (e.g., to assure a continuing supply of goods from the debtor by promising to pay the debtor's obligation to its suppliers), the contract is not within the statute. Therefore, the contract of the promisor is enforceable even though it is oral. In contrast, if the primary purpose is to be a surety for another person's debt (when the promisor is not directly benefited), then the promise must be in writing. For example, A, an infant, obtains goods that are not necessaries from B, a merchant. The sale is a credit transaction. In order to convince B to part with the goods, C (an unrelated adult) agrees with B that A will pay as per the agreed credit terms. If A does not pay, then B can look to C as surety. This agreement must be in writing because it is a promise to answer for the debt of another (see and compare (2), below).

(2)   In contrast, a promise to pay and not answer for the debt of another is not within the statute. For example, when C orally promises to pay the purchase price of goods to be delivered by A to B, the promise is not within the statute. The following are other examples of promises outside the Statute of Frauds:

(a)   Indemnity Contract--A contract between two parties whereby one undertakes and agrees to reimburse the other against loss or damage arising from some contemplated occurrence.

(b)   Novation--A substitution of a new contract between the same or different parties which discharges the old contract and extinguishes the outstanding obligations.

e.   A promise by an executor or administrator to answer for obligations of the decedent's estate.

f.   Agreements in consideration of marriage, except for mutual promises to marry, e.g., an antenuptial contract.

6.   Additional Contracts That Fall Within the Statute (Infrequently Tested)

a.   Contracts for the sale of any face amount of securities.

b. Contracts for the sale of intangible personal property, such as royalty rights, for $5,000 or more.

7. A party may be <u>estopped</u> from pleading the Statute of Frauds. For example, under the theory of promissory estoppel, a party who promises to waive the statute and thereby induces the other party to reasonably rely on that promise to his or her detriment cannot later plead the statute.

D. Capacity of the Parties to Contract

1. Infants (Minors)

   a. Definition--At common law, persons less than 21.

      (1) Currently, 18 is the age of majority in most states. State law supersedes common law.

      (2) A statute may provide that marriage removes the disability of non-age. Court action may also make an infant an adult.

   b. A contract made by an infant is <u>voidable</u> by the infant, i.e., he or she may avoid performance. The one <u>exception</u> to this rule is that an infant may not avoid contracts to supply him or her with necessities, such as food, shelter, and clothing. The other party to a contract with an infant has no power to void the contract on the basis of infancy.

2. Incompetent Persons

   a. Test of Capacity to Contract--Does the disability render the person incapable of understanding the nature and consequences of the transaction?

   b. Two Kinds of Incompetent Persons

      (1) Persons adjudicated insane by a court.

         (a) Contracts made by such persons are void from the beginning.

         (b) Such incompetents are still liable for necessaries furnished to them.

      (2) Persons who are de facto insane. Contracts made by insane persons not judicially declared incompetent are generally voidable.

   c. Intoxicated persons are treated like incompetents; a contract made by an intoxicated individual when he or she is unable to understand the nature of the transaction is generally voidable by the intoxicated individual.

E. Offer--An offer is a proposal made by one party (the offeror) to another (the offeree) which manifests an intent to enter into a contract. The offeree has the power to create the contract by acceptance.

1. Legal Requirements

   a. Intent--The offeror (person making the offer) generally must intend the action to be an offer. Thus, an "offer" that is made in jest or anger is not a true offer. The courts apply the "objective rule"; therefore, they will find intent if a reasonable person would interpret the offeror's action as manifesting actual intent, whether or not the offeror had such actual intent. However, if the offeree (person to whom the offer is made) actually knows there is no intent to offer, then no offer has been made.

b. Mere invitations or inquiries soliciting offers are not offers. Such language as "I would consider selling for $100.00" or "I quote you a price . . ." is usually construed as an invitation to make an offer or commence negotiations. On the other hand, language such as "I offer" or "I will sell X for $100.00" usually is construed as an offer. In determining whether a mere invitation or an offer exists, the courts generally will look not only to the specific language but will also consider the surrounding circumstances, the custom within the industry, and the prior practice between the parties.

    (1) Communications sent to large numbers of people (newspaper advertisements) are normally only invitations. However, when an ad limits the quantities or uses "first come, first served" language, it is probably an offer.

    (2) A reward is an offer to form a unilateral contract; that is, it may be accepted only by performance.

c. Definite and Certain--The "offer" must be sufficiently definite and certain as to allow a court to delineate the terms and requirements of the contract that would result from acceptance. A valid offer may leave one or more terms open. Contracts are often made in which the parties intend to supply the missing terms at a later date. If the parties fail to agree on a term left open, the courts will imply a reasonable term. Terms commonly left open are time and method of delivery, method of payment, and price. **NOTE**: Article 2 of the UCC requires that only the quantity term be certain.

    (1) Identification of the Offeree--A certain offeree or class of offerees must be identifiable by the terms of the offer.

    (2) Subject Matter--The offer must adequately identify the subject matter. For example, an "offer" to sell some of my farmland is not an offer.

2. Types of Offers--Offers may be either written, oral, or implied from the offeror's actions.

a. An offer is either general (addressed to whoever accepts) or specific (addressed to a particular person or persons).

b. Continuing Offer--An offer which may result in a series of contracts by successive acceptances.

c. Illusory Offer--An offer in which the offeror retains the unlimited option to perform the promise. Such an offer generally results in an unenforceable contract.

3. Termination of an offer ends the offeree's power to accept it. If acceptance is attempted after the offer has terminated, it is in effect a new offer. Thus, the original offeror's treatment of it as a valid "acceptance" is actually the offeror's own acceptance of a new offer. Termination of an offer may be effected by the following means:

a. Revocation by the Offeror

    (1) Generally, the offeror can revoke the offer at any time prior to acceptance even if the offeror stated it would be open for a fixed period. However, there are several exceptions to this rule:

        (a) If there is consideration for the offeror's promise to keep the offer open, then that promise becomes an option contract, and it is irrevocable for the period of the option.

    (b)   <u>Firm Offers</u>--These are offers made under the UCC that are irrevocable even though they are not supported by consideration.

    (c)   Partial Performance

        (i)   <u>Unilateral Contract</u>--If an offer can be accepted only by performance so that there is no acceptance until the act is complete, the majority rule is that <u>partial performance</u> makes the offer <u>irrevocable</u>. The usual rationale is that partial performance is consideration for an implied option contract. <u>Minority rule</u>: Revocation is allowed, but the offeree can recover for his or her performance in quasi-contract.

        (ii)   <u>Bilateral Contract</u>--If the offer can be accepted by a promise, then partial performance implies a promise to complete performance, and therefore a bilateral contract results.

(2)   Manner of Revocation

    (a)   Any language or conduct indicating that the offer is revoked is sufficient (e.g., a statement that the property in question has been sold to someone else).

    (b)   Revocation must be communicated to the offeree, and it is not effective until <u>received</u> by the offeree. However, the communication need not be direct. Thus, the offeree cannot accept if he or she learns by any reliable means that the offeror has revoked the offer. If a general offer has been made by public announcement, revocation may be made by any means reasonably certain to reach all who may have heard of the offer. Preferably, the original method of publication should be used to make the revocation. A continuing offer may be revoked as to future contracts even if some binding contracts have already been created.

Cannot accept if he or she learns the offer is revoked

  b.   Lapse of Time

    (1)   If the offeror specifies a time for acceptance, the offer automatically terminates upon the expiration of that time period.

        (a)   If the offeror specifies a mode of communication for acceptance, e.g., "by return mail," this is usually construed to mean that acceptance must arrive as soon as it would if communicated by that mode.

        (b)   If the offer specifies that the offeree must respond within a certain number of days after receiving the offer and the delivery of the offer was delayed by a person other than the offeror, then the following rules apply:

            (i)   If the offeree knows of the delay, he or she must accept within a time period that commences on the date the offer normally would have arrived.

            (ii)   If the offeree has no reason to know of the delay, he or she may accept within a time period which commences on the date of actual delivery.

    (2)   If no time for acceptance is specified, the offer lapses after a reasonable time. What is reasonable under the circumstances depends on factors such as the following:

(a)   The nature of the subject matter.

(b)   The rate at which the price fluctuates, i.e., nature of the market.

(c)   The time within which the offeror's purpose can be accomplished.

(d)   The manner in which the offer is communicated.

c.   Provision of the Offer--The offer may specify that on the occurrence of a specific condition, the offer will automatically terminate.

d.   Rejection by the Offeree--Any conduct communicated to the offeror, either by word or act, that indicates the offeree's intention not to accept constitutes a rejection.

(1)   A rejection is effective only <u>upon receipt</u>. Thus, the offeree can change his or her mind and accept if the offeree does so before the tendered rejection is received.

(2)   A <u>counteroffer</u>, in which the offeree attempts to substitute different terms, is treated as a <u>rejection and a new offer</u>. However, a counteroffer may be worded so as to reserve the original offer for further consideration. Furthermore, a mere inquiry as to the addition of other terms is not treated as a counteroffer.

e.   Death or Disability of the Parties--In general, the death or supervening insanity of the offeror or a specific offeree terminates the offer.

f.   Supervening <u>Illegality</u> or Impossibility--An offer terminates by operation of law if after being made, and prior to acceptance, the object of the contract or either party's performance becomes illegal. Likewise, an offer terminates automatically if a person or thing essential to the performance of the proposed contract dies or is destroyed.

g.   Bankruptcy or insolvency of either the offeror or offeree terminates the offer.

F.   **Legal Subject Matter**

1.   An agreement may be unenforceable if performance of it would be illegal or if the object of the contract is illegal.

2.   Types of Illegality

a.   A contract may be illegal because courts have declared it to be contrary to public policy. Examples:

(1)   Agreements that interfere with the administration of government; for example, an agreement inducing a public official to deviate from his or her duty.

(2)   Agreements that interfere with the administration of justice; for example, agreements tending to hinder prosecution for crime, agreements to give false testimony, and agreements to extend the statute of limitations.

(3)   Agreements that unreasonably restrain trade or interfere with competition.

(4)   Agreements containing exculpatory clauses tending to absolve one from negligence (if the party being exculpated has a superior bargaining position) or from willful wrongdoing.

b.   A contract may be illegal because it violates a statute or a rule of common law. Examples:

   (1)   Contracts for the performance of a crime or tort.

   (2)   Usurious contracts, i.e., those charging more than the statutorily permissible rate of interest for the loan of money.

3.   Related to illegal contracts are <u>unconscionable contracts</u> (see IV.F., below).

G.   **Acceptance**--The intentional manifestation of assent required by an offer to create the contract is termed an acceptance.

1.   Legal Requirements

   a.   Acceptance must be made with <u>knowledge</u> of the offer and with the <u>intention</u> to accept. **NOTE:** This is an exception to the objective rule of contracts; that is, if it is not clear whether an act or forbearance to act is meant as an acceptance, the offeree's actual subjective intent determines whether a contract was created.

   b.   Acceptance must be in the form required by the offer.

   (1)   An offer may call for acceptance by promise. Such acceptance creates a <u>bilateral</u> contract. If the offeree simply begins performance with the offeror's knowledge, a promise to complete the performance may be <u>implied</u> from the offeree's conduct.

   (2)   An offer may call for or permit acceptance by act or forbearance to act. Such acceptance creates a unilateral contract. If the offer requires acceptance by act, acceptance by a promise alone is not an acceptance. While partial performance may end the offeror's right to revoke, acceptance requires full performance.

   (3)   If it is not clear whether a promise or an act is required, the offer is usually interpreted to permit acceptance in either form.

   c.   Acceptance must be unequivocal and unconditional and must comply with any terms set forth in the offer.

   (1)   If the offer sets forth conditions regarding acceptance, such as time, place, or manner, these must be fulfilled for the acceptance to be effective.

   (2)   If an offer merely <u>suggests</u> a time, place, or manner, acceptance by other means may be permitted.

   (3)   A reply that purports to accept an offer but which adds material qualifications or conditions is not an acceptance; rather, it is a rejection and a counter-offer.

   (4)   If the qualification is immaterial or one that would be implied by law, the acceptance is effective.

   (5)   Article 2 of the UCC has materially changed the law stated in (3) and (4), above, as it applies to contracts for the sale of goods.

    d.   Communications

        (1)   <u>Bilateral Contract</u>--Unless the offer provides for acceptance to be made without communication, the offeree must communicate acceptance to the offeror.

        (2)   <u>Unilateral Contract</u>--Unless the offeror has no way of knowing that performance has been completed, the offeree need not communicate acceptance.

2.   When Effective--Generally, acceptance is effective when it is <u>received</u> by the offeror or the offeror's agent.

    a.   However, if acceptance is sent by a mode of communication expressly or impliedly authorized by the offeror (e.g., mail), it is effective when sent, even if it is thereafter delayed or lost. This is known as the <u>mailbox rule</u>. If no mode of acceptance is expressly authorized, the following modes of communication are impliedly authorized:

        (1)   The same mode by which the offer was sent.

        (2)   Any reasonable mode dictated by business custom.

    b.   If the offer is held open under an option contract, acceptance must be received in order to be effective, regardless of the mode of communication.

3.   Who May Accept

    a.   If the offer is made to a specific offeree, a valid acceptance can be made only by that person or his or her agent.

        (1)   If the offeror is mistaken as to the offeree's identity, the offeree may still accept if the offeree reasonably believes the offer was intentionally made to him or her.

        (2)   If the offer requires a promise from a third person as the consideration, acceptance must be made by that third person.

    b.   General offers (reward cases) usually can be accepted by whoever performs the specified act, provided he or she knew of the offer <u>and</u> intended the act to be his or her acceptance.

4.   Silence as Acceptance--Silence is usually not acceptance. However, it may constitute acceptance if the circumstances are such that assent may be implied. The following are some common examples:

    a.   The offeree accepts services that reasonably appear to be offered only for payment, when the offeree could have rejected them.

    b.   The offeree solicits goods "on approval" and retains them for an unreasonable length of time.

    c.   The offeror indicates that silence will be understood as assent, and the offeree subjectively intends his or her silence to be so understood.

    d.   Previous dealings lead the offeror to understand silence as assent.

    e.   Similarly, acceptance of a contractual paper, such as a deed, an insurance policy, or a ticket purporting to be a contract, may be taken to imply assent to its terms.

III. Interpreting the Written Contract

A. <u>General Rules</u>

    1.   Terms in written contracts are assumed to have their ordinary and usual meanings. Technical terms are understood to have their technical meanings.

    2.   If there are ambiguous terms, then the most reasonable meaning under the circumstances is ascribed to them in light of trade customs. Generally, ambiguities are construed against the party who drafted them.

B. <u>Parol Evidence Rule</u>

    1.   Basic Statement--If a contract is completely integrated into a written instrument, any evidence (written or oral) of a <u>prior or contemporaneous agreement</u> offered to modify or contradict the terms of the written instrument is <u>inadmissible</u>.

        a.   Rationale--Parties are presumed to have included every material term in the completed writing.

        b.   A writing is integrated if the parties intended it to represent the complete agreement at the time of writing.

        c.   The parol evidence rule does not exclude the following:

            (1)   Evidence that does not alter, vary, or contradict the terms of the written contract.

            (2)   Evidence showing that the contract never became effective (its taking effect was conditioned on an event that never occurred).

            (3)   Evidence that the contract is void or voidable because of fraud, duress, mistake, lack of capacity, or failure of consideration.

            (4)   Evidence of a clerical mistake in the execution of the contract.

            (5)   Evidence of a party's identity.

            (6)   Evidence of the intended meaning of an ambiguous term.

        d.   The rule does not apply to <u>subsequent</u> agreements varying the terms of a prior integrated written contract.

    2.   With respect to the sale of goods, UCC 2-202 applies. This section allows the written contract to be explained or supplemented, <u>but not contradicted</u>, by evidence relating to course of dealing, usage of trade, or course of performance. In addition, prior or contemporaneous agreements can supplement the integrated written instrument unless the court determines that the written instrument was intended to be the exclusive and complete statement of the terms of the contract.

IV. Actual Assent

If, for one reason or another, a party's assent to an agreement was not actually given, the contract may be voidable.

A.   Mistakes

1. Unilateral Mistake--A mistake made by only one party to the contract. The mistake is usually to the detriment of the mistaken party.

    a.   If the other party had no notice and acted in good faith, the mistaken party cannot avoid the contract.

    b.   If the other party knew or had reason to know of the mistake and attempted to take advantage of it, the mistaken party may be able to avoid the contract.

2. Mutual Mistake--A mistake made by both parties; both parties are mistaken as to the nature or existence of the subject matter, the terms of the contract, or other material facts.

    a.   If the result of the mistake is that there is no real agreement (hence no contract), the purported contract is void.

    b.   If the mistake is related to a material provision and materially increased one party's obligations, the contract is voidable by that party unless

        (1)   An innocent third party would be adversely affected, or

        (2)   The contract can be reformed or the loss can be compensated.

    c.   If the mistake was made in reducing an oral agreement to writing, an equity court may reform the contract to make it conform to the actual agreement.

3. Mistake in the Inducement--If either or both parties were mistaken concerning their reasons for entering into the contract, this is a mistake in the inducement which is not in and of itself a ground for relief.

B.   Innocent Misrepresentation--A misstatement of fact made without intent to defraud. If an innocent misrepresentation is material, such misrepresentation gives rise to the following:

1. A defense to an action to enforce the contract.

2. Grounds for rescission; that is, a restoration of each party to its original position insofar as can equitably be accomplished, including the return of any benefits received.

C.   Fraud

1. Definition--A false representation of material fact made by one party to the other party with the intent to deceive and which induces the other party to justifiably rely on that fact to his or her detriment. In order to find fraud, all of the following elements must be present:

    a.   False Representation--Usually there must be a false statement. However, non-disclosure is a misrepresentation when one of the following occurs:

        (1)   There is a false denial of knowledge of the facts.

        (2)   Truth is suppressed by active concealment or by revealing only part of the facts.

          (3)   Under the circumstances, there is a duty to reveal the facts. For example:

              (a)   There is a confidential or fiduciary relationship between the parties.

              (b)   One party is known to rely upon the special knowledge or skill of the other.

    b.   Material Fact

          (1)   Material--To be material, a fact must be a substantial factor in inducing someone to enter the contract.

          (2)   Statement of Fact--The following are generally not considered to be statements of fact:

              (a)   Statements of opinion, unless made by an expert.

              (b)   Statements of value.

              (c)   Sales "puffing."

              (d)   Statements of law, unless made by an expert (a lawyer).

              (e)   Predictions about the future.

    c.   Intention to Deceive (Scienter)--The knowledge that one's statement is false or made in reckless disregard as to whether it is true or false.

    d.   Justifiable Reliance

          (1)   The misrepresentation must have been a substantial factor inducing the person to enter into the contract.

          (2)   If there are means whereby the accuracy of the statement can be verified and it would be reasonable to do so, justifiable reliance requires such verification.

    e.   Injury results from the deception.

2.   Fraud may occur in the _inducement_ or in the _execution_.

    a.   If fraud in the inducement (i.e., during contract negotiations) is present, the resulting contract is voidable at the option of the defrauded party.

    b.   If fraud in the execution is present (e.g., when one party is induced to sign an instrument different from the one the party intended to sign), the contract is void. It is void because there was never any actual intention to enter into it on the part of the defrauded party.

3.   Remedies

    a.   If the contract is voidable due to fraud, the defrauded party may use the fraud as a defense to an action brought against him or her on the contract.

    b.   If the contract is void, it is of no legal effect. The defrauded party may seek damages in tort.

D. Duress

1. Definition--Duress is the threat of harm to a party or to a member of a party's family which forces him or her to enter into a contract with the person initiating the threat or on whose behalf the threat is made.

2. Examples of duress include the threat of physical violence and the threat of criminal prosecution, whether the victim is guilty or not, but not threat of civil suit. The threat of economic loss is generally not duress, but under some circumstances unlawful detention of another's goods or the threatened destruction of them may constitute duress.

3. Effect--Contract is voidable by the victim.

E. Undue Influence

1. Definition--Undue influence is the mental coercion of one person by another person so that the will of the influencing party is substituted for that of the victim. Consequently, the unduly influenced party's assent to the contract is not voluntary.

2. Usual Case--A person in a position of trust (e.g., an accountant or a lawyer) exerts influence over a person with a weak, susceptible mind who succumbs to such influence.

3. Effect--Contract is voidable by the victim.

F. Unconscionability

1. Definition--Unconscionability occurs when one party takes unfair advantage of another party's ignorance, illiteracy, or greatly inferior bargaining position, so as to cause the party to enter into a contract with oppressive terms.

2. Under UCC 2-302 (regarding contracts for the sale of goods), a court can refuse to enforce an unconscionable contract or an unconscionable clause in a contract, or may limit the application of the unconscionable clause so as to prevent an unconscionable result.

V. Assignment of Rights and Delegations of Duties

One to whom performance under a contract is owed (promisee) has a contract right (the right to receive that performance), while one who must perform under a contract (obligor) has a contractual duty (the duty to perform). Assignment of a contract is rebuttably presumed to mean assignment of rights and delegation of duties.

A. Assignment--A contract right can ordinarily be assigned by the person to whom it is owed (assignor) to another person (assignee).

1. However, a contract right cannot be assigned in the following situations:

a. Without permission of the obligor, if one of the following applies:

(1) The right is personal to the promisee or involves a confidential relationship between the parties.

(2) The duty of the obligor would be materially changed, the burden or risk materially increased, or the chances of obtaining return performance are materially impaired.

b. The contract prohibits assignment. However, in certain cases, the prohibitive clause is void as a matter of law. If a contract for the sale of goods forbids "assignment of the contract" without specifying rights or duties, the prohibition is construed to apply only to the delegation of performance unless the circumstances indicate the contrary [UCC 2-210 (3)].

2. Assignee's Rights Against the Obligor--Generally, the assignee takes whatever rights the assignor had against the obligor but no more.

    a. Rights of Assignor--If the claim was covered by security, the assignee gets the benefit of the security.

    b. "But No More"--The assignee takes subject to any defenses and counterclaims arising from the contract that the obligor had against the assignor.

    c. Payment of the obligation to the assignor is a defense if made before the obligor had notice of the assignment.

    d. Any counterclaims against the assignor arising from collateral transactions may be asserted against the assignee, but if the assignee notifies the obligor of the assignment, the obligor can assert only those collateral counterclaims that accrued before notice was given.

    e. UCC 9-206 provides that in nonconsumer contracts, an agreement by a buyer or lessee of personal property that he or she will not assert any claims or defenses he or she has against the seller or lessor is enforceable by an assignee who takes for value, in good faith, and without notice of any claim or defense.

3. Assignee Vis-a-Vis Assignor

    a. A valid assignment is effective between the parties without notice to the obligor. The assignor no longer owns the right; the assignee does. If the assignor receives the assigned performance, the assignee can recover from him or her. If the assignor causes the obligor not to perform, the assignee can recover from the assignor.

    b. An assignor can revoke a gratuitous (i.e., without consideration) assignment unless one of the following applies:

        (1) There is promissory estoppel.

        (2) The assignor delivers either a tangible document embodying the right assigned or a written assignment.

        (3) The assignee collects the obligation prior to the attempted revocation.

    c. If the assignor wrongfully assigns the same right to two assignees, one of two following rules generally applies:

        (1) The one who first received the assignment prevails over the other.

        (2) The one who first gave notice to the obligor prevails.

B. Delegation

1. Some contract duties may be delegated by the party having the duty (delegator) to another (delegatee), so that performance by the delegatee satisfies the delegator's duty. Duties may be delegated unless

a. The duty requires the personal performance of the original obligor-delegator (e.g., the rendering of professional services), so that the substitute performance would differ materially from that agreed on.

b. A statute, common law, or the contract forbids the delegation of that duty.

2. Effect of Delegation--Delegation does not strip the delegator of duty. The delegator remains liable to the obligee until someone performs.

VI. Third Party Beneficiary Contracts

A. <u>Definition</u>--Contracts that are likely to benefit a person other than the contracting parties.

B. <u>Types of Beneficiaries</u>

cannot sue -- to the dealer
but can sue --

1. <u>Creditor Beneficiary</u>--A third person to whom a debt or other duty is owed by the promisee. The debt or duty will be discharged in whole or in part by the promisor's rendering performance to the third party.

a. Example: If the purchaser of a house (promisor) promises the seller (promisee) that he or she will assume the mortgage (debt owed to third party), the mortgagee is a creditor beneficiary of the contract for the sale of the house.

b. If the promisor fails to perform, the third party creditor beneficiary can do one of the following:

(1) Sue the promisor on the contract.

(2) Recover the original obligation from the promisee, who remains secondarily liable (unless there has been a novation). The promisee, if made to perform, can then recover from the promisor for breach of contract.

2. <u>Donee Beneficiary</u>--A third person to whom the promisee intends to make a gift, by having the promisor render performance to the beneficiary. In a donee beneficiary relationship, there is no debt or duty owed by the promisee to the beneficiary.

Can sue

a. Example: The promisee pays money and the promisor agrees to deliver a car as a gift to a third person, the donee beneficiary.

b. If the promisor fails to perform,

(1) The donee beneficiary can sue the promisor for breach of contract, but cannot sue the promisee because an unexecuted gift cannot be enforced, or

(2) The promisee can sue the promisor for rescission to recover any consideration paid. Alternatively, the promisee can sue the breaching promisor for specific performance. However, in this case the promisee cannot recover damages because he or she suffered no substantial harm as a result of the promisor's nonperformance.

3. <u>Incidental Beneficiary</u>--A third person who benefits from a contract between others made without intent to benefit him or her. Incidental beneficiaries have no contract rights and no cause of action if parties fail to perform. For example, suppose that A contracts to have B build a house and specifies in the contract for B to use a certain type of lumber. If B fails to use the type of wood required in the contract, the local supplier of that kind of lumber has no rights under the contract even though a proper performance by B of his or her duties would have benefited the supplier. The supplier is only an incidental beneficiary.

C. <u>Vesting Rights in Third Party Beneficiaries</u>

1. Life Insurance Contracts--Rights vest in the beneficiary immediately, unless the parties-- insurer and insured--reserve the right to modify or discharge the contract (e.g., the right to change the named beneficiary).

2. Other Contracts--Rights vest in a third party creditor or donee beneficiary when he or she knows of the contract and one of the following applies:

   a. Manifests assent to it.

   b. Materially changes his or her position in justifiable reliance on it.

   c. Sues to enforce it.

3. Until the rights vest in a beneficiary, the parties can modify or discharge the contract without the beneficiary's consent.

D. <u>Defenses to the Contract</u>

1. The promisor's original defenses against the promisee are good against the beneficiary. The promisee's failure to perform a condition precedent to promisor's performance, failure of consideration, incapacity, and failure to comply with the Statute of Frauds are all good against the beneficiary.

2. Defenses against the promisee that arise after the rights vest in the beneficiary are not good as against the beneficiary.

3. Defenses of the promisee against a creditor beneficiary on the original obligation cannot be used by the promisor against the beneficiary.

VII. Joint and Several Obligations

A. <u>Joint Obligors</u>--Two or more persons under a joint duty to a single obligee.

1. The obligee can hold any of them responsible for the entire performance due. Between themselves, joint obligors may agree on how they are to share in the obligation, and if any pays more than his or her share, he or she is entitled to reimbursement from the others.

2. A surety may recover the entire performance from the principal debtor or a pro rata contribution from co-sureties.

3. A principal debtor cannot recover from his or her surety, but is entitled to reimbursement from any other joint principal debtors.

B. <u>Joint Obligees</u>--Two or more persons who are owed performance as a single group.

C. <u>Several Obligors</u>--Two or more persons who separately promise the same performance in the alternative.

1. Discharge of one does not discharge others.

2. The obligee is entitled to only one performance.

3. If one obligor is required to perform more than his or her share, he or she is entitled to reimbursement from the others.

D.   Several Obligees--Two or more persons who are owed individual performance.

VIII. Discharge of Contracts

A.   By Performance--Most contracts are discharged by performance of the promises and acts that the parties have agreed to perform.

1.   Types of Performance

a.   Complete Performance--The obligation is performed exactly as agreed or so close as to satisfy a reasonable person.

b.   Substantial Performance--Performance that is less than complete but which satisfies the contract to the extent that there is not a failure of consideration.

(1)   There must be a substantial, good faith performance of the obligation, with only minor deviations.

(2)   Any loss caused by the breach, or performance as rendered, must be paid to the nonbreaching party or subtracted from the price the party was to pay for complete performance.

c.   Material Breach--A major defect in performance which constitutes a failure of consideration and excuses the other party from his or her duty to perform.

2.   Conditions to Performance

a.   Types of Conditions

(1)   Condition Precedent--An uncertain future event that must occur before there is a duty to perform.

(2)   Condition Subsequent--An uncertain future event that, if it occurs, relieves a party of a previously existing duty to perform.

(3)   Condition Concurrent--Two promises that are to be performed at or about the same time, one in exchange for the other.

b.   A condition may be within the control of one party or neither party.

c.   If a condition is not met, no liability accrues unless the condition was also a promise. If a condition precedent fails to occur, the party whose performance was conditional is simply relieved of having to perform.

3.   Time of Performance

a.   If no time is specified, performance must be made within a reasonable time. What is reasonable depends on the circumstances.

b.   If a time is specified, failure to perform on time is a breach of contract, giving rise to an action for damages.

c.   If time is "of the essence," then failure to perform on time is a failure of a condition, and the other party is relieved of the duty to perform. Time is of the essence if so specified by the parties or if a failure to perform in time would defeat the purpose of the contract.

4.   Performance by Means of Payment

    a.   Payment may be made by either the delivery of money or a negotiable instrument. If payment is made with a negotiable instrument, the acceptance is conditional; that is, the contract is not discharged until the instrument is paid.

    b.   Part Payment

        (1)   The debtor may specify the application of payment (e.g., to one of several debts, to principal, or to interest).

        (2)   If the debtor does not specify, the creditor may choose the application of payment. However, some courts require payment to be applied to interest before principal.

        (3)   If neither party chooses, the law presumes payments go to interest before principal, to older before newer debts, and to unsecured before secured debts.

5.   Tender--An attempt or offer to perform, which is proper in time, place, and manner, is a tender.

    •   Refusal of Tender--If proper performance is tendered, a refusal to accept discharges the promisor and gives the promisor the right to sue for breach of contract. If the tender involves the payment of money, a refusal does not discharge the debt, but it does stop the accrual of interest.

B.   By Agreement--Contracting parties may agree to end or modify liability.

1.   Methods of Ending Liability

    a.   Release--The discharging of a contractual right. To be effective, a release requires one of the following: seal, consideration, detrimental reliance, deed of gift, or gift of evidence of indebtedness. Mutual release discharges both parties from further performance; each release is consideration for the other.

    b.   Waiver--Promise to excuse the breach of promise or failure of condition, often binding without consideration.

    c.   Cancellation--Physical destruction of a written contract with intent to destroy its legal effect.

    d.   Mutual Rescission--Undoing of the contract on both sides and placing the parties in their original position.

2.   Methods of Modifying Liability

    a.   Merger--A contract duty is superseded by a higher duty (e.g., a promissory note for a debt on open account, a judicial judgment for a contract obligation).

    b.   Accord and Satisfaction (Executory Accord)--An agreement to accept a performance in the future in substitution for a performance required under an existing contract. Performance of the substituted duty is the "satisfaction" that discharges the original duty. In the case of disputed or unliquidated debts where there is a question as to the amount actually owed on a contract, an accord can be used to settle the debt. In this situation, use of the words "payment in full" on a check for an amount less than that claimed by the creditor may operate as an accord. Thus, an accord, or an offer to settle for a different sum, will result if the amount is in dispute and the creditor has reasonable notice that the check is being tendered as full satisfaction. A satisfaction and acceptance of the accord occurs upon the cashing of the check.

    c.   Substituted Contract--The parties agree on a different contract which supersedes and replaces the old contract.

    d.   Novation

        (1)   A substitution of a new contract between the same or different parties which discharges the old contract and extinguishes the outstanding obligations.

        (2)   If the promisor of the new contract breaches the new contract, the suit by the promisee must be against the promisor and must be based on the new contract rather than the original contract.

    e.   UCC Revision of Rules for Modification

        (1)   Under common law, the modification of a contract requires consideration. However, UCC 2-209 provides that a good faith modification is binding without consideration.

        (2)   The common law makes unenforceable any clause in a written contract that prohibits a future oral modification or a rescission of the contract. However, UCC 2-209 validates such written clauses providing that, except as between merchants, such a clause on a form supplied by a merchant must be separately signed by the other party.

C.   By Operation of Law--Under certain circumstances, unperformed contracts may be excused by operation of law.

    1.   Impossibility

        a.   Effect--Impossible performance is excused. This means that there is no consideration for the other party's performance, thus the other party is entitled to rescission.

        b.   Objective Impossibility--Performance under the contract must be objectively impossible, that is, it must be impossible for anyone to complete the required performance. There will be no excuse if the required performance is only subjectively impossible, that is, not capable of being performed by the party to the contract (e.g., due to lack of funds).

        c.   Types of Impossibility

            (1)   Subsequent to the formation of the contract, the performance contemplated becomes illegal.

            (2)   Subject matter necessary for performance is destroyed through no fault of promisor.

            (3)   Personal performance is required and the particular person to render or receive it dies or is otherwise incapacitated.

    2.   Frustration of Purpose

        a.   Performance may still be possible, but its value is destroyed by a supervening event not foreseen by the parties.

    b.   The purpose of the performance must be known to both parties.

    c.   Effect--Acts as a failure of consideration.

3.   Impracticality

    a.   Generally, unexpected difficulty or expense does not excuse performance.

    b.   However, in contracts for the sale of goods, UCC 2-615 provides there is no breach if performance becomes impracticable by the occurrence of a contingency that contradicts the assumptions upon which the contract was based.

4.   Statute of Limitations

    a.   Definition--A statute of limitations is a statutorily created period of time within which a party must bring an action to enforce its rights.

    b.   Effect--The expiration of the statute of limitations does not technically discharge a party's performance, but operates to bar the bringing of an action against a nonperforming party.

D.   <u>By Breach</u>--A breach of a contractual promise may excuse the other party's performance.

1.   Definition--An unexcused failure to perform a contractual promise. Failure to perform is a breach whether or not the breaching party was at fault.

2.   <u>Types of Breach</u>

    a.   <u>Renunciation</u> during the course of performance

        (1)   Definition--Any act rendering substantial performance impossible, or a statement that the promisor will not perform.

        (2)   Effect--Promisee is discharged from continuing performance and may immediately sue for breach.

    b.   <u>Anticipatory Breach</u>

        (1)   Definition--The renunciation of a bilateral contract before performance is due.

        (2)   Effect--Promisee has the following options:

            (a)   The promisee may sue immediately for damages, or rescind the contract and sue for restitution.

            (b)   The promisee may wait to see if the obligor will change his or her mind and perform when performance is due.

                (i)   If the obligor changes his or her position in reliance on the breach, the breaching party cannot withdraw his or her renunciation.

                (ii)   If the breaching party withdraws his or her renunciation and performs, there is no breach.

    c.   Action on the part of one party which prevents the other party from performing, discharges the other party and gives him or her the right to sue for the breach.

d. Violation of contract terms

(1) A slight breach entitles the other party to at least nominal damages.

(2) A breach discharges the other party's obligation if either

(a) The breach is material, so that there is essentially a failure of consideration for the other party's promise, or

(b) The breach amounts to the failure of an express condition to the other party's performance.

IX. Remedies for Breach

A. Election of Remedies

1. Under common law, a material breach entitled the other party to either

a. Rescind the contract and sue for restitution, in order to put the nonbreaching party in the position the party was in before the contract, or

b. Affirm the contract and sue for damages or specific performance.

2. UCC 2-720 provides that a breached contract for the sale of goods may be rescinded and damages recovered.

B. Damages--Even if the breach is not material, the other party can sue for damages.

1. Measure of Damages

a. Compensatory Damages--To compensate for losses and lost profits suffered as a result of the breach. If the promisor fails to render the promised service and the promisee must obtain it elsewhere at a higher cost, damages are the difference between the market price and the contract price.

b. Consequential Damages--Damages that predictably follow as a consequence of the breach, e.g., losses resulting from the general or specific needs of the injured party that were known or should have been known by the breaching party.

c. Special Damages--Arising from unusual or special circumstances. Special damages are excluded as not within the contemplation of the parties. They are not excluded if they are provided for in the contract or are foreseeable by the breaching party when the contract is entered into.

d. Punitive Damages--Not allowed even if the breach is willful.

e. Nominal Damages--Allowed if there is a breach of contract but no provable loss.

f. Liquidated Damages--A specific amount provided in the contract to be recoverable in the event of a breach.

(1) They are enforceable if actual damage would be difficult to assess and the amount appears reasonable at time of contracting.

(2) UCC 2-718 allows liquidated damages if the amount is reasonable in light of the anticipated or actual harm caused by the breach.

(3) However, if the liquidated damages are excessive, a court may interpret them as a penalty and refuse enforcement.

2. <u>Mitigation of Damages</u>--The nonbreaching party has a duty to "mitigate" or minimize the losses caused by the breach.

    a. The party cannot recover damages for losses that he or she could have prevented by reasonable action or forbearance to act (e.g., by forbearing from amassing losses after the other party's material breach).

    b. If foreseeable losses result from a reasonable attempt to mitigate damages, they are recoverable.

C. <u>Specific Performance</u>--When the injured party cannot obtain complete relief through the award of damages, a court may order the breaching party to specifically carry out the terms of the breached contract.

    1. Specific performance may be granted when the legal remedy of damages is insufficient. Following are some common examples:

        a. A contract for the sale of unique property (land or goods that are unique or unobtainable elsewhere).

        b. A contract for which damages would be speculative or conjectural (output or requirement contracts).

        c. An enforceable contract not to compete.

    2. However, specific performance may not be granted if one of the following applies:

        a. Specific performance would require close and complicated court supervision of complex matters.

        b. The contract requires personal services or a personal relationship (e.g., marriage or partnership).

D. <u>Injunction</u>--Equitable remedy in which the court orders a party to do something (mandatory injunction) or to refrain from doing something (prohibitory injunction).

CHAPTER 43—CONTRACTS

Problem 43-1 MULTIPLE CHOICE QUESTIONS (110 to 130 minutes)

1. Carson Corp., a retail chain, asked Alto Construction to fix a broken window at one of Carson's stores. Alto offered to make the repairs within three days at a price to be agreed on after the work was completed. A contract based on Alto's offer would fail because of indefiniteness as to the
a. Price involved.
b. Nature of the subject matter.
c. Parties to the contract.
d. Time for performance. (5/91, Law, #12, 0449)

2. Kay, an art collector, promised Hammer, an art student, that if Hammer could obtain certain rare artifacts within two weeks, Kay would pay for Hammer's post-graduate education. At considerable effort and expense, Hammer obtained the specified artifacts within the two-week period. When Hammer requested payment, Kay refused. Kay claimed that there was no consideration for the promise. Hammer would prevail against Kay based on
a. Unilateral contract.
b. Unjust enrichment.
c. Public policy.
d. Quasi-contract. (5/91, Law, #16, 0453)

3. West, an Indiana real estate broker, misrepresented to Zimmer that West was licensed in Kansas under the Kansas statute that regulates real estate brokers and requires all brokers to be licensed. Zimmer signed a contract agreeing to pay West a 5% commission for selling Zimmer's home in Kansas. West did not sign the contract. West sold Zimmer's home. If West sued Zimmer for nonpayment of commission, Zimmer would be
a. Liable to West only for the value of services rendered.
b. Liable to West for the full commission.
c. Not liable to West for any amount because West did **not** sign the contract.
d. Not liable to West for any amount because West violated the Kansas licensing requirements. (5/92, Law, #25, 2838)

4. Blue purchased a travel agency business from Drye. The purchase price included payment for Drye's goodwill. The agreement contained a covenant prohibiting Drye from competing with Blue in the travel agency business. Which of the following statements regarding the covenant is **not** correct?

a. The restraint must be **no** more extensive than is reasonably necessary to protect the goodwill purchased by Blue.
b. The geographic area to which it applies must be reasonable.
c. The time period for which it is to be effective must be reasonable.
d. The value to be assigned to it is the excess of the price paid over the seller's cost of all tangible assets. (11/87, Law, #2, 9911)

5. On September 10, Harris, Inc., a new car dealer, placed a newspaper advertisement stating that Harris would sell 10 cars at its showroom for a special discount only on September 12, 13, and 14. On September 12, King called Harris and expressed an interest in buying one of the advertised cars. King was told that five of the cars had been sold and to come to the showroom as soon as possible. On September 13, Harris made a televised announcement that the sale would end at 10:00 p.m. that night. King went to Harris' showroom on September 14 and demanded the right to buy a car at the special discount. Harris had sold the 10 cars and refused King's demand. King sued Harris for breach of contract. Harris' best defense to King's suit would be that Harris'
a. Offer was unenforceable.
b. Advertisement was **not** an offer.
c. Television announcement revoked the offer.
d. Offer had **not** been accepted.
(5/92, Law, #21, 2834)

6. On February 12, Harris sent Fresno a written offer to purchase Fresno's land. The offer included the following provision: "Acceptance of this offer must be by registered or certified mail, received by Harris no later than February 18 by 5:00 p.m. CST." On February 18, Fresno sent Harris a letter accepting the offer by private overnight delivery service. Harris received the letter on February 19. Which of the following statements is correct?
a. A contract was formed on February 19.
b. Fresno's letter constituted a counteroffer.
c. Fresno's use of the overnight delivery service was an effective form of acceptance.
d. A contract was formed on February 18 regardless of when Harris actually received Fresno's letter. (11/92, Law, #11, 3093)

Revoked before Acceptance.
already accepted & bought

7. On June 15, Peters orally offered to sell a used lawn mower to Mason for $125. Peters specified that Mason had until June 20 to accept the offer. On June 16, Peters received an offer to purchase the lawn mower for $150 from Bronson, Mason's neighbor. Peters accepted Bronson's offer. On June 17, Mason saw Bronson using the lawn mower and was told the mower had been sold to Bronson. Mason immediately wrote to Peters to accept the June 15 offer. Which of the following statements is correct?

a. Mason's acceptance would be effective when received by Peters.

b. Mason's acceptance would be effective when mailed.

c. Peters' offer had been revoked and Mason's acceptance was ineffective.

d. Peters was obligated to keep the June 15 offer open until June 20. (11/92, Law, #13, 3095)

8. On September 27, Summers sent Fox a letter offering to sell Fox a vacation home for $150,000. On October 2, Fox replied by mail agreeing to buy the home for $145,000. Summers did not reply to Fox. Do Fox and Summers have a binding contract?

a. No, because Fox failed to sign and return Summers' letter.

b. No, because Fox's letter was a counteroffer.

c. Yes, because Summers' offer was validly accepted.

d. Yes, because Summers' silence is an implied acceptance of Fox's letter.

(5/90, Law, #12, 0462)

9. Opal offered, in writing, to sell Larkin a parcel of land for $300,000. If Opal dies, the offer will

a. Terminate prior to Larkin's acceptance only if Larkin received notice of Opal's death.

b. Remain open for a reasonable period of time after Opal's death.

c. Automatically terminate despite Larkin's prior acceptance.

d. Automatically terminate prior to Larkin's acceptance. *Death < accept* (5/90, Law, #14, 0464)

10. Martin wrote Dall and offered to sell Dall a building for $200,000. The offer stated it would expire 30 days from April 1. Martin changed his mind and does not wish to be bound by his offer. If a legal dispute arises between the parties regarding whether there has been a valid acceptance of the offer, which one of the following is correct?

a. The offer cannot be legally withdrawn for the stated period of time.

b. The offer will **not** expire before the 30 days even if Martin sells the property to a third person and notifies Dall.

c. If Dall categorically rejects the offer on April 10, Dall cannot validly accept within the remaining stated period of time.

d. If Dall phoned Martin on May 3, and unequivocally accepted the offer, a contract would be created, provided that Dall had **no** notice of withdrawal of the offer. (5/89, Law, #21, 0479)

11. The president of Deal Corp. wrote to Boyd, offering to sell the Deal factory for $300,000. The offer was sent by Deal on June 5 and was received by Boyd on June 9. The offer stated that it would remain open until December 20. The offer

a. Constitutes an enforceable option.

b. May be revoked by Deal any time prior to Boyd's acceptance.

c. Is a firm offer under the UCC but will be irrevocable for only three months.

d. Is a firm offer under the UCC because it is in writing. (11/88, Law, #10, 9911)

12. On June 15, 1990, Alpha, Inc. contracted with Delta Manufacturing, Inc. to buy a vacant parcel of land Delta owned. Alpha intended to build a distribution warehouse on the land because of its location near a major highway. The contract stated that: "Alpha's obligations hereunder are subject to the vacant parcel being rezoned to a commercial zoning classification by July 31, 1991." Which of the following statements is correct?

a. If the parcel is **not** rezoned by July 31, and Alpha refuses to purchase it, Alpha would **not** be in breach of contract.

b. If the parcel is rezoned by July 31, and Alpha refuses to purchase it, Delta would be able to successfully sue Alpha for specific performance.

c. The contract is **not** binding on either party because Alpha's performance is conditional.

d. If the parcel is rezoned by July 31, and Delta refuses to sell it, Delta's breach would **not** discharge Alpha's obligation to tender payment. (11/92, Law, #25, 3107)

13. On July 1, Silk, Inc., sent Blue a telegram offering to sell Blue a building for $80,000. In the telegram, Silk stated that it would give Blue 30 days to accept the offer. On July 15, Blue sent Silk a telegram that included the following statement: "The price for your building seems too high. Would you consider taking $75,000?" This telegram was received by Silk on July 16. On July 19, Tint made an offer to Silk to purchase the building for $82,000. Upon learning of Tint's offer, Blue, on July 27, sent Silk a signed letter agreeing to purchase the building for $80,000. This letter was received by Silk on July 29. However, Silk now refuses to sell Blue the

July 1. Just an offer yet
is going to be revoked

building. If Blue commences an action against Silk for breach of contract, Blue will
a. Win, because Blue effectively accepted Silk's offer of July 1.
b. Win, because Silk was obligated to keep the offer open for the 30-day period.
c. Lose, because Blue sent the July 15 telegram.
d. Lose, because Blue used an unauthorized means of communication.
(5/88, Law, #17, 9911)

14. Able Sofa, Inc. sent Noll a letter offering to sell Noll a custom made sofa for $5,000. Noll immediately sent a telegram to Able purporting to accept the offer. However, the telegraph company erroneously delivered the telegram to Abel Soda, Inc. Three days later, Able mailed a letter of revocation to Noll which was received by Noll. Able refused to sell Noll the sofa. Noll sued Able for breach of contract. Able
a. Would have been liable under the deposited acceptance rule only if Noll had accepted by mail.
b. Will avoid liability since it revoked its offer prior to receiving Noll's acceptance.
c. Will be liable for breach of contract.
d. Will avoid liability due to the telegraph company's error. (5/86, Law, #2, 9911)

15. Stable Corp. offered in a signed writing to sell Mix an office building for $350,000. The offer, which was sent by Stable on April 1, indicated that it would remain open until July 9. On July 5, Mix mailed a letter rejecting Stable's offer. On July 6, Mix sent a telegram to Stable accepting the original offer. The letter of rejection was received by Stable on July 8 and the telegram of acceptance was received by Stable on July 7. Which of the following is correct?
a. Mix's telegram resulted in the formation of a valid contract.
b. Mix's letter of July 5 terminated Stable's offer when mailed.
c. Stable was **not** entitled to withdraw its offer until after July 9.
d. Although Stable's offer on April 1 was a firm offer under the UCC, it will remain open for only three months. (11/86, Law, #12, 9911)

16. In determining whether the consideration requirement to form a contract has been satisfied, the consideration exchanged by the parties to the contract must be
a. Of approximately equal value.
b. Legally sufficient.
c. Exchanged simultaneously by the parties.
d. Fair and reasonable under the circumstances.
(11/92, Law, #12, 3094)

17. Which of the following will be legally binding despite lack of consideration?
a. An employer's promise to make a cash payment to a deceased employee's family in recognition of the employee's many years of service.
b. A promise to donate money to a charity on which the charity relied in incurring large expenditures.
c. A modification of a signed contract to purchase a parcel of land.
d. A merchant's oral promise to keep an offer open for 60 days. (5/92, Law, #23, 2836)

18. In which of the following situations does the first promise serve as valid consideration for the second promise?
a. A police officer's promise to catch a thief for a victim's promise to pay a reward.
b. A builder's promise to complete a contract for a purchaser's promise to extend the time for completion.
c. A debtor's promise to pay $500 for a creditor's promise to forgive the balance of a $600 liquidated debt.
d. A debtor's promise to pay $500 for a creditor's promise to forgive the balance of a $600 disputed debt. (5/92, Law, #24, 2837)

19. Dye sent Hill a written offer to sell a tract of land located in Newtown for $60,000. The parties were engaged in a separate dispute. The offer stated that it would be irrevocable for 60 days if Hill would promise to refrain from suing Dye during this time. Hill promptly delivered a promise not to sue during the term of the offer and to forego suit if Hill accepted the offer. Dye subsequently decided that the possible suit by Hill was groundless and therefore phoned Hill and revoked the offer 15 days after making it. Hill mailed an acceptance on the 20th day. Dye did not reply. Under the circumstances,
a. Dye's offer was supported by consideration and was **not** revocable when accepted.
b. Dye's written offer would be irrevocable even without consideration.
c. Dye's silence was an acceptance of Hill's promise.
d. Dye's revocation, **not** being in writing, was invalid. (5/89, Law, #24, 0482)

20. In deciding whether consideration necessary to form a contract exists, a court must determine whether
a. The consideration given by each party is of roughly equal value.
b. There is mutuality of consideration.

c. The consideration has sufficient monetary value.

d. The consideration conforms to the subjective intent of the parties. (5/88, Law, #18, 0489)

20A. Grove is seeking to avoid performing a promise to pay Brook $1,500. Grove is relying on lack of consideration on Brook's part. Grove will prevail if he can establish that

a. Prior to Grove's promise, Brook had already performed the requested act.

b. Brook's only claim of consideration was the relinquishment of a legal right.

c. Brook's asserted consideration is only worth $400.

d. The consideration to be performed by Brook will be performed by a third party. (5/95, Law, #20, 5354)

21. Dunne and Cook signed a contract requiring Cook to rebind 500 of Dunne's books at 80¢ per book. Later, Dunne requested, in good faith, that the price be reduced to 70¢ per book. Cook agreed orally to reduce the price to 70¢. Under the circumstances, the oral agreement is

a. Enforceable, but proof of it is inadmissible into evidence.

b. Enforceable, and proof of it is admissible into evidence.

c. Unenforceable, because Dunne failed to give consideration, but proof of it is otherwise admissible into evidence.

d. Unenforceable, due to the Statute of Frauds, and proof of it is inadmissible into evidence. (5/91, Law, #18, 0495)

22. Egan, a minor, contracted with Baker to purchase Baker's used computer for $400. The computer was purchased for Egan's personal use. The agreement provided that Egan would pay $200 down on delivery and $200 thirty days later. Egan took delivery and paid the $200 down payment. Twenty days later, the computer was damaged seriously as a result of Egan's negligence. Five days after the damage occurred and one day after Egan reached the age of majority, Egan attempted to disaffirm the contract with Baker. Egan will

a. Be able to disaffirm despite the fact that Egan was **not** a minor at the time of disaffirmance.

b. Be able to disaffirm only if Egan does so in writing.

c. Not be able to disaffirm because Egan had failed to pay the balance of the purchase price.

d. Not be able to disaffirm because the computer was damaged as a result of Egan's negligence. (11/93, Law, #21, 4318)

23. Rail, who was 16 years old, purchased an $800 computer from Elco Electronics. Rail and Elco are located in a state where the age of majority is 18. On several occasions Rail returned the computer to Elco for repairs. Rail was very unhappy with the computer. Two days after reaching the age of 18, Rail was still frustrated with the computer's reliability, and returned it to Elco, demanding an $800 refund. Elco refused, claiming that Rail no longer had a right to disaffirm the contract. Elco's refusal is

a. Correct, because Rail's multiple requests for service acted as a ratification of the contract.

b. Correct, because Rail could have transferred good title to a good faith purchaser for value.

c. Incorrect, because Rail disaffirmed the contract within a reasonable period of time after reaching the age of 18.

d. Incorrect, because Rail could disaffirm the contract at any time. (11/92, Law, #15, 3097)

24. Payne entered into a written agreement to sell a parcel of land to Stevens. At the time the agreement was executed, Payne had consumed alcoholic beverages. Payne's ability to understand the nature and terms of the contract was not impaired. Stevens did not believe that Payne was intoxicated. The contract is

a. Void as a matter of law.

b. Legally binding on both parties.

c. Voidable at Payne's option.

d. Voidable at Stevens' option. (5/90, Law, #17, 0467)

25. Which of the following would be unenforceable because the subject matter is illegal?

a. A contingent fee charged by an attorney to represent a plaintiff in a negligence action.

b. An arbitration clause in a supply contract.

c. A restrictive covenant in an employment contract prohibiting a former employee from using the employer's trade secrets.

d. An employer's promise **not** to press embezzlement charges against an employee who agrees to make restitution. (11/90, Law, #22, 0458)

26. Which of the following statements is true with regard to the Statute of Frauds?

a. All contracts involving consideration of more than $500 must be in writing.

b. The written contract must be signed by all parties.

c. The Statute of Frauds applies to contracts that can be fully performed within one year from the date they are made.

d. The contract terms may be stated in more than one document. (11/92, Law, #16, 3098)

27. On June 1, 1992, Decker orally guaranteed the payment of a $5,000 note Decker's cousin owed Baker. Decker's agreement with Baker provided that Decker's guaranty would terminate in 18 months. On June 3, 1992, Baker wrote Decker confirming Decker's guaranty. Decker did not object to the confirmation. On August 23, 1992, Decker's cousin defaulted on the note and Baker demanded that Decker honor the guaranty. Decker refused. Which of the following statements is correct?

a. Decker is liable under the oral guaranty because Decker did **not** object to Baker's June 3 letter.

b. Decker is **not** liable under the oral guaranty because it expired more than one year after June 1.

c. Decker is liable under the oral guaranty because Baker demanded payment within one year of the date the guaranty was given.

d. Decker is **not** liable under the oral guaranty because Decker's promise was **not** in writing.
    (11/92, Law, #17, 3099)

28. Carson agreed orally to repair Ives' rare book for $450. Before the work was started, Ives asked Carson to perform additional repairs to the book and agreed to increase the contract price to $650. After Carson completed the work, Ives refused to pay and Carson sued. Ives' defense was based on the Statute of Frauds. What total amount will Carson recover?

a. $0
b. $200
c. $450
d. $650
    (5/92, Law, #26, 2839)

29. Nolan agreed orally with Train to sell Train a house for $100,000. Train sent Nolan a signed agreement and a downpayment of $10,000. Nolan did not sign the agreement, but allowed Train to move into the house. Before closing, Nolan refused to go through with the sale. Train sued Nolan to compel specific performance. Under the provisions of the Statute of Frauds,

a. Train will win because Train signed the agreement and Nolan did **not** object.

b. Train will win because Train made a downpayment and took possession.

c. Nolan will win because Nolan did **not** sign the agreement.

d. Nolan will win because the house was worth more than $500. (5/91, Law, #14, 0451)

30. Sand orally promised Frost a $10,000 bonus, in addition to a monthly salary, if Frost would work two years for Sand. If Frost works for the two years, will the Statute of Frauds prevent Frost from collecting the bonus?

a. No, because Frost fully performed.

b. No, because the contract did **not** involve an interest in real estate.

c. Yes, because the contract could **not** be performed within one year.

d. Yes, because the monthly salary was the consideration of the contract.
    (5/90, Law, #18, 0468)

31. Able hired Carr to restore Able's antique car for $800. The terms of their oral agreement provided that Carr was to complete the work within 18 months. Actually, the work could be completed within one year. The agreement is

a. Unenforceable, because it covers services with a value in excess of $500.

b. Unenforceable, because it covers a time period in excess of one year.

c. Enforceable, because personal service contracts are exempt from the Statute of Frauds.

d. Enforceable, because the work could be completed within one year.
    (5/89, Law, #27, 9911)

32. With regard to an agreement for the sale of real estate, the Statute of Frauds

a. Requires that the entire agreement be in a single writing.

b. Requires that the purchase price be fair and adequate in relation to the value of the real estate.

c. Does **not** require that the agreement be signed by all parties.

d. Does **not** apply if the value of the real estate is less than $500. (11/87, Law, #3, 9911)

33. Baker and Able signed a contract which required Able to purchase 600 books from Baker at 90¢ per book. Subsequently, Able, in good faith, requested that the price of the books be reduced to 80¢ per book. Baker orally agreed to reduce the price to 80¢. Under the circumstances, the oral agreement is

a. Unenforceable, because Able failed to give consideration, but proof of it will be otherwise admissible into evidence.

b. Unenforceable, due to the Statute of Frauds, and proof of it will be inadmissible into evidence.

c. Enforceable, but proof of it will be inadmissible into evidence.

d. Enforceable, and proof of it will be admissible into evidence. (5/88, Law, #21, 9911)

34. Which of the following offers of proof are inadmissible under the parol evidence rule when a

written contract is intended as the complete agreement of the parties?

I. Proof of the existence of a subsequent oral modification of the contract.

II. Proof of the existence of a prior oral agreement that contradicts the written contract.

a. I only.
b. II only.
c. Both I and II.
d. Neither I nor II. (11/93, Law, #24, 4321)

35. In negotiations with Andrews for the lease of Kemp's warehouse, Kemp orally agreed to pay one-half of the cost of the utilities. The written lease, later prepared by Kemp's attorney, provided that Andrews pay all of the utilities. Andrews failed to carefully read the lease and signed it. When Kemp demanded that Andrews pay all of the utilities, Andrews refused, claiming that the lease did not accurately reflect the oral agreement. Andrews also learned that Kemp intentionally misrepresented the condition of the structure of the warehouse during the negotiations between the parties. Andrews sued to rescind the lease and intends to introduce evidence of the parties' oral agreement about sharing the utilities and the fraudulent statements made by Kemp. The parol evidence rule will prevent the admission of evidence concerning the

	Oral agreement regarding who pays the utilities	Fraudulent statements by Kemp
a.	Yes	Yes
b.	No	Yes
c.	Yes	No
d.	No	No
		(11/92, Law, #22, 3104)

36. Under the parol evidence rule, oral evidence will be excluded if it relates to
a. A contemporaneous oral agreement relating to a term in the contract.
b. Failure of a condition precedent.
c. Lack of contractual capacity.
d. A modification made several days after the contract was executed. (5/92, Law, #30, 9911)

36A. Where the parties have entered into a written contract intended as the final expression of their agreement, which of the following agreements will be admitted into evidence because they are **not** prohibited by the parol evidence rule?

	Subsequent oral agreements	Prior written agreements
a.	Yes	Yes
b.	Yes	No
c.	No	Yes
d.	No	No
		(5/95, Law, #18, 5352)

37. If a buyer accepts an offer containing an immaterial unilateral mistake, the resulting contract will be
a. Void as a matter of law.
b. Void at the election of the buyer.
c. Valid as to both parties.
d. Voidable at the election of the seller.
(5/92, Law, #29, 2842)

38. A building subcontractor submitted a bid for construction of a portion of a high-rise office building. The bid contained material computational errors. The general contractor accepted the bid with knowledge of the errors. Which of the following statements best represents the subcontractor's liability?
a. Not liable, because the contractor knew of the errors.
b. Not liable, because the errors were a result of gross negligence.
c. Liable, because the errors were unilateral.
d. Liable, because the errors were material.
(5/95, Law, #17, 5351)

39. To prevail in a common law action for innocent misrepresentation, the plaintiff must prove
a. The defendant made the false statements with a reckless disregard for the truth.
b. The misrepresentations were in writing.
c. The misrepresentations concerned material facts.
d. Reliance on the misrepresentations was the only factor inducing the plaintiff to enter into the contract. (5/91, Law, #21, 0455)

40. On May 25, 1991, Smith contracted with Jackson to repair Smith's cabin cruiser. The work was to begin on May 31, 1991. On May 26, 1991, the boat, while docked at Smith's pier, was destroyed by arson. Which of the following statements is correct with regard to the contract?
a. Smith would **not** be liable to Jackson because of mutual mistake.
b. Smith would be liable to Jackson for the profit Jackson would have made under the contract.

c. Jackson would **not** be liable to Smith because performance by the parties would be impossible.

d. Jackson would be liable to repair another boat owned by Smith. (11/91, Law, #25, 2353)

41. To prevail in a common law action for fraud in the inducement, a plaintiff must prove that the

a. Defendant was an expert with regard to the misrepresentations.

b. Defendant made the misrepresentations with knowledge of their falsity and an intention to deceive.

c. Misrepresentations were in writing.

d. Plaintiff was in a fiduciary relationship with the defendant. (11/93, Law, #23, 4320)

42. Long purchased a life insurance policy with Tempo Life Insurance Co. The policy named Long's daughter as beneficiary. Six months after the policy was issued, Long died of a heart attack. Long had failed to disclose on the insurance application a known preexisting heart condition that caused the heart attack. Tempo refused to pay the death benefit to Long's daughter. If Long's daughter sues, Tempo will

a. Win, because Long's daughter is an incidental beneficiary.

b. Win, because of Long's failure to disclose the preexisting heart condition.

c. Lose, because Long's death was from natural causes.

d. Lose, because Long's daughter is a third-party donee beneficiary. (5/93, Law, #23, 3991)

43. Which of the following, if intentionally misstated by a seller to a buyer, would be considered a fraudulent inducement to make a contract?

a. Nonexpert opinion.

b. Appraised value.

c. Prediction.

d. Immaterial fact. (5/92, Law, #28, 2841)

44. Bradford sold a parcel of land to Jones who promptly recorded the deed. Bradford then resold the land to Wallace. In a suit against Bradford by Wallace, recovery will be based on the theory of

a. Bilateral mistake.

b. Ignorance of the facts.

c. Unilateral mistake.

d. Fraud. (11/89, Law, #14, 9911)

45. For a purchaser of land to avoid a contract with the seller based on duress, it must be shown that the seller's improper threats

a. Constituted a crime or tort.

b. Would have induced a reasonably prudent person to assent to the contract.

c. Actually induced the purchaser to assent to the contract.

d. Were made with the intent to influence the purchaser. (11/90, Law, #23, 0459)

46. Baker fraudulently induced Able to sell Baker a painting for $200. Subsequently, Baker sold the painting for $10,000 to Gold, a good faith purchaser. Able is entitled to

a. Rescind the contract with Baker.

b. Recover the painting from Gold.

c. Recover damages from Baker.

d. Rescind Baker's contract with Gold.
(5/87, Law, #19, 9911)

47. Miller negotiated the sale of Miller's liquor store to Jackson. Jackson asked to see the prior year's financial statements. Using the store's checkbook, Miller prepared a balance sheet and profit and loss statement as well as he could. Miller told Jackson to have an accountant examine Miller's records because Miller was not an accountant. Jackson failed to do so and purchased the store in reliance on Miller's financial statements. Jackson later learned that the financial statements included several errors that resulted in a material overstatement of assets and net income. Miller was not aware that the errors existed. Jackson sued Miller, claiming Miller misrepresented the store's financial condition and that Jackson relied on the financial statements in making the decision to acquire the store. Which of the following statements is correct?

a. Jackson will prevail if the errors in the financial statements were material.

b. Jackson will **not** prevail because Jackson's reliance on the financial statements was **not** reasonable.

c. Money damages is the only remedy available to Jackson if, in fact, Miller has committed a misrepresentation.

d. Jackson would be entitled to rescind the purchase even if the errors in the financial statements were **not** material.
(11/92, Law, #20, 3102)

48. Maco, Inc. and Kent contracted for Kent to provide Maco certain consulting services at an hourly rate of $20. Kent's normal hourly rate was $90 per hour, the fair market value of the services. Kent agreed to the $20 rate because Kent was having serious financial problems. At the time the agreement was negotiated, Maco was aware of Kent's financial condition and refused to pay more than $20 per hour for Kent's services. Kent has now sued to rescind the

contract with Maco, claiming duress by Maco during the negotiations. Under the circumstances, Kent will

a. Win, because Maco refused to pay the fair market value of Kent's services.

b. Win, because Maco was aware of Kent's serious financial problems.

c. Lose, because Maco's actions did **not** constitute duress.

d. Lose, because Maco **cannot** prove that Kent, at the time, had **no** other offers to provide consulting services.   (11/92, Law, #18, 3100)

49. Johns leased an apartment from Olsen. Shortly before the lease expired, Olsen threatened Johns with eviction and physical harm if Johns did not sign a new lease for twice the old rent. Johns, unable to afford the expense to fight eviction, and in fear of physical harm, signed the new lease. Three months later, Johns moved and sued to void the lease claiming duress. The lease will be held

a. Void because of the unreasonable increase in rent.

b. Voidable because of Olsen's threat to bring eviction proceedings.

c. Void because of Johns' financial condition.

d. Voidable because of Olsen's threat of physical harm.   (5/91, Law, #20, 0454)

50. On August 1, Neptune Fisheries contracted in writing with West Markets to deliver to West 3,000 pounds of lobsters at $4.00 a pound. Delivery of the lobsters was due October 1 with payment due November 1. On August 4, Neptune entered into a contract with Deep Sea Lobster Farms which provided as follows: "Neptune Fisheries assigns all the rights under the contract with West Markets dated August 1 to Deep Sea Lobster Farms." The best interpretation of the August 4 contract would be that it was

a. Only an assignment of rights by Neptune.

b. Only a delegation of duties by Neptune.

c. An assignment of rights and a delegation of duties by Neptune.

d. An unenforceable third-party beneficiary contract.   (5/90, Law, #22, 0472)

51. Generally, which of the following contract rights are assignable?

	Option contract rights	Malpractice insurance policy rights
a.	Yes	Yes
b.	Yes	No
c.	No	Yes
d.	No	No

(5/95, Law, #21, 5355)

52. On February 1, Burns contracted in writing with Nagel to sell Nagel a used car. The contract provided that Burns was to deliver the car on February 15 and Nagel was to pay the $800 purchase price not later than March 15. On February 21, Burns assigned the contract to Ross for $600. Nagel was not notified of the assignment. Which of the following statements is correct?

a. By making the assignment, Burns impliedly warranted Nagel would pay the full purchase price.

b. The assignment to Ross is invalid because Nagel was **not** notified.

c. Ross will **not** be subject to any contract defenses Nagel could have raised against Burns.

d. By making the assignment, Burns impliedly warranted a lack of knowledge of any fact impairing the value of the assignment.

(5/93, Law, #24, 3992)

53. Baxter, Inc. and Globe entered into a contract. After receiving valuable consideration from Clay, Baxter assigned its rights under the contract to Clay. In which of the following circumstances would Baxter **not** be liable to Clay?

a. Clay released Globe.

b. Globe paid Baxter.

c. Baxter released Globe.

d. Baxter breached the contract.

(5/92, Law, #31, 2844)

54. Egan contracted with Barton to buy Barton's business. The contract provided that Egan would pay the business debts Barton owed Ness and that the balance of the purchase price would be paid to Barton over a 10-year period. The contract also required Egan to take out a decreasing term life insurance policy naming Barton and Ness as beneficiaries to ensure that the amounts owed Barton and Ness would be paid if Egan died. Barton's contract rights were assigned to Vim, and Egan was notified of the assignment. Despite the assignment, Egan continued making payments to Barton. Egan died before completing payment and Vim sued Barton for the insurance proceeds and the other payments on the purchase price received by Barton after the assignment. To which of the following is Vim entitled?

	Payments on purchase price	Insurance proceeds
a.	No	Yes
b.	No	No
c.	Yes	Yes
d.	Yes	No

(5/92, Law, #34, 2847)

55. One of the criteria for a valid assignment of a sales contract to a third party is that the assignment must
a. Be supported by adequate consideration from the assignee.
b. Be in writing and signed by the assignor.
c. Not materially increase the other party's risk or duty.
d. Not be revocable by the assignor.
(5/95, Law, #22, 5356)

56. Yost contracted with Egan for Yost to buy certain real property. If the contract is otherwise silent, Yost's rights under the contract are
a. Assignable only with Egan's consent.
b. Nonassignable because they are personal to Yost.
c. Nonassignable as a matter of law.
d. Generally assignable. (11/91, Law, #24, 9911)

57. On May 2, Kurtz Co. assigned its entire interest in a $70,000 account receivable due in 60 days from Long to City Bank for $65,000. On May 4, City notified Long of the assignment. On May 7, Long informed City that Kurtz had committed fraud in the transaction out of which the account receivable arose and that payment would not be made to City. If City commences an action against Long and Long is able to prove Kurtz acted fraudulently,
a. Long will be able to successfully assert fraud as a defense.
b. City will be entitled to collect $65,000, the amount paid for the assignment.
c. City will be entitled to collect $70,000 since fraud in the inducement is a personal defense which was lost on May 2.
d. City will be entitled to collect $70,000 since Long's allegation of fraud arose after notice of the assignment. (5/87, Law, #21, 9911)

58. Wilcox Co. contracted with Ace Painters, Inc. for Ace to paint Wilcox's warehouse. Ace, without advising Wilcox, assigned the contract to Pure Painting Corp. Pure failed to paint Wilcox's warehouse in accordance with the contract specifications. The contract between Ace and Wilcox was silent with regard to a party's right to assign it. Which of the following statements is correct?
a. Ace remained liable to Wilcox despite the fact that Ace assigned the contract to Pure.
b. Ace would **not** be liable to Wilcox if Ace had notified Wilcox of the assignment.
c. Ace's duty to paint Wilcox's warehouse was nondelegable.
d. Ace's delegation of the duty to paint Wilcox's warehouse was a breach of the contract.
(11/92, Law, #24, 3106)

59. Ferco, Inc. claims to be a creditor beneficiary of a contract between Bell and Allied Industries, Inc. Allied is indebted to Ferco. The contract between Bell and Allied provides that Bell is to purchase certain goods from Allied and pay the purchase price directly to Ferco until Allied's obligation is satisfied. Without justification, Bell failed to pay Ferco and Ferco sued Bell. Ferco will
a. Not prevail, because Ferco lacked privity of contract with either Bell or Allied.
b. Not prevail, because Ferco did **not** give any consideration to Bell.
c. Prevail, because Ferco was an intended beneficiary of the contract between Allied and Bell.
d. Prevail, provided Ferco was aware of the contract between Bell and Allied at the time the contract was entered into.
(11/92, Law, #21, 3103)

60. Egan contracted with Barton to buy Barton's business. The contract provided that Egan would pay the business debts Barton owed Ness and that the balance of the purchase price would be paid to Barton over a 10-year period. The contract also required Egan to take out a decreasing term life insurance policy naming Barton and Ness as beneficiaries to ensure that the amounts owed Barton and Ness would be paid if Egan died. Which of the following would describe Ness' status under the contract and insurance policy?

	Contract	Insurance policy
a.	Donee beneficiary	Donee beneficiary
b.	Donee beneficiary	Creditor beneficiary
c.	Creditor beneficiary	Donee beneficiary
d.	Creditor beneficiary	Creditor beneficiary

(5/92, Law, #33, 2846)

61. Graham contracted with the city of Harris to train and employ high school dropouts residing in Harris. Graham breached the contract. Long, a resident of Harris and a high school dropout, sued Graham for damages. Under the circumstances, Long will
a. Win, because Long is a third-party beneficiary entitled to enforce the contract.
b. Win, because the intent of the contract was to confer a benefit on all high school dropouts residing in Harris.
c. Lose, because Long is merely an incidental beneficiary of the contract.
d. Lose, because Harris did **not** assign its contract rights to Long. (5/91, Law, #22, 0456)

62. Union Bank lent $200,000 to Wagner. Union required Wagner to obtain a life insurance policy

naming Union as beneficiary. While the loan was outstanding, Wagner stopped paying the premiums on the policy. Union paid the premiums, adding the amounts paid to Wagner's loan. Wagner died and the insurance company refused to pay the policy proceeds to Union. Union may

a.   Recover the policy proceeds because it is a creditor beneficiary.
b.   Recover the policy proceeds because it is a donee beneficiary.
c.   Not recover the policy proceeds because it is **not** in privity of contract with the insurance company.
d.   Not recover the policy proceeds because it is only an incidental beneficiary.

(5/90, Law, #19, 0469)

63.   Jones owned an insurance policy on her life, on which she paid all the premiums. Smith was named the beneficiary. Jones died and the insurance company refused to pay the insurance proceeds to Smith. An action by Smith against the insurance company for the insurance proceeds will be

a.   Successful, because Smith is a third party donee beneficiary.
b.   Successful, because Smith is a proper assignee of Jones' rights under the insurance policy.
c.   Unsuccessful, because Smith was **not** the owner of the policy.
d.   Unsuccessful, because Smith did **not** pay any of the premiums.   (11/89, Law, #17, 0477)

64.   Krieg was the owner of an office building encumbered by a mortgage securing Krieg's promissory note to Muni Bank. Park purchased the building subject to Muni's mortgage. As a result of the sale to Park,

a.   Muni is **not** a third party creditor beneficiary.
b.   Krieg is a third party creditor beneficiary.
c.   Park is liable for any deficiency resulting from a default on the note.
d.   Krieg was automatically released from any liability on the note.   (5/87, Law, #23, 9911)

65.   Ordinarily, in an action for breach of a construction contract, the statute of limitations time period would be computed from the date the

a.   Contract is negotiated.
b.   Contract is breached.
c.   Construction is begun.
d.   Contract is signed.   (5/95, Law, #25, 5359)

65A.   On June 1, 1986, Nord Corp. engaged Milo & Co., CPAs, to perform certain management advisory services for nine months for a $45,000 fee. The terms of their oral agreement required Milo to commence performance any time before October 1, 1986. On June 30, 1987, after Milo completed the work to Nord's satisfaction, Nord paid Milo $30,000 by check. Nord conspicuously marked on the check that it constituted payment in full for all services rendered. Nord has refused to pay the remaining $15,000 arguing that although it believes the $45,000 fee is reasonable, it had received bids of $20,000 and $38,000 from other firms to perform the same services as Milo. Milo endorsed and deposited the check. If Milo commences an action against Nord for the remaining $15,000, Milo will be entitled to recover

a. $0, because there has been an enforceable accord and satisfaction.
b. $0, because the Statute of Frauds has **not** been satisfied.
c. $8,000, because $38,000 was the highest other bid.
d. $15,000, because it is the balance due under the agreement.   (11/87, Law, #1, 9911)

66.   Ames Construction Co. contracted to build a warehouse for White Corp. The construction specifications required Ames to use Ace lighting fixtures. Inadvertently, Ames installed Perfection lighting fixtures which are of slightly lesser quality than Ace fixtures, but in all other respects meet White's needs. Which of the following statements is correct?

a.   White's recovery will be limited to monetary damages because Ames' breach of the construction contract was **not** material.
b.   White will **not** be able to recover any damages from Ames because the breach was inadvertent.
c.   Ames did **not** breach the construction contract because the Perfection fixtures were substantially as good as the Ace fixtures.
d.   Ames must install Ace fixtures or White will **not** be obligated to accept the warehouse.

(11/93, Law, #26, 4323)

66A.   Parc hired Glaze to remodel and furnish an office suite. Glaze submitted plans that Parc approved. After completing all the necessary construction and painting, Glaze purchased minor accessories that Parc rejected because they did not conform to the plans. Parc refused to allow Glaze to complete the project and refused to pay Glaze any part of the contract price. Glaze sued for the value of the work performed. Which of the following statements is correct?

a.   Glaze will lose because Glaze breached the contract by **not** completing performance.
b.   Glaze will win because Glaze substantially performed and Parc prevented complete performance.

c. Glaze will lose because Glaze materially breached the contract by buying the accessories.

d. Glaze will win because Parc committed anticipatory breach. (11/90, Law, #25, 0460)

67. Castle borrowed $5,000 from Nelson and executed and delivered to Nelson a promissory note for $5,000 due on April 30. On April 1 Castle offered, and Nelson accepted, $4,000 in full satisfaction of the note. On May 15, Nelson demanded that Castle pay the $1,000 balance on the note. Castle refused. If Nelson sued for the $1,000 balance, Castle would

a. Win, because the acceptance by Nelson of the $4,000 constituted an accord and satisfaction.

b. Win, because the debt was unliquidated.

c. Lose, because the amount of the note in dispute.

d. Lose, because no consideration was given to Nelson in exchange for accepting only $4,000. (11/92, Law, #14, 3096)

68. Which of the following requires consideration to be binding on the parties?

a. Material modification of a contract involving the sale of real estate.

b. Ratification of a contract by a person after reaching the age of majority.

c. A written promise signed by a merchant to keep an offer to sell goods open for 10 days.

d. Material modification of a sale of goods contract under the UCC. (11/90, Law, #21, 0508)

69. To cancel a contract and to restore the parties to their original positions before the contract, the parties should execute a

a. Novation.

b. Release.

c. Rescission.

d. Revocation. (5/92, Law, #32, 2845)

70. Wren purchased a factory from First Federal Realty. Wren paid 20% at the closing and gave a note for the balance secured by a 20-year mortgage. Five years later, Wren found it increasingly difficult to make payments on the note and defaulted. First Federal threatened to accelerate the loan and foreclose if Wren continued in default. First Federal told Wren to make payment or obtain an acceptable third party to assume the obligation. Wren offered the land to Moss, Inc., for $10,000 less than the equity Wren had in the property. This was acceptable to First Federal and at the closing Moss paid the arrearage, assumed the mortgage and note, and had title transferred to its name. First Federal released Wren. The transaction in question is a(an)

a. Purchase of land subject to a mortgage.

b. Assignment and delegation.

c. Third party beneficiary contract.

d. Novation. (5/90, Law, #25, 0475)

71. Which of the following actions will result in the discharge of a party to a contract?

	Prevention of performance	Accord and satisfaction
a.	Yes	Yes
b.	Yes	No
c.	No	Yes
d.	No	No

(5/95, Law, #23, 5357)

72. In 1959, Dart bought an office building from Graco under a written contract signed only by Dart. In 1991, Dart discovered that Graco made certain false representations during their negotiations concerning the building's foundation. Dart could have reasonably discovered the foundation problems by 1965. Dart sued Graco claiming fraud in the formation of the contract. Which of the following statements is correct?

a. The parol evidence rule will prevent the admission into evidence of proof concerning Dart's allegations.

b. Dart will be able to rescind the contract because both parties did **not** sign it.

c. Dart must prove that the alleged misrepresentations were part of the written contract because the contract involved real estate.

d. The statute of limitations would likely prevent Dart from prevailing because of the length of time that has passed. (5/91, Law, #15, 0452)

73. Under a personal services contract, which of the following circumstances will cause the discharge of a party's duties?

a. Death of the party who is to receive the services.

b. Cost of performing the services has doubled.

c. Bankruptcy of the party who is to receive the services.

d. Illegality of the services to be performed. (5/95, Law, #24, 5358)

74. Nagel and Fields entered into a contract in which Nagel was obligated to deliver certain goods to Fields by September 10. On September 3, Nagel told Fields that Nagel had no intention of delivering the goods required by the contract. Prior to September 10, Fields may successfully sue Nagel under the doctrine of

a. Promissory estoppel.
b. Accord and satisfaction.
c. Anticipatory repudiation. *anticipat breach*
d. Substantial performance.

(11/89, Law, #19, 0478)

75. In September 1988, Cobb Company contracted with Thrifty Oil Company for the delivery of 100,000 gallons of heating oil at the price of 75 cents per gallon at regular specified intervals during the forthcoming winter. Due to an unseasonably warm winter, Cobb took delivery on only 70,000 gallons. In a suit against Cobb for breach of contract, Thrifty will

a. Lose, because Cobb acted in good faith.
b. Lose, because both parties are merchants and the UCC recognizes commercial impracticability.
c. Win, because this is a requirements contract.
d. Win, because the change of circumstances could have been contemplated by the parties.

(5/89, Law, #34, 9911)

76. In general, a clause in a real estate contract entitling the seller to retain the purchaser's downpayment as liquidated damages if the purchaser fails to close the transaction, is enforceable

a. In all cases, when the parties have a signed contract.
b. If the amount of the downpayment bears a reasonable relationship to the probable loss.
c. As a penalty, if the purchaser intentionally defaults.
d. Only when the seller cannot compel specific performance. (5/91, Law, #24, 0457)

77. Which of the following types of conditions affecting performance may validly be present in contracts?

	Conditions precedent	Conditions subsequent	Concurrent conditions
a.	Yes	Yes	Yes
b.	Yes	Yes	No
c.	Yes	No	Yes
d.	No	Yes	Yes

(5/95, Law, #19, 5353)

78. Master Mfg., Inc. contracted with Accur Computer Repair Corp. to maintain Master's computer system. Master's manufacturing process depends on its computer system operating properly at all times. A liquidated damages clause in the contract provided that Accur pay $1,000 to Master for each day that Accur was late responding to a service request. On January 12, Accur was notified that Master's computer system failed. Accur did not respond to Master's service request until January 15. If Master sues Accur under the liquidated damage provision of the contract, Master will

a. Win, unless the liquidated damage provision is determined to be a penalty.
b. Win, because under all circumstances liquidated damage provisions are enforceable.
c. Lose, because Accur's breach was **not** material.
d. Lose, because liquidated damage provisions violate public policy. (5/93, Law, #25, 3993)

79. Kaye contracted to sell Hodges a building for $310,000. The contract required Hodges to pay the entire amount at closing. Kaye refused to close the sale of the building. Hodges sued Kaye. To what relief is Hodges entitled?

a. Punitive damages and compensatory damages.
b. Specific performance and compensatory damages.
c. Consequential damages or punitive damages.
d. Compensatory damages or specific performance. (5/92, Law, #35, 2848)

Solution 43-1 MULTIPLE CHOICE ANSWERS

Contract Definitions

1. (a) The contract based on Alto's offer would fail because of indefiniteness as to the price. The contract clearly was definite as to the nature of the subject matter, the parties to the contract, and the time for performance.

2. (a) The offeror made a promise for an act. When the act was performed, a unilateral contract was created and the offeror is bound to pay. Unjust enrichment is generally considered only if there was no contract and the court wishes to provide an "equitable solution." There are no public policy issues involved. A quasi-contract applies only if there was no contract to begin with and the law implies one to

prevent an unjust enrichment. Since there was a unilateral contract, there can be no quasi-contract.

3. (d) There are two types of licensing statutes. First, there are licensing statutes intended primarily for revenue raising. Second, there are licensing statutes (regulatory) intended primarily to protect the public against dishonest or incompetent professionals. An individual without a license can collect his total compensation if the primary purpose of the statute was to raise revenue. However, if the purpose was regulatory in nature (intended to protect the public), the individual can collect nothing since the contract is voidable. Thus, an unlicensed individual who enters into a contract to provide regulated services will not be allowed to enforce the contract or recover even the value of the services rendered.

Offer and Acceptance

4. (d) Covenants not to compete will be enforceable if the purpose of the restraint is to protect a property interest of the promisee, and the restraint is no more extensive than is reasonably necessary to protect that interest. This would include restraints that deal with goodwill, the geographic areas to be covered, and the time periods for which they are to be effective.

5. (b) The general rule is that newspaper advertisements, catalogs, price lists, signs, and price quotations are not offers, but are invitations to negotiate. By advertising, Harris is merely seeking offers. King is the one who makes the offer to Harris, and until Harris accepts, there is no contract.

6. (b) The letter from Fresno (the offeree) constituted a counteroffer, because it was received by Harris (the offeror) on February 19, a day late. If the offeror specifies a time for acceptance, the offer automatically terminates upon the expiration of that time period. The termination of the offer ends the offeree's power to accept it. If acceptance is attempted after the offer has terminated, the acceptance constitutes a new offer. The offer specifically stated that the acceptance must be by registered or certified mail and received by February 18.

7. (c) Peters' offer had been revoked. Since revocation notice can be received either directly or indirectly, Mason, in effect, received the revocation notice when he was told the mower had been sold to Bronson; and therefore, Mason's acceptance was ineffective, even though the specified time of the oral contract had not expired. Peters' offer had been revoked prior to Mason's acceptance. There was no

obligation on the part of Peters to keep the offer open, since there was no consideration for him to do so.

8. (b) Fox's letter was a rejection. Clearly, the difference in price was a *material* difference between Summers' offer and Fox's reply. Fox's letter served as a counteroffer.

9. (d) Death of the offeror (or offeree) will automatically terminate, by operation of law, an offer. The notice of the death is not required to effectuate a termination, and the death *immediately* terminates the offer. However, death cannot undo an offer which has already been accepted. (It is an entirely different question as to the impossibility of *performing* the contract, even though the contract has already been formed.) Thus, the other answers are all in error.

10. (c) Offers are terminated when rejected by the offeree (Dall). Thus, any attempt by Dall to accept an offer after termination will act only as an offer to enter into a new contract. As to this question, the only exception to this rule involves the "option" rule. If consideration is given to hold the offer open for a stated period of time, a rejection by Dall would not terminate the offer during the option period. You can always revoke your offer prior to acceptance *even if you stated you would keep your offer open for a stated period of time*. The only exceptions to this rule are if the "option" rule applies or if the UCC "firm offer" rule applies. An offer terminates by the terms of the offer. In this case, the offer terminated on May 1 and any attempt to accept on May 3 would be too late.

11. (b) Under the law of contracts, an offer that states it will be held open for a period of time may, without consideration, be revoked any time before its acceptance. In contrast, under the UCC, a signed written offer by a merchant to buy or sell goods in which the merchant gives assurance that the offer will be held open is irrevocable, even without consideration, for a period not exceeding three months. However, the UCC does not apply to this situation since a sale of realty is involved and the law of contracts applies instead. An option contract requires that the offeror receive consideration for his promise to keep his offer open.

12. (a) The contract between Alpha and Delta contained the *condition* that the land be rezoned. Since the nonoccurrence of a condition can terminate the existing obligation and, if the condition was not met when the vacant parcel was not rezoned by the deadline set forth in the contract, then the contract was in effect terminated on July 31. If the parcel were rezoned by the deadline and Alpha refused to purchase it, Delta would be able to sue for *breach of*

contract, not specific performance. The rezoning was a reasonable condition set forth in the contract. The condition of the contract would have been met, and Delta's refusal to then sell the property would have breached the contract negating any obligation of Alpha.

13. (a) Blue's telegram on July 15 did not constitute a rejection of Silk's offer since it was so worded as to effectively reserve the original offer. As such, Blue's acceptance through the letter sent on July 27 was effective to create a valid contract. In the absence of an expressly authorized mode of acceptance, any mode dictated by business custom (e.g., mail) is impliedly authorized. The rule concerning firm offers applies to a sale of goods by a merchant in the ordinary course of business and does not apply to this situation.

14. (c) If sent by a mode of communication expressly or impliedly authorized by the offeror (e.g., mail or telegram), acceptance of an offer is normally effective on dispatch, even if subsequently delayed or lost. Noll's telegram was an effective acceptance of the offer by Able. The rule applies to any situation in which acceptance is made in a manner expressly or impliedly authorized. This can include telegraph or telephone as well as mail in most circumstances. In this situation the acceptance was effective on dispatch, before Able's attempted revocation.

15. (a) Mix's telegram accepting Stable's offer was effective to form a valid contract even though it was sent after Mix's letter rejecting the offer, because a rejection is effective only upon receipt. Stable could withdraw its offer anytime up to its acceptance by Mix because there was no consideration involved. The UCC does not apply to the sale of real property.

16. (b) Consideration must be legally sufficient. It is legally irrelevant whether consideration given by one party to the other is of approximately equal value or fair and reasonable under the circumstances. Also, the consideration must be exchanged *contemporaneously;* it need not be simultaneous.

17. (b) Under the concept of promissory estoppel, a promisor is "estopped" or prevented from asserting that his promise is not binding due to lack of consideration if the following elements are present: (1) the promisor makes an express promise; (2) the promisor expects or should expect his promise to induce and it does induce the promisee to act or forbear to act in a substantial way; (3) the promisee did in fact rely on the promise and this reliance was justifiable and; (4) an injustice will result (not merely a legal detriment) to the promisee unless the promise is enforced. It is reasonable to expect a charity to make expenditures in reliance upon promised donations, with a resulting injustice to the charity if such promises are not met.

Consideration

18. (d) Contracts, to be enforceable, must be supported by consideration. The test for consideration is whether a party to a contract suffers a "legal detriment," meaning he or she does something or binds himself or herself to do something that they are not legally or otherwise bound to do. Regarding the performance of a preexisting duty or promise to perform a preexisting duty, there is no legal detriment if one does or promises to do that which he or she is already bound to do. Any change in the preexisting duty may supply sufficient consideration to support the amended contract. A debtor's promise to pay $500 for a creditor's promise to forgive the balance of a $600 disputed debt is enforceable as long as the $500 is tendered before the time the debt is originally due.

19. (a) The general rule is that you can always revoke your offer prior to acceptance unless the UCC "firm offer" rule applies (it does not in this question) or there is an option (consideration has been "paid" to keep the offer open). In this situation, there is a valid option and the offer cannot be revoked during the 60 days. Forbearance to sue on a claim is valid consideration as long as the promisee has a good faith belief in the validity of the claim. The UCC "firm offer" rule does not apply in this situation. Hill's promise not to sue was acceptance of Dye's option offer. Also, silence is never acceptance unless there is a prior agreement or appropriate course of dealing. A revocation of a written offer can be oral and is effective when communicated to the offeree provided the offer is revocable. In this situation, the offer cannot be revoked for 60 days due to the option rule.

20. (b) Mutuality of consideration refers to the obligations imposed upon each party to a contract so that each person is bound to perform in some way. By promising some sort of performance, the parties are furnishing the consideration necessary to form a valid contract. The courts generally do not inquire into whether the amount of consideration given by each party was of roughly the same value or whether the amount of the consideration was adequate. Courts generally do not attempt to determine the subjective intent of the parties to a contract.

20A. (a) Past consideration is not valid consideration because the act was not done in exchange for the promise, but independent of it. Consideration requires that a party suffer a "legal detriment," which may result from the relinquishment of a legal right. Courts generally do not inquire as to the adequacy of the consideration. Contractual duties can generally be delegated to a third party.

21. (c) Contracts for services are governed by common law which specifies that modifications to an agreement must be supported with consideration to be enforceable. The oral agreement is not enforceable. The Statute of Frauds does not apply in this case.

Capacity, Legality, and Public Policy

22. (a) In the case of a contract to which a minor is a party, the contract can generally be disaffirmed by the minor any time before the age of majority or for a reasonable time after the age of majority. In addition, when a minor disaffirms a contract, he or she must return whatever remains regardless of the condition (and the minor is not liable for the condition of the returned item). In this problem, the minor disaffirmed one day after the age of majority which is within the "reasonable" framework described above. Therefore, he or she is able to disaffirm despite the fact that he or she is no longer a minor. There is no requirement that the minor disaffirm in writing. The minor merely needs to communicate his or her wish to disaffirm through actions or words. Failure to pay the balance does not preclude a minor from disaffirming a contract. Egan's negligence does not preclude a minor from disaffirming a contract.

23. (c) Elco's refusal to refund the $800 to Rail was incorrect, since Rail disaffirmed the contract two days after reaching 18, the age of majority. A contract cannot be ratified by a minor until he attains his majority or a reasonable time thereafter, because ratification of a contract by a minor gives rise to another voidable contract. Rail could only ratify the contract after reaching the age of majority. Although Rail does have the ability to transfer title to a good faith purchaser for value, this has no bearing on his ability to disaffirm the contract. Rail has only a reasonable time after reaching the age of majority in which to disaffirm the contract. Failure to disaffirm within a reasonable time serves to act as ratification.

24. (b) Since Payne's capacity was not impaired and Stevens did not believe that Payne was intoxicated, the contract is legally binding on both parties.

25. (d) The law requires reporting of criminal activity. Thus, the promise to not report embezzlement would be unenforceable. Answers (a), (b), and (c) all involve legal activities and thus would be enforceable.

Statute of Frauds

26. (d) The contract terms need not appear in a single document so long as the several documents refer to the same transaction. There is no requirement that the writing contain a monetary amount. Only the signature of the party against whom enforcement is sought is required. If the performance *could* occur within a one-year period, the contract is not within the statute and need not be written.

27. (d) Decker is not liable because his promise was not in writing. When the promisor, Decker, is not directly benefiting in the transaction, but merely acting as the surety for another person's (Decker's cousin) debt, then the promise must be in writing and signed by the person to be charged. The June 3rd letter is irrelevant. The length of the contract is not relevant here.

28. (d) The contract between Carson and Ives does not fall under the Statute of Frauds. The fact that the contract price was renegotiated for an amount over $500 is irrelevant because the contract is not for the *sale of goods*. Hence, Carson is entitled to the full $650 of the contract in exchange for his repair work.

29. (b) Generally, an oral contract for the sale of real property is not enforceable under the Statute of Frauds. However, there are certain exceptions to the statute. For example, if the purchaser takes possession of the property or makes a partial payment on the property, the contract would be enforceable without a writing. Under the Statute of Frauds, the contract must be signed by the party to be charged. Thus, it is irrelevant that Train signed the agreement. In this case, the contract was enforceable without a signing. The sale of real estate is not effected by a $500 benchmark. Under the UCC, contracts for the sale of goods must be in writing if the sales price is $500 or more.

30. (a) Courts generally decide that even if the remedy is not strictly contractual, parties who have fully performed an oral contract should recover under quasi-contract, promissory estoppel, or other such principals. Although the Statute of Frauds requires written evidence for contracts which cannot be performed within one year, it would not be applicable to contracts which have been fully performed.

31. (d) The Statute of Frauds requires that contracts that cannot be performed within one year from the date of the agreement must be in writing to

be enforceable. Although Carr has 18 months to perform, it is possible for Carr to perform within one year from the date of the agreement (this was stated in the question). Thus, this oral contract for services was enforceable without a writing. This particular provision applies to contracts for the sale of goods, not for the performance of services. Personal service contracts may be subject to the Statute of Frauds, for instance, when the contract for personal services is for a two-year time period.

32. (c) The Statute of Frauds does not require that the writing which evidences the agreement be signed by all parties, only those against whom enforcement is sought. Any contract for the sale of real estate falls within the Statute of Frauds. The statute does not require a fair or adequate purchase price, nor does it require a single writing, so long as all of the relevant documents refer to the same transaction.

33. (d) Under the UCC, contracts with a sales price of over $500 are subject to the Statute of Frauds, and therefore must generally be in writing and signed by the party to be charged in order to be enforceable. However, if a contract with a sales price of over $500 is modified so that the sales price involved is now under $500, the Statute of Frauds no longer applies and the agreement as modified need not be in writing to be enforced. The parol evidence rule only prohibits introduction of any evidence of a prior or contemporaneous agreement offered to contradict the terms of a completely integrated written statement, not of any subsequent agreement. Under the UCC, the modification of a contract does not require consideration in order to be valid.

Parol Evidence Rule

34. (b) The parol evidence rule, in general, does not allow the admission into evidence of written or oral evidence to contradict a written contract which was intended to be the final written understanding of the parties. There are three exceptions to this rule: Parole evidence can be introduced to (1) explain an ambiguity, (2) explain a subsequent agreement (not a prior or contemporaneous agreement), or (3) explain why no contract should exist due to lack of consideration, fraud, misrepresentation, duress, etc. Therefore, the rule effectively bars Item II from being admitted into evidence since it is a prior agreement. Item I, however, is not excluded by the rule as it is a subsequent modification of the contract.

35. (c) The parol evidence rule will prevent the admission of evidence concerning the oral agreement regarding who pays the utilities, since the rule excludes evidence of prior or contemporaneous oral agreements which would vary the written contract. However, the parol evidence rule will *not* prevent the admission of the fraudulent statements by Kemp during the original negotiations.

36. (a) If a contract is completely integrated into a written instrument, any evidence, written or oral, of a prior or *contemporaneous* agreement offered to contradict the terms of the written instrument is inadmissible.

36A. (b) Where a contract is completely integrated into a written agreement, the parol evidence rule will apply to prohibit any further evidence except for the following three items: (1) one can introduce evidence to show a subsequent agreement, but not a prior or contemporaneous agreement; (2) one can introduce evidence to explain an ambiguity; and (3) one can introduce evidence to show why no contract should exist due to fraud, lack of consideration, mistake, etc.

Mistake and Misrepresentation

37. (c) A unilateral mistake is a mistake made by only one party to the contract. In most cases the mistake is to the detriment of the mistaken party. Generally, a unilateral mistake does not allow a party to void the contract and it will be binding to both sides. However, an exception to this rule concerns a contract based on a calculation that is so far off that the other party should have known of the mistake, resulting in a voidable contract by the party making the mistake.

38. (a) Where a mistake is made by only one party (a unilateral mistake), the rule is that the mistaken party is bound by the contract unless the nonmistaken party knew of the mistake or should have known of the mistake. In this question, the nonmistaken party knew of the mistake; thus, the mistaken party is not bound by the contract. Whether the mistake was a result of gross negligence is irrelevant.

39. (c) One element necessary to prove misrepresentation is that the misrepresentation involve material facts. It is not necessary to prove that the false statements were made with reckless disregard for the truth. It is not necessary to prove that the misrepresentations were in writing. It is not necessary to prove that the reliance on the misrepresentations was the *only factor* inducing the plaintiff to enter into the contract.

40. (c)   Performance of a contract is objectively impossible if the subject matter necessary for performance is destroyed through no fault of the promisor. Thus, impossible performance is excused, meaning that there is no consideration for the other party's performance and the other party is entitled to rescission.

Fraud, Duress, and Undue Influence

41. (b)   Fraud in the inducement can be defined as follows: A *false representation* of a *fact* that is *material* and made with *knowledge of its falsity* and the *intention to deceive* and which representation is *justifiably relied on*. Only answer (b) addresses the above requirements. Answers (a), (c), and (d) are incorrect because none are requirements for an action for fraud under common law.

42. (b)   Long's daughter is a third-party beneficiary to the insurance contract. The promisor can assert any defenses against third party beneficiaries that he or she has against the promisee. Long's failure to disclose his known preexisting heart condition was an intentional false misrepresentation resulting in fraud in the inducement, and the contract is voidable by Tempo. Thus, Tempo will win if Long's daughter sues. Long's daughter is a third-party donee beneficiary. An incidental beneficiary is a third party whom a contract was not intended to benefit, but who nevertheless may receive an incidental benefit. Although Long's death was from natural causes, the contract is voidable by Tempo due to Long's failure to disclose his known preexisting heart condition. Although Long's daughter is a third-party donee beneficiary, the contract is voidable by Tempo. Tempo can assert any defenses against third party beneficiaries that it has against the promisee (Long).

43. (b)   Fraud is a false representation of *material* fact made by one party to the other party with the intent to deceive and which induces the other party to justifiably rely on that fact to his or her detriment. An appraisal value is generally considered to be a statement of fact. A nonexpert opinion is generally not considered to be a statement of fact. A prediction is not considered to be a statement of fact. An immaterial fact, does not fit the definition of fraud because such a statement of fact must be material in nature.

44. (d)   Fraud is the false representation of a material fact made by one party with the intent to deceive and which induces the other party to justifiably rely on that fact to his or her detriment. Someone who sells land to one party and later sells the same land to another party would be found liable on the theory of fraud.

45. (c)   The test for duress is whether the improper threats actually caused an individual to enter into a contract against his or her will. Duress can involve conduct outside of a tort or a crime. There is no "reasonable person test" in determining duress. The intent of the person making the improper threat is not relevant.

46. (c)   Generally, fraud in the inducement of a contract makes the resulting contract voidable at the option of the defrauded party. The defrauded party may then either affirm or rescind the contract. However, if a third party who is a good faith purchaser acquires an interest in the subject matter of the contract before the defrauded party has elected to rescind, no rescission is permitted. In such a case, the defrauded party's only recourse is to recover damages against the fraudulent party in a tort action.

47. (b)   Jackson will *not* prevail. If there are any means whereby the accuracy of the statement can be verified and it would be reasonable to do so, *justifiable reliance* requires such verification. Miller told Jackson to have an accountant examine Miller's records, which should have indicated to Jackson that verification was in order. Therefore, Jackson could not claim justifiable reliance. To recover, Jackson must not only prove that the errors were material, but also that his reliance on the misstatements was reasonable. If an innocent misrepresentation had occurred, Jackson could rescind the contract but generally would be unable to seek monetary damages.

48. (c)   Kent will lose, because Maco's knowledge of Kent's financial condition did not constitute duress. Duress is the threat of physical harm to a party or to the members of the party's family. The threat of economic loss is generally not considered duress. In this case, Kent was free to refuse the contract. There is no law that a client must pay the fair market value for services. Negotiation between the two parties is certainly allowed, and Maco is able to look elsewhere for its consulting needs. It is irrelevant whether Maco is aware of Kent's financial problems or whether Kent had other offers to provide consulting services.

49. (d)   The lease is voidable because of the landlord's threat of physical harm. Thus, the lease is voidable due to duress. In general, there is nothing wrong with a landlord raising the rent since the tenant, Johns, can move out. Eviction is not improper when the lease has expired. A tenant's financial condition would not cause the lease to be void.

Assignment and Delegation

50. (c)   An assignment is rebuttably presumed to be an assignment of rights *and* a delegation of duties. Here, assignee Deep Sea Lobster Farms presumably could carry out the lobster delivery duties.

51. (b)   Contract rights are generally assignable unless the right is personal to the promisee or the duty of the obligor or the obligor's burden or risk is materially increased. If neither of these are present, option contract rights are clearly assignable. Malpractice insurance policy rights are normally not assignable since the assignee might subject the insurance company to a greater risk, and thus, the insurance company would not agree to such an assignment. It is first necessary to determine who possesses the policy rights. If the right is viewed as being owed by the insurer to the insured, the insured could not assign their rights to another without violating the rules as to assignment. If however, the right is viewed as being owed by the insurer to a claimant injured by the insured's malpractice, the claimant's right to receive compensation should be assignable by the claimant.

52. (d)   An assignor (Burns) for value makes the following implied warranties: (1) the assignor will do nothing to destroy or impair the assigned right, (2) the right exists, (3) the right is not subject to any defense or counterclaim by the obligor (Nagel), and (4) any token or writing the assignor delivers as evidence of the assigned right is genuine. The assignor (Burns) does not warrant that the obligor (Nagel) will perform or pay or that the obligor is solvent. Failure to give notice to the obligor (Nagel) does not invalidate the assignment. The assignee (Ross) takes subject to any defenses and counterclaims arising from the contract which the obligor (Nagel) had against the assignor (Burns).

53. (a)   An assignee is entitled to all the rights his or her assignor had under the assigned contract, including the right to the promisor's performance. Baxter, the assignor, would no longer be liable to Clay, the assignee, if Clay releases Globe, the promisor, from the terms of the contract.

54. (c)   Vim, the assignee is entitled to the payments on the purchase price and the insurance proceeds because the assignee is entitled to all the rights his or her assignor had under the assigned contract--including the right to the promisor's (Egan's) performance. A promisor having notice of an assignment who nevertheless renders performance to the assignor or to any other third party remains liable to the assignee under the assigned contract.

Furthermore, an assignor who accepts performance from the promisor after the assignment receives any benefits as trustee for the assignee.

55. (c)   Contract rights can be assigned unless the assignment would materially increase the obligor's risk or duty. It is not necessary that an assignment be supported by consideration, nor is it necessary to be in writing. An assignor's right to revoke the assignment will not affect its validity.

56. (d)   A contract to purchase real property is assignable. In general, a contract may be assigned unless it involves personal services or a confidential relationship or the duties of the obligor would be materially increased. In this fact situation, there is no evidence given as to why this contract could not be assigned.

57. (a)   The assignee of a claim takes the claim subject to any defenses and counterclaims that the obligor had against the assignor. Since Kurtz acted fraudulently in the transaction out of which the accounts receivable arose, Long will be able to successfully assert a defense of fraud against City.

58. (a)   The delegation of duties does not strip the delegator (Ace) of his duty when the delegate (Pure Painting) fails to perform, but remains liable to the obligee (Wilcox) until someone performs. Notification of the assignment does not bear on the issue of the liability of the delegate. Any duty may be delegated unless the duty requires the personal performance of the original obligor-delegator, so that the substitute performance would differ materially from that agreed on or a statute, common law, or the contract itself forbids delegation.

Beneficiaries

59. (c)   Ferco will prevail because Ferco was the third party creditor beneficiary. The promisor on the contract (Bell) failed to perform and, therefore, Ferco can sue Bell. Ferco does not lack privity of contract. It is an intended creditor beneficiary of the contract between Bell and Allied. The creditor beneficiary need not give consideration to have an enforceable right. Ferco need not have been aware of the contract between Bell and Allied when it was formed in order to prevail in this situation.

60. (d)   A creditor beneficiary is defined as a third person to whom a debt or other duty is owed by the promisee. In a donee beneficiary relationship, there is no debt or duty owed by the promisee to the beneficiary. The primary purpose of entering into the contract and acquiring the insurance was *not* to make

a gift to Ness; Ness, therefore, is not a donee beneficiary with respect to either the contract or the insurance.

61. (c) Long is merely an incidental beneficiary and has no right to enforce the contract. In this case, the purpose of the contract was not to directly benefit Long. Long is an incidental beneficiary of the contract and, as such, has no right to enforce the contract. The assignment of the contract would have no bearing on Long's being able to sue.

62. (a) Wagner is a creditor beneficiary under the insurance policy. It is not a donee or incidental beneficiary. Privity of contract is the issue in this question.

63. (a) In general, the insured can name anyone as the beneficiary of his life insurance policy. Normally, the insured can always modify the beneficiary designation prior to the insured's death. Once the insured dies, the named beneficiary has a vested right to receive the insurance proceeds. If the insurance company does not pay, the beneficiary may successfully sue the insurance company as a third party donee beneficiary.

64. (a) A creditor beneficiary is a third person to whom a debt or other duty is owed by the promisee and promisor. If Park had assumed the mortgage, he would have incurred an obligation to Muni to repay the loan, and Muni would have become a third party creditor beneficiary. However, since Park only took the property subject to the mortgage, he is making no such promise to Muni, and in such a case Muni would not be a third party creditor beneficiary. Since Park only took subject to the mortgage, he is not liable for any deficiency which may result in the event the proceeds of a foreclosure sale are not sufficient to pay the amount due on the mortgage. Krieg was not released from his liability on the mortgage when he sold the property regardless of whether the purchaser either assumed or took subject to the mortgage.

Discharge, Breach, and Remedies

65. (b) The statute of limitations in an action for breach of contract begins to toll from the time the contract is breached.

65A. (d) The oral contract between Nord and Milo is valid since it could be performed within one year of the date it was entered into, and thus it did not fall within the Statute of Frauds. Since the amount owed was not in dispute, the notation on Nord's check that it constituted payment in full had no legal effect. The other bids have no relevance, since the oral contract was valid.

66. (a) For an immaterial breach of contract, the non-breaching party, White Corp., must pay the contract price less monetary damages to compensate for the immaterial breach. Equitable damages such as specific performance and injunction are available only in cases where monetary damages are not adequate. The facts of this problem illustrate an immaterial breach of contract because the injury incurred by White Corp. was relatively insignificant and would not justify an equitable remedy. White Corp. will be able to recover damages regardless of the inadvertent nature of the breach. Failure to install the brand of lighting specified in the contract does constitute a breach of contract. The immaterial nature of the breach limits the recovery to monetary damages.

66A. (b) Glaze will win because he "substantially performed" on the contract. Glaze should receive the contract price less the cost of damages due to minor deviations from the required performance. Glaze can also collect because Parc refused to allow Glaze the opportunity to complete the contract. Glaze can recover for substantial performance of the contract. The breach was a minor breach. Glaze breached the contract by purchasing minor accessories not allowed under the contract. In response, Parc refused to allow Glaze to complete the contract. This is not considered to be anticipatory breach by Parc.

67. (a) An accord and satisfaction is the settlement of a dispute or the satisfaction of a claim through the creation of a new contract between the parties to the original contract. In this case a new contract was created. The consideration given by Castle to Nelson, who agreed to accept $1,000 less than the originally agreed upon amount, was Castle's offer to pay the note on April 1 instead of the originally contracted date of April 30. An unliquidated debt is one in which the specific amount of the debt has not been determined by the parties involved. In this question, an amount of $5,000 had been specified. Castle would win if Nelson sued.

68. (a) To modify a contract, common law consideration is needed. This is related to the "preexisting legal duty rule" where a party to a contract is not bound to modifications unless additional consideration is provided. There is no requirement to provide consideration to ratify a contract upon reaching the age of majority. Under the UCC no consideration is necessary under the "firm offer" rule. Under the UCC, no consideration is required to modify a UCC contract; however, if the

modified contract is for $500 or more, the Statute of Frauds requires written evidence of the modified UCC contract.

69. (c) A rescission involves undoing the contract on both sides and placing the parties in their original positions.

70. (d) The arrangement in question is a novation, with Moss completely replacing Wren under the terms of the Wren-First Federal contract. Moss assumed liability on the mortgage, so answer (a) is incorrect. Wren has been released from liability, something an assignment and delegation does not accomplish.

71. (a) Where one party to a contract prevents the other from rendering performance, the party unable to perform will be discharged from its contractual duties. An accord and satisfaction involves an agreement to accept a substitute future performance for a performance required under an existing contract. Performance of the substituted duty discharges the original duty. Both statements are thus correct.

72. (d) The statute of limitations, which runs from the time the defect could have reasonably been discovered, would likely prevent Dart from prevailing because of the length of time that has passed. The parol evidence rule does not apply to the admission into evidence of the proof of fraud. A contract can be rescinded if there was fraud. It is not necessary for the misrepresentations to be part of the written contract.

73. (d) When a contract is or becomes illegal, that contract becomes void, thus unenforceable. The death of the obligee will not discharge the obligor's duties because the decedent obligee's estate may still receive the services. The fact that the cost of performance has doubled does not render that performance impossible and will not discharge the obligor's duties. Although the bankruptcy of the obligor may discharge the obligor's duties; the bankruptcy of the obligee will not discharge the obligor's duties.

74. (c) The renunciation of a bilateral contract before performance is due is an anticipatory breach which gives the non-breaching party several options (one of which is suing immediately for anticipatory repudiation). Promissory estoppel is an equitable remedy used in situations where your remedy at law is unjust (there is no indication from the facts in this problem that promissory estoppel would apply). The doctrine of accord and satisfaction applies in

circumstances where there is an unliquidated debt and there is a good faith offer to settle this disputed debt. The doctrine involving substantial performance does not apply in this situation.

75. (d) The fact that Cobb no longer needs the 30,000 gallons does not excuse his unilateral modification of the contract (i.e., this is a breach of contract). This contract was not drafted as a "requirements" contract but as a contract for the delivery of 100,000 gallons. The change of circumstances could have been contemplated by the parties and included in the contract but the parties did not do this. There are circumstances which excuse performance by operation of law, for instance, commercial impracticability. However, for it to apply, the performance by Cobb (payment of money) must be physically impossible or impracticable because of extreme and unreasonable expense, difficulty or loss. The facts do not justify this conclusion. An unexcused breach is not cured by good faith. This contract was not worded as a requirements contract since it unequivocally called for 100,000 gallons.

76. (b) A liquidated damages clause will be enforceable if the amount of the penalty bears a reasonable relationship to the probable loss. It is not always necessary to have a signed writing (only if the Statute of Frauds applies). There are no punitive damages for a breach of contract. There is no requirement that liquidated damages apply only when the seller cannot compel specific performance.

77. (a) Conditions precedent, conditions subsequent, and concurrent conditions are all types of conditions which may validly be present in contracts.

78. (a) A liquidated damages provision is a specific amount provided in a contract to be recoverable in the event of a breach. It is enforceable if actual damage would be difficult to assess and the amount appears reasonable at the time of contracting. The UCC 2-718 allows liquidated damages if the amount is reasonable in light of the anticipated or actual harm caused by the breach. However, if the liquidated damages are excessive, a court may interpret them as a penalty and refuse enforcement. Liquidated damage provisions are not enforceable if a court interprets them as a penalty and refuses enforcement. The breach was identified and specified in the contract; thus, materiality is not an issue. Liquidated damage provisions are allowed and enforceable.

79. (d) Under common law, Hodges is entitled to sue for compensatory damages *or* to obtain specific performance. Compensatory damages

compensate for losses and lost profits suffered as a result of the breach. If the promisor fails to render the promised service and the promisee must obtain it *elsewhere* at a higher cost, damages are the difference between the market price and the contract price. Specific performance may be granted in cases where the contract is for the sale of unique property, meaning land or goods that are unique or unobtainable elsewhere. The building Hodges contracted to buy would, in most cases, be considered unique.

PERFORMANCE BY SUBTOPICS

Each category below parallels a subtopic covered in Chapter 43. Record the number and percentage of questions you correctly answered in each subtopic area.

Contract Definitions

Question #	Correct √
1	
2	
3	
# Questions	3

Correct _____
% Correct _____

Offer and Acceptance

Question #	Correct √
4	
5	
6	
7	X
8	
9	
10	
11	
12	X
13	X
14	
15	
16	
17	
# Questions	14

Correct _____
% Correct _____

Consideration

Question #	Correct √
18	
19	X
20	X
20A	
21	X
# Questions	5

Correct _____
% Correct _____

Capacity, Legality, and Public Policy

Question #	Correct √
22	
23	
24	
25	
# Questions	4

Correct _____
% Correct _____

Statute of Frauds

Question #	Correct √
26	
27	
28	
29	
30	
31	
32	
33	
# Questions	8

Correct _____
% Correct _____

Parol Evidence Rule

Question #	Correct √
34	X
35	
36	
36A	X
# Questions	4

Correct _____
% Correct _____

Mistake and Misrepresentation

Question #	Correct √
37	X
38	X
39	X
40	
# Questions	4

Correct _____
% Correct _____

Fraud, Duress, and Undue Influence

Question #	Correct √
41	
42	X
43	
44	
45	X
46	X
47	
48	X
49	
# Questions	9

Correct _____
% Correct _____

Assignment and Delegation

Question #	Correct √
50	
51	X
52	X
53	X
54	X
55	X
56	
57	X
58	
# Questions	9

Correct _____
% Correct _____

Beneficiaries

Question #	Correct √
59	X
60	
61	
62	
63	
64	X
# Questions	6

Correct _____
% Correct _____

Discharge, Breach, and Remedies

Question #	Correct √
65	X
65A	
66	
66A	
67	
68	X
69	
70	X
71	X
72	
73	
74	X
75	
76	
77	
78	X
79	
# Questions	17

Correct _____
% Correct _____

OTHER OBJECTIVE FORMAT QUESTION

Problem 43-2 (Estimated time--10 to 15 minutes)

Problem 43-2 consists of 15 items. Select the **best** answer for each item. **Answer all items.**

On December 15, Blake Corp. telephoned Reach Consultants, Inc. and offered to hire Reach to design a security system for Blake's research department. The work would require two years to complete. Blake offered to pay a fee of $100,000 but stated that the offer must be accepted in writing, and the acceptance received by Blake no later than December 20.

On December 20, Reach faxed a written acceptance to Blake. Blake's offices were closed on December 20, and Reach's fax was not seen until December 21.

Reach's acceptance contained the following language:

> "We accept your $1,000,000 offer. Weaver has been assigned $5,000 of the fee as payment for sums owed Weaver by Reach. Payment of this amount should be made directly to Weaver."

On December 22, Blake sent a signed memo to Reach rejecting Reach's December 20 fax but offering to hire Reach for a $75,000 fee. Reach telephoned Blake on December 23 and orally accepted Blake's December 22 offer.

Required:

a. **Items 1 through 7** relate to whether a contractual relationship exists between Blake and Reach. For each item, determine whether the statement is True (T) or False (F).

1. Blake's December 15 offer had to be in writing to be a legitimate offer. _F_
2. Reach's December 20 fax was an improper method of acceptance. _F_

3. Reach's December 20 fax was effective when sent. _T_
4. Reach's acceptance was invalid because it was received after December 20. _T_
5. Blake's receipt of Reach's acceptance created a voidable contract. _T_
6. Reach's agreement to a $1,000,000 fee prevented the formation of a contract. _T_
7. Reach's December 20 fax was a counteroffer. _T_

b. **Items 8 through 12** relate to the attempted assignment of part of the fee to Weaver. Assume that a valid contract exists between Blake and Reach. For each item, determine whether the statement is True (T) or False (F).

8. Reach is prohibited from making an assignment of any contract right or duty. _F_
9. Reach may validly assign part of the fee to Weaver.
10. Under the terms of Reach's acceptance, Weaver would be considered a third party creditor beneficiary.
11. In a breach of contract suit by Weaver, against Blake, Weaver would not collect any punitive damages.
12. In a breach of contract suit by Weaver, against Reach, Weaver would be able to collect punitive damages.

c. **Items 13 through 15** relate to Blake's December 22 signed memo. For each item, determine whether the statement is True (T) or False (F).

13. Reach's oral acceptance of Blake's December 22 memo may be enforced by Blake against Reach. _F_
14. Blake's memo is a valid offer even though it contains no date for acceptance. _T_
15. Blake's memo may be enforced against Blake by Reach. (11/94, Law, #2, 5238-5252) _T_

_F_

Blake is changed he has to sign or Dr sign it

OTHER OBJECTIVE FORMAT SOLUTION

Solution 43-2 Offer/Acceptance/Assignment

1. (F)   Although Blake's December 15 offer had to be in writing to be *enforceable* against Blake, it is still a legitimate offer and is capable of being accepted. The common law rules of contract require an offer to manifest an <u>intent</u> to be presently bound, be specific as to terms and conditions, and be communicated to the offeree. Blake's offer meets these requirements.

2. (F)   Blake's offer only required that the acceptance be in writing and that the acceptance must be received by December 20. Thus, a fax sent and received on December 20 satisfies the conditions of the offer.

3. (F)   Blake's offer stipulated that the acceptance be received no later than December 20, thus avoiding application of the deposited acceptance (or mail-box) rule.

4. (F)   The fax was received by Blake Corp. shortly after it was sent: i.e., on December 20. The fact that no one saw the fax until December 21 is irrelevant.

5. (F)   The common law rules of contract require that an acceptance mirror the terms of the offer. Reach's memo did *not* mirror the terms of Blake's offer, and thus qualified as a counter-offer and rejection. No contract was formed.

6. (T)   Reach's memo, a counter-offer, presented a new offer which was capable of being accepted. A counter-offer does prevent a contract from being formed from the original offer. The BOE gave credit for both responses.

7. (T)   Reach's December 20 fax was a counter-offer because it did not mirror the terms of Blake's original offer.

8. (F)   There is nothing in the contract between Blake and Reach that prohibits assignment; nor is the right delegated personal or as a result of a confidential relationship between the parties, nor is Blake's duty materially changed. Thus, there is nothing to prevent assignment by Reach.

9. (T)   As stated in the answer to #8, there is nothing to prohibit Blake's assignment of part of the fee to Weaver.

10. (T)   A creditor beneficiary is a third party to whom a debt is owed by the promisee, and who is intended by the contracting parties to benefit from the contract. The debt will be discharged in whole or in part by the promisor's rendering performance to the third party. Weaver meets this definition.

11. (T)   The common law rules of contracts provides that punitive damages are *almost never* available in a breach of contract action.

12. (F)   Punitive damages are *almost never* available in an action for breach of contract.

13. (F)   The Statute of Frauds requires that certain contracts be in writing to be enforceable. Contracts that cannot be performed within one year of the contract date are governed by the statute. Although the Statute of Frauds requires a writing, it only requires that the writing be signed by the party to be charged. Since Reach did not provide a signed writing, the agreement cannot be enforced against Reach.

14. (T)   Although an offer must be sufficiently certain to enable a court to interpret its terms, a valid offer may leave one or more terms open. If the parties fail to agree on a term left open, the courts will imply a reasonable term. Time is a term frequently left open.

15. (T)   As stated above, the Statute of Frauds requires contracts not performable within one year to be in writing and signed by the party to be charged. In this case, Blake is the party to be charged and Blake has signed the written memo.

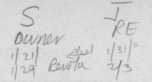

ESSAY QUESTIONS

Essay 43-3 (15 to 25 minutes)

Suburban Properties, Inc. owns and manages several shopping centers.

On May 4, 1993, Suburban received from Bridge Hardware, Inc., one of its tenants, a signed letter proposing that the existing lease between Suburban and Bridge be modified to provide that certain utility costs be equally shared by Bridge and Suburban, effective June 1, 1993. Under the terms of the original lease, Bridge was obligated to pay all utility costs. On May 5, 1993, Suburban sent Bridge a signed letter agreeing to share the utility costs as proposed. Suburban later changed its opinion and refused to share in the utility costs.

On June 4, 1993, Suburban received from Dart Associates, Inc., a signed offer to purchase one of the shopping centers owned by Suburban. The offer provided as follows: a price of $9,250,000; it would not be withdrawn before July 1, 1993; and an acceptance must be received by Dart to be effective. On June 9, 1993, Suburban mailed Dart a signed acceptance. On June 10, before Dart had received Suburban's acceptance, Dart telephoned Suburban and withdrew its offer. Suburban's acceptance was received by Dart on June 12, 1993.

On June 22, 1993, one of Suburban's shopping centers was damaged by a fire, which started when the center was struck by lightning. As a result of the fire, one of the tenants in the shopping center, World Popcorn Corp., was forced to close its business and will be unable to re-open until the damage is repaired. World sued Suburban, claiming that Suburban is liable for World's losses resulting from the fire. The lease between Suburban and World is silent in this regard.

Suburban has taken the following positions:

- Suburban's May 5, 1993, agreement to share equally the utility costs with Bridge is not binding on Suburban.
- Dart could not properly revoke its June 4 offer and must purchase the shopping center.
- Suburban is not liable to World for World's losses resulting from the fire.

Required:

In separate paragraphs, determine whether Suburban's positions are correct and state the reasons for your conclusions. (5/94, Law, #5)

Essay 43-4 (15 to 20 minutes)

The following letters were mailed among Jacobs, a real estate developer, Snow, the owner of an undeveloped parcel of land, and Eljay Distributors, Inc., a clothing wholesaler interested in acquiring Snow's parcel to build a warehouse:

a. **January 21, 1990**--Snow to Jacobs: "My vacant parcel (Lot 2, Birds Addition to Cedar Grove) is available for $125,000 cash; closing within 60 days. You must accept by January 31 if you are interested."

This was received by Jacobs on January 31.

b. **January 29, 1990**--Snow to Jacobs: "Ignore my January 21 letter to you; I have decided not to sell my lot at this time."

This was received by Jacobs on February 3.

c. **January 31, 1990**--Jacobs to Snow: "Per your January 21 letter, you have got a deal."

Jacobs inadvertently forgot to sign the January 31 letter, which was received by Snow on February 4.

d. **February 2, 1990**--Jacobs to Eljay: "In consideration of your promise to pay me $10,000, I hereby assign to you my right to purchase Snow's vacant lot (Lot 2, Birds Addition to Cedar Grove)."

This was received by Eljay on February 5.

All of the letters were signed, except as noted above, and properly stamped and addressed.

Snow has refused to sell the land to Jacobs or Eljay, asserting that no contract exists because:

- Jacobs' acceptance was not received on a timely basis.
- Snow had revoked the January 21 offer.
- Jacobs' acceptance was not signed.
- Jacobs had no right to assign the contract to Eljay.

Required:

For each of Snow's assertions, indicate whether the assertion is correct, setting forth reasons for your conclusion. (11/90, Law, #2)

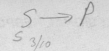

Essay 43-5 (7 to 10 minutes)

Dunn & Co., CPAs, while performing the 1987 year-end audit of Starr Corp.'s financial statements discovered that certain events during 1987 had resulted in litigation.

Starr had purchased a warehouse on March 1, 1987. The contract between Birk and Starr provided for a closing on September 20, 1987. On July 1, 1987, Birk executed a contract to purchase the warehouse from Starr for $200,000. On September 1, 1987, Birk contacted Starr and demanded that the purchase price be reduced to $190,000 because of a sudden rise in interest rates and declining value of real estate. Starr orally agreed to change the price to $190,000. On September 2, 1987, Birk sent Starr a signed memo confirming the reduction in price to $190,000. Starr did not sign the memo or any other agreement reducing the price. On September 15, Starr, by telephone, informed Birk that it would not sell the warehouse for $190,000. Birk refused to pay Starr $200,000 and a closing never occurred.

Starr commenced actions against Birk asserting the following:

• Birk has breached the contract with Starr because Birk failed to close the transaction and buy the warehouse at a price of $200,000.

Required:

Discuss Starr's assertion, indicating whether such an assertion is correct and the reasons therefor.

(11/88, Law, #2)

Essay 43-6 (15 to 20 minutes)

In a signed letter dated March 2, 1991, Stake offered to sell Packer a specific vacant parcel of land for $100,000. Stake had inherited the land, along with several apartment buildings in the immediate vicinity. Packer received the offer on March 4. The offer required acceptance by March 10 and required Packer to have the property surveyed by a licensed surveyor so that exact legal description of the property could be determined.

On March 6, Packer sent Stake a counteroffer of $75,000. All other terms and conditions of the offer were unchanged. Stake received Packer's counteroffer on March 8, and, on that day, telephoned Packer and accepted it. On learning that a survey of the vacant parcel would cost about $1,000, Packer telephoned Stake on March 11 requesting that they share the survey cost equally. During this conversation, Stake agreed to Packer's proposal.

During the course of the negotiations leading up to the March communications between Stake and Packer, Stake expressed concern to Packer that a buyer of the land might build apartment units that would compete with those owned by Stake in the immediate vicinity. Packer assured Stake that Packer intended to use the land for a small shopping center. Because of these assurances, Stake was willing to sell the land to Packer. Contrary to what Packer told Stake, Packer had already contracted conditionally with Rolf for Rolf to build a 48-unit apartment development on the vacant land to be purchased from Stake.

During the last week of March, Stake learned that the land to be sold to Packer had a fair market value of $200,000. Also, Stake learned that Packer intended to build apartments on the land. Because of this information, Stake sued Packer to rescind the real estate contract, alleging that:

• Packer committed fraud in the formation of the contract thereby entitling Stake to rescind the contract.
• Stake's innocent mistake as to the fair market value of the land entitles Stake to rescind the contract.
• The contract was not enforceable against Stake because Stake did not sign Packer's March 6 counteroffer.

Required:

State whether Stake's allegations are correct and give the reasons for your conclusions. (11/91, Law, #3)

Essay 43-7 (15 to 20 minutes)

Bar Manufacturing and Cole Enterprises were arch rivals in the high technology industry and both were feverishly working on a new product which would give the first to develop it a significant competitive advantage. Bar engaged Abel Consultants on April 1, 1983, for one year, commencing immediately, at $7,500 a month to aid the company in the development of the new product. The contract was oral and was consummated by a handshake. Cole approached Abel and offered them a $10,000 bonus for signing, $10,000 a month for nine months, and a $40,000 bonus if Cole was the first to successfully market the new product. In this connection, Cole stated that the oral contract Abel made with Bar was unenforceable and that Abel could walk away from it without liability. In addition, Cole made certain misrepresentations regarding the dollar amount of its commitment to the project, the stage of its development, and the expertise of its research staff. Abel accepted the offer.

Four months later, Bar successfully introduced the new product. Cole immediately dismissed Abel and has paid nothing beyond the first four $10,000 payments plus the initial bonus. Three lawsuits ensured: Bar sued Cole, Bar sued Abel, and Abel sued Cole.

Required:

Answer the following, setting forth reasons for any conclusions stated.

Discuss the various theories on which each of the three lawsuits is based, the defenses which will be asserted, the measure of possible recovery, and the probable outcome of the litigation.   (11/83, Law, #4)

ESSAY SOLUTIONS

Solution 43-3   Elements and Discharge of Contract

Suburban is correct concerning the agreement to share utility costs with Bridge. A **modification** of a contract **requires consideration** to be **binding** on the parties. Suburban is not bound by the lease modification because Suburban did not receive any consideration in exchange for its agreement to share the cost of utilities with Bridge.

Suburban is not correct with regard to the Dart offer. An **offer can be revoked** at any time **prior to acceptance**. This is true despite the fact that the offer provides that it will not be withdrawn prior to a stated time. If **no consideration** is **given in exchange for this promise** not to withdraw the offer, the **promise is not binding** on the offeror. The offer provided that Suburban's acceptance would not be effective until received. Dart's June 10 **revocation terminated Dart's offer**. Thus, Suburban's June 9 acceptance was not effective.

Suburban is correct with regard to World's claim. The general rule is that destruction of, or **damage to, the subject matter** of a contract without the fault of either party **terminates the contract**. In this case, Suburban is not liable to World because Suburban is **discharged from its contractual duties** as a result of the fire, which made **performance** by it under the lease **objectively impossible**.

Solution   43-4   Acceptance/Assignment of Contracts

Snow's assertion that Jacobs' acceptance was not received on a timely basis is incorrect. Jacobs' January 31 acceptance was effective when **dispatched** (mailed) under the **complete-when-posted doctrine** because:

- The letter was an **authorized means of communication** (because Snow's offer was by mail); and
- The letter was properly stamped and addressed.

Therefore, Jacobs' **acceptance was effective on January 31**, the last possible day under Snow's January 21 offer.

Snow's assertion that the January 21 offer was effectively revoked is incorrect because a **revocation is not effective until received**. In this case, the revocation was effective on February 3, and Jacobs' acceptance was effective on January 31.

Snow's assertion that Jacobs' failure to sign the January 31 acceptance prevents the formation of a contract is incorrect. The **Statute of Frauds**, which applies to contracts involving interests in real estate, **requires only the signature of the party to be charged with enforcement of the contract**. Therefore, because Snow had signed the January 21 offer, which was accepted by Jacobs, the contract is enforceable against Snow.

Snow's assertion that Jacobs had no right to assign the contract is incorrect. Contract rights, including the right to purchase real estate, are **generally assignable** unless the assignment:

- Would materially increase the risk or burden of the obligor;
- Purports to transfer highly personal contract rights;
- Is validly prohibited by the contract; or
- Is prohibited by law.

None of these limitations applies to the assignment by Jacobs to Eljay.

Solution 43-5 Oral Agreement Modifying an Enforceable Existing Contract

Starr's assertion, that Birk has breached the contract with Starr because Birk failed to close the transaction and buy the warehouse at a price of $200,000, is correct. An **oral agreement modifying an enforceable existing contract is not enforceable** if the modification is within the **Statute of Frauds**. A contract for the sale of real estate or a modification of such a contract falls within the provisions of the Statute of Frauds and, therefore, a **writing signed by the party to be charged is required**. The fact that Birk sent a signed memo to Starr is not effective because it was not signed by Starr. Furthermore, the agreement to reduce the purchase price to $190,000 is not enforceable because Birk did not give any consideration for the modification. Birk had a **preexisting obligation** to purchase the warehouse for $200,000 and gave no new consideration for the modification of the price. The fact that Birk may have acted in good faith as a result of the decline in value of real estate and rise in interest rates will not be sufficient to make the oral agreement enforceable against Starr. Therefore, Birk's failure to pay $200,000 as required by the July 1 contract constitutes a **breach** of that contract.

Solution 43-6 Fraud/Mistake/Counter-Offer

Stake's first allegation, that Packer committed **fraud in the formation of the contract**, is correct and **Stake may rescind the contract**. Packer has assured Stake that the vacant parcel would be used for a shopping center when, in fact, Packer intended to use the land to construct apartment units that would be in direct competition with those owned by Stake. Stake would not have sold the land to Packer had Packer's real intentions been known. Therefore, the elements of fraud are present:

- A **false representation**;
- Of a **fact**;
- That is **material**;
- **Made with knowledge of its falsity** and **intention to deceive**;
- That is **justifiably relied on**.

Stake's second allegation, that the mistake as to the fair market value of the land entitles Stake to rescind the contract, is incorrect. Generally, **mistakes** as to **adequacy of consideration or fairness of a bargain** are **insufficient grounds** to entitle the aggrieved party **to rescind a contract**.

Stake's third allegation, that the contract was not enforceable against Stake because Stake did not sign the counteroffer, is correct. The contract between Stake and Packer involves real estate and, therefore, the **Statute of Frauds** requirements must be satisfied. The Statute of Frauds requires that a **writing be signed by the party against whom enforcement is sought**. The **counteroffer is unenforceable** against Stake, because Stake did not sign it. As a result, Stake is **not obligated to sell** the land to Packer under the terms of the counteroffer.

Solution 43-7 Wrongful Interference/Breach of Contract

Bar's lawsuit against Cole will be based upon the **intentional tort of wrongful interference with a contractual relationship**. The primary requirement for this cause of action is a **valid contractual relationship** with which the **defendant knowingly interferes**. This requirement is met in the case of Cole. The contract is **not required to be in writing** since it is for exactly one year from the time of its making. It is, therefore, valid even though oral. Cole's knowledge of the contract is obvious. The principal problem, however, is damages.

Since Bar was the first to successfully market the product, it would appear that damages are not present. It is possible there were **actual damages** incurred by Bar (for example, it hired another consulting firm at an increased price). It also might be possible that some courts would permit the recovery of **punitive damages** since this is an **intentional tort**.

Bar's **cause of action** against Abel would be for **breach of contract**. Once again, damages would appear to be a serious problem. Furthermore, **punitive damages would rarely be available in a contract action**. Finally, Bar **cannot recover the same damages twice**. Hence, if it proceeds against Cole and recovers damages caused by Abel's breach of contract, it will not be able to recover a second time.

loss/harm

Abel's lawsuit against Cole will be **based upon fraud and breach of contract**. There were fraudulent statements made by Cole with the **requisite intent** and that were possibly **to Abel's detriment**. The breach of contract by Cole is obvious. However, the contract that Cole induced Abel to enter into and which it subsequently breached was an **illegal contract**, that is, one calling for the commission of a tort. Therefore, both parties are likely to be treated as wrongdoers, and **Abel will be denied recovery**.

NOTES

CHAPTER 44

SALES

I. Sales Transactions 44-3
   A. Condition Precedent 44-3
   B. Condition Subsequent 44-3
   C. Cover 44-3
   D. Goods 44-3
   E. Identification (UCC 2-501) 44-4
   F. Merchant 44-4
   G. Sale 44-4
   H. Tender 44-4

II. Nonsales Transactions 44-4
   A. Bailment 44-4
   B. Gift 44-5

III. Sales and the Uniform Commercial Code 44-5
   A. UCC Article 2 44-5
   B. Effect of the UCC 44-5

IV. Standardized Shipping Terms 44-6
   A. F.O.B. and F.A.S. (UCC 2-319) 44-6
   B. C.I.F. and C&F (UCC 2-320) 44-7
   C. C.O.D. 44-7
   D. No Arrival, No Sale 44-7

V. Conditional Sales (UCC 2-326, -327) 44-8
   A. "Sale on Approval" and "Sale or Return" 44-8
   B. Characteristics of Sales on Approval 44-8
   C. Characteristics of Sale or Return 44-8

VI. Title to Goods 44-8
   A. Importance of Title 44-8
   B. Passage of Title (UCC 2-401) 44-8
   C. Power to Transfer Title (UCC 2-403) 44-9

VII. Risk of Loss 44-10
   A. Express Agreement 44-10
   B. UCC Provisions (UCC 2-509) 44-10

VIII. Warranties 44-11
   A. Types 44-11
   B. Privity 44-12
   C. Disclaimer of Warranties (UCC 2-316) 44-13
   D. Statute of Limitations (UCC 2-725) 44-13

IX. Performance 44-13
   A. Seller's Rights and Duties 44-13
   B. Buyer's Rights and Duties 44-14
   C. Excuses and Substitutes for Performance 44-14

X. Remedies for Breach 44-15
   A.   Buyer's Remedies...44-15
   B.   Seller's Remedies...44-18
   C.   Remedies for Buyer or Seller...44-20
   D.   Statute of Limitations for Breach of Sales Contract (UCC 2-725) 44-21

XI. Products Liability 44-21
   A.   General Characteristics 44-21
   B.   Negligence Actions 44-21
   C.   Strict Liability...44-22
   D.   Breach of Warranty..44-23

CHAPTER 44

SALES

I. Sales Transactions

A.   <u>Condition Precedent</u>--A condition which must be fulfilled before the agreement's promises or covenants are binding on the other party.

B.   <u>Condition Subsequent</u>--A condition, the performance or occurrence of which causes the agreement's promises or covenants to cease being binding on one or both parties.

C.   <u>Cover</u>--The right of the buyer, after a breach by the seller, to buy substitute goods (UCC 2-712).

D.   <u>Goods</u>

    1.   In general, all things moveable at the time of identification to the contract for sale [UCC 2-105(1)].

        a.   Included within the definition of goods are the following:

            (1)   Unborn young of animals.

            (2)   Growing crops and other identified things attached to realty which can be severed without harm (for example, timber).

        b.   Excluded from the definition of goods are the following:

            (1)   Money for payment of the purchase price.

            (2)   Investment securities.

            (3)   Intangible personal property such as accounts receivable, commercial paper, and partnership interests.

    2.   Fungible goods are goods so characterized that a unit of them is by nature, or by trade usage, considered to be equivalent to any other like unit [UCC 1-201(17)]. For example, oil in storage tanks, or wheat in a storage silo, is a fungible good.

    3.   Existing or Future Goods [UCC 2-105(2)]

        a.   Existing goods are those currently owned by the seller.

        b.   Future goods are those to be acquired or produced by the seller. There cannot be a present sale of future goods; an attempt to make such a sale is characterized as a contract to sell in the future.

E.   Identification (UCC 2-501)

    1.   In the absence of an explicit agreement, identification occurs:

        a.   When the contract is made, and the goods already exist and are referred to in the sales contract.

        b.   When the goods are shipped, marked, or otherwise designated by the seller as goods to which the contract refers and the contract is for the sale of future goods (other than crops or unborn young).

        c.   When crops are planted or when young are conceived.

    2.   The buyer obtains a special property right and an insurable interest in goods that are existing and identified.

F.   Merchant--One who either deals in goods similar to the ones involved in the transaction or who, by occupation, represents that he or she has particular knowledge or skill relating to the practices or goods involved in the transaction [UCC 2-104 (1)].

G.   Sale--The transfer of ownership of personal property for a price (consideration) [UCC 2-106(1)].

    •   "Contract for sale" means either of the following:

        a.   A Present Sale of Goods--Sale accomplished by the making of the contract.

        b.   An agreement to sell goods at a future time.

H.   Tender--Tender refers to the requirement that the seller put and hold conforming goods at the buyer's disposition and give the buyer any notification reasonably necessary to take delivery.

II. Nonsales Transactions

A.   Bailment--Present transfer of possession of personal property (but not ownership) for a particular purpose.

    1.   Parties Involved in a Bailment

        a.   Bailor--Party who owns property and delivers it to the bailee.

        b.   Bailee--Party who accepts possession of the bailed property.

        c.   Either party may insure his or her interest in the property.

    2.   Bailment is most often a contractual relationship that may be either expressed or implied. Examples of bailments include the following:

        a.   Consignment--A bailment for sale. Bailee (consignee) becomes bailor's (consignor's) agent to accomplish a sale of the bailor's property to another.

        b.   Bailment for Use--Bailee leases property owned by bailor so that the bailee may use the property for his or her own purposes.

        c.   Pledge--Property is delivered to the bailee as security for the debt of the bailor.

        d.   Bailment With Option to Purchase--Bailor delivers goods on approval. If satisfied, the bailee may buy them; if not satisfied, the bailee returns the goods to the bailor.

B.　<u>Gift</u>--Present transfer of ownership, requiring delivery but not consideration.　Sales, on the other hand, require consideration but not delivery.

III. Sales and the Uniform Commercial Code

A.　<u>UCC Article 2</u>--Sales:　Article 2 deals with contracts for the sale of goods (<u>not</u> real property, investment securities, or services) (UCC 2-102).

B.　<u>Effect of the UCC</u>--The UCC codifies current commercial practices.　These practices may differ from general contract law.

   1.　Thus, a contract for the sale of goods will be found even though some terms are left open, if the parties intended to form a contract and there is a reasonably certain basis for giving an appropriate remedy (UCC 2-204).

      a.　When the price is not agreed upon by the parties, the contract price is deemed to be a "reasonable price at the time of delivery."

      b.　When no place for delivery is specified, delivery shall be made at the seller's place of business; or if the seller has no place of business, then the place for delivery shall be the seller's residence.　However, if the goods identified in the contract of sale are known to be located elsewhere, then that place shall be the place for delivery.

      c.　When no time for delivery is specified, the time is a "reasonable time."

      d.　When no time for payment is specified, and no credit is advanced, payment is due at the place and time the buyer is to <u>receive</u> the goods.　This payment rule applies even though the place of business is the place of delivery (see b., above).

      e.　When not specifically stated in the contract, particulars of performance may be left open to be specified by one of the parties.　As with subsections a. through d., above, the specifying party must exercise good faith in formulating particulars of performance.

   2.　Firm Offer--A firm offer is a signed written offer by a merchant to buy or sell goods in which the merchant gives assurance that the offer will be held open.　Such an offer will be irrevocable (even though it is not supported by consideration) for the time stated or for a reasonable time.　However, in no event may this time period be longer than <u>three months</u>.　Finally, any such term of assurance made on a form supplied by the offeree (party to whom offer is made) must be separately signed by the offeror (party making the offer) (UCC 2-205).

   3.　Acceptance

      a.　Unless otherwise indicated, an acceptance can be made in any manner that is reasonable under the circumstances (UCC 2-206).

      b.　An acceptance containing <u>additional terms</u> is effective unless expressly made conditional on assent to those terms.　The additional terms are treated as proposals for additions to the contract.　<u>Between merchants</u> the additional terms become part of the contract unless one of the following applies (UCC 2-207):

         (1)　The offer expressly limits acceptance to the terms of the offer.

         (2)　They materially alter the offer.

         (3)　Notification of objection to the additional terms is given within a reasonable time after notice of the additional terms is received.

4. Conduct by both parties that recognizes the existence of a contract is sufficient to establish a contract for sale although the writings of the parties (conflicting printed forms) do not otherwise establish a contract [UCC 2-207(3)].

5. An agreement to modify or rescind a sales contract need <u>not</u> be supported by consideration to be binding. However, a signed agreement that precludes modification or rescission except by a signed writing cannot otherwise be modified or rescinded. Finally, except as between merchants, such an agreement precluding modification on a form supplied by a merchant must be separately signed by the other party (UCC 2-209).

   • Common law requires new consideration for any modification.

6. Statute of Frauds--A contract for the sale of goods for a price equal to or greater than <u>$500</u> is <u>unenforceable</u> unless there is a written memorandum <u>signed by the party to be charged</u>. A writing is not insufficient because it omits or incorrectly states a term agreed upon, but the contract is not enforceable under this paragraph beyond the quantity of goods shown in such writing (UCC 2-201).

   a. Between merchants, the Statute of Frauds is satisfied, if within a reasonable time a writing in confirmation of the contract and sufficient against the sender is received and the receiving party has reason to know its contents, unless the receiving party gives a written notice of objection to its contents.

   b. Further, even if an otherwise valid contract does not satisfy the general requirements of the Statute of Frauds, it is still an enforceable contract:

      (1) If the goods are to be <u>specially manufactured</u> for the buyer and are not suitable for sale to others in the ordinary course of the seller's business, and the seller, before notice of repudiation is received and under circumstances which reasonably indicate that the goods are for the buyer, has made either a substantial beginning of their manufacture or commitments for their procurement.

      (2) If the party against whom enforcement is sought <u>admits</u> in his or her pleadings, testimony, or otherwise in court that the contract was made, although the contract is not enforceable beyond the quantity of goods admitted.

      (3) If the contract is <u>partially complete</u>, but only to the extent it has been completed with respect to goods for which payment has been made and accepted or with respect to goods which have been received and accepted.

IV. Standardized Shipping Terms

   A. <u>F.O.B. and F.A.S. (UCC 2-319)</u>

   1. <u>F.O.B.</u> ("free on board") is a contract term indicating that the seller will bear that degree of risk and expense that is appropriate to the F.O.B. terms. F.O.B. terms are generally either <u>F.O.B. shipment</u> or <u>F.O.B. destination</u>.

      a. If the place of shipment is named ("F.O.B. seller's loading dock"), the contract is a "shipment contract."

         (1) Under F.O.B. shipment terms, the seller must bear the risk and expense of delivering the goods to the carrier for their transportation.

         (2) The buyer must pay the costs of transportation from the place of shipment and bear the risks associated with delivery.

(3)   Title passes when the seller puts goods in the possession of the carrier.

b.   If the place of destination is named ("F.O.B. buyer's warehouse"), the contract is a "destination contract." Under F.O.B. destination terms, the seller must bear the risk and cost of transporting goods to the named destination. Title passes on tender at destination.

2.   <u>F.A.S.</u> ("free alongside") is a delivery term indicating that the seller must, at his or her own risk and expense, deliver the goods alongside the vessel or dock named by the buyer and obtain and tender a receipt of the goods in exchange for which the carrier is under a duty to issue a bill of lading.

B.   <u>C.I.F. and C&F (UCC 2-320)</u>

Buyer pays its all without inspection

1.   C.I.F.--Cost, insurance, and freight.

a.   C.I.F. is a contract term indicating that the lump amount paid by the buyer includes the cost of the goods as well as the insurance and freight to the named destination.

b.   Since buyer pays freight, a C.I.F. contract is a <u>shipment</u> contract; thus, the buyer has title and bears risk of loss from the point of shipment after the seller performs his or her C.I.F. duties.

c.   The <u>seller's</u> duties under a C.I.F. contract are as follows:

(1)   Deliver the goods to the carrier and obtain a negotiable bill of lading.

(2)   Pay the freight.

(3)   Obtain insurance for the goods.

(4)   Forward the documents to the buyer, who pays the lump sum cost when the documents are tendered, unless the contract provides otherwise.

d.   The buyer is obligated to pay upon tender of the documents even if the buyer has had no opportunity to inspect the goods first.

2.   C&F--Cost and freight: C&F is a contract term indicating that the seller is under the same obligation as with C.I.F. contracts, except that under C&F contracts the seller has no obligation to insure the goods.

C.   <u>C.O.D.</u>--Collect on Delivery [UCC 2-513(3)(a)]

1.   C.O.D. is a contract term under which the carrier is not to deliver the goods until the purchase price is paid.

2.   The buyer may <u>not</u> inspect the goods before paying for them, <u>unless</u> the contract so provides.

D.   <u>No Arrival, No Sale</u>--Under this type of contract, the seller must properly ship the goods and bear the risk of loss before delivery. However, if the goods are lost or destroyed en route without fault of the seller, he or she is not liable to the buyer for nondelivery (UCC 2-324).

Seller bears it all

V. Conditional Sales (UCC 2-326, -327)

A. "Sale on Approval" and "Sale or Return"

    1.   If the contract provides that goods may be returned by the buyer even though they conform to the contract, this is a <u>conditional sale</u> which is characterized as either a "sale on approval" or a "sale or return."

    2.   If the contract is silent as to the type of conditional sale, then the following rules apply:

        a.   There is a sale on approval if the goods are purchased for use by the buyer.

        b.   There is a sale or return if the goods are purchased for resale by the buyer.

B. Characteristics of Sales on Approval

    1.   The sale is not complete until the buyer has "approved."

    2.   The risk of loss is on the seller until the buyer "accepts" the goods.

    3.   "Acceptance" is defined as either use of the goods in a manner that is inconsistent with the purpose of the trial, or use of the goods coupled with a failure to reasonably notify the seller of the buyer's election to return the goods. Additionally, acceptance of any part of the conforming goods is acceptance of the whole.

    4.   The goods remain free of the claims of the buyer's creditors until acceptance by the buyer.

C. Characteristics of Sale or Return

    1.   The sale is complete from inception but is voidable at the buyer's election. Additionally, the risk and expense of the return are upon the buyer.

    2.   The buyer has the risk of loss while the goods are in his or her possession.

    3.   While in the buyer's possession, the goods are subject to the claims of the buyer's creditors unless the seller files or posts a notice of consignment.

VI. Title to Goods

A. <u>Importance of Title</u>--Under precode law, title had substantial legal effect on many issues, e.g., risk of loss, recovery against third persons for damages, and insurable interests. Although title still determines the buyer's right to transfer the goods, the risk of loss and the right to recover damages are now covered by specific UCC provisions.

B. <u>Passage of Title (UCC 2-401)</u>

    1.   Title cannot pass until goods are <u>identified</u> in the contract. Identification can be made in either of the following ways (UCC 2-501):

        a.   In any fashion explicitly agreed to by the parties.

        b.   In the absence of an explicit agreement:

            (1)   If the goods exist and are identified, identification occurs at the making of the contract.

    (2)   If the goods are not existing and identified, identification occurs when goods are designated by the seller as goods to which the contract refers, e.g., by shipping or marking them.

2.   If goods are identified in the contract at the time of contracting, the parties may agree as to when title passes.

3.   If there is no agreement as to when title passes, then title passes when the seller completes performance with respect to the physical delivery of the goods.

    a.   In a <u>shipment contract</u>, title passes at the time and place of delivery to a carrier for shipment.

    b.   In a <u>destination contract</u>, title passes on tender of delivery at the destination.

    c.   If the goods are not to be moved (e.g., goods in a warehouse) and a document of title is to be delivered, then title passes when the seller <u>delivers</u> such document of title.

    d.   If the goods are not to be moved and there is no delivery of a document, title passes at <u>either</u> of the following times:

        (1)   At the time of contracting if the goods are identified.

        (2)   At the time of identification of the goods in the contract if they have not as yet been so identified.

4.   Rejection of the goods by the buyer revests title in the seller.

C.   <u>Power to Transfer Title (UCC 2-403)</u>

1.   In general, a buyer of goods can acquire no better title than his or her seller, e.g., if a seller steals the goods and thus has no valid title, the seller cannot transfer valid title.

2.   Exceptions

    a.   Voidable Title

        (1)   If the seller has voidable title, he or she may transfer a valid title to a good faith purchaser who takes for value and without notice.

        (2)   Voidable title is created in a person receiving goods if

            (a)   The seller was deceived as to purchaser's identity.

            (b)   The delivery was in exchange for a check that was later dishonored.

            (c)   The delivery was to be for cash and no cash was paid.

            (d)   The delivery was procured through fraud.

    b.   Entrusting the possession of goods to a merchant who deals in goods of that kind in the ordinary course of business gives the merchant the power to transfer all rights of the entruster (bailor) to a buyer who purchases in the ordinary course of the merchant's business. The theory here is that the owner/entruster or (bailor) has clothed the merchant with the <u>apparent authority</u> to sell the goods. Therefore, the owner is estopped from denying that authority as against an innocent buyer. The owner's only remedy is against the merchant.

VII. Risk of Loss

A. <u>Express Agreement</u>--The contract for sale may include an express agreement indicating which party will bear the risk of loss. In the absence of an agreement, UCC provisions determine which party bears the loss.

B. <u>UCC Provisions (UCC 2-509)</u>

1. Shipment Contract--If the seller is to deliver goods to a carrier, risk of loss passes to the buyer on delivery of goods to the carrier.

2. Destination Contract--If the seller is to deliver goods to a particular destination, risk of loss passes to the buyer when the goods are tendered.

3. Goods Held by Bailee--If goods are held by a <u>bailee</u> (e.g., warehouse or carrier) and are to be delivered without being moved, the risk of loss passes to the buyer:

   a. When the bailee acknowledges the buyer's right to possession of the goods.

   b. When the buyer receives a negotiable document of title.

   c. Within a reasonable time after the buyer receives a nonnegotiable document of title. Risk of loss still passes to the buyer even though the buyer does not present the nonnegotiable document to the bailee (to take delivery of the goods).

4. Other Cases

   a. Risk of loss passes to the buyer on receipt of goods if the seller is a merchant.

   b. Risk of loss passes on tender of delivery if the seller is <u>not</u> a merchant.

5. Conditional Sales (UCC 2-327)

   a. Sale on Approval--Risk of loss remains with the seller until the buyer <u>accepts</u> the goods.

   b. Sale or Return--Risk of loss is borne by the buyer while the goods are in his or her possession <u>and</u> during the return of the goods to the seller.

6. Breach of Contract--In most breach situations the risk of loss is on the breaching party (UCC 2-510).

   a. If tender of delivery so fails to conform that the buyer has a right of rejection, the risk of loss remains on the seller until cure or acceptance.

   b. If the buyer rightfully <u>revokes acceptance</u> of the goods, the buyer may treat the risk of loss as having rested on the seller from the beginning, but only to the extent of any deficiency in the <u>buyer's</u> insurance coverage.

   c. If the buyer <u>repudiates</u> as to conforming goods already identified to the contract or otherwise breaches before risk of loss passes to him or her, then the seller may treat the risk of loss as resting on the buyer for a commercially reasonable time. However, the seller may do so only to the extent of the deficiency in the seller's insurance coverage.

VIII. Warranties

A. <u>Types</u>

disclaimer by specific language only

1. Warranty of title and against infringement (UCC 2-312)

   a. Title--In any contract for sale, the seller warrants that

      (1) The title is good and the transfer rightful.

      (2) The goods will be delivered free of any security interest, lien, or encumbrance of which the buyer had no actual knowledge at the time of contracting.

   b. Infringement

      (1) A seller, who is a merchant dealing in goods of the kind sold, warrants that the goods will be delivered free of a third person's rightful claim of infringement of patent or trademark.

      (2) However, if the buyer furnishes specifications to the seller, he or she must hold the seller harmless against any such claim arising from compliance with the specifications.

   c. The warranty of title and against infringement can be disclaimed <u>only</u> by specific language or circumstances that give the buyer reason to know that he or she is not receiving full title. The buyer is under a duty to notify the seller of any breach within a reasonable time.

2. Express Warranties (UCC 2-313)

   a. An <u>express warranty</u> may be created in one of three ways:

      (1) By <u>affirmation of fact or promise</u> made by the seller to the buyer which relates to the goods and becomes part of the basis of the bargain.

      (2) By any description of the goods which is made part of the basis of the bargain, when such description creates a <u>warranty that the goods will conform</u> to the description.

      (3) By any sample or model which is made <u>part of the basis of the bargain</u>.

   b. An express warranty may arise even if the seller does not use language such as "warrant" or "guarantee."

   c. An express warranty is usually not created by the seller's affirmation of value ("these goods are invaluable") or by the seller's opinion as to the quality of the goods ("these goods are the best of their type on the market").

3. Implied Warranty of Merchantability (UCC 2-314)

   a. If the seller is a merchant with respect to the goods sold, the law implies a warranty of merchantability.

   b. <u>The seller impliedly warrants that the goods are "merchantable."</u> To be merchantable, goods must conform to the following requirements:

      (1) Pass without objection in the trade under the contract description.

(2)   If fungible, they are of fair average quality within the description.

(3)   Are fit for the ordinary purposes for which such goods are used.

(4)   Run within the variations permitted by the agreement.

(5)   Are adequately packaged and labeled.

(6)   Conform to any promises or affirmations of fact on the label.

c.   Serving food or drink for consumption on the premises or elsewhere is considered a sale of goods for purposes of this warranty.

4.   Implied Warranty of Fitness for a Particular Purpose--Warranty arises that the goods are fit for a particular purpose if (UCC 2-315)

a.   The seller has actual or constructive knowledge of the particular purpose for which the goods are required.

b.   The buyer relies on the seller's skill or judgment to select goods suitable for that purpose.

B.   Privity--The relationship existing between two contracting parties, e.g., buyer and seller.

1.   Common Law--Under common law, a person seeking to sue another for liability under a warranty had to be "in privity," i.e., have a contractual relationship with the person sued. For example, a buyer could sue the seller, but not the manufacturer or intermediate distributor.

2.   UCC--The Code has enacted three alternatives governing the rights of injured persons not in privity of contract with the seller. They are as follows (UCC 2-318):

a.   A seller's warranty, whether express or implied, extends to any natural person who is in the family or household of the buyer, or who is a guest in the buyer's home if it is reasonable to expect that such person may use, consume, or be affected by the goods, and who is personally injured by breach of the warranty. A seller may not exclude or limit the operation of this section.

b.   A seller's warranty, whether express or implied, extends to any natural person who may reasonably be expected to use, consume, or be affected by the goods and who is personally injured by breach of the warranty. A seller may not exclude or limit the operation of this section.

c.   A seller's warranty, whether express or implied, extends to any person (including any individual or an organization) who may reasonably be expected to use, consume, or be affected by the goods and who is injured by breach of the warranty. A seller may not exclude or limit the operation of this section concerning injury to the person of an individual to whom the warranty extends.

C.   Disclaimer of Warranties (UCC 2-316)

1.   Express warranties, and the warranty of title and against infringement, can be modified or excluded only by specific language or circumstances.

2.   Implied Warranties

a.   To limit or exclude the warranty of merchantability, the disclaimer of liability must specifically mention the word "merchantability." If written, it must be conspicuously presented in the disclaiming document (e.g., bold letter, large print).

b.   Modification of the warranty of fitness for particular use requires a conspicuous writing (no oral modification).

c.   All implied warranties are excluded by language such as "as is" or "with all faults."

d.   If the buyer has an opportunity to inspect the goods or has refused to examine them despite the seller's demand that the buyer examine them, there is no implied warranty as to any defects that should reasonably have been discovered upon such examination.

e.   A course of dealing or trade usage may also modify or exclude an implied warranty.

3.   Parol Evidence Rule--When there is a final written contract, conflicting prior agreements or contemporaneous oral agreements concerning warranties will be excluded from evidence.

D.   Statute of Limitations (UCC 2-725)

1.   An action for breach of warranty must be brought within four years after the cause of action accrues. The cause accrues when either of the following occurs:

a.   When tender of delivery is made.

b.   If the warranty extends to future performance, when the breach is or should have been discovered.

2.   The parties cannot extend the limitations period, but they can agree to reduce it to not less than one year.

IX. Performance

A.   Seller's Rights and Duties

1.   Duty to Tender Delivery of Conforming Goods--Tender is a condition precedent to the buyer's duty to accept and pay for the goods, unless the parties agree otherwise (UCC 2-507).

2.   Right to Cure (UCC 2-508)

a.   If the buyer rejects the seller's tender for nonconformance and the time for performance has not yet expired, the seller may notify the buyer of his or her intention to cure. The seller may then make a delivery of conforming goods provided he or she does so within the time for performance.

b.   If the buyer rejects the seller's tender for nonconformance after the expiration of the time for performance, the seller may cure defects by tendering a conforming delivery within a reasonable time if the seller had reasonable grounds to believe the tender would be acceptable (e.g., the buyer had accepted nonconforming goods in the past).

B.   <u>Buyer's Rights and Duties</u>

    1.   Duty to Accept Conforming Goods

        a.   Acceptance of Goods (UCC 2-606)

            (1)   Acceptance occurs after the buyer has an opportunity to inspect and signify that the goods are conforming or after the buyer agrees to accept them with defects (however, in the latter case, the buyer has the right to sue for damages).

            (2)   Acceptance occurs impliedly when the buyer fails to make an effective rejection after a reasonable opportunity to inspect.

            (3)   Acceptance occurs when the buyer does any act inconsistent with the seller's ownership.

        b.   Effect of Acceptance (UCC 2-607)

            (1)   Duty to pay arises.

            (2)   Goods cannot then be rejected. However, under certain circumstances, the buyer may revoke his or her acceptance. In this case, revocation is functionally the same as a rejection of the goods.

    2.   Duty to Pay (UCC 2-511)

        a.   Tender of payment is a condition to seller's duty to tender delivery, unless otherwise agreed.

        b.   Payment by check is conditional and is defeated by subsequent dishonor.

        c.   If payment is required before inspection, payment does not constitute acceptance.

    3.   Right to Inspect (UCC 2-513)

        a.   Unless otherwise agreed, the buyer may inspect prior to acceptance and payment.

        b.   However, if goods are shipped C.O.D. or the contract provides for payment against documents of title, the buyer may not inspect until after payment, unless otherwise agreed.

C.   <u>Excuses and Substitutes for Performance</u>

    1.   Damage to Goods--If goods identified to the contract are damaged without the fault of either party before the risk of loss passes to the buyer, then either of the following apply (UCC 2-613):

        a.   The contract is avoided if the loss is total.

        b.   If the loss is partial, or the goods have deteriorated so that they no longer conform, the buyer has the option of either of the following:

            (1)   Avoiding the contract.

            (2)   Accepting the goods with due allowance or offset from the contract price. This is in lieu of any further rights against the seller.

2.   Failure of the Means of Payment [UCC 2-614(2)]

    a.   If the agreed method of payment fails because of governmental regulation prior to delivery, the seller may withhold or stop delivery unless the buyer provides a substantially equivalent method of payment.

    b.   If delivery has been made, payment as provided by a foreign governmental regulation discharges the buyer's obligation unless it is discriminatory, oppressive, or predatory.

3.   Failure of the Means of Delivery--Substitute performance must be tendered and accepted if, without the fault of either party, shipping facilities agreed upon become unavailable or commercially impracticable and a commercially reasonable substitute is available [UCC 2-614(1)].

4.   Commercial Impracticability of Seller's Performance (UCC 2-615)

    a.   Delay in delivery or nondelivery is not a breach of the seller's duty if performance has been made impracticable by the occurrence of a contingency, the nonoccurrence of which was a basic assumption on which the contract was made.

    b.   Allocation--If only part of the seller's capacity to perform is affected, the seller must allocate deliveries among the customers, and he or she must give each one reasonable notice of the quota available to him or her.

    c.   Upon notice of material delay, or allocation of deliveries

        (1)   The buyer may do one of the following by written notification as to any delivery concerned:

            (a)   Terminate any unexecuted portion of the contract.

            (b)   Modify the contract by agreeing to take his or her available quota in substitution, but,

        (2)   If the buyer fails to modify within a reasonable time, not exceeding 30 days, the contract lapses with respect to deliveries affected.

X. Remedies for Breach

A.   <u>Buyer's Remedies</u>

1.   If the seller delivers <u>nonconforming goods</u>, the buyer may do one of the following:

    a.   The buyer may reject all or any nonconforming commercial unit(s) (UCC 2-601). Concerning the goods rejected, the following provisions apply:

        (1)   The buyer must reject and give notice of the rejection within a reasonable time after delivery or tender or lose the right to reject [UCC 2-602(1)].

        (2)   Failure to particularize defects ascertainable by reasonable inspection precludes the buyer from relying on those defects to justify rejection or to establish breach in the following cases (UCC 2-605):

            (a)   When the seller could have cured.

(b) As between merchants, when the seller requests in writing a full statement of defects on which the buyer proposes to rely.

(3) The buyer must not exercise ownership over the goods but must hold the goods with reasonable care for a time sufficient to permit the seller to remove them [UCC 2-602(2)].

(4) Disposition of Goods (UCC 2-603)

(a) The merchant buyer has a duty to follow the seller's reasonable instructions as to the disposition of rejected goods.

(b) In the absence of instructions, a merchant buyer must make a reasonable effort to sell the goods for the seller's account if they are perishable or threaten to rapidly decline in value. If the goods are resold, the buyer is entitled to reimbursement for reasonable expenses of caring for and selling them.

b. The buyer may accept any or all nonconforming commercial units (UCC 2-601). With respect to goods accepted

(1) Damages are still available if the buyer reasonably notifies the seller of the breach (UCC 2-714).

(2) Acceptance may be <u>revoked</u> if goods were accepted in either of the following situations (UCC 2-608):

(a) On the reasonable assumption that the nonconformity would be cured and it was not.

(b) Without discovery of the nonconformity, if acceptance was reasonably induced by either of the following:

(i) The difficulty of discovery before acceptance.

(ii) The seller's assurances.

(3) Revocation of acceptance is similar to rejection in that

(a) It must be done within a reasonable time.

(b) It is not effective until the buyer notifies the seller.

(c) A buyer who revokes acceptance has the same duties with regard to the goods as if he or she had rejected them.

2. If the seller <u>unjustifiably</u> fails to deliver or repudiates the contract before delivery, among the remedies available to the buyer are the following [UCC 2-711(2)]:

a. Specific Performance--May be decreed by the court in the following situations [UCC 2-716(1)]:

(1) When the goods are unique.

(2) In "other proper circumstances" (e.g., inability to "cover," see 3.c., below).

b. Replevin--The buyer may be able to recover possession if goods have been identified to the contract, and [UCC 2-716(3)]:

    (1)   The buyer is unable to "cover."

    (2)   The goods have been shipped under reservation (goods shipped to the buyer under a negotiable or a nonnegotiable bill of lading).

c. Rights on Seller's Insolvency--The buyer may recover goods identified to the contract if he or she has paid part or all of their price and the seller becomes insolvent within 10 days after receiving the first payment (UCC 2-502).

3. Buyer's Rights Upon Seller's Breach

a. If the seller fails to deliver or repudiates the contract, or if the buyer rejects nonconforming goods or justifiably revokes his or her acceptance, the buyer may cancel the contract [UCC 2-711(2)]. Furthermore, whether the buyer cancels or not, he or she may recover the price paid and do either of the following:

    (1)   Cover and obtain damages.

    (2)   Recover damages for nondelivery.

b. Cancellation or rescission of the contract does not discharge any claim for damages for an antecedent breach unless the cancellation expressly indicates the intention to renounce rights (UCC 2-720).

c. Cover Under the UCC (UCC 2-712)

    (1)   Cover means to procure substitute goods elsewhere in substitution for those due from the seller.

    (2)   The buyer is under no duty to cover, but if the buyer does so he or she must act reasonably and in good faith.

d. Damages

    (1)   If the buyer "covers," he or she may recover from the seller the difference between the cost of cover and the contract price, plus incidental and consequential damages, less expenses saved because of the breach [UCC 2-712(2)].

    (2)   If the buyer does not cover, he or she may recover damages for nondelivery from the seller. The measure of damage is the difference between the market price of the goods at the place of tender at the time the buyer learned of the breach and the contract price, plus incidental and consequential damages, less expenses saved because of seller's breach (UCC 2-713).

    (3)   If the buyer accepts nonconforming goods and notifies the seller of the breach, the buyer can recover from the seller the loss resulting in the ordinary course of events from the seller's breach, determined in any reasonable manner (UCC 2-714).

    (4)   Incidental and consequential damages (UCC 2-715) are normally recoverable by the buyer.

(a) <u>Incidental damages</u> include expenses reasonably incurred as a result of the seller's delay or other breach (e.g., for inspection, receipt, transportation, care, and custody of rightfully rejected goods) and any commercially reasonable expenses incurred in effecting cover.

(b) <u>Consequential damages</u> include the following:

(i) Losses resulting from requirements and needs the seller had reason to know of at the time of contracting which could not be prevented by cover or otherwise.

(ii) Injuries to persons or property resulting from a breach of warranty.

(5) The buyer may notify the seller and then deduct damages for breach from any part of the price still due under the same contract (UCC 2-717).

B. <u>Seller's Remedies</u>

1. If the seller discovers that the buyer is <u>insolvent</u>, he or she may exercise the following rights where applicable (UCC 2-702):

a. The seller may refuse further delivery of goods, unless payment is in cash. Additionally, the seller may demand payment for all goods previously delivered under the contract.

b. Furthermore, the seller may stop delivery of goods in transit (stoppage) (UCC 2-705).

(1) Generally, delivery may be stopped if the goods are in the possession of a carrier or other bailee.

(2) Stoppage is permitted until one of the following occurs:

(a) Receipt of the goods by the buyer.

(b) Acknowledgment to the buyer by a bailee other than a carrier that the bailee holds the goods for the buyer.

(c) Acknowledgment to the buyer, by a carrier as warehouseman, that he or she holds the goods for the buyer.

(d) Negotiation to the buyer of any negotiable document of title covering the goods.

c. <u>Reclamation</u>--The seller may reclaim any goods received by the buyer on credit when he or she is insolvent.

(1) Demand must be made by the seller within <u>10 days</u> after receipt of the goods.

(2) However, if the buyer <u>misrepresented</u> his or her solvency to the seller in writing within the 3-month period before delivery, the 10-day limitation does <u>not</u> apply.

(3) The seller's right to reclaim is subject to the rights of the purchasers in the ordinary course of buyer's business and other good faith purchasers from the insolvent buyer.

(4) Successful reclamation of goods excludes all other remedies with respect to those goods.

2. If the buyer wrongfully rejects or revokes acceptance of goods, or fails to make a payment due on or before delivery, or repudiates all or part of the contract,

    a. The seller of the affected goods has the following cumulative remedies (UCC 2-703):

        (1) Withhold delivery of such goods.

        (2) Stop delivery by a bailee.

            (a) Generally, the provision regarding stoppage of delivery to an insolvent buyer applies (see 1.b., above).

            (b) However, in cases not involving insolvency, the seller may stop goods in transit only if such goods are in the form of a carload, truckload, planeload, or larger shipments.

        (3) Resell and recover damages.

            (a) The resale may be public or private.

                (i) If private, the seller must give the buyer reasonable notification of his or her intention to resell.

                (ii) If public, goods must generally be identified and sold at a place usually used for such sales. Unless the goods are perishable or subject to a speedy decline in value, the seller must give reasonable notice to the buyer.

            (b) Method, manner, time, place, and terms of resale must be commercially reasonable, and the resale must be identified as referring to the broken contract.

            (c) A purchaser in good faith takes free of any rights of the original buyer, even if the seller fails to comply with any requirements as to resale.

            (d) Damages--The seller has the right to recover from the buyer the difference between the resale price and the contract price, plus incidental damages. However, expenses saved as a consequence of the buyer's breach must be taken into account.

                (i) Incidental damages to a seller include the commercially reasonable costs of stopping delivery, plus those costs relating to transportation. Such damages also include costs involved in the care and custody of goods after the buyer's breach.

                (ii) The seller is not accountable to the buyer for any profit made on resale.

        (4) Choose to recover damages without resale.

            • The purpose of damages is to put the seller in the position he or she would have occupied had the contract been performed.

                (i) Ordinarily, in the absence of resale, the aggrieved seller is entitled to the difference between the market price at the time and place for tender, and the contract price, plus incidental damages, less expenses saved in consequence of the breach.

        (ii)   If the damages above are inadequate to put the seller in as good a position as performance, then the damages are measured by the profit the seller would have made, plus incidental damages and costs reasonably incurred, less credit for payments or any proceeds from resale.

    (5)   Cancel the contract.

b.   The seller may identify to the contract any conforming goods not yet identified if such goods were in the seller's possession when the seller learned of the breach [UCC 2-704(1)].

c.   The seller, with respect to unfinished goods and to avoid a loss in the exercise of reasonable commercial judgment, can choose to do one of the following [UCC 2-704(2)]:

    (1)   Complete the manufacture of unfinished goods and identify them to the contract.

    (2)   Stop manufacture and resell the unfinished goods as scrap.

    (3)   Proceed in any other reasonable manner.

3.   If the buyer fails to pay the price as it becomes due, the seller may bring an action and recover the price of the goods if one of the following applies (UCC 2-709):

a.   Conforming goods were accepted.

b.   Conforming goods were lost or damaged within a commercially reasonable time after the risk of loss passed to the buyer.

c.   Goods were identified to the contract and the seller is unable after a reasonable effort to resell them at a reasonable price, or such effort reasonably appears to be unavailing.

If the seller sues for the price, he or she must hold for the buyer any goods identified to the contract and under his or her control. The seller may resell the goods prior to the collection of a judgment, but any excess proceeds are credited to the buyer. Furthermore, payment of the judgment entitles the buyer to any goods not resold.

C.   Remedies for Buyer or Seller

1.   Right to Assurances of Performance (UCC 2-609)

a.   If reasonable grounds for insecurity arise concerning the performance of either party (that is, it reasonably appears that performance will not be made when and as required), the other party may in writing demand adequate assurance of performance.

b.   Until assurance is received, the insecure party may, if commercially reasonable, suspend any performance for which the party has not already received the agreed return.

c.   If the other party fails to provide the assurances within a reasonable time (but not to exceed 30 days), the party's failure may be treated as a repudiation of the contract.

2.   Anticipatory Repudiation (UCC 2-610)

     a.   Definition--Demonstration by either party of an intention not to perform an obligation not yet due, or an action that renders that performance impossible.

     b.   In case of one party's anticipatory repudiation, the other party may choose to

          (1)   Await performance for a commercially reasonable time.

          (2)   Resort to any remedy for breach, even if he or she has notified the breaching party that he or she would await performance.

          (3)   In any case, suspend his or her own performance.

     c.   The repudiating party may retract his or her repudiation until the time when the next performance is due, unless the other party has since canceled, materially changed his or her position, or otherwise indicated that he or she considers the repudiation final.

D.   Statute of Limitations for Breach of Sales Contract (UCC 2-725)

     1.   An action for breach must be brought within four years after the cause of action accrues. Cause accrues when the breach occurs, regardless of lack of knowledge.

     2.   Parties may agree to reduce the period to one year, but an agreement to extend the period will not be enforced.

XI. **Products Liability**

Sellers and manufacturers may be held liable for damages "caused" by their products. There are three separate theories under which products liability actions may be commenced. The law regarding actions based on the theory of Breach of Warranty has been extensively codified in Article 2 (see VIII., above). This theory, together with the strict liability and negligence theories, will be covered below.

A.   General Characteristics

     1.   Causation--Under any of these theories, the plaintiff must show that the defendant's product was defective or otherwise unreasonably dangerous and that this condition caused the plaintiff harm. The plaintiff must also show that the product was in its defective or unreasonably dangerous condition before it left the defendant's hands.

     2.   Foreseeable or Normal Use--The plaintiff must not only show that the product caused harm or injury, the plaintiff must also show that the harm was caused while the product was being used in a normal or foreseeable manner. For example, if a person loses his or her fingers while picking up a lawn mower to use it to trim the hedge, the person should not be able to collect for these damages.

B.   Negligence Actions--A plaintiff may sue in tort for damages caused by a defective product if the plaintiff can show that the defendant failed to exercise reasonable care under the relevant circumstances. The negligence complained of need not be in the manufacture of the product; it may be in the design, packaging, inspection, or any facet of production or distribution. Negligence may also arise when the manufacturer has failed to adequately warn of inherent dangers or when the manufacturer has failed to supply adequate directions or instructions for use.

     1.   Duty--In some instances, the courts require the plaintiff to show that the defendant owed a duty to the plaintiff. Presently, the law imposes a general duty on manufacturers and sellers to protect all people who may be injured while going about their normal business. However, the law does not always impose the duty to anticipate injuries occurring to a negligent party.

2. Privity--Under the negligence theory, there is no requirement that privity of contract be established between the plaintiff and the defendant. Simply stated, there is <u>no</u> requirement that the plaintiff be a direct purchaser or user of the product. Therefore, any injured person may maintain an action against the negligent party.

3. Defenses

   a. Disclaimer--The defendant may not avoid liability by use of a disclaimer.

   b. Clear Warnings--In certain situations, the defendant may be able to avoid potential liability by providing adequate warning. For example, packaging lye in a protective container with clearly printed warnings and antidotes will insulate the manufacturer from liability due to human ingestion.

   c. Contributory Negligence--In some jurisdictions, the defendant may escape liability if he or she can show that the plaintiff was also careless or at fault.

   d. In jurisdictions that have eliminated the contributory negligence defense, a defendant may still plead assumption of the risk. A plaintiff has assumed the risk when he or she knows of a defect but continues to use a product despite the defect and with full knowledge of the risk.

4. Primary Uses--Negligence actions have largely been superseded by strict liability or breach of warranty actions. However, many negligence suits are still brought on the grounds that the defendant employed a defective design or failed to give adequate warnings or directions.

5. Damages--Negligence actions may be brought to recover personal or property damages. They may not be used to recover mere economic losses caused by a product's failure to perform properly.

C. <u>Strict Liability</u>--A plaintiff may sue under strict liability if he or she can show that the product was sold in a defective or unreasonably dangerous condition and that this condition caused the plaintiff to suffer damages. The plaintiff must further prove that the product was defective or unreasonably dangerous before it left the defendant's hands. The plaintiff need not prove or assert that the defendant was in any way negligent or that any person connected with the manufacture, design, packaging, inspection, etc., of the product was negligent. Furthermore, the plaintiff may sue any and all of the above-mentioned persons so long as the plaintiff can show the product was defective when it left their hands.

1. Defective or Unreasonably Dangerous--Producers and distributors are not insurers; therefore, they are not responsible for all the harm their products inflict. The courts use a subjective test when weighing whether a product is unreasonably dangerous. Some of the factors they consider are as follows:

   a. The usefulness and desirability of the product.

   b. The likelihood and probable extent of injury.

   c. The obviousness of the danger.

   d. The standards within the industry.

   e. The existence or absence of superior, economically feasible safety technology.

f.   The knowledge of the public and efforts taken by the producer to further educate the consumer.

Recently, several states and the United States government have enacted consumer product safety acts.   Typically, these acts (or rules promulgated under their authority) establish minimum safety standards for various products.   Rules may also govern the warnings or instructions that must accompany a product.   Usually, the violation of a standard is <u>prima facie</u> evidence that the product is either defective or unreasonably dangerous.

2.   Privity--The privity requirement for strict liability is similar to that for negligence.   In the case of negligence, a manufacturer will be liable for its failure to exercise reasonable care in the manufacture of goods that, if manufactured negligently, create an unreasonable risk of bodily harm.   This liability attaches regardless of whether there was a sale as long as the manufacturer was proven negligent.   In the case of strict tort liability, the manufacturer need not be proved negligent.   Rather, if the item would create a risk of injury if defectively made, the manufacturer and distributors are liable to specific classes of injured people (see VIII.B.2., above).

3.   Defenses

a.   Disclaimer--The defendant may not escape liability by use of a disclaimer.

b.   Clear Warnings--In certain situations, the defendant may be able to avoid potential liability by providing adequate warning.

c.   Contributory negligence is generally <u>not</u> a defense in strict liability.   [In actions brought under a negligence theory, contributory negligence may be a defense that can be used by the defendant to avoid liability (see B.3., above).]

d.   Assumption of the risk is a valid defense.   (In actions brought under a negligence theory, assumption of the risk may not be a defense.)

4.   Damages--Damages recoverable under strict liability are generally the same as those under negligence.   That is, generally, only personal or property damages are recoverable.

D.   <u>Breach of Warranty</u>--A warranty is a promise or assertion of fact concerning the quality or worth of a product sold.   Warranties may arise in two ways.   <u>Express warranties</u> are those promises actually made by the seller that are a basis of the bargain.   <u>Implied warranties</u> are standards of quality that are established by the law.

1.   Express Warranties--Refer to VIII.A.2., above, regarding the creation of express warranties. These general Code provisions have been supplemented by the Federal Consumer Product Warranty Act (FCPWA).   Consumer product manufacturers and sellers who make written express warranties must comply with the provisions of this Act.   Under the FCPWA, affected parties must label warranties either full, in which case they must meet express federal standards, or limited.

2.   Implied Warranties--Refer to VIII.A.3. and 4., above, regarding the Code's provisions for implied warranties.   In addition to the law as stated in the above Code provisions, implied warranties may arise from a course of dealing or usage of trade.

3.   Disclaimer of Warranties--Refer to VIII.C., above, regarding the disclaimer of warranties. Remedies for breach of warranty can be limited in accordance with the provisions of Article 2 (see X., above).

4.   Privity--Refer to VIII.B., above, regarding the Code's privity requirements.

5.   Liquidation or Limitation of Damages--Damages for breach by either party may be provided for in the agreement by insertion of a "liquidated damages" clause. The liquidated damages shall be limited to an amount that is reasonable considering the anticipated or actual harm caused by the breach, the difficulties of proof of loss, and the inconvenience or unfeasibility of otherwise obtaining an adequate remedy. A term fixing unreasonably large liquidated damages is void as a penalty.

6.   Contractual modification or limitation of remedy [UCC 2-316(4)]

    a.   Subject to the provisions of b. and c., below (UCC 2-719)

        (1)   The agreement may provide for remedies in addition to or in substitution for those provided in Article 2. The agreement may also limit or alter the measure of damages recoverable under Article 2. For example, the agreement might limit the buyer's remedies to return of the goods and repayment of the price or to repair and replacement of nonconforming goods or parts.

        (2)   Furthermore, resorting to a remedy as provided in the contract is optional unless the remedy is expressly agreed upon by the parties as being exclusive. In this case, the contractual remedy is the sole remedy.

    b.   When circumstances cause an exclusive or limited remedy to fail in its essential purpose, then the general Article 2 remedies outlined above are available.

    c.   Consequential damages may be limited or excluded unless the limitation or exclusion is unconscionable. Limitation of consequential damages for injury to the person in the case of consumer goods is prima facie unconscionable. However, limitation of damages when the loss is commercial is not unconscionable.

CHAPTER 44—SALES

Problem 44-1 MULTIPLE CHOICE QUESTIONS (70 to 85 minutes)

1. Under the UCC Sales Article, which of the following statements is correct concerning a contract involving a merchant seller and a nonmerchant buyer?
   a. Only the seller is obligated to perform the contract in good faith.
   b. The contract will be either a sale or return or sale on approval contract.
   c. The contract may **not** involve the sale of personal property with a price of more than $500.
   d. Whether the UCC Sales Article is applicable does **not** depend on the price of the goods involved. (5/91, Law, #43, 0498)

1A. Under the Sales Article of the UCC, which of the following statements is correct?
   a. The obligations of the parties to the contract must be performed in good faith.
   b. Merchants and nonmerchants are treated alike.
   c. The contract must involve the sale of goods for a price of more than $500.
   d. None of the provisions of the UCC may be disclaimed by agreement.
   (11/94, Law, #50, 5227)

2. Under the UCC Sales Article, which of the following conditions will prevent the formation of an enforceable sale of goods contract?
   a. Open price.
   b. Open delivery.
   c. Open quantity.
   d. Open acceptance. (5/94, Law, #41, 4796)

3. Rowe Corp. purchased goods from Stair Co. that were shipped C.O.D. Under the Sales Article of the UCC, which of the following rights does Rowe have?
   a. The right to inspect the goods before paying.
   b. The right to possession of the goods before paying.
   c. The right to reject nonconforming goods.
   d. The right to delay payment for a reasonable period of time. (11/94, Law, #56, 5233)

4. Under the UCC Sales Article, a firm offer will be created only if the
   a. Offeree is a merchant.
   b. Offeree gives some form of consideration.

c. Offer states the time period during which it will remain open.
   d. Offer is made by a merchant in a signed writing. (11/88, Law, #44, 9911)

5. On October 1, Baker, a wholesaler, sent Clark, a retailer, a written signed offer to sell 200 pinking shears at $9 each. The terms were F.O.B. Baker's warehouse, net 30, late payment subject to a 15% per annum interest charge. The offer indicated that it must be accepted no later than October 10, that acceptance would be effective upon receipt, and that the terms were not to be varied by the offeree. Clark sent a telegram which arrived on October 6, and accepted the offer expressly subject to a change of the payment terms to 2/10, net/30. Baker phoned Clark on October 7, rejecting the change of payment terms. Clark then indicated it would accept the October 1 offer in all respects, and expected delivery within 10 days. Baker did not accept Clark's oral acceptance of the original offer. Which of the following is a correct statement?
   a. Baker's original offer is a firm offer, hence irrevocable.
   b. There is **no** contract since Clark's modifications effectively rejected the October 1 offer, and Baker never accepted either of Clark's proposals.
   c. Clark actually created a contract on October 6, since the modifications were merely proposals and did **not** preclude acceptance.
   d. The Statute of Frauds would preclude the formation of a contract in any event.
   (11/83, Law, #53, 9911)

6. On May 2, Mason orally contracted with Acme Appliances to buy for $480 a washer and dryer for household use. Mason and the Acme salesperson agreed that delivery would be made on July 2. On May 5, Mason telephoned Acme and requested that the delivery date be moved to June 2. The Acme salesperson agreed with this request. On June 2, Acme failed to deliver the washer and dryer to Mason because of an inventory shortage. Acme advised Mason that it would deliver the appliances on July 2 as originally agreed. Mason believes that Acme has breached its agreement with Mason. Acme contends that its agreement to deliver on June 2 was not binding. Acme's contention is

Oral agmt modifies existing is binding

a. Correct, because Mason is **not** a merchant and was buying the appliances for household use.
b. Correct, because the agreement to change the delivery date was **not** in writing.
c. Incorrect, because the agreement to change the delivery date was binding.
d. Incorrect, because Acme's agreement to change the delivery date is a firm offer that **cannot** be withdrawn by Acme.

(5/92, Law, #54, 2867)

7. Bond and Spear orally agreed that Bond would buy a car from Spear for $475. Bond paid Spear a $100 deposit. The next day, Spear received an offer of $575, the car's fair market value. Spear immediately notified Bond that Spear would not sell the car to Bond and returned Bond's $100. If Bond sues Spear and Spear defends on the basis of the Statute of Frauds, Bond will probably
a. Lose, because the agreement was for less than the fair market value of the car.
b. Win, because the agreement was for less than $500.
c. Lose, because the agreement was **not** in writing and signed by Spear.
d. Win, because Bond paid a deposit.

(5/91, Law, #17, 9911)

8. To satisfy the UCC Statute of Frauds regarding the sale of goods, which of the following must generally be in writing?
a. Designation of the parties as buyer and seller.
b. Delivery terms.
c. Quantity of the goods.
d. Warranties to be made. (5/90, Law, #40, 0509)

9. On May 2, Lace Corp., an appliance wholesaler, offered to sell appliances worth $3,000 to Parco, Inc., a household appliances retailer. The offer was signed by Lace's president, and provided that it would not be withdrawn before June 1. It also included the shipping terms: "FOB--Parco's warehouse." On May 29, Parco mailed an acceptance of Lace's offer. Lace received the acceptance June 2. Which of the following statements is correct if Lace sent Parco a telegram revoking its offer, and Parco received the telegram on May 25?
a. A contract was formed on May 2.
b. Lace's revocation effectively terminated its offer on May 25.

c. Lace's revocation was ineffective because the offer could **not** be revoked before June 1.
d. No contract was formed because Lace received Parco's acceptance after June 1.

(5/92, Law, #51, 2864)

10. Gray Fabricating Co. and Pine Corp. agreed orally that Pine would custom manufacture a processor for Gray at a price of $80,000. After Pine completed the work at a cost of $60,000, Gray notified Pine that the processor was no longer needed. Pine is holding the processor and has requested payment from Gray. Pine has been unable to resell the processor for any price. Pine incurred storage fees of $1,000. If Gray refuses to pay Pine and Pine sues Gray, the most Pine will be entitled to recover is
a. $60,000.
b. $61,000.
c. $80,000.
d. $81,000. (5/91, Law, #52, 0503)

11. Under a contract governed by the UCC Sales Article, which of the following statements is correct?
a. Unless both the seller and the buyer are merchants, neither party is obligated to perform the contract in good faith.
b. The contract will **not** be enforceable if it fails to expressly specify a time and a place for delivery of the goods.
c. The seller may be excused from performance if the goods are accidentally destroyed before the risk of loss passes to the buyer.
d. If the price of the goods is less than $500, the goods need **not** be identified to the contract for title to pass to the buyer. (5/91, Law, #49, 0500)

11A. Under the Sales Article of the UCC, which of the following events will release the buyer from all its obligations under a sales contract?
a. Destruction of the goods after risk of loss passed to the buyer.
b. Impracticability of delivery under the terms of the contract.
c. Anticipatory repudiation by the buyer that is retracted before the seller cancels the contract.
d. Refusal of the seller to give written assurance of performance when reasonably demanded by the buyer. (11/94, Law, #55, 5232)

12. Which of the following statements applies to a sale on approval under the UCC Sales Article?
a. Both the buyer and seller must be merchants.
b. The buyer must be purchasing the goods for resale.

c. Risk of loss for the goods passes to the buyer when the goods are accepted after the trial period.

d. Title to the goods passes to the buyer on delivery of the goods to the buyer.

(11/93, Law, #49, 4346)

13. Webstar Corp. orally agreed to sell Northco, Inc. a computer for $20,000. Northco sent a signed purchase order to Webstar confirming the agreement. Webstar received the purchase order and did not respond. Webstar refused to deliver the computer to Northco, claiming that the purchase order did not satisfy the UCC Statute of Frauds because it was not signed by Webstar. Northco sells computers to the general public and Webstar is a computer wholesaler. Under the UCC Sales Article, Webstar's position is

a. Incorrect, because it failed to object to Northco's purchase order.

b. Incorrect, because only the buyer in a sale-of-goods transaction must sign the contract.

c. Correct, because it was the party against whom enforcement of the contract is being sought.

d. Correct, because the purchase price of the computer exceeded $500.

(5/94, Law, #46, 4801)

14. Which of the following statements would **not** apply to a written contract governed by the provisions of the UCC Sales Article?

a. The contract may involve the sale of personal property.

b. The obligations of a nonmerchant may be different from those of a merchant.

c. The obligations of the parties must be performed in good faith.

d. The contract must involve the sale of goods for a price of $500 or more. (11/93, Law, #50, 4347)

15. Pulse Corp. maintained a warehouse where it stored its manufactured goods. Pulse received an order from Star. Shortly after Pulse identified the goods to be shipped to Star, but before moving them to the loading dock, a fire destroyed the warehouse and its contents. With respect to the goods, which of the following statements is correct?

a. Pulse has title but **no** insurable interest.

b. Star has title and an insurable interest.

c. Pulse has title and an insurable interest.

d. Star has title but **no** insurable interest.

(5/90, Law, #45, 0513)

16. On May 2, Lace Corp., an appliance wholesaler, offered to sell appliances worth $3,000 to Parco, Inc., a household appliances retailer. The offer was signed by Lace's president, and provided that it

would not be withdrawn before June 1. It also included the shipping terms: "FOB--Parco's warehouse." On May 29, Parco mailed an acceptance of Lace's offer. Lace received the acceptance June 2. If Lace inadvertently ships the wrong appliances to Parco and Parco rejects them two days after receipt, title to the goods will

a. Pass to Parco when they are identified to the contract.

b. Pass to Parco when they are shipped.

c. Remain with Parco until the goods are returned to Lace.

d. Revert to Lace when they are rejected by Parco. (5/92, Law, #53, 0550)

17. Lazur Corp. agreed to purchase 100 radios from Wizard Suppliers, Inc. Wizard is a wholesaler of small home appliances and Lazur is an appliance retailer. The contract required Wizard to ship the radios to Lazur by common carrier, "F.O.B. Wizard Suppliers, Inc., Loading Dock." Under the UCC Sales Article

a. Title to the radios passes to Lazur at the time they are delivered to the carrier, even if the goods are nonconforming.

b. Lazur must inspect the radios at the time of delivery or waive any defects and the right to sue for breach of contract.

c. Wizard must pay the freight expense associated with the shipment of the radios to Lazur.

d. Lazur would have the right to reject any shipment if Wizard fails to notify Lazur that the goods have been shipped.

(5/91, Law, #56, 9911)

18. On September 10, Bell Corp. entered into a contract to purchase 50 lamps from Glow Manufacturing. Bell prepaid 40% of the purchase price. Glow became insolvent on September 19 before segregating, in its inventory, the lamps to be delivered to Bell. Bell will **not** be able to recover the lamps because

a. Bell is regarded as a merchant.

b. The lamps were **not** identified to the contract.

c. Glow became insolvent fewer than 10 days after receipt of Bell's prepayment.

d. Bell did **not** pay the full price at the time of purchase. (5/90, Law, #47, 0515)

19. With respect to the sale of goods, the warranty of title

a. Applies only if the seller is a merchant.
b. Applies only if it is in writing and signed by the seller.
c. Provides that the seller deliver the goods free from any lien of which the buyer lacked knowledge when the contract was made.
d. Provides that the seller cannot disclaim the warranty if the sale is made to a bona fide purchaser for value.   (5/91, Law, #48, 0499)

20. Under the UCC Sales Article, the warranty of title may be excluded by
a. Merchants or non-merchants provided the exclusion is in writing.
b. Non-merchant sellers only.
c. The seller's statement that it is selling only such right or title that it has.
d. Use of an "as is" disclaimer. *does not work*
                              (5/90, Law, #42, 0510)

21. Which of the following factors result(s) in an express warranty with respect to a sale of goods?

I. The seller's description of the goods as part of the basis of the bargain.
II. The seller selects goods knowing the buyer's intended use. *implied warr of fitness*

a. I only.
b. II only.
c. Both I and II.
d. Neither I nor II.   (5/92, Law, #60, 2873)

22. Under the UCC Sales Article, an action for breach of the implied warranty of merchantability by a party who sustains personal injuries may be successful against the seller of the product only when
a. The seller is a merchant of the product involved.
b. An action based on negligence can also be successfully maintained.
c. The injured party is in privity of contract with the seller.
d. An action based on strict liability in tort can also be successfully maintained.
                              (5/92, Law, #57, 2870)

23. Vick bought a used boat from Ocean Marina that disclaimed "any and all warranties" in connection with the sale. Ocean was unaware the boat had been stolen from Kidd. Vick surrendered it to Kidd when confronted with proof of the theft. Vick sued Ocean. Who is likely to prevail and why?

Ocean is resp to Vick

a. Vick, because the implied warranty of title has been breached.
b. Vick, because a merchant **cannot** disclaim implied warranties.
c. Ocean, because of the disclaimer of warranties.
d. Ocean, because Vick surrendered the boat to Kidd.
                              (5/94, Law, #43, 4798)

24. Larch Corp. manufactured and sold Oak a stove. The sale documents included a disclaimer of warranty for personal injury. The stove was defective. It exploded causing serious injuries to Oak's spouse. Larch was notified one week after the explosion. Under the UCC Sales Article, which of the following statements concerning Larch's liability for personal injury to Oak's spouse would be correct?
a. Larch **cannot** be liable because of a lack of privity with Oak's spouse.
b. Larch will **not** be liable because of a failure to give proper notice.
c. Larch will be liable because the disclaimer was **not** a disclaimer of all liability.
d. Larch will be liable because liability for personal injury **cannot** be disclaimed.
                              (5/94, Law, #44, 4799)

25. On May 2, Handy Hardware sent Ram Industries a signed purchase order that stated, in part, as follows:

"Ship for May 8 delivery 300 Model A-X socket sets at current dealer price. Terms 2/10/net 30."

Ram received Handy's purchase order on May 4. On May 5, Ram discovered that it had only 200 Model A-X socket sets and 100 Model W-Z socket sets in stock. Ram shipped the Model A-X and Model W-Z sets to Handy without any explanation concerning the shipment. The socket sets were received by Handy on May 8.

Assuming a contract exists between Handy and Ram, which of the following implied warranties would result?

I. Implied warranty of merchantability.
II. Implied warranty of fitness for a particular purpose.
III. Implied warranty of title.

a. I only.
b. III only.
c. I and III only.
d. I, II, and III.   (11/93, Law, #52, 4349)

26. Which of the following conditions must be met for an implied warranty of fitness for a particular purpose to arise in connection with a sale of goods?

 I. The warranty must be in writing.
 II. The seller must know that the buyer was relying on the seller in selecting the goods.

a. I only.
b. II only.
c. Both I and II.
d. Neither I nor II.   (5/92, Law, #55, 2868)

27. Under the Sales Article of the UCC, which of the following statements is correct regarding the warranty of merchantability arising when there has been a sale of goods by a merchant seller?
a. The warranty must be in writing.
b. The warranty arises when the buyer relies on the seller's skill in selecting the goods purchased.
c. The warranty cannot be disclaimed.
d. The warranty arises as a matter of law when the seller ordinarily sells the goods purchased.
           (11/94, Law, #51, 5228)

28. Lazur Corp. entered into a contract with Baker Suppliers, Inc. to purchase a used word processor from Baker. Lazur is engaged in the business of selling new and used word processors to the general public. The contract required Baker to ship the goods to Lazur by common carrier pursuant to the following provisions in the contract: "F.O.B.--Baker Suppliers, Inc. loading dock." Baker also represented in the contract that the word processor had been used for only 10 hours by its previous owner. The contract included the provision that the word processor was being sold "as is" and this provision was in a larger and different type style than the remainder of the contract. With regard to the contract between Lazur and Baker,
a. An implied warranty of merchantability does **not** arise unless both Lazur and Baker are merchants.
b. The "as is" provision effectively disclaims the implied warranty of title.
c. No express warranties are created by the contract.
d. The "as is" provision would **not** prevent Baker from being liable for a breach of any express warranties created by the contract.
           (5/89, Law, #55, 9911)

29. Under the Sales Article of the UCC, which of the following events will result in the risk of loss passing from a merchant seller to a buyer?

	Tender of the goods at the seller's place of business	Use of the seller's truck to deliver the goods
a.	Yes	Yes
b.	Yes	No
c.	No	Yes
d.	No	No

           (11/94, Law, #54, 5231)

30. Quick Corp. agreed to purchase 200 typewriters from Union Suppliers, Inc. Union is a wholesaler of appliances and Quick is an appliance retailer. The contract required Union to ship the typewriters to Quick by common carrier, "F.O.B. Union Suppliers, Inc. Loading Dock." Which of the parties bears the risk of loss during shipment?
a. Union, because the risk of loss passes only when Quick receives the typewriters.
b. Union, because both parties are merchants.
c. Quick, because title to the typewriters passed to Quick at the time of shipment.
d. Quick, because the risk of loss passes when the typewriters are delivered to the carrier.
           (5/94, Law, #45, 4800)

31. Bond purchased a painting from Wool, who is not in the business of selling art. Wool tendered delivery of the painting after receiving payment in full from Bond. Bond informed Wool that Bond would be unable to take possession of the painting until later that day. Thieves stole the painting before Bond returned. The risk of loss
a. Passed to Bond at Wool's tender of delivery.
b. Passed to Bond at the time the contract was formed and payment was made.
c. Remained with Wool, because the parties agreed on a later time of delivery.
d. Remained with Wool, because Bond had **not** yet received the painting.
           (11/93, Law, #55, 4352)

32. On May 2, Handy Hardware sent Ram Industries a signed purchase order that stated, in part, as follows:

"Ship for May 8 delivery 300 Model A-X socket sets at current dealer price. Terms 2/10/net 30."

Ram received Handy's purchase order on May 4. On May 5, Ram discovered that it had only 200 Model A-X socket sets and 100 Model W-Z socket sets in stock. Ram shipped the Model A-X and Model W-Z sets to Handy without any explanation concerning the shipment. The socket sets were received by Handy on May 8.

Which of the following statements concerning the shipment is correct?
a. Ram's shipment is an acceptance of Handy's offer.
b. Ram's shipment is a counteroffer.
c. Handy's order must be accepted by Ram in writing before Ram ships the socket sets.
d. Handy's order can only be accepted by Ram shipping conforming goods.

(11/93, Law, #51, 4348)

33. Smith contracted in writing to sell Peters a used personal computer for $600. The contract did not specifically address the time for payment, place of delivery, or Peters' right to inspect the computer. Which of the following statements is correct?
a. Smith is obligated to deliver the computer to Peters' home.
b. Peters is entitled to inspect the computer before paying for it.
c. Peters may **not** pay for the computer using a personal check unless Smith agrees.
d. Smith is **not** entitled to payment until 30 days after Peters receives the computer.

(11/93, Law, #56, 4353)

34. Maco Corp. contracted to sell 1,500 bushels of potatoes to LBC Chips. The contract did not refer to any specific supply source for the potatoes. Maco intended to deliver potatoes grown on its farms. An insect infestation ruined Maco's crop but not the crops of other growers in the area. Maco failed to deliver the potatoes to LBC. LBC sued Maco for breach of contract. Under the circumstances, Maco will
a. Lose, because it could have purchased potatoes from other growers to deliver to LBC.
b. Lose, unless it can show that the purchase of substitute potatoes for delivery to LBC would make the contract unprofitable.
c. Win, because the infestation was an act of nature that could **not** have been anticipated by Maco.
d. Win, because both Maco and LBC are assumed to accept the risk of a crop failure.

(5/91, Law, #23, 0496)

35. Under the UCC Sales Article, which of the following legal remedies would a buyer **not** have when a seller fails to transfer and deliver goods identified to the contract?
a. Suit for specific performance.
b. Suit for punitive damages.

c. Purchase substitute goods (cover).
d. Recover the identified goods (capture).

(5/94, Law, #47, 4803)

36. Cara Fabricating Co. and Taso Corp. agreed orally that Taso would custom manufacture a compressor for Cara at a price of $120,000. After Taso completed the work at a cost of $90,000, Cara notified Taso that the compressor was no longer needed. Taso is holding the compressor and has requested payment from Cara. Taso has been unable to resell the compressor for any price. Taso incurred storage fees of $2,000. If Cara refuses to pay Taso and Taso sues Cara, the most Taso will be entitled to recover is
a. $ 92,000.
b. $105,000.
c. $120,000.
d. $122,000.

(11/93, Law, #57, 4354)

37. Jefferson Hardware ordered three hundred Ram hammers from Ajax Hardware. Ajax accepted the order in writing. On the final date allowed for delivery, Ajax discovered it did not have enough Ram hammers to fill the order. Instead, Ajax sent three hundred Strong hammers. Ajax stated on the invoice that the shipment was sent only as an accommodation. Which of the following statements is correct?
a. Ajax's note of accommodation cancels the contract between Jefferson and Ajax.
b. Jefferson's order can only be accepted by Ajax's shipment of the goods ordered.
c. Ajax's shipment of Strong hammers is a breach of contract.
d. Ajax's shipment of Strong hammers is a counteroffer and **no** contract exists between Jefferson and Ajax. (5/90, Law, #46, 0514)

38. Under the UCC Sales Article, a plaintiff who proves fraud in the formation of a contract may
a. Elect to rescind the contract and need **not** return the consideration received from the other party.
b. Be entitled to rescind the contract and sue for damages resulting from the fraud.
c. Be entitled to punitive damages provided physical injuries resulted from the fraud.
d. Rescind the contract even if there was **no** reliance on the fraudulent statement.

(11/91, Law, #22, 2350)

39. Eagle Corporation solicited bids for various parts it used in the manufacture of jet engines. Eagle received six offers and selected the offer of Sky Corporation. The written contract specified a price for 100,000 units, delivery on June 1 at Sky's plant, with

payment on July 1. On June 1, Sky had completed a 200,000 unit run of parts similar to those under contract for Eagle and various other customers. Sky had not identified the parts to specific contracts. When Eagle's truck arrived to pick up the parts on June 1, Sky refused to deliver claiming the contract price was too low. Eagle was unable to cover in a reasonable time. Its production lines were in danger of shutdown because the parts were not delivered. Eagle would probably

a. Have as its only remedy the right of replevin.

b. Have the right of replevin only if Eagle tendered the purchase price on June 1.

c. Have as its only remedy the right to recover dollar damages.

d. Have the right to obtain specific performance.

(5/90, Law, #48, 0516)

40. On May 1, Frost entered into a signed contract for the sale of 5,000 pounds of sugar to Kemp Co. at 30¢ per pound. Delivery was to be made on June 10. Due to a sudden rise in sugar prices, Frost sent Kemp a letter stating that it would not sell the sugar to Kemp. Kemp received the letter on May 15 at which time the market price of sugar was 40¢ per pound. Although Kemp could have reasonably purchased sugar elsewhere in the market, it chose not to do so. On June 10, the market price of sugar was 50¢ per pound. In addition to incidental damages, Kemp is entitled to damages of

a. $ 500.

b. $ 500 plus consequential damages.

c. $1,000.

d. $1,000 plus consequential damages.

(5/86, Law, #36, 9911)

41. Under the UCC Sales Article, if a buyer wrongfully rejects goods, the aggrieved seller may

	Resell the goods and sue for damages	Cancel the agreement
a.	Yes	Yes
b.	Yes	No
c.	No	Yes
d.	No	No

(11/89, Law, #52, 9911)

42. Under the UCC Sales Article, a seller will be entitled to recover the full contract price from the buyer when the

a. Goods are destroyed after title passed to the buyer.

b. Goods are destroyed while risk of loss is with the buyer.

c. Buyer revokes its acceptance of the goods.

d. Buyer rejects some of the goods.

(5/92, Law, #59, 2872)

43. On February 15, Mazur Corp. contracted to sell 1,000 bushels of wheat to Good Bread, Inc. at $6.00 per bushel with delivery to be made on June 23. On June 1, Good advised Mazur that it would not accept or pay for the wheat. On June 2, Mazur sold the wheat to another customer at the market price of $5.00 per bushel. Mazur had advised Good that it intended to resell the wheat. Which of the following statements is correct?

a. Mazur can successfully sue Good for the difference between the resale price and the contract price.

b. Mazur can resell the wheat only after June 23.

c. Good can retract its anticipatory breach at any time before June 23.

d. Good can successfully sue Mazur for specific performance. (5/92, Law, #56, 2869)

Items 44 and 45 are based on the following information:

On April 5, 1987, Anker, Inc., furnished Bold Corp. with Anker's financial statements dated March 31, 1987. The financial statements contained misrepresentations which indicated that Anker was solvent when in fact it was insolvent. Based on Anker's financial statements, Bold agreed to sell Anker 90 computers, "F.O.B.--Bold's loading dock." On April 14, Anker received 60 of the computers. The remaining 30 computers are in the possession of the common carrier and in transit to Anker.

44. If on April 28, Bold discovered that Anker was insolvent, then with respect to the computers delivered to Anker on April 14, Bold may

a. Reclaim the computers upon making a demand.

b. Reclaim the computers irrespective of the rights of any subsequent third party.

c. Not reclaim the computers since ten days have elapsed from its delivery.

d. Not reclaim the computers since it is entitled to recover the price of the computers.

(5/87, Law, #52, 0526)

45. With respect to the remaining 30 computers in transit, which of the following statements is correct if Anker refuses to pay Bold in cash and Anker is **not** in possession of a negotiable document of title covering the computers?

a. Bold may stop delivery of the computers to Anker since their contract is void due to Anker's furnishing of the false financial statements.

b. Bold may stop delivery of the computers to Anker despite the fact that title had passed to Anker.

c. Bold must deliver the computers to Anker on credit since Anker has **not** breached the contract.

d. Bold must deliver the computers to Anker since the risk of loss had passed to Anker.

(5/87, Law, #53, 0527)

46. To establish a cause of action based on strict liability in tort for personal injuries resulting from using a defective product, one of the elements the plaintiff must prove is that the seller (defendant)

a. Failed to exercise due care.
b. Was in privity of contract with the plaintiff.
c. Defectively designed the product.
d. Was engaged in the business of selling the product.   (11/93, Law, #54, 4351)

47. High sues the manufacturer, wholesaler, and retailer for bodily injuries caused by a power saw High

purchased. Which of the following statements is correct under strict liability theory?

a. Contributory negligence on High's part will always be a bar to recovery.

b. The manufacturer will avoid liability if it can show it followed the custom of the industry.

c. Privity will be a bar to recovery insofar as the wholesaler is concerned if the wholesaler did **not** have a reasonable opportunity to inspect.

d. High may recover even if he cannot show any negligence was involved.

(11/94, Law, #53, 5230)

48. Which of the following requirements must be met to create a bailment?

I. Delivery of personal property to the intended bailee.
II. Possession by the intended bailee.
III. An absolute duty on the intended bailee to return or dispose of the property according to the bailor's directions.

a. I and II only.
b. I and III only.
c. II and III only.
d. I, II, and III.   (5/94, Law, #60, 4815)

Solution 44-1 MULTIPLE CHOICE ANSWERS

Sales and the UCC

1. (d) The UCC applies if there is the sale of goods regardless of price, and if no price is stated, price is a reasonable amount at the time of delivery. Both parties are bound by the UCC requirement of "good faith." Under the UCC it is not required that the contract must be either a sale or return or a sale on approval contract. The parties can agree to other types of arrangements since the most important factor in determining risk of loss is the agreement of the parties regarding risk of loss. The UCC Sales Article would apply if the price was $500 or more.

1A. (a) UCC 1-102(3) imposes an obligation on the parties to contract in good faith. Merchants are frequently treated differently under UCC 2 provisions. UCC 2 covers contracts for goods regardless of the contract price, and the UCC permits the parties to a contract to disclaim many of the UCC's provisions.

2. (d) The Uniform Commercial Code (UCC 2-306) provides that a contract for the sale of goods will not be enforceable if the acceptance is open, since if

this term is left open there is no basis for determining contract existence. UCC 2-305 provides that where the price term is left open, the courts will determine a reasonable price at the time of delivery. UCC 2-308 provides that where no delivery terms are stated, the buyer will normally take delivery at the seller's place of business. The quantity may be contingent on seller's production.

3. (c) UCC 2-513(1) provides that a buyer has a right to inspect goods before payment or acceptance occurs. UCC 2-513(3) states that where there is a C.O.D. term, the buyer is not entitled to inspect the goods before payment; however, the buyer still retains the right to inspect before acceptance. A C.O.D. term requires the buyer to pay for the goods immediately upon delivery and before obtaining possession.

4. (d) Under UCC 2-205, a firm offer is a signed written offer by a merchant to buy or sell goods in which the merchant gives assurance that the offer will be held open. If no time period is stated, then it will be considered as irrevocable for a reasonable

period of time not to exceed three months. There are no requirements that the offeree must be a merchant or that consideration must be given in order to have a valid firm offer.

5.   (b)   UCC 2-207 states that terms included with an acceptance which are additional to, or different from, the terms offered will be considered proposals for additions to the new contract except when the offer flatly states that acceptance is limited to the terms of the offer. Baker's offer was not a firm offer under UCC 2-205. Baker's offer specifically limited acceptance to terms of the offer. The Statute of Frauds does not prevent the formation of a contract--it prevents the enforcement of the contract.

6.   (c)   Acme's contention that the agreement to change the delivery date was not binding is incorrect because an oral agreement that modifies an existing contract for the sale of goods does not need new consideration to be binding. Since the contract is for the sale of goods for a price less than $500, the Statute of Frauds does not apply, and the oral modification is enforceable.

7.   (b)   An agreement for the sale of goods under $500 need not be in writing to be enforceable. Thus, Bond and Spear had a valid oral contract, and Spear has breached the contract by agreeing to sell the car to a third party. The adequacy of consideration is not a contract issue. The agreement does not need to be in writing because it was under $500. Paying a deposit is not the deciding factor in this case. The key point is that the agreement was for the sale of goods under $500.

8.   (c)   Under UCC 2-201, a sale falling within the Statute of Frauds is not enforceable beyond the quantity of goods shown in the writing.

9.   (c)   This problem illustrates the concept of a "firm offer." A firm offer is a signed written offer by a merchant to buy or sell goods in which the merchant gives assurance that the offer will be held open. Such an offer is irrevocable, even though it is not supported by consideration, for the time stated or for a reasonable period of time. However, in no event may this time period be longer than three months.

10.   (d)   The Statute of Frauds does not apply to this oral contract, since this was for specifically manufactured goods. If the buyer, Gray, does not take delivery of the custom goods, the seller is entitled to the contract price ($80,000) plus reasonable storage fees ($1,000).

11.   (c)   Under a UCC contract, a seller may be excused from performance if the goods are accidentally destroyed before the risk of loss passes. The UCC requirement of good faith applies even if both parties are not merchants. A contract will be enforceable even if it fails to expressly specify a time and place for delivery of the goods. If no time is stated, delivery will take place in a reasonable time. If place of delivery is not stated, the UCC provides specific rules. In general, delivery will take place at the seller's place of business, or if no place of business, at the seller's residence. If the goods are known to be located at a specific location, delivery will take place at that location unless otherwise agreed. Having goods identified to the contract has nothing to do with risk of loss unless otherwise agreed. Normally, a buyer has an insurable interest in the goods once the goods are identified to the contract. Also, the $500 requirement has nothing to do with risk of loss.

11A.   (d)   UCC 2-609 provides that if reasonable grounds for insecurity arise concerning the performance of either party, the other party may in writing demand adequate assurance of performance. If the other party fails to provide the assurance within a reasonable period of time, then the party's failure to respond may be treated as a repudiation of the contract. The party requesting the assurance may then suspend their own performance. A buyer would not be released of their obligations if delivery has become impractical, nor if the goods are destroyed after risk of loss has passed to them. A repudiating buyer may retract their repudiation until the time before the next performance is due, unless the seller has changed his/her/its position or considered the repudiation to be final.

12.   (c)   Under the UCC Sales Article, a sale on approval is not a sale until the buyer accepts the offer. Until the buyer accepts, the risk of loss and title remain with the seller. Once the buyer accepts, risk of loss and title will pass to the seller. The UCC covers all sales of goods and is not limited to transactions between two merchants. The goods do not have to be for resale. Title does not pass until the offer of sale has been accepted.

13.   (a)   The Statute of Frauds requires that a contract for goods of $500 or more be in writing. UCC 2-207, however, provides that in a contract between merchants, the Statute of Frauds is satisfied if a written confirmation is sent within a reasonable time. The confirmation must be received by the other party who knows or should know the confirmation's contents. If the recipient merchant fails to object to

the confirmation's contents within a reasonable time, they will be bound to the contract.

14. (d) The UCC Sales Article does not specify that a minimum dollar amount be involved in a contract in order for it to be governed by the Sales Article.

Title of Goods

15. (c) Under UCC 2-401(2), title passes to the buyer when the seller completes his or her delivery of the goods. Since the goods did not even get to the place of shipment, title remained with Pulse. Under UCC 2-501(2), seller Pulse retained an insurable interest.

16. (d) The buyer's reasonable rejection of the goods causes title to the goods to revert back to the seller.

17. (a) Under the UCC Sales Article, title to the radios passes to Lazur at the time they are delivered to the carrier, even if the goods are nonconforming. When the nonconforming goods are received by Lazur, the goods may be rejected and title will revert to the seller. There is no requirement that the buyer immediately inspect the goods or lose all right to later reject acceptance. The buyer, in this case, must pay the freight expenses, not the seller. The seller can accept an order by prompt shipment of the goods requested or by a prompt notice of intent to ship followed by a timely shipment. In this case, Lazur would not have the right to reject the shipment if Wizard fails to notify Lazur that the goods have been shipped.

18. (b) Under UCC 2-502(1), buyer Bell Corp. has a right to the goods if it has "a special property" under UCC 2-501. Without an identification of existing goods, no such "special property" arises. Therefore, Bell's rights do not include obtaining the goods themselves after Glow Manufacturing became insolvent.

Warranties

19. (c) With respect to the sale of goods, the warranty of title provides that the seller deliver the goods free from any lien of which the buyer lacked knowledge when the contract was made. In addition, whenever goods are sold, there is an automatic title warranty and this can only be disclaimed with specific language disclaiming the title warranty. The title warranty applies even if the seller is not a merchant.

The title warranty applies even if the sale of goods was not in writing and signed by the seller. The warranty of title can be disclaimed if clear and brought to the attention of the buyer.

20. (c) Warranty of title may be given as well as disclaimed by merchants or non-merchants, orally or in writing. The disclaimer must be by specific language or circumstances, not simply a phrase such as "AS IS."

21. (a) An express warranty may be created in several ways. One is by any description of the goods which is made part of the basis of the bargain when such description creates a warranty that the goods will conform to the description (Part I). The fact that the seller selects goods knowing the buyer's intended use (Part II) concerns the implied warranty of fitness for a particular purpose and not the creation of an express warranty.

22. (a) UCC 2-314 implies a warranty of merchantability when the seller is a merchant with respect to the goods sold.

23. (a) UCC 2-312 provides that all sellers of goods implicitly warrant that the title they are transferring is good. The implied warranty of title can only be disclaimed with very specific language; a general disclaimer is insufficient. In this instance the warranty of title was breached and not properly disclaimed. A merchant can disclaim this as well as other warranties. The general disclaimer used by Ocean was not specific enough to disclaim the implied warranty of title. Kidd was the rightful owner. The surrender of the boat by Vick to Kidd will not affect Vick's rights against Ocean.

24. (d) The liability for personal injury is not subject to disclaimer, exclusion, or modification by contractual agreement. Under strict liability, the manufacturer of a product in a defective condition unreasonably dangerous to the user or consumer is liable for personal injuries and property damage regardless of privity. There was no failure to give proper notice (i.e., notice was given within a reasonable period). Although, Larch Corp. will be liable, the liability results due to the inability to disclaim any liability for personal injury rather than the inadequacy of the disclaimer.

25. (c) An implied warranty of merchantability automatically arises in all sales of goods made by a merchant who deals in such goods. Handy Hardware did not specify a use for the goods or rely on the seller's judgment in making the purchase, so there is

no implied warranty of fitness for a particular purpose. An implied warranty of title arises automatically in most sales contracts. There is no evidence to the contrary in this problem, so we can assume that the warranty of title does exist.

26. (b) The warranty of fitness for a particular purpose is created when the seller has actual or constructive knowledge of the particular purpose for which the goods are required, and also knows that the buyer is relying on the skill and judgment of the seller to select and furnish suitable goods. As this is an implied warranty, there is no requirement that it be in writing.

27. (d) UCC 2-314(1) provides that, unless excluded or disclaimed, "a warranty that the goods shall be merchantable is implied ... if the seller is a merchant with respect to goods of that kind." This warranty need not be in writing, and no requirements exist other than that the seller be a merchant.

28. (d) Most implied warranties are disclaimed when goods are sold with an "as is" provision. An express warranty is not disclaimed with an "as is" provision since it is extremely hard to disclaim an express warranty. Under the Code, in general, it is unreasonable to give an express warranty and then disclaim it. When there is a conflict, the express warranty will prevail. An implied warranty arises if the *seller* is a merchant regardless of whether the *buyer* is a merchant. The only way to disclaim an implied warranty of title is to use specific language clearly indicating the seller does not warrant the title to the goods. Express warranties are affirmations of fact or promises made by the seller to the buyer which relate to the goods and become part of the basis of the bargain. In this question, we have an express warranty that the word processor was "used for only 10 hours by its previous owner."

Risk of Loss

29. (d) UCC 2-509(3) provides that where a contract for the sale of goods is otherwise silent as to the passage of the risk of loss, if the seller is a merchant, risk of loss passes from the seller to the buyer upon the buyer's receipt of the goods. Neither tender of delivery by a merchant seller nor use of the seller's truck for delivery will cause the risk of loss to pass.

30. (d) The contract contains an F.O.B. shipment term which provides that the risk of loss shifts from the seller to the buyer when the seller delivers the goods to a carrier for shipment. With an F.O.B. term it is irrelevant whether the parties to the contract are merchants.

31. (a) Risk of loss passes upon *tender* of delivery when the seller is not a merchant. If the seller was a merchant, risk of loss would pass upon the buyer's receipt of the goods. In this problem, the facts clearly specify that Wool is not a merchant in the goods being sold, so we can determine that risk of loss passed to Bond upon tender of delivery.

Performance

32. (a) The sale of goods is governed by the UCC which states that acceptance occurs if the response indicates a definite acceptance of the offer, even if the response includes different or additional terms. Handy's purchase order was an offer to purchase goods from Ram. When Ram shipped the order he effectively accepted Handy's offer even though he did change the terms of the sale when he shipped sockets of a different model number. An offeree's additional terms are considered proposals and are subject to ratification by the offeror, but they do not preclude an acceptance. The offer does not specify that a written acceptance was required.

33. (b) Unless otherwise agreed between the parties, the buyer normally has a right to inspect the goods before acceptance (there are certain minor exceptions, such as a C.O.D. purchase). Even if you have accepted, you can rightfully reject after inspection if done within a reasonable time. The seller's location is assumed when the contract is silent on the point of delivery. When a contract is silent as to the method of payment, a check is considered an acceptable form of payment. Payment is assumed to be due immediately unless specified in the contract.

34. (a) Maco should have anticipated this problem and provided for it in the contract. Since Maco did not anticipate this problem in the contract, Maco is bound to the contract. Maco can perform by buying potatoes from other farmers and delivering these potatoes. One cannot get out of a contract simply by showing that the contract could be unprofitable to perform. The insect infestation was an act of nature that could have been anticipated. Both parties do not assume the risk of contract failure.

Remedies for Breach

35. (b) Under the common law rules of contract and UCC 2, punitive damages can never be awarded in an action for breach of contract. UCC 2-716(1) provides that the court may order specific performance either when the goods are unique or in

"other proper circumstances" (i.e., inability to obtain cover). UCC 2-712 permits a buyer to cover (i.e., obtain substitute goods elsewhere). UCC 2-502 permits a buyer to recover identified goods if the buyer has made full or partial payment for the goods and the seller becomes insolvent.

36. (d) The UCC provides for the right to recover the purchase price of a contract under the following three circumstances:

1. Buyer accepted goods; title passed.
2. Conforming goods are lost or damaged after risk of loss passed to buyer.
3. Buyer breaches contract after goods are identified to the contract, and seller is unable to resell the goods.

Furthermore, if the goods are specially manufactured goods, the seller is entitled to the contract price plus incidental damages incurred relating to the sale (storage, etc.).

37. (c) The perfect tender rule (UCC 2-601) has not been complied with by Ajax, and thus a breach has occurred. Of course, Jefferson can always decide to accept Ajax's attempted accommodation.

38. (b) Under the UCC Sales Article, if fraud in the inducement (i.e., in the formation of a contract) is present, the resulting contract is *voidable* at the option of the defrauded party, thereby allowing that party to rescind the contract and sue for damages. The plaintiff may elect to rescind the contract, but in doing so must return any consideration received. Punitive damages are normally not allowed. There must have been reliance on the fraudulent statement.

39. (d) Replevin is unavailable because the goods have not been identified to specific contracts [UCC 2-716(3)]. Specific performance is always available when goods are unique or there are "other proper circumstances" [UCC 2-716(1)], so dollar damages may not be the only remedy.

40. (a) UCC 2-713 provides generally that upon the repudiation of a contract by the seller, the buyer is entitled to damages in the amount of the difference between the market price at the time when the buyer learned of the breach and the contract price, along with incidental and consequential damages. Since Kemp was notified of the repudiation on May 15, he is entitled to recover damages of $500, plus incidental damages. Although UCC 2-713 generally provides for consequential damages, Kemp in this instance has not suffered any such injury and is therefore not entitled to receive consequential changes.

41. (a) Under the UCC, if a buyer wrongfully rejects goods, the aggrieved seller may resell and recover damages *or* cancel the contract.

42. (b) Under UCC 2-709 if the buyer fails to pay the price as it becomes due, the seller may bring an action and recover the price of the goods if conforming goods were lost or damaged within a commercially reasonable time after the risk of loss passed to the buyer.

43. (a) An anticipatory repudiation occurs when either party to a contract demonstrates an intention not to perform an obligation not yet due, or an action which renders that performance impossible. In case of one party's (Good Bread Inc.) anticipatory repudiation, the other party (Mazur) may resort to any remedy available for breach. One remedy available to the seller is to sell the goods and to recover damages. Damages are defined in this case as the difference between the resale price and the contract price.

44. (a) When a seller of goods discovers that a buyer is insolvent, he or she may reclaim any goods received by the buyer on credit when the buyer was insolvent if demand is made within 10 days after receipt of the goods. However, if the buyer misrepresented his or her solvency to the seller in writing within the three-month period before delivery, the 10-day limitation does not apply. The seller's right to reclaim is subject to the rights of a buyer in the ordinary course of business or other good faith purchaser. A seller's right to reclaim goods from an insolvent buyer is an alternative remedy open to the seller along with other available remedies under the UCC.

45. (b) A seller may stop the delivery of goods in the possession of a carrier when he or she discovers the buyer to be insolvent. This right to stop delivery terminates when the buyer has received the goods. Thus, even though title and risk of loss have already passed to Anker under the shipment terms (F.O.B. Bold's loading dock), Bold may still stop delivery of the computers.

Products Liability

46. (d) The requirements of an action based on strict liability include the following:

1. Product is defective when sold.
2. Defendant is normally engaged in selling the product.
3. Product is unreasonably dangerous to the user because of its defective condition.
4. Plaintiff incurs physical harm to self or property because of use or consumption of the product.
5. Defective condition is proximate cause of the injury or damages.
6. The product has not been substantially changed from the time it was sold to the time the injury was sustained.

Answer (d) corresponds to requirement #2 listed above. Answers (a), (b), and (c) are not requirements necessary to the establishment of a cause of action based on strict liability in tort.

47. (d) An injured plaintiff may sue any seller of a good under strict liability, if the plaintiff can show that the good was sold in a defective or unreasonably dangerous condition. The plaintiff need not prove fault or wrongdoing by the defendant, thus not having an opportunity to inspect or following industry customs are not defenses available to the defendant. Although contributory negligence is a defense available in negligence, it is generally not a defense in strict liability actions.

Nonsales Transactions

48. (a) In order for there to be a valid bailment, personal property must be delivered to the intended bailee who must then retain possession of the property. Although the bailee has a duty to hold the property for the bailor and to follow any of the bailor's reasonable instructions as to the disposition of the property, the bailee's duty is not an absolute one.

PERFORMANCE BY SUBTOPICS

Each category below parallels a subtopic covered in Chapter 44. Record the number and percentage of questions you correctly answered in each subtopic area.

Sales and the UCC

Question #	Correct √
1	
1A	
2	
3	
4	
5	
6	
7	
8	
9	
10	
11	
11A	
12	
13	
14	
# Questions	16

Correct _____
% Correct _____

Title of Goods

Question #	Correct √
15	
16	
17	
18	
# Questions	4

Correct _____
% Correct _____

Warranties

Question #	Correct √
19	
20	
21	
22	
23	
24	
25	
26	
27	
28	
# Questions	10

Correct _____
% Correct _____

Risk of Loss

Question #	Correct √
29	
30	
31	
# Questions	3

Correct _____
% Correct _____

Performance

Question #	Correct √
32	
33	
34	
# Questions	3

Correct _____
% Correct _____

Remedies for Breach

Question #	Correct √
35	
36	
37	
38	
39	
40	
41	
42	
43	
44	
45	
# Questions	11

Correct _____
% Correct _____

Products Liability

Question #	Correct √
46	
47	
# Questions	2

Correct _____
% Correct _____

Nonsales Transactions

Question #	Correct √
48	
# Questions	1

Correct _____
% Correct _____

OTHER OBJECTIVE FORMAT QUESTION

Problem 44-2 (Estimated time--10 to 15 minutes)

On February 1, 1995, Grand Corp., a manufacturer of custom cabinets, contracted in writing with Axle Co., a kitchen contractor, to sell Axle 100 unique, custom-designed kitchen cabinets for $250,000. Axle had contracted to install the cabinets in a luxury condominium complex. The contract provided that the cabinets were to be ready for delivery by April 15 and were to be shipped F.O.B. sellers loading dock. On April 15, Grand had 85 cabinets complete and delivered them, together with 15 standard cabinets, to the trucking company for delivery to Axle. Grand faxed Axle a copy of the shipping invoice, listing the 15 standard cabinets. On May 1, before reaching Axle, the truck was involved in a collision and all the cabinets were damaged beyond repair.

Required:

Items 1 through 6 refer to the above fact pattern. For each item, determine whether (a), (b), or (c) is correct.

1.
a. The contract between Grand and Axle was a shipment contract.
b. The contract between Grand and Axle was a destination contract.
c. The contract between Grand and Axle was a consignment contract.

V. V. Imp

2. *Imp*

a. The risk of loss for the 85 custom cabinets passed to Axle on April 15.
b. The risk of loss for the 100 cabinets passed to Axle on April 15.
c. The risk of loss for the 100 cabinets remained with Grand.

3.

a. The contract between Grand and Axle was invalid because **no** delivery date was stated.
b. The contract between Grand and Axle was voidable because Grand shipped only 85 custom cabinets.
c. The contract between Grand and Axle was void because the goods were destroyed.

4.

a. Grand's shipment of the standard cabinets was a breach of the contract with Axle.
b. Grand would **not** be considered to have breached the contract until Axle rejected the standard cabinets.
c. Grand made a counteroffer by shipping the standard cabinets.

5.

a. Had the cabinets been delivered, title would **not** transfer to Axle until Axle inspected them.
b. Had the cabinets been delivered, title would have transferred on delivery to the carrier.
c. Had the cabinets been delivered, title would **not** have transferred because the cabinets were nonconforming goods.

6.

a. Axle is entitled to specific performance from Grand because of the unique nature of the goods.
b. Axle is required to purchase substitute goods (cover) and is entitled to the difference in cost from Grand.
c. Axle is entitled to punitive damages because of Grand's intentional shipment of nonconforming

(5/95, Law, #3a)

OTHER OBJECTIVE FORMAT SOLUTION

Solution 44-2 Performance/Remedies for Breach

1. (a) Under the Sales Article of the Uniform Commercial Code, if the place of shipment is named, as "FOB Sellers Location," the contract is a shipment contract.

2. (c) Where a contract for goods includes an FOB shipment term, risk of loss usually passes from seller to buyer when the goods are delivered to the seller's loading dock. However, where a delivery fails to conform to the contract so as to result in a breach, the risk of loss remains on the seller.

3. (b) The failure of a seller to ship conforming goods constitutes a breach of contract and renders the contract voidable. The Sales Article of the Uniform Commercial Code states that if goods identified to a contract are damaged without the fault of either party before the risk of loss passes to the buyer, the contract is avoided if the loss is total (UCC 2-613). However, since the goods do not conform, this is irrelevant. Under the Sales Article of the UCC, failure to include a delivery date in a contract for the sale of goods will not render the contract invalid.

4. (a) The UCC Sales Article states that a shipment of nonconforming goods constitutes a breach of contract. Rejection by the buyer is not a necessary component of the seller's breach. A shipment of nonconforming goods does not result in a counteroffer.

5. (c) The UCC Sales Article provides that where there is a FOB shipment term, title to the goods will transfer to the buyer upon delivery to the carrier. However, when the seller ships nonconforming goods such as to result in a breach of contract, then title and the risk of loss do not leave the seller. A buyer's inspection is not necessary for title to pass.

6. (a) The UCC Sales Article provides that specific performance is an appropriate remedy when the goods are unique (UCC 2-716). Where a contract is breached, the UCC does not require a nonbreaching buyer to purchase substitute goods, since substitute goods may not be available, especially when the goods are unique. Punitive damages are never available in an action for breach of contract.

ESSAY QUESTIONS

Essay 44-3 (15 to 25 minutes)

Victor Corp. engaged Bell & Co., CPAs, to audit Victor's financial statements for the year ended December 31, 1992. Victor is in the business of buying, selling, and servicing new and used construction equipment. While reviewing Victor's 1992 records, Bell became aware of the following disputed transactions:

- On September 8, Victor sent Ambel Contractors, Inc. a signed purchase order for several pieces of used construction equipment. Victor's purchase order described twelve different pieces of equipment and indicated the price Victor was willing to pay for each item. As a result of a mathematical error in adding up the total of the various prices, the purchase price offered by Victor was $191,000 rather than the correct amount of $119,000. Ambel, on receipt of the purchase order, was surprised by Victor's high price and immediately sent Victor a written acceptance. Ambel was aware that the fair market value of the equipment was approximately $105,000 to $125,000. Victor discovered the mistake in the purchase order and refused to purchase the equipment from Ambel. Ambel claims that Victor is obligated to purchase the equipment at a price of $191,000, as set forth in the purchase order.

- On October 8, a Victor salesperson orally contracted to service a piece of equipment owned by Clark Masons, Inc. The contract provided that for a period of 36 months, commencing November 1992, Victor would provide routine service for the equipment at a fixed price of $15,000, payable in three annual installments of $5,000 each. On October 29, Clark's president contacted Victor and stated that Clark did not intend to honor the service agreement because there was no written contract between Victor and Clark.

- On November 3, Victor received by mail a signed offer from GYX Erectors, Inc. The offer provided that Victor would service certain specified equipment owned by GYX for a two-year period for a total price of $81,000. The offer also provided as follows:

  "We need to know soon whether you can agree to the terms of this proposal. You must accept by November 15, or we will assume you can't meet our terms."

- On November 12, Victor mailed GYX a signed acceptance of GYX's offer. The acceptance was not received by GYX until November 17, and by then GYX had contracted with another party to provide service for its equipment. Victor has taken the position that GYX is obligated to honor its November 3 offer. GYX claims that no contract was formed because Victor's November 12 acceptance was not received timely by GYX.

- On December 19, Victor contracted in writing with Wells Landscaping Corp. The contract required Victor to deliver certain specified new equipment to Wells by December 31. On December 23, Victor determined that it would not be able to deliver the equipment to Wells by December 31 because of an inventory shortage. Therefore, Victor made a written assignment of the contract to Master Equipment, Inc. When Master attempted to deliver the equipment on December 31, Wells refused to accept it, claiming that Victor could not properly delegate its duties under the December 19 contract to another party without the consent of Wells. The contract is silent with regard to this issue.

Required:

State whether the claims of Ambel, Clark, GYX, and Wells are correct and give the reasons for your conclusions.   (11/93, Law, #4)

Essay 44-4 (15 to 25 minutes)

Debco Electronics, Inc. sells various brands of computer equipment to retail and business customers. An audit of Debco's 1991 financial statements has revealed the following transactions:

- On September 1, 1991, a Debco salesperson orally agreed to sell Rapid Computers, Inc. eight TMI computers for $11,000, to be delivered on October 15, 1991. Rapid sells computers to the general public. The Debco salesperson sent Rapid a signed confirmation of the sales agreement. Rapid received the confirmation on September 3, but did not respond to it. On October 15, 1991, Debco tendered delivery of the computers to Rapid. Rapid refused to accept delivery, claiming it had no obligation to buy the computers because it had not signed a contract with Debco.

- On October 12, 1991, Debco mailed TMI Computers, Inc. a signed purchase order for certain specified computers for delivery by November 30, 1991. The purchase order also stated the following:

This purchase order will not be withdrawn on or before October 31, 1991. You must accept by that date or we will assume you cannot meet our terms. Ship F.O.B.-- our loading dock.

TMI received the purchase order on October 15, 1991.

- On October 25, Debco mailed the following signed correspondence to TMI, which TMI received on October 29:

Cancel our October 12, 1991, purchase order. We have found a better price on the computers.

- On October 31, 1991, TMI mailed the following signed correspondence to Debco, which Debco received on November 3:

We have set aside the computers you ordered and turned down other offers for them. Therefore, we will ship the computers to you for delivery by November 30, 1991, F.O.B.-- your loading dock with payment terms 2/10; net 30.

There were no further communications between TMI and Debco.

TMI shipped the computers on November 15, and Debco received them on November 29. Debco refused to accept delivery. In justifying its refusal to accept delivery, Debco claimed the following:

- Its October 25 correspondence prevented the formation of a contract between Debco and TMI;
- TMI's October 31 correspondence was not an effective acceptance because it was not received by Debco until November 3;
- TMI's October 31 correspondence was not an effective acceptance because it added payment terms to Debco's purchase order.

Debco, Rapid, and TMI are located in a jurisdiction that has adopted the UCC.

Required:

a.   State whether Rapid's claim is correct and give the reasons for your conclusions.

b.   State whether Debco's claims are correct with regard to the transaction involving TMI and give the reasons for your conclusions.   (11/92, Law, #5)

Essay 44-5 (15 to 20 minutes)

On October 10, Vesta Electronics contracted with Zap Audio to sell Zap 200 18" stereo speakers. The contract provided that the speakers would be shipped F.O.B. seller's loading dock. The contract was silent as to when risk of loss for the speakers would pass to Zap. Delivery was to be completed by November 10.

On October 18, Vesta identified the speakers to be shipped to Zap and moved them to the loading dock. Before the carrier picked up the goods, a fire on Vesta's loading dock destroyed 50 of the speakers. On October 20, Vesta shipped, by common carrier, the remaining 150 18" speakers and 50 16" speakers. The truck carrying the speakers was involved in an accident resulting in damage to 25 of the 16" speakers. Zap received the 200 speakers on October 25, and on October 27 notified Vesta that 100 of the 18" speakers were being accepted but the rest of the shipment was being rejected. Zap also informed Vesta that, due to Vesta's failure to comply with the terms of the contract, Zap would contest paying the contract price and would sue for damages.

The above parties and transactions are subject to the Uniform Commercial Code (UCC).

Required:

Answer the following questions, and give the reasons for your conclusions.

a.   1.   Who bears the risk of loss for the 50 destroyed 18" speakers?
       2.   Who bears the risk of loss for the 25 damaged 16" speakers?

b.   1.   Was Zap's rejection of the 16" speakers valid?
       2.   Was Zap's acceptance of some of the 18" speakers valid?

c. Under the UCC, what duties are required of Zap after rejecting all or part of the shipment?

(11/91, Law, #4)

Essay 44-6 (15 to 20 minutes)

Pharo Aviation, Inc., sells and services used airplanes. Sanders, Pharo's service department manager, negotiated with Secure Equipment Co. for the purchase of a used tug for moving airplanes in and out of Pharo's hangar. Secure sells and services tugs and related equipment. Sanders was unfamiliar with the various models, specifications, and capacities of the tugs sold by Secure; however, Sanders knew that the tug purchased needed to have the capacity to move airplanes weighing up to 10,000 pounds. Sanders and the sales representative discussed this specific need because Sanders was uncertain as to which tug would meet Pharo's requirements. The sales representative then recommended a particular make and model of tug. Sanders agreed to rely on the sales representative's advice and signed a purchase contract with Secure.

About a week after Sanders took delivery, the following occurred:

- Sanders determined that the tug did not have the capacity to move airplanes weighing over 5,000 pounds.
- Sanders was advised correctly by Maco Equipment Distributors, Inc., that Maco was the rightful owner of the tug, which it had left with Secure for repairs.

Pharo has commenced a lawsuit against Secure claiming that implied warranties were created by the contract with Secure and that these have been breached. Maco has claimed that it is entitled to the tug and has demanded its return from Pharo.

Required:

Answer each of the following questions, and set forth the reasons for your conclusions.

a. Were any implied warranties created by the contract between Pharo and Secure and, if so, were any of those warranties breached?

b. Is Maco entitled to the return of the tug?

(11/90, Law, #4a, b)

Essay 44-7 (6 to 8 minutes)

Maple owns 75% of the common stock of Salam Exterminating, Inc. Maple is not an officer or employee of the corporation, and does not serve on its board of directors. Salam is in the business of providing exterminating services to residential and commercial customers.

Dodd performed exterminating services on behalf of Salam. Dodd suffered permanent injuries as a result of inhaling one of the chemicals used by Salam. This occurred after Dodd sprayed the chemical in a restaurant that Salam regularly services. Dodd was under the supervision of one of Salam's district managers and was trained by Salam to perform exterminating services following certain procedures, which he did. Later that day, several patrons who ate at the restaurant also suffered permanent injuries as a result of inhaling the chemical. The chemical was manufactured by Ace Chemical Corp. and sold and delivered to Salam in a closed container. It was not altered by Salam. It has now been determined that the chemical was defectively manufactured and the injuries suffered by Dodd and the restaurant patrons were a direct result of the defect.

Salam has complied with an applicable compulsory workers' compensation statute by obtaining an insurance policy from Spear Insurance Co.

As a result of the foregoing, the following action has been commenced:

- Dodd sued Ace based on strict liability in tort.

Required:

Discuss the merits of the action commenced by Dodd indicating the likely outcome and your reasons therefor.

(11/88, Law, #3)

ESSAY SOLUTIONS

Solution 44-3 Mistake/Statute of Frauds/Acceptance/Assignment

Ambel is incorrect. The general rule is that when a party **knows**, or **reasonably should know, that a mistake has been made** in the making of an offer, the **mistaken party will be granted relief from the offer**. In this case, because Ambel was aware of the approximate fair market value of the equipment, it had **reason to be aware of the mathematical error** made by Victor and will not be allowed to take advantage of it.

Clark is correct. A contract that cannot by its terms be performed within one year from the date it is made must be **evidenced by a writing that satisfies the requirements of the Statute of Frauds**. The contract between Victor and Clark is **not enforceable** by Victor against Clark, because the contract was **oral** and provided for performance by the parties for **longer than one year from the date the contract was entered into**.

GYX is incorrect. An acceptance of an offer is **effective when dispatched** (in this case, when mailed), provided that the **appropriate mode of communication** is used. The **general rule is that an offer shall be interpreted as inviting acceptance in any manner and by any medium reasonable in the circumstances**. In this case, GYX made its offer by mail. An acceptance by mail, if properly addressed with adequate postage affixed, would be considered a **reasonable manner and method of acceptance**. Therefore, Victor's acceptance was **effective** (and a contract was formed) **when the acceptance was mailed** on November 12 and **not when received** by GYX on November 17.

Wells is incorrect. As a general rule, **most contracts are assignable and delegable unless: prohibited** in the contract, the duties are **personal in nature,** or the assignment or delegation is **prohibited by statute or public policy**. Victor was entitled to assign the contract to Master, because none of these exceptions apply to the contract.

Solution 44-4 UCC Sales/Statute of Frauds

a. Rapid's claim is incorrect. Both Debco and Rapid are **merchants under the UCC** because they **both deal in the type of goods involved in the transaction** (computers).

The UCC provides that a **confirmation satisfies the UCC Statute of Frauds**, if an oral contract between merchants is:

- Confirmed **in writing** within a **reasonable period of time,** and
- The confirmation is **signed** by the party sending it and **received** by the other party.

Both parties are bound even though the party receiving the confirmation fails to sign it. This is correct unless the party receiving the confirmation submits a **written objection within 10 days of receipt.** Rapid **will be bound even though it did not sign the confirmation** because no written objection was made.

b. Debco's first claim, that its October 25 correspondence prevented the formation of a contract, is incorrect. Debco's October 12 purchase order will be regarded as a **firm offer under the UCC** because:

- Debco is a **merchant**.
- The purchase order is **in writing and signed**.
- The purchase order **states that it will not be withdrawn for the time specified**.

Because Debco's October 12 purchase order is considered a **firm offer**, Debco **cannot revoke it**, and its October 25 attempt to do so is ineffective.

Debco's second claim, that TMI's October 31 correspondence is not an effective acceptance because it was not received until November 3, is incorrect. An acceptance of an offer is effective **when dispatched** (in this case, when mailed), provided that an **appropriate mode of communication is used.** The UCC provides that an offer shall be construed as inviting acceptance in any manner and by any medium reasonable in the circumstances. In this case, Debco made its offer by mail, which, if adequately addressed with proper postage affixed, would be considered a reasonable manner and medium for acceptance. As a result, TMI's acceptance was **effective when mailed** on October 31.

Debco's third claim, that TMI's acceptance is not effective because it added payment terms to Debco's offer, is also incorrect. The UCC provides that a **definite and timely expression of acceptance of an offer will form a contract,** even if the terms of the acceptance are different from those in the offer, **unless acceptance is expressly made conditional on accepting the different terms**. Therefore, TMI's October 31 correspondence, which expressly stated that TMI would ship the computers ordered by Debco, was an **effective acceptance**, and a contract was formed despite the fact that TMI added payment terms.

Solution 44-5 Risk of Loss/Rejection of Goods

a. **1.** Vesta Electronics would bear the risk of loss for the 18" speakers destroyed by the fire on its loading dock. Even though Vesta **identified and segregated** the goods on its loading dock, the **risk of loss remained with the seller** because the contract's shipping terms "F.O.B. seller's loading dock" made it a **shipping contract**. Thus, **risk of loss does not pass** to Zap until the goods are **delivered to the carrier**.

2. The risk of loss for the 16" speakers also remained with Vesta. Even though the goods were delivered to the common carrier, risk of loss did not pass because Vesta shipped **nonconforming goods**.

b. **1.** Zap may validly reject the 16" speakers because **any buyer may reject nonconforming goods**. To avoid potential liability, the rejection must be made within a **reasonable time** of receipt and must be **communicated to the seller**.

2. Zap may also validly accept some of the 18" speakers. A buyer **may accept none, all, or any commercial unit** of a shipment **when nonconforming goods are shipped**.

c. To be entitled to damages, Zap must comply with the UCC by **notifying Vesta of the rejection of the goods within a reasonable time**; acting in **good faith** with respect to the rejected goods by following any reasonable instructions of the seller; and giving Vesta the **opportunity to cure** until the contract time of performance expires.

Solution 44-6 Implied Warranties

a. Under the UCC Sales Article, the contract between Pharo and Secure creates the following implied warranties:

- Implied warranty of **merchantability**;
- Implied warranty of **fitness for a particular purpose**;
- Implied warranty of **title**.

The implied warranty of merchantability requires the tug to be **merchantable**; that is, **fit for the ordinary purpose intended**. It is probable that the tug was fit for such ordinary purposes and, therefore, the implied warranty of merchantability was not breached.

The implied warranty of fitness for a particular purpose requires that the tug be fit for the **particular purpose for which it was purchased**. To show that the implied warranty of fitness for a particular purpose is present as a result of the contract, Pharo must show that:

- Secure knew of the **particular needs** of Pharo;
- Pharo **relied on** Secure to select a **suitable tug**;
- Secure **knew** that Pharo was relying on Secure to select a tug suitable for Pharo's needs.

The implied warranty of fitness for a particular purpose has been breached because the tug was not suitable for Pharo's particular needs (i.e., to move airplanes weighing up to 10,000 pounds).

The implied warranty of title requires that:

- Secure have **good title**;
- The **transfer** to Pharo would be **rightful**;
- The tug would be delivered **free from any security interest or other lien**.

The implied warranty of title has been breached because Maco was the rightful owner.

b. Maco will not be entitled to recover the tug from Pharo because:

- Maco had entrusted the tug to Secure, which **deals in similar goods**;
- That, as a result of such entrustment, Secure had the **power to transfer** Maco's rights to the tug to a **buyer in the ordinary course of business**;
- Pharo was a **buyer in the ordinary course of business** because Pharo purchased the tug in **good faith** and **without knowledge** of Maco's ownership interest.

Solution 44-7 Strict Liability in Tort

Dodd's action against Ace based on strict liability in tort will be successful. Generally, in order to establish a cause of action based on **strict liability in tort**, it must be shown that: the product was in **defective**

condition when it left the possession or control of the seller; the product was **unreasonably dangerous** to the consumer or user; the **cause of the consumer's or user's injury was the defect**; the **seller engaged in the business of selling such a product**; and the product was one which the **seller expected to, and, did reach the consumer or user without substantial changes in the condition in which it was sold**. Under the facts of this case, Ace will be liable based on strict liability in tort because all of the elements necessary to state such a cause of action have been met. The fact that Dodd is entitled to **workers' compensation benefits does not preclude Dodd from recovering** based on strict liability in tort from a third party (Ace).

---

seller engaged in selling

CHANGE ALERT

UCC Article 3, *Negotiable Instruments*, has undergone revision. The revised Article 3 eliminates the requirement for a <u>check</u> to be payable to order or bearer to be negotiable. The revision contains other changes, which are incorporated in Chapter 45.

CHAPTER 45

COMMERCIAL PAPER

I. **Definitions** 45-3
   A.   Acceptance 45-3
   B.   Accommodation Party 45-3
   C.   Alteration 45-3
   D.   Anomalous Indorsement 45-3
   E.   Check 45-3
   F.   Dishonor 45-3
   G.   Draft 45-3
   H.   Holder 45-3
   I.   Negotiation 45-3
   J.   Note 45-3
   K.   Order 45-3
   L.   Presentment 45-4
   M.   Promise 45-4

II. **The Concept of Negotiability and Holder in Due Course** 45-4

III. **Types of Commercial Paper** 45-4
   A.   Draft 45-4
   B.   Check 45-5
   C.   Certificate of Deposit 45-5
   D.   Note 45-5
   E.   Other Types 45-5

IV. **Formal Requirements of Negotiability** 45-6
   A.   Prerequisites 45-6
   B.   Writing and Signature 45-7
   C.   Unconditional Order or Promise to Pay 45-7
   D.   Payable on Demand or at a Definite Time 45-8
   E.   Words of Negotiability 45-9

V. **Interpretation and Construction** 45-10
   A.   Construction of Ambiguities (UCC 3-118) 45-10
   B.   Dating of Instruments 45-10
   C.   Place of Payment 45-10
   D.   Designation of Payees (UCC 3-116) 45-11
   E.   Incomplete Instruments (UCC 3-115) 45-11
   F.   Modification of Terms (UCC 3-119) 45-11

VI. **Issue and Negotiation** 45-11
   A.   Issue 45-11
   B.   Negotiation (UCC 3-202) 45-11
   C.   Transfer Without Negotiation (UCC 3-201) 45-12
   D.   Rescission of Negotiation (UCC 3-207) 45-12
   E.   Reacquisition of an Instrument (UCC 3-208) 45-12

VII. Endorsement 45-12
    A.   Definition 45-12
    B.   Mechanics of Endorsement 45-13
    C.   Effect of Endorsement 45-13
    D.   Types of Endorsements 45-13

VIII. Holder in Due Course (HDC) 45-15
    A.   Requirements 45-15
    B.   Rights of a Holder in Due Course 45-18

IX. Defenses 45-18
    A.   Personal Defenses (UCC 3-306) 45-18
    B.   Real Defenses [UCC 3-305 (2)] 45-20

X. Liability of the Parties 45-22
    A.   Importance of the Signature 45-22
    B.   Contractual Liability 45-23
    C.   Warranty Liability 45-26
    D.   Effect of Warranty Liability 45-27
    E.   Finality of Acceptance of Payment 45-27
    F.   Statute of Limitations 45-28

XI. Presentment, Dishonor, Notice of Dishonor 45-28
    A.   Presentment 45-28
    B.   Dishonor (UCC 3-507) 45-30
    C.   Notice of Dishonor (UCC 3-508) 45-30
    D.   Protest 45-30
    E.   Excuse (UCC 3-511) 45-31

XII. Discharge From Liability 45-32
    A.   Effect of a Negotiable Instrument on the Underlying Obligation 45-32
    B.   Methods of Discharging a Party's Liability 45-32
    C.   Discharge as a Defense 45-34

XIII. Special Rules Applicable to Checks 45-34
    A.   Checks 45-34
    B.   Relationship Between Drawer-Depositor and Drawee-Bank 45-34
    C.   Duties Owed by the Bank to the Depositor 45-34
    D.   Depositor's Duty to the Bank 45-35

CHAPTER 45

COMMERCIAL PAPER

I. Definitions

A. <u>Acceptance</u>--The drawee's signed engagement to honor a draft as presented (UCC 3-410). It must be written on the draft and becomes operative when completed by delivery or notification.

B. <u>Accommodation Party</u>--One who signs the instrument in any capacity for the purpose of lending his or her name to the instrument [UCC 3-415 (1)].

C. <u>Alteration (Material)</u>--An alteration is material when it changes the contract of any party [UCC 3-407(1)]. <u>Material changes</u> include the following:

    1. Alteration of the number or relationship of parties.

    2. Completion of an incomplete instrument in any manner except as authorized.

    3. Addition to or deletion from a signed writing.

D. <u>Anomalous Indorsement</u>--An indorsement by someone not the holder or the holder's authorized agent is known as an "anomalous indorsement." Such an indorser has the status of an ordinary indorser. However, the anomalous indorsement has no effect on the character of the paper as being order or bearer.

E. <u>Check</u>--A draft drawn on a bank and payable on demand (UCC 3-104).

F. <u>Dishonor</u>--An instrument is dishonored when acceptance or payment cannot be obtained after making any necessary presentment [UCC 3-507(1)].

G. <u>Draft</u>--A draft is an order from one person (drawer) to another person (drawee) to pay a third person (payee) a sum of money. For example, a check is a draft drawn on a bank (drawee) by the drawer and is payable on demand (UCC 3-104).

H. <u>Holder</u>--A person who is in possession of a document of title or an instrument, or of an investment security drawn, issued, or endorsed to the person, his or her order, to bearer, or in blank [UCC 1-201(20)].

I. <u>Negotiation</u>--The transfer of both the title and possession of an instrument in such form that the transferee becomes a holder (UCC 3-202).

J. <u>Note</u>--A written promise by "the maker" to pay a sum of money to "the payee." It may be payable on demand, at a specified future date, or in installments (UCC 3-104).

K. <u>Order</u>--An order is a direction to pay, not a mere authorization or request. It must identify the person to pay with reasonable certainty. It may be addressed to one or more such persons jointly or in the alternative but not in succession [UCC 3-102(1)(b)]. For example, "Pay to the order of Jones" is an order, but "I wish you would pay" is not an order. Checks and drafts must contain an order to pay a sum certain.

L.   <u>Presentment</u>--A demand for acceptance or payment made upon the maker, acceptor, drawee, or other payor by or on behalf of the holder [UCC 3-504(1)].

M.   <u>Promise</u>--A promise is an undertaking to pay, not a mere acknowledgment of a debt or obligation [UCC 3-102(1)(c)]. For example, "I promise to pay" is a promise, but "IOU $500" is not a promise. Notes and certificates of deposit must contain a promise to pay a sum certain.

II. The Concept of Negotiability and Holder in Due Course

The basic idea of commercial paper (negotiable instruments) is to facilitate the transfer and payment of money using a contractual obligation (negotiable instrument) in lieu of the money itself. Implicit in this scheme is the idea that the transferee should obtain at least the same quality of title in the instrument as was possessed by his or her transferor. In order to accomplish this goal, Article 3 (Commercial Paper) and Article 4 (Bank Deposits and Collections) prescribe rules for the orderly transfer and payment of negotiable instruments. The two most important concepts in commercial paper are the concepts of <u>negotiability</u> and <u>holder in due course</u> (HDC). We will develop each of these concepts in detail. Furthermore, you must understand each concept in order to work with Article 3. By way of introduction, we will sketch an outline of negotiability and HDC.

TotalRecall

ELEMENTS OF NEGOTIABILITY	HOLDER IN DUE COURSE
D Payable on **demand** or at a **definite** time.	**V** Takes instrument for **value**.
U **Unconditional** promise to pay.	**F** Takes instrument in good **faith**.
M Promise to pay a certain sum of **money**.	**W** Takes instrument **without** notice of dishonor, defense, or claim.
B Payable to **bearer** or	
O Payable to **order**.	
S In writing, **signed** by the maker or drawer.	

III. Types of Commercial Paper

There are four types of commercial paper covered by Article 3 (UCC 3-104):

• Drafts   • Checks   • Certificates of Deposit   • Notes

A.   <u>Draft</u>--A written order from one person (the <u>drawer</u>) directing a second person (the <u>drawee</u>) to pay a sum certain in money to the order of a third person (the <u>payee</u>) or to the order of the bearer of the draft.

    1.   A draft may be a <u>sight</u> draft (payable on delivery and presentment to the drawer) or a <u>time</u> draft (payable within a certain time).

    2.   Examples of drafts include the following:

        a.   <u>Trade Acceptance</u>--A draft drawn by the seller-drawer on the buyer-drawee that is payable to the seller at some certain future date in the amount of the purchase price. The seller transmits the draft to the buyer for "acceptance," that is, for the buyer's signed engagement written on the draft to honor the draft as presented.

b.   Banker's Acceptance--Similar to trade acceptances <u>except</u> that the check (draft drawn on a bank) is drawn on the buyer's bank rather than on the buyer personally. Banker's acceptances are more marketable than are trade acceptances.

B.   Check--A draft drawn on a bank and payable on demand.

1.   Bank Draft--A draft (check) drawn by one bank on another bank.

<u>Example 1</u>

A purchaser in New York is dealing with a seller in California. In order to assure payment, the seller requires a bank draft. Purchaser obtains a bank draft from his or her bank in New York (drawer-bank). The draft is drawn on a local bank in California (drawee-bank) and is payable to the seller.

---

2.   Cashier's Check--A check drawn by a bank <u>on itself</u>, ordering itself to pay a sum of money to a third person. A check may be either an ordinary check, a cashier's check, or a teller's check. The name on the paper is not controlling. Unless otherwise agreed, the delivery of a certified check, a cashier's check, or a teller's check discharges the debt for which it is given, up to the amount of the check.

C.   Certificate of Deposit--A written acknowledgment by a bank of the receipt of a stated sum of money with an engagement to repay that sum.

D.   Note--A written promise to pay a stated sum of money. The promisor is the "<u>maker</u>," and the person receiving the sum of money is the "<u>payee</u>" or the "<u>bearer</u>." Notes may be made payable on demand or on a stated date.

E.   Other Types of Commercial Paper and Contract Instruments Which May or May Not Be Negotiable--There is a significant difference in the case of transferability of a negotiable instrument as opposed to a nonnegotiable instrument. The former is covered by the UCC while the latter is governed by the contract law of assignments. Furthermore, negotiable instruments may be transferred by negotiation (the usual case) or by assignment (occurs when the transfer falls short of a "negotiation"). Nonnegotiable instruments can only be transferred by assignment. The superiority of "negotiation" as compared to assignment can be illustrated as follows:

ASSIGNMENT	NEGOTIATION
• Nonnegotiable instruments (e.g., contract rights) cannot be assigned if the contract right states that attempted assignments are "void."	• Negotiable instruments are fully transferable; in some cases, by delivery alone; in others, by endorsement and delivery.
• In an assignment, the assignee (person receiving the property) can take no greater interest than was owned by the assignor (person transferring the property). For example, if A steals a car and sells it to C, C can obtain no title to the car, even if C was an innocent purchaser for fair value.	• In a negotiable instrument transfer, the holder (transferee) can acquire greater rights in the property transferred than were possessed by the transferor. For example, if C was a holder in due course of a stolen negotiable instrument signed in blank, C's title would be superior to the original owner's title because the instrument was negotiable by transfer alone.
• In an assignment, the assignee takes the instrument subject to any defenses available against the assignor.	• In a transfer of a negotiable instrument, a holder in due course generally takes free of defenses available against the transferor.
• In an assignment, the assignee must give notice to the obligor (payor) in order to protect him- or herself from defenses the obligor may acquire prior to notice of the assignment.	• In a negotiable instrument transfer, the holder in due course generally takes free of defenses regardless of when they arose.

The following are examples of <u>nonnegotiable instruments</u>:

1. <u>Contract Rights</u>--An interest which is nonnegotiable but which is usually assignable.

2. <u>Letter of Credit</u>--A nonnegotiable instrument that is an engagement (usually by a bank) made at the request of a bank customer which states that the bank issuer will make payments and otherwise honor its customer's obligations. The person in whose favor the letter is prepared may then draw on the bank from the account of the customer who procured the letter.

IV. Formal Requirements of Negotiability

A. <u>Prerequisites</u>--In order to be a negotiable instrument, the writing must possess all of the following four (4) prerequisites (UCC 3-104):

1. The instrument must be <u>in writing and signed</u> by the maker (note) or drawer (draft, check).

2. The instrument must contain an <u>unconditional</u> promise or order to pay a <u>sum certain</u> in money and have no other promise, order, obligation, or power given by the maker or drawer <u>except</u> as authorized by Article 3 of the Uniform Commercial Code.

3. The instrument must be payable on <u>demand</u> or at a <u>definite</u> time.

4. The instrument must be payable to <u>order</u> or to <u>bearer</u> (these are the magic words of negotiability).

   NOTE: These requirements (along with HDC requirements) must be memorized. A detailed discussion of the requirements of negotiability is included in B. through E., below.

B. **Writing and Signature**--The instrument must be in writing and signed by either the maker (if a note or certificate of deposit) or drawer (if a check or other draft).

1. Writing--Handwriting, printing, typewriting, any intentional reduction to written form.

2. Signature--No particular form is required, but there must be some symbol placed somewhere on the instrument. Additionally, the symbol must be intended to operate as a signature (UCC 3-401).

C. **Unconditional Order or Promise to Pay**--The instrument must contain an unconditional promise (note or certificate of deposit) or order (check or draft) to pay a <u>sum certain in money</u>.

1. "Promise"--A promise is an undertaking to pay, not a mere acknowledgment of debt. For example, "I promise to pay" is a promise, but "IOU $500" is not a promise [UCC 3-102(1)(c)].

2. "Order"--An order is a direction to pay, not a mere authorization or request. For example, "Pay to the order of Jones" is an order, but "I wish you (the drawee) would pay" is not an order [UCC 3-102(1)(b)].

3. "Unconditional"--The obligation to pay must be expressed in absolute, unqualified terms.

   a. The promise or order is <u>conditional</u> (and the instrument nonnegotiable) if either of the following is present [UCC 3-105(2)]:

      (1) The instrument states that it is <u>subject to another agreement</u>. For example, a note states on its face that payment is to be made <u>only</u> if a certain act is performed. "Subject to" language will <u>destroy</u> negotiability because the terms of payment of the instrument cannot be determined by looking at the instrument alone; some other document must be consulted. However, if the note made no mention of any condition (e.g., the condition was oral), then the note would be negotiable. This results from the fact that an examination of the note itself indicated that the promise was unconditional.

      (2) The instrument states that it is to be paid <u>only</u> from a certain fund or source. The instrument is conditional because its payment depends on the existence or sufficiency of the fund or source. However, this rule does <u>not apply</u> if the instrument is issued by a governmental entity.

   b. The promise or order is <u>not conditional</u> (it is an "unconditional promise or order") even though the following are present [UCC 3-105(1)]:

      (1) The instrument is subject only to implied or constructive conditions.

      (2) The instrument recites that consideration has been given and/or that the instrument arose from or refers to a separate agreement. For example, if an instrument, which is otherwise negotiable, recites that it is given as payment "as per" or "in accordance with" some other contractual instrument, this reference will not destroy negotiability. Additionally, if the negotiable instrument states that it is drawn "as per a letter of credit" or that "it is secured by a mortgage," negotiability is not destroyed. In contrast, if the instrument expressly recites that it is "subject to" or "governed by" any other agreement, this conditional language will destroy negotiability.

(3) The instrument refers to a particular account or source from which reimbursement is expected. For example, if the instrument merely refers to the account that is later to bear the expense, this will not destroy negotiability (e.g., "charge inventory account"). A different result (nonnegotiability) will occur if the instrument is nongovernmental and that account and no other can be charged.

(4) The instrument is limited to payment out of the entire assets of a partnership, unincorporated association, trust, or estate, or out of a particular government fund.

(5) The instrument recites that it is secured by a mortgage or otherwise.

(6) The instrument recites that other promises have been made so long as payment is <u>not</u> conditioned on those promises.

4. "Sum Certain"

a. The amount to be paid is a sum certain if the holder can determine the amount payable at the <u>time of payment</u>.

b. A sum payable may be certain even if it is to be paid in the following manner (UCC 3-106):

(1) With stated <u>interest</u> or "with interest" (in this case, the rate of interest is that legal judgment rate declared by law).

(2) With a stated <u>discount</u> or addition which is dependent on the date of payment.

(3) With currency <u>exchange rate</u> added or subtracted.

(4) With <u>attorney's fees</u> and/or <u>collection fees</u> on default.

5. "Money"--Money is defined as a medium of exchange accepted as the currency of any domestic or foreign government.

• A promise or order to do something in addition to the payment of money renders the instrument <u>nonnegotiable</u>. However, the following do <u>not</u> affect negotiability (UCC 3-112):

(1) Authorizing the sale of collateral securities on default.

(2) Requiring the maintenance of collateral or the giving of additional collateral.

(3) Authorizing a confession of judgment on default.

(4) Waiving the benefit of a law intended to protect the obligor (e.g., presentment or notice of dishonor).

(5) Stating that the payee acknowledges full satisfaction of the drawer's obligation when the payee endorses a draft.

D. <u>Payable on Demand or at a Definite Time</u>--The instrument must be payable on demand or at a definite time.

1. An instrument is payable on <u>demand</u> (UCC 3-108):

   a. If it states that it is payable at sight or on presentation.

   b. If no time for payment is stated. (Most checks are payable on demand.)

2. An instrument is payable at a <u>definite time</u>, if by its terms, it is payable as follows (UCC 3-109):

   a. On or before a stated date or a fixed period after a stated date.

   b. At a fixed period after sight.

   c. At a definite time subject to any acceleration (e.g., "Full amount due if any delinquency occurs," or "Full amount due 30 days after notice by holder").

   d. At a definite time subject to extension.

      (1) At the option of the holder, or

      (2) At the option of the maker or acceptor, but only to a further definite time, or automatically upon the occurrence of a specified event.

3. An instrument is <u>not</u> payable at a definite time, and hence not negotiable, if it is payable only upon the occurrence of an event <u>uncertain</u> as to time of occurrence (e.g., "Payable at death" is nonnegotiable; however, "Payable on January 1, 1995, or if death occurs before that date, then on the date of death," is negotiable because the date is certain subject to acceleration).

E. <u>Words of Negotiability</u>--All instruments, except checks, <u>must</u> be payable to <u>order</u> or to <u>bearer</u>, or equivalent wording must be used. These are the magic words of negotiability. They must appear on the instrument for it to be negotiable.

NOTE: The Article 3 Revision changed the requirements of negotiability for <u>checks</u>. It is no longer required that <u>checks</u> be payable to order or bearer.

1. Payable to Order

   a. Order paper is payable "to the order of any person" or "to a person or the person's order." The person must be specified with reasonable certainty (e.g., "to the order of A" or "to A or A's order").

   b. An instrument may be payable to the order of the following:

      (1) The maker or drawer.

      (2) The drawee.

      (3) A payee other than the above.

      (4) Two or more payees jointly or in the alternative (jointly, "to A and B"; alternatively, "to A or B").

      (5) An estate, trust, or fund.

    (6)   An office, or an officer by his or her title as such.

    (7)   A partnership or unincorporated association.

  c.   If payable merely to a <u>specific person</u>, it is <u>not</u> payable to order and <u>not negotiable</u> (e.g., "Pay John Doe").

2.   <u>Payable to Bearer</u>--Bearer paper is payable to the following (UCC 3-111):

  a.   "Bearer" or "the order of bearer."

  b.   "A specified person or bearer" (e.g., "to John Jones or bearer"; however, "to John Jones, bearer" is nonnegotiable).

  c.   "Cash," the order of "cash," or any other indication which does not purport to designate a specific payee.

3.   If the instrument states that it is payable to order <u>and</u> to bearer, it is payable to order, <u>unless</u> the bearer words are <u>typed or handwritten</u>, i.e., if the bearer words are printed, the instrument is payable to order [UCC 3-110(3)].

V. Interpretation and Construction

A.   <u>Construction of Ambiguities (UCC 3-118)</u>

  1.   If there is doubt as to whether an instrument is a draft or a note, the holder may treat it as either. If the drawer and drawee of a draft are the same person, the holder may treat it as a note.

  2.   <u>Handwritten</u> terms control typewritten and printed terms. <u>Typewritten</u> terms control printed terms.

  3.   <u>Words</u> control figures unless the words are ambiguous.

  4.   A provision for interest, unless otherwise specified, means interest at the legal judgment rate obtained at the place of payment. Interest runs from the date of the instrument or, if none, the date of issue.

  5.   Two or more persons signing an instrument as part of one transaction in the capacity of maker, acceptor, drawer, or endorser and as part of the same transaction are <u>jointly and severally liable</u>, unless the instrument specifies otherwise, even if the words "I promise to pay" appear.

  6.   Consent to the extension of time for payment authorizes one extension not longer than the original period, unless otherwise specified.

B.   <u>Dating of Instruments</u>--An instrument may be undated, antedated, or post-dated without affecting negotiability. It is payable at the time fixed on the instrument if the instrument is payable on demand or payable at a fixed period after date (UCC 3-114).

C.   <u>Place of Payment</u>

  1.   The omission of a place for payment does not render an instrument nonnegotiable.

2. An instrument "payable through" a bank designates that bank as a collecting bank to make presentment (see XI.A., below), but does not grant the bank authority to pay (UCC 3-120).

3. An instrument "payable at" a bank is, in some states, equivalent to a draft drawn on the bank, but in most states, it is merely the designation of a place of payment (UCC 3-121).

D. Designation of Payees (UCC 3-116)

1. If an instrument is payable to the order of two or more payees in the alternative, the rights with respect to that instrument may be exercised by any of them who has possession.

2. If an instrument is payable to the order of two or more payees not in the alternative ("to A and B"), any rights as to the instrument must be exercised by all of them together (thus, both A and B must endorse the instrument to obtain payment).

E. Incomplete Instruments (UCC 3-115)

1. A signed instrument which is incomplete in any necessary respect (e.g., amount payable) is unenforceable until completed.

2. If completed in accordance with authority to complete, it is effective as completed.

3. If completed in an unauthorized manner, the completion is treated as a material alteration. The burden of showing lack of authority is on the person asserting it.

F. Modification of Terms (UCC 3-119)

1. A transferor and a transferee of a negotiable instrument may modify its terms by a written agreement executed as part of the same transaction.

2. Subsequent holders are bound by the agreement unless they are holders in due course (HDC) without notice of the modifying agreement.

VI. Issue and Negotiation

A. Issue--The initial delivery of a negotiable instrument [UCC 3-102 (1)(a)], usually by the maker or drawer, to a holder who is usually the payee (e.g., a purchaser-maker issues a 30-day promissory note upon taking delivery of goods).

B. Negotiation (UCC 3-202)--Following issue, a negotiable instrument is subsequently transferred by negotiation or assignment. If transfer is by negotiation, the transferee is a holder (or if the transferee qualifies, an HDC). If the transfer is by assignment, the transferee is an assignee (see III.E., above).

1. Bearer paper is negotiated by delivery alone (delivery is defined as the voluntary transfer of possession). Thus, a thief can deliver stolen bearer paper to an HDC. The HDC will have rights in that paper superior to the original true owner. This follows because delivery of bearer paper is negotiation of that paper.

2. Order paper is negotiated by proper endorsement plus delivery. The proper party for endorsement is always the holder or someone authorized to sign on behalf of the holder.

3. The result of negotiation is that the transferee becomes a "holder." (Holder is a person who is in possession of an instrument drawn, issued, or endorsed to him or her, to his or her order, or in blank.)

C. <u>Transfer Without Negotiation (UCC 3-201)</u>--For example, order paper is delivered but not endorsed.

    1. The transferee by assignment obtains possession of the instrument. (Assignment merely requires delivery; negotiation of an order instrument requires endorsement and delivery.) The assignee only obtains the rights held by the transferor. Additionally, the assignee is subject to any claims and defenses against the assignor.

    2. The transferee-assignee has the specifically enforceable right to the unconditional endorsement of the transferor. Only at that time will a transferee for value become a holder and possibly a holder in due course (if other requirements of HDC are satisfied).

D. <u>Rescission of Negotiation (UCC 3-207)</u>

    1. The right to rescind negotiation may exist when negotiation was

        a. Made by one without capacity.

        b. Obtained by fraud, duress, or mistake.

        c. Part of an illegal transaction.

        d. Made in breach of a duty.

    2. Even though the right to rescind exists, the negotiation remains effective until the right is exercised.

    3. Negotiation <u>cannot</u> be rescinded against a subsequent <u>HDC</u>.

E. <u>Reacquisition of an Instrument (UCC 3-208)</u>

    1. A party who reacquires an instrument may cancel any endorsement not necessary to the party's title (e.g., those following the initial endorsement to him or her).

    2. Intervening parties are discharged from liability against any party subsequent to the reacquirer, except an <u>HDC</u>.

    3. If the reacquirer <u>cancels</u> the intervening endorsements, the discharge is effective even against subsequent <u>HDCs</u> because the cancellation is notice of the discharge.

    4. The negotiation of commercial paper cannot be set aside if the paper is held by a person paying the instrument in good faith and without knowledge of the facts on which the rescission claim is based.

VII. Endorsement

A. <u>Definition</u>--Signing one's name on the instrument with or without other words.

B.   Mechanics of Endorsement

    1.   May be typewritten or rubber stamped (UCC 3-401), or an agent may endorse an instrument for the holder (UCC 3-403).

    2.   Endorsement must convey the entire instrument; otherwise, the transfer is considered a partial assignment and not a negotiation.

    3.   If the payee's name is misspelled or is incorrect, the payee may endorse in that name or his or her own or both; a purchaser for value may require his or her signature in both names (UCC 3-203).

    4.   If a signature is so placed that it is not clear in what capacity the person signed, he or she is deemed to be an endorser (UCC 3-402).

C.   Effect of Endorsement

    1.   Endorsement, unless qualified, will establish the endorser's secondary liability; i.e., the endorser is bound to pay the instrument if it is not honored by the maker or drawee (see X., below).

    2.   Endorsement (plus delivery) is necessary to negotiate order paper.

    3.   Endorsement and Bearer Paper

        a.   Bearer paper is paper that is bearer paper on its face (i.e., paper that is payable "to bearer," "to cash," "to a person or bearer," "to order of bearer," or "to order of cash").

        b.   Bearer paper can be transformed into order paper by making the last endorsement in the chain of endorsement a special endorsement [UCC 3-204(1)].

        c.   Order paper can be transformed into bearer paper by making the last endorsement in the chain of endorsement an endorsement in blank [UCC 3-204(2)].

    4.   Forged Endorsement

        a.   A drawee-bank generally does not bear the loss on an instrument with a forged endorsement. A drawee cannot be expected to be able to determine the validity of any endorsements except its drawer-customer's signature. The drawee-bank, after paying a forged instrument, may be indemnified by proceeding against the party who first accepted the forged instrument.

        b.   Distinguish Forged Drawer's Signature--Unlike the case of a forged endorsement, a drawee bank is charged with the recognition of its drawer-customer's signature. Thus, if the bank wrongfully pays an instrument on which the drawer's signature is forged, it has breached its contract with the drawer-customer and will (in the absence of substantial contributory negligence of the drawer) bear the loss.

    5.   See also IX.B.4., below.

D.   Types of Endorsements

    1.   Endorsement may be "in blank" or "special" (UCC 3-204).

a. Blank Endorsement--The transferor's signature appears alone, without specifying any particular endorsee. A blank endorsement converts order paper into bearer paper; further negotiation may be made by delivery only (no further endorsement is necessary).

b. Special Endorsement--Specifies the person to whose order the instrument is now payable. A special endorsement on bearer paper converts it to order paper.

Example 2

Check is payable "to the order of cash." Drawer is A and drawee is bank Z. When A endorses the check, he signs it "A." This is a bearer instrument that has been endorsed in blank. It remains a bearer instrument.

Example 3

Check is payable "to the order of A." A endorses the check by signing "A." The original order paper is now a bearer instrument due to the blank endorsement.

Example 4

Check is payable "to cash." A endorses the check by signing "Pay to the order of B" over her signature "A." The original bearer paper is now order paper due to the special endorsement.

---

2. Restrictive Endorsement

a. Types of restrictive endorsements are as follows (UCC 3-205):

(1) Words indicating a purpose of deposit or collection, e.g., "for deposit" or "pay any bank."

(2) Conditional, e.g., "pay Robert Jones upon the completion of building X."

(3) Purporting to prohibit further transfer or negotiation, e.g., "pay A only."

(4) Payable only for the use or benefit of another, e.g., "pay A in trust for B."

b. Effect of Restrictive Endorsement (UCC 3-206)

(1) Banks in the collection process may ignore restrictive endorsements except for those made by their immediate transferors.

(2) Aside from collecting banks, a transferee who accepts an instrument with a conditional or "deposit or collection" endorsement must give value consistent with the restriction in order to become a holder for value.

(3) A restrictive endorsement that purports to prohibit further negotiation is of no effect.

3.   Qualified Endorsement (UCC 3-414)

    a.   Usually characterized by writing "without recourse" on the instrument.

    b.   Effect

        (1)   Disclaims the endorser's secondary liability to pay the instrument in the event it is dishonored.

        (2)   Does not impair negotiability or prevent the transferee from becoming a holder in due course.

        (3)   Does not prevent the endorser from being liable for breach of warranty, but does limit the endorser's warranty that no defense is good against him or her to a warranty that he or she has no knowledge of a defense of any party [UCC 3-417(3)].

4.   Different types of endorsements may be used together so long as they are not inconsistent.

VIII. Holder in Due Course (HDC)

One who is a holder who takes a negotiable instrument for value, in good faith, and without notice that it is overdue, has been dishonored, or that there is any defense against or claim to it on the part of any person (UCC 3-302).

A.   <u>Requirements</u>--It is important to know about an HDC and what that status means. In order to qualify as an HDC, <u>all</u> of the requirements must be fulfilled.

    1.   HDC Must Be a Holder--A holder is one who takes by negotiation or issue. A holder has the right to transfer, negotiate, enforce payment, or discharge the instrument (UCC 3-301). A holder may strike out any endorsements not necessary to the holder's title. Finally, the holder is entitled to a rebuttable presumption of ownership of the instrument.

    2.   HDC Must Take the Instrument for Value--A holder gives value in the following ways (UCC 3-303):

        a.   To the extent the holder performs the agreed consideration.

            (1)   A promise to perform is not value <u>except</u> to the extent it has been performed.

            (2)   A negotiable instrument given for another instrument is considered to be "value" even though it is an executory promise because it can be negotiated to a holder in due course.

        b.   To the extent the holder acquires a security interest in the instrument, other than by legal process (e.g., the holder perfects a security interest in the instrument by taking possession of it as collateral for another debt).

        c.   By taking the instrument in payment of, or as security for, an antecedent claim against any person.

        d.   By giving a negotiable instrument in exchange for the instrument taken or by giving an irrevocable commitment to a third person in exchange for the negotiable instrument taken by the holder.

e. In the case of a bank, to the extent that the bank credits a depositor <u>and</u> permits a withdrawal of the deposited items. Thus, the bank becomes an HDC only when it permits the depositor to draw against the credited instrument.

   (1) For the purpose of tracing deposits to withdrawals, the first-in, first-out rule (FIFO) is used to determine whether the credit has been withdrawn.

   (2) Similarly, when a bank takes an instrument at a discount, it is giving "value" for the <u>face amount</u> of the discounted instrument.

<u>Example 5</u>

A depositor opens a checking account with a $5,000 check payable to the depositor that is subsequently specially endorsed to the bank (or endorsed in blank). The bank provisionally credits the depositor's account (before collecting on the deposited check) and permits the depositor to immediately draw on the $5,000 balance. To the extent the depositor draws from the $5,000 balance, the bank has given "value" and has become an HDC (assuming the bank knows no defense to the $5,000 check).

---

3. The HDC must take the instrument in good faith, i.e., there must be honesty in fact in the conduct or transaction at hand. This good faith test is a <u>subjective</u> test. The question is, did the holder exercise honesty in fact in taking the instrument?

4. The HDC must take the instrument without notice that it is overdue, has been dishonored, or that any person has a defense against it or claim to it.

   a. Taking Without Notice--In addition to taking for value and in good faith, the holder must take without notice.

      (1) The holder has notice of claim or defense when [UCC 1-201(25)]

         (a) He or she has actual knowledge of it.

         (b) He or she has received notice of it.

         (c) From all the facts or circumstances, he or she has reason to know of its existence.

         To be effective, notice must be received in time and in such manner as to give a reasonable opportunity to act on it.

      (2) One who receives notice after becoming a holder, but before completing his or her performance, takes without notice only to the extent of the performance given before he or she received notice (i.e., it is possible to be a holder in due course as to <u>part</u> of the instrument and a holder not in due course as to the rest).

   b. Overdue (UCC 3-503)

      (1) An instrument payable on a certain date becomes overdue at the beginning of the day after the due date.

      (2) An instrument payable on demand becomes overdue after a reasonable time has lapsed after issue.

      (a)   "Reasonable time" depends on facts and circumstances.

      (b)   A domestic check is presumed overdue thirty days after issue.

(3)   The following are indications that the instrument is overdue [UCC 3-304(3)]:

      (a)   Notice that part of the principal (but not interest) is overdue or that there has been default in payment of another instrument of the same series.

      (b)   Notice that acceleration of the instrument has been made.

      (c)   Notice that demand has been made on a demand instrument.

c.   Dishonored--An instrument is dishonored when <u>either</u> of the following occur [UCC 3-507(1)]:

(1)   Presentment is made and payment or acceptance is refused or cannot be made (in the case of bank collections, a check would be dishonored if it is returned by the midnight deadline).

(2)   Presentment is waived and the instrument is not accepted or paid.

d.   Defense or Claim--A holder cannot be an HDC if he or she takes the instrument with notice that any person has a defense against it or a claim to it.

(1)   The holder is on notice of a defense or claim in the following situations [UCC 3-304(1), (2)]:

      (a)   When the holder has notice that <u>any</u> party's obligation is voidable or that <u>all</u> parties have been discharged.

<u>Example 6</u>

A is induced by fraud to deliver a note to B. B negotiates the note to C who in turn negotiates it to D. D strikes out the endorsements of B and C (discharging them). Because not all of the parties have been discharged (A and D are still liable as maker and endorser, respectively), D's transferee, E, can still become an HDC and cut off A's defense of fraud in the inducement (personal defense).

      (b)   When the instrument is so incomplete or irregular (e.g., bearing evidence of forgery or alteration) as to call into question its validity, terms, or ownership.

      (c)   When the holder has notice that a fiduciary has negotiated it in breach of his or her duty.

      (d)   When a notice preserving consumer defenses is stated in a credit contract, no subsequent person can be a holder in due course.

(2)   The holder is not on notice of a defense or claim in the following situations [UCC 3-304(3)]:

      (a)   When the instrument was antedated or postdated.

(b)   When it was issued or negotiated in return for an executory promise or along with a separate agreement, unless the holder also knows of a defense arising from such promise or agreement.

(c)   When any party has signed as an accommodation party.

(d)   When an incomplete instrument has been completed, unless the holder also knows it was completed improperly.

(e)   When any negotiator of the instrument was a fiduciary.

B.   Rights of a Holder in Due Course

1.   Generally--An HDC takes the instrument free from all claims to it by any person and from all personal defenses of any party with whom he or she has not dealt (UCC 3-305).

2.   The Shelter Provision--Under the "shelter provision," the transfer of an instrument vests in the transferee such rights as the transferors had therein [UCC 3-201(1)]. In other words, because a transferee takes the rights of the transferor, a person who does not qualify as an HDC can, through the shelter provision, enjoy all of the benefits of HDC status if he or she can show that some transferor in his or her chain of ownership was an HDC.

Example 7

A takes a note for value and without notice of the fact that the note was originally induced by fraud by a prior possessor. A thus qualifies as an HDC and, as such, is immune from the personal defense of fraud. A then negotiates the note to B who takes with notice of the fraud. Although B is not an HDC, she nevertheless enjoys all the rights of an HDC because she is sheltered by A, who was an HDC.

•   Exceptions to the shelter provision are as follows:

(1)   A person not a holder in due course cannot acquire those rights by negotiating to a holder in due course and then reacquiring the instrument so as to improve his or her status (UCC 3-208).

(2)   A person who is party to the fraud or illegality affecting the instrument, or who is party to any defense, cannot acquire the rights of a prior holder in due course [UCC 3-201(1)].

3.   One who is neither a holder in due course nor a taker through an HDC is subject to the following (UCC 3-306):

a.   All valid claims to the instrument.

b.   Any real or personal defenses to the instrument.

IX. Defenses

A.   Personal Defenses (UCC 3-306)--Good against persons who are not holders in due course or takers through such holders. However, personal defenses are good against even holders in due course in favor of a person with whom the holder in due course has dealt. They typically do not go to the validity of the instrument, but are reasons that would excuse a promisor from performing the contract under contract law.

1. Absence or failure of consideration or failure of an implied condition precedent. However, the UCC provides that no consideration is necessary for an instrument given in payment for an antecedent obligation (e.g., when the antecedent obligation would be considered "past consideration" under contract law).

2. <u>Fraud in the Inducement</u> (Also Called Fraud in the Procurement)--In this type of fraud, the instrument fraudulently signed is what it purports to be, and the person deceived knows its terms and character (e.g., he or she knows it is a promissory note in the amount of $10,000). The fraud and deception concern some matter other than the instrument (e.g., a person is induced to sign a $10,000 note in payment for a painting that the seller fraudulently misrepresents as a Picasso, but the painting in fact is a cheap imitation worth $50).

   - Distinguished From Fraud in the Factum (Also Called Fraud in the Essence)--This type of fraud is a <u>real defense</u> which is <u>not</u> cut off by an HDC. In fraud in the factum, the misrepresentation concerns the terms and character of the instrument itself (e.g., a person is induced to sign a $10,000 note because the procurer of the signature misrepresents that it is a $1,000 note). Fraud in the factum is a defense <u>if</u> the defrauded party can prove that he or she had no reasonable opportunity to learn the true character or essential terms of the instrument (e.g., the signer was blind and was induced to sign by a trusted relative).

3. Nondelivery of the Instrument--Although a person in possession of an instrument which was not delivered to him or her cannot be a holder, there is a rebuttable presumption that an instrument in the possession of someone other than the maker or drawer has been delivered.

4. Unauthorized Completion of an Instrument--When an instrument is <u>fraudulently completed</u> by a <u>holder</u>, the party whose contract has been <u>materially altered</u> by the unauthorized completion is discharged of all liability on it except against holders in due course (HDC).

Example 8

A writes a check for $50 but fails to name the person to whose order the check is to be paid. S steals the check and writes "S" in the order space. Although A is not liable to S (S is not a holder), A would be liable in the amount of $50 to an HDC who took from S.

---

5. Payment Before Maturity--If a note is paid to a prior holder before maturity, then that payment discharges the instrument to all subsequent holders who are not holders in due course.

6. Discharge of Parties (other than in bankruptcy or insolvency proceedings)

   a. A holder is <u>not</u> barred from being an HDC by having notice upon delivery of the instrument of the discharge of one or more parties. A holder <u>is</u> barred from being an HDC if he or she takes delivery with notice that <u>all</u> parties have been discharged.

   b. An HDC takes free of a discharge of any party <u>if</u> the HDC took delivery of the instrument without notice of such discharge.

   c. If the HDC had notice of such discharge at the time of delivery, then the discharge <u>is</u> good against the HDC.

   - Distinguished from discharge in bankruptcy or insolvency, a discharge in bankruptcy is a real defense and in all cases is a good defense against an HDC.

B. <u>Real Defenses [UCC 3-305(2)]</u>--All holders, including HDCs, take subject to any real defenses of any party, regardless of whether the holder has or has not dealt with that party. Real defenses generally go to the validity of the instrument.

1. Discharge in insolvency proceedings or discharge in bankruptcy.

2. Incapacity

   a. Infancy is a real defense to the extent it is a defense to a simple contract under local law, even though it renders a contract merely voidable, not void.

   b. Any other type of incapacity is a real defense only if it would void a simple contract (e.g., adjudication of incompetence).

```
┌──────────────────────────┐
│  TotalRecall             │
└──────────────────────────┘
```

HOLDER IN DUE COURSE REAL DEFENSES

D Discharge in insolvency proceedings or discharge in bankruptcy.

I Incapacity

F Forgery

F Fraud in the factum (essence)

M Material alteration

I Illegality (if it would render the instrument void under local law)

D Duress (to the extent it would render the obligation void)

3. Forgery

   a. No person is liable, even against an HDC as a maker, drawer, or endorser of an instrument, unless the person's authorized signature appears on it or his or her negligence substantially contributed to an unauthorized signature.

   b. A <u>forged signature</u> creates <u>no</u> liability against the person whose signature it purports to be, but instead operates as the signature of the unauthorized signer, unless the person whose name is forged is estopped by negligence from raising the defense (UCC 3-404). <u>However</u>,

      (1) A valid signature may be made by an authorized representative of the person whose name is to be signed.

      (2) An <u>unauthorized</u> signature may later be ratified, so that the ratifier loses the defense of forgery and becomes liable on the instrument.

   c. Exceptions

      (1) A person whose negligence substantially contributes to the making of a forged signature is estopped from asserting the lack of a valid signature as a defense against a holder in due course or a payor who pays the instrument in good faith (UCC 3-406).

      (2) Any endorsement (forged or not) <u>is</u> effective in the name of the named payee in the following circumstances (UCC 3-405):

         (a) If an imposter induces the maker or drawer to issue the instrument to him or her in the name of the payee.

(b)   If a person signing for the maker or drawer, or supplying the name to the maker or drawer, intends the payee to have no interest (e.g., the fictitious payee will then endorse it him- or herself and appropriate the proceeds).

Example 9

A introduces himself to B Company as C, one of B Company's suppliers. In fact, A is an imposter. A talks B Company into giving him an advance of $1,500 against future billings. The check from B Company is made payable to C. A endorses the check, takes the proceeds, and vanishes. Result: The loss of the $1,500 falls upon the drawer, B Company. The endorsement of an imposter is not considered to be a forgery; accordingly, the forgery rules do not apply.

---

4.   Material Alteration

a.   A material alteration is one that changes the contract of a party who has signed the instrument (UCC 3-407). Material alterations include changes in the following:

(1)   The number or relationship of the parties.

(2)   The date of issue and/or of payment.

(3)   The amount payable and/or medium of payment.

(4)   The place of payment or the addition of one when none is specified.

b.   As a general rule, any material alteration fraudulently made by a holder that changes the original tenor (amount or number of parties) of the instrument discharges all parties whose contract changes, except as against either an HDC or that party whose negligence substantially contributed to the alteration. This general rule is modified as follows:

(1)   If a completed instrument is fraudulently altered without any substantial contributing negligence of a party, then that party whose contract is changed has only a personal defense as to the original tenor, but a real defense (good against an HDC) as to the alteration. Thus, the HDC can only enforce the instrument up to its original amount. However, if a party's negligence substantially contributed to the alteration, that party has no real defense against an HDC [UCC 3-407(2)].

(2)   If an incomplete instrument is fraudulently completed (unauthorized completion), the instrument is assumed not to have had an "original tenor," and a subsequent HDC may enforce the instrument as completed. There is no real defense to the altered portion [UCC 3-407(2),(3)].

(3)   If a party to the instrument substantially contributes to the fraudulent alteration or the unauthorized completion, he or she will be liable for the full amount to subsequent HDCs as well as to drawees and payees who pay on the instrument in good faith.

(4)   See also A.4., above.

c.   An unauthorized completion of an instrument is treated as a material alteration; however, it is not a real defense against an HDC.

    d.   A party whose substantial contributing negligence invites the material alteration is estopped from raising the alteration as a defense.

5.   Illegality, if it would render the instrument void under local law.

6.   Fraud in the Factum (Fraud in the Essence)

    a.   Fraud in the factum (also called fraud in the execution or fraud in the essence) concerns the instrument itself. The fraudulent misrepresentation is of the character or terms of the instrument; it does not concern the misrepresentation of a collateral matter.

    b.   In order for fraud in the factum to be a <u>real defense</u> against a subsequent HDC, the defrauded party signing the instrument must have had no reasonable opportunity to learn the true character or terms of the instrument.

7.   Duress, to the extent it would render the obligation void. If the duress would only render the obligation voidable, it is a personal defense.

X. Liability of the Parties

A.   <u>Importance of the Signature</u>--No person is liable on a negotiable instrument unless his or her signature appears on it [UCC 3-3401(1)].

    1.   An authorized agent may sign for a person and the signature operates as the principal's. The agent must indicate that he or she signs in a representative capacity to avoid being personally liable on the instrument (UCC 3-403).

<u>Example 10</u>

Liability of agent as maker, endorser, acceptor, or drawer results if agent fails to properly sign the instrument as such.

- "P. Ball, by A. Antioch, Agent"
  The principal (P. Ball) is liable as maker, etc.; Agent (A. Antioch) has no liability.

- "P. Ball"
  The principal is liable; the agent is not. Between principal and agent, parol (oral) evidence will be admissible to show agency.

- "A. Antioch"
  The agent is liable as maker, etc., because the agent neither names the person represented nor shows the representative capacity in which she signed. Furthermore, parol evidence is <u>not</u> admissible to show agency. Remember, the general rule is that no one is liable on an instrument unless her signature appears on it.

(continued on next page)

> • "A. Antioch, Agent", or
> "P. Ball
> A. Antioch"
> The agent in both of these cases signs in a representative capacity, and parol evidence will be admissible in litigation between principal and agent to show this agency. In both cases, the agent may also introduce parol evidence of agency in a litigation between the agent and a third party. If, however, in either example, the agent is sued by an HDC, the agent is personally liable because she signed the instrument. However, the agent could then sue the principal for indemnification.

2.   An unauthorized signature (including a forgery) does not bind the person whose signature it purports to be unless that person ratifies the unauthorized signature. If not ratified, the signature operates as the signature of the unauthorized signer. The unauthorized signer is liable to any person who takes the instrument as an HDC (UCC 3-404).

B.   <u>Contractual Liability</u>--Liability on an instrument is borne by primary and secondary parties. In order for a holder to obtain payment from a <u>secondary</u> party, the holder must fulfill certain conditions precedent. These conditions are: presentment for payment, protest if not paid, and notice of dishonor. However, these conditions precedent are <u>not</u> required in order to fix liability upon a <u>primary</u> party.

1.   <u>Primary Parties</u>--Makers (notes) and acceptors (drafts) are the primary parties. The maker of a note is liable on it when the note is executed; however, a drawee on a draft is not liable until he or she accepts (draft) or certifies (check) the instrument.

   a.   <u>The Maker</u>--The maker engages that he or she will pay the instrument according to its original terms or, if incomplete at the time of making, according to its final terms if completed as authorized [UCC 3-413(1)].

   b.   <u>The Drawee-Acceptor</u>--Unlike the maker (who is liable when the instrument is executed), the drawee-acceptor incurs no liability on the instrument <u>until</u> it is presented for acceptance or certification. The drawee then accepts and binds him- or herself by writing "accepted" or "certified" on the draft itself, along with the drawee's signature. Although the word "accepted" or like words ("good") are usually present on such drafts, the drawee's signature is absolutely required for acceptance of certification. After acceptance, the instrument will be operative when completed by delivery or notification (UCC 3-410).

   • Special Rules

      (a)   If a holder obtains the certification of a check then payable, this certification discharges the drawer and all prior endorsers (UCC 3-411). However, endorsers are still bound by their implied warranties (see X.C., below).

      (b)   Usually, the acceptor engages that he or she will pay the draft according to its terms at the time of acceptance. Thus, the acceptor is not liable for a <u>subsequent</u> alteration or unauthorized completion. Furthermore, any such alteration discharges all parties to the instrument, except as against an HDC (UCC 3-407).

      (c)   General Acceptance--Drawee accepts the draft according to its terms as originally drawn or as presented.

(d) Acceptance Varying Draft--Drawee is unwilling to accept the draft as drawn. The drawee may change the terms of the instrument as he or she sees fit. The holder of this draft (usually a seller of goods who has obtained a draft from the purchaser-drawer payable to the seller-payee through a drawee-bank) has two choices (UCC 3-412):

(i) The holder may refuse the varying acceptance and treat the draft as dishonored.

(ii) The holder may assent to the variance. However, such assent discharges each drawer and endorser who has not affirmatively assented to the variance.

Example 11

Purchaser draws a draft for $5,000 payable to seller-payee 30 days after presentment. Seller presents the draft for acceptance and the instrument is accepted and signed by drawee-bank. Seller then negotiates the draft to Forger, who raises the amount to $15,000 and subsequently negotiates the draft to Smith for value and without notice of alteration. Smith becomes an HDC.

Results:

• If Smith was not an HDC, the alteration by Forger, a holder, would discharge all parties (including the acceptor).

• Because Smith is an HDC, he can recover from the acceptor (drawee-bank) the amount of the draft at the time of acceptance ($5,000). Smith can recover the full $15,000 from Forger.

• If the alteration had been made before the acceptance, the drawee-bank acceptor would be liable for the full $15,000 total because that was the amount it "accepted."

• The purchaser and seller are secondarily liable for the unaltered amount ($5,000).

---

2. Secondary Parties--Drawers and endorsers are secondary parties. They are secondarily liable on any instrument if the instrument is not paid by the primary party and conditions precedent to liability have been satisfied by the holder of the instrument. These conditions are presentment for acceptance or payment, notice of dishonor, and protest (in some cases).

a. Liability of the Drawer--By drawing the instrument, the drawer contractually engages that upon dishonor of the draft and after notice of dishonor or protest (if necessary), the drawer will pay the amount of the draft to the holder or to any endorser who takes it up (assumes responsibility through his or her endorser's contract) [UCC 3-413(2)]. A drawer may disclaim such secondary liability by qualifying the endorsement of the instrument using such words as "without recourse."

b. Liability of Endorsers--An endorser (other than a qualified endorser) engages that upon dishonor and any necessary notice of dishonor and protest, the endorser will pay the instrument according to its tenor at the time of his or her endorsement to the holder or to any subsequent holder who takes up the instrument [UCC 3-414(1)]. In the absence of an effective "without recourse" disclaimer, the endorser is jointly and severally (secondarily) liable with the drawer. Thus, a holder is not required (after presentment and dishonor) to make a demand upon or proceed against the drawer before enforcing the endorser's liability. The holder can go against an endorser immediately.

(1)   Unless they agree otherwise, endorsers are liable to one another in the order in which they endorse, i.e., a prior endorser is liable to a subsequent endorser [UCC 3-414(2)].

(2)   A signature appearing on an instrument is considered an endorsement unless the instrument clearly indicates that the signature is made in some other capacity (UCC 3-402).

(3)   When the endorser adds the words "payment guaranteed," it means that when the endorser's secondary liability is triggered, the endorser will become primarily liable automatically upon nonpayment by the primary party. Thus, presentment and notice are not required in a "payment guaranteed" endorsement (UCC 3-416).

(4)   When endorsement is without "payment guaranteed," any unreasonable delay by the holder in fulfilling the conditions precedent to secondary liability completely discharges any endorser. Drawers are discharged only to the extent of any loss covered by the delay (UCC 3-502).

(a)   Presentment of a draft must be by a holder within a reasonable time after the endorsement. There is a rebuttable presumption that "7 days after endorsement" is a reasonable time for presentment of a check payable in the U.S. with respect to the liability of an endorser; 30 days after the date or issue, whichever is later, is considered a reasonable time for presentment of a check payable in the U.S. with respect to the liability of the drawer [UCC 3-503(2)].

(b)   Because an endorsement is essential for negotiation of an order instrument and for the activation of the endorser's contractual liability, it is important to ascertain whether in fact there was an endorsement. If a bearer instrument was negotiated by delivery alone, without endorsement, the transferor bears no contractual liability. However, the transferor is still liable for certain implied warranties, discussed at C., below.

3.   Liability of Accommodation Party--An accommodation party signs an instrument to lend his or her name to some other party to the instrument. An accommodation party may sign as a maker, acceptor, drawer, or endorser. The accommodation party is liable in the capacity in which he or she signed the instrument (UCC 3-415).

a.   If the accommodation party signs as a maker or acceptor, he or she is a primary party and is liable immediately or when accepted; the holder need not first present the instrument to the accommodated party (the party to whom accommodation is made). However, notice that both the accommodation party and the accommodated party must sign the instrument. If the accommodation party signs as an endorser, he or she is only secondarily liable.

b.   The accommodation party is treated as a surety; thus, he or she can be held liable on the instrument without demand being first made on the accommodated party. The normal defenses of a surety are not available to the accommodation party if the holder is an HDC. Finally, the accommodation party is liable on the instrument only and is not liable to the accommodated party. However, if the accommodation party pays the instrument, he or she is entitled to reimbursement from the accommodated party.

c.   Any endorsement out of the chain of title is notice of its accommodation character.

Example 12

B wishes to borrow money from A. However, A requires B to obtain C's signature before the loan will be made. C agrees to sign as an accommodation party to B. C will now be liable to A as an endorser of the instrument. If B later refuses to repay the loan, A can proceed against the accommodation party, C.

C.   Warranty Liability--Distinctly separate from the contractual liabilities of primary and secondary parties are the warranty liabilities of the parties to an instrument. One who endorses or otherwise transfers an instrument creates an implied warranty of certain facts relating to the instrument. There are basically two groups of warranties: transferor's warranties, which run in favor of immediate transferees and subsequent holders, and presenter's warranties, which run in favor of those parties who pay or accept an instrument.

1.   Transferor's Warranties

    a.   Any person who transfers and receives consideration warrants to the transferee, and if the transfer is by endorsement, to any subsequent holder who takes in good faith, the following [UCC 3-417(2)]:

        (1)   He or she has good title to the instrument.

        (2)   All signatures are genuine and authorized.

        (3)   The instrument has not been materially altered.

        (4)   No defense of any party is good against him or her.

        (5)   He or she has no knowledge of any insolvency proceedings instituted with respect to the maker, acceptor, or drawer of an unaccepted instrument.

    b.   Transfer--Transfer means that there was a delivery; the warranties will therefore be imposed even though the transfer was not accompanied by an endorsement (e.g., the bearer instrument was negotiated by delivery only).

    c.   Consideration--The implied warranties attach only if there has in essence been a sale of the instrument through a transfer for value. For this reason, an accommodation endorser cannot be held liable on implied warranties because the accommodating party received no consideration from the transferee.

    d.   It is also important to remember that transferees of HDCs who do not qualify as HDCs nevertheless take the warranty protection of HDCs through the shelter provision (see VIII.B.2., above). However, if there has been a breach of the transferor's warranty of "good title," there cannot again be an HDC who is free of warranty liability when the breach of "good title" is caused by a forgery of one other than the maker or drawer.

2.   Presenter's Warranties

    a.   Any person <u>other than an HDC</u> who presents an instrument for payment or acceptance warrants to the acceptor or payor the following [UCC 3-417(1)]:

        (1)   The presenter has good title to the instrument.

        (2)   The presenter has no knowledge that the signature of the maker or drawer is unauthorized.

        (3)   The presenter warrants that the instrument has not been materially altered. (This is an absolute liability warranty.)

    b.   A <u>holder in due course</u> who presents an instrument for payment or acceptance warrants that he or she has good title to the instrument. **NOTE:** An HDC does not warrant that he or she has no knowledge that the signature of the maker or drawer is unauthorized [UCC 3-417(1)].

    c.   It is important to remember that the presenter's warranties are given not only by those specific parties who receive payment or acceptance, but also by prior transferors.

3.   Effect of Endorsement "Without Recourse"--If the endorsement is <u>qualified</u> ("without recourse"), the following results occur:

    a.   The endorser disclaims his or her contractual secondary liability [UCC 3-414(1)].

    b.   The transferor warrants that he or she has no knowledge of any valid defense (instead of absolute liability as would occur if the transferor endorsed unqualifiedly) [UCC 3-417(3)].

    c.   With the exception of the change in the "any defense" warranty to "no knowledge of any defense" warranty, the qualifying endorser's warranties are the same as any other transferors' warranties (see 1., above).

4.   Warranties run to transferees and all subsequent holders.

D.   <u>Effect of Warranty Liability</u>

1.   A warranty does not go to the payment of the instrument, but to its validity as an instrument. If a warranty is breached, the warrantor is liable for the loss accruing as a result of the defect in the instrument. (Of course, the person liable for breach of warranty may also have contract liability for payment.)

2.   Warranties may be disclaimed by an agreement between the immediate parties which is noted on the instrument.

E.   <u>Finality of Acceptance of Payment</u>--If a holder in due course obtains acceptance or payment of an instrument and the signature of the maker or drawer was forged or unauthorized, the acceptance or payment is nevertheless final, even though the maker or drawee had no obligation to pay or accept (UCC 3-418).

1.   Reasoning--The maker or drawer was negligent in failing to detect the forgery.

2.   This rule does not apply to forged or unauthorized endorsements.

3.   The rule applies not only to holders in due course, but also to any other person who in good faith changed his or her position in reliance on the payment or acceptance.

F.   Statute of Limitations--Requires an action to enforce a liability imposed by Article 4 (*Bank Deposits and Collections*) must be commenced within three years after the cause of action accrued.

XI. Presentment, Dishonor, Notice of Dishonor

As conditions precedent to the activation of the maker's, drawer's, or unqualified endorser's liability, the holder must perform certain acts. The holder must first make a timely presentment of the instrument. Presentment is functionally equivalent to demanding acceptance or payment. If the instrument is dishonored, either through a refusal of the drawee or a refusal to pay on presentment, the holder's duty is fulfilled upon notifying the drawer or endorser of the dishonor. In some cases, these requirements are excused in whole or in part.

A.   Presentment

1.   Presentment for Acceptance--A drawee is not primarily liable on a draft until he or she accepts it. (The requirement for acceptance of a sight or demand draft [check] is excused-- checks are presented for payment, not acceptance.) Time drafts (e.g., "Pay 30 days after sight") are the usual subjects of acceptance. Although such time drafts are usually presented for acceptance before maturity, some time drafts are not accepted until maturity. More specifically, Article 3 of the UCC provides that acceptance is required in order to fix the secondary liability of drawers and endorsers in the following situations (UCC 3-501):

a.   When the draft itself provides that it shall be presented for acceptance.

b.   When the draft is payable at a place other than the place of residence or business of the drawee.

c.   When the date of payment depends upon presentment for acceptance (e.g., draft payable "10 days after sight" means that the draft is payable 10 days after presentment).

2.   Presentment for Payment

a.   Notes and accepted drafts must be presented for payment as a condition precedent to primary and secondary liability of makers and drawers, respectively.

b.   Failure to make presentment for payment discharges any endorsers. Failure to make presentment operates as a discharge of the drawer or acceptor of a draft payable at a bank only to the extent of any loss caused by the delay which is due to the insolvency of the drawee or payor (UCC 3-502).

c.   Generally, payment of an instrument may be deferred without dishonor while it is examined to determine whether it is properly payable, but payment or dishonor of a check must occur by midnight of the next business day after presentment [UCC 3-508(2)].

d.   A check is overdue the day after the demand for payment has been made or 90 days after the date of the check if no demand has been made, whichever date is the earlier. If the holder of the check does not present it for payment or collection within 30 days after an endorsement was made, the endorser is discharged from liability.

e.   Time of Presentment (UCC 3-503)

   (1)   An instrument showing the date payable is due on the stated date (e.g., the primary party can be required to pay on that date). An instrument may show the date payable in the following ways:

      (a)   Payable on a specified date.

      (b)   Payable on a fixed period after a stated date.

      (c)   Payable on a fixed period after sight (accepted instrument).

   (2)   An accelerated instrument must be presented for payment within a reasonable time after acceleration. A reasonable time is deemed to be 30 days after the issue or the date of the instrument, whichever is later, or 30 days after endorsement.

   (3)   A demand instrument presentment date depends on the purpose for which presentment is made.

      (a)   If the purpose is to activate the secondary liability of the drawer or endorser, presentment should be made on the date of issue.

      (b)   If the purpose is to move against the secondary party, presentment is timely if it is made within a reasonable time after the secondary party becomes liable on the instrument (see X.B.2.b.(4)(a), above).

   (4)   If presentment is due on a day which is not a full business day, it is due on the next full business day.

3.   Methods of Presentment--Presentment may be as follows (UCC 3-504):

   a.   By mail, in which case presentment is effective on receipt of the mail.

   b.   Through a clearing house.

   c.   At the place of acceptance or payment specified in the instrument or, if none is specified, the place of business or the residence of the party to accept or pay.

   d.   In the case of a draft accepted or a note made payable at a bank in the United States, at such bank.

4.   Conditions of Presentment--The party receiving presentment may impose certain requirements on the presenting party, which include the following (UCC 3-505):

   a.   Exhibition of the instrument.

   b.   Reasonable identification of the person making presentment and evidence of his or her authority to make it.

   c.   Production of the instrument for acceptance or payment at a place specified in it or, if no place is specified, at any place reasonable under the circumstances.

d.   A signed receipt on the instrument upon full or partial payment and its surrender upon full payment.

The party presenting has a reasonable time in which to comply. Failure to comply invalidates the presentment.

B.   <u>Dishonor (UCC 3-507)</u>

1.   In the case of an instrument required to be presented for acceptance or payment, dishonor occurs when presentment is made and acceptance or payment is refused or cannot be obtained within the time allowed.

2.   In the case of an instrument not required to be presented and not optionally presented, dishonor occurs when the instrument is not duly accepted or paid.

3.   Dishonor gives the holder a right of recourse against parties who are secondarily liable, subject to any requirement of notice of dishonor and protest.

4.   An instrument is not dishonored when it is returned for lack of a proper endorsement.

C.   <u>Notice of Dishonor (UCC 3-508)</u>

1.   Notice of dishonor is necessary unless waived in order to hold the following parties liable: the maker of a bank domiciled note, the acceptor of a bank domiciled draft, any drawer, and any endorser.

a.   Failure to give due notice of dishonor to an endorser discharges the endorser from any liability.

b.   Failure to give due notice of dishonor to any of the other parties named operates as a discharge only to the extent of any loss caused by the delay by reason of the insolvency of the drawee or payor.

2.   Time of Notification of Dishonor

a.   Banks must give notice before their "midnight deadline" (midnight of the next banking day after receipt of item or receipt of notice of dishonor, whichever is later).

b.   Others must give notice within 30 days after dishonor or receipt of notice of dishonor.

3.   Form--Notice of dishonor may be oral or written. It must identify the instrument and state that the instrument has been dishonored.

4.   Effect of Notification of Dishonor

a.   Notice to a party operates for the benefit of any party who has rights on the instrument against the party notified.

b.   Notice of dishonor is effective when sent, regardless of whether it is received.

D.   <u>Protest</u>--A formal certificate of dishonor (UCC 3-509)

1.   Protest is necessary for foreign drafts and <u>optional</u> for any other instrument.

2. Method of Making Protest

   a. Protest is made under the hand and seal of a person authorized to certify dishonor under the law of the jurisdiction (e.g., a United States consul, vice consul, or notary public).

   b. The protest must identify the instrument dishonored and certify that presentment has been made (or excused for some reason) and that notice of dishonor has been given.

3. Protest is due when notice of dishonor is due.

4. Failure to make a necessary protest by the time it is due discharges the drawer and endorsers of the foreign draft.

E. <u>Excuse (UCC 3-511)</u>

1. Delay in making presentment, in giving notice of dishonor, or in making protest <u>is excused</u> under the following circumstances:

   a. When a party is without notice that the instrument is due (e.g., acceleration of a note or demand by a prior holder without the current holder's knowledge).

   b. When caused by circumstances beyond the party's control, so long as he or she exercises reasonable diligence after the cause of delay ceases to operate.

2. Failure to make presentment at all is excused under the following circumstances:

   a. The maker, acceptor, or drawee is dead or in insolvency proceedings that were instituted after the instrument had been issued.

   b. Acceptance or payment has already been refused for a reason other than lack of proper presentment.

3. Failure to make presentment, notice of dishonor, or protest is excused under the following circumstances:

   a. If it is waived by the party to receive presentment or notice.

      (1) Waiver may be oral or written, express or implied, and made before or after presentment, notice of dishonor, or protest is due.

      (2) A waiver embodied in the instrument binds all parties; however, a waiver written above the signature of an endorser binds only the endorser.

   b. It may also be excused if a draft has been dishonored by nonacceptance and is not later accepted.

   c. If a party has dishonored the instrument or has no right to expect it to be accepted or paid; e.g., an accommodated party who breaks the accommodation agreement he or she had with the accommodation party has no right to presentment or notice of dishonor from the latter.

   d. If presentment, notice of dishonor, or protest cannot be made by reasonable diligence.

XII. Discharge From Liability

The issuance of commercial paper changes the form of, and generally suspends, the underlying money obligation for varying periods depending on the negotiable instrument's maturity date. Thus, a purchaser of goods, instead of paying the seller in cash upon delivery of the goods, may convince the seller to take the purchaser's 30-day note at an acceptable interest rate. When the 30-day note is paid (perhaps after it has been negotiated to a bank for discounting), the underlying obligation (payment for goods received) is discharged. If, however, instead of being paid at maturity, the note is dishonored by the purchaser after presentment, the creditor may bring an action on either the note or the obligation underlying the note.

A.   <u>Effect of a Negotiable Instrument on the Underlying Obligation</u>--The following rules summarize the effect of a negotiable instrument on the underlying obligation for which it is given:

   1.   Unless otherwise agreed, the obligation is suspended until the instrument is due or, if it is payable on demand, until its presentment.

   2.   The underlying obligation which is suspended during the prematurity period of the instrument is totally discharged when the obligor is discharged on the instrument.

   3.   The obligation is also discharged if a bank is the drawer, maker, or acceptor of the instrument and there is no recourse on the instrument against the underlying obligor. For example, if the underlying obligor negotiates the instrument without endorsement, the obligation is discharged.

B.   <u>Methods of Discharging a Party's Liability on the Instrument</u>

   1.   <u>Payment or satisfaction</u> of the instrument will discharge a party from liability on the instrument (UCC 3-603).

      a.   Payment or satisfaction must be made to the holder of the instrument.

      b.   However, payment or satisfaction made to a holder will <u>not discharge</u> the liability of a payor who in bad faith pays a holder whom he or she knows obtained the instrument by theft.

<u>Example 13</u>

A holds B's note. After A endorses the note in blank, thief steals the note under facts which do not indicate that A was negligent. Obligor then pays T, the holder of the bearer note, without knowing of the theft. Obligor is discharged because even though the note was stolen, obligor did not act in bad faith. If obligor knew of the theft, he or she would not have been discharged upon payment to thief.

---

   2.   Tender of Payment (UCC 3-604)

      a.   If the maker or acceptor of an instrument payable other than on demand is able and ready to pay at every place of payment specified in the instrument when it is due, it is equivalent to tender.

      b.   If the obligor on an instrument tenders full payment to the holder when or after the instrument is due and the holder improperly refuses payment, the obligation of the party making the tender is not discharged (except as to subsequent liability for interest, costs, and attorney's fees).

c.   The holder's refusal of such tender wholly discharges any party who has a right of recourse against the party making tender.

Example 14

A negotiates obligor's note to B. At maturity, obligor tenders payment to holder B who refuses to accept payment. A is discharged fully. The obligor is discharged to the extent of future interest, costs, and legal fees so long as the obligor continues his tender after the maturity date.

---

3.   Cancellation--The holder may discharge any prior party by cancellation (UCC 3-605). Cancellation may be accomplished by indicating the fact of cancellation on the face of the instrument (e.g., by intentionally canceling the instrument or party's signature by destruction or mutilation) or by striking the endorsement of a party.

  a.   Cancellation is usually effected by writing "paid" on the face of the instrument.

  b.   The prior party whose signature is struck is fully discharged from liability on the instrument.

  c.   No consideration is needed for cancellation.

4.   Renunciation--The holder may discharge any prior party by renunciation (UCC 3-605).

  a.   Renunciation may be accomplished by a signed writing stating that the holder releases the party or by the surrender of the instrument to the party to be discharged.

  b.   An HDC may not be bound by a discharge by renunciation because (unlike cancellation) renunciation will not appear on the face of the instrument.

5.   Reacquisition--When an instrument is returned to or reacquired by a prior party, any intervening party is discharged from liability as against the reacquiring party and as against any subsequent party who is not an HDC without notice of the discharge (UCC 3-208).

Example 15

A, who is payee on a note, negotiates by delivery and endorsement to B, who in turn negotiates the note to the order of C. C then negotiates it to D who negotiates the note back to A. B, C, and D are discharged from liability on the note--they have no secondary liability (they still have transferee's warranty liability). If in these facts A negotiates the note to an HDC and the note is dishonored after presentment, the HDC may recover from _any_ of the above parties.

---

6.   Discharge of any Person as a Surety (UCC 3-606).

  a.   If the holder discharges a party, then any other party who has a right of recourse against the released party is also released.

  b.   If a holder discharges the maker _but_ reserves rights against surety, then the surety's rights against the other parties on the instrument are also reserved.

7.   Activity Affecting the Validity or Terms of the Instrument--As discussed earlier, certain acts by parties to an instrument discharge other parties from liability. These acts which discharge liability are as follows:

   a.   Fraudulent and material alteration (see IX.B.4.b., above).

   b.   Acceptance varying a draft (see X.B.1.b.(d), above).

   c.   Unexcused delay in presentment or notice of dishonor or protest (see XI.A.2., above).

8.   Parties may discharge each other by agreement. Such a discharge only affects the rights as between the parties involved.

C.   Discharge as a Defense--Discharge is a personal defense. It is not effective against a subsequent holder in due course unless the holder has notice of it when he or she takes the instrument. **EXCEPTION**: Discharge in insolvency proceedings, such as bankruptcy, is a real defense.

XIII. Special Rules Applicable to Checks

A.   Checks

1.   Checks are drafts drawn on a bank and payable on demand.

2.   A check is generally a conditional payment; the obligation for which it is given is not discharged until the check has been paid.

3.   Certified Checks (UCC 3-411)

   a.   Certification of a check is the drawee-bank's acceptance; the bank warrants that sufficient funds are on deposit and are set aside for payment.

   b.   Certification procured by the holder discharges the drawer and any prior endorsers; the bank becomes primarily liable.

   c.   Certification procured by the drawer makes the bank primarily liable, but the drawer and any prior endorsers remain secondarily liable.

   d.   The drawee-bank ordinarily owes the depositor no duty to certify his or her checks.

4.   When several checks are received the same day, the bank may decide which checks to charge to the account first.

B.   Relationship Between Drawer-Depositor and Drawee-Bank

1.   The depositor is the drawer of the check (the bank's creditor as to the amount on deposit) and the bank's principal on the contract of deposit agreement.

2.   The bank is the drawee of the check (the depositor's debtor as to the amount on deposit) and the depositor's agent with respect to handling the account.

C.   Duties Owed by the Bank to the Depositor

1.   The bank owes the depositor a duty to honor his or her checks as drawn, providing they are properly drawn and are covered by sufficient funds on deposit (UCC 4-402).

a.   This duty is owed to the drawer, not the payee. If the bank improperly dishonors a check, the payee's action is against the drawer. **EXCEPTION**: If the check has been <u>certified</u>, then the payee can compel payment by the drawee-bank.

b.   The drawee-bank is liable to the depositor for damages caused by its wrongful dishonor. If dishonor occurs by mistake, the bank's liability is limited to actual damages proved.

2.   The bank owes the depositor a duty to follow the depositor's order to stop payment (UCC 4-403).

a.   A stop-payment order must be received by the bank in time to give the bank reasonable time to act.

b.   A stop-payment order may be oral or written.

(1)   A written order is valid for six months unless renewed in writing.

(2)   An oral order is valid for 14 days but may be confirmed in writing before the period expires.

c.   A bank that pays a check while a valid stop-payment order is in effect regarding that check cannot debit the drawer's account.

D.   <u>Depositor's Duty to the Bank</u>--The depositor owes the bank a duty to examine his or her monthly statements and canceled checks for possible alterations and forgeries (UCC 4-406).

1.   If the drawer negligently fails to discover a forgery or material alteration, or fails to notify the bank within 30 days, the drawer will bear the loss of subsequent forgeries or alterations in the same series.

2.   If the bank was negligent, the bank bears the loss even if the drawer was also negligent.

3.   Regardless of the negligence of the drawer or bank, a drawer who fails to report his or her unauthorized signature or any alteration within a <u>year</u> after receiving his or her bank statement, or who fails to report an unauthorized endorsement within three years, bears the loss on the forged or altered check.

4.   The bank ordinarily must recredit the drawer's account after paying a forged or altered check; its remedy is against the person making presentment and the prior transferors for breach of implied warranties.

5.   A customer and a bank may agree that the bank should retain canceled checks and simply provide the customer with a list of paid items. The customer must examine canceled checks or paid items to see if any were improperly paid.

NOTES

CHAPTER 45—COMMERCIAL PAPER

Problem 45-1 MULTIPLE CHOICE QUESTIONS (70 to 85 minutes)

1. One of the requirements to qualify as a holder of a negotiable bearer check is that the transferee must
a. Receive the check that was originally made payable to bearer.
b. Take the check in good faith.
c. Give value for the check.
d. Have possession of the check.
(11/92, Law, #36, 3118)

2. A trade acceptance is an instrument drawn by a
a. Seller obligating the seller or designee to make payment.
b. Buyer obligating the buyer or designee to make payment.
c. Seller ordering the buyer or designee to make payment.
d. Buyer ordering the seller or designee to make payment. (11/89, Law, #40, 0538)

3. Gold is holding the following instrument:

```
To:     Sussex National Bank
        Suffolk, N.Y.
                        October 15, 1988

Pay to the order of Tom Gold    $2,000.00

Two Thousand and xx/100     Dollars
on November 1, 1988

                Lester Davis
                Lester Davis
```

This instrument is a
a. Postdated check.
b. Draft.
c. Promissory note.
d. Trade acceptance.   (11/88, Law, #35, 9911)

3A. Under the Commercial Paper Article of the UCC, which of the following documents would be considered an order to pay?

I.   Draft
II. Certificate of deposit

a. I only.
b. II only.
c. Both I and II.
d. Neither I nor II.   (5/95, Law, #41, 5375)

3B.

```
To:  Middlesex National Bank
     Nassau, N.Y.
                        September 15, 1994

Pay to the order of ___Robert Silver___  $4,000.00

Four Thousand and xx/100          Dollars

on October 1, 1994

                Lynn Dexter
                Lynn Dexter
```

The above instrument is a
a. Draft.
b. Postdated check.
c. Trade acceptance.
d. Promissory note.   (5/95, Law, #42, 5376)

4. Assuming each of the following is negotiable, which qualifies as a draft under the UCC Commercial Paper Article?
a. A warehouse receipt.
b. A demand promissory note.
c. A document of title.
d. A trade acceptance.   (5/88, Law, #47, 0548)

5. A bank issues a negotiable instrument that acknowledges receipt of $50,000. The instrument also provides that the bank will repay the $50,000 plus 8% interest per annum to the bearer 90 days from the date of the instrument. The instrument is a
a. Certificate of deposit.
b. Time draft.
c. Trade or banker's acceptance.
d. Cashier's check.   (11/88, Law, #36, 0545)

6. On February 15, 1993, P.D. Stone obtained the following instrument from Astor Co. for $1,000. Stone was aware that Helco, Inc. disputed liability under the instrument because of an alleged breach by Astor of the referenced computer purchase agreement. On March 1, 1993, Willard Bank obtained the instrument from Stone for $3,900. Willard had no knowledge that Helco disputed liability under the instrument.

February 12, 1993

Helco, Inc. promises to pay to Astor Co. or bearer the sum of $4,900 (four thousand nine hundred and 00/100 dollars) on March 12, 1993, (maker may elect to extend due date to March 31, 1993) with interest thereon at the rate of 12% per annum.

HELCO, INC.

By: *A.J. Help*

A.J. Help, President

Reference: Computer purchase agreement dated February 12, 1993

The reverse side of the instrument is endorsed as follows:

Pay to the order of Willard Bank, without recourse

P.D. Stone

P.D. Stone

The instrument is a
a. Promissory note.
b. Sight draft.
c. Check.
d. Trade acceptance.
(5/93, Law, #36, amended, 4004)

7. Which of the following negotiable instruments is subject to the UCC Commercial Paper Article?
a. Corporate bearer bond with a maturity date of January 1, 2001.
b. Installment note payable on the first day of each month.
c. Warehouse receipt.
d. Bill of lading payable to order.
(11/92, Law, #33, 3115)

8.

May 19, 1991

I promise to pay to the order of A. B. Shark $1,100 (One thousand one hundred dollars) with interest thereon at the rate of 12% per annum.

T. T. Tile

T. T. Tile

Guaranty

I personally guaranty payment by T. T. Tile.

N. A. Abner

N. A. Abner

The instrument is a
a. Promissory demand note.
b. Sight draft.
c. Check.
d. Trade acceptance. (11/91, Law, #46, 2374)

9. A company has in its possession the following instrument:

$500.00	Dayton, October 2, 1987 Ohio

Sixty days after date I promise to pay to the order of

_____Cash_____
_____Five Hundred_____ Dollars
at _____Miami, Florida_____

Value received with interest at the rate of nine percent. This instrument is secured by a conditional sales contract.

No. 11 Due Dec. 1, 1987 *Craig Burk*

Craig Burk

This instrument is
a. Not negotiable until December 1, 1987.
b. A negotiable bearer note.
c. A negotiable time draft.
d. A nonnegotiable note since it states that it is secured by a conditional sales contract.
(11/87, Law, #48, 9911)

10. Following is a note which your client, Best Realtors, obtained from Green in connection with Green's purchase of land located in Rye, N.Y. The note was given for the balance due on the purchase and was secured by a first mortgage on the land.

$90,000.00   Rye, N.Y.
                                                May 1, 1985

For value received, six years after date, I promise to pay to the order of Best Realtors NINETY THOUSAND and 00/100 DOLLARS with interest at 16% compounded annually until fully paid. This instrument arises out of the sale of land located in N.Y. and the law of N.Y. is to be applied to any question which may arise. It is secured by a first mortgage on the land conveyed. It is further agreed that:

1. Purchaser will pay the costs of collection including attorney's fees upon default.
2. Purchaser may repay the amount outstanding on any anniversary date of this note.

                          Ted Green
                          Ted Green

This note is a
a. Negotiable promissory note.
b. Negotiable investment security under the UCC.
c. Nonnegotiable promissory note since it is secured by a first mortgage.
d. Nonnegotiable promissory note since it permits prepayment and requires the maker's payment of the costs of collection and attorney's fees.

(11/85, Law, #40, 9911)

11. Union Co. possesses the following instrument:

Holt, MT $4,000   April 15, 1990

Fifty days after date, or sooner, the undersigned promises to pay to the order of

        Union Co.
        Four Thousand   Dollars
at   Salem Bank, Holt, MT

    Ten percent interest per annum

This instrument is secured by the maker's business inventory.

        EASY, INC.

By: *Thomas Foy*
        Thomas Foy, President

Assuming all other requirements of negotiability are satisfied, this instrument is
a. Not negotiable, because of a lack of a definite time for payment.
b. Not negotiable, because the amount due is unspecified.
c. Negotiable, because it is secured by the maker's inventory.
d. Negotiable, because it is payable in a sum certain in money.   (11/90, Law, #46, 0531)

12. A secured promissory note would be nonnegotiable if it provided that
a. Additional collateral must be tendered if there is a decline in market value of the original collateral.
b. Upon default, the maker waives a trial by jury.
c. The maker is entitled to a 5% discount if the note is prepaid.
d. It is subject to the terms of the mortgage given by the maker to the payee.

(11/88, Law, #38, 9911)

13. On February 15, 1993, P.D. Stone obtained the following instrument from Astor Co. for $1,000. Stone was aware that Helco, Inc. disputed liability under the instrument because of an alleged breach by Astor of the referenced computer purchase agreement. On March 1, 1993, Willard Bank obtained the instrument from Stone for $3,900. Willard had no knowledge that Helco disputed liability under the instrument.

A promissory note can also be negotiable with all neg. terms.

February 12, 1993

Helco, Inc. promises to pay to Astor Co. or bearer the sum of $4,900 (four thousand four hundred and 00/100 dollars) on March 12, 1993, (maker may elect to extend due date to March 31, 1993) with interest thereon at the rate of 12% per annum.

HELCO, INC.

By: *A.J. Help*

A.J. Help, President

Reference: Computer purchase agreement
dated February 12, 1993

The reverse side of the instrument is endorsed as follows:

Pay to the order of Willard Bank, without recourse

P.D. Stone

P.D. Stone

The instrument is
a.   Nonnegotiable, because of the reference to the computer purchase agreement.
b.   Nonnegotiable, because the numerical amount differs from the written amount.
c.   Negotiable, even though the maker has the right to extend the time for payment.
d.   Negotiable, when held by Astor, but nonnegotiable when held by Willard Bank.
(5/93, Law, #37, 4005)

14.   An instrument reads as follows:

$10,000 Ludlow, Vermont   February 1, 1993

I promise to pay to the order of Custer Corp. $10,000 within 10 days after the sale of my two-carat diamond ring. I pledge the sale proceeds to secure my obligation hereunder.

R. Harris

R. Harris

Which of the following statements correctly describes the above instrument?
a.   The instrument is nonnegotiable because it is **not** payable at a definite time.
b.   The instrument is nonnegotiable because it is secured by the proceeds of the sale of the ring.
c.   The instrument is a negotiable promissory note.
d.   The instrument is a negotiable sight draft payable on demand.   (5/93, Law, #40, 4008)

15.

May 19, 1991

I promise to pay to the order of A. B. Shark $1,000 (One thousand one hundred dollars) with interest thereon at the rate of 12% per annum.

T. T. Tile
T. T. Tile

Guaranty

I personally guaranty payment by T. T. Tile.

N. A. Abner
N. A. Abner

The instrument is
a.   Nonnegotiable, even though it is payable on demand.
b.   Nonnegotiable, because the numeric amount differs from the written amount.
c.   Negotiable, even though a payment date is **not** specified.
d.   Negotiable, because of Abner's guaranty.
(11/91, Law, #47, 2375)

16.   The following instrument has been received by Gary Gold:

To: Bill Blake   October 30, 1987
P. O. Box 37
Dubuque, Iowa

Pay to the order of Gary Gold
Five Thousand and no/100 Dollars

Mary Kurke
Mary Kurke

Which of the following is correct?
a. As the drawer, Blake is primarily liable on the instrument.
b. The instrument is a negotiable note.
c. The instrument is payable on demand.
d. As the drawee, Blake is secondarily liable on the instrument. (11/87, Law, #46, 0550)

17. Which of the following conditions, if present on an otherwise negotiable instrument, would affect the instrument's negotiability?
a. The instrument is payable six months after the death of the maker.
b. The instrument is payable at a definite time subject to an accelerated clause in the event of a default.
c. The instrument is postdated.
d. The instrument contains a promise to provide additional collateral if there is a decrease in value of the existing collateral.
(11/92, Law, #34, 3116)

18. Your client has in its possession the following instrument:

No. 1625

FAIR FOOD WHOLESALERS, INC.
22 Woodrow Wilson Hayes Lane
Columbus, Ohio

Jan. 10, 1986

On demand the undersigned promises to pay to

Bearer _____ $1,200.00

Twelve hundred & ten/100 _____ Dollars

Fair Food Wholesalers, Inc.

By: James Duff _____
James Duff, President

For: _____

The instrument is
a. A nonnegotiable promissory note.
b. Nonnegotiable because the instrument is incomplete.
c. A negotiable time draft.
d. Negotiable despite the inconsistency between the amount in words and the amount in numbers. (11/86, Law, #44, 9911)

18A. Under the Commercial Paper Article of the UCC, which of the following circumstances would prevent a promissory note from being negotiable?
a. An extension clause that allows the maker to elect to extend the time for payment to a date specified in the note.
b. An acceleration clause that allows the holder to move up the maturity date of the note in the event of default.
c. A person having a power of attorney signs the note on behalf of the maker.
d. A clause that allows the maker to satisfy the note by the performance of services or the payment of money. (5/95, Law, #44, 5378)

19. Under the Commercial Paper Article of the UCC, for an instrument to be negotiable it must
a. Be payable to order or to bearer.
b. Be signed to the payee.
c. Contain references to all agreements between the parties.
d. Contain necessary conditions of payment.
(5/95, Law, #43, 5377)

20. The following endorsements appear on the back of a negotiable promissory note payable to Lake Corp.:

Pay to John Smith only
Frank Parker, President of Lake Corp.

John Smith

Pay to the order of Sharp, Inc., without recourse, but only if Sharp delivers computers purchased by Mary Harris by March 15, 1993
Mary Harris

Sarah Sharp, President of Sharp, Inc.

Which of the following statements is correct?
a. The note became nonnegotiable as a result of Parker's endorsement.
b. Harris' endorsement was a conditional promise to pay and caused the note to be nonnegotiable.
c. Smith's endorsement effectively prevented further negotiation of the note.
d. Harris' signature was **not** required to effectively negotiate the note to Sharp.
(5/93, Law, #41, 4009)

21. A $5,000 promissory note payable to the order of Neptune is discounted to Bane by blank endorsement for $4,000. King steals the note from Bane and

sells it to Ott who promises to pay King $4,500. After paying King $3,000, Ott learns that King stole the note. Ott makes no further payment to King. Ott is
a.   A holder in due course to the extent of $5,000.
b.   An ordinary holder to the extent of $4,500.
c.   A holder in due course to the extent of $3,000.
d.   An ordinary holder to the extent of $0.

(11/90, Law, #47, 0532)

22.   Under the Commercial Paper Article of the UCC, which of the following requirements must be met for a transferee of order paper to become a holder?

I.   Possession
II.   Endorsement of transferor

a.   I only.
b.   II only.
c.   Both I and II.
d.   Neither I nor II.   (5/95, Law, #45, 5379)

23.   In order to negotiate bearer paper, one must
a.   Endorse the paper.
b.   Endorse and deliver the paper with consideration.
c.   Deliver the paper.
d.   Deliver and endorse the paper. Order

(11/87, Law, #47, 9911)

24.   Under the Commercial Paper Article of the UCC, which of the following statements best describes the effect of a person endorsing a check "without recourse"?
a.   The person has **no** liability to prior endorsers.
b.   The person makes **no** promise or guarantee of payment on dishonor.
c.   The person gives **no** warranty protection to later transferees.
d.   The person converts the check into order paper.   (5/95, Law, #48, 5382)

25.   The following endorsements appear on the back of a negotiable promissory note made payable "to bearer." Clark has possession of the note.

```
Pay to Sam North
    Alice Fox

Sam North             Qualified
(without recourse)
```

Which of the following statements is correct?
a.   Clark's unqualified endorsement is required to further negotiate the note.
b.   To negotiate the note, Clark must have given value for it.
c.   Clark is **not** a holder because North's qualified endorsement makes the note nonnegotiable.
d.   Clark can negotiate the note by delivery alone.

(5/92, Law, #46, 2859)

26.   The following note was executed by Elizabeth Quinton on April 17, 1990 and delivered to Ian Wolf:

```
                   (Face)
                              April 17, 1990

On demand, the undersigned promises to
pay to the order of Ian Wolf

Seven Thousand and 00/100          Dollars

            Elizabeth Quinton
            Elizabeth Quinton
```

```
                   (Back)

    Ian Wolf
            Ian Wolf


Pay: George Vernon

    Samuel Thorn
            Samuel Thorn


Pay: Alan Yule

    George Vernon
            George Vernon

    Alan Yule
            Alan Yule
```

In sequence, beginning with Wolf's receipt of the note, this note is properly characterized as what type of commercial paper?
a.   Bearer, bearer, order, order, order.
b.   Order, bearer, order, order, bearer.
c.   Order, order, bearer, order, bearer.
d.   Bearer, order, order, order, bearer.

(11/90, Law, #49, 0534)

27. Hand executed and delivered to Rex a $1,000 negotiable note payable to Rex or bearer. Rex then negotiated it to Ford and endorsed it on the back by merely signing his name. Which of the following is a correct statement?
a. Rex's endorsement was a special endorsement.
b. Rex's endorsement was necessary to Ford's qualification as a holder.
c. The instrument initially being bearer paper **cannot** be converted to order paper.
d. The instrument is bearer paper and Ford can convert it to order paper by writing "pay to the order of Ford" above Rex's signature.
(11/86, Law, #41, 0556)

28. Jane Lane, a sole proprietor, has in her possession several checks which she received from her customers. Lane is concerned about the safety of the checks since she believes that many of them are bearer paper which may be cashed without endorsement. The checks in Lane's possession will be considered order paper rather than bearer paper if they were made payable (in the drawer's handwriting) to the order of
a. Cash.
b. Ted Tint, and endorsed by Ted Tint in blank.
c. Bearer, and endorsed by Ken Kent making them payable to Jane Lane.
d. Bearer, and endorsed by Sam Sole in blank.
(11/85, Law, #37, 0564)

29. West Corp. received a check that was originally made payable to the order of one of its customers, Ted Burns. The following endorsement was written on the back of the check:

| Ted Burns, without recourse, for collection only |

Which of the following describes the endorsement?

	Special	Restrictive
a.	Yes	Yes
b.	No	No
c.	No	Yes
d.	Yes	No

(11/92, Law, #35, 3117)

30. For a person to be a holder in due course of a promissory note
a. The note must be payable in U.S. currency to the holder.
b. The holder must be the payee of the note.
c. The note must be negotiable.
d. All prior holders must have been holders in due course.
(11/91, Law, #48, 2376)

30A. Under the Commercial Paper Article of the UCC, which of the following requirements must be met for a person to be a holder in due course of a promissory note?
a. The note must be payable to bearer.
b. The note must be negotiable.
c. All prior holders must have been holders in due course.
d. The holder must be the payee of the note.
(5/95, Law, #46, 5380)

31. A purchaser of a negotiable instrument would **least** likely be a holder in due course if, at the time of purchase, the instrument is
a. Purchased at a discount.
b. Collateral for a loan.
c. Payable to bearer on demand.
d. Overdue by three weeks.
(11/88, Law, #40, 9911)

31A. Under the Commercial Paper Article of the UCC, which of the following circumstances would prevent a person from becoming a holder in due course of an instrument?
a. The person was notified that payment was refused.
b. The person was notified that one of the prior endorsers was discharged.
c. The note was collateral for a loan.
d. The note was purchased at a discount.
(5/95, Law, #47, 5381)

32. The value requirement in determining whether a person is a holder in due course with respect to a check will **not** be satisfied by the taking of the check
a. As security for an obligation to the extent of the obligation.
b. As payment for an antecedent debt.
c. In exchange for another negotiable instrument.
d. In exchange for a promise to perform services in the future. (5/88, Law, #48, 0549)

33. Hunt has in his possession a negotiable instrument which was originally payable to the order of Carr. It was transferred to Hunt by a mere delivery by Drake, who took it from Carr in good faith in satisfaction of an antecedent debt. The back of the instrument read as follows, "Pay to the order of Drake in satisfaction of my prior purchase of a new video calculator, signed Carr." Which of the following is correct?

a. Hunt has the right to assert Drake's rights, including his standing as a holder in due course and also has the right to obtain Drake's signature.
b. Drake's taking the instrument for an antecedent debt prevents him from qualifying as a holder in due course.
c. Carr's endorsement was a special endorsement; thus Drake's signature was **not** required in order to negotiate it.
d. Hunt is a holder in due course.

(11/85, Law, #41, 0565)

34. On February 15, 1993, P.D. Stone obtained the following instrument from Astor Co. for $1,000. Stone was aware that Helco, Inc. disputed liability under the instrument because of an alleged breach by Astor of the referenced computer purchase agreement. On March 1, 1993, Willard Bank obtained the instrument from Stone for $3,900. Willard had no knowledge that Helco disputed liability under the instrument.

February 12, 1993

Helco, Inc. promises to pay to Astor Co. or bearer the sum of $4,900 (four thousand nine hundred and 00/100 dollars) on March 12, 1993, (maker may elect to extend due date to March 31, 1993) with interest thereon at the rate of 12% per annum.

HELCO, INC.

By: _A.J. Help_

A.J. Help, President

Reference: Computer purchase agreement dated February 12, 1993

The reverse side of the instrument is endorsed as follows:

Pay to the order of Willard Bank, without recourse

P.D. Stone

P.D. Stone

If Willard Bank demands payment from Helco and Helco refuses to pay the instrument because of Astor's breach of the computer purchase agreement, which of the following statements would be correct?

a. Willard Bank is **not** a holder in due course because Stone was **not** a holder in due course.
b. Helco will **not** be liable to Willard Bank because of Astor's breach.
c. Stone will be the only party liable to Willard Bank because he was aware of the dispute between Helco and Astor.
d. Helco will be liable to Willard Bank because Willard Bank is a holder in due course.

(5/93, Law, #39, amended, 4007)

35. Bond fraudulently induced Teal to make a note payable to Wilk, to whom Bond was indebted. Bond delivered the note to Wilk. Wilk negotiated the instrument to Monk, who purchased it with knowledge of the fraud and after it was overdue. If Wilk qualifies as a holder in due course, which of the following statements is correct?

a. Monk has the standing of a holder in due course through Wilk.
b. Teal can successfully assert the defense of fraud in the inducement against Monk.
c. Monk personally qualifies as a holder in due course.
d. Teal can successfully assert the defense of fraud in the inducement against Wilk.

(5/90, Law, #38, 0536)

36. To the extent that a holder of a negotiable promissory note is a holder in due course, the holder takes the note free of which of the following defenses?

a. Minority of the maker where it is a defense to enforcement of a contract.
b. Forgery of the maker's signature.
c. Discharge of the maker in bankruptcy.
d. Nonperformance of a condition precedent.

personal defense

(5/92, Law, #47, 2860)

37. Cobb gave Garson a signed check with the amount payable left blank. Garson was to fill in, as the amount, the price of fuel oil Garson was to deliver to Cobb at a later date. Garson estimated the amount at $700, but told Cobb it would be no more than $900. Garson did not deliver the fuel oil, but filled in the amount of $1,000 on the check. Garson then negotiated the check to Josephs in satisfaction of a $500 debt with the $500 balance paid to Garson in cash. Cobb stopped payment and Josephs is seeking to collect $1,000 from Cobb. Cobb's maximum liability to Josephs will be

a. $0.
b. $ 500.
c. $ 900.
d. $1,000.

(11/91, Law, #49, 2377)

38. A maker of a note will have a real defense against a holder in due course as a result of any of the following conditions **except**

a. Discharge in bankruptcy.
b. Forgery.
c. Fraud in the execution. *personal defense*
d. Lack of consideration. (11/92, Law, #40, 3122)

39. Robb, a minor, executed a promissory note payable to bearer and delivered it to Dodsen in payment for a stereo system. Dodsen negotiated the note for value to Mellon by delivery alone and without endorsement. Mellon endorsed the note in blank and negotiated it to Bloom for value. Bloom's demand for payment was refused by Robb because the note was executed when Robb was a minor. Bloom gave prompt notice of Robb's default to Dodsen and Mellon. None of the holders of the note were aware of Robb's minority. Which of the following parties will be liable to Bloom?

	Dodsen	Mellon
a.	Yes	Yes
b.	Yes	No
c.	No	No
d.	No	Yes

(5/93, Law, #42, 4010)

40. Frank Supply Co. held the following instrument:

Clark Novelties, Inc.   April 12, 1986
29 State Street
Spokane, Washington

Pay to the order of Frank Supply Co. on April 30, 1986, ten thousand and 00/100 dollars ($10,000.00).

Smith Industries, Inc.

J. C. Kahn
J. C. Kahn, President

ACCEPTED: Clark Novelties, Inc.
By:

Mitchell Clark
Mitchell Clark, President

Date: April 20, 1986

As a result of an audit examination of this instrument which was properly endorsed by Frank to your client, it may be correctly concluded that

a. Smith was primarily liable on the instrument prior to acceptance.
b. The instrument is nonnegotiable and thus **no** one has rights under the instrument.
c. No one was primarily liable on the instrument at the time of issue, April 12, 1986.
d. Upon acceptance, Clark Novelties, Inc., became primarily liable and Smith was released from all liability. (5/86, Law, #28, 9911)

41. Under the Commercial Paper Article of the UCC, in a nonconsumer transaction, which of the following are real defenses available against a holder in due course?

	Material alteration	Discharge in bankruptcy	Breach of contract
a.	No	Yes	Yes
b.	Yes	Yes	No
c.	No	No	Yes
d.	Yes	No	No

(5/95, Law, #49, 5383)

42.

Pay to Ann Tyler
Paul Tyler

Ann Tyler

Mary Thomas

Betty Ash

Pay George Green Only
Susan Town

Susan Town, on receiving the above instrument, struck Betty Ash's endorsement. Under the Commercial Paper Article of the UCC, which of the endorsers of the above instrument will be completely discharged from secondary liability to later endorsers of the instrument?

a. Ann Tyler.
b. Mary Thomas.
c. Betty Ash.
d. Susan Town. (5/95, Law, #50, 5384)

43. Vex Corp. executed a negotiable promissory note payable to Tamp, Inc. The note was collateralized by some of Vex's business assets.

Tamp negotiated the note to Miller for value. Miller endorsed the note in blank and negotiated it to Bilco for value. Before the note became due, Bilco agreed to release Vex's collateral. Vex refused to pay Bilco when the note became due. Bilco promptly notified Miller and Tamp of Vex's default. Which of the following statements is correct?

a. Bilco will be unable to collect from Miller because Miller's endorsement was in blank.
b. Bilco will be able to collect from either Tamp or Miller because Bilco was a holder in due course.
c. Bilco will be unable to collect from either Tamp or Miller because of Bilco's release of the collateral.
d. Bilco will be able to collect from Tamp because Tamp was the original payee.

(5/93, Law, #43, 4011)

44. Which of the following actions does **not** discharge a prior party to a commercial instrument?

a. Good faith payment or satisfaction of the instrument.
b. Cancellation of that prior party's endorsement.
c. The holder's <u>oral</u> renunciation of that prior party's liability. *shd we written*
d. The holder's intentional destruction of the instrument.

(5/92, Law, #48, 2861)

45. A check has the following endorsements on the back:

Paul Frank
without recourse

George Hopkins
payment guaranteed

Ann Quarry
collection guaranteed

Rachell Ott

Which of the following conditions occurring subsequent to the endorsements would discharge all of the endorsers?

a. Lack of notice of dishonor.
b. Late presentment.
c. Insolvency of the maker.
d. Certification of the check.

(11/92, Law, #41, 3123)

46. Blare bought a house and provided the required funds in the form of a certified check from a bank. Which of the following statements correctly describes the legal liability of Blare and the bank?

a. The bank has accepted; therefore, Blare is without liability.
b. The bank has **not** accepted; therefore, Blare has primary liability.
c. The bank has accepted, but Blare has secondary liability.
d. The bank has **not** accepted, but Blare has secondary liability.   (11/89, Law, #43, 0541)

47. In general, which of the following statements is correct concerning the priority among checks drawn on a particular account and presented to the drawee bank on a particular day?

a. The checks may be charged to the account in any order convenient to the bank.
b. The checks may be charged to the account in any order provided **no** charge creates an overdraft.
c. The checks must be charged to the account in the order in which the checks were dated.
d. The checks must be charged to the account in the order of lowest amount to highest amount to minimize the number of dishonored checks.

(11/88, Law, #39, 9911)

Solution 45-1 MULTIPLE CHOICE ANSWERS

Types of Negotiable Instruments

1. (d)   A "holder" is a person who is in possession of a document of title, an instrument, or a certified investment security drawn, issued, or endorsed to him or her, to his or her order, to bearer, or in blank. Although there are good faith and value requirements for a holder in due course, no such requirements apply to a mere holder. A holder could take possession of an order or bearer check.

2. (c)   A trade acceptance is a draft drawn by the seller-drawer on the buyer-drawee which is payable to the seller at some certain future date. The seller transmits the draft to the buyer for "acceptance" by the buyer.

3. (b)   This instrument meets all the requirements of a draft, since it is a written order from one person directing a second person to pay a sum certain in money to the order of a third person. It is also a time draft since it is payable at a certain time and not on demand. This instrument is not a check since it is not payable on demand, but only at a later date. A promissory note is a promise by the maker that *he or she will* pay a sum certain; a promissory note would not be drawn on a bank. On a trade acceptance, the drawer and payee are the same person.

3A. (a)   Under the Commercial Paper Article of the UCC, the nondebt instruments, i.e., checks and drafts, must contain an *order* to pay. The debt instruments, i.e., notes and certificates of deposit, must contain a *promise* to pay. Thus, between the draft and the certificate of deposit, only the draft would be considered an order to pay.

3B. (a)   The instrument depicted is a draft containing a delayed payment, drawn on a bank. Since the instrument indicates three parties, it must be a draft or a check. Since it is not payable on demand, it must be a draft, not a check.

4. (d)   A *draft* is a written order from one person (the drawer) directing a second person (the drawee) to pay a certain sum of money to a third person (the payee) or to the bearer. A *trade acceptance* is a draft drawn by a seller on the buyer-drawee which is payable to the seller at some future date for the amount of purchase (plus interest, if any). Answers (a) and (c) are incorrect because they are covered under Article 7 of the UCC and not under the commercial paper provisions in Article 3. A demand promissory note is a promise to pay a debt, not an order from one person directing another to pay.

5. (a)   A certificate of deposit is a written acknowledgement by a bank of the receipt of a sum of money with an engagement to repay that sum. A time draft is a written order from one person directing a second person to pay a sum certain of money to a third person or to the bearer at a certain future date. The concept of a banker's acceptance is similar to a trade acceptance, except that the draft is drawn on the buyer's bank instead of on the buyer personally. A cashier's check is a check drawn by a bank on itself, ordering itself to pay a sum of money to a third person.

6. (a)   A promissory note is a two-party instrument in which the maker (Helco, Inc.) promises to pay to the order of the payee (Astor Co.) or bearer a certain sum of money ($4,900) on a specified date (March 12, 1993). A sight draft, check, and trade acceptance are all three party instruments requiring a drawee.

7. (b)   Notes can be payable on installment and still be subject to the UCC Commercial Paper Article. Warehouse receipts and bills of lading are documents of title governed by Article 7 of the UCC. Investment bonds, such as corporate bearer bonds, are investment securities subject to Article 8 of the UCC.

8. (a)   Promissory notes are two-party instruments where a maker promises to pay a payee a certain sum of money. This instrument meets that definition. Also, the instrument is payable on demand, because no date of payment is specified. Therefore, this instrument is a promissory demand note. Answers (b), (c), and (d) are incorrect because they are *drafts*, not notes.

Requisites for Negotiability

9. (b)   To be negotiable, an instrument must be in writing, signed by the maker or drawer, contain an unconditional promise or order to pay a sum certain in money on demand or at a specific time, and be payable to order or to bearer. Negotiability is not affected by the fact that the instrument recites the transaction which gave rise to the instrument, and negotiability is not affected by the fact that it is stated with a specific rate of interest. The note is negotiable from the time it is made on October 2, 1987. It is a note (two-party instrument between maker and bearer-payee) and not a draft (which is a three-party instrument).

10. (a) The instrument satisfies all the requirements of negotiability and contains a written promise to pay a certain sum of money. Negotiability is not destroyed if the instrument states that it is secured by a mortgage, *unless* it expressly recites that it is "subject to" or "governed by" the mortgage agreement. Prepayment does not destroy the definite time at which a note is due, and the amount to be paid is still considered to be a "sum certain" even if it includes attorney's fees and collection costs upon default.

11. (d) This instrument is a negotiable note because it has all the requirements to be negotiable: it is in writing, contains an unconditional promise to pay, payable to the order of, a sum certain, payable at a definite time, signed by the maker, and it represents an unconditional promise to pay. Answer (a) is incorrect because this instrument is payable at a definite time. The amount due is specific. It is permissible to state that the instrument is secured by some asset. Had the instrument stated it was subject to some other agreement, the note would be nonnegotiable.

12. (d) An instrument will not be negotiable if it is "subject to" another agreement, since it would then no longer be an *unconditional* promise or order to pay. Negotiability will also be affected by a promise or order to do something in addition to the payment of money. The promises contained in answers (a), (b), and (c) are not considered as violating this requirement.

13. (c) An instrument is payable at a definite time if by its terms it is payable at a definite time subject to extension. If the extension is at the option of the maker or acceptor, it must be at a further definite time, or automatically upon the occurrence of a specified event (e.g., maker may elect to extend due date to March 12, 1993). A reference to the purchase agreement out of which an instrument arose will not prevent it from being negotiable. The instrument would be nonnegotiable if the instrument were subject to the computer purchase agreement. However, if the instrument only makes reference to another agreement, negotiability is not affected. In the case of inconsistencies between words and figures, the words control. Therefore, negotiability is not affected by this discrepancy. Negotiability was not destroyed when the note was transferred to Willard Bank.

14. (a) In order to satisfy the requirements of negotiability, an instrument must be payable at a definite time or on demand. Since the instrument presented in this problem is payable 10 days after the maker sells a diamond ring, it is not payable at a

definite time and, therefore, is not negotiable. Reference to secured collateral does not prevent it from being negotiable. A sight draft is a three-party instrument requiring a drawee. This instrument is a nonnegotiable note that is not payable at a definite time.

15. (c) The lack of a specific payment date will not effect the negotiability of the instrument. When no date is specified, it is considered payable *on demand*. The note is negotiable because, (1) it is in writing and signed by the maker, (2) it contains an unconditional promise to pay a sum certain in money with no other promise, (3) it is payable on demand, and (4) it is payable to order or to bearer. These are the four prerequisites of negotiability. An inconsistency between the amount in words and the amount in numbers does not effect the instrument's negotiability: the written amount will take precedent over the numerical amount. The guaranty by Abner has no bearing on negotiability.

16. (c) The instrument is a draft or bill of exchange which is payable on demand because no time for payment is stated. Therefore, it is payable on sight or upon presentation to the drawee, Bill Blake. Answer (a) is incorrect because Mary Kurke is the drawer of the draft. A note has two parties, the maker and the payee. In this question, there are three parties: the drawer, Mary Kurke, who is secondarily liable; the drawee, Bill Blake, who is primarily liable; and the payee, Gary Gold.

17. (a) To be negotiable, an instrument must be payable on demand or at a definite time. An instrument is *not* payable at a definite time and, hence, not negotiable, if it is payable only upon the occurrence of an event or some fixed time after the occurrence of an event which is uncertain as to time of occurrence. Since one cannot be certain when the maker will die, an instrument payable six months after the death of the maker is not negotiable. However, an instrument is payable at a definite time even though it may contain an acceleration clause in the event of default, e.g., "full payment due if delinquency occurs." A postdated negotiable instrument is still payable at a definite time. If no precise time for payment is specified in the postdated instrument, it is payable on demand on the postdated day. Whether an instrument contains an agreement to secure payment with collateral will not affect the instrument's negotiability. Likewise, an agreement to increase or decrease the securing collateral will have no effect on negotiability.

18. (d) Discrepancies between the figures and words on an instrument do not defeat negotiability

because words control over figures unless the words are ambiguous; thus, the instrument is an acceptable, negotiable promissory note with a "sum certain." The instrument is complete. The instrument does not meet the requirements of a draft nor does it state it is payable within a certain time.

18A. (d)   A clause in a promissory note that allows the maker to satisfy the note by the performance of services or the payment of money defeats the requirement that the instrument be payable in money and will prevent the note from being negotiable. An extension clause that allows the maker to elect to extend the time for payment to a date specified in the note does not defeat the requirement that an instrument be payable at a definite time. Nor does an acceleration clause that allows the holder to move up the maturity date of the note in the event of default. Thus, neither clause will prevent a promissory note from being negotiable. A person having a power of attorney who signs the note on behalf of the maker does not prevent the note from being negotiable.

19. (a)   Under the Commercial Paper Article of the UCC, for an instrument to be negotiable, it must be in writing; signed by the drawer or maker; contain an unconditional promise or order to pay a sum certain in money, on demand, or at an ascertainable time; and be payable to order or to bearer. Answers (b), (c), and (d) do not contain requirements for negotiability.

Transfer and Negotiation

20. (d)   John Smith endorsed the note in blank (did not specify any endorsee), thus, converting the note to bearer paper. Bearer paper may be effectively negotiated by delivery alone. Therefore, Harris' signature was not required. A note (or other instrument) does not become nonnegotiable as a result of an endorsement. A note or other instrument is either negotiable or nonnegotiable on its face and endorsements do not make an instrument negotiable or nonnegotiable. As a representative of the corporation, Parker has express authority to sign the note. Therefore, negotiability was not affected by his endorsement. Harris' conditional endorsement was an effective restrictive endorsement. A restrictive endorsement restricts the rights of the endorsee in some manner, but does not prohibit transfer or negotiation. A qualified endorsement ("without recourse") does not impair negotiability.

21. (c)   If a thief steals a negotiable instrument that has been endorsed in blank so that the instrument can be negotiated by mere delivery alone, a thief can pass good title to a holder in due course. Ott is a holder in due course to the extent of $3,000. Once Ott learns of the theft, King cannot be a holder in due course for any further amount.

22. (c)   In order for a transferee of a negotiable instrument to qualify as a holder, the transferee must take the instrument either by issue or by negotiation. In order to take by negotiation, a transferee of order paper must take by proper endorsement and delivery. Possession results from delivery and a transferee of order paper is entitled to the endorsement of the transferor.

23. (c)   UCC 3-202(1) only requires delivery to negotiate bearer paper. In contrast, order paper requires both endorsement <u>and</u> delivery for negotiation. The negotiability of an instrument, regardless of whether it is order or bearer paper, is not affected by the fact that no consideration is stated in the instrument.

Endorsement

24. (b)   Under the Commercial Paper Article of the UCC, a person endorsing a check "without recourse" disclaims the endorser's secondary liability to pay the check in the event it is dishonored. This qualified endorsement does not prevent the endorser from being liable for breach of warranty. The "without recourse" endorsement does not convert the check into order paper.

25. (d)   Clark may negotiate, by delivery alone, the negotiable promissory note, since the last endorsement did not name a specific endorsee.

26. (b)   When Wolf received the note, it was an "order" instrument. After Wolf signed in blank, the instrument was "bearer" paper. It became an "order" instrument after Thorn gave it a special endorsement, "Pay: Vernon." When Vernon signed it with a special endorsement, "Pay Yule," it continued to be an order instrument. When Yule signed the instrument in blank, it became a "bearer" instrument.

27. (d)   Rex's endorsement did not specify the person to whose order the instrument was then payable; it was, therefore, a blank endorsement. As executed by Hand, the instrument was bearer paper since it was made payable to "Rex or bearer." Ford could, therefore, qualify as a holder without Rex's endorsement. Bearer paper can be converted to order paper by making the last endorsement in the chain of endorsement a special endorsement.

28. (c)   Order paper is payable to a specific person or his or her order. The instrument, although

initially payable to bearer, was endorsed by Kent and made payable to a specific person. An instrument payable to cash is bearer paper. Whether payable to a specific person or to bearer, if an instrument is endorsed in blank, no specific endorsee is indicated and the instrument becomes bearer paper.

29. (c) The endorsement is restrictive, since it is "for collection only," and it is <u>not</u> special, since it does not specify the person to whose order the instrument is now payable. A special endorsement on bearer paper converts it to order paper.

Holders in Due Course

30. (c) A holder in due course is any holder who takes a *negotiable* instrument for value, in good faith, and without notice that it is overdue, has been dishonored, or that there is any defense against or claim to it on the part of any person. The note does not have to be payable in U.S. currency. The holder does not have to be the payee. All prior holders need not have been holders in due course.

30A. (b) Under the Commercial Paper Article of the UCC, in order for a person to qualify as a holder in due course of a promissory note, (1) they must qualify as a holder, (2) the note must be negotiable, and (3) they must take the note for value, in good faith, and without notice that it is overdue, dishonored, or there is a defense against it. Answers (a), (c), and (d) do not contain requirements for becoming a holder in due course.

31. (d) To qualify as a holder in due course, an individual must take the instrument without notice that it is overdue, that it has been dishonored, or that any person has a defense against it or claim to it. In determining whether or not a holder has notice that the instrument is overdue, the holder is bound by what the instrument itself reveals. Thus, if an instrument is payable on March 1, a purchaser cannot become a holder in due course by buying it on March 2. Answer (a), (b), and (c) are incorrect because, by themselves, they are not as likely to put a holder on notice of any defects.

31A. (a) Under the Commercial Paper Article of the UCC, in order for a person to become a holder in due course, they must take the instrument for value, in good faith, and without notice that it is overdue, has been dishonored, or that there is any defense or claim against it. Thus, a person notified that payment was refused would have notice of dishonor and could not become a holder in due course. The fact that the note was collateral for a loan or purchased at a discount

would not affect holder in due course status nor would notice that one of the prior endorsers was discharged.

32. (d) A promise to perform services in the future is not considered "value" for purposes of qualifying as a holder in due course. Answers (a), (b), and (c) all represent the giving of value and are incorrect.

33. (a) Taking an instrument in payment of an antecedent debt satisfies the requirement that an HDC take the instrument for value. A special endorsement converts the instrument to order paper, requiring the endorsee's signature in order to be negotiable. An HDC must take by original issue or by negotiation. Order paper is negotiated by proper endorsement plus delivery. In this situation, Drake delivered the instrument, but did not endorse it.

34. (d) The transfer of a negotiable instrument to a holder in due course cuts off all personal defenses against the HDC. As a holder in due course, Helco would be liable to Willard Bank. Willard Bank, as an HDC, has the right to collect. Helco will have to seek recourse directly from Astor. Note that Helco cannot collect from Stone because Stone endorsed the instrument "without recourse." Willard Bank qualifies as a holder in due course in spite of the fact that he received the instrument from someone (Stone) who was not a holder in due course.

35. (a) Under the "shelter provision" [UCC 3-201(1)], an instrument's transfer vests in the transferee the same rights as the transferor had. Thus, Monk, although not himself a holder in due course, enjoys the benefits of such status, since Wilk had been a holder in due course.

Liabilities, Defenses, and Rights

36. (d) A holder in due course takes an instrument free of personal defenses but is subject to real defenses--those that pertain to the validity of an instrument. Therefore, involving a breach of contract or nonperformance of a condition precedent is correct because it describes a personal defense.

37. (d) An unauthorized completion of an instrument is treated as a material alteration; however, it is not a real defense against a holder-in-due-course. A party whose substantial contributing negligence invites the material alteration is estopped from raising the alteration as a defense. Thus, Cobb is liable for the entire amount of the check to Josephs.

38. (d) A lack of consideration is a personal defense. A maker of a note has a *real* defense

against a holder in due course, but cannot use a *personal* defense. Answers (a), (b), and (c) represent real defenses.

39. (d) Dodsen effectively negotiated the note for value to Mellon by delivery alone and without endorsement. Therefore, he has a warranty liability to Mellon, but not to Bloom. When a person does not endorse an instrument but negotiates it by mere delivery alone, his or her warranty extends only to the person to whom it was given. Thus, Dodsen's warranty extends only to Mellon and not to Bloom. Mellon, however, endorsed the note and thus has contractual liability. Under contractual liability, the endorser guarantees payment of the instrument if the appropriate party for payment dishonors the note. Therefore, Mellon will be liable to Bloom.

40. (c) Smith Industries, as drawer of the instrument, is only secondarily liable for it. Upon Clark's acceptance, it then became primarily liable while Smith remained secondarily liable. The instrument meets all the requirements of negotiability.

41. (b) Under the Commercial Paper Article of the UCC, real defenses available against a holder in due course include material alteration of the instrument and discharge of a person with primary or secondary liability in bankruptcy. Breach of contract is a personal defense not available against a holder in due course.

42. (c) Under the Commercial Paper Article of the UCC, all endorsers of an instrument have secondary liability to later endorsers of the instrument. Since Betty Ash's signature has been stricken from the instrument, she no longer appears as an endorser. Ann Tyler's, Mary Thomas', and Susan Town's unqualified endorsements are all present on the instrument; thus, each of them will have secondary liability for payment.

43. (c) An endorser normally has a right of recourse against primary parties, prior endorsers, or the drawer of a note. If any of the rights of an endorser are affected by the actions of the holder, such as early release of the collateral, that endorser is discharged from liability on the instrument to the extent that the endorser has been injured by the early release of the collateral. In this problem, it appears that the note was 100% collateralized; thus, releasing the collateral without agreement by the endorsers will release Tamp or Miller from liability. Miller's negotiation in blank merely converted the note to bearer paper and will not affect his liability to Bilco.

44. (c) A holder may discharge any prior party by renunciation. However, this renunciation cannot be made orally. It may only be accomplished by a signed writing stating that the holder releases the party or by surrendering the instrument to the party to be discharged.

45. (d) Certification procured by the holder discharges the drawer and any prior endorsers; the bank becomes primarily liable. An endorser might still be held liable for breach of warranty even if the check is presented late. An endorser would have to cause an instrument to be dishonored for the notice of dishonor to be excused. The insolvency of the maker does not affect the responsibilities of the endorsers.

46. (c) Certification of a check is the drawee bank's acceptance of the instrument (and the bank's warranty that funds are set aside for payment). Where certification is obtained by the drawer, the bank is primarily liable and the drawer remains secondarily liable.

47. (a) A bank may charge checks against an account in any order it deems convenient.

Personal Def.
1) Breach of K
2) Nonperformance of a condition precedent
3) Lack of Consideration
4) Misrep of a Condition

PERFORMANCE BY SUBTOPICS

Each category below parallels a subtopic covered in Chapter 45. Record the number and percentage of questions you correctly answered in each subtopic area.

Types of Negotiable Instruments

Question #	Correct √
1	
2	
3	
3A	
3B	
4	
5	
6	
7	
8	
# Questions	10

Correct _____
% Correct _____

Requisites for Negotiability

Question #	Correct √
9	
10	
11	
12	
13	
14	
15	
16	
17	
18	
18A	
19	
# Questions	12

Correct _____
% Correct _____

Transfer and Negotiation

Question #	Correct √
20	
21	
22	
23	
# Questions	4

Correct _____
% Correct _____

Endorsement

Question #	Correct √
24	
25	
26	
27	
28	
29	
# Questions	6

Correct _____
% Correct _____

Holders in Due Course

Question #	Correct √
30	
30A	
31	
31A	
32	
33	
34	
35	
# Questions	8

Correct _____
% Correct _____

Liabilities, Defenses, and Rights

Question #	Correct √
36	
37	
38	
39	
40	
41	
42	
43	
44	
45	
46	
47	
# Questions	12

Correct _____
% Correct _____

OTHER OBJECTIVE FORMAT QUESTION

Problem 45-2 (10 to 15 minutes)

Problem 45-2 consists of 2 parts. Part A consists of 5 items and Part B consists of 8 items. Select the **best** answer for each item.

During an audit of Trent Realty Corp.'s financial statements, Clark, CPA, reviewed the following instruments:

A.

Instrument 1

$300,000   Belle, MD
                                              September 15, 1993

For value received, ten years after date, I promise to pay to the order of Dart Finance Co. Three Hundred Thousand and 00/100 dollars with interest at 9% per annum compounded annually until fully paid.

This instrument arises out of the sale of land located in MD.

It is further agreed that:

1.   Maker will pay all costs of collection including reasonable attorney fees.
2.   Maker may prepay the amount outstanding on any anniversary date of this instrument.

G. Evans

G. Evans

The following transactions relate to Instrument 1.

- On March 15, 1994, Dart endorsed the instrument in blank and sold it to Morton for $275,000.
- On July 10, 1994, Evans informed Morton that Dart had fraudulently induced Evans into signing the instrument.
- On August 15, 1994, Trent, which knew of Evans' claim against Dart, purchased the instrument from Morton for $50,000.

Required:

Items 1 through 5 relate to Instrument 1. For each item, select from List I the correct answer. An answer may be selected once, more than once, or not at all.

1. Instrument 1 is a (type of instrument). *B*

2. Instrument 1 is (negotiability). *G*

3. Morton is considered a (type of ownership). *E*

4. Trent is considered a (type of ownership). *F*

5. Trent could recover on the instrument from (liable party(s)). *I*

_____List I_____
A. Draft
B. Promissory Note
C. Security Agreement
D. Holder
E. Holder in due course
F. Holder with rights of a holder in due course under the Shelter Provision
G. Negotiable
H. Nonnegotiable
I. Evans, Morton, and Dart
J. Morton and Dart
K. Only Dart

B.

Instrument 2

Front

```
To:   Pure Bank
      Upton, VT

                              April 5, 1994

Pay to the order of M. West $1,500.00
One Thousand Five Hundred and 00/100
Dollars on May 1, 1994

          W. Fields
      _____
          W. Fields
```

Back

```
M. West

Pay to C. Larr
T. Keetin

C. Larr
without recourse
```

Required:

Items 6 through 13 relate to Instrument 2. For each item, select from List II the correct answer. An answer may be selected once, more than once, or not at all.

6. Instrument 2 is a (type of instrument). *D*

7. Instrument 2 is (negotiability). *G*

8. West's endorsement makes the instrument (type of instrument). *A*

9. Keetin's endorsement makes the instrument (type of instrument). *H*

10. Larr's endorsement makes the instrument (type of instrument). *A*

11. West's endorsement would be considered (type of endorsement). *B*

12. Keetin's endorsement would be considered (type of endorsement). *g*

13. Larr's endorsement would be considered (type of endorsement). *I*

List II

A. Bearer paper
B. Blank
C. Check
D. Draft
E. Negotiable
F. Nonnegotiable
G. Note
H. Order paper
I. Qualified
J. Special

(11/94, Law, #3)

OTHER OBJECTIVE FORMAT SOLUTION

Solution 45-2 Commercial Paper

1. (B) Instrument I is a promissory note, which is a written promise to pay a stated sum of money.

2. (G) Instrument I is negotiable because it is a writing signed by the maker, containing an unconditional promise to pay a sum certain in money at a definite time. The note also contains the words negotiability, thus, all elements necessary for negotiability are present.

3. (E) Morton is a holder in due course because he is a holder who took the instrument by negotiation. He also took the instrument for value, in good faith and without notice that it is overdue, that it has been dishonored, or that there is a defense against it.

4. (F) Trent is not an ordinary holder in due course because he took the note with notice of Evan's claim against Dart. The Shelter Provision vests in a transferee such rights as the transferor had therein. A person can thus enjoy holder in due course status if any transferor in the chain of ownership was an HDC. Since Trent received the note from Morton, an HDC, Trent has the rights of an HDC.

5. (I) Fraud in the inducement is a personal defense, and personal defenses cannot be asserted against an HDC. Trent is an HDC under the Shelter Provision. Evans is thus liable to Dart. All endorsers of an instrument have secondary liability for payment thereon. If Morton and Dart both endorse the instrument, they would be liable to Trent as well.

6. (D) Instrument II is a bank draft. Although it is drawn on a bank, it is not payable on demand and thus is not a check.

7. (E) The instrument is negotiable because it is in writing and signed by the drawer; it contains an unconditional order to pay a sum certain in money at a definite time. It also contains the words of negotiability; thus, all elements for negotiability are present.

8. (A) A blank endorsement results whenever the transferor's signature appears alone, without specifying a particular endorsee. A blank endorsement results in bearer paper.

9. (H) A special endorsement results when the transferor specifies the person to whose order the paper is to be payable. A special endorsement results in order paper.

10. (A) Larr's signature stands alone, without specifying a particular endorsee. It is, thus, a blank (although qualified) endorsement. A blank endorsement results in bearer paper.

11. (B) A blank endorsement exists where the transferor's signature stands alone, without specifying an endorsee.

12. (J) A special endorsement exists where the transferor specifies the person to whose order the instrument is to be payable.

13. (I) A qualified endorsement (usually characterized by writing "without recourse") disclaims the endorser's secondary liability for payment on the instrument.

ESSAY QUESTIONS

Essay 45-3 (15 to 20 minutes)

On February 12, 1990, Mayfair & Associates, CPAs, was engaged to audit the financial statements of University Book Distributors, Inc. University operates as a retail and wholesale distributor of books, newspapers, magazines, and other periodicals. In conjunction with the audit of University's cash, notes, and accounts receivable, University's controller gave Mayfair's staff accountant certain instruments that University had received from its customers during 1989 in the ordinary course of its business. The instruments are:

• A signed promissory note dated June 30, 1989, in the amount of $3,100 payable "to Harris on December 31, 1989." The maker of the note was Peters and it was endorsed in blank by Harris, who delivered it to University as payment for a shipment of magazines. University demanded that Peters pay the note but Peters refused, claiming that he gave the note as a result of misrepresentations by Harris related to a real estate transaction between the two of them. University advised Harris immediately of Peters' refusal to pay.

• A signed promissory note dated July 31, 1989, in the amount of $1,800 payable "to the order of Able on January 15, 1990." The maker of the note was Cole and it further provided that it was given "pursuant to that certain construction contract dated June 1, 1989." The note had been given to University as payment for books by one of its customers, Baker, who did not endorse it. The note bears Able's blank endorsement. University demanded payment from Cole. Cole refused to honor the note claiming that:

  • The note's reference to the construction contract renders it nonnegotiable; and
  • University has no rights to the note because it was not endorsed by Baker.

University immediately advised Baker of Cole's refusal to pay.

University is uncertain of its rights under the two notes.

Required:

Answer the following questions, setting forth reasons for your conclusions.

a. With regard to the note executed by Peters, is University a holder in due course?

b. Can Peters raise Harris' alleged misrepresentations as a defense to University's demand for payment?

c. Are Cole's claims valid?   (5/90, Law, #5)

Essay 45-4 (15 to 20 minutes)

River Oaks is a wholesale distributor of automobile parts. River Oaks received the promissory note shown below from First Auto, Inc., as security for payment of a $4,400 auto parts shipment. When River Oaks accepted the note as collateral for the First Auto obligation, River Oaks was aware that the maker of the note, Hillcraft, Inc., was claiming that the note was unenforceable because Alexco Co. had breached the license agreement under which Hillcraft had given the note. First Auto had acquired the note from Smith in exchange for repairing several cars owned by Smith. At the time First Auto received the note, First Auto was unaware of the dispute between Hillcraft and Alexco. Also, Smith, who paid Alexco $3,500 for the note, was unaware of Hillcraft's allegations that Alexco had breached the license agreement.

PROMISSORY NOTE

Date: <u>1/14/90</u>

<u> Hillcraft, Inc. </u> promises to pay

<u> Alexco Co. or bearer </u> the sum of <u>$4,400</u>

<u> Four Thousand and 00/100 </u> Dollars on or

before <u> May 15, 1991 (maker may elect to</u>

<u>extend due date by 30 days)</u> with interest

thereon at the rate of <u>9-1/2%</u> per annum.

Hillcraft, Inc.

By:<u> P. J. Hill </u>
     P. J. Hill, President

Reference: <u>Alexco Licensing Agreement</u>

The reverse side of the note was endorsed as follows:

Pay to the order of First Auto with recourse

E. Smith
_____
E. Smith

Pay to the order of River Oaks Co.

G. First
_____
G. First, President

First Auto is not insolvent and unable to satisfy its obligation to River Oaks. Therefore, River Oaks has demanded that Hillcraft pay $4,400, but Hillcraft has refused, asserting:

- The note is nonnegotiable because it references the license agreement and is not payable at a definite time or on demand.
- River Oaks is not a holder in due course of the note because it received the note as security for amounts owed by First Auto.
- River Oaks is not a holder in due course because it was aware of the dispute between Hillcraft and Alexco.
- Hillcraft can raise the alleged breach by Alexco as a defense to payment.
- River Oaks has no right to the note because it was not endorsed by Alexco.
- The maximum amount that Hillcraft would owe under the note is $4,000, plus accrued interest.

Required:

State whether each of Hillcraft's assertions are correct and give the reasons for your conclusions.

(5/91, Law, #3)

Essay 45-5 (15 to 25 minutes)

Williams Co. provides financial consulting services to the business community. On occasion, Williams will purchase promissory notes from its clients. The following transactions involving promissory notes purchased by Williams have resulted in disputes:

- Williams purchased the following promissory note from Jason Computers, Inc.:

January 3, 1992

For value received, Helco Distributors Corp. promises to pay $3,000 to the order of Jason Computers, Inc. with such payment to be made out of the proceeds of the resale of the computer components purchased this day from Jason Computers, Inc. and to be used as part of the customized computer systems sold to our customers. Payment shall be made two weeks after such proceeds become available.

J. Helco
_____
J. Helco, President

Helco executed and delivered the note to Jason in payment for the computer components referred to in the note. Jason represented to Helco that all the components were new when, in fact, a large number of them were used and had been reconditioned. Williams was unaware of this fact at the time it acquired the note from Jason for $2,000. Jason endorsed and delivered the note to Williams in exchange for the $2,000 payment. Williams presented the promissory note to Helco for payment. Helco refused to pay, alleging that Jason misrepresented the condition of the components. Helco also advised Williams that the components had been returned to Jason within a few days after Helco had taken delivery.

Williams commenced an action against Helco, claiming that

- The note is negotiable;
- Williams is a holder in due course; and
- Helco cannot raise Jason's misrepresentation as a defense to payment of the note.

- Williams Co. purchased a negotiable promissory note from Oliver International, Inc. that Oliver had received from Abco Products Corp., as partial payment on the sale of goods by Oliver to Abco. The maker of the note was Grover Corp., which had executed and delivered the note to Abco as payment for services rendered by Abco. When Oliver received the note from Abco, Oliver was unaware of the fact that Grover disputed its obligation under the note because Grover was dissatisfied with the quality of the services Abco rendered. Williams was aware of Grover's claims at the time Williams purchased the note from Oliver. The reverse side of the note was endorsed as follows:

Pay to the order of Oliver
F. Smith
F. Smith, President of Abco Products Corp.
Pay to the order of Williams Co. without recourse
N. Oliver
N. Oliver, President of Oliver International, Inc.

When the promissory note became due, Williams demanded that Grover pay the note. Grover refused, claiming that Abco breached its contractual obligations to Grover and that Williams was aware of this fact at the time Williams acquired the note. Williams immediately advised both Abco and Oliver of Grover's refusal to pay and demanded payment from Oliver in the event Grover fails to pay the note.

Required:

Answer the following questions and give the reasons for your conclusions.

a. Are Williams' claims correct regarding the Helco promissory note?

b. Is Grover correct in refusing to pay its note?

c. What are the rights of Williams against Oliver in the event Grover is not required to pay its note?
(11/93, Law, #5)

Essay 45-6 (15 to 20 minutes)

Prince, Hall, & Charming, CPAs, has been retained to audit the financial statements of Hex Manufacturing Corporation. Shortly before beginning the audit for the year ended December 31, 1986, Mr. Prince received a telephone call from Hex's president indicating that he thought some type of embezzlement was occurring because the corporation's cash position was significantly lower than in prior years. The president

then requested that Prince immediately undertake a special investigation to determine the amount of embezzlement, if any.

After a month of investigation, Prince uncovered an embezzlement scheme involving collusion between the head of payroll and the assistant treasurer. The following is a summary of Prince's findings:

- The head of payroll supplied the assistant treasurer with punched time cards for fictitious employees. The assistant treasurer prepared invoices, receiving reports, and purchase orders for fictitious suppliers. The assistant treasurer prepared checks for the fictitious employees and suppliers which were signed by the treasurer. Then, either the assistant treasurer or the head of payroll would endorse the checks and deposit them in various banks where they maintained accounts in the names of the fictitious payees. All of the checks in question have cleared Omega Bank, the drawee.

- The embezzlement scheme had been operating for 10 months, and more than $120,000 had been embezzled by the time the scheme was uncovered. The final series of defalcations included checks payable directly to the head of payroll and the assistant treasurer. These checks included skillful forgeries of the treasurer's signature that were almost impossible to detect. This occurred while the treasurer was on vacation. These checks have also cleared Omega Bank, the drawee.

Required:

Answer the following, setting forth reasons for any conclusions stated.

Will Hex or Omega bear the loss with respect to the following categories of checks:

a. Those which were signed by the treasurer but payable to fictitious payee?

b. Those which include the forged signature of the treasurer?
(5/87, Law, #2)

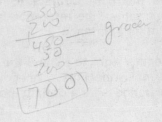

ESSAY SOLUTIONS

Solution 45-3 Holder in Due Course/Misrepresentations by Payee/Negotiability

a. University is **not a holder in due course** (HDC) with regard to Peters' note. To be an HDC, University must:

- Be a **holder** of a negotiable instrument.
- Take it for **value**.
- Take it in **good faith**.
- Take it **without notice** that it is **overdue** or has been **dishonored**.
- Take it **without notice** of any **defense** or **claim** to it.

All of the above requirements are met except the first. Peters' note is **not negotiable** because it is **not made payable to bearer or to the order of a named payee**.

b. University is an **assignee** of Harris' rights under Peters' note. Therefore, University **"stands in the shoes"** of Harris, and Peters can raise Harris' alleged misrepresentations as a defense against University.

c. **1.** Cole's first claim is incorrect. The promissory note Cole executed is **negotiable despite the reference to the construction contract**, because it does not make the note **subject to the other contract**; rather, the reference is only a **recital of that contract's existence**.

2. Cole's second claim is incorrect. University acquired rights to the promissory note without Baker's endorsement because the note had been **converted to a bearer instrument** as a result of Able's **blank endorsement**. Bearer paper can be negotiated by **delivery alone**.

Solution 45-4 Negotiability/Holder in Due Course

Hillcraft's first assertion, that the note is nonnegotiable because it references the license agreement and is not payable at a definite time or on demand, is incorrect. The note is **negotiable despite** the **reference to the license agreement** because it does not make the note **subject to the terms** of the agreement; rather, the **reference** is regarded only as a **recital of its existence**.

Also, Hillcraft's **right to extend the time for payment** does not make the note nonnegotiable because the extension period is for a **definite period of time**.

Hillcraft's second assertion, that River Oaks is not a holder in due course (HDC) because it received the note as security for an existing debt and, therefore, did not give value for it, is incorrect. Under the UCC Commercial Paper Article, a **holder does give value for an instrument when it is taken in payment of, or as security for, an antecedent claim.**

Hillcraft's third assertion, that River Oaks is not an HDC because River Oaks was aware of Alexco's alleged breach of the license agreement, is correct. If a holder of a note is **aware of a dispute** when it acquires the note, that holder **cannot be an HDC** because it **took with notice**.

Hillcraft's fourth assertion, that it can raise the alleged breach by Alexco as a defense to payment of the note, is incorrect. Even though River Oaks is not an HDC under the UCC **"shelter provision,"** it is **entitled to the protection of an HDC** because it took the instrument from First Auto, which was an HDC. Therefore, River Oaks did not take the note subject to Hillcraft's defense based on the alleged breach by Alexco. **Hillcraft's defense** is considered a **personal defense** and can only be used by Hillcraft against Alexco.

Hillcraft's fifth assertion, that River Oaks has no right to the note because it was not endorsed by Alexco, is incorrect. River Oaks acquired rights to the Hillcraft note without Alexco's endorsement because the note was a **bearer instrument** as a result of it being **payable to "Alexco Company or bearer."** A bearer instrument can be **negotiated by delivery alone.**

Hillcraft's final assertion, that the maximum amount Hillcraft would owe under the note is $4,000, plus accrued interest, is correct. If there is a conflict **between a number written in numerals** and also **described by words**, the **words take precedence**. Therefore, Hillcraft's **maximum potential principal liability is $4,000** under the note.

Solution 45-5 Negotiability/Holder in Due Course

a. William's first claim that the promissory note is negotiable is incorrect. The note is **nonnegotiable** because:

- It is **not payable at a definite time or on demand** because payment is not required until two weeks after an event, the occurrence of which is uncertain.

• The note is only payable out of the proceeds of the resale of the computer components making the **promise to pay the note conditional.** This is referred to as the **"particular fund doctrine."**

Williams' second claim that it is a holder in due course is incorrect. Although Williams is a holder of the instrument, it **cannot be a holder in due course** because the **instrument is nonnegotiable.**

Williams' third claim that Helco cannot raise Jason's misrepresentation as a defense to payment of the note is incorrect. This defense is a **personal defense** and would **not be valid against a holder in due course.** Williams only **has the rights of an assignee** of the Helco note. It has no better rights than Jason. Thus, Helco can raise Jason's misrepresentation as a defense.

b. Grover is incorrect in refusing to pay its note. Williams **took the note with notice** of Grover's defense and, therefore, could not be a holder in due course in its own right. Williams took the note from Oliver, who was a holder in due course. Therefore, under the **"shelter provision" of the UCC Commercial Paper Article**, Williams has the **rights of a holder in due course even though it does not qualify as one.** As a result, Williams did not take the note subject to Grover's defense even though Williams was aware of it.

c. Williams will be unable to collect from Oliver in the event Grover is not required to pay the note. Oliver was **unaware of the claims** of Grover, its **endorsement was without recourse** and **violated no transfer warranties.** Therefore, Williams does not have any right to recover from Oliver.

Solution 45-6 Liability for Forged Checks and Checks to Fictitious Employees

a. Checks paid to fictitious payees--Hex will bear the ultimate loss on these items (the fictitious or nonexistent "employees" and the fictitious suppliers). As a general rule, **forged signatures of drawers** and **forged endorsements** are **real defenses** which are **valid even against a holder in due course.**

However, when some of these activities are engaged in by the employees of an employer-drawer of the checks, a different rule is applied. Essentially, this rule negates these real defenses in certain cases thereby **shifting the loss to the employer-drawer.** The key rule is contained in the Uniform Commercial Code's Article on Commercial Paper which deals with "Impostors; Signature of Payee." In essence, this rule makes the endorsement or signature of the agent or employee of the drawer (Hex) "effective" where the agent has supplied the drawer the name of the payee intending the latter to have no such interest.

Insofar as Omega is concerned, it will be treated as if it had honored valid orders to pay and **need not refund to Hex the amounts it paid.** The **orders are valid** since the **forged endorsements are not treated as unauthorized.**

b. Checks which contain the forged signature of the treasurer--From the facts it is apparent that the **treasurer had the authority** to sign checks and not the assistant treasurer or head of payroll. Thus, the forging of the treasurer's signature was an **"unauthorized signature"** under the UCC.

As to these checks, the UCC provides that such **signatures are wholly inoperative** since the guilty parties had no authority to sign the treasurer's or any other authorized party's name as the drawer on behalf of Hex.

As between Hex and Omega, there is an **obligation on the part of the bank to know the signatures of its drawer-depositors.** Since Omega has paid the items, it **cannot recoup the loss from Hex.** However, the bank has two possible ways to escape liability to Hex. First, it can resort to the UCC section which imposes upon a customer to whom items (checks) are returned, a **duty to exercise reasonable care and promptness in discovering and reporting unauthorized signatures.** Another possibility is to establish **negligence** on the part of Hex which **substantially contributed to the forgeries.** Unless the bank can demonstrate that one of these exceptions applies, it will bear the loss.

NOTES

CHAPTER 46

DOCUMENTS OF TITLE AND INVESTMENT SECURITIES

PART ONE: DOCUMENTS OF TITLE 46-2

I. Definitions 46-2
   A. Bailee 46-2
   B. Bill of Lading 46-2
   C. Consignee 46-2
   D. Consignor 46-2
   E. Delivery Order 46-2
   F. Documents of Title 46-2
   G. Issuer 46-2
   H. Warehouse Receipt 46-2

II. Form and Content 46-2
   A. Warehouse Receipt 46-2
   B. Bill of Lading 46-3

III. Negotiability and Effect of Documents of Title 46-3
   A. Negotiable Document 46-3
   B. Nonnegotiable Document 46-3
   C. Effect 46-3
   D. Negotiation and Due Negotiation 46-4
   E. Liability of Endorser or Transferor 46-4
   F. Persons Defeating Holders' and Transferees' Rights 46-5

IV. Duty of Care and Risk of Loss 46-5
   A. Warehouseman 46-5
   B. Carriers 46-5

PART TWO: INVESTMENT SECURITIES 46-5

I. Definitions 46-5
   A. Bona Fide Purchaser 46-5
   B. Broker 46-6
   C. Issuer 46-6
   D. Security 46-6

II. Issuance 46-6
   A. Issuer's Responsibilities 46-6
   B. Issuer's Rights 46-6

III. Purchase and Transfer 46-7
   A. Introduction 46-7
   B. Rights Acquired by Purchaser 46-7
   C. Warranties on Transfer or Presentment 46-7
   D. Purchaser's Right to Endorsement 46-7
   E. Endorser's Liability 46-7
   F. Endorsement Without Delivery 46-7
   G. Effect of Unauthorized Endorsement 46-8

IV. Stolen, Lost, or Destroyed Securities 46-8

CHAPTER 46

DOCUMENTS OF TITLE AND INVESTMENT SECURITIES

PART ONE: DOCUMENTS OF TITLE

I. Definitions

A. <u>Bailee</u>--Person who by a warehouse receipt, bill of lading, or other document acknowledges possession of goods and contracts to deliver them [UCC 7-102(1)(a)].

B. <u>Bill of Lading</u>--Document evidencing the receipt of goods for shipment issued by a person engaged in the business of transporting or forwarding goods. Includes airbills and freight receipts [UCC 1-201(6)].

C. <u>Consignee</u>--Person named in a bill of lading to whom or to whose order the bill promises delivery [UCC 7-102(1)(b)].

D. <u>Consignor</u>--Person named in a bill of lading as the person from whom the goods have been received for shipment [UCC 7-102(1)(c)].

E. <u>Delivery Order</u>--Written order to deliver goods directed to a warehouseman or carrier who issues warehouse receipts or bills of lading in the ordinary course of business [UCC 7-102(1)(d)].

F. <u>Documents of Title</u>--Include bills of lading, dock warrants and receipts, warehouse receipts, orders for the delivery of goods, as well as any other document which in the regular course of business or financing is treated as adequately evidencing that the person in possession of the document is entitled to receive, hold, and dispose of the document and the goods it covers. To be a document of title, a document must purport to be issued by or addressed to a bailee and purport to cover goods in the bailee's possession [UCC 1-201(15)].

G. <u>Issuer</u>--Bailee who issues a document, except that in relation to an unaccepted delivery order, it means the person who orders the possessor of goods to deliver [UCC 7-102(1)(g)].

H. <u>Warehouse Receipt</u>--Receipt issued by a person engaged in the business of storing goods for hire. Even though one cannot become a warehouseman by storing his or her own goods, an owner-storer of goods can issue a document of title that is the equivalent of a receipt [UCC 1-201(45)].

II. Form and Content

A. <u>Warehouse Receipt</u>--Although no particular format is required, it must be in writing and must contain the following terms in order for the warehouseman to avoid liability for damages caused by the terms' omission:

    1. Location of the warehouse in which the goods are stored.

    2. Date of issue of the receipt.

    3. Consecutive number of the receipt.

    4. Statement as to whether goods received will be delivered to the bearer, a specified person, or to a specified person on his or her order.

5.   Rate of storage and handling charges.

6.   Description of the goods.

7.   Signature of the warehouseman.

8.   Statement as to ownership if issued for goods owned by the warehouseman.

9.   Statement of the amount of advances and liabilities on which warehouseman claims a lien.

B.   Bill of Lading--No particular format is required, but it must be in writing and must adequately record the fact that it was issued in receipt for goods to be shipped. Bills are regulated by Article 7 of the UCC to the extent not superseded by federal statutes and treaties. Some types of bills are:

1.   Destination Bills--In the usual shipping situation, the bill is issued by the carrier at the point of shipment. If the goods subsequently arrive at the destination before the document of title, no one would be ready or able to receive them. To solve this problem, the carrier issues a "destination bill." This bill would be issued at the point of destination or other point specified by the consignor. Thus, there is no lag between issue and delivery; rather, the bill is there when the goods arrive (UCC 7-305).

evidence of receipt not title

2.   Through Bills--Issued by a carrier who accepts liability for the transport of goods from the point of shipment through (and over other connecting carriers) to the point of destination. Connecting carriers act as agents for the through bill carrier and are liable for loss while goods are in their possession (UCC 7-302).

3.   Freight-Forwarder Bills--Issued by a middleman who marshals less than carload amounts of goods into carload quantities. Purpose is to provide continuous title documentation while goods are in transit.

III. Negotiability and Effect of Documents of Title

A.   Negotiable Document--A warehouse receipt, bill of lading, or other document of title is negotiable if either of the following applies [UCC 7-104(1)]:

1.   If by its terms, the goods are to be delivered to bearer or to the order of a named person.

2.   Where recognized in overseas trade, the document runs to a named person or assigns.

B.   Nonnegotiable Document--Any document of title not satisfying the requirements of A., above. Furthermore, a bill of lading in which it is stated that the goods are consigned to a named person is not made negotiable by a provision that the goods are to be delivered only against a signed written order by that person. Thus, a straight bill does not become an order bill because a specific person is to be notified and must sign to take possession of goods [UCC 7-104(2)].

C.   Effect--The distinction between negotiable and nonnegotiable documents is the most important aspect of Article 7, because the holder of negotiable documents may acquire more rights than the transferor had in the document. A document of title is "commodity paper"; thus, it represents the underlying goods. (In contrast, commercial paper is "money paper.") It is important to note that a holder to whom a negotiable document has been duly negotiated by endorsement and delivery acquires title to the underlying goods (UCC 7-502). However, a transferee of a negotiable or non--negotiable document to whom the document has been transferred, but not negotiated, acquires only those rights to the underlying goods that the transferor had the power and authority to transfer [UCC 7-504(1)].

D. <u>Negotiation and Due Negotiation</u>--It is important to keep in mind the fact that <u>only</u> a negotiable document can be negotiated (although negotiable documents can also be transferred or assigned). In contrast, a nonnegotiable document can only be transferred or assigned.

1. <u>Negotiation</u>--A special form of transfer that makes the transferee a holder. (Issuance of a negotiable document to a named person has the same effect as negotiation.)

- Rights Acquired by Holder--A holder to whom a document has been duly negotiated acquires title to the document, title to the goods, and right to the goods (if delivered to a bailee). Finally, the issuer of the duly negotiated document has the direct obligation to hold or deliver the goods to the holder according to the terms of the document free of any claim or defense. Moreover, these rights accrue to the holder, even though the negotiation or any prior negotiation constituted a breach of duty, or the document was obtained from a prior possessor by fraud or theft (UCC 7-502).

2. <u>Due Negotiation</u>--In order to obtain the special rights of a holder, there must be either due negotiation or the transferee must take under the shelter principle.

- Due Negotiation of a Negotiable Document--Occurs when the transferee takes <u>in good faith</u>, <u>in the regular course of business</u> of the transferor, and <u>for present (not antecedent) value</u> (UCC 7-501). Note the similarities (and differences) between an Article 7 holder and an Article 3 holder in due course (HDC). An Article 7 holder must take the negotiable instrument running to order of a named person in the ordinary course of business of the transferor (the HDC need not so take). Thus, there could be no due negotiation of an order document running to the order of a person who has no business holding the document. For example, there could be no holder-transferee of a document running to the order of a transient, casual friend, or person not in the business of trading in documents. (However, there would be due negotiation of an Article 3 negotiable instrument from any of the above three people.) This results from the negotiation requirements of <u>order</u> negotiable documents (negotiation accomplished by and only when <u>endorsement and delivery</u> effected) versus <u>bearer</u> negotiable documents (negotiation accomplished upon <u>delivery</u>) (UCC 7-501).

[handwritten margin note: identical to Negotiable except value is not for pre-existing debt]

3. <u>Shelter Principle</u>--A transferee of a negotiable or nonnegotiable document to whom the document has been delivered, but not duly negotiated, acquires the title and rights that the transferor held [UCC 7-504(1)]. In the same way that the shelter principle operates in Article 3, it operates in Article 7. When the transferee receives an unendorsed order document, the transferee has a specifically enforceable right to endorsement from the transferor. However, the transferee becomes a holder only at the instant the endorsement is obtained (UCC 7-506).

E. <u>Liability of Endorser or Transferor</u>--Unlike Article 3 (commercial paper), the endorser of a negotiable document does not have liability if the bailee fails to perform. The holder-transferee's only recourse is against the bailee (UCC 7-505). However, the endorser or transferor does <u>warrant</u> the following (UCC 7-507):

1. The document is genuine.

2. He or she has no knowledge of any fact which would impair its worth.

3. His or her negotiation or transfer is rightful and fully effective with respect to the title of the document and the goods it represents.

F.   <u>Persons Defeating Holders' and Transferees' Rights</u>

1.   A holder who takes an order-negotiable document with a forged endorsement has no rights in either the document or the underlying goods. This is similar to the real defense of forgery, which is good against an HDC in Article 3.

2.   A document of title conveys no rights to underlying goods in a situation in which a thief has deposited the stolen goods in a warehouse and procured a negotiable document (UCC 7-503).

3.   A buyer in the ordinary course of (the issuer's) business (e.g., a grain storer-seller) will defeat the rights of a holder of a negotiable warehouse receipt to fungible goods (UCC 7-205).

IV. Duty of Care and Risk of Loss

A.   <u>Warehouseman</u>

1.   Duty of Care Liable for damages for loss of or injury to goods caused by his or her failure to exercise such care as a reasonably careful person would exercise under like circumstances. Liability may be further limited by written agreement (UCC 7-204). Additionally, a party to, or a purchaser for value in good faith of, a warehouse receipt or other document (except bill of lading) may recover from the issuer damages caused by the nonreceipt or misdescription of the goods. However, no recovery is permitted if the description is qualified by language such as "contents, condition, and quality unknown" or "said to contain," or if the party or purchaser otherwise has notice (UCC 7-203). Furthermore, unless the warehouse receipt provides otherwise, the warehouseman has a duty to keep separate all of the goods covered by each warehouse receipt, although fungible goods may be commingled. The warehouseman will be liable for any loss caused by the commingling of nonfungible goods (UCC 7-207).

2.   Risk of Loss--When goods are held by a warehouseman or other bailee and title to the goods is to be transferred by negotiable warehouse receipt without movement of the goods, the risk of loss passes to the transferee, along with title to the document, at time of receipt of the document.

B.   <u>Carriers</u>

1.   Duty of Care--Carrier must exercise that degree of care which a reasonably careful person would exercise under like circumstances. Although common carriers may limit liability to some extent (in a manner similar to warehousemen), the general view is that common carriers are strictly liable for loss or damage to goods. Contract carriers are liable only for loss or damage caused by negligence.

2.   Risk of Loss--As between buyer and seller, risk of loss is based on whether the contract is a "shipment" or "destination" contract.

PART TWO: INVESTMENT SECURITIES

I. Definitions

A.   <u>Bona Fide Purchaser</u>--Purchaser for value, in good faith, and without notice of any adverse claim, who takes delivery of a security in bearer form or registered form issued or endorsed to him or her or in blank [UCC 8-302(1)].

B. Broker--Person engaged in the business of buying and selling securities, who, in the transaction concerned, acts for, buys a security from, or sells a security to, a customer (UCC 8-303).

C. Issuer--Includes a person who does either of the following (UCC 8-201):

    1. Places his or her (its) name on a security to evidence that it represents a share, participation, or other interest in his or her (its) property.

    2. Directly or indirectly creates fractional interests in his or her (its) property.

D. Security--An instrument that is issued in bearer or registered form and is of a type commonly dealt in upon securities exchanges or is commonly recognized as a medium for investment. A writing that is a security is governed by this Article (Article 8), even though it also meets the requirements of Article 3 and is presumed to be a negotiable instrument.

    • Types of Securities

        a. Security in Registered Form--Specifies a person entitled to the security.

        b. Security in Bearer Form--Runs to bearer according to its terms and not by reason of any endorsement.

II. Issuance

A. Issuer's Responsibilities

    1. The terms of a security include those stated on the security and those made part of the security by reference to another instrument [UCC 8-202(1)].

    2. When a security is issued in registered form and has not been endorsed, the person in whose name it is issued is generally deemed to be the owner.

    3. A security, other than one issued by a governmental unit, is valid in the hands of a purchaser for value and without notice of a particular defect, even if that defect goes to the validity of the security [UCC 8-202(2)]. However, staleness may be sufficient to place purchasers on notice of defects (UCC 8-203). For example, the fact that an interest payment date has been passed without payment is notice of a defect or defense to the security.

B. Issuer's Rights--The issuer has a complete defense to a nongenuine security [UCC 8-202(3)]. This is the only real defense available to the issuer. The following defenses are personal and cannot be asserted against a purchaser for value who is without notice of the defense: (Note the close relationship to the real and personal defenses of an HDC in Article 3.)

    1. Lack of consideration for the issuance.

    2. Nondelivery or conditional delivery [UCC 8-202(4)].

    3. Unauthorized signatures placed on securities during issue if signing done by employee or agent of issuer (UCC 8-205). (Furthermore, if the signature is authorized, but the security contains blanks, any person may fill in the blanks.) Incorrectly filled-in blanks are no defense against a purchaser for value without notice of the incorrectness; however, a complete security that has been improperly, even fraudulently, altered remains enforceable only according to its original tenor (UCC 8-206).

III. Purchase and Transfer

A. Introduction--Generally includes the receipt of the security at original issuance as well as all subsequent transfers in registered or bearer form. This right of transfer is inherent and unless restrictions on transfer are noted conspicuously on the security itself, such restriction is ineffective against a person without actual knowledge of it (UCC 8-204).

B. Rights Acquired by Purchaser--Purchaser acquires the rights held by the transferor, except that a purchaser who has been a party to fraud or illegality or who, as a prior holder, had notice of an adverse claim cannot improve his or her position by subsequently taking from a bona fide purchaser (UCC 8-301). (This is the Article 8 version of the shelter principle.)

1. A bona fide purchaser, in addition to acquiring the rights of a purchaser, also acquires the security free of any adverse claim.

2. A purchaser of a security is charged with notice of adverse claims if the security has been endorsed "for collection," "for surrender," or for some purpose not involving transfer, or if the security is in bearer form, but also has a statement that it is the property of a person other than the transferor (UCC 8-304). Staleness and lapse of stated periods for redemption or distributions also constitute notice of adverse claims (UCC 8-305).

C. Warranties on Transfer or Presentment--These warranties are identical to those in Commercial Paper (Article 3).

1. A person transferring a security to a purchaser for value warrants the following: the person's transfer is effective and rightful, the security is genuine and has not been materially altered, and the person knows of no fact that might impair the validity of the security [UCC 8-306(2)].

2. A person presenting a security for registration of transfer warrants that he or she is entitled to the registration. However, a purchaser for value without notice of adverse claims (bona fide purchaser) who presents a security for registration warrants only that he or she has no knowledge of any unauthorized signature in a necessary endorsement [UCC 8-306(1)].

D. Purchaser's Right to Endorsement--As between the parties, the transfer of the security is complete upon delivery. However, the transferee cannot become a bona fide purchaser of a security in registered form until endorsement is made. The transferee has the specifically enforceable right to compel an endorsement (UCC 8-307).

E. Endorser's Liability--An endorser makes the warranties set forth in C.1., above, to bona fide purchasers. However, there is no secondary liability on the part of an investment security endorser to guarantee that the security will be honored by the issuer. Thus, an endorser warrants only the following:

1. The transfer is effective and rightful.

2. The security is genuine and has not been materially altered.

3. He or she knows of no fact which might impair the validity of the security.

F. Endorsement Without Delivery--An endorsement of a security whether special or in blank does not constitute a transfer until delivery of the security on which the endorsement appears or, if the endorsement is on a separate document, until delivery of both the document and the security (UCC 8-309). Although there is a right to compel an endorsement (see D., above), there is no right to compel delivery of an endorsed security.

1.   Only registered securities need be endorsed (Endorsement + Delivery = Transfer).

2.   A purported endorsement on a bearer security has no effect (Delivery = Transfer) and may indicate presence of adverse claim (for example, endorsement "for collection" or "for surrender" charges purchasers with notice of adverse claim) (UCC 8-310).

G.   Effect of Unauthorized Endorsement--Unless the owner has ratified an unauthorized endorsement or is otherwise precluded from asserting its effectiveness (UCC 8-311):

1.   The owner may assert its ineffectiveness against the issuer or any purchaser other than a purchaser for value without notice of adverse claims who has in good faith received a new, reissued, or reregistered security, and

2.   An issuer who registers the transfer of a security upon the unauthorized endorsement is subject to liability for improper registration.

IV. Stolen, Lost, or Destroyed Securities

Casualties involving investment securities usually involve four persons: the true owner, a forger-thief, a subsequent purchaser, and the issuer.

A.   Generally, the true owner may reclaim the actual stolen securities from the party then holding them, except from an innocent good-faith purchaser [UCC 8-315(1)]. However, if a stolen security has been transferred by a forged endorsement, the true owner may reclaim it even from an innocent good-faith purchaser [UCC 8-315(2)]. (The innocent good-faith purchaser who returns the securities has a course of action for breach of transferor's warranty against his or her seller, the thief.)

B.   If the true owner is unable to reclaim the stolen securities (e.g., cannot locate them), the owner may protect him- or herself by notifying the issuer of the loss within a reasonable time. If such notice is given before the issuer has notice of the loss by presentment by a subsequent good-faith purchaser and the true owner files an indemnity bond with the issuer, the issuer must issue new securities to the true owner to replace the securities lost [UCC 8-405(1),(2)].

C.   If the true owner fails to notify the issuer of the loss within a reasonable time and a subsequent, innocent good-faith purchaser presents the stolen securities (which were either endorsed by the true owner and then stolen, or were simply forged by the thief) for transfer, the subsequent purchaser is entitled to new securities. At this point, the true owner's right to reclaim the original or new securities is cut off [UCC 8-405(1)].

D.   If, after the issuer replaces the true owner's securities (scenario in 2., above), the original (lost or stolen) securities have found their way into the possession of a good-faith purchaser, who now wishes to transfer the shares to his or her own name, the issuer must issue this purchaser new shares. The issuer can then recover the replaced shares now held by the true owner. However, if the true owner has subsequently sold these shares to another good-faith purchaser and an over-issue has occurred (with the transfer to good-faith purchaser), the issuer must either go into the market and purchase the surplus shares or take back replaced shares in exchange for money payment in an amount equal to the value of the shares [UCC 8-405(3)].

CHAPTER 46—DOCUMENTS OF TITLE AND INVESTMENT SECURITIES

Problem 46-1 MULTIPLE CHOICE QUESTIONS (20 to 25 minutes)

1. Which of the following statements is correct concerning a bill of lading in the possession of Major Corp. that was issued by a common carrier and provides that the goods are to be delivered "to bearer"?
a. The carrier's lien for any unpaid shipping charges does **not** entitle it to sell the goods to enforce the lien.
b. The carrier will **not** be liable for delivering the goods to a person other than Major.
c. The carrier may require Major to endorse the bill of lading prior to delivering the goods.
d. The bill of lading can be negotiated by Major by delivery alone and without endorsement.
(11/93, Law, #47, 4344)

2. Which of the following statements is correct concerning a common carrier that issues a bill of lading stating that the goods are to be delivered "to the order of Ajax"?
a. The carrier's lien on the goods covered by the bill of lading for storage or transportation expenses is ineffective against the bill of lading's purchaser.
b. The carrier may **not**, as a matter of public policy, limit its liability for the goods by the terms of the bill.
c. The carrier must deliver the goods only to Ajax or to a person who presents the bill of lading properly endorsed by Ajax.
d. The carrier would have liability only to Ajax because the bill of lading is nonnegotiable.
(5/91, Law, #47, 0568)

3. Under the UCC, a bill of lading
a. Will **never** be enforceable if altered.
b. Is issued by a consignee of goods.
c. Will **never** be negotiable unless it is endorsed.
d. Is negotiable if the goods are to be delivered to bearer. (5/93, Law, #44, 4012)

4. Under the UCC, a warehouse receipt
a. Is negotiable if, by its terms, the goods are to be delivered to bearer or to the order of a named person.
b. Will **not** be negotiable if it contains a contractual limitation on the warehouser's liability.

c. May qualify as both a negotiable warehouse receipt and negotiable commercial paper if the instrument is payable either in cash or by the delivery of goods.
d. May be issued only by a bonded and licensed warehouser. (5/92, Law, #49, 2862)

5. Under a nonnegotiable bill of lading, a carrier who accepts goods for shipment, must deliver the goods to
a. Any holder of the bill of lading. *if negotiable*
b. Any party subsequently named by the seller.
c. The seller who was issued the bill of lading.
d. The consignee of the bill of lading.
(11/92, Law, #43, 3125)

6. Burke stole several negotiable warehouse receipts from Grove Co. The receipts were deliverable to Grove's order. Burke endorsed Grove's name and sold the warehouse receipts to Federated Wholesalers, a bona fide purchaser. In an action by Federated against Grove,
a. Grove will prevail, because Burke **cannot** validly negotiate the warehouse receipts.
b. Grove will prevail, because the warehouser must be notified before any valid negotiation of a warehouse receipt is effective.
c. Federated will prevail, because the warehouse receipts were converted to bearer instruments by Burke's endorsement.
d. Federated will prevail, because it took the negotiable warehouse receipts as a bona fide purchaser for value. (11/92, Law, #42, 3124)

7. Which of the following is **not** a warranty made by the seller of a negotiable warehouse receipt to the purchaser of the document?
a. The document transfer is fully effective with respect to the goods it represents.
b. The warehouseman will honor the document.
c. The seller has **no** knowledge of any facts that would impair the document's validity.
d. The document is genuine.
(11/88, Law, #42, 0571)

8. Field Corp. issued a negotiable warehouse receipt to Hall for goods stored in Field's warehouse. Hall's goods were lost due to Field's failure to exercise such care as a reasonably careful person would under like circumstances. The state in which this transaction occurred follows the UCC rule with

respect to a warehouseman's liability for lost goods. The warehouse receipt is silent on this point. Under the circumstances, Field is

a. Liable, because it is strictly liable for any loss.
b. Liable, because it was negligent.
c. Not liable, because the warehouse receipt was negotiable.
d. Not liable, unless Hall can establish that Field was grossly negligent. (11/93, Law, #46, 4343)

9. Which of the following standards of liability best characterizes the obligation of a common carrier in a bailment relationship?

a. Reasonable care.
b. Gross negligence.
c. Shared liability.
d. Strict liability. (5/95, Law, #58, 5392)

10. Bond Corp. issued a negotiable warehouse receipt to Grey for goods stored in Bond's warehouse. Grey's goods were lost due to Bond's failure to exercise such care as a reasonably careful person would under like circumstances. The state in which this transaction occurred follows the UCC rule with re- spect to a warehouseman's liability for lost goods. The warehouse receipt is silent on this point. Under the circumstances, Bond is

a. Liable, because it was negligent.
b. Liable, because it is strictly liable for any loss.
c. Not liable, unless Grey can establish that Bond was grossly negligent.
d. Not liable, because the warehouse receipt was negotiable. (11/87, Law, #36, 0572)

11. Bell Co. owned 20 engines which it deposited in a public warehouse on May 5, receiving a negotiable warehouse receipt in its name. Bell sold the engines to Spark Corp. On which of the following dates did the risk of loss transfer from Bell to Spark?

a. June 11--Spark signed a contract to buy the engines from Bell for $19,000. Delivery was to be at the warehouse.
b. June 12--Spark paid for the engines.
c. June 13--Bell negotiated the warehouse receipt to Spark.
d. June 14--Spark received delivery of the en- gines at the warehouse.
(11/85, Law, #45, 9911)

12. Assuming all other requirements have been met, which of the following terms generally must be included in a writing in order to satisfy the UCC Statute of Frauds regarding the sale of securities?

	Price	Quantity	Time of payment
a.	Yes	Yes	Yes
b.	No	Yes	No
c.	Yes	No	Yes
d.	Yes	Yes	No

(5/87, Law, #47, 9911)

13. Under the UCC Investment Securities Article, a restriction on the transfer of corporate stock will only be valid against a transferee if the restriction is

a. Contained in a stockholders' agreement.
b. Stated on the face of the stock certificate.
c. Placed on publicly traded stock.
d. Part of a buy-sell contract.
(11/92, Law, #44, 3126)

14. Adams orally agreed to sell certain bearer stock certificates to Mason. Adams delivered the certificates and Mason paid Adams. Mason purchased the securities in good faith and without knowledge of any adverse claims. If Adams had stolen the certificates, which of the following statements would be correct?

a. Mason can rescind the contract because it was oral.
b. Mason's rights to the securities would **not** be superior to those of the rightful owner.
c. By selling the securities to Mason, Adams made an implied warranty that the transfer is effective and does **not** violate the rights of any other person.
d. Mason can require Adams to endorse the certificates in blank. (5/93, Law, #45, 4013)

15. Sims owns a certificate representing 500 shares of Flow Corp.'s preferred stock. The shares were originally issued in Sims' name. If Sims agrees to sell the stock to Lazur for $1.00 per share, which of the following statements would be correct?

a. The sales agreement must be in writing and signed by both Sims and Lazur.
b. Sims must get Flow's consent before transferring the certificate to Lazur.
c. Lazur does **not** become a bona fide purchaser of the shares until Flow has registered the transfer of the stock certificate.
d. By transferring the stock certificate to Lazur, Sims warrants that the certificate is genuine and has **not** been materially altered.
(5/92, Law, #50, 2863)

16. A person who loses a stock certificate is entitled to a new certificate to replace the lost one, provided certain requirements are satisfied. Which of the following is **not** such a requirement?

a. The request for a new certificate is made before the issuer has notice that the lost certificate has been acquired by a bona fide purchaser.

b. The owner files a sufficient indemnity bond with the issuer.

c. The owner satisfies any reasonable requirements of the issuer.

d. The fair market value of the security is placed in escrow with the issuer for six months.

(11/93, Law, #48, 4345)

Solution 46-1 MULTIPLE CHOICE ANSWERS

Documents of Title

1. (d) A bill of lading becomes negotiable bearer paper if, by its terms, the goods are to be delivered to "bearer." Furthermore, "bearer" paper may be negotiated merely by delivery. The carrier's lien does entitle it to sell the goods to cover unpaid shipping charges. The carrier will be liable to whoever "bears" the bill of lading. The bill of lading is bearer paper and may be negotiated without endorsement.

2. (c) An "order" instrument must be delivered to the named person or to the representative of the named person so that the bill of lading can be properly endorsed. To duly negotiate an order document, the document must be properly endorsed and delivered. The carrier's lien would be effective against the bill of lading's purchaser. The carrier may limit its liability for the goods by the terms of the bill. The carrier may have liability to others and because the bill of lading is treated, in this case, as being negotiable.

3. (d) A bill of lading is a document evidencing the receipt of goods for shipment issued by a person engaged in the business of transporting or forwarding goods. A bill of lading is negotiable if the goods are to be delivered to order or bearer. An immaterial alteration will not necessarily render a bill of lading unenforceable. A bill of lading is issued by the carrier, not the consignee. To be negotiable, a bill of lading will need to be endorsed only if it contains a promise to deliver the goods to a named person.

4. (a) A negotiable warehouse receipt is a document issued as evidence of the receipt of goods by a person engaged in the business of storing goods for hire. The warehouse receipt is negotiable if the face of the document contains the words of negotiability (order or bearer).

5. (d) Under a nonnegotiable bill of lading, a carrier who accepts goods for shipment, must deliver the goods to the consignee of the bill of lading. Answers (a), (b), and (c) would be correct if the bill of lading were negotiable.

6. (a) A negotiable warehouse receipt "duly negotiated" can give certain good-faith purchasers greater rights than those possessed by the transferor (similar to the rules of a holder in due course). In this question, the warehouse receipt was not duly negotiated since a proper endorsement was required to negotiate the warehouse receipt, and a forged document is not valid. Grove will prevail since Burke cannot validly negotiate the warehouse receipt. There is no rule that a warehouser must be notified before any valid negotiation of a warehouse receipt is effective. Burke's endorsement is invalid and does not convert the instrument to a bearer instrument. The instrument cannot be negotiated without a proper endorsement.

7. (b) Under Article 7 of the UCC, unless otherwise agreed, a person negotiating a negotiable warehouse receipt for value to his or her immediate purchaser warrants only that the document is genuine, that he or she is without knowledge of any fact which would impair its validity or worth, and that his or her negotiation is rightful and fully effective with respect to the title to the document and the goods it represents. No warranty arises that the warehouse person will honor the document.

8. (b) A warehouse person has a duty of care and is liable for loss or injury to goods caused by his or her failure to exercise such care as a reasonably careful man would exercise under like circumstances. The problem does not specify that liability was limited by a written agreement, so Field would be held liable because he was negligent. A warehouseman is not strictly liable for any loss on goods held in his

warehouse. He need only exercise such care as a reasonably careful person would under like circumstances. The negotiability of the warehouse receipt has no effect on Field's liability or the duty of care he is held to. Hall need only establish that field was negligent, not grossly negligent.

9. (d) A bailee such as a common carrier, must exercise reasonable care with respect to the bailed property. Although common carriers may limit liability to some extent, the general view is that common carriers are strictly liable for loss or damage to goods. Standards of gross negligence and shared liability are inapplicable.

10. (a) Under the UCC, a warehouse person will be liable for damages to, or loss of, goods caused by his or her failure to exercise reasonable care under the circumstances (negligence). The standard for liability is negligence, not strict liability or gross negligence. Negotiability of the warehouse receipt does not affect the warehouse person's liability for negligence.

11. (c) When title is to be transferred by negotiable warehouse receipt without movement of the goods, risk of loss passes to the transferee along with title to the goods at the time of receipt of the document. Therefore, when Bell negotiated the warehouse receipt to Spark, the risk of loss was transferred at that time.

Investment Securities

12. (d) Under UCC 8-319, a sale of securities is generally not enforceable when a writing is involved unless it includes a stated quantity of described securities at a defined or stated price.

13. (b) Unless noted conspicuously on the stock certificate, a restriction on transfer imposed by the issuer, even though otherwise lawful, is ineffective except against a person with actual knowledge of it. A restriction in a stockholder's agreement may not be seen by all transferees. If such a restriction appeared on the stock, it could not be publicly traded. The restrictions need to be written on the face of the stock certificate, not as part of a contract.

14. (c) A seller of securities makes the following implied warranties upon transfer of securities: (1) the right represented by the securities exists, (2) the instrument is genuine, (3) the transferor will do nothing to impair the right, and (4) there are no adverse claims or defenses to the instrument. Rescission involves an undoing of a contract on both sides and placing the parties in their original position. A rightful owner does not have the right to reclaim a security from a bona fide purchaser for value if the wrongful transfer was not due to a forged authentication. Mason would not be able to require Adams to endorse the certificates in blank.

15. (d) According to UCC 8-306(2), a person transferring a security to a purchaser for value, warrants that his or her transfer is effective and rightful, the security is genuine and has not been materially altered, and that no fact is known that might impair the validity of the security.

16. (d) The requirements for the replacement of a lost stock certificate include a provision to indemnify the issuing corporation from incurring liability to both the original owner of the stock certificate and a subsequent bona fide purchaser of the certificate. This is accomplished through the use of an indemnity bond filed with the issuer and not through an escrow account. Answers (a), (b), and (c) are all valid requirements.

PERFORMANCE BY SUBTOPICS

Each category below parallels a subtopic covered in Chapter 46. Record the number and percentage of questions you correctly answered in each subtopic area.

Documents of Title

Question #	Correct √
1	
2	
3	
4	
5	
6	
7	
8	
9	
10	
11	

Questions   11

Correct   _____
% Correct   _____

Investment Securities

Question #	Correct √
12	
13	
14	
15	
16	

Questions   5

Correct   _____
% Correct   _____

NOTES

CHAPTER 47

SECURED TRANSACTIONS

I. **Article 9 of the Uniform Commercial Code**..47-2
   A.   Definitions 47-2
   B.   Scope..47-4
   C.   Purpose 47-4
   D.   Excluded Transactions 47-4

II. **Validity, Attachment, and Enforceability of Security Interests**................................47-5
   A.   Attachment 47-5
   B.   Title 47-5
   C.   Security Agreement Distinguished From Financing Statement....................47-5
   D.   After-Acquired Property and Future Advances..47-6
   E.   Debtor's Use or Disposition of Collateral Without Accounting to the Secured Party 47-6
   F.   Rights and Duties of the Secured Party in Possession of Collateral 47-7
   G.   Debtor-Requested Accounting 47-7

III. **Perfection and Filing** 47-8
   A.   Perfection..47-8
   B.   Perfection by Filing 47-8
   C.   Places for Filing 47-9
   D.   Perfection by Possession 47-9
   E.   Temporary and Permanent Automatic Perfection 47-10

IV. **Rules of Priority Among Creditors** 47-11
   A.   Types of Creditors 47-11
   B.   Priorities Between Secured Parties and Purchasers of Collateral...............47-12
   C.   Transferees of Intangible Collateral..47-13
   D.   Priorities Between Secured Parties and Lien Creditors...............................47-15
   E.   Priorities Among Conflicting Security Interests in the Same Collateral 47-15

V. **Other Secured Transactions**...47-17
   A.   Field Warehousing..47-17
   B.   Consignment 47-18

VI. **Remedies Upon Default and Rights of the Parties** 47-18
   A.   Default Procedures...47-18
   B.   Collection Rights of the Secured Party 47-19
   C.   The Right to Dispose of Collateral After Default and the Effect of Disposition............47-19
   D.   Compulsory Disposition of Collateral and Acceptance of the Collateral as Discharge
        of the Obligation...47-20
   E.   Debtor's Right to Redeem Collateral 47-20
   F.   Secured Party Liability for Failure to Comply With Article 9 47-20

CHAPTER 47

SECURED TRANSACTIONS

I. Article 9 of the Uniform Commercial Code

A. Definitions

1. Accessions--Personal property which by installation or affixation becomes a permanent part of real property (e.g., boiler in an office building) or other personal property (e.g., engine in an automobile).

2. After-Acquired Property Clause--Allows a secured party to have a security interest in goods or other collateral which is not in the possession of the debtor at the time credit is extended. The security interest in such property is deemed to have been taken for new value and not as security for an antecedent debt.

3. Attachment--The specific moment in time when a newly created security interest becomes enforceable against the debtor. Attachment occurs when: (1) value is given by the secured party; (2) the debtor obtains rights in the collateral; and (3) the debtor and creditor acknowledge the creation of a security interest in an agreement signed by the debtor, or the collateral is in the possession of the secured party (UCC 9-203).

4. Buyer in the Ordinary Course of Business (BOC)--A person who buys in good faith and without knowledge that the sale to him or her is in violation of the ownership rights or security interest of another. The buyer also must purchase in the ordinary course from a person in the business of selling goods of that kind [UCC 1-201(3)].

5. Collateral--Property subject to a security interest [UCC 9-105(1)(c)]. For purposes of Article 9, collateral is broken into three main classifications: tangibles, "pure" intangibles, and intangibles.

    a. Tangibles--All goods (except intangibles, documents and money) which are movable at the time the security attaches or which are fixtures. Tangibles may be further classified as follows:

        not real estate

        (1) Consumer Goods--Goods which are used or bought to be used primarily for personal, family, or household purposes [UCC 9-109(1)].

        (2) Equipment--Describes goods which are used or bought primarily for use in a business (including farming or a profession). It also describes goods bought or used by a debtor who is an organization, agency, or government subdivision. Equipment also covers all tangible goods which may not be included as consumer goods, farm products, or inventory [UCC 9-109(2)].

        (3) Inventory--Describes goods which are held by a person for sale or lease. It also describes raw materials, work in progress, or materials used or consumed in a business [UCC 9-109(4)].

        (4) Farm Products--Goods which are used or produced in farming operations as long as they are in their unmanufactured state (such as milk, eggs, crops, or fertilizer). They remain farm products only while they are in the possession of a debtor engaged in farming operations [UCC 9-109(3)].

NOTE: Tangibles are classified according to their use or intended use by the debtor. Additionally, their use or intended use is determined at the time they are acquired by the debtor who is subject to the security agreement.

    b.   <u>Pure Intangibles</u>--Personal property which has no separate physical existence; rather, it is only a right to receive property. Included within this category are accounts, general intangibles, and other property not embodied in a single instrument of title (i.e., patents, literary rights, and rights to performance).

        (1)   <u>Accounts</u>--Any rights to payment for goods sold or leased or for services rendered, which are not evidenced by an instrument or chattel paper. Accounts include earned, as well as unearned, rights to payment (UCC 9-106).

        (2)   <u>General Intangibles</u>--Any personal property other than goods, accounts, chattel paper (mortgages), documents, and money. General intangibles include goodwill, literary rights, and patents (UCC 9-106).

    c.   <u>Intangibles</u>--Any personal property, such as instruments or chattel paper, the ownership rights to which are embodied in an indispensable writing. Transfer of the writing is tantamount to transfer of the underlying rights in that instrument. The following are examples of intangible property:

        (1)   <u>Instruments</u>--Includes negotiable instruments (as defined in UCC 3-104), investment securities (as defined in UCC 8-102), and any other writing which evidences the right to payment of money and is not itself a security interest or lease [UCC 9-105(1)(i)].

        (2)   <u>Documents</u>--Documents of title including warehouse receipts, bills of lading, and dock warrants [UCC 9-105(1)(f)].

        (3)   <u>Chattel Paper</u>--Writings which simultaneously embody a monetary obligation and a security interest [UCC 9-105(1)(b)]. (A promissory note with an appended security agreement together constitute chattel paper. However, the promissory note alone would merely be an instrument, not chattel paper, while the security agreement standing alone may be chattel paper.)

        (4)   <u>Money</u>.

6.   <u>Financing Statement</u>--A document containing required information which is filed by a secured party in a particular location and which indicates that a secured party claims a security interest in specific collateral (UCC 9-402).

7.   <u>Fixtures</u>--Goods which are attached to real estate in such a manner that an interest in them arises under real property law. This includes all goods which are integrally incorporated into the real estate, but excludes ordinary building materials incorporated into an improvement on land [UCC 9-313(1)].

8.   <u>Lien Creditor</u>--Creditor who has acquired a lien on the property involved by attachment, levy, or the like. Included within the definition of a lien creditor are assignees for the benefit of creditors from the time of assignment and trustees in bankruptcy from the date of filing of the petition or from the date of appointment [UCC 9-301(3)].

9.   <u>Mortgage</u>--A consensual lien created by a real estate mortgage, trust deed on real estate, or other like contract [UCC 9-105(1)(j)].

10.   <u>Proceeds</u>--Whatever is received upon the sale, exchange, collection, or other disposition of collateral or proceeds [UCC 9-306(1)].

11. <u>Purchase Money Security Interest</u>--An interest that is taken by either of the following (UCC 9-107):

   a. Taken or retained by the seller of the collateral to secure the amount due on the collateral.

   b. Taken by a person who by making advances or incurring an obligation gives value which enables the debtor to acquire rights in the collateral, to the extent that such value is so used.

12. <u>Secured Party</u>--A lender-seller or other person in whose favor there is a security interest. This includes purchasers of accounts or chattel paper [UCC 9-105(1)(m)].

13. <u>Security Agreement</u>--An agreement which creates or provides for a security interest [UCC 9-105(1)(l)].

14. <u>Security Interest</u>--An interest in personal property or fixtures which secures a payment or the performance of an obligation. A lease or consignment for the purpose of obtaining security creates a security interest [UCC 1-201(37)].

15. <u>Value</u>--A person gives value for rights if he or she acquires them in any of the following situations (UCC 1-201):

   a. In return for a binding commitment to extend credit.

   b. As security for or in satisfaction of a preexisting claim.

   c. By accepting delivery pursuant to a preexisting contract for purchase.

   d. Generally, in return for any consideration sufficient to support a simple contract.

B. <u>Scope</u>--Article 9 of the Uniform Commercial Code applies to any transaction, regardless of its form, which is intended to create a security interest in goods or fixtures. It also applies to any sale of accounts or chattel paper (UCC 9-102).

   1. Types of collateral covered by Article 9 include goods, documents, instruments, general intangibles, chattel paper, and accounts.

   2. Article 9 applies to security interests created by contract including: assignment, chattel mortgage, trust deed, or conditional sales contract or any other lien or title retention contract. It also applies to a lease accounted for as a capital lease under <u>SFAS 13</u> or consignment intended as security.

C. <u>Purpose</u>--The main purpose is to bring all consensual security interests in personal property and fixtures (with specific exceptions) under one uniform codification. The Code presently exists in two versions, the 1962 and 1972 versions. The 1972 version amends or revises over half of the 1962 version's Sections.

D. <u>Excluded Transactions</u>--The following is a partial summary of transactions which are excluded from Article 9 (UCC 9-104):

   1. Transactions involving interests in real estate. Article 9 does not apply to the creation of a real estate mortgage. However, if a promissory note is executed along with the mortgage and the <u>mortgagee</u> later assigns the note as collateral (i.e., "instrument") for a separate loan, this lending transaction between mortgagee and third party is within Article 9.

2. Transfers of interests in timber which are not to be secured and minerals which have not been removed from the land. Conversely, minerals which have been extracted, timber which is under contract to be cut, and growing crops in their unsevered state are within the scope of Article 9.

3. Security interests subject to any statute of the United States to the extent that the statute expressly governs priority rights of the parties.

4. Landlord and artisan liens.

5. Assignments and sales of accounts and chattel paper are excluded to the extent that they are either a part of the sale of the business in which they arose or a part of an assignment for the purpose of collection.

6. Transfers of claims by employees for wages, salary, or other compensation.

7. Transfers of interests in insurance policies as well as transfers of any portion of a tort claim.

II. Validity, Attachment, and Enforceability of Security Interests

A. <u>Attachment</u>--A secured transaction is created when the debtor and creditor enter into a written security agreement giving the creditor rights in the debtor's property as collateral for the debt. However, this security interest is not enforceable against the debtor and third parties until it attaches. Attachment does not occur until and unless all <u>three</u> of the following events occur (UCC 9-203):

1. The collateral must either be in the secured party's possession pursuant to an agreement <u>or</u> the debtor must have signed a security agreement. The security agreement must contain a description sufficient to reasonably identify the collateral.

2. Value must have been given by the secured party (creditor). Value is deemed to have been given if rights to collateral have been received in return for a binding commitment to extend credit or pursuant to a previously existing claim.

> **Example 1**
>
> Debtor farmer borrows $5,000 from bank in return for signing a security agreement reciting which gives creditor a security interest in a tractor as collateral. The security interest attaches when the security agreement is signed by the debtor.

> **Example 2**
>
> Debtor orders inventory from seller on February 1. On February 2, debtor borrows the purchase price from bank giving bank security interest in the inventory. The security interest attaches on February 2, the earliest time of occurrence of all three elements of attachment.

3. Debtor has rights in the collateral. Rights in this context is broadly viewed as any type of ownership right. A debtor therefore has rights in any property which he or she either owns or for which remedies are available in the case of the property's theft, destruction, or nondelivery. For example, a debtor would have rights in earmarked inventory which is still in the possession of the manufacturer or is enroute to the debtor via common or contract carrier.

B. <u>Title</u>--As between debtor and secured party, title to the collateral is immaterial regarding rights, obligations, and remedies under Article 9.

C. <u>Security Agreement Distinguished From Financing Statement</u>--A <u>security agreement</u> must contain a description of the collateral <u>and</u> must be signed by the debtor. A <u>financing statement</u>, on the other hand, must contain the following information (UCC 9-402):

1.   Name and mailing address of debtor.

   a.   Partnership name and address if debtor is a partnership.

   b.   Legal name and address if debtor trades under an assumed name (the assumed name may be added for clarity).

   c.   Corporate name and address if debtor is a corporation.

2.   Name and mailing address of creditor.

3.   Description of collateral such as to assure specific identification of the item.

   a.   Unerring accuracy of identification is not required.

   b.   If collateral is related to real estate (e.g., growing crops or machinery in a building), then legal description of land or address of building is required.

4.   Signature of the debtor.

   •   Signature waived on multiple filings or if debtor not available.

The purpose of the security agreement is to create a validly enforceable security interest between debtor and creditor. In contrast, the financing statement is necessary to protect the interest of the secured party from third party creditors. This protection is effected through perfection by filing of the financing statement. Although not customary, a security agreement containing information required by UCC 9-402 can be filed as a financing statement.

D.   **After-Acquired Property and Future Advances**

1.   A security agreement may provide that any or all obligations covered by the agreement are to be additionally secured by property later acquired by the debtor [UCC 9-204(1)]. For example, assume that a debtor department store signs a security agreement with a bank which gives the bank an interest in "all accounts receivable and proceeds and all inventory owned and to be acquired." As the debtor obtains rights in future receivables and inventory, the bank's interest will attach and be protected from most third parties.

2.   Article 9 also provides limitations on the creditor's power to include after-acquired property as collateral. Thus, a purchase money security interest creditor would be superior to an after-acquired property secured creditor if the purchase money secured creditor followed certain prerequisites. Similarly, no after-acquired interest may attach to consumer goods (except accessions) unless the debtor acquires rights in the consumer goods within 10 days after the secured party gives value.

3.   In addition to after-acquired property, a security interest may extend to obligations which arise subsequent to the agreement. Thus, future advances or other extensions of value which may be provided to the debtor at some later date by the secured party may be included within a present security agreement and therefore secured by the collateral [UCC 9-204(3)].

E.   **Debtor's Use or Disposition of Collateral Without Accounting to the Secured Party**--A security interest can be effected through a financing statement or through possession by the creditor. Regardless of the method used to attach and perfect the secured interest, situations will generally arise when the debtor will have possession of the collateral (for example, inventory on the debtor's showroom floor, or machinery in the debtor's factory). With collateral in the possession of the debtor, the problem becomes one of preventing fraud upon the secured creditor or other (third party) creditors who deal with the debtor, while at the same time permitting the debtor freedom to carry on his or her business activity. The following provisions apply to debtor rights and creditor safeguards in debtor-possession situations:

1. The debtor may voluntarily or involuntarily sell or transfer his or her rights in the collateral, notwithstanding a contrary provision in the security agreement (UCC 9-311).

2. The secured party's interest generally continues in collateral notwithstanding the sale or transfer by the debtor (UCC 9-306), except when the sale was specifically authorized by the secured party in the security agreement, or in other specifically enumerated UCC situations (e.g., sale by debtor to a buyer in the ordinary course of business).

3. Without specific language in the security agreement to the contrary, the secured party has a continuously perfected interest in the proceeds as well as any proceeds of proceeds which result from the debtor's sale or transfer of the collateral (UCC 9-306).

Example 3

Debtor sells nonfarm collateral to purchaser (not in the ordinary course of business); the secured party's perfected interest continues in the collateral in the purchaser's possession. However, the result would favor the purchaser if the sale was in the debtor's ordinary course of business or if the secured party's interest was unperfected.

Example 4

Debtor sells collateral for cash and other noncash property. Because the sale is not made pursuant to a specific right to sell in the security agreement, the secured party's perfected interest generally continues in the cash and noncash proceeds. Additionally, the secured party's interest would continue in any subsequent proceeds from a subsequent sale of the noncash proceeds. (See V., below, for exceptions dealing with proceeds from sale of purchase money security interest collateral.)

F. Rights and Duties of the Secured Party in Possession of Collateral

1. A secured party must use reasonable care in the custody and preservation of collateral in the party's possession. In the case of an instrument or chattel paper, reasonable care includes taking the necessary steps to preserve rights against prior parties [UCC 9-207(1)].

2. Unless otherwise agreed, when collateral is in the secured party's possession, the following apply [UCC 9-207(2)]:

   a. Reasonable expenses incurred in taking and maintaining custody of the collateral are chargeable to the debtor and are secured by the collateral.

   b. The risk of accidental loss or damage is on the debtor to the extent of any deficiency in insurance coverage.

   c. The secured party may hold any increase or profits realized from the collateral but must keep the collateral identifiable.

   d. The secured party may repledge the collateral upon terms which do not impair the debtor's right to redeem it.

3. A secured party is liable for any loss caused by his or her failure to meet any obligation imposed by this Section, but the party does not lose his or her security interest [UCC 9-207(3)].

G. Debtor-Requested Accounting--Upon request, the creditor must provide the debtor with an accounting of the amount of unpaid indebtedness and a list of the collateral which secures the debt.

The secured party must comply with such a request without charge once every six months during the outstanding period of the security interest (UCC 9-208).

III. Perfection and Filing

A. **Perfection**--Although not specifically defined in the UCC, the essence of perfection is the giving of notice to the world that the secured party has an interest in the collateral in question. The importance of having a perfected security interest cannot be overemphasized. An unperfected secured creditor is subjugated to the interests of perfected secured creditors, lien creditors, trustees in bankruptcy, and in some cases mere transferees of the collateral. Perfection occurs in one of three ways: (1) filing a valid financing statement, (2) taking possession of the collateral, or (3) automatically (temporary or permanent automatic perfection).

B. **Perfection by Filing**--Perfection by filing a financing statement is the most common method of perfecting security interests (UCC 9-304). Procedurally, perfection by filing is accomplished by depositing a properly completed financing statement with a filing officer (usually a recorder of deeds). Both the place of filing and the time of filing are important in the consideration of the rights and priorities of conflicting creditors. An insufficient financing statement, or one which is filed in an untimely or inappropriate manner, may deprive the secured party of perfected status.

1. Collateral Which **Must** Be Perfected by Filing--Security interests in pure intangibles (accounts and general intangibles, e.g., goodwill, literary rights, patents) must be perfected by filing (UCC 9-305).

2. Collateral Which **May** Be Perfected by Filing--Generally, all other types of collateral may be perfected by filing or by possession. Thus, along with the types of collateral enumerated in 1., above, inventory, equipment, chattel paper, and negotiable documents of title can be perfected by filing (UCC 9-305). **NOTE**: Some types of collateral can only be permanently perfected by possession. These include money and instruments (see D., below).

3. Perfection of Rights to Proceeds by Filing--Because a security interest continues in collateral proceeds, it is important that this form of secured interest be perfected. As a basic rule, the creditor need not specifically include

---

Example 5

Debtor gives creditor a security interest in a drill press used in her machining business. The financing statement does not indicate that proceeds are covered. Debtor sells the press for cash. The cash proceeds are identifiable and are therefore covered without any additional filing. If, however, debtor received a portion of a crop to be harvested later that month, creditor would have 10 days to file another security in the county where the crop is located.

---

proceeds in the text of the financing statement, since the retention of a secured interest in identifiable proceeds is assumed. However, the creditor is required to file a proceeds financing statement when the proceeds are no longer identifiable or when the proceeds are of a different type or require a different filing place than the collateral from which they emanate. For example, if a debtor uses cash proceeds of a sale of industrial machinery to buy crops, a new financing statement would be required because the machinery financing statement would have been filed in the county of machinery location, while the crops' financing statement would be filed in the county of the crops' location. Therefore, the creditor must file new financing statements in this situation to adequately protect his or her security interest in the proceeds of proceeds. In situations when a new filing is necessary, the secured party's interest is temporarily perfected for 10 days from the day of liquidation of the old collateral. Thus, if a new financing statement is required and is filed within this ten-day grace period, the perfected interest continues unbroken by the liquidation (UCC 9-306).

4. Sufficiency and Duration of Filing--As a general rule, there has been a sufficient filing of the financing statement if a proper statement is presented to the proper filing officer and the filing fee has been paid. Once the financing statement is filed, it remains in force for five years

from the date of filing. If not renewed by means of a continuation statement, the secured interest will become unperfected at the end of this five-year period. The continuation statement must be filed in the same location as the financing statement during a six-month period ending on the expiration date of the five-year period (UCC 9-403).

5. Termination--Upon the satisfaction of the obligation, and not having any commitments to make advances, the debtor may, by written demand, order the secured party to remove the financing statement from the public records. The creditor is required to send the debtor and each filing officer a termination statement to the effect that the creditor no longer claims a security interest (UCC 9-404).

C. Places for Filing--The UCC provides several alternatives regarding the proper places to file financing statements. Generally, a filing is required locally (e.g., in the county where the debtor resides, or in the case of fixtures and farm products, the county wherein the land lies) and/or centrally (e.g., in the office of the Secretary of State). A filing originally made in the proper place usually remains effective even though the debtor's residence or the location of the collateral changes (UCC 9-401).

1. Multiple Local Filing Situations--To fully perfect, the UCC permits states to adopt alternative filing requirements. States may adopt any one or more of these alternative filing procedures. Pursuant to these alternatives a state may require that security interests involving land be filed in the mortgage office of the county wherein the affected land is located. Another filing must usually be made in the county wherein the debtor resides (if different from land location). A third filing may be required in other situations, especially if debtor is a nonresident of the state. This third filing of the financing statement is required to be made with the Secretary of State.

2. Multistate Filing Situations--Local perfection by filing is governed by the law of the jurisdiction where the collateral is located when the last event which controls perfection occurs [UCC 9-103(1)(b)]. Thus, a sale (last event) to a purchaser of consumer goods may require filing with the Secretary of State and/or with the county recorder of deeds where the debtor resides or where the goods are kept, depending on which filing alternative the particular state follows.

D. Perfection by Possession--Although perfection by filing is the most common method of perfection, perfection by possession is equally permissible in certain collateral situations. A basic characteristic of perfection by possession is that, unlike filing, no security agreement is necessary. To clarify the methods of perfection for different types of collateral, the following comparison is presented (UCC 9-304-305).

1. Perfection permitted by possession or filing

a. Goods (immobile or mobile except as covered by certificate of title under state or federal statutes, e.g., automobile registration).

b. Chattel paper (e.g., lease and negotiable instrument; mortgage and negotiable instrument, if transferred together as a package).

c. Letters and advices of credit.

d. Negotiable documents of title (e.g., negotiable bill of lading or negotiable warehouse receipt).

2. Perfection only by possession

a. Instruments--Includes both negotiable and nonnegotiable instruments as well as investment securities. Also included are checks, drafts, and certificates of deposit.

b.   Nonnegotiable documents of title (e.g., straight bill of lading).

c.   Money.

3.   Perfection <u>only</u> by filing

a.   Accounts--Includes any right to payment for goods or services where right is not evidenced by an instrument or chattel paper (e.g., open accounts receivable).

b.   General Intangibles--Includes any intangible which does not fall within the definition of instrument, investment security, documents of title, chattel paper, money, or accounts (e.g., patents, copyrights, trademarks, goodwill, etc.).

E.   <u>Temporary and Permanent Automatic Perfection</u>--In a few specialized situations, perfection by filing or possession is preceded or, in some cases, entirely supplanted by temporary or permanent automatic perfection (UCC 9-302). Automatic perfection occurs upon <u>attachment</u>.

> **Example 6**
>
> Creditor on June 1 gives value to debtor in form of $80,000 loan. Parties agree that creditor will have security interest in a certificate of deposit with a face value of $100,000, currently in possession of debtor. The creditor has a temporary automatically perfected security interest in the CD for 21 days from date of attachment. However, due to the fact that negotiable instruments are a type of collateral that can only be permanently perfected by possession, the creditor must take possession of the CD by June 22, or the security interest will become unperfected.

1.   Temporary Automatic Perfection--A security interest in instruments and negotiable documents of title is automatically perfected effective upon attachment and without filing or possession for a period of 21 days [UCC 9-304(4)].

2.   Temporary Perfection for Release of Possession--A situation may arise wherein the debtor must take possession of collateral over which the secured party has a perfected security interest. In order to protect the creditor during this period of debtor possession, especially if the UCC requires perfection by possession, UCC 9-304 provides for a 21-day perfected security interest in the collateral from the date of release to the debtor. However, this provision is somewhat limited in its scope, as follows:

a.   If the collateral is an instrument, it must have been released to the debtor for sale, presentment for payment (negotiable instrument), or collection.

b.   If the collateral is a document of title over bailed goods, the release of the document (negotiable or nonnegotiable) must have been for sale, transshipment, or manufacturing.

c.   If the collateral consists of proceeds, a slightly different rule prevails: UCC 9-306 provides that if a security interest in collateral is already perfected but proceeds are not fully protected (e.g., proceeds different in character from the collateral), then the secured party has only 10 days from the date the debtor receives the proceeds to fully protect his or her interest in the proceeds.

3. Automatic Perfection in Consumer Goods Purchase Money Security Interests--Any secured party who acquires a purchase money security interest in consumer goods automatically has such interest permanently perfected (UCC 9-302). No filing or possession is required; the automatic perfection occurs upon attachment. However, there are three qualifications to this provision. First, it does not apply to collateral controlled by a title statute (e.g., motor vehicle registration). Second, if the consumer good is to become a fixture, the secured party must file to perfect his or her interest over collateral after it becomes affixed to real property. Third, a purchase money security interest in consumer goods is not good against a subsequent bona fide purchaser who buys the consumer good from the original consumer, unless the purchase money secured party has filed a financing statement covering the goods.

4. Automatic Perfection of Casual or Isolated Assignments of Accounts-- Security interests in accounts are perfected only if effected through a filed financing statement. Thus, any person who regularly takes assignments of debtor's accounts (e.g., accounts receivable) should file to perfect. However, UCC 9-302 provides an exemption from filing requirements for assignments which do not transfer a significant part of the debtor's accounts. Therefore, if assignee-creditor takes an insignificant percentage of debtor's accounts on a casual or isolated basis as collateral, then that casual assignee need not file to perfect his or her security interest.

Example 7

Bank finances debtor's purchase of an air conditioner. Bank has a purchase money security interest to the extent debtor used the loan to purchase the air conditioner. Bank's interest became perfected when the last event for attachment occurred; that is, when debtor purchased the air conditioner. At this point bank's interest is superior to all other creditors. If debtor subsequently affixes the unit to a building (over which another creditor currently has an ownership or a lien interest), the bank must within 10 days of the affixation file a fixture financing statement in order to maintain its secured status over the real property secured creditor.

Example 8

Stereo Showroom gives Bank a security interest on all of its inventory and proceeds in order to borrow money for the purchase of new stereos from the manufacturer. Bank properly files its financing statement. Consumer A buys a stereo system from Stereo Showroom on the installment plan basis. Stereo has an automatically perfected purchase money security interest because A is a buyer in the ordinary course of Stereo's business. Additionally, because A is a buyer in the ordinary course of business, he takes free of the Bank's security interest. If Stereo does not file a financing statement and A subsequently sells the stereo to his neighbor B, a consumer, without telling B of Stereo's security interest, then B will take free of Stereo's interest.

IV. Rules of Priority Among Creditors

UCC 9-201 sets forth the general rule on priorities: "Except as otherwise provided . . . a security agreement is effective according to its terms between the parties, against purchasers of the collateral and against creditors." The remainder of V. will be concerned with the "except as otherwise provided . . ." language. The rules of priority are not simple; to understand them you must understand the preceding material. Additionally, as you read V., be careful to note whether the secured interest in question is perfected (including automatic perfection) or unperfected. If it is unperfected, it will be inferior to all perfected secured creditors and lien creditors. Conversely, if it is perfected before other perfected security interest holders, it will be inferior to only a buyer in the ordinary course of the debtor's business.

A. Types of Creditors--There are several common types of creditors to consider in dealing with priority problems.

1. Lien Creditors--Creditors who have resorted to judicial relief against the debtor.

2.　General Creditors--Creditors not having a secured interest in a claim against debtor.

3.　Real Property Mortgagee--Owner or mortgagee of real property to which fixtures are affixed.

4.　Consignor--Title owner of goods that are transferred to debtor-consignee for purpose of sale.

5.　Trustee-In-Bankruptcy--Person representing interests of all unsecured and general creditors.

B.　<u>Priorities Between Secured Parties and Purchasers of Collateral</u>--The UCC has established rules of priority to protect buyers of tangible and intangible property from overreaching by anxious creditors. Article 9 seeks to effect a balance between the secured interests of creditors and the free flow of goods to buyers in the marketplace. The result is a system of priorities based on such criteria as the identity of the buyer (casual buyer, bulk buyer, buyer in the ordinary course of business), the identity of the collateral (consumer goods, intangibles), and the perfection status of the secured interest (perfected or unperfected).

1.　Buyers of tangible collateral who are other than buyers (except farm buyers) in the ordinary course of business.

　　a.　An unperfected security interest is subordinated to the rights of a person who is not a secured party and who is one of the following:

　　　　(1)　A transferee in bulk.

　　　　(2)　A buyer not in the ordinary course of business.

　　　　(3)　A buyer of farm products in the ordinary course of business, to the extent that the buyer or transferee gives value and takes delivery of the collateral without knowledge of the security interest and before it is perfected [UCC 9-301(1)(c)].

　　b.　Conversely, a perfected security interest is generally not subordinated to the rights of a person who is a buyer other than in the ordinary course of business.

　　<u>Exceptions</u>

　　　　(1)　A consumer goods buyer takes free of a security interest, even if perfected, if the buyer buys without knowledge of the security interest, for value, and for his or her own personal, family, or household purposes, unless prior to the purchase the secured party has filed a financing statement covering such goods [UCC 9-307(2)].

<u>Example 9</u>

Bank makes a loan to newly opened Stationery Store to allow Store to purchase small desktop computers for use in its office. Bank therefore has a purchase money security interest in these goods. Bank, however, does not perfect its security interest by filing. Store subsequently sells several computers to Y who is not a buyer in the ordinary course of business. Additionally, Y is purchasing the computer for use in its business and is therefore not a consumer goods buyer. Y takes free of Bank's security interest because Bank did not file and perfect before the purchase by Y. However, if Bank had perfected its security interest in the computers within 10 days after Store received possession of them, Y would have taken the goods subject to the Bank's interest.

<u>Example 10</u>

X buys a stove for home use from Appliance Store on a revolving charge plan. Store therefore has a purchase money security interest in the stove which is automatically perfected. Store also fails to file a financing statement believing that none is required. X later sells the stove to the neighbor next-door, who does not know of the store's security interest, for home use as a consumer good. Neighbor takes free of the store's security interest because it was purchased for value, without knowledge of store's unfiled purchase money security interest, and for personal, family, or household purposes.

---

(2)   A transferee in bulk or buyer other than in the ordinary course of business takes free of a purchase money secured creditor unless the creditor perfects within 10 days after the debtor (transferor-seller) receives possession of the collateral (UCC 9-301).

(3)   A buyer other than a buyer in the ordinary course of business takes free of a perfected security interest in collateral covering future advances when such advances are made by the secured party after the secured party acquires knowledge of the purchase or when made more than 45 days after the purchase, whichever occurs first, unless the advance is made pursuant to a commitment entered into without knowledge of the purchase and before the expiration of the 45-day period subsequent to the purchase [UCC 9-307(3)].

2.   Buyers of Tangible Collateral in the Ordinary Course of Business--As the rule in 1.a., above, indicates, there are several types of buyers. However, the most favored of all buyers is the buyer in the ordinary course of (the seller's) business. A buyer in the ordinary course of business takes free of a security interest created by the seller even though the security interest is perfected and even though the buyer knows of its existence. He or she takes subject to the security interest only when he or she knows that the sale is in violation of some term in the security agreement. It is also important to note that there cannot be a buyer in the ordinary course of business from a pawnbroker. Furthermore, "buying" does not include transfers in bulk or transfers made as security for or in total or partial satisfaction of a money debt [UCC 9-307(1)].

C.   Transferees of Intangible Collateral--The priority rules applicable to transferees of intangible collateral are in most cases identical to the rules applicable to tangible collateral buyers.

1.   Transferees of Intangibles (Instruments, Documents, and Chattel Paper)--The rules with regard to the ownership rights of these types of transferees vis-a-vis the interests of a secured but unperfected creditor are exactly the same as the priority rules for buyers of tangible collateral as set forth in B.1.a., above. Thus, a transferee who is not a secured party can prevail over an unperfected secured party to the extent the transferee gives value to the debtor and takes

---

Example 11

Bank lends money to debtor-retailer to allow her to purchase inventory and immediately files a financing statement covering its purchase money security interest in the inventory. Retailer subsequently sells an item of inventory to X, a buyer in the ordinary course of business. Bank's filed purchase money security interest is subordinate to the rights of X, even if she knows that the bank has a security interest in the inventory.

Example 12

Assume same facts as in Example 11, except that X knows that the inventory (designer blue jeans) consists entirely of stolen and illegally copied blue jeans. X could not become a buyer in the ordinary course of business due to the fact that X purchased the blue jeans in bad faith and with knowledge that the sale to him was in violation of the ownership rights of a third person (the true owner and designer).

Example 13

Assume same facts as in Example 11, except that the seller is a person engaged in farming operations who also sells farm products (crops, livestock, and products of crops or livestock). Assume further that the buyer is a buyer in the ordinary course of business. Under these facts the bank would prevail. UCC 9-307 excludes from "buyer-in-ordinary-course-of-business" status a person who buys farm products from a person engaged in farming operations. Buyer in this situation is relegated to the status of a buyer other than in the ordinary course of business.

delivery of the intangibles, without knowledge of the security interest, and before the secured party perfects his or her interest [UCC 9-301(1)(c)].

2. Transferees of Pure Intangibles (Accounts and General Intangibles)--Priority rules with regard to these types of transferees vis-a-vis the interests of a secured but unperfected creditor are identical to the rules set forth in B.1.a., above, except there is no delivery requirement imposed upon these transferees. This exception makes sense when one considers that security interests in these types of intangibles can only be perfected by filing [UCC 9-301(1)(d)].

3. Purchaser Transferees of Intangibles When the Secured Party Has a Perfected Security Interest--Although, as a general rule, perfected security interest holders are not subordinated to the rights of buyers other than in the ordinary course of business, we have seen exceptions which favor these nonordinary-course buyers (see B.1.b., above). Another exception favoring buyers over perfected security interest holders occurs in the case of a transferee of intangibles. Thus, a transferee purchaser of intangibles who purchases intangibles in the ordinary course of the purchaser's (not the seller's) business takes free of the secured party's interest. Recall that chattel paper and instruments are intangibles which are commonly used as collateral.

Example 14

Appliance Store gives purchase money security interest in inventory to Bank for loan to enable Store to purchase the inventory. Bank properly perfects its interest in the inventory. (Recall that a financing statement automatically claims proceeds emanating from the collateral.) Appliance Store subsequently sells an appliance to consumer on the installment sale plan. Consumer gives Appliance Store a security agreement and promissory note for the amount due (agreement and note together are chattel paper). Appliance Store immediately sells the chattel paper to Z, a person in the business of purchasing chattel paper. Even though Z knows of Bank's security interest in the inventory and impliedly in the proceeds, she takes free of the interest because she gave new value and took possession of the chattel paper. Conversely, the result would be in favor of Bank if Bank had stamped or noted on the chattel paper that Bank was expressly claiming the paper as proceeds. By this act Bank indicates that it has a right to the proceeds, not merely a claim to the proceeds.

Example 15

A purchaser of a large home appliance may give the seller appliance store a security agreement and a promissory note for the purchase price. The security agreement and the note together are chattel paper. The seller appliance store may either subsequently sell the chattel paper or instead use it as collateral for a bank loan to purchase more inventory. (The bank may then sell it or keep it as assignee.) UCC 9-308 provides that a purchaser of chattel paper or instruments who gives value and receives possession of the intangibles in the ordinary course of business (e.g., a purchaser of mortgages) takes free of any security interest, perfected or unperfected, in those intangibles if the purchaser acts without knowledge that the specific intangibles were subject to a security interest. Alternatively, UCC 9-308 provides that even if the purchaser knows that the particular intangibles are subject to a security interest, the purchaser takes them free of the perfected security interest if the secured party's claim to the chattel paper or instrument is merely as proceeds of inventory subject to a security interest. UCC 9-309 completes the priority rules applicable to purchasers of instruments (including investment securities) and documents of title by providing that a holder in due course of a negotiable instrument, or a bona fide purchaser of an investment security, takes free of an earlier security interest (even though perfected). The rationale for this rule can be found in the perfection rules. Security interests in instruments

(continued on next page)

---

can only be perfected by possession (except for 21-day temporary perfection). Therefore, the UCC in effect holds that if the instrument has legitimately found its way into the stream of commerce, it will stay there free of any interest in it which is no longer perfected by the secured party. The fact that the secured party has filed a financing statement covering the specific instrument or document in question does not constitute "notice of a security interest" to holders in due course or bona fide purchasers (UCC 9-309). Thus, the transferee's status as a holder in due course or bona fide purchaser will not be destroyed by a charge of bad faith in that each purchaser had "notice of a claim or defense" to the instrument (see UCC 3-302).

D. <u>Priorities Between Secured Parties and Lien Creditors</u>--Here we deal with the relatively simple situation of a lien creditor (judicial or artisan lien creditor) who claims some interest in the secured collateral for purposes of satisfying a claim against the debtor.

1. General Rule--A lien creditor who obtains a lien on the collateral in question by attachment, levy, or the like, prevails over an unperfected security interest. If the lien is acquired before the secured party perfects, the secured party's interest is subordinated to the lien creditor [UCC 9-301(1)(b)].

   a. Purchase Money Security Interests--Lien creditor does not take free of purchase money security interest during the 10-day temporary perfection period. If the secured party perfects within the 10-day period, intervening lien creditors are subordinated [UCC 9-301(2)].

   b. Future Advances--Lien creditors are subject to perfected future advance security interests only to the extent that the advance was made before the lien was created or within 45 days thereafter. Additionally, lien creditors are subordinated if advance or commitment to make advance was made without knowledge of the lien [UCC 9-301(4)].

2. Artisan's Lien--A common law artisan's, mechanic's, materialman's, or laborer's lien is superior to perfected or unperfected security interests. However, for such liens to be superior, the lienholder must be in possession of the collateral (UCC 9-310).

E. <u>Priorities Among Conflicting Security Interests in the Same Collateral</u>--In A. through C., above, we dealt with secured parties' rights versus the rights of purchasers and lien creditors. In D., we consider the conflicting rights of two or more parties having secured interests under Article 9.

> **Example 16**
>
> Creditor A gives value on March 1, and debtor obtains rights in collateral on same day. Creditor B gives value on same collateral to same debtor on March 3. Creditor B perfects by filing on March 3, and Creditor A perfects by filing on March 4. Creditor B has priority over Creditor A.

1. General Rule--Except as applies to purchase money security interests, the rules of priority between conflicting secured parties are determined as follows (UCC 9-312):

   a. By the <u>order of filing</u> of the financing statement <u>if</u> both parties perfect by filing.

   b. If both do not perfect by filing, then by the <u>order of perfection</u>.

c.   If neither party's interest is perfected, then by the <u>order of attachment</u>.

NOTE: UCC 9-401(2) provides that an improperly filed financing statement, or a financing statement which is not filed in all of the required locations, will still be effective for perfection purposes to the extent that compliance with local filing rules was followed. Furthermore, such an improperly or incompletely filed financing statement is effective against a person who has knowledge of the contents of the financing statement.

2.   Purchase Money Security Interest in Inventory--A perfected purchase money security interest in inventory has priority over a conflicting security interest in the same inventory [UCC 9-312(2)]. It also has priority as to identifiable cash proceeds received on or before the delivery of the inventory to a buyer if <u>both</u> of the following requirements are met:

a.   The purchase money security interest is perfected at the time the debtor receives possession of the inventory.

b.   The purchase money secured party gives notification in writing to the holder of a filed conflicting security interest if the holder had filed a financing statement covering the same types of inventory before the date of the filing made by the purchase money secured party or before the beginning of the 21-day period when the purchase money security interest is temporarily perfected without filing or possession [UCC 9-312(3)].

3.   Purchase Money Security Interest in Collateral Other Than Inventory--A purchase money security interest in collateral other than inventory has priority over a security interest in the same collateral or its cash and noncash proceeds if the interest is perfected within 10 days after the time the debtor receives possession of the collateral [UCC 9-312(4)].

Example 17

Creditor C gives value to debtor and takes a security interest in negotiable documents of title on April 1. C attempts to perfect by filing on April 1, but the filing is made in the wrong location. Creditor D also gives value on the same collateral and after failing to locate Creditor C's financing statement in any of the proper filing locations, perfects his interest by taking possession of the collateral on April 2. Creditor D takes priority over the defectively filed security interest of Creditor C. When neither of the secured creditors perfect by filing, the first to perfect wins.

Example 18

Pursuant to a commitment to make future advances, Bank X gives value to retailer, taking back a security interest. Bank X perfects by filing. Although not a purchase money security interest, Bank X's security agreement covers present and after-acquired inventory. Subsequently, Bank Y gives value to retailer to enable retailer to purchase inventory. Bank Y has a negotiable warehouse receipt for the inventory which it has perfected by possession. Bank Y will prevail over Bank X if Bank Y: (1) perfects its purchase money security interest at the time retailer takes possession of the inventory, <u>and</u> (2) gives written notification to Bank X of Bank Y's purchase money security interest before Bank Y's 21-day perfection period begins to run. Finally, Bank Y will take priority over identifiable cash proceeds received by retailer on the sale of the inventory to the extent that the proceeds are received by the retailer before the inventory is delivered to the buyer.

Example 19

Bank B gives value to debtor Copy Center and properly files a financing statement covering all of debtor's present and after-acquired copying equipment. Bank C gives value to debtor to enable debtor to purchase a new copier. Bank C's interest in the copier will be superior to Bank B's interest if Bank C perfects its interest by filing either before debtor receives the copier or within 10 days thereafter.

4.   Priority of Security Interests in Fixtures--Perfection of a security interest in fixtures is accomplished by filing a financing statement in the office where a mortgage on the same real estate would be filed or by notation on the real estate records [UCC 9-313(2)].

   a.   A perfected security interest in fixtures has priority over the conflicting interest of an encumbrancer or owner of the real estate when the requirements of either (1) or (2), below, are met [UCC 9-313(4)]:

      (1)   The security interest is a purchase money security interest perfected by filing within ten days after the goods become fixtures. This applies in situations when the interest of the encumbrancer or owner arises before the goods become fixtures and the debtor has an interest in the real estate.

      (2)   The security interest is perfected by a fixture filing before the interest of the encumbrancer or owner is of record.

   b.   An unperfected security interest in fixtures has priority over the conflicting interest of an encumbrancer or owner of the real estate when the following situations exist [UCC 9-313(5)]:

      (1)   The encumbrancer or owner has consented in writing to the security interest or has disclaimed an interest in the goods as fixtures.

      (2)   The debtor has the right to remove the goods.

5.   Priority of Security Interests in Accessions--A security interest which attaches before the goods become affixed takes priority over the claims of a person to the whole except when that person is one of the following [UCC 9-314(3)]:

   a.   A subsequent purchaser for value of any interest in the whole.

   b.   A creditor with a lien on the whole subsequently obtained by judicial proceedings.

   c.   A creditor with a prior perfected security interest in the whole to the extent that he or she makes subsequent advances.

   The purchaser or creditor above must act without knowledge and before the security interest in the accessions are perfected.

V. Other Secured Transactions

A.   Field Warehousing--A unique financing arrangement which provides the necessary security to the creditor while at the same time permitting the debtor to have access to the collateral securing a loan. In the usual field warehousing situation, collateral which is the subject of the security agreement is set aside and placed under the control of a bonded warehouseman who remains on the debtor's premises. The secured party therefore has the alternative of either perfecting the security interest by possession, through his or her warehouseman, or by filing. If by filing, the warehouseman will issue a negotiable warehouse receipt which then becomes the subject of a properly filed financing statement. The advantages of field warehousing are the ease and inexpensiveness with which the debtor may sell the collateral, usually inventory. The disadvantage of field warehousing--especially warehousing which is perfected by possession rather than filing--is that it may result in a fraud upon other creditors. In order to prevent the debtor from misrepresenting the status of the collateral, a field warehousing should be effected with the following safeguards:

1.   Collateral should be clearly segregated from other property of the same type and placed in a secured, limited access portion of the premises.

2. Warehoused area should be under clear control of warehouseman. Warehouseman must be independent of the debtor.

3. Temporary relinquishment to debtor for sale is permissible with proper safeguards. (Recall that the creditor still has 21 days for automatic perfection if field warehouse interest was originally perfected by possession.)

B. Consignment--A type of sales transaction which may be a secured sale under UCC 9-114 or a true consignment or bailment for the purpose of sale under UCC 2-326. In a true consignment the consignor, as title owner, places property in possession of the consignee as his or her agent for the purpose of sale. Upon consummating the sale, the title shifts to the consignee, then to the third party customer. The consignee then remits the proceeds less commission to the consignor. Until the goods are sold, the risk of loss and decrease in value remains with the consignor. If the transaction is in fact a true sale or return consignment, the consignor can insulate the goods from the consignee's creditors by adhering to the requirements of UCC 2-326. Under this provision, goods delivered to the consignee primarily for resale (sale or return) will not be subject to consignee's creditors if the consignor does any of the following:

1. Places signs at the consignee's place of business indicating the consignor's ownership interest in the goods.

2. Establishes that the person conducting the consignee's business is generally known by his or her creditors to be substantially engaged in selling the goods of others.

3. Complies with the filing provisions of Article 9.

If the consignment is in fact a sale of the goods with title retained by the creditor-consignor pending the receipt of the sales price, then the transaction is a secured transaction under Article 9 (UCC 9-114, -408) rather than a bailment for sale under Article 2. If the purpose of the consignment was to provide security for receipt of payment, the consignor must file a financing statement in the appropriate filing place(s) to protect his or her interest from the consignee's creditors.

VI. Remedies Upon Default and Rights of the Parties

A. Default Procedures

1. Upon default, the secured party may reduce the claim to judgment, foreclose, or otherwise enforce the security interest by any available judicial procedure. If the collateral is documents, the secured party may proceed either as to the documents or as to the goods covered thereby [UCC 9-501(1)]. Unless otherwise agreed, a secured party has the right to take possession of the collateral. In taking possession, a secured party may proceed without judicial process if this can be done without breach of the peace. Otherwise, the party must proceed pursuant to judicial process (UCC 9-503).

2. If the security agreement covers both real and personal property, the secured party may proceed under Article 9 as to the personal property. Additionally, the party has the option of proceeding as to both the real and personal property in accordance with his or her rights and remedies in respect to the real property. If this course of action is followed, the provisions of Article 9 do not apply [UCC 9-501(4)].

3. When a secured party has reduced his or her claim to judgment, any lien a party thereafter acquires by execution relates back to the date of the perfection of the security interest [UCC 9-501(5)].

B.   Collection Rights of the Secured Party

 1. When so agreed, and in any event upon default, the secured party is entitled to notify an account debtor or the obligor on an instrument to make payment to him or her. The secured party may also take control of any proceeds to which he or she is entitled [UCC 9-502(1)].

 2. A secured party who undertakes to collect from the account debtor or obligor must proceed in a commercially reasonable manner. The secured party may deduct his or her reasonable expenses from the money he or she realizes through the collections [UCC 9-502(2)].

C.   The Right to Dispose of Collateral After Default and the Effect of Disposition

 1. A secured party, after default, may sell, lease, or otherwise dispose of any or all of the collateral. When necessary, a secured party may prepare the collateral for sale. The proceeds of disposition are applied in the following order [UCC 9-504(1)]:

  a. First, to satisfy the reasonable expenses of retaking and holding the collateral for sale, lease, or disposal.

  b. Second, to satisfy the indebtedness secured by the security interest under which the disposition is made.

  c. Finally, to satisfy the indebtedness secured by any subordinate security interest in the collateral if written notification of demand therefore is received before distribution of the proceeds is completed.

 2. If the security interest secures an indebtedness, the secured party must account to the debtor for any surplus, and, unless otherwise agreed, the debtor is liable for any deficiency. But if the underlying transaction was a sale of accounts or chattel paper, the debtor is entitled to any surplus or is liable for any deficiency only if the security agreement so provides [UCC 9-504(2)].

 3. Disposition may be made by public or private proceedings and by way of one or more contracts. Sale or other disposition may be made on any terms, but every aspect of the disposition must be commercially reasonable. Except when not practical due to the nature of the collateral, the secured party must notify the debtor of the time and place of a public sale or the time after which any private disposition is to be made. The secured party must also furnish such information to any other secured party from whom he or she has received written notice of a claim. The secured party may buy the collateral at any public sale, and if the collateral is of a type for which a standard market or price exists, the secured party may buy at a private sale [UCC 9-504(3)].

 4. When collateral is disposed of by a secured party after default, the disposition transfers to a purchaser, for value, all of the debtor's rights therein. Such sale also discharges the security interest under which it is made and any security interest or lien subordinated thereto. The purchaser takes free of all such rights and interest even though the secured party fails to comply with the requirements of this Section or of any judicial proceedings if either of the following apply [UCC 9-504(4)]:

  a. The purchaser, in the case of a public sale, has no knowledge of any defects in the sale and if the purchaser does not buy in collusion with the secured party, other bidders, or the person conducting the sale.

  b. If the purchaser, in all other cases, acts in good faith.

 5. A person who is liable to a secured party under a guaranty, endorsement, repurchase agreement, or the like, and who receives a transfer of collateral from the secured party or is

subrogated to his or her rights, has thereafter the rights and duties of the secured party. Such a transfer of collateral is not a sale or disposition of the collateral under Article 9 [UCC 9-504(5)].

D.   Compulsory Disposition of Collateral and Acceptance of the Collateral as Discharge of the Obligation

1.   If the debtor has paid 60% of the cash price, in the case of a purchase money security interest in consumer goods, the secured party in possession of the collateral must dispose of it within 90 days after taking possession. If the secured party fails to do so, the debtor may at his or her option recover in conversion or under Article 9 (see F., below). The debtor may waive rights by signing a statement renouncing or modifying these rights. The above provisions also apply when a debtor has paid 60% of a loan secured by an interest in consumer goods [UCC 9-505(1)].

2.   In any other case involving consumer goods or any other collateral, a secured party in possession may, after default, propose to retain the collateral in satisfaction of the obligation. Written notice of such proposal shall be sent to the debtor if he or she has not signed, after default, a statement renouncing or modifying his or her rights under Article 9. In the case of consumer goods, no other notice need be given. In other cases, notice must be sent to any other secured party who has supplied the primary secured party with written notice of his or her claim. If the secured party receives objection in writing from any person entitled to notice, within 21 days after the notice was sent, the secured party must dispose of the collateral as per VI.C., above. In the absence of such written objection, the secured party may retain the collateral in satisfaction of the debtor's obligation [UCC 9-505(2)].

E.   Debtor's Right to Redeem Collateral--At any time before the secured party has disposed of the collateral or otherwise discharged his or her obligations under Article 9, the debtor or any other secured party may redeem the collateral. In order to redeem, that person must tender fulfillment of all obligations secured by the collateral as well as reasonable expenses, including reasonable legal expenses (UCC 9-506).

F.   Secured Party Liability for Failure to Comply With Article 9

1.   If it is established that the secured party is not proceeding in accordance with the provisions of Article 9, disposition may be ordered or restrained on appropriate terms and conditions. If the disposition has occurred, the debtor or any person whose security interest has been made known to the secured party prior to the disposition has a right to recover from the secured party any loss caused by a failure to comply with the provisions of Article 9 [UCC 9-507(1)].

2.   The fact that a better price could have been obtained by a sale at a different time or in a different method from that selected by the secured party is not alone sufficient to establish that the sale was not in a commercially reasonable manner. If the secured party sells the collateral in the usual manner and at the current price, the secured party is selling in a commercially reasonable manner [UCC 9-507(2)].

CHAPTER 47—SECURED TRANSACTIONS

Problem 47-1 MULTIPLE CHOICE QUESTIONS (45 to 55 minutes)

1. On March 1, Green went to Easy Car Sales to buy a car. Green spoke to a salesperson and agreed to buy a car that Easy had in its showroom. On March 5, Green made a $500 downpayment and signed a security agreement to secure the payment of the balance of the purchase price. On March 10, Green picked up the car. On March 15, Easy filed the security agreement. On what date did Easy's security interest attach?
a. March 1.
b. March 5.
c. March 10.
d. March 15.   (5/93, Law, #46, 4014)

2. Under the UCC Secured Transactions Article, which of the following conditions must be satisfied for a security interest to attach?
a. The debtor must have title to the collateral.
b. The debtor must agree to the creation of the security interest.
c. The creditor must be in possession of part of the collateral.
d. The creditor must properly file a financing statement.   (11/92, Law, #45, 3127)

2A. Under the UCC Secured Transactions Article, which of the following after-acquired property may be attached to a security agreement given to a secured lender?

	Inventory	Equipment
a.	Yes	Yes
b.	Yes	No
c.	No	Yes
d.	No	No

(5/94, Law, #49, 4804)

2B. Under the Secured Transactions Article of the UCC, which of the following requirements is necessary to have a security interest attach?

	Debtor has rights in the collateral	Proper filing of a security agreement	Value given by the creditor
a.	Yes	Yes	Yes
b.	Yes	Yes	No
c.	Yes	No	Yes
d.	No	Yes	Yes

(11/94, Law, #57, 5234)

3. Under the UCC Secured Transactions Article, when collateral is in a secured party's possession, which of the following conditions must also be satisfied to have attachment?
a. There must be a written security agreement.
b. The public must be notified.
c. The secured party must receive consideration.
d. The debtor must have rights to the collateral.

(11/92, Law, #46, 3128)

4. Pix Co., which is engaged in the business of selling appliances, borrowed $18,000 from Lux Bank. Pix executed a promissory note for that amount and pledged all of its customer installment receivables as collateral for the loan. Pix executed a security agreement that described the collateral, but Lux did not file a financing statement. With respect to this transaction,
a. Attachment of the security interest did **not** occur because Pix failed to file a financing statement.
b. Perfection of the security interest occurred despite Lux's failure to file a financing statement.
c. Attachment of the security interest took place when the loan was made and Pix executed the security agreement.
d. Perfection of the security interest did **not** occur because accounts receivable are intangibles.

(5/91, Law, #57, 0580)

4A. Winslow Co., which is in the business of selling furniture, borrowed $60,000 from Pine Bank. Winslow executed a promissory note for that amount and used all of its accounts receivable as collateral for the loan. Winslow executed a security agreement that described the collateral. Winslow did not file a financing statement. Which of the following statements best describes this transaction?
a. Perfection of the security interest occurred even though Winslow did **not** file a financing statement.
b. Perfection of the security interest occurred by Pine having an interest in accounts receivable.
c. Attachment of the security interest did **not** occur because Winslow failed to file a financing statement.
d. Attachment of the security interest occurred when the loan was made and Winslow executed the security agreement.

(11/93, Law, #58, 4355)

5. Which of the following requirements is **not** necessary in order to have a security interest attach?
a. There must be a proper filing.
b. Value must be given by the creditor.
c. Either the creditor must take possession or the debtor must sign a security agreement that describes the collateral.
d. The debtor must have rights in the collateral.
(5/87, Law, #58, 9911)

5A. Under the UCC Secured Transactions Article, which of the following events will always prevent a security interest from attaching?
a. Failure to have a written security agreement.
b. Failure of the creditor to have possession of the collateral.
c. Failure of the debtor to have rights in the collateral.
d. Failure of the creditor to give present consideration for the security interest.
(5/94, Law, #48, 4803)

6. On June 3, Muni Finance loaned Page Corp. $20,000 to purchase four computers for use in Page's trucking business. Page contemporaneously executed a promissory note and security agreement. On June 7, Page purchased the computers with the $20,000, obtaining possession that same day. On June 10, Mort, a judgment creditor of Page, levied on the computers. Which of the following statements is correct?
a. Muni failed to qualify as a purchase money secured lender.
b. Muni's security interest attached on June 3.
c. Muni's security interest attached on June 7.
d. Muni's security interest did **not** attach.
(5/85, Law, #44, 9911)

7. Frey Products, Inc., leased ten lathes from Tri Corp., a manufacturer of lathes. The lease provided for monthly payments of $2,000 per month for 60 months. Frey has an option to purchase the ten lathes for $200 upon completion of the 60 payments. Tri has accounted for this lease as a sales-type lease and Frey has accounted for this lease as a capital lease. Assuming Frey exercises the option, which of the following statements is correct?
a. Frey lacks an insurable interest in the lathes until it exercises the option to purchase them.
b. The lease agreement represents a purchase money security interest which is automatically perfected without the necessity of filing a financing statement.

c. In order to have an enforceable lease, Tri must file a security agreement.
d. Title to the lathes passed to Frey prior to the time Frey exercised the option.
(5/86, Law, #45, 0602)

8. A secured creditor wants to file a financing statement to perfect its security interest. Under the UCC Secured Transactions Article, which of the following must be included in the financing statement?
a. A listing or description of the collateral.
b. An after-acquired property provision.
c. The creditor's signature.
d. The collateral's location.
(11/92, Law, #48, 3130)

9. Under the UCC Secured Transactions Article, what is the effect of perfecting a security interest by filing a financing statement?
a. The secured party can enforce its security interest against the debtor.
b. The secured party has permanent priority in the collateral even if the collateral is removed to another state.
c. The debtor is protected against all other parties who acquire an interest in the collateral after the filing.
d. The secured party has priority in the collateral over most creditors who acquire a security interest in the same collateral after the filing.
(11/92, Law, #47, 3129)

10. If a manufacturer assigns 90% of its accounts receivable to a factor, perfection will occur by

	Filing a financing statement	Possession	Attachment
a.	Yes	Yes	No
b.	Yes	No	No
c.	No	No	Yes
d.	No	Yes	No

(5/87, Law, #59, 9911)

11. On June 15, Harper purchased equipment for $100,000 from Imperial Corp. for use in its manufacturing process. Harper paid for the equipment with funds borrowed from Eastern Bank. Harper gave Eastern a security agreement and financing statement covering Harper's existing and after-acquired equipment. On June 21, Harper was petitioned involuntarily into bankruptcy under Chapter 7 of the Federal Bankruptcy Code. A bankruptcy trustee was appointed. On June 23, Eastern filed the financing statement. Which of the parties will have a superior security interest in the equipment?

a. The trustee in bankruptcy, because the filing of the financing statement after the commencement of the bankruptcy case would be deemed a preferential transfer.

b. The trustee in bankruptcy, because the trustee became a lien creditor before Eastern perfected its security interest.

c. Eastern, because it had a perfected purchase money security interest without having to file a financing statement.

d. Eastern, because it perfected its security interest within the permissible time limits.

(5/91, Law, #59, 0582)

12. Under the UCC Secured Transactions Article, which of the following actions will best perfect a security interest in a negotiable instrument against any other party?

a. Filing a security agreement.

b. Taking possession of the instrument.

c. Perfecting by attachment.

d. Obtaining a duly executed financing statement.

(5/94, Law, #50, 4805)

13. Grey Corp. sells computers to the public. Grey sold and delivered a computer to West on credit. West executed and delivered to Grey a promissory note for the purchase price and a security agreement covering the computer. West purchased the computer for personal use. Grey did not file a financing statement. Is Grey's security interest perfected?

a. Yes, because Grey retained ownership of the computer.

b. Yes, because it was perfected at the time of attachment.

c. No, because the computer was a consumer good.

d. No, because Grey failed to file a financing statement. (11/93, Law, #59, 4356)

14. Mars, Inc. manufactures and sells VCRs on credit directly to wholesalers, retailers, and consumers. Mars can perfect its security interest in the VCRs it sells without having to file a financing statement or take possession of the VCRs if the sale is made to

a. Retailers.

b. Wholesalers that sell to distributors for resale.

c. Consumers.

d. Wholesalers that sell to buyers in the ordinary course of business. (5/93, Law, #47, 4015)

15. Carr Corp. sells VCRs and video tapes to the public. Carr sold and delivered a VCR to Sutter on credit. Sutter executed and delivered to Carr a promissory note for the purchase price and a security agreement covering the VCR. Sutter purchased the VCR for personal use. Carr did not file a financing statement. Is Carr's security interest perfected?

a. No, because the VCR was a consumer good.

b. No, because Carr failed to file a financing statement.

c. Yes, because Carr retained ownership of the VCR.

d. Yes, because it was perfected at the time of attachment. (5/91, Law, #58, 0581)

16. Which of the following transactions would illustrate a secured party perfecting its security interest by taking possession of the collateral?

a. A bank receiving a mortgage on real property.

b. A wholesaler borrowing to purchase inventory.

c. A consumer borrowing to buy a car.

d. A pawnbroker lending money.

(5/93, Law, #48, 4016)

17. Under the Secured Transactions Article of the UCC, which of the following purchasers will own consumer goods free of a perfected security interest in the goods?

a. A merchant who purchases the goods for resale.

b. A merchant who purchases the goods for use in its business.

c. A consumer who purchases the goods from a consumer purchaser who gave the security interest.

d. A consumer who purchases the goods in the ordinary course of business.

(11/94, Law, #58, 5235)

This was PMSI but it also filed so it protected

Wine

18. Wine purchased a computer using the proceeds of a loan from MJC Finance Company. Wine gave MJC a security interest in the computer. Wine executed a security agreement and financing statement, which was filed by MJC. Wine used the computer to monitor Wine's personal investments. Later, Wine sold the computer to Jacobs, for Jacobs' family use. Jacobs was unaware of MJC's security interest. Wine now is in default under the MJC loan. May MJC repossess the computer from Jacobs?

a. No, because Jacobs was unaware of the MJC security interest.

b. No, because Jacobs intended to use the computer for family or household purposes.

c. Yes, because MJC's security interest was perfected before Jacobs' purchase.

d. Yes, because Jacobs' purchase of the computer made Jacobs personally liable to MJC. (5/91, Law, #60, 0583)

19. Under the UCC Secured Transactions Article, perfection of a security interest by a creditor provides added protection against other parties in the event the debtor does not pay its debts. Which of the following parties is **not** affected by perfection of a security interest?
a. Other prospective creditors of the debtor.
b. The trustee in a bankruptcy case.
c. A buyer in the ordinary course of business.
d. A subsequent personal injury judgment creditor.
(5/94, Law, #51, 4806)

20. On July 8, Ace, a refrigerator wholesaler, purchased 50 refrigerators. This comprised Ace's entire inventory and was financed under an agreement with Rome Bank that gave Rome a security interest in all refrigerators on Ace's premises, all future-acquired refrigerators, and the proceeds of sales. On July 12, Rome filed a financing statement that adequately identified the collateral. On August 15, Ace sold one refrigerator to Cray for personal use and four refrigerators to Zone Co. for its business. Which of the following statements is correct?
a. The refrigerators sold to Zone will be subject to Rome's security interest.
b. The refrigerator sold to Cray will **not** be subject to Rome's security interest.
c. The security interest does **not** include the proceeds from the sale of the refrigerators to Zone.
d. The security interest may **not** cover after-acquired property even if the parties agree.
(11/92, Law, #49, 3131)

21. Under the UCC Secured Transactions Article, what is the order of priority for the following security interests in store equipment?

I. Security interest perfected by filing on April 15, 1994.
II. Security interest attached on April 1, 1994.
III. Purchase money security interest attached April 11, 1994 and perfected by filing on April 20, 1994.

a. I, III, II.
b. II, I, III.
c. III, I, II.
d. III, II, I.
(5/94, Law, #52, 4807)

22. Larkin is a wholesaler of computers. Larkin sold 40 computers to Elk Appliance for $80,000. Elk paid $20,000 down and signed a promissory note for the balance. Elk also executed a security agreement giving Larkin a security interest in Elk's inventory,

including the computers. Larkin perfected its security interest by properly filing a financing statement in the state of Whiteacre. Six months later, Elk moved its business to the state of Blackacre, taking the computers. On arriving in Blackacre, Elk secured a loan from Quarry Bank and signed a security agreement putting up all inventory (including the computers) as collateral. Quarry perfected its security interest by properly filing a financing statement in the state of Blackacre. Two months after arriving in Blackacre, Elk went into default on both debts. Which of the following statements is correct?
a. Quarry's security interest is superior because Larkin's time to file a financing statement in Blackacre had expired prior to Quarry's filing.
b. Quarry's security interest is superior because Quarry had **no** actual notice of Larkin's security interest.
c. Larkin's security interest is superior even though at the time of Elk's default Larkin had **not** perfected its security interest in the state of Blackacre.
d. Larkin's security interest is superior provided it repossesses the computers before Quarry does.
(5/94, Law, #53, 4808)

23. In what order are the following obligations paid after a secured creditor rightfully sells the debtor's collateral after repossession?

I. Debt owed to any junior security holder.
II. Secured party's reasonable sale expenses.
III. Debt owed to the secured party.

a. I, II, III.
b. II, I, III.
c. II, III, I.
d. III, II, I.
(11/93, Law, #53, 4350)

24. Noninventory goods were purchased and delivered on June 15, 1993. Several security interests exist in these goods. Which of the following security interests has priority over the others?
a. Security interest in future goods attached June 10, 1993.
b. Security interest attached June 15, 1993.
c. Security interest perfected June 20, 1993.
d. Purchase money security interest perfected June 24, 1993.
(11/93, Law, #60, 4357)

25. Under the UCC Secured Transactions Article, which of the following statements is correct concerning the disposition of collateral by a secured creditor after a debtor's default?

a. A good faith purchaser for value and without knowledge of any defects in the sale takes free of any subordinate liens or security interests.

b. The debtor may **not** redeem the collateral after the default.

c. Secured creditors with subordinate claims retain the right to redeem the collateral after the collateral is sold to a third party.

d. The collateral may only be disposed of at a public sale. (5/93, Law, #50, 4018)

26. Burn Manufacturing borrowed $500,000 from Howard Finance Co., secured by Burn's present and future inventory, accounts receivable, and the proceeds thereof. The parties signed a financing statement that described the collateral and it was filed in the appropriate state office. Burn subsequently defaulted in the repayment of the loan and Howard attempted to enforce its security interest. Burn contended that Howard's security interest was unenforceable. In addition, Green, who subsequently gave credit to Burn without knowledge of Howard's security interest, is also attempting to defeat Howard's alleged security interest. The security interest in question is valid with respect to

a. Both Burn and Green.

b. Neither Burn **nor** Green.

c. Burn but **not** Green.

d. Green but **not** Burn. (5/89, Law, #60, 0590)

27. Under the Secured Transactions Article of the UCC, what would be the order of priority for the following security interests in consumer goods?

I. Financing agreement filed on April 1.

II. Possession of the collateral by a creditor on April 10.

III. Financing agreement perfected on April 15.

a. I, II, III.

b. II, I, III.

c. II, III, I.

d. III, II, I. (11/94, Law, #59, 5236)

28. A party who filed a security interest in inventory on April 1, 1993, would have a superior interest to which of the following parties?

a. A holder of a mechanic's lien whose lien was filed on March 15, 1993.

b. A holder of a purchase money security interest in after-acquired property filed on March 20, 1993.

c. A purchaser in the ordinary course of business who purchased on April 10, 1993.

d. A judgment lien creditor who filed its judgment on April 15, 1993. (5/93, Law, #49, 4017)

29. Roth and Dixon both claim a security interest in the same collateral. Roth's security interest attached on January 1, 1989, and was perfected by filing on March 1, 1989. Dixon's security interest attached on February 1, 1989, and was perfected on April 1, 1989, by taking possession of the collateral. Which of the following statements is correct?

a. Roth's security interest has priority because Roth perfected before Dixon perfected.

b. Dixon's security interest has priority because Dixon's interest attached before Roth's interest was perfected.

c. Roth's security interest has priority because Roth's security interest attached before Dixon's security interest attached.

d. Dixon's security interest has priority because Dixon is in possession of the collateral. (11/89, Law, #54, 0587)

30. Under the UCC Secured Transactions Article, if a debtor is in default under a payment obligation secured by goods, the secured party has the right to

	Peacefully repossess the goods without judicial process	Reduce the claim to a judgment	Sell the goods and apply the proceeds toward the debt
a.	Yes	Yes	Yes
b.	No	Yes	Yes
c.	Yes	Yes	No
d.	Yes	No	Yes

(11/92, Law, #50, 3132)

31. Under the UCC, which of the following is correct regarding the disposition of collateral by a secured creditor after the debtor's default?

a. It is improper for the secured creditor to purchase the collateral at a public sale.

b. The collateral must be disposed of at a public sale.

c. A good faith purchaser for value and without knowledge of any defects in the sale takes free of any subordinate liens or security interests.

d. Secured creditors with subordinate claims retain the right to redeem the collateral after the disposition of the collateral to a third party. (11/86, Law, #49, 9911)

Items 32 and 33 are based on the following:

Drew bought a computer for personal use from Hale Corp. for $3,000. Drew paid $2,000 in cash and signed a security agreement for the balance. Hale properly filed the security agreement. Drew defaulted in paying the balance of the purchase price. Hale asked Drew to pay the balance. When Drew refused, Hale peacefully repossessed the computer.

32. Under the UCC Secured Transactions Article, which of the following rights will Drew have?
a. Redeem the computer after Hale sells it.
b. Recover the sale price from Hale after Hale sells the computer.
c. Force Hale to sell the computer.
d. Prevent Hale from selling the computer.

(5/94, Law, #55, 4810)

33. Under the UCC Secured Transactions Article, which of the following remedies will Hale have?
a. Obtain a deficiency judgment against Drew for the amount owed.
b. Sell the computer and retain any surplus over the amount owed.
c. Retain the computer over Drew's objection.
d. Sell the computer without notifying Drew.

(5/94, Law, #54, 4809)

34. Under the Federal Fair Debt Collection Practices Act, which of the following would a collection service using improper debt collection practices be subject to?
a. Abolishment of the debt.
b. Reduction of the debt.
c. Civil lawsuit for damages for violating the Act.
d. Criminal prosecution for violating the Act.

(11/94, Law, #26, 5203)

35. Under the Secured Transactions Article of the UCC, which of the following remedies is available to a secured creditor when a debtor fails to make a payment when due?

	Proceed against the collateral	Obtain a general judgment against the debtor
a.	Yes	Yes
b.	Yes	No
c.	No	Yes
d.	No	No

(11/94, Law, #60, 5237)

Solution 47-1 MULTIPLE CHOICE ANSWERS

Attachment of Security Interest

1. (c) Attachment occurs when (1) value is given by the secured party, (2) the debtor attains rights in the collateral, and (3) the debtor and creditor acknowledge the creation of a security interest by a signed security agreement or by collateral in the possession of the secured party. In this situation, attachment occurred on March 10 because the following occurred on or before that date: (1) Easy picked up the car, (2) the car had been identified to the contract, therefore Green had a right in the property, and (3) Green signed a security agreement.

2. (b) Attachment occurs when (1) value is given by the secured party, (2) the debtor obtains rights in the collateral, and (3) the debtor and the creditor acknowledge the creation of a security interest by a signed security agreement or by collateral in the possession of the secured party. The debtor must have rights, but need not have title. It is not *always* required that the creditor take possession for the security interest to attach, and filing a financing statement has nothing to do with attachment, only perfection.

2A. (a) UCC 9-204 permits a creditor to attach to a security agreement both after-acquired inventory and after-acquired equipment.

2B. (c) UCC 9-203 states that attachment occurs when (1) the creditor has given value, (2) the debtor has rights in the collateral, and (3) when the creditor either obtains a security agreement signed by the debtor or obtains possession of the collateral. The filing of a security agreement is not necessary for attachment.

3. (d) Attachment occurs when (1) value is given by the secured party, (2) the debtor obtains rights in the collateral, and (3) the debtor and the creditor acknowledge the creation of a security interest by a signed security agreement or by collateral in the possession of the secured party. The security agreement may be oral if the collateral is in the secured party's possession. Notification of the public is one of the requirements of perfection, not attachment. The collateral in the possession of the secured party serves as the consideration.

4. (c) Attachment takes place with accounts receivables once the security agreement was signed and the loan took place. Failure to file a financing

statement has nothing to do with attachment, only perfection. Perfection cannot occur when the financing statement is not filed. To perfect a security interest in accounts receivables, a financing statement must be filed. The reason perfection of the security interest did not occur was because there was a failure to file a financing statement.

4A. (d)   The requirements for attachment include the following:

1. Creditor gives value to debtor.
2. Debtor has rights in the collateral.
3. Agreement in writing, unless creditor has possession of the collateral.

5. (a)   Under 9-203(1) of the UCC, a security interest attaches when the last of the following events occurs: (1) the collateral is in the secured party's possession pursuant to an agreement or the debtor has signed a security agreement, (2) value has been given to the debtor, and (3) the debtor has rights in the collateral.

5A. (c)   UCC 9-203 requires that in order for attachment to take place, (1) the creditor must give value, (2) the debtor must have rights in the collateral, and (3) the creditor must either take possession of the collateral or obtain a signed security agreement from the debtor. The creditor may either take possession or obtain a signed security agreement. The Secured Transactions Article does not require that the creditor give present consideration for the security interest, only that the creditor give value.

6. (c)   Attachment occurs when all three of the following events occur: (1) value is given by the secured party, (2) the debtor obtains rights in the collateral, and (3) the debtor and creditor acknowledge the creation of a security interest. In this instance, attachment occurred when the last of these events occurred (i.e., on June 7 when the debtor purchased and took possession of the computers and obtained rights in the collateral). On June 3, although value had been given by the secured party and the parties had acknowledged the creation of a security interest by executing a security agreement, the debtor had *not* yet acquired rights in the collateral and attachment could not occur until all these conditions had been met. A person who gives value which enables the debtor to acquire rights in the collateral qualifies as a purchase money lender.

7. (d)   Article 9, as a general rule, applies to any transaction regardless of its form which is intended to create a security interest, including a lease intended as security. In this instance, the lease provided for substantial payments which approximately equaled the value of the lathes, with a purchase option requiring only a nominal payment at the end of the lease term. The lease was most likely therefore intended as a type of disguised sale and security agreement with the intent that title to the lathes would pass prior to the exercise of the option. As a security interest, Tri Corp. would need to file a financing statement in order to perfect its interest since it is not one of the types of interests that is automatically perfected upon attachment. Therefore, answer (b) is incorrect. A lessee does possess an insurable interest in the items leased. A lease does not require a security agreement in order to be enforceable.

8. (a)   Included in the financing statement must be the names of the debtor and the secured party, the signature of the debtor, an address of the secured party from which information concerning the security interest may be obtained, a mailing address of the debtor, and a statement indicating the types, or describing the items of collateral. An after-acquired property provision and the location of the collateral are not required to be included in the financing statements. The financing statement must contain the debtor's, not the creditor's, signature.

Perfection of Security Interest

9. (d)   Perfecting a security interest by filing a financing statement serves to protect the secured party's interest in the collateral against most creditors who acquire a security interest in the same collateral after the filing. Subsequent creditors may still obtain security interests in the same collateral although they will normally obtain a lower priority. Moving the property to another state and a debtor with a perfected security interest may both affect the priority of the secured party's interest in the collateral.

10. (b)   A security interest in accounts receivable may be perfected only by the filing of a financing statement.

11. (d)   If a creditor takes a purchase money security interest in equipment and files a financing statement within ten days of attachment, the creditor will have priority over other secured creditors. In this situation, Eastern filed the financing statement within the ten-day period and, thus, Eastern will have priority over the trustee in bankruptcy. A trustee will lose to Eastern since Eastern filed the financing statement

within the ten-day period. In addition, filing the financing statement after commencement of the bankruptcy case is not a preferential transfer. This represents a contemporaneous exchange since value was given in exchange for the perfected security interest. Eastern, a purchase money secured creditor, filed the financing statement within ten days. Eastern must file to have a perfected security interest in equipment.

12. (b)   UCC 9-304/5 provides that a security interest in negotiable instruments can only be perfected by possession.

13. (b)   Automatic perfection occurs when a purchase money security interest is in *consumer goods* and the requirements of attachment have been met. The facts of the problem indicate that a purchase money security interest does exist and attachment had occurred when the security agreement was delivered. Grey did not retain ownership but it did perfect its security interest since it had an attached purchase money security interest in consumer goods. Grey's purchase money security interest in a consumer good *was* perfected upon attachment without the need for the filing of a financing statement.

14. (c)   A purchase money security interest in consumer goods is automatically perfected. A filing is necessary whenever goods are sold to wholesalers and other retailers.

15. (d)   Carr's security interest is perfected automatically with attachment since the seller had a purchase money security interest in consumer goods and there is no need to file a financing statement for perfection. There is a perfected security interest in consumer goods automatically with attachment. There is a perfected security interest without filing because this is a purchase money security interest in consumer goods that is perfected with attachment. The fact that Carr retained ownership of the VCR does not perfect Carr's security interest.

16. (d)   Perfection by possession occurs when the secured party takes possession of the collateral, such as when a pawnbroker lends money after taking possession of the debtor's property. A mortgage is a conveyance of an interest in land. A wholesaler borrowing to purchase inventory is a purchase money security interest in inventory. A consumer borrowing to buy a car is an example of a secured transaction where perfection would not occur until a financing statement was filed.

17. (d)   UCC 9-307 provides that a buyer in the ordinary course of business will own goods free of a perfected security interest, even if the buyer knows of its existence. A merchant who purchases goods, for resale or for use in its business would not take free of a perfected security interest in the goods, nor would a consumer who purchases the goods from a consumer purchaser (a good faith purchaser for value) take the goods free of a perfected security interest.

18. (c)   Jacob should have been constructively aware of MJC's financing statement. If MJC had relied upon automatic perfection (no financing statement was filed), MJC would have lost to Jacob. The key to this type of problem is determining if the creditor had filed a financing statement prior to the purchase by a good faith purchaser for personal use. It does not matter if Jacob was unaware of the MJC security interest since Jacob had constructive knowledge of the filing (you are deemed to know what has been filed). MJC can repossess the computer even if it is used for household purposes. MJC can repossess since a financing statement was filed prior to the purchase by Jacob. Jacob has no personal liability to MJC when Jacob purchases the computer.

Priorities

19. (c)   UCC 9-307(2) provides that a perfected security interest is not enforceable against a buyer in the ordinary course of business, even if the buyer had knowledge of the secured interest. A perfected security interest is enforceable against other prospective creditors of the debtor, the trustee in bankruptcy and a subsequent personal injury judgment creditor.

20. (b)   Under UCC 9-307, a buyer in the ordinary course of business takes free of a security interest created by his or her seller even though the security interest is perfected and even though the buyer knows of its existence. Neither Cray nor Zone is subject to the security interest. A security agreement may provide that any or all obligations covered by the agreement are to be additionally secured by property later acquired by the debtor. Unless otherwise provided in the security agreement, the secured party has a continuously perfected security interest in the proceeds that result from the debtor's sale or transfer of the collateral.

21. (c)   UCC 9-301 states that where there are conflicting interests in the same collateral, the first to have perfected its interest will prevail. This section also provides that creditors who have perfected their security interests will prevail over those who have

merely attached. UCC 9-301(2) provides that where there is a purchase money security interest (PMSI) in equipment, the creditor has a 10-day period after attachment to perfect its interest. If the creditor properly perfects within the 10-day period, then perfection will be held to have occurred retroactively on the date of attachment. In this instance a PMSI exists and the security interest was perfected effective April 11, 1994. This precedes the April 15, 1994, filing of Creditor I. Creditor II never perfected its interest and would thus fall behind those creditors who have perfected. Creditor III would prevail over Creditor I, who would in turn prevail over Creditor II.

22. (c) UCC 9-103(1) provides that when collateral such as inventory is properly perfected in one jurisdiction and is then removed to another jurisdiction, the creditor will have a four-month period in which to perfect its interest in the new jurisdiction. The collateral remains perfected during the four-month period, and is thus perfected against creditors who perfected their interests before the expiration of the four months.

23. (c) Proceeds from the disposition of collateral must be applied in the following order:

1. Reasonable expenses incurred in retaking, holding, and selling the collateral.
2. Satisfaction of the debt owed the secured party.
3. Subordinate security interests in the property.
4. Any surplus goes back to the debtor.

24. (d) A purchase money security interest in noninventory collateral takes priority over other perfected interests if the purchase money interest is perfected at the time the debtor takes possession of the collateral or within 10 days of receipt.

25. (a) A good faith purchaser for value and without knowledge of any defects in the sale takes free of any subordinate liens or security interests but remains subject to security interests which are senior to that being discharged at the sale. A debtor has a right to redeem collateral before a secured party disposes of it by paying the entire debt and the secured party's reasonable expenses. A good faith purchaser for value and without knowledge of any defects in the sale takes free of any subordinate liens or security interests. Disposition may be made by public or private proceedings.

26. (a) UCC 9-312 states that except as it applies to purchase money security interests, the rules of priority between conflicting secured parties are determined by the order of filing, and if no filing, then by order of perfection, and if no perfection, then

by order of attachment. Therefore, assuming Green does not have a purchase money security interest, answers (b), (c), and (d) are incorrect because Howard filed before Green did. Green's lack of knowledge is immaterial as he is deemed to have knowledge (constructive notice) under the statute due to Howard's prior filing. Under UCC 9-203(1) a security interest attaches against the debtor, *Burn*, when: (1) the collateral is in the secured party's possession pursuant to a signed security agreement, (2) value has been given to the debtor, and (3) the debtor has rights in the collateral.

27. (a) UCC 9-312(5)(a) states that conflicting security interests rank according to priority in time of filing or perfection. UCC 9-305 states that a security interest is perfected by possession from the time possession is taken. Possession is as valid a means of perfection as any other. In this instance the conflicting interests are all perfected, thus they would rank in order of perfection, by date.

28. (d) A security interest perfected before a lien has priority. A lien creditor has priority over an unperfected security interest or a security interest perfected after attachment of the lien. In addition, it is the general rule that a mechanic's lien has priority over a prior perfected security interest. A purchase money security interest in after-acquired property has priority over an after-acquired property secured creditor. Buyers in the ordinary course of business take free of any security interest whether perfected or not.

29. (a) The general rule is that, except as applies to purchase money security interests where both perfected interests are by filing, the first to file has priority. Second, if both do not perfect by filing (as in this question), the first to perfect has priority. Since Roth was the first to perfect, Roth has priority.

Remedies Upon Default and Rights of the Parties

30. (a) Under Article 9, upon default, the secured party has the right to reduce the claim to a judgment, sell the goods and apply the proceeds toward the debt, or take possession of the goods without judicial process.

31. (c) Among other types of disposition allowed are both public and private sales, and the secured party may buy the collateral at either type of sale. The purchaser of the collateral takes free of all security interests and subordinated liens if he or she

acts in good faith and without knowledge of any defects in the sale.

32. (c) UCC 9-505 requires the creditor to sell the collateral where there has been a purchase money security interest (PMSI) in consumer goods and the debtor has paid 60% or more of the purchase price. Both of these elements are satisfied here. UCC 9-506 provides that a debtor may redeem collateral at any time before the collateral is sold, but after its sale the purchaser will have superior rights. The UCC Secured Transactions Article has no provision to permit a debtor to either recover the sales price from the creditor or to prevent the creditor from selling the computer.

33. (a) UCC 9-503 permits a secured party to peacefully repossess the collateral. UCC 9-504(1) permits the secured party to sell the collateral, and if the proceeds from the sale do not satisfy the obligation, the creditor may obtain a deficiency judgment against the debtor for the balance.

34. (c) The Fair Debt Collection Practices Act, which is largely enforced by the Federal Trade Commission, permits debtors to recover civil damages, including attorney's fees, from a collection service for violations of the Act. There are no provisions for criminal liability for violating the Act, nor does the Act provide that reduction or abolishment of the debt are appropriate remedies.

35. (a) UCC 9-501(1) states that when a debtor defaults, a secured creditor may repossess the collateral or reduce his/her/its claim to judgment. In the latter case, the creditor can obtain a judgment against the perfected collateral, and, then can obtain a general judgment against the debtor, which would enable a creditor to proceed against any nonexempt property of the debtor.

PERFORMANCE BY SUBTOPICS

Each category below parallels a subtopic covered in Chapter 47. Record the number and percentage of questions you correctly answered in each subtopic area.

Attachment of Security Interest		Perfection of Security Interest		Priorities		Remedies Upon Default and Rights of the Parties	
Question #	Correct √	Question #	Correct √	Question #	Correct √		
1		9		19			
2		10		20			
2A		11		21		Question #	Correct √
2B		12		22		30	
3		13		23		31	
4		14		24		32	
4A		15		25		33	
5		16		26		34	
5A		17		27		35	
6		18		28		# Questions	6
7		# Questions	10	29			
8				# Questions	11	# Correct	_____
# Questions	12	# Correct	_____			% Correct	_____
		% Correct	_____	# Correct	_____		
# Correct	_____			% Correct	_____		
% Correct	_____						

OTHER OBJECTIVE FORMAT QUESTION

Problem 47-2 (10 to 15 minutes)

a. On January 2, 1994, Gray Interiors Corp., a retailer of sofas, contracted with Shore Furniture Co. to purchase 150 sofas for its inventory. The purchase price was $250,000. Gray paid $50,000 cash and gave Shore a note and security agreement for the balance. On March 1, 1994, the sofas were delivered. On March 10, 1994, Shore filed a financing statement.

On February 1, 1994, Gray negotiated a $1,000,000 line of credit with Float Bank, pledged its present and future inventory as security, and gave Float a security agreement. On February 20, 1994, Gray borrowed $100,000 from the line of credit. On March 5, 1994, Float filed a financing statement.

On April 1, 1994, Dove, a consumer purchaser in the ordinary course of business, purchased a sofa from Gray. Dove was aware of both security interests.

Required:

Items 1 through 6 refer to the above fact pattern. For each item, determine whether (a), (b), or (c) is correct.

1. Shore's security interest in the sofas attached on
a. January 2, 1994.
b. March 1, 1994.
c. March 10, 1994.

2. Shore's security interest in the sofas was perfected on
a. January 2, 1994.
b. March 1, 1994.
c. March 10, 1994.

3. Float's security interest in Gray's inventory attached on
a. February 1, 1994.
b. March 1, 1994.
c. March 5, 1994.

4. Float's security interest in Gray's inventory was perfected on
a. February 1, 1994.
b. February 20, 1994.
c. March 5, 1994.

5.
a. Shore's security interest has priority because it was a purchase money security interest.
b. Float's security interest has priority because Float's financing statement was filed before Shore's.
c. Float's security interest has priority because Float's interest attached before Shore's.

6.
a. Dove purchased the sofa subject to Shore's security interest.
b. Dove purchased the sofa subject to both the Shore and Float security interests.
c. Dove purchased the sofa free of either the Shore or Float security interests.

(5/95, Law, #3b)

OTHER OBJECTIVE FORMAT SOLUTION

Solution 47-2 Perfection and Priority

1. (b) The UCC's Article on Secured Transaction provides that a security interest attaches when the creditor has given value, the debtor has rights in the collateral, and the debtor has signed a security agreement or the collateral is in the possession of the secured party. Since Shore did not give value until March 1, 1994, all three elements necessary for attachment were not present until that date.

2. (c) Shore's security interest was perfected as of March 10, 1994, the date on which Shore filed a financing statement.

3. (a) The UCC's Article on Secured Transactions states that attachment occurs when the creditor has given value, when the debtor has rights in the collateral, and when the debtor has signed a security agreement or the collateral is in the creditor's possession. Since Gray could have accessed the line of credit with Float Bank on February 1, 1994, all elements necessary for attachment occurred on that date.

4. (c) Float's security interest in Gray's inventory was perfected on March 5, 1994, when the financing statement was filed.

5. (b) Shore Furniture Company is a Purchase Money Security Interest (PMSI) inventory creditor of Gray. A PMSI in inventory collateral has priority over a conflicting security interest in the same collateral if (1) it is perfected when the debtor gets possession, and (2) written notice is given to all other secured parties before the debtor takes possession of the inventory. Since Shore did not perfect until after Gray received the inventory and since Shore did not give written notice to Float, Shore does not have a priority as a result of its PMSI. Where more than one party has perfected their security interest by filing, priority is determined by ascertaining which party filed or otherwise perfected their interest first. When the party's interest attached is, at that point, irrelevant.

6. (c) The Secured Transactions Article of the UCC provides that a buyer in the ordinary course of business purchases property free of a security interest, even if perfected.

ESSAY QUESTIONS

Essay 47-3 (15 to 20 minutes)

Mead, a junior member of a CPA firm's audit staff, was assigned to assist in auditing Abco Electronics, Inc.'s financial statements. Abco sells various brands of computer equipment to the general public, and to distributors who sell the equipment to retail customers for personal and business use. One of Mead's assignments was to evaluate the following transactions:

- On September 1, Abco sold a CDM computer out of its inventory to Rice, who intended to use it for business purposes. Rice paid 25% of the purchase price and executed and delivered to Abco a promissory note for the balance. A security agreement was signed only by the Abco sales representative. Abco failed to file a financing statement. Rice is in default under the promissory note. Rice claimed that Abco does not have an effective security interest in the computer because Rice did not sign the security agreement, and because Abco did not file a financing statement.

- On August 18, Abco sold a computer to Baker, who intended to us it for business inventory and accounts payable control, and payroll processing. Baker paid 20% of the purchase price and executed and delivered to Abco a promissory note for the balance and a security agreement covering the computer. Abco filed a financing statement on August 27. On August 25, Baker borrowed $5,000 from Condor Finance Co., giving Condor a promissory note for the loan amount and a security agreement covering the computer. Condor filed a financing statement on August 26. Baker defaulted on the promissory note given to Abco and its obligation to Condor. Condor has asserted that its security interest in the computer is superior to Abco's.

Required:

State whether the claims of Rice and Condor are correct and give the reasons for your conclusions.

(11/91, Law, #5)

Essay 47-4 (15 to 20 minutes)

Dunn & Co., CPAs, is auditing the 1987 financial statements of its client, Safe Finance. While performing the audit, Dunn learned of certain transactions that occurred during 1987 that may have an adverse impact on Safe's financial statements. The following transactions are of most concern to Dunn:

- On May 5, Safe sold certain equipment to Lux, who contemporaneously executed and delivered to Safe a promissory note and security agreement covering the equipment. Lux purchased the equipment for use in its business. On May 8, City Bank loaned Lux $50,000, taking a promissory note and security agreement from Lux that covered all of Lux's existing and after-acquired equipment. On May 11, Lux was involuntarily petitioned into bankruptcy under the liquidation provisions of the Bankruptcy Code and a trustee was appointed. On May 12, City filed a financing statement covering all of Lux's equipment. On May 14, Safe filed a financing statement covering the equipment it had sold to Lux on May 5.

- On July 10, Safe loaned $600,000 to Cam Corp., which used the funds to refinance existing debts. Cam duly executed and delivered to Safe a promissory note and a security agreement covering Cam's existing and after-acquired inventory of machine parts. On July 12, Safe filed a financing statement covering Cam's inventory of machine parts. On July 15, Best Bank loaned Cam $200,000. Contemporaneous with the loan, Cam executed and delivered to Best a promissory note and security agreement covering all of Cam's inventory of machine parts and any after-acquired inventory. Best had already filed a financing statement covering Cam's inventory on June 20 after Best agreed to make the loan to Cam. On July 14, Dix, in good faith, purchased certain machine parts from Cam's inventory and received delivery that same day.

Required:

Define a purchase money security interest. In separate paragraphs, discuss whether Safe has a priority security interest over:

- The trustee in Lux's bankruptcy with regard to the equipment sold by Safe on May 5. *Yes*
- City with regard to the equipment sold by Safe on May 5.
- Best with regard to Cam's existing and after-acquired inventory of machine parts.
- Dix with regard to the machine parts purchased on July 14 by Dix.   (5/88, Law, #4)

Essay 47-5 (15 to 20 minutes)

Rustic Equipment, Inc. manufactures lathes and other woodworking equipment. It sells these products to hardware stores, often on credit. Rustic usually requires its credit customers to place large signs in their stores indicating that Rustic products are made available through financing provided by Rustic.

On February 1, 1992, Rustic sold and delivered five lathes to Friendly Hardware Corp. for $25,000. Friendly sells woodworking tools and equipment, among other things, to the general public. Friendly made a 10% down payment and delivered a promissory note for the balance, along with a security agreement and a financing statement covering the lathes. Rustic properly filed the financing statement on February 9, 1992. Rustic required Friendly to display a sign in its store indicating that Rustic provided financing for the lathes. *has constr. notice*

On February 6, 1992, Friendly borrowed $100,000 from National Bank, and gave National a promissory note, a security agreement, and a financing statement covering Friendly's inventory, fixtures, and equipment. Friendly intended to use the loan proceeds to remodel its store. National properly filed the financing statement on February 7, 1992. National was not aware of Rustic's security interest in the lathes included in Friendly's inventory. *doesn't matter*

On March 8, 1992, Friendly sold one of the Rustic lathes to Karry, whose hobby was woodworking. Karry paid 20% of the purchase price, and gave Friendly a promissory note for the balance and a security agreement covering the lathes. Karry, at the time of the purchase, saw the sign publicizing the financing arrangement between Rustic and Friendly. Friendly did not file a financing statement.

The following is the promissory note Karry gave to Friendly:

March 8, 199 2

I promise to pay Friendly Hardware Corp. or bearer $900.00, with interest thereon at 12% per annum.

S. J. Karry
Maker

Reference: Sale of Lathe
                    Invoice #6734

On March 10, 1992, Friendly delivered Karry's promissory note, without endorsement, to Queen Bank in exchange for $750. Queen, a holder in due course, was unaware that Karry had advised Friendly that the lathe was not operating properly and that Karry had no intention of paying the note. Queen then delivered the note to Abcor Factors, Inc. in exchange for $800. At the time Abcor acquired the note from Queen, it knew that Karry disputed any obligation under the note because the lathe was not working properly.

Friendly has experienced serious financial difficulties and defaulted on its obligations to Rustic and National. Abcor has demanded that Karry pay the note given to Friendly, but Karry has refused to do so. Rustic and Karry have taken the following positions:

- Rustic claims that its security interest in the lathes, including the one sold to Karry, is superior to that of National and that Karry purchased the lathe subject to Rustic's security interest.
- Karry refuses to honor the note held by Abcor, claiming that:
  - It is nonnegotiable because it is not payable at a definite time and it references the sales invoice.
  - Abcor has no rights under the note because it was not endorsed by Friendly.
  - Abcor was aware of Karry's claim that the lathe was not working properly and, therefore, took the note subject to that claim.

R invent. (filed) 2/9

didn't Friendly (inv.) 2/7
file sold   filed National
Karry
Queen   Abcor
HDC   HHDC

Required:

State whether the claims of Rustic and Karry are correct and give the reasons for your conclusions.

(5/92, Law, #5)

ESSAY SOLUTIONS

Solution 47-3 Validity and Priority of Security Interests

Rice's assertion that Abco does not have an effective security interest in the CDM computer purchased by Rice is correct. For Abco to have an **enforceable security interest in the collateral, the security interest claimed must have attached.** Attachment requires that:

- The secured party (Abco) has **given value**;
- The debtor (Rice) has **rights in the collateral**; and
- The debtor (Rice) has **executed** and **delivered to the creditor** (Abco) a **security agreement covering the collateral**.

In this case, all but one of the requirements are met. The security agreement is ineffective because it was **not signed** by the debtor (Rice). Abco's **failure to perfect** its security interest by filing a financing statement would have **no effect** on the **enforceability** of the security interest against Rice.

Condor's assertion that its security interest in the computer is superior to Abco's is incorrect. Both Condor's and Abco's security interests are perfected. Condor's security interest was **perfected when it filed** its financing statement on August 26. Because Abco's security interest was a **purchase money security interest in collateral other than inventory**, its security interest was **perfected at the time of the sale** to Baker (August 18), provided it filed a financing statement at the time Baker **took possession** of the computer or **within the UCC time period for perfection**. Abco's security interest was perfected on August 18 before Condor's was perfected (on August 26), because Abco filed a financing statement within the applicable UCC time period. Therefore, Abco's security interest is superior to Condor's.

Solution 47-4 Purchase Money Security Interest/ Priority

A purchase money security interest is an **interest in personal property** or **fixtures that secures payment or performance** of an obligation and that is (1) taken or retained **by the seller of the collateral to secure all or part of its price**, or (2) taken by a person who by **making advances** or **incurring an obligation** gives value to **enable the debtor to acquire rights** in or the **use of** collateral if such value is in fact so used.

Safe's security interest has priority over the rights of the trustee in bankruptcy. The UCC Article on Secured Transactions states that a **lien creditor includes a trustee in bankruptcy from the date of the filing of the petition.** Under the general rule, an **unperfected security interest is subordinate** to the rights of a person who becomes a **lien creditor before the security interest is perfected**. However, if the secured party files with respect to a purchase money security interest **before or within 10 days** after the debtor receives **possession** of the collateral, he takes **priority over** the rights of a **lien creditor** that arise **between the time** the security interest **attaches** and the **time of filing**. Under the facts of our case, Safe has a purchase money security interest in the equipment because the security interest was taken by Safe **to secure the price**. Therefore, because Safe filed a financing statement on May 14 (within 10 days after Lux received possession of the equipment), it has priority security interest over the trustee in bankruptcy (lien creditor) whose claim arose between the time the security interest attached (May 5) and the time of filing (May 14).

Safe has a priority security interest in the equipment over City. A purchase money security interest in **collateral other than inventory** has **priority** over a **conflicting security interest in the same collateral** if the purchase money security interest is **perfected at the time the debtor receives possession** of the collateral **or within 10 days** thereafter. Because Safe has a purchase money security interest in the equipment that was perfected by filing a financing statement on May 14 (within 10 days after Lux received possession of the equipment on May 5), Safe has a priority security interest over City despite City's perfection of its security interest on May 12.

Best's security interest in the inventory has priority over Safe's security interest. In general, conflicting perfected security interests **rank according to priority in time of filing or perfection**. **Priority dates** from the time **a filing is first made** covering the collateral or the time the security interest is **first perfected, whichever is earlier**, provided that there is no period thereafter when there is neither a filing nor perfection. In this case, because **both** Best's and Safe's security interests were **perfected by filing**, the **first to file** (Best) will have a priority security interest. The fact that Best filed a financing statement prior to making the loan will not affect Best's priority.

Safe will not have a priority security interest over Dix because Dix is a **buyer in the ordinary course of business** and will **take free** of Safe's perfected security interest. Dix is a buyer in the ordinary course of business because Dix **acted in good faith** when purchasing the machine parts **in the regular course of** Cam's **business**. The UCC Article on Secured Transactions states that a buyer in the ordinary course of business takes free of a security interest created by his seller even though the security interest is perfected and even though the buyer knows of its existence. Therefore, Dix will take the machine parts purchased from Cam's inventory on July 14, free from Safe's security interest which was perfected on July 12.

Solution 47-5 Priority of Security Interests

Rustic's first claim, that its security interest is superior to National's, is incorrect. Rustic's security interest was **perfected at the time it filed its financing statement**, February 9, 1992, because it was a **purchase money security interest in inventory**. National filed its financing statement on February 7, 1992, therefore, National's security interest was perfected before, and is superior to, Rustic's security interest.

Rustic's second claim, that Karry purchased the lathe subject to Rustic's security interest, is incorrect. Karry, as a buyer **in the ordinary course of** Friendly's **business**, purchased the lathe **free of any security interest** given by Friendly. The fact that Karry was aware of Rustic's security interest does not affect this conclusion.

Karry's first claim, that the note is nonnegotiable, is incorrect. For a promissory note to be negotiable, it must be **payable on demand** or **at a definite time**. An instrument is payable on demand when it states that it is so payable, or when it provides no specific time for payment. Therefore, the note would be considered payable on demand.

Also, Karry's promissory note is negotiable despite the **reference** to the sales invoice because the reference does not make the note **subject to the sales contract**; rather, the reference only notes the existence of the invoice.

Karry's second claim, that Abcor has no rights to Karry's note because Friendly did not endorse it, is incorrect. The note is a **bearer instrument** because it is made **payable to** Friendly **or bearer**. Bearer instruments may be negotiated **by delivery** of the instrument **alone**.

Karry's third claim, that Abcor took the note subject to Karry's dispute with Friendly, is incorrect. Karry's dispute with Friendly was a **personal defense** to Karry. Even though Abcor took the note knowing of Karry's dispute and, therefore, could not ordinarily be a **holder in due course**, Abcor did take the note from Queen, which was a holder in due course. Under the **"shelter provision"** of the UCC Commercial Paper Article, Abcor has the **rights of a holder in due course even though it does not qualify as one**. As a result, Abcor did not take the note subject to Karry's personal defense, despite knowing of Karry's claim.

CHANGE ALERT

The Federal Bankruptcy Reform Act of 1994, passed on October 22, 1994, has changed the dollar amounts for allowable exemptions and the amount of debt to initiate a bankruptcy proceeding. These changes are incorporated into Chapter 48.

CHAPTER 48

BANKRUPTCY

I. **Federal Bankruptcy Definitions** 48-2
   A.   Claim 48-2
   B.   Community Claim 48-2
   C.   Creditor 48-2
   D.   Custodian 48-2
   E.   Debt 48-2
   F.   Debtor 48-2
   G.   Entity 48-2
   H.   Equity Security 48-2
   I.   Equity Security Holder 48-2
   J.   Estate 48-2
   K.   Execution 48-2
   L.   Exempt Property 48-2
   M.   Garnishment 48-2
   N.   Insolvent 48-2
   O.   Judicial Lien 48-2
   P.   Lien 48-2
   Q.   Transfer 48-2

II. **Application of Remedies Under State Law Prior to Bankruptcy** 48-3
   A.   Legal Actions Available to Creditors 48-3
   B.   Creditors' Actions to Set Aside Fraudulent Conveyances 48-3
   C.   Collective Actions by Creditors 48-3

III. **An Overview of Federal Bankruptcy Law** 48-5
   A.   The Federal Bankruptcy Code 48-5
   B.   Federal Bankruptcy Law Emphasis 48-5
   C.   Federal Bankruptcy Law 48-5
   D.   The Four Operative Chapters of the Code 48-5

IV. **Bankruptcy Case Administration** 48-6
   A.   The Debtor 48-6
   B.   The Commencement of a Bankruptcy Case 48-7
   C.   The Role and Capacity of the Trustee 48-8
   D.   Specific Administrative Duties and Responsibilities Imposed Upon the Trustee and the Debtor .. 48-8
   E.   Administrative Powers 48-9

V. **Creditors, the Debtor, and the Estate** 48-10
   A.   Creditors and Claims 48-10
   B.   The Debtor's Benefits 48-14
   C.   The Estate 48-18

CHAPTER 48

BANKRUPTCY

I. Federal Bankruptcy Definitions

A.   Claim--Any right to payment.

B.   Community Claim--A claim against community property.

C.   Creditor--An entity which has a claim against the debtor that arose before the filing of bankruptcy or is treated by the Bankruptcy Code as arising before such filing, or an entity that has a community claim.

D.   Custodian--A nonbankruptcy receiver, trustee, assignee for the benefit of creditors, or other agent appointed to take charge of the debtor's property.

E.   Debt--A liability on a claim.

F.   Debtor--An entity liable to a creditor.

G.   Entity--A person, estate, trust, or governmental unit.

H.   Equity Security--A share in a corporation, an interest in a limited partnership, or a warrant or right to purchase, sell, or subscribe to such share or interest.

I.   Equity Security Holder--Holder of an equity security of the debtor.

J.   Estate--A collective term referring to all of the debtor's legal and equitable interests in property at the time bankruptcy is commenced.

K.   Execution--The legal process by which a debtor's property is levied upon or otherwise seized and exposed to sale for the payment of his or her debts.

L.   Exempt Property--Property which, under either federal or state exemption laws, is exempt from seizure and sale for the payment of the debtor's debts. In bankruptcy, exempt property does not become part of the bankrupt's estate.

M.   Garnishment--The legal process of attaching or gaining access to assets of the debtor held by a third party (e.g., attaching a debtor's bank account by having an order of garnishment issued to the debtor's bank).

N.   Insolvent--Financial condition of an entity wherein the debts exceed the assets, at a fair valuation. Also, a debtor who cannot pay his or her debts as they come due.

O.   Judicial Lien--Lien obtained by judgment, levy, or other legal or equitable process.

P.   Lien--An interest in property securing payment or other performance for an underlying obligation.

Q.   Transfer--Every mode of disposing of property or an interest in property.

II. Application of Remedies Under State Law Prior to Bankruptcy

A. <u>Legal Actions Available to Creditors</u>--When a debtor defaults on its payments or obligations owed to an unsecured creditor, the unsecured creditor may institute legal action to enforce its rights. The creditor may do any of the following:

   1. Obtain a statutory <u>writ of attachment</u>, whereby the debtor's property will be seized to secure payment either prior or subsequent to a judgment being rendered for the creditor.

   2. Garnish a debt owed to the debtor by a third person and apply the garnished debt to the claim owed by the debtor.

   3. Obtain a judgment and enforce it by execution, whereby the debtor's nonexempt property will be seized and sold to satisfy the judgment. A statutory supplementary proceeding may be instituted if the judgment is not satisfied by execution and the proceeding may give access to the debtor's nonexempt property which is not subject to execution.

   These types of legal actions encourage a "race of diligence" among creditors, pitting one against the other in an effort to reach the debtor's usually limited and insufficient assets.

B. <u>Creditors' Actions to Set Aside Fraudulent Conveyances</u>--In most states, a creditor may bring an action to set aside a fraudulent conveyance of a debtor or to levy on and sell fraudulently conveyed property.

   1. A fraudulent conveyance is a conveyance made by a debtor with intent to delay, hinder, or defraud creditors, or one made without fair consideration by a person who is or will thereby become insolvent.

   2. A transfer of exempt property cannot be a fraudulent conveyance.

   3. Generally, a creditor to whom the conveyance is fraudulent needs only a matured, valid claim to challenge the transfer. A judgment is not required.

C. <u>Collective Actions by Creditors</u>

   1. The debtor may make an assignment for the benefit of creditors (an "ABC").

      a. An ABC is a voluntary transfer of all the debtor's nonexempt assets to another person in trust, the assignee, who liquidates the assets and distributes the proceeds to the creditors.

      b. Generally, creditor consent is not a precondition to the assignment.

      c. Legal title to the assets, generally subject to valid liens or claims, passes to the assignee and bars the creditors from levying on the assets.

      d. If an interest or benefit in the property conveyed is reserved in the debtor, it is usually construed as a fraudulent conveyance.

      e. Generally, the debtor is not fully discharged if deficiencies in the debts owed remain after distribution of the proceeds to the creditors.

      f. ABCs affect all general creditors.

      g. ABCs are regulated by specific statutes in most states. In the absence of a statute, the general legal principles of the law of trusts apply.

2. The debtor and its creditors may enter into a <u>composition</u> or <u>extension agreement</u>.

    a. A <u>composition agreement</u> is an agreement between a debtor and its creditors in which the participating creditors agree to accept an immediate or early payment of a lesser sum in full satisfaction of the debt due them. An <u>extension</u> is an agreement between a debtor and its creditors in which the participating creditors take full payment of their claims, but extended over a period of time beyond the original due date.

    b. Such agreements are contractual.

        (1) Thus, all essential elements of a contract must be present to make the agreement valid.

        (2) The element of consideration.

            (a) The consideration given by the participating creditors is their mutual promises to accept less than the full amount of their claims. Because there must be such mutual promises among the participating creditors, a composition or extension agreement requires the participation of at least two or more creditors.

            (b) The consideration given by the debtor is the immediate or future payments stipulated in the agreement.

    c. Generally, creditors unwilling to accept the terms of a composition or extension agreement are not required to do so. Creditors who do not agree to the agreement are not affected by it.

    d. The participating creditors may void the agreement if either of the following applies:

        (1) They are not made aware of any creditors who are not participating in the agreement.

        (2) Any participating creditor is given secret preferential treatment by the debtor.

    e. The debtor is discharged from all debts which it pays under the agreement.

    f. The debtor retains all of its property following the agreement, except as provided in the agreement.

3. Creditors may petition the state court for an <u>equity receivership</u>.

    a. An equity receivership is a court supervised liquidation or reorganization.

    b. A receiver is appointed by the court to administer and take charge of the debtor's property. The receiver may liquidate, or hold and preserve property, and continue to operate any business of the debtor.

    c. Equity receivership as an equitable remedy will not apply if there is an adequate remedy at law (e.g., collection suit).

    d. The receiver takes possession but not title to the debtor's property. Existing liens on the property remain valid but cannot be enforced during receivership. Creditors who petition for receivership do not thereby gain a lien on the debtor's property.

    e. An equity receivership does not discharge the debtor from debts.

III. An Overview of Federal Bankruptcy Law

A. <u>The Federal Bankruptcy Code</u>--The law of bankruptcy is federal law, consisting primarily of the Federal Bankruptcy Code. Thus, under principles of federal supremacy, state insolvency laws have generally been superseded. The result is one uniform bankruptcy law. However, not all state law is inapplicable in a bankruptcy proceeding; the Bankruptcy Code in many of its provisions specifically incorporates certain aspects of state law (such as contract law, real property law, etc.).

B. <u>Federal Bankruptcy Law Emphasis</u>--Unlike state debtor-creditor law, with its emphasis on prompt action by creditors to enforce their rights against the debtor's limited and insufficient assets, federal bankruptcy law emphasizes equality of treatment among creditors within the same class. Once a bankruptcy proceeding is commenced, a creditor cannot improve his or her position vis-a-vis other creditors by resorting to such remedies as attaching the debtor's property, executing on the property, etc.

C. <u>Federal Bankruptcy Law</u>--Federal bankruptcy law is administered by bankruptcy courts, which constitute adjuncts of the United States District Courts.

D. <u>The Four Operative Chapters of the Code</u>--There are four operative chapters under the Federal Bankruptcy Code. They represent the four types of bankruptcy proceedings. All bankruptcy cases must be filed under one of the following four chapters:

1. <u>Chapter 7</u>: <u>Straight Bankruptcy or Liquidation</u>--The majority of bankruptcy proceedings will be commenced under Chapter 7. This chapter applies equally to business and consumer bankruptcy cases. Such a case is in the nature of a liquidation proceeding. It basically involves the collection of the debtor's nonexempt property, the liquidation or sale of such property, and the distribution of the proceeds to the creditors by the trustee in the manner provided by the Federal Bankruptcy Code.

   • The three remaining bankruptcy proceedings are known as "debtor rehabilitation proceedings." They differ from a Chapter 7 proceeding in that the debtor looks to rehabilitation and reorganization rather than liquidation. Generally, the creditors look to future earnings of the debtor for satisfaction of their claims instead of property held by the debtor at the commencement of the bankruptcy case.

2. <u>Chapter 9</u>: <u>Adjustment of Debts of a Municipality</u>--Chapter 9 provides a procedure so that a municipality which has encountered financial difficulty may work with its creditors to adjust its debts. This is accomplished by having the debtor work out a plan with its creditors for the adjustment, refinancing, and payment of its claims and by having the court confirm the plan.

3. <u>Chapter 11</u>: <u>Reorganizations</u>--Although Chapter 11 is designed primarily for business cases, it may be used by individuals. It is the chapter to be followed for all business reorganizations. The purpose of a Chapter 11 reorganization, unlike a Chapter 7 liquidation, is to restructure a business' finances so that it may continue to operate, pay its creditors, and generate a return for its stockholders, if any. The goal of the Chapter 11 case is to formulate and confirm a plan of reorganization for the debtor. This plan determines the amount and the manner in which the creditors will be paid, in what form the business will continue, and any other necessary details.

4. <u>Chapter 13</u>: <u>Adjustment of Debts of an Individual With Regular Income</u>--The purpose of Chapter 13 is to enable a debtor who is an individual to formulate and perform a plan for the repayment of his or her creditors over an extended period. Such a plan might provide for full repayment or may offer creditors only a percentage of their claims in full settlement. The benefit of the Chapter 13 repayment plan is that it allows the debtor to retain his or her property, even that which is nonexempt, unless he or she otherwise agrees in the plan.

NOTE: The material discussed in IV. and V., below, generally applies to Chapter 7, Chapter 11, and Chapter 13 proceedings. The material generally does not apply to a Chapter 9 proceeding, unless specific reference is made to Chapter 9.

IV. Bankruptcy Case Administration

A.   The Debtor--The debtor is the person or municipality which is the subject of a bankruptcy.

    1.   Person includes an individual, partnership, or corporation but not a governmental unit, a decedent's estate, or a trust.

    2.   Municipality means a political subdivision, public agency, or instrumentality of a state but does not include the District of Columbia or U.S. territories.

    3.   Eligibility to be a debtor

        a.   The general eligibility rule provides that only the following may be a debtor:

            (1)   A person who either resides in the United States or has a domicile, a place of business, or property in the United States.

            (2)   A municipality.

        b.   Additionally, specific eligibility rules and exclusions apply in specific chapters of the Bankruptcy Code.

            (1)   Any person may be a debtor under Chapter 7 liquidation except:

                (a)   Railroads,

                (b)   Domestic insurance companies, banks, or other specified lending institutions.

            (2)   A debtor under Chapter 7 liquidation may be a debtor under Chapter 11 reorganization except for:

                (a)   Railroads (restricted to special provisions of Chapter 11), and

                (b)   Stockbrokers and commodity brokers (restricted to special provisions of Chapter 7).

            (3)   Chapter 13 is limited to an individual who has:

                (a)   Regular income,

                (b)   Less than $100,000 unsecured debts, and

                (c)   Less than $350,000 secured debts.

            (4)   In Chapter 11 cases, the court is required to select a creditors' committee from unsecured creditors. In Chapter 13 cases, the court must appoint a trustee.

B.   The Commencement of a Bankruptcy Case

1.   Voluntary Bankruptcy

a.   A voluntary case may be commenced by the filing of a petition in bankruptcy court involving either Chapter 7, 11, or 13. The petitioner must be an eligible entity under the chapter invoked.

b.   Filing of the petition constitutes an order for relief under the invoked chapter.

c.   The debtor need not be insolvent, just needs to state that he or she has debts.

2.   Joint Bankruptcy

a.   The petition may be filed jointly by a husband and wife. Neither may undertake it without the other's knowledge and consent.

b.   A joint case is commenced by the filing of a single petition for the individual and his or her spouse in bankruptcy court invoking either Chapter 7, 11, or 13. The individual must be eligible under the chapter invoked.

c.   Filing of the petition constitutes an order for relief under the invoked chapter.

d.   In a joint case the court must consider the consolidation of the two debtors' estates; that is, to what extent, if at all, the assets and liabilities of the debtors will be combined to pay creditors. Factors included in the court's determination are the extent of jointly held property and the amount of jointly owed debts.

3.   Involuntary Bankruptcy

a.   Involuntary proceedings may be commenced only under Chapter 7 liquidation or Chapter 11 reorganization against a Chapter 7 or 11 debtor but not against:

(1)   A farmer (a person who derives more than 80% of his or her gross income from farming, ranching, or the raising of poultry or livestock), or

(2)   A church, school, or charitable foundation.

b.   An involuntary case is commenced by the filing of a petition in the bankruptcy court.

(1)   Three or more creditors may file the petition if the debtor has 12 or more creditors with claims that are not contingent and, in the aggregate, the claims of the petitioners exceed any security they hold in the debtor's property by at least $10,000.

(2)   One or more creditors may file the petition if the debtor has fewer than 12 such creditors, provided that the unsecured portion of the petitioner's claims is equal in the aggregate to at least $10,000.

(3)   Filing of an involuntary petition against a partnership.

(a)   Less than all of the general partners may file the petition notwithstanding a contrary agreement, state law, or local law.

(b)   If relief has been ordered under any chapter of the Bankruptcy Code with respect to all of the general partners in a partnership, but not as to their partnership, then the trustee of the estate of a general partner or a holder of a claim against the partnership may file an involuntary petition against the partnership.

c. The debtor, or a general partner in a partnership debtor that did not join in the petition, may file an answer to an involuntary petition which has been filed against the debtor or the partnership (i.e., controverted).

d. Except to the extent that the bankruptcy court orders otherwise, and until an order for relief is entered in the involuntary case, any business of the debtor may continue to operate. Furthermore, the debtor may continue to use, acquire, or dispose of property as if the involuntary case had not been commenced.

e. If the petition is not timely controverted by the debtor (the Rules of Bankruptcy Procedure will fix the time limit), the bankruptcy court will enter an order for relief against the debtor under the chapter under which the petition was filed. If the petition is timely controverted, the bankruptcy court will, after trial, enter an order for relief against the debtor only if it is found that:

(1) The debtor is generally not paying its debts as they become due, or

(2) Within 120 days before the date of the filing of the petition, a custodian was appointed or took possession of the debtor's property.

f. If the involuntary petition is timely controverted and neither of the two requisite grounds for entry of an order of relief is established, the petition will be dismissed by the bankruptcy court.

C. <u>The Role and Capacity of the Trustee</u>

1. The trustee is appointed or elected to be the representative of the bankruptcy estate. The trustee can sue and be sued. A trustee is required in <u>Chapter 7 and 13</u> proceedings but **not** in <u>Chapter 9 and 11</u> proceedings.

2. The trustee is charged with the administration of the estate.

3. The trustee may, with the bankruptcy court's approval, employ one or more attorneys, accountants, appraisers, or other professional persons to assist the trustee in carrying out its duties.

D. <u>Specific Administrative Duties and Responsibilities Imposed Upon the Trustee and the Debtor</u>

1. Generally, in bankruptcy proceedings a meeting of creditors is held in which the trustee presides.

a. The debtor must appear and submit to examination under oath.

b. A creditor trustee or examiner may examine the debtor.

c. The purpose of the examination is to determine if assets have improperly been disposed of, concealed, or if there are grounds for objection to the debtor's discharge.

d. The scope of such examination includes the debtor's acts, conduct, property, or any matter that may affect the administration of the estate or the debtor's right to a discharge.

2.   The debtor must

    a.   File with the bankruptcy court a list of creditors, a schedule of assets and liabilities, and a statement of financial affairs.

    b.   Cooperate with the trustee in the performance of the trustee's duties.

    c.   Surrender to the trustee all property of the estate.

    d.   Attend the hearing on discharge.

E.   Administrative Powers

    1.   Automatic Stay--A fundamental debtor protection is the automatic stay which stops all collection efforts, all harassment, and all foreclosure or other legal proceedings. It also protects creditors in that no one creditor can obtain an advantage to the detriment of the others by expediting nonbankruptcy remedies against the debtor.

        a.   In general, the filing of a bankruptcy petition operates as a stay, applicable to all entities, of the following:

            (1)   The commencement or continuation of a judicial, administrative, or other proceeding.

            (2)   The enforcement, against the debtor or property of the estate, of an existing judgment.

            (3)   Any act to obtain possession of property of the estate.

            (4)   Any act to create, perfect, or enforce any lien against property of the estate.

            (5)   Any act to create, perfect, or enforce any lien against property of the debtor (property that the debtor acquires after the date of the filing of the petition, property that is exempt, or property that does not pass to the estate) to the extent that the lien secures a claim that arose before the commencement of the bankruptcy case.

            (6)   Any act to collect, assess, or recover a claim against the debtor that arose before the commencement of the bankruptcy case.

            (7)   The setoff of any prebankruptcy debt owing to the debtor.

            (8)   The commencement or continuation of any proceeding concerning the debtor before the United States Tax Court.

        An automatic stay does not vitiate the rights of creditors. It puts them on hold pending an orderly examination of the debtor's and creditor's rights.

        b.   The filing of a bankruptcy petition does not operate as a stay under a., above, of the following:

            (1)   The commencement or continuation of a criminal proceeding against the debtor.

            (2)   The collection of alimony, maintenance, or support payments from property that is not property of the estate.

(3) Any act to perfect an interest in property to the extent that the trustee's rights and powers are subject to such perfection.

(4) The commencement of any action by the Secretary of Housing and Urban Development to foreclose or take possession in a case of a loan insured under the National Housing Act.

(5) The issuance of a notice of tax deficiency.

c. The Duration of the Automatic Stay

(1) Generally, the stay of an act against property of the estate continues until such property ceases to be property of the estate, such as by sale, abandonment, or exemption.

(2) Generally, the stay of any other act as enumerated in a., above, continues until the earliest of the time the case is closed, the case is dismissed, or a discharge is granted or denied.

2. The Use, Sale, or Lease of Property of the Estate

a. Upon notice to interested parties, and a hearing if there are objections, the trustee (debtor or debtor in possession if there is no trustee) may use, sell, or lease, other than in the ordinary course of business, property of the estate.

b. Without notice or hearing, a trustee who has been authorized to operate a business of the debtor may generally use, sell, or lease property in the ordinary course of business.

3. Executory Contracts and Unexpired Leases--The Bankruptcy Code provides for the assumption or rejection of such contracts and leases by the trustee subject to court approval.

a. An executory contract is generally unperformed to some extent by both sides. Thus, a promissory note is usually not an executory contract.

b. Rejection constitutes a breach and gives rise to a claim for damages -against the estate.

V. Creditors, the Debtor, and the Estate

A. <u>Creditors and Claims</u>

1. Filing of Proofs of Claims or Interests

a. A creditor presents his or her claim to the bankruptcy court by filing a proof of claim, and an equity security holder does so by filing a proof of interest.

b. An entity, such as a surety, co-debtor, or guarantor, that is liable with a debtor to a creditor may file a proof of claim if the creditor does not timely do so.

c. If a creditor does not file a timely proof of claim, the debtor or trustee may do so for such creditor.

2. The Allowance of Claims or Interests--Generally, only allowed claims may share in the distribution of the property of the estate.

a.   A proof of claim or a proof of interest is prima facie evidence of the claim or interest and is allowed unless a party in interest objects to its allowance.

b.   Generally, once an objection to a claim is made, the bankruptcy court must determine the amount of the claim as of the date of the filing of the petition and must either allow or disallow the claim in whole or in part.

c.   All claims against the debtor must be converted into dollar amounts. Thus, contingent or unliquidated claims must be estimated.

d.   The bankruptcy court must disallow the entire claim of any entity that fails to pay or turn over money or property to the estate which the trustee is entitled to recover. One example of such an entity is the transferee of a voidable transfer.

e.   Claims of co-debtors, sureties, and guarantors.

   (1)   The bankruptcy court must disallow any claim for reimbursement or contribution of a co-debtor, surety, or guarantor that is liable with the debtor on, or that has secured, the claim of a creditor, to the extent that the creditor's claim against the estate is disallowed.

   (2)   Generally, a co-debtor, surety, or guarantor is permitted a claim for reimbursement or contribution only if he or she has paid the assured creditor in full.

   (3)   The claim for reimbursement or contribution must be disallowed, however, to the extent the co-debtor, surety, or guarantor chooses to be subrogated to the rights of the creditor.

   (4)   The thrust of (2) and (3), above, is that the co-debtor, surety, or guarantor has a choice since he or she may not be allowed both a claim for contribution or reimbursement and a claim as subrogee to the rights of the creditor whom he or she has paid.

f.   In an involuntary bankruptcy case, a claim arising in the ordinary course of the debtor's business or financial affairs <u>after</u> the filing of the petition, but <u>before</u> the order for relief, must be treated as a prepetition claim.

3.   The Allowance of Administrative Expenses--The distinction between treatment of a claim as a prepetition claim and treatment as an administrative expense is important because administrative expenses take priority over other unsecured claims in the distribution of the assets of the estate.

a.   An administrative expense claimant must file a request for payment of the expense with the bankruptcy court, not with the trustee.

b.   The following are allowed as administrative expenses:

   (1)   The actual, necessary costs and expenses of preserving the estate, including wages, salaries, or commissions for services rendered after the commencement of the case.

   (2)   Generally, most taxes incurred by the estate.

   (3)   Any fine, penalty, or reduction in credit, relating to any tax that is allowed as an administrative expense.

(4) Compensation and reimbursement awarded to trustees, examiners, professional persons hired by the trustee, and the debtor's attorney.

(5) The actual and necessary expenses incurred by:

(a) A creditor that files an involuntary bankruptcy petition.

(b) A creditor that, with court approval, recovers for the benefit of the estate any property transferred or concealed by the debtor.

(c) A creditor that acts in connection with the prosecution of a criminal offense relating to the case.

(d) A custodian upon being superseded by the representative of the estate.

(6) Reasonable compensation for professional services rendered by an attorney or an accountant of an entity whose expense is allowed under (5), above.

(7) Witness fees and mileage.

4. Determination of Secured Claims

a. An allowed claim of a creditor which is secured by a lien on property in which the estate has an interest is a secured claim to the extent of the value of the creditor's interest in the collateral. It is an unsecured claim to the extent that the value of the creditor's interest in the collateral is less than the amount of the creditor's allowed claim.

b. An allowed claim of a creditor that is subject to setoff under the Bankruptcy Code is a secured claim to the extent of the amount subject to setoff. It is an unsecured claim to the extent that the amount so subject to setoff is less than the creditor's claim.

c. Generally, a lien passes through the bankruptcy case unaffected. However, if a claim secured by a lien is disallowed, then the lien is void <u>unless</u>:

(1) There was no objection to the claim by a party in interest, **or**

(2) The only reason the claim was disallowed was because such claim was one for reimbursement or contribution by a co-debtor or surety who chose to be subrogated.

5. Priority Claims--Although, in bankruptcy, equality of distribution among creditors is the policy, certain claims have priority based on a priority ranking system for distribution. Thus, under a Chapter 7 liquidation, since assets must be utilized to satisfy priority claims until depleted, if the assets are insufficient to satisfy all claims, higher ranking claims may be satisfied in full while lower ranking claims receive nothing. The order of priority for claims is as follows:

a. Secured Claims--A creditor holding an allowed claim secured by a lien on property is entitled to this first priority only in the distribution of the proceeds from the liquidation of its collateral and only to the extent of its secured claim. Collateral must be applied first to satisfy the claim that it secures.

b. Allowed administrative expenses.

c. Unsecured claims for debts incurred after the commencement of an involuntary bankruptcy case but before the order of relief (holders of these claims are known as "involuntary gap creditors," see 2.f., above).

d.   Allowed unsecured claims for wages, salaries, or commissions earned by an individual employee of the debtor within 90 days before the date of the filing of the petition or 90 days before the date of cessation of the debtor's business, whichever occurs first, but only to the extent of $4,000 for each individual.

e.   Certain allowed unsecured claims for contributions to employee benefit plans arising from services rendered by the debtor's employees within 180 days before the date of the filing of the petition or the date of the cessation of the debtor's business, whichever occurs first.

f.   Farm producers and fishermen against debtors who operate grain storage facilities or fish produce storage up to $4,000 per claim.

g.   Allowed unsecured claims of individuals to the extent of $1,800 for each individual who, prior to the commencement of the case, deposited money with the debtor in connection with the purchase or rental of property for the personal, family, or household use of the individual, and who never received such goods or property.

h.   Allowed claims for debts to a spouse, former spouse, or child of the debtor for alimony, maintenance, or support of such spouse or child.

i.   Allowed unsecured claims of a governmental unit (whether federal, state, or local) for certain taxes.

  (1)   Such taxes generally include income taxes, property taxes, withholding taxes, excise taxes, employment taxes, and customs duties.

  (2)   The claims which are given priority here do not include fines or penalties which are not compensation for actual pecuniary loss.

NOTE: Each claim must be paid in full before any lower claim is paid anything. If a class of claim cannot be paid in full, the claims in that class will be paid on a pro rata basis.

6.   Distribution Rules in a Chapter 7 Case

a.   There are general distribution rules in addition to those priority distribution rules discussed in 5., above, which are applicable only in a Chapter 7 case. After the property of the estate, which has usually been reduced to money by the trustee in the liquidation case, has been distributed to satisfy all of the priority claims (in the order specified in 5., above), the remaining property is then distributed in the following order:

  (1)   In payment of any allowed unsecured claim, proof of which was timely filed.

  (2)   In payment of any allowed unsecured claim, proof of which was tardily filed.

  (3)   In payment of any allowed claim, whether secured or unsecured, for any fine, penalty, or forfeiture or for multiple, exemplary, or punitive damages, which arose before the order for relief and which is not compensation for actual pecuniary loss suffered by the holder of such claim.

  (4)   In payment of any interest, accruing from the date of the filing of the bankruptcy petition, on any paid claim.

(5)   In payment (of any surplus) to the debtor.

b.   Claims within a particular class are to be paid pro rata when there are inadequate funds to pay in full.

c.   Community property in the estate must be segregated from noncommunity property. Such community property is then subject to its own distribution rules (and not those distribution rules discussed in a., above).

B.   The Debtor's Benefits

1.   The Debtor's Exemptions--To give an individual debtor a fresh start after bankruptcy, certain property may be claimed by the individual as exempt and retained by him or her.

a.   An individual debtor may choose between two exemption systems.

(1)   The debtor may exempt from the estate any property that is exempt under federal nonbankruptcy law and the law of the state of domicile and any interest in property which he or she had as a tenant by the entirety or joint tenant before the commencement of bankruptcy proceedings that is exempt under nonbankruptcy law.

(a)   State exemption laws are, generally, those laws which give the debtor a right or privilege to retain a portion of his or her property free from seizure and sale by creditors under judicial process.

(b)   Examples of federal nonbankruptcy law exemptions are social security payments, veterans' benefits, and certain civil service retirement benefits.

(2)   In lieu of the exemptions described in (1), above, the debtor may choose the Federal Bankruptcy Code exemptions but only if these are allowed by the law of the debtor's state of domicile. The Bankruptcy Code exemptions include:

(a)   Up to $15,000 of real or personal property of the residence used by the debtor or the debtor's dependent(s).

(b)   Up to a $2,400 interest in one motor vehicle.

(c)   Household goods, furnishings, clothing, appliances, books, animals, and crops, that are held primarily for the personal, family, or household use of the debtor or the debtor's dependent(s) but not to exceed $400 in value in any particular item.

(d)   Up to $1,000 in jewelry held primarily for the personal, family, or household use of the debtor or the debtor's dependent(s).

(e)   Up to $800, plus any unused amount of the exemption provided in paragraph (a), above, in any property.

(f)   Up to $1,500 in any implements, professional books, or tools of the trade of the debtor or the debtor's dependent(s).

(g)   Any unmatured life insurance contract owned by the debtor, other than a credit life insurance contract.

(h)   Up to $8,000 in any accrued dividend or interest under, or loan value of, any unmatured life insurance contract owned by the debtor and insuring either the debtor or an individual of whom the debtor is a dependent(s).

(i)   Any professionally prescribed health aids for the debtor or the debtor's dependent(s).

(j)   The debtor's right to receive social security benefits; unemployment compensation; veterans' benefits; disability or illness benefits; reasonable alimony, support, or separate maintenance; and certain stock bonus, pension, profit sharing, or annuity payments.

(k)   The debtor's right to receive certain compensation for losses, such as crime victim's reparation benefits, wrongful death benefits, and payments under a life insurance contract that insured the life of an individual of whom the debtor was a dependent on the date of such individual's death.

b.   Unless the bankruptcy case is dismissed, exempt property may not be seized during or after the case for any debt of the debtor that arose, or that is treated as if it had arisen (see A.2.f., above), before the commencement of the case, except for:

(1)   Debt for taxes not discharged in bankruptcy;

(2)   Debt for alimony, maintenance, or child support; and

(3)   Valid liens not avoided by the trustee.

c.   To protect the debtor's exemptions, any waiver of exemptions executed in favor of a creditor that holds an unsecured claim against the debtor is unenforceable in the bankruptcy case.

d.   The debtor must file a list of property that he or she claims as exempt. Absent an objection by a party in interest, the property claimed as exempt is exempt. If there is an objection, the court will rule on the exemption.

e.   Under a joint bankruptcy case, each debtor is entitled to his or her own election of exemptions.

2.   Discharge of the Debtor

a.   Exceptions to Discharge

(1)   Under Chapters 7, 11, and 13, certain debts of an individual are <u>not</u> discharged.

(a)   Tax Debts

•   Entitled to priority under A.5., above, which were due within 3 years of filing of bankruptcy petition.

•   Which were the subject of a fraudulent return or which the debtor willfully attempted to evade.

(b)   A debt for obtaining money, property, services, or an extension or renewal of credit, by means of false pretenses, false representations, actual fraud, or by means of a materially false written financial statement, made by the debtor with intent to deceive and reasonably relied upon by the creditor.

(c)   Debts which were not included on the schedules required to be filed by the debtor or were not included in time to permit timely action by the creditor unless such creditor had notice or actual knowledge of the case.

(d)   Debts for fraud while the debtor was acting in a fiduciary capacity, and debts for embezzlement or larceny.

(e)   Debts to a spouse, former spouse, or child of the debtor for alimony, maintenance, or support.

(f)   Debts for willful and malicious injury by the debtor to another person or to the property of another person.

(g)   Debts for fines, penalties, or forfeitures payable to and for the benefit of a governmental unit, which are not compensation for actual pecuniary loss, other than certain tax penalties.

(h)   Debts to a governmental unit, or a nonprofit institution of higher education, for an educational loan, unless the loan first becomes due more than 7 years before the date of filing the petition or unless excepting the debt from discharge would impose undue hardship on the debtor.

(i)   Debts that survived an earlier bankruptcy proceeding because the debtor was denied a discharge other than on the basis of elapsed time since a prior discharge or because the debtor waived discharge.

(j)   As a general rule, a debtor is entitled to only one discharge from bankruptcy during a 6-year period running from a prior petition in which debtor was then discharged.

(2)   A creditor who is owed one of the debts that may be exempted from discharge under (b), (d), or (f), above, must initiate proceedings in the bankruptcy court for a determination of the nondischargeability of such debt. If the creditor does not act, the debt is discharged. However, if the debtor has not listed the creditor, then the creditor does not have to initiate such proceedings, and the debtor is not discharged from such debts.

b.   The Effect of Discharge

(1)   A discharge in a bankruptcy case under any chapter:

(a)   Voids any existing and future judgments that are determinations of the personal liability of the debtor with respect to any discharged debt.

(b)   Operates as an injunction against the commencement or continuation of an action at law, the employment of legal process, or any act (including telephone calls and letters) to recover, collect, or offset any discharged debt as a personal liability of the debtor or from the property of the debtor.

(c)   Generally operates as an injunction against the commencement or continuation of an action at law. Finally, a discharge is effective against community creditors of the nondebtor spouse as well as the debtor spouse.

These three results are not defeated even if the debtor waives the discharge of any particular debt.

(2)   Generally, the discharge of a debt does not affect the liability of any co-debtors, sureties, or guarantors for such debt.

c.   Additional Rules of Discharge Applicable to Chapter 7 Cases:

(1)   An order to discharge releases the debtor from all dischargeable debts arising or treated as arising before commencement of bankruptcy whether a proof of claim has been filed or allowed.

(2)   Bankruptcy Offenses--The court must grant a discharge unless:

(a)   The debtor is not an individual.

(b)   The debtor, with intent to hinder, delay, or defraud a creditor or an officer of the estate, has transferred, removed, destroyed, mutilated, or concealed property of the debtor or the estate within a year before or after commencement of bankruptcy, respectively.

(c)   The debtor has concealed, falsified, or failed to preserve any books or records from which his or her financial condition might be ascertained, unless the act or failure to act was justified.

(d)   The debtor knowingly and fraudulently:

- Made a false oath or account;

- Presented or used a false claim;

- Gave, offered, received, or attempted to obtain money, property, or advantage, or a promise therefor, for acting or forbearing to act; or

- Withheld recorded information from an officer of the estate entitled to possession of such information when the information related to the debtor's financial affairs.

(e)   The debtor has failed to explain satisfactorily any loss of assets or deficiency of assets to meet the debtor's liabilities.

(f)   The debtor has refused, in the case, to obey any lawful order of the court or to testify after having been granted immunity or after having improperly invoked the constitutional privilege against self-incrimination.

(g)   The debtor has committed any of the above acts on or within 1 year before the date of the filing of the bankruptcy petition.

(h)   The debtor has incurred, within 60 days of the order for relief, both of the following:

- A consumer debt owed to a single creditor totaling more than $1,000 for luxury goods or services; and

- Cash advances totaling more than $1,000, based on consumer open-end credit, such as a credit card.

(i)   The discharge is for loans used to pay taxes (including those paid on credit cards).

(j)   Generally, the debtor has been granted a discharge in a bankruptcy case commenced within 6 years preceding the present bankruptcy case.

(k)   The bankruptcy court approves a written waiver of discharge executed by the debtor after the order of relief.

(3)   The trustee or a creditor may object to discharge, and upon request of a party in interest, the court may order the trustee to examine the debtor to determine whether grounds exist to deny discharge.

d.   Revocation of a Discharge--The bankruptcy court may revoke an order of discharge if such order was procured by fraud.

C.   The Estate

1.   The property of the estate consists of the debtor's assets administered in bankruptcy.

a.   On commencement of bankruptcy, an estate is created of:

(1)   All legal and equitable interests in property and, with certain limitations, in community property.

(2)   Proceeds, product, offspring, rents, and profits of estate property.

(3)   Property interests acquired by the estate after commencement.

(4)   Property interests acquired by the debtor within 180 days after commencement by bequest, devise, inheritance, as a result of a property settlement agreement with a spouse, or as a beneficiary of a life insurance policy or health benefit plan.

(5)   Any interest in property received by the trustee through the debtor's avoiding power.

(6)   Any interest in property recovered from a nonbankruptcy receiver, assignee (of an ABC), trustee, agent, or other custodian.

b.   Property which does not become a part of the estate includes:

(1)   Earnings from services of an individual after bankruptcy commencement, except under Chapter 13.

(2)   Any power, such as a power of appointment, exercisable by the debtor for the benefit of another.

(3)   Property held in trust by the debtor.

(a)   Bare legal title held by the debtor comes into the estate, but not a beneficial interest of another person.

(b)   Constructive trust property, such as insurance payments received for an unpaid doctor bill, does not become estate property.

c.   The debtor's property interests become a part of the estate despite any provisions restricting transfer or despite any forfeiture provisions contingent on bankruptcy filing or appointment of a receiver or trustee.

d.   The estate acquires the same rights as were held by the debtor. For example, if the debtor held a beneficial interest, the estate would hold the debtor's interest.

2.   The Trustee's Avoiding Powers--To implement the policy of fair and equitable treatment of creditors, the bankruptcy laws grant the trustee avoiding powers to set aside certain conveyances and liens including the following:

   a.   Statutory Liens

   (1)   Liens that first become effective upon the insolvency or bankruptcy of the debtor.

   (2)   Liens that, on the date of bankruptcy filing, are unperfected or unenforceable against a bona fide purchaser.

   (3)   Liens for rent or of distress for rent, whether statutory or common law.

   b.   Preferential Transfers

   NOTE: All of the 5 tests below must be satisfied to establish a preferential transfer.

   (1)   A preferential transfer is a transfer of the property of the debtor:

      (a)   To or for the benefit of a creditor.

      (b)   For or on account of an antecedent debt owed by the debtor.

      (c)   Made while the debtor was insolvent (debtor presumed insolvent in the 90-day period immediately preceding the filing of bankruptcy).

      (d)   Made

         •   On or within 90 days before the date of bankruptcy filing.

         •   Between 90 days and 1 year before the filing date, if the creditor at the time of transfer was an insider and had reason to believe the debtor was insolvent.

         •   To an insider and which, in turn, is transferred to a non-insider transferee is not subject to recovery by the trustee.

      (e)   That enables the creditor to receive more than it would receive as a distributive share under a Chapter 7 liquidation.

   NOTE: Insiders are relatives, officers, directors, and controlling shareholders of the debtor.

   (2)   Exceptions--The trustee cannot avoid as preferential the following transfers:

      (a)   A contemporaneous exchange for new value given to the debtor.

      (b)   Payment in the ordinary course of business in financial affairs of the debtor and transferee made not later than 45 days after the debt was incurred.

    (c)   A transfer of a security interest in property acquired by the debtor which enables the debtor to purchase the property (i.e., a purchase money security interest).

    (d)   Generally, transfers of security interests by the debtor which are offset by new value which the creditor subsequently gave to the debtor. (These transfers are usually found in those settings involving after-acquired property clauses and future advance clauses contained in security agreements.)

    (e)   Generally, certain transfers by the debtor of security interests in its inventory or accounts receivable.

    (f)   A transfer that is the fixing of a statutory lien that is not avoidable by the trustee under his or her second avoiding power.

    (g)   Child support and alimony payments are not subject to the preferential provisions.

c.   Fraudulent Transfers

    (1)   A fraudulent transfer is the transfer of an interest of the debtor in property, or any obligation incurred by the debtor, that was made or incurred within one year before the date of the filing of the petition and that was made or incurred by the debtor with actual intent to hinder, delay, or defraud any present or future creditor.

    (2)   It is also a transfer of an interest of the debtor in property, or any obligation incurred by the debtor, that was made or incurred within one year before the date of the filing of the petition and that was made or incurred under circumstances whereby the debtor received less than a reasonably equivalent value in exchange for the transfer or obligation and whereby the debtor:

        (a)   Was insolvent at the time or became insolvent as a result thereof.

        (b)   Was engaged in business, or was about to engage in business, for which the debtor's remaining property was unreasonably small capital.

        (c)   Intended to incur, or believed that he or she would incur, debts that would be beyond the debtor's ability to pay as they matured.

    (3)   When the debtor is a partnership, a transfer can be avoided by the trustee if it was made to a general partner within a year before bankruptcy filing and at the time the partnership was insolvent or if by the transfer the partnership became insolvent.

3.   Offset--Generally, the Bankruptcy Code leaves unaffected any right of a creditor to offset a mutual debt it owes to the debtor against a claim it possesses against the debtor, so long as both the claim and the debt arose before the commencement of the bankruptcy case.

CHAPTER 48—BANKRUPTCY

Problem 48-1 MULTIPLE CHOICE QUESTIONS (65 to 80 minutes)

1. Robin Corp. incurred substantial operating losses for the past three years. Unable to meet its current obligations, Robin filed a petition for reorganization under Chapter 11 of the Federal Bankruptcy Code. Which of the following statements is correct?
a. The creditors' committee must select a trustee to manage Robin's affairs.
b. The reorganization plan may only be filed by Robin.
c. A creditors' committee, if appointed, will consist of unsecured creditors.
d. Robin may continue in business only with the approval of a trustee. (11/93, Law, #32, 4329)

2. Under the reorganization provisions of Chapter 11 of the Federal Bankruptcy Code, after a reorganization plan is confirmed, and a final decree closing the proceedings entered, which of the following events usually occurs?
a. A reorganized corporate debtor will be liquidated.
b. A reorganized corporate debtor will be discharged from all debts except as otherwise provided in the plan and applicable law.
c. A trustee will continue to operate the debtor's business.
d. A reorganized individual debtor will **not** be allowed to continue in the same business. (11/94, Law, #37, 5214)

Items 3 and 4 are based on the following:

Strong Corp. filed a voluntary petition in bankruptcy under the reorganization provisions of Chapter 11 of the Federal Bankruptcy Code. A reorganization plan was filed and agreed to by all necessary parties. The court confirmed the plan and a final decree was entered.

3. Which of the following parties ordinarily must confirm the plan?

	1/2 of the secured creditors	2/3 of the shareholders
a.	Yes	Yes
b.	Yes	No
c.	No	Yes
d.	No	No

(5/95, Law, #34, 5368)

4. Which of the following statements best describes the effect of the entry of the court's final decree?
a. Strong Corp. will be discharged from all its debts and liabilities.
b. Strong Corp. will be discharged only from the debts owed creditors who agreed to the reorganization plan.
c. Strong Corp. will be discharged from all its debts and liabilities that arose before the date of confirmation of the plan.
d. Strong Corp. will be discharged from all its debts and liabilities that arose before the confirmation of the plan, except as otherwise provided in the plan, the order of confirmation, or the Bankruptcy Code. (5/95, Law, #35, 5369)

5. Under Chapter 11 of the Federal Bankruptcy Code, which of the following would **not** be eligible for reorganization?
a. Retail sole proprietorship.
b. Advertising partnership.
c. CPA professional corporation.
d. Savings and loan corporation. (11/92, Law, #32, 3114)

6. Which of the following statements is correct under the reorganization provisions of the Bankruptcy Code?
a. The court is required to appoint a trustee or an examiner in all cases.
b. The creditors must appoint a trustee or an examiner after the bankruptcy petition is filed.
c. The bankruptcy petition may only be filed voluntarily by the debtor.
d. The court is required to appoint a committee of unsecured creditors. (11/88, Law, #29, 9911)

6A. Which of the following statements is correct with respect to the reorganization provisions of Chapter 11 of the Federal Bankruptcy Code?
a. A trustee must always be appointed.
b. The debtor must be insolvent if the bankruptcy petition was filed voluntarily.
c. A reorganization plan may be filed by a creditor anytime after the petition date.
d. The commencement of a bankruptcy case may be voluntary or involuntary. (11/93, Law, #34, 4331)

7. Which of the following statements is correct concerning the voluntary filing of a petition in bankruptcy?
a. If the debtor has 12 or more creditors, the unsecured claims must total at least $10,000.
b. The debtor must be insolvent.
c. If the debtor has less than 12 creditors, the unsecured claims must total at least $10,000.
d. The petition may be filed jointly by spouses.

(11/91, Law, #28, amended, 2356)

7A. Deft, CPA, is an unsecured creditor of Golf Co. for $11,000. Golf has a total of 10 creditors, all of whom are unsecured. Golf has not paid any of the creditors for three months. Under Chapter 11 of the Federal Bankruptcy Code, which of the following statements is correct?
a. Golf may **not** be petitioned involuntarily into bankruptcy because there are less than 12 unsecured creditors.
b. Golf may **not** be petitioned involuntarily into bankruptcy under the provisions of Chapter 11.
c. Three unsecured creditors must join in the involuntary petition in bankruptcy.
d. Deft may file an involuntary petition in bankruptcy against Golf.

(11/94, Law, #32, amended, 5209)

8. To file for bankruptcy under Chapter 7 of the Federal Bankruptcy Code, an individual must
a. Have debts of any amount.
b. Be insolvent.
c. Be indebted to more than three creditors.
d. Have debts in excess of $10,000.

(11/91, Law, #29, amended, 2357)

8A. Which of the following conditions, if any, must a debtor meet to file a voluntary bankruptcy petition under Chapter 7 of the Federal Bankruptcy Code?

	Insolvency	Three or more creditors
a.	Yes	Yes
b.	Yes	No
c.	No	Yes
d.	No	No

(11/93, Law, #29, 4326)

8B. The filing of an involuntary bankruptcy petition under the Federal Bankruptcy Code
a. Terminates liens on exempt property.
b. Terminates all security interests in property in the bankruptcy estate.
c. Stops the debtor from incurring new debts.
d. Stops the enforcement of judgment liens against property in the bankruptcy estate.

(11/93, Law, #27, 4324)

8C. Which of the following actions between a debtor and its creditors will generally cause the debtor's release from its debts?

	Composition of creditors	Assignment for the benefit of creditors
a.	Yes	Yes
b.	Yes	No
c.	No	Yes
d.	No	No

(11/94, Law, #27, 5204)

Items 9 through 9E are based on the following:

Dart, Inc., a closely held corporation, was petitioned involuntarily into bankruptcy under the liquidation provisions of Chapter 7 of the Federal Bankruptcy Code. Dart contested the petition.

Dart has not been paying its business debts as they became due, has defaulted on its mortgage loan payments, and owes back taxes to the IRS. The total cash value of Dart's bankruptcy estate after the sale of all assets and payment of administration expenses is $100,000.

Dart has the following creditors:

- Fracon Bank is owed $75,000 principal and accrued interest on a mortgage loan secured by Dart's real property. The property was valued at and sold, in bankruptcy, for $70,000.
- The IRS has a $12,000 recorded judgment for unpaid corporate income tax.
- JOG Office Supplies has an unsecured claim of $3,000 that was timely filed.
- Nanstar Electric Co. has an unsecured claim of $1,200 that was not timely filed.
- Decoy Publications has a claim of $14,000, of which $2,000 is secured by Dart's inventory that was valued and sold, in bankruptcy, for $2,000. The claim was timely filed.

9. Which of the following creditors must join in the filing of the involuntary petition?

I. JOG Office Supplies
II. Nanstar Electric Co.
III. Decoy Publications

a. I, II, and III.
b. II and III.
c. I and II.
d. III only.

(5/95, Law, #28, 5362)

9A. Which of the following statements would correctly describe the result of Dart's opposing the petition?
a. Dart will win because the petition should have been filed under Chapter 11.
b. Dart will win because there are **not** more than 12 creditors.
c. Dart will lose because it is **not** paying its debts as they become due.
d. Dart will lose because of its debt to the IRS.
(5/95, Law, #29, 5363)

9B. Which of the following events will follow the filing of the Chapter 7 involuntary petition?

	A trustee will be appointed	A stay against creditor collection proceedings will go into effect
a.	Yes	Yes
b.	Yes	No
c.	No	Yes
d.	No	No

(5/95, Law, #30, 5364)

For items 9C through 9E assume that the bankruptcy estate was distributed.

9C. What dollar amount would Nanstar Electric Co. receive?
a. $0
b. $ 800
c. $1,000
d. $1,200
(5/95, Law, #31, 5365)

9D. What total dollar amount would Fracon Bank receive on its secured and unsecured claims?
a. $70,000
b. $72,000
c. $74,000
d. $75,000
(5/95, Law, #32, 5366)

9E. What dollar amount would the IRS receive?
a. $0
b. $ 8,000
c. $10,000
d. $12,000
(5/95, Law, #33, 5367)

10. Unger owes a total of $50,000 to eight unsecured creditors and one fully secured creditor. Quincy is one of the unsecured creditors and is owed $11,000. Quincy has filed a petition against Unger under the liquidation provisions of Chapter 7 of the Federal Bankruptcy Code. Unger has been unable to pay debts as they become due. Unger's liabilities exceed Unger's assets. Unger has filed papers opposing the bankruptcy petition. Which of the following statements regarding Quincy's petition is correct?
a. It will be dismissed because the secured creditor failed to join in the filing of the petition.
b. It will be dismissed because three unsecured creditors must join in the filing of the petition.
c. It will be granted because Unger's liabilities exceed Unger's assets.
d. It will be granted because Unger is unable to pay Unger's debts as they become due.
(5/91, Law, #29, amended, 0606)

11. Green owes unsecured creditors: Rice, $2,000; Vick, $6,000; Young, $11,000; and Zinc, $2,500. Green has not paid any creditor since January 1, 1992. On March 15, 1992, Green's sole asset, a cabin cruiser, was seized by Xeno Marine Co. the holder of a perfected security interest in the boat. On July 1, 1992, Rice, Vick, and Zinc involuntarily petitioned Green into bankruptcy under Chapter 7 of the Federal Bankruptcy Code. If Green opposes the involuntary petition, the petition will be
a. Upheld, because the three filing creditors are owed more than $10,000.
b. Upheld, because one creditor is owed more than $10,000.
c. Dismissed, because there are less than 12 creditors.
d. Dismissed, because the boat was seized more than 90 days before the filing.
(11/92, Law, #29, amended, 3111)

12. Which of the following transfers by a debtor, within ninety days of filing for bankruptcy, could be set aside as a preferential payment?
a. Making a gift to charity.
b. Paying a business utility bill.
c. Borrowing money from a bank secured by giving a mortgage on business property.
d. Prepaying an installment loan on inventory.
(11/93, Law, #30, 4327)

13. Which of the following acts by a debtor could result in a bankruptcy court revoking the debtor's discharge?

I. Failure to list one creditor.
II. Failure to answer correctly material questions on the bankruptcy petition.

a. I only.
b. II only.
c. Both I and II.
d. Neither I nor II.
(11/93, Law, #31, 4328)

14. By signing a reaffirmation agreement on April 15, 1991, a debtor agreed to pay certain debts that would be discharged in bankruptcy. On June 20, 1991, the debtor's attorney filed the reaffirmation agreement and an affidavit with the court indicating that the debtor understood the consequences of the reaffirmation agreement. The debtor obtained a discharge on August 25, 1991. The reaffirmation agreement would be enforceable only if it was

a. Made after discharge.
b. Approved by the bankruptcy court.
c. Not for a household purpose debt.
d. Not rescinded before discharge.

(11/91, Law, #31, 2359)

15. On June 5, 1989, Gold rented equipment under a four-year lease. On March 8, 1990, Gold was petitioned involuntarily into bankruptcy under the Federal Bankruptcy Code's liquidation provisions. A trustee was appointed. The fair market value of the equipment exceeds the balance of the lease payments due. The trustee

a. May **not** reject the equipment lease because the fair market value of the equipment exceeds the balance of the lease payments due.
b. May elect **not** to assume the equipment lease.
c. Must assume the equipment lease because its term exceeds one year.
d. Must assume and subsequently assign the equipment lease. (11/90, Law, #27, 0613)

16. A debtor may attempt to conceal or transfer property to prevent a creditor from satisfying a judgment. Which of the following actions will be considered an indication of fraudulent conveyance?

	Debtor remaining in possession after conveyance	Secret conveyance	Debtor retains an equitable benefit in the property conveyed
a.	Yes	Yes	Yes
b.	No	Yes	Yes
c.	Yes	Yes	No
d.	Yes	No	Yes

(5/94, Law, #21, 4776)

17. Which of the following claims would have the highest priority in the distribution of a bankruptcy estate under the liquidation provisions of Chapter 7 of the Federal Bankruptcy Code if the petition was filed June 1, 1991?

a. Federal tax lien filed May 15, 1991.
b. A secured debt properly perfected on February 10, 1991.

c. Trustee's administration costs filed September 30, 1991.
d. Employee wages due March 30, 1991.

(11/91, Law, #30, 2358)

18. Which of the following types of claims would be paid first in the distribution of a bankruptcy estate under the liquidation provisions of Chapter 7 of the Federal Bankruptcy Code if the petition was filed July 15, 1993?

a. A secured debt properly perfected on March 20, 1993.
b. Inventory purchased and delivered August 1, 1993.
c. Employee wages due April 30, 1993.
d. Federal tax lien filed June 30, 1993.

(11/93, Law, #39, 4336)

19. A party involuntarily petitioned into bankruptcy under Chapter 7 of the Federal Bankruptcy Code who succeeds in having the petition dismissed could recover

	Court costs and attorney's fees	Compensatory damages	Punitive damages
a.	Yes	Yes	Yes
b.	Yes	Yes	No
c.	No	Yes	Yes
d.	Yes	No	No

(11/92, Law, #30, 3112)

20. Peters Co. repairs computers. On February 9, 1991, Stark Electronics Corp. sold Peters a circuit tester on credit. Peters executed an installment note for the purchase price, a security agreement covering the tester, and a financing statement that Stark filed on February 11, 1991. On April 13, 1991, creditors other than Stark filed an involuntary petition in bankruptcy against Peters. What is Stark's status in Peters' bankruptcy?

a. Stark will be treated as an unsecured creditor because Start did **not** join in the filing against Peters.
b. Stark's security interest constitutes a voidable preference because the financing statement was **not** filed until February 11.
c. Stark's security interest constitutes a voidable preference because the financing statement was filed within 90 days before the bankruptcy proceeding was filed.
d. Stark is a secured creditor and can assert a claim to the circuit tester that will be superior to the claims of Peters' other creditors.

(5/91, Law, #32, 0609)

21. Which of the following prejudgment remedies would be available to a creditor when a debtor owns **no** real property?

	Writ of attachment	Garnishment
a.	Yes	Yes
b.	Yes	No
c.	No	Yes
d.	No	No

(11/94, Law, #28, 5205)

22. Which of the following claims will **not** be discharged in bankruptcy?
a. A claim that arises from alimony or maintenance.
b. A claim that arises out of the debtor's breach of a contract.
c. A claim brought by a secured creditor that remains unsatisfied after the sale of the collateral.
d. A claim brought by a judgment creditor whose judgment resulted from the debtor's negligent operation of a motor vehicle.

(11/94, Law, #33, 5210)

23. Which of the following requirements must be met for creditors to file an involuntary bankruptcy petition under Chapter 7 of the Federal Bankruptcy Code?
a. The debtor must owe one creditor more than $10,000.
b. The debtor has **not** been paying its *bona fide* debts as they become due.
c. There must **not** be more than 12 creditors.
d. At least one fully secured creditor must join in the petition. (11/93, Law, #28, amended, 4325)

24. Which of the following methods will allow a creditor to collect money from a debtor's wages?
a. Arrest.
b. Mechanic's lien.
c. Order of receivership.
d. Writ of garnishment. (5/94, Law, #23, 4778)

25. Which of the following claims would have the highest priority in the distribution of a bankruptcy estate under the liquidation provisions of Chapter 7 of the Federal Bankruptcy Code if the petition was filed June 1, 1995?
a. Federal tax lien filed May 15, 1995.
b. A secured debt properly perfected on February 10, 1995.

c. Trustee's administration costs filed September 30, 1995.
d. Employee wages due March 30, 1995.

(11/91, Law, #30, amended, 2358)

26. A homestead exemption ordinarily could exempt a debtor's equity in certain property from post-judgment collection by a creditor. To which of the following creditors will this exemption apply?

	Valid home mortgage lien	Valid IRS tax lien
a.	Yes	Yes
b.	Yes	No
c.	No	Yes
d.	No	No

(5/94, Law, #22, 4777)

read back

27. In general, which of the following debts will be discharged under the voluntary liquidation provisions of Chapter 7 of the Federal Bankruptcy Code?
a. A debt due to the negligence of the debtor arising before filing the bankruptcy petition.
b. Alimony payments owed the debtor's spouse under a separation agreement entered into two years before the filing of the bankruptcy petition.
c. A debt incurred more than 90 days before the filing of the bankruptcy petition and **not** disclosed in the petition.
d. Income taxes due within two years before the filing of the bankruptcy petition.

(5/91, Law, #31, 0608)

28. A bankrupt who filed voluntarily and received a discharge in bankruptcy under the provisions of Chapter 7 of the Federal Bankruptcy Code
a. May obtain another voluntary discharge in bankruptcy under Chapter 7 after five years have elapsed from the date of the prior filing.
b. Will receive a discharge of any and all debts owed.
c. Is precluded from owning or operating a similar business for two years.
d. Must surrender for distribution to the creditors any amount received as an inheritance if received within 180 days after filing the petition.

(11/90, Law, #35, 0619)

28A. Under the liquidation provisions of Chapter 7 of the Federal Bankruptcy Code, which of the following statements applies to a person who has voluntarily filed for and received a discharge in bankruptcy?

a. The person will be discharged from all debts.
b. The person can obtain another voluntary discharge in bankruptcy under Chapter 7 after three years have elapsed from the date of the prior filing.
c. The person must surrender for distribution to the creditors amounts received as an inheritance, if the receipt occurs within 180 days after filing the bankruptcy petition.
d. The person is precluded from owning or operating a similar business for two years.
(11/94, Law, #34, 5211)

Items 29 through 31 are based on the following:

On August 1, 1995, Hall filed a voluntary petition under Chapter 7 of the Federal Bankruptcy Code.

Hall's assets are sufficient to pay general creditors 40% of their claims.

The following transactions occurred before the filing:

- On May 5, 1995, Hall gave a mortgage on Hall's home to National Bank to secure payment of a loan National had given Hall two years earlier. When the loan was made, Hall's twin was a National employee.
- On June 1, 1995, Hall purchased a boat from Olsen for $10,000 cash.
- On July 1, 1995, Hall paid off an outstanding credit card balance of $500. The original debt had been $2,500.

29. The National mortgage was
a. Preferential, because National would be considered an insider.
b. Preferential, because the mortgage was given to secure an antecedent debt.
c. Not preferential, because Hall is presumed insolvent when the mortgage was given.
d. Not preferential, because the mortgage was a security interest.
(11/92, Law, #37, amended, 3119)

30. The payment to Olsen was
a. Preferential, because the payment was made within 90 days of the filing of the petition.
b. Preferential, because the payment enabled Olsen to receive more than the other general creditors.

c. Not preferential, because Hall is presumed insolvent when the payment was made.
d. Not preferential, because the payment was a contemporaneous exchange for new value.
(11/92, Law, #38, amended, 3120)

31. The credit card payment was
a. Preferential, because the payment was made within 90 days of the filing of the petition.
b. Preferential, because the payment was on account of an antecedent debt.
c. Not preferential, because the payment was for a consumer debt of less than $600.
d. Not preferential, because the payment was less than 40% of the original debt.
(11/92, Law, #39, amended, 3121)

32. On February 28, 1991, Master, Inc. had total assets with a fair market value of $1,200,000 and total liabilities of $990,000. On January 15, 1991, Master made a monthly installment note payment to Acme Distributors Corp., a creditor holding a properly perfected security interest in equipment having a fair market value greater than the balance due on the note. On March 15, 1991, Master voluntarily filed a petition in bankruptcy under the liquidation provisions of Chapter 7 of the Federal Bankruptcy Code. One year later, the equipment was sold for less than the balance due on the note to Acme.

Master's payment to Acme could
a. Be set aside as a preferential transfer because the fair market value of the collateral was greater than the installment note balance.
b. Be set aside as a preferential transfer unless Acme showed that Master was solvent on January 15, 1991.
c. Not be set aside as a preferential transfer because Acme was oversecured.
d. Not be set aside as a preferential transfer if Acme showed that Master was solvent on March 15, 1991. (11/91, Law, #44, 2372)

Items 33 and 34 are based on the following:

On May 1, 1991, two months after becoming insolvent, Quick Corp., an appliance wholesaler, filed a voluntary petition for bankruptcy under the provisions of Chapter 7 of the Federal Bankruptcy Code. On October 15, 1990, Quick's board of directors had authorized and paid Erly $50,000 to repay Erly's April 1, 1990, loan to the corporation. Erly is a sibling of Quick's president. On March 15, 1991, Quick paid Kray $100,000 for inventory delivered that day.

33. Which of the following is **not** relevant in determining whether the repayment of Erly's loan is a voidable preferential transfer?
a. Erly is an insider.
b. Quick's payment to Erly was made on account of an antecedent debt.
c. Quick's solvency when the loan was made by Erly.
d. Quick's payment to Erly was made within one year of the filing of the bankruptcy petition.
(5/91, Law, #33, 0610)

34. Quick's payment to Kray would
a. Not be voidable, because it was a contemporaneous exchange. *Value for value*
b. Not be voidable, unless Kray knew about Quick's insolvency.
c. Be voidable, because it was made within 90 days of the bankruptcy filing.
d. Be voidable, because it enabled Kray to receive more than it otherwise would receive from the bankruptcy estate. (5/91, Law, #34, 0611)

35. Which of the following assets would be included in a debtor's bankruptcy estate in a liquidation proceeding?
a. Proceeds from a life insurance policy received 90 days after the petition was filed.
b. An inheritance received 270 days after the petition was filed.

c. Property from a divorce settlement received 365 days after the petition was filed.
d. Wages earned by the debtor after the petition was filed. (11/89, Law, #27, 0625)

36. Flax, a sole proprietor, has been petitioned involuntarily into bankruptcy under the Federal Bankruptcy Code's liquidation provisions. Simon & Co., CPAs, has been appointed trustee of the bankruptcy estate. If Simon also wishes to act as the tax return preparer for the estate, which of the following statements is correct?
a. Simon is prohibited from serving as both trustee and preparer under any circumstances because serving in that dual capacity would be a conflict of interest.
b. Although Simon may serve as both trustee and preparer, it is entitled to receive a fee only for the services rendered as a preparer.
c. Simon may employ itself to prepare tax returns if authorized by the court and may receive a separate fee for services rendered in each capacity.
d. Although Simon may serve as both trustee and preparer, its fee for services rendered in each capacity will be determined solely by the size of the estate. (11/90, Law, #28, 9911)

Solutions 48-1 MULTIPLE CHOICE ANSWERS

Reorganizations

1. (c) Section 1102 of Chapter 11 in the Federal Bankruptcy Code specifies that the court is required to appoint a committee of creditors holding *unsecured* claims. A trustee does not have to be appointed under a Chapter 11 filing. Any interested party may propose a plan after the first 120 days following the order for relief. Robin may continue in business without the approval of a trustee and a trustee may not even have been appointed.

2. (b) Chapter 11 of the Federal Bankruptcy Code permits corporations and individuals to restructure finances so that a business may continue to operate, pay its creditors, and generate a return for any stockholders. The purpose of Chapter 11 is to formulate a plan of reorganization that determines the amount and manner in which creditors will be paid, in what form the business will continue, and other necessary details. The Bankruptcy Code

requires a trustee to be appointed or elected in Chapters 7 and 13; however, no trustee is required in Chapter 11 proceedings. The debtor is thus permitted to continue to operate the business, both during and after the bankruptcy proceedings.

3. (d) Under the provisions of Chapter 11 of the Federal Bankruptcy Code, a reorganization plan must always be confirmed by the court. Prior to court confirmation, *approval* of the plan is generally required by creditors holding two-thirds in amount and one-half in number of each class of claims. It is not necessary that any creditors or any shareholders *confirm* the reorganization plan.

4. (d) Under Chapter 11 of the Federal Bankruptcy Code, a corporation will be discharged from all its debts and liabilities that arose before the confirmation of the plan, except as otherwise provided in the plan, the order of confirmation, or the bankruptcy code. If there are exceptions, Strong Corp. will not be discharged from all its debts and

liabilities. Creditor approval of the reorganization plan is not a prerequisite to the discharge of debts.

5. (d)   A savings and loan is not eligible for reorganization under Chapter 11. A retail sole proprietorship, an advertising partnership, and a CPA professional corporation are permitted to file for reorganization under Chapter 11 of the Code.

6. (d)   Under the reorganization provisions of Chapter 11, the court will appoint a committee of unsecured creditors as soon as practicable after the order of relief for purposes of formulating the plan of reorganization. The court is not required to appoint a trustee or examiner except in certain instances (such as fraud, dishonesty, incompetency, or gross mismanagement of the debtor's affairs) and if generally such an appointment is in the interests of the creditors or equity security holders of the debtor. A petition under Chapter 11 may be either voluntary or involuntary.

6A. (d)   Like a liquidation proceeding, a reorganization may be either voluntary or involuntary. The appointment of a trustee is not required under Chapter 11. A debtor is not precluded from filing for bankruptcy if the debtor is solvent. During the first 120 days after the order of relief, *only* the debtor may file a plan of reorganization.

Effects of Bankruptcy on Debtors and Creditors

7. (d)   A joint voluntary bankruptcy petition can be filed by a husband and wife. Answers (a) and (c) are incorrect because they pertain to an involuntary petition. There is no rule that a debtor be insolvent to file a petition in bankruptcy.

7A. (d)   Under Chapter 11 of the Bankruptcy Code, an involuntary petition may be commenced against a debtor. If the debtor has fewer than 12 creditors, any one creditor may file the petition if the unsecured portion of the amount due that creditor is at least $10,000. Since Deft is owed $11,000 in unsecured debt, he may file the petition.

8. (a)   To file for bankruptcy under Chapter 7 of the Federal Bankruptcy Code, an individual must have debt, the amount of which is irrelevant. The debtor need not be insolvent, be indebted to a minimum number of creditors, or have debt above a specified amount, in order to file under Chapter 7.

8A. (d)   A debtor does *not* have to be insolvent in order to declare bankruptcy. Almost all debtors are allowed to file a petition in bankruptcy as long as there is a full and honest disclosure of all the debtor's assets and liabilities.

8B. (d)   The filing of a petition of bankruptcy, either voluntary or involuntary, stops the enforcement of judgment liens against property in the bankruptcy estate, and it, in general, stops all other legal actions against the debtor except for legal actions involving alimony, child support, and criminal actions. Bankruptcy proceedings act to protect the assets of the debtor until an equitable distribution of those assets among all creditors can be achieved. A discharge of debt under the Federal Bankruptcy Code has no effect on exempt property. The Federal Bankruptcy Code considers security interests in property in the bankruptcy estate when it assigns priority to creditors for the distribution of assets. The Federal Bankruptcy Code has no power to limit the debtor's actions regarding new debt.

8C. (b)   A composition agreement involves a modification of the original credit agreement/contract whereby the creditors agree to accept an immediate payment of a lesser amount in satisfaction of the debt. If the debtor makes the payments due, then the debtor will be released from the debt. An Assignment for the Benefit of Creditors (ABC) involves a voluntary transfer of the debtor's nonexempt assets to an assignee who liquidates the assets and distributes the proceeds to the creditors. All of the debtor's general creditors participate; however, the debtor is not released from its debts if these are not satisfied as a result of the distribution.

9. (d)   An involuntary bankruptcy case is commenced by the filing of a petition with the bankruptcy court. One creditor may file the petition if the debtor has fewer than twelve such creditors, provided that the unsecured portion of the petitioner's claims is equal to at least $5,000. Since Dart has fewer than twelve creditors, any one creditor owed at least $5,000 may file the petition. Since Decoy has an unsecured claim for $12,000, Decoy alone may file the petition.

9A. (c)   When an involuntary petition is filed, the debtor may oppose/controvert the petition upon proof that the debtor is paying its debts as they become due. Dart will thus lose because it is not paying its debts as they become due. There is no reason that the petition should have been filed under Chapter 11, nor is there a requirement that there be more than twelve creditors. Dart's debt to the IRS has no effect on Dart's ability to controvert the petition.

9B. (a)   Following the filing of a Chapter 7 involuntary petition, the court issues a stay against creditor collection proceedings and, in most cases, a trustee will be appointed.

9C. (a)   The distribution rules for a Chapter 7 case require that all priority claims be satisfied first. Any remaining property is then distributed as follows: (1) in payment of any unsecured claim, proof of which was timely filed; (2) in payment of any unsecured claim, proof of which was not timely filed. Since there is insufficient property to satisfy the unsecured claims which were timely filed, Nanstar, whose claim was not timely filed, would receive nothing.

9D. (c)   After payments to secured creditors (Fracon $70,000; Decoy $2,000), and after payment of $12,000 to the IRS, there is only $16,000 remaining in the bankruptcy estate. The claims of unsecured creditors whose claims were timely filed is $20,000. Each unsecured creditor would receive 80% of their claim. Fracon would thus receive $70,000 as a secured creditor and $4,000 as an unsecured creditor.

9E. (d)   After payments to secured creditors (Fracon $70,000; Decoy $2,000), $28,000 remains in the bankruptcy estate. Of Dart's creditors, the IRS has the next highest priority after payment of administration expenses; its $12,000 claim will be satisfied in full.

10.   (d)   One requirement for an involuntary bankruptcy petition is that the debtor is unable to pay debts as they become due. Another requirement is having the right number of creditors sign the petition. If there are less than 12 creditors, only one creditor need sign the petition as long as the creditor has at least $10,000 of unsecured debt. If there are 12 or more creditors, at least three creditors having unsecured debt of $10,000 must sign the petition. It is not necessary for a secured creditor to sign the involuntary petition. Three creditors need not sign the petition. It is only necessary for one creditor having at least $10,000 of unsecured debt to sign. It does not matter if liabilities exceed assets. The requirements only provide that the debtor must be unable to pay his/her debts as they become due.

11.   (a)   An involuntary petition may be filed with the bankruptcy court when the debtor has fewer than 12 creditors, provided that the unsecured portion of the petitioners' claims is equal in the aggregate to at least $10,000. There is no stipulation that one creditor must be owed more than $10,000. The debtor need not have more than 12 creditors. Answer (d) is not applicable.

12.   (d)   A "preferential transfer" is any payment or transfer of property from an insolvent debtor to a creditor for a *preexisting* debt within 90 days of filing a petition in bankruptcy court. There was no preexisting debt in answer (a). The courts generally assume that payments for services rendered within ten to fifteen days prior to the payment represent current consideration and are not a preference. There was a contemporaneous exchange in answer (c) (mortgage in exchange for money). A debtor making a payment to one creditor on a preexisting debt meets the criteria of a preferential transfer.

13.   (b)   Revocation of the discharge may be granted by the court if it was obtained through fraud. Failure to answer material questions correctly on the bankruptcy petition would most probably be considered a fraudulent act. However, the failure to list one creditor may be considered unintentional and thus non-fraudulent. While this failure to list one creditor will not, in general, disqualify the debtor from filing for bankruptcy, that one debt will not be discharged in bankruptcy since it was "unscheduled."

14.   (d)   The reaffirmation of a debt is a commitment to pay a debt that can be discharged in bankruptcy. To be enforceable, a reaffirmation must be implemented under state law and the debtor must have received adequate notice on the effects of signing the reaffirmation. If the reaffirmation is rescinded before discharge, then it is not enforceable.

15.   (b)   In the administration of the bankrupt's estate, the trustee can assume or reject executory contracts and unexpired leases subject to the approval of the court/bankruptcy judge. A trustee may elect not to assume the equipment lease. The lease may be rejected even if it is for more than one year.

16.   (a)   A debtor's remaining in possession of property transferred, a debtor's retention of an equitable benefit in property conveyed, and the fact that a conveyance occurred in secret are all indicators of a fraudulent conveyance.

17.   (b)   Under a Chapter 7 liquidation, assets must be utilized to satisfy priority claims until depleted. The highest priority would be given to secured claims, then administrative expenses and unsecured claims.

18. (a) Creditor's claims are ranked according to guidelines established by the Federal Bankruptcy Code. Secured creditors are paid on their security interests before those with junior claims. In this problem, the first to perfect a secured interest in the bankruptcy estate will be paid first. The federal tax lien is a non-dischargeable debt so it will not be paid with the liquidation proceeds. Therefore, the first security interest to be perfected, takes priority over the other unperfected, later interests.

19. (a) Judgment may be granted against the petitioning creditors for court costs and attorney's fees incurred by the debtor in defending against an involuntary petition which is dismissed by the court. Also, if the petition is filed in bad faith, both compensatory and punitive damages can be awarded for injury to the debtor's reputation.

Creditors and Claims

20. (d) Stark has a purchase money security interest in equipment and the financing statement was filed within ten days. As a result, Stark is a secured creditor and can assert a claim to the circuit tester that will be superior to the claims of other creditors. It is not necessary for a secured creditor to sign the involuntary petition against the debtor to protect the creditor's security interest. A contemporaneous exchange of value for value would not create voidable preferences, which involve paying one creditor to the detriment of others.

21. (a) Attachment involves a prejudgment, court-ordered seizure of property (including personal property) that is in controversy because of a debt. Garnishment is also a prejudgment remedy that permits a creditor to proceed against property or property rights held by a third person. Garnishments and writs of attachment are *both* prejudgment remedies available to a creditor where the debtor owns no real property.

22. (a) Under Chapters 7, 11, and 13 of the Bankruptcy Code, certain debts are excepted from discharge. These include claims that arise from alimony or maintenance. Claims arising from a breach of contract, from an unsecured creditor, or from an action in negligence are all dischargeable.

23. (b) There are two basic requirements that must be met in filing an involuntary petition against the debtor. First, there must be an indication that the debtor is not paying his or her bona fide debts as they become due or that a custodian, general receiver, or assignee was appointed or took possession of substantially all of the debtor's property within 120 days before the filing of the petition. Second, the proper number of creditors must sign the petition. If there are 12 or more creditors, three creditors having unsecured debt totaling at least $10,000 must sign the petition. If less than 12 creditors, only one creditor having at least $10,000 of unsecured debt need sign.

24. (d) A writ of garnishment is served upon a debtor's employer, which results in part of the debtor's wages being paid to the creditor. The arrest of a debtor will not allow a creditor to attach a debtor's wages. A mechanics lien is a device that enables someone who has rendered services to real property to place a lien against the real property to secure payment for labor, materials or services provided. An order of receivership pertains to a debtor's assets, not the debtor's income.

25. (b) Under a Chapter 7 liquidation, assets must be utilized to satisfy priority claims until depleted. The highest priority would be given to secured claims, then administrative expenses and unsecured claims.

Debtor's Benefits

26. (d) Homestead exemption legislation protects a debtor's property from seizure by unsecured creditors, such as the IRS, but the IRS debt would not be discharged. A secured creditor with a valid home mortgage lien could also seize the property.

27. (a) Debts due to negligence arising before the petition was filed are dischargeable in bankruptcy as long as the debtor lists the debt on his/her bankruptcy petition. Alimony payments are not dischargeable in bankruptcy. Unscheduled debts (debts not listed in the bankruptcy petition) are not dischargeable in bankruptcy. Income taxes due within three years before the filing of the bankruptcy petition are not dischargeable in bankruptcy.

The Estate

28. (d) An inheritance, life insurance proceeds, or property from a divorce decree settlement received within 180 days after the filing of a petition in bankruptcy must be surrendered for distribution to the creditors of the bankrupt. A debtor can declare bankruptcy only every six years. Not all debts are discharged in bankruptcy. There is no rule such as in answer (c).

28A. (c) The Bankruptcy Code defines property of the bankruptcy estate to include certain property interests that the debtor has a right to receive within 180 days after filing the bankruptcy petition, including a right to receive an inheritance, a property settlement pursuant to a divorce, or life insurance proceeds. Certain debts (such as alimony) are excepted from discharge. A debtor is entitled to only one discharge from bankruptcy during a six-year period. There are no provisions in the Code to preclude a debtor from owning or operating a similar business for any time period.

29. (b) To constitute a preference that may be recovered, an insolvent debtor must have transferred property, for a pre-existing, or antecedent debt, within 90 days of the filing of the petition. Hall gave the mortgage to National Bank 75 days after he filed his petition, so he was insolvent at the time. A preferential transfer may be made to an insider (National) if the transfer did not occur within 12 months prior to the filing of the petition and because secured creditors are not considered insiders for purposes of a preferential transfer. Answer (d) is incorrect because National was an unsecured creditor at the time of the payment.

30. (d) Hall's purchase of the boat from Olsen is a contemporaneous exchange for new value given and no antecedent debt was involved; therefore, a preference is not present. The payment was not preferential. Hall's insolvency is not a factor in a contemporaneous exchange.

31. (c) The credit card payment was not preferential, because Chapter 7 of the Federal Bankruptcy Code specifically states that a payment does not constitute a preferential transfer if it is for a consumer debt of less than $600. The credit card payment was not preferential. The exception is stated as payments of $600 or less rather than 40% of the original debt. _Read_

32. (c) The bankruptcy laws grant the trustee avoiding powers to set aside certain conveyances, including preferential transfers. A preferential transfer is a property transfer: (1) to or for the benefit of a creditor; (2) for or on account of an antecedent debt owed by the debtor; (3) made while the debtor was insolvent; (4) on or within 90 days before the date of bankruptcy filing; and (5) that enables the creditor to receive more than it would receive as a distributive share under a Chapter 7 liquidation. All five tests must be met to establish a preferential

transfer. The fifth test in this case is not met because secured creditors have priority over other creditors, and Acme was oversecured at the time of the monthly installment payment.

33. (c) Quick's solvency when the loan was made by Erly is not a relevant factor in determining whether the repayment of Erly's loan is a voidable transfer. Quick's solvency when the loan is repaid is a relevant factor. The fact that Erly is an insider is an important factor in determining if a voidable preferential transfer was made. Quick's payment to Erly for an antecedent debt would be a relevant factor in determining if a voidable preferential transfer was made. Quick's payment to Erly within one year of the filing of the petition would be an important factor in determining if a voidable preferential transfer was made.

34. (a) Quick's payment to Kray would be considered a contemporaneous exchange and not a voidable preferential transfer. When Quick paid Kray $100,000, Quick received $100,000 of inventory. Thus, a contemporaneous exchange took place: value for value. This transaction is not voidable even if Kray knew about Quick's insolvency since this transaction is a contemporaneous exchange. This is a contemporaneous exchange, not a voidable preferential transfer. Thus, it does not matter if the transaction took place within 90 days of filing of the petition. This is a contemporaneous exchange, not a voidable preferential transfer. Thus, it does not matter if Kray received more than it would have received in bankruptcy.

35. (a) A debtor's bankruptcy estate includes property interests acquired by the debtor within 180 days after the filing of the bankruptcy petition. These property interests include inheritances and life insurance proceeds (where the debtor is the beneficiary of a life insurance policy). It must be within 180 days--not 270 days. There is no such rule. Bankruptcy gives the debtor a "fresh start" and wages earned after the petition is filed are not subject to creditors' claims.

36. (c) A CPA may serve as both a trustee of an estate and act as its tax return preparer if authorized by the bankruptcy court (and receive a separate fee for each service). A separate fee may be obtained for each service. The fee is determined by the type of work performed and not by the size of the estate (although the size of the estate will be a factor).

PERFORMANCE BY SUBTOPICS

Each category below parallels a subtopic covered in Chapter 48. Record the number and percentage of questions you correctly answered in each subtopic area.

Reorganizations

Question #	Correct √
1	
2	
3	
4	
5	
6	
6A	
# Questions	7
# Correct	
% Correct	

Effects of Bankruptcy on Debtors and Creditors

Question #	Correct √
7	
7A	
8	
8A	
8B	
8C	
9	
9A	
9B	
9C	
9D	
9E	
10	
11	
12	
13	
14	
15	
16	
17	
18	
19	
# Questions	22
# Correct	
% Correct	

Creditors and Claims

Question #	Correct √
20	
21	
22	
23	
24	
25	
# Questions	6
# Correct	
% Correct	

Debtor's Benefits

Question #	Correct √
26	
27	
# Questions	2
# Correct	
% Correct	

The Estate

Question #	Correct √
28	
28A	
29	
30	
31	
32	
33	
34	
35	
36	
# Questions	10
# Correct	
% Correct	

OTHER OBJECTIVE FORMAT QUESTIONS

Problem 48-2 (10 to 15 minutes)

Items 1 through 6 are based on the following:

On May 1, 1994, Able Corp. was petitioned involuntarily into bankruptcy under the provisions of Chapter 7 of the Federal Bankruptcy Code.

When the petition was filed, Able had the following unsecured creditors:

Creditor	Amount owed
Cole	$10,000
Lake	4,000
Young	3,500
Thorn	2,000

The following transactions occurred before the bankruptcy petition was filed:

- On January 15, 1994, Able paid Vista Bank the $1,000 balance due on an unsecured business loan.
- On February 28, 1994, Able paid $1,000 to Owen, an officer of Able, who had lent Able money.
- On March 1, 1994, Able bought a computer for use in its business from Core Computer Co. for $2,000 cash.

Required:

Items 1 through 3 refer to the bankruptcy filing. For each item, determine whether the statement is True (T) or False (F).

1. Able can file a voluntary petition for bankruptcy if it is solvent.
2. Lake, Young, and Thorn can file a valid involuntary petition.
3. Cole alone can file a valid involuntary petition.

Drs Solvency / Insolvency Irrelevant Voluntary. Needs only Unsec. Cros does not pay dues - involant

BANKRUPTCY

Items 4 through 6 refer to the transactions that occurred before the filing of the involuntary bankruptcy petition. Assuming the bankruptcy petition was validly filed, for each item determine whether the statement is True (T) or False (F).

4. The payment to Vista Bank would be set aside as a preferential transfer.

5. The payment to Owen would be set aside as a preferential transfer.

6. The purchase from Core Computer Co. would be set aside as a preferential transfer.

(5/94, Law, #2, 67-72, amended)

Problem 48-3 (15 to 25 minutes)

This problem consists of 15 items. Select the **best** answer for each item. **Answer all items**.

On April 15, 1992, Wren Corp., an appliance wholesaler, was petitioned involuntarily into bankruptcy under the liquidation provisions of Chapter 7 of the Federal Bankruptcy Code.

When the petition was filed, Wren's creditors included:

Secured creditors	Amount owed
Fifth Bank--1st mortgage on warehouse owned by Wren	$50,000
Hart Manufacturing Corp.--perfected purchase money security interest in inventory	30,000
TVN Computers, Inc.--perfected security interest in office computers	15,000

Unsecured creditors	Amount owed
IRS--1990 federal income taxes	$20,000
Acme Office Cleaners--services for January, February, and March 1992	750
Ted Smith (employee)--February and March 1992 wages	4,400
Joan Sims (employee)--March 1992 commissions	1,500
Power Electric Co.--electricity charges for January, February, and March 1992	600
Soft Office Supplies--supplies purchased in 1991	2,000

The following transactions occurred before the bankruptcy petition was filed:

- On December 31, 1991, Wren paid off a $10,000 loan from Mary Lake, the sister of one of Wren's directors.

- On January 30, 1992, Wren donated $2,000 to Universal Charities.
- On February 1, 1992, Wren gave Young Finance Co. a security agreement covering Wren's office fixtures to secure a loan previously made by Young.
- On March 1, 1992, Wren made the final $1,000 monthly payment to Integral Appliance Corp. on a two-year note.
- On April 1, 1992, Wren purchased from Safety Co., a new burglar alarm system for its factory, for $10,000 cash.

All of Wren's assets were liquidated. The warehouse was sold for $75,000, the computers were sold for $12,000, and the inventory was sold for $25,000. After paying the bankruptcy administration expenses of $8,000, secured creditors, and priority general creditors, there was enough cash to pay each non-priority general creditor 50 cents on the dollar.

Required:

a. **Items 1 through 5** represent the transactions that occurred before the filing of the bankruptcy petition. For each transaction, determine if the transaction would be set aside as a preferential transfer by the bankruptcy court. Answer "Yes" if the transaction would be set aside or "No" if the transaction would **not** be set aside.

1. Payment to Mary Lake
2. Donation to Universal Charities
3. Security agreement to Young Finance Co.
4. Payment to Integral Appliance Corp.
5. Purchase from Safety Co.

b. **Items 6 through 10** represent creditors claims against the bankruptcy estate. Select from List I each creditor's order of payment in relation to the other creditors named in items 6 through 10.

		List I
6.	Bankruptcy administration expense	A. First
7.	Acme Office Cleaners	B. Second
8.	Fifth Bank	C. Third
9.	IRS	D. Fourth
10.	Joan Sims	E. Fifth

c. **Items 11 through 15** also represent creditor claims against the bankruptcy estate. For each of the creditors listed in Items 11 through 15, select from List II the amount that creditor will receive.

Mortgage Pymt OK - Sec loan (Unsec) Ls Pref for antecedent debt

		List II	
11.	TVN Computers, Inc.	A.	$0
12.	Hart Manufacturing Corp.	B.	$ 300
13.	Ted Smith	C.	$ 600
14.	Power Electric Co.	D.	$ 1,000
15.	Soft Office Supplies	E.	$ 1,200
		F.	$ 2,000
		G.	$ 4,200
		H.	$ 4,400
		I.	$12,000
		J.	$13,500
		K.	$15,000
		L.	$25,000
		M.	$27,500
		N.	$30,000

(5/93, Law, #2, (61-75), amended)

OTHER OBJECTIVE FORMAT SOLUTIONS

Solution 48-2 Creditor Claims

1. (T) In order to file a voluntary petition for bankruptcy, a debtor (Able) only need have unsecured debts of any amount. The debtor's solvency/ insolvency is irrelevant.

2. (F) If a debtor has fewer than 12 creditors owed unsecured debts, then one or more creditors may file an involuntary petition for bankruptcy against the debtor provided that the unsecured portion of the creditor/petitioner's claims is equal in the aggregate to at least $10,000. The unsecured amounts owed in the aggregate to Lake, Young and Thorn are only $9,500.

3. (T) If a debtor has fewer than 12 creditors owed unsecured debts, then one or more creditors may file an involuntary petition for bankruptcy against the debtor provided that the unsecured portion of the creditor's claims is equal in the aggregate to at least $10,000. Since Cole is owed $10,000 in unsecured debt, he can file the involuntary petition alone.

4. (F) A preferential transfer is a transfer of property or an interest in property that meets all the following criteria: (1) to or for the benefit of a creditor; (2) for or on account of an antecedent debt; (3) made while the debtor was insolvent; (4) made within 90 days of the bankruptcy filing; and (5) that enables the creditor to receive more in the bankruptcy distribution than it would have without the transfer. The payment to Vista Bank occurred more than 90 days after the bankruptcy filing, and thus would not qualify as a preferential transfer.

5. (T) A preferential transfer is a transfer of property or an interest in property that meets all the following criteria: (1) to or for the benefit of a creditor; (2) for or on account of an antecedent debt; (3) made while the debtor was insolvent; (4) made within 90 days of the bankruptcy filing; and (5) that enables the creditor to receive more in the bankruptcy distribution than it would have without the transfer. The payment to Owen meets all five of these requirements and thus would be set aside as a preferential transfer.

6. (F) A preferential transfer is a transfer of property or an interest in property that meets all the following criteria: (1) to or for the benefit of a creditor; (2) for or on account of an antecedent debt; (3) made while the debtor was insolvent; (4) made within 90 days of the bankruptcy filing; and (5) that enables the creditor to receive more in the bankruptcy distribution than it would have without the transfer. The purchase of the computer will not be set aside as a preferential transfer because it does not meet the antecedent debt requirement. The purchase would be regarded as a contemporaneous exchange for new value.

Solution 48-3 Creditor Claims

1. (Yes) A transfer is considered preferential if made between 90 days and 1 year before the filing date if the creditor at the time was an insider. Insiders are relatives, officers, directors, and controlling shareholders of the debtor. Mary Lake, the sister of one of Wren's directors, is considered an insider, and the transaction occurred on December 31, 1991, within a year of the petition date of April 15, 1992.

2. (No) A preferential transfer is a property transfer that meets all five of the following: (1) to or for the benefit of a creditor; (2) for or on account of an antecedent debt owed by the debtor; (3) made while the debtor was insolvent; (4) on or within 90 days before the date of bankruptcy filing; and (5) that enables the creditor to receive more than it would receive as a distributive share under a Chapter 7 liquidation. A donation to charity would not meet the five characteristics of a preferential transfer. Therefore, it would not be set aside.

3. (Yes) A preferential transfer is a property transfer that meets all five of the following: (1) to or for the benefit of a creditor; (2) for or on account of an antecedent debt owed by the debtor; (3) made while the debtor was insolvent; (4) on or within 90 days before the date of bankruptcy filing; and (5) that enables the creditor to receive more than it would receive as a distributive share under a Chapter 7 liquidation. The security agreement to Young covering Wren's office fixtures to secure a loan previously made by Young meets all five of these requirements and would be set aside.

4. (No) A preferential transfer is a property transfer that meets all five of the following: (1) to or for the benefit of a creditor; (2) for or on account of an antecedent debt owed by the debtor; (3) made while the debtor was insolvent; (4) on or within 90 days before the date of bankruptcy filing; and (5) that enables the creditor to receive more than it would receive as a distributive share under a Chapter 7 liquidation. The payment to Integral Appliance Corp. made on March 1, 1992 on a two-year note is considered a normal payment that did not have the intent of favoring one creditor over another.

5. (No) Wren's purchase from Safety would be considered a contemporaneous exchange for new value and not a voidable preferential transfer. When Wren paid $10,000 cash, Wren received a new alarm system. Thus, a contemporaneous exchange took place.

6. (B) Bankruptcy administrative expenses are second in the order of payment behind secured claims.

7. (E) The payment to Acme Office Cleaners for services for January, February, and March 1992 would be last in the order of payment because it represents a payment to a general unsecured creditor.

8. (A) The payment to Fifth Bank represents a secured claim; therefore, it would be first in the order of payment.

9. (D) The payment to the IRS represents 1990 federal income taxes and would be fourth in the order of payment.

10. (C) The payment to Joan Sims for March 1992 commissions represents wages of the bankrupt's employees ($4,000 maximum each) accrued within 3 months before the petition is filed, and would be third in the order of payment.

11. (J) As a secured creditor, TVN Computers, Inc. would be entitled to the proceeds from the sale of the collateral of $12,000. The remainder is considered as part of the nonpriority general creditors. There was enough to pay 50 cents on the dollar; therefore, TVN would get an additional $15,000 − $12,000 = $3,000 x 1/2 or $1,500, for a total of $13,500.

12. (M) As a secured creditor, Hart Manufacturing Corp. would be entitled to the proceeds from the sale of the inventory of $25,000. The remainder is considered as part of the nonpriority general creditors. There was enough to pay 50 cents on the dollar, therefore, Hart would get an additional $30,000 − $25,000 = $5,000 x 1/2 or $2,500, for a total of $27,500.

13. (G) Wages, salaries, or commissions earned by an individual employee of the debtor within 90 days before the date of the filing of the petition have a priority, but only to the extent of $4,000. Any excess is treated as a general claim. Therefore, Ted Smith would receive $4,000 plus 1/2 x ($4,400 − $4,000) for a total of $4,200.

14. (B) Payment to Power Electric Co. for electricity charges for January, February, and March 1992 represents an amount owed to a general unsecured creditor. Therefore, they would receive 1/2 x $600 = $300.

15. (D) Payment to Soft Office Supplies for supplies purchased in 1991 represents an amount owed to a general unsecured creditor. Therefore, Soft would receive 1/2 x $2000 = $1,000.

ESSAY QUESTIONS

Essay 48-4 (15 to 20 minutes)

Techno, Inc. is a computer equipment dealer. On February 3, 1992, Techno was four months behind in its payments to Allied Building Maintenance, Cleen Janitorial Services, Inc., and Jones and Associates, CPAs, all of whom provide monthly services to Techno. In an attempt to settle with these three creditors, Techno offered each of them a reduced lump-sum payment for the past due obligations and full payment for future services. These creditors rejected Techno's offer and on April 9, 1992, Allied, Cleen, and Jones filed an involuntary petition in bankruptcy against Techno under the provisions of Chapter 7 of the Federal Bankruptcy Code. At the time of the filing, Techno's liability to the three creditors was $9,100, all of which was unsecured.

Techno, at the time of the filing, had liabilities of $229,000 (owed to 23 creditors) and assets with a fair market value of $191,000. During the entire year before the bankruptcy filing, Techno's liabilities exceeded the fair market value of its assets.

Included in Techno's liabilities was an installment loan payable to Dollar Finance Co., properly secured by cash registers and other equipment.

The bankruptcy court approved the involuntary petition.

On April 21, 1992, Dollar filed a motion for relief from automatic stay in bankruptcy court claiming it was entitled to take possession of the cash registers and other equipment securing its loan. Dollar plans to sell these assets immediately and apply the proceeds to the loan balance. The fair market value of the collateral is less than the loan balance and Dollar claims it is entitled to receive a priority distribution, before distribution to unsecured creditors, for the amount Techno owes Dollar less the proceeds from the sale of the collateral.

During the course of the bankruptcy proceeding, the following transactions were disclosed:

- On October 6, 1991, Techno paid its president $9,900 as repayment of an unsecured loan made to the corporation on September 18, 1989.
- On February 19, 1992, Techno paid $1,150 to Aiexis Computers, Inc. for eight color computer monitors. These monitors were delivered to Techno on February 9, 1992, and placed in inventory.
- On January 12, 1992, Techno bought a new delivery truck from Maple Motors for $7,900 cash. On the date of the bankruptcy filing, the truck was worth $7,000.

Required:

Answer the following questions and give the reasons for your conclusions.

a. What circumstances had to exist to allow Allied, Cleen, and Jones to file an involuntary bankruptcy petition against Techno?

b. 1. Will Dollar's motion for relief be granted?
2. Will Dollar's claim for priority be approved by the bankruptcy court?

c. Are the payments to Techno's president, Alexis, and Maple preferential transfers?

(5/92, Law, #4)

Essay 48-5 (15 to 20 minutes)

On July 1, 1986, Mix was petitioned by Able into bankruptcy under the liquidation provisions of the Bankruptcy Code. Able and Baker are unsecured creditors of Mix, owed $20,000 and $40,000 respectively. Mix also owes Carr $80,000, secured by a valid perfected security interest in bankruptcy on Mix's machinery, valued at $20,000. Mix has no other debts, except for 1986 federal income taxes.

Shortly after the filing of the petition Lang was appointed trustee in Mix's bankruptcy. In Lang's capacity as trustee, Lang:

- Engaged Ring & Co., CPAs, as the accountants for the bankruptcy estate.
- Included as part of the bankruptcy estate an inheritance that Mix became entitled to receive on December 15, 1986 and that Mix actually received on January 15, 1987.

Lang has sold the property in the estate (including the sale of Mix's machinery for $20,000, which Carr consented to) and now the sole asset of the estate is $60,000 cash. Lang wishes to distribute the $60,000 so as to satisfy the following claims and expenses of the estate:

- Unsecured claim for 1986
  federal income taxes $ 6,000
- Carr's claim   80,000
- Able's and Baker's claims   60,000
- Expenses necessary to maintain
  and sell the unsecured
  property of the estate   1,000
- Ring's fee for services rendered 3,000

There are no other claims.

Required:

Answer the following, setting forth reasons for any conclusions stated.

a. Under the facts, were the requirements necessary for the filing of a valid petition in bankruptcy met? Discuss.

b. Discuss whether Lang's actions in engaging Ring and including the inheritance in the bankruptcy estate were proper.

c. Indicate the order in which the $60,000 should be distributed to satisfy the claims and expenses of the bankruptcy estate, assuming all necessary court approvals have been obtained.   (11/87, Law, #3)

Essay 48-6 (15 to 20 minutes)

Ultra Corporation is engaged in the metal stamping business. On March 2, 1986, it filed a voluntary petition in bankruptcy seeking relief in the form of a liquidation of the business pursuant to Chapter 7 of the Bankruptcy Code. A trustee was appointed on March 10, 1986 and has commenced amassing the debtor's property. Much of Ultra's property was leased from various third parties. One of Ultra's punch presses was rented from Van Equipment

Rental and Sales Corporation under a 40-month lease arrangement.

The lease was heavily front loaded and provided for purchase of the punch press for $100 upon expiration of the lease. The fair market value of the punch press at the expiration of the lease is estimated at $4,500. Van failed to file a financing statement or its equivalent with respect to this lease. In addition, Ultra has a 15-year lease on a warehouse which has 13 years of its term remaining. Payments on the lease are current. Dann Corp. has offered to assume all obligations under the warehouse lease and to pay Ultra $8,000 for an assignment of that lease. There is no applicable state law affecting such an assignment and the lease itself is silent in this regard.

Specifically, the trustee in bankruptcy asserts that:

- The punch press lease is in essence a secured installment sales contract for which Van has an unperfected security interest and therefore the punch press should be included in the bankruptcy estate.
- As trustee she has the right to assume and assign to Dann Corp. the warehouse lease and include the $8,000 in the bankruptcy estate.

Required:

Answer the following, setting forth reasons for any conclusions stated.

a. Briefly discuss what property should be included in a corporate debtor's estate in bankruptcy.

b. What rights does a trustee in bankruptcy have regarding property leased by a debtor?

c. Are the trustee's assertions concerning the punch press lease and the warehouse lease correct?
                                    (11/86, Law, #5)

read answers of others

ESSAY SOLUTIONS

Solution 48-4 Involuntary Bankruptcy/Preferential Transfers

a. An involuntary bankruptcy petition may be filed against a debtor having **12 or more creditors** by **at least three creditors having unsecured claims of at least $10,000**, provided the debtor is **not paying its undisputed debts as they become due**.

b. **1.** Dollar's motion for relief will be granted. Dollar's claim that it is entitled to take possession of the collateral securing its loan is correct. Generally, a **secured creditor is allowed to take possession of its collateral if there is no equity in it** (that is, the debt balance exceeds the collateral's fair market value). Dollar would then be entitled to sell the collateral and apply the proceeds to the loan balance.

2. Dollar's claim that it is entitled to a **priority distribution** to the extent that the proceeds from the sale of its collateral are less than the loan balance will not be approved by the bankruptcy court. Dollar is entitled to the value of its collateral. As to any **deficiency**, Dollar will be treated as an **unsecured creditor**.

c. The payment to Techno's president would be regarded as a **preferential transfer**. Because the president is an **"insider,"** any payments made on the unsecured loan during the year preceding the bankruptcy filing would be considered a preferential transfer.

The payment to Alexis was not a preferential transfer because it was made **in the ordinary course of business** and under ordinary business terms.

The $7,900 payment to Maple for the truck was not a preferential transfer because it was not made on account of an **antecedent debt**, but as a **contemporaneous exchange for new value**.

Solution 48-5 Involuntary Bankruptcy--Requirements and Priority of Claims

a. Yes. The requirements necessary for the filing of a valid petition in bankruptcy have been met. An involuntary case may be commenced against a person by the filing of a petition where the aggregate amount of **unsecured claims is at least $10,000** and a sufficient number of creditors join in the filing of the petition. **Where there are fewer than 12 creditors, only one creditor need file the petition.** Under the facts, the petition was validly filed against Mix because Able's unsecured claim was more than $10,000 and because there were fewer than 12 creditors.

b. Lang's action as trustee to appoint Ring as the accountant for the bankruptcy estate was proper if such action was with the bankruptcy court's approval. **The trustee, with the court's approval, may engage professional persons** such as accountants on any reasonable terms and conditions.

Lang's inclusion of the inheritance in the property of the estate was also correct because property of the estate **includes property** that the debtor acquires or becomes entitled to acquire by inheritance **within 180 days after the filing of the petition**. By acquiring the right to inherit the property on December 15, 1986, which was less than 180 days after the filing of the petition on July 1, 1986, Mix's inheritance was properly included in the bankruptcy estate. Thus, Mix's receipt of the inheritance more than 180 days after the filing of the petition does not prevent the inclusion of the inheritance in the property of the estate.

c. The $60,000 will be distributed to satisfy the claims and expenses of the bankruptcy estate in the following order of priority:

1. Carr's claim to the extent of the sale proceeds of the machinery in which Carr had a **valid perfected security interest in bankruptcy**. $20,000

2. **Administrative expenses** including the expenses to maintain and sell the unsecured property of the estate ($1,000) and Ring's fee for services rendered ($3,000). 4,000

3. **Unsecured claim** for federal income taxes. 6,000

4. The unsecured claims of Able and Baker and the balance of Carr's claim, which have **equal priority**, will be **paid proportionately** as follows:

Able -- $\dfrac{\$\ 20,000}{\$120,000}$ x $30,000 5,000

Baker -- $\dfrac{\$\ 40,000}{\$120,000}$ x $30,000 10,000

Carr -- $\dfrac{\$\ 60,000}{\$120,000}$ x $30,000 15,000

Total distributions $ 60,000

Solution 48-6 Property of an Estate in Bankruptcy/ Trustee's Rights

a. In general, property of the estate in bankruptcy is comprised of **all legal and equitable interests of the debtor** in property **as of the commencement of the case**, i.e., the filing of the bankruptcy petition. Property of the estate also includes **post-petition income** or **proceeds from the property** of the estate after the commencement of the case. In addition, certain property acquired by the debtor or which the debtor becomes entitled to acquire within 180 days after the filing of the bankruptcy petition will be included in the estate. Also the estate may include certain property interests that can be recovered by the trustee from third parties.

b. The legal effect of the filing of a bankruptcy petition on a debtor's leases permits a bankruptcy trustee to:

1. **Assume** and **retain** the debtor's **leases**, or
2. **Assume** and **assign** such leases, or
3. **Reject** the debtor's leases.

A trustee's assumption or rejection of a lease is **subject to court approval**. In a Chapter 7 case, a lease is **deemed rejected by operation of law** unless it is assumed by the trustee **within 60 days** after the order for relief.

c. The trustee's first assertion with regard to the punch press lease is correct. Where the agreement entered into between the parties is a true lease and **not a disguised secured installment sales contract**, the subject matter of the lease will not be included in the bankruptcy estate.

Whether a lease is intended as security and thereby treated as a secured installment sales contract is determined by the facts of each case. The inclusion of an option to purchase does not of itself make the lease one intended as security. However, where by the terms of the lease the lessee will become or has the option to become the owner of the property for **no additional consideration** or for a **nominal consideration**, the lease is likely one intended for security.

Under the facts of our case, the option to purchase the punch press for $100 at the expiration of the lease would be deemed nominal consideration since the fair market value of the punch press at that time is estimated at $4,500. Thus, the lease is one intended as security and a security interest arises. In order for Van to perfect its security interest, it must file a financing statement. In this case, Van did not file a financing statement or its equivalent and thus Van has an **unperfected security interest** in the punch press. The UCC Article on Secured Transactions states that an unperfected security interest is **subordinate** to a person who becomes a **lien creditor** before the security interest is perfected. It defines, in part, a lien creditor as a trustee in bankruptcy from the date of the filing of the bankruptcy petition. In addition, the Bankruptcy Code gives the trustee in bankruptcy the **power to avoid any transfer of property of the debtor** that under nonbankruptcy law is **voidable as to a creditor who extended credit** and **obtained a judicial lien** on the date of the filing of the bankruptcy petition. Even though the UCC uses the term subordinate instead of voidable, a security interest that would be subordinate to a creditor that obtained a judicial lien on the date of the filing of the bankruptcy petition is **voidable by the trustee**. Thus, Van's unperfected security interest may be avoided by the trustee in bankruptcy and the punch press should be included in the debtor's estate in bankruptcy.

The trustee's second assertion is correct. Since there is no applicable state law affecting such an assignment and the lease itself is silent in this regard, the trustee may **assume** and **assign** the lease. In this case, the warehouse lease has a **substantial value** to other potential lessees and therefore due to the **favorable circumstances** indicated commands a substantial premium of $8,000. The debtor's estate in bankruptcy will receive this upon assignment (sale) of the lease to Dann.

NOTES

CHAPTER 49

SURETYSHIP

I. **Definitions** 49-2
   A. Exoneration 49-2
   B. Subrogation 49-2
   C. Surety Bond 49-2

II. **Nature and Characteristics of Suretyship** 49-2
   A. Suretyship Contract 49-2
   B. Three Party Relationship 49-2
   C. Suretyship vs. Guaranty 49-2
   D. Types of Guaranties 49-3
   E. Suretyship vs. Indemnification and Endorsement 49-3
   F. Characteristics of Surety Bonds 49-3

III. **Formation of Suretyship Contracts** 49-4
   A. Offer and Acceptance 49-4
   B. Consideration 49-4
   C. Statute of Frauds 49-4
   D. Capacity 49-4

IV. **Rights of the Creditors** 49-4
   A. Against the Debtor 49-4
   B. Against the Surety 49-5
   C. Against the Collateral 49-5

V. **Rights of the Surety** 49-5
   A. Before Payment 49-5
   B. After Payment 49-6

VI. **Defenses of the Surety** 49-6
   A. Defenses Which Are Derived From the Debtor 49-6
   B. Personal Defenses 49-7
   C. Defenses Arising out of the Creditor's Actions 49-7
   D. Defenses Not Available to the Surety 49-8

VII. **Co-Suretyship** 49-8
   A. Common Law Rules 49-8
   B. Right of Contribution Between Co-Sureties 49-8
   C. Co-Suretyship vs. Sub-Suretyship 49-9
   D. Release of a Co-Surety by the Creditor 49-9

CHAPTER 49

SURETYSHIP

I. Definitions

Action S — D.

A. <u>Exoneration</u>--An action by the surety against the debtor which seeks to force the debtor to pay his or her creditor. The surety must show that the debtor is wrongfully withholding assets sufficient to satisfy the debt.

B. <u>Subrogation</u>--The substitution of the surety, who has paid the debt of another, in place of the creditor to whom the debt was paid. Subrogation allows the surety to succeed to all of the creditor's rights against the debtor.

CR ← pay S — D

C. <u>Surety Bond</u>--A written acknowledgement of a duty to make good the performance by another of some obligation or responsibility.

II. Nature and Characteristics of Suretyship

A. <u>Suretyship Contract</u>--An agreement whereby a person secures the debt of another by assuring performance upon the debtor's default. In a broad sense, contracts of guarantors, indemnitors, and endorsers are forms of suretyship contracts.

B. <u>Three Party Relationship</u>--All suretyship contracts involve three persons: the principal debtor, the creditor, and the surety or guarantor.

   1. The <u>principal debtor</u> (<u>principal</u>) is the party who owes the ultimate burden of performing the obligation. The principal debtor owes a duty to both the creditor and surety.

   2. The <u>creditor</u> is the party to whom the obligation is owed and to whom the surety is bound.

   3. The <u>surety</u> is the party who agrees to be answerable for the obligation. The surety is primarily liable; i.e., his or her duty is not strictly conditioned on the default of the principal debtor. The surety is liable if the debtor fails to perform for any reason.

C. <u>Suretyship vs. Guaranty</u>--These two terms are often used interchangeably in law. However, they technically denote different contractual arrangements.

   1. A <u>suretyship contract</u> is generally created simultaneously with the primary contract and is considered part of the same transaction. Therefore, there is no need for separate consideration to support the suretyship contract. This follows because the consideration supporting the principal contract is deemed to also support the suretyship contract. The surety is primarily liable to the creditor without any demand first being made on the debtor after default.

   2. A <u>guaranty contract</u>, on the other hand, is generally created separately from the primary contract; it is considered to be an agreement distinct from the main contract. By virtue of the fact that there are two distinct agreements, there is usually a separate consideration supporting the guaranty. The guarantor's liability is secondary, or conditioned, on the default of the debtor. However, unless otherwise provided (a "collection guaranteed"), no demand need be made on the guarantor to activate his or her liability. Thus, from a mechanical point of view, guaranty liability may at times be activated merely by debtor default.

D.   Types of Guaranties

1.   A conditional guaranty subjects the creditor's right to proceed against the guarantor to some condition precedent. Usually, this means that the creditor must first exhaust his or her remedies against the principal debtor or must show that the pursuit of any remedies would be futile (e.g., guarantor of collection).

2.   An unconditional guaranty places no conditions on the right of the creditor to proceed against the guarantor. The guarantor is bound to perform when the debtor defaults (e.g., guarantor of payment).

3.   A temporary guaranty is limited by its terms to a specific duration or transaction.

4.   A continuing guaranty is not limited to any specific time period or number of transactions.

5.   A special guaranty is one addressed to a particular person.

6.   A general guaranty is extended to anyone who knows and relies on the contract of guaranty.

E.   Suretyship vs. Indemnification and Endorsement--These two terms describe agreements which are very similar to suretyship contracts.

1.   An indemnification contract is a direct, original, two party contract in which the indemnitor agrees to keep another harmless from a specific consequence. The indemnitor ordinarily has no right to reimbursement from the protected party. Most insurance contracts are indemnification contracts. Indemnity contracts are not within the Statute of Frauds, whereas suretyship and guaranty contracts are; this is due to the fact that surety and guaranty contracts are promises to answer for the debt or default of another.

2.   An endorsement contract creates only secondary liability on the part of the endorser. The endorser agrees to pay the holder of the instrument only after a demand has been made on the maker and notice of a dishonor is given to the endorser. An endorser is also liable for all warranties he or she makes to subsequent holders.

F.   Characteristics of Surety Bonds--A surety bond is a written acknowledgment of a duty to make good the performance by another of some obligation or responsibility. Surety bonds are usually issued by companies that, for a stated consideration, assume the risk of performance by the bonded party. Surety bonds are usually classified in the following manner:

1.   Performance or construction bonds guarantee the faithful performance of a contract. They are most often used in connection with supply and/or construction contracts. Courts have uniformly held that construction bonds cover the performance of the actual contract work. However, there is a split of authority on whether such bonds also cover payment of the construction workers' wages. For this reason, surety companies today also provide a payment bond.

2.   Fidelity bonds guarantee the faithful performance of duties by an employee. The surety has a right of subrogation if the employee commits any act in violation of the provisions, of the bond. Any significant change in the employee's duties may serve to release the surety from his or her obligation.

3.   Official bonds guarantee the faithful performance of duties by a public official. These bonds are often required by law for all public officials who administer public funds.

4.   Judicial bonds include all bonds used in judicial proceedings (for example, bail bonds or attachment bonds).

III. Formation of Suretyship Contracts

Generally, these contracts must contain all the elements of the traditional contract.

A. <u>Offer and Acceptance</u>--All suretyship contracts must have a valid offer and acceptance, but the acceptance need not always be by express notice to the surety.

1. In most jurisdictions, an <u>absolute guaranty</u> may be accepted without any formal notice. On the other hand, a <u>continuing guaranty</u> may usually be accepted only by an express notice.

2. An express notice is not necessary if circumstances exist whereby the nature of the transaction itself informs the guarantor of the acceptance. Additionally, an express notice of acceptance is not needed when the guarantor waives notice in the letter of guaranty, or when he or she enters into a guaranty agreement in exchange for an extension of time.

B. <u>Consideration</u>--When the surety contract is contemporaneous with the primary contract, there is no need for any separate consideration beyond that supporting the primary contract. When the surety contract is entered into subsequent to the primary contract, it must be supported by its own consideration.

C. <u>Statute of Frauds</u>--Generally, suretyship and guaranty contracts are agreements to "answer for" the debt of another, and thus they are within the Statute of Frauds. They must be in writing to be enforceable. There are two exceptions to this general rule:

1. Indemnification Contracts--Indemnification contracts (insurance contracts) are agreements to hold another harmless. They are outside the Statute of Frauds because they are two party contracts (not three party contracts as are surety agreements), and because they operate independently of any default by the principal debtor.

2. Primary Suretyship Contracts--Contracts which are entered into primarily for the benefit of the surety, rather than the debtor, are held to be outside the Statute of Frauds. For example, a del credere agent (a sales agent who guarantees the payment of his or her purchasers) is the primary beneficiary of his or her guaranty. His or her guaranty is not a ". . . promise to answer for the debt of another." Thus, it is not within the Statute.

D. <u>Capacity</u>--Generally, the rules that govern an individual's capacity to contract also govern the surety's capacity.

1. Partnerships--Unless specifically prohibited by the partnership agreement, a partnership has the capacity to enter into a suretyship contract.

2. Corporations--Ordinarily, corporations may not enter into suretyship contracts unless such powers are specifically authorized.

3. Partners--A partner does not have the power to bind the partnership to a suretyship contract unless that power is expressly authorized in the articles of co-partnership or a separate partnership agreement.

IV. Rights of the Creditors

A. <u>Against the Debtor</u>

1. Unless otherwise agreed, the creditor may proceed immediately against the debtor upon his or her default. There is no requirement that the creditor first allow the surety to make good.

2. In cases in which the debtor owes more than one debt, the creditor may apply any payment received to the debt of his or her choice. Thus, if two debts are owed and only one of which

is guaranteed, the creditor is free to apply funds solely towards the satisfaction of the unsecured debt.

B.   Against the Surety

1.   Unless otherwise agreed, the creditor may proceed immediately against the surety upon default. The surety is immediately liable, and there is no duty on the part of the creditor to first ask the debtor for payment or to notify the surety of the debtor's default.

2.   When the surety is a guarantor, a creditor usually must give notice of the debtor's default before proceeding against the guarantor.

C.   Against the Collateral

1.   Collateral Pledged With the Creditor

a.   If the debtor fully pays, the collateral must be returned.

b.   Upon default, the creditor is not bound to resort to the collateral; the creditor may proceed immediately against the surety.

c.   If the creditor chooses to resort to the collateral, any amount realized by its disposal, which is in excess of the amount due, must be returned to the debtor. If the collateral is insufficient, the creditor has the right to proceed against the debtor and the surety for the balance due. If the creditor holds collateral pledged by both the debtor and the surety, the creditor must first look to the debtor's collateral for satisfaction of the debt.

d.   If the creditor voluntarily surrenders or intentionally destroys the collateral he or she holds, the creditor reduces the surety's obligation by that amount.

e.   If the surety satisfies the principal debtor's obligation, the surety becomes subrogated to the creditor's rights in the collateral.

2.   Collateral Pledged With the Surety

a.   Creditor's Rights in the Collateral Before Default--Prior to default, the creditor has an interest in the collateral, even if both the primary debtor and the surety are solvent. Thus, the creditor may, if necessary, seek equitable relief to enjoin the surety from wasting, releasing, or otherwise impairing the collateral. This is true even when the collateral has been pledged with the intent that it only benefit the surety. Generally, the surety maintains possession of the collateral as a trustee for the benefit of the creditor.

b.   Creditor's Rights in Collateral After Default--Upon default, the creditor may use the collateral to satisfy the debtor's duty, or the creditor may proceed directly against the surety on his or her promise. After the debt is paid in full, the surety may use the collateral to satisfy his or her right to reimbursement.

V. Rights of the Surety

A.   Before Payment

1.   A surety may request the creditor to proceed first against the debtor. The creditor is not normally bound to do so, and the creditor's failure to try to enforce the debt against the debtor will not discharge the surety's obligation. However, when the suretyship contract is conditional, or whenever the surety requests the creditor to proceed against the debtor, the surety is entitled to any damages caused by the creditor's noncompliance.

2. A surety may request the creditor to resort first to any collateral security if he or she can show that the collateral is seriously depreciating in value, or if he or she can show undue hardship will otherwise result.

3. Exoneration--A surety may seek exoneration from the debtor or co-sureties. A surety does this by bringing a suit in equity to require the debtor or co-sureties to pay so that he or she will not be required to satisfy his or her obligation.

B. <u>After Payment</u>

1. Reimbursement or Indemnity--This is the right of the surety to recover from the principal debtor for the obligation performed by the surety. The surety's rights under various circumstances are as follows:

    a. When the principal debtor has consented to the retention of a surety, the surety may recover from the debtor in the amount that the surety has actually paid. The statute of limitations on such actions runs from the date of payment and <u>not</u> the date of default.

    b. When the surety is retained without the consent of the principal debtor, the surety is entitled to recover from the debtor only to the extent that the debtor has been unjustly enriched.

    c. When the surety's payment is voluntary, the surety is not entitled to reimbursement. This situation may arise when both the surety and the debtor have a legal defense, such as the statute of limitations, and the surety voluntarily performs.

2. Subrogation is the surety's right to succeed to the rights of the creditor once the surety has made good on the debtor's obligation. Thus, the surety has the right to enforce any lien, pledge, or mortgage securing the principal debt to the extent that an excess exists after the creditor has been satisfied.

3. Contribution--A surety has a right of contribution against co-sureties (see VII., below).

VI. Defenses of the Surety

A. <u>Defenses Which Are Derived From the Debtor</u>--The debtor's defenses, except for personal defenses, are generally available to the surety.

1. Fraud or Duress--If a creditor obtains the debtor's promise by use of fraud, duress, misrepresentation, concealment, etc., and the debtor elects to rescind, then the surety may assert the defense of fraud. If the debtor affirms the contract, the surety is likewise bound. Additionally, if the creditor uses fraud and the surety knows of the fraud, he or she may not avail himself or herself of that defense.

2. Consideration--A material failure by the creditor to render the agreed-upon consideration discharges the surety's liability.

3. Proper Tender of Performance--A proper tender of performance by the debtor discharges the surety even though it may not discharge the debtor.

4. Impossibility or Illegality--If the debtor's performance is impossible because of illegality or otherwise, the surety's liability is discharged.

5. Performance--If the debtor properly performs, meeting all requirements of the contract, the surety is discharged.

[handwritten: forgery, fraud and duress, illegality — real def. will discharge surety, but not personal defense — incapacity, bankruptcy, death of]

B. **Personal Defenses**

1. Suretyship Contract Is Void--For example, if the signature is a forgery, the suretyship contract would be void.

2. Contract Is Unenforceable Due to the Failure of a Necessary Element--Recall that a suretyship contract must have all the elements of a normal contract. Review III. Formation of Suretyship Contracts, above, for discussion of the particular problems caused by acceptance, consideration, and the Statute of Frauds.

3. Fraud or Duress--If the creditor obtains the surety's promise through fraud, duress, misrepresentation, etc., the contract is voidable by the surety. If the principal debtor obtains the surety's promise through fraud, the contract is not voidable unless the creditor knew of the fraud.

4. Failure of the Creditor to Disclose Facts Material to Determining the Surety's Risk--The creditor must disclose all material facts concerning the debtor and bearing upon his or her ability to perform. If the creditor fails to notify the surety of any material facts in his or her possession, the surety may avoid liability.

5. Legal Remedies Render the Contract Unenforceable--For example, if the statute of limitations has run, the surety may avoid liability.

C. **Defenses Arising out of the Creditor's Actions**

1. Release of Collateral--Any release of collateral by the creditor before satisfaction of the debtor's obligation, releases the surety to the extent of the collateral released.

2. Release of a Co-Surety--Rights and duties under a co-suretyship agreement are discussed in VII., below.

3. Release of the Principal Debtor--A release of the principal without the consent of the surety releases the surety, unless the creditor specifically reserves his or her rights against the surety. An agreement to release a debtor while retaining rights against a surety is treated as a covenant not to sue rather than a release. When a debtor fraudulently effects his or her release, the surety is excused only to the extent that he or she has been prejudiced.

4. Alteration of the Principal Contract--Under old common law, any variance in the suretyship contract, no matter how minor, discharged the surety. The prevailing rule today is that only material changes in the principal contract will discharge the surety.

    a. The following is a list of material variances which will cause a discharge:

        (1) A change in the identity of the debtor.

        (2) An extension of the time for payment or other change in the amount, rate, or manner of payment.

        (3) A substantial change in the duties of the debtor (for example, from a teller to loan officer).

        (4) A surrender or impairment of the security.

    b. Consent by the surety to any variation waives the right to release.

c.   The modern trend is to make a distinction between a gratuitous and a compensated surety. Current cases generally hold that only a variation which is injurious to a compensated surety will discharge him or her.

D.   <u>Defenses Not Available to the Surety</u>--These situations, which do not discharge the surety's duty to perform, have been mentioned elsewhere throughout the chapter and are repeated here in summary.

   1.   Any personal defenses of the debtor or co-surety, such as death, insolvency, or incapacity, are not available to the surety. (However, personal defenses of the surety against the creditor will provide the surety with a defense to the suretyship agreement.)

   2.   The surety's own insolvency will not discharge his or her estate's liability.

   3.   Generally, the surety is not discharged because the creditor either failed to proceed against the debtor or failed to notify the surety of the debtor's default.

   4.   Failure on the part of the creditor to resort to any collateral security that he or she holds will not discharge the surety. A creditor's surrender or waste of the collateral may discharge the surety in the amount that the security is depreciated.

   5.   Fraudulent representations by the debtor (without knowledge of the creditor) to the surety to induce a suretyship agreement will not provide the surety a defense against the creditor.

VII. Co-Suretyship

When two or more sureties are liable on the same obligation to the same creditor, the obligation is shared by each surety. Generally, the rights and duties as between co-sureties are fixed by the contract.

A.   <u>Common Law Rules</u>--In the absence of any agreement to the contrary, the following rules apply:

   1.   Generally, co-sureties are jointly and severally liable to the creditor; however, as between co-sureties, each is individually liable only in the amount that has been personally guaranteed.

   2.   Two or more persons may be co-sureties even if they do not know of each other's existence and even though they are bound for different amounts. They need only share the same burden.

B.   <u>Right of Contribution Between Co-Sureties</u>

   1.   Each co-surety has a right of contribution from his or her co-sureties to the extent he or she has paid more than his or her proportionate share. This amount is determined as follows:

$$\frac{\textit{Dollar amount of liability assumed by co-surety}}{\textit{Total dollar amount of liability assumed by all co-sureties}} \times \textit{Dollar amount of liability paid by co-surety} = \textit{Dollar amount of contribution entitled each co-surety}$$

Example 1

A, B, and C are co-sureties of a $25,000 debt owed by D. A is liable for $5,000, B for $8,000, and C for $12,000. After making payments of $5,000, D defaults on the debt and C pays the remaining $20,000. C's proportionate share of the liability paid is $9,600; he is entitled to recover a total of $10,400: $4,000 from A and $6,400 from B. These amounts are computed as follows:

Co-surety A: ($5,000 ÷ $25,000)   x $20,000 = $4,000

Co-surety B: ($8,000 ÷ $25,000)   x $20,000 = $6,400

Co-surety C: ($12,000 ÷ $25,000)   x $20,000 = $9,600

---

2.   Each co-surety is entitled to share in any collateral pledged to any of the co-sureties in proportion to his or her liabilities.

Example 2

Assume the same facts as in Example 1, above, except that C is in possession of collateral pledged by D worth $12,000. Since C has assumed 48% of the total amount of the debt, she is entitled to $5,760 of the collateral. A would be entitled to 20%, or $2,400, and B would be entitled to 32%, or $3,840.

C.   Co-Suretyship vs. Sub-Suretyship--A sub-suretyship usually requires an express agreement. The principal surety is primarily liable and bears the entire burden of performance. The sub-surety is in effect a surety for the principal surety.

D.   Release of a Co-Surety by the Creditor--Unless the creditor specifically reserves his or her rights, a release of a co-surety releases the other co-sureties in the amount of the released surety's share.

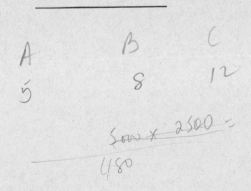

NOTES

Surety needs consideration

CHAPTER 49—SURETYSHIP

Problem 49-1 MULTIPLE CHOICE QUESTIONS (30 to 35 minutes)

1. A party contracts to guaranty the collection of the debts of another. As a result of the guaranty, which of the following statements is correct?
   a. The creditor may proceed against the guarantor without attempting to collect from the debtor.
   b. The guaranty must be in writing.
   c. The guarantor may use any defenses available to the debtor.
   d. The creditor must be notified of the debtor's default by the guarantor. (5/94, Law, #24, 4779)

2. If a debtor defaults and the debtor's surety satisfies the obligation, the surety acquires the right of
   a. Subrogation.
   b. Primary lien.
   c. Indemnification.
   d. Satisfaction. (11/89, Law, #21, 0639)

3. Which of the following events will release a noncompensated surety from liability?
   a. Release of the principal debtor's obligation by the creditor but with the reservation of the creditor's rights against the surety.
   b. Modification by the principal debtor and creditor of their contract that materially increases the surety's risk of loss.
   c. Filing of an involuntary petition in bankruptcy against the principal debtor.
   d. Insanity of the principal debtor at the time the contract was entered into with the creditor. (5/94, Law, #25, 4780)

4. Which of the following defenses by a surety will be effective to avoid liability?
   a. Lack of consideration to support the surety undertaking.
   b. Insolvency in the bankruptcy sense by the debtor.
   c. Incompetency of the debtor to make the contract in question.
   d. Fraudulent statements by the principal debtor which induced the surety to assume the obligation and which were unknown to the creditor. (5/82, Law, #23, 9911)

5. Sorus and Ace have agreed, in writing, to act as guarantors of collection on a debt owed by Pepper to Towns, Inc. The debt is evidenced by a promissory note. If Pepper defaults, Towns will be entitled to recover from Sorus and Ace unless

   a. Sorus and Ace are in the process of exercising their rights against Pepper.
   b. Sorus and Ace prove that Pepper was insolvent at the time the note was signed.
   c. Pepper dies before the note is due.
   d. Towns has **not** attempted to enforce the promissory note against Pepper. (11/90, Law, #26, 0637)

6. Which of the following defenses would a surety be able to assert successfully to limit the surety's liability to a creditor?
   a. A discharge in bankruptcy of the principal debtor.
   b. A personal defense the principal debtor has against the creditor.
   c. The incapacity of the surety.
   d. The incapacity of the principal debtor. (11/94, Law, #29, 5106)

7. Queen paid Pax & Co. to become the surety on a loan which Queen obtained from Squire. The loan is due and Pax wishes to compel Queen to pay Squire. Pax has not made any payments to Squire in its capacity as Queen's surety. Pax will be most successful if it exercises its right to
   a. Reimbursement (Indemnification).
   b. Contribution.
   c. Exoneration.
   d. Subrogation. (11/86, Law, #28, 0642)

8. Which of the following rights does a surety have?

	Right to compel the creditor to collect from the principal debtor	Right to compel the creditor to proceed against the principal debtor's collateral
a.	Yes	Yes
b.	Yes	No
c.	No	Yes
d.	No	No

(11/94, Law, #30, 5107)

9. Which of the following acts will always result in the total release of a compensated surety?
   a. The creditor extends the principal debtor's time to pay.
   b. The principal debtor's performance is tendered.
   c. The place of payment is changed.
   d. The principal debtor's obligation is partially released. (11/92, Law, #27, 3109)

10. Ingot Corp. lent Flange $50,000. At Ingot's request, Flange entered into an agreement with Quill and West for them to act as compensated co-sureties on the loan in the amount of $100,000 each. Ingot released West without Quill's or Flange's consent, and Flange later defaulted on the loan. Which of the following statements is correct?

a. Quill will be liable for 50% of the loan balance.
b. Quill will be liable for the entire loan balance.
c. Ingot's release of West will have **no** effect on Flange's and Quill's liability to Ingot.
d. Flange will be released for 50% of the loan balance. (11/94, Law, #31, 5108)

11. Green was unable to repay a loan from State Bank when due. State refused to renew the loan unless Green provided an acceptable surety. Green asked Royal, a friend, to act as surety on the loan. To induce Royal to agree to become a surety, Green fraudulently represented Green's financial condition and promised Royal discounts on merchandise sold at Green's store. Royal agreed to act as surety and the loan was renewed. Later, Green's obligation to State was discharged in Green's bankruptcy. State wants to hold Royal liable. Royal may avoid liability

a. If Royal can show that State was aware of the fraudulent representations.
b. If Royal was an uncompensated surety.
c. Because the discharge in bankruptcy will prevent Royal from having a right of reimbursement.
d. Because the arrangement was void at the inception. (5/95, Law, #26, 5360)

12. Wright cosigned King's loan from Ace Bank. Which of the following events would release Wright from the obligation to pay the loan?

a. Ace seeking payment of the loan only from Wright.
b. King is granted a discharge in bankruptcy.
c. Ace is paid in full by King's spouse.
d. King is adjudicated mentally incompetent. (5/95, Law, #27, 5361)

13. A distinction between a surety and a co-surety is that only a co-surety is entitled to

a. Reimbursement (Indemnification).
b. Subrogation.
c. Contribution. only to Co-Surety
d. Exoneration. (11/92, Law, #28, 3110)

14. West promised to make Noll a loan of $180,000 if Noll obtained sureties to secure the loan.

Noll entered into an agreement with Carr, Gray, and Pine to act as co-sureties on his loan from West. The agreement between Noll and the co-sureties provided for compensation to be paid to each of the co-sureties. It further indicated that the maximum liability of each co-surety would be as follows: Carr, $180,000; Gray, $60,000; and Pine, $120,000. West accepted the commitment of the sureties and made the loan to Noll. After paying nine installments totaling $90,000, Noll defaulted. Gray's debts (including his surety obligation to West on the Noll loan) were discharged in bankruptcy. Subsequently, Carr properly paid the entire debt outstanding of $90,000. What amounts may Carr recover from the co-sureties?

	Gray	Pine
a.	$0	$30,000
b.	$0	$36,000
c.	$15,000	$30,000
d.	$30,000	$30,000	(11/85, Law, #32, 9911)

15. Nash, Owen, and Polk are co-sureties with maximum liabilities of $40,000, $60,000 and $80,000, respectively. The amount of the loan on which they have agreed to act as co-sureties is $180,000. The debtor defaulted at a time when the loan balance was $180,000. Nash paid the lender $36,000 in full settlement of all claims against Nash, Owen, and Polk. The total amount that Nash may recover from Owen and Polk is

a. $0.
b. $ 24,000.
c. $ 28,000.
d. $140,000. (11/93, Law, #25, 4322)

16. Ivor borrowed $420,000 from Lear Bank. At Lear's request, Ivor entered into an agreement with Ash, Kane, and Queen for them to act as co-sureties on the loan. The agreement between Ivor and the co-sureties provided that the maximum liability of each co-surety was: Ash, $84,000; Kane, $126,000; and Queen, $210,000. After making several payments, Ivor defaulted on the loan. The balance was $280,000. If Queen pays $210,000 and Ivor subsequently pays $70,000, what amounts may Queen recover from Ash and Kane?

a. $0 from Ash and $0 from Kane.
b. $42,000 from Ash and $63,000 from Kane.
c. $70,000 from Ash and $70,000 from Kane.
d. $56,000 from Ash and $84,000 from Kane. (11/92, Law, #26, 3108)

Solution 49-1 MULTIPLE CHOICE ANSWERS

Surety Contracts and Creditor's Rights

1. **(b)** The Statute of Frauds requires that all promises to be liable for the debt of another be in writing; thus, in order for the guarantor to be liable the agreement must be in writing and signed by the guarantor. A guarantor has secondary liability, and thus the creditor must attempt to collect from the debtor first. Although a guarantor may use some defenses available to the debtor, the debtor's lack of capacity, or bankruptcy, are defenses personal to the debtor and thus not available to a guarantor. It is not necessary that the guarantor notify the creditor of the debtor's default.

2. **(a)** Once the surety pays the debtor's obligation to the creditor, the surety has a right of subrogation. Subrogation is the surety's right to succeed to the rights of the creditor once the surety has made good on the debtor's obligation. Some might argue that answer (c) is also correct because once the surety pays the debtor's obligation, the surety has a right of reimbursement (indemnity) from the debtor (debtor must now pay the surety), but when the surety's payment is voluntary he is not entitled to reimbursement. There are no rules such as those in answers (b) and (d).

3. **(b)** The general rule of law is that a material change in the suretyship contract will release a noncompensated surety from liability. The release of the principal debtor by the creditor will release the surety as well, unless the creditor specifically reserves his/her rights against the surety. The bankruptcy of the principal debtor is not a defense available to a surety. The principal debtor's lack of capacity is not a defense available to a surety.

4. **(a)** A suretyship agreement is a contract which must be supported by consideration. When the suretyship agreement is contemporaneous with the primary contract, there is no need for separate consideration. The surety may exercise any real defenses on the contract which are available to the debtor. Thus, fraud, duress, illegality, forgery, etc., will discharge both surety and debtor. However, the surety may not rely on the debtor's personal defenses (e.g., incapacity, insolvency, or death) to avoid the suretyship obligation. The surety is also discharged from liability if the surety agreement was procured by duress or fraudulent misrepresentation by the *creditor*. Thus, if the creditor fraudulently contracts with the debtor or fraudulently procures the suretyship agreement itself, the agreement is voidable. However, if the debtor procures the suretyship agreement by fraudulent misrepresentation, the surety remains liable to the creditor.

Rights and Defenses of the Surety

5. **(d)** If a suretyship problem involves a "guarantor of collection," the creditor is required to proceed against the debtor first, and only when the creditor is unable to collect from the debtor, is the creditor allowed to go after the surety. In this problem, the surety is a "guarantor of collection." Thus, the creditor (Towns) must proceed against the debtor (Pepper) prior to proceeding against Sorus and/or Ace.

6. **(c)** A surety may not avail him-/her-/itself of any personal defenses of the debtor against the creditor, such as the debtor's incapacity or bankruptcy. The incapacity of the surety, however, is a personal defense of the surety against the creditor and can be asserted successfully to limit the surety's liability to the creditor.

7. **(c)** The right of exoneration allows a surety to bring a suit in equity against the debtor in order to force the debtor to pay the matured debt so that the surety will not be required to satisfy the obligation. Answer (a) refers to the surety's right to recover from the debtor after the surety has paid the debt. Answer (b) describes the surety's right to recover from any co-surety to the extent the surety has paid more than his proportionate share. Subrogation is the surety's right to succeed to the rights of the creditor once the surety has satisfied the debtor's obligation.

8. **(d)** A surety (as opposed to a guarantor) has primary liability to the creditor, and thus does not have the right to either compel the creditor to collect from the principal debtor or to proceed against the principal debtor's collateral.

9. **(b)** A proper tender of performance by the debtor discharges the surety even though it may not discharge the debtor. Generally, a change or alteration in the contract does not discharge a *compensated* surety, unless the change is injurious to the surety. Answers (a), (c), and (d) do not represent changes which would normally be considered injurious to the surety.

10. **(a)** Unless a creditor specifically preserves his/her/its rights, a release of a cosurety releases the other cosureties in the amount of the released surety's share. Thus, Quill will only be liable for 50%

of the loan balance. Release of a co-surety will have no effect on the debtor's liability.

11. (a) If a creditor obtains a surety's promise through fraud, the contract is voidable by the surety. If the principal debtor obtains the surety's promise through fraud, the contract is <u>not</u> voidable unless the creditor knew of the fraud. Thus, if Royal can show that State was aware of the fraud, Royal will have a defense against liability. The fact that Royal was an uncompensated surety will not relieve him or her of liability. The debtor's discharge in bankruptcy is a risk the surety assumes and will have no affect on the surety's liability. There is nothing to indicate that the arrangement was void at its inception.

12. (c) If the debtor, or someone acting on behalf of the debtor, fully performs all requirements of the contract, the surety is discharged. Thus, if King's spouse satisfies the debt to Ace, Wright will be released from liability. A surety has primary liability upon the debtor's default. Therefore, the creditor may seek payment exclusively from the surety. The debtor's discharge in bankruptcy is a risk the surety assumes, as is the debtor's adjudication of mental incompetence. Neither releases the surety from liability.

Co-suretyship

13. (c) The legal rights of a surety and a co-surety are identical, because both are sureties. A surety is called a co-surety when two or more sureties are liable on the same obligation. Thus, only a co-surety has a right to *contribution*, which allows him/her to recover from the co-sureties amounts paid in excess of his/her proportionate share. Both sureties and co-sureties are entitled to reimbursement from the debtor if the surety pays the obligation. The right of subrogation (the right to succeed to the creditor's rights against the principal debtor) applies to all sureties and co-sureties. The right of exoneration applies to all sureties and co-sureties. This right allows the surety to compel the creditor to take action against the debtor in order to collect the debt. If the creditor fails to proceed against the debtor, the surety is exonerated from the liability to the extent he or she is injured by the creditor's failure to proceed.

14. (b) Each co-surety has a right of contribution from his/her co-sureties to the extent he/she has paid more than his/her proportionate share. However, in this situation, Gray's obligation has been released through his bankruptcy. Therefore, Carr's and Pine's obligations must be computed based upon the proportionate amount that each of the two are now liable for. The two of them are co-sureties of an aggregate amount of $300,000, with Carr's proportionate share being 60% ($180,000 ÷ $300,000) and Pine's share being 40% ($120,000 ÷ $300,000). Since Carr paid all of the $90,000 defaulted amount, he is entitled to receive 40% of that amount, or $36,000, from Pine.

15. (c) When there are two or more sureties (co-sureties), the right of contribution requires that a surety who pays more than his or her proportionate share on a debtor's default, may recover from the co-sureties the amount paid above his or her obligation. Nash paid $36,000 in full settlement of the claims against the co-sureties. To determine each co-surety's proportionate share of the $36,000 liability, look at their maximum liabilities under the surety contract. Then divide the liability among the co-sureties according to their respective pro rata share in the surety contract. Nash had a maximum liability of $40,000 on a surety contract with total liability of $180,000. Nash's share of the liability is $8,000 ($40,000 / $180,000 × $36,000 = $8,000). Therefore, Nash may recover from Owen and Polk, the co-sureties, the amount by which he overpaid his obligation, $28,000 ($36,000 − $8,000 = $28,000).

16. (b) The right of contribution arises when one co-surety, in performance of the principal debtor's obligation, pays more than his/her proportionate share of the total liability. The right of contribution allows the performing co-surety to receive reimbursement from the other co-sureties for their pro-rata shares of the liability. Queen paid his maximum liability of $210,000, or 50% of the debt; then Ivor paid $70,000, reducing the balance to $210,000. Ash's liability was $84,000 representing 20%, so Queen may collect 20% of the remainder, or $42,000 from Ash. Kane's liability was $126,000 representing 30%, so Queen may collect $63,000 from Kane.

PERFORMANCE BY SUBTOPICS

Each category below parallels a subtopic covered in Chapter 49. Record the number and percentage of questions you correctly answered in each subtopic area.

Surety Contracts and Creditor's Rights

Question #	Correct √
1	
2	
3	
4	
# Questions	4
# Correct	_____
% Correct	_____

Rights and Defenses of the Surety

Question #	Correct √
5	
6	
7	
8	
9	
10	
11	
12	
# Questions	8
# Correct	_____
% Correct	_____

Co-suretyship

Question #	Correct √
13	
14	
15	
16	
# Questions	4
# Correct	_____
% Correct	_____

ESSAY QUESTION

Essay 49-2 (15 to 20 minutes)

Hardaway Lending, Inc., had a 4-year $800,000 callable loan to Superior Metals, Inc., outstanding. The loan was callable at the end of each year upon Hardaway's giving 60 days written notice. Two and one-half years remained of the four years. Hardaway reviewed the loan and decided that Superior Metals was no longer a prime lending risk and it therefore decided to call the loan. The required written notice was sent to and received by Superior 60 days prior to the expiration of the second year. Merriweather, Superior's chief executive officer and principal shareholder, requested Hardaway to continue the loan at least for another year. Hardaway agreed, provided that an acceptable commercial surety would guarantee $400,000 of the loan and Merriweather would personally guarantee repayment in full. These conditions were satisfied and the loan was permitted to continue.

The following year the loan was called and Superior defaulted. Hardaway released the commercial surety but retained its rights against Merriweather and demanded that Merriweather pay the full amount of the loan. Merriweather refused, asserting the following:

- There was no consideration for his promise. The loan was already outstanding and he personally received nothing.
- Hardaway must first proceed against Superior before it can collect from Merriweather.
- Hardaway had released the commercial surety, thereby releasing Merriweather.

Required:

Answer the following, setting forth reasons for any conclusions stated.

Discuss the validity of each of Merriweather's assertions. (11/80, Law, #3a)

ESSAY SOLUTION

Solution 49-2   Consideration/Liability of Debtor and Surety

The first two defenses asserted by Merriweather are invalid. The third defense is partially valid.

Consideration on Hardaway's part consisted of **foregoing the right to call** the Superior Metals loan. The fact that the loan was already outstanding is irrelevant. By permitting the loan to remain outstanding for **an additional year** instead of calling it, Hardaway **relinquished a legal right**, which is **adequate consideration** for Merriweather's surety promise. **Consideration need not pass to the surety**; in fact, it usually primarily benefits the principal debtor.

There is no requirement that the creditor first proceed against the debtor before it can proceed against the surety, unless the surety undertaking **expressly provides such a condition**. Basic to the usual surety undertaking is the **right of the creditor to proceed immediately against the surety**. Essentially, that is the reason for the surety.

Hardaway's release of the commercial surety from its $400,000 surety undertaking **partially released** Merriweather. The release had the legal effect of **impairing Merriweather's right of contribution against its co-surety** (the commercial surety). Thus, Merriweather is **released to the extent of 1/3** [$400,000 (commercial surety's guarantee) ÷ $1,200,000 (the aggregate of the co-sureties' guarantees)] of the principal amount ($800,000), or $266,667.

CHAPTER 50

AGENCY

I. **General Characteristics** 50-2
   A. Definitions 50-2
   B. Consensual Relationship 50-2
   C. Contractual Arrangement 50-2
   D. Fiduciary Relationship 50-2

II. **Capacity** 50-2
   A. To Be a Principal..50-2
   B. To Be an Agent 50-3

III. **Types of Agents** 50-3
   A. General or Special 50-3
   B. Sub-Agent 50-3
   C. Gratuitous Agent 50-3
   D. Agency Coupled With an Interest 50-3
   E. Del Credere Agent 50-3
   F. Exclusive Agent 50-3
   G. Factor..50-3

IV. **Creation of the Agency Relationship** 50-4
   A. By Appointment..50-4
   B. By Approval or Ratification..50-4
   C. By Operation of Law 50-5

V. **Authority of the Agent to Bind the Principal** 50-5
   A. Agent's Authority 50-5
   B. Apparent or Ostensible Authority 50-5
   C. Agent's Authority With Respect to Notice, Knowledge, and Admissions 50-6

VI. **Liability of the Principal for Torts of the Agent**...50-6
   A. Respondeat Superior 50-6
   B. Liability of the Principal for the Crimes of the Agent 50-6

VII. **Contractual Liability of the Principal to Third Parties** 50-7
   A. Disclosed Principal...50-7
   B. Partially Disclosed Principal 50-7
   C. Undisclosed Principal...50-7

VIII. **Liability of the Agent to Third Parties** 50-7
   A. Agent's Liability for Torts...50-7
   B. Agent's Liability on Contracts 50-7

IX. **Duties Between Principal and Agent**..50-8
   A. Principal's Duties Owed to the Agent...50-8
   B. Duties of the Agent to the Principal..50-8

X. **Termination of the Agency Relationship** 50-9
   A. Methods...50-9
   B. Notice..50-10

CHAPTER 50

AGENCY

II. General Characteristics

A. <u>Definitions</u>

1. <u>Independent Contractor</u>--One who contracts to do a particular job for another. An independent contractor is subject to the control or supervision of his or her employer only as to the result; that is, the independent contractor works according to his or her own methods.

2. <u>Respondeat Superior</u>--A maxim which means that a master is liable in certain cases for the wrongful acts of his or her servant, and a principal is liable for the wrongs of his or her agent. Under this doctrine, the master is responsible for want of care on the servant's part toward those to whom the master owes a duty of care, provided the servant's failure to exercise due care occurred during the course of that servant's employment.

3. <u>Servant</u>--One who is in the employ of another (the master). A servant's physical conduct in the performance of his or her work is controlled or is subject to the right of control by the master. The servant has no authority to legally bind the master.

B. <u>Consensual Relationship</u>--Agency is a consensual relationship whereby one person, the agent, agrees to act on behalf and under the control of another, the principal. An agent has the authority to represent the principal in contractual matters so as to affect the legal relationships between the principal and third parties.

C. <u>Contractual Arrangement</u>--When an agency arises from a contractual arrangement, as it normally does, the law of contracts applies. However, agency may arise solely from the consent of the principal to have the agent represent him or her.

D. <u>Fiduciary Relationship</u>--Agency is a fiduciary relationship. An agent acting for the benefit of the principal is distinguished from a servant and an independent contractor.

II. Capacity

A. <u>To Be a Principal</u>

1. A principal must have sufficient legal capacity to consent to the agency.

   a. Infants may appoint agents in most jurisdictions and may <u>void</u> the appointment of an agent, <u>unless</u> that agent acts as an agent for securing necessities (food, clothing, shelter, education).

   b. Insane persons' appointments of agents are <u>voidable</u> if made prior to judicial determination of insanity and are <u>void</u> if made after such judicial determination.

2. Marriage does not prevent spouses from acting as principal and agent for each other.

3. Corporations must act through agents; partnerships, on the other hand, may act through partners or through outside agents. Unincorporated associations are not legal entities and, thus, cannot appoint agents. Only their individual members, as principals, may appoint agents.

B. <u>To Be an Agent</u>--Anyone who has the ability to carry out instructions may be an agent. The agent need not possess the legal capacity to contract, because contracts properly negotiated as an agent will not personally bind the agent.

III. Types of Agents

A. <u>General or Special</u>

   1. <u>General Agent</u>--Has broad authority to act for the principal in a variety of transactions.

   2. <u>Special Agent</u>--Has authority that is limited to a single transaction or series of related transactions (e.g., attorneys, auctioneers, brokers, etc.). **NOTE:** A principal is less likely to be liable for a special agent's unauthorized acts than he or she would be for a general agent's unauthorized acts.

B. <u>Sub-Agent</u>--An agent appointed by another agent who is authorized to appoint sub-agents in connection with his or her performance of the principal's business. Sub-agency is to be distinguished from the following:

   1. Co-Agent--An agent hired by another agent to act as an ancillary agent for the principal. The co-agent is subject to the principal's control; the co-agent is not subject to the employing agent's control.

   2. Agent of an Agent--An agent appointed by another agent who has not been given the authority by the principal to appoint other agents. He or she is an agent for the appointing agent, not a sub-agent for the principal.

C. <u>Gratuitous Agent</u>--One who agrees to act as agent without compensation. The agent is not bound to perform, but if the agent begins to perform he or she must not act negligently.

D. <u>Agency Coupled With an Interest</u>--An <u>irrevocable</u> agency in which the principal gives the agent a property (or security) interest in the thing subject to the power of the agency. For example, P agrees with A that if A will lend P $5,000, A shall have a one-half interest in P's property, and A shall have the exclusive authority to sell the property, with A's loan to be repaid out of the sales proceeds. A's agency power is irrevocable. However, an agency coupled with an interest is to be distinguished from a situation in which the agent is merely entitled to receive some of the proceeds or profits from the sale of the property. For example, a real estate agent who merely receives a commission from the sale of property does not have an agency coupled with an interest.

E. <u>Del Credere Agent</u>--A sales agent who promises to pay the principal if the principal's customer fails to pay. If the debt is not paid when due, the principal's action is against the agent. Though the agent guarantees to pay the debt of another, the agent's promise does not come within the statute of frauds because the promise is made for his or her own benefit (usually, a higher commission from the principal).

F. <u>Exclusive Agent</u>--An agent is an exclusive agent if he or she is the only agent a principal will deal with for a particular purpose. For example, a principal who appoints an exclusive real estate agent for the purpose of procuring a buyer for his or her property may not sell to a buyer procured by another agent; however, the principal may sell to a buyer he or she procures without any broker assistance.

G. <u>Factor</u>--A commercial agent for the sale or other disposition of goods for a commission ("factorage"). The factor is a bailee in possession of goods whose title remains in the principal. Because the factor has the appearance of ownership, the factor may sell the goods in his or her own name. Furthermore, the factor has the power to convey title to a good faith purchaser for value, and this title transfer is valid as against the principal, even if the conveyance exceeds the factor's authority.

IV. Creation of the Agency Relationship

A. <u>By Appointment</u>--A principal may appoint an agent.

    1. Express or Implied Agency

        a. Express--By written or oral agreement between the parties that one shall act for and be subject to the control of the other.

        b. Implied--By conduct of the principal which manifests the intention that the agency relationship should exist.

    2. Consideration is not necessary.

    3. Writing

        a. The principal may create an agency by a written instrument called a <u>power of attorney</u>, authorizing another, the "attorney in fact," to act as his or her agent.

        b. Most agency relationships need not be in writing to be valid. However, some are required by statute to be evidenced by a written memorandum. For example, if the agent's duties involve the making of a contract governed by the statute of frauds, such as a sale of real property, the agent's authority usually must be in writing. Also, the agreement must be in writing if the agency contract cannot be completed within one year.

    4. One may <u>not</u> appoint an agent to perform certain duties:

        a. Those which the principal is bound to perform personally (nondelegable duties).

        b. Those precluded by statute. For example, the execution of a will.

        c. Those that the principal cannot perform. For example, a minor cannot appoint an agent to convey real estate since he or she can void the conveyance.

B. <u>By Approval or Ratification</u>--Acts performed by one who is not an agent, or unauthorized acts performed by an agent, may be ratified by the principal.

    1. Ratification may be either express or implied, depending on the circumstances.

    2. Ratification requires the following:

        a. An act capable of ratification (for example, a tort may be ratified, but a crime may not be ratified) that is performed on behalf of the principal.

        b. A principal who:

            (1) Has the capacity to appoint the agent,

            (2) Has knowledge of the material facts of the transaction, and

            (3) Was in existence at the time the act was done (for example, a corporation cannot ratify the acts of its promoters done before it came into existence; however, it may later adopt those acts).

- and -

        c. Any formalities that would be required for an appointment.

3. A single transaction must be ratified in its entirety or not at all.

4. Timing--If the purported agent contracts with a third party on the principal's behalf, the third party can withdraw at any time prior to ratification. His or her withdrawal cuts off the principal's power to ratify. Alternatively, if the principal impairs the third party's rights by waiting too long, the principal may also lose his or her power to ratify.

5. Effect of Ratification--After ratification, the parties stand in the same position as if the agent had authority to do the act at the time it was done. The ratification "relates back" to the time the act was performed; thus, it is as if the act were authorized when performed.

    a. The principal cannot charge the agent with exceeding his or her authority nor can the third party hold him or her liable for breach of warranty of authority.

    b. The principal cannot retract his or her ratification.

C. <u>By Operation of Law</u>--The law may operate so as to create an agency relationship.

1. Agency by Estoppel--No actual agency relationship in fact exists. However, because the acts of the principal cause a third party to reasonably believe in the existence of the agency, and to reasonably rely on the existence of the agency, the principal is estopped from denying its existence.

2. Agency by Representation or Appearance--A person who represents to a third party that another is his or her agent may be bound to that party by his or her "agent's" actions, whether or not the third party acted in reliance.

3. Agency by Necessity--The law implies an agency in certain situations, such as emergencies.

V. Authority of the Agent to Bind the Principal

A. <u>Agent's Authority</u>

1. An agent's <u>actual authority</u> is that power consented to by the principal which affects the principal's legal relations.

2. This authority may be express or implied from the principal's conduct. <u>Implied authority</u> includes the authority to do acts reasonably necessary to accomplish an authorized act. Implied authority may also arise from customary practices in the business community.

B. <u>Apparent or Ostensible Authority</u>

1. If the conduct of the principal leads a third party to believe that an agent has authority beyond that which the principal has actually consented to, the agent is said to have <u>apparent authority</u>. For example, if a principal places an agent with limited authority in a position usually held by an agent with greater authority, the principal may lead others to believe the agent has greater authority than is actually the case.

2. Legal Effect of Apparent Authority

    a. Between the principal and the third party, it is as if the agent's authority were actual; neither can deny it.

    b. If losses to the principal result, the principal can hold the agent liable for exceeding his or her actual authority.

C. Agent's Authority With Respect to Notice, Knowledge, and Admissions

1. Notice by a third person to an agent is considered notice to the principal if the agent has actual or apparent authority to receive the notice. However, if the third person has knowledge that the agent's personal interest is adverse to the principal's interest, then notice to the agent is not notice to the principal.

2. Similarly, the agent's knowledge is imputed to the principal if the agent has the authority to represent the principal in the matter, unless the agent's personal interest is adverse to the principal's interest.

3. Out-of-court statements by an agent to a third person, which are within the scope of his or her employment, may be treated as admissions of the principal and introduced into evidence against the principal.

VI. Liability of the Principal for Torts of the Agent

A. Respondeat Superior--The principal is vicariously liable (i.e., liable regardless of whether he or she is at fault) for the torts of the agent if they are committed within the scope (actual or apparent) of the agent's employment.

1. The rule is the same for master and servant.

2. The question of whether the person committing the tortious act is the principal's agent (or servant) is a question of fact.

3. The act falls within the scope of the agent's employment if it is the type of act the agent is authorized to perform, if it takes place substantially within the time and place that is authorized, and if it is intended to serve the principal in some way.

a. Even if the agent violated the principal's instructions in committing the tort, the rule of respondeat superior applies.

b. However, if the agent or servant departs from the performance of his or her duties and acts on his or her own ("independent journey," "frolic and detour"), the principal is not liable. **NOTE:** An intentionally tortious act is not likely to be performed within the scope of employment. It is usually for the agent's own benefit.

4. The agent remains liable for his or her own tort and the injured third person can choose to hold the agent or the agent's principal liable. However, the injured party is entitled to only one recovery.

B. Liability of the Principal for the Crimes of the Agent

1. Ordinarily, a principal is not liable for his or her agent's crimes even when they are committed in the course of the agent's employment. However, the principal is liable if:

a. The principal participated in the crime in some way (i.e., the principal planned, directed, ordered, or acquiesced in its commission), or
b. If a statute makes the principal liable (e.g., the sale of liquor to minors).

2. A principal cannot ratify the crimes of the agent after their commission.

VII. Contractual Liability of the Principal to Third Parties

A. <u>Disclosed Principal</u>--If the third party dealing with the agent knows of the existence of the agency and the identity of the principal, then contracts made by the agent in the exercise of his or her actual or apparent authority will bind the <u>principal</u> only.

B. <u>Partially Disclosed Principal</u>--If the third party dealing with the agent knows of the existence of the agency but <u>not</u> the identity of the principal, then contracts made by the agent bind <u>both</u> the agent <u>and</u> the principal.

C. <u>Undisclosed Principal</u>--If the third party dealing with the agent has no knowledge of either the existence of the agency or the identity of the principal, then contracts made by the agent bind the <u>agent</u> only.

1. After discovering the identity of the principal, the third party may choose to hold him or her liable for acts either actually or apparently authorized unless:

   a. The contract is a negotiable or sealed instrument,

   b. The agent has already performed,

   c. The third party has already elected to hold the agent liable after discovering the principal's identity, or

   d. The contract provides that no undisclosed principal shall be liable.

2. The undisclosed principal has the right to enforce the contract against the third party, so long as it does not involve personal service, trust, or confidence.

   a. The principal takes the contract subject to:

      (1) Any defenses the third party has arising from the transaction,

      (2) Any personal defenses or set-offs the third party has against the principal, and

      (3) In cases where it is impliedly authorized, any set-offs the third party has against the agent.

   b. Defenses the agent has against the third party which arose from the transaction and are not personal to the agent are available to the principal.

3. A material misrepresentation of the facts inducing the third party to enter into the contract may be grounds for his or her rescission.

VIII. Liability of the Agent to Third Parties

A. <u>Agent's Liability for Torts</u>--An agent is liable to third parties for his or her own torts, even if the agent's principal is also vicariously liable for them. However, the third party is entitled to only one recovery. **NOTE:** Unless varied by statute, the agent is solely liable for his or her own crimes.

B. <u>Agent's Liability on Contracts</u>

1. An agent who is authorized to act by a disclosed principal is personally liable to third parties if:

   a. The agent contracts in his or her own name (for example, by carelessly signing his or her name to a written contract without indicating his or her representative capacity),

      b.   The agent makes him- or herself a party to the contract between the principal and the third party,

      c.   The agent personally guarantees the principal's performance and the principal does not perform, or

      d.   The agent signs a negotiable or sealed instrument on which the principal's name does not appear.

2.   When an agent is representing a partially disclosed principal, the agent is liable on contracts for that principal unless:

      a.   The agent and third party agree that the agent is not to be bound, and

      b.   The identity of the principal is indicated so that it can become known.

3.   An agent who fails to bind his or her principal because his or her act is unauthorized is generally liable on the contract unless the third party knew of the "agent's" lack of authority.

      a.   The agent is liable to a third party for breaching his or her implied warranty of authority. Damages are limited to those which the third party could have recovered from the principal had the agent been bound. For example, if the principal is insolvent, damages obtainable from the agent are nominal.

      b.   The agent may also be liable in tort for fraud and deceit.

4.   A person who purports to contract as an agent for a principal the person knows to be nonexistent or incompetent is liable on the contract so long as the person:

      a.   Knows the third party is ignorant of the nonexistence or incompetence, or

      b.   Represents to the third party that the principal exists or is competent.

IX. Duties Between Principal and Agent

A.   <u>Principal's Duties Owed to the Agent</u>--The principal owes the agent the following duties:

    1.   To compensate the agent for services rendered, either according to their agreement or, if there is no agreement, in an amount that reasonably reflects the value of the services.

    2.   To reimburse the agent for reasonable expenses incurred in the course of the agency.

    3.   To indemnify the agent against loss or liability for acts performed at the principal's direction, unless they are unlawful.

    4.   To compensate the agent for physical injury (for example, workers' compensation).

B.   <u>Duties of the Agent to the Principal</u>

    1.   An agent has a fiduciary duty to be loyal to his or her principal.

      a.   The agent cannot act for two principals with conflicting interests unless both principals consent.

      b.   The agent cannot deal for his or her own interest (for example, to make a profit at the principal's expense), and if the agent does, he or she is a constructive trustee for the principal of whatever should have been acquired for the principal.

c.   The agent cannot compete with his or her principal without the principal's consent.

d.   The agent cannot disclose to others any confidential information learned during the agency relationship.

e.   An agent who violates the duty of loyalty is subject to liability for any losses caused thereby and is not entitled to compensation, reimbursement, or indemnification.

2.   An agent must follow the principal's lawful instructions, using reasonable care and skill.

a.   The agent cannot delegate duties involving discretion, except with the principal's permission.

b.   The agent is liable to the principal for losses resulting from his or her own negligence.

3.   An agent has the duty to communicate notice of any material facts that come to the agent's attention while he or she is acting in his or her agency capacity.

4.   An agent must account for any property or money he or she receives through the agency. The agent may not commingle his or her own funds with those of the principal. If the agent does, he or she is liable for any resulting loss.

X. Termination of the Agency Relationship

A.   <u>Methods</u>

Terminate any time by any one

1.   Termination by Agreement Between the Parties

a.   The agency agreement may specify that it will terminate at a particular date, that it will end when an objective is accomplished, or that either party may terminate the relationship at will.

b.   The parties may mutually consent to terminate their relationship at any time.

2.   Termination by Revocation or Renunciation

a.   In most cases, the principal has the power to revoke the agency, but:

(1)   If the principal has given an "agency coupled with an interest," it is irrevocable, i.e., he or she has neither the right nor the power to revoke.

(2)   In all other cases, the principal has the power to revoke, but if the principal has no right to revoke (for example, the principal has contracted not to revoke) the principal will be subject to liability for breach of the agency contract.

(3)   If the agent violates his or her duties to the principal, the principal has the right to revoke the agency.

b.   The agent always has the power to renounce the agency. However, the agent may be liable to the principal for breach, unless the principal violated his or her duties or the agency was gratuitous.

3.   Termination by Operation of Law--On the occurrence of certain events, most agencies will terminate by operation of law. A partial list of these events includes the following:

automatically
no need for any notice

a.   Death or insanity of either party.

b.   Bankruptcy or insolvency of the principal.

c.   Bankruptcy of the agent if it affects the agency relationship.

d.   Illegality or impossibility.

B.   Notice

1.   No notice is required if the agency terminates by operation of law.

2.   In all other cases, notice must be given.

a.   If the principal revokes or the agent renounces, each must notify the other.

b.   Third parties who have dealt with the agent must be given actual notice; otherwise, if they have no knowledge of the termination, their transactions with the agent will still bind the principal.

c.   Third parties who have not previously dealt with the agent may be given constructive notice (for example, by publication).

_____

CHAPTER 50—AGENCY

Problem 50-1 MULTIPLE CHOICE QUESTIONS (40 to 50 minutes)

1. A principal and agent relationship requires a
a. Written agreement.
b. Power of attorney.
c. Meeting of the minds and consent to act.
d. Specified consideration.   (5/92, Law, #6, 2819)

1A. Trent was retained, in writing, to act as Post's agent for the sale of Post's memorabilia collection. Which of the following statements is correct?

I. To be an agent, Trent must be at least 21 years of age.
II. Post would be liable to Trent if the collection was destroyed before Trent found a purchaser.

a. I only.
b. II only.
c. Both I and II.
d. Neither I nor II.   (5/95, Law, #6, 5340)

2. Noll gives Carr a written power of attorney. Which of the following statements is correct regarding this power of attorney?
a. It must be signed by both Noll and Carr.
b. It must be for a definite period of time.
c. It may continue in existence after Noll's death.
d. It may limit Carr's authority to specific transactions.   (11/93, Law, #11, 4308)

3. Which of the following actions requires an agent for a corporation to have a written agency agreement?
a. Purchasing office supplies for the principal's business.
b. Purchasing an interest in undeveloped land for the principal.
c. Hiring an independent general contractor to renovate the principal's office building.
d. Retaining an attorney to collect a business debt owed the principal.   (11/94, Law, #16, 5193)

4. Able, on behalf of Pix Corp., entered into a contract with Sky Corp., by which Sky agreed to sell computer equipment to Pix. Able disclosed to Sky that she was acting on behalf of Pix. However, Able had exceeded her actual authority by entering into the contract with Sky. If Pix wishes to ratify the contract with Sky, which of the following statements is correct?
a. Pix must notify Sky that Pix intends to ratify the contract.
b. Able must have acted reasonably and in Pix's best interest.

c. Able must be a general agent of Pix.
d. Pix must have knowledge of all material facts relating to the contract at the time it is ratified.
(5/88, Law, #5, 9911)

5. Orr gives North power of attorney. In general, the power of attorney
a. Will be valid only if North is a licensed attorney at law.
b. May continue in existence after Orr's death.
c. May limit North's authority to specific transactions.
d. Must be signed by both Orr and North.
(11/91, Law, #13, 2341)

6. Easy Corp. is a real estate developer and regularly engages real estate brokers to act on its behalf in acquiring parcels of land. The brokers are authorized to enter into such contracts, but are instructed to do so in their own names without disclosing Easy's identity or relationship to the transaction. If a broker enters into a contract with a seller on Easy's behalf,
a. The broker will have the same actual authority as if Easy's identity had been disclosed.
b. Easy will be bound by the contract because of the broker's apparent authority.
c. Easy will not be liable for any negligent acts committed by the broker while acting on Easy's behalf.
d. The broker will not be personally bound by the contract because the broker has express authority to act.   (11/94, Law, #18, 5195)

7. Frost's accountant and business manager has the authority to
a. Mortgage Frost's business property.
b. Obtain bank loans for Frost.
c. Insure Frost's property against fire loss.
d. Sell Frost's business.   (5/91, Law, #3, 0649)

8. A principal will **not** be liable to a third party for a tort committed by an agent
a. Unless the principal instructed the agent to commit the tort.
b. Unless the tort was committed within the scope of the agency relationship.
c. If the agency agreement limits the principal's liability for the agent's tort.
d. If the tort is also regarded as a criminal act.
(11/89, Law, #2, 0655)

8A. An agent will usually be liable under a contract made with a third party when the agent is acting on behalf of a(an)

	Disclosed principal	Undisclosed principal
a.	Yes	Yes
b.	Yes	No
c.	No	Yes
d.	No	No

(11/94, Law, #19, 5196)

9. Pine, an employee of Global Messenger Co., was hired to deliver highly secret corporate documents for Global's clients throughout the world. Unknown to Global, Pine carried a concealed pistol. While Pine was making a delivery, he suspected an attempt was being made to steal the package, drew his gun and shot Kent, an innocent passerby. Kent will **not** recover damages from Global if

a. Global discovered that Pine carried a weapon and did nothing about it.
b. Global instructed its messengers **not** to carry weapons.
c. Pine was correct and an attempt was being made to steal the package.
d. Pine's weapon was unlicensed and illegal.

(5/90, Law, #2, 0651)

10. Which of the following rights will a third party be entitled to after validly contracting with an agent representing an undisclosed principal?

a. Disclosure of the principal by the agent.
b. Ratification of the contract by the principal.
c. Performance of the contract by the agent.
d. Election to void the contract after disclosure of the principal. (11/93, Law, #14, 4311)

11. When an agent acts for an undisclosed principal, the principal will **not** be liable to third parties if the

a. Principal ratifies a contract entered into by the agent.
b. Agent acts within an implied grant of authority.
c. Agent acts outside the grant of actual authority.
d. Principal seeks to conceal the agency relationship. (11/91, Law, #12, 2340)

11A. When a valid contract is entered into by an agent on the principal's behalf, in a nondisclosed principal situation, which of the following statements concerning the principal's liability is correct?

	The principal may be held liable once disclosed	The principal must ratify the contract to be held liable
a.	Yes	Yes
b.	Yes	No
c.	No	Yes
d.	No	No

(5/95, Law, #8, 5342)

12. Frey entered into a contract with Cara Corp. to purchase televisions on behalf of Lux, Inc. Lux authorized Frey to enter into the contract in Frey's name without disclosing that Frey was acting on behalf of Lux. If Cara repudiates the contract, which of the following statements concerning liability on the contract is **not** correct?

a. Frey may hold Cara liable and obtain money damages.
b. Frey may hold Cara liable and obtain specific performance.
c. Lux may hold Cara liable upon disclosing the agency relationship with Frey.
d. Cara will be free from liability to Lux if Frey fraudulently stated that he was acting on his own behalf. (11/87, Law, #24, 0662)

13. Generally, a disclosed principal will be liable to third parties for its agent's unauthorized misrepresentations if the agent is an

	Employee	Independent Contractor
a.	Yes	Yes
b.	Yes	No
c.	No	Yes
d.	No	No

(11/93, Law, #13, 4310)

14. North, Inc. hired Sutter as a purchasing agent. North gave Sutter written authorization to purchase, without limit, electronic appliances. Later, Sutter was told not to purchase more than 300 of each appliance. Sutter contracted with Orr Corp. to purchase 500 tape recorders. Orr had been shown Sutter's written authorization. Which of the following statements is correct?

a. Sutter will be liable to Orr because Sutter's actual authority was exceeded.
b. Sutter will **not** be liable to reimburse North if North is liable to Orr.
c. North will be liable to Orr because of Sutter's actual and apparent authority.
d. North will **not** be liable to Orr because Sutter's actual authority was exceeded.

(11/93, Law, #15, 4312)

15. Able, as agent for Baker, an undisclosed principal, contracted with Safe to purchase an antique car. In payment, Able issued his personal check to Safe. Able could not cover the check but expected Baker to give him cash to deposit before the check was presented for payment. Baker did not do so and the check was dishonored. Baker's identity became known to Safe. Safe may **not** recover from
a. Baker individually on the contract.
b. Able individually on the contract.
c. Baker individually on the check.
d. Able individually on the check.
(5/90, Law, #4, 0653)

16. Bolt Corp. dismissed Ace as its general sales agent and notified all of Ace's known customers by letter. Young Corp., a retail outlet located outside of Ace's previously assigned sales territory, had never dealt with Ace. Young knew of Ace as a result of various business contacts. After his dismissal, Ace sold Young goods, to be delivered by Bolt, and received from Young a cash deposit for 20% of the purchase price. It was not unusual for an agent in Ace's previous position to receive cash deposits. In an action by Young against Bolt on the sales contract, Young will
a. Lose, because Ace lacked any implied authority to make the contract.
b. Lose, because Ace lacked any express authority to make the contract.
c. Win, because Bolt's notice was inadequate to terminate Ace's apparent authority.
d. Win, because a principal is an insurer of an agent's acts. (11/94, Law, #17, 5194)

17. Generally, an agency relationship is terminated by operation of law in all of the following situations **except** the
a. Principal's death.
b. Principal's incapacity.
c. Agent's renunciation of the agency.
d. Agent's failure to acquire a necessary business license. (5/90, Law, #1, 0650)

18. Pell is the principal and Astor is the agent in an agency coupled with an interest. In the absence of a contractual provision relating to the duration of the agency, who has the right to terminate the agency before the interest has expired?

	Pell	Astor
a.	Yes	Yes
b.	No	Yes
c.	No	No
d.	Yes	No

(5/89, Law, #11, 0657)

19. Simmons, an agent for Jensen, has the express authority to sell Jensen's goods. Simmons also has the express authority to grant discounts of up to 5% of list price. Simmons sold Hemple goods with a list price of $1,000 and granted Hemple a 10% discount. Hemple had not previously dealt with either Simmons or Jensen. Which of the following courses of action may Jensen properly take?
a. Seek to void the sale to Hemple.
b. Seek recovery of $50 from Hemple only.
c. Seek recovery of $50 from Simmons only.
d. Seek recovery of $50 from either Hemple or Simmons. (5/89, Law, #13, 9911)

20. Thorp was a purchasing agent for Ogden, a sole proprietor, and had the express authority to place purchase orders with Ogden's suppliers. Thorp placed an order with Datz, Inc. on Ogden's behalf after Ogden was declared incompetent in a judicial proceeding. Thorp was aware of Ogden's incapacity. Which of the following statements is correct concerning Ogden's liability to Datz?
a. Ogden will be liable because Datz was **not** informed of Ogden's incapacity.
b. Ogden will be liable because Thorp acted with express authority.
c. Ogden will **not** be liable because Thorp's agency ended when Ogden was declared incompetent.
d. Ogden will **not** be liable because Ogden was a nondisclosed principal. (5/95, Law, #7, 5341)

21. Young Corp. hired Wilson as a sales representative for six months at a salary of $5,000 per month plus 6% of sales. Which of the following statements is correct?
a. Young does **not** have the power to dismiss Wilson during the six-month period without cause.
b. Wilson is obligated to act solely in Young's interest in matters concerning Young's business.
c. The agreement between Young and Wilson is **not** enforceable unless it is in writing and signed by Wilson.
d. The agreement between Young and Wilson formed an agency coupled with an interest.
(5/95, Law, #9, 5343)

Solution 50-1 MULTIPLE CHOICE ANSWERS

Creation of Agency Relationship

1. (c) Agency is a consensual relationship whereby one person, the agent, agrees to act on behalf of another, the principal. Generally, the agency need not be in writing (exceptions are the sale of real property or the appointment of an agent for more than one year). A power of attorney (a written authorization to act) is not necessary. A specified consideration is not always necessary (for example, in the case of a gratuitous agent).

1A. (d) In order to be an agent, a person need not possess legal capacity to contract because contracts properly negotiated as an agent will not personally bind the agent. Impossibility of performance would terminate the agency relationship by operation of law and releases Post from any liability to Kent. Thus, neither of the statements is correct.

2. (d) A power of attorney may be either "special" or "general" in nature. A "special" power of attorney permits the agent to do specified acts only. Therefore, a power of attorney can be written in such a way as to limit Carr's authority to specific transactions. A power of attorney is effective when signed by the person transferring power. A power of attorney may be established for a period of indefinite duration. A power of attorney expires upon the death of the person transferring power.

3. (b) It is generally not necessary for an agent to have a written agency agreement. An exception to the general rule exists if the agent's duties will involve the buying and selling of real property, or if the agency agreement is to last more than one year.

4. (d) In order for a principal to ratify a contract entered into by its agent, the principal generally must have the capacity to appoint an agent, knowledge of the material facts of the transaction, and have been in existence at the time the agent entered into the contract. A valid ratification does not require the principal to make any type of notification so as to be effective since the ratification may be implied from the principal's actions. A principal may ratify any act of its agent, however unreasonable, so long as it is not unlawful. There is no requirement that the agent must have acted reasonably and in the principal's best interest. Pix could ratify the act of someone who is not an agent as long as all of the requirements for ratification are met.

5. (c) A power of attorney creates an agency relationship. Therefore, the principal, Orr, has the power to limit North's authority to specific transactions. There is no requirement that one party be a licensed attorney. An agency relationship, including a power of attorney, ends with the death of either the principal or the agent. The power of attorney needs to be signed only by the party granting the authority.

Agent's Authority

6. (a) Actual authority is granted by the principal to the agent and is not affected by the principal's status as disclosed or undisclosed. Easy will be bound by the contract because of the brokers' actual authority. Where a principal is undisclosed, there can be no apparent authority. A principal's liability under the doctrine of *Respondeat Superior* is not affected by the principal's status as disclosed or undisclosed. Agents for undisclosed principals are always liable on the contracts that they negotiate on their principal's behalf, regardless of whether the agent has express authority.

7. (c) The accountant and business manager has authority to do "normal" or "reasonable" business activities. Answer (c) is the activity that would be the most "reasonable" for a business manager to perform. The others all involve activities that would not generally happen within "normal" business activities. An agent would not have the apparent authority to mortgage the business property, obtain bank loans, or sell the business. In those situations, he would need specific authorization.

Liability of Principal

8. (b) The general rule is that the principal is vicariously liable for the torts of his agent if the tort is committed within the scope of the employment (the doctrine of respondeat superior). The principal is generally liable whether the principal instructed the agent to commit the tort or not. A limitation of liability in an agency agreement has no bearing on the right of the third party to sue the principal. It is possible for a principal to be liable for a tort that is also a criminal act (for example, where the principal instructs the agent to injure a customer if the customer does not pay).

8A. (c) An agent will not usually be liable under a contract made with a third party if the principal is disclosed and if the agent acts within the scope of his or her agency. Agents for undisclosed principals always have contract liability.

9. (d) Tort liability under respondeat superior arises when the agent is acting within the scope of his employment. Conduct was motivated by service to the principal. Thus, only if Pine's weapon was unlicensed and illegal is Global not liable.

10. (c) When neither the agency relationship nor the identity of the principal is disclosed, a third party is deemed to be dealing with the agent personally, and the agent is liable as a party to the contract. A third party is not entitled to disclosure of the principal or ratification by the principal. A third party may <u>not</u> elect to void the contract after disclosure of the principal.

11. (c) Actual authority is that power consented to by the principal which affects the principal's legal relations. If a third party dealing with an agent has no knowledge of either the existence of the agency or the identity of an undisclosed principal, then contracts made by the agent *bind the agent only*, and the principal will not be liable.

11A. (b) When an agent enters into a contract on behalf of a nondisclosed principal, the agent may be held liable on the contract. If the agent acted with authority, the principal may also be held liable upon disclosure. It is not necessary for a principal to ratify a contract in order to be held liable.

12. (b) Specific performance is appropriate only when the subject matter is so unique that the aggrieved party cannot be fairly compensated with money damage. The agent of an undisclosed principal binds himself and has the right to sue the third person in his own name; money damages are the appropriate remedy. If the principal discloses himself and asserts his rights under the contract, he may also sue the third party as long as the contract does not involve personal services, trust, or confidence.

13. (b) As a general rule, an independent contractor is hired to accomplish a specific task and is not subject to the supervision and control of the principal. Thus, generally, a principal is not liable for the misrepresentations of the independent contractor. On the other hand, the employee is subject to the supervision and control of the employer. In general, principals are liable for the misrepresentations of their employees.

14. (a) Sutter had actual authority to purchase 300 of the tape recorders. Sutter also had apparent authority due to the fact that the third party, Orr, was aware of the written authorization giving Sutter unlimited power to purchase electronic appliances. However, Orr was not informed that this authority had

been revoked by North. Therefore, the apparent authority of Sutter existed with respect to Orr. This combination of actual and apparent authority effectively bound North to the contract and makes North liable to Orr. Sutter *would* be liable for breaching the implied warranty of authority. An agent with apparent authority *can* bind a principal and third party to a contract even though he or she has exceeded his or her actual authority. Therefore, both North and Sutter would be liable to the third party on the contract, but the best answer is (c) because the third party would be more likely to pursue the party with more assets, usually the principal. If losses to the principal result, the principal *can* hold the agent liable for exceeding his or her actual authority. North will be held liable to Orr due to the fact that Sutter's apparent authority does bind North to contract.

15. (c) Not being a signatory to the check, Baker cannot be held liable on it. As the check's drawer, Able can be held liable on the check. The third party can elect to hold either the agent or the principal liable when the agent makes a contract.

Agent's Duties and Termination of Agency Relationship

16. (c) Where an agency relationship terminates for any reason other than by operation of law, the principal must give actual notice of the termination to all third parties who have previously dealt with the agent and constructive notice to all other parties to terminate the agent's apparent authority. Since Bolt did not give constructive notice, and since Young had no knowledge of the termination, Young will be able to hold Bolt liable for the Ace contract. It is irrelevant that Ace lacked any express or implied authority since apparent authority to act was still present.

17. (c) The agent's renunciation of the agency does not automatically terminate by *operation of law*. The other answers listed *do* terminate an agency.

18. (b) The general rule is that a principal always has the *power* to terminate an agency but not necessarily the *right*. The only exception is where the agency is coupled with an interest. In this situation the principal has neither the *power* nor the *right* to terminate the agency. The agent, however, can terminate the agency as it is the agent's interest that the law seeks to protect. If the agent wishes to waive such interest, the agent is free to do so.

19. (c) The principal (Jensen) may seek recovery from the agent (Simmons) since an agent has a fiduciary duty to follow the instructions of the principal. Agents must pay damages to the principal

when the agent fails to use reasonable care and skill in carrying out their duties. The principal may not void the sale to the third party (Hemple) nor seek recovery of the $50. The principal is liable for the action of the agent when the agent has either actual or apparent authority. In this situation, the agent has the apparent authority to grant a 10% discount. Apparent authority is derived from the conduct of the principal which leads a third party to reasonably believe that the agent has the authority represented. A third party may believe the agent has authority represented. A third party may believe the agent has authority by the usual activity of the agent or the custom of the industry. Since the principal allowed the agent to give discounts, a secret limitation as to the amount of the discount will not be effective against a third party.

20. (c) A declaration of incompetency terminates the agency relationship by operation of law. Notice to third parties is not required when the agency terminates by operation of law. Odgen will not be liable because Thorp's authority ended upon the declaration of incompetency. The agent would be liable on the contract since an agent guarantees the principal's capacity to enter into the contract.

21. (b) An agent's duties to a principal include an obligation to act solely in the principal's interest in matters concerning the principal's business. Unless there is an agency coupled with an interest, the principal has the power to terminate the agency relationship, although the principal may not have the right to do so. The Statute of Frauds does not apply to the agreement between Young and Wilson, since the contract was for less than one year. Thus, their oral agreement is enforceable. An agency coupled with an interest results when the principal gives the agent a property or security interest in the subject matter of the agency. The paying of a commission does not create a property or security interest.

PERFORMANCE BY SUBTOPICS

Each category below parallels a subtopic covered in Chapter 50. Record the number and percentage of questions you correctly answered in each subtopic area.

Creation of Agency Relationship

Question #	Correct √
1	
1A	
2	
3	
4	
5	
# Questions	6
# Correct	
% Correct	

Agent's Authority

Question #	Correct √
6	
7	
# Questions	2
# Correct	
% Correct	

Liability of Principal

Question #	Correct √
8	
8A	
9	
10	
11	
11A	
12	
13	
14	
15	
# Questions	10
# Correct	
% Correct	

Agent's Duties and Termination of Agency Relationship

Question #	Correct √
16	
17	
18	
19	
20	
21	
# Questions	6
# Correct	
% Correct	

ESSAY QUESTIONS

Essay 50-2 (15 to 25 minutes)

Exotic Pets, Inc. hired Peterson to be the manager of one of its stores. Exotic sells a wide variety of animals. Peterson was given considerable authority by Exotic to operate the store, including the right to buy inventory. Peterson was told that any inventory purchase exceeding $2,000 required the approval of Exotic's general manager.

On June 1, 1992, Peterson contracted with Creatures Corp. to buy snakes for $3,100. Peterson had regularly done business with Creatures on Exotic's behalf in the past, and on several occasions had bought $1,000 to $1,750 worth of snakes from Creatures. Creatures was unaware of the limitation on Peterson's authority to buy inventory.

Peterson occasionally would buy, for Exotic, a certain breed of dog from Premier Breeders, Inc., which was owned by Peterson's friend. Whenever Exotic bought dogs from Premier, Premier paid Peterson 5% of the purchase price as an incentive to do more business with Premier. Exotic's management was unaware of these payments to Peterson.

On June 20, 1992, Mathews went to the Exotic store managed by Peterson to buy a ferret. Peterson allowed Mathews to handle one of the ferrets. Peterson knew that this particular ferret had previously bitten one of the store's clerks. Mathews was bitten by the ferret and seriously injured.

On July 23, 1992, Peterson bought paint and brushes for $30 from Handy Hardware. Peterson charged the purchase to Exotic's account at Handy. Peterson intended to use the paint and brushes to repaint the pet showroom. Exotic's management had never specifically discussed with Peterson whether Peterson had the authority to charge purchases at Handy. Although Exotic paid the Handy bill, Exotic's president believes Peterson is obligated to reimburse Exotic for the charges.

On August 1, 1992, Exotic's president learned of the Creatures contract and advised Creatures that Exotic would neither accept delivery of the snakes, nor pay for them, because Peterson did not have the authority to enter into the contract.

Exotic's president has also learned about the incentive payments Premier made to Peterson.

Exotic has taken the following positions:

- It is not liable to Creatures because Peterson entered into the contract without Exotic's consent.
- Peterson is obligated to reimburse Exotic for the charges incurred by Peterson at Handy Hardware.
- Peterson is liable to Exotic for the incentive payments received from Premier.

Mathews has sued both Peterson and Exotic injuries sustained from the ferret bite.

Required:

a. State whether Exotic's positions are correct and give the reasons for your conclusions.

b. State whether Mathews will prevail in the lawsuit against Exotic and Peterson and give the reasons for your conclusions. (11/92, Law, #4)

Essay 50-3 (7 to 10 minutes)

John Nolan, a partner in Nolan, Stein, & Wolf partnership, transferred his interest in the partnership to Simon and withdrew from the partnership. Although the partnership will continue, Stein and Wolf have refused to admit Simon as a partner.

Subsequently, the partnership appointed Ed Lemon as its agent to market its various product lines. Lemon entered into a two-year written agency contract with the partnership which provided that Lemon would receive a 10% sales commission. The agency contract was signed by Lemon and, on behalf of the partnership, by Stein and Wolf.

After six months, Lemon was terminated without cause. Lemon asserts that:

- He is an agent coupled with an interest.
- The agency relationship may not be terminated without cause prior to the expiration of its term.
- He is entitled to damages because of the termination of the agency relationship.

Required:

Answer the following, setting forth reasons for any conclusions stated.

Discuss the merits of Lemon's assertions.
(11/85, Law, #3b)

ESSAY SOLUTIONS

Solution 50-2 Agents Authority and Liability/Liabilities of Principal

a. Exotic's first position is incorrect. Although Peterson lacked actual authority to bind Exotic to the Creatures contract, from Creatures' perspective

Peterson did have **apparent authority** to do so. Peterson was a store manager and had **previously contracted with Creatures on Exotic's behalf**. Creatures **would not be bound by the limitation** on Peterson's authority unless **Creatures was aware of it.**

Exotic's second position is incorrect. Although Peterson did not have express authority to charge purchases at Handy Hardware, Peterson had the **implied authority** as store manager to enter into **contracts incidental to the express grant of authority to act as manager**. Buying paint and brushes to improve Exotic's store would fall within Peterson's implied grant of authority.

Exotic's third position is correct. An **agent owes a duty of loyalty to his or her principal. An agent may not benefit directly or indirectly from an agency relationship at the principal's expense.** If an agent receives any profits from the principal/agent relationship without consent of the principal, the agent must pay the profits to the principal. In this case, Peterson's incentive payments constituted a **violation of** Peterson's **fiduciary duty** to Exotic. Peterson must turn over all incentive payments to Exotic.

b. Peterson was negligent by allowing Mathews to handle a ferret that Peterson knew was dangerous. An **employer is held liable for the torts of its employees** if the tort occurs **within the scope of employment** and if the employee is **subject to the employer's control**. At the time of the accident, Peterson was acting within the scope of employment and subject to Exotic's control because this conduct occurred while on the job, during normal working hours, and with the intention of benefiting Exotic. Exotic, therefore, will be liable to Mathews because the accident occurred within the scope of Peterson's employment.

Peterson also will be liable to Mathews because **all persons are liable for their own negligence.**

Solution 50-3 Agency Coupled With an Interest/ Termination

Lemon's first assertion that he is an agent coupled with an interest is incorrect. An **agency coupled with an interest in the subject matter arises when the agent has an interest in the property that is the subject of the agency.** The fact that Lemon entered into a two year written agency agreement with the partnership that would pay Lemon a commission clearly will not establish an interest in the subject matter of the agency. The **mere expectation of profits** to be realized or proceeds to be derived from the sale of the partnership's products is **not sufficient** to create an agency coupled with an interest. As a result, the principal-agency relationship **may be terminated at any time**.

Lemon's second assertion that the principal-agency relationship may not be terminated without cause prior to the expiration of its term is incorrect. When a **principal-agency relationship is based upon a contract** to engage the agent **for a specified period of time**, the **principal may discharge the agent despite the fact such discharge is wrongful**. Although the principal **does not have the right to discharge the agent**, he does **have the power to do so**. Thus, Lemon may be discharged without cause.

Lemon's third assertion that he is entitled to damages because of the termination of the agency relationship is correct. When a principal **wrongfully discharges** its agent, **the principal is liable for damages based on breach of contract.** Under the facts, Lemon's discharge by the partnership without cause constitutes a breach of contract for which Lemon **may recover damages**.

CHAPTER 51

PARTNERSHIPS

I. **Definitions** 51-2
    A.   Fiduciary 51-2
    B.   Joint Liability 51-2
    C.   Joint and Several Liability 51-2
    D.   Partnership Property 51-2

II. **Nature and Classification of Partnerships** 51-2
    A.   The Uniform Partnership Act (UPA) 51-2
    B.   Entity vs. Aggregate Theories of Partnership 51-3
    C.   Partnerships Distinguished From Corporations and Joint Ventures.............. 51-3
    D.   Classifications of Partnerships and Partners.. 51-3

III. **Formation, Rules of Construction, and Property Rights of a Partnership**.......... 51-4
    A.   Formation of a Partnership 51-4
    B.   Rules for Determining the Existence of a Partnership.................................. 51-5
    C.   Partnership by Estoppel... 51-5
    D.   Partnership Property.. 51-6

IV. **Relations Among Partners** 51-7
    A.   Partners as Fiduciaries 51-7
    B.   Rights and Duties of Partners to One Another and to the Partnership........... 51-7
    C.   Rights of a Partner in Actions Between Self and the Partnership 51-8

V. **Relations of Partners to Third Persons** 51-9
    A.   Authority of Partners to Bind the Partnership 51-9
    B.   Partnership Liability... 51-10

VI. **Dissolution of a Partnership** 51-10
    A.   Causes.. 51-10
    B.   Rights of Partners... 51-12
    C.   Effect on the Partner's Authority and Rights to Bind the Partnership Thereafter 51-13
    D.   Effect on a Partner's Liability 51-14
    E.   Rules for the Distribution of a Partnership's Assets 51-14
    F.   Liability of Persons Continuing the Partnership's Business 51-15
    G.   Rights of a Retiring Partner or the Estate of a Deceased Partner When the Business
        Is Continued.. 51-15

VII. **Limited Partnerships** 51-15
    A.   General Nature 51-15
    B.   Formation 51-16
    C.   Dissolution 51-16
    D.   Distribution.. 51-16
    E.   Revised Uniform Limited Partnership Act... 51-17

VIII. **Federal Income Tax Ramifications**.. 51-17
    A.   Partnership as Conduit 51-17
    B.   Taxable Entity Status of a Partnership 51-17

CHAPTER 51

PARTNERSHIPS

I. Definitions

A. <u>Fiduciary</u>--A person who occupies a position of trust and confidence in relation to another and, thus, owes that person a duty to exercise care.

B. <u>Joint Liability</u>--All partners in a partnership are jointly liable for any contract actions against the partnership. A creditor must name all the partners in any suit where the creditor wishes to obtain a judgment good against each partner's individual property. Failure on the part of the creditor to name all the partners will result in dismissal of the case.

C. <u>Joint and Several Liability</u>--All partners are jointly and severally liable for all actions in tort or fraud against any member of the partnership. The other partners are liable only when the cause of action arises out of partnership business. A person with a cause of action against a partnership may sue any number of partners he or she wishes, collectively or separately. Each partner is liable for the entire amount of damages arising out of such a cause of action. However, a partner may have either a right to contribution from all the other partners or a right to indemnification from the wrongdoing partner.

D. <u>Partnership Property</u>--All property originally brought into the partnership or subsequently acquired on account of the partnership.

II. Nature and Classification of Partnerships

A. <u>The Uniform Partnership Act (UPA)</u>--defines a partnership as an association of two or more persons to carry on a business for profit as co-owners.

   1. "To carry on a business" includes almost any type of profitable, legal activity.

   2. The persons engaged in a partnership must be co-owners. This requirement distinguishes a partnership from an agency. An agent may at times receive a share of the profits of a business. However, an agent does not have a partner's proprietary interest in the business. There is a fiduciary relationship among the partners, and between them and the partnership. Thus, each partner is an agent for the partnership and for all other partners.

   3. A Partnership Must Be Carried on for a Profit--Nonprofit, unincorporated associations such as religious or charitable groups, labor unions, or clubs, are not partnerships.

   4. Capacity to Be a Partner--Generally, any person (entity) who is competent to contract may be a partner.

      a. An infant may be a partner, but only to the extent of the infant's power to contract. Therefore, an infant may at any time withdraw his or her investment unless, and to the extent that, the partnership is subject to creditors' claims. Furthermore, if liable for debts, an infant is liable only up to the amount of his or her contribution.

      b. A corporation may become a partner only where permitted by state corporation laws.

      c. A partnership may become a partner in another partnership provided all the partners agree to the arrangement.

d. A trustee may become a partner if to do so would be prudent and in the best interest of the trust.

B. <u>Entity vs. Aggregate Theories of Partnership</u>

1. The UPA generally follows the aggregate theory; that is, it treats a partnership as an aggregate of individual partners rather than as an entity unto itself. Thus, the partnership itself is not taxed; rather, each partner pays income tax on his or her share of the profits or losses. Generally, a suit against a partnership must be brought against the individual partners. In those states which do permit a suit to be brought against the partnership as an entity, most require that the partners be individually joined if the plaintiff desires to reach beyond the partnership assets.

2. For certain purposes, a partnership is treated as an entity. Real property may be bought and sold in the partnership name.

C. <u>Partnerships Distinguished From Corporations and Joint Ventures</u>

1. Corporations

    a. The advantages of a corporation as compared to a general partnership are:

        (1) The liability of stockholders is limited to the amount of their investment, whereas partners have unlimited liability.

        (2) A corporation allows continuity of business operations despite changes in ownership or management; a partnership is of limited duration (for example, the death of a partner dissolves a partnership).

        (3) A corporation may utilize a centralized management of professional managers, whereas a partnership is run co-equally by all the partners.

        (4) The ownership rights in a corporation are readily transferable; however, a partner may not transfer interest and rights in the partnership without the approval of all other partners.

    b. The advantages of a partnership as compared to a corporation are:

        (1) A partnership may be easily and cheaply organized, whereas a corporation must be organized in accordance with specific statutory procedures and must have sufficient capitalization.

        (2) A partnership is generally less burdened by government supervision and reporting requirements than is a corporation.

2. <u>Joint Ventures</u>--A joint venture resembles a partnership except that it is formed for only one transaction or series of transactions, rather than for a general purpose.

D. <u>Classifications of Partnerships and Partners</u>

1. A <u>General Partnership</u>--An ordinary partnership formed under the UPA or common law (see II.A., above) and which consists only of general partners.

    • A <u>general partner</u> has the right to share in the management and profits of the partnership and has unlimited liability to partnership creditors.

2. A <u>Limited Partnership</u>--An arrangement specially created by the Uniform Limited Partnership Act (ULPA) which consists of one or more general partners and one or more limited partners.

- A <u>limited partner</u> is one who contributes capital to the partnership but does not have any authority or voice in the management of the business. The limited partner's liability to partnership creditors is limited to the amount of capital contributed.

3. A Silent Partner--One who has unlimited liability but does not share in the management of the partnership.

4. An Ostensible or Nominal Partner--One who is not actually a partner, but who may become a partner by estoppel insofar as he or she is held out to appear to be a partner.

5. A Dormant Partner--One who is a partner with the right to management participation, but who is undisclosed and generally inactive. Once disclosed, the dormant partner has the same liability as a general partner.

6. A Secret Partner--One who actually participates in the management of the partnership but is undisclosed. If the secret partner's connection with the business is disclosed, he or she has unlimited liability.

III. Formation, Rules of Construction, and Property Rights of a Partnership

A. <u>Formation of a Partnership</u>

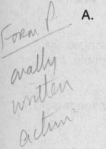
Form P
orally
written
action

1. A partnership may be formed by either an express or implied agreement. Except in specific instances (see 2., below), there is no need for a partnership agreement to be in writing, and the acts of the parties alone may establish a partnership.

2. A writing is needed in the formation of a partnership only when the partnership would otherwise be in violation of the Statute of Frauds. For example, any partnership agreement which necessitates the transfer of real property or to carry on a business for a term in excess of one year must be in writing.

3. Important provisions contained in the Articles of Partnership are the following:

a. Firm name.

b. Names and addresses of all the partners.

c. Date the partnership becomes effective, as well as the intended duration of the partnership.

d. Nature, purpose, and scope of partnership activity.

e. Procedure for admission of new partners.

f. Computation of interest on partnership capital.

g. Computation of profits and the proportionate share of profits and losses attributable to each partner.

h. Powers and duties of the partners.

i. Dissolution procedures and rights.

j.   Procedure for distribution of surplus, including the disposition of the firm name and goodwill.

4.   In most states, when a partnership is doing business under a fictitious name, it must file a certificate with the Secretary of State. This certificate must list the names and addresses of the partners and the fictitious name of the business.

      a.   Failure to comply with the statutes does not invalidate the partnership, but may result in fines.

      b.   The purpose of requiring registration is to allow third parties to know who is in the partnership.

B.   <u>Rules for Determining the Existence of a Partnership</u>

1.   The receipt by a person of a share of the profits of a business is prima facie evidence that the person is a partner in the business, but no such inference shall be drawn if the profits were received in payment:

      a.   Of a debt by installments or otherwise,

      b.   As wages of an employee or rent to a landlord,

      c.   As an annuity to a widow or representative of a deceased partner,

      d.   As interest on a loan, though the amount of payment varies with the profits of the business, or

      e.   As the consideration for the sale of goodwill of a business or other property by installments or otherwise.

2.   The sharing of gross revenues, by itself, does not establish a partnership.

3.   Joint tenancy, tenancy in common, tenancy by the entireties, or any other type of joint ownership of property does not in itself establish a partnership. This is true regardless of whether the co-owners share any profits made through use of the property.

4.   The contribution of capital to a business endeavor does not establish a partnership, and it is not essential to the existence of a partnership that all the partners contribute capital.

5.   The designation of a business relationship as a "partnership" does not conclusively establish a partnership, nor can the parties avoid partnership liability merely by denouncing the existence of a partnership.

6.   Combining the above principles with the UPA definition of a partnership, the determining test is whether or not the parties intended to carry on together as partners, a business for profit. It must appear that the parties intended joint responsibility in the management and operation of the business and intended to share in its profits and losses.

C.   <u>Partnership by Estoppel</u>--The relationship among the partners is governed by the express or implied partnership agreement. In dealings with third parties, however, the conduct of a party or parties may bind him or her or them as partners.

1.   One who holds him- or herself out as a partner in an actual or apparent partnership is liable to another who in good faith and in reliance on the misrepresentation extends credit to the apparent partner. An actual partner who either expressly or impliedly consents to a misrepresentation is likewise liable to third parties.

2.   When an actual partner represents that another is a member of the partnership, when in fact he or she is not, the partner makes the other person his or her agent. The "agent" then has the power to bind the partner to third parties as though the "agent" were actually a partner. **NOTE:** Any liability resulting from such a misrepresentation extends only to the partners who consented to the misrepresentation.

D.   <u>Partnership Property</u>--Rights of the individual partners vis-a-vis the partnership.

1.   All property originally brought into the partnership, or subsequently acquired by purchase or otherwise on account of the partnership, is partnership property. Included within this description is the partnership's capital and name and the goodwill of the partnership.

2.   In construing the phrase "acquired . . . on account of the partnership," the courts look to the intent of the parties as evidenced by the facts and circumstances surrounding each acquisition. The following are of particular importance:

a.   Title--The fact that an asset is acquired or held in the partnership name may be considered by the court, but is not usually a major indication.

b.   Improvement by the Partnership--Again, the fact that partnership funds were used to improve an asset may be considered, but it is not a major indication.

c.   Use of the Property--The fact that an asset is used in the partnership business is indicative of partnership ownership if that fact combined with others (for example, a. & b., above) tends to establish the asset as partnership property.

d.   Partnership Purpose--The fact that an asset is closely connected with the operation of a partnership is of particular importance when there is a dispute between one of the partners and the firm. In recognition of the fiduciary responsibilities inherent in a partnership, courts often view assets acquired by a partner which are necessary for or related to partnership operations as actually held in trust for the firm.

3.   Under the UPA, any estate in real property may be acquired in the partnership name, and title so acquired may be conveyed in the partnership name. A partner may convey title to the property by a conveyance executed in the partnership name. If the partner in fact has no authority to so convey and the person with whom the partner is dealing has knowledge of the fact that he or she has no authority, the partnership may recover the property conveyed. However, when the purchaser or the purchaser's assignee is a holder for value who is without knowledge that the partner has exceeded his or her authority, then the partnership may not recover the property.

4.   A Partner's Property Rights--The direct property rights of a partner are the partner's interest in the partnership, the partner's right to participate in the management of the partnership, and the partner's rights in specific partnership property.

a.   Interest in the Partnership--A partner's interest in the partnership is his or her share of the profits and surplus. This interest is classified as personal property. Profits and losses are shared equally unless the agreement specifies otherwise, even if the amount of contributed capital is not equal. If the partners agree on unequal profit sharing percentages, but are silent as to loss sharing percentages, losses are to be shared using the profit sharing proportions.

(1)   Inheritance--On his or her death, a partner's interest descends as personal property regardless of the form in which the firm's assets exist.

(2)   Assignment--Unless otherwise agreed, a partner's interest is freely assignable. The assignee is only entitled to receive the profits and capital to which the partner would have been entitled. He or she does not become a partner and is not entitled to exercise control over the partnership or use partnership property. The assignor remains liable on all partnership debts. An assignment does not dissolve the partnership.

do not need permission

(3)   Rights of an Individual Partner's Creditor to Partnership Assets--The creditor of an individual partner may not execute on or attach partnership assets. The creditor's only remedy, once his or her claim has been reduced to a judgment, is to obtain a charging order against the debtor-partner's interest. The creditor is then entitled to all future distributions of assets or surplus due the partner until the judgment is satisfied.

(4)   Family Rights--Generally, the partner's interest is treated as community property and is subject to a family allowance (statutory right of a widow to certain portions of the deceased husband's property).

b.   Right to Participate in Management--Unless there is a specific agreement to the contrary, all partners have equal rights in the management and control of the partnership business.

c.   Rights to Specific Partnership Property--Each partner in a partnership has the right to possess and use the partnership property for partnership purposes.

(1)   This right is not assignable except in connection with the assignment of rights of all the partners in the same property.

(2)   This right is not subject to execution or attachment on a claim arising against the individual partner.

(3)   This right is not community property, nor is it subject to family allowance or dower rights.

(4)   On the death of the partner, this right vests in the surviving partners who are then under a duty to account to the estate of the deceased for the value of his or her rights in the property.

IV. Relations Among Partners

A.   <u>Partners as Fiduciaries</u>--Every partner is a fiduciary and must account to the partnership for any benefit derived by him or her from his or her association in the partnership. Likewise, the partner must hold in trust any funds realized from any transaction connected with the information, conduct, or liquidation of the partnership. A partner must also generally account for any benefit, or hold in trust any profit, realized from the partner's use of partnership property.

B.   <u>Rights and Duties of Partners to One Another and to the Partnership</u>--The rights and duties of each partner in relation to the partnership are governed by any agreement among them. If there is no agreement, the UPA imposes the following rules:

1.   All partners have equal rights in the management and conduct of the partnership business. Any differences concerning ordinary matters connected with the partnership business may be decided by a majority of the partners, but no act in contravention of any agreement among the partners may be done rightfully without the consent of all the partners.

2.   A partner's share in profits and losses and rights to assets upon dissolution of the partnership is covered by the following rules:

    a.   Each partner is entitled to repayment of his or her capital contributions or advances made to the partnership. All partners are entitled to an equal share in profits and any surplus remaining after all liabilities (including those to the partners) are satisfied. A partner must contribute to the losses sustained by the partnership proportionately according to the partner's share in the profits.

    b.   The partnership must indemnify every partner for payments made or liabilities incurred by him or her in the ordinary conduct of the partnership business or in the preservation of its business or property.

    c.   A partner is entitled to interest on any sums advanced by him or her in furtherance of partnership business beyond the amount of capital the partner agreed to contribute.

    d.   A partner is not entitled to compensation for acting in the partnership business other than sharing in its profits, unless otherwise agreed. However, a surviving partner is entitled to reasonable compensation for his or her services in winding up the partnership affairs.

3.   Partnership Books and Duties of Partners to Render Information--The partnership must keep its books at a central, agreed-to location. Each partner is entitled to have access to them at all times. A partner has the right to demand from the other partners full and true information of all things affecting the partnership. A partner's legal representative has the same right to such information.

4.   Any partner has the right to a formal accounting of partnership affairs:

    a.   When the partner is wrongfully excluded from the partnership or possession of its property,

    b.   If the right is provided for under the agreement,

    c.   When another partner breaches his or her fiduciary duty, or

    d.   At any other reasonable time.

C.   <u>Rights of a Partner in Actions Between Self and the Partnership</u>

1.   Suit in Equity--The principal remedy available to a partner against his or her co-partners is a suit in equity for a dissolution and an accounting. This topic will be discussed at length in V., below.

2.   Action at Law--Disputes between partners almost invariably involve a conflict as to partnership assets, which necessitates an accounting of assets. Additionally, any suit by a partner against the partnership creates a conflict of interest for the plaintiff partner between his or her individual interest as plaintiff and his or her interest as a defendant member of the partnership. For these reasons, actions at law are seldom permitted except in a few situations. Typically, these situations involve controversies in which no complex accounting is necessary or in which the partner's activity is outside the scope of the partnership business. Thus, the courts will allow an action at law involving a dispute which arose at the outset of the partnership, a suit between partners not related to partnership business, or a suit for fraud or conversion of partnership assets.

V. Relations of Partners to Third Persons

A. <u>Authority of Partners to Bind the Partnership</u>--Generally, the rules of agency apply in determining whether or not the partnership is bound by the dealings of one of its members with a third party. Thus, for the purpose of conducting partnership business, every partner is an agent for the partnership and for every other partner. The act of a partner committed within the scope of the partner's actual or apparent authority will, therefore, bind the partnership.

1. Partner's Actual Authority

   a. Express--A partner's express authority includes that authority specifically set forth in an agreement among the partners. It may also arise from decisions made by a majority of the partners regarding the conduct of the partnership business.

   b. Implied--This type of authority has not been expressly granted to a partner, but instead arises from the nature and business of the partnership. It is essentially that type of authority which is reasonably necessary for a partner to perform his or her duties. For example, if a partner is in charge of the partnership's personnel, it would be reasonable and necessary to imply that he or she has the power to hire and fire employees even though this authority is not expressly granted.

2. Partner's Apparent Authority--The actions of a partner which are apparently for the carrying on of the partnership's business in the usual way, but which are not actually authorized, will still bind the partnership if the third party does not know of the partner's lack of actual authority. However, if the third party knows that a partner's dealings exceed the partner's authority or is outside of the scope of the partner's apparent authority, the other partners are not liable. For example, A is a partner in ABC partnership and is in charge of purchasing. However, by agreement, his authority to contract is limited to $1 million. A enters into a contract on behalf of ABC with Z Company, which does not know of the limitation on A's authority. ABC is still liable on the entire contract.

3. Limitations on a Partner's Authority--In addition to any limitations imposed by agreement, there are several limitations imposed by the UPA. Without authorization to the contrary, no partner may:

   a. Assign the partnership property in trust for the benefit of creditors or on the assignee's promise to pay the debts of the partnership,

   b. Dispose of the goodwill of the business or do any other act that would make it impossible to carry on the ordinary business of a partnership,

   c. Confess a judgment, or

   d. Submit a partnership claim or liability to arbitration.

4. Termination of Authority--The majority of partners may terminate the authority of a partner, or minority of partners, unless this action would be contrary to a previous agreement. Some cases have allowed one partner to terminate the authority of a co-partner when the partnership is limited to two persons.

5. Notice, Knowledge, and Admissions

   a. In regard to any matter affecting partnership affairs, notice to any individual partner is imputed to all other partners.

   b. The knowledge of any partner gained while working on partnership matters is also imputed to all other members of the partnership. However, any knowledge gained by a partner who is engaged in a fraud as to the partnership is not imputed to the partnership. Normally, knowledge acquired by one before he or she becomes a partner is not imputed to the partnership.

    c.   An admission or representation made by any partner while the partner is acting within the scope of his or her authority is admissible as evidence against the partnership.

B. Partnership Liability

1. Contract Liability--Partners are jointly liable for all debts and contract obligations of the partnership.

    a.   This liability extends to all "in fact" partners (for example, dormant partners) whether or not the creditor relied upon the fact that such a person was a partner.

    b.   An incoming partner is jointly liable for all debts of the partnership, including those incurred before the partner's admission. The partner is held to have assumed all existing liabilities, and this presumption may not be altered by an agreement among the partners. However, the partner's liability as to pre-existing claims may be satisfied only out of partnership property.

    c.   Effect of Joint Liability--A creditor may not proceed against one or several of the partners without joining all the partners. In most jurisdictions, a release of one partner has the effect of releasing all partners. A creditor has the option of suing the partnership as an entity, but the judgment obtained in such a suit would bind only the partnership assets.

    d.   Remedies--Liability for partnership debts extends beyond the partnership interest of each partner and includes the partner's personal assets. Partnership assets are subject to attachment and execution only when the action is on a partnership debt. A partner's rights in partnership property are not subject to claims against the partner as an individual.

2. Tort Liability--All partners are liable jointly and severally for actions in tort.

    a.   Tort liability may arise from the wrongful act or omission of a partner arising out of activity which was authorized by the other partners or within the partner's normal course of business. The partnership is also liable for funds misapplied by one of the partners.

    b.   Since the partners are severally liable, an action may be brought against any one of the partners.

    c.   Any partner adjudicated guilty of tortious conduct towards an outsider is liable to his or her co-partner(s).

        •   Generally, a partnership has no right to recover from third persons who inflict injuries on an individual partner.

VI. Dissolution of a Partnership

The change in the relation of the partners caused by a partner ceasing to be associated with the carrying on of the business. The partnership does not terminate on dissolution, but continues until the winding up of the partnership is complete.

A. Causes--Dissolution may be accomplished either without violating the partnership agreement or in violation of the partnership agreement.

1. Dissolution without violating the partnership agreement may occur by the following four methods:

   a. Termination of the Partnership Period or Particular Undertaking--When the partnership agreement specifies that the partnership will terminate on a certain date or when a particular project is completed, the expiration of the term or completion of the undertaking dissolves the partnership. The partners may, if they choose, continue beyond the term as partners at will.

   b. Express Decision of Any Partner When the Partnership Is At Will--Under these circumstances, a partner may dissolve the partnership at anytime without liability to the other partners even if the dissolution causes a loss to the firm. However, pursuant to the partner's fiduciary duty, a partner must act in good faith. Thus, if a partner chooses to exercise his or her right to dissolve in order to exclude the partner's co-partners from a lucrative business opportunity, his or her act of dissolution would be wrongful, and his or her rights on dissolution would change accordingly.

   c. Express Will of All the Partners Who Have Not Assigned Their Interests or Had Them Claimed in Satisfaction of a Personal Debt--When all the partners agree to dissolve, it is immaterial that the partnership is for a term and not at will.

   d. Expulsion of a Partner From the Firm When the Partnership Agreement Provides for Dissolution in This Manner--The expulsion must be both authorized by the agreement and bona fide. Under these circumstances, the expelling partners are not liable for any resulting damages.

2. Alternate methods of dissolution which violate the partnership agreement:

   a. The Express Decision of Any Partner Which Violates the Agreement--Every partner has the power to dissolve the partnership whether or not the partner has that right under the partnership agreement. When the dissolving partner acts in violation of the agreement, the partner may be held liable for any losses caused by the dissolution. The following acts by a partner have been construed by the courts as evidencing the partner's intent to discontinue:

      (1) Assignment of Partnership Interests--A partner's transfer of his or her partnership property to a third party may be indicative, but is not conclusive, of an intent to dissolve.

      (2) Levy of a Charging Order--The levy of a charging order on the partnership interest of a debtor/partner does not by itself produce a dissolution. However, the assignee or holder of a charging order can obtain a judicial dissolution of the partnership after expiration of the term or, if it is a partnership at will, whenever the interest is acquired.

   b. Illegality--Dissolution of a partnership results automatically upon the occurrence of any event that makes it unlawful for the business of the partnership to be carried on. The partners may change their business to avoid the illegality and thus continue the partnership relationship.

   c. Death, Withdrawal, or Admission of a Partner--Unless the partnership agreement provides otherwise, these changes in the makeup of the partnership will result in its dissolution. When the partnership is dissolved by the death of a partner, the surviving partners have the right to wind up partnership affairs.

d.   Bankruptcy of a Partner or Partnership--A partner's credit and that of the partnership are essential to the operation of the partnership; therefore, bankruptcy normally results in dissolution.

e.   Judgment--The court has the power to adjudicate dissolution on application by or for a partner when the following circumstances exist:

    (1)   A partner has been declared a lunatic in a judicial proceeding or is otherwise shown to be of unsound mind.

    (2)   A partner otherwise becomes incapable of performing his or her part of the partnership contract (generally, the incapacity must be of such a nature as to materially affect the partner's ability to discharge his or her duties).

    (3)   A partner has been guilty of conduct that tends to prejudicially affect the carrying on of the business.

    (4)   A partner willfully or persistently commits a breach of the partnership agreement.

    (5)   The business of the partnership can only be carried on at a loss.

    (6)   Whenever the dissolution would be equitable.

f.   Upon the application of a partner's assignee or creditor with a charging order, the court may adjudge dissolution as stated in a.(2), above. Normally, the following procedures are followed when a court decrees dissolution:

    (1)   Accounting--A suit for dissolution is generally a suit in equity for dissolution and accounting. An accounting is necessary so that the court can determine the credits or debits of each partner and supervise the distribution of partnership assets.

    (2)   Method of Distribution--Usually, the court orders a sale of all partnership assets and applies the proceeds first to satisfy debts, and then to repay each partner's capital account. Any proceeds still remaining are paid to the partners as current earnings in proportion to each partner's share of the profits.

        (a)   If there are no debts, the court may distribute the partnership assets in kind.

        (b)   If there are losses, each partner must contribute in proportion to his or her share of the profits. If one partner is insolvent or refuses to contribute, the remaining partners are liable for his or her share. They then will have a cause of action against the noncontributing partner.

B.   <u>Rights of Partners</u>

1.   Not in Contravention of the Partnership Agreement--As against the partner's co-partners and persons claiming through them, each partner has the right (unless otherwise agreed) to have the partnership property applied to discharge its liabilities and the surplus applied to pay in cash the amount owing to the partner. An expelled partner who is discharged from all partnership liabilities receives only the net amount due the partner from the partnership.

2. Contravention of the Partnership Agreement

   a. Partners who have not caused the wrongful dissolution have all the rights specified in 1., above, and the right to damages from the breaching partner or partners.

   b. If all nonbreaching partners desire to continue the business in the same name, they may do so. They are entitled to possess the partnership property but must pay to any partner who caused the wrongful dissolution the value of the partner's interest.

   c. A partner who has wrongfully caused dissolution has the rights and liabilities as provided in 1., above, when the business is not continued. The partner has the rights as provided under a. and b., above, when the business is continued by the nonbreaching partners. However, a partner who wrongfully causes dissolution is liable for all damages to the partnership caused by the partner's action.

3. Caused by Fraud--When a partnership contract is rescinded on the grounds of fraud or misrepresentation, the party entitled to rescission has the following rights:

   a. The partner has the right to a lien on, or a right to retention of, the surplus of the partnership to secure his or her capital investment and any advances.

   b. After all liabilities to third persons have been satisfied, the partner has the right to stand in the place of creditors for his or her payments made on partnership liabilities.

   c. The partner has the right to be indemnified by the person who is guilty of the fraud or the misrepresentation. This indemnity is good against all the debts and liabilities of the partnership.

4. Right of Partners to Wind Up--Unless otherwise agreed, any nonbankrupt partner who has not wrongfully dissolved the partnership, or the legal representative of the last surviving partner, has the right to wind up the partnership affairs. Any partner, the partner's legal representative, or the partner's assignee may petition for a winding up by the court.

C. Effect on the Partner's Authority and Rights to Bind the Partnership Thereafter

1. Contribution From Co-Partners After Dissolution--When the dissolution is caused by the act, death, or bankruptcy of a partner, each partner is liable to his or her co-partners as though the partnership had not been dissolved. However, the nondealing partners are not liable to any partner who has actual knowledge of the dissolution before the partner acts on "behalf of the partnership."

2. A partner has the power to bind the partnership as to third persons as follows:

   a. By an act appropriate for winding up partnership affairs or completing unfinished transactions, or

   b. By a transaction that would bind the partnership if dissolution had not taken place, provided the third party has no knowledge of the dissolution.

3. The partnership is not bound by acts of any partner after dissolution when:

   a. The partnership is dissolved because it is unlawful to carry on the business, except when the act is appropriate to wind up partnership affairs, or

   b. The partner is bankrupt or has no authority to wind up partnership affairs.

D. <u>Effect on a Partner's Liability</u>--Generally, the dissolution of a partnership does not discharge the existing liability of any partner.

1. A partner may be discharged from any existing liability upon dissolution of the partnership by an agreement to that effect. The agreement must include as parties the partner him- or herself, the partnership creditor, and the person or partnership continuing the business. The agreement may be inferred from the course of dealing between the creditor having knowledge of the dissolution and the person or partnership continuing the business.

2. When a person agrees to assume the existing obligations of a dissolved partnership, the withdrawing partner is thereby discharged from any liability to creditors who agree to the substitution.

3. A deceased partner's nonpartnership property is subject to all the partnership's obligations which were incurred while he or she was a partner. However, the claims of a decedent's individual creditors have priority over those of any partnership creditors as against the nonpartnership property.

E. <u>Rules for the Distribution of a Partnership's Assets</u>--Subject to any agreement among the partners the following rules apply:

1. The liabilities of the partnership rank in order of payment as follows:

   a. Those owing to creditors other than the partners,

   b. Those owing to partners other than for capital and profits,

   c. Those owing to the partners for capital, and

   d. Those owing to the partners for profit.

2. The partnership's assets (which are the partnership property and the contributions of the partners necessary for the payment of all liabilities) are applied in the order above.

3. The partners are liable for the amount necessary to satisfy all the claims. If a partner is insolvent or beyond the reach of judicial process, the other partners are responsible for his or her liabilities. Such contributing partners are liable in the proportion in which they share in the profits.

4. An assignee for the benefit of creditors or any person appointed by the court may enforce the contributions specified in 3., above.

5. Any partner or the partner's legal representative may enforce the contributions specified in 3., above, to the extent of the amount the partner has paid in excess of his or her share.

6. The individual property of a deceased partner is liable for contributions required in 3., above.

7. Once the partnership property and the property of the individual partners are in the hands of the court for distribution, the priorities are as follows:

   a. Partnership creditors have priority as to partnership property,

   b. Individual creditors have priority as to individual property, and

   c. The rights of secured or lien creditors are provided for as previously discussed.

8. If a partner becomes bankrupt or if the partner's estate is insolvent, the claims against his or her separate property rank as follows:

    a. Those owing to personal creditors,

    b. Those owing to partnership creditors, and

    c. Those owing to partners who have made advances for the benefit of the partnership.

F. <u>Liability of Persons Continuing the Partnership's Business</u>

    1. Generally, anytime a partnership is dissolved and the same business is carried on by a newly formed partnership, creditors of the dissolved partnership are also creditors of the partnership continuing the business.

    2. The liability of a third person who becomes a partner in the new partnership for debts owed to creditors of the dissolved partnership may be satisfied only out of partnership property.

G. <u>Rights of a Retiring Partner or the Estate of a Deceased Partner When the Business Is Continued</u>-- When a partner retires or dies and the business is continued without any settlement of accounts, the partner or his or her legal representative has the option of taking either:

    1. The value of the partner's interest in the partnership as of the date of dissolution plus any interest accruing until the date of discharge, or

    2. The value of the partner's partnership interest and, instead of interest, the profits attributable to the use of that interest in continuing the business.

VII. Limited Partnerships

The purpose of a limited partnership is to allow persons, who do not have the desire or ability to assume the responsibilities of a general partner, to invest in a partnership business.

A. <u>General Nature</u>--A limited partnership is a partnership formed by two or more persons having as members one or more general partners and one or more limited partners.

    1. A general partner is analogous to a partner in a general partnership. The partner is responsible for the management and control of the partnership and is personally liable for its debts. There must be at least one general partner in any limited partnership.

    2. A limited partner is one who makes a capital contribution to the partnership and thereby obtains an interest in that partnership. **NOTE:** A limited partner's contribution may not be in the form of personal services.

        a. A limited partner has all the rights of a general partner except that the partner has no right to manage or control the partnership. Nevertheless, the partner has the right to inspect the books, demand an accounting, and have a dissolution and winding-up decree by the court.

        b. A limited partner's surname may not appear in the partnership name unless there is sufficient designation attached to the partner's name to indicate that he or she is a limited partner.

        c. A limited partner's liability is limited to the amount of the partner's contribution in the partnership unless he or she takes part in the management of the business or violates b., above.

d. A limited partner may loan money to and transact other business with the partnership. The partner also receives payment on any resulting claims on an equal, pro rata basis with third party creditors.

e. A limited partner may receive a share of the profits or other compensation as stipulated in the certificate, provided, however, that after such payment, the partnership assets are in excess of all liabilities to creditors.

f. Generally, a limited partner may demand or receive cash in repayment of his or her contribution. However, the partner may not do so until all partnership liabilities to creditors have been paid or the partnership has sufficient assets to pay them.

g. A limited partner's interest is considered personal property and it is freely assignable. A limited partner's rights are not assignable unless they are assigned to a substituted limited partner. For a person to become a substituted limited partner, all partners must be in agreement, and the certificate (see VII.B.1., below) must be amended to reflect the substitution of limited partners.

h. The death of a limited partner does not dissolve the partnership.

i. A limited partner is liable to the partnership for any difference between his or her contribution as actually made and that which the partner agreed to make in the certificate. A limited partner holds, as trustee for the partnership, property stated in the certificate as contributed by the partner, but which in fact he or she possesses, and any money or property wrongfully paid or conveyed to the partner on account of his or her contribution.

j. Any creditor of a limited partner may obtain, through the court, a charge against the debtor's interest in the partnership.

B. Formation--In contrast to the formation of a general partnership, the formation of a limited partnership must be in accordance with strict statutory requirements. Additionally, limited partnerships may be formed only in those jurisdictions which have enacted enabling statutes.

1. The partners must execute a certificate which states the following: the name of the partnership, the character of the business, the location of the business, the term for which the partnership is to exist, a description of the capital, and the name and residence of each partner or limited partner together with a list of each member's status and rights. The certificate must be filed with the Secretary of State, and a copy must be filed with the clerk of the court in the county of the principal place of business. The certificate may be amended or canceled only if the above formalities are observed. The purpose of the certificate is to put creditors on notice of the limited liability of the limited partners.

2. There is a requirement that the certificate substantially comply with the requirements listed in 1., above. If a certificate contains a false statement, anyone who suffers a loss through reliance thereon may hold all the partners liable.

C. Dissolution--A limited partnership may be dissolved in any of the ways discussed previously for general partnerships. However, the death or assignment of interest of a limited partner does not dissolve the partnership.

D. Distribution--In settling accounts after dissolution, the liabilities of the partnership shall be entitled to payment in the following order:

1. To creditors (including limited partners who are creditors), except claims to limited partners on account of their capital contributions;

2. To limited partners in respect of their share of undistributed profits and other compensation by way of income on their capital contributions;

3. To limited partners for the amount of their capital contributions;

4. To general partners' claims for loans, etc., but not for capital contributions and profits;

5. To general partners in respect to profits; and

6. To general partners in respect to their capital contributions.

E. Revised Uniform Limited Partnership Act--The Uniform Limited Partnership Act was amended in 1985 and the Revised Uniform Limited Partnership Act (RULPA) provides for the following distribution of partnership assets (this rule should be followed in states that have adopted the RULPA:

1. First, to partnership creditors including partners (general and limited) who are creditors, except for "unpaid distributions" to partners.

2. Second, to partners who have previously withdrawn from the partnership, payments to these partners for "unpaid distributions" plus the return of capital. Unpaid distributions are any distributions a partner is entitled to upon withdrawal from the firm.

3. Third, to partners (general and limited) to the extent of their capital contribution.

4. Fourth, to partners (general and limited) as to profits.

VIII. Federal Income Tax Ramifications

A. Partnership as Conduit--General and limited partnerships are not tax-paying entities. Rather, they are reporting entities which pass through distributive shares of gain and loss as well as partnership ordinary income or loss to the individual partners. The partnership's return is made on Form 1065 and is for information purposes only. The individual partners are taxable on their distributive shares of partnership gain and income regardless of whether the distributive share is actually distributed.

B. Taxable Entity Status of a Partnership--A general or limited partnership which does not possess a majority of the attributes of a corporation will be accorded the tax status and treatment described in A., above. To be characterized as a partnership rather than an association (corporation), an entity must not have a majority of the following corporate attributes:

1. Free transferability of ownership interest.

2. Centralized management.

3. Continuity of existence.

4. Limited liability.

NOTES

CHAPTER 51—PARTNERSHIPS

Problem 51-1 MULTIPLE CHOICE QUESTIONS (55 to 65 minutes)

1. A general partnership must
   a. Pay federal income tax.
   b. Have two or more partners.
   c. Have written articles of partnership.
   d. Provide for apportionment of liability for partnership debts. (11/91, Law, #14, 2342)

2. For which of the following is a partnership recognized as a separate legal entity?
   a. The liability for and payment of taxes on partnership gains from the sale of capital assets.
   b. In respect to contributions and advances made by partners to the partnership.
   c. The recognition of net operating losses.
   d. The status of the partnership as an employer for workers' compensation purposes. (11/81, Law, #20, 9911)

3. A joint venture is a(an)
   a. Association limited to no more than two persons in business for profit.
   b. Enterprise of numerous co-owners in a nonprofit undertaking.
   c. Corporate enterprise for a single undertaking of limited duration.
   d. Association of persons engaged as co-owners in a single undertaking for profit. (11/89, Law, #4, 0669)

4. Which of the following statements is correct with respect to the differences and similarities between a corporation and a limited partnership?
   a. Directors owe fiduciary duties to the corporation and limited partners owe such duties to the partnership.
   b. A corporation and a limited partnership may be created only pursuant to a state statute, and a copy of its organizational document must be filed with the proper state agency.
   c. Shareholders may be entitled to vote on corporate matters, whereas limited partners are prohibited from voting on any partnership matters.
   d. Stock of a corporation may be subject to the federal securities laws registration requirements, whereas limited partnership interests are automatically exempt from such requirements. (11/88, Law, #5, 9911)

5. Noll Corp. and Orr Co. are contemplating entering into an unincorporated joint venture. Such a joint venture

   a. Will be treated as a partnership in most important legal respects.
   b. Must be dissolved upon completion of a single undertaking.
   c. Will be treated as an association for federal income tax purposes and taxed at the prevailing corporate rates.
   d. Must file a certificate of limited partnership with the appropriate state agency. (5/86, Law, #58, 0684)

6. Downs, Frey, and Vick formed the DFV general partnership to act as manufacturers' representatives. The partners agreed Downs would receive 40% of any partnership profits and Frey and Vick would each receive 30% of such profits. It was also agreed that the partnership would not terminate for five years. After the fourth year, the partners agreed to terminate the partnership. At that time, the partners' capital accounts were as follows: Downs, $20,000; Frey, $15,000; and Vick, $10,000. There also were undistributed losses of $30,000. Which of the following statements about the form of the DFV partnership agreement is correct?
   a. It must be in writing because the partnership was to last for longer than one year.
   b. It must be in writing because partnership profits would **not** be equally divided.
   c. It could be oral because the partners had explicitly agreed to do business together.
   d. It could be oral because the partnership did **not** deal in real estate. (5/93, Law, #11, 3980)

7. Which of the following requirements must be met to have a valid partnership exist?

   I. Co-ownership of all property used in a business.
   II. Co-ownership of a business for profit.

   a. I only.
   b. II only.
   c. Both I and II.
   d. Neither I nor II. (11/93, Law, #16, 4313)

8. To which of the following parties may a CPA partnership provide its working papers, without being lawfully subpoenaed or without the client's consent?
   a. The IRS.
   b. The FASB.

Read *Automatic dissolution of change of partners*

c. Any surviving partner(s) on the death of a partner.

d. A CPA before purchasing a partnership interest in the firm. (11/94, Law, #15, 5192)

Read

9. Which of the following is **not** necessary to create an express partnership? *only if > 1 yr*

a. Execution of a written partnership agreement.

b. Agreement to share ownership of the partnership.

c. Intention to conduct a business for profit.

d. Intention to create a relationship recognized as a partnership. (11/90, Law, #11, 0665)

10. Many states require partnerships to file the partnership name under laws which are generally known as fictitious name statutes. These statutes

a. Require a proper filing as a condition precedent to the valid creation of a partnership.

b. Are designed primarily to provide registration for tax purposes.

c. Are designed to clarify the rights and duties of the members of the partnership.

d. Have little effect on the creation or operation of a partnership other than the imposition of a fine for noncompliance. (11/83, Law, #15, 0690)

11. For which of the following purposes is a general partnership recognized as an entity by the Uniform Partnership Act?

a. Recognition of the partnership as the employer of its partners.

b. Insulation of the partners from personal liability.

c. Taking of title and ownership of property.

d. Continuity of existence. (5/83, Law, #3, 0693)

12. Cobb, Inc., a partner in TLC Partnership, assigns its partnership interest to Bean, who is not made a partner. After the assignment, Bean asserts the rights to

I. Participate in the management of TLC.

II. Cobb's share of TLC's partnership profits.

Bean is correct as to which of these rights?

a. I only.

b. II only.

c. I and II.

d. Neither I **nor** II. (5/93, Law, #15, 3984)

13. In a general partnership, a partner's interest in specific partnership property is

a. Transferable to a partner's individual creditors.

b. Subject to a partner's liability for alimony.

c. Transferable to a partner's estate upon death.

d. Subject to a surviving partner's right of survivorship. (11/91, Law, #16, 2344)

14. Unless otherwise provided in a general partnership agreement, which of the following statements is correct when a partner dies?

	The deceased partner's executor would automatically become a partner	The deceased partner's estate would be free from any partnership liabilities	The partnership would be dissolved automatically
a.	Yes	Yes	Yes
b.	Yes	No	No
c.	No	Yes	No
d.	No	No	Yes

(11/94, Law, #20, 5197)

Items 15 and 16 are based on the following:

Dowd, Elgar, Frost, and Grant formed a general partnership. Their written partnership agreement provided that the profits would be divided so that Dowd would receive 40%; Elgar, 30%; Frost, 20%; and Grant, 10%. There was no provision for allocating losses. At the end of its first year, the partnership had losses of $200,000. Before allocating losses, the partners' capital account balances were: Dowd, $120,000; Elgar, $100,000; Frost, $75,000; and Grant, $11,000. Grant refuses to make any further contributions to the partnership. Ignore the effects of federal partnership tax law.

15. What would be Grant's share of the partnership losses?

a. $ 9,000

b. $20,000

c. $39,000

d. $50,000 (5/92, Law, #12, 2825)

16. After losses were allocated to the partners' capital accounts and all liabilities were paid, the partnership's sole asset was $106,000 in cash. How much would Elgar receive on dissolution of the partnership?

a. $37,000

b. $40,000

c. $47,500

d. $50,000 (5/92, Law, #13, 2826)

17. The partnership agreement for Owen Associates, a general partnership, provided that profits be paid to the partners in the ratio of their financial contribution to the partnership. Moore contributed $10,000, Noon contributed $30,000, and Kale contributed $50,000. For the year ended December 31, 1993, Owen had losses of $180,000.

What amount of the losses should be allocated to Kale?

a. $ 40,000
b. $ 60,000
c. $ 90,000
d. $100,000   (11/94, Law, #22, 5199)

18. Gillie, Taft, and Dall are partners in an architectural firm. The partnership agreement is silent about the payment of salaries and the division of profits and losses. Gillie works full-time in the firm, and Taft and Dall each work half-time. Taft invested $120,000 in the firm, and Gillie and Dall invested $60,000 each. Dall is responsible for bringing in 50% of the business, and Gillie and Taft 25% each. How should profits of $120,000 for the year be divided?

a. Gillie $60,000, Taft $30,000, Dall $30,000.
b. Gillie $40,000, Taft $40,000, Dall $40,000.
c. Gillie $30,000, Taft $60,000, Dall $30,000.
d. Gillie $30,000, Taft $30,000, Dall $60,000.
          (11/89, Law, #6, 0671)

19. Locke and Vorst were general partners in a kitchen equipment business. On behalf of the partnership, Locke contracted to purchase 15 stoves from Gage. Unknown to Gage, Locke was not authorized by the partnership agreement to make such contracts. Vorst refused to allow the partnership to accept delivery of the stoves and Gage sought to enforce the contract. Gage will

a. Lose, because Locke's action was **not** authorized by the partnership agreement.
b. Lose, because Locke was **not** an agent of the partnership.
c. Win, because Locke had express authority to bind the partnership.
d. Win, because Locke had apparent authority to bind the partnership.   (5/93, Law, #14, 3983)

20. The apparent authority of a partner to bind the partnership in dealing with third parties

a. Will be effectively limited by a formal resolution of the partners of which third parties are aware.
b. Will be effectively limited by a formal resolution of the partners of which third parties are unaware. (actual)
c. Would permit a partner to submit a claim against the partnership to arbitration.
d. Must be derived from the express powers and purposes contained in the partnership agreement.   (11/93, Law, #12, 4309)

21. Acorn and Bean were general partners in a farm machinery business. Acorn contracted, on behalf of the partnership, to purchase 10 tractors from Cobb Corp. Unknown to Cobb, Acorn was not authorized by the partnership agreement to make such contracts. Bean refused to allow the partnership to accept delivery of the tractors and Cobb sought to enforce the contract. Cobb will

a. Lose, because Acorn's action was beyond the scope of Acorn's implied authority.
b. Prevail, because Acorn had implied authority to bind the partnership.
c. Prevail, because Acorn had apparent authority to bind the partnership.
d. Lose, because Acorn's express authority was restricted, in writing, by the partnership agreement.   (11/90, Law, #13, 0667)

22. Eller, Fort, and Owens do business as Venture Associates, a general partnership. Trent Corp. brought a breach of contract suit against Venture and Eller individually. Trent won the suit and filed a judgment against both Venture and Eller. Trent will generally be able to collect the judgment from

a. Partnership assets only.
b. The personal assets of Eller, Fort, and Owens only.
c. Eller's personal assets only after partnership assets are exhausted.
d. Eller's personal assets only.
          (11/90, Law, #12, 0666)

23. In a general partnership, the authorization of all partners is required for an individual partner to bind the partnership in a business transaction to

a. Purchase inventory.
b. Hire employees.
c. Sell goodwill.
d. Sign advertising contracts.
          (11/91, Law, #15, 2343)

24. Unless the partnership agreement prohibits it, a partner in a general partnership may validly assign rights to

	Partnership property	Partnership distributions
a.	Yes	Yes
b.	Yes	No
c.	No	Yes
d.	No	No

(11/93, Law, #18, 4315)

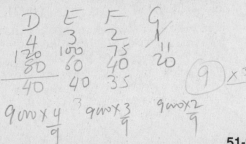

25. A general partner of a mercantile partnership
a. Can, by virtue of his or her acts, impose tort liability upon the other partners.
b. Has **no** implied authority if the partnership agreement is contained in a formal and detailed signed writing.
c. Can have his or her apparent authority effectively negated by express limitations in the partnership agreement.
d. **Cannot** be sued individually for a tort he or she has committed in carrying on partnership business until the partnership has been sued and a judgment returned unsatisfied.

(11/83, Law, #16, 0691)

26. Which of the following statements is correct concerning liability when a partner in a general partnership commits a tort while engaged in partnership business?
a. The partner committing the tort is the only party liable.
b. The partnership is the only party liable.
c. Each partner is jointly and severally liable.
d. Each partner is liable to pay an equal share of any judgment.   (11/94, Law, #21, 5198)

27. Lark, a partner in DSJ, a general partnership, wishes to withdraw from the partnership and sell Lark's interest to Ward. All of the other partners in DSJ have agreed to admit Ward as a partner and to hold Lark harmless for the past, present, and future liabilities of DSJ. As a result of Lark's withdrawal and Ward's admission to the partnership, Ward
a. Acquired only the right to receive Ward's share of DSJ profits.
b. Has the right to participate in DSJ's management.
c. Is personally liable for partnership liabilities arising before and after being admitted as a partner.
d. Must contribute cash or property to DSJ to be admitted with the same rights as the other partners.   (11/94, Law, #23, 5200)

28. The partners of College Assoc., a general partnership, decided to dissolve the partnership and agreed that none of the partners would continue to use the partnership name. Under the Uniform Partnership Act, which of the following events will occur on dissolution of the partnership?

	Each partner's existing liability would be discharged	Each partner's apparent authority would continue
a.	Yes	Yes
b.	Yes	No
c.	No	Yes
d.	No	No

(11/94, Law, #24, 5201)

Items 29 and 30 are based on the following:

Downs, Frey, and Vick formed the DFV general partnership to act as manufacturers' representatives. The partners agreed Downs would receive 40% of any partnership profits and Frey and Vick would each receive 30% of such profits. It was also agreed that the partnership would not terminate for five years. After the fourth year, the partners agreed to terminate the partnership. At that time, the partners' capital accounts were as follows: Downs, $20,000; Frey, $15,000; and Vick, $10,000. There also were undistributed losses of $30,000.

29. If Frey died before the partnership terminated,
a. Downs and Vick, as a majority of the partners, would have been able to continue the partnership.
b. The partnership would have continued until the five year term expired.
c. The partnership would automatically dissolve.
d. Downs and Vick would have Frey's interest in the partnership.   (5/93, Law, #13, 3982)

30. Vick's share of the undistributed losses will be
a. $ 0.
b. $ 1,000.
c. $ 9,000.
d. $10,000.   (5/93, Law, #12, 3981)

31. On dissolution of a general partnership, distributions will be made on account of:

I. Partners' capital accounts.
II. Amounts owed partners with respect to profits.
III. Amounts owed partners for loans to the partnership.

in the following order:
a. III, I, II.
b. I, II, III.
c. II, III, I.
d. III, II, I.

(11/91, Law, #17, 2345)

32. Which of the following statements regarding a limited partner is(are) generally correct?

	The limited partner is subject to personal liability for partnership debts	The limited partner has the right to take part in the control of the partnership
a.	Yes	Yes
b.	Yes	No
c.	No	Yes
d.	No	No

(11/89, Law, #5, 0670)

33. Which of the following statements is correct with respect to a limited partnership?

a. A limited partner may **not** be an unsecured creditor of the limited partnership.

b. A general partner may **not** also be a limited partner at the same time.

c. A general partner may be a secured creditor of the limited partnership.

d. A limited partnership can be formed with limited liability for all partners. (5/92, Law, #11, 2824)

34. Cavendish is a limited partner of Custer Venture Capital. He is extremely dissatisfied with the performance of the general partners in making investments and managing the portfolio. He is contemplating taking whatever legal action may be appropriate against the general partners. Which of the following rights would Cavendish **not** be entitled to assert as a limited partner?

a. To have a formal accounting of partnership affairs whenever the circumstances render it just and reasonable.

b. To have the same rights as a general partner to a dissolution and winding up of the partnership.

c. To have reasonable access to the partnership books and to inspect and copy them.

d. To have himself elected as a general partner by a majority vote of the limited partners in number and amount. (5/82, Law, #4, 9911)

35. Unless otherwise provided in the limited partnership agreement, which of the following statements is correct?

a. A general partner's capital contribution may **not** consist of services rendered to the partnership.

b. Upon the death of a limited partner, the partnership will be dissolved.

c. A person may own a limited partnership interest in the same partnership in which he or she is a general partner.

d. Upon the assignment of a limited partner's interest, the assignee will become a substituted limited partner if the consent of two-thirds of all partners is obtained. (11/84, Law, #11, 0689)

36. In general, which of the following statements is correct with respect to a limited partnership?

a. A limited partner has the right to obtain from the general partner(s) financial information and tax returns of the limited partnership.

b. A limited partnership can be formed with limited liability for all partners.

c. A limited partner may **not** also be a general partner at the same time.

d. A limited partner may hire employees on behalf of the partnership. (11/88, Law, #4, 9911)

Items 37 and 38 are based on the following:

White, Grey, and Fox formed a limited partnership. White is the general partner and Grey and Fox are the limited partners. Each agreed to contribute $200,000. Grey and Fox each contributed $200,000 in cash while White contributed $150,000 in cash and $50,000 worth of services already rendered. After two years, the partnership is insolvent. The fair market value of the assets of the partnership is $150,000, and the liabilities total $275,000. The partners have made no withdrawals.

37. Unless otherwise provided in the certificate of limited partnership, which of the following is correct if Grey dies?

a. Grey's executor will automatically become a substituted limited partner.

b. Grey's executor will have all the rights of a limited partner for the purpose of settling the estate.

c. The partnership will automatically be dissolved.

d. Grey's estate will be free from any liabilities which may have been incurred by Grey as a limited partner. (5/87, Law, #9, 0680)

38. Unless otherwise provided in the certificate of limited partnership, which of the following is correct if Fox assigns her interest in the partnership to Barr and only White consents to Barr's admission as a limited partner?

a. Barr will **not** become a substituted limited partner unless Grey also consents.

b. Barr will have the right to inspect the partnership's books.

c. The partnership will be dissolved.

d. Barr will become a substituted limited partner because White, as general partner, consented. (5/87, Law, #8, 0679)

39. Vast Ventures is a limited partnership. The partnership agreement does not contain provisions dealing with the assignment of a partnership interest. The rights of the general and limited partners

regarding the assignment of their partnership interests are

a. Determined according to the common law of partnerships as articulated by the courts.

b. Basically the same with respect to both types of partners.

c. Basically the same with the exception that the limited partner must give ten days' notice prior to the assignment.

d. Different in that the assignee of the general partnership interest does not become a substituted partner, whereas the assignee of a limited partnership interest automatically becomes a substituted limited partner.

(11/83, Law, #18, 0692)

Solution 51-1 MULTIPLE CHOICE ANSWERS

Nature and Classification of Partnerships

1. (b) By definition of the Uniform Partnership Act, a partnership is "an association of *two or more persons* to carry on a business for profit as co-owners." In general, a partnership does not pay federal income tax. Instead it passes through, to the individual partners, separately stated items of income and deductions for inclusion on the partners' personal returns. A partnership does not have to be evidenced by a writing. There is no requirement that a partnership must provide for the apportionment of liability for partnership debts.

2. (d) For most employment purposes, a partnership is regarded as a separate legal entity; it must withhold a portion of its nonpartner employees' incomes for FICA contributions. Similarly, the partnership must make deductible contributions to FUTA and state unemployment plans for its nonpartner employees. Additionally, premiums paid by the partnership for workers' compensation are deductible if for nonpartner employees but are *nondeductible if for partner employees*. The partnership does not make FICA, FUTA, or FIT payments for employee-partners; however, as stated above, the partnership will make nondeductible contributions to state workers' compensation plans for its employee-partners. With the exception of these workers' compensation payments, the partnership is not an entity vis-a-vis the partners; rather, the partnership is a conduit through which items of revenue, loss, and credit are passed through to the individual partners. The partners themselves are responsible for FICA payments through the self-employment tax and FIT through estimated tax payments.

3. (d) A joint venture resembles a partnership except that it is formed for only one transaction (or in some cases, a *limited* number of transactions). It is possible to have more than two persons as part of the joint venture. A joint venture is for a profit undertaking *not* a nonprofit undertaking. A joint venture is treated as a partnership and not as a corporate enterprise.

4. (b) Both a limited partnership and a corporation can only be created pursuant to state statute, and each must file a copy of its certificate with the proper state authorities. Furthermore, both a corporation's stock and a limited partnership interest are subject to the federal securities laws registration requirements if they are "securities" under the federal securities laws. A limited partner is not an agent of the partnership as a general partner is, and so would not occupy a fiduciary relationship with the partnership. A limited partner is not prohibited from voting on *any* partnership matter. He or she must, however, take care to prevent becoming involved in the management or operation of the partnership so as not to lose his or her status as a limited partner.

5. (a) A joint venture is essentially very similar in its characteristics to a partnership and is generally governed by the law of partnerships. Although a joint venture is generally formed to carry out a single business venture, it is not necessary for it to dissolve upon the completion of its task. A joint venture does not possess the requisite corporate characteristics in order to be taxed as an association. A joint venture is not a limited partnership and thus need not comply with a state's limited partnership act.

Formation and Existence

6. (a) A partnership agreement may be either expressed or implied depending on the activities and conduct of the parties. A partnership agreement can be oral unless the agreement falls within the Statute of Frauds, e.g., partnership that cannot be completed within one year.

7. (b) A partnership is defined as an association of two or more persons to carry on, as co-owners, a business for profit. Item II is clearly a basic requirement of a partnership as it is virtually the

definition of a partnership. Item I, however, is not a requirement in a partnership as certain property used in a partnership may be owned individually by one or more partners.

8. **(c)** The working papers of a partnership may be provided to any partner without the consent of the client because all partners are entitled to participate in the management of the partnership. **NOTE:** Answer (d) also has merit. ET 301.04 states that Rule 301 allows "a review in conjunction with a prospective purchase, sale, or merger of all or part of a member's practice," provided that appropriate precautions are taken to prevent disclosure of client information by the prospective purchaser.

9. **(a)** To create an express partnership, there must be some agreement to share ownership in the business, an intention to conduct the business for profit, and some intention to create a relationship recognized as a partnership. What is not normally needed to create an express partnership is a written partnership agreement. The only time a written partnership agreement is required is when the partners agree to be partners for more than one year (the Statute of Frauds would require the agreement to be in writing). Otherwise a written partnership agreement is not necessary.

10. **(d)** Fictitious name statutes have no operational effect on partnerships. Partnership operations and the rights and duties of partners are affected by the partnership agreement, state statutes codifying the Uniform Partnership Act (UPA), and the Revised Uniform Limited Partnership Act (RULPA). A general partnership comes into existence when the partners intend its creation to begin. Such intent can be found in the partnership agreement or from the circumstances surrounding the operation of the firm (ULPA §7). Partnership existence for tax purposes is determined under the Internal Revenue Code, not state statute.

11. **(c)** The Uniform Partnership Act defines a partnership as an association of two or more persons to carry on a business for profit. In order to achieve its business purposes, a partnership may own property. Partners are not considered employees, but are co-owners of the partnership. General partners are always personally liable for the acts of the partnership. It is only the corporate form of ownership that insulates owners from personal liability. The death of one partner will dissolve a partnership.

12. **(b)** Unless otherwise agreed, a partner's interest is freely assignable. The assignee is entitled to receive only profits and capital to which the partner would have been entitled. He or she does not become a partner and is not entitled to exercise control over the partnership.

13. **(d)** Partnership property is held in a form of joint tenancy known as "tenancy in partnership." Consequently, a partner's interest in specific partnership property is subject to a surviving partner's right of survivorship upon the death of an individual partner.

14. **(d)** Since a partnership is viewed as an aggregate of the partners, there is an automatic dissolution of the partnership any time there is a change in partners. A deceased partner's executor would <u>not</u> automatically become a partner, since no person can become a partner without the express consent of all other partners. Since a decedent's estate continues to be liable for the debts of the decedent, the estate would not be free from any partnership liabilities that were incurred while the decedent was still a partner.

15. **(b)** When a partnership arrangement is set forth allocating profits, but does not mention how losses are to be divided, an assumption is made that losses will be shared in the same manner as profits. Since Grant has a 10 percent profit share percentage, he or she is also attributed with 10 percent of the losses. In this case, Grant's losses total $20,000 ($200,000 X .10). The capital balances given in the question play no part in calculating the loss attributable to Grant.

16. **(a)** It is important to note that when a partnership agreement is silent regarding the allocation of the partnership losses, the losses are allocated in the same manner as partnership profits. Accordingly, Elgar is saddled with 30% of the $200,000 loss, or $60,000. He is also responsible for one-third of the deficit capital balance of Grant. Grant, who began with an $11,000 contribution to capital, sustained 10% of the loss, or $20,000, and as a result, has a negative capital balance of $9,000. It is Grant's responsibility to contribute an additional $9,000 towards the elimination of the deficit, however, the question states that Grant refuses to make any further contribution to the partnership. Therefore, the other partners must make up the difference, but are free to go after Grant for the additional amount each contributes. Thus, Elgar's one-third share of this deficit is $3,000 which leaves his capital account at $37,000 ($100,000 – $60,000 – $3,000).

17. **(d)** The partners of Owen Associates have entered into an enforceable agreement providing that a partner's distributive share of profits would

represent each partner's percentage of capital contribution. The Uniform Partnership Act provides that a partner's liability for losses is the same percentage as their right to profits. Kale contributed 5/9 of all capital, thus is entitled to 5/9 of all profits and for 5/9 of all losses. $180,000 x 5/9 = $100,000.

18. (b) Unless agreed otherwise, partnership profits and losses are shared equally even if contributed capital is unequal and even if services provided are unequal.

Partner's Authority and Liability

19. (d) In a general partnership, any partner may bind the partnership and other partners to all transactions within the apparent scope of the partnership business. Each partner is an agent for the other partners and for the partnership and may bind the partnership based upon apparent authority, such as what is customary in the business or by previous dealings. A partner would have apparent authority to purchase stoves for a kitchen equipment business. Even if Locke's action was not authorized by the partnership agreement, Locke had the apparent authority to conduct business with Gage. For the purpose of conducting partnership business, every partner is an agent for the partnership and every other partner. The problem stated that Locke was not authorized by the partnership agreement to make such contracts, thus there would be no express authority.

20. (a) Apparent authority depends upon what third parties believe about the authority of an agent. Answer (a) is correct because it addresses what third parties are "aware of." The partnership can effectively limit the apparent authority of a partner if it makes the third parties "aware" of the limitation. A resolution which third parties are unaware of will have an effect on the partner's actual authority but will not affect the apparent authority of the partner since third parties are not informed of the change. A partner's authority is limited to preclude any partner from submitting a claim or liability to arbitration without all partners' concurrence. Apparent authority is derived from the implied powers associated with the operation of a partnership and not expressly contained in the partnership agreement.

21. (c) In a general partnership, any partner may bind the partnership and other partners to all transactions within the apparent scope of the partnership business. Each partner is an agent for the other partners and for the partnership and may bind the partnership based upon apparent authority, such as what is customary in the business or by previous dealings. Note how there is no apparent authority if the third party is aware of the partner's limitation, *and* there is no apparent authority to transact business outside the normal scope of the business. A partner would have apparent authority to do normal partnership business, such as order tractors for a farm machinery business. There can be no implied authority if there is no actual authority. Express limitations in a partnership agreement have no bearing on apparent authority unless the third party was aware of the limitation.

22. (c) Under the "Marshaling of Assets Rule," partnership creditors have first claim on partnership assets before proceeding against individual partners' personal assets. In this problem, Trent, a partnership creditor, must go after partnership assets first and, once partnership assets are exhausted, proceed after the individual assets of Eller. Partners have unlimited liability for partnership debts, and Trent can proceed against those individual partners the creditor has individually sued.

23. (c) The Uniform Partnership Act provides several limitations on the ability of an individual partner to bind the partnership, in addition to any limitations spelled out in the written partnership agreement. One such limitation indicates that, without authorization to the contrary, no partner may dispose of the goodwill of the business or do any other act that would make it impossible to carry on the ordinary business of the partnership. Answers (a), (b), and (d) are examples of transactions frequently performed by individual partners, in carrying on partnership business, that will bind the partnership.

24. (c) A partner may assign his or her partnership interest and thus the partnership distributions. Each partner also has a right to possess and use the partnership property for partnership purposes, but this right is not assignable except in connection with the assignment of rights of all the partners in the same property. Therefore, only the distributions can be assigned by a partner.

25. (a) Each partner is an agent for every other partner in the firm and is liable for acts performed within the scope of the partnership business. Therefore, under UPA §15, all partners are liable jointly as well as severally (individually) for torts committed in the course of the partnership business. A general partner has the power to bind the partnership, even if he or she lacks actual authority pursuant to the partnership agreement, if the binding act is apparently within the scope of the partnership's business and the third party does not know that the partner lacks authority. Tort liability is joint and several. No

unsatisfied demand need first be made against the partnership.

26. (c) All partners in a general partnership are jointly and severally liable for torts committed by any partner while engaged in partnership business. Since the rule of *Respondeat Superior* applies, partners may be held liable for each other's torts. Answer (b) is incorrect because of the word "only." A partnership could be liable for the torts committed by a partner; however, partners are jointly and severally liable as well. "Several liability" means that one partner can be liable for the entire judgment amount. After paying the entire judgment, that partner would have the right of contribution from other solvent partners.

27. (b) The Uniform Partnership Act provides that the only element necessary to confer partnership status is mutual consent by all partners. Since all the partners in DSJ agreed to admit Ward, Ward is a partner in DSJ with all the rights and duties which accompany partnership status, including the right to participate in management. Since DSJ has agreed to admit Ward as a substitute partner, there has been a transfer from Lark to Ward of more than a mere assignment of Lark's interest in the partnership. The Uniform Partnership Act (UPA) provides that a partner entering a partnership has only limited liability for partnership liabilities arising before being admitted as a partner. In this instance, it was the other partners of DSJ, not Ward, who promised to hold Lark harmless for past liabilities of DSJ. The UPA does <u>not</u> require an incoming partner to contribute cash or property to the partnership.

28. (c) The Uniform Partnership Act (UPA) provides that all partners have personal liability for partnership liabilities incurred while they were partners. Their liability would continue even after dissolution. The UPA also provides that unless a partnership dissolves by operation of law, the partnership, to terminate the partners' apparent authority, must give actual notice to all third parties who have had dealings with the partners and constructive notice to all others. Since College Assoc. has not provided any notice, the partners will continue to have apparent authority.

Dissolution

29. (c) Dissolution terminates all authority of each partner to act on behalf of the partnership, except authority to wind up partnership affairs and complete pending transactions. Death, by operation of law, results in the dissolution of a partnership. Even if the agreement provides for the continuation of the business, it does not prevent dissolution; it merely

eliminates the necessity of the winding-up process. Dissolution is a change in the relation of partners, as when a partner dies. This does not mean that the partnership will "wind up" and terminate.

30. (c) When a partnership agreement is silent regarding the allocation of partnership losses, the losses are allocated in the same manner as partnership profits. Vick's share of the undistributed losses would be 30% of $30,000 or <u>$9,000</u>.

31. (a) On dissolution of a general partnership, there is a specific order of distributions to be made to the partners. Of the alternatives listed in this question, the first distribution to be made would be on account of amounts owed partners for loans to the partnership. Although not given as one of the answer choices, amounts owed to creditors, other than the partners, is the first distribution made when applicable. Following the payments of amounts owed to partners for loans to the partnership is payment of the partner's capital accounts and amounts owed partners with respect to profits, respectively.

Limited Partnerships

32. (d) A limited partner is not subject to personal liability for partnership debts, because a limited partner's liability is limited to the amount of his or her capital contribution. In addition, generally, a limited partner has no right to control (manage) the partnership (there are a few limited exceptions).

33. (c) It is permissible for a general partner to be a secured creditor of the limited partnership. A limited partner may loan money to and transact other business with a partnership. A general partner may be a limited partner at the same time. Only limited partners have limited liability; the general partners are personally liable for the partnership debts.

34. (d) A limited partnership is a statutorily created association for the purpose of conducting a business for profit. It is composed of one or more general partners who manage the affairs of the business and one or more limited partners who remain passive investors in the partnership. Limited partners have essentially the same rights as general partners: to inspect the books, to receive profits, and to cause an accounting and dissolution. However, limited partners are not personally liable for partnership debts beyond their capital contributions. However, this shield lasts only as long as the limited partners do not participate in the management of the enterprise or allow their names to be used in the firm name. Limited partners are not elected as general partners by a majority vote of limited partners.

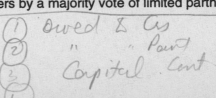

35. (c)   A person may be a general partner and a limited partner in the same partnership at the same time. Although a limited partner may not contribute services, a general partner may contribute services. The death of a limited partner will not dissolve a partnership. A limited partner's interest is freely assignable. However, unless otherwise provided in the partnership agreement, an assignee can become a substitute limited partner only if all members of the limited partnership consent.

36. (a)   A limited partner has all of the rights of a general partner *except* that he has no right to manage or control the partnership. This would include the right to obtain financial information and tax returns of the partnership. However, a limited partner would not be able to hire employees without losing his or her status as a limited partner since this type of activity is closely associated with managing the partnership. Only the limited partners have limited liability; the general partners are personally liable for the partnership debts. A limited partner may also be a general partner.

37. (b)   Under §20 of the Revised Uniform Limited Partnership Act, the executor of an estate of a deceased limited partner is provided with all the rights of a limited partner for the purpose of settling the partner's estate, although he or she does not automatically become a substituted limited partner. Furthermore, the estate is liable for all of the deceased partner's liabilities as a limited partner. The death of a limited partner does not dissolve the partnership.

38. (a)   The assignment of a limited partnership interest, unless otherwise agreed, entitles the assignee only to receive the profits and capital to which the assigning partner would have been entitled. To become a substituted limited partner, *all* of the partners must agree to Barr's admission as a limited partner and the certificate of limited partnership must be amended to reflect the substitution of limited partners. Since Barr is not a partner, he is not entitled to any partnership rights Fox had, such as examining the partnership books. Furthermore, assignment of a partnership interest does not dissolve the partnership.

39. (b)   Under UPA §27 and RULPA §19, an assignee does not automatically become a substituted partner or limited partner. Answers (a), (c), and (d) are incorrect statements of the Uniform Acts relating to the assignment of a partner's interest.

PERFORMANCE BY SUBTOPICS

Each category below parallels a subtopic covered in Chapter 51. Record the number and percentage of questions you correctly answered in each subtopic area.

Nature and Classification of Partnerships		Formation and Existence		Partner's Authority and Liability		Dissolution	
Question #	Correct √	Question #	Correct √	Question #	Correct √	Question #	Correct √
1		6		19		29	
2		7		20		30	
3		8		21		31	
4		9		22		# Questions	3
5		10		23			
# Questions	5	11		24		# Correct	____
		12		25		% Correct	____
# Correct	____	13		26			
% Correct	____	14		27			
		15		28		**Limited Partnerships**	
		16		# Questions	10	Question #	Correct √
		17				32	
		18		# Correct	____	33	
		# Questions	13	% Correct	____	34	
						35	
		# Correct	____			36	
		% Correct	____			37	
						38	
						39	
						# Questions	8
						# Correct	____
						% Correct	____

OTHER OBJECTIVE FORMAT QUESTION

Problem 51-2 (Estimated time--10 to 15 minutes)

In 1992, Anchor, Chain, and Hook created ACH Associates, a general partnership. The partners orally agreed that they would work full time for the partnership and would distribute profits based on their capital contributions. Anchor contributed $5,000; Chain $10,000, and Hook $15,000.

For the year ended December 31, 1993, ACH Associates had profits of $60,000 that were distributed to the partners. During 1994, ACH Associates was operating at a loss. In September 1994, the partnership dissolved.

In October 1994, Hook contracted in writing with Ace Automobile Co. to purchase a car for the partnership. Hook had previously purchased cars from Ace Automobile Co. for use by ACH Associates partners. ACH Associates did not honor the contract with Ace Automobile Co., and Ace Automobile Co. sued the partnership and the individual partners.

Required:

Items 1 through 6 refer to the above facts. For each item, determine whether (a) or (b) is correct.

1.
a. The ACH Associates oral partnership agreement was valid.
b. The ACH Associates oral partnership agreement was invalid because the partnership lasted for more than one year.

2.
a. Anchor, Chain, and Hook jointly owning and conducting a business for profit establishes a partnership relationship.
b. Anchor, Chain, and Hook jointly owning income producing property establishes a partnership relationship.

3.
a. Anchor's share of ACH Associates' 1993 profits was $20,000.
b. Hook's share of ACH Associates' 1993 profits was $30,000.

4.
a. Anchor's capital account would be reduced by 1/3 of any 1994 losses.
b. Hook's capital account would be reduced by 1/2 of any 1994 losses.

5.
a. Ace Automobile Co. would lose a suit brought against ACH Associates because Hook, as a general partner, has no authority to bind the partnership.
b. Ace Automobile Co. would win a suit brought against ACH Associates because Hook's authority continues during dissolution.

6.
a. ACH Associates and Hook would be the only parties liable to pay any judgment recovered by Ace Automobile Co.
b. Anchor, Chain, and Hook would be jointly and severally liable to pay any judgment recovered by Ace Automobile Co.   (5/95, Law, #2a)

OTHER OBJECTIVE FORMAT SOLUTION

Solution 51-2 Liabilities

1. (a) The Statute of Frauds requires that contracts which are not performable within one year of execution be in writing. ACH Associates partnership agreement could be performed within one year; thus, the Statute of Frauds is not applicable and the oral agreement is valid.

2. (a) The Uniform Partnership Act defines a partnership as an association of two or more persons who jointly carry on a business for profit. Merely owning property jointly, without active involvement in management of the business, does not create a partnership.

3. (b) The Uniform Partnership Act specifies that partnership profits are shared equally unless the partnership agreement specifies otherwise. The ACH Associates partnership agreement specifies that partners will share in profit distributions based on their capital contributions. As a result, Hook's share of ACH Associates' 1993 profits was $30,000. Anchor's share of ACH Associates' 1993 profits was $10,000.

4. (b) The Uniform Partnership Act provides that if partners agree on unequal profit percentages, but are silent as to loss-sharing percentages, losses are to be shared using the profit sharing proportions. Since Hook's share of partnership profits is 50%, Hook's capital account would be reduced by one-half of any 1994 losses.

5. (b) The Uniform Partnership Act provides that upon the dissolution of a partnership for any reason other than by operation of law, the partnership must provide actual notice to third parties with whom the partners have dealt in order to sever the apparent authority of partners or other agents. Since ACH Associates failed to provide Ace Automobile Company with notice of the partnership's dissolution and since Ace was not aware of the dissolution, Hook's apparent authority to conduct partnership business will continue, and ACH will be bound.

6. (b) Since all partners are agents of one another, Anchor, Chain, and Hook will all be liable to pay any judgment recovered by Ace Automobile Company.

ESSAY QUESTIONS

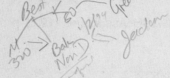

Essay 51-3 (15 to 25 minutes)

Best Aviation Associates is a general partnership engaged in the business of buying, selling and servicing used airplanes. Best's original partners were Martin and Kent. They formed the partnership on January 1, 1992, under an oral partnership agreement which provided that the partners would share profits equally. There was no agreement as to how the partners would share losses. At the time the partnership was formed, Martin contributed $320,000 and Kent contributed $80,000.

On December 1, 1993, Best hired Baker to be a salesperson and to assist in purchasing used aircraft for Best's inventory. On December 15, 1993, Martin instructed Baker to negotiate the purchase of a used airplane without disclosing that Baker was acting on Best's behalf. Martin thought that a better price could be negotiated by Baker if Jackson was not aware that the aircraft was being acquired for Best. The agreement provided that Jackson would deliver the airplane to Baker on January 2, 1994, at which time the purchase price was to be paid. On January 2, 1994, Jackson attempted to deliver the used airplane purchased for Best by Baker. Baker, acting on Martin's instructions, refused to accept delivery or pay the purchase price.

On December 20, 1993, Kent assigned Kent's partnership interest in Best to Green. On December 31, 1993, Kent advised Martin of the assignment to Green. On January 11, 1994, Green contacted Martin and demanded to inspect the partnership books and to participate in the management of partnership affairs, including voting on partnership decisions.

On January 13, 1994, it was determined that Best had incurred an operating loss of $160,000 in 1993.

Martin demanded that Kent contribute $80,000 to the partnership to account for Kent's share of the loss. Kent refused to contribute.

On January 28, 1994, Laco Supplies, Inc., a creditor of Best, sued Best and Martin for unpaid bills totalling $92,000. Best had not paid the bills because of a cash shortfall caused by the 1993 operating loss.

Jackson has taken the following position:

- Baker is responsible for any damages incurred by Jackson as a result of Best's refusal to accept delivery or pay the purchase price.

Martin has taken the following positions:

- Green is not entitled to inspect the partnership books or participate in the management of the partnership.
- Only the partnership is liable for the amounts owed to Laco, or, in the alternative, Martin's personal liability is limited to 50% of the total of the unpaid bills.

Kent has taken the following positions:

- Only Martin is liable for the 1993 operating loss because of the assignment to Green of Kent's partnership interest.
- Any personal liability of the partners for the 1993 operating loss should be allocated between them on the basis of their original capital contributions.

Required:

a. Determine whether Jackson's position is correct and state the reasons for your conclusions.

b. Determine whether Martin's positions are correct and state the reasons for your conclusions.

c. Determine whether Kent's positions are correct and state the reasons for your conclusions.

(5/94, Law, #4)

Essay 51-4 (15 to 20 minutes)

Prime Cars Partnership is a general partnership engaged in the business of buying, selling, and servicing used cars. Prime's original partners were Baker and Mathews, who formed the partnership three years ago under a written partnership agreement, which provided that:

- Profits and losses would be allocated 60% to Baker and 40% to Mathews.
- Baker would be responsible for supervising Prime's salespeople and for purchasing used cars for inventory. Baker could not, without Mathews' consent, enter into a contract to purchase more than $15,000 worth of used cars at any one time.
- Mathews would be responsible for supervising Prime's service department.

On May 1, 1990, Baker entered into a contract on Prime's behalf with Jaco Auto Wholesalers, Inc., to purchase 11 used cars from Jaco for a total purchase price of $40,000. Baker's agreement with Jaco provided that the cars would be delivered to Prime on September 1. Baker did not advise Mathews of the terms and conditions of the contract with Jaco. Baker had regularly done business with Jaco on behalf of Prime in the past, and on several occasions had purchased $12,000 to $15,000 of used cars from Jaco. Jaco was unaware of the limitation on Baker's authority.

Baker also frequently purchased used cars for Prime from Top Auto Auctions, Ltd., a corporation owned by Baker's friend. Whenever Prime purchased cars from Top, Baker would personally receive up to 5% of the total purchase price from Top as an incentive to do more business with Top. Baker did not tell Mathews about these payments.

On August 1, 1990, Baker and Mathews agreed to admit KYA Auto Restorers, Inc., as a partner in Prime to start up and supervise a body shop facility. KYA made a $25,000 capital contribution and Prime's partnership agreement was amended to provide that Prime's profits and losses would be shared equally by the partners.

On September 1, 1990, Mathews learned of the Jaco contract and refused to accept delivery of the cars. Mathews advised Jaco that Baker had entered into the contract without Mathews' consent as required by their agreement. Jaco has demanded a payment of $10,000 from Prime for Jaco's lost profits under the contract.

Mathews has also learned about the incentive payments made to Baker by Top.

Mathews has taken the following positions:

- Prime is not liable to Jaco because Baker entered into the contract without Mathews' consent.
- In any event, Mathews is not liable to Jaco for more than 40% of Jaco's lost profits because of the original partnership provisions concerning the sharing of profits and losses.
- Baker is liable to Mathews for any liability incurred by Mathews under the Jaco contract.
- Baker is liable to Prime for accepting the incentive payments from Top.

KYA contends that none of its $25,000 capital contributions should be applied to the Jaco liability and that, in any event, KYA does not have any responsibility for the obligation.

Required:

a. State whether Mathews' positions are correct and give the reasons for your conclusions.

b. State whether KYA's contentions are correct and give the reasons for your conclusions.

(5/91, Law, #2)

Essay 51-5 (15 to 20 minutes)

On January 5, Stein, Rey, and Lusk entered into a written general partnership agreement by which they agreed to operate a stock brokerage firm. The agreement stated that the partnership would continue upon the death or withdrawal of a partner. The agreement also provided that no partner could reduce the firm's commission below 2% without the consent of all of the other partners. On March 10, Rey, without the consent of Stein and Lusk, agreed with King Corp. to reduce the commission to 1-1/2% on a large transaction by King. Rey believed this would entice King to become a regular customer of the firm. King was unaware of any of the terms of the partnership agreement.

On May 15, Stein entered into a contract conveying Stein's partnership interest to Park and withdrew from the partnership. That same day, all of the partners agreed to admit Park as a general partner. Notice of Stein's withdrawal and Park's admission as a partner was properly published in two newspapers. In addition, third parties who had conducted business with the partnership prior to May 15 received written notice of Stein's withdrawal.

Required:

a. In separate paragraphs, discuss whether:
    1. The partnership could recover the 1/2% commission from King.
    2. The partnership could recover the 1/2% commission from Rey.

b. In separate paragraphs, discuss:
    1. Park's liability for partnership obligations arising both before and after being admitted to the partnership.
    2. Stein's liability for partnership obligations arising both before and after withdrawing from the partnership.
                                     (11/88, Law, #4)

Essay 51-6 (15 to 20 minutes)

Edna Slavin intends to enter into a limited partnership with three of her business associates. Slavin wishes to know the advantages and disadvantages of being a general partner as opposed to a limited partner in a limited partnership. The issues of most concern to Slavin are:

- Her right as a general or limited partner to participate in the daily management of the partnership.
- Her liability as a general or limited partner for debts incurred on behalf of or by the partnership.
- Her right as a general or limited partner to assign her partnership interest and substitute a third party as a partner.
- The effect of a clause in the certificate of limited partnership which permits the partnership to continue after the death of one of the general or limited partners.

Required:

Answer the following, setting forth reasons for any conclusions stated.

What are the essential differences in the formation of a general partnership and a limited partnership? Discuss in separate paragraphs the issues raised by Slavin.   (11/86, Law, #2)

ESSAY SOLUTIONS

Solution 51-3 Assignment of Partnership/Agents

a. Jackson is correct. Baker, as an **agent** acting on behalf of an **undisclosed principal** (Best), is **personally liable** for any contracts entered into in that capacity.

b. Martin's first position that Green is not entitled to inspect the partnership books or participate in partnership management is correct. Green, as an **assignee** of Kent's **partnership interest**, is entitled to receive Kent's share of partnership profits only. Green is not entitled, as an assignee of Kent's partnership interest, to **inspect** the partnership **records** or to **participate in the management** of the partnership.

Martin's second position that only the partnership is responsible for the debt owed Laco is incorrect. Although the partnership is **primarily liable** for the unpaid bills, both Martin and Kent, as Best's partners, are personally liable for the **unpaid** amount of the debt. Laco will be entitled to seek recovery against Martin or Kent for the full amount owed.

c. Kent's first position that only Martin is liable for the 1993 operating loss because of the **assignment** of Kent's partnership interest to Green is incorrect. A partner's assignment of a partnership interest does **not terminate** that partner's **liability** for the partnership's losses and debts.

Kent's second position that any personal liability of the partners for the 1993 operating loss should be allocated on the basis of their original capital contributions is incorrect. The 1993 loss will be **allocated in the same way** that **profits were to be allocated** between the parties, that is, equally, because Martin and Kent had not agreed on the method for allocating losses between themselves.

Solution 51-4 Partnership Liability/Consequences for Violation of Authority

a. 1. Mathews' first position is incorrect. A **partner is considered an agent** of the partnership in carrying out its **usual business.** In this case, Baker **lacked actual authority to bind** Prime to the Jaco contract; however, Baker did have, from Jaco's perspective, **apparent authority** to do so because of the **general character** of Prime's business and, more important, because Baker had previously purchased cars from Jaco on Prime's behalf. Jaco was **not bound by the limitation** on Baker's authority unless Jaco was aware of it.

2. Mathews' second position is also incorrect. As a general rule, a **partner is liable for the debts of the partnership,** and a **third party** is **not bound by the profit and loss sharing agreements** between partners because the third party is **not a party to** the partnership agreement. Therefore, Jaco can look to Prime's assets and Mathews' personal assets to satisfy the obligation.

3. Mathews' third position is correct. A **partner is liable to other partners for any liability associated** with contracts entered into ostensibly **on behalf of the partnership** but **outside the partner's actual authority.** In this case, because Baker **violated the agreement** with Mathews concerning the $15,000 limitation on used car purchases, Baker will be liable to Mathews for any liability that Mathews may have to Jaco.

4. Mathews' fourth position is also correct. A **partner owes a fiduciary duty** (that is, a duty of loyalty) to the partnership and every other partner. A **partner may not benefit** directly or indirectly at the expense of the partnership. A partner must account to the partnership for any benefits derived from the partnership's business without the consent or knowledge of the other partners. In this case, Baker was **not entitled to accept and retain the incentive payments** made by Top. Doing so violated Baker's fiduciary duty to Prime and Mathews. Baker must account to Prime for all the incentive payments received.

b. KYA's contention that its $25,000 capital contribution cannot be used to satisfy Prime's obligation to Jaco is incorrect. A **new partner is liable for partnership liabilities that arose prior** to the new partner's **admission,** but the liability is **limited to the partner's capital contribution** and **interest** in partnership property. Therefore, KYA's liability is limited to its capital contribution and its interest as a partner in Prime's assets.

Solution 51-5 Liabilities of Partners

a. 1. The partnership cannot recover the 1/2% commission from King because Rey had the **apparent authority** to reduce the commission to 1-1/2%. The Uniform Partnership Act states that **every partner is an agent** of the partnership for the purpose of its business, and the act of every partner for apparently carrying on in the usual way the business of the partnership, **binds the partnership,** unless the partner so acting has in fact no authority to act for the partnership in the particular matter, and the person with whom the partner is dealing has **knowledge of the fact that the partner has no such authority.** In determining whether Rey had the apparent authority to bind the partnership, one must examine the circumstances and conduct of the parties and whether King **reasonably believed such authority to exist.** Because brokerage commissions are generally not uniform, it would be reasonable for King to believe that Rey had the authority to perform the transaction at 1-1/2% commission. Furthermore, King **lacked knowledge** of the restriction in the partnership agreement that prohibited Rey from reducing a commission below 2% without the other partners' consent. Therefore, King will not be liable for the 1/2% commission.

2. The partnership can recover the 1/2% commission from Rey because Rey **violated the partnership agreement** by reducing the commission to 1-1/2% without the partners' consent. Rey **owes a duty to act in accordance with the partnership agreement.**

b. 1. Under the Uniform Partnership Act, a person admitted as a partner into an existing partnership is liable for all the obligations of the partnership arising before being admitted as though that person had been a partner when such obligations were incurred, except that this liability may be satisfied **only out of partnership property.** Thus, Park **will not be personally liable** for the partnership obligations arising prior to being admitted as a partner but would be liable based upon the extent of partnership interests held. Park **will be personally liable for partnership obligations arising after being admitted to the partnership.**

2. Stein will continue to be personally liable for partnership obligations arising prior to withdrawing from the partnership, unless Stein obtains a release from the existing creditors. Stein will have **no liability** for partnership obligations arising **after actual and constructive notice of withdrawing** was properly given. However, Stein may be personally liable for partnership obligations arising after withdrawing but prior to notice being given. **Actual notice** of Stein's

withdrawal was **given by written notification** to partnership creditors that had conducted business with the partnership prior to May 15. **Constructive notice** of Stein's withdrawal was given by **proper publication** in two newspapers to those third parties who had not dealt with the partnership, but may have known of its existence.

Solution 51-6 Advantages and Disadvantages of a General Partnership vs. a Limited Partnership

Typically, a **general partnership** is formed by an **agreement between** or **among two or more persons**, whether the agreement is written, oral, or implied. **No filing of a partnership agreement is necessary** in order to legally create the general partnership. In contrast, a **limited partnership** can be **formed only where a state statute permits** such formation. In addition, a duly signed **certificate of limited partnership** must be completed and **filed** with the appropriate state or local agency. A limited partnership, like a general partnership, is formed by two or more persons. However, unlike a general partnership, the **limited partnership must have** as members **one or more general partners** and **one or more limited partners.**

As a limited partner, Slavin would not be able to participate in the **daily management** of the partnership's business if she wishes to **limit her liability** to her investment in the partnership. Thus, if Slavin intends to be involved in the daily operations of the partnership and to participate in the **control** of the partnership, she should consider becoming a **general partner** since general partners have rights in the **management** and **conduct** of the partnership's business.

In her capacity as a limited partner, Slavin's **liability** would be **limited** to her investment in the partnership for partnership debts if her interest is fully paid and nonassessable. However, if Slavin were to become a **general partner,** she would have **unlimited liability** which would allow partnership creditors to satisfy the debts of the partnership out of Slavin's **personal** assets.

Unless otherwise provided in the partnership agreement, Slavin has the **right to assign** her limited partnership interest and may also **substitute** the third party as a limited partner if **all** the members (except the assignor) **consent** thereto. Similarly, as a general partner, Slavin may **assign** her interest in the partnership and the **third party** may become a **general partner** if **all** of the partners consent.

A clause providing for the partnership to continue **after the death** of a general partner is **valid** and the partnership will continue. The clause has relatively **little** if any **effect** where a limited partner dies since the limited partnership continues upon the death of one of the limited partners, whether or not the clause is contained in the certificate.

General

2 or More Persons
Written oral or implied
No filing of PA nec

Can participate in daily

Unlimit liab
Rts in Mgt & Conduct
                  trust
Rt to have p-int
All Partners consent
Can Continue after

Ltd.

must have a G.P & Ltd P.
State statute permits
Signed Cert of Ltd P
  & filed with State

Not particip in dailyng'

Ltd liab
Rts in cut or profit of bus
Rt to Assy
No Need
Ltd dies Can continue
but not without G.

CHAPTER 52

CORPORATIONS

I. **Definitions** 52-3
  A. Domestic Corporation 52-3
  B. Foreign Corporation 52-3
  C. Limited Liability Company 52-3
  D. Piercing the Corporate Veil 52-3
  E. Preemptive Rights 52-3
  F. Proxy 52-3
  G. Ultra Vires 52-3
  H. Watered Stock 52-3
  I. Professional Corporation 52-3

II. **General Characteristics** 52-3
  A. Attributes of a Corporation 52-3
  B. Disadvantages of a Corporation 52-4

III. **Formation** 52-4
  A. Promoter 52-4
  B. Incorporation 52-5
  C. Defects in Formation 52-5

IV. **Financing the Corporation** 52-6
  A. Capital Stock 52-6
  B. Subscription Agreements 52-6
  C. Authorized Capital 52-6
  D. Consideration for Shares 52-8
  E. Issuance of Stock 52-8
  F. Transfer 52-8

V. **Powers of the Corporation** 52-8
  A. Express Powers 52-8
  B. Implied Powers 52-8
  C. Particular Powers 52-9

VI. **Corporate Liabilities** 52-9
  A. Respondeat Superior 52-9
  B. Ultra Vires Doctrine 52-9
  C. Piercing the Corporate Veil 52-9

VII. **Directors and Officers** 52-10
  A. Directors 52-10
  B. Officers 52-11

VIII. **Regulation of Securities Trading by Persons Within the Corporation** 52-12
  A. Common Law 52-12
  B. Federal Securities Law 52-12

IX. **Stockholders' Rights and Liabilities** 52-12
  A. Voting Rights 52-12
  B. Right to Inspect Books and Records 52-12
  C. Fundamental Changes 52-12

D.   Miscellaneous Rights...52-13
E.   Liabilities of Shareholders..52-13
F.   Shareholder Control Devices...52-13
G.   Fiduciary Duty of Shareholders 52-13
H.   Dividends...52-13

X. Fundamental Changes 52-13
A.   Corporate Reorganization..52-13
B.   Quasi-Reorganization 52-14
C.   Dissolution 52-14
D.   Liquidation 52-14

XI. Federal Income Tax Ramifications...52-14
A.   Corporate Attributes..52-14
B.   Contribution to Capital of Corporation 52-15
C.   Corporate Distributions 52-15
D.   Corporate Reorganizations...52-16

CHAPTER 52

CORPORATIONS

I. Definitions

A. <u>Domestic Corporation</u>--A corporation which does business in the state in which it is incorporated.

B. <u>Foreign Corporation</u>--A corporation doing business in any state except the one in which it is incorporated. This type of corporation is subject to the requirements and administrative controls of the states in which it is doing business.

C. <u>Limited Liability Company</u>--An LLC's tax treatment depends on the existence of corporate characteristics. An LLC possessing more than two attributes of a corporation (see II.A., below) will be taxed as a corporation, while an LLC with two or less of these characteristics will be taxed as a partnership. LLCs are formed at the state level, and LLCs have been approved for formation in almost all fifty states.

D. <u>Piercing the Corporate Veil</u>--The act of disregarding the shareholders' general shield from liability for corporate debts. This occurs when the court finds corporate fraud and desires to hold shareholders liable.

E. <u>Preemptive Rights</u>--The stockholders' right to acquire the number of newly authorized shares necessary to allow them to maintain their proportional equity in the corporation.

F. <u>Proxy</u>--The shareholder's right to delegate authority to another person, as agent, to vote his or her shares at a meeting of shareholders. A general proxy allows the agent to vote the shares only as directed by the record shareholder.

G. <u>Ultra Vires</u>--Acts by the corporation or its management which are beyond the scope of corporate authority as granted by its charter, bylaws, and state law. *unauthorized acts*

H. <u>Watered Stock</u>--Stock which is issued for less than its par or stated value.

I. <u>Professional Corporation</u>--A corporation under state law which allows professionals such as doctors, attorneys, and accountants to incorporate. Usually shares are owned only by the professionals who retain personal liability for their professional acts.

II. General Characteristics

A corporation is an artificial person or legal entity created by or under the authority of a state statute. It may be owned by one or more persons, but is considered to be a single, separate legal entity. It is vested with the capacity of continuous succession, irrespective of changes in its membership or operating management. In carrying out its purpose, a corporation is limited by the provisions of its charter as well as state and federal regulating statutes. The Revised Model Business Corporation Act (RMBCA) governs the formation, activities, and termination of corporations in many, but not all, states.

A. <u>Attributes of a Corporation</u>

1. Centralization--The corporation's management is centralized in the board of directors, elected by the shareholders.

2. Limited Liability--Generally, a shareholder is not personally liable for the debts and obligations of the corporation. Risk of loss extends only to the shareholder's actual investment in the corporation.

3. Continuous Life--A corporation is customarily regarded as having a perpetual life. Although it may be terminated by such acts as merger or dissolution, it continues independently of changes in ownership and management.

4. Transferability of Interest--A shareholder's interest in the corporation may be bought or sold with little effect on the operation of the corporate business.

B. Disadvantages of a Corporation

1. Taxation--A corporation suffers double taxation on its profits. Taxation occurs once on the corporate level and again when profits pass into the hands of the shareholders.

2. Costs--Initially, a corporation must incur the cost of formally incorporating. Subsequent to formation and throughout its life, a corporation must remain cognizant of and responsive to a variety of procedural and administrative regulations.

III. Formation

A. Promoter--The individual who is primarily responsible for forming, arranging for capitalization, and initiating the general business of the corporation. The promoter's duties also include drawing up the corporate charter and promoting stock subscriptions.

1. Fiduciary Duty--A promoter is said to be a fiduciary of the not-yet-formed corporation. This special relationship imposes a duty on the promoter to act in good faith and in the corporation's best interest. The promoter is barred from making secret profits (self-dealing) at the expense of either the corporation or those subscribing to it. The promoter must make full disclosure of his or her dealings with the corporation to anyone with an interest in the corporation who is in a position to legally consent to his or her activities. In the event of any self-dealing, the promoter is required to turn his or her secret profits over to the corporation.

2. Contracts of the Promoter--The general rule is that a corporation is not liable on pre-incorporation contracts entered into on behalf of the corporation by the promoter. The rationale is that there can be no ratification of the promoter's contract by a nonexisting entity. However, a corporation may become liable on such contracts by adoption.

    a. Adoption--To circumvent the harsh results of placing the complete financial burden on the promoter for pre-incorporation contracts, the courts formulated the theory of adoption. Adoption is the act of corporate acceptance of the promoter's pre-incorporation contract. It may occur in three ways:

        (1) Statute--The corporation may be forced by state statute to adopt the contracts made by the promoter.

        (2) Agreement--Adoption may occur by an express agreement, entered into after incorporation, between the promoter and the corporation.

        (3) Implied--The corporation may implicitly adopt a pre-incorporation contract by accepting the benefits of the contract.

    b. Continuing Promoter Liability--Even if the corporation adopts the contract, the promoter remains personally liable unless one of the following occurs:

        (1) The promoter states in the contract that he or she is not personally liable.

        (2) A novation occurs when a third party creditor agrees to look to the corporation for satisfaction of the contract.

3. Securities Act of 1933--A promoter has a duty to comply with the Securities Act of 1933. The Act requires the filing of a registration statement with the Securities and Exchange Commission (SEC) if securities are to be offered through the mail or through some other means of interstate commerce. In addition, the Act requires the promoter to provide each potential purchaser with a prospectus containing detailed information about the corporation. The registration statement must include information relating to such matters as management, control, capitalization, and financial conditions of the corporation.

B. Incorporation--Corporations are regulated by state laws which usually allow their formation for the purpose of carrying on lawful activity. The primary statutory requirement is the execution and filing of articles of incorporation.

   1. Incorporators--Incorporators sign the articles of incorporation. Frequently, the incorporators and promoters are the same persons.

   2. Articles of Incorporation--Under state law, the articles of incorporation (corporate charter) must contain certain mandatory provisions. Thus, the articles normally include the name of the corporation, corporate purpose, capital stock authorized, location of the principal office, number of directors, capital structure, and duration. Additionally, some states require that a minimum amount of capital be paid into the corporation and that the board of directors elect officials and adopt bylaws before the certificate of incorporation is valid.

   1) location of office
   2) names of incorp
   3) names of 1st BOD's.
   4) classes of stock
   do not have names of officers

   3. Procedure--After the articles of incorporation are signed and acknowledged by the persons named as directors, the document, accompanied by the appropriate fee, must be filed with the designated state office. Under common law, the corporation does not come into existence until that office files a certificate of incorporation. However, under the modern trend, corporate existence begins at the time of filing and before the certificate is issued.

C. Defects in Formation--Under former common law, a corporation which did not follow the above procedure for formation might not achieve corporate status. This allowed third persons an alternative to performing contracts entered into with the corporation; that is, if there were no corporation, then there would be no duty to perform. Also, without corporate status, a third party could hold the shareholders directly liable for any contract entered into in the corporate name. To avoid this result, the courts adopted several doctrines to deal with defects in the incorporation process.

   1. De Jure Corporation--Under current common law, any corporation that substantially complies with the mandatory statutory requirements of incorporation is deemed a de jure corporation. Such corporate status cannot be attacked by anyone, including the state.

   2. De Facto Corporation--If the corporation fails to substantially comply with mandatory requirements, the courts might nevertheless recognize its existence as de facto. This status forces third parties to perform on corporate contracts and shields shareholders from direct liability. However, the state may still bring a suit challenging the corporate existence through a "quo warranto" proceeding. The essential elements of a de facto corporation are as follows:

      a. A valid statute under which the business could have been legally incorporated.

      b. Existence of a corporate charter.

      c. A good faith effort to incorporate.

      d. Some good faith business dealings in the corporate name.

3.   Corporation by Estoppel--Many courts in the absence of even a de facto corporation have protected shareholders from third-party suits. If the third party entered into a contract believing he or she was dealing with a corporation, the courts will not allow the third party to hold shareholders liable on the contract.

4.   Noncorporation--If a corporation fails to obtain any status mentioned above, it may be attacked by anyone. Generally, in such cases the shareholders are liable for the debts of the corporation in the same manner as partners if they have actively participated in the venture.

IV. Financing the Corporation

A.   Capital Stock--Capital is the consideration or other property received by a corporation in exchange for issued and outstanding stock. The original capital may be contributed in the form of money, property, or services. In a state with a minimum capitalization requirement, the fair market value of the property or services contributed will determine whether the corporation has met its requirement.

B.   Subscription Agreements--A subscription agreement is a contract by which the subscriber agrees to purchase a number of shares of corporate stock at a subscription price specified in the agreement.

1.   Pre-Incorporation Subscribers--The major problem with pre-incorporation subscribers is determining at what point the subscriber becomes bound by his or her commitment to buy stock. Generally, the courts have held that a subscription for shares in a corporation not yet formed is an unenforceable contract due to the lack of parties. Therefore, some act of acceptance by the corporation, after incorporation, is required before pre-incorporation subscription agreements will become binding.

a.   Enforceable Pre-Incorporation Subscriptions--If individuals agreed to subscribe to corporate stock, and it appears that each party's promise was dependent on the other parties also subscribing, then an enforceable contract exists. The subscription is enforceable not between the corporation and each subscriber, but rather among the subscribers themselves.

b.   Model Business Corporation Act--Under this Act, pre-incorporation stock subscriptions are deemed to be continuing offers that are irrevocable for purposes of administrative convenience for a period of six months.

2.   Post-Incorporation Subscribers--Any agreement to subscribe that comes into existence after the corporation is formed constitutes a binding obligation to sell or purchase stock.

3.   Conditional Subscription--Normally, a subscriber may condition a purchase on any event or occurrence he or she chooses. Generally, any such condition must appear in writing on the face of the subscription agreement. However, courts have long held that the stock subscription contract contains both of the following implied conditions:

a.   The corporation has achieved a de jure status.

b.   The corporation has complied with all applicable securities laws.

C.   Authorized Capital--The articles of incorporation must specify the types and number of shares that a corporation may issue. Although fewer shares may be issued than specified, it is unlawful to issue a greater number than is authorized in the articles.

1.   Equity Definitions

a.   Authorized Stock--The stock that is authorized to be issued in the articles of incorporation.

b.   Issued Stock--That portion of authorized stock that has actually been issued to shareholders.

c.   Outstanding Stock--That portion of authorized stock that has actually been issued to and is still owned by shareholders.

d.   Treasury Stock--Stock that has been issued, but that is no longer outstanding because the corporation has redeemed it (reacquired it). Treasury stock may only be purchased with surplus. Additionally, it carries no right to vote or receive dividends, it may be resold without regard to par value, and it may be distributed as a stock dividend. If treasury stock is canceled, the effect is to reduce stated capital by the amount represented by the shares, and such canceled shares are restored to the status of authorized but unissued shares.

e.   Paid-In Surplus--Any amount paid for stock above the par (stated) value.

f.   Earned Surplus (Retained Earnings)--The total net profits of a corporation minus any dividends paid out in past years plus or minus any prior period adjustments.

g.   Legal Capital (Stated Capital)--The number of shares issued times their par value or stated value. This fund is primarily used for the payment of creditors. Dividends may not come from this source.

h.   Surplus--Earned surplus combined with paid-in surplus, also stated as net assets minus stated or legal capital.

i.   Contributed Capital--The total amount paid for stock when issued; i.e., stated capital plus paid-in surplus.

2.   Common Stock--Stock which entitles its owner to share in any dividends declared by the board of directors. Additionally, common stock is entitled to share in liquidating distributions of corporate assets. Common stock may be either voting or nonvoting.

3.   Preferred Stock--Preferred stock has certain rights and preferences, which are defined in the articles of incorporation, the bylaws, or the share contract itself. The shares may be either voting or nonvoting. At liquidation, holders of preferred stock receive the par value of their stock before the common stock holders are entitled to any value. Other rights and preferences of preferred stock vary depending on the class of preferred held.

a.   Cumulative Preferred--The holders of cumulative preferred have the right to receive fixed yearly dividends. If the corporation fails in its payment for year one, the stockholder's rights cumulate to year two. Additionally, preferred shareholders must receive full payment of all arrearages before common shareholders receive their dividends.

b.   Straight Preferred--Shareholders are entitled to be paid a fixed dividend before any dividends are paid to holders of common stock. This class of stock does not include the rights to any other profits.

c.   Participating Preferred--Participating preferred shareholders share ratably with common shareholders in any profit distribution beyond the prescribed preferred rate. Fully participating preferred holders share equally with common holders in excess profit distribution, while partially participating preferred holders share in a more limited manner in such excess.

d.   Convertible Preferred--Holders of this stock may convert into common stock after a stipulated time.

4. Par Value--Par value is the nominal value assigned to the stock, which is established by the corporation. However, the corporation may sell the stock at par value or any price above par value. The par value is allocated to the capital account; all value received in excess of par value is allocated to capital surplus accounts. Corporations may issue no-par stock, i.e., a stock that has no established par value. State statutes usually require that a certain portion of the value received for no-par stock be allocated to the capital account.

5. Voting Stock--Any class of stock may be designated as voting or nonvoting. A shareholder is entitled to one vote for each share that he or she owns.

D. Consideration for Shares--A corporation may receive only certain types and quantities of consideration for its shares.

1. Types of Consideration--A corporation may issue its stock in return for cash or property, including promissary notes. It may also accept past services and contracts for future services as consideration for the issuance of stock.

2. Quantity of Consideration--A corporation may issue its no-par stock at a price determined by the board of directors. Par value shares may not be issued for less than par value.

E. Issuance of Stock--The Uniform Commercial Code sets forth the measure of liability to be borne by a corporation with regard to its issued securities. Furthermore, a corporation is liable to good faith purchasers for damages caused by its employees or agents who have forged or signed corporate securities without corporate authority.

F. Transfer--Stock may be transferred by endorsement and delivery. If a stock certificate is endorsed in blank, it may be transferred by delivery alone. A transfer becomes legally effective against the corporation only when the security is presented to the corporation, or a duly appointed agent, for registration. The corporation is bound to accept such stock for registration as long as the stock was properly endorsed and all other formalities of transfer were complied with. The corporation may place certain restrictions on the transfer of stock. For example, it may require the holder to offer the corporation the right of first refusal on a repurchase of the stock before any sale is permitted to anyone else. However, in order to be enforceable, such restrictions must be reasonable and must be conspicuously noted on the face of the certificate.

V. Powers of the Corporation

A. Express Powers--A corporation has the express power to perform any act authorized by state law, the articles of incorporation, or the bylaws.

B. Implied Powers--A corporation also possesses those powers which are reasonably necessary to promote and carry out the express corporate powers. These powers may be implied if the transaction undertaken is in furtherance of the objectives and purposes for which the corporation was formed. Examples of implied powers are as follows:

1. Power to sue and be sued in the corporate name.

2. Power to make or amend corporate bylaws.

3. Power to acquire, mortgage, and transfer property for corporate purposes.

4. Power to issue corporate bonds.

C.   Particular Powers--Certain powers may not be implied to exist in a corporation due to public policy considerations:

    1.   Gifts--As a general rule, a corporation has no implied power to give away its money or other assets at the expense of the shareholders. However, in certain situations, such as when a gift promotes the purpose for which the corporation was formed, the courts may recognize an implied power to make such a gift.

    2.   Partnerships--A corporation has no implied power to enter into a partnership with a person or another entity. The rationale is that the corporation should not be bound by the acts of partners who are not its duly appointed agents and officers. However, a corporation may enter into a partnership if authorized to do so by the corporate charter or state corporation statute.

    3.   Surety--Generally, a corporation may not lend money unless specifically authorized to do so by charter or statute. However, a corporation may become a surety on a particular customer's debt if this action promotes the corporate business. A corporation may not pledge its credit or assets as an accommodation.

    4.   Acquiring and Reacquiring Shares--Most courts hold that a corporation may purchase its own shares and the shares of other corporations, provided such action promotes the corporate business. Such purchases must normally be made from accumulated profits, or surplus.

VI. Corporate Liabilities

A corporation is liable on the contracts of its employees and, in particular situations, for torts committed by employees. Additionally, under certain circumstances individual shareholders may be held personally liable for the debts of the corporation.

A.   Respondeat Superior--Under this doctrine, a corporation is liable for the tortious acts of its employees, provided that the acts were committed within the course and scope of employment.

B.   Ultra Vires Doctrine--A corporation may not act or contract in any way that is not authorized either expressly or impliedly by state statute, the articles of incorporation, or the bylaws. Such acts or contracts are termed "ultra vires," and while they are not illegal, they are void or unenforceable under common law. In most jurisdictions today, the ultra vires doctrine may not be asserted by either the corporation or a third party to nullify an action or contract. However, it can be asserted by the shareholders of the ultra vires corporation. These shareholders, as well as the state, can sue the corporation to enjoin it from acting in violation of its charter or state statute.

C.   Piercing the Corporate Veil--Occasionally, a corporation is formed by its owners for the purpose of committing frauds, circumventing the law, or for pursuing, in some other way, illegal objectives. If a court determines that such is the case, it will pierce the corporate veil and hold the shareholders personally liable for a loss suffered by a third party. Some of the factors examined by the courts in making their determination are whether there is a bona fide corporate purpose, whether the corporate funds are carefully segregated from the shareholders' funds, and whether the formalities of corporate existence have been followed (such as shareholders and directors meetings). Other common situations that may cause a court to pierce the corporate veil are as follows:

    1.   Undercapitalization--The courts will examine the amount of capital present at the formation of the corporation. If that amount is inadequate to meet the reasonably foreseeable financial needs of the corporation, it is undercapitalized and shareholders may be held personally liable upon the insolvency of the corporation.

    2.   Subsidiary Corporations--Normally, a subsidiary is treated as a unique entity distinct from the parent corporation. However, if the subsidiary is inadequately capitalized, its activities are substantially intermingled with the parent's, or if it exists solely for the benefit of the parent,

the courts will treat the two entities as one and hold the parent liable for the debts of the subsidiary.

3. Loans--Shareholders will often contribute money at the inception of the corporation in the form of loans. Contributors do this in hopes of elevating their position to that of creditors, with rights superior to those of other shareholders in the event of corporate liquidation. Such shareholder loans are suspect. In cases of undercapitalization and bankruptcy, courts will subordinate insider loans to loans of outside creditors or transform insider "loans" into capital contributions (stock).

VII. Directors and Officers

A. <u>Directors</u>--The right to manage the affairs of the corporation is vested in the board of directors. Although the directors are elected by the shareholders, they have a statutory right to manage the corporation independent of any direct shareholder influence.

   1. Appointment of Directors--The original board of directors is named in the articles of incorporation. Subsequently, directors are elected at shareholder meetings, with the board having the power to fill vacancies which occur during the term. Traditionally, the number of directors prescribed by various statutes was three; however, the modern trend is to allow as few as one.

   2. Elections--Directors usually hold office for a given statutory period, unless a shorter term is specified by the articles. Board members are elected by a plurality or through cumulative voting. The articles may also provide that the terms of various directors be staggered.

   3. Removal--Under common law, directors could only be removed for cause, e.g., fraud, incompetency. However, under many modern statutes a director may be removed at any time during his or her term, with or without cause, with the consent of the shareholders.

   4. Meetings--Corporate board powers are usually exercised at a properly-noticed board meeting attended by the necessary number of directors.

      a. Notice--The general rule is that a director must receive notice of an impending meeting within a reasonable time before each meeting. However, notice of a meeting may be waived before or after the meeting. Many jurisdictions have modified these requirements by prescribing specific board meeting procedures.

      b. Quorum--In order for board action to be binding, a simple majority of the directors must be present at the meeting. Furthermore, a simple majority of those present is sufficient to legally bind the corporation, unless the articles call for a higher percentage.

      c. Without Meeting--Some state statutes allow the board of directors to act without a meeting if all of the directors consent in writing to the proposed action and such consent is filed in the minutes book of the corporation.

      d. Delegation of Authority--It is a common practice in many jurisdictions for the board of directors to appoint an "executive committee" to handle specific matters or the day-to-day affairs of the corporation. This committee must be composed of directors. However, it is important to note that there are certain statutory duties which the directors may not delegate to such a committee, e.g., declaring dividends, amending bylaws.

   5. Powers--Generally, the board of directors has the power to manage the business of the corporation, initiate fundamental changes subject to final approval by the shareholders, fill vacancies on the board, adopt and amend the bylaws, elect and fix the compensation of

officers, remove officers, and declare dividends. However, directors are personally liable for dividends which are wrongfully or unlawfully paid.

6. Rights--Directors have the right to be reimbursed for their expenses, to inspect the corporate books, and to rely on reports and statements made by management and personnel. Normally, a director does not have the right to compensation for services unless specifically stated in the bylaws.

7. Duties of the Directors--Directors are fiduciaries of the corporation and have the duty to act with reasonable care and loyalty.

    a. Duty of Due Care--Directors must exercise the care and skill that an ordinarily prudent person would exercise under similar circumstances. While a director may not delegate duties by appointing another to act in his or her place, a director may rely on information given to him or her by others associated with the corporation. A director who fails to act with due care may be negligent and liable to the corporation in damages for losses or injuries suffered as a result of his or her breach.

        • Business Judgment Rule--Finding directors guilty of negligence for their breach of duty of due care discouraged many qualified people from serving as directors. In order to mitigate this result, courts adopted the rule that when the acts or omissions involve a question of policy or business judgment, a director who acted in good faith will not be held personally liable for "mere errors of judgment or want of prudence, short of clear and gross negligence."

    b. Duty of Loyalty--A director often has a personal stake in some aspect of the corporation's business. Common law generally prohibited a director from having any personal dealings with his or her corporation. However, today most jurisdictions allow individual dealings with the corporation if full disclosure is made to the other board members and they approve of the action. In addition, the courts will examine such transactions to determine their fundamental fairness. If any contract is determined not to be in the corporation's best interest, it may be rescinded. The breaching director may also be liable for any losses or damages resulting to the corporation from the transaction.

    c. Corporate Opportunity Doctrine--A director may not divert to him- or herself a business opportunity belonging to the corporation (i.e., one in which the corporation has a right, interest, or expectancy) without first giving the corporation a chance to act. Failure to give the corporation this opportunity will result in the director's being liable in damages for any profit made on the venture.

B. Officers--In most jurisdictions, the major officers are elected by the board of directors and serve at the board's pleasure. The same individuals may be both officers and directors, and a person can hold more than one office.

1. Authority to Contract--Officers are granted the express authority to contract by virtue of statute, articles, and bylaws. They also possess that degree of implied authority which is reasonably necessary to carry out their duties. As with other corporate agents, officers may bind the corporation by apparent authority, even though they are acting beyond their actual authority.

2. Tort Liability--The usual rules of agency apply to officers. The corporation is liable for the torts of its officers if they are committed within the course and scope of the employment relationship, even if the act itself is unauthorized.

3. Fiduciary Duties--Officers are held to the same fiduciary standards as directors.

VIII. Regulation of Securities Trading by Persons Within the Corporation

A.   Common Law--Under common law, corporate directors and officers had no fiduciary duty directly to shareholders. While insiders were liable for fraud and deceit, they generally had no duty to disclose inside information concerning the sale and purchase of stock. An exception to this rule existed when an insider was dealing face to face with a buyer or seller of stock. Under these circumstances, an insider was required to disclose any known facts of an unusual nature.

B.   Federal Securities Law--Today, insider trading is subject to regulation under federal securities law, primarily under the Securities Exchange Act of 1934.

   1.   SEC Rule 10b-5--This rule makes it unlawful to (a) employ any device, scheme, or artifice to defraud; (b) make any untrue statement of a material fact or to omit a material fact necessary in order to make the statement made not misleading; or (c) engage in any act, practice, or course of business which operates as fraud or deceit upon any person in connection with the purchase or sale of any security in interstate commerce.

   2.   Rule 16b., Insider Trading--This rule applies to officers, directors, and holders of more than 10% of the company's stock. It makes it unlawful for these individuals to buy and sell stock for a profit within any 6-month period.

IX. Stockholders' Rights and Liabilities

Although a stockholder may not exercise any direct control over corporate management, there are several ways a stockholder may affect the corporation indirectly through the exercise of stock ownership rights.

A.   Voting Rights--The right to vote is held by shareholders of record. The articles or bylaws may designate some classes of stock as nonvoting, but at least one class of stock at all times must have the right to vote.

   1.   Straight Voting--Under this method of voting, a shareholder is entitled to one vote for every share held. When there are several classes of shares, one class may be given multiple votes (weighted voting). A simple majority determines the outcome.

   2.   Cumulative Voting for Directors--This type of voting is designed to give minority shareholders a greater say on the board of directors. Cumulative voting means that each shareholder receives votes equal to the number of his or her shares times the number of directors to be elected. For example, if S holds 100 shares and there are 5 directors to be elected, S holds 500 votes. His or her chances for electing a board member are increased because all 500 votes may be cast for one candidate if he or she so desires.

B.   Right to Inspect Books and Records--Corporations are required to keep records pertaining to such things as shareholder names and addresses and minutes of corporate-related meetings. Under the common law, a shareholder had a right to inspect these records provided he or she could prove to the court that the inspection was for a proper purpose. In most jurisdictions today, shareholders have statutory rights to inspect the corporate books or records. However, in most states the right is qualified, and the shareholder must demonstrate that the purpose for inspecting the materials is reasonably related to his or her interest as a shareholder.

C.   Fundamental Changes--Certain types of changes, such as amendments to the articles, merger, consolidation, dissolution, or sale of a substantial part of the corporate assets, require approval by an absolute majority of the shareholders, unless a greater proportion is required by the articles. In addition, if the rights of one particular class of shareholders are to be affected, an absolute majority of that class must also approve.

D.   Miscellaneous Rights--In addition to the above rights, a shareholder has the right to share in dividends if and when declared by the board of directors, receive notice of and attend meetings, share in corporate assets upon dissolution, and maintain his or her proportionate interest in the outstanding stock of the corporation (preemptive right) unless withheld by charter, law, or statute. Stockholders also have the right to sue for their own benefit (direct action suit) or for the benefit of the corporation (derivative suit).

E.   Liabilities of Shareholders--The liability of a shareholder is generally limited to his or her capital investment. However, a shareholder may be liable for so called "watered stock" which was issued for less than lawful consideration. The liability here is the difference between what was actually paid and what lawfully should have been paid. Also, a shareholder is liable to the corporation or its creditors for any unpaid portion of his or her stock subscription contract. A shareholder, knowingly or unknowingly, who receives illegally-declared dividends is liable for repayment of the dividend amount to an insolvent corporation.

F.   Shareholder Control Devices--Shareholders may agree to vote their stock in a particular way in order to maximize their effect on corporate policy.

1.   Voting Trust--One effective means of controlling votes is through the use of a voting trust. Under such a trust, shareholders turn over their voting rights to a trustee for a period not exceeding 10 years. The trustee has a copy of the trust agreement which is also filed with the corporation, and he or she becomes the record holder, entitled to vote the shares. The shareholder receives a voting trust certificate from the trustee, and all dividends received on the stock are paid to the shareholder. Upon termination of the trust, the shares are transferred back to the certificate holder.

2.   Pooling Agreements--Any two or more shareholders may agree to vote their shares in a given way. Such agreements must be in writing and signed by the shareholders. At common law, many courts refused to recognize pooling agreements, but today most jurisdictions recognize them if instituted for a proper purpose. A primary difference between pooling agreements and voting trusts is that in a pooling agreement, title to the shares pooled remains with the individual shareholders, while in a voting trust, title to the shares in trust is transferred to the trustee.

G.   Fiduciary Duty of Shareholders--Generally, a shareholder owes no fiduciary duty to the corporation; the shareholder's primary concern is his or her own self-interest. An exception to this rule is the duty of the majority or controlling shareholders to the minority shareholders. The courts have held that a group in de facto control of a corporation may not use that control to injure, oppress, or defraud the minority shareholders.

H.   Dividends--The board of directors has the discretionary right to declare dividends, and stockholders generally have no inherent right to force a dividend declaration. One important exception to this rule is when there is a surplus and stockholders can convince a court of equity that the directors have acted fraudulently, oppressively, or arbitrarily in refusing to declare a dividend. Dividends may always be paid out of a corporation's unrestricted and unreserved earned surplus (retained earnings) and, depending on the state, may also be paid out of its paid-in surplus. However, legal capital (stated capital) is never an appropriate source for the payment of dividends.

X. Fundamental Changes

A.   Corporate Reorganization

1.   Merger--A merger is a process by which two (or more) companies join together, with one company losing its identity, while the other company retains its corporate identity. (A + B = A)

2.   Consolidation--Consolidation is a process by which two or more companies join together. All the old companies disappear and are absorbed by a completely new corporation. (A + B = C)

3.   Procedure--As a minimum, a merger or consolidation requires approval by an absolute majority of the shareholders of each corporation involved. Moreover, it is not uncommon for the charter or bylaws to require a super majority (e.g., 66%) vote of approval for fundamental corporate changes such as mergers and consolidations.

B.   Quasi-Reorganization--A quasi-reorganization is a reorganization or revision of the capital structure, which is permitted in some states. This procedure eliminates an accumulated deficit as if the company had been legally reorganized without much of the cost and difficulty of a legal reorganization. Thus, the corporation will be able to pay dividends again. It involves the following steps:

1.   Assets are revalued at net realizable value, but there is no net asset increase. (Any loss on revaluation increases the deficit.)

2.   A minimum of the amount of the adjusted deficit must be available in paid-in capital (PIC). This might be created by donation of stock from shareholders or reduction of the par value.

3.   The deficit is charged against PIC and thus is eliminated.

C.   Dissolution--Dissolution involves the termination of a corporation's status as a legal entity.

1.   Voluntary Dissolution--For voluntary dissolution to occur, most jurisdictions require a vote by the board of directors recommending dissolution. This must be followed with approval of at least an absolute majority of the shareholders and filing of a certificate of dissolution with the appropriate state court.

2.   Involuntary Dissolution--Involuntary dissolution may be brought about by an individual shareholder or the state.

     a.   Quo Warranto Action--If a corporation exceeds the authority conferred on it under statutory law, the state may bring an action for dissolution.

     b.   Shareholder Action--A shareholder may bring an action for dissolution if the board of directors has committed fraud, waste, oppression, or misapplication of corporate funds. Also, dissolution may be sought by shareholders if the board of directors is deadlocked and the corporate business may no longer be conducted in a manner advantageous to the shareholders.

     c.   Miscellaneous Grounds--Dissolution of a corporation may arise by expiration of the time period set out in the charter, consolidation, or merger.

D.   Liquidation--After dissolution, the affairs of the corporation must "wind up" or be liquidated. This process entails paying off creditors and distributing among the shareholders any remaining assets or proceeds from those assets.

XI. Federal Income Tax Ramifications

A.   Corporate Attributes--An association of persons engaged in a business for profit will be found to be a corporation if (in addition to having a desire to reduce taxes) the entity possesses three of the following four attributes:

1. Centralized management.

2. Limited liability.

3. Free transferability of interest.

4. Continuity of life notwithstanding the death of a shareholder.

B. **Contribution to Capital of Corporation**

1. Shareholder--If one or more shareholders own 80% of the stock immediately after contribution of property (including money) to the corporation, solely in exchange for stock, the shareholder(s) in general recognize no gain or loss in the transaction. The basis of the stock equals the basis of property contributed to the corporation. If a shareholder is not in control immediately after the exchange, gain or loss is recognized to the extent of fair market value minus the basis of property exchanged for the stock. The basis of stock in the shareholder's hands is its fair market value.

2. Corporation--No gain or loss is recognized by the corporation. If the contribution was tax-free to the shareholder, the corporation carries over the shareholder's basis in property transferred for stock. If the contribution creates a recognized gain, the corporation's basis in property received is the stockholder's basis plus the gain recognized on the exchange of property for stock.

C. **Corporate Distributions**

1. Cash and Other Property Dividend Distributions--Ordinary dividend income to shareholder to the extent of the corporation's current and accumulated earnings and profits. The corporation will generally recognize gain or loss on any nonliquidating or liquidating distribution of property.

2. Stock Dividend Distributions--Stock dividends are additional shares issued to shareholders in proportion to their existing holdings. They neither reduce total assets nor affect stockholder's equity, and the effect of a stock dividend is to reduce retained earnings and increase legal capital. Distributions by a corporation of its common stock to its common shareholders is tax free to the shareholders. The distributing corporation may also use unissued or treasury stock for this common-on-common dividend. Generally, dividends of any other type of property (money, preferred stock) on common stock will be taxable to the shareholder. A tax-free stock dividend will also have no effect on earnings and profits of the corporation for federal income tax purposes. The corporation making the distribution does not generally recognize gain on stock dividend distributions.

   • In contrast to a stock dividend, a stock split simply increases the number of shares outstanding and proportionately decreases the par or stated value of the stock. There is no change in the dollar amount of capital stock, retained earnings, or total stockholders' equity.

3. Constructive Dividends--Corporations and other business entities are entitled to a deduction from gross income for reasonable salaries paid to employees. If the IRS finds that a salary is unreasonable in amount, it will disallow the deduction for the portion of salary found to be unreasonable. In closely-held corporations, such disallowance may have the effect of recharacterizing the salary into ordinary dividend income to the extent of current and accumulated earnings and profits.

D.   Corporate Reorganizations--As a general rule, reorganizations effected under the tax-free reorganization provisions (e.g., stock for stock mergers and consolidations effected under state statutes) of the Internal Revenue Code (§§354-374) will be tax free to the corporations and shareholders involved.

CHAPTER 52—CORPORATIONS

Problem 52-1 MULTIPLE CHOICE QUESTIONS (50 to 60 minutes)

1. Under the Revised Model Business Corporation Act, which of the following must be contained in a corporation's articles of incorporation?
a. Quorum voting requirements.
b. Names of stockholders.
c. Provisions for issuance of par and nonpar shares.
d. The number of shares the corporation is authorized to issue. (5/94, Law, #11, 4766)

2. The corporate veil is most likely to be pierced and the shareholders held personally liable if
a. The corporation has elected S corporation status under the Internal Revenue Code.
b. The shareholders have commingled their personal funds with those of the corporation.
c. An ultra vires act has been committed.
d. A partnership incorporates its business solely to limit the liability of its partners. (11/93, Law, #20, 4317)

3. Which of the following provisions must a for-profit corporation include in its Articles of Incorporation to obtain a corporate charter?

I. Provision for the issuance of voting stock.
II. Name of the corporation.

a. I only.
b. II only.
c. Both I and II.
d. Neither I nor II. (11/93, Law, #19, 4316)

4. A parent corporation owned more than 90% of each class of the outstanding stock issued by a subsidiary corporation and decided to merge that subsidiary into itself. Under the Revised Model Business Corporation Act, which of the following actions must be taken?
a. The subsidiary corporation's board of directors must pass a merger resolution.
b. The subsidiary corporation's dissenting stockholders must be given an appraisal remedy.
c. The parent corporation's stockholders must approve the merger.
d. The parent corporation's dissenting stockholders must be given an appraisal remedy. (11/94, Law, #25, 5202)

5. Assuming all other requirements are met, a corporation may elect to be treated as an S corporation under the Internal Revenue Code if it has

a. Both common and preferred stockholders.
b. A partnership as a stockholder.
c. Thirty-five or fewer stockholders.
d. The consent of a majority of the stockholders. (5/92, Law, #15, 2828)

6. Which of the following statements is correct concerning the similarities between a limited partnership and a corporation?
a. Each is created under a statute and must file a copy of its certificate with the proper state authorities.
b. All corporate stockholders and all partners in a limited partnership have limited liability.
c. Both are recognized for federal income tax purposes as taxable entities.
d. Both are allowed statutorily to have perpetual existence. (11/92, Law, #1, 3083)

7. Rice is a promoter of a corporation to be known as Dex Corp. On January 1, 1985, Rice signed a nine-month contract with Roe, a CPA, which provided that Roe would perform certain accounting services for Dex. Rice did not disclose to Roe that Dex had not been formed. Prior to the incorporation of Dex on February 1, 1985, Roe rendered accounting services pursuant to the contract. After rendering accounting services for an additional period of six months pursuant to the contract, Roe was discharged without cause by the board of directors of Dex. In the absence of any agreements to the contrary, who will be liable to Roe for breach of contract?
a. Both Rice and Dex.
b. Rice only.
c. Dex only.
d. Neither Rice nor Dex. (11/85, Law, #5, 0710)

8. Bixler obtained an option on a building he believed was suitable for use by a corporation he and two other individuals were organizing. After the corporation was successfully promoted, Bixler met with the Board of Directors who agreed to acquire the property for $200,000. Bixler deeded the building to the corporation and the corporation began business in it. Bixler's option contract called for the payment of only $155,000 for the building and he purchased it for that price. When the directors later learned that Bixler paid only $155,000, they demanded the return of Bixler's $45,000 profit. Bixler refused, claiming the building was worth far more than $200,000 both when he secured the option and when he deeded it to the corporation. Which of the following statements correctly applies to Bixler's conduct?

a. It was improper for Bixler to contract for the option without first having secured the assent of the Board of Directors.

b. If, as Bixler claimed, the building was fairly worth more than $200,000, Bixler is entitled to retain the entire price.

c. Even if, as Bixler claimed, the building was fairly worth more than $200,000, Bixler nevertheless must return the $45,000 to the corporation.

d. In order for Bixler to be obligated to return any amount to the corporation, the Board of Directors must establish that the building was worth less than $200,000.

(5/81, Law, #23, 9911)

9. Which of the following securities are corporate debt securities?

	Convertible bonds	Debenture bonds	Warrants
a.	Yes	Yes	Yes
b.	Yes	No	Yes
c.	Yes	Yes	No
d.	No	Yes	Yes

(11/93, Law, #17, 4314)

10. Price owns 2,000 shares of Universal Corp.'s $10 cumulative preferred stock. During its first year of operations, cash dividends of $5 per share were declared on the preferred stock but were never paid. In the second year, dividends on the preferred stock were neither declared nor paid. If Universal is dissolved, which of the following statements is correct?

a. Universal will be liable to Price as an unsecured creditor for $10,000.

b. Universal will be liable to Price as a secured creditor for $20,000.

c. Price will have priority over the claims of Universal's bond owners.

d. Price will have priority over the claims of Universal's unsecured judgment creditors.

(5/92, Law, #19, 9911)

11. Which of the following statements concerning treasury stock is correct?

a. Cash dividends paid on treasury stock are transferred to stated capital.

b. A corporation may **not** purchase its own stock unless specifically authorized by its articles of incorporation.

c. A duly appointed trustee may vote treasury stock at a properly called shareholders' meeting.

d. Treasury stock may be resold at a price less than par value. (5/84, Law, #9, 0715)

12. Sandy McBride, president of the Cranston Corporation, inquired about the proper method of handling the expenditures incurred in connection with the recent incorporation of the business and sale of its shares to the public. In explaining the legal or tax treatment of these expenditures, which of the following is correct?

a. The expenditures may be paid out of the consideration received in payment for the shares without rendering such shares not fully paid or assessable.

b. The expenditures are comparable to goodwill and are treated accordingly for nontax and tax purposes.

c. The expenditures must be capitalized and are nondeductible for federal income tax purposes since the life of the corporation is perpetual.

d. The expenditures may be deducted for federal income tax purposes in the year incurred or amortized at the election of the corporation over a five-year period. (5/82, Law, #11, 9911)

13. Golden Enterprises, Inc., entered into a contract with Hidalgo Corporation for the sale of its mineral holdings. The transaction proved to be ultra vires. Which of the following parties, for the reason stated, may properly assert the ultra vires doctrine?

a. Golden Enterprises to avoid performance.

b. A shareholder of Golden Enterprises to enjoin the sale.

c. Hidalgo Corporation to avoid performance.

d. Golden Enterprises to rescind the consummated sale. (5/80, Law, #12, 9911)

14. The limited liability of a stockholder in a closely held corporation may be challenged successfully if the stockholder

a. Undercapitalized the corporation when it was formed.

b. Formed the corporation solely to have limited personal liability.

c. Sold property to the corporation.

d. Was a corporate officer, director, or employee. (5/91, Law, #6, 0697)

15. Under the Revised Model Business Corporation Act, which of the following statements is correct regarding corporate officers of a public corporation?

a. An officer may **not** simultaneously serve as a director.

b. A corporation may be authorized to indemnify its officers for liability incurred in a suit by stockholders.

c. Stockholders always have the right to elect a corporation's officers. *No*

d. An officer of a corporation is required to own at least one share of the corporation's stock. *No*

(5/94, Law, #12, 4767)

16. Absent a specific provision in its articles of incorporation, a corporation's board of directors has the power to do all of the following, **except**

a. Repeal the bylaws.
b. Declare dividends. *2/3 vote of shareholder*
c. Fix compensation of directors.
d. Amend the articles of incorporation.

(5/90, Law, #7, 0704)

17. Jane Cox, a shareholder of Mix Corp., has properly commenced a derivative action against Mix's Board of Directors. Cox alleges that the Board breached its fiduciary duty and was negligent by failing to independently verify the financial statements prepared by management upon which Smart & Co., CPAs, issued an unqualified opinion. The financial statements contained inaccurate information which the Board relied upon in committing large sums of money to capital expansion. This resulted in Mix having to borrow money at extremely high interest rates to meet current cash needs. Within a short period of time, the price of Mix Corp. stock declined drastically. Which of the following statements is correct?

a. The Board is strictly liable, regardless of fault, since it owes a fiduciary duty to both the corporation and the shareholders.
b. The Board is liable since any negligence of Smart is automatically imputed to the Board.
c. The Board may avoid liability if it acted in good faith and in a reasonable manner.
d. The Board may avoid liability in all cases where it can show that it lacked scienter.

(11/85, Law, #3, 9911)

18. Which of the following rights is a holder of a public corporation's cumulative preferred stock always entitled to?

a. Conversion of the preferred stock into common stock.
b. Voting rights.
c. Dividend carryovers from years in which dividends were **not** paid, to future years.
d. Guaranteed dividends. (5/94, Law, #13, 4768)

19. Under the Revised Model Business Corporation Act, a merger of two public corporations usually requires all of the following **except**

a. A formal plan of merger.
b. An affirmative vote by the holders of a majority of each corporation's voting shares.

c. Receipt of voting stock by all stockholders of the original corporations. *No*

d. Approval by the board of directors of each corporation. (5/94, Law, #14, 4769)

20. Knox, president of Quick Corp., contracted with Tine Office Supplies, Inc., to supply Quick's stationery on customary terms and at a cost less than that charged by any other supplier. Knox later informed Quick's board of directors that Knox was a majority stockholder in Tine. Quick's contract with Tine is

a. Void, because of Knox's self-dealing.
b. Void, because the disclosure was made after execution of the contract.
c. Valid, because of Knox's full disclosure.
d. Valid, because the contract is fair to Quick.

(11/90, Law, #15, 0712)

21. A stockholder's right to inspect books and records of a corporation will be properly denied if the stockholder

a. Wants to use corporate stockholder records for a personal business.
b. Employs an agent to inspect the books and records. *OK*
c. Intends to commence a stockholder's derivative suit. *OK*
d. Is investigating management misconduct. *OK*

(11/92, Law, #2, 3084)

22. Unless prohibited by the organization documents, a stockholder in a publicly held corporation and the owner of a limited partnership interest both have the right to

a. Ownership of the business' assets.
b. Control management of the business.
c. Assign their interest in the business.
d. An investment that has perpetual life. *shareholder*

(5/92, Law, #17, 2830)

23. Fairwell is executive vice president and treasurer of Wonder Corporation. He was named as a party in a shareholder derivative action in connection with certain activities he engaged in as a corporate officer. In the lawsuit, it was determined that he was liable for negligence in performance of his duties. Fairwell seeks indemnity from the corporation for his liability. The board would like to indemnify him. The articles of incorporation do not contain any provisions regarding indemnification of officers and directors. Indemnification

a. Is **not** permitted since the articles of incorporation do **not** so provide.
b. Is permitted only if he is found **not** to have been grossly negligent.

c. **Cannot** include attorney's fees since he was found to have been negligent.

d. May be permitted by court order despite the fact that Fairwell was found to be negligent.

(5/82, Law, #10, 9911)

24. Ambrose purchased 400 shares of $100 par value original issue common stock from Minor Corporation for $25 a share. Ambrose subsequently sold 200 of the shares to Harris at $25 a share. Harris did not have knowledge or notice that Ambrose had not paid par. Ambrose also sold 100 shares of this stock to Gable for $25 a share. At the time of this sale, Gable knew that Ambrose had not paid par for the stock. Minor Corporation became insolvent and the creditors sought to hold all the above parties liable for the $75 unpaid on each of the 400 shares. Under these circumstances

a. The creditors can hold Ambrose liable for $30,000.

b. If $25 a share was a fair value for the stock at the time of issuance, Ambrose will have no liability to the creditors.

c. Since Harris acquired the shares by purchase, he is not liable to the creditors and his lack of knowledge or notice that Ambrose paid less than par is immaterial.

d. Since Gable acquired the shares by purchase, he is not liable to the creditors, and the fact that he knew Ambrose paid less than par is immaterial. (11/83, Law, #24, 9911)

25. Which of the following must take place for a corporation to be voluntarily dissolved?

a. Passage by the board of directors of a resolution to dissolve.

b. Approval by the officers of a resolution to dissolve.

c. Amendment of the certificate of incorporation.

d. Unanimous vote of the stockholders.

(11/92, Law, #3, 3085)

26. A corporate stockholder is entitled to which of the following rights?

a. Elect officers.

b. Receive annual dividends.

c. Approve dissolution.

d. Prevent corporate borrowing.

(5/92, Law, #18, 2831)

27. Which of the following would be grounds for the judicial dissolution of a corporation on the petition of a shareholder?

a. Refusal of the board of directors to declare a dividend.

b. Waste of corporate assets by the board of directors.

c. Loss operations of the corporation for three years.

d. Failure by the corporation to file its federal income tax returns. (5/84, Law, #6, 0714)

28. All of the following distributions to stockholders are considered asset or capital distributions, **except**

a. Liquidating dividends.

b. Stock splits.

c. Property distributions.

d. Cash dividends. (11/90, Law, #17, 0701)

29. Opal Corp. declared a 9% stock dividend on its common stock. The dividend

a. Requires a vote of Opal's stockholders.

b. Has **no** effect on Opal's earnings and profits for federal income tax purposes.

c. Is includible in the gross income of the recipient taxpayers in the year of receipt.

d. Must be registered with the SEC pursuant to the Securities Act of 1933.

(11/90, Law, #18, 0702)

30. The stock of Crandall Corporation is regularly traded over the counter. However, 75% is owned by the founding family and a few of the key executive officers. It has had a cash dividend record of paying out annually less than 5% of its earnings and profits over the past 10 years. It has, however, declared a 10% stock dividend during each of these years. Its accumulated earnings and profits are beyond the reasonable current and anticipated needs of the business. Which of the following is correct?

a. The shareholders can compel the declaration of a dividend only if the directors' dividend policy is fraudulent.

b. The Internal Revenue Service **cannot** attack the accumulation of earnings and profits since the Code exempts publicly held corporations from the accumulations provisions.

c. The fact that the corporation was paying a 10% stock dividend, apparently in lieu of a cash distribution, is irrelevant insofar as the ability of the Internal Revenue Service to successfully attack the accumulation.

d. Either the Internal Revenue Service or the shareholders could successfully obtain a court order to compel the distribution of earnings and profits unreasonably accumulated.

(5/81, Law, #25, 9911)

Solution 52-1 MULTIPLE CHOICE ANSWERS

Corporate Formation and Characteristics

1. (d) The Revised Model Business Corporation Act (RMBCA) requires that the articles of incorporation set forth a corporate name, the street address of the corporation and its registered agent, the name and address of each incorporator, and the number of shares the corporation is authorized to issue (MBCA 2.02). Answers (a), (b), and (c) are incorrect because it is not necessary to list shareholder names, provide for the issuance of par and non-par shares, or list state quorum voting requirements. Inclusion of this information in the articles of incorporation is optional.

2. (b) Four factors that frequently cause the courts to pierce the corporate veil are listed below:

1. Fraudulently inducing someone into dealing with the corporation rather than the individual.
2. "Thinly capitalized" corporations.
3. Failure to act as a corporation.
4. Commingling personal and corporate assets to the extent that the corporation has no identity of its own.

Answer (b) falls within the description of Factor #4; thus, it would be most likely to cause the courts to pierce the corporate veil.

3. (c) Under state law, the article of incorporation (corporate charter) must contain certain mandatory provisions. Thus, the articles normally include the *name of the corporation*, corporate purpose, *capital stock authorized*, location of the principal office, number of directors, capital structure, and duration. Item I refers to the provision for the authorization of capital stock, and Item II, the corporation name, is also clearly required.

4. (b) The Revised Model Business Corporation Act (RMBCA) 11.01 provides that one or more corporations may merge into another corporation if the board of directors of the *parent* corporation approve a plan of merger. Under RMBCA 11.04, it is not necessary for the shareholders of the parent or the subsidiary to approve the merger, if the parent's board of directors has already done so. Under 13.02, the RMBCA states that only shareholders with voting rights on the merger have a right to dissent; thus, the shareholders of the parent have appraisal rights. Under 13.02, dissenting shareholders of a subsidiary corporation merged with its parent under 11.04 have the right to obtain payment for the fair market value of their shares.

5. (c) An S corporation is allowed to have no more than 35 stockholders, is allowed only one class of stock, and is not allowed to have a partnership as a stockholder. *All* stockholders, not just the majority, must consent to the election to be treated as an S corporation.

6. (a) Both a limited partnership and a corporation may be created only under a state statute, and each must file a copy of its certificate with the proper state authorities. Further, both a corporation's stock and a limited partnership interest are subject to the federal securities laws registration requirements if they are "securities" under the federal securities laws. General partners in a limited partnership do not have limited liability. Partnerships are not recognized for federal income tax purposes as taxable entities. Instead, the income flows through to the partners and is taxed on their individual returns. Partnerships do not have perpetual existence. Their existence can be affected by the death of a partner.

7. (a) The promoter of a corporation is liable on a preincorporation contract made with a third party, unless he specifically states in the contract that he is not personally liable or there is a novation, by which the third party creditor agrees to release the promoter and look only to the corporation for satisfaction of the contract. Neither of these circumstances are present here; therefore, Rice remains liable on the contract. Generally, a corporation is not liable on preincorporation contracts entered into on behalf of the corporation by the promoter, *unless* the corporation "adopts" or accepts the contract. Here, by accepting the benefits of the contract after February 1, Dex Corp. adopted the preincorporation contract and is also liable for breach of contract.

8. (c) In this situation, Bixler is a promoter. As a promoter, he has a fiduciary duty to the not-yet-formed corporation and is thereby barred from making secret profits in his dealings with the corporation. Bixler should have made a full disclosure of his private dealings; however, because he did not divulge the details and obtain approval of the directors, he must return the $45,000 profit to the corporation.

Financing the Corporation and Corporate Liabilities

9. (c) Convertible bonds are classified as debt securities as long as they are not converted into stock shares (equity). Debenture bonds are debt securities by definition. Warrants, however, represent the right to buy a given number of shares of stock, usually

within a set time period, and are classified as equity instruments.

10. (a) A cash dividend on preferred stock becomes a legal debt of the corporation when the dividend is declared. Afterward the preferred shareholder becomes an unsecured creditor of the corporation. However, dividends not paid in any year concerning cumulative preferred stock are not a liability of the corporation until they are declared. Therefore, Universal will be liable to Price as an unsecured creditor for $10,000, which is the amount of the declared dividends. Answer (b) is incorrect because undeclared dividends do not become a legal liability to the corporation. Answers (c) and (d) are incorrect because Price has become a general unsecured creditor for the declared dividends and will have the same priority as the bond owners and the unsecured judgment creditors.

11. (d) *Newly* issued stock must be issued at par or above, but treasury stock may be sold below par. No dividends are paid on treasury stock. A corporation has the right to purchase its own stock unless specifically denied by statute or by specific provision in the articles of incorporation. Treasury stock does not have any voting rights. (Otherwise, management could take control of the corporation away from its owners simply by purchasing enough treasury stock and then voting it according to management's wishes.)

12. (a) Organization expenses made by a forming corporation may be paid out of proceeds of stock subscriptions. Moreover, share subscribers will not be liable for assessments by creditors if their subscriptions were fully paid at the time of share issuance. Answers (b), (c), and (d) are incorrect because incorporation expenditures are not characterized as goodwill with an unlimited life for tax purposes. Rather, they are characterized as deferred expenses which are amortizable over a period of not less than 60 months, beginning with the month in which the business begins.

13. (b) The doctrine of ultra vires states that a corporation may not act or contract in any way that is not authorized either expressly or implied by state statute, the articles of incorporation, or the bylaws. If an action or contract is ultra vires, it is void or unenforceable under common law. However, the doctrine may be raised by a person harmed by it, such as a shareholder. It may not be raised by either the corporation or a third party to nullify an action or contract.

14. (a) Courts may "pierce the corporate veil" and hold a shareholder personally liable under the following circumstances: the corporation was undercapitalized when formed, the shareholders commingle personal assets/transactions with business assets/transactions, or the corporation is used to perpetrate a fraud on others. Answer (b) is incorrect since there is nothing wrong with forming a corporation to limit personal liability. Answer (c) is incorrect since there is nothing wrong with selling property to a corporation. Answer (d) is incorrect since a shareholder does not lose his/her limited liability just by being an officer, director, or employee of the corporation.

Directors and Officers

15. (b) Under the Revised Model Business Corporations Act (RMBCA 8.50 and 8.56), a corporation may be authorized to indemnify its officers and directors for liability incurred in a suit by shareholders. The RMBCA does not prohibit a person from serving as both an officer and director in a corporation. Corporate officers are chosen by the corporation's directors. The RMBCA does not require that an officer also be a shareholder.

16. (d) The amendment of the articles of incorporation is a task ultimately left to the *shareholders*, via a majority or perhaps even greater (e.g., two-thirds) vote.

17. (c) The business judgment rule, as used to explain the board of director's duty of due care, means that directors will not be held liable for acts or omissions involving a question of policy or business judgment, so long as they acted in good faith and without gross negligence. A director may reasonably rely on information given him or her by others associated with the organization. Scienter is an element of knowing, reckless behavior, and directors *can* be held liable in cases where they were sufficiently negligent, but lacked scienter. Smart and Co. is an independent contractor performing specialized services, and its negligence cannot be imputed to the directors.

Stockholders' Rights and Liabilities

18. (c) Cumulative preferred stock is stock that entitles its holders to future year dividend carryovers from years in which dividends were not paid. The right to convert preferred stock to common stock is a matter of contract, and thus is not always present. Preferred stock may be either voting or non-voting. A corporation cannot declare a dividend distribution if such would render the corporation insolvent. Thus,

there is no guarantee that dividends will be declared or paid.

19. (c) The Revised Model Business Corporations Act requires a formal plan of merger (RMBCA 11.01) and requires that the board of directors and the shareholders of each corporation approve the merger (RMBCA 11.03). The RMBCA does not require that all stockholders of the original corporations be issued voting stock.

20. (d) Corporate officers are fiduciaries and are ordinarily prohibited from engaging in self-dealing or making a secret profit from contracts with the corporation. However, most states make an exception where the self-interest is disclosed and fair to the corporation.

21. (a) Corporations are required to keep books and records pertaining to such things as stockholder names and addresses and minutes of corporate-related meetings. Under common law, a stockholder has the right to inspect these books and records, in person or by his or her attorney, agent, or accountant [answer (b)], if there is a proper purpose, such as gathering information to commence a stockholder's derivative suit [answer (c)], to solicit stockholders to vote for a change in the board of directors, or to investigate possible management misconduct [answer (d)]. Therefore, answer (a), to use stockholder records for a personal business, is not a proper purpose.

22. (c) A limited partner's interest is considered personal property and is freely assignable. Likewise, a shareholder's interest in a corporation may be bought or sold with little effect on the operation of the corporate business. Answer (a) is incorrect because neither has the right to direct ownership of the business assets. Answer (b) is incorrect because neither a limited partner nor a stockholder of a publicly held company can directly control the management of the business. Answer (d) is incorrect because only the stockholder is entitled to an investment characterized by perpetual life.

23. (d) There are two types of shareholder suits: representative suits (direct suits against the corporation by shareholders to prevent a corporate act) and derivative suits (indirect suits brought by shareholders as representatives of the corporation against directors, officers, or outside partners). In the absence of any contrary provision in the articles, indemnification of officers and directors found to be negligent will be made only by court order.

24. (a) Under the general rule, a subscriber who pays less than par or stated value for stock ("watered stock") as well as a transferee with knowledge of the deficiency are liable jointly and/or severally for the deficiency to creditors of the corporation. Answers (b), (c), and (d) are incorrect statements of the general rule relating to watered stock.

25. (a) For voluntary dissolution to occur, most jurisdictions require a vote by the board of directors recommending dissolution. This must be followed by the approval of at least an absolute majority of the stockholders and the filing of a certificate of dissolution with the appropriate state court. Answers (b) and (c) are incorrect because they are not requirements of a voluntary dissolution. Answer (d) is incorrect because the dissolution must be approved by at least an absolute majority of the stockholders. A unanimous vote is not required.

26. (c) Certain types of changes, such as amendments to the articles, merger, consolidation, *dissolution*, or sale of a substantial part of the corporate assets, require approval by an absolute majority of the shareholders, unless a greater proportion is required by the articles of incorporation. Answers (a) is incorrect because the board of directors is responsible for electing officers. Answer (b) is incorrect because stockholders do not have a right to receive *annual* dividends. Answer (d) is incorrect because stockholders have no right to prevent corporate borrowing.

27. (b) A shareholder may bring an action for dissolution if the board of directors has committed fraud, waste [answer (b)], oppression, or misapplication of corporate funds. Dissolution may also be sought by the shareholders if the board of directors is deadlocked and the corporate business may no longer be conducted in a manner advantageous to the shareholders.

28. (b) A stock split does not represent an asset or capital distribution to shareholders. A stock split simply increases the number of shares outstanding and proportionately decreases the par or stated value of the stock. There is no change in the dollar amount of capital stock, retained earnings, or total stockholders' equity. Answers (a), (c), and (d) all represent asset or capital distributions to shareholders.

Federal Income Tax Ramifications

29. (b) A stock dividend (compared to a cash dividend) has no effect on the earnings and profits of a company for federal income tax purposes. Only the

board of directors is required to vote on declaration of dividends. Stock dividends are not includable in gross income for federal income tax purposes. There is no rule that stock dividends be registered with the Securities and Exchange Commission.

30. (c) Every corporation (except personal holding companies and charitable associations) is liable for the accumulated earnings tax on sums of accumulated taxable income in excess of $250,000. The board of directors controls the timing, amount, and character of lawful dividends as long as it does not abuse its discretion. The IRS cannot compel distribution by court order; however, the mere presence of the accumulated earnings tax has some influence on frequency of cash dividend distributions. Stock dividends will not reduce amounts subject to the tax.

PERFORMANCE BY SUBTOPICS

Each category below parallels a subtopic covered in Chapter 52. Record the number and percentage of questions you correctly answered in each subtopic area.

Corporate Formation and Characteristics

Question #	Correct √
1	
2	
3	
4	
5	
6	
7	
8	
# Questions	8

Correct _____
% Correct _____

Financing the Corporation and Corporate Liabilities

Question #	Correct √
9	
10	
11	
12	
13	
14	
# Questions	6

Correct _____
% Correct _____

Directors and Officers

Question #	Correct √
15	
16	
17	
# Questions	3

Correct _____
% Correct _____

Stockholders' Rights and Liabilities

Question #	Correct √
18	
19	
20	
21	
22	
23	
24	
25	
26	
27	
28	
# Questions	11

Correct _____
% Correct _____

Federal Income Tax Ramifications

Question #	Correct √
29	
30	
# Questions	2

Correct _____
% Correct _____

ESSAY QUESTIONS

Essay 52-2 (15 to 25 minutes)

Edwards, a director and a 10% stockholder in National Corp., is dissatisfied with the way National's officers, particularly Olsen, the president, have been operating the corporation.

Edwards has made many suggestions that have been rejected by the board of directors, and has made several unsuccessful attempts to have Olsen removed as president.

National and Grand Corp. had been negotiating a merger that Edwards has adamantly opposed. Edwards has blamed Olsen for initiating the negotiation and has urged the board to fire Olsen. National's board refused to fire Olsen. In an attempt to defeat the merger, Edwards approached Jenkins, the president of Queen Corp., and contracted for Queen to purchase several of National's assets. Jenkins knew Edwards was a National director, but had never done business with National. When National learned of the contract, it notified Queen that the contract was invalid.

Edwards filed an objection to the merger before the stockholders' meeting called to consider the merger proposal was held. At the meeting, Edwards voted against the merger proposal.

Despite Edward's efforts, the merger was approved by both corporations. Edwards then orally demanded that National purchase Edwards' stock, citing the dissenters rights provision of the corporation's by-laws, which reflects the Model Business Corporation Act.

National's board has claimed National does not have to purchase Edward's stock.

As a result of the above:

- Edwards initiated a minority stockholder's action to have Olsen removed as president and to force National to purchase Edward's stock.
- Queen sued National to enforce the contract and/or collect damages.
- Queen sued Edwards to collect damages.

Required:

Answer the following questions and give the reasons for your answers.

a. Will Edwards be successful in a lawsuit to have Olsen removed as president? *No*

b. Will Edwards be successful in a lawsuit to have National purchase the stock? *Yes*

c. 1. Will Queen be successful in a lawsuit against National?
2. Will Queen be successful in a lawsuit against Edwards? (5/93, Law, #3)

Essay 52-3 (15 to 20 minutes)

On May 1, 1987, Cray's board of directors unanimously voted to have Cray reacquire 100,000 shares of its common stock. On May 25, 1987, Cray did so, paying current market price. In determining whether to reacquire the shares, the board of directors relied on reports and financial statements that were negligently prepared by Cray's internal accounting department under the supervision of the treasurer and reviewed by its independent accountants. The reports and financial statements indicated that, as of April 30, 1987, Cray was solvent and there were sufficient funds to reacquire the shares. Subsequently, it was discovered that Cray had become insolvent in March 1987 and continued to be insolvent after the reacquisition of the shares. As a result of the foregoing, Cray experienced liquidity problems and losses during 1987 and 1988.

The board of directors immediately fired the treasurer because of the treasurer's negligence in supervising the preparation of the reports and financial statements. The treasurer had three years remaining on a binding five-year employment agreement which, among other things, prohibited the termination of the treasurer's employment for mere negligence.

Required:

Discuss the following assertions, indicating whether such assertions are correct and the reasons therefor.

- It was improper for the board of directors to authorize the reacquisition of Cray's common stock while Cray was insolvent.
- The members of the board of directors are personally liable because they voted to reacquire shares while Cray was insolvent.
- Cray will be liable to the treasurer as a result of his termination by the board of directors.

(5/89, Law, #4)

Essay 52-4 (15 to 20 minutes)

Mace, Inc., wishes to acquire Creme Corp., a highly profitable company with substantial retained earnings. Creme is incorporated in a state that recognizes the concepts of stated capital (legal capital) and capital surplus.

In conjunction with the proposed acquisition, Mace engaged Gold & Co., CPAs, to audit Creme's financial statements. Gold began analyzing Creme's stated capital account and was provided the following data:

- Creme was initially capitalized in 1980 by issuing 40,000 shares of common stock, 50¢ par value, at $15 per share. The total number of authorized shares was fixed at 100,000 shares.
- Costs to organize Creme were $15,000.
- During 1982, Creme's board of directors declared and distributed a 5% common stock dividend. The fair market value of the stock at that time was $20 per share.
- On June 1, 1983, the president of Creme exercised a stock option to purchase 1,000 shares of common stock at $21 per share when the market price was $25 per share.
- During 1984, Creme's board of directors declared and distributed a 2-for-1 stock split on its common stock when the market price was $28 per share.
- During 1985, Creme acquired as treasury stock 5,000 shares of its common stock at a market price of $30 per share. Creme uses the cost

52-25

method of accounting and reporting for treasury stock.

- During 1986, Creme reissued 3,000 shares of the treasury stock at the market price of $32 per share.

Required:

Answer the following, setting forth reasons for any conclusions stated.

a. Discuss what effect each of the transactions described above would have on stated capital (legal capital), indicating the dollar amount of change.

b. Discuss the requirements necessary to properly declare and pay cash dividends. (11/87, Law, #5)

Essay 52-5 (15 to 20 minutes)

Major formed the Dix Corp. for the purpose of operating a business to repair, install, and sell used refrigerators. Major is the sole shareholder and president of Dix. Major owns 2,000 shares of $10 par value common stock. He paid for 1,000 of these shares by transferring to Dix property with a fair market value of $3,500 and his promissory note for $2,500 due and payable on June 1, 1988. He also received at a later date 1,000 shares in consideration of services rendered to Dix fairly valued at $7,000 and his agreement to render specific additional services starting with January 1, 1987 which are fairly valued at $1,000. The promissory note has not been paid nor have the additional services been rendered.

Fox, a customer of Dix, was seriously injured when a refrigerator negligently repaired by Major on behalf of Dix caught fire. Dix has $500,000 of liability insurance covering itself and its employees for such occurrences. Fox wishes to hold Major personally liable since Dix has insufficient assets and insurance to pay Fox's claim.

Pine, one of Dix's largest creditors, has asserted claims against Major, individually, claiming that Major is:

- Personally liable to the extent of $6,000 for the common shares issued to him.
- Personally liable for all of the debts of Dix because he instructed several of Dix's customers to make checks payable to the order of Major which were deposited in his individual account and not recorded on the corporate books.

Required:

Answer the following, setting forth reasons for any conclusions stated.

a. Discuss Major's liability and the liability of Dix for the injuries sustained by Fox. What effect does the insurance carried by Dix have on Major's and Dix's liability to Fox?

b. Discuss the assertions of Pine and reach a conclusion for each. (5/86, Law, #4)

ESSAY SOLUTIONS

Solution 52-2 Rights of Stockholders

a. Edwards will not win the suit to have Olsen removed as president. The **right to hire and fire** officers is held by the **board of directors**. **Individual stockholders**, regardless of the size of their holding, **have no vote in the selection of officers**. Individual stockholders may exert influence in this area by voting for directors at the annual stockholders' meeting.

b. Edwards will lose the suit to have National purchase the stock. A stockholder who **dissents from a merger** may require the corporation to purchase his or her shares if the statutory requirements are met and would be entitled to the fair value of the stock **(appraisal remedy)**. To **compel the purchase**, Edwards would have had to **file an objection** to the merger before the stockholders

meeting at which the merger proposal was considered, **vote against** the merger proposal, and make a **written demand** that the corporation purchase the stock at an appraised price. Edwards will lose because the first two requirements were met but Edwards failed to make a written demand that the corporation purchase the stock.

c. **1.** Queen will lose its suit against National to enforce the contract, even though Edwards was a National director. Jenkins may have assumed that Edwards was **acting as National's agent**, but Edwards had **no authority** to contract with Queen. A director has a **fiduciary duty** to the stockholders of a corporation but, unless **expressly authorized** by the board of directors or the officers of the corporation, has **no authority to contract on behalf of the**

corporation. There is **no implied agency authority** merely **by being a director**.

     2.   Queen will win its suit against Edwards because Edwards had **no authority to act** for National. Edwards will be **personally liable** for Queen's damages.

Solution 52-3 Authority and Liability of Board of Directors

The assertion that it was improper for the board of directors to authorize the reacquisition of Cray's common stock while Cray was insolvent is correct. A board of directors may authorize and the corporation may reacquire its shares of stock subject to any restriction in the articles of incorporation, except that **no reacquisition may be made if,** after giving effect thereto, **either the corporation would be unable to pay its debts as they become due** in the usual course of business **or the corporation's total assets would be less than its total liabilities**. Because Cray was **insolvent** before and after the reacquisition of Cray's common stock, it was improper for the board of directors to authorize the reacquisition.

The assertion that the members of Cray's board of directors are personally liable because Cray reacquired its own shares of Cray stock while Cray was insolvent is incorrect. In general, directors who vote or assent to a reacquisition by the corporation of its own shares while the corporation is insolvent will be **jointly** and **severally liable** to the corporation. However, the directors will not be liable if they **acted in good faith**, in a manner they reasonably believed to be in the best interests of the corporation, and with such care as an **ordinarily prudent person** in a like position would use under similar circumstances. In performing their duties, **directors are entitled to rely on information, opinions, reports, or statements**, including financial statements and other financial data prepared or **presented by one or more officers or employees of the corporation** whom the directors reasonably believe to be reliable and competent in the matters presented. The directors may rely on the same information prepared or presented by independent accountants that the directors reasonably believe to be within such person's professional competence. Based on the facts of this case, the directors' reliance on the reports and financial statements prepared by Cray's internal accounting department under the supervision of the treasurer and reviewed by its independent accountants was proper so long as the directors **exercised due care, acted in good faith,** and **acted without knowledge** that would cause such reliance to be unwarranted. In addition, the courts are precluded from substituting their business judgment for that of the board of directors if the directors have acted with due care and in good faith.

The assertion that Cray will be liable to the treasurer as a result of his termination by the board of directors is correct. **An officer may be removed** by the board of directors **with or without cause** whenever in its judgment the best interests of the corporation will be served by the removal. However, such removal is **without prejudice to the contract rights** of the person so removed. Thus, the board of directors had the power to remove the treasurer. The treasurer will prevail in a breach of contract action for damages against Cray because **the firing violated the employment agreement.**

Solution 52-4 Stated Capital/Cash Dividends

a.   The initial capitalization of Creme in 1980 would result in $20,000 being allocated to stated capital. **Stated capital includes the par value of all shares of the corporation** having a par value that have been issued. Therefore, the $20,000 is calculated as follows: **40,000 shares issued x 50 cents par value = $20,000.**

The $15,000 of expenses incurred in organizing Creme would not affect stated capital. The **model Business Corporation Act permits payment of organization expenses out of the consideration received by it in payment for its shares** if the payment does not render such shares assessable or unpaid. Thus, stated capital remains at $20,000.

The 5% stock dividend would increase stated capital by $1,000 calculated as follows: **40,000 shares x 5% stock dividend = 2,000 shares x 50** cents par value = **$1,000.** The market price of the shares would have no effect on stated capital. Thus, stated capital is $21,000.

The exercise of the stock option by Creme's president would increase stated capital by $500 calculated as follows: 1,000 shares x 50 cents par value = $500. **Neither the price paid** by Creme's president **nor the market price** of the shares on the date the option was exercised **would affect stated capital**. Thus, stated capital is $21,500.

The 2-for-1 stock split would not affect stated capital. Instead the **par value** of 50 cents per share would be **reduced to 25 cents per share** and the **43,000 shares of stock issued** would be **increased to 86,000** shares. Thus, stated capital remains at $21,500.

The acquisition of 5,000 shares as treasury stock at $30 per share by Creme would have **no effect on stated capital under the cost method.** Thus, stated capital remains at $21,500.

The reissuance of the 3,000 shares of treasury stock at $32 per share would also have **no effect on stated capital under the cost method.** Thus, stated capital remains at $21,500.

b.   Cash dividends may be declared and paid if the corporation is **solvent** and payment of the dividends would not render the corporation insolvent. Furthermore, each state imposes **additional restrictions** on what funds are **legally available** to pay dividends. One of the more restrictive tests adopted by many states permits the payment of dividends only out of **unrestricted** and **unreserved earned surplus** (retained earnings). The Model Business Corporation Act **prohibits dividend distributions** if, after giving effect to the distribution, the **corporation's total assets would be less than its total liabilities.**

Solution 52-5 Liability of Stockholders

a.   Although officers are **generally insulated** from personal liability for the negligence of the corporation or its employees, they are subject to personal liability **in tort** for their **own negligent conduct** or **participation**, even while engaged in corporate business activities. **Shareholders** generally **will not be held liable** for the negligence of the corporation unless they have in some way **participated in the negligent act.** Based on the facts presented, Major is **personally liable** to Fox for his **own negligence** even though the negligent acts were committed **while engaged in corporate business activities.** Major **may also be liable** because of his status as a shareholder if the **corporate veil is pierced.**

A corporation is **liable** under the doctrine of **respondeat superior** for the **torts committed by its agents and employees** (officers) **in the course of their employment.** Thus, Dix will also be liable to Fox for the negligence of Major.

The liability insurance carried by Dix will provide **coverage of Dix and Major up to $500,000 of liability to Fox.** If Fox were to obtain a judgment in excess of $500,000, Major and Dix would be **liable for the uninsured balance.**

b.   Pine's assertion that Major is personally liable to the extent of $6,000 for the common shares issued to Major is incorrect as to the dollar amount of his potential liability. Where a corporation issues par value stock in return for property or services rendered having a fair market value less than the par value, the **shareholder purchasing the stock at the discounted price** will remain **potentially liable to the creditors of the corporation.** The potential liability is the **difference between** the **fair market value** of the consideration given and the **total par value** of the stock. Stock issued at such a discounted price is commonly referred to as **"watered stock."** In this case, Major's part payment by a promissory note and future services is **insufficient consideration.** Therefore, Major is **potentially liable** to Pine and the other corporate creditors for **$9,500,** calculated as follows:

First Acquisition
Total par value
   (1,000 shares x $10 par value) $ 10,000
Less: Consideration given (fair market value of property)   (3,500)
Potential liability on first acquisition $ 6,500

Second Acquisition
Total par value
   (1,000 shares x $10 par value) $ 10,000
Less: Consideration given (services rendered)   (7,000)
Potential liability on second acquisition   3,000
        Total Potential Liability $ 9,500

Pine's assertion that Major may be personally liable as a result of his directing customers to make checks payable to him in his individual capacity and depositing the checks in his individual account without recording the checks on the corporation's books is correct. Although a corporation may be established to limit the liability of the shareholders, the courts will **pierce the corporate veil** (disregard the corporate entity) and hold the shareholders personally liable when the corporation is **used to perpetuate a fraud** or in a closely held corporation when the shareholders fail to treat the corporation as a separate business entity. The **commingling** of the corporation's funds with Major's own funds amounts to a disregard of the corporate entity and will likely **subject Major to personal liability for the debts of Dix.**

CHAPTER 53

ESTATES AND TRUSTS

I. **Definitions**..53-2
   A.   Administrator..53-2
   B.   Beneficiary 53-2
   C.   Charitable Trust 53-2
   D.   Devise 53-2
   E.   Executor...53-2
   F.   Intestate Succession...53-2
   G.   Legacy 53-2
   H.   Per Capita 53-2
   I.   Per Stirpes 53-2
   J.   Probate 53-2
   K.   Trust...53-2

II. **Estates**...53-2
   A.   Definition and Functions 53-2
   B.   Administration 53-4

III. **Trusts** 53-5
   A.   Definition and Characteristics 53-5
   B.   Allocation of Principal and Income..53-10

IV. **Overview of the Federal Estate Tax** 53-12

CHAPTER 53

ESTATES AND TRUSTS

I. Definitions

A.   Administrator--A person who is appointed by the court to administer the estate of an individual who died intestate.

B.   Beneficiary--The holder of the equitable title to trust property.

C.   Charitable Trust--A trust created for the purpose of benefiting the public at large or some particular class of the public indefinite in number. In order for a trust to be classified as charitable, the trust purpose must be exclusively charitable.

D.   Devise--A disposition by will of real property.

E.   Executor--A person who is appointed by the testator to carry out the testator's directions concerning the disposition of property under his or her will.

F.   Intestate Succession--The disposition and distribution of the assets of an estate when the assets are not disposed of or distributed by a valid will. If an individual dies testate, the laws of intestate succession will still govern the distribution of any assets not disposed of by the will.

G.   Legacy--A disposition by will of personal property.

H.   Per Capita--The manner of distribution of property in which the heirs to an intestate's estate share and share alike.

I.   Per Stirpes--The manner of distribution of property in which a class or group of distributees take the share which their deceased would have been entitled to. For example: A dies leaving one son, B, and two grandchildren of deceased daughter, C. B takes one-half and the two grandchildren each take one-quarter (they share equally in what their deceased parent would have taken, if living).

J.   Probate--The process of proving the validity of a will by demonstrating that an instrument purporting to be a will was executed in accordance with legal requirements.

K.   Trust--The legal relationship between the trustee and beneficiary in which the trustee holds legal title to the trust property for the benefit and use of the beneficiary.

II. Estates

A.   Definition and Functions--An estate is a legal entity which comes into existence upon the death of an individual and succeeds to the title of property owned by the individual at the time of death. The estate also assumes liability for all debts owed by the decedent at the time of death.

   1.   An individual may control the distribution of the assets of the estate by means of a valid will.

      a.   A will is a legal declaration of an individual's intentions and desires with respect to the distribution of property after his or her death.

         (1)   An individual who dies with a valid will in existence is said to die "testate."

         (2)   The person who makes a will and whose intentions are reflected in the will is called a "testator."

(3)   In order to make a valid will, a testator must have legal capacity; that is, the testator must be of legal age and sound mind when the will is executed.

(4)   In order to be valid, a will must be properly executed; that is, it must be signed by the testator in the presence of witnesses who then sign in the presence of each other.

(5)   A will is ambulatory; that is, during the testator's lifetime, the testator has the power to alter, amend, or revoke the will.

(6)   A will is a testamentary instrument; that is, it becomes effective only upon the death of the testator.

b.   A valid will has the effect, upon the testator's death, of distributing the decedent's assets to those beneficiaries who are named in the will.

(1)   A <u>legacy</u> is a gift of personal property under a will.

(a)   A general legacy is a gift of personal property payable out of the general assets of the estate; for example, a gift of $500.

(b)   A specific legacy is a gift of a specified item or personalty; for example, a particular painting.

(2)   A <u>devise</u> is a gift of real property under a will.

(a)   A general devise is a gift of an unspecified piece of realty; for example, a gift of an unidentified 100 acres.

(b)   A specific devise is a gift of a particular piece of real estate; for example, a gift of a house and lot at a specified address.

(3)   The residuary estate is what remains after all other gifts have been distributed.

(a)   Most wills include a residuary clause which expressly disposes of property not distributed as general and specific gifts.

(b)   The content of the residuary estate is not normally determined until all other gifts have been distributed or accounted for.

2.   An individual is said to die "intestate" if the person dies without having a valid will in existence. Distribution of the assets of an individual who dies intestate is controlled by state law. State statutes of intestate succession vary from state to state, but certain features and provisions are common to virtually all intestate succession statutes.

a.   Most state statutes give first consideration to the surviving spouse of a decedent who dies intestate.

(1)   The surviving spouse is generally the recipient of a stated percentage (often one-half) of the decedent's estate.

(2)   Additionally, in many states the surviving spouse of an individual who dies testate may elect to receive a stated percentage (often one-third) of the decedent's estate instead of taking under the will.

      b.   After the surviving spouse has been provided for, the usual order of distribution of the remaining assets of the estate is as follows:

          (1)   The descendants (children and grandchildren) of the deceased; or if none survive,

          (2)   The ascendants (parents and grandparents) of the deceased; or if none survive,

          (3)   The collaterals (such as brothers and sisters) of the deceased.

B.   <u>Administration</u>--The administration of the estate includes the entire process of assembling the assets of the estate, paying off claims against the estate (including taxes), and distributing the assets of the estate according to the testator's intentions or the law of intestate succession.

     1.   The probate court has jurisdiction to determine and approve the validity of a will and to supervise the administration of the estate. Probating a will involves proving that an instrument which purports to be a will was in fact signed, witnessed, and otherwise executed in accordance with the requirements of the law.

        a.   Probate is generally initiated by filing the will in the proper court along with a petition for probate.

          (1)   The petition normally includes an estimate of the value of the estate and a list of the names of the beneficiaries.

          (2)   The petition is usually accompanied by the sworn statements of the original witnesses attesting to their belief that the will is valid.

        b.   Admission of the will to probate is accompanied by the execution of letters testamentary in which the court empowers the executor to administer the estate.

     2.   The administration of the estate is carried out by the executor or the administrator of the estate.

        a.   The executor or administrator acts as the representative of the estate.

        b.   An executor named in the decedent's will need not serve if he or she does not wish to do so. In such a case, the court will appoint an administrator who will have the same powers and duties as an executor.

     3.   The general duty of an executor or administrator is to use reasonable diligence and to act in good faith on behalf of the estate and in accordance with the terms of the will (if one exists).

        a.   In fulfilling this general duty, the executor or administrator usually possesses the following powers:

          (1)   He or she may contract on behalf of the estate (with the approval of the court).

          (2)   He or she may engage attorneys, accountants, appraisers, etc., to perform services necessary to the administration of the estate.

          (3)   He or she may sell the assets of the estate to pay debts.

             (a)   Generally, he or she must sell personalty first; realty may be sold only with court approval if all debts cannot be satisfied by selling personalty.

        (b)   However, the testator may in his or her will empower the executor to sell realty for any and all purposes.

    b.   In addition, the following duties are imposed on the executor or administrator:

        (1)   He or she must use reasonable care and diligence in promptly collecting and preserving the assets of the estate.

            (a)   Personal liability may be imposed on the executor or administrator for negligent failure to discover and collect assets.

            (b)   Personal liability may also be imposed for any shrinkage of the assets of the estate caused by the negligence of the executor or administrator.

        (2)   He or she must refrain from commingling the assets of the estate with his or her own funds or property. Personal liability may result from any shrinkage of the assets of the estate due to commingling. In addition, such commingling is punishable in some states as a misdemeanor.

        (3)   He or she must represent the estate in lawsuits brought against it.

          •   The executor is generally not personally liable on any contracts entered into in his or her capacity as such, unless the executor fails to reveal his or her representative capacity and identify the estate.

    4.   Once an executor or administrator has been appointed, the general steps in the administration of an estate are as follows:

        a.   The executor must collect and preserve all of the assets of the estate and file with the court an inventory of the property.

        b.   The executor will publish a notice of the administration of the decedent's estate that will require all claims against the estate to be filed within a certain period of time. If a creditor does not file the claim on time, he or she will be barred from collecting on the debt.

        c.   Once the claims have been filed and proved, the executor will pay the debts in accordance with their statutory priority.

            (1)   <u>Abatement</u> is the process of determining the distribution of the estate when the total available assets in the estate are insufficient to satisfy the provisions of the will.

            (2)   <u>Ademption</u> occurs when a specific bequest or devise becomes impossible to perform due to circumstances or events occurring after the execution of the will.

        d.   At the conclusion of his or her duties, the executor must file with the court a final accounting of the administration of the estate.

        e.   The final step in the administration of a decedent's estate is for the executor to be discharged by the court and the estate closed.

III. Trusts

    A.   <u>Definition and Characteristics</u>--A trust is a fiduciary relationship with respect to property in which one person (a trustee) holds legal title to the property for the benefit of another (a beneficiary).

Thus, a trust involves two forms of ownership--one legal, the other equitable--in the same property at the same time.

1. There are four elements that are essential to the existence of a valid trust: a settlor, a trustee, trust property, and a beneficiary.

   a. A <u>settlor</u> (or trustor) is the person who causes the trust to come into existence.

      (1) The settlor may also be a trustee or beneficiary, but not both.

         • The merger doctrine states that if the sole trustee and the sole beneficiary are the same person, the trust will go out of existence because the legal title (held by the trustee) and the equitable title (held by the beneficiary) have "merged."

      (2) Even though the settlor creates the trust, the settlor may generally terminate the trust only if he or she is empowered to do so by the trust instrument.

   b. A <u>trustee</u> holds the legal title to the trust property for the benefit of the beneficiaries.

      (1) Trustees stand in a fiduciary relationship to beneficiaries. As a fiduciary, a trustee may not use his or her position for personal advantage.

      (2) A trustee manages the trust property and distributes the trust income to the beneficiaries as directed by the trust instrument.

         (a) In addition to the powers expressly conferred upon the trustee by the trust instrument, a trustee possesses those powers which are necessary and appropriate to carry out the trust purposes.

         (b) A trustee may not delegate his or her control over the administration of the trust. However, the trustee may seek advice from such professionals as lawyers, accountants, and appraisers, and contract for their services.

         (c) Generally, a trust which satisfies all other requirements will not fail due to the refusal or incapacity of the trustee to serve. In such cases, the court will appoint a trustee.

      (3) In administering a trust, the trustee must exercise that degree of care and skill which a reasonably prudent businessperson would exercise in dealing with his or her own property.

         (a) A trustee has a duty to the beneficiaries to preserve the assets of the trust and to make the trust property productive.

         (b) A trustee may not invest trust assets in speculative ventures, and he or she must rid the trust of assets that are nonproductive.

         (c) A trustee must strive for diversity in investing the assets of the trust.

         (d) A trustee has a duty to enforce all rights and claims belonging to the trust, and is required to defend suits brought against the trust.

         (e) A trustee must keep trust assets separate from his or her personal assets and from the assets of any other trust which he or she is administering.

c. The trust property (or trust res) is the property interest that the trustee holds for the benefit of the beneficiaries. The trust property must be an existing interest in identifiable property which is capable of being owned and conveyed.

    (1) An interest which has not yet come into existence (i.e., an expectancy) cannot be held in trust.

        (a) For example, property which the settlor may later inherit cannot be the subject of a present trust, since the settlor has only an expectancy, not an existing interest, in the trust res.

        (b) However, a future interest in property may be held in trust so long as it is a presently-existing and transferable interest.

    (2) The trust res must be identified or at least described with sufficient specificity so that it can be identified with certainty.

        (a) For example, a declaration that "a large part of my assets shall be held in trust" is too indefinite to establish a trust.

        (b) However, a declaration that "all of my real property except my current residence shall be held in trust" is probably sufficiently specific to adequately identify the trust res.

    (3) Since a trust is created by a transfer of ownership from the settlor, the trust res must be capable of being owned and sold.

    (4) The rule against perpetuities limits the duration of a trust to a life in being plus 21 years.

d. A beneficiary is the person for whose benefit the trust property is held by the trustee. The beneficiary holds the equitable interest in the trust property, and is empowered to enforce the terms of the trust.

    (1) Any ascertainable person or group of persons may be beneficiaries.

    (2) Corporations, clubs, churches, and other entities may be beneficiaries so long as they are sufficiently identifiable to permit a determination of who is empowered to enforce the terms of the trust.

2. The various types of trusts are classified according to the duties imposed upon the trustees, the purpose of the trust, and the manner in which the trust was created.

a. An active trust imposes affirmative duties of management and administration on the trustees. A passive trust imposes no real duties on the trustees; they are mere holders of the legal title to the trust property until ownership passes to the beneficiaries.

b. A trust which is intended to confer a benefit on the public at large or on a large segment of the public is a charitable trust. All other trusts are private trusts.

    (1) Special rules apply to charitable trusts. These rules are designed to give the most liberal effect to the settlor's intentions.

        (a) Charitable trusts are valid even though they may be indefinite in identifying specific beneficiaries.

(b) The <u>doctrine of cy pres</u> is applied by the courts when the stated purpose of a charitable trust is impossible or impractical to carry out. Under this doctrine, a court will apply the trust assets to a purpose as nearly like the stated purpose as possible.

(c) Charitable trusts are not subject to the rule against perpetuities (see A.1.c.(4) above).

(2) Private trusts are subject to more rigid substantive rules. They will be allowed to fail for indefiniteness in some situations, while a similarly-vague charitable trust would be upheld.

c. An <u>express trust</u> is created by the settlor's expression of his or her intention to establish a division of legal and equitable title in property. In an <u>implied trust</u>, the intention to create the trust is inferred or presumed by law. There are two types of implied trusts: (1) a resulting trust and (2) a constructive trust.

(1) A <u>resulting trust</u> arises due to the presumed intention of a settlor to create a trust when the intent to do otherwise is not adequately expressed. A resulting trust may be implied in law under the following circumstances:

(a) Failure of an express trust for any reason.

(b) Fulfillment of the trust purpose and trust property still remains.

(c) The title to property is taken in the name of one who did not furnish consideration. For example: A politician pays the purchase price of a parcel of land, but the title is taken in the name of her associate without the intention of making it a gift. The presumption here is that the parties intended the associate to hold the property for the politician's benefit, and the associate will be treated as a trustee upon a resulting trust.

(2) A <u>constructive trust</u> is a remedy in the form of a trust created by operation of law to prevent unjust enrichment. The court converts the legal owner into a trustee for the party who is entitled to beneficial enjoyment. A constructive trust is imposed whenever the court establishes that the one who acquired title to property is obligated to transfer it because acquisition was by breach of fiduciary duty, wrongful killing, fraud, duress, or undue influence.

d. An <u>inter vivos trust</u> is created by the settlor while he or she is living and comes into existence during his or her lifetime.

e. A <u>testamentary trust</u> is generally created in a testamentary instrument (usually a will) and comes into existence only upon the settlor's death.

f. A <u>spendthrift trust</u> may be either inter vivos or testamentary. This type of trust prohibits any transfer of a beneficiary's rights by assignment or otherwise. It is often created to protect a beneficiary from creditors or from his or her squandering of the trust's assets. If the trust is irrevocable, it may not be terminated by the settlor during the term of the trust. A spendthrift trust is terminated at the end of the term of trust or when all beneficiaries die.

g. A <u>"tentative" or "Totten" trust</u> is created when the settlor opens a bank account in his or her own name "as trustee" for another.

(1) Such a trust may be revoked by the settlor simply by withdrawing the funds from the account.

(2)   The trust becomes irrevocable upon the settlor's death.

(3)   If the beneficiary dies before the settlor, the trust terminates.

h.   A <u>Real Estate Investment Trust (REIT)</u> is authorized by the provisions of the Real Estate Investment Trust Act of 1960. It is created by a transfer of the legal title to real estate to a trustee. The trustee manages the trust property for the benefit of specified beneficiaries. A qualifying trust need not pay corporate taxes, preventing double taxation of trust income.

(1)   Qualification--To qualify as a REIT, the following provisions must be met:

(a)   The certificates of ownership must be freely transferable.

(b)   There must be 100 or more certificate holders during each year and no fewer than 6 may own 50 percent of all outstanding certificates.

(c)   The trust's primary business cannot be to buy and sell real estate.

(d)   The major portion of the trust's income must be derived from real estate; i.e., rent, interest on mortgages, and gains on sale of real property.

(e)   The trustee must have centralized control.

(f)   The trust must distribute at least 90 percent of taxable income to certificate holders each year.

Failure to meet these provisions results in the trust being taxed as a corporation.

(2)   Statute of Frauds--A REIT falls within the provisions of the Statute of Frauds and must be in writing to be enforceable.

(3)   Limited Liability--Certificate holders (beneficiaries) are not personally liable for debts and other obligations of the trust. Their liability is limited to their investment in the trust.

(4)   Tax Treatment--Ordinary income and capital gains distributed by the trust are taxable only to the beneficiaries. Depreciation and other losses do not pass through to the beneficiaries.

3.   In order to create a trust, the settlor must indicate his or her present intention to establish the separation of legal and equitable title.

a.   This intention is usually expressed in writing (a trust instrument); however, the requisite intent to create a trust may be manifested orally or by conduct.

(1)   When the trust res is real property, the trust must be evidenced by a writing to satisfy the statute of frauds.

(2)   The writing need only be signed by the settlor in order to create a valid trust of real property.

b.   The beneficiaries of the trust and the trust property must be adequately identified.

c.　No consideration is necessary for the present creation of a trust. However, an agreement to create a trust in the future is subject to the same requirements of consideration as any other contract.

d.　A trust must be created for a lawful purpose. Any trust which is created for an illegal purpose is invalid. For example, a trust is invalid if it is created for the purpose of fraudulently avoiding payment of the settlor's creditors.

4.　Generally, a validly-created trust may be terminated either by those methods provided in the trust instrument or by operation of law.

   a.　Under certain limited circumstances, the parties to a trust may terminate the trust.

     (1)　The settlor may unilaterally terminate the trust only if the trust instrument expressly reserves to the settlor the right of termination.

     (2)　Similarly, the trustee has only such powers of termination as are conferred upon him or her by the trust instrument.

     (3)　If all of the beneficiaries (including potential future beneficiaries) join in a suit to terminate a trust, the trust may be terminated if termination would not defeat a material trust purpose.

   b.　A trust terminates by its own effect when the instrument specifies a definite period of duration or a termination date.

   c.　A trust may terminate when the purposes for which the trust was created are completely fulfilled or upon complete failure of the trust purpose.

     (1)　For example, a trust created exclusively for the purpose of sending the settlor's daughter through college would terminate upon her completion of college.

     (2)　A trust established for the purpose of sending the settlor's daughter through college would also terminate if the daughter died or became mentally incompetent before she completed college.

B.　<u>Allocation of Principal and Income</u>--The most frequent target of questions involving trusts on past exams has been the area of principal and income allocation. The following rules and principles are generally applicable to the administration of estates as well as trusts.

1.　The allocation of principal and income is generally governed by the provisions of the Uniform Principal and Income Act.

   a.　The Uniform Act has been adopted by more than two-thirds of the states and represents the majority view.

   b.　The provisions of the Uniform Act are applicable to both estates and trusts.

2.　Problems involving the allocation of principal and income frequently occur when a will or trust instrument provides for the income to be distributed to one or several beneficiaries and for the principal to be distributed to others. For example, problems of principal and income allocation might arise when a trust instrument creates a life estate in one beneficiary and a remainder interest in another. (A remainder is a future interest created in a third person which takes effect at the end of the prior possessory interest, the life estate.)

a. In such a situation, the trustee must make decisions bearing on the allocation of the benefits (receipts) and burdens (expenses) between the income beneficiary and the remainderman.

    (1) If the trust instrument expressly empowers the trustee to determine what is principal and what is income, his or her determination is usually conclusive.

    (2) When the instrument is silent, the trustee's decisions are generally governed by the Uniform Act.

b. The trustee may be held personally liable to the income beneficiary and/or remainderman for commingling or misallocating costs and benefits.

3. In allocating benefits between the income beneficiary and the remainderman, the general rule is that ordinary receipts are treated as income, while extraordinary receipts are treated as additions to principal.

  a. Ordinary receipts include the following:

    (1) Net rents received from property owned by the estate or trust, as well as the net income from a partnership or proprietorship managed by the executor or trustee (operating losses from such an enterprise are allocated solely to principal).

    (2) Cash dividends (regular or extraordinary).

    (3) Rights to subscribe to shares of another corporation, as well as distributions of stock in another corporation.

    (4) Interest on notes and bonds held by the estate or trust (including discount portion of treasury bills).

    (5) Royalties from property subject to depletion (depletion allowance chargeable to principal).

  b. Extraordinary receipts include the following:

    (1) Stock dividends and stock splits (but not cash dividends).

    (2) Proceeds from the sale or exchange of trust assets.

    (3) Sums received in settlement of claims for injury to trust property.

    (4) Income earned on property prior to the formation of the trust.

4. In allocating the burdens (expenses) between the income account and the principal account, the general rule is that current administration expenses incurred to keep the trust property productive should be paid out of trust income, while extraordinary expenses and those which primarily benefit the remainderman should be borne by the principal account.

  a. Examples of ordinary expenses incurred in the production or collection of income, and chargeable to the income account, include the following:

    (1) The cost of insuring trust property.

    (2) Interest on loans and mortgages secured by trust assets.

    (3) Ordinary income taxes and real estate taxes.

        (4)   The cost of repairing and preserving trust property.

        (5)   Depreciation allowance.

   b.   Examples of extraordinary expenses and expenses incurred in the improvement of trust principal chargeable to principal include the following:

        (1)   The cost of permanent (capital) improvements.

        (2)   Losses sustained in the operation of businesses owned by the trust.

        (3)   Mortgage and loan principal payments.

        (4)   Costs incurred in the purchase or sale of trust property.

        (5)   Real estate taxes on improvements.

5.   Some types of receipts and expenses are equitably apportioned between income and principal, for example:

   a.   Administrative expenses, including trustees' fees.

   b.   Annuities.

IV. Overview of the Federal Estate Tax

The estate tax is a transfer tax (not an income tax) imposed on the value of property "transferred" by a decedent at death. The gift tax is also a transfer tax based on the same tax rate schedule as the estate tax. However, the gift tax is imposed on inter vivos transfers of property. Thus, a transfer tax cannot be avoided simply by giving property away before death.

The first step in determining the estate tax due is to obtain the value of the gross estate (Item A. in the diagram, below). The gross estate includes not only property actually owned by the decedent, but also property constructively owned by the decedent. In addition, certain gifts made within three years of death may be includable in the gross estate (see Item A., below). The gross estate is reduced by certain nondiscretionary deductions [Item B.] to arrive at adjusted gross estate. The adjusted gross estate is further reduced by discretionary deductions [Item C.] to obtain the taxable estate. To the taxable estate we must add post-1976 adjusted taxable gifts [Item D.] other than gifts which were included in the gross estate. This equals the tentative tax base, on which a tentative estate tax is determined, based on the table provided in §2001(c). The next step [Item E.] is to subtract from this tentative tax the amount of taxes that would have been payable (at the §2001(c) rates in effect at date of death) on gifts included in the tentative tax base (i.e., pursuant to Items A. and D.). The objective of this whole scheme is to increase the marginal rates at which the estate is taxed (i.e., by increasing the tax base by the amount of gifts made); however, double taxation of gifts is prevented by providing for the reduction of the tentative estate tax by the amount of gift taxes that would have been payable on the gifts themselves. The last two items in the tax computation are credits against the estate tax: the unified credit and other miscellaneous tax credits. These adjustments taken together produce the estate tax due [Items F. and G.].

In the diagram which follows, we will expand upon the overview by summarizing each block in the flow chart with textual material to the right of the chart. As you read down the chart, keep in mind the main objective of the estate tax--to identify, value, and levy an appropriate tax on the transfer of all of a decedent's property.

Determination of Federal Estate Tax

```
┌─────────────┐
│   Gross     │
│   Estate    │
└─────────────┘
```

A.   The gross estate of a decedent who is a citizen or resident includes the value at the date of death (or alternate valuation date--six months after date of death) of all of the decedent's worldwide property, both real and personal, tangible and intangible (§2031).

This all inclusive definition of property identified to the gross estate includes the following:

1.   The value of all property to the extent of the decedent's beneficial interest, including income due to the decedent at the time of death in the form of salary, rents, royalties, dividends, insurance proceeds, and business interests (§2033).

2.   The value of any interest in property gratuitously transferred by the decedent during life, but over which the decedent retained control during his or her life. Thus, if the decedent transferred securities, real rental property, or other income-producing property, but retained the right to control the property and/or its income stream, the entire value of the property is included in the gross estate (§2036). Similarly included are gratuitous transfers conditioned on the transferee's surviving the decedent (§2037).

3.   The value of property gratuitously transferred during life to the extent of the portion of the property over which the decedent had a right to revoke. Thus, if the decedent during life gifted securities to his or her son with income to his or her daughter with a right to revoke the income gift, the discounted value of the income, but not the value of the security will be included (§2038).

(Less)

4.   The value of a joint and survivor annuity purchased by the decedent for him- or herself and another is included (§2039).

```
┌─────────────────┐
│ Nondiscretionary│
│   Deductions    │
└─────────────────┘
```

B.   The gross estate, as identified and valued above, is reduced by the following nondiscretionary deductions:

1.   Funeral expenses

2.   Administration expenses

3.   Claims against the estate

4.   Casualty and theft losses

5.   Indebtedness of property included in gross estate

6.   Certain taxes (however, income taxes accrued after death and state estate or inheritance taxes are not deductible)

Value of the gross estate – Nondiscretionary deductions = Adjusted gross estate

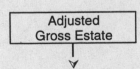
```
┌─────────────┐
│  Adjusted   │
│ Gross Estate│
└─────────────┘
```

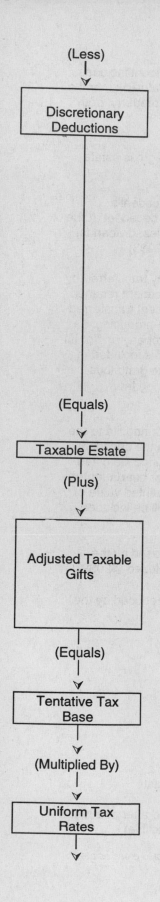

(Less)

Discretionary Deductions

(Equals)

Taxable Estate

(Plus)

Adjusted Taxable Gifts

(Equals)

Tentative Tax Base

(Multiplied By)

Uniform Tax Rates

C. The adjusted gross estate is diminished by the discretionary deductions. The most common discretionary deductions are the following:

1. Transfers to or for the use of any charitable, scientific, educational, religious, or literary entity qualified under §501(c)(3). The amount of the transfer is limited only by the value of the gross estate (§2055).

2. The marital deduction, which is generally unlimited. Thus, as with the charitable deduction, the decedent could give the entire net estate after expenses to his or her surviving spouse. The only limitation on the marital deduction is that the marital deduction interest consist of a nonterminable interest in property included in the gross estate. A terminable interest is an interest in property given to the surviving spouse which will lapse after a certain time (e.g., life estate or term for years) or upon the occurrence of an event or contingency or its failure to occur (e.g., until wife's remarriage, or only if decedent's daughter does not marry by age 30) (§2056).

D. In 1976, the Unified Transfer Tax System was introduced. Under this system, one transfer tax schedule [§2001(c)] is used to compute gift tax as well as estate tax. The system also requires the inclusion of all lifetime gifts in the determination of the tentative tax base. The adjusted taxable gifts inclusion brings into the computation all taxable gifts (net of the annual exclusion and net of all gifts made within 3 years of death).

The tentative tax base is applied against the appropriate rates set forth in §2001(c).

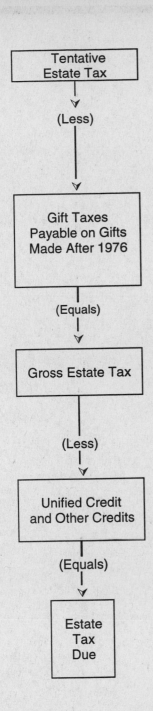

E.   The tentative tax as computed above is then reduced by gift taxes payable on gifts made after 1976. Since adjusted taxable gifts (gifts not included in the gross estate by §2035) were pulled into the tentative tax base for the estate tax computation using the uniform tax rates, to avoid double taxation a reduction is allowed for gift taxes payable on such gifts.

F.   The tentative estate tax is further reduced by the unified credit against estate tax. In the case of decedents dying in 1994, the credit is $192,800. Additionally, a limited credit is allowed the estate for certain state death taxes paid (§§2010, 2011).

G.   The executor or administrator of the estate is required to file the estate tax return (§6018) and pay any estate tax due (§2002). When no executor or administrator has been named in the will and/or appointed by the court, property transferees receiving property from the estate may be liable for the return and tax due.

NOTES

CHAPTER 53—ESTATES AND TRUSTS

Problem 53-1 MULTIPLE CHOICE QUESTIONS (35 to 45 minutes)

1. A descendant's will provided that the estate was to be divided among the decedent's issue, per capita and not per stirpes. If there are two surviving children and three grandchildren who are children of a predeceased child at the time the will is probated, how will the estate be divided?
a. 1/2 to each surviving child.
b. 1/3 to each surviving child and 1/9 to each grandchild. *per stirpes*
c. 1/4 to each surviving child and 1/6 to each grandchild.
d. 1/5 to each surviving child and grandchild.
(11/92, Law, #9, 3091)

2. Generally, an estate is liable for which debts owed by the decedent at the time of death?
a. All of the decedent's debts.
b. Only debts secured by the decedent's property.
c. Only debts covered by the Statute of Frauds.
d. None of the decedent's debts.
(5/89, Law, #17, 0862)

3. A personal representative of an estate would breach fiduciary duties if the personal representative
a. Combined personal funds with funds of the estate so that both could purchase treasury bills.
b. Represented the estate in a lawsuit brought against it by a disgruntled relative of the decedent.
c. Distributed property in satisfaction of the decedent's debts.
d. Engaged a non-CPA to prepare the records for the estate's final accounting.
(5/89, Law, #19, 9911)

4. Rita Ryan died leaving a will naming her children, John and Dale, as the sole beneficiaries. In her will, Rita designated John as the executor of her estate and excused John from posting a bond as executor. At the time of Rita's death, she owned a parcel of land with her sister, Ann, as joint tenants with right of survivorship. In general, John as executor, must
a. Post a bond despite the provision to the contrary in Rita's will.
b. Serve without compensation because John is also a named beneficiary in the will.
c. File a final account of the administration of the estate.
d. Relinquish the duties because of the conflict of interest as executor and beneficiary.
(11/87, Law, #18, 0866)

5. Which of the following is **not** necessary to create an express trust?
a. A successor trustee.
b. A trust corpus.
c. A beneficiary.
d. A valid trust purpose. (5/94, Law, #15, 4770)

6. In a written trust containing **no** specific powers, the trustee will have all of the following implied powers **except**
a. Sell trust property.
b. Pay management expenses.
c. Accumulate income.
d. Employ a CPA to prepare trust tax returns.
(5/94, Law, #17, 4772)

7. On the death of the grantor, which of the following testamentary trusts would fail?
a. A trust created to promote the public welfare.
b. A trust created to provide for a spouse's health care.
c. A trust created to benefit a charity.
d. A trust created to benefit a childless person's grandchildren. (5/95, Law, #10, 5344)

8. An irrevocable testamentary trust was created by Park, with Gordon named as trustee. The trust provided that the income will be paid to Hardy for life with the principal then reverting to Park's estate to be paid to King. The trust will automatically end on the death of
a. Park.
b. Gordon.
c. Hardy.
d. King. (5/94, Law, #19, 4774)

9. Which of the following events will terminate an irrevocable spendthrift trust established for a period of five years?
a. Grantor dies.
b. Income beneficiaries die.
c. Grantor decides to terminate the trust.
d. Income beneficiaries agree to the trust's termination. (5/94, Law, #20, 4775)

Items 10 and 11 are based on the following:

Arno plans to establish a spendthrift trust naming Ford and Sims as life income beneficiaries, Trip residuary beneficiary, and Bing as trustee. Arno plans to fund the trust with an office building.

10. For the trust to be enforceable, Arno must
a. Execute a written trust instrument.
b. Provide for Bing's trustee fees.
c. Designate a successor trustee.
d. Deed the property to Bing as trustee.
(5/93, Law, #16, 9911)

For item 11, assume an enforceable trust was formed.

11. Sims has the following personal creditors:

I. Bank holding a home mortgage note deficiency judgment.
II. Judgment creditor as a result of an automobile accident.

To which of these creditors can Bing pay Sims' share of trust income?
a. I only.
b. II only.
c. Both I and II.
d. Neither I **nor** II. (5/93, Law, #17, 3985)

12. An irrevocable trust that contains **no** provision for change or termination can be changed or terminated only by the
a. Courts.
b. Income beneficiaries.
c. Remaindermen.
d. Grantor. (5/95, Law, #11, 5345)

13. Which of the following situations would cause a resulting trust to be created?

I. Failure of an express trust.
II. Application of the *cy pres* doctrine.
III. Fulfillment of the trust purpose.

a. I and II.
b. I and III.
c. II and III.
d. I, II, and III. (11/92, Law, #5, 3087)

14. To properly create an inter vivos trust funded with cash, the grantor must
a. Execute a written trust instrument.
b. Transfer the cash to the trustee.
c. Provide for payment of fees to the trustee.
d. Designate an alternate trust beneficiary.
(5/91, Law, #8, 0856)

15. Cord's will created a trust to take effect on Cord's death. The will named Cord's spouse as both the trustee and personal representative (executor) of the estate. The will provided that all of Cord's securities were to be transferred to the trust and named Cord's child as the beneficiary of the trust. Under the circumstances,
a. Cord has created an inter vivos trust.
b. Cord has created a testamentary trust.
c. The trust is invalid because it will **not** become effective until Cord's death.
d. Cord's spouse may **not** serve as both the trustee and personal representative because of the inherent conflict of interest.
(5/95, Law, #15, 5349)

16. A distinguishing feature between the making of an inter vivos gift and the creation of a trust is that
a. A gift may be made orally whereas a trust must be in a signed writing.
b. Generally, a gift is irrevocable whereas a trust may be revoked in certain cases.
c. In order to create a valid trust, the creator must receive some form of consideration.
d. The beneficiary of a trust must be notified of the trust's creation. (11/88, Law, #58, 9911)

17. If **not** expressly granted, which of the following implied powers would a trustee have?

I. Power to sell trust property.
II. Power to borrow from the trust.
III. Power to pay trust expenses.

a. I and II.
b. I and III.
c. II and III.
d. I, II, and III. (11/92, Law, #7, 3089)

18. Mason's will created a testamentary trust for the benefit of Mason's spouse. Mason's sister and Mason's spouse were named as co-trustees of the trust. The trust provided for discretionary principal distributions to Mason's spouse. It also provided that, on the death of Mason's spouse, any remaining trust property was to be distributed to Mason's children. Part of the trust property consisted of a very valuable coin collection. After Mason's death, which of the following statements would be correct?
a. Mason's spouse may **not** be a co-trustee because the spouse is also a beneficiary of the trust.
b. Mason's sister may delegate her duties as co-trustee to the spouse and thereby **not** be liable for the administration of the trust.

c. Under **no** circumstances could the spouse purchase the coin collection from the trust without breaching fiduciary duties owed to the trust and Mason's children.

d. The co-trustees must use the same degree of skill, judgment, and care in managing the trust assets as reasonably prudent persons would exercise in managing their own affairs.

(5/91, Law, #10, 0858)

19. Which of the following fiduciary duties may be violated by the trustee if the trustee, without express direction in the trust instrument, invests trust assets in unsecured loans to a co-trustee?

I.   Duty to invest prudently.
II. Duty of loyalty to the trust.

a. I only.
b. II only.
c. Both I and II.
d. Neither I nor II.   (5/95, Law, #13, 5347)

20. To which of the following trusts would the rule against perpetuities **not** apply?
a. Charitable.
b. Spendthrift.
c. Totten.
d. Constructive.   (11/92, Law, #8, 3090)

21. Which of the following expenditures resulting from a trust's ownership of commercial real estate should be allocated to the trust's principal?
a. Building management fees.
b. Insurance premiums.
c. Sidewalk assessments.
d. Depreciation.   (5/94, Law, #16, 4771)

22. Arno plans to establish a spendthrift trust naming Ford and Sims life income beneficiaries, Trip residuary beneficiary, and Bing as trustee. Arno plans to fund the trust with an office building. Assume an enforceable trust was formed.

Which of the following will be allocated to trust principal?

	Annual property tax	Monthly mortgage principal payment
a.	Yes	Yes
b.	Yes	No
c.	No	Yes
d.	No	No

(5/93, Law, #18, 3986)

23. Cox transferred assets into a trust under which Smart is entitled to receive the income for life. After Smart's death, the remaining assets are to be given to Mix. In 1991, the trust received rent of $1,000, stock dividends of $6,000, interest on certificates of deposit of $3,000, municipal bond interest of $4,000, and proceeds of $7,000 from the sale of bonds. Both Smart and Mix are still alive. What amount of the 1991 receipts should be allocated to trust principal?
a. $ 7,000
b. $ 8,000
c. $13,000
d. $15,000   (11/92, Law, #6, 3088)

24. Which of the following would ordinarily be distributed to a trust income beneficiary?

I.   Royalties.
II.   Stock received in a stock split.
III. Cash dividends.
IV.   Settlements of claims for damages to trust property.

a. I and II.
b. I and III.
c. II and III.
d. II and IV.   (11/92, Law, #10, 3092)

25. Frost's will created a testamentary trust naming Hill as life income beneficiary, with the principal to Brown when Hill dies. The trust was silent on allocation of principal and income. The trust's sole asset was a commercial office building originally valued at $100,000 and having a current market value of $200,000. If the building was sold, which of the following statements would be correct concerning the allocation of the proceeds?
a. The entire proceeds would be allocated to principal and retained.
b. The entire proceeds would be allocated to income and distributed to Hill.
c. One half of the proceeds would be allocated to principal and one half to income.
d. One half of the proceeds would be allocated to principal and one half distributed to Brown.

(5/95, Law, #12, 5346)

26. Jay properly created an inter vivos trust naming Kroll as trustee. The trust's sole asset is a fully rented office building. Rental receipts exceed expenditures. The trust instrument is silent about the allocation of items between principal and income. Among the items to be allocated by Kroll during the year are insurance proceeds received as a result of fire damage to the building and the mortgage interest payments made during the year. Which of the following items is(are) properly allocable to principal?

	Insurance proceeds on building	Current mortgage interest payments
a.	No	No
b.	No	Yes
c.	Yes	No
d.	Yes	Yes

(5/90, Law, #10, 9911)

27. On January 1, 1988, Dix transferred certain assets into a trust. The assets consisted of Lux Corp. bonds with a face amount of $500,000 and an interest rate of 12%. The trust instrument named Dix as trustee, Dix's child as life beneficiary, and Dix's grandchild as remainderman. Interest on the bonds is payable semiannually on May 1 and November 1. Dix had purchased the bonds at their face amount. As of January 1, 1988, the bonds had a fair market value of $600,000. The accounting period selected for the trust is a calendar year. The trust instrument is silent as to whether Dix may revoke the trust. Assuming the trust is valid, how should the amount of interest received in 1988 be allocated between principal and income if the trust instrument is otherwise silent?

	Principal	Income
a.	$0	$60,000
b.	$0	$72,000
c.	$10,000	$50,000
d.	$12,000	$60,000 (11/89, Law, #9, 9911)

28. Absent specific directions, which of the following parties will ordinarily receive the assets of a terminated trust?
a. Income beneficiaries.
b. Remaindermen.
c. Grantor.
d. Trustee.   (5/95, Law, #14, 5348)

Solution 53-1 MULTIPLE CHOICE ANSWERS

Estates

1. (d) For a per capita distribution of an estate, each person takes an equal share of the estate. Since, in this case, there are a total of five issues (two surviving children and three grandchildren of a predeceased child), the estate would be divided into five equal parts. Answers (b) would be correct if the distribution were to be made on a per stirpes basis.

2. (a) An estate is a legal entity which comes into existence upon the death of an individual and succeeds to the title of all property owned by the individual. It also assumes liability for all debts owed by the decedent at the time of his death.

3. (a) The personal representative of an estate would breach fiduciary duties by commingling the assets of the estate with his own property. Personal liability may result from any shrinkage of estate assets due to commingling. Answers (b), (c), and (d) are incorrect because the personal representative of an estate could be involved in these activities without violating the fiduciary duties required of all personal representatives.

4. (c) Generally, the terms of a valid will control its administration. Thus, John need not post bond. Whether the named executor is a beneficiary does not affect his potential right to reasonable compensation, nor does it require him to relinquish the duties of the appointment.

Characteristics of Trusts

5. (a) It is not necessary that the grantor appoint a trustee or a successor trustee. If no trustee is stipulated, the courts will appoint one. In order for there to be a valid express trust, there must be a valid trust purpose, a trust corpus and at least one beneficiary.

6. (c) A written trust containing no specific powers does not grant the trustee the implied power to accumulate income. The most common implied powers are the power to sell assets, the power to lease assets and the power to incur reasonable expenses.

7. (d) The rule against perpetuities limits the duration of a trust to a life in being plus 21 years; thus, a trust created to benefit a childless person's grandchildren would fail. Trusts created to promote the public welfare, to provide for a spouse's health care, and/or to benefit a charity are valid and would not fail.

8. (c) A trust will terminate by operation of law when there are no longer any income beneficiaries. Since Hardy is the only beneficiary, the trust will terminate upon his death. Hardy's life is the measuring life of the trust, and he is the trust's only income beneficiary. The timing of the deaths of Park, Gordon and King are irrelevant to the trust's termination.

9. (b) All trusts, including spendthrift trusts, terminate when there are no longer any income beneficiaries. The death of the grantor will have no impact on trust termination. The trust in this instance is irrevocable. Spendthrift trusts are created to protect the beneficiaries from their own careless actions, and cannot be terminated by the beneficiaries.

10. (d) The AICPA's unofficial answer is (d). The trustee holds legal title to property in a trust for the benefit of the beneficiaries and is a requirement for the trust to be valid. However, our editorial board also feels (a) is correct. A trust may be created orally or in writing. However, for an express trust of real property to be enforceable, it must be in writing under the Statute of Frauds. Because this trust is funded by an office building (real property), it must be in writing. There is no rule that for a trust to be enforceable, there must be a provision for trustee fees. A trust will never fail for lack of a trustee.

11. (d) A spendthrift trust is often created to protect a beneficiary from creditors or from his or her squandering of the trusts' assets. This type of trust prohibits any transfer of beneficiary's rights by assignment or otherwise, and prevents creditors of the beneficiary from obtaining trust principal or its income until it is actually paid to the beneficiary.

12. (a) An irrevocable trust that contains no provision for change or termination can be changed or terminated only by the courts. The grantor, income beneficiaries, and remaindermen have no power to change or terminate the trust.

13. (b) A resulting trust may arise where an express trust has been created gratuitously and it fails (I) because it is impossible to carry out. Also, the fulfillment of a trust purpose (III) could result in the creation of a resulting trust if trust property still remained. The application of the cy pres doctrine (II) would not cause a resulting trust to be created. It is applied in those situations in which a gift to a charitable trust cannot be carried out in the manner specified by the donor. In that case, the doctrine would allow that the trust be carried out as closely as possible to the intent of the donor.

14. (b) Trust property must exist at the time of the creation of the trust and must be transferred to the trustee during the grantor's lifetime. An inter vivos trust is not required to be in writing. It is not necessary to provide for payment of fees to the trustee since it is implied that a trustee can collect a reasonable fee for his/her services. There is no requirement that an alternate trust beneficiary be designated.

15. (b) A testamentary trust is generally created in a testamentary instrument such as a will and comes into existence only upon the settlor's death. The fact that a trust will not become effective until the settlor's death does not render the trust invalid. An inter vivos trust comes into existence during the settlor's lifetime. There is nothing to preclude a person from serving as both the trustee of a trust and the personal representative of an estate.

16. (b) Once the necessary elements of a gift are present, the gift may not be involved. A trust may be revoked if the settlor has reserved the power to revoke the trust or if the settlor and beneficiaries of an irrevocable trust mutually agree to terminate the trust. The requisite intent to create a trust may be manifested orally or in writing. No consideration is necessary for the present creation of a valid trust; however, an agreement to create a trust in the future would require consideration. Though there must be identifiable beneficiaries of a private trust, they need not be notified of the trust or of its creation.

17. (b) A trustee has express powers conferred upon him by the trust instrument and those implied powers which are reasonably necessary to enable the trustee to carry out the purpose of the trust. If not expressly granted, the power to sell trust property (I) and the power to pay trust expenses (III) would be considered reasonably necessary, but implied powers would not extend to mortgaging the trust property or to borrowing money from the trust (II).

18. (d) A trustee has a fiduciary duty. As a result, a trustee or co-trustees must use the same degree of skill, judgment, and care in managing the trust assets as reasonably prudent persons would exercise in managing their own affairs. A spouse can be a co-trustee even if the spouse is a beneficiary. The "merger doctrine" states that if the sole trustee and the sole beneficiary are the same person, the trust will go out of existence because the legal title (held by the trustee) and the equitable title (held by the beneficiary) have "merged." Since the wife is not the sole trustee, there is no problem presented. A trustee will not escape liability by delegating duties to someone else. A trustee could purchase trust property under certain circumstances, such as when the trust document does not prevent it, there is full disclosure, and the fair market value is paid. Also, the court would have to grant its approval.

19. (c) A trustee must act with honesty, good faith, and prudence in administering the trust. A trustee is held to the standard of care that a prudent person would exercise in conducting his or her personal affairs. A trustee is also charged with a duty of loyalty that requires the trustee to act in the exclusive interest of the beneficiary. Thus, a trustee who invests trust assets in unsecured loans to a co-trustee may violate both duties.

20. (a) Charitable trusts are **not** subject to the rule against perpetuities. The rule against perpetuities limits the duration of a private trust to a life in being plus 21 years. This rule does apply to spendthrift trusts, totten trusts, and constructive trusts.

Allocation of Principal and Income

21. (c) The Uniform Principal and Income Act allocates extraordinary expenses to trust principal. Extraordinary expenses are those which are not ordinary and include the cost of capital improvements such as sidewalk assessments. The Act provides that ordinary and current operating expenses are chargeable to income. Current and ordinary operating expenses would include building management fees, insurance premiums and depreciation.

22. (c) In general, current administration expenses incurred to keep the trust property productive, such as annual property tax, should be paid out of trust income. Extraordinary expenses and expenses incurred in the improvement of trust principal, such as mortgage principal payments, should be allocated to trust principal.

23. (c) In allocating benefits between the income beneficiary (Smart) and the remainderman (Mix), the general rule is that *ordinary* receipts, such as rents, interest on certificates of deposit, and municipal bond interests, are treated as income, and *extraordinary* receipts, such as stock dividends and the proceeds from the sale of bonds, are treated as additions to principal. Therefore, the amount of 1991 receipts which should be allocated to trust principal is $13,000 ($6,000 from stock dividends plus $7,000 from the sale of bonds).

24. (b) A trust income beneficiary would receive the ordinary receipts, or income, of the trust. Royalties (I) and cash dividends (III) are considered income; stock received in a stock split (II) and settlements of claims for damages to trust property (IV) are considered extraordinary receipts, or allocation of principal.

25. (a) In allocating benefits between principal and income, the general rule is that ordinary receipts are treated as income, while extraordinary receipts are treated as additions to principal. Extraordinary receipts include proceeds from the sale of trust assets. If the building, a trust asset, was sold, the entire proceeds would be allocated to principal.

26. (c) The insurance proceeds constitute sums received in settlement of claims for injury to the trust property (i.e., an extraordinary receipt). It should be allocated to principal. On the other hand, mortgage *interest* payments (as opposed to mortgage principal payments) are an ordinary expense, properly allocated to trust income.

27. (c) Generally, in the absence of any contrary directions in the trust instrument, income generated from trust assets is allocated to income and not principal. Thus, income accruing after the assets were transferred to the trust is allocated to trust income, ($500,000 x 12% x 10 months/12 months = $50,000) while interest accruing prior to the transfer is allocated to principal ($500,000 x 12% x 2 months/12 months = $10,000).

28. (b) Trust income is distributed to, or held for the benefit of, the income beneficiaries during the lifetime of the trust. Upon termination of a trust, any remaining assets/principal will go to the remaindermen.

PERFORMANCE BY SUBTOPICS

Each category below parallels a subtopic covered in Chapter 53. Record the number and percentage of questions you correctly answered in each subtopic area.

Estates		Characteristics of Trusts		Allocation of Principal and Income	
Question #	Correct √	Question #	Correct √	Question #	Correct √
1		5		21	
2		6		22	
3		7		23	
4		8		24	
# Questions 4		9		25	
		10		26	
# Correct _____		11		27	
% Correct _____		12		28	
		13		# Questions 8	
		14			
		15		# Correct _____	
		16		% Correct _____	
		17			
		18			
		19			
		20			
		# Questions 16			
		# Correct _____			
		% Correct _____			

ESSAY QUESTIONS

Essay 53-2 (15 to 25 minutes)

In 1990, Park, after consulting a CPA and an attorney, decided to have an *inter vivos* trust and will prepared. Park wanted to provide for the welfare of three close relatives: Archer, Book, and Cable, during Park's lifetime and after Park's death.

The trust was funded by cash and real estate transfers. The trust contained spendthrift provisions directing the trustees to pay the income to only the trust beneficiaries, Archer, Book, and Cable. Park also provides for $10,000 "sprinkling" provisions allowing for the annual distribution of up to $10,000 of principal to each beneficiary at the trustees' discretion.

Park's will provided for a "pour-over" transfer of any residuary estate to the trust.

Young, a CPA, and Zack, a stockbroker, were named trustees of the trust and executors of the will. Young and Zack were directed to perform their duties as "prudent business people" in investing and protecting the assets of the trust and estate.

During 1991, Young and Zack properly allocated income and principal and paid the trust income to Park's relatives as directed. They also made $5,000 principal payments to two of the beneficiaries for a medical emergency and to pay college tuition.

During 1992, Zack, with Young's consent, borrowed $10,000 from the trust. Zack agreed to repay the loan at a higher interest rate than the trust normally received on its investments. Archer, one of the trust beneficiaries, asked for and received a $15,000 principal payment. The money was used to enable Archer to invest in a joint venture with Zack.

In January 1993, Park died and the will was probated. After payment of all taxes, debts, and bequests, the residuary estate was transferred to the trust. Archer, Book, and Cable sued:

- To have the court allow distribution of the residuary estate instead of the residuary being transferred to the trust.
- To have the spendthrift trust terminated.
- To remove Young and Zack as trustees for making the $5,000 principal payments.
- To remove Young and Zack as trustees for allowing Zack to borrow money from the trust.
- To remove Young and Zack as trustees for making the $15,000 principal payment to Archer.

Required:

Determine whether Archer, Book, and Cable will be successful in the lawsuits and give the reasons for your conclusions. (11/93, Law, #3)

Essay 53-3 (15 to 25 minutes)

On January 1, 1993, Stone prepared an *inter vivos* spendthrift trust. Stone wanted to provide financial security for several close relatives during their lives, with the remainder payable to several charities. Stone funded the trust by transferring stocks, bonds, and a commercial building to the trust. Queen Bank was named as Trustee. The trust was to use the calendar year as its accounting period. The trust instrument contained no provision for the allocation of receipts and disbursements to principal and income.

The following transactions involving trust property occurred in 1993:

- The trust sold stock it owned for $50,000. The cost basis of the stock was $10,000. $40,000 was allocated to income and $10,000 to principal.
- The trust received a stock dividend of 500 shares of $10 par value common stock selling, at the time, for $50 per share. $20,000 was allocated to income and $5,000 to principal.
- The trust received bond interest of $18,000, which was allocated to income. The interest was paid and received semiannually on May 1 and November 1.
- The trust made mortgage amortization payments of $40,000 on the mortgage on the commercial building. The entire amount was allocated to principal.

On December 3, 1993, all the income beneficiaries and the charities joined in a petition to have the court allow the trust to be terminated and all trust funds distributed.

Required:

a. State the requirements to establish a valid *inter vivos* spendthrift trust and determine whether the Stone trust meets those requirements.

b. State whether the allocations made in the four transactions were correct and, if not, state the proper allocation to be made under the majority rule. Disregard any tax effect of each transaction.

c. State whether the trust will be terminated by the court and give the reasons for your conclusion. (11/94, Law, #4)

Essay 53-4 (15 to 20 minutes)

Ted and his wife Judy own Redacre in a tenancy by the entirety. Redacre is a lot by the seaside on which they plan someday to build a summer home. Ted also owns Bigacre in a joint tenancy with Lois, Clark, and Jeff, each owning a 1/4 undivided interest. Bigacre is a large parcel of investment acreage which produces no current income. Ted and Judy have had several arguments about the raising of their son Peter, now age 18, who Judy believes has exhibited a tendency toward irresponsibility. Ted, as a result, has decided to take certain steps on his own to protect Peter's future financial security.

Ted plans to establish a trust with Guardem Trust Company and Peter as co-trustees. He plans to transfer Redacre to the trust along with $100,000 cash. The $100,000 is to be used to purchase Ted's interest in Bigacre. Although Judy knows of the steps being taken, she has not agreed to them. Accordingly, Ted does not plan to have her participate in the establishment of the trust or in any of the transactions or paperwork involved.

The trust will provide that all income is to be paid to Peter, with final distribution of all trust assets to Peter upon his reaching age 40. The trust will also permit Peter, after reaching age 21, to remove Guardem as trustee leaving himself as successor sole trustee.

Required:

Answer the following, setting forth reasons for any conclusions stated.

If Ted's plans are carried out:

1. What interest will the trust have in Redacre and Bigacre?
2. What interests will the remaining three parties have in Bigacre, if Clark dies subsequent to the transfer of Ted's interest in Bigacre to the trust?
3. Will the requirements of a valid trust be met?
4. Will the purchase of Bigacre from Ted be a proper exercise of the trustees' duties?
5. What effect would Peter's exercise of his right to remove Guardem as a trustee, after he reaches 21, have on the trust and the ownership of Bigacre? (5/84, Law, #4)

Solution 53-2 Spendthrift Trust/Termination/Trustees

Archer, Book, and Cable will:

- Lose their lawsuit to have the residuary estate distributed. Park's inclusion of a **"pour-over" provision** in the will is a **binding transfer** of the residuary estate to the **preexisting spendthrift trust.**

- Lose their lawsuit to have the trust terminated. Whereas a trust may **ordinarily be terminated at the request of all beneficiaries**, Park created the trust to protect the beneficiaries from their own possible financial mismanagement and to provide for their welfare during Park's lifetime and after Park's death. **Terminating the trust at the request of the beneficiaries would defeat the purpose of the trust.**

- Lose their lawsuit to have Young and Zack removed as trustees for making the $5,000 principal payments. **Ordinarily** trustees **may not distribute trust principal** to income beneficiaries. However, Park **specifically authorized** Young and Zack to make limited principal payments by providing **"sprinkling" provisions** in the trust instrument.

- Win their lawsuit to have Young and Zack removed as trustees for allowing Zack to borrow $10,000 from the trust. A trustee **does not have the right to borrow money** from a trust unless that right is **specifically granted** in the trust instrument. By allowing Zack to borrow the $10,000, Young and Zack **violated their fiduciary duty of loyalty.**

- Win their lawsuit to have Young and Zack removed as trustees for making the $15,000 principal payment to Archer. The payment **exceeded the trustees' authority** to make limited principal payments. By exceeding their authority, they **violated their fiduciary duties** to **safeguard** the trust, **properly manage** the trust, and **have loyalty to** the trust.

Solution 53-3 Spendthrift Trust/Allocation/Termination

a. The requirements to establish a valid *inter vivos* spendthrift trust are as follows:

- Grantor

- Trust Res

- Intent to create a trust

- Lawful purpose

- Trustee and separate beneficiaries

Stone created a valid spendthrift trust. As grantor, Stone transferred stocks, bonds, and real estate (res) to the trust with a present intent to create the trust for the express lawful purpose of providing income for life to close relatives with the remainder left to charity. Stone designated Queen Bank as trustee.

b.

- Incorrect. The entire proceeds from the sale of the stock should be allocated to principal.

- Incorrect. The entire amount of the stock dividend should be allocated to principal.

- Incorrect. One-third of the semiannual payment of bond interest received on May 1 had already accrued when the trust was created on January 1, 1993. Therefore, $3,000 should be allocated to principal and $15,000 to income.

- Correct/Incorrect. All mortgage payments representing a repayment of a mortgage debt should be allocated to principal. However, if any portion of the payment includes interest on the mortgage, that amount should be allocated to income.

c. The petition to have the trust terminated and distributed will fail. Even though all beneficiaries and remaindermen joined in the petition, termination of the trust, while any of the income beneficiaries is alive, would defeat the intent of the grantor in establishing a spendthrift trust.

Solution 53-4 Formation/Trustees

1. The trust will have no interest in Redacre but would have a one-quarter interest as tenant in common in Bigacre. The attempted transfer of realty held as tenants by the entirety without the co-owner's consent **does not transfer the property.** Therefore, Ted is unable to transfer any portion of Redacre since Judy has not consented to the transfer. A **joint tenant may transfer** his interest in the tenancy **without the consent of the co-tenants.** However, such a transfer **destroys the joint tenancy** of the interest transferred. Therefore, the purchase of Ted's interest in Bigacre gives the trust a one-quarter interest in the property as tenant in common with

Clark, Lois, and Jeff remaining as joint tenants of three-quarters of the property.

2.   Despite the trust's one-quarter interest in Bigacre, it acquires no additional interest due to Clark's death since there is **no right of survivorship with respect to a tenant-in-common**. However, Jeff and Lois will acquire Clark's one-quarter interest **by operation of law,** due to the **right-of-survivorship feature among joint tenants.** Therefore, Jeff and Lois will each own a three-eighths interest in Bigacre as joint tenants, whereas the trust will retain its one-quarter interest as tenant in common.

3.   A valid trust has been created. Ted, as **grantor or settlor,** has **transferred property** (res) to Guardem and Peter **for the benefit of** Peter. **Intent** to create a trust is evident, and the trust is **established for a lawful purpose**. It is proper for the **sole beneficiary to act as co-trustee.**

4.   The trustees have a **fiduciary duty** to manage the trust for the benefit of the beneficiaries.

In the absence of trust provisions otherwise, the trustees are **required to invest in accordance with the standard of a prudent man** in the conduct of his own investments. A trustee should ordinarily invest in income-producing property. However, the purchase of Bigacre by the trustees could meet this standard even though Bigacre is not currently earning income if the amount paid is fair and the future value may be expected to increase.

5.   The trust would terminate and the interest in Bigacre would vest in Peter if he exercises his right to remove Guardem as trustee. As **sole trustee** Peter would **hold legal title**, and as **sole beneficiary** he would **hold equitable title**. A trust **terminates** when the **sole beneficiary** and **sole trustee** are the **same person**, as **legal and equitable title will be merged.**

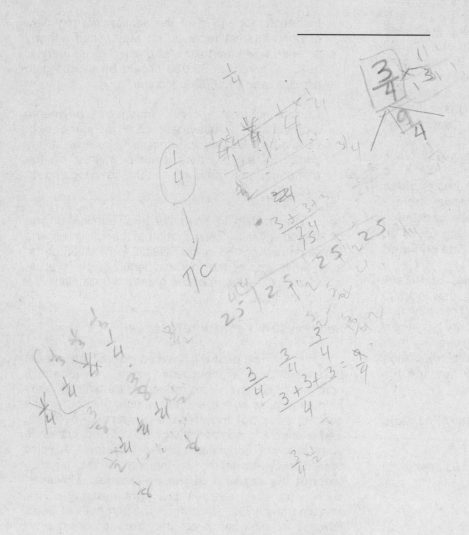

CHAPTER 54

REGULATION OF EMPLOYMENT

I. **The Federal Social Security Act** 54-2
   A. Social Insurance Programs 54-2
   B. Financing the Act's Social Insurance Programs 54-2
   C. Coverage 54-3
   D. Benefits 54-4

II. **Workers' Compensation** 54-5
   A. Purpose 54-5
   B. Elective vs. Compulsory Statutes 54-6
   C. Uniform Provisions 54-6
   D. Insurance Requirements 54-6
   E. Benefits 54-6
   F. Administration of Claims 54-7
   G. Employees' Claims Under Workers' Compensation Laws 54-7

III. **Employee Safety--Occupational Safety and Health Act (OSHA)** 54-8
   A. Purpose 54-8
   B. Coverage 54-8
   C. Enforcement 54-8
   D. Penalties 54-8

IV. **Equal Employment Opportunity Commission (EEOC)** 54-9
   A. Title VII of the Civil Rights Act of 1964 54-9
   B. The Age Discrimination in Employment Act 54-9
   C. The Rehabilitation Act of 1973 54-9
   D. The Equal Pay Act 54-9
   E. The Americans With Disabilities Act of 1990 54-9
   F. The Civil Rights Act of 1991 54-9
   G. Reverse Discrimination 54-9

V. **The Federal Fair Labor Standards Act (Wage-Hour Law)** 54-10

VI. **Pensions--Employee Retirement Security Act of 1974 (ERISA)** 54-10

VII. **Federal Income Tax Ramifications** 54-10
   A. Social Security 54-10
   B. Workers' Compensation 54-11
   C. Unemployment Compensation 54-11

CHAPTER 54

REGULATION OF EMPLOYMENT

I. The Federal Social Security Act

A. <u>Social Insurance Programs</u>--The Social Security Act contains provisions for several social insurance programs which affect employer-employee relationships.

    1. The most familiar of the Act's social insurance programs provides for old-age, survivors, and disability insurance coverage.

    2. The Act also provides for a program of hospital insurance coverage.

    3. In addition, an unemployment insurance program has been established by the Social Security Act.

B. <u>Financing the Act's Social Insurance Programs</u>

    1. The unemployment insurance program is financed through payments made by employers under federal and state unemployment insurance laws.

        a. Employers are required to contribute to the Social Security Act's unemployment insurance program through the payment of state unemployment taxes.

            (1) The state unemployment tax may be adjusted according to the number and frequency of claims filed against the employer.

            (2) Employers, in states with acceptable claims levels, may credit their state unemployment tax payments against the federal unemployment tax for up to 90% of the federal unemployment tax liability.

        b. An employer must pay the federal unemployment tax if he or she pays $1,500 or more in wages during any calendar quarter or if he or she employs one or more persons at least one day per week for 20 weeks during a calendar year.

            (1) Only the first $7,000 in wages paid to each covered employee is taxable under the Federal Unemployment Tax Act (FUTA).

            (2) The tax rate is 6.2% for wages paid in 1995 and 1996, with a maximum state unemployment tax offset credit of 5.4%.

    2. The old-age, survivors, disability, and hospital insurance programs are financed through payments made under the provisions of the Federal Insurance Contributions Act (FICA) and the Self-Employment Contributions Act.

        a. Under FICA, both the employer and employee are taxed.

            (1) The FICA tax rate for employer and employee is 7.65%, consisting of a 6.2% component for Social Security and a 1.45% component for Medicare.

            (2) For 1995, the maximum wage base for tax imposition is $61,200. Beginning in 1994, there is no limit on the amount of earnings subject to the Medicare portion of the tax.

(3) FICA requires that the employer must withhold the employee's share from the employee's wages as they are paid.

    (a) The employer is required to furnish the employee with a written statement of wages paid and contributions withheld during the calendar year.

    (b) The employer's failure to withhold the employee's contribution may cause the employer to be responsible for both the employee's and employer's share of taxes, i.e., a double tax liability.

b. The Self-Employment Contributions Act imposes a tax of 15.3% for 1992 and later years, consisting of a 12.4% component for Social Security and a 2.9% component for Medicare. The maximum wage base against which the Social Security portion operates for 1995 is $61,200; there is no limitation for the Medicare portion.

• Individuals may deduct one-half of their self-employment taxes for income tax purposes.

indep. contra. pays FICA on net earnings
employee FICA - pays on gross. earnings

C. Coverage

1. To be covered under the Social Security Act, a person must be an "employee," the services the person performs must be "employment," and the compensation the person receives must be "wages."

a. An "employee" is a person whose performance is subject to the control of an employer. This control extends not only to the result, but to the details and means by which the result is accomplished.

    (1) Part-time as well as full-time employees are included under the coverage of the Act.

    (2) Partners, independent contractors, and self-employed persons are not covered by the unemployment compensation provisions since they are not "employees." They are treated as self-employed persons for purposes of coverage under the old-age, survivors, and disability programs.

    (3) Corporate officers and directors may qualify as "employees" depending upon the services they perform and the remuneration they receive.

b. "Employment" includes all services performed by an employee for the person employing him or her.

    (1) Certain services are expressly exempted from the Act's definition of "employment." For example, services performed by ministers, student nurses, nonresident aliens, and certain public employees are not considered "employment" for purposes of coverage under the Social Security Act.

    (2) In order to constitute "employment," the services provided must be of a continuing or recurring nature.

c. "Wages" generally include all remuneration for employment, including remuneration paid in a medium other than cash.

    (1) Such items as vacation and severance pay, bonuses, commissions, and tips (if amounting to $20 per month or more) are included in "wages."

    (2)   "Wages" does not include the following:

        (a)   Insurance premiums paid by the employer.

        (b)   Employer-paid retirement benefits.

        (c)   Tips (if not in cash or if less than $20 per month).

        (d)   Compensation exceeding $60,600 in 1994.

        (e)   Reimbursed travel expenses.

    (3)   For purposes of the employer's share of FICA taxes, wages includes all cash tips subject to the employee FICA tax. An employer must thus pay FICA taxes on the total amount of cash tips and other remuneration (up to the amount of compensation included as wages, e.g., $60,600 in 1994).

  d.   Coverage under the Social Security Act is mandatory.

    (1)   Employees qualifying for coverage are not permitted to exchange their coverage for other benefits.

    (2)   Employees cannot elect not to be covered.

2.   The Act also provides for coverage of self-employed persons.

  a.   A person is "self-employed" if he or she carries on a trade or business either as an individual or in a partnership.

    •   Carrying on a trade or business means engaging in extensive or repeated business activity for profit.

  b.   Self-employment income generally means the <u>net</u> compensation from self-employment and does <u>not</u> include earnings in excess of $60,600 in 1994.

D. <u>Benefits</u>

1.   Old-Age, Survivors, and Disability Insurance Benefits

  a.   The availability of benefits under these programs depends upon the attainment by the individual of "insured status."

    (1)   Certain lengths of working time are required to attain "insured status."

    (2)   An individual who is "fully" insured is eligible for the following benefits:

        (a)   Survivors' benefits for dependents.

        (b)   Benefits for dependents of retired disabled workers.

        (c)   Lump-sum death benefits.

        (d)   Old age retirement benefits (at age 62). Retirement benefits may be reduced if an individual's earnings exceed certain annual limitations.

        (e)   Divorced spouses may receive benefits.

      b.   The amount of benefits paid under these programs generally depends on the following:

          (1)   The average monthly earnings of the employee or self-employed individual.

          (2)   The relationship of the beneficiary to the retired, deceased, or disabled worker.

          (3)   Increased benefits based on the cost of living.

          (4)   Increased benefits for delayed retirement.

          (5)   Receipt of payments under a private pension plan will not limit the payment of social security benefits to an otherwise qualifying individual.

      c.   A reduction of social security benefits can occur in the following situations:

          (1)   Early retirement results in reduced benefits.

          (2)   Returning to work can reduce social security benefits.

             •   Social security retirement benefits are reduced $1 for every $2 of earned income above a base amount that varies from year to year.

2.   Benefits Under the Unemployment Insurance Program

      a.   State laws govern eligibility for unemployment benefits and the amount of such benefits.

          (1)   All states require substantial past employment and, generally, unemployment benefits are provided to workers who are discharged through no fault of their own.

          (2)   The amount of benefits varies from state to state.

      b.   Unemployment benefits are <u>not</u> available to the self-employed.

      c.   Unemployment benefits are funded by contributions from employers only and are considered to be deductible as a business expense for federal income tax purposes.

      d.   The Federal Consolidated Budget Reconciliation Act (COBRA) provides that former employees, whether they quit, are fired, or laid-off, may retain their health insurance coverage for a period of up to 18 months, at their own expense.

II. Workers' Compensation

A.   <u>Purpose</u>--Workers' compensation statutes were enacted to enable employees to recover for injuries regardless of negligence. Every state in the country has some form of workers' compensation law; federal employees are covered by a federal statute. These laws have four generally recognized objectives:

1.   To provide prompt, reasonable benefits and compensation to work-related accident victims or their dependents.

2.   To provide a single, relatively simple remedy for victims of work-related accidents. The remedy generally provided by workers' compensation laws does <u>not</u> require a finding of fault.

3.   To shift the financial burden of industrial accidents from public and private charities to the industry itself.

4.   To encourage employer interest in safety.

B.   Elective vs. Compulsory Statutes--There are two general types of workers' compensation statutes:

1.   Elective workers' compensation statutes permit the employer to either accept or reject the provisions of the statute. An employer who rejects the elective statute loses the three common law defenses--assumption of risk, negligence of fellow employees, and contributory negligence. As a practical matter, this means that all workers' compensation laws are compulsory, since the loss of these defenses seriously impairs an employer's overall legal defense when an employee sues for damages.

2.   Compulsory workers' compensation laws require employers to accept the laws' provisions and provide the specified benefits. The current trend among the states is toward compulsory workers' compensation laws and away from elective laws.

C.   Uniform Provisions--The workers' compensation laws that have been enacted in the various states are fairly uniform in the scope of their coverage.

1.   None of the state workers' compensation laws extend coverage to all employees. Some of the more common exceptions include the following:

a.   Domestic workers.

b.   Agricultural workers.

c.   Casual employees.

d.   Employees of common carriers.

2.   Most workers' compensation laws extend coverage to minors.

3.   When an employee accepts the benefits of the workers' compensation laws, he or she is generally barred from suing the employer for damages.

a.   The employee's acceptance of benefits does not bar a suit against a third party whose negligence caused the injury.

b.   However, if the employee recovers from the third party, the employer is entitled to compensation for the benefits paid to the employee. If the employee's recovery exceeds the benefits paid to him or her by the employer, the employee may keep the excess.

D.   Insurance Requirements

1.   The laws of most states permit employers to purchase insurance from either a private insurance company or a competitive state fund. However, several states require employers to purchase insurance from a state fund.

2.   Virtually all states permit employers to assume liability for workers' compensation claims. However, these "self-insurers" are required to demonstrate financial responsibility before they are permitted to forego the purchase of insurance.

E.   Benefits--Benefits under workers' compensation laws usually fall into four categories: cash benefits, medical benefits, death benefits, and rehabilitation benefits.

1.   Cash benefits are based on a percentage of the employee's regular weekly wage. They are limited with regard to the amount and number of payments. They include the following:

    a.   Impairment benefits which are paid whenever the injury results in physical impairment.

    b.   Disability benefits which are paid whenever there is physical impairment and wage loss.

2.   <u>Medical benefits</u> furnish the employee with medical care for job-related injuries or disease. There are usually no dollar or time limitations on medical benefits.

3.   <u>Death benefits</u> generally include a burial allowance plus the payment of a percentage of the worker's former weekly wage. Payments are generally directed to the deceased worker's spouse and minor children; however, payments normally cease upon the spouse's remarriage.

4.   <u>Rehabilitation benefits</u> include the following:

    a.   Medical rehabilitation to facilitate a more complete recovery.

    b.   Vocational rehabilitation, when the nature or severity of the injury necessitates retraining.

5.   In addition, some workers' compensation plans provide payment schedules for the loss of a limb or an eye.

F.   <u>Administration of Claims</u>

1.   Workers' compensation claims are normally handled by a state compensation board or commission. However, a few states delegate the administration of claims to the state judicial system.

2.   Employers are required, under the penalty of law, to report all injuries.

3.   Employees are required to notify their employer promptly (usually within 30 days) of any injury.

4.   Employees are also required to file their claims with the appropriate state authority within a specified period (usually 60 days to two years).

    a.   In some states, the failure of the employee to file the claim on time bars his or her recovery.

    b.   In other states, the failure to file on time will bar the claim only if the delay has been prejudicial to the employer.

5.   The time periods for reporting injuries and filing claims generally begin to run from the time the injury is first noticed rather than from the time of the accident.

G.   <u>Employees' Claims Under Workers' Compensation Laws</u>

1.   Unless the workers' compensation coverage is inadequate, an employer who is covered by the workers' compensation laws may <u>not</u> be sued by his or her employees for unintentional job-related injuries.

2.   Workers' compensation laws provide coverage for injuries which occur on the job or in the course of employment.

    a.   The fact that the injury was caused by the injured employee's own negligence is <u>not</u> a bar to recovery.

      b.   Employees are usually <u>not</u> covered during transit to and from the job. Coverage generally begins when the employee arrives on the employer's premises.

      c.   Under most programs, coverage is <u>not</u> extended to injuries which are intentionally self-inflicted and injuries resulting from the employee's intoxication.

    3.   Employers may be sued for damages in excess of or in lieu of workers' compensation recoveries if the employer intentionally injured the employee.

III. Employee Safety--Occupational Safety and Health Act (OSHA)

    A.   <u>Purpose</u>--OSHA was enacted by Congress in 1970 in order to ensure a safe working environment for employees.

    B.   <u>Coverage</u>--Applies to all employees of businesses that affect interstate commerce.

    C.   <u>Enforcement</u>--The Occupational Safety and Health Administration is in charge of administering the act. OSHA allows inspectors to enter the workplace.

      1.   OSHA regulations require that an inspector have a warrant in order to inspect a business.

         •   The legal standard, "probable cause," is necessary to obtain a warrant.

           (1)   Probable cause is not a "high standard."

           (2)   Employee complaints may be sufficient for probable cause.

           (3)   Employees making complaints may have names withheld upon request.

      2.   OSHA requires that employers keep records of accidents and report serious accidents to the Occupational Safety and Health Administration.

    D.   <u>Penalties</u>--The Occupational Safety and Health Administration can issue citations, impose fines, and assess civil penalties for violations to the act.

      1.   Repeat or willful violations may result in fines up to $70,000 for each violation.

      2.   Serious violations, or violations which involve "a substantial probability" that an accident resulting from the violation will lead to death or serious harm, can result in fines up to $7,000 for each serious violation.

      3.   Willful violations that lead to an employee's death may result in criminal prosecution.

      4.   Employers can be forced to correct violations.

         a.   Penalties and citations may be appealed to the Occupational Safety and Health Review Commission.

         b.   Employers may obtain temporary exemptions from some OSHA standards when an inability to comply within required time can be demonstrated.

         c.   Permanent exemptions from some OSHA standards may sometimes be given to employers if they can show that their own safety methods comply with the safety standards of OSHA.

IV. Equal Employment Opportunity Commission (EEOC)

The following employment laws are under the jurisdiction of the EEOC.

A.   <u>Title VII of the Civil Rights Act of 1964</u> (amended by the Civil Rights Act of 1991)--Prohibits sexual harassment and employment discrimination on the basis of race, color, religion, sex, or national origin.

    1.   Title VII applies to the following:

        a.   Employers and labor organizations whose businesses affect interstate commerce and who employ at least 15 people for at least 20 weeks a year.

        b.   Employment agencies.

        c.   Federal, state, and local governments were added by amendment in 1972.

    2.   Illegal discrimination, as described under Title VII, includes the following:

        a.   Employer uses prescribed rules, which affect a protected class, in making an employment decision: hiring, firing, promoting, etc.

        b.   Employer engages in conduct that perpetuates past discriminatory practices.

        c.   Employer adopts rules that adversely affect a protected class and are not necessary for business.

    3.   Defenses to alleged Title VII violations are limited to the following:

        a.   Bona fide occupational qualification. This may be a defense to allegations of discrimination involving religion, sex, and national origin, but not race.

        b.   National security.

        c.   Seniority or merit system.

        d.   Professionally-developed ability test.

B.   <u>The Age Discrimination in Employment Act</u>--Protects workers, age 40 to 70, from discrimination on the basis of age.

C.   <u>The Rehabilitation Act of 1973</u>--Directs federal contractors to take affirmative action with respect to hiring "otherwise qualified" handicapped individuals.

D.   <u>The Equal Pay Act</u>--Prohibits wage discrimination on the basis of sex.

E.   <u>The Americans With Disabilities Act of 1990</u>--Protects disabled individuals from discrimination and guarantees equal access to services.

F.   <u>The Civil Rights Act of 1991</u>--Reaffirms the rights of complainants alleging employment discrimination.

G.   <u>Reverse Discrimination</u>--There have been a growing number of challenges to employer's affirmative action plans that remedy the under-representation of a protected class by considering a person's race or gender as a hiring criteria.

    1.   Challenges to private employer's affirmative action plans are brought under Title VII.

2. Challenges to affirmative action plans imposed by government agencies are brought under the Equal Protection Clause in the fourteenth amendment of the United States Constitution.

V. The Federal Fair Labor Standards Act (Wage-Hour Law)

- The Fair Labor Standards Act of 1938 is applicable to all employers engaged in interstate commerce. It covers maximum hours, minimum wages, and child labor.

  1. Maximum Hours--Any employee who works over forty hours per week must be paid no less than one and one half times his or her regular pay for those hours exceeding forty. An exception exists for certain employees whose duties necessitate irregular working hours and who also meet other criteria.

  2. Minimum Wage--As of April 1, 1991, the minimum wage specified by Congress is $4.25 per hour for employees in covered industries. This amount is periodically revised by Congress.

  3. Child Labor--Children under the age of sixteen cannot be employed full-time except by a parent under certain circumstances. Also, children between the ages of sixteen and eighteen cannot be employed in hazardous jobs or perform tasks detrimental to their health and well-being.

VI. Pensions--Employee Retirement Security Act of 1974 (ERISA)

- The act does not require employers to set up a pension plan for their employees, but it does set standards which employers must follow if they choose to implement a plan.

  1. Employee contributions to the pension plan must vest immediately.

  2. Employee's rights to employer's contributions must vest after five years of employment.

  3. Investment of pension funds are subject to certain standards in order to avoid mismanagement.

VII. Federal Income Tax Ramifications

A. Social Security--FICA contributions made by the employer for employee services are generally deductible as a business expense.

  1. If the services rendered by the employee are not business oriented (e.g., household help), no deduction by the employer is allowed.

  2. The share of contributions paid by the employee is not deductible by the employer.

  3. For the employee, social security benefits are excludable from gross income to the extent that the sum of the taxpayer's "modified adjusted gross income" plus one-half of the benefits received (provisional income) does not exceed a "base amount." If the base amount is exceeded, the taxpayer includes in gross income the lesser of one-half of the excess over the base amount or one-half of the benefits received, unless the provisional income exceeds a second base amount, in which case up to 85% of the benefits may be taxable income. Modified adjusted gross income means adjusted gross income determined without the deduction for two-earner married couples or any amounts earned in a foreign country, a U.S. possession, or Puerto Rico that are excluded from gross income, and increased by any tax-exempt interest received or accrued during the taxable year. The base amount for married taxpayers filing jointly is $32,000; for married filing separately, $0; and for all other individuals, $25,000. The second base amounts are $44,000 for married taxpayers filing jointly; $0 for married taxpayers filing separately; and $34,000 for all others.

• Disability retirement payments in lieu of wages to employees under age 65 who are permanently and totally disabled receive a 15% tax credit.

B. Workers' Compensation--Amounts received under state workers' compensation acts are fully excludable. Similarly, amounts received as a result of suit for injury or from employee paid health or accident insurance plans are also excludable. However, amounts received from employer paid health and accident insurance plans to the extent they are not reimbursements for expenses paid are includible in the employees' gross income.

C. Unemployment Compensation--Benefits received as unemployment compensation are fully includible in gross income.

———————————

NOTES

CHAPTER 54—REGULATION OF EMPLOYMENT

Problem 54-1 MULTIPLE CHOICE QUESTIONS (40 to 50 minutes)

1. Under the Federal Consolidated Budget Reconciliation Act of 1985 (COBRA), when an employee voluntarily resigns from a job, the former employee's group health insurance coverage that was in effect during the period of employment with the company
   a. Automatically ceases for the former employee and spouse, if the resignation occurred before normal retirement age.
   b. Automatically ceases for the former employee's spouse, but continues for the former employee for an 18-month period at the former employer's expense.
   c. May be retained by the former employee at the former employee's expense for at least 18 months after leaving the company, but must be terminated for the former employee's spouse.
   d. May be retained for the former employee and spouse at the former employee's expense for at least 18 months after leaving the company.
   (5/94, Law, #30, 4785)

2. An employer who fails to withhold Federal Insurance Contributions Act (FICA) taxes from covered employees' wages, but who pays both the employer and employee shares would
   a. Be entitled to a refund from the IRS for the employees' share.
   b. Be allowed **no** federal tax deduction for any payments.
   c. Have a right to be reimbursed by the employees for the employees' share.
   d. Owe penalties and interest for failure to collect the tax. (5/92, Law, #36, 2849)

3. Tower drives a truck for Musgrove Produce, Inc. The truck is owned by Musgrove. Tower is paid on the basis of a formula that takes into consideration the length of the trip, cargo, and fuel consumed. Tower is responsible for repairing or replacing all flat tires. Musgrove is responsible for all other truck maintenance. Tower drives only for Musgrove. If Tower is a common law employee and **not** an independent contractor, which of the following statements is correct?

a. All social security retirement benefits are fully includible in the determination of Tower's federal taxable income if certain gross income limitations are exceeded.
b. Musgrove remains primarily liable for Tower's share of FICA taxes if it fails to withhold and pay the taxes on Tower's wages.
c. Musgrove would **not** have to withhold FICA taxes if Tower elected to make FICA contributions as a self-employed person.
d. Bonuses or vacation pay that are paid to Tower by Musgrove are **not** subject to FICA taxes because they are **not** regarded as regular compensation. (5/90, Law, #26, 9911)

4. During the calendar year 1994, Nix estimates having $5,000 of gross earnings from self-employment and $4,800 of allowable deductions attributable to such income. Nix expects to earn the self-employment income as a sole proprietor rendering management advisory services. If Nix receives in 1994 wages of $40,000 as an employee of Pace Corp., the amount of self-employment earnings subject to social security taxes would be
   a. $0.
   b. $ 200.
   c. $3,800.
   d. $5,000. (11/87, Law, #13, amended, 9911)

5. An employer having an experience unemployment tax rate of 3.2% in a state having a standard unemployment tax rate of 5.4% may take a credit against a 6.2% federal unemployment tax rate of
   a. 3.0%.
   b. 3.2%.
   c. 5.4%.
   d. 6.2%. (5/91, Law, #37, 0717)

6. Social security benefits may include all of the following **except**
   a. Payments to divorced spouses.
   b. Payments to disabled children.
   c. Medicare payments.
   d. Medicaid payments. (5/91, Law, #36, 0716)

7. Under the Federal Insurance Contributions Act (FICA), all of the following are considered wages **except**

a.   Contingent fees.
b.   Reimbursed travel expenses.
c.   Bonuses.
d.   Commissions.   (11/90, Law, #36, 0719)

8.   For the entire year 1993, Ral Supermarket, Inc. conducted its business operations without any permanent or full-time employees. Ral employed temporary and part-time workers during each of the 52 weeks in the year. Under the provisions of the Federal Unemployment Tax Act (FUTA), which of the following statements is correct regarding Ral's obligation to file a federal unemployment tax return for 1993?
a.   Ral must file a 1993 FUTA return only if aggregate wages exceeded $100,000 during 1993.
b.   Ral must file a 1993 FUTA return because it had at least one employee during at least 20 weeks of 1993.
c.   Ral is obligated to file a 1993 FUTA return only if at least one worker earned $50 or more in any calendar quarter of 1993.
d.   Ral does not have to file a 1993 FUTA return because it had **no** permanent or full-time employees in 1993.   (11/94, Law, #35, 5212)

9.   Which of the following statements is **not** correct concerning federal unemployment insurance?
a.   Federal law provides general guidelines, standards, and requirements for the program.
b.   The states administer the benefit payments under the program.
c.   The program is funded by taxes imposed on employers and employees.
d.   The federal unemployment tax is calculated as a fixed percentage of each covered employee's salary up to a stated maximum.
          (11/89, Law, #31, 0723)

10.   Under the Federal Insurance Contributions Act (FICA) and the Social Security Act (SSA),
a.   Persons who are self-employed are **not** required to make FICA contributions.
b.   Employees who participate in private retirement plans are **not** required to make FICA contributions.
c.   Death benefits are payable to an employee's survivors only if the employee dies before reaching the age of retirement.
d.   The receipt of earned income by a person who is also receiving social security retirement benefits may result in a reduction of such benefits.   (5/89, Law, #37, 0725)

11.   Social security may be obtained by
a.   Qualifying individuals who are also receiving benefits from a private pension plan.
b.   Qualifying individuals or their families only upon such individual's disability or retirement.
c.   Children of a deceased worker who was entitled to benefits until such children reach age 25 or complete their education, whichever occurs first.
d.   Only those individuals who have made payments while employed. (11/86, Law, #39, 0731)

12.   Unemployment tax payable under the Federal Unemployment Tax Act (FUTA), is
a.   Payable by all employers.
b.   Deducted from employee wages.
c.   Paid to the Social Security Administration.
d.   A tax deductible employer's expense.
          (5/92, Law, #37, 2850)

12A.   Which of the following payments are deducted from an employee's salary?

	Unemployment compensation insurance	Workers' compensation insurance
a.	Yes	Yes
b.	Yes	No
c.	No	Yes
d.	No	No

          (5/95, Law, #36, 5370)

13.   An unemployed CPA generally would receive unemployment compensation benefits if the CPA
a.   Was fired as a result of the employer's business reversals.
b.   Refused to accept a job as an accountant while receiving extended benefits.
c.   Was fired for embezzling from a client.
d.   Left work voluntarily without good cause.
          (11/91, Law, #33, 2361)

14.   Workers' Compensation Acts require an employer to
a.   Provide coverage for all eligible employees.
b.   Withhold employee contributions from the wages of eligible employees.
c.   Pay an employee the difference between disability payments and full salary.
d.   Contribute to a federal insurance fund.
          (5/92, Law, #38, 2851)

15. The primary purpose for enacting workers' compensation statutes was to
a. Eliminate all employer-employee negligence lawsuits.
b. Enable employees to recover for injuries regardless of negligence.
c. Prevent employee negligence suits against third parties.
d. Allow employees to recover additional compensation for employer negligence.
(5/91, Law, #38, 0718)

16. Which one of the following statements concerning workers' compensation laws is generally correct?
a. Workers' compensation laws are very narrowly construed against employees.
b. The amount of damages recoverable is based on comparative negligence.
c. Employers are strictly liable without regard to whether or not they are at fault.
d. Workers' compensation benefits are **not** available if the employee is grossly negligent.
(5/89, Law, #38, 9911)

17. Which of the following provisions is basic to all workers' compensation systems?
a. The injured employee must prove the employer's negligence.
b. The employer may invoke the traditional defense of contributory negligence.
c. The employer's liability may be ameliorated by a co-employee's negligence under the fellow-servant rule.
d. The injured employee is allowed to recover on strict liability theory. (11/94, Law, #36, 5213)

18. Under which of the following conditions is an on-site inspection of a workplace by an investigator from the Occupational Safety and Health Administration (OSHA) permissible?
a. Only if OSHA obtains a search warrant after showing probable cause.
b. Only if the inspection is conducted after working hours.
c. At the request of employees.
d. After OSHA provides the employer with at least 24 hours notice of the prospective inspection.
(5/95, Law, #37, 5371)

19. Kroll, an employee of Acorn, Inc., was injured in the course of employment while operating a forklift manufactured and sold to Acorn by Trell Corp. The forklift was defectively designed by Trell. Under the state's mandatory workers' compensation statute, Kroll will be successful in

	Obtaining workers' compensation benefits	A negligence action against Acorn
a.	Yes	Yes
b.	Yes	No
c.	No	Yes
d.	No	No

(5/93, Law, #28, 3996)

20. Which of the following statements is correct regarding the scope and provisions of the Occupational Safety and Health Act (OSHA)?
a. OSHA requires employers to provide employees a workplace free from risk.
b. OSHA prohibits an employer from discharging an employee for revealing OSHA violations.
c. OSHA may inspect a workplace at any time regardless of employer objection.
d. OSHA preempts state regulation of workplace safety. (5/94, Law, #27, 4782)

21. If an employee is injured, full workers' compensation benefits are **not** payable if the employee
a. Was injured because of failing to abide by written safety procedures.
b. Was injured because of the acts of fellow employees.
c. Intentionally caused self-inflicted injury.
d. Brought a civil action suit against a third party who caused the injury. (11/90, Law, #38, 0721)

22. Syl Corp. does **not** withhold FICA taxes from its employees' compensation. Syl voluntarily pays the entire FICA tax for its share and the amounts that it could have withheld from the employees. The employees' share of FICA taxes paid by Syl to the IRS is
a. Deductible by Syl as additional compensation that is includible in the employees' taxable income.
b. Not deductible by Syl because it does **not** meet the deductibility requirement as an ordinary and necessary business expense.
c. A nontaxable gift to each employee, provided that the amount is less than $1,000 annually to each employee.
d. Subject to prescribed penalties imposed on Syl for its failure to withhold required payroll taxes.
(5/94, Law, #26, 4781)

23. Taxes payable under the Federal Unemployment Tax Act (FUTA) are
a. Deductible by the employer as a business expense for federal income tax purposes.
b. Payable by employers for all employees.

c. Withheld from the wages of all covered employees.

d. Calculated as a fixed percentage of all compensation paid to an employee.

(5/93, Law, #27, 3995)

24. Which of the following forms of income, if in excess of the annual exempt amount, will cause a reduction in a retired person's social security benefits?

a. Annual proceeds from an annuity.

b. Director's fees.

c. Pension payments.

d. Closely held corporation stock dividends.

(5/93, Law, #26, 4783)

25. Under the Federal Age Discrimination in Employment Act, which of the following practices would be prohibited?

	Compulsory retirement of employees below the age of 65	Termination of employees between the ages of 65 and 70 for cause
a.	Yes	Yes
b.	Yes	No
c.	No	Yes
d.	No	No

(11/94, Law, #38, 5215)

26. Under Title VII of the 1964 Civil Rights Act, which of the following forms of discrimination is **not** prohibited?

a. Sex.

b. Age.

c. Race.

d. Religion.   (5/94, Law, #28, 4783)

27. Under the provisions of the Americans With Disabilities Act of 1990, in which of the following areas is a disabled person protected from discrimination?

	Public transportation	Privately operated public accommodations
a.	Yes	Yes
b.	Yes	No
c.	No	Yes
d.	No	No

(5/95, Law, #38, 5372)

28. When verifying a client's compliance with statutes governing employees' wages and hours, an auditor should check the client's personnel records against relevant provisions of which of the following statutes?

a. National Labor Relations Act.

b. Fair Labor Standards Act.

c. Taft-Hartley Act.

d. Americans With Disabilities Act.

(5/95, Law, #39, 5373)

29. Under the Federal Fair Labor Standards Act, which of the following would be regulated?

	Minimum wage	Overtime	Number of hours in the workweek
a.	Yes	Yes	Yes
b.	Yes	No	Yes
c.	Yes	Yes	No
d.	No	Yes	Yes

(11/94, Law, #39, 5216)

30. Which of the following statements correctly describes the funding of noncontributory pension plans?

a. All of the funds are provided by the employees.

b. All of the funds are provided by the employer.

c. The employer and employee each provide 50% of the funds.

d. The employer provides 90% of the funds, and each employee contributes 10%.

(11/94, Law, #40, 5217)

31. Under the provisions of the Employee Retirement Income Security Act of 1974 (ERISA), which of the following statements is correct?

a. Employees are entitled to have an employer established pension plan.

b. Employers are prevented from unduly delaying an employee's participation in a pension plan.

c. Employers are prevented from managing retirement plans.

d. Employees are entitled to make investment decisions.   (5/95, Law, #40, 5374)

Solution 54-1 MULTIPLE CHOICE ANSWERS

Federal Social Security Act

1. (d) The Federal Consolidated Budget Reconciliation Act of 1985 (COBRA) provides that when an employee voluntarily resigns from a job, the former employee's group health insurance coverage may be retained for the former employee and spouse at the employee's expense for at least 18 months after leaving the job.

2. (c) Employers are required to withhold FICA taxes on covered employees' taxable wages, and file quarterly FICA tax returns. The liability to make the tax deposits begins when the wages are paid. In this case, since the employer paid both its share and the employees' share, the employer's obligation to pay the FICA taxes has been fulfilled. The employer is then entitled to reimbursement of the employee FICA taxes for the employees' share.

3. (b) Under the provisions of FICA, the employer's failure to withhold the employee's contribution may cause the employer to be responsible for both the employee's and employer's share of taxes. Musgrove can be made to pay because it failed to withhold and pay FICA taxes on Tower's wages.

4. (a) Under IRC §1402(b)(2), "self-employment income" does not include the net earnings from self-employment if such earnings for the taxable year are less than $400. Since Nix's net earnings from self-employment are only $200, none of those earnings are subject to social security taxes.

5. (c) The employer is allowed a credit of 90% of the taxes paid into a state unemployment program. Because the state unemployment tax rate (5.4%) is less than 90% of the federal rate (6.2%), the entire state unemployment rate would qualify as a credit.

6. (d) Social security benefits may include payments to divorced spouses, payments to disabled children, and Medicare payments, but not Medicaid payments.

7. (b) Under the Federal Insurance Contributions Act (FICA), wages generally include all remuneration for employment including bonuses, commissions, and contingent fees. "Wages" does not include reimbursed travel expenses.

8. (b) The Federal Unemployment Tax Act (FUTA) requires an employer to file a federal unemployment tax return if the employer pays wages of $1,500 or more in any calendar quarter or employs one or more persons at least one day per week for 20 weeks during a calendar year. Ral Supermarket clearly meets the latter requirement and must file.

9. (c) Unemployment benefits are funded by contributions from employers only, not employers and employees. Answers (a), (b), and (d) represent correct statements regarding unemployment insurance.

10. (d) Social security retirement benefits are reduced $1 for every $2 of *earned income* above a base amount which varies from year to year. Self-employed individuals are taxed on their *net income* if over $400. Participation in the social security retirement system is mandatory even though the employee also participates in a private retirement plan. Death benefits are payable if death occurs after retirement in certain situations.

11. (a) Receipt of payments under a private pension plan will not limit the payment of social security benefits to an otherwise qualifying individual. An individual (or his or her family) may also qualify for benefits if the individual reaches age 62, whether or not he or she is disabled or retired, so long as his or her earned income is below the qualifying level. Normally the benefits paid to a deceased worker's child cease when the child reaches age 18. If the child is a full-time high school student, he or she may continue to receive benefits until three months after reaching age 19 or until he or she stops full-time school attendance, whichever occurs first. Benefit payments may be made to the spouse or dependents of an otherwise qualifying individual in certain situations.

12. (d) Federal unemployment taxes made by an employer are considered to be deductible as a business expense for federal income tax purposes.

12A. (d) Unemployment compensation insurance is financed through payments made by employers under federal and state unemployment insurance laws. Workers' compensation insurance is also financed by payments made by employers under state workers' compensation laws. No payments are deducted from an employees salary for either type of insurance.

13. (a) Generally, unemployment compensation is provided to workers who are discharged through no fault of their own. As a result, a CPA who is fired as a result of an employer's business reversals qualifies to receive benefits. The accountant could not continue to receive unemployment compensation if he or she refused a job that he or she was qualified to perform. Being fired for embezzlement is the fault of the worker. Voluntarily leaving work, without adequate cause, does not qualify one for unemployment benefits.

Workers' Compensation

14. (a) The majority of states have compulsory workers' compensation laws. As a result, employers must carry workman's compensation insurance on their eligible employees. The employer is required to cover the cost of injuries to the employee, at no cost to the employee. Workers that are generally not covered by workman's compensation insurance includes certain domestic and agriculture workers, "casual" workers, and employees who work for a business not meeting a threshold number of total workers employed.

15. (b) The primary purpose for enacting workers' compensation statutes was to enable employees to recover for injuries regardless of negligence. The primary purpose for enacting workers' compensation statutes was not to eliminate *all* employer-employee negligence lawsuits. Workers' compensation statutes do not prevent lawsuits against third parties. The purpose of workers' compensation statutes is not to allow employees to recover *additional* compensation for employer negligence.

16. (c) The general rule is that when an employee suffers a work-related injury, the employer is strictly liable regardless of the reason. The only exception to this rule involves the rare situation of where an employee intentionally injures himself or when an employer intentionally injures the employee. By making workers' compensation the exclusive remedy for injured employees, employers have given up their traditional defenses of contributory negligence, assumption of risk, and the fellow-servant rule. Workers' compensation laws are *liberally* construed to protect the injured employee. Damages are set up by statutory formula, and ignore the comparative negligence of the employee. The employee's own negligence (even gross negligence) is not a bar to recovery (with an exception for intentionally self-inflicted injury).

17. (d) Workers' compensation systems require an employer to insure workers for job-related injuries. An employee may recover damages without proof of fault or negligence on the part of the employer; thus, an employer is strictly liable for the job-related injuries of an employee. The negligence of an employee or a co-employee does not affect the employee's right to recover.

18. (c) An on-site inspection of a workplace by an investigator from the Occupational Safety and Health Administration (OSHA) is permissible after a request by employees. Employee requests provide OSHA with the probable cause necessary to obtain a warrant. Since OSHA may conduct an on-site inspection without a warrant if the owner consents, it is not true that OSHA can *only* inspect the premises with a search warrant. It is not necessary that an on-site inspection be conducted after working hours, nor that the employer be given any prior notice of the inspection.

19. (b) The workers' compensation statutes enable employees to recover for job-related injuries or diseases whether the employer is negligent or not. When an employee accepts the benefits of the workers' compensation laws, he or she is generally barred from suing the employer for damages. The employee's acceptance of benefits does not bar suit against a third party whose negligence caused the injury. Thus, Kroll will be successful in obtaining workers' compensation benefits but not in a negligence action against Acorn. However, Kroll would be able to sue Trell, the third party whose negligence caused the accident.

20. (b) OSHA prohibits an employer's firing an employee for reporting OSHA violations. OSHA requires an employer to maintain a work environment free from recognized hazards. It does not require that the employer provide a completely risk-free environment. Agency such as OSHA must obtain an administrative warrant to inspect the premises if the employer does not give permission for the site search. OSHA is a federal law and thus is only applicable when the employer is engaged in interstate commerce or an activity affecting interstate commerce. States are not prohibited from also enacting legislation to protect worker health and safety.

21. (c) Workers' compensation benefits are allowed to employees who are injured "on the job" even if the employee is negligent. However, if an employee intentionally causes the self-inflicted injury, the employee cannot collect. Failing to abide by safety procedures will not preclude the injured worker

from collecting workers' compensation. An injured employee can collect even if the injury was caused by a fellow employee. An injured worker can collect workers' compensation and still maintain a civil suit against a third party who caused the injury.

Federal Tax Ramifications

22. (a)   Where an employer pays an employee's share of FICA taxes, the amount of FICA taxes paid on behalf of that employee qualifies as taxable income to the employee and as an ordinary and necessary business expense to the employer. The FICA requires an employer to withhold and pay both the employer's and the employee's share of FICA taxes. An employer who fails to withhold the employee's share will be liable for payment of both the employer's and employee's share. There are no additional penalties imposed on an employer who voluntarily pays its employee's share.

23. (a)   Unemployment benefits are funded by contributions from employers only and are considered to be deductible as a business expense for federal income tax purposes. Only those employers who paid wages of $1,500 or more during a calendar quarter or who employed at least one employee for at least one day a week for 20 weeks must pay FUTA taxes. The employer, not the employee, pays the FUTA tax. Only the first $7,000 in wages paid to each covered employee is taxable under FUTA. The tax rate is 6.0% with a maximum state unemployment tax offset of 5.4%.

24. (b)   Earned income such as director's fees after retirement, which exceeds an annual limitation, results in reduced benefits of $1 for each $2 of earnings above a specified amount of annual earned income. Annual proceeds from an annuity, pension payments, and closely held corporation stock dividends all represent unearned income and do not affect benefits.

Employment Discrimination

25. (b)   The federal Age Discrimination in Employment Act prohibits employment discrimination on the basis of age against persons forty years of age and older; thus, compulsory retirement of employees below the age of 65 would violate the Act.

Terminating employees for cause is not age-based discrimination and does not violate the Act.

26. (b)   Title VII of the Civil Rights Act of 1964 prohibits discrimination in employment on the bases of race, sex, religion, color, and national origin. The Age Discrimination in Employment Act protects workers between the ages of forty and seventy from discrimination.

27. (a)   Under the provisions of the Americans With Disabilities Act, a disabled person is protected from discrimination by providers of public transportation, as well as privately operated public accommodations. Thus, the Act protects a disabled person in both areas.

Wage-Hour Law

28. (b)   The Fair Labor Standards Act is the Federal Statute that governs employees' wages and hours. The National Labor Relations and Taft-Hartley Act govern employees' rights to bargain collectively. The Americans With Disabilities Act protects persons with disabilities from discrimination.

29. (a)   The Fair Labor Standards Act (FLSA) requires covered employers to pay a legally specified minimum wage. The FLSA does not establish the number of hours to be worked in a workweek; however, it does regulate the compensation rate of hours worked in excess of 40, which is a regulation of the number of hours.

Pensions

30. (b)   A noncontributory pension fund is one to which only the employer contributes. Employees make no contributions.

31. (b)   Under the Employee Retirement Income Security Act (ERISA), employers are prevented from unduly delaying an employee's participation in a pension plan. ERISA does not establish an employee's right to an employer-established pension plan. Although ERISA establishes rules on how funds must be invested, the Act neither prevents employers from managing investment plans nor entitles employees to make investment decisions.

PERFORMANCE BY SUBTOPICS

Each category below parallels a subtopic covered in Chapter 54. Record the number and percentage of questions you correctly answered in each subtopic area.

Federal Social Security Act

Question #	Correct √
1	
2	
3	
4	
5	
6	
7	
8	
9	
10	
11	
12	
12A	
13	
# Questions	14

Correct _____
% Correct _____

Workers' Compensation

Question #	Correct √
14	
15	
16	
17	
18	
19	
20	
21	
# Questions	8

Correct _____
% Correct _____

Federal Tax Ramifications

Question #	Correct √
22	
23	
24	
# Questions	3

Correct _____
% Correct _____

Employment Discrimination

Question #	Correct √
25	
26	
27	
# Questions	3

Correct _____
% Correct _____

Wage-Hour Law

Question #	Correct √
28	
29	
# Questions	2

Correct _____
% Correct _____

Pensions

Question #	Correct √
30	
31	
# Questions	2

Correct _____
% Correct _____

ESSAY QUESTION

Essay 54-2 (6 to 8 minutes)

Maple owns 75% of the common stock of Salam Exterminating, Inc. Maple is not an officer or employee of the corporation, and does not serve on its board of directors. Salam is in the business of providing exterminating services to residential and commercial customers.

Dodd performed exterminating services on behalf of Salam. Dodd suffered permanent injuries as a result of inhaling one of the chemicals used by Salam. This occurred after Dodd sprayed the chemical in a restaurant that Salam regularly services. Dodd was under the supervision of one of Salam's district managers and was trained by Salam to perform exterminating services following certain procedures, which he did. Later that day several patrons who ate at the restaurant also suffered permanent injuries as a result of inhaling the chemical. The chemical was manufactured by Ace Chemical Corp. and sold and delivered to Salam in a closed container. It was not altered by Salam. It has now been determined that the chemical was defectively manufactured and the injuries suffered by Dodd and the restaurant patrons were a direct result of the defect.

Salam has complied with an applicable compulsory workers' compensation statute by obtaining an insurance policy from Spear Insurance Co.

As a result of the foregoing, the following actions have been commenced:

- Dodd sued Spear to recover workers' compensation benefits.
- Dodd sued Salam based on negligence in training him.

Required:

Discuss the merits of the actions commenced by Dodd indicating the likely outcomes and your reasons therefor. (11/88, Law, #3)

ESSAY SOLUTION

Solution 54-2 Workers' Compensation Act

Dodd is entitled to recover workers' compensation benefits from Spear because Dodd was an **employee** of Salam, the injury was **accidental**, and the **injury occurred out of and in the course of his employment** with Salam. Based on the facts of this case, Dodd would be considered an employee and **not an independent contractor** because Salam had **control over the details of Dodd's work** by training Dodd to perform the services in a specified manner and Dodd was **subject** to Salam's **supervision.**

Dodd will be unsuccessful in his action against Salam based on **negligence** in training him because Dodd is an **employee** of Salam, and Salam has complied with the applicable compulsory workers' compensation statute by obtaining workers' compensation insurance. Under workers' compensation, an **employee who receives workers' compensation benefits cannot successfully maintain an action for negligence against his employer seeking additional compensation.** Therefore, whether Salam was negligent in training Dodd is irrelevant.

CHANGE ALERT

The SEC has amended **Rule 504 of Regulation D**, dealing with transactions exempt from registration under the Securities Act of 1933. These changes are discussed in Section III.C.2.a.(1) on page 55-6.

- Rule 504 now permits offerings of up to $1 million worth of securities **regardless of registration under state law**.

- The ban on general solicitations and the requirement that the securities be restricted has been **eliminated**.

- There are **no longer** restrictions on resale of securities purchased in a Rule 504 offering.

CHAPTER 55

FEDERAL SECURITIES REGULATIONS

I. **Definitions** 55-2
    A.   Beneficial Ownership 55-2
    B.   Controlling Person 55-2
    C.   Dealer 55-2
    D.   Equity Security 55-2
    E.   Insider 55-2
    F.   Interstate Commerce 55-2
    G.   Issuer 55-2
    H.   Person 55-2
    I.   Prospectus... 55-2
    J.   Registration Statement 55-3
    K.   Sale or Sell 55-3
    L.   Security 55-3
    M.   Shelf Registration 55-3
    N.   Underwriter 55-3

II. **The Securities and Exchange Commission (SEC)** 55-3
    A.   Purpose 55-3
    B.   Composition.. 55-3
    C.   Powers and Functions 55-3

III. **The Securities Act of 1933** 55-4
    A.   Purpose, Structure, and Prohibitions.. 55-4
    B.   Exempted Securities.. 55-4
    C.   Exempted Transactions 55-6
    D.   Registration Process 55-9
    E.   Fraudulent Conveyances... 55-11
    F.   Criminal Penalties.. 55-11
    G.   Civil Liability 55-11

IV. **The Securities Exchange Act of 1934** 55-12
    A.   Overview of the Exchange Act of 1934 55-12
    B.   Reporting Requirements.. 55-13
    C.   Anti-Fraud Provisions 55-13
    D.   Proxy Solicitation 55-15
    E.   Tender-Offers 55-16

V. **State "Blue Sky" Laws**... 55-16

CHAPTER 55

FEDERAL SECURITIES REGULATIONS

I. Definitions

A. Beneficial Ownership--Holder of securities, in the name of his or her spouse and minor children; in a trust in which the insider or any member of his or her family has an interest in either the corpus or income; or in a trust created by an insider and over which he or she has retained a power to revoke, when that trust contains 20% or more of a security subject to reporting requirements.

B. Controlling Person--Any person directly or indirectly controlling the issuer or under direct or indirect common control with the issuer. Factors indicating control are the following: stock ownership and actual or practical control ("control" is broadly construed and includes any person capable of influencing the management or policies of the issuer). Thus, a 5%-or-less owner who is an officer or director could be a controlling person.

C. Dealer--Any person who engages either for all or part of his or her time, directly or indirectly, as agent, broker, or principal in the business of offering, buying, selling, or otherwise dealing or trading in securities issued by another.

D. Equity Security--Any stock or similar security, or any security convertible into such a security, or carrying any warrant or right to subscribe to or purchase such warrant or right, or any security which the SEC shall prescribe to treat as an equity security.

E. Insider--Directors and officers of the issuer and every person who is directly or indirectly the beneficial owner of more than 10% of any class of an equity security which is registered pursuant to the 1934 Act.

F. Interstate Commerce--Trade or commerce in securities or any transportation or communication relating thereto among or between the states and territories of the United States, or between those states and territories and foreign countries.

G. Issuer--Every person who issues or proposes to issue any security. For the purposes of registration, controlling persons are considered to be issuers. Thus, controlling persons who make secondary offerings are issuers.

H. Person--An individual, a corporation, a partnership, an association, etc.

I. Prospectus--Any notice, circular, advertisement, letter, or any communication written or broadcast, which offers any security for sale or confirms the sale of any security.

- Exceptions

    a. A communication sent after the effective date of the registration statement shall not be deemed a prospectus if a written prospectus has been previously or is being contemporaneously provided to the person to whom the communication was made.

    b. A notice, circular, advertisement, letter, or communication shall not be deemed a prospectus if it states from whom a written prospectus may be obtained and, in addition, does no more than identify the security, state the price thereof, state by whom offers will be executed, and contain other information deemed appropriate by the SEC.

J.   Registration Statement--The disclosure document required to be filed by the 1933 Act in connection with a registered offering. It includes any amendment thereto and any report, document, or memorandum filed as part of such statement or incorporated therein by reference.

K.   Sale or Sell--Includes every contract of sale or disposition of a security for value. The terms offer to sell or offer to buy shall include every offer to dispose of or purchase, or any solicitation of an offer to buy or sell, a security or interest in a security. The above terms do not include preliminary negotiations or agreements between an issuer and any underwriter or among underwriters who are to be in privity of contract with an issuer.

L.   Security--The statutory definition includes conventional securities such as stocks, bonds, or notes and any interest or instrument commonly known as a "security." It also includes any certificate or interest or participation in, temporary or interim certificate for, receipt for, guarantee of, or warrant or right to subscribe to or purchase, any of the foregoing. Courts have defined a security as requiring (1) an investment in (2) a common enterprise (3) premised on a reasonable expectation of profits (4) to be derived from the managerial efforts of others.

M.   Shelf Registration--An established issuer may file a registration statement and hold the securities until an opportune time to offer them arises. The statement must be continuously updated.

N.   Underwriter--Any person who has purchased from an issuer with a view to, or offers or sells for an issuer in connection with, the distribution of any security, or who participates in such undertaking. An underwriter does not include a person whose interest is limited to a commission from an underwriter or a dealer not in excess of the usual and customary distributor's or seller's commission.

II. The Securities and Exchange Commission (SEC)

A.   Purpose--The SEC was created by the 1934 Act to administer all federal security law, which includes those provided in both the 1933 and 1934 Acts as well as the Public Utility Holding Company Act of 1935, the Trust Indenture Act of 1939, the Investment Company Act of 1940, and the Investment Advisor Act of 1940.

B.   Composition--The SEC is composed of five commissioners appointed by the President. No more than three of the commissioners may be of the same political party. The SEC is an independent agency.

C.   Powers and Functions

1.   Rulemaking--Under the 1933 and 1934 Acts, Congress has vested the SEC with the power to enact rules to construe and implement the law contained in those Acts. The SEC must publish these proposed rules, solicit comments, and in rare instances conduct public hearings before finalizing these rules. However, once finalized, the rules have the force and effect of law.

2.   Administrative Interpretations--The SEC may issue formal and informal opinions construing and interpreting the Acts as applied to proposed actions by natural persons and entities.

3.   Investigations--The SEC has broad subpoena powers which enable it to investigate practices within the securities market.

4.   Enforcement

a.   In order to investigate potential violations, the SEC holds quasi-judicial proceedings to determine compliance with the Acts and the rules which it administers. All such rulings are subject to judicial review.

      b.   Remedies

          (1)   The SEC may suspend or revoke the registration of persons, exchanges, or securities, as required by the 1933 and 1934 Acts.

          (2)   The SEC may seek preliminary and final injunctions in order to prevent violations of the Acts or rules.

          (3)   In appropriate circumstances, the SEC may institute criminal proceedings against violators of the Acts. These proceedings are tried in the Federal District Court and may result in imprisonment and/or fines.

III. The Securities Act of 1933

A.   <u>Purpose, Structure, and Prohibitions</u>

    1.   The 1933 Act is intended to provide the interested public with the information necessary to evaluate the merits of various securities being offered and to protect the potential investor from fraudulent acts, misleading statements, or omissions by the selling party.

    2.   Coverage--The 1933 Act is concerned with the original issuance of securities intended for sale to the public, provided the transaction or any communication relating thereto involves interstate commerce.

    3.   The 1933 Act makes it unlawful for any person, directly or indirectly, to make use of any means or instruments of interstate commerce or the mails to do the following:

      a.   Sell, carry, or transmit for the purpose of sale any security, unless a registration statement is in effect as to such security.

      b.   Carry or transmit for the purpose of sale any security, unless such security is accompanied or preceded by a prospectus that meets the requirements of the Act.

      c.   Offer to sell or offer to buy any security unless a registration statement has been filed as to such security, or offer to sell or buy while the registration statement is subject to a refusal order or stop order.

      d.   Employ any fraudulent schemes or devices, make any misstatement of a material fact, or omit any material facts so as to defraud a purchaser. This provision covers all securities, whether or not registration of such securities is required.

    4.   The 1933 Act provides for civil liabilities for failure to meet the registration and/or prospectus requirements of the Act. The Act also provides for a variety of administrative proceedings for violations of any rule or regulation promulgated by the SEC. Included in these administrative proceedings are stop orders, injunctions, and criminal sanctions for violation of any rule or regulation promulgated by the SEC. Liability extends to the underwriters, issuers, directors, partners, and all experts (including accountants) who have prepared or certified any part of the registration statement.

    5.   Under the 1933 Act, the SEC is empowered to seek writs of mandamus commanding any person to comply with the provisions of the Act or any rules promulgated under the Act.

B.   <u>Exempted Securities</u>--The 1933 Act exempts certain types of securities from its registration requirements. Such securities may be sold and resold any number of times and never be subject to the registration and/or prospectus requirements of the Act. These exemptions are granted because (1) it is felt that registration is not necessary to protect the public interest, (2) the securities are regulated by another government agency, or (3) the nature of the security (for example, commercial paper) necessitates that it be exempt. However, exempt securities are subject to the anti-fraud provisions of the Act (see A.3.d., above). The following is a list of exempt securities:

1. Securities issued by federal, state, territorial, and local governments or by any entities acting as instrumentalities of the government, such as banks, carriers, building and loan associations, and farm cooperatives. (Securities of public utilities are not exempt.)

2. Securities of nonprofit, religious, educational, or charitable organizations.

3. Any security which is part of an issue offered and sold only to persons within a single state by an issuer resident (or incorporated) and doing business within that same state. This is the so-called "Intrastate Offering Exemption."

   a. The issuer of the security must be organized and "doing business" (i.e., 80% of its gross revenue must be derived from operations in that state, and 80% of the sale proceeds must be used in connection with its business operations in that state) in the same state of residence as all offerees and purchasers.

   b. All offers and sales must be limited to residents of the state in which the issuer is organized and doing business.

   c. Resales of the issue may only be made to residents of the issuer's state of residence for nine months following the last sale by the issuer.

   d. A violation of the above rules voids the intrastate exemption for the entire issue.

4. Insurance policies or conventional variable annuity contracts subject to other governmental supervision.

5. Any security exchanged by the issuer with its existing security holders exclusively where no commission or other remuneration is given. (For example, stock splits or any security offered partly in exchange and partly for cash where such transaction is approved by the appropriate government agency.)

6. Commercial paper, such as checks, notes, and bills of exchange, arising out of current transactions or the proceeds of which have been or are to be used for current transactions, which have a maturity date not exceeding 9 months.

7. Small Issues (Regulation A)--Securities that are part of an issue not exceeding $5,000,000 when it finds that registration is not necessary to protect the public interest. These securities must be issued in accordance with SEC Regulation A. "Reg. A," promulgated pursuant to Section 3 of the 1933 Act, is a less restrictive method of registration than is a full registration under Section 5 of the 1933 Act. Under "Reg. A," sales must be made using an "offering circular" rather than a prospectus. "Reg. A" permits an issuer to offer up to $5,000,000 of securities in any 12-month period without Section 5 registration if the issuer files a notification and offering circular with the SEC regional office. Each purchaser must be supplied with an offering circular. Securities issued under "Reg. A" are not "restricted." Thus, they may be freely traded after sale.

8. Securities offered in any reorganization subject to court control (e.g., bankruptcy).

9. Securities issued by an investment company under the Small Business Investment Act of 1958 when it finds that registration is not necessary to protect the public interest.

10. Any security sold prior to or within 60 days after May 27, 1933, the date of enactment of the 1933 Act.

C. <u>Exempted **Transactions**</u>--The Act exempts certain transactions from its registration requirements. When only the particular transaction is exempt, a resale of the same security may not be exempt from the Act's registration and prospectus requirements. This is in contrast to exempted securities which are exempt for all transactions. The scope of the transaction exemptions is very broad, allowing the vast majority of security sales by investors to take place without any registration. The following is a list of the major exempted transactions:

1. Certain Transactions by Any Person Other Than an Issuer, Underwriter, or Dealer Under Section 4(1) of the 1933 Act--The term "underwriter" includes (a) a controlling person who sells on behalf of the issuer, (b) in many instances lenders who sell securities which have been pledged by a control person, and (c) persons who purchase from a controlling person for the purpose of distribution or who sell or offer for sale securities in connection with a distribution.

2. Certain Transactions by an Issuer Involving Public and Nonpublic Companies--<u>Regulation D</u> sets the standards applicable to certain private offerings to be made during any one twelve (12)-month period.

   a. Substantive Rules

      (1) <u>Rule 504</u> permits nonpublic companies not registered under the 1934 Act (usually closely held companies) to offer securities for sale without fulfilling the Section 5 (1933 Act) registration and disclosure requirements. The exemption extends to offerings of securities up to $1,000,000 in a 12-month period. It is important to keep in mind that the anti-fraud provisions of the 1933 and 1934 Acts are applicable in every case.

> **Change Alert**
>
> The SEC has amended Rule 504, resulting in the following changes:
>
> - Rule 504 now permits offerings of up to $1 million worth of securities **regardless of registration under state law**.
>
> - The ban on general solicitations and the requirement that the securities be restricted has been **eliminated**.
>
> - There are **no longer** restrictions on resale of securities purchased in a Rule 504 offering.

      (2) <u>Rule 505</u> permits nonpublic and public companies to offer, without fulfilling the Section 5 (1933 Act) registration requirements, up to $5 million in a 12-month period. Sales can be made to up to 35 "nonaccredited purchasers" and an unlimited number of "accredited investors." The issuer must "reasonably believe" that there are no more than 35 purchasers. (In counting this number related persons are excluded.) "Accredited investors" include institutional investors, any executive of the issuer, and an individual with a net worth or annual income figure in excess of certain levels. Unlike Rule 504, Rule 505 requires that certain information be provided to offerees if there are <u>any</u> nonaccredited purchases within the offering group. Included among the required information are a set of audited financial statements for the most recent year or, if a public issuer, its most recent shareholder's annual report or the most recent Form 10-K or Form S-1. Finally, all anti-fraud provisions apply to Rule 505 offerings.

(3) Rule 506 permits nonpublic and public companies to raise, without full Section 5 (1933 Act) registration, an unlimited amount of money from an unlimited number of "accredited purchasers" and 35 "nonaccredited investors." Under Rule 506, there are simpler offeree sophistication tests, and there are no specific net worth requirements beyond the "accredited purchaser" tests. More specifically, as to the "accredited purchasers," they are simply assumed to be sophisticated. As to the 35 "nonaccredited purchasers," the issuer must reasonably believe that each purchaser "has such knowledge and . . . financial experience as to be capable of evaluating the offering's merits and risks . . ." Toward this end, the nonpublic and public issuer must provide offerees with the same information as is required in Rule 505, at 2.a.(2), above. Finally, the anti-fraud provisions of the 1933 and 1934 Acts apply in every Rule 506 offering.

b. Procedural Rules--In order to comply with Regulation D and fit into one of the three substantive rules, issuers must comply with three general conditions contained in Rules 501, 502, and 503.

(1) No general advertising or solicitation may be used to offer or sell the securities involved in Rules 505 or 506. "General advertising or solicitation" is defined to include any advertisement or notice by any medium under Rules 505 and 506.

(2) The issuer must exercise reasonable care to ensure that purchasers are not underwriters under Rules 505 and 506. Thus, there must be reasonable inquiry into the motive for purchase (i.e., must not be for resale), and there must be a disclosure made to each purchaser to the effect that the securities have not been registered for public sale as required by Section 5 of the 1933 Act. Finally, the issuer must place a legend on each certificate indicating the restrictions on transferability and resale. These restrictions on the resale of securities, however, no longer apply to an offer or sale of securities under Rule 504.

(3) Notification of the offering must be sent to the SEC within 15 days of the first sale of securities in the offering.

3. Private Offerings Under Section 4(2) of the 1933 Act

a. The issuer must demonstrate that the potential offerees and purchasers are sufficiently sophisticated so that they do not need the protection of the Act.

(1) Pursuant to showing that the offerees are sophisticated, the issuer must demonstrate that information sufficient to allow for an intelligent appraisal is readily available to the offerees.

(2) Certain courts have required that the above information actually be placed into the hands of the purchasers.

b. Other important factors which have been considered by the courts include the following:

(1) The number and diversity of the potential investors.

(2) The amount of the offering and the extent to which the securities are readily marketable (for example, when a large number of securities are offered in small denominations, it is more likely that the intent is to distribute to the public at large).

(3) The manner of the offering and whether or not advertising was used.

(4)   The purpose for which the securities are purchased. When they are quickly resold rather than retained as an investment, the presumption is that the original sale was public.

4.   Certain Post-Distribution Transactions by a Dealer

a.   These exemptions for dealers are available only after the distribution period has ended. The 1933 Act defines the distribution period as follows:

(1)   Old Companies--When the securities being offered are by a company that has previously issued securities to the public, the distribution period commences with either the effective date of the registration statement or the start of the offering, whichever date occurs later, and continues for a period of 40 days.

(2)   New Companies--When the securities are being offered by a company that is issuing securities to the public for the first time, the distribution period runs for 90 days.

b.   Once the distribution period has run, dealers need not deliver a prospectus to an offeree or purchaser.

(1)   The above exemption does <u>not</u> apply to dealers who are participating in the original distribution and have not yet sold their original allotment.

(2)   The exemption does apply to dealers transacting in securities in the post-distribution period even though a registration statement was never filed. This prevents innocent dealers selling illegally unregistered securities from being found in violation of the Act.

c.   When the dealer is not participating in the original distribution and the issuing company is filing periodic reports with the SEC pursuant to the 1934 Act, the prospectus requirements do not apply to the dealer.

5.   Resale of Restricted Securities and Certain Sales of Controlled Securities Pursuant to Rule 144

a.   When a person meets the requirements of Rule 144, he or she may resell <u>restricted securities</u>. Restricted securities are securities received in a private offering (e.g., securities sold pursuant to Reg. D). Restricted securities may not be resold unless they are registered or they are exempted from registration (e.g., under Section 4 or Rule 144).

b.   The Sale of "Controlled Securities"--Securities sold by "controlling persons." A control person can sell either restricted securities (above) or nonrestricted securities acquired by a controlling person as part of a registered public distribution. If the latter is the case, the controlling person need not conform with Rule 144's two-year holding period (see c.(2), below).

c.   Rule 144 establishes the following safe harbor criteria which must be met by persons claiming this exemption.

(1)   Adequate information concerning the issuer must be made publicly available. **NOTE:** When a company is required to report and has been reporting, under the 1934 Act, such adequate information is presumed available.

(2)   A person must have been the beneficial owner and have borne the risk of ownership in the securities for a period of at least two years prior to sale, and the person must have fully paid for the securities by the date of sale. This rule attempts to make certain that the person purchased the securities for the purpose of investment rather than for resale to the public. **NOTE:** Controlling persons who sell nonrestricted securities need not comply with this requirement.

(3)   During a three-month period, only the following amounts of securities may be sold. **NOTE:** This applies to both "listed" and "unlisted" securities.

    (a)   1% of all outstanding shares of that class, or

    (b)   The average weekly reported volume of trading in such securities for all security exchanges through which the securities are traded for the four calendar weeks preceding the sale.

(4)   The seller must file a notice with the SEC of his or her intention to sell the restricted securities.

(5)   Generally, all sales must take place in "brokers' transactions," the requirements of which are as follows:

    (a)   The broker must receive only the ordinary brokerage commission.

    (b)   The broker may not solicit any offers to buy, but may publish a bid and ask prices if he or she has been regularly dealing in the security to be sold.

    (c)   The broker must reasonably inquire into whether the seller is entitled to the Rule 144 exception.

    (d)   A recent amendment to the Rule provides for certain exceptions to these general requirements.

        •   Besides brokers' transactions, the sale may also take place directly with a market maker.

        •   Estates and beneficiaries are exempt from the brokers' transaction requirement.

(6)   When there is no public market for the securities, Rule 144 is of little benefit. In these situations, Rule 237 provides an exemption for sales of restricted securities. However, the Rule 237 resale safe harbor applies only to noncontrolling persons and only to the lesser of $50,000 or 1% of the outstanding securities in a one-year period. Moreover, the securities resold pursuant to Rule 237 must have been held for 5 years.

D.   Registration Process--Prior to the initial issuance of any security, the Act requires that a registration statement be filed with the SEC. The registration statement contains all the information necessary to enable the potential investors to determine the desirability of the offered securities. This information, condensed to the essentials, is also used to make up the prospectus which must be provided to all offerees.

1. Information Requirements for Registration Statements

    a. The registration statement must contain all information specified in Schedule A of the Act, unless abrogated by the SEC. A summary of the requirements of Schedule A is as follows:

        (1) Basic Information--Such as names and addresses of the issuer, directors, controlling persons, and underwriters. The statement must also disclose the percentage amount of securities under the control of individual directors or controlling persons.

        (2) Financial Information--The statement must include detailed information of the securities to be issued and securities previously issued, a balance sheet of the issuer not more than 90 days old at the time of filing, a profit and loss statement for the last fiscal year and at least two preceding years, unless the issuer has been in business less than three years, then for such time as the issuer has been in business, and a statement of all material contracts entered into by the issuer during the two years before the filing.

    b. Written Consent of Any Experts (Including Accountants)--All experts who are listed as having prepared or certified any of the information contained in the registration statement must consent to their listing in writing.

    c. Other facts deemed material by the SEC, such as any difference in value that may exist between the offering price and actual book value of the securities, any information concerning directors or top executives tending to demonstrate lack of integrity or potential conflicts of interest, and any information which would serve to put a person on notice that the securities being offered may be "high risk" securities.

    d. The prospectus must contain most of the basic information concerning the issuer, directors, executives, controlling persons, underwriters, and all financial information required under Schedule A. However, any information which the SEC designates as not being necessary to protect the public may be omitted from the prospectus.

2. Once the registration statement and prospectus are filed with the SEC, persons may, through use of "red herring" prospectuses or other limited preliminary prospectuses, announce proposed offerings. Persons may also make offers to sell or buy securities during this "waiting period" (the period after filing and before the effective date of the registration statement).

    a. All written offers must be accompanied by a "red herring" or other preliminary prospectus. A preliminary prospectus must contain most of the information required in a final prospectus, but may exclude such items as the price of the securities, which usually is not decided until just before the effective date. Such a prospectus may be used only during the waiting period.

    b. No prospectus is needed for verbal offers and agreements to sell or buy entered into during the waiting period.

3. Procedures for Processing the Registration Statement

    a. Unless it is subjected to an SEC refusal or stop order, a registration statement becomes effective 20 days after filing. The SEC may also issue an acceleration order to advance the effective date.

    b. Once filed, a registration statement is reviewed by the SEC. The SEC has two primary methods of suspending the effectiveness of a registration statement.

(1)   The SEC may issue a refusal order, which will delay the effective date in order to allow the SEC to further review the security. However, the SEC must issue such an order within 10 days after the filing.

(2)   The SEC may issue a stop order, which has the same effect as a refusal, at any time. However, the SEC may issue such an order only when there are material deficiencies in the registration statement and only after a hearing with notice.

(3)   Alternatively, the SEC has the power to issue letters of deficiency to the issuer. The issuer is then allowed to cure such deficiencies by making amendments to the registration statement.

E.   <u>Fraudulent Conveyances</u>--The 1933 Act generally prohibits the use of fraud by any person who offers or sells a security in interstate commerce. This prohibition applies to all securities, whether or not those securities must be registered. The Act specifically prohibits the following practices:

1.   The use of any device, scheme, or artifice to defraud.

2.   The obtaining of money or property by means of an untrue statement of material fact or by an omission of a material fact.

3.   The engaging in any transaction or practice which would operate as a fraud or deceit on the purchaser.

F.   <u>Criminal Penalties</u>--The Act establishes criminal penalties of a fine of not more than $10,000 and/or imprisonment of up to 5 years for anyone who willfully (1) violates any provision of the Act or the rules and regulations promulgated by the SEC, or (2) makes any untrue statement of a material fact or omits to state any material fact.

G.   <u>Civil Liability</u>--In addition to criminal penalties, the Act provides for civil liabilities.

1.   A person who sues under the anti-fraud provisions (e.g., schemes to defraud, material omissions, and false or misleading statements) must prove the following:

a.   The registration statement contained false or misleading information or material omissions.

b.   The securities purchased were covered by the defective statement.

The injured purchaser need not prove reliance on the statement. Furthermore, the injured person need not prove negligence or fraud. Rather, the burden of persuasion shifts away from the person injured to the experts (attorneys, accountants, officers, directors) who must prove that they exercised due diligence in dealing with the defective statement.

2.   Due Diligence Defense--No person, other than the issuer, shall be liable when he or she can prove the following:

a.   Before the effective date of the statement he or she resigned, or advised the SEC and the issuer that he or she planned to resign, and would not be responsible for such a statement, or, if the statement became effective without his or her knowledge, the SEC was contacted and given reasonable public notice of the fact upon becoming aware of the issuance.

b.   In regard to any part of the statement not purporting to be made on the authority of an expert, he or she had, after reasonable investigation, reasonable grounds to believe and did believe the statement to be true and without material omissions.

c.   In regard to any part of the statement made upon his or her authority as an expert, he or she had, after reasonable investigation, reasonable grounds to believe the statement to be true and without material omissions.

d.   In regard to any part of the statement purporting to be made upon the authority of an expert other than him- or herself, there were no reasonable grounds to believe and he or she did not believe that the statement was untrue or contained material omissions.

The issuer's only defense is that the injured person knew of the misleading or omitted information before the purchase of the securities.

•   The standard of reasonableness is that of a prudent man in the management of his or her own property.

3.   All or any of the persons specified as being liable are jointly and severally liable. Generally, they have the right of contribution.

4.   In no case may the amount recoverable under this section exceed the price at which the security was offered to the public.

5.   In addition to the above liabilities arising from an improper registration statement, the 1933 Act provides that any person who sells or offers to sell a security in violation of the Act's registration requirement, or who offers or sells a security in interstate commerce by use of any communication which makes an untrue statement or omits to state a material fact, shall be liable to the purchaser. This liability can take the form of either the consideration paid for the security with interest, less the amount of any income received thereon, or damages if he or she no longer owns the security. The defendant may escape liability by showing that he or she did not know and in the exercise of reasonable care could not have known of such untruth or omission.

6.   Statute of Limitations--The Act has the following statute of limitations regarding civil liability:

a.   In most instances, an action must be brought within <u>one year</u> of the discovery of an untruth or omission or one year after the discovery <u>should have been made</u> by the exercise of due diligence. Actions based on a violation of the Act's registration requirements must be brought within one year of the violation.

b.   In no event may an action be brought later than <u>three years</u> after a security was offered in good faith to the public.

IV. The Securities Exchange Act of 1934

A. Overview of the Exchange Act of 1934

1.   Purpose--As stated in the 1934 Act, its purpose is to regulate and control security transactions in order to protect interstate commerce, the national credit, banking systems, and the Federal Reserve System, and to ensure the maintenance of fair and honest markets. The 1934 Act takes over where the Securities Act of 1933 leaves off, focusing on secondary offerings of securities.

2.   Scope of Registration Requirements Under the 1934 Act--The following are required to register under the 1934 Act:

a.   Corporations whose securities are traded on a national security exchange or whose assets are in excess of $5 million, and which have a class of equity security held on record by 500 or more persons.

b.   National securities exchanges.

c.   Brokers and dealers transacting business in interstate commerce.

3.   Content of the Registration Statement--The following are required disclosures in the registration:

    a.   The nature of the business.

    b.   The names of officers and directors.

    c.   The financial structure of the firm.

    d.   Any bonus and profit-sharing arrangements.

4.   Margin Requirements--The SEC regulates the amount of credit which may be initially extended or subsequently maintained on any security.

5.   Manipulative and Deceptive Practices--The 1934 Act regulates practices intended to manipulate the price of securities and prohibits deceptive practices.

6.   Regulation of Certain Practices Affecting or Relating to Stock Ownership

    a.   Tender-Offers--The 1934 Act regulates stock purchases and tender-offers by persons acquiring 5% or more of a company's equity securities (see E., below).

    b.   Proxy Solicitations--The 1934 Act regulates the manner by which proxy votes may be solicited from company shareholders.

B.   <u>Reporting Requirements</u>

1.   Corporations

    a.   A company registering under the 1934 Act must supply information similar to, but less extensive than, the information required in a 1933 Act registration statement.

    b.   Every issuer registered under the 1934 Act must file annual reports with the SEC for each fiscal year within 90 days of the close of that year (Form 10-K). These reports must contain financial statements certified by independent public accountants.

    c.   Uncertified reports must be filed quarterly (Form 10-Q), and current reports (Form 8-K) must be filed within 10 days of the close of any month during which certain specific events have occurred.

    d.   Certain specified events must be reported to the SEC. These events include a change in auditor, newly appointed officers, or the resignation of a director, bankruptcy, default of a debt instrument, or a sale of assets not in the ordinary course of business.

2.   National securities exchanges must file reports with the SEC advising of any changes in their rules or regulations.

3.   Directors, Officers, and 10% Security Holders--See C.4., below, for reporting requirements of insiders.

C.   <u>Anti-Fraud Provisions</u>--Section 10(b) of the 1934 Act makes it unlawful for any person to use interstate commerce or any facility of any national security exchange to directly or indirectly effect a short sale. It also makes it unlawful for any person to use or employ in connection with the purchase or sale of any security any deceptive or manipulative practice in contrary to the rules or regulations prescribed by the SEC as necessary to protect the public interest.

1. Coverage--Section 10(b) was broadly written so as to give the SEC power to regulate substantially all securities transactions over which the federal government may exercise control. Of special importance are provisions relating to the following:

   a. Securities--This provision covers transactions in both registered and unregistered securities.

   b. Persons--This provision covers all persons transacting in securities (not just insiders, issuers, or dealers).

   c. Transactions--This provision covers both sales and purchases, thus protection is extended to defrauded sellers. Additionally, the wording "in connection with any sale or purchase" has been held to cover not only situations in which the person engaged in "fraud" is buying or selling, but also situations in which reasonable investors would rely on the "fraud" in making investment decisions. For example, a corporation may not release false information which may influence the decision of a reasonable investor to buy or sell.

2. Pursuant to its rulemaking authority, the SEC promulgated Rule 10b-5 in an attempt to clarify the meaning of Section 10(b). Rule 10b-5 makes it unlawful for any person (in connection with the purchase or sale of any security) to use interstate commerce, the mails, or any facility of any national securities exchange to do the following:

   a. Employ any device, scheme, or artifice to defraud.

   b. Make any untrue statement of a material fact or to omit to state a material fact.

   c. Engage in any act, practice, or course of business which operates or would operate as a fraud or deceit upon any person.

3. A material fact has been defined by the court as follows:

   a. The basic test of materiality is whether a reasonable man would attach importance to that fact in determining a choice of action in the transaction in question.

   b. Material facts include not only the information disclosing the earnings and distributions of a company, but also those facts which affect the future of the company and those which may affect the desire of investors to buy, sell, or hold the company's securities.

   c. Courts will balance both the indicated probability that an event will occur and the anticipated magnitude of the event in light of the totality of the company's activity.

   d. Courts may look to the importance attached to the event by those who knew about it and were in a position to evaluate it. For instance, a substantial mineral find and a pending merger have been held to be material facts.

4. Disclosure Requirements--There is no direct requirement that corporations or their directors or experts disclose important developments within the corporation. However, insiders in possession of such information must either disclose that information or refrain from trading the corporation's stock. For purposes of the above prohibition, insiders include all persons as defined in I.E., above, and also anyone in possession of material inside information, that is, anyone privy to a (secret) "tip."

5. Liability--Persons found to be in violation of Section 10 of the 1934 Act or Rule 10b-5 may be liable to private parties and/or the SEC as follows:

    a. Actions by the SEC

        (1) The SEC may bring an action in any United States District Court to enjoin any activity in violation of the anti-fraud provisions, or to compel, by a writ of mandamus, any person to comply with these provisions or any order issued by the SEC. Pursuant to this power, the SEC may subpoena witnesses, compel their attendance, and require the production of relevant material.

        (2) The SEC may base the above actions under Section 10(b) on a showing of reckless disregard of the truth; it has no duty to establish specific fraudulent intent.

        (3) Persons who willfully violate any provision of Section 10(b) may be held criminally liable and subject to a fine of up to $100,000 or imprisonment of not more than 5 years or both.

        (4) In an enforcement action brought by the SEC to enjoin future violations of Section 10(b), the conduct complained of can be judged under a negligence standard.

    b. Actions by Private Parties

        (1) Any person who, in reliance on any statement in violation of Section 10(b) of the 1934 Act and with no knowledge of the falsity of such statement, buys or sells a security and thereby suffers a loss, may bring an action in law or equity. **NOTE:** Only purchasers or sellers may bring an action. Persons who hold or refrain from buying have no cause of action.

        (2) Persons suing under this section must allege fraud on the part of the persons in violation of the Act. Scienter must be proven. However, there is no requirement to establish privity between those defrauded and the violating parties.

D. Proxy Solicitation--It is unlawful for any person, by use of interstate commerce, the mails, or any facility of a national security exchange, to solicit from holders of securities required to be registered under the 1934 Act a proxy in violation of SEC rules. A proxy is an authorization from a shareholder to vote his or her shares.

1. Subject to several exemptions, before any proxy may be solicited, each person contacted must be furnished with a written proxy statement. This statement must contain the following:

    a. A statement as to whether or not the proxy is revocable.

    b. The identity of the person (or persons) making the solicitation and a statement by him or her as to his or her interest in any matter to be acted upon.

    c. Information relevant to voting for new directors.

    d. A list of matters to be acted upon and whether they are proposed by the management or a security holder.

2.   The form of proxy presented to the security holders must contain the following:

    a.   Whether or not the proxy is solicited on behalf of the management.

    b.   A specially designated blank space for dating the proxy.

    c.   A list of each matter intended to be acted upon.

    d.   A means to express a view on each matter.

3.   If the solicitation is made on behalf of the management of the issuer and relates to an annual meeting of security holders at which directors are to be elected, an annual report must accompany the proxy statement. This report shall contain a financial statement for the last two fiscal years certified by an independent accountant.

4.   The proxy statement, form of proxy, and annual reports shall be filed with the SEC at least 10 days before such information is sent to the holders.

5.   Under the 1934 Act, the SEC has promulgated Rule 14a-9 which prohibits false or misleading statements in any material required to be filed with the SEC. Violation of this rule gives rise to a private cause of action. In some instances, a mere showing of negligence is sufficient to establish liability. However, in the majority of cases, intent or reckless disregard must be shown.

E.   Tender-Offers--In 1968, the 1934 Act was amended (Rule 13) so as to make it unlawful for anyone, directly or indirectly, by use of interstate commerce, the mails, or any facility of a national securities exchange, to acquire or to make a tender-offer of any class of equity security (required to be registered under the 1934 Act) if, after acquisition of those securities, he or she would become the beneficial owner of 5% or more of such class of security unless he or she first does the following:

1.   Files a report (Schedule 13D) with the SEC, with the pertinent security exchange, and with the issuer, and if a tender offer is made, to holders of that class of security.

2.   The report generally must include information about the purchaser, the source and amount of funds or other consideration used in making the purchases, and the purpose for the purchase (for example, to take over control of the business or to liquidate the business). It must also include the number of shares actually owned (by the offeror) and any related activity (tender-offers) planned.

V. State "Blue Sky" Laws

In addition to the federal scheme of securities regulation, most states have their own laws regulating the offer and sale of securities in their state. These laws are often called "blue sky" laws. These laws typically regulate the offer and sale of securities within the geographical borders of the state and/or to residents of the state. Issuers must comply with both the state and the SEC. Furthermore, exemptions from federal laws are not exemptions from state laws.

CHAPTER 55—FEDERAL SECURITIES REGULATIONS

Problem 55-1 MULTIPLE CHOICE QUESTIONS (70 to 85 minutes)

1. Which of the following is **least** likely to be considered a security under the Securities Act of 1933?
   a. Stock options.
   b. Warrants.
   c. General partnership interests.
   d. Limited partnership interests.

   (5/93, Law, #30, 3998)

2. When a common stock offering requires registration under the Securities Act of 1933,
   a. The registration statement is automatically effective when filed with the SEC.
   b. The issuer would act unlawfully if it were to sell the common stock without providing the investor with a prospectus.
   c. The SEC will determine the investment value of the common stock before approving the offering.
   d. The issuer may make sales 10 days after filing the registration statement.

   (11/91, Law, #36, 2364)

3. Under the Securities Act of 1933, which of the following statements most accurately reflects how securities registration affects an investor?
   a. The investor is provided with information on the stockholders of the offering corporation.
   b. The investor is provided with information on the principal purposes for which the offering's proceeds will be used.
   c. The investor is guaranteed by the SEC that the facts contained in the registration statement are accurate.
   d. The investor is assured by the SEC against loss resulting from purchasing the security.

   (11/94, Law, #41, 5218)

4. The registration requirements of the Securities Act of 1933 are intended to provide information to the SEC to enable it to
   a. Evaluate the financial merits of the securities being offered.
   b. Ensure that investors are provided with adequate information on which to base investment decisions.
   c. Prevent public offerings of securities when management fraud or unethical conduct is suspected.
   d. Assure investors of the accuracy of the facts presented in the financial statements.

   (11/90, Law, #39, 0743)

5. If securities are exempt from the registration provisions of the Securities Act of 1933, any fraud committed in the course of selling such securities can be challenged by

	SEC	Person defrauded
a.	Yes	Yes
b.	Yes	No
c.	No	Yes
d.	No	No

   (5/94, Law, #39, 4794)

6. The Securities Act of 1933 provides an exemption from registration for

	Bonds issued by a municipality for governmental purposes	Securities issued by a not-for-profit charitable organization
a.	Yes	Yes
b.	Yes	No
c.	No	Yes
d.	No	No

   (5/93, Law, #33, 4001)

7. Which of the following securities is exempt from registration under the Securities Act of 1933?
   a. Shares of nonvoting common stock, provided their par value is less than $1.00.
   b. A class of stock given in exchange for another class by the issuer to its existing stockholders without the issuer paying a commission.
   c. Limited partnership interests sold for the purpose of acquiring funds to invest in bonds issued by the United States.
   d. Corporate debentures that were previously subject to an effective registration statement, provided they are convertible into shares of common stock. (5/93, Law, #34, 4002)

8. Which of the following securities would be regulated by the provisions of the Securities Act of 1933?
   a. Securities issued by not-for-profit, charitable organizations.
   b. Securities guaranteed by domestic governmental organizations.
   c. Securities issued by savings and loan associations.
   d. Securities issued by insurance companies.

   (11/94, Law, #42, 5219)

9. Which of the following statements concerning an initial intrastate securities offering made by an issuer residing in and doing business in that state is correct?
a. The offering would be exempt from the registration requirements of the Securities Act of 1933.
b. The offering would be subject to the registration requirements of the Securities Exchange Act of 1934.
c. The offering would be regulated by the SEC.
d. The shares of the offering could **not** be resold to investors outside the state for at least one year. (11/94, Law, #52, 5229)

10. The registration requirements of the Securities Act of 1933 apply to
a. The issuance of a stock dividend without commissions or other consideration paid.
b. The issuance of stock warrants.
c. Securities issued by a federally chartered savings and loan association.
d. Securities issued by a common carrier regulated by the Interstate Commerce Commission. (5/87, Law, #41, 0774)

11. Exemption from registration under the Securities Act of 1933 would be available for
a. Promissory notes maturing in 12 months.
b. Securities of a bank.
c. Limited partnership interests.
d. Corporate bonds. (11/91, Law, #35, 2363)

12. Which of the following transactions will be exempt from the full registration requirements of the Securities Act of 1933?
a. All intrastate offerings.
b. All offerings made under Regulation A.
c. Any resale of a security purchased under a Regulation D offering.
d. Any stockbroker transaction.
(5/94, Law, #37, 4782)

13. Lux Limited Partnership intends to offer $300,000 of its limited partnership interests under Rule 504 of Regulation D of the Securities Act of 1933. Which of the following statements is correct?
a. The resale of the limited partnership interests by a purchaser generally will **not** be restricted.
b. The limited partnership interests may be sold only to accredited investors.
c. The exemption under Rule 504 is **not** available to an issuer of limited partnership interests.
d. The limited partnership interests may **not** be sold to more than 35 investors.
(11/93, Law, #38, 4335)

14. Regulation D of the Securities Act of 1933
a. Restricts the number of purchasers of an offering to 35.
b. Permits an exempt offering to be sold to both accredited and nonaccredited investors.
c. Is limited to offers and sales of common stock that do **not** exceed $1.5 million.
d. Is exclusively available to small business corporations as defined by Regulation D.
(5/93, Law, #35, 4003)

14A. Securities available under a private placement made pursuant to Regulation D of the Securities Act of 1933
a. Cannot be subject to the payment of commissions.
b. Must be sold to accredited institutional investors.
c. Must be sold to fewer than 20 non-accredited investors.
d. Cannot be the subject of an immediate unregistered reoffering to the public.
(11/89, Law, #38, 0755)

14B. For an offering to be exempt under Regulation D of the Securities Act of 1933, Rules 504, 505, and 506 each require that
a. The SEC be notified within 10 days of the first sale.
b. The offering be made without general advertising.
c. All accredited investors receive the issuer's financial information.
d. There be a maximum of 35 investors.
(11/94, Law, #49, 5226)

15. Data, Inc. intends to make a $375,000 common stock offering under Rule 504 of Regulation D of the Securities Act of 1933. Data
a. May sell the stock to an unlimited number of investors.
b. May not make the offering through a general advertising.
c. Must offer the stock for a period of more than 12 months.
d. Must provide all investors with a prospectus.
(5/92, Law, #44, amended, 2857)

16. Which of the following facts will result in an offering of securities being exempt from registration under the Securities Act of 1933?
a. The securities are nonvoting preferred stock.
b. The issuing corporation was closely held prior to the offering.

c. The sale or offer to sell the securities is made by a person other than an issuer, underwriter, or dealer.

d. The securities are AAA-rated debentures that are collateralized by first mortgages on property that has a market value of 200% of the offering price. (11/94, Law, #48, 5225)

17. Kamp is offering $10 million of its securities. Under Rule 506 of Regulation D of the Securities Act of 1933,

a. The securities may be debentures.

b. Kamp must be a corporation.

c. There must be more than 35 purchasers.

d. Kamp may make a general solicitation in connection with the offering. (11/91, Law, #40, 2368)

18. Taso Limited Partnership intends to offer $400,000 of its limited partnership interests under Rule 504 of Regulation D of the Securities Act of 1933. Which of the following statements is correct?

a. The exemption under Rule 504 is **not** available to an issuer of limited partnership interests.

b. The limited partnership interests may be sold only to accredited investors.

c. The total number of nonaccredited investors who purchase the limited partnership may **not** exceed 35.

d. The resale of the limited partnership interests by a purchaser generally will not be restricted. (11/91, Law, #41, amended, 2369)

19. Under the Securities Act of 1933, an initial offering of securities must be registered with the SEC, unless

a. The offering is made through a broker-dealer licensed in the states in which the securities are to be sold.

b. The offering prospectus makes a fair and full disclosure of all risks associated with purchasing the securities.

c. The issuer's financial condition meets certain standards established by the SEC.

d. The type of security or the offering involved is exempt from registration. (11/91, Law, #37, 2365)

19A. Under the Securities Act of 1933, which of the following statements concerning an offering of securities sold under a transaction exemption is correct?

a. The offering is exempt from the anti-fraud provisions of the 1933 Act.

b. The offering is subject to the registration requirements of the 1933 Act.

c. Resales of the offering are exempt from the provisions of the 1933 Act.

d. Resales of the offering must be made under a registration or an exemption provision of the 1933 Act. (11/94, Law, #44, amended, 5221)

20. Imperial Corp. is offering $450,000 of its securities under Rule 504 of Regulation D of the Securities Act of 1933. Under Rule 504, Imperial is required to

a. Provide full financial information to all nonaccredited purchasers.

b. Make the offering through general solicitation.

c. Register the offering under the provisions of the Securities Exchange Act of 1934.

d. Notify the SEC within 15 days after the first sale of the securities. (11/90, Law, #43, 0747)

21. Hamilton Corp. is making a $4,500,000 securities offering under Rule 505 of Regulation D of the Securities Act of 1933. Under this regulation, Hamilton is

a. Required to provide full financial information to accredited investors only.

b. Allowed to make the offering through a general solicitation.

c. Limited to selling to **no** more than 35 nonaccredited investors.

d. Allowed to sell to an unlimited number of investors both accredited and nonaccredited. (11/90, Law, #44, 0748)

21A. Frey, Inc. intends to make a $2,000,000 common stock offering under Rule 505 of Regulation D of the Securities Act of 1933. Frey

a. May sell the stock to an unlimited number of investors.

b. May make the offering through a general advertising.

c. Must notify the SEC within 15 days after the first sale of the offering.

d. Must provide all inspectors with a prospectus. (11/93, Law, #45, 4243)

22. A $10,000,000 offering of corporate stock intended to be made pursuant to the provisions of Rule 506 of Regulation D of the Securities Act of 1933 would **not** be exempt under Rule 506 if

a. The offering was made through a general solicitation or advertising.

b. Some of the investors are nonaccredited.

c. There are more than 35 accredited investors.

d. The SEC was notified 14 days after the first sale of the securities. (11/90, Law, #45, 0749)

Items 23 and 23A are based on the following:

Pix Corp. is making a $6,000,000 stock offering. Pix wants the offering exempt from registration under the Securities Act of 1933.

23. Which of the following provisions of the Act would Pix have to comply with for the offering to be exempt?
a. Regulation A.
b. Regulation D, Rule 504.
c. Regulation D, Rule 505.
d. Regulation D, Rule 506.
(11/93, Law, #43, 4340)

23A. Which of the following requirements would Pix have to comply with when selling the securities?
a. No more than 35 investors.
b. No more than 35 nonaccredited investors.
c. Accredited investors only.
d. Nonaccredited investors only.
(11/93, Law, #44, 4341)

24. Which of the following statements concerning the prospectus required by the Securities Act of 1933 is correct?
a. The prospectus is a part of the registration statement.
b. The prospectus should enable the SEC to pass on the merits of the securities.
c. The prospectus must be filed after an offer to sell.
d. The prospectus is prohibited from being distributed to the public until the SEC approves the accuracy of the facts embodied therein.
(5/94, Law, #31, 4786)

25. A preliminary prospectus, permitted under SEC Regulations, is known as the
a. Unaudited prospectus.
b. Qualified prospectus.
c. "Blue-sky" prospectus.
d. "Red-herring" prospectus.
(5/94, Law, #32, 4787)

26. A tombstone advertisement
a. May be substituted for the prospectus under certain circumstances.
b. May contain an offer to sell securities.
c. Notifies prospective investors that a previously-offered security has been withdrawn from the market and is therefore effectively "dead."
d. Makes known the availability of a prospectus.
(5/94, Law, #33, 4788)

27. Under the Securities Act of 1933, which of the following statements is correct concerning a public issuer of securities who has made a registered offering?
a. The issuer is required to distribute an annual report to its stockholders.
b. The issuer is subject to the proxy rules of the SEC.
c. The issuer must file an annual report (Form 10-K) with the SEC.
d. The issuer is **not** required to file a quarterly report (Form 10-Q) with the SEC, unless a material event occurs. (5/94, Law, #36, 4791)

27A. Under Regulation D of the Securities Act of 1933, which of the following conditions apply to private placement offerings? The securities
a. Cannot be sold for longer than a six month period.
b. Cannot be the subject of an immediate unregistered reoffering to the public.
c. Must be sold to accredited institutional investors.
d. Must be sold to fewer than 20 nonaccredited investors. (5/94, Law, #40, 4795)

27B. An offering made under the provisions of Regulation A of the Securities Act of 1933 requires that the issuer
a. File an offering circular with the SEC.
b. Sell only to accredited investors.
c. Provide investors with the prior four years' audited financial statements.
d. Provide investors with a proxy registration statement. (11/93, Law, #40, 4337)

Items 28 and 29 are based on the following:

World Corp. wanted to make a public offering of its common stock. On May 10, World prepared and filed a registration statement with the SEC. On May 20, World placed a "tombstone ad" announcing that it was making a public offering. On May 25, World issued a preliminary prospectus and the registration statement became effective on May 30.

28. On what date may World first make oral offers to sell the shares?
a. May 10.
b. May 20.
c. May 25.
d. May 30. (5/92, Law, #39, 2852)

29. On what date may World first sell the shares?
a. May 10.
b. May 20.
c. May 25.
d. May 30. (5/92, Law, #40, 2853)

30. Which of the following requirements must be met by an issuer of securities who wants to make an offering by using shelf registration?

	Original registration statement must be kept updated	The offeror must be a first-time issuer of securities
a.	Yes	Yes
b.	Yes	No
c.	No	Yes
d.	No	No

(11/94, Law, #43, 5220)

31. Under the liability provisions of Section 11 of the Securities Act of 1933, a CPA may be liable to any purchaser of a security for certifying materially misstated financial statements that are included in the security's registration statement. Under Section 11, a CPA usually will **not** be liable to the purchaser
a. If the purchaser is contributorily negligent.
b. If the CPA can prove due diligence.
c. Unless the purchaser can prove privity with the CPA.
d. Unless the purchaser can prove scienter on the part of the CPA. (11/94, Law, #12, 5189)

32. Ivor and Associates, CPAs, audited the financial statements of Jaymo Corporation. As a result of Ivor's negligence in conducting the audit, the financial statements included material misstatements. Ivor was unaware of this fact. The financial statements and Ivor's unqualified opinion were included in a registration statement and prospectus for an original public offering of stock by Jaymo. Thorp purchased shares in the offering. Thorp received a copy of the prospectus prior to the purchase but did not read it. The shares declined in value as a result of the misstatements in Jaymo's financial statements becoming known. Under which of the following Acts is Thorp most likely to prevail in a lawsuit against Ivor?

	Securities Act of 1933, Section 11	Securities Exchange Act of 1934, Section 10(b), Rule 10b-5
a.	Yes	Yes
b.	Yes	No
c.	No	Yes
d.	No	No

(11/93, Law, #8, 4305)

33. One of the elements necessary to recover damages if there has been a material misstatement in a registration statement filed under the Securities Act of 1933 is that the

a. Issuer and plaintiff were in privity of contract with each other.
b. Issuer failed to exercise due care in connection with the sale of the securities.
c. Plaintiff gave value for the security.
d. Plaintiff suffered a loss. (11/93, Law, #37, 4334)

34. Jay, CPA, gave an unqualified opinion on Nast Power Co.'s financial statements. Larkin bought Nast bonds in a public offering subject to the Securities Act of 1933. The registration statement filed with the SEC included Nast's financial statements. Larkin sued Jay for misstatements contained in the financial statements under the provisions of Section 11 of the Securities Act of 1933. To prevail, Larkin must prove

	Scienter	Reliance
a.	Yes	No
b.	Yes	Yes
c.	No	No
d.	No	Yes

(11/91, Law, #8, 2336)

35. Under the Securities Exchange Act of 1934, which of the following types of instruments is excluded from the definition of "securities"?
a. Investment contracts.
b. Convertible debentures.
c. Nonconvertible debentures.
d. Certificates of deposit. (5/94, Law, #38, 4793)

36. Under the Securities Exchange Act of 1934, a corporation with common stock listed on a national stock exchange
a. Is prohibited from making private placement offerings.
b. Is subject to having the registration of its securities suspended or revoked.
c. Must submit Form 10-K to the SEC except in those years in which the corporation has made a public offering.
d. Must distribute copies of Form 10-K to its stockholders. (5/93, Law, #32, 4000)

37. Under the Securities Exchange Act of 1934, which of the following individuals would **not** be subject to the insider reporting provisions?
a. An owner of ten percent of a corporation's stock.
b. An owner of five percent of a corporation's voting stock.
c. The vice president of marketing.
d. A member of the board of directors. (5/90, Law, #31, 9911)

37A. Which of the following persons is **not** an insider of a corporation subject to the Securities Exchange Act of 1934 registration and reporting requirements?

a. An attorney for the corporation.
b. An owner of 5% of the corporation's outstanding debentures.
c. A member of the board of directors.
d. A stockholder who owns 10% of the outstanding common stock.

(11/93, Law, #42, 4339)

38. Adler, Inc. is a reporting company under the Securities Exchange Act of 1934. The only security it has issued is voting common stock. Which of the following statements is correct?
a. Because Adler is a reporting company, it is **not** required to file a registration statement under the Securities Act of 1933 for any future offerings of its common stock.
b. Adler need **not** file its proxy statements with the SEC because it has only one class of stock outstanding.
c. Any person who owns more than 10% of Adler's common stock must file a report with the SEC.
d. It is unnecessary for the required annual report (Form 10K) to include audited financial statements. (11/93, Law, #41, 4338)

39. For a CPA to be liable for damages under the antifraud provisions of Section 10(b) and Rule 10b-5 of the Securities Exchange Act of 1934, a plaintiff must prove all of the following **except** that
a. The plaintiff relied on the financial statements audited by the CPA.
b. The CPA violated generally accepted auditing standards.
c. There was a material misrepresentation of fact in the financial statements audited by the CPA.
d. The CPA acted with scienter.

(11/91, Law, #7, 2335)

Items 40 through 41A are based on the following:

Link Corp. is subject to the reporting provisions of the Securities Exchange Act of 1934.

40. Which of the following situations would require Link to be subject to the reporting provisions of the 1934 Act?

	Share listed on a national securities exchange	More than one class of stock
a.	Yes	Yes
b.	Yes	No
c.	No	Yes
d.	No	No

(11/94, Law, #45, 5222)

41. Which of the following documents must Link file with the SEC?

	Quarterly reports (Form 10-Q)	Proxy statements
a.	Yes	Yes
b.	Yes	No
c.	No	Yes
d.	No	No

(11/94, Law, #46, 5223)

41A. Which of the following reports must also be submitted to the SEC?

	Report by any party making a tender offer to purchase Link's stock	Report of proxy solicitations by Link stockholders
a.	Yes	Yes
b.	Yes	No
c.	No	Yes
d.	No	No

(11/94, Law, #47, 5224)

42. Universal Corp. intends to sell its common stock to the public in an interstate offering that will be registered under the Securities Act of 1933. Under the Act,
a. Universal can make offers to sell its stock before filing a registration statement, provided that it does **not** actually issue stock certificates until after the registration is effective.
b. Universal's registration statement becomes effective at the time it is filed, assuming the SEC does **not** object within 20 days thereafter.
c. A prospectus must be delivered to each purchaser of Universal's common stock unless the purchaser qualifies as an accredited investor.
d. Universal's filing of a registration statement with the SEC does **not** automatically result in compliance with the "blue-sky" laws of the states in which the offering will be made.

(5/91, Law, #40, 0737)

43. Wool, Inc. is a reporting company under the Securities Exchange Act of 1934. The only security it has issued is its voting common stock. Which of the following statements is correct?
a. It is unnecessary for the required annual report (Form 10-K) to include audited financial statements.
b. Any person who owns more than 5% of Wool's common stock must file a report with the SEC.

c. Because Wool is a reporting company, it is **not** required to file a registration statement under the Securities Act of 1933 for any future offerings of its common stock.

d. Wool need **not** file its proxy statements with the SEC because it has only one class of stock outstanding. (11/91, Law, #27, 2355)

44. The reporting and registration provisions of the Securities Exchange Act of 1934

a. Do **not** require registration by a corporation if its stock was originally issued under an offering exempt from registration under the Securities Act of 1933.

b. Do **not** require registration by a corporation unless its stock is listed on a national securities exchange.

c. Require a corporation reporting under the Act to register any offering of its securities under the Securities Act of 1933.

d. Require a corporation reporting under the Act to file its proxy statements with the SEC even if it has only one class of stock outstanding. (11/91, Law, #39, 2367)

45. Jay and Co., CPAs, audited the financial statements of Maco Corp. Jay intentionally gave an unqualified opinion on the financial statements even though material misstatements were discovered. The financial statements and Jay's unqualified opinion were included in a registration statement and prospectus for an original public offering of Maco stock. Which of the following statements is correct regarding Jay's liability to a purchaser of the offering under Section 10(b) and Rule 10b-5 of the Securities Exchange Act of 1934?

a. Jay will be liable if the purchaser relied on Jay's unqualified opinion on the financial statements.

b. Jay will be liable if Jay was negligent in conducting the audit.

c. Jay will **not** be liable if the purchaser's loss was under $500.

d. Jay will **not** be liable if the misstatement resulted from an omission of a material fact by Jay. (11/93, Law, #6, 4303)

46. Corporations that are exempt from registration under the Securities Exchange Act of 1934 are subject to the Act's

a. Antifraud provisions.

b. Proxy solicitation provisions.

c. Provisions dealing with the filing of annual reports.

d. Provisions imposing periodic audits.
(5/93, Law, #31, 3999)

47. The antifraud provisions of Rule 10b-5 of the Securities Exchange Act of 1934

a. Apply only if the securities involved were registered under either the Securities Act of 1933 or the Securities Exchange Act of 1934.

b. Require that the plaintiff show negligence on the part of the defendant in misstating facts.

c. Require that the wrongful act must be accomplished through the mail, any other use of interstate commerce, or through a national securities exchange.

d. Apply only if the defendant acted with intent to defraud. (5/91, Law, #44, 0740)

Solution 55-1 MULTIPLE CHOICE ANSWERS

Securities Act of 1933

1. (c) Under the Securities Act of 1933, securities are defined broadly as any security that allows an investor to make a profit on an investment through the efforts of others rather than through his or her own efforts. Therefore, a general partnership interest would not likely be considered a security under the 1933 Act since partners in a general partnership have a right to manage and are considered active in the management of the business. Under the 1933 Act, securities are broadly defined to include stock options, warrants, and limited partnership interests.

2. (b) The 1933 Act makes it unlawful for any person, directly or indirectly, to make use of any means or instruments of interstate commerce to carry or transmit for the purpose of sale, any security, including common stock, unless such security is accompanied or preceded by a prospectus that meets the requirements of the Act.

3. (b) Under the Securities Act of 1933, registration of certain securities is required to provide investors with information material to making an investment decision. The registration statement will generally include a description of the issuer's business and property, a description of management, a description of the security to be issued and its relationship to the issuer's other securities, and the

issuer's most recent certified financial statement. The investor is generally not provided information on the stockholders of the offering corporation. The SEC does not guarantee the accuracy of the information in registration statements, nor does it assure against loss.

4. (b) The registration requirements of the Securities Act of 1933 are intended to ensure that investors are provided with adequate information on which to base investment decisions. The SEC does not evaluate the financial merits of the securities being offered or prevent public offerings of securities when management fraud or *unethical* conduct is *suspected*. The SEC makes no representation of the accuracy of the facts presented in the financial statements.

Exempted Securities

5. (a) Securities exempt from the registration requirements of the Securities Act of 1933 are not exempt from the Act's fraud provisions. The 1933 Act provides that both the SEC and persons defrauded may challenge fraudulent activities.

6. (a) Certain securities are exempt from registration under the Securities Act of 1933. Included in those listed are bonds issued by a municipality for governmental purposes and securities issued by a not-for-profit charitable organization. Also, if bonds are issued by a municipality for nongovernmental purposes, the bonds would not be exempt. Thus, not all municipal bonds are exempt.

7. (b) Among those securities that are exempt from registration under the 1933 Act is a class of stock given in exchange for another class by the issuer to its existing stockholders without the issuer paying a commission. Answers (a), (c), and (d) are not among the specified exempt securities.

8. (d) The Securities Act of 1933 exempts certain securities from its registration requirements. These exempted securities include those issued by not-for-profit, charitable organizations, those guaranteed by domestic governmental organizations, and those issued by savings and loan associations. Although the Act exempts insurance policies and annuity contracts, securities issued by insurance companies are not exempt.

9. (a) The Securities Act of 1933 provides an exemption from its registration requirements for intrastate offerings. In order to qualify for this exemption, all securities that are part of the issue must be sold to persons residing within the same state as the issuer. Also, resales of the offering may only be made to residents of the issuer's state of residence for a period of at least nine months.

10. (b) The issuance of stock warrants is subject to the §5 registration requirements of the Securities Act of 1933. Security swaps or distributions by the issuer with its existing security holders exclusively, where no commission or other remuneration is given, are exempted from the registration requirements of the 1933 Act. Securities issued by governments or quasi-governmental authorities, such as banks, carriers, building and loan associations, and farm cooperatives, are exempted from the Act's registration requirements.

11. (b) Securities of a bank are specifically listed as being exempt from registration under the Securities Act of 1933. Exempt securities may be sold and resold any number of times and never be subject to the registration and/or prospectus requirements of the Act. These exemptions are granted because (1) it is felt that registration is not necessary to protect the public interest, (2) the securities are regulated by another government agency, or (3) the nature of the security, for example commercial paper, necessitates that it be exempt. Answers (a), (c), and (d) are all securities or offerings that are not specifically listed as exempt, and must be registered under the 1933 Act.

12. (b) Offerings made under Regulation A are exempt from the *full* registration requirement of the 1933 Act. Answer (a) is incorrect because intrastate *securities* are exempt and the question asks for exempt *transactions*. Note: This is not a well-worded question, thus answer (a) could potentially be correct because under the 1933 Act, there are no registration requirements where a valid intrastate offering is made. Resales of securities purchased pursuant to a Regulation D offering are restricted and subject to full registration requirements. Stockholder transactions are not specifically exempt from compliance with the 1933 Act's filing requirements.

Exempted Transactions

13. (a) The SEC has amended Rule 504 of Regulation D, so that there are no longer restrictions on the resale of securities purchased in a Rule 504 offering. Rule 504 does not disallow the sale of securities to any class of investors. The Rule 504 exemption is available to the issuers of limited partnership interests. Rule 504 does not place restrictions on the class or number of investors to whom the securities may be sold.

14. (b) Regulation D of the Securities Act of 1933 permits an exempt offering to be sold to both accredited and nonaccredited investors. Rule 504 of Regulation D does not restrict the number of purchasers. Rule 505 restricts the sale to up to 35 "nonaccredited investors" and an unlimited number of "accredited investors" within 12 months. Rule 506 restricts the sale to an unlimited number of "accredited investors" and up to 35 sophisticated "unaccredited investors." Rule 504 of Regulation D restricts the sale to $1,000,000. Rule 505 restricts the sale to $5,000,000 and Rule 506 is unlimited. Regulation D does not restrict sales to $1.5 million. Regulation D is not restricted to small business corporations.

14A. (d) Investors in a private placement pursuant to Regulation D must buy the securities for investment purposes and not with the intention of an immediate reoffering to the public. Normally, securities purchased pursuant to Regulation D should be held for two years. Answer (a) is incorrect because there is no such rule. Regulation D permits sales to 35 non-accredited investors plus an unlimited number of accredited investors.

14B. (The BOE gave credit for all responses.) Under Regulation D of the Securities Act of 1933, only Rules 505 and 506 require that the offering be made without general advertising. Regulation D does not require that the SEC be notified within 10 days, nor that there be a maximum of investors, nor that accredited investors receive financial information.

15. (a) Rule 504 of the Securities Act of 1933 permits the sale of up to $1 million of securities to an unlimited number of investors. The offering may be publicly promoted.

16. (c) The Securities Act of 1933 exempts transactions made by any person other than an issuer, underwriter, or dealer. There are no provisions in the Act to exempt securities that are nonvoting preferred stock, nor to exempt securities of a closely held corporation, nor AAA-rated debentures.

17. (a) There is no restriction concerning debentures being offered under Rule 506 of Regulation D of the Securities Act of 1933. There is no requirement that the issuing company be incorporated. Rule 506 permits an unlimited amount of money from an unlimited number of "accredited purchasers" and 35 "nonaccredited investors." A general solicitation is not permitted under Rule 506.

18. (d) Rule 504 permits nonpublic companies not registered under the Securities Act of 1934 to offer securities for sale without fulfilling the Section 5 (1933 Act) registration and disclosure requirements. *Resale restrictions* no longer apply to securities sold under Rule 504 of Regulation D. There is no restriction on the type of security offered for sale under Rule 504. Unlike Rules 505 and 506, Rule 504 does not place any restrictions on the type or number of investors to whom the securities may be sold.

19. (d) The 1933 Act is concerned with the original issuance of securities intended for sale to the public, provided the transaction or any communication relating to it involves interstate commerce. There are, however, some types of securities or offerings that are specifically exempt. Therefore, unless specifically exempt, an initial offering of securities must be registered with the SEC.

19A. (d) Under the Securities Act of 1933, certain transactions in securities are exempt from the Act's registration requirements. Resales of the securities, however, may not be exempt from registration, or resales may be exempt from registration by a different exemption provision, such as the "safe harbor" provisions of SEC Rule 144. Where a specified transaction is exempt, it is not subject to the Act's registration requirements. A transaction that is exempt from the Act's registration requirements is not exempt from the Act's anti-fraud provisions.

20. (d) Under Rule 504 of Regulation D, Imperial is required to notify the SEC within 15 days after the first sale of the securities. No specific disclosure is required under Rule 504. Under Rule 504 of Regulation D, a general solicitation is allowed, but not required. The purpose of meeting the requirements of Regulation D is to avoid the general registration of the 1934 Act.

21. (c) Under Rule 505, sales can be made to no more than 35 nonaccredited investors and to an unlimited number of accredited investors. An audited balance sheet and other financial statements must be supplied to the nonaccredited investors. No general solicitation is allowed under Rule 505. Sales to non-accredited investors cannot exceed 35 in number.

21A. (c) Rule 505 of Regulation D requires that the offering be reported to the SEC within 15 days after the first sale of the offering. The number of nonaccredited purchasers is limited to 35. Rule 505 specifically prohibits general advertisement. The required information includes audited financial statements and not a prospectus.

22. (a)   Rule 506 (also Rule 505) does not allow a general solicitation. Rule 506 allows sales to nonaccredited investors who are "sophisticated investors" (cannot exceed 35 in number). Under Rule 506, sales can be made to an unlimited number of accredited investors. Under Rule 506, the SEC must be notified within 15 days after the first sale of the securities. Thus, notifying the SEC 14 days after the first sale would not cause the securities to lose their exemption.

23. (d)   The amount of the stock offering eliminates all possibilities except for Rule 506, which has no limit. Any offering exceeding $5,000,000 will be required to use Rule 506.

23A. (b)   Rule 506 places a limit on the number of nonaccredited investors eligible to purchase securities in the stock offering. The 35 nonaccredited investors must also "have such knowledge and...financial experience as to be capable of evaluating the offering's merits and risks..."

Registration Process--1933 Act

24. (a)   Under the Federal Securities Act of 1933, a prospectus is part of the registration statement and must be filed with the Securities and Exchange Commission (SEC). The SEC does not pass on the merits of securities offered for sale. The SEC merely requires that certain information be provided to security purchasers to enable them to make knowledgeable investment decisions. The prospectus and registration statement must be filed with the SEC before any offer to sell can be made. A preliminary prospectus may be distributed during the 20-day waiting period. Furthermore, although the SEC looks for material deficiencies in the financial statement, it does not approve the accuracy of the facts contained therein.

25. (d)   A "red herring" prospectus is a limited preliminary prospectus that must accompany any written offers to sell an initial issue of a security after the filing of the registration period and during the 20-day waiting period. Although the financial statement which is part of the registration statement must be audited, and the audit should be unqualified, there is no such thing as an unaudited, qualified, or "Blue Sky" prospectus.

26. (d)   A tombstone advertisement is a written advertisement that informs potential investors where and how they may obtain a prospectus. Normally, this is the only type of post-waiting period advertising permitted under the 1933 Federal Securities Act. The tombstone advertisement does not serve as a substitute for a prospectus nor may it contain an offer to sell.

27. (c)   Under the Securities Act of 1933, an issuer of securities who has made a registered offering is required to distribute an annual report with the SEC. The 1933 Act does not require the issuance of an annual report to the stockholders. The requirements for filing form 10-Q as well as rules pertaining to proxy solicitation are all governed by the Securities Exchange Act of 1934, not the 1933 Act.

27A. (b)   Regulation D, Rule 506 of the Securities Act of 1933 provides for an exemption from registration for private placement offerings of an unlimited number of securities made within a 12 month period to up to 35 sophisticated unaccredited investors and to an unlimited number of accredited investors. Resale of securities purchased pursuant to Rules 505 and 506 are restricted and thus cannot be the subject of an immediate unregistered public offering. The securities may be sold to more than 35 unaccredited investors in a 12 month period. Securities may be sold to up to 35 sophisticated unaccredited investors.

27B. (a)   "Reg. A" is a less restrictive method of registration than is a full registration under Section 5 of the 1933 Act. Under "Reg. A," sales must be made using an "offering circular" rather than a prospectus. Each purchaser must be provided with an "offering circular." There are no restrictions placed on the purchasers of the securities. "Reg. A" does not require that this [answer (c)] information be provided to the purchasers. The only information required to be distributed to the purchaser is the offering circular.

28. (a)   Once the registration statement and prospectus are filed with the SEC, oral offers and/or written offers (note, however, that written offers can only be made through a statutory prospectus) may be made to sell the shares. These offers may be extended throughout the "waiting period," which in this question begins on May 10th (the filing date) and ends on May 30th (the effective date).

29. (d)   Securities subject to the Securities Act of 1933 may only be sold after the effective date, provided that the buyer has received a final prospectus. The effective date is that date on which the SEC declares the registration effective. In this question it was stated that the registration became effective on May 30.

30. (b)   Securities and Exchange Commission (SEC) Rule 415 permits shelf registration of securities. A shelf registration is only available to

established (as opposed to first-time) issuers and enables the issuer to file a registration statement and then put the securities "on the shelf" until an opportune time to offer the securities arises. Rule 415 requires that the original registration statement be continuously updated.

Civil Liability--1933 Act

31. (b)   Under the provisions of Section 11 of the Securities Act of 1933, a CPA will be liable to a purchaser of securities if the financial statement either omits or misstates a material fact. The CPA may avoid liability by showing that he or she acted with due diligence. Pursuant to the 1933 Act, the purchaser need not prove privity or scienter to impose liability. Contributory negligence by the purchaser is not a defense under Section 11.

32. (b)   This problem describes an original public offering of stock and is thus governed by the rules of the Securities Act of 1933, Section 11. The 1934 Act covers subsequent trading of securities and so is not applicable to the facts of this problem. The 1933 Act does not require that a purchaser rely on the registration in order to recover damages, and Thorp appears to have satisfied the remaining requirements to file suit. He was a purchaser of the security, and he suffered an economic loss. Thus, it is likely that Thorp will prevail against Ivor under the 1933 Act.

33. (d)   An action brought under the 1933 Securities Act does not require that the injured party prove that he or she relied on the misleading information, but he or she is required to prove he or she actually incurred a loss. Privity of contract is not a requirement as the 1933 Act is designed to protect the "investing public." The plaintiff does not have to prove negligence in the issuance of the securities, only that the misleading information was material. Any person acquiring securities covered by the registration statement is covered by the Act. There is no requirement that value be given for the security.

34. (c)   Under the 1933 Act, the investor, in bringing a suit against a CPA for misstatements in the financial statements, is only required to prove the existence of a false statement or material omission and that the security he purchased was offered through the inaccurate registration statement. He does not have the burden of proving that the accountant was fraudulent or negligent. Also, it is not necessary for the purchaser to prove that he relied on the accountant's error.

Securities Act of 1934

35. (d)   The statutory definition of a security includes conventional securities, such as stocks, bonds, or notes and any interest or instrument commonly known as a "security." It also includes any certificate or interest or participation in, temporary or interim certificate for, receipt for, guarantee of, or warrant or right to subscribe to or purchase, any of the foregoing. A certificate of deposit is a written acknowledgement by a bank of the receipt of a stated sum of money with an engagement to repay that sum. A certificate of deposit does not represent an interest in or participation in a company and, therefore, does not meet the definition of a security.

36. (b)   A corporation with stock listed on a national stock exchange is required to register under the 1934 Act. The Securities Exchange Commission may suspend or revoke the registration of persons, exchanges, or securities, as required by the 1933 and 1934 Acts. Rules 505 and 506 of Regulation D allow publicly listed companies to make private placements if they meet certain requirements. An issuer of securities under the 1934 Act must file Form 10-K annually, regardless of whether it has made a public offering in a certain year. Form 10-K should not be confused with reports to shareholders. Companies are not required under the 1934 Act to distribute Form 10-K to their stockholders.

Reporting Requirements--1934 Act

37. (b)   An owner of five percent of a corporation's voting stock is not subject to the insider reporting provisions of the Securities Exchange Act of 1934. The other answers are all subject to insider trading provisions. An insider is an officer, director, or owner of 10% or more of the stock.

37A. (b)   Insiders are directors, officers, employees, and agents of the issuer, as well as others privy to information that is not available to the general public. An owner of debenture bonds does not gain access to corporate information which is unavailable to the general public. Therefore, the owner of debenture bonds is not an insider with respect to the corporation. An attorney is an agent of the corporation and is privy to corporate information not available to the general public so he/she qualifies as an insider. A director is specifically designated an insider due to the position he/she holds and information he/she has access to. Those stockholders owning 10% of equity securities registered under Section 12 of the 1934 Act are designated insiders by the SEC.

38. (c) The 1934 Act requires that every issuer registered under the 1934 Act file annual reports. It also requires that certain specified events be reported. National securities exchanges must file reports, and directors and officers must report to the SEC. Finally, any persons having a 10% interest in a registered entity must file a report with the SEC. Answer (a) is an entity which the 1934 Act specifically requires to file. Adler is required to file its proxy statements with the SEC regardless of the number of classes of stock outstanding. The 1934 Act specifically requires that audited financial statements be included in the Form 10K.

39. (b) A plaintiff who sues a CPA for damages under the anti-fraud provisions of the 1934 Act need not prove that the CPA violated generally accepted auditing standards, for this could be evidence of ordinary negligence, not scienter. Under the 1934 Act, the plaintiff would have to prove that he relied on the statements, that there was a material misstatement in the statements, and that the CPA acted with scienter (intent to deceive or defraud).

40. (b) The Securities Exchange Act of 1934 requires corporations whose securities are traded on a national exchange to comply with the reporting provisions of the Act. The Act's reporting requirements are not based on the number of classes of stock.

41. (a) An issuer registered under the 1934 Securities Exchange Act must file quarterly reports (Form 10-Q). The 1934 Act also requires that before any proxy may be solicited, each person solicited must be provided with a proxy statement. The proxy statement must also be filed with the SEC at least 10 days prior to being sent to the shareholders.

41A. (a) Rule 13 of the 1934 Securities Exchange Act requires any party making a tender offer to file a report (Schedule 13D) with the SEC. The Act also requires that, prior to soliciting a proxy from any shareholder, a proxy statement, form of proxy, and annual reports be filed with the SEC.

Proxy Solicitation and Tender Offers

42. (d) The filing of a registration statement with the SEC does not automatically result in compliance with the "blue-sky" laws of the states in which the offering will be made. Each state will have their own securities laws ("blue-sky" laws) and compliance is necessary with both the state and with the SEC. There is no automatic state exemption just because the SEC has approved the offering. There can be no offers to sell until the registration statement is filed with the SEC. Once the registration is filed with the SEC, offers to sell may be made during the 20-day "waiting period." The registration does not become effective until the end of the 20-day period, assuming the SEC does not object. A prospectus must be delivered to each purchaser regardless if they are accredited or not.

43. (b) The Securities Exchange Act of 1934 regulates stock purchases and tender-offers by persons acquiring more than 5% of a company's equity securities. Hence, any person who owns more than 5% of a reporting company's common stock must file a report with the SEC. The required annual report (Form 10-K) must contain financial statements audited by independent public accountants. A reporting company under the 1934 Act is not exempt from the filing requirements of the 1933 Act. Wool is required to file its proxy statements with the SEC at least 10 days before such information is sent to the stockholders.

44. (d) For a proper proxy registration, the proxy statements must be filed with the SEC. The number of classes of stock is immaterial for filing purposes.

Anti-Fraud Provisions

45. (a) Among the requirements for an action under Section 10(b) and Rule 10b-5 of the Securities Act of 1934 are intent, material misstatement or omission, and justifiable reliance by the innocent party. The facts of the problem stipulate all of these requirements except "reliance." Therefore, reliance is the element which must be proven by the purchaser. Negligence is not a required component in a fraud action under the securities act. There is no minimum dollar amount on losses covered by the Securities Act of 1934. The facts of the problem stipulate that the misstatements were discovered by the auditor. The client's knowledge has no effect on the accountant's liability.

46. (a) Even if a corporation is exempt from registration under the Securities Exchange Act of 1934, it is still subject to the Act's antifraud provisions. Provisions dealing with proxy solicitation, filing of annual reports, and imposing periodic audits do not apply if the corporation is exempt from registration under the 1934 Act.

47. (c) The Securities Exchange Act of 1934 applies (including the antifraud provisions) if "interstate" commerce is involved, such as where transactions use the mail, or any other use of interstate commerce, or through the use of a national securities exchange. The antifraud provisions of the

'34 Act will apply even if the securities were not required to be registered under the 1933 or 1934 Securities Act. There is no requirement that the plaintiff must show negligence on the part of the defendant in misstating facts. It is not necessary to show that the defendant acted with intent to defraud. Gross negligence would be enough for the antifraud provisions to apply. However, in order to recover a loss, a seller or purchaser of securities must prove the defendant acted with the intent to defraud (scienter).

PERFORMANCE BY SUBTOPICS

Each category below parallels a subtopic covered in Chapter 55. Record the number and percentage of questions you correctly answered in each subtopic area.

Securities Act of 1933

Question #	Correct √
1	
2	
3	
4	
# Questions	4
# Correct	_____
% Correct	_____

Exempted Securities

Question #	Correct √
5	
6	
7	
8	
9	
10	
11	
12	
# Questions	8
# Correct	_____
% Correct	_____

Exempted Transactions

Question #	Correct √
13	
14	
14A	
14B	
15	
16	
17	
18	
19	
19A	
20	
21	
21A	
22	
23	
23A	
# Questions	16
# Correct	_____
% Correct	_____

Registration Process--1933 Act

Question #	Correct √
24	
25	
26	
27	
27A	
27B	
28	
29	
30	
# Questions	9
# Correct	_____
% Correct	_____

Civil Liability--1933 Act

Question #	Correct √
31	
32	
33	
34	
# Questions	4
# Correct	_____
% Correct	_____

Securities Act of 1934

Question #	Correct √
35	
36	
# Questions	2
# Correct	_____
% Correct	_____

Reporting Requirements--1934 Act

Question #	Correct √
37	
37A	
38	
39	
40	
41	
41A	
# Questions	7
# Correct	_____
% Correct	_____

Proxy Solicitation and Tender Offers

Question #	Correct √
42	
43	
44	
# Questions	3
# Correct	_____
% Correct	_____

Anti-Fraud Provisions

Question #	Correct √
45	
46	
47	
# Questions	3
# Correct	_____
% Correct	_____

10% Insider   Tender offer
                          5%
must file report with SEC

OTHER OBJECTIVE FORMAT QUESTIONS

Problem 55-2 (10 to 15 minutes)

Items 1 through 6 are based on the following:

Under Section 11 of the Securities Act of 1933 and Section 10(b), Rule 10b-5 of the Securities Exchange Act of 1934, a CPA may be sued by a purchaser of registered securities.

Required:

Items 1 through 6 relate to what a plaintiff who purchased securities must prove in a civil liability suit against a CPA. For each item determine whether the statement must be proven under Section 11 of the Securities Act of 1933, under Section (10)b, Rule 10b-5 of the Securities Exchange Act of 1934, both Acts, or neither Act.

- If the item must be proven **only** under Section 11 of the Securities Act of 1933, select (A).
- If the item must be proven **only** under Section 10(b), Rule 10b-5, of the Securities Exchange Act of 1934, select (B).
- If the item must be proven under **both** Acts, select (C).
- If the item must be proven under **neither** of the Acts, select (D).

The plaintiff security purchaser must allege or prove:

1. Material misstatements were included in a filed document. C
2. A monetary loss occurred. C
3. Lack of due diligence by the CPA. D
4. Privity with the CPA. D
5. Reliance on the document. B
6. The CPA had scienter. B (5/94, Law, #61-65)

Problem 55-3 (15 to 25 minutes)

Butler Manufacturing Corp. planned to raise capital for a plant expansion by borrowing from banks and making several stock offerings. Butler engaged Weaver, CPA, to audit its December 31, 1989, financial statements. Butler told Weaver that the financial statements would be given to certain named banks and included in the prospectuses for the stock offerings.

In performing the audit, Weaver did not confirm accounts receivable and, as a result, failed to discover a material overstatement of accounts receivable. Also, Weaver was aware of a pending class action product liability lawsuit that was not disclosed in Butler's financial statements. Despite being advised by Butler's legal counsel that Butler's potential liability under the lawsuit would result in material losses, Weaver issued an unqualified opinion on Butler's financial statements.

In May 1990, Union Bank, one of the named banks, relied on the financial statements and Weaver's opinion in giving Butler a $500,000 loan.

Butler raised an additional $16,450,000 through the following stock offerings, which were sold completely:

- June 1990--Butler made a $450,000 unregistered offering of Class B nonvoting common stock under Rule 504 of Regulation D of the Securities Act of 1933. This offering was sold over two years to 30 nonaccredited investors and 20 accredited investors by general solicitation. The SEC was notified eight days after the first sale of this offering.

- September 1990--Butler made a $10,000,000 unregistered offering of Class A voting common stock under Rule 506 of Regulation D of the Securities Act of 1933. This offering was sold over two years to 200 accredited investors and 30 nonaccredited investors through a private placement. The SEC was notified 14 days after the first sale of this offering.

- November 1990--Butler made a $6,000,000 unregistered offering of preferred stock under Rule 505 of Regulation D of the Securities Act of 1933. This offering was sold during a one-year period to 40 nonaccredited investors by private placement. The SEC was notified 18 days after the first sale of this offering.

Shortly after obtaining the Union loan, Butler began experiencing financial problems but was able to stay in business because of the money raised by the offerings. Butler was found liable in the product liability suit. This resulted in a judgment Butler could not pay. Butler also defaulted on the Union loan and was involuntarily petitioned into bankruptcy. This caused Union to sustain a loss and Butler's stockholders to lose their investments.

As a result:

- The SEC claimed that all three of Butler's offerings were made improperly and were not exempt from registration.

- Union sued Weaver for
  - Negligence
  - Common Law Fraud
- The stockholders who purchased Butler's stock through the offerings sued Weaver, alleging fraud under Section 10(b) and Rule 10b-5 of the Securities Exchange Act of 1934.

These transactions took place in a jurisdiction providing for accountant's liability for negligence to known and intended users of financial statements.

Required:

a. **Items 1 through 5** are questions related to the June 1990 offering made under Rule 504 of Regulation D of the Securities Act of 1933.

1. Did the offering comply with the dollar limitation of Rule 504?
2. Did the offering comply with the method of sale restrictions?
3. Was the offering sold during the applicable time limit?
4. Was the SEC notified timely of the first sale of the securities?
5. Was the SEC correct in claiming that this offering was not exempt from registration?

b. **Items 6 through 10** are questions related to the September 1990 offering made under Rule 506 of Regulation D of the Securities Act of 1933.

6. Did the offering comply with the dollar limitation of Rule 506?
7. Did the offering comply with the method of sale restrictions?
8. Was the offering sold to the correct number of investors?
9. Was the SEC notified timely of the first sale of the securities?
10. Was the SEC correct in claiming that this offering was not exempt from registration?

c. **Items 11 through 15** are questions related to the November 1990 offering made under Rule 505 of Regulation D of the Securities Act of 1933.

11. Did the offering comply with the dollar limitation of Rule 505?
12. Was the offering sold during the applicable time limit?
13. Was the offering sold to the correct number of investors?
14. Was the SEC notified timely of the first sale of the securities?
15. Was the SEC correct in claiming that this offering was not exempt from registration?

(11/92, Law, #2)

OTHER OBJECTIVE FORMAT SOLUTIONS

Solution 55-2   Securities Acts of 1933 and 1934

1. **(C)** A purchaser of securities may bring a civil suit for fraud under Section 11 of the Securities Act of 1933. A purchaser or seller of securities may bring a civil action for fraud under Section 10(b), Rule 10b-5 of the Securities Exchange Act of 1934. Under both statutes, a plaintiff must prove that there were material misstatements or omissions in the filed document(s).

2. **(C)** A plaintiff bringing a civil suit for fraud under either Section 11 of the Securities Act of 1933 or Section 10(b) of the Securities Exchange Act of 1934 must prove that they sustained a loss. If no loss can be proven, then there is nothing on which a court can base a damage award.

3. **(D)** Lack of due diligence on the part of the CPA need not be proven by a plaintiff in a civil suit under either Section 11 of the 1933 Act or Rule 10(b) of the 1934 Act. Due diligence is a defense available to CPAs and others who are sued for violation of Section 11 of the Securities Act of 1933.

4. **(D)** Neither Section 11 of the Securities Act of 1933 nor Rule 10(b) of the Securities Exchange Act of 1934 requires that a plaintiff in a civil suit prove that he or she was in privity of contract with the CPA.

5. **(B)** Under Section 11 of the Securities Act of 1933, it is not necessary for a plaintiff in a civil action to prove reliance on the document. Material omissions or misstatements in the filed document are sufficient to trigger liability where a plaintiff has suffered a loss. However, under Rule 10(b) of the Securities Exchange Act of 1934, it is necessary that a plaintiff prove his or her reliance on the document.

6. **(B)** Under Section 11 of the Securities Act of 1933 it is not necessary for a plaintiff in a civil action to prove that the CPA had scienter. Material omissions or misstatements in the filed documents are sufficient to trigger liability where a plaintiff has

suffered a loss. However, under Rule 10(b) of the Securities Exchange Act of 1934 it is necessary that a plaintiff prove that the CPA had scienter.

Solution 55-3 Securities Act of 1933/Issuance of Securities

1.   (Yes) Rule 504 allows up to $1,000,000 in interstate sales. In this case the offering was for $450,000.

2.   (Yes) Rule 504 allows an offering by general solicitation.

3.   (No) Rule 504 specifies that the sale must be completed within 12 months. In this case the sale took place over two years.

4.   (Yes) Under Rule 504 the issuer must notify the SEC within 15 days of the sale. In this case the notification was made eight days after the first sale.

5.   (Yes) This offering was not exempt because the offering was not sold during the applicable time limit.

6.   (Yes) Rule 506 does not set a dollar limit on the amount of the sale.

7.   (Yes) Rule 506 does not prohibit a sale made by private placement.

8.   (Yes) Rule 506 limits the sale to 35 nonaccredited investors and an unlimited number of accredited investors. In this case, the offering was sold to 30 nonaccredited investors and 200 accredited investors.

9.   (Yes) Under Rule 506 the issuer must notify the SEC within 15 days of the sale. In this case the notification was made 14 days after the sale.

10.   (No) This offering would be permitted under Rule 506, since it did not violate any of the applicable requirements.

11.   (No) Rule 505 sets a dollar limit of $5,000,000 for a sale. In this case, the sale was for $6,000,000.

12.   (Yes) Rule 505 specifies that the sale must take place within twelve months. In this case it was stated that the sale took place during a one-year time period.

13.   (No) Rule 505 limits the sale to 35 nonaccredited investors. In this case the sale was made to 40 nonaccredited investors.

14.   (No) Under Rule 505 the issuer must notify the SEC within 15 days of the sale. In this case the notification was made 18 days after the sale.

15.   (Yes) This offering was not exempt because it did not comply with the dollar limit of the sale, the limits on the number of nonaccredited investors, or with the requirement governing notification of the SEC.

ESSAY QUESTION

Essay 55-4 (15 to 20 minutes)

One of your firm's clients, Fancy Fashions, Inc., is a highly successful, rapidly expanding company. The company is owned predominantly by the Munn family and key corporate officers. Although additional funds would be available on a short-term basis from its bankers, this would only represent a short-term solution to the company's need for capital to fund its expansion plans. In addition, the interest rates being charged are not appealing. Therefore, John Munn, Fancy's chairman of the board, in consultation with the other shareholders, has decided to explore raising additional equity capital of approximately $5.5 to $6 million which will provide the funds necessary to continue the growth and expansion of the company.

This will be Fancy's first offering to persons other than the Munn family and key management personnel.

At a meeting of Fancy's major shareholders, its attorneys and a CPA from your firm, the advantages and disadvantages of "going public" and registering an offering of its stock were discussed. One of the participants suggested that Regulation D under the Securities Act of 1933 might be a preferable alternative.

Required:

Answer the following, setting forth reasons for any conclusions stated. [**NOTE**: Certain changes were made to reflect current law--Ed.]

a. What are the elements or factors which will determine whether Fancy's offering is required to be registered pursuant to the provisions of the Securities Act of 1933?

b. Assume there is a public offering for $5.5 million and, as a result, more than 500 persons own shares of Fancy. What implications, if any, will these facts have in respect to the Securities Exchange Act of 1934?

c. What federal civil and criminal liabilities may apply in the event that Fancy sells the securities without a registration and an exemption to registration is not available?

d. Discuss the exemption applicable to offerings of up to $5 million (under Rule 505 of Regulation D) in terms of:

  1. What are the two kinds of and the number of investors who may participate?
  2. Are audited financial statements required?
  3. What restrictions apply to the manner or way the securities may be sold?   (11/85, Law, #5)

ESSAY SOLUTION

Solution 55-4 Securities Acts of 1933 and 1934/ Exemptions

a. There are four elements or factors to be considered in determining whether an offering of securities is subject to the registration requirements of the Securities Act of 1933. These are:

- The **use of interstate commerce**, e.g., the mail, in connection with the offer to sell or the sale of securities.
- The **offering** of said securities is to the "**public.**"
- The **offering** or sale is **made by an issuer, controlling person, or "statutory" underwriter.**
- There is **no relevant exemption** available.

b. Since the sale of equity securities results in **more than 500 persons** owning Fancy stock, coupled with the fact that Fancy will have **more than $5 million of assets**, the corporation will be **subjected to the full application of the Securities Exchange Act of 1934.** As such, it will be **required to register** pursuant to the Act and thereby become **subject to the Act's reporting, insider trading, proxy, and other requirements.**

c. The Securities Act of 1933 provides that if there is a violation of the Act as a **result of the failure to file a registration statement**, the parties responsible shall be liable upon tender of the securities purchased for the **amount paid, plus interest, less any distributions received. Damages are recoverable even if the party no longer owns the securities. Criminal penalties of a fine or imprisonment or both** are applicable to any person who willfully violates the Securities Act of 1933.

d. An **offering pursuant to Regulation D is exempt from registration**. Regulation D is intended to permit exemption from registration of **limited offers and sales by small businesses in need of capital**.

  1. There are two kinds of investors under Rule 505 of Regulation D: **accredited investors** as defined in the Regulation and all others who are designated as **non-accredited investors**. An **unlimited number of accredited investors** is permitted, but a **maximum of 35 non-accredited investors** is permitted.
  2. Under Rule 505, if **non-accredited investors are involved** and Fancy is a nonreporting company under the Securities Exchange Act of 1934, it **must supply audited financial statements** for one year. If an audit of the most recent year would involve unreasonable effort or expense, an **audited balance sheet only, dated within 120 days of the start of the offering**, is permitted.
  3. Rule 505 **prohibits** any **general solicitation or general advertising** of the securities **within a 12-month period.**

NOTES

CHAPTER 56

REAL AND PERSONAL PROPERTY

I. Definitions 56-2

II. Overview 56-2

III. Freehold Estates 56-3
    A. Fee Simple 56-3
    B. Life Estate 56-4

IV. Future Interests 56-5
    A. Possibility of Reverter 56-5
    B. Reversion 56-5
    C. Right of Reentry 56-5
    D. Remainder 56-5
    E. Executory Interest 56-5

V. Concurrent Estates in Land 56-6
    A. Joint Tenancy 56-6
    B. Tenancy in Common 56-6
    C. Tenancy by the Entirety 56-6
    D. Rights and Duties Among Co-Tenants 56-7

VI. Acquisition of Real Property 56-7
    A. Executory Contract for the Sale of Land 56-7
    B. The Deed 56-9
    C. Recording Statutes 56-10
    D. Covenants of Title 56-10
    E. Adverse Possession 56-10

VII. Landlord and Tenant 56-11
    A. Types of Tenancies 56-11
    B. Rights, Duties, and Liabilities of the Landlord 56-12
    C. Rights, Duties, and Liabilities of the Tenant 56-14
    D. Termination of the Leasehold Estate 56-15

VIII. Mortgages 56-16
    A. Formalities in the Execution of a Mortgage Agreement 56-16
    B. Recording of a Mortgage 56-16
    C. Common Provisions of a Mortgage Agreement 56-17
    D. Rights of the Parties 56-17
    E. Sale of Mortgaged Property 56-18
    F. Termination of the Mortgage Interest 56-18

IX. Environmental Protection 56-18

X. Personal Property 56-19
    A. Methods of Acquisition and Transfer 56-19
    B. Bailment 56-20

CHAPTER 56

REAL AND PERSONAL PROPERTY

I. Definitions

Most of the terms pertinent to this topic are complex and closely tied to a particular subtopic. For these reasons, they will be defined as they arise within this outline. Several of the more common terms, which will be encountered in multiple areas, are defined below.

A.   Alienable--An alienable right or interest may be properly transferred from the holder to another person.

B.   Condition Precedent--A condition which must be fulfilled before the agreement's promises or covenants are binding on the other party. Generally, a condition precedent is a future and uncertain event, the happening of which depends on the existence of an obligation.

C.   Condition Subsequent--A condition, the performance or happening of which causes the agreement's currently enforceable promises or covenants to cease being binding on one or both parties.

D.   Convey--To pass or transmit the title to property from one to another.

E.   Devest (Divest)--To deprive, take away, or withdraw. Usually it is spoken of as an authority or power. Property subject to such a power is said to be subject to devestment (divestment).

F.   Devise--A testamentary (pertaining to a will) disposition of land or realty.

G.   Encumbrance (Incumbrance)--Any right to, or interest in, land which subsists in another. This includes any claim, lien, or liability which binds an estate.

H.   Subsequent Bona Fide Purchaser--A purchaser who, without actual or constructive notice of any prior interest in a piece of property, pays value for an interest in such property.

II. Overview

This topic includes both personal and real property. The major subtopics under real property are freehold estates, concurrent estates, landlord and tenant, and mortgages.

A.   Definition--In the strict legal sense, property is an aggregate of rights that are guaranteed and protected by law. The essence of property is exclusive ownership, i.e., the right to dispose of a thing in every legal way: to possess it, use it, and exclude everyone else from interfering with it. The term extends to every species of valuable right and interest. It includes both tangibles (land, goods, documents, and instruments) and intangibles (accounts, contract rights, and generally any rights to payment).

B.   Classifications of Property--For purposes of this outline, property will be broken down into real and personal property and fixtures.

1.   Real Property--Land and generally whatever is erected, growing upon, or affixed in a permanent or semipermanent manner to the land.

2.   Personal Property--In the broadest sense, everything that is the subject of ownership and not real property.

3.   Fixtures--A chattel or item of personal property which is affixed to the land. This is a hybrid term which encompasses both personal and real property. The Uniform Commercial Code defines a fixture as a good so related to particular real estate that an interest in it arises under real estate law. On the other hand, the so-called trade fixtures doctrine classifies several types of fixtures as personal property and allows the tenant to remove any fixtures which he or she has attached for the purpose of conducting business. The tenant's right is limited to the extent that his or her action in removing the fixture may not materially damage the realty. This doctrine has been extended to include easily removable agricultural (farming equipment) and consumer or domestic (large appliances) fixtures. The basic test used by the courts to determine whether a fixture is real or personal property is the <u>objective intent test</u>. The test is phrased as a question asking the following: "Would the ordinary reasonable person be justified in assuming that the person attaching the chattel intended it to become a part of the real estate?" This question is usually answered by examining the chattel's method of annexation, the degree to which the chattel is adapted to the use of the realty, and the prevailing custom of the time, place, and business.

   a.   By definition, there must be at least some annexation. The general rule is that a chattel becomes part of the realty when it cannot be removed without causing material injury to the realty.

   b.   A chattel's appropriateness to the use or purpose of the realty is particularly important in trade or business cases. The test may become two-fold in these situations. First, a chattel is generally considered a part of the realty when it is necessary to the commonly accepted use of the realty. Second, a chattel that is necessary to the business which happens to be conducted on the premises, but which could be as easily or profitably used at another location, is usually considered personal property.

   c.   Considerations bearing on whether or not a fixture has become a part of the realty also depend on the custom at the place of affixing, the length of time of affixation, and the particular industry involved in the affixation.

III. Freehold Estates

A freehold estate is the highest form of estate. A freeholder <u>possesses and owns</u> his or her estate. By comparison, a nonfreeholder or a leaseholder only has <u>possession</u>. Additionally, freehold estates are to be distinguished from future interests. A <u>future interest</u> is an interest in property where the right to possession and use of the property is postponed until some future time. Freehold estates are classified according to their potential duration.

A.   <u>Fee Simple</u>

   1.   <u>Fee Simple Absolute</u>--An estate of potentially infinite duration. There are no limitations on its inheritability, and it is not subject to a power of divestment.

   •   Creation--At common law, it was necessary to use the words "to A and his heirs" to create a fee simple estate. Under modern law, a deed is presumed to convey a fee simple absolute or the largest estate that can be owned by the grantor. Thus, any words of conveyance, not expressly limited, will pass the grantor's entire estate.

   2.   <u>Defeasible Fee Simple</u>--A fee simple may be created so that it is defeasible upon the occurrence of a particular event. There are three classifications of defeasible estates.

   a.   <u>Fee Simple Determinable</u>--An estate which automatically terminates upon the occurrence of a particular event. If and when the specified event occurs, the land automatically reverts to the grantor.

   (1)   A fee simple determinable is freely transferable, but the transferred estate remains subject to the condition.

(2)   A fee simple determinable may be created by words such as "so long as," "until," or "while." Example: "A to B, so long as she shall continue to farm Blackacre."

b.   **Fee Simple Subject to a Condition Subsequent**--An estate which does not automatically terminate, but may terminate at the election of the grantor. If and when the specified event occurs, the grantor has the right to reenter the land and terminate the estate.

    (1)   A fee simple subject to a condition subsequent is freely transferable, but the transferred estate remains subject to the condition.

    (2)   A fee simple subject to a condition subsequent is created by words such as "but if," "upon the condition that," or "provided, however." Example: "A to B, but if B shall ever use Blackacre other than as a farm . . ."

c.   **Fee Simple Subject to an Executory Interest**--An estate which automatically terminates upon the occurrence of a particular event. However, the estate transfers to a third person and not to the grantor or the heirs.

    (1)   A fee simple subject to an executory interest is freely transferable, but the transferred estate remains subject to the condition.

    (2)   A fee simple subject to an executory interest is created by using the same words as those used to create a fee simple determinable. The only difference is that upon the occurrence of the event, the property transfers to a third party.

B.   <u>Life Estate</u>--An estate limited in duration to the life of some particular person specified in the deed. This person may be referred to as the measuring life.

1.   **Types of Life Estates**--A life estate may be either for the life of the grantee or "pour autre vie," i.e., for the life of another. Under the modern view, if A is the grantee and B is the measuring life of the estate, and if A predeceases B, then A's estate descends to his or her heirs. A's heirs own the estate until B's death.

2.   **Defeasible Life Estates**--These estates may be defeasible in the same manner as a defeasible fee simple estate.

3.   **Alienability**--A life estate is freely transferable. However, the transferred estate is still limited in duration by the original measuring life.

4.   **Rights and Duties of the Life Tenant**--Generally, a life tenant has all the rights and duties of a fee simple owner. However, the life tenant's rights and duties are limited by the concept of waste.

    a.   A life tenant has the right to use and enjoy the land and to exclude others from the land. A life tenant also has the duties of a fee simple holder, such as the duty to pay taxes and assessments for public improvements. However, if the public improvement is of a permanent nature so that the holder of the future interest will also benefit from it, then the life tenant and future interest holders must apportion the assessment.

    b.   **Waste**--A life tenant's rights and duties are limited by the concept of waste. Waste is conduct by the life tenant which impairs the value of the land and, therefore, the interest of the future interest holder.

5. Life Estates Created by Operation of Law--At common law, if possible, certain estates were created to protect the survivors or heirs of a decedent. These estates, as they existed at common law, have been almost wholly abolished or altered by state statutes.

    a. Dower--The right a wife has in her husband's property. Dower is either <u>inchoate</u> (while the husband is alive) or <u>choate</u> (upon his death).

    b. Statutory Forced Share--The right of a surviving spouse (sometimes limited to a surviving wife) to an absolute share of all the decedent's property owned by the decedent at his or her death. Usually, this share applies to real and personal property.

    c. Community Property--The 1/2 interest each spouse has in all property acquired during their relationship from earnings or investment of community property.

IV. Future Interests

A future interest is an interest in property where the right to possession is postponed until some future time. While the topic of future interests is no longer covered in depth on the CPA Exam, an awareness of its concepts will facilitate your understanding of the remaining topics in the area of property that are tested. There are five classifications of future interests: possibility of reverter, reversion, right of reentry, remainder, and executory interest.

A. <u>Possibility of Reverter</u>--The reversionary interest which is left in the grantor after his or her conveyance of a fee simple determinable is a possibility of reverter.

B. <u>Reversion</u>--The interest left in the grantor when he or she conveys away less than the entire estate is a reversion. For example, if O (the owner of Blackacre in fee simple) conveys Blackacre to A for life, A has a life estate, and O has a reversion. A reversion interest is freely alienable.

C. <u>Right of Reentry</u>--A right of reentry is the future interest left to the grantor when he or she conveys a fee simple subject to a condition subsequent.

D. <u>Remainder</u>--The future interest created in a third-person transferee which otherwise would be a reversion is a remainder. For example, if O (owner of Blackacre in fee simple) conveys Blackacre to A for life, remainder to B, B's future interest is a vested remainder. Remainders may be either vested or contingent.

    1. A vested remainder is similar to a reversion in that it is not subject to a condition precedent (see the example in B., above). It must also be in the possession of an ascertained person.

    2. A remainder is contingent if it is either subject to a condition precedent (not subsequent) or limited to an unascertained person.

        a. Subject to a Condition Precedent--A condition precedent is an event which must occur before the interest vests. For example, O conveys to A for life, then to B if B attains the age of 30. B has a contingent remainder which vests when he becomes 30.

        b. Limited to an Unascertained Person--For example, O conveys to A for life, then to the children of B (B now has no children). There is a contingent remainder which will vest as soon as B has her first child.

E. <u>Executory Interest</u>--The future interest created in a third-person transferee which corresponds to a grantor's possibility of reverter is an executory interest.

V. Concurrent Estates in Land

The freehold estates covered in III., above, may be held singly or jointly. There are five classifications of concurrent or joint estates: joint tenancy, tenancy in common, tenancy by the entirety, community property, and tenancy in partnership.

A.   Joint Tenancy--A concurrent estate with the right of survivorship is a joint tenancy.

    1.   Characteristics--The most important characteristic of a joint tenancy is the right of survivorship. On the death of any joint tenant, his or her interest in the estate terminates, and the estate is held by the surviving joint tenants. There may be any number of co-tenants, so long as there are at least two. Each co-tenant has a share in the whole, subject to each other tenant's share.

    2.   Creation--Under modern law, a person seeking to convey a joint tenancy must use specific words of conveyance such as "O to A and B as joint tenants with right of survivorship." If the language is in any way ambiguous, the courts will construe it so as to create the legally preferred tenancy in common. Additionally, a joint tenancy may not be created in the absence of the four unities. The four unities are as follows: (a) the unity of time, which means each joint tenant's interest must arise at the same time; (b) the unity of title, which means each joint tenant must acquire his or her interest by the same instrument; (c) the unity of interest, which means each joint tenant's interest must be of the same type and duration; and (d) the unity of possession, which means that each joint tenant must have an undivided right to use the whole property.

    3.   Termination--A joint tenancy may be terminated by the unilateral action of any joint tenant, during his or her lifetime, which destroys one of the required unities.

        a.   An inter vivos conveyance (transferred during life) by one joint tenant terminates the joint tenancy, because it affects the grantee. The grantee's interest is a tenancy in common with the remaining joint tenants. However, the remaining joint tenants' interests still represent a joint tenancy.

        b.   Termination may also be accomplished by the co-tenants' agreeing to revoke their rights of survivorship or by a judicial severance proceeding.

B.   Tenancy in Common--A concurrent estate with no right of survivorship.

    1.   Characteristics--There is no right of survivorship in the co-tenants of a tenancy in common. Therefore, each co-tenant's interest is inheritable. A tenancy in common may be shared by any number of co-tenants, so long as there is more than one. Each co-tenant has an undivided interest in the whole property.

    2.   Creation--Under modern statutes, a tenancy in common is the preferred type of co-tenancy. The only required unity is the unity of interest.

    3.   Termination--A tenancy in common may be terminated by agreement of all the co-tenants or by a court-ordered partition.

C.   Tenancy by the Entirety--A joint tenancy created by a husband and wife is a tenancy by the entirety.

    1.   Characteristics--A tenancy by the entirety's characteristics are generally similar to those of a joint tenancy except that it may only be created by a husband and wife.

    2.   Creation--All the requirements which need to be met to create a joint tenancy must be met to create a tenancy by the entirety; plus, it may only be created by a husband and wife. **NOTE:** Some states have relaxed the requirements of the four unities.

3.   Termination--A tenancy by the entirety may not be terminated by the unilateral action of one spouse. It may be terminated only by death, divorce, or agreement.

D.   <u>Rights and Duties Among Co-Tenants</u>

1.   Right to Use and Possess the Property--Generally, each co-tenant may occupy or use the whole of a joint estate, so long as his or her use does not act to exclude the other co-tenants. A tenant in possession has no duty to account to or reimburse co-tenants not in possession. There are several <u>exceptions</u> to this generalization.

a.   Ouster--The action of one co-tenant which denies another co-tenant's title or right to use or possess the land, or action which denies another the rightful share of any proceeds. This is a tortious or wrongful act. The ousted tenant may maintain an action for the value of the reasonable use of the land or for his or her share of the profits.

b.   A co-tenant is accountable for any profit realized by him or her from activity which reduces the value of the land. Thus, that co-tenant must reimburse each co-tenant a proportionate share of all profits realized from the exploitation of minerals.

c.   A co-tenant is liable for any voluntary waste (see III.B.4.b., above). Voluntary, destructive waste is a tortious act and the co-tenant may be liable for double or treble damages.

2.   Duty to Maintain the Joint Estate--Each tenant is bound to pay his or her share of the taxes and his or her share of the interest on any outstanding mortgage. A co-tenant has no duty to make repairs or improvements.

VI. Acquisition of Real Property

The most common method of acquiring title to real property is by deed of conveyance. The grantor, or previous owner, conveys the estate or other interest in the land to the grantee. This transaction is represented by a deed. The deed is filed in a land records office, which is open to the public, in order to put all persons on notice of the owner's interest in the property. Normally, the sale of real property is a two-step process. The parties first contract for the sale of the land and, second, at some later date, "close." At the "closing," the deed is exchanged for the agreed consideration.

A.   <u>Executory Contract for the Sale of Land</u>--This is the first step in most real property transactions.

1.   The Statute of Frauds requires that all contracts for the sale of real property must be in writing and signed by the party to be charged (the grantor). The writing may be a memorandum or some other informal writing and need not be a formal document.

a.   The writing must contain the following essential terms: identification of the parties, a description of the property sufficient to identify it, and the terms and conditions such as price or consideration and manner of payment.

b.   In rare instances, the courts will enforce an oral contract. The usual situation involves a part performance or activity which occurs as a result of a party's detrimental reliance on the terms of an oral contract. For example, if O orally contracts to sell Blackacre to A, and A, in reliance, erects substantial improvements on Blackacre, the courts may (in an equity proceeding) enforce specific performance.

c.   A written contract for the sale of land may be revoked or modified by an oral agreement between the parties.

d.   Unless the contract states that "time is of the essence," the parties have a reasonable time in which to perform.

2. Marketable Title--Unless the contract specifies otherwise, it is implied that the seller will furnish a marketable title. A marketable title is one that is free from plausible or reasonable objections; it need not be perfect. It must be free from private encumbrances not otherwise specified in the title, such as easements or mortgages. However, zoning laws or subdivision restrictions generally will not render a title unmarketable. Unless so stated, marketable title does not have to be record title; therefore, a title based on adverse possession (see VI.E., below) may be marketable. Finally, the seller usually contracts to furnish title at closing. The seller is not required to have title when he or she contracts.

3. Title Insurance--Covers losses resulting from defects or failure of title to real property. Any exceptions not insured must be shown on the face of the policy. This type of insurance is usually issued to the purchaser or mortgagor. Most state statutes require that the policy indicate on its face the extent of the risk assumed. Many statutes also establish specific premium schedules. Unlike other types of insurance, no title insurance policy or guarantee of title may be issued on a casualty basis (issued without regard to the possible extent of adverse matters or defects of title). Thus, the issuer of a title insurance policy must first examine the title abstract which summarizes the conveyances, mortgages, and known encumbrances and liabilities affecting the property. Only if the title examiner believes that there are no material defects of title may the insurer issue a policy. In this respect, title insurance resembles a guaranty in which the insurer warrants the validity of the title. As a practical matter, most title insurance policies exclude coverage of any defect which is not of record.

4. Payment of the purchase price and delivery of the deed are concurrent conditions. Neither party may hold the other in breach unless he or she is capable of tendering performance.

5. Remedies Upon Breach of Contract for Sale

    a. Buyer's Remedies

    (1) Specific Performance--Because land is considered to be "unique" property, the buyer is entitled to specific performance.

    (2) Abatement in Price--In situations when the estate is less than what the seller contracted to sell, the buyer may complete the sale and seek an abatement in price.

    (3) Damages--If the seller is unable to deliver the land, the buyer may seek monetary damages.

    b. Seller's Remedies

    (1) Specific Performance--The seller is allowed to sue for specific performance of the sales contract.

    (2) Damages--If the seller chooses to sue for damages, he or she is entitled to the difference between the contract price and the current market price.

    (3) Liquidated Damages--The contract may call for liquidated damages, usually forfeiture of the down payment. These clauses are enforceable only when the seller can show some connection between the liquidated damages and the actual damages.

6. Equitable Conversion and Risk of Loss--After the contract for sale has been executed and before the closing, the majority of courts place the risk of loss on the buyer. This is based on the doctrine of equitable conversion. The seller's right to the real estate is converted into a right to receive the purchase price for the real estate (equitable conversion).

B.   The Deed

1.   Formalities--The formal requirements of the deed differ from those of the sales contract. It is important to understand these differences.

   a.   The Statute of Frauds requires a writing signed by the grantor for the transfer of an interest in real property. Usually, this writing takes the form of a deed. There is no requirement that a transfer of land be supported by consideration; therefore, a deed need not contain a statement of the consideration. If the deed fails to clearly state what interest it purports to convey, it will be presumed to convey the grantor's entire interest.

   b.   The deed must name a grantee and sufficiently describe him or her.

   c.   The land must be described sufficiently to furnish some means of identification. The description is usually by bounds, reference to a government survey, or by reference to a plat or street name and number. Parol evidence is generally admissible to clarify any ambiguities. Parol evidence is extraneous evidence which is not furnished by the deed or other document itself. Rather, it originates from other sources, such as witnesses or outside documents.

2.   Delivery--There is no effective transfer of an interest in land until the grantor has delivered the deed or other writing.

   a.   "Delivery" means more than simply the physical transfer of the deed out of the hands of the grantor. The grantor must intend to transfer an immediate interest in the property. Actual intent rather than physical action controls. Any type of evidence, including parol evidence and evidence of the grantor's conduct or statements before and after delivery of the deed, is admissible to prove this intent.

   b.   The grantor need not deliver the deed to the grantee; the grantor may deliver it to a third party so long as the third party is not wholly under his or her control.

   c.   A delivery of a deed, valid on its face, but which is subject to an oral condition, effectively transfers the interest to the grantee, whether or not he or she fulfills the condition. Parol evidence is inadmissible to establish the existence of the condition.

3.   Types of Deeds

   a.   General Warranty Deed--A deed which contains all five of the usual covenants is a general warranty deed (see D., below). This deed warrants the title good against all encumbrances arising prior to the transfer.

   b.   Special Warranty Deed--A deed which contains all five of the usual covenants, but limits its coverage to defects arising while the grantor owned the property.

   c.   Quitclaim Deed--A transfer by the grantor of all his or her interest in the land, whatever it might be. However, a quitclaim deed makes no warranties.

4.   Contents--Generally, real property deeds contain the following clauses. **NOTE:** All of these provisions are not required.

   a.   The premise clause includes the date of delivery, names of the parties, purpose of the conveyance, and a statement of the consideration.

   b.   The granting clause includes a description of the land and the words of conveyance.

   c.   The habendum or "to have" clause sets forth the estate conveyed.

    d.   The <u>reddendum clause</u> contains any conditions or reservations.

    e.   The <u>covenants clause</u> contains the seller's title warranties.

    f.   The <u>conclusion</u> contains the signatures of the parties and any witnesses and the seal.

C.   <u>Recording Statutes</u>--In order to protect his or her title against subsequent conflicting interests, the grantee must record his or her deed in the appropriate land records office. Recording or lack of recording only affects the rights of the grantor as against subsequent recorded parties in interest.

    1.   Types of Recording Statutes

        a.   Race-Notice--Once he or she records, a subsequent bona fide purchaser is protected against any prior unrecorded parties in interest.

        b.   Notice--A subsequent bona fide purchaser is protected, whether or not he or she records against prior unrecorded parties in interest.

        c.   Race--The first party to record prevails.

    2.   Effects of Recordation--The only purpose of recording is to put subsequent purchasers on notice. Thus, recording protects the rights of the grantee from interference by subsequent purchasers. It does not validate an invalid deed or protect the grantee from conflicting interests which arise by operation of law.

D.   <u>Covenants of Title</u>--The following covenants may be expressed or implied in a deed:

    1.   The Covenant of Seizen--The grantor warrants that he or she owns the property and has a right to convey it.

    2.   The Covenant of Quiet Enjoyment--The grantee will not be disturbed in his or her possession of the property by the grantor or some third party's lawful claim of ownership.

    3.   The Covenant Against Encumbrances--The grantor promises that there are no existing encumbrances on the title to the property.

    4.   The Covenant of Further Assurance--The grantor will execute or obtain any further documents or assurances necessary to perfect the title.

    5.   The Covenant of Warranty Forever--The grantor will forever warrant title to the property.

E.   <u>Adverse Possession</u>--Mere possession of property alone tends to raise an inference that the possessor has legal title. Therefore, the law has developed in such a manner that proof of long continued possession will establish title. This method of acquiring legal title is termed adverse possession. Most states have established a statute of limitations which bars others from ousting the possessor after a certain period of time. Once this statute of limitations has run, the possessor has valid title by adverse possession, and, if so desired, the possessor may bring a quiet title action and obtain title of record. In order for possession to ripen into title, it must be open, notorious, continuous, exclusive, adverse, and with claim of right for the statutory period (usually 20 years).

    1.   Open and Notorious--For possession to be open and notorious, it must be visible and in the usual manner that such property would be possessed, so as to put the real owner and the community at large on notice.

    2.   Continuous and Exclusive--The possession must be continuous for the entire statutory period; short, disconnected periods of use may not be added together to establish the required number of years. The possession must be to the exclusion of all other persons.

3. Adverse--The possession must be adverse to the interests of the real owner, i.e., without permission or acquiescence.

4. Claim of Right--Normally, this requirement demands only that the possessor hold him- or herself out, by words and actions, as the true owner of the land. Some states require that an adverse possessor have some instrument purporting to be a title or that the adverse possessor pay taxes on the land for the statutory period.

VII. Landlord and Tenant

This property topic covers nonfreehold or leasehold estates. Landlord and tenant law has undergone more recent development than any other area of real property law. The courts and state legislatures have not only changed much of the common law concerning the rights and duties of landlords and tenants, they have also added whole new bodies of law to expand the recognized rights of the various parties.

A. <u>Types of Tenancies</u>--There are four recognized tenancies.

1. <u>Tenancy for Years</u>--A tenancy for years is a tenancy for a specified duration, even if the period is less than a year. There is usually a specific termination date. However, a tenancy for years may also run until a certain event occurs. For example, a tenancy for years may run until a construction contract is completed.

   a. Generally, the Statute of Frauds requires that a tenancy for years which will run for more than 1 year must be in writing to be enforceable.

   b. A tenancy for years may be limited by conditions or covenants. However, remember that, traditionally, covenants associated with leases are assumed to be independent of the lease.

2. <u>Tenancy From Period to Period</u>--A tenancy which continues from year to year, month to month, or any other fraction of a year, is a tenancy from period to period. Usually, the measuring period is the same as the rent period. **NOTE**: Every tenancy from period to period must originate as a tenancy for a fixed term. For example, if L and T agree to a month-to-month tenancy, with T paying each month's rent on the first, then the first month's tenancy is a fixed term, i.e., neither party may terminate within the first month (see b., below).

   a. A tenancy from period to period may be created by an express agreement or by operation of law.

      (1) Express Agreement--The parties may agree on a lease from month to month or for any other period. If the parties agree to a rent period but do not set a lease termination date, they have created a tenancy from period to period.

      (2) Operation of Law--In some jurisdictions, if the tenant holds over after the end of the term, the landlord may elect to hold him or her liable for rent for an additional rent period. In addition, if the purported lease agreement is invalid (for example, because it violates the Statute of Frauds) and the tenant pays rent periodically, the courts will imply a tenancy from period to period.

   b. A distinctive feature of a tenancy from period to period is that it continues until termination by proper notice. Under common law, notice must be given in the same amount of time as the rent period or tenancy period. For example, if tenancy is from month to month, then the tenant or landlord must give at least one month's notice.

      • In addition, the terminating party may terminate a lease only at the end of a period. Finally, it is important to note that many states have enacted statutory modifications to these common law rules.

3. <u>Tenancy at Will</u>--A tenancy at will is one that continues until either party terminates. It is distinguished from a tenancy from period to period because there is no requirement that the terminating party give notice. However, most states have enacted statutes which require some notice. This in effect transforms a tenancy at will into a tenancy from period to period.

   a. The parties may terminate a tenancy at will by any action which manifests an intent to terminate. Thus, if the tenant abandons or assigns, he or she has terminated the lease.

   b. A tenancy at will is considered to be a personal relationship, and thus it will terminate by operation of law whenever the personal relationship ceases. Thus, if the landlord dies or sells the rental property, the tenancy at will terminates.

4. <u>Tenancy at Sufferance</u>--If the tenant holds over after the expiration of the tenancy term without the consent of the landlord, there is a tenancy at sufferance. This tenancy continues until the landlord terminates it by an action for eviction, by reentering the premises and treating the holdover tenant as a trespasser, or by creating a new lease.

B. <u>Rights, Duties, and Liabilities of the Landlord</u>--This area of landlord and tenant law has undergone substantial statutory modification in recent years. These changes are in response to the change from a rural, agrarian society to an urban, industrial society. At early common law, the landlord's only duty was to grant an interest in the land. Most tenants were farmers and all-around handymen; it was their responsibility to put and maintain the premises in a habitable condition.

   1. The majority rule at modern common law is that the landlord has the duty to transfer to the tenant both the legal right to enter the premises and actual possession of the premises. This change results from the legal concept that the tenant bargains for use of the property, not the legal right to evict a prior tenant.

   2. A covenant of quiet enjoyment is implied in all leases.

      a. If the tenant is physically evicted from the entire premises, the duty to pay rent ceases.

      b. If the tenant is physically evicted from any part of the premises through the fault of the landlord, the duty to pay rent also ceases entirely. However, if the tenant is evicted from a part of the premises by a third party, the duty to pay rent abates in proportion to the extent of the eviction.

      c. If the tenant's use and enjoyment of the premises is substantially interfered with through the fault of the landlord, the duty to pay rent ceases. The interference must be such that a reasonable person would feel compelled to vacate the premises.

   3. At old common law, the landlord had no right to enter the premises. However, under modern law the landlord may enter the premises to inspect, repair, or exhibit them to potential renters or purchasers. The landlord must give the tenant notice of intent to enter, and the landlord may only enter during reasonable hours.

   4. Landlord's Duty to Deliver Habitable Premises

      a. At common law, there is no general duty on the part of the landlord to deliver the premises in a habitable condition. There are <u>three exceptions</u> to this general principle:

         (1) If the lease is a short-term lease for furnished premises, there is an implied covenant of habitability.

         (2) If there are hidden defects known to the landlord, he or she must either repair those defects or disclose them to the tenant.

(3)   If a building is being constructed for a particular use and the tenant enters into a lease agreement before construction is finished, there is an implied covenant of habitability.

b.   Recently, many jurisdictions have held that there is an implied covenant of habitability for urban dwellings and commercial buildings. If the premises are not habitable the tenant may terminate the lease. In the case of a dwelling, the tenant also has the contract remedy for damages. If the tenant knows of the defect, and freely bargains for a special rent rate, he or she is estopped from asserting the covenant of habitability.

c.   Most states have enacted statutes which require the premises to be delivered in a habitable condition. Usually, habitable is defined as complying with the relevant housing code.

5.   Landlord's Duty to Repair After Entry by the Tenant

a.   Under old common law, there is no implied duty to repair. The duty to maintain is placed on the tenant. The tenant's failure to maintain is known as permissive waste.

b.   Recently, many jurisdictions have implied a continuing covenant of habitability. Modern courts hold that the duty to pay rent is dependent on the landlord's duty to repair. Thus, where the landlord fails to repair, the tenant may either terminate the lease or repair and deduct the costs from the rent due.

c.   Several states have enacted landlord and tenant acts which require the landlord to maintain dwellings in a habitable condition. These acts usually state what constitutes habitable. Upon breach, the tenant has the duty to terminate, repair, and subtract the cost from the rent due, or pay the rent into escrow until the repairs are affected. The law is split as to whether or not the lease may include an exculpatory clause which shifts the duty to repair back to the tenant. Some jurisdictions hold such clauses absolutely void; others require that the lessee freely bargain away his or her right in a separately signed clause.

6.   Landlord's Tort Liability

a.   At old common law, there is generally no liability on the landlord for injuries to the tenant or his or her guest which occurred on the leased premises. There are three exceptions to this general premise:

(1)   One exception to this general statement is that the landlord may be held liable when the injury is caused by a hidden defect of which the landlord had knowledge or had reason to know.

(2)   Another exception arises when the lessor negligently makes repairs which cause an injury to the tenant or his or her guest. The landlord may be held liable under these circumstances even if he or she had no duty to repair but did so voluntarily.

(3)   A landlord has the duty to inspect and repair common areas (hallways, stairways, etc.). Any injuries which result from a breach of this duty may result in the landlord's being held liable.

b.   The modern trend is to impose liability on the landlord for all injuries resulting from any unsafe conditions on the premises. This follows from the concurrent trend requiring the landlord to maintain the premises in a habitable condition. Some cases have gone so far as to hold a lessor strictly liable for any injuries occurring on the leased premises. As a general rule, the landlord is not liable for injuries caused by the negligent acts of the tenant. However, the landlord may be liable when the tenant's use of the premises is inherently dangerous. For example, if the tenant mines the property, the landlord may be vicariously liable for nuisance actions against the tenant.

C. <u>Rights, Duties, and Liabilities of the Tenant</u>

1. Duty to Repair--As stated earlier, under old common law, the tenant is accountable for waste.

   a. Permissive Waste--In the past, the tenant was bound to maintain the premises in the same condition as they were at the commencement of the lease. The tenant was under a duty not only to repair defects caused by use, but the tenant also had the affirmative duty to protect the property from damages caused by the elements. The tenant's failure to meet this duty was termed permissive waste.

   b. Affirmative Waste--The tenant is still liable for any affirmative or voluntary waste. Affirmative waste consists of any activity which either damages the premises or which substantially changes the leased premises. However, many modern long-term leases do give the tenant the right to alter the premises.

2. Duty to Pay Rent--Rent payment is an inherent obligation of the landlord and tenant relationship. Practically speaking, the landlord's prime remedy for nonpayment is eviction. At common law, eviction terminates the lease and excuses the tenant from any further liability. In recent years, several additional remedies have been fashioned to further protect the landlord in the event the tenant defaults.

   a. Landlord Liens--Several states have enacted statutes which create a lien in favor of the landlord on all the tenant's personal property. Other states allow the landlord to peaceably enter the premises and seize the tenant's personal property, except his or her life's necessities, as security for the unpaid rent.

   b. Lease Deposits and Damage Clause--Many leases now require some sort of advance payment which provides security for the landlord. The most common forms these prepayments take are as follows:

      (1) Advance Rent--Many leases require that the tenant prepay a certain period's rent. For example, the lease may require 1 month's rent be paid in advance. If the lease is terminated prematurely, the landlord may retain this fee.

      (2) Security Deposit--Other leases require an advance as a security deposit. Should the lease be prematurely terminated, the deposit may be retained only to cover the landlord's actual expenses or damages; any excess must be returned to the tenant.

      (3) Liquidated Damages--Commercial leases often contain a clause requiring a deposit for liquidated damages. Courts will uphold these clauses if the sum deposited is reasonably related to the actual damages.

3. Right to Assign or Sublet the Lease--If there is no restrictive clause, the tenant has the right to assign his or her leasehold or to sublet any portion of the estate.

   a. Assignment--If the tenant transfers the entire interest in the estate and retains no reversionary interest, he or she has assigned the estate. The majority view is that the primary tenant may retain a right of reentry, in the event the assignee-tenant fails to pay the rent, without transforming the assignment into a sublease. Other jurisdictions hold that the retention of any interest, including a right of reentry, creates a sublease and not an assignment.

(1)   An assignment establishes privity of estate between the lessor and assignee; therefore, the assignee becomes personally liable for the rent.

(2)   The original lessee remains in privity of contract with the lessor, unless released by the lessor. Therefore, he or she remains personally liable for all covenants.

b.   Sublease--If the tenant retains a reversionary interest (for example, the tenant leases less than the entire premises or leases all the property for less than the full term of the lease), the tenant has subleased the estate.

(1)   The sublessee does not come into privity of estate with the lessor; therefore, he or she is not personally liable for the rent. If the rent is not paid, the lessor may terminate the lease and oust the sublessee, but the lessor may not proceed against the sublessee for back rent.

(2)   The original lessee remains personally liable for the rent and all the covenants contained in the lease agreement.

c.   Covenants Against Assignment and Sublease--Most jurisdictions consider covenants against assignment and/or sublease enforceable. However, these covenants are strictly construed, and a covenant against assignment does not prohibit a sublease and vice versa.

D.   Termination of the Leasehold Estate--Leasehold estates may be terminated.

1.   Lessor's Termination Upon Tenant's Breach of Covenant--At common law and under most statutes, the lessor has a right to terminate the lease if the tenant fails to pay rent. Generally, the lessor may not terminate if the tenant breaches other covenants. In response to this, most leases today contain express clauses giving the lessor the right to terminate upon breach of any enumerated covenant. These clauses are enforceable.

2.   Lessor's right to terminate upon tenant's surrender or abandonment.

a.   Surrender--If the tenant voluntarily gives up possession to the landlord and the landlord accepts with the intent that the estate be terminated, a surrender has occurred. **NOTE**: The lessor's acceptance of an assignment or sublease does not connote a surrender.

b.   Abandonment--If the tenant abandons the property without the consent of the landlord, the landlord has two options. The landlord may keep the property unoccupied and sue for the rent as it becomes due, or the landlord may relet the premises and sue for damages. There is no general duty on the part of the landlord to relet the premises and thereby mitigate his or her damages.

3.   Tenant's Right to Terminate Upon Landlord's Breach of Covenant--The landlord's breach of most covenants does not entitle the tenant to terminate the lease. However, the breach of the following covenants does entitle the tenant to terminate:

a.   The landlord's breach of the covenant of quiet enjoyment, by actual or constructive eviction, terminates the lease as a matter of law.

b.   The modern trend is that the landlord's breach of the covenant of habitability entitles the tenant to terminate.

c.   Generally, the landlord's breach of any covenant that materially supports the value of the estate entitles the tenant to terminate.

4. Third-Party Eviction by Title Paramount--If the lessee is evicted by a third party who has superior title, the lessee may terminate the lease and hold the lessor liable for damages.

5. Destruction of the Premises--If the premises are destroyed in any manner other than by the tenant's negligence, the tenant may surrender possession and terminate the lease. Under the old common law and in situations where the tenant has agreed to bear the risk, he or she may not terminate upon destruction.

6. Eminent Domain Condemnation--If the estate is entirely and permanently taken in an eminent domain proceeding, the leasehold is extinguished. Less than a total taking creates only a right for damages in favor of both the tenant and landlord.

7. Frustration of Purpose--If the premises are leased for a particular purpose recognized by both the landlord and tenant and that purpose is later frustrated (i.e., it becomes illegal or impossible to perform), the tenant usually has the power to terminate. For example, if the premises are rented as a brewery and the manufacture of alcoholic beverages is later outlawed, the tenant would have the power to terminate.

8. Illegal Use of Property--A landlord may terminate a lease if the tenant uses the leased property for a purpose that is illegal.

VIII. Mortgages

Under the common law, any estate created by a conveyance absolute in its form, but intended to secure a debt or obligation, is a mortgage. It is a conditional estate, however, in that it becomes absolutely void once the obligation is performed in accordance with the terms of the mortgage agreement. The modern trend, which is in force in many states, is to treat a mortgage as a mere lien and not as an estate.

A. Formalities in the Execution of a Mortgage Agreement--Even in those jurisdictions which do not treat a mortgage as an estate, it is considered to be an interest in real property. Therefore, it is required by the Statute of Frauds to be in writing and signed by the party to be charged (mortgagor). Generally, a mortgage must meet the requirements of a deed; it is unenforceable against subsequent bona fide parties at interest unless it is recorded or unless it is noted on the property's deed or title which is recorded in the land records office.

B. Recording of a Mortgage--A mortgage may be recorded to give constructive notice of the mortgage and protect against subsequent mortgages. A recorded mortgage takes priority over any subsequent interests which may be acquired in the mortgaged property. There are three types of recording statutes:

1. Notice-Type Statute--A subsequent bona fide mortgagee is protected, whether or not he or she records, as against prior unrecorded mortgagees.

2. Race-Notice-Type Statute--Once he or she records, a subsequent bona fide mortgagee is protected as against any prior unrecorded mortgagees.

3. Race-Type Statute--The first party to record a mortgage prevails.

C. Common Provisions of a Mortgage Agreement--Usually the agreement contains the following clauses:

1. The names of the parties.

2. The amount of the principal secured by the mortgage, the date it is due, the payment schedule, and the interest rate.

3. A complete legal description of the mortgaged property.

4. A statement to the effect that the mortgagor has the sole possessory right to the property.

5. A list of the mortgagor's covenants.

   a. A promise to pay the debt under the agreed to conditions,

   b. A promise to insure the property and to not "waste" the property without the mortgagee's consent, and

   c. An Acceleration Clause--This last clause allows the mortgagee to demand full payment in the event the mortgagor defaults.

D. Rights of the Parties--The parties to a mortgage are the mortgagee, the person to whom the obligation is owed, and the mortgagor, who owes the obligation.

1. The mortgagee has the following rights:

   a. The mortgagee has either a lien on the land or actual title subject to defeasance, i.e., the title terminates upon satisfactory completion of the obligation.

   b. The mortgagee may freely assign his or her right to a third party.

   c. The mortgagee may foreclose his or her mortgage upon the mortgagor's default. If the foreclosure is successful, the court will direct that the property be sold at a foreclosure sale. A foreclosure sale serves to extinguish the mortgagee's interest in the property, and the mortgagee must return any amount realized which is in excess of that necessary to cover the obligation and expenses. If the proceeds from the sale are insufficient to satisfy the debt in full, the mortgagor remains liable for any deficiency. If there is more than one mortgage on the property, the mortgage which has priority (as determined under the state's recording statute) will be satisfied in full first before any proceeds may go towards satisfying the second mortgage.

2. The mortgagor's rights are as follows:

   a. The mortgagor has the right to possess the premises and make any reasonable use of them.

   b. The mortgagor may lease the land.

   c. The mortgagor may sell the land; however, a sale does not extinguish the mortgage unless the mortgagee releases him or her.

   d. The mortgagor has the right of redemption. This right entitles him or her to retain the property even after foreclosure, but before the foreclosure sale, by paying the amount due plus interest and any other costs.

E. <u>Sale of Mortgaged Property</u>--The mortgagor has the right to sell the mortgaged property. This sale does not extinguish his or her personal liability nor does it affect the status of the mortgaged property. The grantee of the property may take in two ways:

    1. Subject to the Mortgage--A grantee who takes subject to the mortgage does not assume any personal liability for the mortgage. However, the grantee's interest in the property is "subject to" the outstanding mortgage for which the mortgagor remains liable. The property continues to secure a debt, and the mortgagee retains the power to foreclose.

    2. Assume the Mortgage--If a grantee expressly "assumes" the mortgage, he or she thereby becomes personally liable for it. The grantee's interest in the land is also subject to the outstanding mortgage. The grantor/mortgagor remains personally liable, unless the mortgagee releases him or her. He or she is treated as a surety. Generally, a grantee is better off buying subject to the mortgage because he or she thereby avoids personal liability.

F. <u>Termination of the Mortgage Interest</u>--Under the title theory of mortgage, termination extinguishes the mortgage estate. Under the lien theory, termination frees the property from the mortgage lien. Termination may occur in the following ways:

    1. Performance--Once the mortgagor has performed his or her obligation according to the provisions of the agreement, the mortgage is extinguished.

    2. Tender--If the mortgagor tenders proper performance and the mortgagee refuses, the mortgage is extinguished. The debt or obligation remains outstanding.

    3. Merger--If the mortgagee acquires the mortgagor's interest or vice versa, the mortgage is extinguished by merger.

IX. Environmental Protection

In an attempt to combat the ever increasing problem of environmental deterioration, the government has increased federal regulation over the past several decades.

A. National Environmental Policy Act (NEPA)

    1. This act established the Council on Environmental Quality (CEQ) which helps insure that various environmental laws are followed.

    2. NEPA also requires an environmental impact statement before any federal laws can be adopted or activities undertaken that might affect the environment.

B. The Environmental Protection Agency (EPA)

    1. Established in 1970 by presidential executive order, this agency enforces all laws whose design is to protect the environment.

    2. The EPA may use both civil and criminal prosecution.

C. Clean Air Act of 1963--Covers stationary emission sources, mobile emission sources, acid rain, and toxic industrial emissions.

D. Clean Water Act--Designed to improve the quality of our nation's waterways by making the water safe for recreational use and protecting wildlife associated with the waterways.

E. Safe Drinking Water Act of 1986--Empowers the EPA to set standards for drinking water.

F. Common Law (Nuisance)--Under common law, if one's enjoyment of one's own property were interfered with by another person, then that person could be sued.

G.   Comprehensive Environmental Response, Compensation, and Liability Act (CER-CLA) or Superfund

    1.   This act was passed by Congress in 1980 and amended in 1986 by the Superfund Amendments and Reauthorization Act. It provides for severe penalties.

    2.   The EPA has the authorization to clean up a site that has released or threatens to release hazardous waste.

        a.   The following are jointly and severally liable for the cleanup costs: (1) the person who created the waste, (2) the person who transported the waste to the site, (3) the owner or operator of the site at disposal time, and (4) the <u>current</u> owner or operator.

        b.   This leads to some unusual results:

            (1)   A person who created only a fraction of the waste at a site may be held liable for all cleanup costs at that site.

            (2)   Corporations' officers, shareholders, and secured creditors, who had the authority to exercise control over the financial management of the facility to a degree indicating influence on the corporation's handling of hazardous waste, have been included in the definition of owners or operators and have been found liable.

X. Personal Property

All property which is not included within real property is classified as personal property. Personal property may be divided into: (1) tangible personal property, which includes movable things such as cars, furniture, merchandise, etc., and (2) intangible personal property, which consists of such rights as personal annuities, invested securities, patents, and copyrights. Intangible personal property is often referred to as a <u>chose in action</u>.

A.   <u>Methods of Acquisition and Transfer</u>--The following are the principal modes by which title to personal property may be transferred or acquired:

    1.   Purchase--A transfer of property from one person to another by voluntary act and agreement, founded on a valuable consideration, is a purchase. This is perhaps the most common form of transfer.

    2.   Finding Lost or Mislaid Property--One who discovers and takes possession of another's lost personal property is a finder. Lost property is that which the owner has involuntarily parted with and does not know where to find or recover. A finder's right to the property is superior to that of any other person except the original owner.

    3.   Abandonment--The giving up of a thing absolutely, without reference to any particular person or purpose, and with the intention of not retrieving it. The first person who recovers abandoned property with the intent of reducing it to his or her control acquires that property.

    4.   Capture--Anyone may capture a wild animal from his or her own land, the sea, or in certain cases public land, and acquire ownership by confining or killing it.

    5.   Creation--A person may acquire the ownership of something by producing or creating it. This concept covers inventions and original writings, etc., which may be the subject of patents and/or copyrights.

6.   Merger or Confusion--When goods of a similar nature owned by more than one person are commingled so that a precise separation is impossible, the goods and rights in them are held to be merged. The law recognizes a co-tenancy in the commingled whole. The shares in the co-tenancy may be equal or unequal, depending on the relevant facts.

7.   Accession--The right to all which one's property produces and the right to that which is united or added to it, either naturally or artificially. Generally, an owner is entitled to another's additions to his or her property only when their value is much less than the value of the whole. For example, a bank which repossesses a car upon the purchaser's default may recover any accessories which the purchaser has added, unless they could be removed without damaging the car. On the other hand, the possessor of property may become entitled to it, as against the original owner, when the addition made to it by his or her skill or labor is of greater value than the property itself. This method of acquisition is also called accession.

8.   Gift--A voluntary transfer of personal property without consideration is a gift. The essential requisites of a gift are: capacity of the donor, intention of the donor to make a gift, complete delivery to or for the donee, and acceptance of the gift by the donee. Gifts may be one of the following:

   a.   Inter Vivos, i.e., Between the Living--This is an absolute gift by which the donee becomes the owner of the thing given within the lifetime of the donor.

   b.   Causa Mortis, i.e., in Contemplation of Death--This is a gift, the completion of which is conditioned upon the occurrence of the donor's death. In addition, the donor must in fact be in danger of dying and must be aware of his or her condition.

9.   Inheritance--A person who acquires property which has descended from another has acquired the property by inheritance.

B.   Bailment--A delivery of goods or other personal property for some purpose upon a contract, express or implied, is a bailment. The goods are held for the benefit of another and must be dealt with according to the instructions of the deliverer. The person who delivers the goods is termed a bailor. The person who holds the goods is termed the bailee. In a bailment, only possession or control of the goods passes; title does not pass.

   1.   Duties of the Bailee

      a.   The bailee must exercise reasonable care with respect to the bailed property. If the goods are lost, damaged or destroyed during the bailment, the bailee may be liable for negligence.

         (1)   If the bailment is for the benefit of the bailor, the bailee is liable only for gross negligence.

         (2)   If the bailment is for the benefit of the bailee, the bailee is liable for even slight negligence.

      b.   The bailee has a duty to return the bailed property to the bailor upon termination of the bailment or to deliver it elsewhere according to the bailor's instructions. The bailee is liable for conversion if he or she refuses to deliver the property to the bailor or if he or she delivers it to someone other than the person designated by the bailor.

   2.   Rights of Third Parties--One who in good faith and in the ordinary course of business purchases bailed goods acquires good title superior to that of the bailor. For this result to occur, the bailee must be a merchant who regularly deals in goods of the type which were bailed.

CHAPTER 56—REAL AND PERSONAL PROPERTY

Problem 56-1 MULTIPLE CHOICE QUESTIONS (65 to 75 minutes)

1. Which of the following would change if an asset is treated as personal property rather than as real property?

	Requirements for transfer	Creditor's rights
a.	Yes	No
b.	No	Yes
c.	Yes	Yes
d.	No	No

(11/92, Law, #51, 3133)

1A. Which of the following factors help determine whether an item of personal property has become a fixture?

	Manner of affixation	Value of the item	Intent of the annexor
a.	Yes	Yes	Yes
b.	Yes	Yes	No
c.	Yes	No	Yes
d.	No	Yes	Yes

(5/95, Law, #55, 5389)

2. Which of the following items is tangible personal property?
a. Share of stock.
b. Trademark.
c. Promissory note.
d. Oil painting. (5/95, Law, #57, 5391)

3. Which of the following unities (elements) are required to establish a joint tenancy?

	Time	Title	Interest	Possession
a.	Yes	Yes	Yes	Yes
b.	Yes	Yes	No	No
c.	No	No	Yes	Yes
d.	Yes	No	Yes	No

(5/93, Law, #52, 4020)

4. Sklar, Rich, and Cey own a building as joint tenants with the right of survivorship. Sklar gave Sklar's interest in the building to Marsh by executing and delivering a deed to Marsh. Neither Rich nor Cey consented to this transfer. Rich and Cey subsequently died. After their deaths, Marsh's interest in the building would consist of
a. A 1/3 interest as a tenant in common.
b. A 1/3 interest as a joint tenant.
c. Total ownership due to the deaths of Rich and Cey.
d. No interest, because Rich and Cey did **not** consent to the transfer. (11/92, Law, #52, 3134)

5. A person may own property as a joint tenant with the right of survivorship with any of the following **except** a(an)
a. Divorced spouse.
b. Related minor child.
c. Unaffiliated corporation.
d. Unrelated adult. (5/90, Law, #50, 9911)

6. Green and Nunn own a 40-acre parcel of land as joint tenants with the right of survivorship. Nunn wishes to sell the land to Ink. If Nunn alone executes and delivers a deed to Ink, what will be the result?
a. Green will retain a 1/2 undivided interest in the 40-acre parcel, and will be unable to set aside Nunn's conveyance to Ink.
b. Ink will obtain an interest in 1/2 of the parcel, or 20 acres.
c. Ink will share ownership of the 40 acres with Green as a joint tenant with a right of survivorship.
d. The conveyance will be invalid because Green did **not** sign the deed. (11/88, Law, #56, 0823)

7. Boch and Kent are equal owners of a warehouse. Boch died leaving a will that gave his wife all of his right, title, and interest in his real estate. If Boch and Kent owned the warehouse at all times as joint tenants with the right of survivorship, Boch's interest
a. Will pass to his wife after the will is probated.
b. Will **not** be included in his gross estate for federal estate tax purposes.
c. Could **not** be transferred before Boch's death without Kent's consent.
d. Passed to Kent upon Boch's death.
(5/88, Law, #53, 0828)

8. Court, Fell, and Miles own a parcel of land as joint tenants with right of survivorship. Court's interest was sold to Plank. As a result of the sale from Court to Plank,
a. Fell, Miles, and Plank each own one-third of the land as joint tenants.
b. Fell and Miles each own one-third of the land as tenants in common.

c.   Plank owns one-third of the land as a tenant in common.

d.   Plank owns one-third of the land as a joint tenant.   (5/94, Law, #56, 4811)

9.   On August 15, 1994, Tower, Nolan, and Oak were deeded a piece of land as tenants in common. The deed provided that Tower owned 1/2 the property and Nolan and Oak owned 1/4 each. If Oak dies, the property will be owned as follows:

a.   Tower 1/2, Nolan 1/4, Oak's heirs 1/4.

b.   Tower 1/3, Nolan 1/3, Oak's heirs 1/3.

c.   Tower 5/8, Nolan 3/8.

d.   Tower 1/2, Nolan 1/2.   (5/95, Law, #51, 5385)

10.   Which of the following remedies is available against a real property owner to enforce the provisions of federal acts regulating air and water pollution?

	Citizen suits against the Environmental Protection Agency to enforce compliance with the laws	State suits against violators	Citizen suits against violators
a.	Yes	Yes	Yes
b.	Yes	Yes	No
c.	No	Yes	Yes
d.	Yes	No	Yes

(5/94, Law, #59, 4814)

11.   Under the Comprehensive Environmental Response, Compensation, and Liability Act (CER-CLA), commonly known as Superfund, which of the following parties would be liable to the Environmental Protection Agency (EPA) for the expense of cleaning up a hazardous waste disposal site?

I.   The current owner or operator of the site.

II.   The person who transported the wastes to the site.

III.   The person who owned or operated the site at the time of the disposal.

a.   I and II.

b.   I and III.

c.   II and III.

d.   I, II, and III.   (5/95, Law, #56, 5390)

12.   Which of the following is a defect in marketable title to real property?

a.   Recorded zoning restrictions.

b.   Recorded easements referred to in the contract of sale.

c.   Unrecorded lawsuit for negligence against the seller.

d.   Unrecorded easement.   (5/94, Law, #57, 4812)

13.   A standard title insurance policy will generally insure that

a.   There are **no** other deeds to the property.

b.   The purchaser has good record title as of the policy's date.

c.   All taxes and assessments are paid.

d.   The insurance protection will be transferable to a subsequent purchaser. (5/93, Law, #54, 4022)

14.   A purchaser who obtains real estate title insurance will

a.   Have coverage for the title exceptions listed in the policy.

b.   Be insured against all defects of record other than those excepted in the policy.

c.   Have coverage for title defects that result from events that happen after the effective date of the policy.

d.   Be entitled to transfer the policy to subsequent owners.   (11/91, Law, #54, 2382)

15.   For a deed to be effective between the purchaser and seller of real estate, one of the conditions is that the deed must

a.   Contain the signatures of the seller and purchaser.

b.   Contain the actual sales price.

c.   Be delivered by the seller with an intent to transfer title.

d.   Be recorded within the permissible statutory time limits.   (11/92, Law, #54, 3136)

15A.   For a deed to be effective between a purchaser and seller of real estate, one of the conditions is that the deed must

a.   Be recorded within the permissible statutory time limits.

b.   Be delivered by the seller with an intent to transfer title.

c.   Contain the actual sales price.

d.   Contain the signatures of the seller and purchaser.   (5/95, Law, #53, 5387)

16.   Which of the following deeds will give a real property purchaser the greatest protection?

a.   Quitclaim.

b.   Bargain and sale.

c.   Special warranty.

d.   General warranty.   (11/90, Law, #56, 0817)

17.   On February 2, Mazo deeded a warehouse to Parko for $450,000. Parko did not record the deed. On February 12, Mazo deeded the same warehouse

to Nexis for $430,000. Nexis was aware of the prior conveyance to Parko. Nexis recorded its deed before Parko recorded. Who would prevail under the following recording status?

	Notice statute	Race statute	Race-Notice statute
a.	Nexis	Parko	Parko
b.	Parko	Nexis	Parko
c.	Parko	Nexis	Nexis
d.	Parko	Parko	Nexis

(5/90, Law, #55, 9911)

18. Which of the following warranties is (are) contained in a general warranty deed?

I. The grantor has the right to convey the property.
II. The grantee will **not** be disturbed in possession of the property by the grantor or some third party's lawful claim of ownership.

a. I only.
b. II only.
c. I and II.
d. Neither I **nor** II.   (5/93, Law, #53, 4021)

19. Which of the following warranty (warranties) is (are) given by a general warranty deed?

I. The grantor owns the property being conveyed.
II. The grantee will **not** be disturbed in her possession of the property by the grantor or some third party's lawful claim of ownership.
III. The grantor has the right to convey the property.

a. I only.
b. I, II, and III.
c. I and III only.
d. II and III only.   (11/86, Law, #58, 9911)

20. Which of the following forms of tenancy will be created if a tenant stays in possession of the leased premises without the landlord's consent, after the tenant's one-year written lease expires?
a. Tenancy at will.
b. Tenancy for years.
c. Tenancy from period to period.
d. Tenancy at sufferance. (11/92, Law, #53, 3135)

21. Which of the following provisions must be included in a residential lease agreement?
a. A description of the leased premises.
b. The due date for payment of rent.

c. A requirement that the tenant have public liability insurance.
d. A requirement that the landlord will perform all structural repairs to the property.
(5/95, Law, #52, 5386)

22. Bronson is a residential tenant with a 10-year written lease. In the absence of specific provisions in the lease to the contrary, which of the following statements is correct?
a. The premises may **not** be sublet for less than the full remaining lease term.
b. Bronson may **not** assign the lease.
c. The landlord's death will automatically terminate the lease.
d. Bronson's purchase of the property will terminate the lease.   (11/90, Law, #52, 0813)

23. Delta Corp. leased 60,000 square feet in an office building from Tanner under a written 25-year lease. Which of the following statements is correct?
a. Tanner's death will terminate the lease and Delta will be able to recover any resulting damages from Tanner's estate.
b. Tanner's sale of the office building will terminate the lease unless both Delta and the buyer consented to the assumption of the lease by the buyer.
c. In the absence of a provision in the lease to the contrary, Delta does **not** need Tanner's consent to assign the lease to another party.
d. In the absence of a provision in the lease to the contrary, Delta would need Tanner's consent to enter into a sublease with another party.
(5/90, Law, #54, 9911)

24. Tell, Inc., leased a building from Lott Corp. Tell paid monthly rent of $500 and was also responsible for paying the building's real estate taxes. On January 1, 1987, Vorn Co. and Tell entered into an agreement by which Vorn was entitled to occupy the building for the remainder of the term of Tell's lease in exchange for monthly payments of $600 to Tell. For the year 1987, neither Tell nor Vorn paid the building's real estate taxes and the taxes are delinquent. Learning this, Lott demanded that either Tell or Vorn pay the delinquent taxes. Both refused to do so and Lott has commenced an action against them. Lott will most likely prevail against
a. Vorn, because the lease was assigned to it.
b. Tell and Vorn, because both are jointly and severally liable for the delinquent taxes.
c. Tell without Vorn, because their January 1 agreement constituted a sublease.
d. Vorn, but only to the extent of $100 for each month that it occupied the building during 1987.
(11/88, Law, #57, 9911)

25. Drake Corp. entered into a five-year lease with Samon that provided for Drake's occupancy of three floors of a high-rise office building at a monthly rent of $16,000. The lease provided that "lessee may sublet the premises but only with the landlord's (Samon's) prior written consent." The lease was silent as to whether Drake could assign the lease. Which of the following statements is correct?
a. Subletting of the premises with Samon's consent will relieve Drake from its obligation to pay rent.
b. Assignment of the lease with Samon's consent will relieve Drake from its obligation to pay rent.
c. Samon may refuse to consent to a subsequent sublet even if she has consented to a prior sublet.
d. Subletting of the premises without Samon's consent is void. (11/87, Law, #56, 0836)

26. A tenant renting an apartment under a three-year written lease that does **not** contain any specific restrictions may be evicted for
a. Counterfeiting money in the apartment.
b. Keeping a dog in the apartment.
c. Failing to maintain a liability insurance policy on the apartment.
d. Making structural repairs to the apartment. (5/90, Law, #53, 9911)

27. Which of the following conditions must be met to have an enforceable mortgage?
a. An accurate description of the property must be included in the mortgage.
b. A negotiable promissory note must accompany the mortgage.
c. Present consideration must be given in exchange for the mortgage.
d. The amount of the debt and the interest rate must be stated in the mortgage. (5/94, Law, #58, 4813)

28. A mortgage on real property must
a. Be acknowledged by the mortgagee.
b. State the exact amount of the debt.
c. State the consideration given for the mortgage.
d. Be delivered to the mortgagee. (11/91, Law, #55, 2383)

29. Gilmore borrowed $60,000 from Dix Bank. The loan was used to remodel a building owned by Gilmore as investment property and was secured by a second mortgage that Dix did not record. FCA Loan Company has a recorded first mortgage on the building. If Gilmore defaults on both mortgages, Dix

a. Will **not** be entitled to any mortgage foreclosure sale proceeds, even if such proceeds are in excess of the amount owed to FCA.
b. Will be unable to successfully claim any security interest in the building.
c. Will be entitled to share in any foreclosure sale proceeds *pro rata* with FCA.
d. Will be able to successfully claim a security interest that is subordinate to FCA's security interest. (11/90, Law, #59, 0819)

30. Fern purchased property from Nix for $150,000. Fern obtained a $90,000 loan from Jet Bank to finance the purchase, executing a promissory note and mortgage. By recording the mortgage, Jet protects its
a. Priority against a previously filed real estate tax lien on the property.
b. Priority against all parties having earlier claims to the property.
c. Rights against the claims of subsequent bona fide purchasers for value.
d. Rights against Fern under the promissory note. (5/93, Law, #56, 4024)

31. On May 1, 1991, Chance bought a piece of property by taking subject to an existing unrecorded mortgage held by Hay Bank. On April 1, 1992, Chance borrowed money from Link Finance and gave Link a mortgage on the property. Link did not know about the Hay mortgage and did not record its mortgage until July 1, 1992. On June 1, 1992, Chance borrowed money from Zone Bank and gave Zone a mortgage on the same property. Zone knew about the Link mortgage but did not know about the Hay mortgage. Zone recorded its mortgage on June 15, 1992. Which mortgage would have priority if these transactions took place in a race-notice jurisdiction?
a. The Hay mortgage, because it was first in time.
b. The Link mortgage, because Zone had notice of the Link mortgage.
c. The Zone mortgage, because it was the first recorded mortgage.
d. The Zone and Link mortgages share priority because neither had notice of the Hay mortgage. (5/93, Law, #57, 4025)

Items 32 and 33 are based on the following:

On February 1, Frost bought a building from Elgin, Inc. for $250,000. To complete the purchase, Frost borrowed $200,000 from Independent Bank and gave Independent a mortgage for that amount; gave Elgin a second mortgage for $25,000; and paid $25,000 in cash. Independent recorded its mortgage on

February 2, and Elgin recorded its mortgage on March 12.

The following transaction also took place:

- On March 1, Frost gave Scott a $20,000 mortgage on the building to secure a personal loan Scott had previously made to Frost.
- On March 10, Scott recorded this mortgage.
- On March 15, Scott learned about both prior mortgages.
- On June 1, Frost stopped making payments on all the mortgages.
- On August 1, the mortgages were foreclosed. Frost, on that date, owed Independent, $195,000; Elgin, $24,000; and Scott, $19,000.

A judicial sale of the building resulted in proceeds of $220,000 after expenses were deducted. The above transactions took place in a race-notice jurisdiction.

32. What amount of the proceeds will Scott receive?
a. $0
b. $ 1,000
c. $12,500
d. $19,000   (11/92, Law, #58, 3140)

33. Why would Scott receive this amount?
a. Scott knew of the Elgin mortgage.
b. Scott's mortgage was recorded before Elgin's and before Scott knew of Elgin's mortgage.
c. Elgin's mortgage was first in time.
d. After Independent is fully paid, Elgin and Scott share the remaining proceeds equally.
(11/92, Law, #59, 3141)

34. If a mortgagee fails to record its mortgage in a jurisdiction with a race-notice recording statute,
a. A subsequent recording mortgagee who has **no** knowledge of the prior mortgage will have a superior security interest.
b. A subsequent recording mortgagee who has knowledge of the prior mortgage will have a superior security interest.
c. A subsequent purchaser for value who has **no** knowledge of the mortgage will take the property subject to the mortgage.
d. A subsequent purchaser for value who has knowledge of the mortgage will take the property free of the prior security interest.
(11/91, Law, #56, 2384)

35. Wyn bought real estate from Duke and gave Duke a purchase money mortgage. Duke forgot to record the mortgage. Two months later, Wyn gave a mortgage on the same property to Goode to secure a property improvement loan. Goode recorded this mortgage nine days later. Goode knew about the Duke mortgage. If these events took place in a race-notice statute jurisdiction, which mortgage would have priority?
a. Duke's, because it was the first mortgage given.
b. Duke's, because Goode knew of the Duke mortgage.
c. Goode's, because it was the first mortgage recorded.
d. Goode's, because it was recorded within ten days.   (11/91, Law, #58, 2386)

36. On April 6, Ford purchased a warehouse from Atwood for $150,000. Atwood had executed two mortgages on the property: a purchase money mortgage given to Lang on March 2, which was not recorded; and a mortgage given to Young on March 9, which was recorded the same day. Ford was unaware of the mortgage to Lang. Under the circumstances,
a. Ford will take title to the warehouse subject only to Lang's mortgage.
b. Ford will take title to the warehouse free of Lang's mortgage.
c. Lang's mortgage is superior to Young's mortgage because Lang's mortgage is a purchase money mortgage.
d. Lang's mortgage is superior to Young's mortgage because Lang's mortgage was given first in time.   (5/90, Law, #56, 9911)

37. Bell obtained a $30,000 loan from Arco Bank, executing a promissory note and mortgage. The loan was secured by a building that Bell purchased from Marx for $50,000. Arco's recording of the mortgage
a. Generally does **not** affect the rights of Bell and Arco against each other under the promissory note.
b. Generally creates a possessory security interest in Arco.
c. Cuts off the rights of all prior and subsequent lessees of the building.
d. Transfers legal title to the building to Arco.
(5/88, Law, #56, 0831)

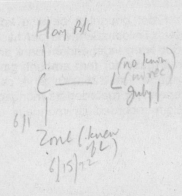

38. Generally, which of the following federal acts regulate mortgage lenders?

	Real Estate Settlement Procedures Act (RESPA)	Federal Trade Commission Act
a.	Yes	Yes
b.	Yes	No
c.	No	Yes
d.	No	No

(5/95, Law, #54, 5388)

39. Generally, in addition to being in writing, a real estate mortgage must
a. Be signed by both the mortgagor and mortgagee.
b. Be recorded to validate the mortgagee's rights against the mortgagor.
c. Contain a description of the real estate covered by the mortgage.
d. Contain the actual amount of the underlying debt and the interest rate.

(11/92, Law, #55, 3137)

40. In general, which of the following statements is correct with respect to a real estate mortgage?
a. The mortgage may **not** be given to secure an antecedent debt.
b. The mortgage must contain the actual amount of the underlying debt.
c. The mortgage must be signed by both the mortgagor (borrower) and mortgagee (lender).
d. The mortgagee may assign the mortgage to a third party without the mortgagor's consent.

(5/93, Law, #55, 4023)

41. A mortgagor's right of redemption will be terminated by a judicial foreclosure sale unless
a. The proceeds from the sale are **not** sufficient to fully satisfy the mortgage debt.
b. The mortgage instrument does **not** provide for a default sale.
c. The mortgagee purchases the property for market value.
d. The jurisdiction has enacted a statutory right of redemption.

(5/93, Law, #58, 4026)

42. On February 1, Frost bought a building from Elgin, Inc. for $250,000. To complete the purchase, Frost borrowed $200,000 from Independent Bank and gave Independent a mortgage for that amount; gave Elgin a second mortgage for $25,000; and paid $25,000 in cash. Independent recorded its mortgage on February 2 and Elgin recorded its mortgage on March 12.

The following transactions also took place:

- On March 1, Frost gave Scott a $20,000 mortgage on the building to secure a personal loan Scott had previously made to Frost.
- On March 10, Scott recorded this mortgage.
- On March 15, Scott learned about both prior mortgages.
- On June 1, Frost stopped making payments on all the mortgages.
- On August 1, the mortgages were foreclosed. Frost, on that date, owed Independent, $195,000; Elgin, $24,000; and Scott, $19,000.

A judicial sale of the building resulted in proceeds of $220,000 after expenses were deducted. The above transactions took place in a race-notice jurisdiction.

Frost may redeem the property before the judicial sale only if
a. There is a statutory right of redemption.
b. It is probable that the sale price will result in a deficiency.
c. All mortgages are paid in full.
d. All mortgagees are paid a penalty fee.

(11/92, Law, #60, 3142)

43. Which of the following is correct regarding foreclosure of a purchase money mortgage by judicial sale of the property?
a. The mortgagor has the right to any remaining sale proceeds after the mortgagee is paid.
b. The purchaser at the sale is liable for any deficiency owed the mortgagee.
c. The court must confirm any price received at the sale.
d. The mortgagor can never be liable for a deficiency owed the mortgagee.

(11/91, Law, #57, 2385)

44. Lusk borrowed $20,000 from Marco Finance. The loan was secured by a mortgage on a four-unit apartment building owned by Lusk. The proceeds of the loan were used by Lusk to purchase a business. The mortgage was duly recorded 60 days after Marco loaned the money to Lusk. Six months after borrowing the money from Marco, Lusk leased one of the apartments to Rudd for $800 per month. Neither Rudd nor Lusk notified Marco of the lease. Subsequently, Lusk defaulted on the note to Marco and Marco has commenced foreclosure proceedings. Under the circumstances,

a. Marco's mortgage is junior to Rudd's lease because the mortgage was **not** a purchase money mortgage.

b. Marco's mortgage is junior to Rudd's lease because Marco failed to record the mortgage for 60 days after the closing.

c. Rudd's lease is subject to Marco's mortgage because Marco recorded its mortgage prior to the time Rudd's leasehold interest arose.

d. Rudd's lease is subject to Marco's mortgage because of the failure to notify Marco of the lease. (11/87, Law, #52, 0834)

45. Wilk bought an apartment building from Dix Corp. There was a mortgage on the building securing Dix's promissory note to Xeon Finance Co. Wilk took title subject to Xeon's mortgage. Wilk did not make the payments on the note due Xeon and the building was sold at a foreclosure sale. If the proceeds of the foreclosure sale are less than the balance due on the note, which of the following statements is correct regarding the deficiency?

a. Xeon must attempt to collect the deficiency from Wilk before suing Dix.

b. Dix will **not** be liable for any of the deficiency because Wilk assumed the note and mortgage.

c. Xeon may collect the deficiency from either Dix or Wilk.

d. Dix will be liable for the entire deficiency. (5/91, Law, #19, 0810)

46. Omega Corp. owned a factory that was encumbered by a mortgage securing Omega's note to Eagle Bank. Omega sold the factory to Spear, Inc., which assumed the mortgage note. Later, Spear defaulted on the note, which had an outstanding balance of $15,000. To recover the outstanding balance, Eagle

a. May sue Spear only after suing Omega.

b. May sue either Spear or Omega.

c. Must sue both Spear and Omega.

d. Must sue Spear first and then proceed against Omega for any deficiency. (11/90, Law, #24, 0811)

47. Ritz owned a building on which there was a duly recorded first mortgage held by Lyn and a recorded second mortgage held by Jay. Ritz sold the building to Nunn. Nunn assumed the Jay mortgage and had no actual knowledge of the Lyn mortgage. Nunn defaulted on the payments to Jay. If both Lyn and Jay foreclosed, and the proceeds of the sale were insufficient to pay both Lyn and Jay,

a. Jay would be paid after Lyn was fully paid.

b. Jay and Lyn would be paid proportionately.

c. Nunn would be personally liable to Lyn but **not** to Jay.

d. Nunn would be personally liable to Lyn and Jay. (11/90, Law, #58, 0818)

Solution 56-1 MULTIPLE CHOICE ANSWERS

Realty vs. Personalty

1. (c) Requirements for transfer and creditor's rights would differ based on whether an asset was treated as personal property or real property. Requirements for transfer would differ because transfer of real property would require the transfer of the related deed for the property whereas transfer of personal property would not require a deed. Creditor's rights would differ in that rules for foreclosure on real property differ from those for repossession of personal property.

1A. (c) In order to determine whether an item of personal property has become a fixture, it is necessary to determine the degree and/or manner of affixation/attachment and/or whether the owner/annexor intended for the item to be a fixture. The value of an item is irrelevant in determining whether it is a fixture.

2. (d) Tangible personal property is property that has physical substance such as a car, a television set, or an oil painting. A share of stock, a trademark, and a promissory note represent intangible property interests, i.e., those that have no real physical existence.

Joint Tenancy

3. (a) A joint tenancy requires the following four unities: (1) time, (2) title, (3) interest, and (4) possession.

4. (a) Sklar's *inter vivos* conveyance to Marsh terminated the joint tenancy with respect to the grantee, Marsh. Therefore, Marsh's interest is that of a tenant in common, a one-third interest with no rights of survivorship. The interest in the building can be transferred without the consent of the other joint tenants.

5.   (c)   Rights of survivorship involve natural persons.   A corporation is not such a person. (Indeed, corporations generally opt for "perpetual existence" in the corporate documents.) Therefore, a joint tenant with the right of survivorship cannot involve an unaffiliated corporation.

6.   (a)   If a joint tenant with right of survivorship wants to convey his interest in the property to another, he may do so without the consent of any of the other joint owners. The result of such a transfer is to sever the joint tenancy as between the owners retaining their interests and the new owner, and instead create between them a tenancy in common in the entire property with no right of survivorship. This means that Green and Ink will each own an undivided interest in the entire 40 acres.

7.   (d)   Since Boch's and Kent's interests are as joint tenants with the right of survivorship, upon the death of Boch, his interest will automatically pass to Kent. This interest is not subject to the terms of Boch's will, nor is it included in his probate estate. However, the interest will be included in Boch's estate for purposes of the federal estate tax. An interest in a joint tenancy with a right of survivorship may be transferred by its owner, although by doing so the joint tenancy will be severed.

Tenancy in Common

8.   (c)   If one joint tenant in a joint tenancy with rights of survivorship makes an *inter vivos* conveyance of his share, the grantee of that share would be a tenant in common with the remaining joint tenants. The joint tenants who do not make such an *inter vivos* transfer continue to hold their interests as joint tenants.

9.   (a)   A distinguishing feature of a tenancy in common is that there is no right of survivorship; therefore, each co-tenant's interest is inheritable. Oak's death will not affect the shares of the other co-tenants and Oak's heirs will inherit Oak's share.

Environmental Protection

10.   (a)   The federal acts regulating air and water pollution permit citizens or states to enforce the provisions of these acts either by bringing private suits against violators or by suing the Environmental Protection Agency to enforce compliance with the laws.

11.   (d)   Under the Comprehensive Environmental Response, Compensation, and Liability Act (CERCLA), known as Superfund, current and prior owners or operators of a site, as well as any person who transported waste to the site, would be liable to the Environmental Protection Agency for the expense of cleaning up a hazardous waste disposal site.

Real Property Transfers

12.   (d)   A marketable title is one which is free from reasonable objections. It must be free from private encumbrances not otherwise specified in the title, such as easements or mortgages. Zoning laws will generally not render a title unmarketable. The easements are recorded on the title. A recorded lawsuit against the seller would not qualify as a lien, mortgage or other encumbrance to the property.

13.   (b)   Title insurance generally insures that the purchaser has good title as of the policy's date, covering losses that result from defects or failure of title to real property. Title insurance covers only defects of record, does not ensure that all taxes and assessments are paid, and does not pass to subsequent purchasers.

14.   (b)   Title insurance covers losses resulting from defects or failure of title to real property. As a practical matter, most title insurance policies *exclude* coverage of any defect which is not of record. Title exceptions listed in the policy are *not* covered. Coverage is only for defects of record that exist as of the effective date of the policy. Title insurance is not transferable.

15.   (c)   The necessary requirements for a valid deed are: (1) the names of the seller and purchaser; (2) a legally sufficient description of the land; (3) the seller's (and the spouse's, where appropriate) signature; (4) words indicating an intent to convey; and (5) delivery of the deed. Answers (a), (b), and (d) are items not required for a deed to be effective.

15A. (b)   In order for a deed to be effective between a purchaser and seller of real estate, the deed must be delivered by the seller with the intent to transfer title. The deed must be in writing and signed by the seller/grantor, must name the grantee and describe him or her, and must contain a description of the land. It is not necessary for the deed to contain the sales price or the signature of the purchaser/grantee. The recording of the deed is effective between the purchaser and third parties and not between the purchaser and the seller of real estate.

16. (d) A general warranty deed gives the purchaser the greatest protection when purchasing property, and a quitclaim deed gives the buyer the least amount of protection.

17. (b) Nexis knew about the prior conveyance and thus was not a bona fide (good faith) purchaser. Nexis' lack of good faith prevents his prevailing under a notice statute or a race-notice statute. However, under a purely race statute, where good faith is not an issue (simply a question of who recorded first), Nexis would prevail.

18. (c) A general warranty deed contains the following covenants: (1) the grantor warrants that he or she owns the property and has a right to convey it, (2) the grantee will not be disturbed in possession of the property by the grantor or some third party's lawful claim of ownership, (3) the grantor promises that there are no existing encumbrances on the title to the property, (4) the grantor will execute or obtain further documents or assurances necessary to perfect title, and (5) the grantor will forever warrant title to the property.

19. (b) A general warranty deed contains all six of the usual covenants. Among the possibilities stated, item I is the covenant of seisin; item II is the covenant of quiet enjoyment, and item III is the covenant of right to convey.

Landlord/Tenant Relationship

20. (d) If the tenant holds over after the expiration of the tenancy term without the consent of the landlord, there is a tenancy at sufferance. A tenancy at will is one that continues until either party terminates. A tenancy for years is a tenancy for a specified duration, even if the period is less than a year. A tenancy from period to period is one which continues from year to year, month to month, or any other fraction of a year.

21. (a) A residential lease agreement must contain a description of the leased premises. A residential lease agreement need not include a due date for payment of rent, a requirement that the tenant have liability insurance, or a requirement that the landlord will perform all structural repairs to the property.

22. (d) A tenant has a possessory interest in property according to the lease, and the landlord has a reversionary interest (i.e., once the lease expires, the possession of the property "reverts" to the landlord). If a tenant purchases the building so that the tenant and the landlord are the same party, the lease is terminated since the tenant and landlord are the same. If a lease does not prohibit assigning or subletting, the tenant is free to assign or sublet without the permission of the landlord. The landlord's death does not terminate the lease.

23. (c) Unless there is a clause restricting or prohibiting assignments and/or subleases, a tenant has the right to assign or sublease to another party. Therefore, Delta does not need Tanner's consent to assign the lease to another party.

24. (c) The January 1 agreement between Tell and Vorn was a sublease since it resulted in the creation of a new lease effective as between those parties and was not merely an assignment of the original lease between Tell and Lott. As a sublease, Vorn did not become liable to Lott for the rent or taxes, and upon their nonpayment, Lott could only proceed against Tell and not Vorn.

25. (c) An assignment transfers the entire leasehold interest of the tenant-assignor to the assignee. A sublease, in contrast, transfers less than all of the tenant's rights in the lease. Samon, by consenting to a prior sublet, has not waived his right to deny a subsequent sublease. Despite the sublease, Drake is still primarily liable under the lease to Samon. Drake is also still liable as a surety under his covenant to payment despite the assignment of his entire interest. Samon could waive the prohibition against subletting by accepting rent from the sub-lessee.

26. (a) A landlord may terminate the lease (and of course, evict the tenant) if the tenant uses the leased property for a purpose that is illegal and the landlord is not a party to that illegal use. Even if the landlord were a party to the illegal use, and intended for the property to be so used, the enforceability of the lease is quite doubtful and thus the tenant could most likely be evicted. Since counterfeiting money is illegal, that would be cause for eviction.

Mortgage Characteristics

27. (a) In order for a mortgage to be enforceable, there must be a description of the property sufficiently accurate to furnish some means of identification. It is not necessary that a negotiable promissory note accompany the mortgage, or that present consideration be given in exchange for the mortgage, or that the amount of the debt and the interest rate be stated.

28. (d) Generally, a mortgage must meet the requirements of a deed, including its delivery to the mortgagee. Since a mortgage is considered an interest in real property, it must be in writing and signed by the *mortgagor*. There is no requirement of acknowledgment by the *mortgagee*. It is not mandatory for a mortgage to contain the amount of the debt or consideration given to be valid.

29. (d) If a mortgage is not recorded, the owner of the mortgage can still bring a claim for payment when the debtor defaults. In this question, Dix is entitled to payment after the first mortgage has been satisfied. Dix's second priority status would be lost if a subsequent lender in good faith loaned money and recorded another mortgage. Dix can claim a security interest in the property even if the mortgage was not recorded. There is no pro rata sharing of proceeds when a debtor defaults. Money is distributed to the first recorded mortgage and when this interest is paid in full, the second mortgage is entitled to payment.

Mortgage Recording Requirements

30. (c) A mortgage is recorded to give constructive notice of the mortgage and protect against the claims of subsequent bona fide purchasers for value. Recording a mortgage does not protect against previously filed real estate tax liens on the property, parties having earlier claims to the property, or rights against Fern under the promissory note.

31. (b) A mortgage is recorded to give constructive notice of the mortgage and protect against subsequent mortgagees. Under a race-notice statute, if the first mortgage is not recorded, a subsequent mortgagee who has no knowledge of the first mortgage will have priority once he or she records. However, if the subsequent mortgagee did have notice of the first mortgage he or she can't get priority. Thus, the Link mortgage has priority because Zone had notice of the Link mortgage. The first mortgage in time has priority only if it is recorded first. The Zone mortgage can't have priority since Zone knew about the Link mortgage. Although neither Zone nor Link had notice of the Hay mortgage, Link has priority because Zone had notice of the Link mortgage.

32. (d) In a race-notice jurisdiction, the recording of the mortgages would determine the priority of the creditors. Here, Independent recorded on February 2, Scott recorded on March 10, while Elgin recorded on March 12. Therefore, the $220,000 would be divided as follows: Independent $195,000,

Scott $19,000, and Elgin the remaining $8,000. Scott would get the full amount Frost owed him.

33. (b) In a race-notice jurisdiction the recording of the mortgages would determine the priority of the creditors. Here, Independent recorded on February 2, Scott recorded on March 10, while Elgin recorded on March 12. Therefore, the $220,000 would be divided as follows: Independent $195,000, Scott $19,000, and Elgin the remaining $8,000. Answer (a) is incorrect because Scott was not aware of the prior mortgages until after he had recorded his own mortgage. Thus, this had no effect on the priority of the mortgages. Although Elgin's mortgage was the first in time it would have priority only if it had been recorded before Scott's. The mortgages are paid in the order of their priority. The proceeds are not split equally.

34. (a) In states with race-notice recording statutes, the first mortgagee to file prevails. In order to have a superior security interest, however, the mortgagee must <u>not</u> have knowledge of a prior mortgage.

35. (b) In states with race-notice recording statutes, the first mortgagee to file prevails. In order to have a superior security interest, however, the mortgagee must not have knowledge of a prior mortgage. Because Goode knew of the Duke mortgage, Duke's mortgage has priority.

36. (b) Ford was unaware of the mortgage to Lang. Because Ford is a subsequent bona fide party at interest, he takes the property free of Lang's *unrecorded* mortgage.

37. (a) The recording of the mortgage serves to protect Arco's interests as against third parties who subsequently acquire rights in the property. It does not affect the rights and liabilities as between Bell and Arco. Answers (b), (c), and (d) each represent an incorrect statement concerning the recording of mortgages.

Mortgage Provisions, Rights of Parties, and Sale of Mortgaged Property

38. (b) The Real Estate Settlement Procedures Act (RESPA) regulates the activities of mortgage lenders. The Federal Trade Commission Act generally regulates nonreal estate consumer credit transactions.

39. (c) A complete legal description of the property is required in the mortgage. The mortgage is required to be signed by the mortgagor only and not

the mortgagee. Recording is necessary to make the mortgage enforceable against subsequent bona fide parties at interest, but <u>not</u> between a mortgagor and a mortgagee. It is not mandatory that the mortgage contain the amount of the debt and the rate of interest in order to be valid.

40. (d) A mortgage is generally freely transferable and, in the absence of any restrictions in the document, the mortgagee may assign the mortgage to a third party without the mortgagor's consent. A mortgage may be given to secure an antecedent debt. It is not mandatory for the mortgage to contain the amount of the debt and the rate of interest in order to be valid. The mortgage is required to be signed only by the mortgagor and not the mortgagee.

41. (d) Right of redemption is a statutory right that occurs after the judicial sale. States that have enacted a right of redemption allow a mortgagor a period of time, usually one year after the foreclosure sale, to reinstate the debt and mortgage by paying to the purchaser at the judicial sale the amount of the purchase price plus the statutory interest rate. The mortgagor has the right to redeem the property prior to the judicial sale by paying the mortgage in full plus interest and other costs. Foreclosure requires a judicial action; the mortgage instrument does not need to provide for a default sale. The mortgagor, not the mortgagee, can redeem the property by paying interest, outstanding debt, and expenses.

42. (c) Frost's right of redemption entitles him to retain the property even after foreclosure, but before the foreclosure sale, by paying the amount due plus interest and any other costs. A statutory right of redemption occurs after a judicial sale. This right entitles the mortgagor a period of time, usually one year, to reinstate the debt and mortgage by paying to the purchaser at the judicial sale the amount of the purchase price plus the statutory rate of interest. Frost may redeem the property before the judicial sale by paying all mortgages in full. The probable sales price of the property is irrelevant. Frost would not have to pay any penalty fees to the mortgagees.

43. (a) In a judicial sale of property, proceeds are first applied to the foreclosure costs (such as court filing fees and advertising) and then toward payment of the debt. Any surplus after the sale goes to the mortgagor. When the proceeds from the sale

do not cover the debt, the mortgagor (not the subsequent purchaser) is responsible for the deficiency. It is only the foreclosure sale *proceedings* that are court approved; the sales *price* need not be approved or "confirmed" by the court.

44. (c) The recording of a mortgage has no effect on the mortgagor-mortgagee relationship. Recordation is merely meant to protect the mortgagee's rights against other persons who acquire an interest in the mortgagor's property. Because Rudd's lease was executed after Marco recorded his mortgage, Rudd takes subject to the mortgage. The type of mortgage is not important in categorizing competing interests in the same property. Any notification given by Rudd to Marco would be irrelevant.

45. (d) Wilk, the buyer, purchased the property "subject to the mortgage." Since the buyer never assumed the liability of the mortgage, only the mortgagor, Dix, will be liable.

46. (b) When a mortgagor sells his or her property and the buyer assumes the mortgage debt, unless otherwise agreed, the mortgagor remains liable to the mortgagee (the bank), and the bank becomes the creditor beneficiary of the buyer's agreement to assume the mortgage. Thus, in the event of default, the bank can proceed against either the original mortgagor or the buyer who assumed the mortgage. The bank can go after either the mortgagor (Omega) or after the individual who assumed the mortgage (Spear). There is no requirement that the bank proceed against one or the other first since no order or priority is necessary. There is no need to sue both.

47. (a) Since both mortgages were recorded, the purchaser (Nunn) of the property is constructively aware of the first mortgage held by Lyn. While Nunn assumed the second mortgage, Nunn purchases the property subject to the first mortgage. If Nunn defaults, proceeds from the sale of the property will go toward paying the first mortgage held by Lyn, and if any money remains, the money will be paid to Jay, the second mortgage holder. A first mortgage is paid in full before a second mortgage receives anything. Nunn has no personal liability to Lyn since the first mortgage was never assumed.

PERFORMANCE BY SUBTOPICS

Each category below parallels a subtopic covered in Chapter 56. Record the number and percentage of questions you correctly answered in each subtopic area.

Realty vs. Personalty

Question #	Correct √
1	
1A	
2	
# Questions	3

Correct _____
% Correct _____

Joint Tenancy

Question #	Correct √
3	
4	
5	
6	
7	
# Questions	5

Correct _____
% Correct _____

Tenancy in Common

Question #	Correct √
8	
9	
# Questions	2

Correct _____
% Correct _____

Environmental Protection

Question #	Correct √
10	
11	
# Questions	2

Correct _____
% Correct _____

Real Property Transfers

Question #	Correct √
12	
13	
14	
15	
15A	
16	
17	
18	
19	
# Questions	9

Correct _____
% Correct _____

Landlord/Tenant Relationship

Question #	Correct √
20	
21	
22	
23	
24	
25	
26	
# Questions	7

Correct _____
% Correct _____

Mortgage Characteristics

Question #	Correct √
27	
28	
29	
# Questions	3

Correct _____
% Correct _____

Mortgage Recording Requirements

Question #	Correct √
30	
31	
32	
33	
34	
35	
36	
37	
# Questions	8

Correct _____
% Correct _____

Mortgage Provisions, Rights of Parties, and Sale of Mortgaged Property

Question #	Correct √
38	
39	
40	
41	
42	
43	
44	
45	
46	
47	
# Questions	10

Correct _____
% Correct _____

OTHER OBJECTIVE FORMAT QUESTIONS

Problem 56-2 (10 to 15 minutes)

On June 1, 1990, Anderson bought a one family house from Beach for $240,000. At the time of the purchase, the house had a market value of $200,000 and the land was valued at $40,000. Anderson assumed the recorded $150,000 mortgage Beach owed Long Bank, gave a $70,000 mortgage to Rogers Loan Co., and paid $20,000 cash. Rogers did not record its mortgage. Rogers did not know about the Long Mortgage.

Beach gave Anderson a quitclaim deed that failed to mention a recorded easement on the property held by Dalton, the owner of the adjacent piece of property. Anderson purchased a title insurance policy from Edge Title Insurance Co. Edge's policy neither disclosed nor excepted Dalton's easement.

On August 1, 1992, Anderson borrowed $30,000 from Forrest Finance to have a swimming pool dug. Anderson gave Forrest a $30,000 mortgage on the property. Forrest, knowing about the Long mortgage but not the Rogers mortgage, recorded its mortgage on August 10, 1992. After the digging began, Dalton sued to stop the work claiming violation of the easement. The court decided in Dalton's favor.

At the time of the purchase, Anderson had taken out two fire insurance policies; a $120,000 face value policy with Harvest Fire Insurance Co., and a $60,000 face value policy with Grant Fire Insurance Corp. Both policies contained a standard 80% coinsurance clause.

On December 1, 1992, a fire caused $180,000 damage to the house. At that time, the house had a market value of $250,000. Harvest and Grant refused to honor the policies claiming that the house was under insured.

Anderson made no mortgage payments after the fire and on June 1, 1993, after the house had been rebuilt, the mortgages were foreclosed. The balances due for principal and accrued interest were as follows: Long, $140,000; Rogers, $65,000; and Forrest, $28,000. At a foreclosure sale, the house and land were sold. After payment of all expenses, $200,000 of the proceeds remained for distribution. As a result of the above events, the following actions took place:

* Anderson sued Harvest and Grant for the face values of the fire insurance policies.
* Anderson sued Beach for failing to mention Dalton's easement in the quitclaim deed.
* Anderson sued Edge for failing to disclose Dalton's easement.
* Long, Rogers, and Forrest all demanded full payment of their mortgages from the proceeds of the foreclosure sale.

The preceding took place in a "Race-Notice" jurisdiction.

Required:

a. **Items 1 through 3** relate to Anderson's suit against Beach. For each item, determine whether that statement is True or False.

1. Anderson will win the suit against Beach. *F*
2. A quitclaim deed conveys only the grantor's interest in the property. *T*
3. A warranty deed protects the purchaser against any adverse title claim against the property.

b. **Items 4 through 6** relate to Anderson's suit against Edge. For each item, determine whether the statement is True or False.

4. Anderson will win the suit against Edge. *F No*

5. Edge's policy should insure against all title defects of record. *T*
6. Edge's failure to disclose Dalton's easement voids Anderson's contract with Beach. *F*

c. **Items 7 through 9** relate to the demands Long, Rogers, and Forrest have made to have their mortgages satisfied out of the foreclosure proceeds. For each items, select from *List I* the dollar amount to be paid.

7. What dollar amount of the foreclosure proceeds will Long receive? *G*
8. What dollar amount of the foreclosure proceeds will Rogers receive? *C*
9. What dollar amount of the foreclosure proceeds will Forrest receive? *B*

	List I
A.	$ 0
B.	$ 28,000
C.	$ 32,000
D.	$ 65,000
E.	$107,000
F.	$135,000
G.	$140,000

(11/93, Law, #2)

Problem 56-3 (15 to 25 minutes)

On June 10, 1990, Bond sold real property to Edwards for $100,000. Edwards assumed the $80,000 recorded mortgage Bond had previously given to Fair Bank and gave a $20,000 purchase money mortgage to Heath Finance. Heath did not record this mortgage. On December 15, 1991, Edwards sold the property to Ivor for $115,000. Ivor bought the property subject to the Fair mortgage but did not know about the Heath mortgage. Ivor borrowed $50,000 from Knox Bank and gave Knox a mortgage on the property. Knox knew of the unrecorded Heath mortgage when its mortgage was recorded. Ivor, Edwards, and Bond defaulted on the mortgages. Fair, Heath, and Knox foreclosed and the property was sold at a judicial foreclosure sale for $60,000. At the time of the sale, the outstanding balance of principal and accrued interest on the Fair mortgage was $75,000. The Heath mortgage balance was $18,000 and the Knox mortgage was $47,500.

Fair, Heath, and Knox all claim that their mortgages have priority and should be satisfied first from the sale proceeds. Bond, Edwards, and Ivor all claim that they are not liable for any deficiency resulting from the sale.

The above transactions took place in a jurisdiction that has a race-notice recording statute and allows foreclosure deficiency judgments.

Required:

a.   Items 1 through 3. For each mortgage, select from List A the priority of that mortgage. A priority should be selected only once.

List A

1.	Knox Bank. *C*	A.	First Priority.
2.	Heath Finance. *B*	B.	Second Priority.
3.	Fair Bank. *A*	C.	Third Priority.

b.   Items 4 through 6. For each mortgage, select from List B the reason for its priority. A reason may be selected once, more than once, or not at all.

List B

4.	Knox Bank. *B*	A.	An unrecorded mortgage has priority over any subsequently recorded mortgage.
5.	Heath Finance. *D*	B.	A recorded mortgage has priority over any unrecorded mortgage.
6.	Fair Bank. *C*	C.	The first recorded mortgage has priority over all subsequent mortgages.
		D.	An unrecorded mortgage has priority over a subsequently recorded mortgage if the subsequent mortgagee knew of the unrecorded mortgage.
		E.	A purchase money mortgage has priority over a previously recorded mortgage.

c.   Items 7 through 9. For each mortgage, select from List C the amount of the sale proceeds that each mortgagee would be entitled to receive. An amount may be selected once, more than once, or not at all.

List C

7.	Knox Bank. *A*	A.	$0.
8.	Heath Finance. *X*	B.	$12,500.
9.	Fair Bank. *G*	C.	$18,000.
		D.	$20,000.
		E.	$42,000.
		F.	$47,500.
		G.	$60,000.

d.   Items 10 through 12. Determine whether each party would be liable to pay a mortgage foreclosure deficiency judgment on the Fair Bank mortgage. If the party would be held liable, select from List D the reason for the party's liability. A reason may be selected once, more than once, or not at all.

List D

10.	Edwards. *B*	A.	Original mortgagor.
11.	Bond. *A*	B.	Assumed the mortgage.
12.	Ivor. *C*	C.	Took subject to the mortgage.
		D.	Not liable.

e.   For items 13 through 15, determine whether each party would be liable to pay a mortgage foreclosure deficiency judgment on the Heath Finance mortgage. If the party would be held liable, select from List E the reason for that party's liability. A reason may be selected once, more than once, or not at all.

List E

13.	Edwards. *A*	A.	Original mortgagor.
14.	Bond. *D*	B.	Assumed the mortgage.
15.	Ivor. *D*	C.	Took subject to the mortgage.
		D.	Not liable.

f.   For items 16 through 18, determine whether each party would be liable to pay a mortgage foreclosure deficiency judgment on the Knox Bank mortgage. If the party would be held liable, select from List F the reason for that party's liability. A reason may be selected once, more than once, or not at all.

List F

16.	Edwards. *D*	A.	Original mortgagor.
17.	Bond. *D*	B.	Assumed the mortgage.
18.	Ivor. *A*	C.	Took subject to the mortgage.
		D.	Not liable.

(5/92, Law, #2)

OTHER OBJECTIVE FORMAT SOLUTIONS

Solution 56-2 Mortgage Priorities and Liability

1. (F) Anderson will not win in his suit against Beach because Beach gave Anderson a quitclaim deed which does not guarantee that other parties do not have claims on the property. The quitclaim deed only transfers whatever interest the grantor may have in the property.

2. (T) A quitclaim deed transfers whatever interest the grantor has in the property.

3. (T) A warranty deed promises the grantee that the grantor has valid title to the property and obliges the grantor to make the grantee whole if the grantee suffers damage because of defective title. Other covenants are also usually included such as title, against encumbrances, quiet enjoyment, and warranty. All of these assurances act to protect the purchaser against any adverse title claims that could arise.

4. (T) Title insurance guarantees the owner against any loss due to defects, liens, or encumbrances on the title of the property which are not disclosed on the insurance policy. The court will find that Edge is liable to Anderson for damages incurred as a result of the failure to disclose the easement on the property.

5. (T) Title insurance only guarantees the owner against title defects *of record*.

6. (F) Title insurance provides for monetary damages to the insured party only. The policy has no power to affect the contract between Anderson and Beach.

7. (G) Proceeds of the foreclosure sale after expenses were $200,000. This must be paid out to the creditors according to their order of priority. Long will be the first to be paid since its security interest was the first to be perfected in the property. So, Long's claim of $140,000 is paid first. The remaining proceeds go to the next creditor to perfect a security interest in the property. This would be Forrest, since Rogers failed to record its mortgage. Forrest is paid on its claim of $28,000, and the remaining proceeds of $32,000 go to Rogers in partial satisfaction of its $65,000 claim.

8. (C) Proceeds of the foreclosure sale after expenses were $200,000. This must be paid out to the creditors according to their order of priority. Long will be the first to be paid since its security interest was the first to be perfected in the property. So, Long's claim of $140,000 is paid first. The remaining proceeds go to the next creditor to perfect a security interest in the property. This would be Forrest, since Rogers failed to record its mortgage. Forrest is paid on its claim of $28,000, and the remaining proceeds of $32,000 go to Rogers in partial satisfaction of its $65,000 claim.

9. (B) Proceeds of the foreclosure sale after expenses were $200,000. This must be paid out to the creditors according to their order of priority. Long will be the first to be paid since its security interest was the first to be perfected in the property. So, Long's claim of $140,000 is paid first. The remaining proceeds go to the next creditor to perfect a security interest in the property. This would be Forrest, since Rogers failed to record its mortgage. Forrest is paid on its claim of $28,000, and the remaining proceeds of $32,000 go to Rogers in partial satisfaction of its $65,000 claim.

Solution 56-3 Mortgage Priorities and Liability

1. (C) Knox bank has third priority because Knox knew of the unrecorded Heath Finance mortgage when it recorded its mortgage. A subsequent mortgagee who records has priority over a prior mortgagee who does not record only if he or she has no knowledge of the unrecorded mortgage.

2. (B) Heath Finance has second priority to Fair Bank because the first mortgagee to obtain a mortgage and to record it has priority over all subsequent mortgages. However, Heath has priority over Knox Bank because Knox knew of the unrecorded Heath mortgage when it recorded its mortgage.

3. (B) Fair Bank has first priority because the first mortgagee to obtain a mortgage and to record it has priority over all subsequent mortgages.

4. (D) Knox bank has third priority (behind Heath Finance), because Knox knew of the unrecorded Heath mortgage when it recorded its mortgage. A subsequent mortgagee who records has priority over a prior mortgagee who does not record only if he or she has no knowledge of the unrecorded mortgage.

5. (D) Heath Finance has priority over Knox Bank because Knox knew of the unrecorded Heath mortgage when it recorded its mortgage.

6. (C) Fair Bank has first priority because the first mortgagee to obtain a mortgage and to record it has priority over all subsequent mortgages.

7. (A) Where there is more than one mortgage on property which is subject to a foreclosure sale, a mortgage which has priority is satisfied in full before proceeds are applied to satisfying mortgages of lower priority. Before any proceeds from the sale could be applied to satisfaction of Knox Bank's claim, the priority claims of Fair Bank, in the amount of $75,000 and Heath Finance, in the amount of $18,000, would have to be satisfied in full. Because the property was sold for only $60,000, Knox bank is not entitled to any of the foreclosure sale proceeds.

8. (A) Where there is more than one mortgage on property which is subject to a foreclosure sale, a mortgage which has priority is satisfied in full before proceeds are applied to satisfying mortgages of lower priority. Before any proceeds from the sale could be applied to satisfaction of Heath's claim, the priority claim of Fair Bank, in the amount of $75,000, would have to be satisfied in full. Because the property was sold for only $60,000, Heath Finance is not entitled to any of the foreclosure sale proceeds.

9. (G) Where there is more than one mortgage on property which is subject to a foreclosure sale, a mortgage which has priority is satisfied in full before proceeds are applied to satisfying mortgages of lower priority. Because Fair Bank's mortgage has priority, and because the property was sold for less than Fair Bank's claim of $75,000, the entire amount of $60,000 is applied to Fair Bank's claim. Nothing remains to be applied to the claims of Heath Finance or Knox Bank.

10. (B) If the proceeds from a foreclosure sale are insufficient to satisfy the obligation, the mortgagor (Bond) is still indebted to the mortgagee for the deficiency. A grantee of the mortgagor (Edwards) who expressly assumes the mortgage is also personally liable for it.

11. (A) If the proceeds from a foreclosure sale are insufficient to satisfy the obligation, the mortgagor (Bond) is still indebted to the mortgagee for the deficiency. Even though Edwards assumed the mortgage and is personally liable for it, Bond (the original mortgagor) remains personally liable unless the mortgagee (Fair Bank) releases him.

12. (D) A grantee (Ivor) who takes subject to the mortgage does not assume any personal liability for the mortgage.

13. (A) If the mortgage is not recorded, the mortgage is still valid between the mortgagor and mortgagee. Edwards, therefore, is personally liable (as the original mortgagor) if the proceeds from a foreclosure sale are insufficient to satisfy the obligation.

14. (D) Edwards is the original mortgagor on the Heath finance mortgage. Bond had no part in that mortgage and is therefore not liable if the proceeds from a foreclosure sale are insufficient to satisfy the obligation.

15. (D) If the mortgage is not recorded, the mortgage is still valid between the mortgagor (Edwards) and mortgagee (Heath Finance), but it is not valid against a subsequent bona fide purchaser (Ivor) if the subsequent purchaser is unaware of the unrecorded mortgage.

16. (D) Ivor is the original mortgagor on the Knox Bank mortgage. Edwards had no part in that mortgage and is therefore not liable if the proceeds from a foreclosure sale are insufficient to satisfy the obligation.

17. (D) Ivor is the original mortgagor on the Knox Bank mortgage. Bond had no part in that mortgage and is therefore not liable if the proceeds from a foreclosure sale are insufficient to satisfy the obligation.

18. (A) If the proceeds from a foreclosure sale are insufficient to satisfy the obligation, the mortgagor (Ivor) is still indebted to the mortgagee for the deficiency.

ESSAY QUESTIONS

Essay 56-4 (15 to 20 minutes)

On February 1, 1998, Tower and Perry, as tenants in common, purchased a two-unit apartment building for $250,000. They made a downpayment of $100,000, and gave a $100,000 first mortgage to Midway Bank and a $50,000 second mortgage to New Bank.

New was aware of Midway's mortgage but, as a result of clerical error, Midway did not record its mortgage until after New's mortgage was recorded.

At the time of purchase, a $200,000 fire insurance policy was issued by Acme Insurance Co. to Tower and Perry. The policy contained an 80% coinsurance clause and a standard mortgagee provision.

Tower and Perry rented an apartment to Young under a month-to-month oral lease. They rented the other apartment to Zimmer under a three-year written lease. On December 8, 1989, Perry died leaving a will naming the Dodd Foundation as the sole beneficiary of Perry's estate. The estate was distributed on January 15, 1990. That same date, the ownership of the fire insurance policy was assigned to Tower and Dodd with Acme's consent. On January 21, 1990, a fire caused $180,000 in structural damage to the building. At that time, its market value was $300,000 and the Midway mortgage balance was $80,000 including accrued interest. The New mortgage balance was $40,000 included accrued interest.

The fire made Young's apartment uninhabitable and caused extensive damage to the kitchen, bathrooms, and one bedroom of Zimmer's apartment. On February 1, 1990, Young and Zimmer moved out. The resulting loss of income caused a default on both mortgages.

On April 1, 1990, Acme refused to pay the fire loss claiming that the required insurable interest did not exist at the time of the loss and that the amount of the insurance was insufficient to provide full coverage for the loss. Tower and Dodd are involved in a lawsuit contesting the ownership of the building and the claims they have both made for any fire insurance proceeds.

On June 1, 1990, Midway and New foreclosed their mortgages and are also claiming any fire insurance proceeds that may be paid by Acme.

On July 1, 1990, Tower sued Zimmer for breach of the lease and is seeking to collect the balance of the lease term rent.

The above events took place in a race-notice statute jurisdiction.

Required:

Answer the following questions and give the reasons for your conclusions.

a. Who had title to the building on January 21, 1990? *Tower + Dodd*

b. Did Tower and/or Dodd have an insurable interest in the building when the fire occurred? If so, when would such an interest have arisen? *1/15/90*

(5/91, Law, #4a,b)

Essay 56-5 (15 to 20 minutes)

On March 2, 1988, Ash, Bale, and Rangel purchased an office building from Park Corp. as joint tenants with right of survivorship. There was an outstanding note and mortgage on the building, which they assumed. The note and mortgage named Park as the mortgagor (borrower) and Vista Bank as the mortgagee (lender). Vista has consented to the assumption.

Wein, Inc., a tenant in the office building, had entered into a 10-year lease dated May 8, 1985. The lease was silent regarding Wein's right to sublet. The lease provided for Wein to take occupancy on June 1, 1985, and that the monthly rent would be $5,000 for the entire 10-year term. On March 10, 1989, Wein informed Ash, Bale, and Rangel that it had agreed to sublet its office space to Nord Corp. On March 17, 1989, Ash, Bale, and Rangel notified Wein of their refusal to consent to the sublet. The following assertions have been made:

- The sublet from Wein to Nord is void because Ash, Bale, and Rangel did not consent.
- If the sublet is not void, Ash, Bale, and Rangel have the right to hold either Wein or Nord liable for payment of the rent.

On April 4, 1989, Ash transferred his interest in the building to his spouse.

Required:

Answer the following, setting forth reasons for any conclusions stated.

a. **For this item only**, assume that Ash, Bale, and Rangel default on the mortgage note, that Vista forecloses, and a deficiency results. Discuss the personal liability of Ash, Bale, and Rangel to Vista and the personal liability of Park to Vista.

b. Discuss the assertions as to the sublet, indicating whether such assertions are correct and the reasons therefor.

c. **For this item only**, assume that Ash and Rangel died on April 20, 1989. Discuss the ownership interest(s) in the office building as of April 5, 1989, and April 21, 1989. (5/89, Law, #3)

Essay 56-6 (15 to 20 minutes)

On June 1, 1972, Fein, Inc., leased a warehouse to Ted Major for use in his trucking business. Among the essential terms of the lease are the following:

- The lease term is 15 years.
- The monthly rent is $1,500.
- Major was required to replace the outside wood surface of the warehouse with aluminum siding by December 31, 1972 and, in consideration of this, Fein reduced the monthly rent from its market rate of $1,700 to $1,500.

On June 10, 1972, Major had the aluminum siding installed on the warehouse at a cost of $17,000. On June 15, 1982, Major installed a mainframe computer and several computer terminals in the warehouse at a cost of $250,000.

The lease on the warehouse is silent with respect to Major's right to remove the aluminum siding or computer and terminals upon the expiration of the lease.

Fein has asserted the following with respect to the above facts:

- That it is entitled to retain ownership of the aluminum siding at the expiration of the lease.
- That it is entitled to retain ownership of the computer and terminals at the expiration of the lease.

Required:

Discuss Fein's assertions indicating whether such assertions are correct. (5/87, Law, #4)

Essay 56-7 (15 to 25 minutes)

On May 15, 1993, Strong bought a factory building from Front for $500,000. Strong assumed Front's $300,000 mortgage with Ace Bank, gave a $150,000 mortgage to Lane Finance Co., and paid $50,000 cash.

The Ace mortgage had never been recorded. Lane knew of the Ace mortgage and recorded its mortgage on May 20, 1993.

Strong bought the factory for investment purposes and, on June 1, 1993, entered into a written lease with Apex Mfg. for seven years. On December 1, 1993, Apex subleased the factory to Egan Corp. without Strong's permission. Strong's lease with Apex was silent concerning the right to sublease.

On May 15, 1993, Strong had obtained a fire insurance policy from Range Insurance Co. The policy had a face value of $400,000. Apex and Egan obtained fire insurance policies from Zone Insurance Co. Each policy contained a standard 80% coinsurance clause. On May 1, 1994, when the factory had a fair market value of $600,000, a fire caused $180,000 damage.

Strong made no mortgage payments after the fire and on September 1, 1994, after the factory had been repaired, the mortgages were foreclosed. The balances due for principal and accrued interest were: Ace, $275,000; and Lane, $140,000. At a foreclosure sale, the factory and land were sold. After payment of all expenses, $400,000 of the proceeds remained for distribution.

As a result of the above events, the following actions took place:

- Strong sued Apex for subleasing the factory to Egan without Strong's permission.
- Zone refused to honor the Apex and Egan fire insurance policies claiming neither Apex nor Egan had an insurable interest in the factory.
- Strong sued Range to have Range pay Strong's $180,000 loss. Range refused claiming Strong had insufficient coverage under the coinsurance clause.
- Ace and Lane both demanded full payment of their mortgages from the proceeds of the foreclosure sale.

The preceding took place in a "Notice-Race" jurisdiction.

Required:

Answer the following questions and give the reasons for your conclusions.

a. Would Strong succeed in the suit against Apex for subletting the factory to Egan without Strong's permission?

b. Is Zone correct in claiming that neither Apex nor Egan had an insurable interest in the factory at the time of the fire?

c. What amount will Strong be able to recover from Range?

d. What amount of the foreclosure proceeds will Lane recover? (11/94, Law, #5)

ESSAY SOLUTIONS

Solution 56-4 Title of Property Upon Death/ Insurable Interest

a. Tower and Perry owned the property as **tenants in common.** This form of ownership allows either party to dispose of his or her undivided interest by sale or on death. **Any person purchasing or inheriting Perry's interest would become a tenant in common with Tower.** Thus, on January 21, 1990, **Tower and Dodd are tenants in common,** each owning a one-half undivided interest in the house.

b. **Both Tower and Dodd have an insurable interest in the house.** Tower's interest arose when the **property** was **purchased,** continued when the **insurance policy was purchased,** and still existed at the **time of the fire loss.** Dodd's interest arose when Dodd inherited Perry's interest in the house. **Acme's consent to the assignment of the policy to Tower and Dodd entitled Dodd to a share of the proceeds of the policy.**

Solution 56-5 Foreclosure/Sublease/Joint Tenancy

a. **Ash, Bale, and Rangel will be personally liable to Vista for the deficiency** resulting from the foreclosure sale because they became the **principal debtors when they assumed the mortgage. Park will remain liable for the deficiency.** Although Vista consented to the assumption of the mortgage by Ash, Bale, and Rangel, such **assumption does not relieve Park from its obligation to Vista unless Park obtains a release from Vista** or there is a novation.

b. The assertion that the sublet from Wein to Nord is void because Ash, Bale, and Rangel must consent to the sublet is incorrect. **Unless the lease provides otherwise, a tenant may sublet the premises without the landlord's consent.** Since the lease was silent regarding Wein's right to sublet, **Wein may sublet to Nord without the consent of Ash, Bale, and Rangel.**

The assertion that if the sublet was not void Ash, Bale, and Rangel have the right to hold either Wein or Nord liable for payment of rent is incorrect. **In a sublease, the sublessee/subtenant (Nord) has no obligation to pay rent to the landlord (Ash, Bale, and Rangel).**

The **subtenant** (Nord) **is liable to the tenant** (Wein), but the **tenant** (Wein) **remains solely liable to the landlord** (Ash, Bale, and Rangel) for the rent stipulated in the lease.

c. Ash's *inter vivos* transfer of his 1/3 interest in the office building to his spouse on April 4, 1989 resulted in his **spouse obtaining a 1/3 interest in the office building as a tenant in common.** Ash's **wife did not become a joint tenant** with Bale and Rangel because the **transfer of a joint tenant's interest to an outside party destroys the joint tenancy nature of the particular interest transferred.** Bale and Rangel will remain as joint tenants with each other.

As of April 21, 1989, the office building was owned by **Ash's spouse who had a 1/3 interest as tenant in common and Bale who had a 2/3 interest as tenant in common.**

Ash's death on April 20, 1989 will have no effect on the ownership of the office building because **Ash had already transferred all of his interest to his wife** on April 4, 1989.

Rangel's death on April 20, 1989 **resulted in his interest being acquired by Bale because of the right of survivorship feature in a joint tenancy.**

Because there are **no surviving joint tenants, Bale will become a tenant in common** who owns 2/3 of the office building. **Ash's spouse will not acquire any additional interest** due to Rangel's death because she was a **tenant in common** with Rangel.

Solution 56-6 Lessor's Rights to Lessee's Improvements to Leased Property

Fein's first assertion that it is **entitled to retain ownership of the aluminum siding at the expiration of the lease is correct**. The ownership of the aluminum siding will remain with Fein since it was **converted from personal property to real property** by virtue of it becoming a **fixture**. Since the lease between Fein and Major is silent as to Major's right to remove the aluminum siding, the facts and circumstances surrounding the installation of the aluminum siding must be evaluated. One significant factor which indicates that the parties may have impliedly agreed that the aluminum siding is to remain with Fein after the lease expires is the **reduction in the monthly rent** by $200 over 15 years **in exchange for the installation of the aluminum siding** by Major. In the absence of an agreement, the most important factor is the annexor's (Major's) objective intent in having added the aluminum siding to the real property. Major's intent may be inferred from such things as the following: the **manner by which the item is attached to the realty**, the **extent of damage** to the realty **caused by the removal** of the item, the **nature or purpose of the item**, and the **interest of the annexor in the realty** at the time of the annexation of the item. Under the foregoing tests, it is likely that the aluminum siding has become a fixture which is so **permanently affixed** to the warehouse that it probably could not be removed without doing substantial damage to the warehouse. Thus, the aluminum siding has become a part of the realty (warehouse).

Fein's second assertion that it is **entitled to retain ownership of the computer and computer terminals at the expiration of the lease is incorrect**. Although the computers may also have become a fixture under the tests mentioned above, they were **installed in order for the lessee** (Major) **to pursue its trade or business** and were likely **not intended to be permanent**. Thus, the computers would be classified as **trade fixtures** which may be **removed** by Major **at the expiration of the lease** if it can be accomplished **without doing material damage** to the warehouse.

Solution 56-7 Real Property

a. Strong will lose its suit against Apex for subletting the factory to Egan without Strong's permission. **Unless a lease provides otherwise**, a tenant may sublet the premises without the landlord's consent.

b. Zone is incorrect in claiming that neither Apex nor Egan had an insurable interest in the factory. Apex has an insurable interest because it was the original lessee of the factory. Apex has a financial interest both in receiving rent from Egan and its liability to Strong under the original lease. Egan has an **insurable interest and a financial interest** as tenant in possession.

c. Strong will only recover $150,000 from Range. Strong's recovery is based on the coinsurance formula:

$$\frac{\textit{Insurance carried (policy amount)}}{\textit{Insurance required (coinsurance \% x fair market value of the property at the time of the loss)}} \times \textit{The amount of loss} = \textit{Recovery}$$

$$\frac{400,000}{.80 \times 600,000} \times 180,000 = \$150,000$$

Strong will be able to recover $150,000 from Range, despite having insufficient coverage.

d. Lane will recover $125,000 of the foreclosure proceeds. Lane's recovery is limited to the amount left after the satisfaction of the Ace mortgage. In a **"Notice-Race" jurisdiction**, Lane's recorded mortgage **will not have priority** over Ace's earlier unrecorded mortgage because Lane **knew of** the Ace mortgage.

CHAPTER 57

FIRE AND CASUALTY INSURANCE

I. Definitions 57-2
    A.   Assured 57-2
    B.   Hazard 57-2
    C.   Insured 57-2
    D.   Insurer 57-2
    E.   Peril 57-2
    F.   Policy 57-2
    G.   Premium 57-2

II. Classification, Formation, and Nature of the Insurance Contract 57-2
    A.   Classifications 57-2
    B.   Formation 57-4
    C.   Nature 57-6

III. Insurable Interests 57-6

IV. Representations and Warranties 57-6
    A.   Representations 57-6
    B.   Warranties 57-6
    C.   Importance of the Distinction 57-6

V. Waiver, Estoppel, and Election 57-7
    A.   Waiver 57-7
    B.   Estoppel 57-7
    C.   Election 57-7

VI. Assignment of Insurance Contracts 57-7
    A.   Fire or Property Insurance 57-7
    B.   Marine Insurance 57-7

VII. Subrogation 57-7
    A.   Applicability 57-8
    B.   Release 57-8

VIII. Coinsurance 57-8
    A.   Formula 57-8
    B.   Pro Rata Recovery 57-8
    C.   Over-Insurance Clauses 57-9

CHAPTER 57

FIRE AND CASUALTY INSURANCE

I. Definitions

A.   Assured--The party for whose benefit the contract was made. Often, the terms "assured" and the "insured" are used synonymously.

B.   Hazard--A condition or situation that causes or increases the risk or chance of loss.

C.   Insured--The party who is protected by insurance from certain risks.

D.   Insurer--The party (such as an insurance company) who, in return for a premium, agrees to undertake the risk of loss from certain specified perils.

E.   Peril--The particular active harm which may cause the economic damage that insurance seeks to protect against. For example: fire, wind, or water.

F.   Policy--The written insurance contract.

G.   Premium--The consideration (money) paid by the assured in return for insurance.

II. Classification, Formation, and Nature of the Insurance Contract

A.   Classifications--Insurance may be purchased to cover losses or liabilities arising from an array of perils. The major classifications are listed and briefly described below.

   1.   Fire and Property Insurance--Generally, fire and property insurance covers losses arising from accidental damage to property caused by certain stipulated perils. Fire insurance minimally covers all damage directly or indirectly resulting from a fire (including smoke and water). Fire insurance policies often cover losses resulting from other named perils such as wind, flooding, and lightning.

      a.   Types of Fire Insurance

         (1)   A valued policy is one that stipulates the value of the insured property. Upon total destruction, this value is conclusive unless the insurer can show fraud.

         (2)   An open policy is one that does not stipulate the value of the property; instead, only a maximum liability is specified. The value of the property and the extent of damages must be proved at the time a claim is filed.

         (3)   A blanket policy is one under which several items are insured and a maximum overall liability is stipulated. The value and liability for each item is not specified.

         (4)   A specific policy specifies the insurer's maximum liability for the destruction of each individual item.

         (5)   A floating policy is one that covers constantly changing property such as inventory or stock.

b.   Standard Provisions--The most important provisions will be covered under separate headings elsewhere in the outline. Below are some less important, but commonly found provisions.

    (1)   Friendly Fire Exemptions--Precludes recovery for damages resulting from "friendly" or planned fires that occur during normal operation. For example, if fireplace masonry cracks from excessive heat developing in the fireplace, repairs would not be covered. However, losses arising from friendly fires that have become hostile are covered. Thus, for example, a fireplace fire which spreads to the carpet, etc., eventually causing extensive room damage is a hostile fire and repairs are covered.

    (2)   Increase of Hazard Clause--Relieves the insurer from liability if the insured has done something which increases the risk of loss. For example, if the insured, in an effort to provide adequate fuel for the family vehicle during an energy shortage, begins storing drums of gasoline in his or her garage, the resultant increase in the risk of loss may cause his or her insurance policy to be voidable by the insurer.

    (3)   Proof of Loss--Usually, a policy will require "satisfactory" proof of loss within a reasonable time (60 to 90 days) after the occurrence of the damages or the date of notification. To comply, an insured must file a written and verified statement containing all of the information required by the policy.

    (4)   Cancellation--Most policies allow either the insured or the insurer to cancel after giving notice.

c.   Payment of Proceeds--In cases where only one party has an interest, the insurer merely pays the proceeds due that party. Often, however, more than one party has an insurable interest in the insured property.

    (1)   Mortgagor vs. Mortgagee--Most mortgage agreements require the mortgagor to insure the property for the benefit of both parties. (The mortgagor is the party who borrows funds from the mortgagee, who is the lender.)

        •   The mortgagor and mortgagee each have a separate insurable interest (see III., below), and they may each insure for their own benefit.

    (2)   Creditors vs. Possessor/Insured--Generally, a creditor has no rights in the possessor's insurance before the property is destroyed or damaged.

        (a)   Article 9 of the Uniform Commercial Code provides that secured creditors automatically have a security interest in proceeds. Proceeds is defined so as to include insurance proceeds.

        (b)   As was the case for mortgagees, secured creditors have an insurable interest in collateral; thus, they may procure their own insurance.

        (c)   General creditors have no special rights to any of the debtor's insurance, nor do they have an insurable interest in any of the debtor's property.

    (3)   Seller vs. Buyer--Some jurisdictions follow the rule that the risk of loss is on the buyer from the moment the contract is entered into. In these jurisdictions, the buyer has a right to any insurance proceeds the seller has realized for damaged or destroyed property during the time that the buyer bore the risk of loss.

(4)   Life Tenant vs. Remainderman--The law of insurance in this area is very similar to that covering mortgagees and mortgagors.

    (a)   When a policy is purchased for the benefit of both parties, the proceeds usually go first to rebuilding principal so as to protect the interest of each party.

    (b)   Each party has an insurable interest and may purchase insurance for his or her own benefit.

2.   Liability Insurance--Covers the liability of the insured for damages to other persons or property caused by unintentional acts of the insured or the insured's agents.

    a.   Automobile Liability Insurance--Provides coverage for damages to other persons and their property caused either by the insured or those for whom the insured is held liable. For example, A is negligently driving his car and accidentally injures B. Although A is at "fault," because the accident was unintentional, A's liability insurance will pay for the damages to B and B's property.

    •   "No-Fault" Insurance--Certain states have adopted forms of no-fault insurance. Basically, each vehicle owner's insurer pays his or her insured's own expenses which result from an automobile accident, whether or not the insured was at fault. Generally, the party who is not at fault cannot sue the party at fault for damages unless the accident causes certain specified serious physical injuries.

    b.   Personal Liability--Various kinds of personal liability insurance are available to protect against losses associated with injuries to other persons for which the insured is liable.

    (1)   For example, most homeowner's policies cover liability for accidents to others which occur in the insured's home. If A is visiting B in B's home, and while walking up the steps slips and falls, B's liability insurance will pay for A's injuries.

    (2)   Malpractice insurance is another type of liability insurance which protects against liability for errors and omissions in connection with professional work. For example, A is a stockholder in Company X, which B audits. If B negligently makes a material error in connection with the audit of X's financial statements, and if A sues B for B's negligent audit, B's malpractice insurance will pay A's damages.

B.   Formation

1.   Elements--Essentially the same elements are required for an insurance contract as are necessary for any other enforceable agreement.

    a.   Agreement--For an insurance contract to be binding, there must be an agreement between the parties, i.e., a meeting of the minds. The components of an agreement are typically phrased as "offer" and "acceptance."

    (1)   The "offer" is generally made by the applicant in his or her application for insurance.

    (2)   The "acceptance" of the offer is made by the insurer when it acknowledges that it agrees to insure the applicant. This is generally accomplished by the issuance of a policy. The policy contains all the terms, conditions, and exclusions of the insurance contract.

b.   Consideration is that money paid by the insured in return for the insurer's promises to cover certain risks. Recall that this consideration is called a "premium." The insurer's consideration is his or her promise to make payment in the event of a loss.

c.   Capacity--Both parties to the insurance contract must have the legal capacity to enter into a contract (sanity, age, authority).

d.   Legality of Subject Matter--A policy is void if the subject matter is either illegal or not in existence at the time the policy is issued, and if this fact is known by one of the parties. For example, insurance which covers losses associated with criminal activities is void. In addition, a policy which insures property not in existence usually will be issued only pursuant to a misrepresentation or a fraud. It is thus an illegal contract and would therefore be void.

e.   Writing--Although insurance contracts are not required by the Statute of Frauds to be in writing, most states have enacted statutes which now require such. However, some property insurance contracts may be consummated by verbal agreement.

f.   Delivery--In insurance law, delivery of the policy is primarily a matter of intent. That is, actual physical delivery of the policy is not necessary to the creation of a valid contract. However, there must be an intention to deliver the policy to the applicant or his or her agents.

   (1)   Constructive delivery occurs when the insurance company unconditionally accepts the application of the insured and takes steps to communicate this to the insured. For example, there is constructive delivery when the insurance company executes and mails the policy to the insured. Additionally, when the insurer mails and/or delivers the policy to the local agent of the insurer, courts have generally held that constructive delivery has occurred. The insurance policy is held to be effective as of the date of the mailing or delivery to the agent.

   (2)   Property insurance contracts are generally held to be effective even without delivery. For example, oral contracts, such as those made over the telephone, are valid and effective when the agreement is reached or at the time otherwise agreed to by the parties.

   (3)   A "binder" or "binding slip" is a written memorandum which an insurer's agent will often issue to signify that the contract is to become effective prior to the actual physical delivery of a policy.

2.   Other Aspects of Insurance Contracts

a.   Voidable--The insurance contract is voidable by the insurer if the applicant has concealed information or misrepresented a material fact. (Representations and warranties are discussed in IV., below.) "Voidable" means that the policy is valid, but may be invalidated by the insurer, at his or her option, upon discovery of the misrepresentation or concealment.

b.   Ambiguities--Because most insurance contracts are written by the insurer and generally include certain standardized language, any ambiguities in the contract (or policy) are construed against the insurer. That is, any question about the meaning of any terms or conditions used in the policy will be resolved in favor of the insured.

c.   Agents--Because insurance companies generally act through agents, the rules of agency law apply to this aspect of the law of insurance.

C.   <u>Nature</u>--Insurance contracts are considered to be "personal" because they typically cover specified property (property insurance). Therefore, they are assignable only under limited circumstances (see VI., below).

III. Insurable Interests

In general, there must exist such a relationship between the assured/insured and the risk covered that if specified events occur, the assured will suffer some substantial loss or injury.

- Fire or Property Insurance--The rule with respect to insurable interests in these types of contracts requires that there be both a legally recognized interest and the possibility of a pecuniary (financial or economic) loss in the event the property is damaged or destroyed.

     1.   Legal interests include ownership and possessory interests (including equitable interests), future interests, and the interests of secured creditors, including mortgagees. For example, tenants have an insurable interest in their leaseholds, stockholders have an interest in their corporation's property, and bailees have an interest in bailed property.

     2.   In addition to legal interest in the insured property, an insured must have a pecuniary interest, i.e., the insured must stand to suffer an economic or financial loss if the property is damaged or destroyed. Insurance provides only monetary protection; therefore, only those with a pecuniary interest are protected.

     3.   Under the broad common law rule, the insured is required to have an insurable interest (1. and 2., above) both at the time of issuance and at the time the loss is incurred. However, under a substantial body of minority opinion, an insurable interest under a fire or property insurance policy must exist only at the time of loss. More importantly, <u>for CPA Exam purposes, an insurable interest must exist only at the time of loss</u>.

IV. Representations and Warranties

A.   <u>Representations</u>--Representations are statements made by the applicant to the prospective insurer concerning facts and conditions, and on the basis of which the insurance policy is written. These statements may be made orally or in writing. Representations are inducements to enter into the contract.

B.   <u>Warranties</u>--Warranties are statements (conditions precedent) which must be true before the insurer will be liable. They appear in, and are considered a part of, the insurance contract. As in general contract law, a breach of a warranty by one party excuses the other party from performing. For example, if a warranty made by the insured is not true, or is "breached," the insurer is excused from paying the claim. However, the falsity of an immaterial representation will not excuse the insurer's performance.

C.   <u>Importance of the Distinction</u>--Because the breach of a statement, which is a warranty, excuses the insurer from paying, it is important that the false statement be properly classified as either a "warranty" or a "representation." As stated above, the chief distinction between representations and warranties is that representations are inducements <u>to enter into</u> a contract, while warranties are made <u>a part of</u> the contract. Many insurance contracts specifically make all statements "warranties."

     1.   State Statutes--Most states have statutes which provide that all statements made by an applicant are to be deemed representations, not warranties.

     2.   Materiality of Statement--Most statutes provide that those misstatements made in good faith and without fraud do not void the policy unless the misstatement relates to a matter which is material to the risk of the insured. In addition, only omissions that materially increase the risk borne by the insurer are grounds for excused performance.

3. Fraud--Note, however, that even those statements that are immaterial but fraudulently made void the policy and excuse performance by the insurer. The same is true for fraudulent omissions.

V. Waiver, Estoppel, and Election

The following rule applies in situations where the insurer knows that the insured has made a misrepresentation or breached a warranty. If the insurer has knowledge of a misrepresentation, but nevertheless elects to issue the policy or allow the policy to remain in effect in spite of the misrepresentation, the insurer has then waived the fraud defense. The insurer is thereafter estopped from asserting that defense; he or she must perform his or her obligations under the contract.

A. Waiver--The voluntary relinquishment of a known right. For example, an agent of the insurer may properly waive certain requirements of the policy, such as the requirement that a claim be submitted in writing within 30 days of the loss.

B. Estoppel--A barrier raised by the law which prevents the insurer from asserting or denying certain facts that are inconsistent with its previous acts or allegations. For example, the insurer may be estopped from asserting the fact that the claim was not submitted in writing within 30 days if the insurer waived this requirement.

C. Election--The voluntary exercise of a right to choose one alternative over another. An election has the same effect as a waiver in that the party, once it has made its choice, forever loses its rights under the other alternative. For example, assume that A has failed to report several car accidents in breach of one of the provisions of her policy. Once Big Rock Insurance discovers the breach, it may choose to cancel her insurance or excuse the breach and continue to accept premium payments. If it chooses the latter, Big Rock cannot subsequently assert the breach to avoid liability.

VI. Assignment of Insurance Contracts

Because the contract of insurance is a personal contract between the insured and the insurer, the assignment of insurance contracts is subject to certain rules and restrictions.

A. Fire or Property Insurance--Historically, property insurance contracts are not assignable without the consent of the insurer because the risk assumed by the insurer varies with the person protected. However, there are exceptions as follows:

1. Assignment as Collateral--An insured may assign a fire policy as collateral. For example, an insured may assign her policy to a person who has acquired the mortgage on the insured property. In this circumstance, the insured retains an interest in the property insured (because she is still the owner).

2. Assignment of Loss Proceeds--The prohibition against the assignment of a fire policy without the permission of the insurer does not preclude the assignment of proceeds due or payable following a loss. Just as any other claim for money is assignable, so is the claim for the proceeds of an insurance policy. Moreover, provisions in policies which prohibit the assignment of these claims are not enforceable.

B. Marine Insurance--Marine insurance is generally assignable unless the policy specifically requires the consent of the insurer.

VII. Subrogation

The right of the insurer, upon paying the loss, to recover from some third person who actually caused the loss is known as subrogation. In essence, the insurance company "stands in the shoes" of the insured in order to recover from the person who is legally liable for the loss.

A. <u>Applicability</u>--In fire or property insurance policies, there is generally a right of subrogation.

B. <u>Release</u>--If the damaged insured party releases the party causing the injury prior to the payment of the loss by the insured, he or she also releases the insurer from any duty to pay on the policy. In addition, if the insured releases the party, causing the loss subsequent to the payment by the insurer, he or she forfeits the right to retain the insurance proceeds. The reason for these two rules is that the insured, by releasing the party causing the loss, has terminated the insurer's right to subrogation.

VIII. Coinsurance

A coinsurance clause provides that if the insured fails to carry an amount of insurance equal to a stated percentage (usually 80%) of the value of the property insured, then the insured becomes a coinsurer and must proportionally bear the loss. The share of the loss borne by the insurer will be the lower of (1) the face value of the policy, (2) fair market value of property at date of loss, or (3) the coinsurance amount. If there is a total loss, the insured will collect the full amount of the insurance if it is the lowest of the three measures of recovery.

A. <u>Formula</u>--The amount of recovery for a partial loss is equal to (1) the face value of the insurance policy, divided by the coinsurance percent times the actual fair value of the property, times (2) the actual loss. Mathematically, this formula appears as follows:

$$Recovery = \frac{Face\ value\ of\ insurance}{Coinsurance\ \%\ \times\ FV\ of\ property} \times Actual\ loss$$

Example 1

Assume A carries only $35,000 of insurance on property worth $100,000, and that his policy contains a coinsurance clause which requires that the property must be insured at 80% of its fair market value. Given these facts, if a fire inflicts actual damages in the amount of $25,000, A's recovery will be $10,937.50. This figure is derived as follows:

$$\frac{\$35,000}{80\% \times \$100,000} \times \$25,000 = \$10,937.50$$

Thus, A will be liable, as the co-insurer, for $14,062.50. If A had been insured in the amount of $80,000 or more, he would have recovered the full $25,000 and not been personally liable for any damages.

B. <u>Pro Rata Recovery</u>--When the insured has several policies with different insurance companies all covering the same property and the aggregate insurance exceeds the actual loss, he or she may collect from each company only its proportionate or pro rata share. A proportionate share is that percentage of an insured's total insurance which is carried with an individual company.

Example 2

Assume A has two fire insurance policies covering the same property, one for $10,000 and the other for $15,000. If the property is damaged in the amount of $20,000, A will collect $8,000 from the first insurer and $12,000 from the second insurer. This is calculated as follows:

$$\frac{\$10,000}{\$25,000} \times \$20,000 = \$8,000; \quad \frac{\$15,000}{\$25,000} \times \$20,000 = \$12,000$$

C.   <u>Over-Insurance Clauses</u>--Serve the same general purpose as do the rules governing pro rata or proportionate recovery, i.e., they prohibit a double or excessive recovery. This clause prohibits an insured from procuring other or additional insurance to cover losses for which the insured is completely insured. If the insured violates such a clause, the policy is voidable by the insurer. Thus, over-insurance provisions may act to totally preclude the insured from collecting any proceeds. **NOTE**: An over-insurance clause does not prohibit another party who has the requisite insurable interest from insuring his or her interest. For example, both a mortgagor and mortgagee may separately insure their individual interests.

———————

NOTES

CHAPTER 57—FIRE AND CASUALTY INSURANCE

Problem 57-1 MULTIPLE CHOICE QUESTIONS (25 to 30 minutes)

1. Daly tried to collect on a property insurance policy covering a house that was damaged by fire. The insurer denied recovery, alleging that Daly had no insurable interest in the house. In which of the following situations will the insurer prevail?
a. The house belongs to a corporation of which Daly is a 50% stockholder.
b. Daly is **not** the owner of the house but a long-term lessee.
c. The house is held in trust for Daly's mother and, on her death, will pass to Daly.
d. Daly gave an unsecured loan to the owner of the house to improve the house.

(11/92, Law, #57, 3139)

2. On February 1, Papco Corp. entered into a contract to purchase an office building from Merit Company for $500,000 with closing scheduled for March 20. On February 2, Papco obtained a $400,000 standard fire insurance policy from Abex Insurance Company. On March 15, the office building sustained a $90,000 fire loss. On March 15, which of the following is correct?

I. Papco has an insurable interest in the building.
II. Merit has an insurable interest in the building.

a. I only.
b. II only.
c. Both I and II.
d. Neither I nor II.

(11/90, Law, #60, 0848)

3. Which of the following parties has an insurable interest?

I. A corporate retailer in its inventory.
II. A partner in the partnership property.

a. I only.
b. II only.
c. Both I and II.
d. Neither I nor II.

(5/95, Law, #60, 5394)

4. To recover under a property insurance policy, an insurable interest must exist.

	When the policy is purchased	At the time of loss
a.	Yes	Yes
b.	Yes	No
c.	No	Yes
d.	No	No

(11/89, Law, #60, 0849)

5. Beal occupies an office building as a tenant under a 25-year lease. Beal also has a mortgagee's (lender's) interest in an office building owned by Hill Corp. In which capacity does Beal have an insurable interest?

	Tenant	Mortgagee
a.	Yes	Yes
b.	Yes	No
c.	No	Yes
d.	No	No

(5/88, Law, #60, 9911)

6. With respect to property insurance, the insurable interest requirement
a. Need only be satisfied at the time the policy is issued.
b. Must be satisfied both at the time the policy is issued and at the time of the loss.
c. Will be satisfied only if the insured owns the property in fee simple absolute.
d. Will be satisfied by an insured who possesses a leasehold interest in the property.

(11/87, Law, #59, 0851)

7. The earliest time a purchaser of existing goods will acquire an insurable interest in those goods is when
a. The purchaser obtains possession.
b. Title passes to the purchaser.
c. Performance of the contract has been completed or substantially completed.
d. The goods are identified to the contract.

(11/86, Law, #59, 0853)

8. Jerry's House of Jewelry, Inc., took out an insurance policy with the Old Time Insurance Company which covered the stock of jewelry displayed in the store's windows. Old Time agreed to indemnify Jerry's House for losses due to window smashing and theft of the jewels displayed. The application contained the following provision: "It is hereby warranted that the maximum value of the jewelry displayed shall not exceed $10,000." The insurance policy's coverage was for $8,000. The application was initialed alongside the warranty and attached to the policy. Subsequently, thieves smashed the store window and stole $4,000 worth of jewels. The total value of the display during that week, including the day of the robbery, was $12,000. Which of the following is correct?

a. Jerry's House will recover nothing.

b. Jerry's House will recover $2,000, the loss less the amount in excess of the $10,000 display limitation.

c. Jerry's House will recover the full $4,000 since the warranty will be construed as a mere representation.

d. Jerry's House will recover the full $4,000 since attaching the application to the policy is insufficient to make it a part thereof.

(11/81, Law, #55, 9911)

9. One of the primary purposes of including a coinsurance clause in a property insurance policy is to

a. Encourage the policyholder to insure the property for an amount close to its full value.

b. Make the policyholder responsible for the entire loss caused by some covered perils.

c. Cause the policyholder to maintain a minimum amount of liability insurance that will increase with inflation.

d. Require the policyholder to insure the property with only one insurance company.

(11/90, Law, #57, 0847)

10. Hart owned a building with a fair market value of $400,000. The building was covered by a $300,000 fire insurance policy containing an 80% coinsurance clause. What amount would Hart recover if a fire totally destroyed the building?

a. $0

b. $240,000

c. $256,000

d. $300,000

(11/92, Law, #56, 3138)

Items 11 and 12 are based on the following:

In 1988, Pod bought a building for $220,000. At that time, Pod purchased a $150,000 fire insurance policy with Owners Insurance Co. and a $50,000 fire insurance policy with Group Insurance Corp. Each policy contained a standard 80% coinsurance clause. In 1992, when the building had a fair market value of $250,000, it was damaged in a fire.

11. How much would Pod recover from Owners and Group if the fire totally destroyed the building?

a. $160,000

b. $200,000

c. $220,000

d. $250,000

(5/93, Law, #60, 4028)

12. How much would Pod recover from Owners if the fire caused $180,000 in damage?

a. $ 90,000

b. $120,000

c. $135,000

d. $150,000

(5/93, Law, #59, 4027)

13. Clark Corp. owns a warehouse purchased for $150,000 in 1990. The current market value is $200,000. Clark has the warehouse insured for fire loss with Fair Insurance Corp. and Zone Insurance Co. Fair's policy is for $150,000 and Zone's policy is for $75,000. Both policies contain the standard 80% coinsurance clause. If a fire totally destroyed the warehouse, what total dollar amount would Clark receive from Fair and Zone?

a. $225,000

b. $200,000

c. $160,000

d. $150,000

(5/95, Law, #59, 5393)

14. The coinsurance clause with regard to property insurance

a. Prohibits the insured from obtaining an amount of insurance which would be less than the coinsurance percentage multiplied by the fair market value of the property.

b. Encourages the insured to be more careful in preventing losses since the insured is always at least partially at risk when a loss occurs.

c. Permits the insured to receive an amount in excess of the policy amount when there has been a total loss and the insured carried the required coverage under the coinsurance clause.

d. Will result in the insured sharing in partial losses when the insured has failed to carry the required coverage under the coinsurance clause.

(5/85, Law, #59, 9911)

15. Lawfo Corp. maintains a $200,000 standard fire insurance policy on one of its warehouses. The policy includes an 80% coinsurance clause. At the time the warehouse was originally insured, its value was $250,000. The warehouse now has a value of $300,000. If the warehouse sustains $30,000 of fire damage, Lawfo's insurance recovery will be a maximum of

a. $20,000.

b. $24,000.

c. $25,000.

d. $30,000.

(5/90, Law, #59, 9911)

16. Mason Co. maintained two standard fire insurance policies on one of its warehouses. Both policies included an 80% coinsurance clause and a typical "other insurance" clause. One policy was with Ace Fire Insurance, Inc., for $24,000, and the other was with Thrifty Casualty Insurance Co., for $16,000.

At a time when the warehouse was worth $100,000, a fire in the warehouse caused a $40,000 loss. What amounts can Mason recover from Ace and Thrifty, respectively?

a. $0 and $0.
b. $10,000 and $10,000.
c. $12,000 and $8,000.
d. $24,000 and $16,000.   (11/91, Law, #60, 2388)

17. On May 5, Sly purchased a warehouse for $100,000. Sly immediately insured the warehouse in the amount of $40,000 with Riff Insurance Co. Six months later, Sly obtained additional fire insurance on the warehouse in the amount of $10,000 from Beek Insurance Co. Both policies contained an 80% coinsurance clause. Sly failed to notify Riff of the policy with Beek. Two years later, while both policies were still in effect, a fire caused by Sly's negligence resulted in $20,000 of damage to the warehouse. At the time of the loss, the warehouse had a fair market value of $50,000. Which of the following will prevent Sly from obtaining the full $20,000 from Riff?

a. Sly's negligence in causing the fire.
b. Sly's failure to satisfy the coinsurance clause.
c. Sly's failure to notify Riff of the policy with Beek.
d. Sly's purchase of insurance from Beek.
(11/87, Law, #60, 0852)

Solution 57-1 MULTIPLE CHOICE ANSWERS

Insurable Interests

1. (d)   Generally, there must be a relationship between the insured and the risk covered such that, if specified events occur, the insured will suffer substantial loss or injury. With regard to property insurance, there must be a legally recognized interest and the possibility of financial or economic loss, which would not occur in this case, when the only interest Daly had in the property was having given an unsecured loan to the owner of the house. Stockholders have a legally insurable interest in corporation property. Possessory interests, such as leaseholds, are legally insurable interests.

2. (c)   To recover under a property insurance contract, the insured must have an insurable interest in the property at the time of the loss. An insurable interest exists when an entity has both a legal interest in the property and the possibility of a monetary loss if the property is damaged. In this question, the seller of the building has an insurable interest in the building until the seller receives the entire purchase price. The buyer has an insurable interest in the building as soon as the buyer enters into a contract to purchase the building.

3. (c)   The rule with respect to fire or property insurance contracts requires that there be both a legally recognized interest and the possibility of economic loss if the property is damaged or destroyed. Both the corporate retailer and the partner have an ownership interest in their respective property and would suffer possible economic loss if the property were damaged or destroyed. Thus, each has an insurable interest.

4. (c)   To recover under a property insurance policy, an insurable interest must exist at the time of the loss, not at the time the policy is purchased.

5. (a)   For an insurable interest to arise, there must exist such an interest between the insured and the risk covered, so that if specified events occur, the insured will suffer some substantial loss or injury. Such an interest includes the possessory interest of a tenant of property and the interests of secured creditors, including mortgagees.

6. (d)   Property insurance requires that there be an insurable interest only at the time of the loss. Any person who has a possessory interest in property may obtain property casualty insurance. Thus, the insurable interest requirement may be satisfied by a person other than the legal owner of the property.

7. (d)   UCC 2-501(1) provides that the earliest time that a purchaser of existing goods may acquire an insurable interest in those goods is when the goods are identified to the contract.

Warranties

8. (a)   The written clause limiting the value of displayed jewelry to $10,000 was a statement of fact which became a basis for the insurance company's risk in writing this theft policy. As such, it was a warranty rather than a mere representation. More importantly, the continued compliance with this warranty was a condition precedent to the insurer's liability for any theft loss. At the time of loss the warranty was not being complied with; therefore, no recovery.

Coinsurance

9. (a) One of the primary purposes of the coinsurance clause is to encourage the insured to maintain a certain amount of insurance on the property in relation to the fair market value of the property. For example, if there is an 80% coinsurance clause, the insurance company encourages the insured to maintain insurance on the property equal to at least 80% of the fair market value of the property. In the event the policy holder does not maintain sufficient insurance, the insured will not receive 100% of his or her partial losses. The coinsurance clause has nothing to do with excluding certain types of perils. The coinsurance clause does not "cause the policyholder to maintain a minimum amount of *liability* insurance that will increase with inflation." The coinsurance clause encourages the policyholder to maintain a certain amount of property insurance, not liability insurance. The insured can insure with more than one insurance company; however, the insured can collect only once (i.e., one cannot profit from insurance).

10. (d) Under a fire insurance policy with an 80% coinsurance clause, when there is a *total loss*, the insured will collect the full amount of the insurance, if it is the *lowest* of the three measures of recovery: (1) the face value of the policy ($300,000); (2) the fair market value of the property at date of loss ($400,000); or (3) the coinsurance amount ($320,000) [$400,000 x 80% = $320,000]. In this case, $300,000, the face value of the policy, is the lowest.

11. (b) Since Pod has met the coinsurance requirements, Pod can collect 100% of his total loss, up to the face amount of his policies. Thus, Pod can collect a total of $200,000. This amount will be prorated between the two insurance companies.

12. (c) Pod's recoverable loss is calculated using the coinsurance formula:

$$\text{Actual Loss} \times \frac{\text{Amount of Insurance}}{\text{Coinsurance \% x } \frac{\text{FV of Property}}{\text{at Time of Loss}}}$$

$$\$180,000 \times \frac{\$200,000}{80\% \times \$250,000} = \$180,000$$

The amount recoverable from Owners is calculated as follows:

$$\$180,000 \times \frac{\$150,000}{\$200,000} = \$135,000$$

13. (b) These coinsurance clauses provide that if Clark fails to carry an amount of insurance equal to 80% of the value of the property insured, the insured becomes a coinsurer and must proportionally bear the loss. The share of the loss born by the insurer will be the lower of (1) the face value of the policy, (2) the fair market value of the property at the date of loss, or (3) the coinsurance amount. The coinsurance rules only apply to partial losses, and since this was a total loss, the insured is paid the total amount of the insurance policies, up to the fair market value of the property. (One can not profit by insurance, only recover one's actual loss.)

14. (d) A coinsurance clause provides that if the insured failed to carry an amount of insurance equal to a stated percentage of the value of the property insured, then the insured becomes a coinsurer and must proportionally bear the loss. A coinsurance clause does not *prohibit* the insured from underinsuring his or her property, but *encourages* against underinsuring by denying policy face value benefits where property is underinsured. If the insured has insured his or her property for at least the amount of the stated percentage, he or she will not be at risk if a loss occurs. The insured can never receive an amount in *excess* of his or her policy amount.

15. (c) The formula is:

$$\frac{\text{Face Value of Insurance}}{\text{Coinsurance } \times \text{ Fair Market}}{\text{Percentage} \times \text{Value of}}{\text{Property}} \times \text{Actual Loss}$$

Lawfo's insurance recovery will be:

$$\frac{\$200,000}{80\% \times \$300,000} \times \$30,000 = \$25,000$$

16. (c) A coinsurance clause provides that if the insured fails to carry an amount of insurance equal to the stated percentage (80% in this case) of the value of the property insured, then the insured becomes a coinsurer and must proportionally bear the loss. The *total* amount of loss borne by the insurers is the lower of (1) the face value of the policies ($40,000), (2) fair market value of property at date of loss ($100,000), or (3) the coinsurance amount of $20,000 [$40,000/$80,000 x $40,000]. Thus, the loss borne by the insurers is $20,000. Ace is responsible for 60% of the loss ($12,000) because it provided 60% of the total insurance [$24,000/$40,000]. Thrifty is responsible for 40% of the loss ($8,000) because it provided 40% of the total insurance [$16,000/$40,000].

17. (d) Riff will bear 80% of the insured loss after operation of the coinsurance formula, and Beek will bear 20% of the insured loss after application of the formula. Sly's simple negligence in causing the fire will not void coverage. The coinsurance formula is used to measure what part of the loss Sly may have to bear through his underinsurance. Notification to other insurers is not required to put coverage in force.

PERFORMANCE BY SUBTOPICS

Each category below parallels a subtopic covered in Chapter 57. Record the number and percentage of questions you correctly answered in each subtopic area.

Insurable Interests

Question #	Correct √
1	
2	
3	
4	
5	
6	
7	
# Questions	7
# Correct	_____
% Correct	_____

Warranties

Question #	Correct √
8	
# Questions	1
# Correct	_____
% Correct	_____

Coinsurance

Question #	Correct √
9	
10	
11	
12	
13	
14	
15	
16	
17	
# Questions	9
# Correct	_____
% Correct	_____

OTHER OBJECTIVE FORMAT QUESTIONS

Problem 57-2 (10 to 15 minutes)

Items 1 through 6 are based on the following:

On January 12, 1994, Frank, Inc. contracted in writing to purchase a factory building from Henderson for $250,000 cash. Closing took place on March 15, 1994. Henderson had purchased the building in 1990 for $225,000 and had, at that time, taken out a $180,000 fire insurance policy with Summit Insurance Co.

On January 15, 1994, Frank took out a $140,000 fire insurance policy with Unity Insurance Co. and a $70,000 fire insurance policy with Imperial Insurance, Inc.

On March 16, 1994, a fire caused $150,000 damage to the building. At that time the building had a market value of $250,000. All fire insurance policies contain a standard 80% coinsurance clause. The insurance carriers have refused any payment to Frank or Henderson alleging lack of insurable interest and insufficient coverage. Frank and Henderson have sued to collect on the policies.

Required:

Items 1 through 6 relate to the suits by Frank and Henderson. For each item, determine whether the statement is True (T) or False (F).

1. Frank had an insurable interest at the time the Unity and Imperial policies were taken out.
2. Henderson had an insurable interest at the time of the fire.
3. Assuming Frank had an insurable interest, Frank's coverage would be insufficient under the Unity and Imperial coinsurance clauses.
4. Assuming Henderson had an insurable interest, Henderson's coverage would be insufficient under the Summit coinsurance clause.
5. Assuming only Frank had an insurable interest, Frank will recover $100,000 from Unity and $50,000 from Imperial.
6. Assuming only Henderson had an insurable interest, Henderson will recover $135,000 from Summit.

(5/94, Law, #3b)

Problem 57-3 (4 to 6 minutes)

On June 1, 1990, Anderson bought a one-family house from Beach for $240,000. At the time of the purchase, the house had a market value of $200,000 and the land was valued at $40,000. Anderson assumed the recorded $150,000 mortgage Beach owed Long Bank, gave a $70,000 mortgage to Rogers Loan Co., and paid $20,000 cash. Rogers did not record its mortgage. Rogers did not know about the Long Mortgage.

Beach gave Anderson a quitclaim deed that failed to mention a recorded easement on the property held by Dalton, the owner of the adjacent piece of property. Anderson purchased a title insurance policy from Edge Title Insurance Co. Edge's policy neither disclosed nor excepted Dalton's easement.

On August 1, 1992, Anderson borrowed $30,000 from Forrest Finance to have a swimming pool dug. Anderson gave Forrest a $30,000 mortgage on the property. Forrest, knowing about the Long mortgage but not the Rogers mortgage, recorded its mortgage on August 10, 1992. After the digging began, Dalton sued to stop the work claiming violation of the easement. The court decided in Dalton's favor.

At the time of the purchase, Anderson had taken out two fire insurance policies; a $120,000 face value policy with Harvest Fire Insurance Co., and a $60,000 face value policy with Grant Fire Insurance Corp.

Both policies contained a standard 80% coinsurance clause.

On December 1, 1992, a fire caused $180,000 damage to the house. At that time, the house had a market value of $250,000. Harvest and Grant refused to honor the policies claiming that the house was underinsured.

Anderson made no mortgage payments after the fire and on June 1, 1993, after the house had been rebuilt, the mortgages were foreclosed. The balances due for principal and accrued interest were as follows: Long, $140,000; Rogers, $65,000; and Forrest, $28,000. At a foreclosure sale, the house and land were sold. After payment of all expenses, $200,000 of the proceeds remained for distribution. As a result of the above events, the following actions took place:

- Anderson sued Harvest and Grant for the face values of the fire insurance policies.
- Anderson sued Beach for failing to mention Dalton's easement in the quitclaim deed.
- Anderson sued Edge for failing to disclose Dalton's easement.
- Long, Rogers, and Forrest all demanded full payment of their mortgages from the proceeds of the foreclosure sale.

The preceding took place in a "Race-Notice" jurisdiction.

Required:

a. **Items 1 through 3** relate to Anderson's suit against Harvest and Grant. For each item, select from *List I* the dollar amount Anderson will receive.

1. What will be the dollar amount of Anderson's total fire insurance recovery?
2. What dollar amount will be payable by Harvest?
3. What dollar amount will be payable by Grant?

	List I	
A.	$	0
B.	$	20,000
C.	$	48,000
D.	$	54,000
E.	$	60,000
F.	$	80,000
G.	$	96,000
H.	$108,000	
I.	$120,000	
J.	$144,000	
K.	$162,000	
L.	$180,000	

(11/93, Law, #2, 61-63)

OTHER OBJECTIVE FORMAT SOLUTIONS

Solution 57-2 Insurable Interest and Coverage

1. (T)   The common law provides that a person who obtains property insurance must have an insurable interest in that property.   In most jurisdictions it is necessary that this interest exist at the time of the loss.   A person has an insurable interest in property if they have any legal or equitable interest in the property and will suffer economic loss from its destruction.   Frank obtained an insurable interest on January 12, 1994 as a result of the enforceable contract for the purchase of the property entered into with Henderson.

2. (F)   The common law provides that a person who has property insurance must have an insurable interest in the property at the time of the loss.   A person has an insurable interest in property if he or she has a legal or equitable interest in the property and will suffer an economic loss from its destruction.   Although Henderson had an insurable interest in the property at the time the insurance was purchased in 1990, that interest expired upon closing of the sale to Frank on March 15, 1994. Henderson no longer had an insurable interest when the loss occurred one day later.

3. (F)   A 80% coinsurance clause requires the insured to carry an amount of insurance equal to 80% of the market value of the insured property. If the insured fails to do so, he or she becomes a coinsurer and must bear a proportionate share of the loss. At the time of the loss the building had a fair market value of $250,000, 80% of which is $200,000. Frank had insured the building for a total of $210,000, which exceeds 80%.

4. (T)   An 80% coinsurance clause requires the insured to carry an amount of insurance equal to 80% of the market value of the insured property. If the insured fails to do so, he or she becomes a coinsurer and must bear a proportionate share of the loss. At the time of the loss, the building had a fair market value of $250,000, 80% of which is $200,000.

5. (T)   If an insured has multiple fire insurance policies covering the same property, then each insurer will be liable for a pro rate share of the loss. A proportionate share is that percentage of an insured's total insurance which is carried with an individual company.   Thus Frank will be able to collect $100,000 from Unity computed as follows:

$$\frac{\$140,000}{\$120,000} \times \$150,000 = \$100,000$$

Frank will collect $50,000 from Imperial, computed as follows:

$$\frac{\$70,000}{\$210,000} \times \$150,000 = \$50,000$$

6. (T)   An 80% coinsurance clause requires an insured to carry an amount of insurance equal to 80% of the market value of the property.   If the insured fails to do so, he or she will be a coinsurer and must proportionately bear the loss.   Recovery is calculated as follows:

$$\frac{\text{Face value of insurance}}{\text{Coinsurance \% } \times \text{ FMV of property}} \times \text{Actual loss} = \text{Recovery}$$

In Henderson's case, the calculation would be as follows:

$$\frac{\$180,000}{80\% \times \$250,000} \times \$150,000 = \$135,000$$

Solution 57-3 Recovery

1. (K)   Anderson's recovery is calculated using the coinsurance formula as follows:

$$\frac{\text{Face value of insurance}}{\text{Coinsurance \% } \times \frac{\text{FMV of property}}{\text{at time of loss}}} \times \text{Actual Loss} = \text{Recovery}$$

Harvest:

$$\frac{\$120,000}{80\% \times \$250,000} \times \$180,000 = \$108,000$$

Grant:

$$\frac{\$60,000}{80\% \times \$250,000} \times \$180,000 = \$54,000$$

Total Recovery for Fire Insurance = $162,000

2. (H)   The amount recoverable from Harvest is calculated as follows:

$$\frac{\text{Face value of insurance}}{\text{Coinsurance \% } \times \frac{\text{FMV of property}}{\text{at time of loss}}} \times \text{Actual Loss} = \text{Recovery}$$

$$\frac{\$120,000}{80\% \times \$250,000} \times \$180,000 = \$108,000$$

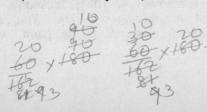

3. (D) The amount recoverable from Grant is calculated as follows:

$$\frac{\text{Face value of insurance}}{\text{Coinsurance \% x} \begin{array}{c} \text{FMV of property} \\ \text{at time of loss} \end{array}} \times \text{Actual Loss} = \text{Recovery}$$

$$\frac{\$60,000}{80\% \times \$250,000} \times \$180,000 = \underline{\$\ 54,000}$$

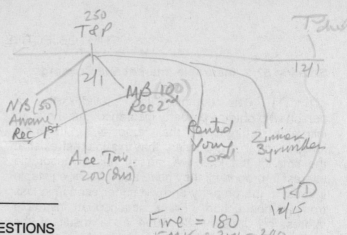

ESSAY QUESTIONS

Essay 57-4 (7 to 10 minutes)

On February 1, 1988, Tower and Perry, as tenants in common, purchased a two-unit apartment building for $250,000. They made a downpayment of $100,000, and gave a $100,000 first mortgage to Midway Bank and a $50,000 second mortgage to New Bank.

New was aware of Midway's mortgage, but as a result of clerical error, Midway did not record its mortgage until after New's mortgage was recorded.

At the time of purchase, a $200,000 fire insurance policy was issued by Acme Insurance Co. to Tower and Perry. The policy contained an 80% coinsurance clause and a standard mortgagee provision.

Tower and Perry rented an apartment to Young under a month-to-month oral lease. They rented the other apartment to Zimmer under a three-year written lease.

On December 8, 1989, Perry died, leaving a will naming the Dodd Foundation as the sole beneficiary of Perry's estate. The estate was distributed on January 15, 1990. That same date, the ownership of the fire insurance policy was assigned to Tower and Dodd with Acme's consent. On January 21, 1990, a fire caused $180,000 in structural damage to the building. At that time, its market value was $300,000 and the Midway mortgage balance was $80,000 including accrued interest. The New mortgage balance was $40,000 including accrued interest.

The fire made Young's apartment uninhabitable and caused extensive damage to the kitchen, bathrooms, and one bedroom of Zimmer's apartment. On February 1, 1990, Young and Zimmer moved out. The resulting loss of income caused a default on both mortgages.

On April 1, 1990, Acme refused to pay the fire loss claiming that the required insurable interest did not exist at the time of the loss and that the amount of the insurance was insufficient to provide full coverage for the loss. Tower and Dodd are involved in a lawsuit contesting the ownership of the building and the claims they have both made for any fire insurance proceeds.

On June 1, 1990, Midway and New foreclosed their mortgages and are also claiming any fire insurance proceeds that may be paid by Acme.

On July 1, 1990, Tower sued Zimmer for breach of the lease and is seeking to collect the balance of the lease term rent.

The above events took place in a race-notice statute jurisdiction.

Required:

Answer the following questions and give the reasons for your conclusions.

a. Does Acme have to pay under the terms of the fire insurance policy? If so, how much?

b. Assuming the fire insurance proceeds will be paid, what would be the order of payment to the various parties and in what amounts?

c. Would Tower succeed in the suit against Zimmer? (5/91, Law, #4c, d, e)

Essay 57-5 (7 to 10 minutes)

While auditing the financial statements of Jackson Corporation for the year ended December 31, 1981, Harvey Draper, CPA, desired to verify the balance in the insurance claims receivable account. Draper obtained the following information:

- On November 4, 1981, Jackson's Parksdale plant was damaged by fire. The fire caused $200,000 damage to the plant, which was purchased in 1970 for $600,000. When the plant was purchased, Jackson obtained a loan secured by a mortgage from Second National Bank of Parksdale. At the time of the fire the loan balance, including accrued interest, was $106,000. The plant was insured against fire with Eagle Insurance Company. The policy contained a "standard mortgagee" clause and an 80% coinsurance clause. The face value of the policy was $600,000 and the value of the plant was $1,000,000 at the time of the fire.

- On December 10, 1981, Jackson's Yuma warehouse was totally destroyed by fire. The warehouse was acquired in 1960 for $300,000. At the time of the fire, the warehouse was unencumbered by any mortgage; it was insured against fire with Eagle for $300,000; and it had a value of $500,000. The policy contained an 80% coinsurance clause.

- On December 26, 1981, Jackson's Rye City garage was damaged by fire. At the time of the fire, the garage had a value of $250,000 and was unencumbered by any mortgage. The fire caused $60,000 damage to the garage, which was constructed in 1965 at a cost of $50,000. In 1975, Jackson expanded the capacity of the garage at an additional cost of $50,000. When the garage was constructed in 1965, Jackson insured the garage against fire for $50,000 with

Eagle, and this policy was still in force on the date of the fire. When the garage was expanded in 1975, Jackson obtained $100,000 of additional fire insurance coverage from Queen Insurance Company. Each policy contains an 80% coinsurance clause and a standard pro rata clause.

Required:

Answer the following, setting forth reasons for any conclusions stated.

a. How much of the fire loss relating to the Parksdale plant will be recovered from Eagle?

b. How will such recovery be distributed between Second National and Jackson?

c. How much of the fire loss relating to the Yuma warehouse will be recovered from Eagle?

d. How much of the fire loss relating to the Rye City garage will be recovered from the insurance companies?

e. What portion of the amount recoverable in connection with the Rye City garage loss will Queen be obligated to pay?   (11/82, Law, #5a)

ESSAY SOLUTIONS

Solution 57-4   Liability With Assigned Policy/ Order of Proceeds/Liability for Breach

a. Acme would have to honor the insurance contract and **pay part of the loss**. Despite Tower and Perry not maintaining insurance coverage of **80%** of the **property's market value**, the **coinsurance clause allows for a percentage of recovery**. The formula is as follows:

$$\frac{Amount\ of\ Coverage}{Actual\ Market\ Value \times Coinsurance\ \%} \times \begin{array}{c}Amount\\of\ Loss\end{array}$$

This would allow a recovery as follows:

$$\frac{\$200,000}{\$300,000 \times .8} \times \$180,000 = \mathbf{\$150,000}$$

b. The conflict between Midway and New would be resolved in favor of Midway. In a **race-notice**

statute jurisdiction, New's **knowledge of Midway's first mortgage would give Midway priority despite New's earlier filing**. The insurance proceeds would be distributed as follows:

- $80,000 to Midway representing the balance due on the mortgage including accrued interest. This is due because **Midway as a mortgagee is included as a contingent beneficiary** in the policy.
- $40,000 to New for the same reasons as above but **not paid unless and until Midway is fully paid**.
- $30,000 to be **divided equally** between Tower and Dodd **as tenants in common**.

c. Tower would not be able to collect rent from Zimmer for the balance of the term of the lease because Zimmer moved as a result of the extensive fire damage to the apartment. The **implied warranty of habitability** would be considered breached by the landlord and a **constructive eviction** of Zimmer would be deemed to have taken place because the **premises could no longer be used for their intended purpose. Constructive eviction releases both the landlord and the tenant from their obligations under the lease.**

Solution 57-5 Coinsurance

a. The recoverable loss is determined by reference to the following formula:

$$\frac{Insurance\ carried}{Insurance\ required} \times The\ amount\ of\ the\ loss$$

The insurance required is defined as the value of the property at the time of the loss multiplied by the coinsurance percentage. Applying the foregoing formula, the **amount of the loss recovered** is as follows:

$$\frac{\$600,000}{\$1,000,000 \times .8} \times \$200,000 = \mathbf{\$150,000}$$

b. The $150,000 will be distributed as follows: $106,000 to Second National and $44,000 to Jackson. This is because **Second National's**

insurable interest equals the extent of its mortgage outstanding, which is limited to debt outstanding plus accrued interest, and is paid first. The **remaining** $44,000 would then be **paid to Jackson.**

c. **Jackson will recover $300,000,** the face amount of the policy. The **coinsurance clause does not apply to a total loss.**

d. **Jackson will recover $45,000.** The formula for determination of the total amount recoverable under the 80% coinsurance clause is as follows:

$$\frac{\$150,000}{\$250,000 \times .8} \times \$60,000 = \$45,000$$

e. **Jackson will recover $30,000 from Queen.** This amount is determined as follows:

$$\frac{\$100,000}{(Queen's\ coverage)}\ \frac{}{\$150,000}\ \times \$45,000 = \$30,000$$
$$(Total\ coverage)$$

CHAPTER 58

ETHICS AND PROFESSIONAL RESPONSIBILITIES

PART ONE: PROFESSIONAL ETHICS 58-3

I. **AICPA Code of Professional Conduct** 58-3

II. **Principles of Conduct** 58-3
    A.   Responsibilities 58-3
    B.   The Public Interest 58-3
    C.   Integrity 58-3
    D.   Objectivity and Independence 58-3
    E.   Due Care 58-4
    F.   Scope and Nature of Services 58-4

III. **Rules of Conduct and Interpretations of Rules of Conduct** 58-4
    A.   Applicability of Rules of Conduct (ET 91) 58-4
    B.   Definitions (ET 92) 58-4
    C.   Interpretations of Rules of Conduct 58-5

IV. **Rules of Conduct and Interpretations on the Concepts of Independence, Integrity, and Objectivity** 58-5
    A.   *Independence* (ET 101) 58-5
    B.   Interpretations of Rule 101 58-5
    C.   *Integrity and Objectivity* (ET 102) 58-12

V. **Rules of Conduct and Interpretations on the Concepts of General and Technical Standards** 58-12
    A.   *General Standards* (ET 201) 58-12
    B.   *Compliance With Standards* (ET 202) 58-12
    C.   *Accounting Principles* (ET 203) 58-12
    D.   Interpretations of Rule 203 58-13

VI. **Rules of Conduct and Interpretations on the Concepts of Responsibilities to Clients** 58-14
    A.   *Confidential Client Information* (ET 301) 58-14
    B.   *Contingent Fees* (ET 302) 58-14
    C.   Interpretation of Rule 302 58-14

VII. **Rules of Conduct and Interpretations: Other Responsibilities and Practices** 58-14
    A.   *Acts Discreditable* (ET 501) 58-14
    B.   Interpretations of Rule 501 58-15
    C.   Forms of Solicitation 58-15
    D.   Interpretations of Rule 502 (ET 502) 58-15
    E.   *Commission* (ET 503) 58-16
    F.   *Form of Practice and Name* (ET 505) 58-16
    G.   Interpretations of Rule 505 (ET 505) 58-16

VIII. Ethics Rulings 58-17
   A.   Applicability 58-17
   B.   Independence, Integrity, and Objectivity (ET 191) 58-17
   C.   General and Technical Standards (ET 291) 58-24
   D.   Responsibilities to Clients (ET 391) 58-24
   E.   Other Responsibilities and Practices (ET 591) 58-25

PART TWO: STATEMENTS ON RESPONSIBILITIES IN TAX PRACTICE 58-28

I. Background 58-28
   A.   Significance 58-28
   B.   Objectives 58-28
   C.   Purpose 58-28

II. Statements on Responsibilities in Tax Practice 58-28
   A.   No. 1: Tax Return Positions 58-28
   B.   No. 2: Answers to Questions on the Tax Return 58-29
   C.   No. 3: Certain Procedural Aspects of Preparing Returns 58-29
   D.   No. 4: Use of Estimates 58-29
   E.   No. 5: Departure From a Position Previously Concluded in an Administrative
           Proceeding or Court Decision 58-30
   F.   No. 6: Knowledge of Error--Preparation of Return 58-30
   G.   No. 7: Knowledge of Error--Administrative Proceeding 58-30
   H.   No. 8: Advice to Clients 58-31

PART THREE: DEFINITIONS AND STANDARDS FOR CONSULTING SERVICES (SSCS1) 58-31

I. Background 58-31

II. Definitions 58-31
   A.   Consulting Process 58-31
   B.   Consulting Services 58-32

III. General Standards for Consulting Services 58-32
   A.   Professional Competence 58-32
   B.   Due Professional Care 58-32
   C.   Planning and Supervision 58-32
   D.   Sufficient Relevant Data 58-32

IV. Additional General Standards 58-33
   A.   Client Interest 58-33
   B.   Understanding With Client 58-33
   C.   Communication 58-33

CHAPTER 58

ETHICS AND PROFESSIONAL RESPONSIBILITIES

PART ONE: PROFESSIONAL ETHICS

I. AICPA Code of Professional Conduct

A.   The current version was adopted in 1988, and amended January 1992.

B.   The AICPA recognizes that a distinguishing mark of a profession is its acceptance of a high degree of responsibility to the public.

C.   The Code supports GAAS and provides a basis for their enforcement.

D.   Consists of the following four parts:

    1.   Principles of Conduct

    2.   Rules of Conduct

    3.   Interpretations of Rules of Conduct

    4.   Ethics Rulings

II. Principles of Conduct

Six articles compose the Principles of Conduct section of the AICPA Code of Professional Conduct. They stress the CPA's responsibility to the public, to clients, and to colleagues. Their purpose is to provide a level of conduct toward which CPAs should strive, and to provide a basis for the Rules of Conduct.

A.   Responsibilities--In carrying out their responsibilities as professionals, members should exercise sensitive professional and moral judgments in all their activities.

Members have a responsibility to cooperate with each other to continually improve the art of accounting and maintain the public's confidence.

B.   The Public Interest--Members should accept the obligation to act in a way that will serve the public interest, honor the public trust, and demonstrate a commitment to professionalism.

Members have a duty to discharge their responsibilities with integrity, objectivity, due professional care, and a genuine interest in serving the public. The public relies on the integrity and objectivity of certified public accountants to maintain the orderly functioning of commerce.

C.   Integrity--To maintain and broaden public confidence, members should perform all professional responsibilities with the highest sense of integrity.

Integrity requires a member to be honest and candid within the constraints of client confidentiality. Integrity also requires a member to observe the principles of objectivity and independence and of due care. Service and the public trust should not be subordinated to personal gain and advantage.

D.   Objectivity and Independence--A member should maintain objectivity and be free of conflicts of interest in discharging professional responsibilities. A member in public practice should be independent in fact and appearance when providing auditing and other attestation services. It is of utmost importance to the profession that the general public maintain confidence in the auditor's independence. Public confidence would be impaired by evidence that independence was actually impaired <u>and</u> it might also be impaired by the existence of circumstances which reasonable people might believe likely to influence independence.

E. <u>Due Care</u>--Everyone in a CPA firm engaged in auditing has the duty to abide by the fieldwork and reporting standards. Due care mandates critical review at all supervision levels of judgments made by audit assistants.

F. <u>Scope and Nature of Services</u>--A member in public practice should observe the Principles of the Code of Professional Conduct in determining the scope and nature of services to be provided.

To be satisfied that they are meeting the spirit of the Principles, members of the AICPA should:

1. Practice in firms that have in place internal quality control procedures to ensure that services are competently delivered and adequately supervised.

2. Determine, in their individual judgments, whether the scope and nature of other services provided to an audit client would create a conflict of interest in the performance of the audit function for that client.

3. Assess, in their individual judgments, whether an activity is consistent with their role as professionals.

III. Rules of Conduct and Interpretations of Rules of Conduct

A. <u>Applicability of Rules of Conduct (ET 91)</u>

1. The Rules of Conduct that follow apply to all professional services performed except (a) where the wording of the rule indicates otherwise and (b) that a member who is practicing outside the U.S. will not be subject to discipline for departing from any of the rules stated herein as long as the member's conduct is in accord with the rules of the organized accounting profession in the country in which the member is practicing. However, where a member's name is associated with financial statements under circumstances that would entitle the reader to assume that U.S. practices were followed, the member must comply with the requirements of Rules 202 and 203.

2. A member may be held responsible for compliance with the rules of all colleagues in the practice of public accounting who are either under the member's supervision or are the member's partners or shareholders in the practice.

B. <u>Definitions (ET 92)</u>

1. Client--A client is any person, enterprise, or entity, other than the member's employer, that engages a member or a member's firm to perform professional services, or a person or entity with respect to which professional services are performed. The term "employer" for these purposes does not include those entities engaged in the practice of public accounting.

2. Financial Statements--Statements and footnotes related thereto that purport to show financial position that relates to a point in time or changes in cash flows that relate to a period of time, and statements that use a cash or other basis of accounting. Balance sheets, statements of income, statements of retained earnings, statements of cash flows, and statements of changes in owners' equity are financial statements.

   • Tax returns and supporting schedules and incidental data that the CPA includes in consulting services reports to support the CPA's recommendations are not considered to be financial statements as the term is used in the Rules and Interpretations of the Code of Professional Conduct.

3. Firm--A proprietorship, partnership, or professional corporation or association engaged in the practice of public accounting, including individual partners or shareholders thereof.

4. Institute--The AICPA.

5. Member--A member or international associate of the AICPA.

6. Practice of Public Accounting--The practice of public accounting consists of the performance for a client by a member or a member's firm, while holding out as CPA(s), of the professional services of accounting, tax, personal financial planning, litigation support services, and those professional services for which standards are promulgated by bodies designated by Council, such as Statements of Financial Accounting Standards, Statements on Auditing Standards, Statements on Standards for Accounting and Review Services, Statements on Standards for Consulting Services, Statement on Standards for Attestation Engagements, and Statement on Standards for Accountants' Services on Prospective Financial Information.

However, a member or a member's firm, while holding out as CPA(s), is not considered to be in the practice of public accounting if the member or the member's firm does not perform, for any client, any of the professional services described in the preceding paragraph.

7. Professional Services--Professional services include all services performed by a member while holding him- or herself out as a CPA.

8. Holding Out--In general, any action initiated by a member that informs others of the member's status as a CPA or AICPA-accredited specialist constitutes holding out as a CPA. This would include, for example, any oral or written representation to another regarding CPA status, use of the CPA designation on business cards or letterhead, the display of a certificate evidencing a member's CPA designation, or listing as a CPA in local telephone directories.

C. Interpretations of Rules of Conduct--Pronouncements that provide guidelines as to the scope and application of the Rules of Conduct. A CPA who departs from these guidelines shall have the burden of justifying such departures in any disciplinary hearing.

IV. Rules of Conduct and Interpretations on the Concepts of Independence, Integrity, and Objectivity

A. *Independence (ET 101)*--A member in public practice shall be independent in the performance of professional standards promulgated by bodies designated by Council.

B. Interpretations of Rule 101

1. Financial Interest--The following will impair independence:

a. Direct or Material Indirect--If the member or the member's firm had or was committed to acquire any direct or material indirect financial interest in the enterprise. In other words, a direct financial interest will impair independence even if it is immaterial.

b. Trustee, Executor, or Administrator--If the member or the member's firm is trustee, executor, or administrator of any estate that had or was committed to acquire any direct or material indirect financial interest in the enterprise.

c. Business Investment--If the member or the member's firm had any joint closely held business investment with the enterprise or with any of its officers, directors, or principal stockholders that is material in relation to the member's net worth.

d. Loan--If a member or a member's firm had any loan to or from the enterprise or any officer, director, or principal stockholder of the enterprise except as specifically permitted in Interpretation 101-5.

2. Involvement in a Managerial (or Employee) Relationship--Since a CPA who is either a manager or an employee of an entity does not have the appearance of independence, independence will be impaired. Two examples are as follows:

   a. Promoter, Etc.--The member or the member's firm is a promoter, underwriter, voting trustee, a director, or an officer.

   b. Trustee--The member or the member's firm is a trustee for any pension or profit sharing trust of the client.

3. Honorary Directorships and Trusteeships (101-1)--A not-for-profit organization that limits its activities to performing charitable, religious, civic, or similar functions may seek to gain the prestige of a member's name by asking the member to serve on its board of directors or trustees. The member may do so and be associated with the organization's financial statements as long as (a) the position is purely honorary, (b) all letterheads and material circulated to outside parties that identify the member as a director or trustee clearly indicate that the position is honorary, (c) the member's only participation is the use of the member's name, and (d) the member does not vote or in any other way participate in management functions. This Interpretation applies only to those cases where the boards of directors or trustees are sufficiently large so that the member is able to limit participation as called for in the Interpretation.

4. Former Practitioners and Firm Independence (101-2)--A former practitioner is defined as a proprietor, partner, shareholder, or equivalent who leaves by resignation, termination, retirement, or sale of all or part of the practice. For purposes of compliance with Rule 101 and its interpretations, a former practitioner is not included in the term "a member or a member's firm."

   a. Payment of amounts owed to a former practitioner for an interest in the firm or for unfunded, vested retirement benefits should be such that there is not cause for substantial doubt about the firm's ability to continue as a going concern for a reasonable period of time. Amounts and payment dates should be fixed. Retirement benefits may be adjusted only for inflation.

   b. The former practitioner may not participate in the firm's business or professional activities whether or not compensated for the participation. This proscription does not apply to consultations on an advisory basis for a reasonable period of time during the transition period upon leaving the firm.

   c. The former practitioner may not <u>appear</u> to participate in the activities of or be <u>associated</u> with the former firm.

   d. A former practitioner in a position of significant influence with the client must no longer be provided with office space and related amenities by the former firm.

5. Accounting Services (101-3)--Members in public practice often perform manual or automated bookkeeping or data processing services for clients who are not large enough to have their own internal accounting staff. The member <u>must be careful</u> not to appear to be an employee of the client. The Interpretation also provides guidance for members who sell "block computer time" on their computers to clients and on the status of accounting services when a client registers with the Securities and Exchange Commission.

a. Performing Accounting Services for an Audit Client--The member must be careful not to appear to be an employee of the client. <u>Four requirements that prevent this are as follows</u>:

    (1) No Conflict of Interest--The CPA cannot have any relationship with the client or any conflict of interest that would impair the CPA's integrity or objectivity.

    (2) Client Responsible for Financial Statements--Even though the CPA may be keeping the accounting records and preparing the financial statements, the client must have a sufficient knowledge of the business and the applicable accounting standards to permit acceptance of responsibility for the financial statements.

    (3) No Participation in Operations--The CPA must not participate in the operations of the business as an employee or a manager. <u>For example</u>, the CPA should not consummate transactions, have custody of the client's assets, or act as the client's agent.

    (4) Accordance With GAAS--When performing an audit, the CPA must still be in accordance with GAAS even though personally performing some or all of the accounting work. The CPA is not relieved from the obligation to perform sufficient audit tests.

b. Selling "Block Time"--Sometimes a CPA rents time on a personally owned computer (i.e., "block time") to a client but does not become involved in the processing of the client's transactions or in maintaining the client's accounting records. In this case, the sale of "block time" is viewed as a <u>business relationship</u> with the client--not as a professional relationship. Therefore, independence is not usually impaired.

c. SEC Regulation--Once a client becomes subject to SEC or other federal or state regulations, the CPA can no longer keep the accounting records nor rent block time to the client.

6. Loans From Financial Institution Clients and Related Terminology (101-5)--This Interpretation concerns the specifically permitted loans allowed under Interpretation 101-A.4. Specifically, certain "grandfathered" loans and other permitted loans from financial institution clients will not impair independence.

    a. Grandfathered Loans--The following loans from a financial institution will not impair independence.

        (1) Home mortgages.

        (2) Other secured loans in which the collateral equals or exceeds the balance of the loan at January 1, 1992, and at all times afterwards.

        (3) Loans that are immaterial in relation to the member's net worth.

    b. Specified Conditions to Qualify--The loans above must meet certain conditions in order to qualify for the "grandfathering" provision.

    c. Other Permitted Loans--The following personal loans, from a financial institution client, are generally permitted under normal lending procedures as long as the loans are kept current as to all terms.

        (1) Car loans and leases collateralized by the vehicle.

(2)   Loans of the surrender value under terms of an insurance policy.

(3)   Borrowings fully collateralized by cash deposits.

(4)   Credit cards and cash advances on checking accounts with a current balance of no more than $5,000.

7.   The Effect of Actual or Threatened Litigation on Independence (101-6).

a.   Litigation Between Client and Auditor--Threatened or actual litigation may create an adverse relationship between the client and the CPA. This situation may affect management's willingness to disclose data to the CPA, as well as the CPA's objectivity in regard to the client. Since this is a complex area, it is impossible to pinpoint where independence becomes impaired. However, the Interpretation offers the following guidelines:

(1)   Independence would be impaired when current management begins litigation alleging deficiencies in the audit work the CPA performed for the client.

(2)   Independence would be impaired when the auditor begins litigation against current management alleging management fraud or deceit.

(3)   Independence will be impaired when current management has expressed the intention to begin litigation against the auditor alleging deficiencies in the audit work the CPA performed for the client as long as the CPA feels there is a strong possibility that the claim will be filed.

(4)   Independence will usually not be impaired in the case of threatened or actual litigation that is not related to the audit performed for the client for an amount that is not material to the CPA's firm or to the financial statements of the client.

Examples include disputes over billings for services and for tax or consulting advice.

b.   Litigation by Security Holders--Independence is not impaired solely because of primary litigation in which the CPA and the client company (or its management) are defendants, for example, in the case of a "class action" suit. However, if there are cross-claims alleging that the auditor is responsible for the deficiencies that gave rise to the suit or alleging fraud or deceit by current management, the area of impairment of independence should be examined carefully. The Interpretation provides the following guidelines:

(1)   Cross-claims filed to protect a right to legal redress in the event of a future adverse decision in the primary litigation would not normally impair independence unless there is a significant risk that the cross-claim will result in a settlement or judgment that is a material amount to either the CPA's firm or the financial statements.

(2)   Independence is not usually impaired by the assertion of cross-claims against the auditor by underwriters if no such claims are asserted by the company or its current management.

(3)   If a cross-claim is filed against the auditor by someone who is also an officer or director of one of the auditor's other clients, the auditor's independence with respect to such other client will usually not be impaired.

c. Other Third-Party Litigation--Independence usually will <u>not</u> be impaired because of third-party litigation against the auditor by a lending institution, other creditor, security holder, or insurance company alleging reliance on the financial statements examined by the auditor as a basis for extending credit or insurance coverage to the client. In cases where the real party in interest in the litigation (e.g., the other creditor) is also a client of the auditor ("the plaintiff client"), independence with respect to the <u>plaintiff client</u> may be impaired if the litigation involves an amount that would be <u>material</u> to either the CPA's firm or the plaintiff client's financial statements.

d. Effects of Impairment of Independence--When the auditor concludes that independence is impaired, the auditor should either (1) resign from the engagement or cease any audit work then in progress until the issues can be resolved between the parties, or (2) disclaim an opinion because of a lack of independence.

e. Termination of Impairment--Independence is no longer impaired when a resolution is reached and the matters at issue no longer have any effect on the relationship between the auditor and the client.

f. Actions Permitted When Independence Is Impaired--An auditor may issue a report when independent and then, at a later time when the auditor's independence has become impaired, be asked to reissue it or consent to its use. This is permitted as long as the auditor has not performed any post-audit work during the time that independence was impaired. In this particular Interpretation, "post-audit work" does <u>not</u> include inquiries of subsequent auditors, reading of subsequent financial statements, or such other procedures the auditor feels are needed to properly consider subsequent events.

8. Meaning of Certain Independence Terminology and the Effect of Family Relationships on Independence (101-9)

   a. Terminology--Certain terms are defined below as they are used in relation to Rule 101.

      (1) The term "a member or a member's firm" includes the following:

         (a) The member's firm and its proprietors, partners, or shareholders. A member's firm is defined as a proprietorship, partnership, or professional corporation or association engaged in the practice of public accounting.

         (b) All individuals participating in the engagement, except those who perform only routine clerical functions, such as typing and photocopying.

         (c) All individuals with a managerial position located in an office participating in a significant portion of the engagement.

         (d) Any entity (for example, partnership, corporation, trust, joint venture, or pool) whose operating, financial, or accounting policies can be controlled by one or more of the persons described in (a) through (c) or by two or more such persons if they choose to act together.

      The term "a member and a member's firm" does not include an individual solely because of a former association with the client above, if such individual has become disassociated from the client and does not participate in the engagement for the client covering any period of association with the client.

      The term "a member and a member's firm" does include a professional employee who is associated with the client in any capacity described in Rule

101 if the professional employee is located in an office participating in a significant portion of the engagement.

    (2)   A <u>managerial employee</u> is a professional employee who has either of the following positions:

        (a)   A position generally similar to that of a partner, including an employee having the final authority to sign or give final approval to the issuance of reports in the firm's name.

        (b)   A management position, in contrast to a nonmanagement position, with the firm.

The organization of firms varies; therefore, whether an employee has a management position depends on that employer's normal responsibilities and how the employer or the position itself is held out to clients and third parties. Some, but not necessarily all, of the responsibilities that suggest that an employee has a management position are (1) continuing responsibility for the overall planning and supervision of engagements, (2) authority for determining that an engagement is complete, (3) responsibility for client relationships, (4) responsibility for overall management of the firm, and (5) existence of profit-sharing as a significant feature of total compensation.

    (3)   A person or entity can exercise significant influence over the operating, financial, or accounting policies of another entity if, for example, the person or entity

        (a)   Is connected with the entity as a promoter, underwriter, voting trustee, general partner, or director.

        (b)   Is connected with the entity in a policy-making position related to the entity's primary operating, financial, or accounting policies.

        (c)   Meets the criteria established in par. 17 of <u>APB 18</u>, *The Equity Method of Accounting for Investments in Common Stock*, to determine the ability of an investor to exercise such influence.

b.   Effect of Family Relationships

    (1)   The term "member" includes spouses (whether or not dependent) and dependent persons (whether or not related) <u>except</u> that the independence of the member and the member's firm will not normally be impaired solely because of employment of a spouse or dependent person by a client provided that the employment is in a position that does not allow "significant influence" over the client's operating, financial, or accounting policies. However, if such employment is in a position where the person's activities are "audit sensitive," the member should not participate in the engagement.

        (a)   A person's activities would be considered <u>audit sensitive</u> if such activities are normally an element of, or subject to, significant internal controls.

        (b)   For example, the positions of cashier, internal auditor, general accounting clerk, purchasing agent, or inventory warehouse supervisor.

    (2)   Nondependent Close Relatives--The term "member" excludes nondependent close relatives of the members. Nevertheless, the independence of a member or a firm may be impaired because of a nondependent close relative. <u>Close</u>

relatives are nondependent children, brothers, sisters, grandparents, parents, parents-in-law, and their respective spouses. The independence of a member and his or her firm is impaired with respect to an enterprise if

(a) A proprietor, partner, shareholder, or professional employee participating in the engagement has a close relative who (1) can exercise significant influence over the operating, financial, or accounting policies of the client, (2) is otherwise employed in a position where the person's activities are "audit sensitive," or (3) has a financial interest in the client which is material to the close relative and of which the proprietor, partner, shareholder, or professional employee has knowledge.

(b) A proprietor, partner, shareholder, or managerial employee located in an office participating in a significant portion of the engagement has a close relative who can exercise significant influence over the operating, financial, or accounting policies of the client.

(3) Other Considerations--In situations involving assessment of the association of any relative or dependent person with a client, members must consider whether the strength of personal and business relationships between the member and the relative or dependent person, considered in conjunction with the specified association with the client, would lead a reasonable person aware of all the facts and taking into consideration normal strength of character and normal behavior under the circumstances to conclude that the situation poses an unacceptable threat to the member's objectivity and appearance of independence.

9. The Effect on Independence of Relationships With Entities Included in the Governmental Financial Statements (101-10)

a. Oversight entities are entities that can exercise influence over the component units of a government. Such oversight entities can influence the component unit's financial interdependency, selection of governing authority, designation of management, operations, and accountability for fiscal matters.

b. Component units are entities that have substantial authority exercised over them by an oversight entity.

c. Accountants issuing a report on financial statements of a government reporting entity must be independent of the following:

(1) The responsible oversight entity.

(2) Each component unit included in the reporting entity's financial statements.

d. Accountants who audit material components must be independent of all components because of the impact on the oversight entity which has significant influence over all the other component units.

e. Accountants who audit immaterial component units need to be independent only of those units.

f. If several immaterial components are audited, and when aggregated are material, the accountant should be independent of the oversight entity and each component entity.

10. Independence and Attest Engagements (101-11)--Rule 101 provides that "a member in public practice shall be independent in the performance of professional services as required

by standards promulgated by bodies designated by the Council." The Statement on Standards for Attestation Engagements [AT 100] requires independence in the performance of engagements covered by that statement.

C. *Integrity and Objectivity* (ET 102)--In the performance of any professional service, a member shall maintain objectivity and integrity, shall be free of conflicts of interest, and shall not knowingly misrepresent facts or subordinate his or her judgment to others.

    1. Knowing Misrepresentations in the Preparation of Financial Statements (102-1)--Knowingly making, permitting, or directing another to make false and misleading entries in an entity's financial statements or records is in violation of Rule 102.

    2. Conflicts of Interest (102-2)--A conflict of interest may occur if a member performs a professional service for a client or employer and the member or the member's firm has a significant relationship that could be viewed as impairing the member's objectivity. If the significant relationship is disclosed to, and consent is obtained from, the client or appropriate parties, the rule shall not prohibit the performance of the professional service. However, independence impairments under Rule 101 and its interpretations cannot be eliminated by such disclosure and consent.

V. Rules of Conduct and Interpretations on the Concepts of General and Technical Standards

A. *General Standards* (ET 201)

    1. General Standards--A CPA must comply with the following general standards as interpreted by bodies designated by the Council of the AICPA.

        a. Professional Competence--A CPA will undertake only those professional services which the CPA or the CPA's firm has reasonable expectations of being able to complete with professional competence.

        b. Due Professional Care--A CPA must exercise due professional care in the performance of professional services.

        c. Planning and Supervision--A CPA will adequately plan and supervise the performance of professional services.

        d. Sufficient Relevant Data--A CPA must obtain sufficient relevant data to provide a reasonable basis for reaching conclusions or making recommendations in relation to any professional services performed.

    2. Interpretations of Rule 201--Competence (201-1)--The CPA does not assume responsibility for infallibility of knowledge or judgment. Competence involves the technical knowledge of the CPA and the staff, the ability to apply this knowledge to the particular engagement, and the ability to supervise and evaluate the work performed. If the CPA does not possess the required knowledge when undertaking the engagement, additional research and/or consultation with others must be undertaken. If the CPA cannot acquire the knowledge, the client should be advised that a competent individual must be engaged to perform the service either independently or as an associate.

B. *Compliance With Standards* (ET 202)--A member who performs auditing, review, compilation, consulting, tax, or other professional services shall comply with standards promulgated by bodies designated by Council.

C. *Accounting Principles* (ET 203)--A CPA will not express an opinion that financial statements are presented in conformity with GAAP or state that the CPA is not aware of any material modifications that should be made to such statements or data in order for them to be in conformity with GAAP, if the statements contain a deviation from GAAP that has a <u>material</u> effect on the financial statements taken as a whole, <u>unless</u> the CPA can demonstrate that because of unusual circumstances the financial statements would have been misleading.

D.   <u>Interpretations of Rule 203</u>

1.   Departures From Established Accounting Principles (203-1)--Proper accounting treatment is that which will render the financial statements <u>not misleading</u>. While GAAP will usually do this, there will be unusual cases where GAAP would render the financial statements misleading. The CPA must use <u>professional judgment</u> in deciding when a deviation is appropriate. Circumstances which <u>may</u> justify a departure include new legislation or the evolution of a new form of business transaction.

2.   Status of FASB Interpretations (203-2)--The <u>FASB</u> has been designated as the body to establish accounting principles. <u>FASB Statements of Financial Accounting Standards</u> and those <u>Accounting Research Bulletins</u> and <u>APB Opinions</u> which have not been superseded by action of the FASB, constitute accounting principles. <u>FASB Interpretations</u> also constitute GAAP and are similarly covered by Rule 203.

3.   New GAAP Hierarchy--In January 1992, the Auditing Standards Board issued <u>SAS 69</u>, which established a hierarchy for applying accounting principles to financial statements that the auditor's report represents are presented fairly in conformity with GAAP. According to <u>SAS 69</u>, the auditor's opinion that the financial statements present fairly the financial position, results of operations, and cash flows in conformity with GAAP in all material respects, requires the auditor to exercise judgment in determining whether: (a) the accounting principles selected and applied have general acceptance; (b) the accounting principles are appropriate for the entity's circumstances and operations; (c) the financial statements and related notes contain adequate disclosure of all matters that may affect the use, understanding, and interpretation of that information; (d) the information presented in the financial statements is properly classified and summarized in a reasonable way; and (e) the financial statements reflect the underlying transactions and events of the entity, such that the resulting financial statements present information within an acceptable range. The new hierarchy is presented in the following exhibit:

Exhibit 1

NEW GAAP HIERARCHY	OLD GAAP HIERARCHY
a. FASB Statements and Interpretations, APB Opinions, and AICPA Accounting Research Bulletins	a. FASB Statements and Interpretations, APB Opinions, AICPA Accounting Research Bulletins
b. FASB Technical Bulletins, AICPA Industry Audit and Accounting Guides, and AICPA Statements of Position cleared by the FASB	b. FASB Technical Bulletins, AICPA Industry Audit and Accounting Guides, and AICPA Statements of Position
c. Consensus positions of the FASB EITF, and AcSEC Practice Bulletins cleared by the FASB	
d. AICPA accounting interpretations, "Qs&As" published by the FASB staff, as well as industry practices widely recognized and prevalent	c. AICPA accounting interpretations as well as industry practices widely recognized and prevalent
e. Other accounting literature, including FASB Concepts Statements; APB Statements; AICPA Issues Papers; International Accounting Standards Committee Statements; GASB Statements, Technical Bulletins and Interpretations; pronouncements of other professional associations and regulatory agencies; AICPA Technical Practice Aids; and other accounting textbooks and articles	d. Other accounting literature, including FASB Concepts Statements; APB Statements; AICPA Issues Papers; AcSEC Practice Bulletins; minutes of FASB EITF; International Accounting Standards Committee Statements; pronouncements of other professional associations or regulatory agencies; and accounting articles and textbooks

In assessing the appropriateness of the accounting principles used, the auditor must bear in mind that the financial statements should capture the <u>economic substance</u> of business transactions and not just their legal form. As a result, in assessing whether the financial statements are presented fairly, in conformity with GAAP, the auditor must make a two-fold determination. First, a determination must be made that the accounting principles used are generally accepted. Second, the auditor must be satisfied that the accounting principles used capture the <u>economic substance</u> of those business transactions that materially affect the entity to which the auditor's report relates.

VI. Rules of Conduct and Interpretations on the Concepts of Responsibilities to Clients

A. <u>*Confidential Client Information* (ET 301)</u>--A CPA will not disclose confidential information obtained in the course of the professional engagement without the <u>consent</u> of the client. This Rule <u>DOES NOT</u> (1) relieve the CPA of obligations under Rule 202 (GAAS) and Rule 203 (GAAP); (2) affect the CPA's compliance with a subpoena or a summons enforceable by court order; (3) prohibit review of a CPA's professional practices as a part of an AICPA authorized voluntary quality review program; or (4) preclude a CPA from initiating or responding to inquiries by the Ethics Division or Trial Board of the AICPA, by any disciplinary body of the state CPA society, or under state statutes.

1. Disclosure of Confidential Client Information in Certain Circumstances (301-2)--Exemption 4 of Rule 301 is interpreted to state that Rule 301 shall not be construed to preclude a member from initiating a complaint with or responding to any inquiry made by a recognized investigative or disciplinary body of the AICPA or other participant in the Joint Ethics Enforcement Program. Exemption 2 is interpreted to provide that Rule 301 should not be construed to prohibit or interfere with a member's compliance with applicable laws and government regulations.

2. Confidential Information and the Purchase, Sale, or Merger of a Practice (301-3)--Rule 301 prohibits a member in public practice from disclosing any confidential client information without the specific consent of the client. Hence, a CPA, without consent, should not disclose information contained in working papers to a CPA firm that has purchased the CPA's accounting practice. However, the rule provides that it shall not be construed to prohibit the review of a member's professional practice under AICPA or state CPA society authorization.

B. <u>*Contingent Fees* (ET 302)</u>--A CPA will not offer or render services under an agreement whereby the fee is <u>contingent</u> upon the findings. A CPA's fees may depend on the complexity of the service rendered. Fees which are fixed by the courts or public authorities or which are determined in tax matters by judicial proceedings or governmental agency findings are <u>not</u> considered contingent and are therefore permitted. Specified services that a member in public practice or the member's firm shall not perform for a contingent fee include an audit or review of a financial statement, a compilation of a financial statement when the member might reasonably expect that a third party will use the statement, or an examination of prospective financial information. A member is also precluded from preparing an original or amended tax return or claim for a tax refund for a contingent fee.

C. <u>Interpretation of Rule 302</u>--Contingent Fees in Tax Matters (302-1)--A contingent fee would be permitted when a member represents a client in an examination by a revenue agent of the client's federal or state income tax return, when the member represents a client in connection with obtaining a private letter ruling, or when filing an amended return claiming a refund which exceeds the threshold for review by the appropriate taxing authority.

VII. Rules of Conduct and Interpretations: Other Responsibilities and Practices

A. <u>*Acts Discreditable* (ET 501)</u>--A CPA will not commit an act which is discreditable to the profession. (This is one of the two rules that a CPA who is not engaged in the practice of public accounting must follow.)

B.   Interpretations of Rule 501

1.   Retention of Client's Records (501-1)--A CPA violates Rule 501 by <u>refusing</u> to return a client's records <u>after</u> the client has demanded them.

a.   A client's records are any accounting or other records belonging to the client that were provided to the member by or on behalf of the client. If an engagement is terminated prior to completion, the member is required to return only client records.

b.   A member's working papers--including, but not limited to, analyses and schedules prepared by the client at the request of the member--are the member's property, not client records, and need not be made available.

c.   In some instances, a member's workpapers contain information that is not reflected in the client's books and records, with the result that the client's financial information is incomplete. This would include (1) adjusting, closing, combining, or consolidating journal entries and (2) information normally contained in books of original entry and general ledgers or subsidiary ledgers. In those instances when an <u>engagement has been completed</u>, such information should also be made available to the client upon request. However, the member may require that fees due the member with respect to such completed engagements be paid before such information is provided.

d.   Once the member has complied with the foregoing requirements, the member need not comply with any subsequent requests to again provide such information.

2.   Discrimination in Employment Practices (501-2)--It is to be presumed that discrimination based on race, color, religion, sex, age, or national origin is an act discreditable to the profession and is, therefore, a <u>violation</u> of Rule 501.

3.   Failure to Follow Standards and/or Procedures in Government Audits (501-3)--In audits of government grants, government units, or other recipients of government monies, the auditor is obligated to follow government audit standards, guides, procedures, statutes, rules, and regulations.

4.   Negligence in the Preparation of Financial Statements or Records (501-4)--A CPA who, by virtue of negligence, makes, or permits or directs another to make, false and misleading entries in the financial statements or records of an entity is considered to have committed an act discreditable to the profession.

5.   Failure to Follow Requirements of Governmental Bodies, Commissions, or Other Regulatory Agencies in Performing Attest or Similar Services (501-5)--When a CPA agrees to perform an attest or similar service for the purpose of reporting to governmental bodies, commissions, or other regulatory agencies, the CPA should follow such requirements, in addition to GAAS. Failure to follow such requirements is an act discreditable to the profession, unless the CPA discloses that such requirements were not followed and includes the reasons in the report. Failure to substantially follow requirements for additional disclosures is also an act discreditable to the profession.

C.   Forms of Solicitation--A CPA will not seek to obtain clients by advertising or other forms of solicitation in a manner that is <u>false</u>, <u>misleading</u>, or <u>deceptive</u>.

D.   Interpretations of Rule 502 (ET 502)

1.   False, Misleading, or Deceptive Acts (502-2)--Advertising or other forms of solicitation that are false, misleading, or deceptive are prohibited since they are not in the <u>public interest</u>. Examples of such activities include those that (a) create false or unjustified expectations of favorable results, (b) imply the ability to influence any court, tribunal, regulatory agency, or

similar body or official, (c) contain a representation that specific professional services in current or future periods will be performed for a stated fee, estimated fee, or fee range when it was likely at the time of representation that such fees would be substantially increased and the prospective client was not advised of that likelihood, or (d) contain any other representations that would be likely to cause a reasonable person to misunderstand or be deceived.

2. Engagements Obtained Through Efforts of Third Parties (502-5)--A CPA may be asked to render professional services to clients or customers of third parties who were obtained through the advertising and solicitation efforts of the third parties. The CPA may do so, but has the responsibility to determine that all promotional efforts are <u>consistent</u> with the Code of Professional Conduct. The reason is that the CPA will receive the benefits of the advertising and solicitation efforts of the third parties, and a CPA cannot do through others what the CPA cannot do him- or herself.

E. *Commission (ET 503)*--A CPA is prohibited from recommending, for a commission, any product or service to a client or any product or service to be supplied by a client, when that member or member's firm provides certain services to the client. Specified services that a member in public practice or the member's firm shall not perform for a commission include an audit or review of a financial statement, a compilation of a financial statement when the member might reasonably expect that a third party will use the statement, or an examination of prospective financial information.

1. Disclosure of Commissions--A member who receives or expects to receive a commission from a nonprohibited act should disclose that fact to the client.

2. Fees--Fees paid to a member for referring a client to a particular person or service should be disclosed. Likewise, the fact that a referral fee was paid to obtain a client should also be disclosed.

F. *Form of Practice and Name* (ET 505)--A CPA may practice public accounting in the form of a <u>proprietorship</u>, a <u>partnership</u>, or a <u>professional corporation</u> whose characteristics conform to AICPA guidelines.

1. Firm Name--The name of the firm will <u>not</u> be misleading as to the <u>type of organization structure</u> being used (for example, using a name that implies a proprietorship in a partnership). The names of one or more past partners or shareholders may be included in the firm name. A partner who survives the death or withdrawal of all of the other partners may continue to practice under the firm name for <u>up to two years after becoming a sole practitioner</u>.

2. Designation--A firm cannot designate itself as "Members of the AICPA" unless <u>all</u> of its partners or shareholders belong to the AICPA.

G. Interpretations of Rule 505 (ET 505)

1. Investment in Accounting Organization (505-1)--A member in the practice of public accounting may have an unlimited investment in an accounting organization as long as the practice of public accounting through that form of organization is permitted by state law or regulation and the organization's characteristics conform to regulations of council.

2. Application of Rules of Conduct to Members Who Operate a Separate Business (505-2)--Members in public practice who also operate a separate business offering to clients one or more of the types of services rendered by public accountants must observe all the Rules of Conduct in the operation of the separate business.

Members not otherwise in the practice of public accounting, but who hold out to the public as being CPAs, must also observe the Rules of Conduct in the operations of a business providing one or more of the types of services rendered by public accountants.

VIII. Ethics Rulings

A. Applicability--Ethics rulings are formal rulings promulgated by the executive committee of the AICPA Professional Ethics Division after exposure to state societies and local boards. They summarize the application of Rules of Conduct and Interpretations to a particular set of circumstances. CPAs who depart from them in similar circumstances should be prepared to justify their departure.

B. Independence, Integrity, and Objectivity (ET 191)--Ruling numbers not represented below have been superseded, deleted, or withdrawn.

1. Acceptance of a Gift--Independence may be impaired if an employee or partner accepts more than a token gift from a client.

2. Association Membership--A CPA can join a trade association that is a client without impairing the CPA's independence as long as the CPA does not serve in a capacity equivalent to management.

3. Member as a Cosigner of Checks--Independence would be impaired if a CPA accepts the responsibility of co-signing checks with a designated employee of a client in emergency situations.

4. Payroll Preparation Services--Independence is impaired if a CPA takes over a client's payroll function.

6. Member's Spouse as Bookkeeper of Client--Independence is not impaired as long as spouse does only bookkeeping work. If scope of responsibilities and activities of spouse extend into areas requiring management decisions, independence would be impaired.

7. Member as Contract Bookkeeper--Independence is impaired if a CPA contracts with a client to supervise office personnel, approve vouchers for payment, and prepare monthly and quarterly reports since the CPA is performing management functions.

8. Member Providing Accounting and Consulting Services--Independence is not impaired by providing extensive accounting and consulting services as long as the requirements of Interpretation 101-3 are met.

9. Member as Representative of Creditors' Committee--Independence with respect to the debtor corporation would be impaired if the CPA co-signs checks issued by the debtor corporation, co-signs its purchase orders, or exercises general supervision to ensure compliance with budgetary controls and pricing formulas aimed at the liquidation of deferred indebtedness.

10. Member as Legislator--Independence is impaired if a CPA serves as an elected legislator in a municipal body while the CPA (or CPA firm) is the auditor of the body.

11. Member as Executor or Trustee--Independence is not impaired if a CPA is merely designated to become executor or trustee of the estate of an individual who owns majority stock ownership of a closely held corporation. Actual service impairs independence.

12. Member as a Trustee--Independence is impaired if a CPA is a trustee of a foundation.

13. Member as Bank Stockholder--Independence is not impaired if a CPA holds an immaterial stock interest in a bank. A CPA's independence is not impaired with respect to a client who has borrowings from a bank in which the CPA has immaterial stock holdings.

14. Member on Board of Directors of Federated Fund-Raising Organization--Independence is not impaired in regard to groups receiving funds from the United Way or similar organization if a CPA serves as a director or officer of the organization as long as the organization does not exercise managerial control over the groups.

16. Member on Board of Directors of Nonprofit Social Club--Independence is impaired if a member serves on the board of directors of a nonprofit social club when the board assumes important administrative or financial responsibilities.

17. Member of Social Club--Independence is not impaired as long as the CPA does not take part in the management of the club.

19. Member on Deferred Compensation Committee--If a CPA serves on a committee that provides general supervisory services over the client's deferred compensation program, the CPA's independence would be impaired.

20. Member Serving on Governmental Advisory Unit--Independence is not considered to be impaired with respect to the governmental unit.

21. Member as Director and Auditor of the Entity's Profit-Sharing Trust--A CPA's independence is impaired if the CPA serves as director of an enterprise and also as auditor of that enterprise's profit sharing and retirement trust.

29. Member as Bondholder--Independence is impaired if a CPA owns bonds of a municipal authority, since the member has a loan to the authority/client.

31. Financial Interest in a Cooperative, Condominium Association, Planned Unit Development, Homeowners Association, Time-Share Development, or Other Common Interest Realty Association--Independence of a CPA or the CPA's firm would be considered impaired with respect to an engagement to perform services for a cooperative, condominium association, planned unit development, homeowners association, time-share development, or other common interest realty association if the CPA or the CPA's firm owned a unit in such an entity.

32. Mortgage Loan to Member's Corporation--The independence of a CPA who is president and substantial stockholder of a company which is indebted to a financial institution on a loan secured by a first mortgage on a company building would not be impaired with respect to the financial institution provided the mortgage loan was made under normal lending procedures, terms, and requirements of the financial institution.

33. Retirement Plan Offer--Independence is impaired if a CPA joins in a client's employee benefit plan.

35. Stockholder in Mutual Funds--Independence in regard to the clients is usually not impaired if a CPA owns shares in a mutual fund that holds shares in the CPA's audit clients, unless the indirect financial interest becomes material to the member or the member has significant influence over the mutual fund.

36. Stockholder in Investment Club--Independence with respect to a client is impaired if a CPA is a member of an investment club which holds shares in the CPA's client.

38. Member as Co-Fiduciary With Client Bank--Independence of a firm is not impaired with respect to the bank or its trust department if a CPA serves with a client bank in a co-fiduciary

capacity with respect to the estate or trust as long as the assets in the estate or trust are not material in relation to the total assets of the bank and/or trust department.

39. Member as Stock Transfer Agent and/or Registrar--Independence is impaired, because such services would be considered equivalent to that of a member of management or of an employee.

41. Member as Auditor of Insurance Company--Independence is not impaired if a CPA audits an insurance company that provides a retirement plan for the member's employees as long as the contributions are invested and managed in a pooled separate account, not part of the general assets of the insurance company.

48. Faculty Member as Auditor of a Student Fund--A CPA who is a faculty member is not independent with respect to a Student Senate Fund because the CPA would be auditing several of the management functions performed by the university that is the CPA's employer.

51. Member Providing Legal Services--Independence is impaired if a CPA who is also an attorney provides legal services to a client.

52. Unpaid Fees--Independence is impaired if fees for professional services rendered for prior years are not collected before the issuance of the CPA's report for the current year. Such amounts assume the characteristics of a loan.

54. Member Providing Appraisal, Valuation, or Actuarial Services--Independence is not impaired if a firm renders appraisal, valuation, or actuarial services to a client as long as a client can make informed judgments on the results.

55. Independence During Consulting Services Systems Implementation--Independence is not impaired during a consulting services systems implementation if a CPA arranges interviews for the client's hiring of new personnel and instructs and oversees the training of current client personnel as long as the client makes all significant management decisions. The CPA must restrict supervisory activities to initial instruction and training of personnel.

56. Executive Search--Independence is impaired if a CPA recruits and hires a controller and a cost accountant for a client. It is not impaired if the CPA recommends a position description and candidate specifications, searches for and initially screens candidates, and recommends qualified candidates to the client, provided client management is responsible for the ultimate hiring decision.

57. Consulting Services Engagement to Evaluate Service Bureaus--Under Rule 102, if, when a client asks a member's firm to evaluate and recommend service bureaus in which partners of the member's firm have material financial interests, and the interests are disclosed to the client and the client's consent is obtained for performance of the engagement, the member is not precluded from evaluating and recommending, if appropriate, the service bureau to the client.

58. Member as Lessor--Independence is impaired when a CPA leases space to a client in a building owned by the CPA.

60. Employee Benefit Plans--A potential problem may arise for a member auditing an employee benefit plan with multiple participating employers. With certain exceptions, a member must remain independent with respect to the employers for whom the plan has a material financial impact.

61. Participation of Member's Spouse in Employee Stock Ownership Plan of Client--When a CPA's spouse participates in an employee stock ownership plan of a client, independence is

not impaired until the right of possession of the stock exists, unless the indirect financial interest is material to the member's net worth.

64. Member as Director of Agency for Which Client Raises Funds--A member's independence would be considered to be impaired with respect to a fund-raising foundation if the member serves on the board of directors of the entity for whose sole benefit the foundation exists unless the position is purely honorary and the member restricts participation to the use of the member's name.

65. Use of CPA Designation by Member Not in Public Practice

   a. A member who is not in public practice may use the CPA designation in connection with the employer's financial statements of the member's employer issued for internal or external distribution provided that the following occur:

      (1) Such CPA designation appears on the employer's letterhead.

      (2) The member's employment status or title is clearly indicated.

      (3) The member makes reference neither to an audit nor to generally accepted auditing standards, nor states that the member has reviewed the financial statements. When a member states that the financial statements have been compiled, the member should specifically make reference to a lack of independence.

   b. The correspondence of a member who is not in public practice may contain the member's CPA designation provided that the correspondence appears on or with the employer's letterhead and the member's employment status or title is clearly indicated.

   c. Business cards of a member who is not in public practice that indicate the member's CPA designation should clearly display the member's employer and the member's employment status or title.

66. Member's Retirement or Savings Plan Has Financial Interest in Client--Independence is impaired if a CPA's retirement or savings plan has any direct or material indirect financial interest in a client company.

67. Servicing of Loan--Independence of a CPA with respect to a financial institution is not impaired by the mere servicing of the CPA's loan as long as there was not risk of material loss to the client with respect to the loan being serviced.

68. Blind Trust--Independence is impaired if a CPA has a direct financial interest in an enterprise, whether or not the financial interest is placed in a blind trust.

69. Investment With a General Partner--A CPA's or CPA firm's independence is impaired with respect to a limited partnership when the CPA or CPA firm has a financial interest in another limited partnership of the same general partner which is material to the CPA's or CPA firm's net worth.

70. Member's Depository Relationship With Client Financial Institution--Independence of a CPA with respect to a financial institution is not impaired if checking account, savings account, certificates of deposit, or money market accounts are fully insured by the appropriate state or federal insurance agency. Uninsured deposits would not impair independence unless material to the CPA or CPA's firm.

71. Use of Nonindependent CPA Firm on an Engagement--A CPA firm's independence is impaired by the use of partners, shareholders, or professional employees from another firm

which is not independent with respect to a client, as part of the engagement team. The work of such individuals in a manner similar to internal auditors is permitted if there is compliance with the Statements on Auditing Standards.

72. Member on Advisory Board of Client--A CPA and the CPA's firm's independence would be impaired by the CPA's service on an advisory board of a client unless all of the following criteria are met: (a) the responsibilities of the advisory board are, in fact, advisory in nature; (b) the advisory board has no authority to make, nor does it appear to make, management decisions on behalf of the client; and (c) the advisory board and those having authority to make management decisions (including the board of directors or its equivalent) are distinct groups with minimal, if any, common membership.

73. Meaning of the Period of a Professional Engagement--The period of a professional engagement starts when the CPA begins to perform professional services requiring independence and ends with the notification of the termination of that professional relationship either by the CPA or by the client.

74. Audits, Reviews, or Compilations and Lack of Independence--A CPA may not issue an audit opinion or review report if the CPA is not independent with respect to the client. A CPA may issue a compilation report for a client with respect to which the CPA is not independent. However, the CPA must specifically disclose this lack of independence without giving reasons for the impairment.

75. Member Joining Client Credit Union--Membership in a credit union does not impair the member's independence with respect to the credit union as long as all of the following criteria are met:

a. A member and/or that member's partners or employees must individually qualify to join the credit union other than by virtue of the professional services provided to the credit union.

b. The exercise of the member's vote or other activities must not have significant influence over the operating, financial, or accounting policies of the credit union.

c. Any loans from the credit union must meet the conditions specified in Interpretation 101-1 and be made under normal lending procedures, terms, and requirements.

d. Any deposits with the credit union must meet the conditions specified in Ruling No. 70 under Rule 101 (ET section 191).

77. Individual Considering or Accepting Employment With the Client--When an engagement is one requiring independence, an individual participating in the engagement who is offered employment by, or seeks employment with, that client during the conduct of the engagement must withdraw from the engagement until the employment offer is rejected or employment is no longer being sought. If a member becomes aware that an individual participated in the engagement while employment with the client was being considered or after it had been accepted, the member should consider what, if any, additional procedures may be necessary to ensure that all work had been performed with objectivity and integrity as required under Rule 102.

78. Services on Government Board--A member is prohibited from serving on a governmental board (for example, board of tax appeals, zoning commission) if, at the same time the member provides professional services for a client or employer who comes before the board unless the member: (a) discloses this to the client or employer, the board, and any other appropriate parties; and (b) receives consent from all parties to participate as a board member with respect to matters involving the client or employer.

79. Member's Investment in a Partnership That Invests in Member's Client--A member who is a general partner, or functions in the capacity of a general partner, in a partnership that invests in a client of the member's firm is considered to have a direct financial interest in the client and, therefore, independence is impaired.

80. The Meaning of Joint Closely Held Business Investment--A joint closely held business investment is a business investment that is subject to control (as defined in FAS 94), by a member, the client, its officers, or principal stockholders, individually or in any combination. A member's independence is considered impaired if during the time of the engagement or expressing an opinion, the member or member's firm had any joint closely held business investment with the client or director, stockholder or officer thereof, that was material in relation to the member or member firm's net worth.

81. Member's Investment in a Limited Partnership

   a. If a member is a limited partner in a limited partnership (LP), including a master limited partnership, and a client of the member is a general partner in the same LP, the member's limited partnership interest in the LP is considered a direct financial interest in the LP which would impair independence.

   b. Assuming the same situation above, the LP is an investee of the client because the client is a general partner in the LP. Therefore, under Interpretation 101-8, the member's independence with respect to the client would be impaired if the investment in the LP is material to the client. The member's independence would not be impaired with respect to the client if the investment is immaterial.

   c. Assuming the same situation, since the member is a limited partner in the LP, the member is considered to have an indirect financial interest in all subsidiaries of the LP. The member's independence would be considered to be impaired with respect to the subsidiaries only if the indirect interest is material.

82. Member as Campaign Treasurer--The independence of a member serving as the campaign treasurer for a mayoral candidate is not considered impaired with respect to the political party with which the candidate is associated, nor with the municipality of which the candidate may become mayor. Due to the member's role as the treasurer, however, the member is not independent with respect to the campaign organization.

83. Member on Board of Component Unit and Auditor of Oversight Entity--A member who serves on the governing board of a local transit authority, which is a component unit of the city (the oversight entity), is not independent with respect to the city's general-purpose financial statements. Members who report on general-purpose financial statements must be independent of the oversight entity and any component units of the entity.

84. Member on Board of Material Component Unit and Auditor of Another Material Component Unit--A member retains independence when he or she is a member of a material component unit of the oversight entity and the auditor of another material component unit of the oversight entity. The member is not independent with respect to the oversight entity such as a county due to membership in a material component unit, for example, the economic development authority.

85. Member as Bank Director--Members in public practice can serve as the director of a bank, but must consider the following implications of doing so if clients are customers of the bank:

   a. Under Rule 301, confidential client information cannot be released without the consent of the client even if failure to release information violates the member's fiduciary responsibility as director.

b.   A conflict of interest may occur when a member performs a professional service and also has a significant relationship with another entity that could be viewed as impairing the member's objectivity. As long as the significant relationship is disclosed and consent is obtained from all parties, performance of the service is not prohibited.

86.   Partially Secured Loans--A loan is grandfathered if, at all times after the member is required to be independent with respect to the client, the portion of the loan that exceeds the value of the collateral is not material to the member's net worth, under Interpretation 101-5.

87.   Loan Commitment or Line of Credit--For purposes of applying the grandfathered loans provisions of Interpretation 101-5 the date of the loan commitment or line of credit may be used rather than the date a transaction would close or the date the funds would be obtained, as long as the loan would have met the conditions of Interpretation 101-5 on the date the loan commitment or line of credit was extended. If the loan commitment or line of credit was renegotiated subsequent to the time the member was required to be independent, independence would be impaired.

88.   Loans to Partnership in Which Members are Limited Partners--A member who is a limited partner in a limited partnership that has obtained a loan from a financial institution client, will not be considered independent with respect to the financial institution if the members have a combined interest exceeding 50 percent of the total limited partnership as this would be considered a loan to those members.

89.   Loan to Partnership in Which Members are General Partners--If a general partner can control the partnership, the loan to that partnership is considered to be a loan to the member. The loan is ascribed to the member on the basis of his or her legal liability as a general partner, which is usually the entire loan because of the joint and several liability usually assumed by a general partner.

90.   Credit Card Balances and Cash Balances--If a member has credit cards and cash advances from a client financial institution and the aggregate balance outstanding exceeds $5,000, independence would not be considered to be impaired if the aggregate outstanding balance is reduced to $5,000 or less on a current basis.

91.   Member Leasing Property From a Client--A member leasing property from a client would be considered independent if, at the time the lease transaction is entered into, it meets the criteria of an operating lease made under normal leasing procedures, terms, and requirements. Independence would be considered to be impaired for a leasing transaction if, at the time the transaction is entered into, it meets the criteria of a capital lease, unless the lease is in compliance with Interpretations 101-1.A.4 and 101-5, because the lease would be considered to be a loan from the client.

92.   Joint Interest in Vacation Home--A member holding a joint interest in a vacation home along with an officer, director, or principal stockholder of an entity for which the member performs services requiring independence, even if solely intended for the personal use of the owners, the vacation home would be considered a joint closely held business investment and the materiality provisions of Interpretation 101-1.A.3 must be considered.

93.   Service on Board of Directors of Federated Fund-Raising Organization--A conflict of interest may occur if a member performs a professional service for a client such as serving as director or officer of a local United Way that operates as a federated fund-raising organization from which local charities that are clients of the member receive funds. If this significant relationship is disclosed and consent is obtained from the appropriate parties, performance of the service shall not be prohibited.

C. <u>General and Technical Standards (ET 291)</u>--Ruling numbers not represented below have been superseded.

1. Association of Name With Unaudited Statements Where Member Is Not Independent--A CPA who prepares an unaudited financial statement for a corporation in which the CPA is a corporate officer (and shareholder) must disclaim an opinion with respect to the statements because of lack of independence.

3. Controller, Preparation of Financial Statements--A CPA cannot accept the report of a controller (who is a CPA) on the financial statements of a subsidiary corporation as meeting the requirements of GAAS.

4. Two-Year Opinion, Prior Year Previously Unaudited--A CPA may express an opinion on financial statements for a prior year in which the CPA previously was engaged to prepare unaudited financial statements, provided the audit is in accordance with GAAS, and the CPA performed the necessary audit procedures.

5. Interim Financial Statements--A CPA is considered to be associated with a client's unaudited interim reports if the CPA's name is listed anywhere on or in the report. Consequently, each statement should be marked "unaudited."

6. Letterhead--A CPA who is treasurer of a private club and performs accounting services for that club may issue financial statements on the CPA's firm's letterhead with proper disclaimer for lack of independence although the club's letterhead is preferable.

7. Non-CPA Partner--A CPA who is in partnership with non-CPAs may sign reports with the firm name and the CPA's own signature with the designation "Certified Public Accountant" providing it is clear that the partnership is not being represented as being entirely composed of CPAs.

8. Subcontractor Selection for Consulting Services Engagements--A CPA must select sub-contractors who are professionally qualified for consulting services engagements.

9. Supervision of Technical Specialist on Consulting Services Engagements--A CPA must be qualified to supervise and evaluate the work of consulting services specialists employed. The CPA must be able to define the tasks and evaluate the end product.

D. <u>Responsibilities to Clients (ET 391)</u>--Ruling numbers not represented below have been deleted.

1. Computer Processing of Clients' Returns--A CPA may utilize outside service bureaus to process clients' tax returns as long as the CPA takes the necessary precautions to prevent the release of confidential information.

2. Distribution of Client Information to Trade Associations--A CPA may distribute the client's profit and loss percentages to its trade association if the client gives permission.

3. Information to Successor Accountant About Tax Return Irregularities--A CPA who has with-drawn from an engagement because of discovering irregularities in the client's tax return should urge the successor (upon contact from the successor) to request that the client permit a free discussion of all matters.

5. Records Retention Agency--A CPA may use a records-retention agency to store clients' records, working papers, etc.

6. Revealing Client Information to Competitors--A CPA firm does not violate Rule 301, Confidential Client Information, merely by being employed by a municipality for the purpose

of examining the books and records of competing businesses so that the proper values have been declared for personal property tax purposes.

7. Revealing Names of Clients--A CPA may disclose the name of a client, whether publicly or privately owned, without the client's specific consent unless the disclosure of the client's name constitutes the release of confidential information.

14. Use of Confidential Information on Consulting Services Engagements--A CPA should not disclose the source and details of information provided by a nonclient if the agreement is not to disclose. If the client will not accept this arrangement, the CPA may have to withdraw from the consulting services engagement.

15. Earlier Similar Consulting Services Study With Negative Outcome--A CPA may advise a potential client of an unfavorable outcome anticipated for a potential consulting services engagement based on information acquired while performing an assignment for a client competitor, as long as the earlier relationship is not disclosed. However, if the earlier relationship would be obvious, the information should not be disclosed without the permission of the competitor.

16. Disclosure of Confidential Client Information--Rule 301 does not prohibit the release of confidential information held by the member in relation to the joint tax returns of a couple undergoing divorce proceedings. Regardless of which spouse originally retained the member, both spouses are considered clients in regard to previous tax returns. As a result, either spouse may access information for prior tax returns. Because of the divorce proceedings, however, the legal implication of disclosure of such information should be reviewed with an attorney.

17. Definition of the Receipt of Contingent Fees--A contingent fee or a commission is deemed to be received when the performance of the related services is complete and the fee or the commission is determined.

18. Bank Director--See Ruling No. 85 under Rule 102; Integrity and Objectivity; at B. 85., above.

19. Receipt of Contingent Fees by Member's Spouse--The spouse of a member may provide services to the member's attest client for a contingent fee, and may refer products or services for a commission without causing the member to violate Rules 302 and 503. The activities of the spouse must be separate from the member's practice, and the member may not be significantly involved in the activities.

E. Other Responsibilities and Practices (ET 591)--Many of these rulings have been suspended because of the lifting of the prohibitions against advertising and solicitation. The following listing includes only those rulings that are still in effect:

2. Fees: Collection of Notes Issued in Payment--A CPA may make arrangements with a bank to collect notes issued by a client in payment of a fee due.

3. Employment by Non-CPA Firm--A CPA may be employed by a public accounting firm made up of one or more non-CPA practitioners. The CPA must comply with the Rules of Conduct, and upon becoming a partner, the CPA will be held responsible for compliance by all colleagues.

33. Course Instructor--A CPA who is conducting an adult education tax course has the responsibility to be sure the promotional efforts used in connection with the course conform to Rule 502; Advertising and Other Forms of Solicitation, at VII.C., above.

38. CPA Title, Controller of Bank--A CPA who is not in public practice but who is controller of a bank may use the CPA title on bank stationery and in paid advertisements of the bank that list the officers and directors.

78. Letterhead: Lawyer-CPA--A CPA who practices accounting and law may use either a single or separate letterhead.

82. Newsletter--Publisher may engage a CPA to write a monthly newsletter under the CPA's name that would be sold for a yearly fee. The CPA is responsible for being sure the promotional efforts comply with Rule 502.

108. Member Interviewed by the Press--A member interviewed by a writer or reporter should observe the limitations imposed by the Rules of Conduct. The member may not provide the press with any information for publication that could not be published by the member.

115. Actuary--A CPA firm may perform actuarial and administrative services in connection with employee benefit plans.

117. Consumer Credit Company Director--A CPA may serve as a director or officer of a consumer credit company that purchases installment sales contracts as long as the CPA does not audit the corporation or participate in matters which would constitute a conflict of interest.

134. Association of Accountants Not Partners--CPAs should not use a letterhead which shows the names of two accountants when a partnership does not in fact exist.

135. Association of Firms Not Partners--CPA firms that are not a partnership cannot use a letterhead that would give the impression they are a partnership.

136. Audit With Former Partner--Two practitioners, one a CPA and one not a CPA, who have dissolved their partnership may continue to service an account; however, the signatures on the audit report should make it clear that a partnership does not exist.

137. Nonproprietary Partners--The title "nonproprietary partner" should not be used since it may be misleading.

138. Partner Having Separate Proprietorship--A CPA may be a partner in a firm of public accountants, in which all other members are noncertified and, at the same time, retain a practice as a CPA.

139. Partnership With Non-CPA--The Institute's code does not prohibit a member from forming a partnership with a non-CPA (although some state boards and CPA societies may prohibit such partnerships) as long as all partners conform to the Code, and the partnership does not represent itself as a partnership of CPAs.

140. Political Election--The remaining partners of a partnership which uses the name of the managing partner may use the firm name (followed by the designation "and Company") if the managing partner is elected to high public office and withdraws from the partnership.

141. Responsibility for Non-CPA Partner--A CPA who has formed a partnership with a noncertified public accountant is responsible for any violations of the Code by the noncertified accountant.

144. Title: Partnership Roster--A CPA firm may use an established firm name in a different state where there is some difference in the roster of partners.

145. Firm Name of Merged Partnerships--A newly merged firm may practice under a title which includes the name of a partner who had retired from one of the two firms prior to the merger.

146. Membership Designation--A CPA firm may not designate itself as "Members of the AICPA" unless all of its partners or shareholders are members of the Institute. Individual members may be so designated.

155. Data Processing: Computer Corporation--A CPA firm and a firm of computer consultants could set up a computer corporation which is designed to provide services only to the clients of the CPA firm (not directly to the public).

156. Data Processing: Consultant to Service Bureau--A CPA in public practice may assist a corporation in developing a tabulating service to be offered to the public where the CPA has no financial interest in the corporation and where no representations would be made that the CPA assisted in the development.

158. Data Processing: Employee-Shareholder in Public Practice--A CPA who has a public accounting practice is also president and a shareholder of a corporation whose main business is financing but which also engages in adjunct data processing services for the public. The CPA's relationship to the corporation should be strictly that of an investor, with a financial interest not material in relation to the corporation's net worth. The CPA's association with the data processing corporation should be limited to that of a consultant.

175. Bank Director--Before accepting a bank directorship, a CPA should consider the implications of (a) confidentiality of information, (b) possible conflict of interest (between duty to the bank and duty to a client who may be a customer of the bank), (c) independence (may be impaired if a client obtains a large bank loan in relation to its worth), and (d) solicitation of clients through the CPA's position as a bank director. It will often be more appropriate for a CPA in public practice to serve as a consultant to the bank's board.

176. Newsletters and Publications Prepared by Others--A CPA may permit the firm name of the CPA to be imprinted on a newsletter, tax booklet, or similar publication provided that there is a reasonable basis to conclude that the information contained therein is not false, misleading, or deceptive.

177. Data Processing: Billing Services--A separate business formed by a member to perform centralized billing services constitutes a service of the type performed by public accountants; consequently, the member can provide this service only if the operation is conducted in accordance with the Institute's Rules of Conduct.

178. Location of Separate Business--The simultaneous operation of an accounting practice and another business or occupation, either in the same or separate offices, does not by itself violate Rule 504 unless a conflict of interest exists in rendering professional services.

179. Practice of Public Accounting Under Name of Association or Group--CPA firms belonging to an association or group for the purpose of joint advertising, training, professional development, and management assistance may not practice public accounting under the name of the association or group. Each firm should practice under its own name. It may indicate the association or group name elsewhere on the firm stationery.

180. Side Businesses Which Offer Services of a Type Performed by CPAs--A member may not conduct a separate estate planning business in the form of a commercial corporation, nor utilize a fictitious name indicating a specialization. Estate planning is a service of a type performed by public accountants; therefore, the member will be able to provide that service only in the form of a proprietorship, a partnership, or a professional corporation. In addition, the member must observe all Rules of Conduct in that business.

182. Termination of Engagement Prior to Completion--When a CPA has been engaged to prepare a tax return and the client or the CPA terminates the engagement before the tax return is

delivered to the client, the CPA's responsibility is to return only those records originally provided to the CPA by the client.

183. Use of the AICPA Accredited Personal Financial Specialist Designation--The designation "Accredited Personal Financial Specialists" (APFS) can be used on a firm's letterhead and in marketing materials only if all partners or shareholders of the firm currently have the AICPA-awarded designation. An individual member is permitted to use the designation after that member's name.

184. Definition of the Receipt of a Commission--See Ruling 17 under Rule 302--*Contingent Fees*; See VI. B. for a summary.

185. Sale of Products to Clients--Members who purchase products from a third party supplier and then resell the product to clients are not in violation of Rule 503--*Commissions* (see VII. E., above.) The purchase of a product indicates ownership and all its associated risks.

186. Billing for Subcontractors' Services--A commission does not exist when a member subcontracts work and then charges the client a higher service fee for the subcontracted service than the fee paid by the member for the subcontracted service.

187. Receipt of Commissions by Member's Spouse--See Ruling 19 under Rule 302.

188. Referral of Products of Others--A member may not refer a client to a product produced by a third party if a commission will be paid to the member by the third party upon purchase of the product by the client. Under section 502.06 of the Code of Professional Conduct, a member may not permit others to perform acts on behalf of a member, if, had the act been carried out by the member, the member would be in violation of the rules.

PART TWO: STATEMENTS ON RESPONSIBILITIES IN TAX PRACTICE

I. Background

A. Significance--Set standards of tax practice which define the CPA's responsibility to the client, the government, and the public accounting profession.

B. Objectives--Identify and develop appropriate standards of responsibility in tax practice and to promote their uniform application by CPAs, encourage an increased understanding of the CPA's responsibilities, and foster an increased compliance with, and confidence in, the tax system by the public.

C. Purpose--The primary purpose of the Statements is educational. Their authority depends on general acceptability. They are issued by the AICPA's Federal Taxation Executive Committee.

II. Statements on Responsibilities in Tax Practice

NOTE: TX 111, *Signature of Preparer*, and TX 121, *Signature of Reviewer: Assumption of Preparer's Responsibility*, have been withdrawn by the Executive Committee of the Federal Tax Division of the AICPA because of their potential conflict with the Internal Revenue Code's definition of a "tax return preparer" at IRC §7701(a)(36).

A. No. 1: Tax Return Positions

1. Standards--A CPA should comply with the following standards:

    a. A CPA should not recommend a position be taken unless the CPA has a good faith belief that the position is warranted in existing law or can be supported by a good faith argument for an extension, modification, or reversal of existing law.

    b.   A CPA should not prepare or sign a return if the return takes a position the CPA could not recommend.

    c.   A CPA can recommend a position that the CPA concludes is not frivolous as long as the position is adequately disclosed on the return.

    d.   In recommending certain tax return positions, the CPA should advise the client as to potential penalty consequences.

2.   <u>Objectives</u>--The CPA should not recommend a tax return position that does the following:

    a.   Exploits the IRS audit selection process.

    b.   Serves as a mere "arguing" position advanced solely to obtain leverage in the bargaining process of settlement negotiation with the IRS.

3.   <u>Disclosure</u>--Disclosure should be considered when the CPA believes it would decrease the likelihood of an audit or a taxpayer penalty. The CPA should advise the client concerning disclosure, but it is the <u>client's responsibility to</u> decide whether and how to <u>disclose</u>.

B.   <u>No. 2: Answers to Questions on the Tax Return</u>--A CPA should make a reasonable effort to obtain from the client, and provide appropriate answers to all questions on a tax return before signing as preparer. Omitting an answer just because it is <u>disadvantageous</u> to the client is <u>not justified</u>. A CPA is <u>not</u> required to provide on the return an explanation of the reason for the omission.

•   Reasonable Grounds--Reasonable grounds for unanswered questions include the following: (1) the data is neither readily <u>available</u> nor <u>significant</u> to the tax liability, (2) the data is significant to the tax liability but <u>genuine uncertainty</u> exists and the data is not sufficiently reliable to report, or (3) the answer is <u>voluminous</u> but is available at the client's office.

C.   <u>No. 3: Certain Procedural Aspects of Preparing Returns</u>

1.   <u>Client-Provided Data</u>--The CPA may in good faith rely <u>without verification</u> on information furnished by the client or by third parties. However, the CPA should make reasonable inquiries if the information appears to be <u>incorrect</u>, <u>incomplete</u>, or <u>inconsistent</u> either on its face or on the basis of other facts known to the CPA, including information from returns of other clients. The client should be <u>encouraged</u> to provide appropriate supporting data.

2.   <u>Returns of Prior-Year</u>--The CPA should make use of the client's prior-year returns whenever feasible for comparison purposes to (a) provide information as to the client's general tax status, (b) avoid the omission or duplication of items, and (c) afford a basis for the treatment of similar or related transactions.

3.   <u>Responsibility</u>--Although the CPA has certain responsibilities in exercising <u>due diligence</u> in preparing a return, the <u>client has ultimate responsibility</u> for the contents of the return.

D.   <u>No. 4: Use of Estimates</u>

1.   <u>CPA's Responsibility</u>--The CPA may advise on estimates used in the preparation of a tax return, but <u>responsibility for estimated data</u> is that of the <u>client</u>, who should provide the estimated data.

2.   <u>Use</u>--Estimates may be used if (a) the required data is unavailable or impracticable to obtain, (b) the amounts are <u>reasonable</u>, and (c) they are presented in a manner which avoids the implication of greater accuracy than exists.

3. <u>Disclosure</u>--Although specific disclosure that an estimate is used for an item in the return is not required in most instances, the following <u>unusual circumstances</u> need to be disclosed to avoid misleading the IRS:

   a. The taxpayer has died or is ill at the time the return must be filed.

   b. The taxpayer has not received a K-1 for a flow-through entity at the time the tax return is to be filed.

   c. There is litigation pending which bears on the return.

   d. Fire or computer failure destroyed the relevant records.

E. <u>No. 5: Departure From a Position Previously Concluded in an Administrative Proceeding or Court Decision</u>--A CPA will usually recommend a position regarding the tax treatment of an item that is the same as was consented to by the taxpayer for a similar item as a result of an administrative proceeding or that was subject to a court decision concerning a prior year's return of the taxpayer. However, though the IRS will usually act consistently in its judgment of an item, it is not bound to do so, and the taxpayer is not bound by the treatment of an item as consented to in an earlier administrative proceeding; hence, it is possible that <u>justifiable grounds</u> exist for the departure from a prior position:

   1. The prior consent to the treatment in the administrative proceeding was based on a lack of documentation, whereas adequate documentation now exists.

   2. The client yielded to the treatment even though the position met the applicable standards.

   3. Court decisions, rulings or other authorities that are more favorable to the taxpayer's current position may have developed since the prior proceeding or court decision.

F. <u>No. 6: Knowledge of Error--Preparation of Return</u>

   1. <u>Procedures</u>--When the CPA learns of errors in the return of a prior period or learns that a return was not filed in a prior period, the IRS requires the CPA to <u>notify the client</u> of the error and to <u>recommend</u> appropriate action. If it appears that the IRS might assert the charge of fraud or other criminal misconduct, the client should be advised to consult legal counsel before taking any actions. The CPA <u>cannot</u> notify the IRS of the error <u>without</u> the client's permission. If the client refuses to correct the return, the CPA may be forced to withdraw and should consider whether to continue a professional relationship with the client. If the CPA does continue, reasonable steps should be taken to ensure that the error is not repeated on subsequent returns. In cases where the CPA learns the client is using an erroneous method of accounting, when it is past the due date to request IRS permission to change to an acceptable method, the CPA may sign the return for the current year, provided the previous use of the erroneous method is properly disclosed.

   2. <u>Meaning of the Term "Error"</u>--The term "error" includes any position, omission, or method of accounting that, at the time the return was filed, fails to meet the standards set out in SRTP No. 1. Also included is a position taken on a return of a prior year that no longer meets these standards due to legislation, judicial decisions, or administrative pronouncements having retroactive effect. Not included within this definition are those items that have an insignificant effect on the client's tax liability.

G. <u>No. 7: Knowledge of Error--Administrative Proceeding</u>

   1. <u>Procedures</u>--When the CPA learns of an error in a return that is the subject of an administrative proceeding, the CPA should <u>inform</u> the client promptly and <u>recommend</u> appropriate actions. If it appears that the IRS might assert a charge of fraud or other criminal

misconduct, the client should be advised to consult legal counsel. The CPA is not obligated to inform the IRS of the error and should not inform them without the client's permission. If the client refuses to inform the IRS, the CPA should consider whether to withdraw from representing the client and whether to continue a professional relationship with the client. Once the CPA and the client agree to disclose the error, they should do so promptly, as a delay might be considered a failure to act in good faith or an attempt to provide misleading information.

    2.   <u>Meaning of the Term "Error"</u>--(See F.2., above)

H.   <u>No. 8: Advice to Clients</u>--The CPA should use judgment to ensure that the advice given reflects professional competence and appropriately serves the client's needs.

    1.   <u>Considerations</u>--In reaching this assurance, the CPA should consider (1) the <u>importance</u> of the transaction and the amounts, (2) the <u>specific or general</u> nature of the inquiry, (3) the <u>time available</u> to develop and submit the advice, (4) <u>technical</u> complications, (5) the existence of <u>authority</u> and <u>precedents</u>, (6) the <u>tax sophistication</u> of the client, and (7) the need to seek legal advice.

    2.   <u>Form of Advice</u>--Written advice is recommended for important, unusual, or complex transactions; otherwise, oral advice is acceptable.

    3.   <u>Subsequent Developments</u>--If the CPA assists the client in implementing procedures or plans associated with the advice offered and continues to advise, the CPA should review and revise such advice as warranted by subsequent developments and events. If the CPA does not assist in the implementation or planning associated with the advice, the CPA cannot be expected to communicate later developments that affect such advice unless the CPA undertakes this obligation by special agreement with the client.

PART THREE: DEFINITIONS AND STANDARDS FOR CONSULTING SERVICES (SSCS 1)

I. Background

A.   This Standard supersedes the previous series of Statements on Standards for Management Advisory Services (SSMAS Nos. 1 - 3), and provides standards for practice for a wider variety of professional services.

B.   Consulting services provided by CPAs have steadily grown in the overall importance of the activity to the CPA profession, and the scope of services performed. Services are no longer limited to advice on accounting related matters, but now include a tremendous range of technical disciplines, industry knowledge, and consulting skills.

C.   The understanding established with the client may impose some constraints within which the services are to be performed. Because of these constraints, professional judgment is to be used in applying the Standards for Consulting Services to specific situations.

D.   A consulting service performed for an attest client does not, of itself, impair independence.

II. Definitions

A.   <u>Consulting Process</u>--This process includes the analytical approach and process applied in a consulting service. It involves some combination of activities relating to a determination of client objectives, definition of problems and solutions, fact finding, evaluation of alternatives, formulation of proposed actions, communication of results, implementation, and follow-up.

B.   Consulting Services--These services are composed of professional services that use the CPAs technical skills, education, observations and experience, and knowledge of the consulting process. Such services include the following:

1.   Consultations--Consultations are based mostly, if not entirely, on existing personal knowledge about the client, the circumstances, the technical matters involved, and the mutual intent of the parties. It generally involves advice or information given by a practitioner in a short time frame. Examples of consultations include reviewing and commenting on a client prepared business plan and making recommendations for computer software for further analysis by the client.

2.   Advisory Services--These services are primarily used to develop findings, conclusions, and recommendations for client consideration and decision making. Examples include operational review and improvement study, analysis of an accounting system, assistance with strategic planning, and defining requirements for an information system.

3.   Implementation Services--Implementation services consist of the practitioner putting an action plan into effect. In an engagement of this type, client personnel may be pooled with those of the practitioners. The overall responsibility of all the activities rests with the practitioner. Examples include providing computer support, effecting steps to improve productivity, and assisting with the merger of organizations.

4..   Transaction Services--A type of service that concerns a specific client transaction, usually with a third party. Insolvency services are one type of transaction service, as well as valuation services, preparation of information to secure financing, and litigation services.

5.   Staff and Other Support Services--The role of the practitioner is to provide staff and other support, as needed, to accomplish tasks specified by the client. Examples include the management of data processing facilities, computer programming, trustees in a bankruptcy situation, and controllership activities.

6.   Product Services--The practitioner provides a product to the client along with professional services to support, use, or maintain the product provided. Two examples of product services are the sale of a packaged training program or the sale and implementation of computer software.

III. General Standards for Consulting Services

The following general standards apply to all services performed by members of the AICPA. These are contained in Rule 201 of the AICPA Rules of Conduct and apply to all services performed in the practice of public accounting.

A.   Professional Competence--A member shall undertake only those professional services which the member or the member's firm can reasonably expect to complete with professional competence.

B.   Due Professional Care--A member shall exercise due professional care in the performance of professional services.

C.   Planning and Supervision--A member shall adequately plan and supervise the performance of professional services.

D.   Sufficient Relevant Data--A member shall obtain sufficient relevant data to afford a reasonable basis for conclusions or recommendations in relation to any professional services performed.

IV. Additional General Standards

The following general standards address the distinctive nature of consulting services. These Standards are established under Rule 202 of the AICPA Code of Professional Conduct.

A. <u>Client Interest</u>--Serve the client's interest by seeking to accomplish the objectives established by the understanding with the client while maintaining integrity and objectivity.

B. <u>Understanding With Client</u>--An oral or written understanding should be reached with the client concerning the nature, scope, and limitations of the services to be performed, and modifications should be made to the understanding if circumstances require a significant change during the engagement.

C. <u>Communication</u>--The client should be informed of the following:

1. Conflicts of interest that may occur pursuant to interpretations of Rule 102 of the Code of Professional Conduct.

2. Significant reservations concerning the scope or benefits of the engagement.

3. Significant engagement findings or events.

NOTES

CHAPTER 58—ETHICS AND PROFESSIONAL RESPONSIBILITIES

Problem 58-1 MULTIPLE CHOICE QUESTIONS (30 to 40 minutes)

1. Which of the following statements best explains why the CPA profession has found it essential to promulgate ethical standards and to establish means for ensuring their observance?
a. Vigorous enforcement of an established code of ethics is the best way to prevent unscrupulous acts.
b. Ethical standards that emphasize excellence in performance over material rewards establish a reputation for competence and character.
c. A distinguishing mark of a profession is its acceptance of responsibility to the public.
d. A requirement for a profession is to establish ethical standards that stress primarily a responsibility to clients and colleagues.

(11/88, Aud., #5, 9911)

1A. Which of the following statements best explains why the CPA profession has found it essential to promulgate ethical standards and to establish means for ensuring their observance?
a. A distinguishing mark of a profession is its acceptance of responsibility to the public.
b. A requirement for a profession is to establish ethical standards that stress primary responsibility to clients and colleagues.
c. Ethical standards that emphasize excellence in performance over material rewards establish a reputation for competence and character.
d. Vigorous enforcement of an established code of ethics is the best way to prevent unscrupulous acts.

(5/94, Law, 2, 4757)

2. Which of the following best describes what is meant by the term generally accepted auditing standards?
a. Rules acknowledged by the accounting profession because of their universal application.
b. Pronouncements issued by the Auditing Standards Board.
c. Measures of the quality of the auditor's performance.
d. Procedures to be used to gather evidence to support financial statements.

(5/95, Law, #2, 5336)

3. The concept of materiality would be **least** important to an auditor when considering the
a. Adequacy of disclosure of a client's illegal act.
b. Discovery of weaknesses in a client's internal control structure.

c. Effects of a direct financial interest in the client on the CPA's independence.
d. Decision whether to use positive or negative confirmations of accounts receivable.

(5/91, Aud., #52, 0003)

3A. According to the standards of the profession, which of the following circumstances will prevent a CPA performing audit engagements from being independent?
a. Obtaining a collateralized automobile loan from a financial institution client.
b. Litigation with a client relating to billing for consulting services for which the amount is immaterial.
c. Employment of the CPA's spouse as a client's internal auditor.
d. Acting as an honorary trustee for a not-for-profit organization client. (5/95, Law, #1, 5335)

4. A violation of the profession's ethical standards most likely would have occurred when a CPA
a. Issued an unqualified opinion on the 1992 financial statements when fees for the 1991 audit were unpaid.
b. Recommended a controller's position description with candidate specifications to an audit client.
c. Purchased a CPA firm's practice of monthly write-ups for a percentage of fees to be received over a three-year period.
d. Made arrangements with a financial institution to collect notes issued by a client in payment of fees due for the current year's audit.

(5/93, Aud., #1, 3897)

4A. Which of the following actions by a CPA most likely violates the profession's ethical standards?
a. Arranging with a financial institution to collect notes issued by a client in payment of fees due.
b. Compiling the financial statements of a client that employed the CPA's spouse as a bookkeeper.
c. Retaining client records after the client has demanded their return.
d. Purchasing a segment of an insurance company's business that performs actuarial services for employee benefit plans.

(5/94, Law, #1, 4756)

4B. The profession's ethical standards most likely would be considered to have been violated when a CPA represents that specific consulting services will

be performed for a stated fee, and it is apparent at the time of the representation that the
a. Actual fee would be substantially higher.
b. Actual fee would be substantially lower than the fees charged by other CPAs for comparable services.
c. CPA would **not** be independent.
d. Fee was a competitive bid.
(11/94, Law, #1, 5178)

5. Without the consent of the client, a CPA should **not** disclose confidential client information contained in working papers to a
a. Voluntary quality control review board.
b. CPA firm that has purchased the CPA's accounting practice.
c. Federal court that has issued a valid subpoena.
d. Disciplinary body created under state statute.
(5/87, Aud., #29, 9911)

5A. A CPA is permitted to disclose confidential client information without the consent of the client to

I. Another CPA firm if the information concerns suspected tax return irregularities.
II. A state CPA society voluntary quality control review board.

a. I only.
b. II only.
c. Both I and II.
d. Neither I nor II. (5/95, Law, #5, 5339)

6. The auditor with final responsibility for an engagement and one of the assistants have a difference of opinion about the results of an auditing procedure. If the assistant believes it is necessary to be disassociated from the matter's resolution, the CPA firm's procedures should enable the assistant to
a. Refer the disagreement to the AICPA's Quality Review Committee.
b. Document the details of the disagreement with the conclusion reached.
c. Discuss the disagreement with the entity's management or its audit committee.
d. Report the disagreement to an impartial peer review monitoring team. (11/93, Aud., #4, 4241)

6A. Which of the following statements best describes whether a CPA has met the required standard of care in conducting an audit of a client's financial statements?
a. The client's expectations with regard to the accuracy of audited financial statements.
b. The accuracy of the financial statements and whether the statements conform to generally accepted accounting principles.

c. Whether the CPA conducted the audit with the same skill and care expected of an ordinarily prudent CPA under the circumstances.
d. Whether the audit was conducted to investigate and discover all acts of fraud.
(11/93, Law, #2, 4299)

6B. To exercise due professional care, an auditor should
a. Critically review the judgment exercised by those assisting in the audit.
b. Examine all available corroborating evidence supporting management's assertions.
c. Design the audit to detect all instances of illegal acts.
d. Attain the proper balance of professional experience and formal education.
(11/94, Law, #3, 5180)

7. Which of the following is required for a CPA partnership to designate itself "Member of the American Institute of Certified Public Accountants" on its letterhead?
a. All partners must be members.
b. The partners whose names appear in the firm name must be members.
c. At least one of the partners must be a member.
d. The firm must be a dues-paying member.
(5/85, Aud., #8, 0038)

7A. Which of the following reports may be issued only by an accountant who is independent of a client?
a. Standard report on an examination of a financial forecast.
b. Report on consulting services.
c. Compilation report on historical financial statements.
d. Compilation report on a financial projection.
(5/94, Law, #3, 4756)

8. A violation of the profession's ethical standards would most likely have occurred when a CPA
a. Performed actuarial and administrative services in connection with employee benefit plans.
b. Made arrangements with a bank to collect notes issued by a client in payment of fees due.
c. Named Smith formed a partnership with two other CPAs and used "Smith & Co." as the firm name.
d. Issued an unqualified opinion on the 1992 financial statements when fees for the 1991 audit were unpaid.
(5/88, Aud., #53, amended, 0018)

9. In which of the following situations would a CPA's independence be considered to be impaired?

I. The CPA maintains a checking account that is fully insured by a government deposit insurance agency at an audit-client financial institution.

II. The CPA has a direct financial interest in an audit client, but the interest is maintained in a blind trust.

III. The CPA owns a commercial building and leases it to an audit client. The rental income is material to the CPA.

a. I and II.
b. II and III.
c. I and III.
d. I, II, and III.   (11/92, Aud., #2, 2936)

9A. According to the profession's ethical standards, an auditor would be considered independent in which of the following instances?

a. The auditor's checking account, which is fully insured by a federal agency, is held at a client financial institution.

b. The auditor is also an attorney who advises the client as its general counsel.   *No*

c. The auditor is an official stock transfer agent for the client.   *No*

d. The client owes the auditor fees for two consecutive annual audits.   *No*
            (5/89, Aud., #3, amended, 9911)

10. Which of the following acts by a CPA who is **not** in public practice would most likely be considered a violation of the ethical standards of the profession?

a. Using the CPA designation without disclosing employment status in connection with financial statements issued for external use by the CPA's employer.

b. Distributing business cards indicating the CPA designation and the CPA's title and employer.

c. Corresponding on the CPA's employer's letterhead, which contains the CPA designation and the CPA's employment status.

d. Compiling the CPA's employer's financial statements and making reference to the CPA's lack of independence.   (11/88, Aud., #3, 0016)

11. May a CPA hire for the CPA's public accounting firm a non-CPA systems analyst who specializes in developing computer systems?

a. Yes, provided the CPA is qualified to perform each of the specialist's tasks.

b. Yes, provided the CPA is able to supervise the specialist and evaluate the specialist's end product.

c. No, because non-CPA professionals are **not** permitted to be associated with CPA firms in public practice.

d. No, because developing computer systems is **not** recognized as a service performed by public accountants.   (11/93, Aud., #3, 4240)

12. According to the AICPA Code of Professional Conduct, may a CPA who is in partnership with non-CPAs sign a report with the firm name and below it affix the CPA's own signature with the designation "Certified Public Accountant"?

a. No, because a CPA should **not** form a partnership with non-CPAs.

b. No, because it would appear that all partners were associated with the report when only one actually is associated.

c. Yes, provided the non-CPA partners adhere to the professional standards concerning quality control.

d. Yes, provided it is clear that the partnership itself is **not** being held out as composed entirely of CPAs.   (11/87, Aud., #21, 0021)

13. Must a CPA in public practice be independent in fact and appearance when providing the following services?

	Compilation of personal financial statements	Preparation of a tax return	Compilation of a financial forecast
a.	Yes	No	No
b.	No	Yes	No
c.	No	No	Yes
d.	No	No	No

            (11/94, Law, #4, 5181)

14. According to the profession's standards, which of the following is **not** required of a CPA performing a consulting engagement?

a. Complying with Statements on Standards for Consulting Services.

b. Obtaining an understanding of the nature, scope, and limitations of the engagement.

c. Supervising staff who are assigned to the engagement.

d. Maintaining independence from the client.
            (11/94, Law, #5, 5182)

15. When a CPA prepares a client's federal income tax return, the CPA has the responsibility to

a. Take a position of independent neutrality.

b. Argue the position of the Internal Revenue Service.

c. Be an advocate for the entity's realistically sustainable position.
d. Verify the data to be used in preparing the return. (5/91, Aud., #56, 0416)

15A. Kopel was engaged to prepare Raff's 1994 federal income tax return. During the tax preparation interview, Raff told Kopel that he paid $3,000 in property taxes in 1994. Actually, Raff's property taxes amounted to only $600. Based on Raff's word, Kopel deducted the $3,000 on Raff's return, resulting in an understatement of Raff's tax liability. Kopel had no reason to believe that the information was incorrect. Kopel did not request underlying documentation and was reasonably satisfied by Raff's representation that Raff had adequate records to support the deduction. Which of the following statements is correct?
a. To avoid the preparer penalty for willful understatement of tax liability, Kopel was obligated to examine the underlying documentation for the deduction.
b. To avoid the preparer penalty for willful understatement of tax liability, Kopel would be required to obtain Raff's representation in writing.
c. Kopel is **not** subject to the preparer penalty for willful understatement of tax liability because the deduction that was claimed was more than 25% of the actual amount that should have been deducted.
d. Kopel is **not** subject to the preparer penalty for willful understatement of tax liability because Kopel was justified in relying on Raff's representation. (5/95, Law, #4, 5338)

16. According to the profession's ethical standards, a CPA preparing a client's tax return may rely on unsupported information furnished by the client, without examining underlying information, unless the information
a. Is derived from a pass-through entity.
b. Appears to be incomplete on its face.
c. Concerns dividends received.
d. Lists charitable contributions.
(5/94, Law, #7, 4762)

17. According to the profession's standards, which of the following statements is correct regarding the standards a CPA should follow when recommending tax return positions and preparing tax returns?
a. A CPA may recommend a position that the CPA concludes is frivolous as long as the position is adequately disclosed on the return.
b. A CPA may recommend a position in which the CPA has a good faith belief that the position has a realistic possibility of being sustained if challenged.

c. A CPA will usually **not** advise the client of the potential penalty consequences of the recommended tax return position.
d. A CPA may sign a tax return as preparer knowing that the return takes a position that will **not** be sustained if challenged.
(11/94, Law, #7, 5184)

18. According to the profession's standards, which of the following actions should be taken by a CPA tax preparer who discovers an error in a client's previously filed tax return?
a. Advise the IRS.
b. Correct the error.
c. Advise the client.
d. End the relationship with the client.
(11/94, Law, #8, 5185)

19. According to the standards of the profession, which of the following events would require a CPA performing a consulting services engagement for a nonaudit client to withdraw from the engagement?

I. The CPA has a conflict of interest that is disclosed to the client and the client consents to the CPA continuing the engagement.
II. The CPA fails to obtain a written understanding from the client concerning the scope of the engagement.

a. I only.
b. II only.
c. Both I and II.
d. Neither I nor II. (5/95, Law, #3, 5337)

20. Which of the following services may a CPA perform in carrying out a consulting service for a client?

I. Analysis of the client's accounting system.
II. Review of the client's prepared business plan.
III. Preparation of information for obtaining financing.

a. I and II only.
b. I and III only.
c. II and III only.
d. I, II, and III. (5/94, Law, #5, 4760)

21. Nile, CPA, on completing an audit, was asked by the client to provide technical assistance in implementing a new EDP system. The set of pronouncements designed to guide Nile in this engagement is the Statement(s) on
a. Quality Control Standards.
b. Auditing Standards.

c.   Standards for Accountants' EDP Services.
d.   Standards for Consulting Services.

(5/94, Law, #6, 4761)

22.   Which of the following statements applies to consultation services engagements?
a.   A practitioner should obtain an understanding of the internal control structure to assess control risk.
b.   A practitioner is **not** permitted to compile a financial forecast.
c.   A practitioner should obtain sufficient relevant data to complete the engagement.
d.   A practitioner is to maintain an appearance of independence.   (11/93, Aud., #14, 4251)

23.   According to the profession's standards, which of the following would be considered consulting services?

	Advisory services	Implementation services	Product services
a.	Yes	Yes	Yes
b.	Yes	Yes	No
c.	Yes	No	Yes
d.	No	Yes	Yes

(11/94, Law, #6, 5183)

Solution 58-1 MULTIPLE CHOICE ANSWERS

Code of Professional Conduct

1. (c)   ET 51.02 states, "These principles of the Code of Professional Conduct of the American Institute of Certified Public Accountants express the profession's recognition of its responsibilities to the public, to clients and to colleagues."

1A. (a)   The AICPA's Code of Professional Conduct states that a distinguishing mark of a profession is its acceptance of responsibility to the general public.

2. (c)   AU 150.01 states, "Auditing standards differ from auditing procedures in that *procedures* relate to acts to be performed, whereas *standards* deal with measures of the quality of the performance of those acts and the objectives to be attained by the use of the procedures undertaken."

3. (c)   Independence will be considered to be impaired if during the period of the professional engagement, or at the time of expressing his or her opinion, the auditor or his or her firm had or was committed to acquire any direct or material indirect financial interest in the enterprise (ET 101.10). In other words, if a direct financial interest exists, materiality is not a factor as it relates to the auditor's independence. Materiality would be important in consideration of answers (a), (b), and (d).

3A. (c)   ET 101-9 states that independence is impaired if a spouse's employment is in a position where the spouse's activities are audit sensitive, and specifically mentions *internal auditors*.

4. (a)   Independence is considered to be impaired if, when the report on the client's current year is issued, fees remain unpaid for professional services provided more than one year prior to the date of the report. Such amounts assume the characteristics of a loan within the meaning of Rule 101. ET 191.104. Recommending a controller's position description is not a violation of the ethical standards as long as the final hiring decision is made by management of the client. Purchasing a CPA firm's practice of monthly write-ups does not violate any provisions of the Code or client confidentiality. A member firm making arrangements with a bank to collect notes issued by a client in payment of fees due does not violate any provision of the Code, per ET 591.004.

4A. (c)   Rule of Conduct No. 501 specifically states that a CPA would be in violation of Rule 501 should the CPA refuse to return a client's records after the client has demanded them. Rule ET 591 allows note collection for fees. Rule ET 191 allows a CPA to retain independence if the client employed the CPA's spouse as a bookkeeper or if the CPA purchased that segment of an insurance company's business that performs actuarial services.

4B. (a)   ET 502.03 provides, "Advertising or other forms of solicitation that are false, misleading, or deceptive are not in the public interest and are prohibited." A prohibited activity is one that contains a representation that specific professional services in current or future periods will be performed for a stated fee, estimated fee, or fee range when it is likely at the time of representation that such fees would be substantially increased and the prospective client was not advised of such likelihood.

5. (b) Rule 301 of the AICPA Code of Professional Conduct (ET 301.01) prohibits the disclosure of confidential client information without the client's consent. This rule, however, does *not* (1) relieve the CPA of his or her obligations under Rule 202 (GAAS) and Rule 203 (GAAP); (2) affect the CPA's compliance with a subpoena or a summons enforceable by court order; (3) prohibit review of a CPA's professional practices as a part of an AICPA or state society authorization; or (4) preclude a CPA from responding to inquiries made by a recognized investigative or disciplinary body.

5A. (b) ET 301 prohibits the disclosure of confidential information obtained in the course of the professional engagement without the consent of the client, but does not prohibit review of a CPA's professional practices (including pertinent information) as a part of an AICPA authorized voluntary quality review program.

6. (b) QC 90.14(2)(d) addresses consultation policies and procedures and recommends designating individuals as specialists to serve as authoritative sources, and defining their authority in consultative situations. A procedure to implement this objective would be to provide procedures for resolving differences of opinion between personnel and specialists and to require documentation of the considerations involved in the resolution of differences of opinion. Therefore, answers (a), (c), and (d) are incorrect.

6A. (c) The basic duty of care standard is that of the reasonable man. However, since CPAs have knowledge and skill beyond that of the ordinary person, they must act with a level of care of similarly situated professionals.

6B. (a) The third general standard states, "Exercise of due care requires critical review at every level of supervision of the work done and the judgment exercised by those assisting in the audit" (AU §230.02).

7. (a) "A firm may not designate itself as 'members of the AICPA' unless *all* of its partners or shareholders are members" (ET 505.01).

7A. (a) Rule ET 191 states that a CPA who is not independent with respect to the client may not issue an audit opinion or review report. The Rule also states that a CPA who is not independent may issue

compilation reports for the client as long as the lack of independence is specifically disclosed without giving the reasons for the impairment of independence.

8. (d) Independence is impaired if fees for professional services rendered for prior years are not collected *before the issuance of the CPA's report for the current year* (ET 191.104). Answers (a) and (b) are acceptable practices by a CPA according to Ethics rulings on Other Responsibilities and Practices No. 115 and No. 2, respectively. Answer (c) is an acceptable practice by a CPA according to Rule 505, Form of Practice and Name, of the Code of Professional Conduct, because the name of the firm is not misleading.

Ethics Rulings

9. (b) The independence of the CPA would be considered impaired whether or not the financial interest is placed in a blind trust. Further, a CPA should ensure that a blind trust does not hold a direct or material indirect financial interest in clients for which the CPA provides services requiring independence (ET 191.137) (Part II). Leasing property to a client results in an indirect financial interest in that client. Therefore, a CPA's independence would be considered to be impaired if the indirect financial interest in a client is material to the CPA (ET 191.116) (Part III). A CPA's independence would **not** be considered to be impaired by his or her maintaining a checking account that is fully insured by a government deposit insurance agency at an audit-client financial institution (ET 191.040) (Part I).

9A. (a) An auditor's independence would not be considered to be impaired by his or her having a checking account in a fully insured client financial institution (ET 191.140). An auditor who also functions as general counsel for a client would not be considered independent because the legal services rendered result in undue identification with the management of the client or involvement with the client's affairs to such a degree as to place him or her virtually in the position of being an employee (ET 191.101). Independence of the auditor would also be impaired if he or she also serves as the client's officially appointed stock transfer agent or registrar (ET 191.077). "Independence of the member's firm may be impaired if more than one year's fees due from a client for professional services remain unpaid for an extended period of time" (ET 191.104). Such amounts, when they are long past due, take on characteristics of a loan. Under these conditions, it may appear that the practitioner is providing working capital for his or her client and that the collection of past due amounts may depend on the nature of the auditor's report on the client's financial statements.

10. (a) ET 191.131 states, "The use of the CPA designation by a member who is not in public practice in a manner to imply that the member is independent of the employer will be considered a knowing misrepresentation of fact. Therefore, such a member may use the CPA designation in connection with financial statements issued for internal and external distribution provided that . . . the member's employment status or title is clearly indicated." Answers (b), (c), and (d) are not violations of the profession's ethical standards.

11. (b) The service in question constitutes a type of service performed by public accountants, and the member may hire such an employee as long as the CPA is able to supervise the specialist and evaluate his or her results. The CPA is not required to be a specialist outside of the realm of accounting and tax services. The CPA is permitted to be associated with non-CPA professionals, as long as the association is not misleading and the client is aware of the relationship.

12. (d) A member who is in partnership with non-CPAs may sign reports with the firm name and below it affix his or her own signature with the designation "Certified Public Accountant," provided it is clear that the partnership itself is not being held out as composed entirely of CPAs (ET 291.013-.014).

13. (d) A CPA who provides auditing and other attestation services should be independent in fact and appearance. In providing all other services, an accountant should maintain objectivity and avoid conflicts of interest (ET 55.03). Thus, an accountant need not be independent when providing compilation services or when preparing a tax return.

14. (d) Rule 201 of the AICPA's Rules of Conduct requires a CPA performing a consulting engagement to comply with Standards on Consulting Services and to supervise staff assigned to the engagement. Rule 202 of the AICPA's Code of Professional Conduct requires that the CPA obtain an understanding of the nature, scope, and limitations of the engagement. Rule 202 also states that performing a consulting service does not, of itself, impair independence.

Responsibilities in Tax Practice

15. (c) A CPA has both the right and responsibility to be an advocate for the client with respect to any return positions for which the CPA has a good faith belief that the position has a realistic possibility of being sustained administratively or judicially on its merit if challenged (TX 112.02). The CPA is not neutral or an agent of the IRS. TX 132.02 states, "In preparing or signing a return, the CPA may in good faith rely without verification upon information furnished by the client or by third parties." However, the CPA should make reasonable inquiries if the information furnished appears to be incorrect, incomplete, or inconsistent either on its face or on the basis of other facts known to the CPA.

15A. (d) The CPA may in good faith rely, without verification, on information furnished by the client. However, the CPA should make reasonable inquiries if the information appears to be incorrect, incomplete, or inconsistent either on its face or on the basis of other facts known to the CPA, including information from prior years' returns and other clients' returns.

16. (b) The Statement on Responsibilities in Tax Practice, No. 3, states that a CPA may rely in good faith and without verification on information provided by clients or third parties unless the information appears to be incorrect, incomplete, or inconsistent on its face.

17. (b) A CPA should not recommend a position unless the CPA has a good faith belief that the position is warranted or can be supported if challenged. A CPA may recommend a position that is not frivolous as long as the position is adequately disclosed on the return. The CPA should advise the client as to potential penalty consequences. A CPA should not prepare or sign a return if the return takes a position the CPA knows will not be sustained if challenged.

18. (c) When a CPA discovers an error in a client's previously filed tax return, the CPA should notify the client and recommend appropriate action. The CPA cannot correct the error or notify the IRS without client consent and it is not necessary that the CPA end the relationship with the client.

Consulting Services

19. (d) Rule 202 of the AICPA Code of Professional Conduct requires that the client be informed of any conflict of interest or significant reservations concerning the scope or benefits of the engagement. However, independence is *not* required. This rule also requires a written *or oral* understanding between consultant and client.

20. (d) Definitions for consulting services (SSCS1) identify an analysis of a client's accounting system as an example of advisory services; identifies a review of a client's prepared business plan as an example of consultations; and identifies the preparation of information for obtaining financing as an example of a transaction service. Advisory, consultation and transaction services are all considered consulting services.

21. (d) Under the Standards for Consulting Services, advisory services are used to develop findings, conclusions and recommendations for client consideration and decision making. A stated example of advisory services is the defining of requirements for an information system.

22. (c) CS 100.06 states that the CPA should obtain sufficient relevant data to afford a reasonable basis for conclusions or recommendations in relation to any professional services performed. An understanding of the internal control structure and independence is not required (as they are in an audit). A CPA may compile a financial forecast and then perform consultation services for the engagement, because most practitioners also provide business and management consulting services to their clients, regardless of the work performed.

23. (a) The Statement of Standards for Consulting Services (SSCS 1) defines advisory services, implementation services, and product services as consulting services.

PERFORMANCE BY SUBTOPICS

Each category below parallels a subtopic covered in Chapter 58. Record the number and percentage of questions you correctly answered in each subtopic area.

Code of Professional Conduct

Question #	Correct √
1	
1A	
2	
3	
3A	
4	
4A	
4B	
5	
5A	
6	
6A	
6B	
7	
7A	
8	
# Questions	16

Correct _____
% Correct _____

Ethics Rulings

Question #	Correct √
9	
9A	
10	
11	
12	
13	
14	
# Questions	7

Correct _____
% Correct _____

Responsibilities in Tax Practice

Question #	Correct √
15	
15A	
16	
17	
18	
# Questions	5

Correct _____
% Correct _____

Consulting Services

Question #	Correct √
19	
20	
21	
22	
23	
# Questions	5

Correct _____
% Correct _____

CHAPTER 59

ACCOUNTANT'S PROFESSIONAL LIABILITY

I. **Definitions** 59-2
   A.   Actual Damages 59-2
   B.   Actual Fraud 59-2
   C.   Constructive Fraud 59-2
   D.   Negligence.. 59-2
   E.   Punitive Damages... 59-2
   F.   Third-Party Beneficiary 59-2

II. **Accountant's Civil Liability to Clients**.. 59-2
   A.   Contractual Liability.. 59-2
   B.   Liability for Negligence.. 59-3
   C.   Liability for Fraud 59-4
   D.   Foreign Corrupt Practices Act of 1977 59-4

III. **Accountant's Civil Liability to Third Parties**... 59-4
   A.   Contractual Liability.. 59-5
   B.   Liability for Negligence.. 59-5
   C.   The Ultramares Doctrine 59-5
   D.   Damages (Common Law Liability).. 59-5
   E.   Accountant's Liability to Third Parties Under Federal Statutes................ 59-5

IV. **Accountant's Criminal Liability** 59-7
   A.   Under Federal Securities Acts... 59-7
   B.   Under the Internal Revenue Code 59-7
   C.   Under State Criminal Laws.. 59-8
   D.   Other State and Federal Criminal Laws 59-8

V. **Accountant's Duty of Nondisclosure** 59-8
   A.   Working Papers... 59-8
   B.   Privileged Communications 59-8
   C.   Ethical Protection From Disclosure 59-8

VI. **Typical Practical Situations in Which Accountants May Incur Legal Liability** 59-9
   A.   Audit Liability... 59-9
   B.   Duty to Discover Irregularities... 59-9
   C.   Liability for Another Auditor's Work 59-9
   D.   Inadequate Disclosure.. 59-9
   E.   Subsequent Changes 59-9
   F.   Unaudited Financial Statements.. 59-9
   G.   Preparation of Tax Returns 59-10

CHAPTER 59

ACCOUNTANT'S PROFESSIONAL LIABILITY

I. Definitions

A. <u>Actual Damages</u>--Those losses which can be proven to have been directly caused by the wrongful acts of the defendant.

B. <u>Actual Fraud</u>--A material misrepresentation made with the intent to deceive another. To form the basis for a lawsuit, the misrepresentation must have been relied upon by another with resulting injury.

C. <u>Constructive Fraud</u>--A material misrepresentation, innocently made, that is relied upon by another to his or her detriment.

D. <u>Negligence</u>--The failure to exercise that degree of care which a reasonable man would exercise under the same or similar circumstances. Negligent conduct falls below the standard established by law for the protection of others against unreasonable risk of loss or damage.

E. <u>Punitive Damages</u>--Compensation in excess of actual damages, usually awarded as a means of punishing the wrongdoer.

F. <u>Third-Party Beneficiary</u>--A person who may enforce the terms of a contract even though he or she is not a party to the contract. In order to create a valid third-party beneficiary contract, the parties to the contract must intend that the third party receive the primary benefit of performance under the contract.

II. Accountant's Civil Liability to Clients

A. <u>Contractual Liability</u>--Generally, an accountant occupies the position of an independent contractor in his or her relationships with clients. Consequently, an accountant's liability to a client usually stems from a violation of a contractual duty owed to the client.

   1. An accountant's contractual duties may be either express or implied.

      a. Express duties are those which are spelled out by the terms of the contract. For example, if the terms of the engagement letter call for the accountant to perform particular services for the client, the accountant has an express contractual duty to perform those services.

      b. Implied duties are those which the courts have determined to be a part of every contract, whether or not the duty is expressed in the terms of the contract. For example, an accountant normally has an implied contractual duty not to perform in a negligent or fraudulent manner. This duty exists even though it is not mentioned in the contract.

   2. An accountant's duty to perform under a contract may not be delegated. That is, since the contract is one for a personal service, an accountant cannot escape liability by delegating to another the duty to perform under the contract. Therefore, partners in accounting firms may be held liable for the wrongful acts of their subordinates or employees committed in the course of their employment.

3.   An accountant will generally be held liable for his or her failure to fulfill the terms of a contract with a client. Failure to fulfill the terms of a contract usually constitutes a breach of the contract and may subject the accountant to liability in the form of money damages.

    a.   If the accountant's failure to fulfill his or her contractual duties is so substantial that the client receives no real benefit from the accountant's performance, a material breach of contract has occurred.

        (1)   For example, a material breach is committed when an accountant fails to complete an audit or finishes late when time is of the essence.

        (2)   Minor inaccuracies and insignificant errors or omissions will not normally constitute a material breach of contract.

        (3)   When an accountant commits a material breach, he or she is not entitled to compensation for whatever work may have been performed.

    b.   If the accountant's breach of contract is a minor one, he or she is entitled to be compensated for his or her services. However, the client will probably be permitted to reduce or offset the accountant's compensation by the amount of damage or loss attributable to the breach.

    c.   In determining the adequacy of an accountant's performance under the terms of a contract, the law imposes upon the accountant the profession's generally accepted standards of competence and care. Thus, an accountant must demonstrate the average degree of learning and skill generally possessed by accountants.

4.   An accountant's duties under a contract with a client do not normally include a duty to discover fraud, unless the accountant's own negligence prevents him or her from discovering the fraud. For example, in an audit, a CPA would be negligent if he or she did not perform tests of controls to verify controls on which he or she planned to rely.

5.   An accountant will not incur contractual liability if his or her performance under the contract was prevented by the client's interference. The client has an implied contractual duty not to interfere with or prevent the accountant's performance.

6.   An accountant who breaches his or her contract with a client may be subject to liability for damages and losses which the client suffers as a direct result of the breach. However, punitive damages will not normally be awarded for a simple breach of contract. In contrast, punitive damages may be awarded in a tort action for negligence or constructive fraud against the accountant.

B.   <u>Liability for Negligence</u>--As a general rule, an accountant may incur liability to a client for negligence. Liability may be based on an accountant's failure to exercise reasonable care under the circumstances.

1.   The standard of reasonable care to which accountants are held is measured by that degree of quality, accuracy, and completeness which is demonstrated by the average accountant when performing his or her work with reasonable care.

    a.   Honest inaccuracies and judgmental errors will not give rise to negligence liability so long as the accountant exercised reasonable care in performing his or her work.

    b.   It is not necessary that an error or inaccuracy be <u>intentional</u> in order to give rise to negligence liability. Negligence may be based on unintentional errors resulting from failure to exercise reasonable care.

2. An accountant's liability for negligence may be reduced or eliminated if it can be shown that the client's own negligence contributed to the error or inaccuracy. For example, if an inaccuracy in a financial statement is due to the client's own error or omission, and the nature of it is such that the CPA cannot reasonably be expected to find it, the client's error may amount to contributory negligence which may mitigate the accountant's potential liability.

3. Damages for negligence are usually calculated on the basis of the amount of loss or damage which would have been avoided by the exercise of reasonable care. As a general rule, punitive damages are not normally awarded in simple negligence cases.

C. Liability for Fraud--An accountant may be held liable for acts or omissions which amount to actual (intentional) fraud or constructive (unintentional) fraud.

1. Actual fraud consists of an intentional act or omission which is designed to deceive. In order to constitute actual fraud the following must occur:

a. The act or omission itself must have been intentionally committed.

b. The act or omission must have been accompanied by an intent to deceive.

2. Constructive fraud consists of acts or omissions characterized by gross negligence or lack of even slight care.

a. In order to prove constructive fraud, it is not necessary to prove a conscious intent to deceive; in situations involving gross negligence, the law infers an intent to deceive. For example, an accountant who takes an unauthorized shortcut in order to save time may be guilty of gross negligence and constructive fraud, but not of actual fraud, since there was a lack of conscious intent to deceive.

b. Gross negligence (constructive fraud) has also been defined as "reckless disregard for the truth" (scienter).

3. Punitive damages may be imposed on an accountant who has committed actual fraud or constructive fraud.

D. Foreign Corrupt Practices Act of 1977

1. Antibribery Provisions--The Act makes it illegal for any U.S. business engaged in interstate commerce to offer a bribe to foreign official. Companies are subject to a fine of up to $1,000,000, while individuals are subject to a maximum fine of $10,000 and/or up to 5 years imprisonment.

2. Recordkeeping and Internal Control--The Act requires entities to maintain books, records, and accounts which accurately reflect the transactions and dispositions of the assets of the entity. Entities must also maintain a system of accounting control sufficient to provide reasonable assurance that (1) transactions are executed in accordance with management's authorization, (2) transactions are properly recorded in conformity with GAAP, (3) access to assets is restricted only to those authorized by management, and (4) the recorded accountability for assets is periodically compared to, and reconciled with, the existing assets. The Act does not require the auditor to issue a special report on internal control.

III. Accountant's Civil Liability to Third Parties

Under certain circumstances, an accountant may be held civilly liable to persons who are not clients. Such liability to third parties generally arises under the common law notions of negligence and fraud or under federal statutes. In addition, an accountant may incur contractual liability to third parties in some cases.

A.   Contractual Liability--An accountant's contractual liability to persons who are not parties to the contract extends only to third-party beneficiaries of the contract. A third-party beneficiary of a contract is a person whom the contracting parties intended to receive the primary benefits of the accountant's services. For example, if an accountant is hired by a client to prepare financial statements for purposes of securing a loan from a particular bank, the bank is an intended third-party beneficiary of the contract between the accountant and his or her client.

B.   Liability for Negligence--An accountant's tort liability to third parties for ordinary negligence normally extends only to those third parties whom the accountant knew (or should have known) would be users or beneficiaries of the accountant's work product. Thus, an accountant will not normally be held liable to third parties for ordinary negligence if the accountant was unaware that the particular third parties would be using his or her work product. For example, if a CPA prepares financial statements for the client's personal use only, there would be no contractual or tort liability to a bank for misstatements or omissions, as the bank was an unknown and unintended user. Conversely, if the financial statements were prepared to enable the client to obtain a bank loan, there would be contractual liability (bank is intended beneficiary), as well as tort liability (use by bank was foreseeable at time of engagement).

C.   The Ultramares Doctrine--In the Ultramares case (1931), the courts decided that accountants owe a duty to all third parties to make their reports without fraud (actual or constructive). This third-party liability for fraud exists regardless of whether the work product was intended primarily for the benefit of third parties or for the benefit of the client.

   1.   In order for a third party to recover damages from an accountant for actual or constructive fraud, the third party must show that he or she reasonably relied on the accountant's work.

   2.   There is no need for the third party to show privity of contract in the case of fraud or gross negligence.

D.   Damages (Common Law Liability)--Damages recoverable by third parties under the common law doctrines consist of actual damages and, in some cases, punitive damages.

   1.   A third party may recover actual damages to the extent that he or she can prove the losses were caused by the accountant's fraud, negligence, or breach of contract.

   2.   Punitive damages may be awarded for an accountant's fraudulent or grossly negligent acts. Usually, however, ordinary negligence or breach of contract will not support an award of punitive damages.

E.   Accountant's Liability to Third Parties Under Federal Statutes--The Securities Act of 1933 and the Securities Exchange Act of 1934.

   1.   The Securities Act of 1933 ("Truth in Securities Law") is designed to provide the investing public with sufficient information to enable them to adequately evaluate the merits of new securities.

      a.   The Act requires the filing of a registration statement with the Securities and Exchange Commission (SEC) prior to the public offering of any securities in interstate commerce. The registration statement must make a full disclosure of all material facts concerning the securities to be issued and must include financial statements certified by independent public accountants.

      b.   In addition, each potential investor must be furnished with a prospectus which must contain essentially the same financial information as is required in the registration statement.

c. Liability Under Section 11 of the 1933 Act--The Securities Act of 1933 makes an accountant liable for any false statements concerning material facts or material omissions in these financial statements or in the prospectus. The risk and extent of liability under the 1933 Act is quite significant.

(1) Any purchaser of the initial issue of securities covered by the registration statement may sue the accountant. This includes third parties (investors) who are not clients of the accountant.

(2) The investor is only required to prove the existence of a false statement or material omission and that the security purchased was offered through the inaccurate registration statement. The investor does not have the burden of proving that the accountant was fraudulent or negligent.

 (a) An accountant charged under this Act may assert the "due diligence defense" (see E.1.(c)(3), below).

 (b) It is not necessary for the purchaser to prove that he or she relied on the accountant's error or that he or she had a contractual relationship with the accountant.

(3) The accountant's defense of "due diligence" is established by proving that after reasonable investigation, the accountant had a reasonable basis for the belief that all statements in the registration statement were accurate and complete. A "reasonable investigation" is measured against the standard of care observed by a prudent person in the management of his or her own financial affairs.

(4) The truth and accuracy of the registration statement is determined as of the date the statement becomes effective, not as of the date the accountant prepared the statement. As a result, the accountant is responsible for errors resulting from changes that occurred between the time he or she prepared the statement and its effective date.

(5) The following statutory periods of limitation are applicable to suits brought under the Securities Act of 1933:

 (a) An action against an accountant must be commenced within one year of the time when the error or omission was (or should have been) discovered.

 (b) In any event, an action against an accountant must be commenced no later than three years after the initial offering of the security.

(6) The amount of damages generally recoverable under the Act is measured by the difference between the amount paid for the security and the market value of the security at the time of the suit.

 (a) If the investor has already sold the security at the time he or she brings suit, the damages are measured by the difference between the amounts that he or she paid and sold.

 (b) In no event can the amount of damages exceed the price at which the security was offered to the public.

 (c) The investor's recovery does not include any decrease in the price of the security during the course of the suit.

2.   The Securities Exchange Act of 1934 regulates the national securities exchanges and the securities that are traded on the national exchanges. In addition, most provisions of the Act apply to securities of companies that have more than $5,000,000 in assets and equity stock that is held by 500 or more persons as of the last day of the fiscal year.

    a.   The Act requires each company to submit to the SEC an annual report (Form 10-K) which includes financial statements that have been certified by an independent public accountant. These financial statements are the chief source of an accountant's liability under the Act. Form 10-K differs from the company's annual report to shareholders. (The provisions of the Securities Exchange Act do not apply to reports to shareholders.)

    b.   The Act imposes civil liability on any person (including the certifying accountant) who, in any SEC annual report, makes a false or misleading statement with respect to a material fact.

    c.   Unlike the Securities Act of 1933, the 1934 Act places the burden on the investor to prove the following:

        (1)   That he or she bought or sold the security at a price that was affected by the false or misleading statement.

        (2)   That he or she was not aware that the statement was false or inaccurate.

        (3)   That he or she relied on the statement.

    d.   Liability under the 1934 Act requires proof that the accountant made the false or misleading statement with the intent to deceive or defraud (scienter).

        (1)   As a result, the accountant's good faith or lack of knowledge of his or her statement's falsity are valid defenses under the 1934 Act.

        (2)   In addition, mere negligence will not give rise to liability under the 1934 Act.

    e.   The statutory limitations periods for the 1934 Act are the same as under the 1933 Act (see E.1.c.(5), above).

IV. Accountant's Criminal Liability

A.   <u>Under Federal Securities Acts</u>--Willful violations of the provisions of either the Securities Act of 1933 or the Securities Exchange Act of 1934 can subject the offender to criminal penalties of fines and/or imprisonment. [For more information, see the Federal Securities Regulations chapter, 1934 Act, Anti-Fraud Provisions (Chapter 55, IV.C.)]

B.   <u>Under the Internal Revenue Code</u>--The Internal Revenue Code provides criminal penalties (fines and/or imprisonment) for persons convicted of violating its provisions. Examples of types of violations particularly applicable to accountants include the following:

    1.   Willfully preparing false returns (perjury) and willfully assisting others to evade taxes.

    2.   Fraudulently executing or procuring the fraudulent execution of documents required to be executed under the Internal Revenue Code.

    3.   Removing and/or concealing goods with the intent to evade taxes.

    4.   Willfully delivering documents that the accountant knows to be fraudulent or false.

C. Under State Criminal Laws--Each state has enacted laws imposing criminal sanctions on certain activities closely connected with an accountant's normal duties. For example, criminal penalties may be imposed in most states for activities such as the following:

   1. Knowingly certifying false or fraudulent reports.

   2. Falsifying, altering, or destroying books of account.

   3. Obtaining property or credit through the use of false financial statements.

D. Other State and Federal Criminal Laws--In addition, federal and state laws impose severe criminal penalties for such activities as perjury, conspiracy to defraud, and fraudulent use of the mails.

V. Accountant's Duty of Nondisclosure

A. Working Papers--An accountant's working papers generally include the notes, computations, memoranda, copies, and other papers that represent the by-product of the accountant's services to the client.

   1. At common law and in the absence of an express agreement to the contrary, ownership of an accountant's working papers rests with the accountant.

   2. The accountant's ownership, however, is in the nature of a custodial interest, since the accountant may not normally disclose the contents of his or her working papers without the consent of the client. This custodial arrangement serves the dual purpose of permitting the client to control the confidentiality of the information contained in the papers, while at the same time permitting the accountant to retain possession of the papers for use as evidence of the nature and extent of his or her services.

   3. An accountant must relinquish possession of the working papers in response to an enforceable subpoena or court order.

B. Privileged Communications--A few states have promulgated statutes asserting that communications between an accountant and his or her clients may be regarded as privileged. This privilege protects the accountant from being compelled to testify in court with regard to privileged matters. However, the purpose of the privilege is to protect the client, and therefore, the client is free to waive it.

C. Ethical Protection From Disclosure--In addition to the protection of legal privilege, confidential communications between accountants and their clients are also protected from unauthorized disclosure by professional ethical considerations.

   1. Confidential communications include both written and oral communications between an accountant and a client relating to professional advice and services.

   2. Professional ethics discourage disclosure by an accountant of confidential information except in the following circumstances:

      a. Where disclosure is pursuant to a voluntary quality review under AICPA authorization or in response to an AICPA trial board request.

      b. Where disclosure is in compliance with an enforceable subpoena or court order.

      c. Where the client consents to the disclosure.

      d. Where disclosure is in compliance with generally accepted accounting principles or generally accepted auditing standards.

VI. Typical Practical Situations in Which Accountants May Incur Legal Liability

A. Audit Liability--An accountant may incur civil liability for acts or omissions occurring in the course of an audit.

B. Duty to Discover Irregularities--Unless such performance is specifically contracted for, an accountant has no contractual duty to discover irregularities.

   1. An accountant may be held liable for failure to discover irregularities only if the failure to discover was the result of the accountant's own negligence or fraud. For example, if an accountant fails to adequately investigate an obvious indication of fraud, he or she may be liable for negligence or fraud.

   2. Where an accountant has expressly contracted to discover shortages and defalcations, his or her failure to take reasonable and adequate discovery measures may be treated as either a breach of contract or negligence.

C. Liability for Another Auditor's Work--An accountant may be held liable for the work of another auditor if he or she relies on the other auditor's work and no mention is made of the other auditor in the audit report.

   1. However, if the audit report clearly indicates that responsibility for the audit was divided, then each auditor may be held liable only for his or her own inaccuracies.

   2. An auditor may not rely on unaudited data. If such data is included in audited financial statements, he or she must qualify or disclaim an opinion.

D. Inadequate Disclosure--An accountant may incur liability for inadequate disclosure.

   1. For example, liability may result if the accountant fails to reveal the existence of inadequate insurance or excessive political contributions.

   2. However, liability may be avoided through the issuance of a qualified, adverse, or disclaimed opinion.

E. Subsequent Changes--An accountant is not generally liable for inaccuracies resulting from changes that occur after the last day of field work.

   1. However, liability may result If the report is dated subsequent to the changes that caused the inaccuracy.

   2. Under the Securities Act of 1933, the accountant is responsible for changes occurring up to the effective date of the registration statement.

   3. An accountant may be held liable if subsequently discovered facts indicate that the statements were misleading at the time they were issued. Such liability may be avoided in certain conditions:

      a. An immediate investigation is conducted.

      b. The statements are promptly revised.

      c. The SEC and persons known to be relying on the statements are promptly notified.

F. Unaudited Financial Statements--An accountant may incur liability in the preparation of an unaudited financial statement.

1. A financial statement is considered unaudited if no auditing procedures have been applied or if insufficient procedures have been applied to justify an opinion.

2. Liability in conjunction with an unaudited financial statement may arise in certain conditions:

   a. The accountant fails to mark each page "unaudited."

   b. The accountant fails to issue a disclaimer.

   c. The accountant fails to inform the client of discrepancies or defalcations.

G. Preparation of Tax Returns--Under the Internal Revenue Code, accountants and others face potential liability in the preparation of tax returns.

1. A tax preparer is defined as anyone who accepts compensation to prepare all or any substantial part of an income tax (not estate, gift, or excise tax) return or claim for refund [§7701(a)(36)].

   a. A person who merely types a return is not a tax preparer. Similarly, one who completes a return for free or as a "gift" is not a preparer.

   b. In determining whether a "substantial" part of a return has been prepared, consideration will be given to both the length and complexity of the portion prepared, as well as to the amount of the tax.

2. Requirements of a Tax Preparer

   a. The return must be signed by the preparer.

   b. The returns and claims for refunds must contain the identification number of the preparer and the preparer's employer or partnership (if applicable).

   c. The preparer must furnish a copy of the completed return to the client.

   d. An employer of tax preparers must retain specific information on all preparers employed by him or her.

   e. The preparer must retain a copy of the completed return, or a list of all taxpayers for whom returns have been prepared, for three years.

   f. The preparer is required to advise the client of errors found in previously-filed returns while performing services for the client (Treasury Department Circular 230).

3. Preparer Penalties

   a. Negligent or Intentional Disregard of Rules and Regulations [§6694(a)]--If any part of any understatement (understatement of net amount payable or overstatement of net amount creditable or refundable) of liability is due to negligence by the return preparer, a penalty of $100 per return or claim may be levied.

      (1) Once the negligence penalty has been proposed, the return preparer must rebut the inference of negligence.

      (2) Negligence is determined by the nature, frequency, and materiality of the errors causing the understatement.

b. Willful Understatement of Liability [§6694(b)]--If any part of any understatement is due to preparer <u>willfulness</u> (knowing disregard of information, absence of preparer diligence in questioning obvious irregularities), <u>a penalty of $500 per return</u> may be imposed.

   (1) Once proposed, the IRS has the burden of proving a willful understatement by the preparer.

   (2) Amounts assessed under the willful understatement penalty will be reduced by amounts paid under the negligent or intentional disregard penalty.

c. Penalties for Aiding and Abetting Understatement of Tax Liability (§6701)--Any person who aids in the preparation of any portion of a return, affidavit, or claim which is used in any material matter arising under the tax laws, where that person knows that the portion will result in an understatement of liability, will be subject to a penalty of $1,000 per document ($10,000 per corporate document).

   (1) Only one penalty per taxpayer per taxable year. Thus, the same preparer can be penalized only once for each taxpayer, regardless of the number of documents filed by that taxpayer during a particular taxable year.

   (2) "Aiding and abetting" does not include typing, reproducing, or other rendering of mechanical assistance to a taxpayer.

   (3) If this penalty is imposed, no penalty under either §6694(a) or (b) will be imposed with respect to the same document.

d. False and Fraudulent Statements (§7201)--Any person who willfully aids or assists in, or procures, counsels, or advises the preparation or presentation in connection with any matter arising under the internal revenue laws, of a return, affidavit, claim, or other document which is fraudulent or false in any material matter shall be guilty of a felony and subject to imprisonment of not more than 3 years and a fine of not more than $100,000 ($500,000 in the case of a corporation).

e. Other Assessable Penalties With Respect to Return Preparation (§6695)--In addition to the foregoing, several additional penalties apply with respect to the record-keeping functions which must be performed by preparers or others:

   (1) Failure to furnish a copy of completed return to client ($25 penalty for each failure).

   (2) Failure to sign return ($25 penalty for each failure).

   (3) Failure to furnish preparer I.D. number ($25 penalty for each failure). A preparer's I.D. number is his or her social security number (§6109).

   (4) Failure to retain a copy of completed return for 3 years ($50 penalty for each failure, not to exceed $25,000).

   (5) Failure to file correct information return ($100 penalty for each failure to file a return; $5 penalty for each failure to include an item, not to exceed $20,000).

NOTES

CHAPTER 59—ACCOUNTANT'S PROFESSIONAL LIABILITY

Problem 59-1 MULTIPLE CHOICE QUESTIONS (60 to 70 minutes)

1. A CPA's duty of due care to a client most likely will be breached when a CPA
   a. Gives a client an oral instead of a written report.
   b. Gives a client incorrect advice based on an honest error of judgment.
   c. Fails to give tax advice that saves the client money.
   d. Fails to follow generally accepted auditing standards. (5/93, Law, #4, 3973)

2. Cable Corp. orally engaged Drake & Co., CPAs, to audit its financial statements. Cable's management informed Drake that it suspected the accounts receivable were materially overstated. Though the financial statements Drake audited included a materially overstated accounts receivable balance, Drake issued an unqualified opinion. Cable used the financial statements to obtain a loan to expand its operations. Cable defaulted on the loan and incurred a substantial loss. If Cable sues Drake for negligence in failing to discover the overstatement, Drake's best defense would be that Drake did **not**
   a. Have privity of contract with Cable.
   b. Sign an engagement letter.
   c. Perform the audit recklessly or with an intent to deceive.
   d. Violate generally accepted auditing standards in performing the audit. (11/91, Law, #1, 2329)

3. When performing an audit, a CPA
   a. Must exercise the level of care, skill, and judgment expected of a reasonably prudent CPA under the circumstances.
   b. Must strictly adhere to generally accepted accounting principles.
   c. Is strictly liable for failing to discover client fraud.
   d. Is **not** liable unless the CPA commits gross negligence or intentionally disregards generally accepted auditing standards. (11/91, Law, #2, 2330)

4. When CPAs fail in their duty to carry out their contracts for services, liability to clients may be based on

	Breach of contract	Strict liability
a.	Yes	Yes
b.	Yes	No
c.	No	No
d.	No	Yes

(5/89, Law, #6, 0791)

5. Sun Corp. approved a merger plan with Cord Corp. One of the determining factors in approving the merger was the financial statements of Cord that were audited by Frank & Co., CPAs. Sun had engaged Frank to audit Cord's financial statements. While performing the audit, Frank failed to discover certain irregularities that later caused Sun to suffer substantial losses. For Frank to be liable under common law negligence, Sun at a minimum must prove that Frank
   a. Knew of the irregularities.
   b. Failed to exercise due care.
   c. Was grossly negligent.
   d. Acted with scienter. (5/93, Law, #1, 3970)

6. A CPA will most likely be negligent when the CPA fails to
   a. Correct errors discovered in the CPA's previously issued audit reports.
   b. Detect all of a client's fraudulent activities.
   c. Include a negligence disclaimer in the CPA's engagement letter.
   d. Warn a client's customers of embezzlement by the client's employees. (5/93, Law, #2, 3971)

7. One of the elements necessary to hold a CPA liable to a client for conducting an audit negligently is that the CPA
   a. Acted with scienter or guilty knowledge.
   b. Was a fiduciary of the client.
   c. Failed to exercise due care.
   d. Executed an engagement letter. (11/87, Law, #28, 0799)

8. Which of the following elements, if present, would support a finding of constructive fraud on the part of a CPA?
   a. Gross negligence in applying generally accepted auditing standards.
   b. Ordinary negligence in applying generally accepted accounting principles.
   c. Identified third party users.
   d. Scienter. *actual fraud* (5/93, Law, #3, 3972) *reckless disregard for truth*

9. If a stockholder sues a CPA for common law fraud based on false statements contained in the financial statements audited by the CPA, which of the following, if present, would be the CPA's best defense?
   a. The stockholder lacks privity to sue.
   b. The false statements were immaterial.

[handwritten top margin: Negligence = Privity - Ultram. False sts. immater.]

c. The CPA did **not** financially benefit from the alleged fraud.

d. The contributory negligence of the client.

(5/89, Law, #2, 0787)

10. If a CPA recklessly departs from the standards of due care when conducting an audit, the CPA will be liable to third parties who are unknown to the CPA based on

a. Negligence.

b. Gross negligence.

c. Strict liability.

d. Criminal deceit. (5/94, Law, #9, 4764)

[handwritten: needed privity]

11. In a common law action against an accountant, lack of privity is a viable defense if the plaintiff

a. Is the client's creditor who sues the accountant for negligence. *[handwritten: Ultramares]*

b. Can prove the presence of gross negligence that amounts to a reckless disregard for the truth.

c. Is the accountant's client.

d. Bases the action upon fraud.

(11/94, Law, #9, 5187)

12. Beckler & Associates, CPAs, audited and gave an unqualified opinion on the financial statements of Queen Co. The financial statements contained misstatements that resulted in a material overstatement of Queen's net worth. Queen provided the audited financial statements to Mac Bank in connection with a loan made by Mac to Queen. Beckler knew that the financial statements would be provided to Mac. Queen defaulted on the loan. Mac sued Beckler to recover for its losses associated with Queen's default. Which of the following must Mac prove in order to recover?

I. Beckler was negligent in conducting the audit.

II. Mac relied on the financial statements.

a. I only.

b. II only.

c. Both I and II.

d. Neither I nor II. (11/93, Law, #1, 4298)

Items 13 and 14 are based on the following:

While conducting an audit, Larson Associates, CPAs, failed to detect material misstatements included in its client's financial statements. Larson's unqualified opinion was included with the financial statements in a registration statement and prospectus for a public offering of securities made by the client. Larson knew that its opinion and the financial statements would be used for this purpose.

13. In a suit by a purchaser against Larson for common law negligence, Larson's best defense would be that the

a. Audit was conducted in accordance with generally accepted auditing standards.

b. Client was aware of the misstatements.

c. Purchaser was **not** in privity of contract with Larson.

d. Identity of the purchaser was **not** known to Larson at the time of the audit.

(11/93, Law, #4, 4301)

14. In a suit by a purchaser against Larson for common law fraud, Larson's best defense would be that

a. Larson did **not** have actual or constructive knowledge of the misstatements.

b. Larson's client knew or should have known of the misstatements.

c. Larson did **not** have actual knowledge that the purchaser was an intended beneficiary of the audit.

d. Larson was **not** in privity of contract with its client. (11/93, Law, #5, 4302)

15. Which of the following is the best defense a CPA firm can assert in defense to a suit for common law fraud based on their unqualified opinion on materially false financial statements?

a. Lack of privity.

b. Lack of scienter.

c. Contributory negligence on the part of the client.

d. A disclaimer contained in the engagement letter. (11/93, Law, #7, 4304)

[handwritten: No Contractual Relationship]

16. Hark, CPA, failed to follow generally accepted auditing standards in auditing Long Corp.'s financial statements. Long's management had told Hark that the audited statements would be submitted to several banks to obtain financing. Relying on the statements, Third Bank gave Long a loan. Long defaulted on the loan. In a jurisdiction applying the *Ultramares* decision, if Third sues Hark, Hark will

[handwritten: not intended beneficiary, foreseen not foreseen]

a. Win, because there was **no** privity of contract between Hark and Third.

b. Lose, because Hark knew that banks would be relying on the financial statements.

c. Win, because Third was contributorily negligent in granting the loan.

d. Lose, because Hark was negligent in performing the audit. (11/91, Law, #4, 2332)

17. Krim, President and CEO of United Co., engaged Smith, CPA, to audit United's financial statements so that United could secure a loan from First Bank. Smith issued an unqualified opinion on

Gross Neg :- Actual & Const. Knowledge of Mis

May 20, 1988, but the loan was delayed. On August 5, 1988, on inquiry to Smith by First Bank, Smith, relying on Krim's representation, made assurances that there was no material change in United's financial status. Krim's representation was untrue because of a material change which took place after May 20, 1988. First relied on Smith's assurances of no change. Shortly thereafter, United became insolvent. If First sues Smith for negligent misrepresentation, Smith will be found

a. Not liable, because Krim misled Smith, and a CPA is not responsible for a client's untrue representations.
b. Liable, because Smith should have undertaken sufficient auditing procedures to verify the status of United.
c. Not liable, because Smith's opinion covers only the period up to May 20.
d. Liable, because Smith should have contacted the chief financial officer rather than the chief executive officer. (5/89, Law, #1, 0786)

18. In general, the third party (primary) beneficiary rule as applied to a CPA's legal liability in conducting an audit is relevant to which of the following causes of action against a CPA?

	Fraud	Constructive fraud	Negligence
a.	Yes	Yes	No
b.	Yes	No	No
c.	No	Yes	Yes
d.	No	No	Yes

(11/87, Law, #29, 9911)

18A. Which of the following facts must be proven for a plaintiff to prevail in a common law negligent misrepresentation action?

a. The defendant made the misrepresentations with a reckless disregard for the truth.
b. The plaintiff justifiably relied on the misrepresentations.
c. The misrepresentations were in writing.
d. The misrepresentations concerned opinion. (5/95, Law, #16, 5350)

19. Ford & Co., CPAs, issued an unqualified opinion on Owens Corp.'s financial statements. Relying on these financial statements, Century Bank lent Owens $750,000. Ford was unaware that Century would receive a copy of the financial statements or that Owens would use them to obtain a loan. Owens defaulted on the loan. To succeed in a common law fraud action against Ford, Century must prove, in addition to other elements, that Century was

a. Free from contributory negligence.
b. In privity of contract with Ford.
c. Justified in relying on the financial statements.
d. In privity of contract with Owens. (11/91, Law, #3, 2331)

20. Under common law, which of the following statements most accurately reflects the liability of a CPA who fraudulently gives an opinion on an audit of a client's financial statements?

a. The CPA is liable only to third parties in privity of contract with the CPA.
b. The CPA is liable only to known users of the financial statements.
c. The CPA probably is liable to any person who suffered a loss as a result of the fraud.
d. The CPA probably is liable to the client even if the client was aware of the fraud and did **not** rely on the opinion. (11/94, Law, #10, 5188)

21. To be successful in a civil action under Section 11 of the Securities Act of 1933 concerning liability for a misleading registration statement, the plaintiff must prove the

	Defendant's intent to deceive	Plaintiff's reliance on the registration statement
a.	No	Yes
b.	No	No
c.	Yes	No
d.	Yes	Yes

(5/93, Law, #5, 3974)

22. An accountant will be liable for damages under Section 10(b) and Rule 10b-5 of the Securities Exchange Act of 1934 only if the plaintiff proves that

a. The accountant was negligent.
b. There was a material omission.
c. The security involved was registered.
d. The security was part of an original issuance. (5/93, Law, #10, 3979)

23. Under the provisions of Section 10(b) and Rule 10b-5 of the Securities Exchange Act of 1934, which of the following activities must be proven by a stock purchaser in a suit against a CPA?

I. Intentional conduct by the CPA designed to deceive investors.
II. Negligence by the CPA.

a. I only.
b. II only.
c. Both I and II.
d. Neither I and II. (11/94, Law, #11, 5189)

24. Under the liability provisions of Section 11 of the Securities Act of 1933, a CPA may be liable to any purchaser of a security for certifying materially misstated financial statements that are included in the security's registration statement. Under Section 11, which of the following must be proven by a purchaser of the security?

	Reliance on the financial statements	Fraud by the CPA
a.	Yes	Yes
b.	Yes	No
c.	No	Yes
d.	No	No

(11/94, Law, #13, 5191)

Items 25 and 26 are based on the following:

Dart Corp. engaged Jay Associates, CPAs, to assist in a public stock offering. Jay audited Dart's financial statements and gave an unqualified opinion, despite knowing that the financial statements contained misstatements. Jay's opinion was included in Dart's registration statement. Larson purchased shares in the offering and suffered a loss when the stock declined in value after the misstatements became known.

25. If Larson succeeds in the Section 11 suit against Dart, Larson would be entitled to
a. Damages of three times the original public offering price.
b. Rescind the transaction.
c. Monetary damages only.
d. Damages, but only if the shares were resold before the suit was started.

(5/92, Law, #3, 2816)

26. If Larson succeeds in the Section 10(b) and Rule 10b-5 suit, Larson would be entitled to
a. Only recover the original public offering price.
b. Only rescind the transaction.
c. The amount of any loss caused by the fraud.
d. Punitive damages. (5/92, Law, #5, 2818)

27. Which of the following statements concerning an accountant's disclosure of confidential client data is generally correct?
a. Disclosure may be made to any state agency without subpoena.
b. Disclosure may be made to any party on consent of the client.
c. Disclosure may be made to comply with an IRS audit request.
d. Disclosure may be made to comply with generally accepted accounting principles.

(11/94, Law, #14, 5192)

28. Which of the following statements is correct with respect to ownership, possession, or access to a CPA firm's audit working papers?
a. Working papers may **never** be obtained by third parties unless the client consents.
b. Working papers are **not** transferable to a purchaser of a CPA practice unless the client consents.
c. Working papers are subject to the privileged communication rule which, in most jurisdictions, prevents any third-party access to the working papers.
d. Working papers are the client's exclusive property. (5/94, Law, #10, 4765)

29. A CPA's working papers
a. Need **not** be disclosed under a federal court subpoena.
b. Must be disclosed under an IRS administrative subpoena.
c. Must be disclosed to another accountant purchasing the CPA's practice even if the client hasn't given permission.
d. Need **not** be disclosed to a state CPA society quality review team. (11/93, Law, #10, 4307)

30. Pym, CPA, was engaged to audit Silo Co.'s financial statements. During the audit, Pym discovered that Silo's inventory contained stolen goods. Silo was indicted and Pym was subpoenaed to testify at the criminal trial. Silo claimed accountant-client privilege to prevent Pym from testifying. Silo will be able to prevent Pym from testifying
a. If the action is brought in a federal court.
b. About the nature of the work performed in the audit.
c. Due to the common law in the majority of the states.
d. Where a state statute has been enacted creating such a privilege. (5/93, Law, #9, 3978)

31. A CPA is permitted to disclose confidential client information without the consent of the client to

I. Another CPA who has purchased the CPA's tax practice.
II. Another CPA firm if the information concerns suspected tax return irregularities.
III. A state CPA society voluntary quality control review board.

a. I and III only.
b. II and III only.
c. II only.
d. III only. (5/93, Law, #6, 3975)

32. Which of the following acts by a CPA will **not** result in a CPA incurring an IRS penalty?
a. Failing, without reasonable cause, to provide the client with a copy of an income tax return.
b. Failing, without reasonable cause, to sign a client's tax return as preparer.
c. Understating a client's tax liability as a result of an error in calculation.
d. Negotiating a client's tax refund check when the CPA prepared the tax return.

(5/94, Law, #8, 4763)

33. Clark, a professional tax return preparer, prepared and signed a client's 1992 federal income tax return that resulted in a $600 refund. Which one of the following statements is correct with regard to an Internal Revenue Code penalty Clark may be subject to for endorsing and cashing the client's refund check?
a. Clark will be subject to the penalty if Clark endorses and cashes the check.
b. Clark may endorse and cash the check, without penalty, if Clark is enrolled to practice before the Internal Revenue Service.
c. Clark may **not** endorse and cash the check, without penalty, because the check is for more than $500.
d. Clark may endorse and cash the check, without penalty, if the amount does **not** exceed Clark's fee for preparation of the return.

(11/93, Law, #9, 4306)

34. A CPA will be liable to a tax client for damages resulting from all of the following actions **except**
a. Failing to timely file a client's return.
b. Failing to advise a client of certain tax elections.
c. Refusing to sign a client's request for a filing extension.
d. Neglecting to evaluate the option of preparing joint or separate returns that would have resulted in a substantial tax savings for a married client. (5/93, Law, #7, 3976)

35. Starr, CPA, prepared and signed Cox's 1992 federal income tax return. Cox informed Starr that Cox had paid doctors' bills of $20,000 although Cox actually had paid only $7,000 in doctors' bills during 1992. Based on Cox's representations, Starr computed the medical expense deduction that resulted in an understatement of tax liability. Starr had no reason to doubt the accuracy of Cox's figures and Starr did not ask Cox to submit documentation of the expenses claimed. Cox orally assured Starr that sufficient evidence of the expenses existed. In connection with the preparation of Cox's 1992 return, Starr is
a. Liable to Cox for interest on the underpayment of tax.
b. Liable to the IRS for negligently preparing the return.
c. Not liable to the IRS for any penalty or interest.
d. Not liable to the IRS for any penalty, but is liable to the IRS for interest on the underpayment of tax. (5/93, Law, #8, 3977)

36. A CPA who prepares clients' federal income tax returns for a fee must
a. File certain required notices and powers of attorney with the IRS before preparing any returns.
b. Keep a completed copy of each return for a specified period of time.
c. Receive client documentation supporting all travel and entertainment expenses deducted on the return.
d. Indicate the CPA's federal identification number on a tax return only if the return reflects tax due from the taxpayer. (11/91, Law, #9, 2337)

37. A CPA owes a duty to
a. Provide for a successor CPA in the event death or disability prevents completion of an audit.
b. Advise a client of errors contained in a previously filed tax return.
c. Disclose client fraud to third parties.
d. Perform an audit according to GAAP so that fraud will be uncovered. (11/90, Law, #2, 0779)

38. In preparing Watt's 1986 individual income tax return, Stark, CPA, took a deduction contrary to a Tax Court decision that had disallowed a similar deduction. Stark's position was adopted in good faith and with a reasonable belief that the Tax Court decision failed to conform to the Internal Revenue Code. Under the circumstances, Stark will
a. Not be liable for a preparer penalty unless the understatement of taxes is at least 25% of Watt's tax liability.
b. Not be liable for a preparer penalty if Stark exercised due diligence.
c. Be liable for the preparer's negligence penalty.
d. Be liable for the preparer's penalty because of Stark's intentional disregard of the Tax Court decision. (11/87, Law, #33, 0802)

Solution 59-1 MULTIPLE CHOICE ANSWERS

Accountant's Civil Liability to Clients

1. (d) An auditor has a responsibility to exercise due professional care in the performance of the audit and the preparation of the report. CPAs are expected to comply with generally accepted auditing standards (GAAS). Although adherence to GAAS does not guarantee that there is no negligence, failure to follow GAAS would be a breach of a CPA's duty of due care. An oral report is not necessarily a breach of due care. Depending on the type of engagement involved, an oral report may be appropriate. Honest inaccuracies and judgmental errors will not give rise to negligence liability so long as the CPA exercised reasonable care in performing his or her work. A CPA in tax practice has a responsibility to use judgment to ensure that advice given reflects professional competence and appropriately serves the clients' needs. While one goal of tax advice is to save the client money, failure to do so does not necessarily result in a breach of a CPA's duty of due care.

2. (d) An auditor's best defense when sued for negligence is proof that the auditor did not violate generally accepted auditing standards in performing the audit. Lack of privity is not a valid defense with the client who engaged the auditor. A signed engagement letter is not a required part of the audit and the lack of such a letter would not be a valid defense for the auditor. Even if the auditor did not perform the audit recklessly or with an intent to deceive, it is still possible that the auditor failed to exercise reasonable care, under the circumstances, in conducting the audit.

3. (a) The law imposes upon the accountant the profession's generally accepted standards of competence and care. Thus, an accountant must demonstrate the average degree of learning and skill possessed by accountants generally. It is the financial statements that must be in conformity with GAAP. An accountant's duties under a contract with a client do not normally include a duty to discover fraud, unless the accountant's own negligence prevents him from discovering the fraud. The CPA could also be held liable for ordinary negligence.

4. (b) A CPA's contract for services to his client is governed by general common law contract rules. Therefore, the CPA's failure to perform as promised is a breach of contract. A CPA is not liable to his client under the concept of strict liability because this legal concept normally applies to merchant sellers. Strict liability provides that a merchant seller is strictly liable for the physical harm or property damage experienced by the ultimate consumer if the product was in a defective condition and unreasonably dangerous to the user.

5. (b) For an accountant to be held liable under common law negligence, a client must prove that the accountant failed to exercise due care under the circumstances. Sun need not prove that Frank knew of the irregularities, only that he failed to exercise due care. Gross negligence involves a reckless disregard for the truth and is an element of constructive fraud. Scienter is an element of fraud.

6. (a) Failing to correct errors discovered in the CPA's previously issued audit report is a failure to exercise due care, and the CPA would most likely be negligent. A CPA is not liable for detecting fraud unless the CPA's own negligence prevents him from discovering the fraud. An engagement letter does not include reference to a negligence disclaimer, rather it ensures that the auditor and client clearly understand the services the auditor is to perform. In general, it is against public policy to attempt to exclude the accountant's liability for negligence. Thus, a negligence disclaimer would most likely be unenforceable. Disclosure of irregularities to parties other than the client's senior management and its audit committee or board of directors is not ordinarily part of the auditor's responsibility, and would be precluded by the auditor's ethical obligation of confidentiality unless the matter affects his opinion on the financial statements.

7. (c) An accountant may be held liable to a client for negligence if he fails to exercise reasonable care (due care) under the circumstances. This liability may be imposed even if the errors were unintentional. Furthermore, the accountant need not be a fiduciary of the client for the client to charge him with negligence. The accountant's execution of an engagement letter is not one of the elements of a charge of negligence.

8. (a) The elements of constructive fraud are: (1) misrepresentation or omission of a material fact, (2) reckless disregard for the truth, (3) reasonable reliance by the injured party, and (4) injury. Proof of reckless disregard for the truth (gross negligence) satisfies the scienter requirement to support a finding of constructive fraud. All four of these elements must be present to support a finding of constructive fraud, as is the case when a CPA is grossly negligent in applying generally accepted auditing standards. Ordinary negligence is not sufficient to support a finding of constructive fraud. Third party users may

recover for fraud once they establish the elements of fraud, but the identification of the third party users is not an actual element of fraud. Scienter indicates that the misrepresentation was "knowingly made" and there was actual knowledge of the misrepresentation as compared to constructive knowledge. However, in general, reckless disregard for the truth will normally support a finding of scienter for purposes of a 1934 SEC violation.

9. (b) In a suit based on fraud, the plaintiff must prove: (1) false statements of a *material* fact knowingly made (scienter) or made with reckless disregard for the truth (constructive fraud), and (2) the plaintiff relied on the false statements and suffered damages thereby. The suit is not based on negligence where privity is an essential element. It does not matter if the CPA benefited from the alleged fraud or not. This is not a defense. The amount of damages suffered by the third party (the stockholder) is the important factor. Answer (d) applies only if the suit is based on negligence.

Liability to Third Parties--Common Law

10. (b) A CPA's liability to third parties who are unknown to the CPA will usually arise only if the CPA was grossly negligent. A CPA is not normally liable for ordinary negligence to third parties of whose existence the CPA is unaware. A CPA would normally be held liable for ordinary negligence to those third parties whom the CPA knew (or should have known) to be using the CPA's work product. CPAs are not strictly liable to anyone since they are neither engaged in an ultrahazardous activity nor sellers of a good in the stream of commerce (UCC 2). There is no standard of criminal deceit by which a CPA would have liability to unknown third parties.

11. (a) An accountant's liability to third parties for ordinary negligence normally extends only to those parties who the accountant specifically knew would be users of the work product. Thus, if the accountant did not know that the creditor would use the work product, privity would be a viable defense. Under the *Ultramares* doctrine, accountants owe a duty to all third parties to make their reports without actual or constructive fraud. Gross negligence amounting to a reckless disregard for the truth constitutes constructive fraud. Accountants have a contractual relationship with their clients, thus privity would <u>not</u> be a defense.

12. (c) In order to prove negligence under common law, Mac must prove the following:

1. A duty of care existed.
2. That duty of care was breached.
3. The injury was proximately caused by the defendant's breach of the duty of care.
4. The plaintiff suffered an injury.

Item I corresponds to the second element--"duty of care." Item II corresponds to the third element--"proximate cause." Thus, both items I and II are necessary in order for Mac to recover.

13. (a) Under common law (not under the Securities Act), the duty of care required for accountants is compliance with GAAP and GAAS. As long as an accountant conforms to generally accepted auditing standards in good faith, he or she will not be held liable to the client for incorrect judgment. Compliance with GAAS, however, does not *necessarily* relieve an accountant from all potential legal liability. Therefore, the editorial board feels that this answer is not entirely correct. "Awareness" of the misstatements is not a requirement in a negligence suit under common law. Most courts have adopted the position taken by the Restatement of Torts (in place of the *Ultramares* rule), which states that accountants will be subject to a suit by any *foreseen,* or *known,* users or class of users of the accountant's work product. The erosion of the *Ultramares* rule eliminates the necessity of privity of contract. Larson will be subject to a suit by any third party whom the accountant *knew* or *should have known* would be users of the accountant's work product.

14. (a) The four elements required in a fraud action include the following: (1) misrepresentation of a material fact; (2) intent to deceive or reckless disregard for the truth (constructive knowledge); (3) justifiable reliance by the injured party; (4) innocent party is injured. Thus, the best defense would be that the CPA did not have actual or constructive knowledge of the misstatements and so had no "intent to deceive." The client's knowledge of the misstatements does not affect the accountant's liability. Under the common law, a third party need only prove that he or she reasonably relied on the accountant's work. Privity of contract is never a defense to fraud under common law.

15. (b) The four elements of a common law fraud action include the following: (1) misrepresentation of a material fact; (2) intent to deceive; (3) justifiable reliance by the injured party; (4) innocent party is injured. Thus, lack of scienter is the best defense as there can be no "intent to deceive" if the CPA had no knowledge (scienter) of the misstatements. Privity of contract is not required in an action for common law fraud. Contributory negligence

is not considered in an action of common law fraud. An auditor can not disclaim liability to third parties through statements contained in an engagement letter.

16. (a) In order to prevail in a suit under the *Ultramares* doctrine the third party must show privity of contract when ordinary negligence took place. Since, under common law, for privity of contract to exist a person must have a contractual relationship with the person sued, in this case there is no privity of contract between Hark and Third.

17. (b) The general rule is that a CPA is not liable to third parties for injury caused by breach of contract between the CPA and his client (unless fraud or gross negligence is involved). The defense by the CPA is known as lack of privity between the CPA and the third party plaintiff. An exception exists, however, under the doctrine of "third party beneficiary." This exception exists where the third party is known by the CPA to be an intended user of the CPA's services. Therefore, First Bank can sue Smith for breach of Smith's contract with United. The breach here is Smith's negligence in not using reasonable care in independently confirming whether any material changes occurred between May 20 and August 5.

18. (d) A third party need not be an intended beneficiary in order to bring a charge of actual or constructive fraud. However, a third party must be an intended beneficiary, or one whom the accountant knew or should have known would be a user or beneficiary of the work product, before the third party may bring a charge of negligence.

18A. (b) Negligent misrepresentation requires proof of a misstatement of material fact upon which the other party relies to their detriment. It is not necessary to show that the misrepresentations were made with a reckless disregard for the truth nor that they be in writing.

19. (c) The *Ultramares* doctrine provides that an accountant may be liable to a third party for fraud in the accountant's reports regardless of whether or not the work was intended for use by the third party or for the accountant's clients. To recover damages, the third party must show that he or she reasonably relied on the accountant's work. The third party is not required to show privity with either the client or the accountant. Contributory negligence is not a defense to a charge of fraud.

20. (c) Under the *Ultramares* doctrine accountants owe a duty to ALL third parties to make their reports without actual or constructive fraud. It is

not necessary that the CPA have knowledge of or be in privity of contract with third parties to incur liability for fraud. The CPA will <u>not</u> be liable to a client who is aware of the fraud and did not rely on the opinion.

Liability to Third Parties--Federal Law

21. (b) To be successful under Section 11 of the Securities Act of 1933, the plaintiff must establish that he or she purchased securities which had been issued under a registration statement containing a false statement or an omission of a material fact and that he or she suffered an economic loss. The plaintiff need not prove reliance on the registration statement or the defendant's intent to deceive.

22. (b) In an action brought under Section 10(b) and Rule 10b-5 of the Securities Act of 1934, a plaintiff must prove the following: (1) there was a material misrepresentation or omission, (2) the plaintiff suffered damages, (3) the plaintiff relied on the fraudulent statement, and (4) existence of scienter. Negligence alone will not subject an accountant to liability under this section. Answer (c) is incorrect because this section covers transactions in both registered and unregistered securities. Section 10(b) and Rule 10b-5 apply to transactions involving the purchase or sale of any security within the jurisdiction of the SEC.

23. (a) Section 10(b) and Rule 10b-5 of the Securities Exchange Act of 1934 impose liability on anyone (including a CPA) who intentionally (or with reckless disregard) makes an untrue statement of fact or omits a material fact in an SEC annual report. It is <u>not</u> necessary that the stock purchaser prove negligence.

24. (d) To impose liability under Section 11 of the Securities Act of 1933, a purchaser of securities can hold a CPA liable upon proof that the financial statement either omitted or misstated a material fact. It is not necessary that the purchaser prove reliance or fraud, which requires proof of intent or scienter.

25. (c) The amount of damages generally recoverable under the Act is measured by the difference between the amount paid for the security and the market value of the security at the time of the suit. In no event can the amount of damages exceed the price at which the security was offered to the public. Treble damages are not permitted in such cases. The transaction cannot be rescinded. There is no requirement that the shares must have been resold before the suit was commenced.

26. (c) Where the defendant has violated the antifraud provisions [Section 10(b) and Rule 10b-5] of the Securities and Exchange Act of 1934, the plaintiff may recover the amount of loss caused by the fraud. The plaintiff would not be entitled to punitive damages.

Workpapers, Privileged Communications, and Confidentiality

27. (b) An accountant may disclose confidential client information to any party with the consent of the client. An accountant may not make disclosure to the IRS or state agencies except in response to an enforceable subpoena or court order. Answer (d) is also potentially correct since disclosure can be make in compliance with generally accepted accounting principles. Answer (b) is a better answer than answer (d) because an accountant may always disclose information with the client's consent.

28. (b) A CPA may not transfer working papers to a purchaser of his/her practice without the client's consent. Third parties may obtain working papers if they have an enforceable subpoena or court order. Federal law and the laws of most states do not recognize an accountant-client privilege. Under the common law working papers are held to be the accountant's property, although the client has a right to access them.

29. (b) A CPA may disclose working papers under the following circumstances:

- When the client gives permission to do so or when a client brings an action against the accountant.
- When a valid court order is served.
- When a CPA quality review board requests the information as part of a CPA quality review audit process.

An IRS administrative subpoena is considered a valid court order.

30. (d) Accountant-client privileged communications do not exist at common law. To be considered privileged, accountant-client communications must be located in a jurisdiction where a state statute has been enacted creating such a privilege. Federal law does not recognize privileged communications. Privileged communication refers to any communication intended to be confidential at the time of the communication, not just the nature of the work performed in the audit. Silo will be able to prevent Pym from testifying only if a state statute has been enacted creating such a statute. Accountant-client privilege does not exist at common law.

31. (d) The Code of Professional Conduct prohibits disclosure by a CPA of confidential information except in the following circumstances: (1) Where disclosure is pursuant to a voluntary quality review under AICPA authorization, (2) where disclosure is in compliance with an enforceable subpoena or court order, (3) where the client consents to the disclosure, and (4) to comply with GAAP or GAAS. A CPA must have permission from the client to disclose confidential information to another CPA who has purchased the CPA's tax practice or another CPA firm if the information concerns suspected tax return irregularities.

Tax Return Preparer's Liability

32. (c) A CPA will not incur an IRS penalty for an error resulting from an honest error in calculation. A CPA will incur a $25 penalty for each failure to provide a client with a copy of an income tax return, and a $25 penalty for each failure to sign a tax return as a preparer. A preparer of a tax return is liable for a $500 penalty per check for endorsing or otherwise negotiating a client's income tax refund check. (IRC §6695)

33. (a) Section 6695 of the IRC states that any income tax return preparer who endorses or otherwise negotiates any check which is issued to a taxpayer shall pay a penalty of $500 for each check.

34. (c) A CPA will not be liable to a tax client for refusing to sign a client's request for a filing extension. This extension can be signed by either the client or the preparer. The CPA has a primary responsibility to the client to see that the client pays the proper amount of tax and no more. The CPA must adhere to the same standard of truth and personal integrity in tax work as in all other professional activities. Failure to timely file a client's return or advise a client of certain tax elections, and neglecting to evaluate an option that would result in substantial tax savings would all violate the responsibilities of the CPA to exercise due care.

35. (c) According to TX §132, in preparing or signing a return, the CPA may in good faith rely without verification upon information furnished by the client or by third parties in most cases where the CPA has a reasonable belief in the information supplied by the client or third party. Therefore, Starr would not be liable to the IRS for any penalty or interest. Although the CPA has certain responsibilities in exercising due diligence in preparing a return, the client has the

ultimate responsibility for the contents of the return. Cox would be liable to the IRS for any penalty.

36. (b)   A CPA who prepares a client's federal income tax return for a fee must keep a copy of the completed return for three years or a penalty will be assessed. It is not necessary for the preparer to file notices and powers of attorney to enable him to prepare returns. The preparer is not required to receive client documentation supporting *all* travel and entertainment expenses. The preparer must furnish his preparer ID number on all returns for which he receives a fee.

37. (b)   While performing services for a client, a CPA may become aware of an error in a previously filed tax return. The CPA is required to advise the client of such error as required by Treasury Department Circular 230. A CPA has no duty as suggested by alternatives (a), (c), and (d).

38. (b)   Though an accountant will be subject to criminal penalties for willful preparation of a false return, if after due diligence in his research and analysis, an accountant has a reasonable, good faith belief in the correctness of his position, he will not be held liable. The percentage of understatement of taxes is not relevant in these circumstances. Any penalty for an understatement of liability due to a preparer's negligent or intentional disregard of rules or regulations does not extend to Tax Court decisions.

PERFORMANCE BY SUBTOPICS

Each category below parallels a subtopic covered in Chapter 59. Record the number and percentage of questions you correctly answered in each subtopic area.

Accountant's Civil Liability to Clients		Liability to Third Parties--Common Law		Liability to Third Parties--Federal Law		Workpapers, Privileged Communications, and Confidentiality		Tax Return Preparer's Liability	
Question #	Correct √	Question #	Correct √	Question #	Correct √			Question #	Correct √
1								32	
2		10		21		Question #	Correct √	33	
3		11		22		27		34	
4		12		23		28		35	
5		13		24		29		36	
6		14		25		30		37	
7		15		26		31		38	
8		16		# Questions	6	# Questions	5	# Questions	7
9		17							
# Questions	9	18		# Correct		# Correct		# Correct	
		18A		% Correct		% Correct		% Correct	
# Correct		19							
% Correct		20							
		# Questions	12						
		# Correct							
		% Correct							

ESSAY QUESTIONS

Essay 59-2 (15 to 25 minutes)

Butler Manufacturing Corp. planned to raise capital for a plant expansion by borrowing from banks and making several stock offerings. Butler engaged Weaver, CPA, to audit its December 31, 1989 financial statements. Butler told Weaver that the financial statements would be given to certain named banks and included in the prospectuses for the stock offerings.

In performing the audit, Weaver did not confirm accounts receivable and, as a result, failed to discover a material overstatement of accounts receivable. Also, Weaver was aware of a pending class action product liability lawsuit that was not disclosed in Butler's financial statements. Despite being advised by Butler's legal counsel that Butler's potential liability under the lawsuit would result in material losses, Weaver issued an unqualified opinion on Butler's financial statements.

[handwritten margin notes: "Negligency", "Violation of duty to comply with GAAS", "Gross. Neg.", "material - intentional"]

In May 1990, Union Bank, one of the named banks, relied on the financial statements and Weaver's opinion in giving Butler a $500,000 loan.

Butler raised an additional $16,450,000 through the following stock offerings, which were sold completely:

- June 1990--Butler made a $450,000 unregistered offering of Class B nonvoting common stock under Rule 504 of Regulation D of the Securities Act of 1933. This offering was sold over two years to 30 nonaccredited investors and 20 accredited investors by general solicitation. The SEC was notified eight days after the first sale of this offering.
- September 1990--Butler made a $10,000,000 unregistered offering of Class A voting common stock under Rule 506 of Regulation D of the Securities Act of 1933. This offering was sold over two years to 200 accredited investors and 30 nonaccredited investors through a private placement. The SEC was notified 14 days after the first sale of this offering.
- November 1990--Butler made a $6,000,000 unregistered offering of preferred stock under Rule 505 of Regulation D of the Securities Act of 1933. This offering was sold during a one-year period to 40 nonaccredited investors by private placement. The SEC was notified 18 days after the first sale of this offering.

Shortly after obtaining the Union loan, Butler began experiencing financial problems but was able to stay in business because of the money raised by the offerings. Butler was found liable in the product liability suit. This resulted in a judgment Butler could not pay. Butler also defaulted on the Union loan and was involuntarily petitioned into bankruptcy. This caused Union to sustain a loss and Butler's stockholders to lose their investments.

As a result:

- The SEC claimed that all three of Butler's offerings were made improperly and were not exempt from registration. *True*
- Union sued Weaver for
  - Negligence
  - Common Law Fraud
- The stockholders who purchased Butler's stock through the offerings sued Weaver, alleging fraud under Section 10(b) and Rule 10b-5 of the Securities Exchange Act of 1934.

These transactions took place in a jurisdiction providing for accountant's liability for negligence to known and intended users of financial statements.

Required:

Answer the following questions and give reasons for your conclusions.

a.   Will Union be successful in its suit against Weaver for:
1. Negligence?
2. Common law fraud?

b.   Will the stockholders who purchased Butler's stock through the 1990 offerings succeed against Weaver under the anti-fraud provisions of Section 10(b) and Rule 10b-5 of the Securities Exchange Act of 1934?   (11/92, Law, #3)

Essay 59-3 (15 to 20 minutes)

Goodwin, a CPA, and Jensen, a banker, were the trustees of the Moore Family Trust. The trust was created as a spendthrift trust and provided for distribution of income annually to the four Moore adult children for life, with the principal to be distributed to their issue after the death of the last income beneficiary. The trust was funded with commercial and residential real estate and a stock portfolio.

Goodwin, in addition to being a trustee, was lawfully employed as the trust's accountant. Goodwin, as the trust's accountant, prepared and signed all trust tax returns, kept the trust's accounting records, and supervised distributions to the income beneficiaries.

In 1990, Goodwin and Jensen, as trustees, sold a building owned by the trust for $400,000, its fair market value. The building had been valued at $250,000 when acquired by the trust. The $150,000 gain was allocated to income. In addition, the trust had rental, interest, and dividend income of $1,500,000 in 1990. Expenses for taxes, replacement of plumbing fixtures, roof repairs, utilities, salaries, and fees and commissions totaled $1,050,000.

On December 31, 1990, Goodwin and Jensen prepared and signed four $150,000 trust account checks and sent three of them to three of the income beneficiaries and the fourth one to a creditor of the fourth beneficiary. This beneficiary had acknowledged that the creditor was owed $200,000.

In February 1991, Goodwin discovered that Jensen had embezzled $200,000 by secretly selling part of the trust's stock portfolio. Goodwin agreed not to reveal Jensen's embezzlement if Jensen would pay Goodwin $25,000.

In April 1991, Goodwin prepared the 1990 trust income tax return. The return was signed by Goodwin as preparer and by Jensen and Goodwin as trustees and was filed with the IRS. Goodwin also prepared the 1990 income tax returns for the income beneficiaries. In an attempt to hide the embezzlement, Goodwin, in preparing the trust tax return, claimed nonexistent losses and improper credits. The beneficiaries' returns reflected the same nonexistent losses and improper credits. Consequently, the beneficiaries' taxes were underpaid. As a result of an IRS audit, the embezzlement was uncovered, the nonexistent losses and improper credits were disallowed, and the beneficiaries were assessed additional taxes, penalties, and interest.

Jensen cannot be located.

As a result of the above, the income beneficiaries sued Goodwin for negligence, fraud, and breach of fiduciary duty.

Required:

Answer the following questions and give the reasons for your conclusions.

Will the income beneficiaries win their suits against Goodwin for:

a. Accountant's negligence?

b. Actual fraud?

c. Breach of fiduciary duty as a trustee?

(5/92, Law, #3)

Essay 59-4 (15 to 20 minutes)

Sleek Corp. is a public corporation whose stock is traded on a national securities exchange. Sleek hired Garson Associates, CPAs, to audit Sleek's financial statements. Sleek needed the audit to obtain bank loans and to make a public stock offering so that Sleek could undertake a business expansion program.

Before the engagement, Fred Hedge, Sleek's president, told Garson's managing partner that the audited financial statements would be submitted to Sleek's banks to obtain the necessary loans.

During the course of the audit, Garson's managing partner found that Hedge and other Sleek officers had embezzled substantial amounts of money from the corporation. Those embezzlements threatened

Sleek's financial stability. When these findings were brought to Hedge's attention, Hedge promised that the money would be repaid and begged that the audit not disclose the embezzlements.

Hedge also told Garson's managing partner that several friends and relatives of Sleek's officers had been advised about the projected business expansion and proposed stock offering, and had purchased significant amounts of Sleek's stock based on this information.

Garson submitted an unqualified opinion on Sleek's financial statements, which did not include adjustments for or disclosures about the embezzlements and insider stock transactions. The financial statements and audit report were submitted to Sleek's regular banks including Knox Bank. Knox, relying on the financial statements and Garson's report, gave Sleek a $2,000,000 loan.

Sleek's audited financial statements were also incorporated in a registration statement prepared under the provisions of the Securities Act of 1933. The registration statement was filed with the SEC in conjunction with Sleek's public offering of 100,000 shares of its common stock at $100 per share.

An SEC investigation of Sleek disclosed the embezzlements and the insider trading. Trading in Sleek's stock was suspended and Sleek defaulted on the Knox loan.

As a result, the following legal actions were taken:

- Knox sued Garson.
- The general public purchasers of Sleek's stock offering sued Garson.

Required:

Answer the following questions and give the reasons for your conclusions.

a. Would Knox recover from Garson for fraud?

b. Would the general public purchasers of Sleek's stock offerings recover from Garson
    1. Under the liability provisions of Section 11 of the Securities Act of 1933?
    2. Under the anti-fraud provisions of Rule 10b-5 of the Securities Exchange Act of 1934?

(5/91, Law, #5)

Essay 59-5 (15 to 20 minutes)

In order to expand its operations, Dark Corp. raised $4 million by making a private interstate offering of $2 million in common stock and negotiating a $2 million loan from Safe Bank. The common stock was properly offered pursuant to Rule 505 of Regulation D.

In connection with this financing, Dark engaged Crea & Co., CPAs to audit Dark's financial statements. Crea knew that the sole purpose for the audit was so that Dark would have audited financial statements to provide to Safe and the purchasers of the common stock. Although Crea conducted the audit in conformity with its audit program, Crea failed to detect material acts of embezzlement committed by Dark's president. Crea did not detect the embezzlement because of its inadvertent failure to exercise due care in designing its audit program for this engagement.

After completing the audit, Crea rendered an unqualified opinion on Dark's financial statements. The financial statements were relied upon by the purchasers of the common stock in deciding to purchase the shares. In addition, Safe approved the loan to Dark based on the audited financial statements.

Within 60 days after the sale of the common stock and the making of the loan by Safe, Dark was involuntarily petitioned into bankruptcy. Because of the president's embezzlement, Dark became insolvent and defaulted on its loan to Safe. Its common stock became virtually worthless. Actions have been commenced against Crea by:

- The purchasers of the common stock who have asserted that Crea is liable for damages under Section 10(b) and Rule 10b-5 of the Securities Exchange Act of 1934.
- Safe, based upon Crea's negligence.

Required:

In separate paragraphs, discuss the merits of the actions commenced against Crea, indicating the likely outcomes and the reasons therefor. (11/88, Law, #5)

Essay 59-6 (5 to 8 minutes)

Birk Corp. is interested in acquiring Apple & Co. Birk engaged Kaye & Co., CPAs, to audit the 1987 financial statements of Apple. Both Birk and Apple are engaged in the business of providing management consulting services. While reviewing certain contracts entered into by Apple, Kaye became concerned with the proper reporting of the following matter:

- On December 5, 1987, Apple entered into an oral agreement with Cream, Inc., to perform certain management advisory services for Cream for a fee of $150,000 per month. The services were to have commenced on February 15, 1988 and to have ended on December 20, 1988. Apple reported all of the revenues related to the contract on its 1987 financial statements. This constituted 30% of Apple's income for 1987.

On February 1, 1988, Birk acquired all of Apple's outstanding stock. Birk's decision was based on the unqualified opinion issued by Kaye on Apple's 1987 financial statements. Within 10 days after the merger, Cream decided not to honor the agreement with Apple and gave notice that it had selected another management consulting firm. This caused the market value of the Apple stock acquired by Birk to decrease drastically.

Based on the foregoing, Birk has commenced an action against Kaye alleging negligence in performing the audit of Apple's financial statements.

Required:

Answer the following, setting forth reasons for any conclusions stated.

Discuss whether Birk will prevail in its action against Kaye & Co., CPAs. (5/88, Law, #5c)

Essay 59-7 (15 to 25 minutes)

Verge Associates, CPAs, were retained to perform a consulting service engagement by Stone Corp. Verge contracted to advise Stone on the proper computers to purchase. Verge was also to design computer software that would allow for more efficient collection of Stone's accounts receivable. Verge prepared the software programs in a manner that allowed some of Stone's accounts receivable to be erroneously deleted from Stone's records. As a result, Stone's expense to collect these accounts was increased greatly.

During the course of the engagement, a Verge partner learned from a computer salesperson that the computers Verge was recommending to Stone would be obsolete within a year. The salesperson suggested that Verge recommend a newer, less expensive model that was more efficient. Verge intentionally recommended, and Stone purchased, the more expensive model. Verge received a commission from the computer company for inducing Stone to purchase that computer.

BUSINESS LAW & PROFESSIONAL RESPONSIBILITIES

Stone sued Verge for negligence and common law fraud.

Required:

a.   State whether Stone will be successful in its negligence suit against Verge and describe the elements of negligence shown in the above situation that Stone should argue.

b.   State whether Stone will be successful in its fraud suit against Verge and describe the elements of fraud shown in the above situation that Stone should argue.

ESSAY SOLUTIONS

Solution 59-2 Accountant's Liability for Negligence/Common Law Fraud/Securities Act of 1934 Rule 10b-5

a.   1.   Union Bank will be successful in its negligence suit against Weaver. To be successful in a lawsuit for accountant's **negligence** there must be:

- **duty**
- **breach**
- **plaintiff must be a known intended user**
- **reliance**
- **loss**

Weaver was negligent in performing the audit by failing to confirm accounts receivable, which resulted in failing to discover the overstatement of accounts receivable. Weaver's failure to confirm accounts receivable was a **violation of Weaver's duty to comply with generally accepted auditing standards**. Weaver knew that Union would receive the financial statements and was thereby an **intended user**. Union relied on Weaver's opinion in granting the loan and, as a result, **suffered a loss**.

2.   Union will be successful in its common-law **fraud** suit against Weaver. To be successful in a lawsuit for common law fraud there must be:

- an **intentional material misstatement or omission**
- **reliance**
- **loss**

Weaver was **grossly negligent** for failing to qualify its opinion after being advised of Butler's potential material losses from the product liability lawsuit by legal counsel. Weaver will be liable to anyone who **relied** on Weaver's opinion and **suffered a loss** as a result of this **fraudulent omission**.

b.   Butler's stockholders who purchased stock under the 1990 offerings will also be successful in their suit against Weaver under Section 10(b) and Rule 10b-5 of the Securities Exchange Act of 1934. Under the Act stock purchaser must show:

- **intentional material misstatement** or **omission (scienter)**
- **reliance**
- **loss**

Weaver's failure to qualify its opinion for Butler's potential legal liability was **material** and done intentionally (**scienter**). Weaver will be liable for losses sustained by the purchasers who **relied** on Weaver's opinion.

Solution 59-3 Accountant/Trustee's Liability to Income Beneficiaries

a.   The income beneficiaries will win their suit for **negligence** against Goodwin. Goodwin was negligent in **improperly allocating trust income** and in **paying a beneficiary's creditor**. The beneficiaries sustained losses due to Goodwin's **failure to exercise the due care** required of a reasonable accountant.

b.   The income beneficiaries will win their suit for **fraud** against Goodwin. Goodwin **intentionally concealed the embezzlements** and **made material misstatements in the tax returns**. These actions are considered fraud and will permit the beneficiaries who relied on Goodwin to prepare the returns, to recover their losses.

c.   The income beneficiaries will win their suit for **breach of fiduciary duty** against Goodwin. The following fiduciary duties were breached by Goodwin:

- The fiduciary **duty of loyalty** by personally benefiting from and concealing the embezzlements.
- The fiduciary **duty of obedience** by paying the beneficiary's creditor.

- The fiduciary **duty of due care** by misallocating trust principal and income, paying the creditor, and falsifying tax returns.
- The fiduciary **duty to notify** by failing to inform the beneficiaries of the embezzlements.
- The fiduciary **duty to account** by maintaining improper records and profiting from the embezzlements.

Solution 59-4 Common Law Fraud/Under Securities Act 1933/Securities Act of 1934 Rule 10b-5

a. Knox would recover from Garson for fraud. The elements of fraud are: the **misrepresentation of a material fact** (because Garson issued an unqualified opinion on misleading financial statements. Garson's opinion did not include adjustments for or disclosures about the embezzlements and insider stock transactions); with knowledge or **scienter** (because Garson was aware of the embezzlements and insider stock transactions); and a **loss** sustained by Knox (because of Sleek's default on the loan).

b. 1. The general public purchasers of Sleek's stock offerings would recover from Garson under the liability provisions of Section 11 of the Securities Act of 1933. Section 11 of the Act provides that anyone, such as an accountant, who submits or contributes to a registration statement or allows **material misrepresentations or omissions** to appear in a **registration statement** is liable to **anyone purchasing the security who sustains a loss**. Under the facts presented, Garson could not establish a **"due diligence"** defense to a Section 11 action because it knew that the registration statement failed to disclose material facts.

2. The general public purchasers of Sleek's stock offerings would also recover from Garson under the **anti-fraud provisions** of Section 10(b) and Rule 10b-5 of the Securities Exchange Act of 1934. Under Rule 10b-5, Garson's knowledge that the registration statement **failed to disclose a material fact**, such as the insider trading and the embezzlements, is considered a **fraudulent action**. The **omission was material.** Garson's **action was intentional** or, at a minimum, a result of **gross negligence** or recklessness (**scienter**). These purchasers **relied** on Garson's opinion on the financial statements and **incurred a loss**.

Solution 59-5 Statutory Liability to Third Parties

Crea will not be liable to the purchasers of the common stock. Although an offering of securities made pursuant to Regulation D is exempt from the registration requirements of the Securities Act of 1933, the **antifraud provisions** of the federal securities acts continue to apply. In order to establish a cause of action under Section 10(b) and rule 10b-5 of the Securities Exchange Act of 1934, the purchasers generally must show that: Crea made a **material misrepresentation or omission** in connection with the purchase or sale of a security; Crea acted with some element of **scienter** (intentional or willful conduct); Crea's wrongful conduct was material; the purchasers **relied** on Crea's wrongful conduct; and, that there was a **sufficient causal connection** between the purchasers loss and Crea's wrongful conduct. Under the facts of this case, Crea's inadvertent **failure** to exercise due care, which resulted in Crea's not detecting the president's embezzlement, will not be sufficient to satisfy the scienter element because such conduct merely amounts to **negligence**. Therefore, Crea will not be liable for damages under Section 10(b) and rule 10b-5 of the Securities Exchange Act of 1934.

Crea is likely to be held liable to Safe Bank based on Crea's **negligence** despite the fact that Safe is **not in privity of contract with Crea**. In general, a CPA will not be liable for negligence to creditors if its auditor's report was primarily for the benefit of the client, for use in the development of the client's business, and only incidentally or collaterally for the use of those to whom the client might show the financial statements. However, a CPA is generally **liable for ordinary negligence to third parties if the audit report is for the identified third party's primary benefit**.

In order to establish Crea's negligence, Safe must show that Crea had a legal duty to protect Safe from unreasonable risk; Crea failed to perform the audit with the **due care or competence** expected of members of its profession; there was a **causal relationship** between Safe's loss and Crea's failure to exercise due care; **actual damage or loss resulted** from Crea's failure to exercise due care. On the facts of this case, Crea will be liable based on negligence since the audited financial statement reports were for the **primary benefit of Safe, an identified third party**, and Crea **failed to exercise due care** in detecting the president's embezzlement, which resulted in Safe's loss, i.e., Dark's default in repaying the loan to Safe.

Solution 59-6 Accountant's Liability for Negligence

Birk will prevail in its action against Kaye based on **negligence**. Kaye owed a duty to Birk to conduct the audit with **due care**. Kaye failed to conduct the audit with due care by issuing an unqualified opinion on Apple's 1987 financial statements when, in fact, Apple had made a **material error by reporting all of the revenues** related to the unenforceable December 5 agreement on its 1987 financial statements. Kaye's issuance of an unqualified opinion despite the material error caused Birk to **suffer damages** as evidenced by the **drastic decrease in the market value of Apple stock**.

Solution 59-7 Accountant's Liability--Consulting Service

a. **Stone will be successful in its negligence suit** against Verge. The elements of negligence are as follows:

- **duty of care owed**
- **breach of the duty**
- **loss caused by the breach of duty**

Verge Associates, CPAs **owed a duty** to its client, Stone Corp., **to perform** the consulting services engagement in a **competent manner** with the **expertise necessary** to perform the engagement.

Verge breached this duty by **incompetently preparing** the computer software programs. **As a result of the breach**, Stone **sustained damages** through increased accounts receivable collection costs.

b. **Stone will be successful in its fraud suit** against Verge. The elements of fraud are as follows:

- **false representation of a material fact**
- **done intentionally or with gross negligence**
- **justifiable reliance by the plaintiff**
- **resultant damages sustained by the plaintiff**

Verge Associates **falsely represented** that it was **recommending the best possible computer** to Stone when, in fact, it was recommending an inferior product. The computer to be purchased was **material** to the entire engagement. Verge made its recommendation **knowing that a better, less expensive computer was available**. Stone, as Verge's client, **justifiably relied** on Verge's recommendation. Stone was **damaged because** it spent more money for an inferior computer.

_____

APPENDIX A
BUSINESS LAW & PROFESSIONAL RESPONSIBILITIES FINAL EXAM

Problem 1 MULTIPLE CHOICE QUESTIONS (90 to 110 minutes)

1. Jackson Enterprises dismissed its auditors for cause. The CPA firm failed to complete its audit within the time stipulated due to its own inefficiency. Under the circumstances
a. The client has the right to all of the CPA's working papers relating to the engagement which are retained by the CPA.
b. The CPA firm is entitled to recover the full fee agreed upon less a per diem diminution of 5% for each day delayed.
c. Recovery by the CPA firm in quasi-contract will not be available if as a result of the delay the audit is worthless to Jackson.
d. If Jackson sues the CPA firm for damages for breach of contract, recovery will be denied because it is commonly recognized that unless the contract so stipulates, time is not of the essence.

2. Franklin engaged in extensive negotiations with Harlow in connection with the proposed purchase of Harlow's factory building. Which of the following must Franklin satisfy to establish a binding contract for the purchase of the property in question?
a. Franklin must obtain an agreement signed by both parties.
b. Franklin must obtain a formal, detailed, all-inclusive document.
c. Franklin must pay some earnest money at the time of final agreement.
d. Franklin must have a writing signed by Harlow which states the essential terms of the understanding.

Items 3 and 4 are based on the following information:

Bates ordered 1,000 units of merchandise from Watson, a wholesaler, at a unit price of $50 each, with delivery to be made at Bates' warehouse after April 11 but in no event later than April 15 with payment to be made 30 days after delivery. Watson accepted Bates' offer.

3. If Watson notifies Bates on April 1, that he will not be able to deliver the merchandise until May 2,

a. Bates may notify Watson that he is treating the contract as terminated immediately, but if he does so, he waives any right to damages for breach of contract.
b. If Bates elects to do nothing, he will be bound if Watson subsequently tenders the goods on April 15.
c. Watson's notification is without legal effect until actual breach occurs.
d. Watson's action gives Bates no right to recovery if Watson can show that a sudden drop in the market occurred and Watson would have suffered a greater loss if the contract had been performed.

4. If Watson ships the goods to Bates and the shipment arrives on April 12,
a. Bates must inspect all items at the time delivery is tendered or waive any defects.
b. Bates may inspect the goods prior to accepting delivery but may not accept conforming goods while rejecting the nonconforming goods if he wishes to preserve his remedies for any breach of contract as to the latter.
c. If Watson delivers 1,000 units of a newer model of the merchandise ordered, reasonably believing it to be acceptable, and Bates rejects the merchandise as nonconforming, Watson may hold Bates to the contract terms by reasonably notifying Bates of his intention to cure, and delivering conforming units by April 15.
d. If the goods are damaged but salable as damaged merchandise, Bates must immediately seek to sell them and then he may recover any loss as damages from Watson.

5. Joe Walters was employed by the Metropolitan Department Store as a driver of one of its delivery trucks. Under the terms of his employment, he made deliveries daily along a designated route and brought the truck back to the store's garage for overnight storage. One day instead of returning to the garage as required, he drove the truck twenty miles north of the area he covered expecting to attend a social function unrelated to his employment or to his employer's affairs. Through his negligence in operating the truck while en route, Walters seriously injured Richard Bunt. Walters caused the accident and

was solely at fault. Bunt entered suit in tort against the store for damages for personal injuries, alleging that the store, as principal, was responsible for the tortious acts of its agents. Under these circumstances

a. Metropolitan is not liable because Walters was an independent contractor.

b. Metropolitan is not liable because Walters had abandoned his employment and was engaged in an independent activity of his own.

c. Metropolitan is liable based upon the doctrine of respondeat superior.

d. Bunt can recover damages from both Walters and Metropolitan.

6. After proper incorporation of Alpha, it was decided to purchase a plant site. Gold, a newly elected director, has owned a desirable site for many years. He purchased the property for $60,000, and its present fair value is $100,000. What would be the result if Gold offered the property to Alpha for $100,000 in an arm's-length transaction with full disclosure at a meeting of the seven directors of the corporation?

a. The sale would be proper only upon requisite approval by the appropriate number of directors and at no more than Gold's cost, thus precluding his profiting from the sale to the corporation.

b. The sale would be void under the self-dealing rule.

c. The sale would be proper and Gold would not have to account to the corporation for his profit if the sale was approved by a disinterested majority of the directors.

d. The sale would not be proper, if sold for the present fair value of the property, without the approval of all of the directors in these circumstances.

Items 7 and 8 are based on the following information:

Jackson paid Brady $100 for a 90-day option to purchase Brady's 160 acre farm for $32,000. The option agreement was in writing and signed by both parties. The agreement referred only to the option, its period, a legal description of the farm, and the purchase price. Thirty days later, Jackson wrote Brady:

7. "I hereby exercise my option to purchase your farm for $32,000, subject to your replacing the well pump and related plumbing fixtures." Jackson's letter

a. Rejects Brady's offer and terminates the option agreement.

b. Accepts Brady's offer leaving customary details to be worked out during formalization of the contract.

c. Accepts Brady's offer leaving a matter to be negotiated during formalization of the contract.

d. Has no effect on the option agreement.

8. "I hereby exercise my option to purchase your farm for $32,000, subject to closing details to be worked out by you and my attorney." Jackson's letter

a. Rejects Brady's offer and terminates the option agreement.

b. Accepts Brady's offer leaving customary details to be worked out during formalization of the contract.

c. Accepts Brady's offer leaving a matter to be negotiated during formalization of the contract.

d. Has no effect on the option agreement.

9. Baker Loan Company made secured loans to Smith, Jack, and Roe. Smith gave Baker a security interest in his household furniture. Jack delivered Baker his rare coin collection as a pledge. Roe's loan is evidenced by his promissory note, payable over three years in monthly payments and secured by a security interest in the inventory of Roe's Clothing Store, a sole proprietorship owned by Roe. Proper security agreements were made and financing statements were duly executed and filed with respect to all of these transactions.

a. A filing of a financing statement is **not** required to perfect the security interest in Smith's household furniture.

b. Baker's security interest in Jack's coin collection was perfected before a financing statement was filed.

c. On filing a financing statement covering Roe's inventory, Baker's security interest herein was perfected for a maximum period of one year.

d. The financing statement for Roe's inventory must include an itemization and valuation of the inventory if the financing statement is to be valid.

10. Which of the following problems are within the competency of a CPA?

a. The validity of a will to be admitted to probate.

b. The parties who would have the standing in court to contest the validity of the will.

c. The validity of a trust created under the terms of the will.

d. The value of a decedent's gross estate at the time of death and alternate valuation date.

11. A client has joined other creditors of the Ajax Demolition Company in a composition agreement seeking to avoid the necessity of a bankruptcy proceeding against Ajax. Which statement describes the composition agreement?

a. It provides for the appointment of a receiver to take over and operate the debtor's business.

b. It must be approved by all creditors.

c. It does not discharge any of the debts included until performance by the debtor has taken place.

d. It provides a temporary delay, not to exceed six months, insofar as the debtor's obligation to repay the debts included in the composition.

12. Carter fraudulently misrepresented the quality and capabilities of certain machinery he sold to Dobbins. Carter obtained a check for $2,000, the amount agreed upon, at the time he made delivery. The machinery proved to be virtually worthless. Dobbin promptly stopped payment on the check. Carter negotiated the check to Marvel in satisfaction of a prior loan of $600 and received $1,400 in cash. Marvel, who had accepted the check in good faith, presented the check for payment which was refused by Dobbins' bank.

a. Even if Marvel is a holder in due course, Dobbins has a real defense.

b. Marvel can only collect for $1,400 in cash since he did not give new value beyond that amount.

c. Marvel will be able to collect the full amount from Dobbins.

d. Dobbins' timely stop order eliminates his liability on the check.

13. Philpot purchased the King Pharmacy from Golden. The contract contained a promise by Golden that he would not engage in the practice of pharmacy for one year from the date of the sale within one mile of the location of King Pharmacy. Six months later Golden opened the Queen Pharmacy within less than a mile of the King Pharmacy. Which of the following is a correct statement?

a. Golden has **not** breached the above covenant since he did not use his own name or the name King in connection with the new pharmacy.

b. The covenant is enforceable if it does not unreasonably restrain trade.

c. The covenant is unenforceable if Golden can prove that the opening of the Queen Pharmacy had no impact on the King Pharmacy's business.

d. The covenant is contrary to public policy and is illegal and void.

14. Harris is the trustee named in Filmore's trust. The trust named Filmore as the life beneficiary, with the remainder to his children at age 21. The trust consists of stocks, bonds, and three pieces of rental income property. Which of the following statements **best** describes the trustee's legal relationships or duties?

a. The trustee has legal and equitable title to the rental property.

b. The trustee must automatically reinvest the proceeds from the sale of one of the rental properties in like property.

c. The trust is a fiduciary with respect to the trust and the beneficiaries.

d. The trustee must divide among all the beneficiaries any insurance proceeds received in the event the real property is destroyed.

15. Which of the following defenses asserted by a surety should be effective in a suit by a creditor?

a. Insolvency of the creditor and the principal debtor.

b. Death of the principal debtor.

c. Failure of the creditor to foreclose a mortgage on property which he holds to secure the principal debtor's performance.

d. A material variance of the surety's undertaking as a result of a modification in the principal debtor's obligation.

16. Jack Gordon, a general partner of Visions Unlimited, is retiring. He sold his partnership interest to Don Morrison for $80,000. Gordon assigned to Morrison all his rights, title, and interests in the partnership and named Morrison as his successor partner in Visions. In this situation

a. The assignment to Morrison dissolves the partnership.

b. Absent any limitation regarding the assignment of a partner's interest, Gordon is free to assign it at his will.

c. Morrison is entitled to an equal voice and vote in the management of the partnership, and he is entitled to exercise all the rights and privileges that Gordon had.

d. Morrison does **not** have the status of a partner, but he can, upon demand, inspect the partnership accounting records.

17. Issuer, Inc., a New York corporation engaged in retail sales within New York City, was interested in raising $2,000,000 in capital. In this connection it approached, through personal letters, 88 people in New York, New Jersey, and Connecticut, and then followed up with face-to-face negotiations where it seemed promising to do so. After extensive efforts in which Issuer disclosed all the information that these people requested, 19 people from these areas purchased Issuer's securities. Issuer did **not** limit its offers to insiders, their relatives, or wealthy or sophisticated investors. In regard to this securities issuance,

a. The offering is probably exempt from registration under federal securities law as a private placement.

b. The offering is probably exempt from registration under federal securities law as a small offering.

c. The offering is probably exempt from registration under federal securities law as an intrastate offering.

d. The offering probably is **not** exempt from registration under federal securities law.

18. A CPA is subject to criminal liability if the CPA

a. Refuses to turn over the working papers to the client.

b. Performs an audit in a negligent manner.

c. Willfully omits a material fact required to be stated in a registration statement.

d. Willfully breaches the contract with the client.

19. Olson conveyed real property to his sons, Sampson and David, but the deed was ambiguous as to the type of estate created and the interest each son had in relation to the other. David died intestate shortly after Olson. David's widow and children are contending that they have rights in the property. Which of the following would be the widow's and children's best argument to claim valid rights in the real property?

a. The conveyance by Olson created a life estate in Sampson with a contingent remainder interest in David.

b. The conveyance by Olson created a joint tenancy with a right to survivorship.

c. The conveyance by Olson created a tenancy in common.

d. The widow is entitled to a percentage interest in the estate under state law.

20. Filmore hired Stillwell as his agent to acquire Dobbs' land at a price **not** to exceed $50,000; the land is badly needed to provide additional parking space for Filmore's shopping center. In order to prevent Dobbs from asking for an exorbitant price, Filmore told Stillwell **not** to disclose his principal. Stillwell subsequently purchased the land for $45,000. Under these circumstances

a. Stillwell and Filmore committed fraud when they did **not** disclose the fact that Stillwell was Filmore's agent.

b. Absent an agreement regarding the compensation to be paid Stillwell, he is entitled to the difference between the $50,000 limitation and the $45,000 he paid for the land, i.e., $5,000 based upon quasi-contract.

c. Dobbs may rescind the contract upon his learning the truth as long as the conveyance has **not** been accomplished.

d. Dobbs may sue either Filmore or Stillwell on the contract in the event of default by Filmore.

21. Seymore was recently invited to become a director of Buckley Industries, Inc. If Seymore accepts and becomes a director, he along with the other directors will **not** be personally liable for

a. Lack of reasonable care.

b. Honest errors of judgment.

c. Declaration of a dividend which the directors know will impair legal capital.

d. Diversion of corporate opportunities to themselves.

22. Forward Motor, Inc., is a franchised automobile dealer for National Motors. National provides the financing for the purchase of its automobiles by Forward. It sells Forward 25 to 50 automobiles at a time and takes back promissory notes, a security agreement, and a financing statement on each sale. The financing statement covering this revolving inventory has been duly filed.

a. Each automobile sold to Forward must be described and the serial number listed on the financing statement.

b. Sales by Forward to bona fide purchasers for value in the ordinary course of business will be subject to the rights of National.

c. No filing is required against the creditors of Forward since the automobiles are "consumer goods" in its hands.

d. As against the creditors of Forward, National has a valid "floating lien" against the automobiles and the proceeds from their sale.

23. The normal types of questions relating to estates and trusts which might be referred from a law firm to a CPA firm would include problems which involve

a. The order of distribution under the intestate succession laws.

b. Whether an ancillary proceeding is required.

c. The amount of property or money to be received by the income beneficiaries as contrasted with the amount to be accumulated for the remainderman.

d. Whether a will has been effectively revoked.

24. In the course of your audit of Baxter Corporation, you discover a claim against Willis, Inc., which is in bankruptcy. The approximate amount of recovery on this claim depends on the validity of the other claims against Willis. Which of the following statements is valid concerning the other claims against Willis?

a. The claims of secured creditors may be disregarded.

b. Priorities are of no importance since equity rule applies.

c. Judgments obtained as of the date of bankruptcy are legitimate claims against the bankrupt estate.

d. Anticipatory breaches of contract can be disregarded in assessing your client's position.

25. The good faith purchaser of a stolen stock certificate will defeat the claims of the prior owner(s)

a. Even though the certificate bears the forged endorsement of the prior owner.

b. Provided the certificate was endorsed in blank by the prior owner.

c. If the certificate contains **no** endorsement whatsoever.

d. If the certificate contains the full endorsement of one of the two prior joint owners.

26. A holder in due course will take an instrument free from which of the following defenses?

a. Discharge in insolvency proceedings.

b. Infancy of the maker or drawer.

c. Claims of ownership on the part of other persons.

d. The forged signature of the maker or drawer.

27. The intestate succession distribution rules

a. Do **not** apply to property held in joint tenancy.

b. Do **not** apply to real property.

c. Effectively prevent a decedent from totally disinheriting his wife and children.

d. Apply to situations where the decedent failed to name an executor.

28. Parker owed Charles $100,000 secured by a first mortgage on Parker's plant and land. Simons was the surety on the obligation but his liability was limited to $50,000. Parker defaulted on the debt and Charles demanded and received payment of $50,000 from Simons. Charles subsequently foreclosed the mortgage and upon sale of the mortgaged property netted $75,000. Simons claims a right of subrogation for his loss. Under the right of subrogation Simons should receive

a. Nothing.

b. $25,000.

c. $37,500.

d. $50,000.

29. Josephs & Paul is a growing medium-sized partnership of CPAs. One of the firm's major clients is considering offering its stock to the public. This will be the firm's first client to go public. Which of the following is true with respect to this engagement?

a. If the client is a service corporation, the Securities Act of 1933 will not apply.

b. If the client is not going to be listed on an organized exchange, the Securities Exchange Act of 1934 will not apply.

c. The Securities Act of 1933 imposes important additional potential liability on Josephs & Paul.

d. As long as Josephs & Paul engages exclusively in intrastate business, the federal securities law will not apply.

30. Kimball, Thompson, and Darby formed a partnership. Kimball contributed $25,000 in capital and loaned the partnership $20,000; he performed no services. Thompson contributed $15,000 in capital and part-time services. The partnership agreement provided that all profits and losses would be shared equally. Three years after the formation of the partnership, the three partners agreed to dissolve and liquidate the partnership. Firm creditors, other than Kimball, have bona fide claims of $65,000. After all profits and losses have been recorded there are $176,000 of assets to be distributed to creditors and partners. When the assets are distributed

a. Darby receives nothing since he did not contribute any property.
b. Thompson receives $45,333 in total.
c. Kimball receives $62,000 in total.
d. Each partner receives one-third of the remaining assets after all the firm creditors, including Kimball, have been paid.

31. Maurice sent Schmit Company a telegram offering to sell a one acre tract of commercial property located adjacent to Schmit's warehouse for $8,000. Maurice stated that Schmit had three days to consider the offer and in the meantime the offer would be irrevocable. The next day Maurice received a better offer from another party, and he telephoned Schmit informing him that he was revoking the offer. The offer was
a. Irrevocable for three days upon receipt by Schmit.
b. Effectively revoked by telephone.
c. Never valid, since the statute of frauds applies.
d. Not effectively revoked because Maurice did not use the same means of communication.

32. Martin agreed to purchase a two acre home site from Foxworth. The contract was drafted with great care and meticulously set forth the alleged agreement between the parties. It was signed by both parties. Subsequently, Martin claimed that the contract did not embody all of the agreements that the parties had reached in the course of their negotiations. Foxworth has asserted that the parol evidence rule applies. As such, the rule
a. Applies to both written and oral agreements relating to the contract made prior to the signing of the contract.
b. Does not apply to oral agreements made at the time of the signing of the contract.
c. Applies exclusively to written contracts signed by both parties.
d. Is not applicable if the statute of fraud applies.

33. Joseph Manufacturing, Inc., received an order from Raulings Supply Company for certain valves it manufactured. The order called for prompt shipment. In respect to Joseph's options as to the manner of acceptance, which of the following is incorrect?
a. Joseph can accept only by prompt shipment since this was the manner indicated in the order.
b. The order is construed as an offer to enter into either a unilateral or bilateral contract and Joseph may accept by a promise or by prompt shipment.

c. If Joseph promptly ships the goods, Raulings must be notified within a reasonable time.
d. Joseph may accept by mail, but he must make prompt shipment.

34. Base Electric Co. has entered an agreement to buy its actual requirements of copper wiring for six months from the Seymour Metal Wire Company and Seymour Metal has agreed to sell all the copper wiring Base will require for six months. The agreement between the two companies is
a. Unenforceable, because it is too indefinite.
b. Unenforceable, because it lacks mutuality of obligation.
c. Unenforceable, because of lack of consideration.
d. Valid and enforceable.

35. Monrad is contemplating making a contract for the purchase of certain real property. Which of the following is incorrect insofar as such a contract is concerned?
a. It must meet the requirements of the statute of frauds.
b. If the agreement is legally consummated Monrad could obtain specific performance.
c. The contract is nonassignable as a matter of law.
d. An implied covenant of marketability applies to the contract.

36. Milgore, the vice president of Deluxe Restaurants, telephoned Specialty Restaurant Suppliers and ordered a made-to-order dishwashing unit for one of its restaurants. Due to the specifications, the machine was not adaptable for use by other restaurateurs. The agreed price was $2,500. The machine **was** constructed as agreed but Deluxe has refused to pay for it. Which of the following is correct?
a. Milgore obviously lacked the authority to make such a contract.
b. The statute of frauds applies and will bar recovery by Specialty.
c. Specialty can successfully maintain an action for the price.
d. Specialty must resell the machine and recover damages based upon the resale price.

37. Gibbons Manufacturing shipped 300 designer navy blue blazers to Custom Clothing Emporium. The blazers arrived on Friday, earlier than Custom had anticipated and on an exceptionally busy day for its receiving department. They were perfunctorily examined and sent to a nearby warehouse for storage until needed. On Monday of the following week, upon closer examination, it was

discovered that the quality of the linings of the blazers was inferior to that specified in the sales contract. Which of the following is correct insofar as Custom's rights are concerned?

a. Custom can reject the blazers upon subsequent discovery of the defects.

b. Custom must retain the blazers since it accepted them and had an opportunity to inspect them upon delivery.

c. Custom's only course of action is rescission.

d. Custom had no rights if the linings were of merchantable quality.

38. The Balboa Custom Furniture Company sells fine custom furniture. It has been encountering difficulties lately with some customers who have breached their contracts after the furniture they have selected has been customized to their order or the fabric they have selected has been cut or actually installed on the piece of furniture purchased. The company therefore wishes to resort to a liquidated damages clause in its sales contract to encourage performance or provide an acceptable amount of damages. Regarding Balboa's contemplated resort to a liquidated damages clause, which of the following is correct?

a. Balboa may not use a liquidated damages clause since it is a merchant and is the preparer of the contract.

b. Balboa can simply take a very large deposit which will be forfeited if performance by a customer is not made for any reason.

c. The amount of the liquidated damages stipulated in the contract must be reasonable in light of the anticipated or actual harm caused by the breach.

d. Even if Balboa uses a liquidated damages clause in its sales contract, it will nevertheless have to establish that the liquidated damages claimed did not exceed actual damages by more than 10%.

39. Fifteen years ago Madison executed a valid will. He named his son, Walker, as the executor of his will and left two-thirds of his estate to his wife and the balance equally to his children. Madison is now dead and the approximate size of his estate is one million dollars. Which of the following statements is correct?

a. The will is invalid because it was executed at a time which is beyond the general statute of limitations.

b. The estate is **not** recognized as a taxable entity for tax purposes.

c. All the property bequeathed to his wife will be excluded from the decedent's estate for federal estate tax purposes.

d. Walker must, in addition to being named in the will, be appointed or approved by the appropriate state court to serve as the executor.

40. Barstow Hardware Company received an order for $850 of assorted hardware from Flanagan & Company. The shipping terms were F.O.B. Mannix Freight Line, seller's place of business, 2/10, net/30. Barstow packed and crated the hardware for shipment and it was loaded upon Mannix Freight's truck. While the goods were in transit to Flanagan, Barstow learned that Flanagan was insolvent in the equity sense (unable to pay its debts in the ordinary course of business). Barstow promptly wired Mannix Freight's office in Pueblo, Colorado, and instructed them to stop shipment of the goods to Flanagan and to store them until further instructions. Mannix complied with these instructions. Regarding the rights, duties, and liabilities of the parties, which of the following is correct?

a. Barstow's stoppage in transit was improper if Flanagan's assets exceeded its liabilities.

b. Flanagan is entitled to the hardware if it pays cash.

c. Once Barstow correctly learned of Flanagan's insolvency, it had no further duty or obligation to Flanagan.

d. The fact that Flanagan became insolvent in no way affects the rights, duties, and obligations of the parties.

41. Which of the following receipts should be allocated by a trustee exclusively to income?

a. A stock dividend.

b. An extraordinary year-end dividend.

c. A liquidating dividend whether in complete or partial liquidation.

d. A stock split.

42. Ford bought a used typewriter for $625 from Jem Typewriters. The contract provided that the typewriter was sold "with all faults, as is, and at the buyer's risk." The typewriter broke down within a month. Ford took it back to Jem, and after prolonged arguing and negotiations, Jem orally agreed to reduce the price by $50 and refund that amount. Jem has reconsidered its rights and duties and decided not to refund the money. Under the circumstances, which of the following is correct?

a. The disclaimer of the implied warranties of merchantability and fitness is invalid.

b. The agreement to reduce the price is valid and binding.

c. Jem's promise is unenforceable since Ford gave no new consideration.

d. Since the contract as modified is subject to the statute of frauds, the modification must be in writing.

43. Target Company, Inc., ordered a generator from Maximum Voltage Corporation. A dispute has arisen over the effect of a provision in the specifications that the generator have a 5,000 kilowatt capacity. The specifications were attached to the contract and were incorporated by reference in the main body of the contract. The generator did not have this capacity but instead had a maximum capacity of 4,800 kilowatts. The contract had a disclaimer clause which effectively negated both of the implied warranties of quality. Target is seeking to avoid the contract based upon breach of warranty and Maximum is relying on its disclaimer. Which of the following is a correct statement?

a. The 5,000 kilowatt term contained in the specifications does not constitute a warranty.

b. The disclaimer effectively negated any and all warranty protection claimed by Target.

c. The description language (5,000 kilowatt) contained in the specifications is an express warranty and has not been effectively disclaimed.

d. The parol evidence rule will prevent Target from asserting the 5,000 kilowatt term as a warranty.

44. Wilcox works as a welder for Miracle Muffler, Inc. He was specially trained by Miracle in the procedures and safety precautions applicable to installing replacement mufflers on automobiles. One rule of which he was aware involved a prohibition against installing a muffler on any auto which had heavily congealed oil or grease or which had any leaks. Wilcox disregarded this rule, and as a result an auto caught fire causing extensive property damage and injury to Wilcox. Which of the following statements is true?

a. Miracle is **not** liable because its rule prohibited Wilcox from installing the muffler in question.

b. Miracle is **not** liable to Wilcox under the workers' compensation law.

c. Miracle is liable irrespective of its efforts to prevent such an occurrence and the fact that it exercised reasonable care.

d. Wilcox does **not** have any personal liability for the loss because he was acting for and on behalf of his employer.

45. Smith has been engaged as a general sales agent for the Victory Medical Supply Company. Victory, as Smith's principal, owes Smith several duties which are implied as a matter of law. Which of the following duties is owed by Victory to Smith?

a. **Not** to compete.

b. To reimburse Smith for all expenditures as long as they are remotely related to Smith's employment and **not** specifically prohibited.

c. Not to dismiss Smith without cause for one year from the making of the contract if the duration of the contract is indefinite.

d. To indemnify Smith for liability for acts done in good faith upon Victory's orders.

46. In which of the following circumstances would a CPA who audits XM Corporation lack independence?

a. The CPA and XM's president are both on the board of directors of COD Corporation.

b. The CPA and XM's president each owns 25% of FOB Corporation, a closely held company.

c. The CPA has a home mortgage from XM, which is a savings and loan organization.

d. The CPA reduced XM's usual audit fee by 40% because XM's financial condition was unfavorable.

47. Gladstone has been engaged as sales agent for the Doremus Corporation. Under which of the following circumstances may Gladstone delegate his duties to another?

a. Where an emergency arises and the delegation is necessary to meet the emergency.

b. Where it is convenient for Gladstone to do so.

c. Only with the express consent of Doremus.

d. If Doremus sells its business to another.

48. Musgrove Manufacturing Enterprises is subject to compulsory workers' compensation laws in the state in which it does business. It has complied with the state's workers' compensation provisions. State law provides that where there has been compliance, workers' compensation is normally an exclusive remedy. However, the remedy will **not** be exclusive if

a. The accident was entirely the fault of a fellow-servant of the employee.

b. The employee dies as a result of his injuries.

c. The employee has been intentionally injured by the employer personally.

d. The employer was only slightly negligent and the employee's conduct was grossly negligent.

49. Yeats Manufacturing is engaged in the manufacture and sale of convertible furniture in interstate commerce. Yeats' manufacturing facilities are located in a jurisdiction which has a compulsory workers' compensation act. Hardwood, Yeats' president, decided that the company should, in light of its safety record, choose to ignore the requirement of providing workers' compensation insurance. Instead, Hardwood indicated that a special account should be created to provide for such contingencies. Basset was severely injured as a result of his negligent operation of a lathe which accelerated and cut off his right arm. In assessing the potential liability of Yeats, which of the following is a correct answer?

a. Federal law applies since Yeats is engaged in interstate commerce.

b. Yeats has **no** liability since Basset negligently operated the lathe.

c. Since Yeats did **not** provide workers' compensation insurance, it can be sued by Basset and cannot resort to the usual common law defenses.

d. Yeats is a self-insurer, hence it has **no** liability beyond the amount of the money in the insurance fund.

50. The third general standard states that due care is to be exercised in the performance of the audit. This standard means that a CPA who undertakes an engagement assumes a duty to perform each audit

a. As a professional possessing the degree of skill commonly possessed by others in the field.

b. In conformity with generally accepted accounting principles.

c. With reasonable diligence and without fault or error.

d. To the satisfaction of governmental agencies and investors who rely upon the audit.

51. Johnson lost a check that he had received for professional services rendered. The instrument on its face was payable to Johnson's order. He had endorsed it on the back by signing his name and printing "for deposit only" above his name. Assuming the check was found by Alcatraz, a dishonest person who attempts to cash it, which of the following is correct?

a. Any transferee of the instrument must pay or apply any value given by him for the instrument consistent with the endorsement.

b. The endorsement is a blank endorsement and a holder in due course who cashed it for Alcatraz would prevail.

c. The endorsement prevents further transfer or negotiation by anyone.

d. If Alcatraz simply signs his name beneath Johnson's endorsement, he can convert it into bearer paper and a holder in due course would take free of the restriction.

52. A client company has not paid its 19X3 audit fees. According to the AICPA Code of Professional Conduct, for the auditor to be considered independent with respect to the 19X4 audit, the 19X3 audit fees must be paid before the

a. 19X3 report is issued.

b. 19X4 fieldwork is started.

c. 19X4 report is issued.

d. 19X5 fieldwork is started.

53. Troy fraudulently induced Casper to make a negotiable instrument payable to the order of Troy in exchange for goods he never intended to deliver. Troy negotiated it to Gorden, who took with notice of the fraud. Gorden in turn negotiated it to Wagner, a holder in due course. Wagner presented it for payment to Casper, who refused to honor it. Wagner contacted Gorden who agreed to reacquire the instrument by negotiation from Wagner. Which of the following statements is correct?

a. Casper would have been liable if Wagner had pursued his rights on the negotiable instrument.

b. Gorden was initially a holder in due course as a result of the negotiation to him from Troy.

c. Casper is liable to all parties except Troy in that it was his fault that the instrument was issued to Troy.

d. Gorden can assert the rights of his prior holder in due course, Wagner, as a result of the repurchase.

54. Franco & Sons, Inc., was engaged in the furniture manufacturing business. One of its biweekly paychecks was payable to Stein, who negotiated it to White in payment of a gambling debt. White proceeded to raise the amount of the check from $300 to $800 and negotiated it to Carson, a holder in due course, for cash. Upon presentment by Carson at the drawee bank, the teller detected the raising of the amount and contacted Franco who stopped payment on the

check. Franco refuses to pay Carson. Carson is seeking to recover the $800. Under the circumstances, which of the following is a correct statement?

a. Franco is liable, but only for $300.
b. Franco is liable for the $800.
c. Stein is liable for the $800.
d. Franco has **no** liability to Carson.

55. Migrane Financial does a wide variety of lending. It provides funds to manufacturers, middlemen, retailers, consumers, and home owners. In all instances it intends to create a security interest in the loan transactions it enters into. To which of the following will Article 9 (Secured Transactions) of the Uniform Commercial Code **not** apply?

a. A second mortgage on the borrower's home.
b. An equipment lease.
c. The sale of accounts.
d. Field warehousing.

56. Bigelow manufactures mopeds and sells them through franchised dealers who are authorized to resell them to the ultimate consumer or return them. Bigelow delivers the mopeds on consignment to these retailers. The consignment agreement clearly states that the agreement is intended to create a security interest for Bigelow in the mopeds delivered on consignment. Bigelow wishes to protect itself against the other creditors of and purchasers from the retailers who might assert rights against the mopeds. Under the circumstances, Bigelow

a. Must file a financing statement and give notice to certain creditors in order to perfect his security interest.
b. Will have rights against purchasers in the ordinary course of business who were aware of the fact that Bigelow had filed.
c. Need take **no** further action to protect himself, since the consignment is a sale or return and title is reserved in Bigelow.
d. Will have a perfected security interest in the mopeds upon attachment.

57. Johnson loaned money to Visual, Inc., a struggling growth company, and sought to obtain a security interest in negotiable stock certificates which are traded on a local exchange. To perfect his interest against Visual's other creditors, Johnson

a. Need do nothing further in that his security interest was perfected upon attachment.
b. May file or take possession of the stock certificates.

c. Must take possession of the stock certificates.
d. Must file and give the other creditors notice of his contemplated security interest.

58. Jones, CPA, prepared Smith's 19X1 federal income tax return and appropriately signed the preparer's declaration. Several months later, Jones learns that Smith improperly altered several figures before mailing the tax return to the IRS. Jones should communicate disapproval of this action to Smith and

a. Take no further action with respect to the 19X1 tax return but consider the implications of Smith's actions upon any future relationship.
b. Inform the IRS of the unauthorized alteration.
c. File an amended tax return.
d. Refund any fee collected, return all relevant documents, and refuse any further association with Smith.

59. Donaldson, Inc., loaned Watson Enterprises $50,000 secured by a real estate mortgage which included the land, buildings, and "all other property which is added to the real property or which is considered as real property as a matter of law." Star Company also loaned Watson $25,000 and obtained a security interest in all of Watson's "inventory, accounts receivable, fixtures, and other tangible personal property." There is insufficient property to satisfy the two creditors. Consequently, Donaldson is attempting to include all property possible under the terms and scope of its real property mortgage. If Donaldson is successful in this regard, then Star will receive a lesser amount in satisfaction of its claim. What is the probable outcome of Donaldson's action?

a. Donaldson will **not** prevail if the property in question is detachable trade fixtures.
b. Donaldson will prevail if Star failed to file a financing statement.
c. Donaldson will prevail if it was the first lender and duly filed its real property mortgage.
d. The problem will be decided by taking all of Watson's property (real and personal) subject to the two secured creditors' claims and dividing it in proportion to the respective debts.

60. Gladstone Warehousing, Inc. is an independent bonded warehouse company. It issued a warehouse receipt for 10,000 bales of cotton belonging to Travis. The word "NEGOTIABLE" was conspicuously printed on the warehouse receipt it issued to Travis. The warehouse receipt also contained a statement in large, clear print that the cotton would only be surrendered upon return of the

receipt and payment of all storage fees. Travis was a prominent plantation owner engaged in the cotton growing business. Travis pledged the warehouse receipt with Southern National Bank in exchange for a $50,000 personal loan. A financing statement was **not** filed. Under the circumstances, which of the following is correct?

a. Travis' business creditors **cannot** obtain the warehouse receipt from Southern National unless they repay Travis' outstanding loan.

b. The bank does **not** have a perfected security interest in the cotton since it did **not** file a financing statement.

c. Travis' personal creditors have first claim, superior to all other parties, to the cotton in question because the loan was a personal loan and constituted a fraud upon the personal creditors.

d. The fact that the word "NEGOTIABLE" and the statement regarding the return of the receipt were conspicuously printed upon the receipt is not binding upon anyone except Travis.

SOLUTIONS

Solution 1   MULTIPLE CHOICE ANSWERS

1. (c)   If the audit was worthless to Jackson, then time was probably of the essence, and the CPA firm is not entitled to compensation for the value of its performance. Time may be of the essence even though it is not stipulated in the contract. The accountant, not the client, owns and has the right to possess his or her working papers. Absent an express provision in the contract, there is no legal basis for a 5% diminution of compensation as a measure of damages.

2. (d)   Contracts for the sale of real property are required by the statute of frauds to be written and signed by the party to be <u>charged</u> (Harlow, the grantor). The statute of frauds applies to all sales of real property. The writing must only include the <u>essential terms</u>, such as the identity of the parties, a description of the property, and the terms and conditions of payment.

3. (b)   Watson's action is an anticipatory repudiation. Unless Bates materially changes his position, or indicates that he considers the repudiation final, the repudiating party can retract his repudiation until his performance is due. Bates could, on the other hand, cancel <u>and</u> recover damages, even if they would be nominal.

4. (c)   When a buyer rejects nonconforming goods, the seller has the right to "cure" by delivering conforming goods within the time specified, after notifying the buyer of his or her intention to cure. A buyer may inspect goods within a reasonable time after accepting them.

5. (b)   The principal is vicariously liable through the doctrine of respondeat superior for its agent's or employee's torts when they are committed within the scope of the agent's employment. Walters departed from the performance of his duties and acted on his own, not in the scope of his employment, so Metropolitan is not liable either vicariously or for any other reason. Walters is an employee and not an independent contractor.

6. (c)   The sale would be proper and Gold would not have to account to the corporation for his profit if the sale was approved by a disinterested majority of the directors. The directors are then answerable to the stockholders for any wrongdoing.

7. (d)   Jackson's action raises a matter that will have to be settled <u>prior</u> to formalization of the contract; therefore, (b) and (c) are incorrect. His communication does not terminate the option agreement because he contracted to have the offer kept open for 90 days. His acceptance, adding new terms, may be a rejection and counter-offer sufficient to terminate an ordinary offer, but not sufficient to terminate an irrevocable option.

8. (b)   Jackson's letter accepts the offer leaving only the usual details to be worked out. It does not reject the offer or leave anything to negotiate. The option is effected; Jackson's letter exercises it.

9. (b)   Baker's security interest in Jack's coin collection was perfected by possession. Under Article 9, security interests in tangibles may be perfected without filing a security agreement by taking possession of the collateral.

10. (d)   A CPA should be competent to value a decedent's gross estate although he or she may need the assistance of an appraiser. Questions involving the validity of a will or trust are legal problems that should be handled by an attorney. Similarly, the issue of standing to challenge a will is a legal problem.

11. (c)   A composition agreement is an agreement between a debtor and its creditors in which the participating creditors agree to accept an immediate or early payment of a lesser sum in full satisfaction of the debt due them. The debtor must make all payments as contemplated by the composition agreement before it is discharged from any of the debts which are included in the agreement.

12. (c)   Marvel is a holder in due course because he took the check by negotiation, for value, in good faith, and without notice of the defense Dobbins had against Carter. As such, he will be able to collect the full amount of the check, since the defense of fraud in the inducement is a personal defense and not good against a holder in due course. Marvel gave value in the amount of $2,000 since the satisfaction of an antecedent claim is considered as value. Dobbin's stop-payment order will not affect his liability to the holder.

13. (b)   A covenant by the seller of a business not to directly compete with the purchaser (i.e., sell the same products in the immediate area for a limited period of time) is enforceable as long as its terms are reasonable. In this situation, the prohibition against practicing pharmacy within a one mile radius for one year is reasonable and therefore is valid.

14. (c)   A trustee stands in a fiduciary relationship with the trust and the beneficiaries. A trustee has a certain amount of discretion with regard to the investment and reinvestment of trust funds.

15. (d)   Any variance in the principal contract which materially changes the surety's position creates a defense in favor of the surety. The surety may not assert any of the debtor's personal defenses. A creditor is under no obligation to proceed first against any collateral security.

16. (b)   A partner may assign his or her partnership interest without dissolving the partnership. The assignee receives the assignor/partner's interest in the partnership property but not his or her right to participate in the management or control of the partnership.

Therefore, the assignee has no right to an accounting or to inspect the books.

17. (d)   This offering is a public offering because it is to more than 35 people who are not insiders or sophisticated investors able to take financial risks. The amount of the offering is in excess of that permitted under the small offering exception.

18. (c)   The Securities Act of 1933 and the Securities Exchange Act of 1934 provide criminal penalties for willful violations. Ordinary negligence and willful breach of contract do not give rise to criminal sanctions.

19. (c)   A tenancy in common is a joint estate with no right of survivorship. The interest in the estate descends to the heirs of the deceased (in this case, David's widow and children). The purpose of providing a widow with a stated percentage interest in the estate under state law is to protect her from action taken by her deceased husband. It does not affect a conveyance from him.

20. (d)   The third party may hold either the agent or the undisclosed principal liable on contracts made between the third party and the agent. Nondisclosure of the principal is neither fraud nor a ground for rescission. In the absence of an agreement for compensation, the amount of compensation is the reasonable value of the services rendered.

21. (b)   The directors will not be personally liable for honest errors of judgment. The fiduciary relationship does not require perfection on the part of the directors. Such a liability would deter the directors from ever taking any risks at all and corporate growth and advancement would be stifled.

22. (d)   Article 9 allows inventory financing. The secured party need only file a financing statement which adequately describes the collateral (inventory). Such a secured party also has a perfected interest in all proceeds of inventory sales for a minimum of ten days.

23. (c)   A CPA firm would normally handle problems involving the allocation of principal and income. An attorney should deal with problems involving revocation of a will, probate procedure, and the laws of intestate succession.

24. (c)   Judgments obtained as of the date of bankruptcy are valid claims and, thus, are allowable against the bankrupt's estate.

25. (b) Forgery is a real defense which would defeat the claim of a good faith purchaser. One of two joint owners cannot transfer an instrument. The endorsement of each joint owner is necessary. If the certificate were endorsed in blank, however, the purchaser's claim would defeat the prior owner, since the purchaser would have no notice of any problem, and there would be no real defense against him or her.

26. (c) A holder in due course (HDC) takes an instrument free from all claims to it by others (UCC 3-305). An HDC also takes free of all defenses of any party with whom he or she has not dealt except the following defenses: (1) infancy; (2) incapacity; (3) misrepresentation; (4) discharge in insolvency proceedings and (5) any other discharge the holder has notice of when he or she takes the instrument (UCC 3-305). Therefore, answers (a) and (b) are incorrect. Answer (d) is incorrect because all HDC's take subject to the defense of unauthorized signature of the maker or drawer where maker/drawer is not negligent.

27. (a) The survivor succeeds to the title of property held in joint tenancy regardless of whether or not there was a will. A decedent may disinherit his wife and children in spite of the intestate succession laws simply by executing a valid will or other estate planning device.

28. (b) Once a surety has completely discharged his or her obligation, he or she succeeds to the rights of the creditor. This right to subrogation includes the creditor's rights in the collateral. The creditor retains the primary rights to first satisfy the debt owed to him or her. Once Charles has taken the $50,000, Simons has the right to receive the remaining $25,000.

29. (c) Under the Securities Act of 1933, public offerings in interstate commerce may only take place after a registration statement has been filed with and accepted by the SEC. A financial statement certified by an independent public accountant must be included in each statement. The accountants preparing these statements are liable to any parties relying thereon for any statements which are knowingly false. Unlike common law actions, those based on the above provisions are not subject to any privity requirements as between the plaintiff and the accountants.

30. (c) The firm has $176,000 in assets which is distributed in the following manner: First, the creditors' claims (including Kimball's advance of $20,000) are paid, leaving $91,000. The partners are then reimbursed for their capital contributions, which leaves $51,000 in profits to be split three ways. In total, Kimball receives payment of his advance, $20,000, plus the amount of his capital contributions, $25,000, and his share of the profits, $17,000, for a total of $62,000.

31. (b) An offer can be revoked at anytime prior to acceptance even if it states that it will remain open for a fixed period of time, unless there was consideration given for the offer to remain open or unless the offer was a "firm offer" to sell goods by a merchant (UCC 2-205). There is no requirement that an offer be revoked by the same means as it was made as long as the revocation is received by the offeree before it is in fact accepted. Furthermore, there is no requirement that an offer to transfer real property be in writing but only that the eventual contract satisfies the requirements of the statute of frauds.

32. (a) The parol evidence rule states that if a contract is completely integrated into a written agreement, any other evidence--whether written or oral--of a prior or contemporaneous agreement is inadmissible if offered to contradict the terms of the written agreement. However, contradictory expressions made subsequent to the written agreement are admissible.

33. (a) The order placed by Raulings Supply is in fact an offer to Joseph Manufacturing. One of the terms set forth in this offer is the "prompt shipment" of the equipment; however, this does not mean that the offer may only be accepted by promptly shipping the goods. When it is unclear from the terms of the offer whether an act or a promise is required for acceptance, the offer is usually interpreted to permit acceptance by either a prompt promise to ship or by the prompt shipment of the goods (UCC 2-206).

34. (d) A requirement contract is an agreement by one party to buy his or her "requirements" of a given product from a certain supplier. The supplier's consideration is his or her promise to meet the buyer's requirements. The buyer provides consideration in that, generally, the buyer gives up his or her right to buy his or her requirements from other suppliers. Thus, answers (b) and (c) are incorrect because both Base Electric and Seymour Wire have given consideration in the form of their obligation to respectively buy and sell Base Electric's wire requirements. The contract is not too indefinite since it is for a stated period (six months), and the term "requirements" is defined by

law to mean the purchaser's good faith requirements.

35. (c)   Contracts for the transfer of an interest in real property must be in writing and signed by the party to be charged or bound by the contract. Furthermore, unless the contract specifies otherwise, it is implied that the seller will furnish a marketable title. In addition, because land is considered "unique," the buyer is entitled to specific performance. Answer (c) represents the only incorrect statement because, as a general rule, a contract is presumed assignable unless specifically stated to the contrary or unless assignment would materially affect the rights or duties of the other parties to the contract.

36. (c)   The statute of frauds does not apply to a sale involving goods specifically designed for a customer. Under the general rule applicable to seller's damages for repudiation, Specialty could attempt to sell the machine elsewhere and recover damages measured by the difference between the market price at the time and place of tender and the unpaid contract price together with incidental damages. However, the machine in this question was not adaptable for use by other restaurateurs; thus, the general rule is inapplicable and the seller can maintain an action for the price of the machine (UCC 2-709).

37. (a)   A seller has the duty to tender conforming goods, and the buyer has the duty to accept them. The buyer has "accepted" the goods when he or she:

(i)   Has an opportunity to inspect and signify that the goods are conforming, or if the buyer agrees to accept them with defects (in which case he or she has the right to sue for damages);
(ii)   Fails to make an effective rejection after a reasonable time; or
(iii) Does any act inconsistent with the seller's ownership of the goods.

Thus, in this problem there was no real acceptance since the goods were rejected and the seller was notified within a reasonable time after delivery. Answer (c) is incorrect since the buyer of noncomforming goods may accept them and sue for damages or agree to let the seller "cure" by delivering conforming goods. A buyer has the right to specify in the sales contract the quality of the goods to be provided.

38. (c)   A liquidated damages clause to a contract provides for a specific amount to be recoverable in the event of a breach of the contract. This clause will be enforceable if actual damages will be difficult to assess and the amount appears reasonable at the time of contracting. However, if the amount of the liquidated damages is deemed excessive, a court will probably interpret them as punitive damages and refuse enforcement. (Punitive damages are not allowed for a simple breach of contract, even if willful.)

39. (d)   An executor must be approved by the appropriate state court. There is no statutory limitation period beyond which a will becomes invalid.

40. (b)   If a seller discovers that a buyer is insolvent, he or she may stop delivery of goods in transit--regardless of whether the original contract called for F.O.B. shipping or destination terms--and demand payment in cash. This right can be exercised as long as the goods (or negotiable instrument of title) have not been delivered to the buyer or to a bailee who acknowledges their receipt and availability to the buyer. In determining whether the buyer is "solvent," the criterion used is whether the buyer is able to pay his or her debts as they become due, rather than whether the buyer's assets exceed his or her liabilities; thus, answer (a) is incorrect. Answer (c) is incorrect because Barstow has the duty to notify Flanagan of his stoppage and demand for cash payment. He must then wait a reasonable time before selling the goods elsewhere.

41. (b)   Cash dividends, whether extraordinary or not, should be allocated to income. Stock dividends and stock splits should be allocated to principal. Liquidating dividends are another example of the types of receipts which should be added to the trust corpus.

42. (d)   Jem Typewriters is a merchant with respect to the type of goods sold. Therefore, as a general rule, the law would imply a warrant of merchantability unless disclaimed by the seller. In this situation, all implied warranties were excluded by the language of the contract. The agreement reducing the sales price needs no consideration in order to be binding since it is under the Uniform Commercial Code. However, because the total reduced price was still over $500, the contract must comply with the statute of frauds before it will be enforceable.

43. (c)   The specification requiring a "5,000 kilowatt capacity" was an affirmation of fact which related to the goods and became a basis for the contract. As such, the quoted language constituted an express warranty. Answer (b) is incorrect

because the warranty was express, not implied. Answer (a) is patently erroneous. Answer (d) misstates the parol evidence rule; the quoted language was integrated into the written contract.

44. (c) Under the doctrine of respondeat superior, the employer is vicariously liable for the negligence of its employee, even though the employer, him- or herself is not at fault. Wilcox, as an employee, is covered by workers' compensation laws even though he was at fault. He is personally liable to third parties for his tort even though his employer is vicariously liable for the same tort. An injured third party may proceed against either Wilcox or Miracle, or both; however, he or she is only entitled to recover once.

45. (d) The principal owes his or her agent the duty to compensate him or her, to reimburse his or her reasonable expenses incurred in the course of the agency, and to indemnify him or her against loss for lawful acts performed at the principal's direction. The agent owes his or her principal the duty not to compete, but, in the absence of an agreement otherwise, the reverse is not true. An agency contract for an indefinite duration does not preclude a dismissal without cause for any particular period.

46. (b) ET 101.02 states that independence is impaired with respect to an entity if the CPA or his or her firm had any joint closely held business investment with such entity or any officer, director, or principal stockholder of the entity. This is the case in answer (b). Answer (a) is incorrect because the CPA's nonfinancial relationship to COD cannot impair his or her independence with respect to XM. Answer (c) is incorrect because CPAs can have home mortgages from clients that are financial institutions (ET 101.02). The CPA is not precluded from decreasing his or her audit fee [answer (d)].

47. (a) Ordinarily, the consent of the principal is necessary before an agent can delegate his or her duties. In the case of an emergency, however, a delegation may be made without the principal's consent.

48. (c) Workers' compensation recoveries are usually the exclusive remedy available to an employee injured in the workplace when there is no intentional infliction of injury. Thus, in workplaces where the employer has elected coverage (or where coverage is mandatory), the employee is left to the statutory amounts provided by state workers' compensation laws. An exception to this exclusive remedy rule occurs when the employer him- or herself intentionally inflicts injury on the employee.

In this situation, the employee may sue the employer directly for any injury sustained.

49. (c) A company which has complied with the Workers' Compensation Act may not be sued by an injured employee. However, if the company fails to comply with the Act, not only is the company open to suit, but it also loses the common law defenses. Thus, the employees' negligence is immaterial. Federal law does not apply to private industry injuries; all workers' compensation acts are state laws.

50. (a) Due care implies that if a professional offers his or her services, that professional is understood as holding him- or herself out to the public as possessing the degree of skill commonly possessed by others in the same employment (AU 230.03). Answer (b) is incorrect because GAAP relates to the presentation of the financial statements--not the conduct of an audit. Answer (c) is incorrect. Due care implies that the auditor performs the audit with good faith and integrity. It does not imply infallibility. Answer (d) is incorrect. An auditor's exercise of due care has no relation to the satisfaction of governmental agencies and investors.

51. (a) Words written above an endorsement indicating a purpose of deposit make the endorsement a "restrictive" one. A transferee who accepts an instrument with such an endorsement must give value consistent with the restriction in order to become a holder in due course. Thus, one who cashed the check for Alcatraz could not become a holder in due course. Alcatraz's signature would not convert the check into bearer paper because it is not payable to his order. Even if the restriction had purported to prohibit further transfer or negotiation, it would not have had that effect.

52. (c) ET 191.104 states that independence is considered to be impaired if fees for all professional services rendered for prior years are not collected before the issuance of the members' report for the current year. Thus, the 19X3 fees must be paid before the 19X4 report is issued.

53. (a) Since Wagner was a holder in due course, Casper's personal defense against Troy, fraud in the inducement, would not have been good against him. In an action on the instrument, Wagner would have prevailed against Casper. Gorden was not a holder in due course because he took the instrument from Troy with notice of the defense Casper has against him. Though ordinarily

the transferee of a holder in due course acquires the rights of the holder in due course, a person cannot improve his position by negotiating the instrument to, and then reacquiring it from, a holder in due course. Casper would not be liable to Troy on the instrument since it was Troy who dealt fraudulently with him.

54. (a) An alteration of the instrument that changes the contract of one who has signed it, e.g., a change in the amount payable, is a material alteration. Any material alteration gives the person liable on the instrument a real defense (good against holders in due course) as to the change; liability is only according to the instrument's original tenor--$300 in this case. Franco, as drawer, is primarily liable in the amount of $300, and Stein, as endorser, is secondarily liable for the same amount.

55. (a) Article 9 does not apply to any transactions in real property, and a mortgage is an interest in real property.

56. (a) A purchase money security interest in inventory may have priority over a conflicting security interest in the same inventory. To have priority, the secured party must file and must give notice to creditors who have a perfected security interest in the same types of inventory.

57. (c) Stock certificates are considered securities and are, therefore, instruments under Article 9. A security interest in instruments may only be perfected by taking possession.

58. (a) It is the client's responsibility to decide whether an error is to be corrected. The CPA is neither obligated to inform the IRS, nor may he or she do so without his or her client's permission. Thus answers (b) and (c) are incorrect. Answer (d) is also incorrect because the fee was properly collected for work performed and also because the CPA should advise the client about possibly amending the altered return.

59. (a) Detachable trade fixtures are not sufficiently attached to real estate for an interest in them to arise under real property law. Therefore, Donaldson's mortgage will not be secured by the trade fixtures.

60. (a) A proper method of perfecting an interest in a negotiable warehouse receipt is by taking possession. The bank need not surrender its security until the debt it secures (Travis' loan) is repaid.

ESSAY QUESTIONS

Essay 2 (15 to 20 minutes)

a. The Decimile Corporation is a well-established, conservatively managed, major company. It has consistently maintained a $3 or more per share dividend since 1940 on its only class of stock, which has a $1 par value. Decimile's board of directors is determined to maintain a $3 per share annual dividend distribution to maintain the corporation's image in the financial community, to reassure its shareholders, and to prevent a decline in the price of the corporation's shares which would occur if there were a reduction in the dividend rate. Decimile's current financial position is not encouraging although the corporation is legally solvent. Its cash flow position is not good and the current year's earnings are only $0.87 per share. Retained earnings amount to $17 per share. Decimile owns a substantial block of Integrated Electronic Services stock which it purchased at $1 per share in 1950 and which has a current value of $6.50 per share. Decimile has paid dividends of $1 per share so far this year and contemplates distributing a sufficient number of shares of Integrated to provide an additional $2 per share.

Required:

Answer the following, setting forth reasons for any conclusions stated.

1. May Decimile legally pay the $2 per share dividend in the stock of Integrated?
2. As an alternative, could Decimile pay the $2 dividend in its own authorized but unissued shares of stock? What would be the legal effect of this action upon the corporation?
3. What are the federal income tax consequences to the noncorporate shareholders:

(a) If Decimile distributes the shares of Integrated?

(b) If Decimile distributes its own authorized but unissued stock?

b. Clayborn is the president and a director of Marigold Corporation. He currently owns 1,000 shares of Marigold which he purchased several years ago upon joining the company and assuming the presidency. At that time, he received a stock option for 10,000 shares of Marigold at $10 per share. The option is about to expire but Clayborn does not have the money to exercise his option. Credit is very tight at present and most of his assets have already been used to obtain loans. Clayborn spoke to the chairman of Marigold's board about his plight and told the chairman that he is going to borrow $100,000 from Marigold in order to exercise his option. The chairman was responsible for Clayborn's being hired as the president of Marigold and is a close personal friend of Clayborn. Fearing that Clayborn will leave unless he is able to obtain a greater financial interest in Marigold, the chairman told Clayborn: "It is okay with me and you have a green light." Clayborn authorized the issuance of a $100,000 check payable to his order. He then negotiated the check to Marigold in payment for the shares of stock.

Required:

Answer the following, setting forth reasons for any conclusions stated.

What are the legal implications, problems, and issues raised by the above circumstances?

c. Towne is a prominent financier, the owner of 1% of the shares of Toy, Inc., and one if its directors. He is also the chairman of the board of Unlimited Holdings, Inc., an investment company in which he owns 80% of the stock. Toy needs land upon which to build additional warehouse facilities. Toy's president, Arthur, surveyed the land sites feasible for such a purpose. The best location in Arthur's opinion from all standpoints, including location, availability, access to transportation, and price, is an eight acre tract of land owned by Unlimited. Neither Arthur nor Towne wishes to create any legal problems in connection with the possible purchase of the land.

Required:

Answer the following, setting forth reasons for any conclusions stated.

1. What are the legal parameters within which this transaction may be safely consummated?

2. What are the legal ramifications if there were to be a $50,000 payment "on the side" to Towne in order that he use his efforts to "smooth the way" for the proposed acquisition?

Essay 3 (15 to 20 minutes)

a. Strom, Lane, and Grundig formed a partnership on July 1, 1990, and selected "Big M Associates" as their partnership name. The partnership agreement specified a fixed duration of ten years for the partnership. Business went well for the partnership for several years and it established an excellent reputation in the business community. In 1994, Strom, much to his amazement, learned that Grundig was padding his expense accounts by substantial amounts each month and taking secret kickbacks from certain customers for price concessions and favored service. Strom informed Lane of these facts and they decided to seek an accounting of Grundig, a dissolution of the firm by ousting Grundig, and the subsequent continuation of the firm by themselves under the name, "Big M Associates."

Required:

Answer the following, setting forth reasons for any conclusions stated.

1. Were there any filing requirements to be satisfied upon the initial creation of the partnership?

2. What will be the basis for the accounting and dissolution and should such actions be successful?

3. Can Strom and Lane obtain the right to continue to use the firm name if they prevail?

b. Palmer is a member of a partnership. His personal finances are in a state of disarray, although he is not bankrupt. He recently defaulted on a personal loan from the Aggressive Finance Company. Aggressive indicated that if he did not pay within one month, it would obtain a judgment against him and levy against all his property including his share of partnership property and any interest he had in the partnership. Both Palmer and the partnership are concerned about the effects of this unfortunate situation upon Palmer and the partnership.

Required:

Answer the following, setting forth reasons for any conclusions stated.

1. Has a dissolution of the partnership occurred?
2. What rights will Aggressive have against the partnership or Palmer concerning Palmer's share of partnership property or his interest in the partnership?
3. Could Palmer legally assign his interest in the partnership as security for a loan with which to pay off Aggressive?

Essay 4 (15 to 20 minutes)

a. A CPA firm was engaged to audit the financial statements of Martin Manufacturing Corporation for the year ending December 31, 1994. The facts revealed that Martin was in need of cash to continue its operations and agreed to sell its common stock investment in a subsidiary through a private placement. The buyers insisted that the proceeds be placed in escrow because of the possibility of a major contingent tax liability that might result from a pending government claim. The payment in escrow was completed in late November 1994. The president of Martin told the audit partner that the proceeds from the sale of the subsidiary's common stock, held in escrow, should be shown on the balance sheet as an unrestricted current account receivable. The president was of the opinion that the government's claim was groundless and that Martin needed an "uncluttered" balance sheet and a "clean" auditor's opinion to obtain additional working capital from lenders. The audit partner agreed with the president and issued an unqualified opinion on the Martin financial statements which did not refer to the contingent liability and did not properly describe the escrow arrangement.

The government's claim proved to be valid, and pursuant to the agreement with the buyers, the purchase price of the subsidiary was reduced by $450,000. This adverse development forced Martin into bankruptcy. The CPA firm is being sued for deceit (fraud) by several of Martin's unpaid creditors who extended credit in reliance upon the CPA firm's unqualified opinion on Martin's financial statements.

Required:

Answer the following, setting forth reasons for any conclusions stated.

Based on these facts, can Martin's unpaid creditors recover from the CPA firm?

b. A CPA firm has been named as a defendant in a class action by purchasers of the shares of stock of the Newly Corporation. The offering was a public offering of securities within the meaning of the Securities Act of 1933. The plaintiffs alleged that the firm was either negligent or fraudulent in connection with the preparation of the audited financial statements which accompanied the registration statement filed with the SEC. Specifically, they allege that the CPA firm either intentionally disregarded, or failed to exercise reasonable care to discover, material facts which occurred subsequent to January 31, 1994, the date of the auditor's report. The securities were sold to the public on March 16, 1994. The plaintiffs have subpoenaed copies of the CPA firm's working papers. The CPA firm is considering refusing to relinquish the papers, asserting that they contain privileged communication between the CPA firm and its client. The CPA firm will, of course, defend on the merits irrespective of the questions regarding the working papers.

Required:

Answer the following, setting forth reasons for any conclusions stated.

1. Can the CPA firm rightfully refuse to surrender its working papers?
2. Discuss the liability of the CPA firm in respect to events which occur in the period between the date of the auditor's report and the effective date of the public offering of the securities.

ESSAY SOLUTIONS

Solution 2

a. 1. Yes. The Model Business Corporation Act authorizes the declaration and payment of dividends in cash, property, or the shares of the corporation as long as the corporation is **not insolvent** and would **not be rendered insolvent by the dividend payment.** The Act **limits the payment** of dividends in cash or property to the **unreserved** and **unrestricted earned surplus** of the corporation. Decimile meets this requirement since it has retained earnings of $17 per share. Thus, payment of the dividend in the shares of Integrated is **permitted.**

2. Yes. The Model Business Corporation Act permits dividends to be declared and paid in the shares of the corporation. However, when the dividend is paid in its authorized but unissued shares, the payment must be out of **unreserved** and **unrestricted surplus.** Furthermore, they must be issued at **not less than par value. Concurrent** with the **dividend payment,** an amount of **surplus equal to** the **aggregate par value of the shares issued** as a dividend must be **transferred to stated capital.**

3. (a) If the shares of Integrated stock are paid as a dividend to the noncorporate shareholders, the shareholders must include the fair market value of the Integrated shares as **dividend income received,** and such income is **ordinary income.** The recipient taxpayer will have as a tax basis for the Integrated shares an amount equal to the **fair market value** of the stock received.

(b) If the shares of Decimile stock are paid as a dividend, the recipient taxpayer is not subject to tax upon receipt of the shares. Internal Revenue Code §305 provides that such stock dividends are **not taxable.** However, the recipient must **allocate** his or her **basis** (typically his or her cost) for the shares he or she originally owned to the **total number** he or she **owned after the distribution.**

b. The Model Business Corporation Act specifically deals with loans to employees and directors. If the loan is **not for the benefit of the corporation,** then such a loan must be **authorized by the shareholders.** However, the **board of directors may authorize** loans to employees when and if the board decides that such loan or assistance may **benefit the corporation.** It would appear that the loan was made for the benefit of the corporation so the latter rules apply. However, the chairman's individual authorization clearly does not meet these statutory requirements and could subject him to personal liability. Therefore, a meeting of the board should be called to consider the ratification or recall of the loan.

c. 1. The Model Business Corporation Act allows such transactions between a corporation and one or more of its directors or another corporation in which the director has a financial interest. The transaction is neither void nor voidable even though the director is present at the board meeting which authorizes the transaction or because his vote is counted for such purpose if--

- The fact of such relationship or interest is **disclosed** or **known to the board of directors** or committee that authorizes, approves, or ratifies the contract or transaction by a vote or consent sufficient for the purpose without counting the votes or consents of such interested directors; or

- The fact of such relationship or interest is **disclosed** or **known to the shareholders** entitled to vote and they authorize, approve, or ratify such contract or transaction by vote or written consent; or the contract or transaction is fair and reasonable to the corporation.

- **Common** or **interested directors may be counted in determining** the presence of a **quorum** at a meeting of the board of directors or a committee thereof that authorizes, approves, or ratifies such contract or transaction.

2. A $50,000 payment to Towne would be a **violation** of his **fiduciary duty** to the corporation. In addition, it might be **illegal** depending upon the criminal law of the jurisdiction. In any case, he would be obligated to return the amount to the corporation. Furthermore, the payment would constitute grounds for permitting Toy to treat the transaction as **voidable.**

Solution 3

a. 1. Yes. Although no filing of the partnership agreement is required, virtually all states have statutes that **require registration of fictitious** or **assumed names used in trade or business.** The purpose of such statutes is to **disclose** the **real parties** in interest to creditors and those doing business with the company. This is typically accomplished by filing in the proper office of public records the names and addresses of the parties doing business under an assumed name. The states vary greatly in detail (e.g., some states require newspaper publication).

2. The facts indicate a clear **breach of fiduciary duty** by Grundig. Section 21 of the Uniform Partnership Act holds every partner accountable as a fiduciary. It provides that "every partner must account to the partnership for any benefit, and hold as trustee for it any profits derived by him [or her] without consent of other partners from any transaction connected with the . . . conduct . . . of the partnership or from any use by him [or her] of its property." Grundig's conduct is squarely within the Act's language. Section 22 of the Act gives any partner a **right to a formal accounting of partnership affairs** if there is a breach of fiduciary duty by a fellow partner.

Section 32(c) and (d) of the Act provides for a **dissolution by court decree** upon application of a partner whenever--

- A partner has been **guilty of conduct** that tends to **prejudicially affect the business**.
- A partner **willfully** or **persistently commits** a **breach** of the partnership agreement or otherwise so conducts him- or herself in matters relating to the partnership business that it is **not reasonably practicable** to carry on the business in partnership with him.
- Certainly, Grundig's conduct would appear to fall within one or both of the above categories. He **breached** his fiduciary duty, was **dishonest** with his fellow partners, and was in fact **stealing** from his partners. Thus, the grant of application for dissolution would be appropriate.

3. Probably yes. Section 32(2)(b) of the Uniform Partnership Act relating to the right to continue the business in the same firm name, under the circumstances described, is narrowly drawn. This provision was designed to cover situations where the partnership has a fixed duration and one of the partners has caused a **dissolution wrongfully "in contravention of the partnership agreement."** The facts indicate that Big M Associates did have a **fixed duration** (10 years); consequently, this requirement is met. While the acts by Grundig are not in contravention of any specific express language of the partnership agreement, as would be the case where a partner wrongfully withdraws, the courts treat other types of wrongful conduct to be in contravention of the partnership agreement and, thus, to be the **basis for dissolution**. Strom and Lane could obtain the right to continue to use the firm name for the duration of the partnership agreement if Grundig's conduct was deemed **both wrongful and in contravention of the agreement**.

b. 1. No. Since the facts clearly indicate that Palmer is **not bankrupt**, his financial problems will **not precipitate a dissolution of the partnership**. However, if Palmer were bankrupt, the Uniform Partnership Act [§3(5)] specifically provides that the **bankruptcy of one of the partners causes a dissolution**. The fact that creditors take action against a delinquent partner's interest in the partnership, although annoying and inconvenient, does not result in a dissolution.

2. Aggressive will have **no rights to the partnership property** either directly or indirectly by asserting Palmer's rights. In fact, Palmer only has the right to the use of partnership property for partnership purposes. Since partnership property is insulated from attack by Aggressive, Aggressive will assert its right against Palmer's partnership interest. The method used to reach this interest is to reduce its claim against Palmer to a judgment and then obtain from a court a **"charging order"** to enable Aggressive to **collect on the judgment**. In effect, Aggressive has obtained a right comparable to a lienholder against Palmer's interest in the partnership. The "charging order" would provide Aggressive with the **right to payments** (earnings or capital distributions) that would ordinarily go to Palmer, the partner-debtor.

3. Yes. There is **nothing** in the Uniform Partnership Act that **prevents** a partner from **assigning all** or **part** of his or her interest in a partnership. The assignment may be outright or for the more common purpose of securing a loan. If there is to be any such restriction on a partner's right to assign his partnership interest, the partnership agreement must so provide. Section 27 of the Uniform Partnership Act specifically provides that a partner's **assignment** of his or her partnership interest **does not cause a dissolution. The Act limits such an assignment to the partner's right to share in profits and capital distributions** but does not make the assignee a partner.

Solution 4

a. Yes. The CPA firm is guilty of **common law deceit**, commonly referred to as **"fraud."** The CPA firm was associated with financial statements that were not in conformity with generally accepted accounting principles because of the failure to disclose the restriction on the cash received, as well as the contingent liability. This association constitutes the commission of an **actionable tort** (**deceit**) upon the creditors. The fact that there was no privity of contract between the creditors and the accountants is **immaterial** in relation to an action based on deceit. When deceit is involved, the defense of **lack of privity** is **not available**. Deceit is an **intentional tort**, and those who engage in it must bear the burden of their wrongdoing, even though they may not have intended harm to those affected. The common law elements of deceit in general are:

1. A **false representation** of a **material fact** made by the defendant.
2. **Knowledge** or **belief of falsity**, technically described as "**scienter**."
3. An **intent** that the plaintiff **rely upon** the false representation.
4. **Damage** as a result of the reliance.

Clearly, the elements of deceit are present. The only element that needs further elaboration is the "scienter" requirement. About the only defense available to the CPA firm would be that it honestly believed that the government's claim was groundless based upon the president's statement. However, even if this were true, the CPA firm did not have sufficient basis to express an unqualified opinion that the financial statements were fairly presented. The law includes not only representations made with actual knowledge or belief of falsity, but also those made with a **reckless disregard for the truth**. The fact that the CPA firm **did not intend to harm anyone** is **irrelevant**. The CPA firm must be considered liable in light of its training, qualifications, and responsibility and its duty to those who would read, and might act upon, financial statements with which the firm is associated.

b. 1. No. **Neither federal nor common law recognizes** the validity of the **privilege rule** insofar as accountants are concerned. Furthermore, even when the privilege rule is applicable, it can only be claimed by the client. Only a limited number of jurisdictions have by statute overridden the common law rule which does not consider such communications to be within the privilege rule. The privilege rule applies principally to the attorney-client and doctor-patient relationships.

2. The Securities Act of 1933 **requires** a review by the auditor who reported on the financial statements accompanying the registration statement of events in the period between the date of the auditor's report and the date of the public sale of the securities. The auditors must show that they made a **reasonable investigation**, had a **reasonable basis** for their belief, and they did believe the financial statements were true as of the time the registration statement became effective. The auditor-defendants have the **burden of proving** that the requisite standard was met. Therefore, unless the auditors can satisfy the foregoing tests, they will be liable.

NOTES

BUSINESS LAW AND PROFESSIONAL RESPONSIBILITIES INDEX

A

Abandonment, Leasehold 56-15
Abatement, Defined 53-5
Acceptance
    Commercial Paper 45-3, 45-27
    Insurance Contracts 57-4
Accessions
    Defined 47-2
    Security Interests in 47-17
Accommodation Party 45-3, 45-25
Accord and Satisfaction 43-24
Accountant's Professional Liability
    Audit Liability 59-9
    Civil Liability to Clients 59-2
    Civil Liability to Third Parties 59-4
    Communications, Privileged/Confidential 59-8
    Contractual Duties 59-2
    Contractual Liability 59-2, 59-5
    Criminal Liability 59-7
    Damages 59-2, 59-5
    Defense, Due Diligence 59-6
    Duty of Nondisclosure 59-8
    Duty to Discover Irregularities 59-9
    Ethical Protection From Disclosure 59-8
    Ethics 59-8
    Federal Criminal Laws 59-8
    Financial Statements, Unaudited 59-9
    Fraud 59-2, 59-4
    Fraudulent Execution of Documents 59-7
    Gross Negligence 59-4
    Inadequate Disclosure 59-9
    Internal Revenue Code 59-7
    Liability for Another Auditor's Work 59-9
    Negligence 59-3
    Negligence Liability 59-5
    Penalties, Preparer 59-10
    Standard of Reasonable Care 59-3
    State Criminal Laws 59-8
    Subsequent Changes 59-9
    Tax Returns, Preparation of 59-10
    Third Parties Under Federal Statutes, to 59-5
    Third-Party Beneficiary 59-2
    Ultramares Doctrine 59-5
    Working Papers 59-8
Actual Authority
    Express 51-9
    Implied 51-9
Ademption, Defined 53-5
Administration
    Bankruptcy 48-6
    Estates 53-4
    Workers' Compensation 54-7
Adverse Possession 56-11
After-Acquired Property Clause
    Defined 47-2
    Security Agreement 47-6
Agency
    Appointment 50-4
    Approval or Ratification 50-4
    Capacity 50-2
    Contractual Arrangement 50-2

    Corporations 50-2
    Coupled With an Interest 50-3, 50-9
    Creation of 50-4
    Defined 50-2
    Duties Between Principal and Agent 50-8
    Estoppel 50-5
    Express 50-4
    Fiduciary Relationship 50-2
    Implied 50-4
    Irrevocable 50-3
    Liability of the Principal 50-6
    Necessity 50-5
    Operation of Law 50-5
    Partnerships 50-2
    Power of Attorney 50-4
    Principal 50-7
    Property Interest 50-3
    Ratification 50-5
    Renunciation 50-9
    Representation or Appearance by 50-5
    Respondeat Superior 50-6
    Revocation 50-9
    Sub-agency 50-3
    Termination 50-9, 50-10
    Third Parties 50-7
    Torts 50-7
    Types of Agents 50-3
    Writing 50-4
Agent
    Agent, of an 50-3
    Authority 50-5, 50-6
    Bankruptcy of the 50-10
    Capacity To Be an 50-3
    Co-Agent 50-3
    Criminal Liability of 50-6
    Defenses 50-7
    Del Credere 50-3
    Del Credere (Suretyship) 49-4
    Duties 50-4, 50-8
    Exclusive 50-3
    Factor 50-3
    Fire and Casualty Insurance 57-5
    General 50-3
    Gratuitous 50-3
    Independent Contractor 50-2
    Legal Effect of Apparent Authority 50-5
    Liability 50-7
    Misrepresentation 50-7
    Negligence 50-9
    Respondeat Superior 50-2
    Servant 50-2
    Special 50-3
    Sub-Agent 50-3
Alienable Right (Alienable Interest) 56-2
Americans With Disabilities Act of 1990 54-9
Antibribery 59-4
Anticipatory Breach 43-26
Anticipatory Repudiation 44-21
Apparent Authority
    Agent, of 50-5
    Partner, of 51-9

Article 1 (UCC)..45-3, 45-16
Article 2 (UCC)..44-5
Article 3 (UCC)..........................45-3, 46-4, 46-6
Article 4 (UCC)..45-4, 45-35
Article 7 (UCC)..46-3, 44-4
Article 8 (UCC)..46-6, 46-7
Article 9 (UCC)..57-3
Articles of Incorporation
    Authorized Capital.............................52-6
    Defined..52-5
Articles of Partnership................................51-4
Ascendants, Defined..................................53-4
Assignment
    Defined..43-19
    Delegation, Compared.....................43-20
    Insurance Contracts..........................57-7
    Prohibition Against............................43-19
Assured, Defined.......................................57-2
Automatic Stay...48-9
Automobile Liability Insurance.................57-4

B

Bailee
    Defined..44-4, 46-2
    Duties of...56-20
    Goods Held by...................................44-10
Bailment
    Defined..44-4
    Elements of..56-20
    Parties Involved in............................44-4
Bailor...44-4, 56-20
Bank Draft..45-5
Banker's Acceptance.................................45-5
Bankruptcy
    Administration of Cases....................48-6
    Chapter 11..48-5
    Chapter 13..48-5
    Chapter 7..48-5
    Chapter 9..48-5
    Creditor...48-2
    Creditors' Committee.........................48-6
    Custodian..48-2
    Debtor..48-2
    Debtor Rehabilitation Proceedings...48-5
    Debts of an Individual.......................48-5
    Distribution Rules..............................48-13
    Federal Nonbankruptcy Law.............48-14
    Insolvency...48-2
    Involuntary..48-7
    Joint...48-7
    Municipality..48-5
    Offenses..48-17
    Overview...48-5
    Partnerships, of.................................51-12
    Person, Defined.................................48-6
    Petition..48-7
    Priority Claims...................................48-12
    Proofs of Claims or Interests...........48-10
    Remedies Under State Law Prior to Bankruptcy.....48-3
    Reorganizations................................48-5
    Secured Claims.................................48-12
    Straight Bankruptcy or Liquidation..48-5
    Voluntary..48-7
Bankruptcy Estate
    Administration of...............................48-8
    Administrative Expenses..................48-11
    Claims Against..................................48-9
    Community Property...........................48-14

Compensation for Professional Services...............48-12
Custodian..48-18
Damages Against 48-10
Debtor or Debtor in Possession.................48-10
Defined...48-2, 48-18
Exceptions to Transfers.............................48-19
Exempt Property...48-14
Exemption Laws...48-14
Fraudulent Transfers..................................48-20
Joint Tenant..48-14
Liens Against..48-9
Preferential Transfers.................................48-19
Preserving the Estate.................................48-11
Promissory Note...48-10
Property Not a Part of................................48-18
Rights Acquired..48-19
Statutory Liens...48-19
Taxes Incurred by.......................................48-11
Tenant by the Entirety................................48-14
Use, Sale, or Lease of Property................48-10
Bankruptcy, Administration of Cases
    Administrative Powers......................48-9
    Alimony, Maintenance, or Support Payments..........48-9
    Automatic Stay...................................48-9
    Chapter 11 Reorganizations.............48-6
    Chapter 13 for Individuals................48-6
    Chapter 7 Liquidation.............48-6, 48-13
    Custodian..48-8
    Debtor..48-6
    Discharge of the Debtor....................48-15
    Discharge, Bankruptcy Offenses......48-17
    Discharge, Effect of..........................48-16
    Discharge, Exceptions to..................48-15
    Discharge, Revocation of..................48-18
    Discharge, Rules Applicable to Chapter 7 Cases..48-17
    Duties and Responsibilities of Trustee and
        Debtor...48-8
    Involuntary Bankruptcy......................48-7
    Joint Bankruptcy................................48-7
    Liens..48-9
    Municipality..48-6
    Notice of Tax Deficiency...................48-10
    Partnership...48-7
    Petition..48-7
    Tax Debts...48-15
    Trustee..48-8
    Voluntary Bankruptcy.........................48-7
    Waiver of Discharge..........................48-18
    Witness Fees......................................48-12
Bankruptcy, Remedies Prior to
    Collective Actions..............................48-3
    Composition or Extension Agreement.....................48-4
    Creditor's Petition.............................48-4
    Creditors' Actions to Set Aside Fraudulent
        Conveyances................................48-3
    Equity Receivership...........................48-4
    Execution..48-3
    Fraudulent Conveyance....................48-3
    Judgment..48-3
    Legal Actions Available to Creditors.......................48-3
    Transfer of Exempt Property.............48-3
    Writ of Attachment.............................48-3
Beneficial Ownership, Defined..................55-2
Beneficiary
    Also see Estates; Trusts...................53-7
    Creditor...43-21
    Donee..43-21
    Incidental..43-21
    Third Party..................................43-22, 59-2
    Will or Trust of...................................53-2

Benefits
    Social Security 54-4
    Unemployment Insurance 54-5
    Workers' Compensation.......................................54-6
Bill of Lading
    Consignee...46-2
    Consignor 46-2
    Defined 46-2
    Destination Bill 46-3
    Form and Content of 46-3
    Freight Forwarder Bill 46-3
    Negotiability of 46-3
    Through Bill...46-3
Binder 57-5
Blue Sky Laws 55-16
Board of Directors
    Appointment of..52-10
    Corporate Opportunity Doctrine............................52-11
    Delegation of Authority 52-10
    Duties of 52-11
    Elections 52-10
    Meetings 52-10
    Powers of..52-10
    Quorum...52-10
    Removal of 52-10
    Rights of 52-11
Bonds
    See Surety Bonds 49-2
Breach
    Anticipatory 43-26
    Contract, of 43-21, 43-23, 44-10, 56-8, 59-3
    Covenant, of 56-15
    Remedies for 44-15
    Warranty, of 44-23, 46-8, 57-7
Bribery 59-4
Broker..46-6, 55-9
Business Judgment Rule 52-11
Buyer in the Ordinary Course of Business 47-2, 47-11

C

Capacity
    Agent 50-3
    Contract, of Parties to 43-10
    Principal..50-2
Carrier
    Duty of Care 46-5
    Risk of Loss 46-5
Cashier's Check...45-5
Certificate of Deposit 45-5
Charitable Trusts 53-2, 53-7
Chattel 56-3
Chattel Paper
    Defined 47-3
Checks
    Article 4 (UCC)..45-35
    Bank Draft...45-5
    Cashier's Check..45-5
    Certified 45-34
    Defined 45-3, 45-5
    Depositor 45-34
    Endorsement 45-13
    Special Rules 45-34
    Stop-Payment Order 45-35
Child Labor 54-10
Choate Dower...56-5

Claims
    Adverse 46-7
    Negotiable Instruments 45-18
    Workers' Compensation.......................................54-7
Claims (Bankruptcy)
    Administrative Expense Claimant.........................48-11
    Allowance of 48-10
    Claims Against Estate..48-9
    Co-Debtors 48-11
    Collateral...48-12
    Creditor...48-2
    Defined 48-2
    Equity Security..48-2
    Equity Security Holder....................48-2, 48-10
    Guarantors 48-11
    Involuntary Bankruptcy Cases...............................48-11
    Objections to..48-11
    Prepetition...48-11
    Prima Facie Evidence 48-11
    Priority 48-12
    Proofs of Claims or Interests................................48-10
    Secured Claims, Determination of.........................48-12
    Set-Off..48-20
    Sureties 48-11
    Taxes 48-13
    Unliquidated Claims 48-11
    Unsecured 48-12
Co-Debtor 48-11
Co-Suretyship
    Common Law Rules...49-8
    Defined 49-8
    Right of Contribution 49-8
    Sub-Suretyship vs...49-9
Co-Tenants...56-6
Code of Professional Conduct
    Ethics Rulings 58-17
    Principles of Conduct 58-3
    Rules of Conduct 58-4
Coinsurance
    Formula for the Recovery of 57-8
    Pro Rata Recovery of 57-8
Collateral 49-5
    Assignment of Insurance Contract 57-7
    Contracts 43-9
    Creditor's Rights Against......................................49-5
    Intangibles...47-3
    Proceeds of Disposition 47-19
    Purchasers of...47-12
    Pure Intangibles...47-3
    Secured Claims (Bankruptcy) 48-12
    Tangibles 47-2
Collaterals, Defined...53-4
Collect on Delivery (C.O.D.) 44-7
Commercial Paper
    Absence of Consideration 45-19
    Acceptance..45-3
    Accommodation Party..45-3
    Alteration (Material)...45-3
    Article 1 (UCC)...45-3
    Article 3 (UCC)...45-3
    Article 4 (UCC)...45-4
    Certificate of Deposit..45-5
    Check 45-5
    Consideration...43-6
    Contractual Liability..45-23
    Defenses 45-18, 45-20
    Discharge From Liability.......................................45-32

Dishonor 45-3, 45-28
Drafts 45-3, 45-4
Duress 45-22
Endorsement 45-12
Endorser 45-10
Exempted Securities 55-5
Fraud 45-19
Holder in Due Course (HDC) 45-15
Interpretation and Construction 45-10
Issue and Negotiation 45-11
Liability of the Parties 45-22
Money 45-8
Negotiability 45-4, 45-6
Negotiation 45-3, 45-12
Note 45-3, 45-5
Order 45-3
Presenter's Warranties 45-27
Presentment 45-4, 45-28
Primary Parties 45-23
Promise 45-4
Special Rules Applicable to Checks 45-34
Transfer 45-12
Transferor's Warranties 45-26
Types of 45-4
Unauthorized Completion 45-19
Warranty Liability 45-26
Commodity Paper
    Also see Documents of Title 46-3
    Defined 46-3
Community Claim 48-2
Community Property 56-5
Compensatory Damages 43-27
Concurrent (Joint) Estates in Land 56-6
    Classifications 56-6
    Rights and Duties Among Co-Tenants 56-7
    Tenancy by the Entirety 56-6
    Tenancy in Common 56-6
    Termination 56-6
Conditional Sales 44-8
Conditions
    Contracts, Performance of 43-23
    Offer, of 43-14
    Precedent 56-2, 56-5
    Sales, Defined 43-26
    Subsequent 56-2
Consequential Damages 43-27, 44-18
Consideration
    Absence of 45-19
    Acquisition of Real Property 56-7
    Adequacy of 43-5
    Commercial Paper 43-6
    Conditional Promise 43-5
    Contracts 43-3, 49-2, 57-5
    Creditors, of (Bankruptcy) 48-4
    Criminal or Tortious Conduct 43-5
    Exceptions 43-6
    Forbearance as 43-4
    Fraud 43-5
    Illusory Promise 43-5
    Legal Detriment 43-4
    Moral Obligation 43-6
    Nominal 43-5
    Past Consideration 43-6
    Promissory Estoppel 43-6
    Quid Pro Quo 43-4
    Shares, for 52-8
    Types of 43-4
    Warranties 45-26
Consignee 44-4, 46-2
Consignment 44-4, 47-18

Consignor 44-4, 46-2, 47-12
Consolidation
    Approval of 52-14
    Defined 52-14
Constructive Fraud 59-2, 59-4
Consulting Services
    Advisory Services, Defined 58-32
    Background 58-31
    Consultations 58-32
    Consulting Process, Defined 58-31
    Defined 58-32
    Definitions and Standards 58-31
    Implementation Services, Defined 58-32
    Product Services, Defined 58-32
    Staff and Other Support Services, Defined 58-32
    Transaction Services, Defined 58-32
Contingent Remainder 56-5
Continuing Offer 43-11
Contracts
    Acceptance of 57-4
    Accord and Satisfaction 43-24
    Agency 50-2
    Agreement 43-4, 57-4
    Alteration of 49-7
    Ambiguities 57-5
    Article 2 (UCC) 43-7, 43-16, 43-19, 43-25
    Article 9 (UCC) 43-20
    Assent 43-17
    Assignee Vis-a-Vis Assignor 43-20
    Assignee's Rights Against the Obligor 43-20
    Assignment 57-7
    Assignment of Loss Proceeds 57-7
    Assignment of Rights 43-19
    Beneficiaries, Types of 43-21
    Bilateral 43-3, 43-12, 43-15
    Binder or Binder Slip 57-5
    Breach of 43-21
    Breach, Remedies for 43-27
    Cancellation 43-24
    Capacity of 43-10, 57-5
    Collateral 43-9
    Collect on Delivery (C.O.D.) 44-7
    Consideration of 49-2, 49-4, 49-6, 57-5
    Corporations Capacity to 49-4
    Counterclaims 43-20
    Damages 43-27
    Damages, Mitigation of 43-28
    Defenses to 43-22
    Defined 43-3
    Delegation of Rights 43-20
    Delivery of 57-5
    Discharge of 43-23
    Duress 43-19
    Elements of 43-4, 57-4
    Endorsement 49-3
    Exclusive Dealing 43-6
    Exculpatory Clauses 43-13
    Executed, Defined 43-3
    Executory Accord 43-24
    Executory, Defined 43-3
    Executory, for the Sale of Land 56-7
    Express Agreement 44-10
    Express, Defined 43-3
    False Representation 43-17
    Formation of 57-4
    Fraud 43-17
    Free Alongside (F.A.S.) 44-7
    Free on Board (F.O.B.) 44-6
    Frustration of Purpose 43-25
    Guarantor's Liability 49-2

Guarantor, Indemnitor, and Endorser of 49-2
Guaranty...49-2
Illegality...43-13
Implied, Defined...43-3
Incompetent Persons...43-10
Indemnification..49-3, 49-4
Indemnity Contract...43-9
Individual's Capacity to 49-4
Injunction 43-28
Innocent Misrepresentation.................................43-17
Insurance Contracts, Classifications of 57-2
Intention to Deceive (Scienter)............................43-18
Interpreting the Written Contract 43-16
Joint and Several Obligations...............................43-22
Joint Obligors/Obligees.......................................43-22
Justifiable Reliance 43-18
Legal Detriment..43-4
Legality of Subject Matter..........................43-13, 57-5
Life Insurance 43-22
Material Fact..43-18
Material Variances 49-7
Merger 43-24
Methods of Modifying Liability 43-24
Mirror Acceptance Rule...43-4
Mistake in the Inducement 43-17
Mutual Mistake..43-17
Nature of..57-6
No Arrival, No Sale 44-7
Novation...43-9, 43-25
Objective Rule of Contracts 43-4
Offer..43-10, 49-4, 57-4
Option..43-11
Output Contract 43-6
Parol Evidence Rule 43-16
Partner's Capacity to...49-4
Partnership's Capacity to 49-4
Performance 43-23, 43-24, 43-25
Primary Suretyship...49-4
Privity...44-12, 44-22
Promissory Estoppel..43-6
Quasi-Contract..43-3, 43-12
Real Property 43-8
Rejection of Offer...43-13
Remedies Upon Breach 56-8
Renunciation..43-26
Requirement Contract...43-6
Rescission 43-4, 43-17, 43-21, 43-25
Restitution..43-26
Rights of Assignor..43-20
Signature Requirement 43-7
Statute of Frauds 43-7, 43-10
Statute of Limitations...43-26
Suretyship..49-2
Third Party Beneficiary Contracts.........................43-21
Three Party Relationship..49-2
Tort, Contract to Commit......................................43-14
Unconscionability...43-19
Under Seal..43-6
Undue Influence...43-19
Unenforceable, Defined 43-3
Unilateral..........................43-3, 43-12, 43-15
Unilateral Mistake 43-17
Usurious 43-14
Vesting Rights..43-22
Void 43-3, 43-17, 49-7
Voidable......................................43-4, 43-17, 57-5
Writing of..57-5
Writing Requirement 43-7
Contractual Liability...45-23
Controlling Person 55-2, 55-8

Conveyance
    Deed of 56-7
    Defined 56-2
    Inter Vivos...56-6
    Property 56-3
Corporate Opportunity Doctrine 52-11
Corporations
    Articles of Incorporation 52-5
    Attributes of 52-3
    Authorized Capital...52-6
    Board of Directors..52-10
    Consideration for Shares 52-8
    Consolidation 52-14
    Continuous Life 52-4
    Contribution to Capital....................................52-15
    De Facto Corporation.......................................52-5
    De Jure Corporation...52-5
    Defects in Formation..52-5
    Defined 52-3
    Disadvantages of 52-4
    Dissolution 52-14
    Distributions...52-15
    Dividends 52-13
    Domestic, Defined 52-3
    Estoppel, by 52-6
    Federal Securities Law...................................52-12
    Financing 52-6
    Foreign, Defined 52-3
    Formation of...52-4
    Incorporation 52-5
    Incorporators...52-5
    Insider Trading 52-12
    Liabilities...52-9
    Limited Liability Company 52-3
    Liquidation 52-14
    Merger 52-13
    Officers 52-10, 52-11
    Piercing the Corporate Veil 52-3, 52-9
    Powers of...52-8
    Professional Corporation..................................52-3
    Promoter..52-4
    Proxy 52-3
    Reorganizations....................................52-13, 52-16
    Respondeat Superior 52-9
    Stock 52-6
    Stockholders' Rights and Liabilities.................52-12
    Subscription Agreements 52-6
    Subsidiaries 52-9
    Surety 52-9
    Tort Liability 52-11
    Ultra Vires 52-3, 52-9
    Undercapitalization 52-9
Cost, Insurance, and Freight (C.I.F.)........................44-7
Counter-Offer..43-13
Covenants of Title 56-10
Cover...44-3, 44-17
Creditor
    Assignment for the Benefit of Creditors...................48-3
    Composition or Extension Agreement.....................48-4
    Consideration (Bankruptcy).....................................48-4
    Defined 48-2, 49-2
    Failure to Disclose Material Facts 49-7
    Insurance..57-3
    Petition..48-4
    Pre-Bankruptcy Actions Available to 48-3
    Race of Diligence...48-3
    Rights Against the Collateral...................................49-5
    Rights Against the Debtor 49-4
    Rights Against the Surety..49-5
    Rights of (Suretyship) 49-4

Transfer of Exempt Property 48-3
Custodian (Bankruptcy) 48-8
Cy Pres Doctrine, Defined..................................53-8

D

Damages
    Actual, Defined 59-2
    Common Law Liability..................................59-5
    Compensatory 43-27
    Consequential 43-27, 44-18
    Incidental 44-18
    Liquidated 43-27
    Nominal 43-27
    Property Buyer's Remedy, as.....................56-8
    Punitive...59-2
Dealer, Securities 55-2
Debt, Defined...48-2
Debtor
    Appearance and Examination of 48-8
    Creditor's Rights 49-4
    Defined 48-2
    Discharge..48-15
    Eligibility To Be a 48-6
    Fraudulent Conveyance 48-3
    Fraudulent Transfers 48-20
    Petition...48-8
    Preferential Transfers 48-19
    Property Held In Trust by 48-18
    Protection 48-9
    Schedule Filing 48-9
    Under Chapters 7, 11, 13 48-6
    Waiver of Exemptions................................48-15
Deeds
    Contents (Clauses) of 56-9
    Delivery...56-9
    Effects of Recordation.................................56-10
    Formal Requirements 56-9
    General Warranty...56-9
    Grantee...56-9
    Grantor 56-9
    Notice 56-10
    Parol Evidence...56-9
    Quitclaim...56-9
    Race 56-10
    Race-Notice 56-10
    Recording Statutes 56-10
    Special Warranty 56-9
    Statute of Frauds 56-9
Delivery Order...46-2
Descendants, Defined.......................................53-4
Destination Bill, Defined...................................46-3
Devest (Divest), Defined 56-2
Devise..53-2, 56-2
Discharge
    Contracts, of 43-23
    Defense, as a...45-34
    Endorser; Drawer 45-24
    Holder in Due Course (HDC), of.................45-19
    Liability from 45-32
    Surety, of 45-33, 49-5
Dishonor
    Defined 45-3
    Instrument, of..45-28
    Protest 45-30
Dissolutions
    Involuntary 52-14
    Miscellaneous Grounds for 52-14
    Partnerships, of...51-10

Quo Warranto Action 52-14
        Shareholder Action 52-14
        Voluntary...52-14
Divest (Devest), Defined 56-2
Dividends
    Cash Distributions......................................52-15
    Constructive..52-15
    Property Distributions.................................52-15
    Stock Distributions 52-15
Documents of Title
    Defeating Holders' and Transferees' Rights 46-5
    Definition and Types of 46-2
    Delivery Order...46-2
    Destination Bill 46-3
    Due Negotiation 46-4
    Duty of Care..46-5
    Effects of...46-3
    Endorser..46-4
    Forgery 46-5
    Freight Forwarder Bill 46-3
    Holder in Due Course (HDC)......................46-4
    Holder of Negotiable Documents 46-3
    Negotiable Document 46-3
    Negotiation..46-4
    Nonnegotiable Document............................46-3
    Risk of Loss 46-5
    Shelter Principle..46-4
    Through Bill...46-3
    Transferee 46-4
    Transferor 46-4
    Warehouse Receipt 46-2
Dower 56-5
Drafts
    Acceptance..45-3
    Bank Draft...45-5
    Banker's Acceptance 45-5
    Check 45-5
    Defined 45-3, 45-4
    Drawee 45-4
    Drawer 45-4
    Payee 45-4
    Sight 45-4
    Time 45-4
    Trade Acceptance 45-4
Drawee
    Defined 45-4
    Liability of...45-23
Drawer
    Defined 45-4
    Discharge of..45-24
    Liability of...45-24
    Negligence 45-35
Duress
    Contracts 43-19
    Suretyship...49-6

E

Eminent Domain 56-16
Employee...54-3
Employee Retirement Security Act of 1974 (ERISA).....54-10
Employee Safety
    See Occupational Safety and Health Act (OSHA) ...54-8
Employer 54-2
Employment...54-3
Encumbrance (Incumbrance), Defined............56-2
Endorse...45-12
Endorsement
    Blank Endorsement......................................45-14

Cancellation of 45-12
Conditional Endorsement.................................45-14
Conveyance...45-13
Defined 45-12
Effect of 45-13
Forgery 45-13
Mechanics of...45-13
Qualified Endorsement 45-15
Restrictive Endorsement..................................45-14
Signature 45-13
Special Endorsement.......................................45-14
Without Recourse 45-27
Endorser
Discharge of..45-24
Documents of Title, Liability of 46-4, 46-7
Documents of Title, Warranties of....................46-7
Liability of.......................................45-13, 45-24, 45-27
Negotiable Instruments, of 45-10, 45-12
Entity, Defined 48-2
Environmental Protection
Clean Air Act of 1963 56-18
Clean Water Act..56-18
Common Law (Nuisance).................................56-18
Environmental Protection Agency 56-18
National Environmental Policy Act (NEPA) 56-18
Safe Drinking Water Act of 1986.....................56-18
Environmental Protection Agency (EPA)..............56-18
Equal Employment Opportunity Commission (EEOC)
Age Discrimination in Employment Act 54-9
Americans With Disabilities Act of 1990.................54-9
Equal Pay Act 54-9
The Rehabilitation Act of 1973 54-9
Equity Receivership 48-4
Equity Security...55-2
Estate Tax, Federal.......................................53-12, 53-13
Estates
Abatement 53-5
Ademption 53-5
Adjusted Taxable Gifts 53-12
Administration 53-4
Administrator...53-2, 53-4
Ascendants..53-4
Assets, Distribution of 53-3
Beneficiary 53-2
Collaterals...53-4
Deductions...53-12, 53-13
Definition and Functions..................................53-2
Descendants..53-4
Devise..53-2
Discretionary Deductions 53-12
Executor...53-2
Federal Estate Tax...53-12
Gift Tax 53-12
Gross Estate..53-12, 53-13
Intestate...53-3
Intestate Succession..53-2
Legacy 53-2
Letters Testamentary 53-4
Objective of the Estate Tax..............................53-12
Probate...53-2, 53-4
Probate Court 53-4
Property 53-13
Representative..53-4
Residuary...53-3
State Statutes..53-3
Tax Return 53-15
Taxable Estate 53-12
Tentative Estate Tax...53-12
Tentative Tax Base 53-12
Transfers of Property 53-12

Unified Credit 53-12, 53-15
Will, Defined 53-2
Estates and Trusts
See Estates; Trusts 53-2
Estoppel
Agency by..50-5
Corporation by 52-6
Fire and Casualty Insurance 57-7
Partnership by..51-5
Promissory...43-6, 43-10
Ethics Rulings
Applicability...58-17
General and Technical Standards.........................58-24
Independence, Integrity, and Objectivity 58-17
Other Responsibilities and Practices....................58-25
Responsibilities to Clients 58-24
Exculpatory Clauses 43-13
Executor 53-2, 53-4
Exoneration
Defined 49-2
Surety's Rights to..49-6

F

Factor 50-3
Fair Labor Standards Act 54-10
Federal Bankruptcy Code 48-5, 48-14
Federal Estate Tax...53-12
Federal Insurance Contributions Act (FICA)
See Social Security...54-2
Federal Reserve System 55-12
Federal Securities Law 52-12
Federal Securities Regulations 55-2
See Securities...55-2
Federal Unemployment Tax Act (FUTA)
See Social Security...54-2
Fee Simple Estates
Conveyance...56-3
Creation 56-3
Subject to a Condition Subsequent 56-4
Subject to an Executory Interest 56-4
Fiduciary Duty
Partners...51-7
Promoters 52-4
Shareholders 52-13
Fiduciary Relationship
Agent 50-8
Defined 51-2
Partnerships...51-7
Trusts...53-5
Financing Statement
Contents of 47-5
Defined 47-3
Places for Filing 47-9
Purpose of 47-6
Sufficiency and Duration of Filing...........................47-8
Termination...47-9
Fire and Casualty Insurance
See Insurance, Fire and Casualty 57-2
Firm Offer 44-5
Fixtures...47-3, 56-3
Forbearance
Acceptance, as 43-14
Consideration, as 43-4
Foreign Corrupt Practices Act of 1977 59-4
Forgery
Documents of Title...46-5
Endorsement 45-13
Holder in Due Course, Defense Against.................45-20

Fraud
    Accountant's Liability for 59-4
    Actual..59-2
    Commercial Paper 45-12
    Constructive.....................................59-2, 59-4
    Contracts 43-17
    Dissolution Caused by 51-13
    Fire and Casualty Insurance 57-2, 57-7
    Suretyship..49-6
Fraudulent Conveyance
    Bankruptcy.......................................48-3, 48-20
    Securities..55-11
Free Alongside (F.A.S.) 44-7
Free on Board (F.O.B.) 44-6
Freehold Estates
    Defined 56-3
    Fee Simple Estates 56-3
    Freeholder 56-3
    Future Interests..56-3
    Life Estates..56-4
Freeholder 56-3
Freight Forwarder Bill, Defined..........................46-3
Frustration of Purpose
    Contracts 43-25
    Rental Agreement 56-16
Fungible Goods 44-3
Future Interests
    Executory Interest 56-5
    Freehold Estates..56-3
    Possibility of Reverter 56-5
    Property, Real and Personal 56-5
    Remainder 56-5
    Reversion 56-5
    Right of Reentry...56-5

G

Garnish; Garnishment..............................48-2, 48-3
General Warranty Deed 56-9
Gift Tax...53-12
Gifts
    Causa Mortis..56-20
    Defined 56-20
    Inter Vivos..56-20
Goods
    Damages to 44-17
    Defined 44-3
    Disposition of 44-16
    Fungible Goods...44-3
    Held by Bailee...44-10
    Identification of...44-4
    Reclamation of..44-18
    Title to 44-8
Grantor 56-7
Gross Estate 53-12
Guaranties
    Conditional..49-3
    Continuing...49-3
    General..49-3
    Special..49-3
    Temporary 49-3
    Unconditional..49-3

H

Hazard, Defined..57-2
Holder
    Also see Holder in Due Course (HDC) 46-3
    Defense or Claim 45-17
    Defined 45-3, 45-15
    Real Defenses 45-20
    Rights of 46-4
    Subsequent Holder 45-11
Holder in Due Course (HDC)
    Acceptance of Payment.............................45-27
    Article 1 (UCC)..45-16
    Article 3 (UCC)..45-16
    Defense or Claim 45-17
    Defined 45-15, 46-4
    Discharge..45-19
    Good Faith Test 45-16
    Notice 45-16
    Real Defenses 45-20
    Requirements 45-15
    Rights of 45-18
Homeowner's Policies.......................................57-4

I

Illusory Offer 43-11
Illusory Promise 43-5
Implied Authority of Agent..................................50-4
Inchoate Dower 56-5
Incidental Damages 44-18
Incorporation
    Defined 52-5
    Procedure for 52-5
Incorporators...52-5
Incumbrance (Encumbrance), Defined................56-2
Indemnification 49-3
Independence 58-5
Independence and Attest Engagements 58-11
Independent Contractor
    Accountant as 59-2
    Defined 50-2
Infancy
    Minors, To Contract 43-10
    Principal, Capacity To Be...........................50-2
    Real Defense, as 45-20
Inheritance
    Partner's Interest, of..................................51-6
    Personal Property 56-20
    Taxes 53-13
Injunction 43-28
Innocent Misrepresentation...............................43-17
Insider...55-2
Insider Trading...52-12
Insolvency..48-2
Insurable Interests 57-6
Insurance, Fire and Casualty
    Agent 57-5
    Article 9 (UCC)...57-3
    Assignment of..57-7
    Assured, Defined 57-2
    Automobile Liability 57-4
    Coinsurance...57-8
    Consideration...57-5
    Creditors vs. Possessor 57-3
    Election...57-7
    Estoppel..57-7
    Fraud 57-7
    Hazard 57-2
    Insurable Interests 57-6
    Insurance Proceeds 57-8
    Insured..57-2
    Insurer 57-2
    Legal Interests 57-6

Liability Insurance 57-4
Life Tenant vs. Remainderman 57-4
Malpractice Insurance 57-4
Marine Insurance 57-7
Materiality of Statement.................................... 57-6
Mortgagor vs. Mortgagee 57-3
No-Fault 57-4
Over-Insurance Clauses.................................... 57-9
Payment of Proceeds 57-3
Pecuniary Interest 57-6
Peril 57-2
Personal Liability 57-4
Policy, Defined.. 57-2
Premium 57-2
Pro Rata Recovery 57-8
Release 57-8
Representations 57-6
Seller vs. Buyer 57-3
State Statutes 57-6
Subrogation... 57-7
Time of Loss 57-6
Types of Fire Insurance.................................... 57-2
Waiver.. 57-7
Warranties.. 57-6
Insured, Defined.. 57-2
Insurer, Defined.. 57-2
Inter Vivos
    Conveyance 56-6
    Gifts 56-20
    Trust.. 53-8
Internal Control.. 59-4
Interstate Commerce (Securities)......................... 55-2
Intestate, Defined.. 53-3
Investment Securities
    Adverse Claim.. 46-7
    Beneficial Ownership...................................... 55-2
    Broker 55-9
    Consideration, Lack of.................................... 46-6
    Defined.. 46-6
    Delivery Order 46-2
    Delivery, Endorsement Without...................... 46-7
    Endorsement... 46-3
    Equity 55-2
    Exempted Securities 55-4
    Issuance.. 46-6
    Issuer 46-6
    Private Offerings 55-7
    Prospectus.. 55-2, 55-4
    Purchase and Transfer.................................... 46-7
    Purchaser, Bona Fide...................................... 46-5
    Registration Statement....................... 55-3, 55-4
    Restricted Securities 55-8
    Sale or Sell.. 55-3
    Stolen, Lost, or Destroyed.............................. 46-8
    Transfer or Presentment, Warranties on 46-7
    Unauthorized Signature.................................. 46-6
    Warranties... 46-7
Issue of Negotiable Instruments.......................... 45-11
Issuer
    Documents of Title, Defined 46-2
    Securities 46-6, 55-2

J

Joint and Several Contracts 43-22
Joint and Several Liability...................................... 51-2
Joint Liability
    Defined.. 51-2
    Effect on Partners 51-10

Joint Tenancy... 56-6
Joint Venture.. 51-3

L

Landlord
    Breach of Covenant.. 56-15
    Covenant of Habitability.................................. 56-13
    Duties... 56-12, 56-13
    Lease Deposits and Damage Clause 56-14
    Liens 56-14
    Privity of Estate 56-15
    Rights, Duties, and Liabilities 56-12
    Termination 56-15
    Tort Liability of... 56-13
Leasehold Estates
    Breach of Covenant.. 56-15
    Destruction of the Premises 56-16
    Eminent Domain Condemnation...................... 56-16
    Frustration of Purpose.................................... 56-16
    Rights, Duties, and Liabilities of the Tenant.... 56-14
    Termination of 56-15
    Third-Party Eviction by Title Paramount 56-16
    Types of Tenancies 56-11
Legacy, Defined.. 53-2, 53-3
Liability
    Accountant..................... 59-2, 59-4, 59-7, 59-9
    Audit.. 59-9
    Commercial Paper 45-22
    Contractual, to Third Parties.......................... 59-5
    Documents of Title 46-4
    Principal for Agent's Acts 50-6
    Products Liability (Sales) 44-21
    Third Parties Under Federal Statutes 59-5
    Ultramares Doctrine 59-5
    Warranty 45-26
Lien Creditor 47-3
Liens
    Defined.. 48-2
    Judicial 48-2
    Statutory.. 48-19
    Unperfected... 48-19
Life Estates
    Alienability.. 56-4
    Community Property... 56-5
    Created by Operation of Law........................... 56-5
    Defeasible 56-4
    Dower.. 56-5
    Life Tenant 56-4
    Statutory Forced Share 56-5
    Types 56-4
Life Tenant 56-4
Limited Liability Company 52-3
Limited Partnerships
    Dissolution 51-16
    Distribution of Assets 51-16
    Formation.. 51-16
Liquidated Damages 56-8
Liquidation
    Bankruptcy.. 48-5
    Corporations.. 52-14

M

Malpractice Insurance 57-4
Marine Insurance 57-7
Marketable Title... 56-8
Medicare
    See Social Security 54-2

Merchant
    Acceptance of Offer 44-5
    Defined 44-4
    Firm Offer 44-5
Merger
    Approval of..52-14
    Defined 52-13
Minimum Wage...54-10
Mirror Acceptance Rule 43-4
Money, Defined 45-8
Mortgage Agreements
    Execution of 56-16
    Fire and Casualty Insurance 57-3
Mortgagee
    Defined 56-17, 57-3
    Real Property 47-12
Mortgages
    Defined 47-3, 56-16
    Grantee...56-18
    Rights of the Parties...............................56-17
    Sale of Mortgaged Property 56-18
    Termination of the Mortgage Interest 56-18
Mortgagor
    Default of 56-17
    Defined 56-17, 57-3
    Merger 56-18
    Rights of 56-17
    Tender 56-18

N

National Housing Act 48-10
Negligence
    Accountant's Liability for 59-2, 59-3, 59-5
    Bank 45-35
    Drawer, Depositor 45-35
Negligence Actions
    Damages 44-22
    Defenses 44-22
    Duty 44-21
    Primary Uses 44-22
    Privity...44-22
Negotiability
    Also see Negotiable Instruments 45-4
    Cash 45-10
    Concept 45-4
    Contract Law of Assignments 45-5
    Fraud, Duress, Mistake 45-12
    Money...45-8
    Order, Defined 45-7
    Payable at a Definite Time 45-8
    Payable on Demand 45-8
    Prerequisites..45-6
    Promise, Defined 45-7
    Requirements of 45-6
    Rescission of Negotiation.......................45-12
    Sum Certain 45-8
    Unconditional Order or Promise to Pay 45-7
    Words of 45-9
    Writing and Signature 45-7
Negotiable Document
    Also See Negotiable Instruments............46-3
    Defined 46-3
Negotiable Instruments
    Accelerated Instrument 45-29
    Ambiguities 45-10
    Assignment..45-11
    Cancellation 45-33
    Claims...45-18

Contract Rights 45-6
    Dating of 45-10
    Delivery...45-11, 45-12
    Demand Instrument 45-29
    Designation of Payees 45-11
    Dishonored 45-17
    Endorsement and Bearer Paper..............45-13
    Forgery 45-20
    Incomplete 45-11
    Issue 45-11
    Letter of Credit 45-6
    Liability...45-10
    Material Alteration 45-21
    Methods of Discharging Liability.............45-32
    Modification of Terms.............................45-11
    Overdue 45-16
    Place of Payment...................................45-10
    Reacquisition 45-12, 45-33
    Renunciation 45-33
    Shelter Provision....................................45-18
    Signature, Importance of........................45-22
    Types of Endorsements 45-13
    Underlying Obligation.............................45-32
    Validity 45-20
    Void 45-22
Negotiation, Defined 45-3
No-Fault Insurance 57-4
Nonnegotiable Document...............................46-3
Note
    Bearer...45-5
    Defined 45-3, 45-5
    Maker..45-5
    Payee 45-5
    Promisor 45-5
Novation 43-9

O

Occupational Safety and Health Act (OSHA)
    Coverage Under......................................54-8
    Enforcement 54-8
    Penalties...54-8
    Purpose 54-8
Offer
    Acceptance of...43-14
    Article 2 (UCC)..43-11
    Bankruptcy or Insolvency 43-13
    Bilateral Contract 43-15
    Conditions...43-14
    Consideration..................................43-4, 43-11
    Continuing...43-11
    Counter-Offer..43-13
    Death or Disability of the Parties.............43-13
    Defined 43-10
    Definite and Certain 43-11
    Firm Offer 43-12, 44-5
    Forbearance To Act 43-14
    General Offer 43-15
    Identification of the Offeree 43-11
    Illegality or Impossibility 43-13
    Illusory 43-11
    Insurance Contract..................................57-4
    Intent..43-10
    Knowledge and Intent 43-14
    Lapse of Time 43-12
    Legal Requirements.......................43-10, 43-14
    Partial Performance 43-12
    Promise 43-14
    Provision of 43-13

Receipt of 43-13
Rejection of...43-13
Reply 43-14
Revocation by the Offeror 43-11
Revocation, Manner of 43-12
Reward 43-11
Silence as Acceptance.................................43-15
Subject Matter, Identification of.....................43-11
Termination of 43-11, 43-12
Types of..43-11
Unilateral Contract 43-15

Officers of a Corporation
    Authority to Contract 52-11
    Fiduciary Duties 52-11
    Tort Liability 52-11

Order
    Defined 45-3
    Endorsement and Delivery..........................45-11
    Negotiation...45-13

Other Professional Services
    Statements on Responsibilities in Tax Practice.....58-28

P

Parol Evidence...............................43-16, 56-9
Parol Evidence Rule 44-13

Partners
    Action at Law 51-8
    Actual Authority..51-9
    Apparent Authority 51-9
    Assignment of Interest 51-7
    Bankruptcy..51-12
    Capacity To Be 51-2
    Death, Withdrawal, or Admission 51-11
    Dormant Partners......................................51-4
    Family Rights to Interest 51-7
    Fiduciaries, as..51-7
    General Partners.......................................51-3
    Inheritance of Interest 51-6
    Interest in the Partnership 51-6
    Limited Partners.......................................51-4
    Participation in Management.........................51-7
    Property Rights...51-6
    Rights and Duties......................................51-7
    Secret Partners..51-4
    Silent Partners 51-4
    Suit in Equity...51-8

Partnerships
    Action at Law 51-8
    Admission of a Partner...............................51-11
    Articles of Partnership 51-4
    Assignment of Interests 51-7, 51-11
    Bankruptcy..51-12
    Books..51-8
    Classifications of Partners 51-3
    Conduit, as..51-17
    Contract Liability 51-10
    Corporations, Distinguished 51-3
    Death of a Partner.....................................51-11
    Dissolution 51-10
    Distribution of Assets 51-14
    Estoppel, by..51-5
    Existence, Determination of 51-5
    Expulsion of a Partner................................51-11
    Fictitious Name 51-5
    Fiduciary 51-2
    Formation 51-4
    General Partnerships..................................51-3
    Joint and Several Liability 51-2

Joint Liability 51-2
Joint Ventures, Distinguished........................51-3
Levy of a Charging Order 51-11
Limited Partnerships 51-4, 51-15
Property 51-2, 51-6
Relations Among Partners 51-7
Revised Uniform Limited Partnership Act
    (RULPA) 51-17
Rights and Duties of Partners 51-7
Suit in Equity...51-8
Taxation...51-17
Tort Liability 51-10
Withdrawal of a Partner 51-11

Penalties, Tax Preparer 59-10
Pensions...54-10
Per Capita, Defined......................................53-2
Per Stirpes, Defined.....................................53-2

Perfection
    Automatic...47-10
    Filing, by..47-8
    Possession, by...47-9

Performance
    Complete 43-23
    Conditions to...43-23
    Discharge by 43-23
    Excuses and Substitutes for.........................44-14
    Frustration of Purpose 43-25
    Impossibility 43-25
    Means of Payment, by 43-24
    Sales..44-13
    Statute of Limitations 43-26
    Substantial...43-23
    Tender by..43-24
    Time of..43-23

Peril, Defined 57-2
Person, Defined (Securities Regulations)....................55-2
Personal Liability Insurance 57-4

Policy
    Blanket..57-2
    Cancellation of 57-3
    Defined 57-2
    Exemptions, Friendly Fire 57-3
    Floating 57-2
    Hazard Clause 57-3
    Homeowner's...57-4
    Open..57-2
    Premium, Defined 57-2
    Proof of Loss...57-3
    Provisions, Standard 57-3
    Specific...57-2
    Time of Loss 57-6
    Valued 57-2

Pooling Agreements 52-13

Powers of the Corporation
    Express..52-8
    Implied 52-8
    Particular 52-9

Preemptive Rights 52-3, 52-13
Preferential Transfers, Defined 48-19
Premium, Defined 57-2

Presentment
    Acceptance, for..45-28
    Conditions of...45-29
    Defined 45-4
    Delay 45-31
    Dishonor, Notice of 45-30
    Excuse 45-31
    Failure To Make 45-31
    Methods of 45-29
    Payment, for 45-28

Time of...45-29
Waived...45-17
Principal
   Bankruptcy or Insolvency of the 50-10
   Capacity To Be a 50-2
   Contractual Liability................................50-7
   Disclosed..50-7
   Duties Owed to the Agent 50-8
   Liability of...50-6
   Material Misrepresentation of the Facts 50-7
   Partially Disclosed.................................50-7
Principles of Conduct
   Due Care 58-4
   Integrity..58-3
   Objectivity and Independence 58-3
   Public Interest.......................................58-3
   Responsibilities.....................................58-3
   Scope and Nature of Services.................58-4
Pro Rata Recovery...57-8
Probate, Defined.................................53-2, 53-4
Proceeds, Defined 47-3
Products Liability
   Causation...44-21
   Foreseeable or Normal Use 44-21
Professional Ethics.......................................58-3
Promise, Defined..43-3
Promisee, Defined 43-3
Promisor, Defined...43-3
Promissory Note 48-10
Promoter
   Continuing Liability................................52-4
   Contracts of 52-4
   Defined 52-4
   Fiduciary Duty.......................................52-4
Property, Distribution of
   Abatement 53-5
   Per Capita...53-2
   Per Stirpes 53-2
Property, Personal
   Abandonment 56-19
   Accession 56-20
   Bailee...56-20
   Bailment...56-20
   Capture 56-19
   Creation 56-19
   Defined 56-2
   Finding Lost or Mislaid Property..............56-19
   Gift..56-20
   Inheritance 56-20
   Intangible 56-19
   Merger or Confusion 56-20
   Methods of Acquisition and Transfer.......56-19
   Overview...56-19
   Purchase of...56-19
   Rights of Third Parties 56-20
   Tangible..56-19
Property, Real
   Abatement in Price 56-8
   Acquisition of 56-7
   Buyer's Remedies..................................56-8
   Concurrent Conditions 56-8
   Covenants of Title.................................56-10
   Damages 56-8
   Deed...56-7, 56-9
   Defined 56-2
   Delivery of the Deed..............................56-8
   Equitable Conversion 56-8
   Executory Contract for the Sale of Land...56-7
   Grantor 56-7
   Marketable Title 56-8

Mortgages..56-16
Parol Evidence...56-9
Payment of the Purchase Price.......................56-8
Possession, Adverse 56-10
Possession, Claim of Right.............................56-11
Possession, Continuous and Exclusive.............56-10
Possession, Open and Notorious.....................56-10
Remedies Upon Breach of Contract.................56-8
Risk of Loss 56-8
Seller's Remedies 56-8
Statute of Frauds 56-7
Title Insurance 56-8
Property, Real and Personal
   Also see Property, Personal; Property, Real ...56-2
   Annexation..56-3
   Chattel 56-3
   Classifications 56-2
   Concurrent Estates in Land.....................56-6
   Encumbrance (Incumbrance)....................56-2
   Fixtures 56-3
   Freehold Estates...................................56-3
   Future Interests.....................................56-5
   Intangibles 56-2
   Landlord and Tenant..............................56-11
   Objective Intent Test..............................56-3
   Overview...56-2
   Tangibles 56-2
   Uniform Commercial Code.......................56-3
Prospectus...............................55-2, 55-4, 55-10
Proxy 52-3
Proxy Solicitations 55-13, 55-15
Punitive Damages...59-2
Purchase Money Security Interest 47-4
Purchaser (Bona Fide) of Investment Securities
   Adverse Claims.....................................46-7
   Defined 46-5
   Right to Endorsement 46-7
   Rights Acquired by.................................46-7
Purchaser (Bona Fide), Subsequent, of Property...56-2

Q

Qualified Endorsement 45-15
Quasi-Contract...43-3
Quasi-Reorganization 52-14
Quitclaim Deed...56-9
Quo Warranto Action 52-14
Quorum..52-10

R

Real Estate Investment Trust (REIT) 53-9
Real Estate Investment Trust Act of 1960..........53-9
Recordkeeping...59-4
Red Herring...55-10
Registration Statement 55-3, 55-4, 55-9
Regulations of Securities, Federal 55-2
Remainder 53-10, 56-5
Remainderman 53-11
Replevin...44-17
Representations (Insurance)...........................57-6
Respondeat Superior, Defined.........................50-2
Reversion 56-5
Revised Model Business Corporation Act (RMBCA) ...52-3
Revised Uniform Limited Partnership Act (RULPA)...51-17
Right of Reentry...56-5

Royalties...53-11
Rules of Conduct and Interpretations
    Accounting Principles....................58-12
    Accounting Services........................58-6
    Advertising 58-15
    Applicability......................................58-4
    Client, Defined 58-4
    Commissions 58-16
    Competence 58-12
    Compliance With Standards 58-12
    Confidential Client Information..........58-14
    Contingent Fees..............................58-14
    Discreditable Acts...........................58-14
    Discrimination in Employment Practices 58-15
    Engagements Obtained Through Third Parties 58-16
    False, Misleading, or Deceptive Acts 58-15
    Family Relationships.......................58-10
    Financial Interest 58-5
    Financial Statements, Defined 58-4
    Firm, Defined 58-5
    Form of Practice and Name 58-16
    Former Practitioners and Firm Independence 58-6
    GAAP Hierarchy..............................58-13
    General Standards...........................58-12
    Government Standards....................58-15
    Governmental Financial Statements 58-11
    Holding Out, Defined........................58-5
    Honorary Directorships and Trusteeships 58-6
    Independence 58-5
    Independence and Attest Engagements 58-11
    Institute, Defined.............................58-5
    Integrity and Objectivity..................58-12
    Litigation 58-8
    Loans..58-7
    Managerial (or Employee) Relationship...................58-6
    Member, Defined 58-5
    Negligence 58-15
    Practice of Public Accounting, Defined 58-5
    Professional Services, Defined 58-5
    SEC Regulation 58-7

S

Sales
    Acceptance 44-5
    Anticipatory Repudiation 44-21
    Bailment...44-4
    Breach of Contract..........................44-10
    Breach of Warranty.........................44-23
    Buyer's Rights and Duties...............44-14
    Collect on Delivery (C.O.D.)............44-7
    Condition Precedent 44-3
    Condition Subsequent......................44-3
    Conditional Sales 44-8
    Cover 44-3
    Damages to Goods.........................44-17
    Express Agreement 44-10
    Firm Offer 44-5
    Free Alongside (F.A.S.) 44-7
    Free on Board (F.O.B.) 44-6
    Gifts, Distinguished.........................44-5
    Goods 44-3
    Identification.....................................44-4
    Merchant..44-4
    Negligence Actions 44-21
    No Arrival, No Sale 44-7
    Performance 44-13
    Products Liability..............................44-21
    Reclamation of Goods 44-18

    Remedies for Breach 44-15
    Replevin...44-17
    Risk of Loss 44-10
    Seller's Rights and Duties 44-13
    Statute of Frauds 44-6
    Strict Liability...................................44-22
    Tender 44-4
    Title to Goods 44-8
    Uniform Commercial Code (UCC)....................44-5
    Warranties 44-11
Secured Party
    Compliance With Article 9................47-20
    Debtor-Requested Accounting 47-7
    Default Procedures 47-18
    Disposition of Collateral 47-19
    Rights of 47-18
Secured Transactions
    Accessions 47-2
    After-Acquired Property Clause........47-2
    Attachment 47-2, 47-5
    Buyer in the Ordinary Course of Business.............47-2
    Collateral...47-2
    Consignment...................................47-18
    Debtor's Right to Redeem Collateral 47-20
    Field Warehousing 47-17
    Lien Creditor 47-3
    Mortgage...47-3
    Proceeds 47-3
    Purchase Money Security Interest 47-4
    Secured Party 47-4, 47-7
    Security Agreement 47-4
    Security Interest...............................47-4
Securities
    Also see Investment Securities........46-6
    Defined 55-3
    Equity Security Holder.....................48-2
    Equity, Defined 48-2
    Types..46-6
Securities Act of 1933
    Accountant's Liability 59-6
    Accredited Investors 55-6
    Accredited Purchasers....................55-7
    Anti-Fraud Provisions......................55-5, 55-11
    Broker..55-9
    Civil Liability 55-11
    Commercial Paper 55-5
    Controlled Securities 55-8
    Controlling Persons.........................55-8
    Coverage 55-4
    Criminal Penalties...........................55-11
    Due Diligence Defense 55-11
    Exempted Securities 55-4
    Exempted Transactions 55-6
    Fraudulent Conveyances 55-11
    Interstate Commerce 55-4, 55-11
    Letters of Deficiency 55-11
    Liability of Offeror or Seller.............55-12
    Nonaccredited Investors 55-7
    Nonaccredited Purchasers..............55-7
    Post-Distribution Transactions 55-8
    Private Offerings 55-7
    Procedural Rules 55-7
    Promoter Compliance With 52-5
    Prospectus.......................................55-4
    Purpose, Structure, and Prohibitions...............55-4
    Refusal Order or Stop Order 55-4, 55-11
    Registration Process........................55-9
    Registration Statement 55-4
    Regulation A 55-5
    Regulation D 55-6

Restricted Securities 55-8
Rule 144 55-8
Rule 237 55-9
Rule 504 55-6
Rule 505 55-6
Rule 506 55-7
Safe Harbor 55-8
Schedule A 55-10
Section 4(1) 55-6
Section 4(2) 55-7
Small Business Investment Act of 1958 55-5
Standard of Reasonableness 55-12
Statute of Limitations 55-12
Underwriter 55-6
Violation of Registration Requirement 55-12
Violations 55-4
Writ of Mandamus 55-4

Securities and Exchange Commission (SEC)
Accountant's Liability 59-5
Administrative Interpretations 55-3
Enforcement 55-3
Investigations 55-3
Letters of Deficiency 55-11
Powers and Functions 55-3
Purpose 55-3
Refusal Order 55-11
Remedies 55-4
Rulemaking 55-3
Schedule 13D 55-16

Securities Exchange Act of 1934
Anti-Fraud Provisions 55-13
Coverage 55-14
Disclosure Requirements 55-14
Federal Reserve System 55-12
Fraud 55-15
Interstate Commerce 55-13
Liability 55-15
Manipulative and Deceptive Practices 55-13
Margin Requirements 55-13
Materiality 55-14
Overview 55-12
Private Parties 55-15
Proxy Solicitations 55-13, 55-15
Purpose of 55-12
Registration Requirements 55-12
Reporting Requirements 55-13
Rule 10b-5 55-14
Rule 13 55-16
Rule 14a-9 55-16
Schedule 13D 55-16
Section 10(b) 55-13
Short Sale 55-13
Tender-Offers 55-13, 55-16
Transactions 55-14
Violations 55-15, 55-16
Writ of Mandamus 55-15

Security Agreement
After-Acquired Property 47-6
Contents of 47-5
Defined 47-4
Future Advances 47-6
Purpose of 47-6

Security Interest
Accessions, in 47-17
Attachment 47-5
Defined 47-4
Fixtures, in 47-17
Perfection 47-8
Secured Party 47-7

Self-Employment Contributions Act
See Social Security 54-3
Servant, Defined 50-2
Settlor (Trustor), Defined 53-6

Shareholders
Control Devices 52-13
Cumulative Voting 52-12
Fiduciary Duties 52-13
Inspection Rights 52-12
Liabilities of 52-13
Loans 52-10
Preemptive Rights 52-3
Proxy 52-3
Voting Rights 52-12

Shelf Registration 55-3
Shelter Principle 46-4
Shelter Provision 45-18
Small Business Investment Act of 1958 55-5

Social Security
Federal Income Tax Ramifications 54-10
Federal Insurance Contributions Act (FICA) 54-2
Federal Unemployment Tax Act (FUTA) 54-2
Financing 54-2
Introduction 54-2
Medicare 54-2
Self-Employment Contributions Act 54-3
Social Security Act 54-2
State Unemployment Taxes 54-2
Workers' Compensation 54-5

Social Security Act
Benefits 54-4
Coverage 54-3
Employee, Defined 54-3
Employment, Defined 54-3
Insurance Programs 54-2
Old-Age, Survivors, and Disability Insurance 54-2
Self-Employed Persons, Defined 54-4
Taxes, FICA 54-4
Tips 54-4
Wages, Defined 54-3

Special Warranty Deed 56-9
Standard of Reasonableness 55-12

Statements on Responsibilities in Tax Practice
Knowledge of Error--Administrative Proceeding ... 58-30
Knowledge of Error--Preparation of Return 58-30
Objectives 58-28
Procedural Aspects of Preparing Returns 58-29
Purpose 58-28
Significance 58-28
Tax Return Positions 58-28
Use of Estimates 58-29
Withdrawal Due to Conflict With Internal
    Revenue Code 58-28

Statute of Frauds
Compliance With 43-7
Sale of Real Property 56-7
Sales Contracts 44-6
Suretyship 49-4

Stock
Authorized 52-6
Capital 52-6
Common 52-7
Contributed Capital 52-7
Convertible Preferred 52-7
Cumulative Preferred 52-7
Dividend Distributions 52-15
Earned Surplus (Retained Earnings) 52-7
Issuance of 52-8
Issued 52-7
Legal Capital (Stated Capital) 52-7

No-Par 52-8
Outstanding 52-7
Paid-In Surplus 52-7
Par Value 52-8
Participating Preferred 52-7
Preferred..52-7
Stock Split..52-15
Straight Preferred...52-7
Surplus...52-7
Transfer of 52-8
Treasury...52-7
Watered 52-3
Strict Liability
    Damages 44-23
    Defenses 44-23
    Privity...44-23
Sublease...56-14
Subrogation
    Fire and Casualty Insurance 57-7
    Suretyship.....................................49-2, 49-6
Subscription Agreements
    Conditional Subscription 52-6
    Defined 52-6
    Enforceable Pre-Incorporation Subscriptions 52-6
    Model Business Corporation Act.................52-6
    Post-Incorporation Subscribers...................52-6
    Pre-Incorporation Subscribers.....................52-6
Surety
    Accommodation Party, as 45-25
    Claims in Bankruptcy 48-11
    Contribution 49-6
    Corporations 52-9
    Defense, Personal 49-7
    Defenses Not Available to............................49-8
    Defenses, Derived From the Debtor.............49-6
    Defined 49-2
    Discharge..49-7
    Exoneration..................................49-2, 49-6
    Fraud or Duress.............................49-6, 49-7
    Insolvency...49-8
    Liability of.....................................49-6, 49-7
    Reimbursement or Indemnity 49-6
    Release of a Co-Surety...................49-7, 49-9
    Release of Collateral....................................49-7
    Release of the Principal Debtor....................49-7
    Rights After Payment 49-6
    Rights Before Payment 49-5
    Subrogation of the........................49-2, 49-6
Surety Bonds
    Characteristics of 49-3
    Defined 49-2
    Fidelity Bonds 49-3
    Judicial Bonds..49-3
    Official Bonds...49-3
    Payment Bonds 49-3
    Performance or Construction Bonds 49-3
Suretyship
    Agent, Del Crede 49-4
    Also see Co-Suretyship................................49-8
    Guaranties, Types of....................................49-3
    Guaranty, vs. 49-2
    Nature and Characteristics of......................49-2
    Principal Debtor (Principal), Defined 49-2
    Statute of Frauds 49-4
    Sub-Suretyship 49-9

T

Tax Preparer, Defined.......................................59-10
Tenancies, Types of 56-11
Tenancy, Freehold
    Accountability..56-7
    Co-Tenancy 56-6
    Duty to Maintain Joint Estate 56-7
    Four Unities of Tenancy...............................56-6
    Inter Vivos Conveyance 56-6
    Joint Tenancy 48-14, 56-6
    Liability...56-7
    Ouster...56-7
    Right of Survivorship...................................56-6
    Rights and Duties Among Co-Tenants 56-7
    Rights and Duties of the Life Tenant 56-4
    Tenancy by the Entirety 48-14, 56-6
    Tenancy in Common.....................................56-6
    Termination...56-6
    Waste..56-4
Tenancy, Leasehold
    Abandonment 56-15
    Advance Rent 56-14
    Covenant of Habitability...............................56-13
    Covenant of Quiet Enjoyment 56-12
    Covenants Against Assignment and Sublease......56-15
    Damages 56-14
    Duty to Pay Rent..56-14
    Duty to Repair 56-14
    Exculpatory Clause 56-13
    Express Agreement 56-11
    Lease Deposits and Damage Clause 56-14
    Negligent Acts of the Tenant.......................56-14
    Operation of Law..56-11
    Privity of Estate 56-15
    Right to Assign or Sublet the Lease 56-14
    Right to Terminate Upon Landlord's Breach of
      Covenant 56-15
    Rights, Duties, and Liabilities of the Tenant 56-14
    Security Deposit...56-14
    Statute of Frauds 56-11
    Sublease...56-15
    Surrender..56-15
    Tenancy at Sufferance 56-12
    Tenancy at Will..56-12
    Tenancy for Years..56-11
    Tenancy From Period to Period 56-11
    Waste..56-14
Tender..44-4
Tender-Offers 55-13, 55-16
Testate, Defined 53-3
Third-Party Beneficiary
    Contracts 43-21
    Defined 59-2
Through Bill, Defined 46-3
Title Insurance 56-8
Title to Goods
    Identification...44-8
    Importance of...44-8
    Passage of..44-8
    Power to Transfer 44-9
Title VII of the Civil Rights Act of 1964
    Illegal Discrimination 54-9
Torts
    Agent's Liability for.......................................50-7
    Partnership's Liability for 51-10
    Principal's Liability for...................................50-7

Trade Acceptance..45-4
Transfer of Shares
    Free Transferability 46-7
    Registration of Transfer............................46-7
    Stolen, Lost, or Destroyed.......................46-8
Transferor, Documents of Title.......................46-4
Trustee
    Avoiding Powers 48-19
    Bankruptcy.............................48-8, 48-12
    Defined 53-6
Trusts
    Active..53-7
    Administrative Expenses............................53-12
    Administrator...53-2
    Allocation of Benefits 53-11
    Allocation of Principal and Income 53-10
    Annuities..53-12
    Beneficiary..53-2, 53-7
    Burdens (Expenses)..................................53-11
    Cash Dividends 53-11
    Charitable 53-2, 53-7
    Constructive...53-8
    Cy Pres Doctrine...53-8
    Definition and Characteristics 53-2, 53-5
    Devise...53-2
    Express...53-8
    Extraordinary Expenses 53-12
    Extraordinary Receipts...............................53-11
    Inter Vivos...53-8
    Invalid 53-10
    Lawful Purpose 53-10
    Ordinary Expenses....................................53-11
    Ordinary Receipts 53-11
    Passive 53-7
    Private 53-8
    Real Estate Investment Trust (REIT) 53-9
    Real Estate Investment Trust Act of 1960..............53-9
    Remainder; Remainderman 53-10
    Resulting..53-8
    Royalties...53-11
    Separation of Legal and Equitable Title.................53-9
    Settlor (Trustor)..53-6
    Spendthrift 53-8
    Termination..53-10
    Testamentary..53-8
    Totten 53-8
    Trust Property (Trust Res) 53-7
    Trustee 53-6
    Types..53-7
    Uniform Principal and Income Act...........53-10

U

Ultra Vires Doctrine......................................52-9
Ultramares Doctrine......................................59-5
Underwriter......................................55-3, 55-6
Unified Credit.............................53-12, 53-15
Uniform Commercial Code (UCC)
    Article 1.............................45-3, 45-16
    Article 2...................43-11, 43-19, 44-5
    Article 3...................45-3, 45-20, 46-4
    Article 4..45-4
    Article 7..46-3
    Article 8..46-7
    Article 9..43-20
    Issuance of Stock 52-8
    Perfection 47-8
    Property 56-3
    Rules of Priority 47-11

Uniform Partnership Act (UPA)
    Aggregate Theory 51-3
    Profits and Losses 51-8
    Real Property...51-6
Uniform Principal and Income Act................53-10

V

Value, Defined...47-4
Vested Remainder..56-5
Voidable Title...44-9
Voting Trust...52-13

W

Wage-Hour Law
    Child Labor 54-10
    Fair Labor Standards Act 54-10
    Maximum Hours..54-10
    Minimum Wage...54-10
Wages 54-3
Waiver (Insurance) 57-7
Warehouse Receipt
    Defined 46-2
    Form and Content......................................46-2
    Fungible Goods...46-5
    Negotiability of 46-3
    Warehouseman 46-5
Warehouseman
    Duty of Care..46-5
    Risk of Loss...46-5
Warranties (Insurance) 57-6
Warranties (Sales)
    Breach of 44-23
    Disclaimer of..44-13
    Express Warranties....................................44-11
    Implied Warranty of Merchantability 44-11
    Privity...44-12
    Statute of Limitations 44-13
    Types of..44-11
Warranties (Securities)
    Breach of 46-8
    Endorsement 46-7
    Endorser's Liability....................................46-7
    Transfer and Presentment 46-7
Watered Stock.............................52-3, 52-13
Will
    Abatement 53-5
    Ademption 53-5
    Ambulatory, Defined 53-3
    Assets, Distribution of 53-3
    Devise..53-3
    Executor...53-2
    Gift, Defined 53-3
    Intestate Succession.................................53-2
    Intestate, Defined......................................53-3
    Legacy 53-3
    Probate 53-2, 53-4
    Probate Court 53-4
    Testate, Defined 53-2
    Testator, Defined 53-2
    Valid...53-3

Workers' Compensation
    Administration 54-7
    Cash Benefits 54-6
    Claims.. 54-7
    Compulsory Statute 54-6
    Death Benefits 54-7
    Elective Statute... 54-6
    Exceptions to Coverage 54-6
    Federal Income Tax Ramifications......................... 54-11
    Impairment Benefits.. 54-7
    Insurance Requirements.. 54-6
    Intoxication of Employee.. 54-8
    Medical Benefits 54-7
    Negligence of Employee 54-6
    Provisions 54-6
    Purpose 54-5
    Rehabilitation Benefits 54-7
    Self-Inflicted Injuries... 54-8
    Unemployment Compensation............................... 54-11
Working Papers 59-8
Writ of Attachment.. 48-3
Writ of Mandamus 55-4, 55-15

NOTES

NOTES

NOTES

NOTES

NOTES

NOTES

NOTES

NOTES

NOTES

APPENDIX B

NOVEMBER 1995 UNIFORM CPA EXAMINATION

BUSINESS LAW & PROFESSIONAL RESPONSIBILITIES

Number 1 (Estimated time--90 to 100 minutes)

1. According to the ethical standards of the profession, which of the following acts is generally prohibited?
a. Purchasing a product from a third party and reselling it to a client.
b. Writing a financial management newsletter promoted and sold by a publishing company.
c. Accepting a commission for recommending a product to an audit client.
d. Accepting engagements obtained through the efforts of third parties.

2. According to the ethical standards of the profession, which of the following acts is generally prohibited?
a. Issuing a modified report explaining a failure to follow a governmental regulatory agency's standards when conducting an attest service for a client.
b. Revealing confidential client information during a quality review of a professional practice by a team from the state CPA society.
c. Accepting a contingent fee for representing a client in an examination of the client's federal tax return by an IRS agent.
d. Retaining client records after an engagement is terminated prior to completion and the client has demanded their return.

3. According to the standards of the profession, which of the following activities may be required in exercising due care?

	Consulting with experts	Obtaining specialty accreditation
a.	Yes	Yes
b.	Yes	No
c.	No	Yes
d.	No	No

4. According to the standards of the profession, which of the following activities would most likely **not** impair a CPA's independence?
a. Providing extensive advisory services for a client.
b. Contracting with a client to supervise the client's office personnel.

c. Signing a client's checks in emergency situations.
d. Accepting a luxurious gift from a client.

5. Under the Statements on Standards for Consulting Services, which of the following statements best reflects a CPA's responsibility when undertaking a consulting services engagement? The CPA must
a. Not seek to modify any agreement made with the client.
b. Not perform any attest services for the client.
c. Inform the client of significant reservations concerning the benefits of the engagement.
d. Obtain a written understanding with the client concerning the time for completion of the engagement.

6. According to the standards of the profession, which of the following sources of information should a CPA consider before signing a client's tax return?

I. Information actually known to the CPA from the tax return of another client.

II. Information provided by the client that appears to be correct based on the client's returns from prior years.

a. I only.
b. II only.
c. Both I and II.
d. Neither I nor II.

7. According to the standards of the profession, which of the following statements is(are) correct regarding the action to be taken by a CPA who discovers an error in a client's previously filed tax return?

I. Advise the client of the error and recommend the measures to be taken.

II. Withdraw from the professional relationship regardless of whether or not the client corrects the error.

a. I only.
b. II only.
c. Both I and II.
d. Neither I nor II.

8. Under the "Ultramares" rule, to which of the following parties will an accountant be liable for negligence?

	Parties in privity	Foreseen parties
a.	Yes	Yes
b.	Yes	No
c.	No	Yes
d.	No	No

9. When performing an audit, a CPA will most likely be considered negligent when the CPA fails to
a.   Detect all of a client's fraudulent activities.
b.   Include a negligence disclaimer in the client engagement letter.
c.   Warn a client of known internal control weaknesses.
d.   Warn a client's customers of embezzlement by the client's employees.

10. Which of the following is the best defense a CPA firm can assert in a suit for common law fraud based on its unqualified opinion on materially false financial statements?
a.   Contributory negligence on the part of the client.
b.   A disclaimer contained in the engagement letter.
c.   Lack of privity.
d.   Lack of scienter.

11. Under the anti-fraud provisions of Section 10(b) of the Securities Exchange Act of 1934, a CPA may be liable if the CPA acted
a.   Negligently.
b.   With independence.
c.   Without due diligence.
d.   Without good faith.

12. Under Section 11 of the Securities Act of 1933, which of the following standards may a CPA use as a defense?

	Generally accepted accounting principles	Generally accepted fraud detection standards
a.	Yes	Yes
b.	Yes	No
c.	No	Yes
d.	No	No

13. Ocean and Associates, CPAs, audited the financial statements of Drain Corporation. As a result of Ocean's negligence in conducting the audit, the financial statements included material misstatements.

Ocean was unaware of this fact. The financial statements and Ocean's unqualified opinion were included in a registration statement and prospectus for an original public offering of stock by Drain. Sharp purchased shares in the offering. Sharp received a copy of the prospectus prior to the purchase but did not read it. The shares declined in value as a result of the misstatements in Drain's financial statements becoming known. Under which of the following Acts is Sharp most likely to prevail in a lawsuit against Ocean?

	Securities Exchange Act of 1934, Section 10(b), Rule 10b-5	Securities Act of 1933, Section 11
a.	Yes	Yes
b.	Yes	No
c.	No	Yes
d.	No	No

14. Which of the following statements is correct regarding a CPA's working papers? The working papers must be
a.   Transferred to another accountant purchasing the CPA's practice even if the client hasn't given permission.
b.   Transferred permanently to the client if demanded.
c.   Turned over to any government agency that requests them.
d.   Turned over pursuant to a valid federal court subpoena.

15. Thorp, CPA, was engaged to audit Ivor Co.'s financial statements. During the audit, Thorp discovered that Ivor's inventory contained stolen goods. Ivor was indicted and Thorp was subpoenaed to testify at the criminal trial. Ivor claimed accountant-client privilege to prevent Thorp from testifying. Which of the following statements is correct regarding Ivor's claim?
a.   Ivor can claim an accountant-client privilege only in states that have enacted a statute creating such a privilege.
b.   Ivor can claim an accountant-client privilege only in federal courts.
c.   The accountant-client privilege can be claimed only in civil suits.
d.   The accountant-client privilege can be claimed only to limit testimony to audit subject matter.

16. Generally, under the Uniform Partnership Act, a partnership has which of the following characteristics?

	Unlimited duration	Obligation for payment of federal income tax
a.	Yes	Yes
b.	Yes	No
c.	No	Yes
d.	No	No

17. Which of the following statements is(are) usually correct regarding general partners' liability?

I. All general partners are jointly and severally liable for partnership torts.

II. All general partners are liable only for those partnership obligations they actually authorized.

a. I only.
b. II only.
c. Both I and II.
d. Neither I nor II.

18. Which of the following statements is correct regarding the division of profits in a general partnership when the written partnership agreement only provides that losses be divided equally among the partners? Profits are to be divided
a. Based on the partners' ratio of contribution to the partnership.
b. Based on the partners' participation in day to day management.
c. Equally among the partners.
d. Proportionately among the partners.

19. Which of the following statements best describes the effect of the assignment of an interest in a general partnership?
a. The assignee becomes a partner.
b. The assignee is responsible for a proportionate share of past and future partnership debts.
c. The assignment automatically dissolves the partnership.
d. The assignment transfers the assignor's interest in partnership profits and surplus.

20. Park and Graham entered into a written partnership agreement to operate a retail store. Their agreement was silent as to the duration of the partnership. Park wishes to dissolve the partnership. Which of the following statements is correct?

a. Park may dissolve the partnership at any time.
b. Unless Graham consents to a dissolution, Park must apply to a court and obtain a decree ordering the dissolution.
c. Park may **not** dissolve the partnership unless Graham consents.
d. Park may dissolve the partnership only after notice of the proposed dissolution is given to all partnership creditors.

21. Which of the following facts is(are) generally included in a corporation's articles of incorporation?

	Name of registered agent	Number of authorized shares
a.	Yes	Yes
b.	Yes	No
c.	No	Yes
d.	No	No

22. Which of the following statements best describes an advantage of the corporate form of doing business?
a. Day to day management is strictly the responsibility of the directors.
b. Ownership is contractually restricted and is **not** transferable.
c. The operation of the business may continue indefinitely.
d. The business is free from state regulation.

23. To which of the following rights is a stockholder of a public corporation entitled?
a. The right to have annual dividends declared and paid.
b. The right to vote for the election of officers.
c. The right to a reasonable inspection of corporate records.
d. The right to have the corporation issue a new class of stock.

24. Carr Corp. declared a 7% stock dividend on its common stock. The dividend
a. Must be registered with the SEC pursuant to the Securities Act of 1933.
b. Is includable in the gross income of the recipient taxpayers in the year of receipt.
c. Has **no** effect on Carr's earnings and profits for federal income tax purposes.
d. Requires a vote of Carr's stockholders.

25. Which of the following statements is a general requirement for the merger of two corporations?
a. The merger plan must be approved unanimously by the stockholders of both corporations.
b. The merger plan must be approved unanimously by the boards of both corporations.
c. The absorbed corporation must amend its articles of incorporation.
d. The stockholders of both corporations must be given due notice of a special meeting, including a copy or summary of the merger plan.

26. Which of the following statements is(are) correct regarding debtors' rights?

I. State exemption statutes prevent all of a debtor's personal property from being sold to pay a federal tax lien.

II. Federal social security benefits received by a debtor are exempt from garnishment by creditors.

a. I only.
b. II only.
c. Both I and II.
d. Neither I nor II.

27. Which of the following liens generally require(s) the lienholder to give notice of legal action before selling the debtor's property to satisfy the debt?

	Mechanic's lien	Artisan's lien
a.	Yes	Yes
b.	Yes	No
c.	No	Yes
d.	No	No

28. Which of the following rights does one cosurety generally have against another cosurety?
a. Exoneration.
b. Subrogation.
c. Reimbursement.
d. Contribution.

29. Which of the following acts always will result in the total release of a compensated surety?
a. The creditor changes the manner of the principal debtor's payment.
b. The creditor extends the principal debtor's time to pay.
c. The principal debtor's obligation is partially released.
d. The principal debtor's performance is tendered.

30. When a principal debtor defaults and a surety pays the creditor the entire obligation, which of the following remedies gives the surety the best method of collecting from the debtor?
a. Exoneration.
b. Contribution.
c. Subrogation.
d. Attachment.

31. Under the Federal Insurance Contributions Act (FICA), which of the following acts will cause an employer to be liable for penalties?

	Failure to supply taxpayer identification numbers	Failure to make timely FICA deposits
a.	Yes	Yes
b.	Yes	No
c.	No	Yes
d.	No	No

32. Taxes payable under the Federal Unemployment Tax Act (FUTA) are
a. Calculated as a fixed percentage of all compensation paid to an employee.
b. Deductible by the employer as a business expense for federal income tax purposes.
c. Payable by employers for all employees.
d. Withheld from the wages of all covered employees.

33. Which of the following claims is(are) generally covered under workers' compensation statutes?

	Occupational disease	Employment aggravated pre-existing disease
a.	Yes	Yes
b.	Yes	No
c.	No	Yes
d.	No	No

34. Generally, which of the following statements concerning workers' compensation laws is correct?
a. The amount of damages recoverable is based on comparative negligence.
b. Employers are strictly liable without regard to whether or **not** they are at fault.
c. Workers' compensation benefits are **not** available if the employee is negligent.
d. Workers' compensation awards are payable for life.

35. Under the Age Discrimination in Employment Act, which of the following remedies is(are) available to a covered employee?

	Early retirement	Back pay
a.	Yes	Yes
b.	Yes	No
c.	No	Yes
d.	No	No

36. Which of the following Acts prohibit(s) an employer from discriminating among employees based on sex?

	Equal Pay Act	Title VII of the Civil Rights Act
a.	Yes	Yes
b.	Yes	No
c.	No	Yes
d.	No	No

37. Under the Fair Labor Standards Act, which of the following pay bases may be used to pay covered, nonexempt employees who earn, on average, the minimum hourly wage?

	Hourly	Weekly	Monthly
a.	Yes	Yes	Yes
b.	Yes	Yes	No
c.	Yes	No	Yes
d.	No	Yes	Yes

38. Under the Fair Labor Standards Act, if a covered, nonexempt employee works consecutive weeks of 45, 42, 38, and 33 hours, how many hours of overtime must be paid to the employee?
a. 0
b. 7
c. 18
d. 20

39. Under the Employee Retirement Income Security Act of 1974 (ERISA), which of the following areas of private employer pension plans is(are) regulated?

	Employee vesting	Plan funding
a.	Yes	Yes
b.	Yes	No
c.	No	Yes
d.	No	No

40. Which of the following employee benefits is(are) exempt from the provisions of the National Labor Relations Act?

	Sick pay	Vacation pay
a.	Yes	Yes
b.	Yes	No
c.	No	Yes
d.	No	No

41. Under the Sales Article of the UCC, a firm offer will be created only if the
a. Offer states the time period during which it will remain open.
b. Offer is made by a merchant in a signed writing.
c. Offeree gives some form of consideration.
d. Offeree is a merchant.

42. Under the Sales Article of the UCC, when a written offer has been made without specifying a means of acceptance but providing that the offer will only remain open for ten days, which of the following statements represent(s) a valid acceptance of the offer?

I. An acceptance sent by regular mail the day before the ten-day period expires that reaches the offeror on the eleventh day.

II. An acceptance faxed the day before the ten-day period expires that reaches the offeror on the eleventh day, due to a malfunction of the offeror's printer.

a. I only.
b. II only.
c. Both I and II.
d. Neither I nor II.

43. Under the Sales Article of the UCC, the warranty of title
a. Provides that the seller cannot disclaim the warranty if the sale is made to a bona fide purchaser for value.
b. Provides that the seller deliver the goods free from any lien of which the buyer lacked knowledge when the contract was made.
c. Applies only if it is in writing and signed by the seller.
d. Applies only if the seller is a merchant.

44. To establish a cause of action based on strict liability in tort for personal injuries that result from the use of a defective product, one of the elements the injured party must prove is that the seller
a. Was aware of the defect in the product.
b. Sold the product to the injured party.
c. Failed to exercise due care.
d. Sold the product in a defective condition.

45. Under the Sales Article of the UCC, which of the following factors is most important in determining who bears the risk of loss in a sale of goods contract?
a. The method of shipping the goods.
b. The contract's shipping terms.
c. Title to the goods.
d. How the goods were lost.

46. Under the Sales Article of the UCC, in an F.O.B. place of shipment contract, the risk of loss passes to the buyer when the goods
a. Are identified to the contract.
b. Are placed on the seller's loading dock.
c. Are delivered to the carrier.
d. Reach the buyer's loading dock.

47. Under the Sales Article of the UCC, which of the following rights is(are) available to the buyer when a seller commits an anticipatory breach of contract?

	Demand assurance of performance	Cancel the contract	Collect punitive damages
a.	Yes	Yes	Yes
b.	Yes	Yes	No
c.	Yes	No	Yes
d.	No	Yes	Yes

48. Under the Sales Article of the UCC, and unless otherwise agreed to, the seller's obligation to the buyer is to
a. Deliver the goods to the buyer's place of business.
b. Hold conforming goods and give the buyer whatever notification is reasonably necessary to enable the buyer to take delivery.
c. Deliver all goods called for in the contract to a common carrier.
d. Set aside conforming goods for inspection by the buyer before delivery.

49. Under the Sales Article of the UCC, which of the following statements regarding liquidated damages is(are) correct?

I. The injured party may collect any amount of liquidated damages provided for in the contract.

II. The seller may retain a deposit of up to $500 when a buyer defaults even if there is no liquidated damages provision in the contract.

a. I only.
b. II only.
c. Both I and II.
d. Neither I nor II.

50. Under the Sales Article of the UCC, which of the following rights is available to a seller when a buyer materially breaches a sales contract?

	Right to cancel the contract	Right to recover damages
a.	Yes	Yes
b.	Yes	No
c.	No	Yes
d.	No	No

51. Long, Fall, and Pear own a building as joint tenants with the right of survivorship. Long gave Long's interest in the building to Green by executing and delivering a deed to Green. Neither Fall nor Pear consented to this transfer. Fall and Pear subsequently died. After their deaths, Green's interest in the building would consist of
a. A 1/3 interest as a joint tenant.
b. A 1/3 interest as a tenant in common.
c. No interest because Fall and Pear did **not** consent to the transfer.
d. Total ownership due to the deaths of Fall and Pear.

52. A method of transferring ownership of real property that most likely would be considered an arm's-length transaction is transfer by
a. Inheritance.
b. Eminent domain.
c. Adverse possession.
d. Sale.

53. Which of the following provisions must be included to have an enforceable written residential lease?

	A description of the leased premises	A due date for the payment of rent
a.	Yes	Yes
b.	Yes	No
c.	No	Yes
d.	No	No

54. Which of the following elements must be contained in a valid deed?

	Purchase price	Description of the land
a.	Yes	Yes
b.	Yes	No
c.	No	Yes
d.	No	No

55. Rich purchased property from Sklar for $200,000. Rich obtained a $150,000 loan from Marsh Bank to finance the purchase, executing a promissory note and a mortgage. By recording the mortgage, Marsh protects its
a. Rights against Rich under the promissory note.
b. Rights against the claims of subsequent bona fide purchasers for value.
c. Priority against a previously filed real estate tax lien on the property.
d. Priority against all parties having earlier claims to the property.

56. Which of the following factors help determine whether an item of personal property is a fixture?

I. Degree of the item's attachment to the property.

II. Intent of the person who had the item installed.

a. I only.
b. II only.
c. Both I and II.
d. Neither I nor II.

57. Which of the following activities is(are) regulated under the Federal Water Pollution Control Act (Clean Water Act)?

	Discharge of heated water by nuclear power plants	Dredging of wetlands
a.	Yes	Yes
b.	Yes	No
c.	No	Yes
d.	No	No

58. Which of the following methods of obtaining personal property will give the recipient ownership of the property?

	Lease	Finding abandoned property
a.	Yes	Yes
b.	Yes	No
c.	No	Yes
d.	No	No

59. A common carrier bailee generally would avoid liability for loss of goods entrusted to its care if the goods are
a. Stolen by an unknown person.
b. Negligently destroyed by an employee.
c. Destroyed by the derailment of the train carrying them due to railroad employee negligence.
d. Improperly packed by the party shipping them.

60. Which of the following statements correctly describes the requirement of insurable interest relating to property insurance? An insurable interest
a. Must exist when any loss occurs.
b. Must exist when the policy is issued and when any loss occurs.
c. Is created only when the property is owned in fee simple.
d. Is created only when the property is owned by an individual.

Number 2 (Estimated time--10 to 15 minutes)

Question Number 2 consists of two parts. Each part consists of five items. Select the **best** answer for each item.

a. Items 61 through 65 are based on the following.

Lace Computer Sales Corp. orally contracted with Banks, an independent consultant, for Banks to work part-time as Lace's agent to perform Lace's customers' service calls. Banks, a computer programmer and software designer, was authorized to customize Lace's software to the customers' needs, on a commission basis, but was specifically told not to sell Lace's computers.

On September 15, Banks made a service call on Clear Co. to repair Clear's computer. Banks had previously called on Clear, customized Lace's software for Clear, and collected cash payments for the work performed. During the call, Banks convinced Clear to buy an upgraded Lace computer for a price much lower than Lace would normally charge. Clear had previously purchased computers from other Lace agents and had made substantial cash down payments to the agents. Clear had no knowledge that the price was lower than normal. Banks received a $1,000 cash down payment and promised to deliver the computer the next week. Banks never turned in the down payment and left town. When Clear called the following week to have the computer delivered, Lace refused to honor Clear's order.

Required:

Items 61 through 65 relate to the relationship between the parties. For each item, select from List I whether only statement I is correct, whether only statement II is correct, whether both statements I and II are correct, or whether neither statement I nor II is correct.

List I
(A)	I only.
(B)	II only.
(C)	Both I and II.
(D)	Neither I nor II.

61.
  I. Lace's agreement with Banks had to be in writing for it to be a valid agency agreement.
  II. Lace's agreement with Banks empowered Banks to act as Lace's agent.

62.
  I. Clear was entitled to rely on Banks' implied authority to customize Lace's software.
  II. Clear was entitled to rely on Banks' express authority when buying the computer.

63.
  I. Lace's agreement with Banks was automatically terminated by Banks' sale of the computer.
  II. Lace must notify Clear before Banks' apparent authority to bind Lace will cease.

64.
  I. Lace is **not** bound by the agreement made by Banks with Clear.
  II. Lace may unilaterally amend the agreement made by Banks to prevent a loss on the sale of the computer to Clear.

65.
  I. Lace, as a disclosed principal, is solely contractually liable to Clear.
  II. Both Lace and Banks are contractually liable to Clear.

b. Items 66 through 70 are based on the following:

Under the provisions of Glenn's testamentary trust, after payment of all administrative expenses and taxes, the entire residuary estate was to be paid to Strong and Lake as trustees. The trustees were authorized to invest the trust assets, and directed to distribute income annually to Glenn's children for their lives, then distribute the principal to Glenn's grandchildren, per capita. The trustees were also authorized to make such principal payments to the income beneficiaries that the trustees determined to be reasonable for the beneficiaries' welfare. Glenn died in 1992. On Glenn's death there were two surviving children, aged 21 and 30, and one two-year old grandchild.

On June 15, 1995, the trustees made the following distributions from the trust:

- Paid the 1992, 1993, and 1994 trust income to Glenn's children. This amount included the proceeds from the sale of stock received by the trust as a stock dividend.
- Made a $10,000 principal payment for medical school tuition to one of Glenn's children.
- Made a $5,000 principal payment to Glenn's grandchild.

Required:

For each item, select from List II whether only statement I is correct, whether only statement II is correct, whether both statements I and II are correct, or whether neither statement I nor II is correct.

List II
(A)	I only.
(B)	II only.
(C)	Both I and II.
(D)	Neither I nor II.

66.
  I. Glenn's trust was valid because it did **not** violate the rule against perpetuities.
  II. Glenn's trust was valid even though it permitted the trustees to make principal payments to income beneficiaries.

67.
  I. Glenn's trust would be terminated if both of Glenn's children were to die.
  II. Glenn's trust would be terminated because of the acts of the trustees.

68.
  I. Strong and Lake violated their fiduciary duties by making any distributions of principal.
  II. Strong and Lake violated their fiduciary duties by failing to distribute the trust income annually.

69.
  I. Generally, stock dividends are considered income and should be distributed.
  II. Generally, stock dividends should be allocated to principal and remain as part of the trust.

70.
  I. The $10,000 principal payment was an abuse of the trustees' authority.
  II. The $5,000 principal payment was valid because of its payment to a non-income beneficiary.

Number 3 (Estimated time--10 to 15 minutes)

Question Number 3 consists of two parts. Each part consists of five items.

a. **Items 71 through 75** are based on the following:

On June 1, 1995, Rusk Corp. was petitioned involuntarily into bankruptcy. At the time of the filing, Rusk had the following creditors:

- Safe Bank, for the balance due on the secured note and mortgage on Rusk's warehouse.
- Employee salary claims.
- 1994 federal income taxes due.
- Accountant's fees outstanding.
- Utility bills outstanding.

Prior to the bankruptcy filing, but while insolvent, Rusk engaged in the following transactions:

- On February 1, 1995, Rusk repaid all corporate directors' loans made to the corporation.
- On May 1, 1995, Rusk purchased raw materials for use in its manufacturing business and paid cash to the supplier.

Required:

Items 71 through 75 relate to Rusk's creditors and the February 1 and May 1 transactions. For each item, select from List I whether only statement I is correct, whether only statement II is correct, whether both statements I and II are correct, or whether neither statement I nor II is correct.

List I	
(A)	I only.
(B)	II only.
(C)	Both I and II.
(D)	Neither I nor II.

71.
I. Safe Bank's claim will be the first paid of the listed claims because Safe is a secured creditor.
II. Safe Bank will receive the entire amount of the balance of the mortgage due as a secured creditor regardless of the amount received from the sale of the warehouse.

72.
I. The employee salary claims will be paid in full after the payment of any secured party.
II. The employee salary claims up to $4,000 per claimant will be paid before payment of any general creditors' claims.

73.
I. The claim for 1994 federal income taxes due will be paid as a secured creditor claim.
II. The claim for 1994 federal income taxes due will be paid prior to the general creditor claims.

74.
I. The February 1 repayments of the directors' loans were preferential transfers even though the payments were made more than 90 days before the filing of the petition.
II. The February 1 repayments of the directors' loans were preferential transfers because the payments were made to insiders.

75.
I. The May 1 purchase and payment was **not** a preferential transfer because it was a transaction in the ordinary course of business.
II. The May 1 purchase and payment was a preferential transfer because it occurred within 90 days of the filing of the petition.

b. **Items 76 through 80** are based on the following:

Coffee Corp., a publicly-held corporation, wants to make an $8,000,000 exempt offering of its shares as a private placement offering under Regulation D, Rule 506, of the Securities Act of 1933. Coffee has more than 500 shareholders and assets in excess of $1 billion, and has its shares listed on a national securities exchange.

Required:

Items 76 through 80 relate to the application of the provisions of the Securities Act of 1933 and the Securities Exchange Act of 1934 to Coffee Corp. and the offering. For each item, select from List II whether only statement I is correct, whether only statement II is correct, whether both statements I and II are correct, or whether neither statement I nor II is correct.

List II	
(A)	I only.
(B)	II only.
(C)	Both I and II.
(D)	Neither I nor II.

76.

I.   Coffee Corp. may make the Regulation D, Rule 506, exempt offering.

II. Coffee Corp., because it is required to report under the Securities Exchange Act of 1934, may **not** make an exempt offering.

77.

I.   Shares sold under a Regulation D, Rule 506, exempt offering may only be purchased by accredited investors.

II. Shares sold under a Regulation D, Rule 506, exempt offering may be purchased by any number of investors provided there are **no** more than 35 non-accredited investors.

78.

I.   An exempt offering under Regulation D, Rule 506, must **not** be for more than $10,000,000.

II. An exempt offering under Regulation D, Rule 506, has **no** dollar limit.

79.

I.   Regulation D, Rule 506, requires that all investors in the exempt offering be notified that for nine months after the last sale **no** resale may be made to a nonresident.

II. Regulation D, Rule 506, requires that the issuer exercise reasonable care to assure that purchasers of the exempt offering are buying for investment and are **not** underwriters.

80.

I.   The SEC must be notified by Coffee Corp. within 5 days of the first sale of the exempt offering securities.

II. Coffee Corp. must include an SEC notification of the first sale of the exempt offering securities in Coffee's next filed Quarterly Report (Form 10-Q).

NOVEMBER 1995 UNIFORM CPA EXAMINATION
BUSINESS LAW & PROFESSIONAL RESPONSIBILITIES UNOFFICIAL SOLUTIONS

1. (c) Rule 503 prohibits a CPA from accepting a commission for recommending a product to an audit client. The other activities are not prohibited.

2. (d) Retaining a client's records after an engagement is terminated prior to completion and the client has demanded their return is prohibited by the ethical standards of the profession. Issuing a modified report explaining a failure to follow a governmental agency's standards and revealing confidential client information during a state review of a professional practice are not ethically prohibited. Interpretation of Rule 302 provides that a contingency fee is permissible when a CPA represents a client in an *examination* by a revenue agent.

3. (b) According to the standards of the profession, an exercise in due care may require consulting with experts, but would not require obtaining specialty accreditation.

4. (a) According to the standards of the profession (ET 191), providing extensive advisory services for a client would not impair the CPA's independence. Contracting with a client to supervise the client's office personnel, signing client checks, and accepting luxurious gifts would all impair a CPA's independence.

5. (c) Under the Statements of Standards for Consulting Services, a CPA has the responsibility to inform the client of significant reservations concerning the benefits of the engagement. The Standards for Consulting Services do not require a CPA to obtain a written understanding with the client concerning the time for completion of the engagement. Nor do the Standards prohibit a CPA from modifying a client agreement or from performing attest services.

6. (c) According to the standards of the profession, a CPA may consider both information provided by the client that appears to be correct based on prior year filings and information actually known to the CPA from the tax return of another client.

7. (a) According to professional standards, a CPA who discovers an error in a client's previously filed tax return must advise the client of the error and recommend the measures to be taken. It is not necessary for the CPA to withdraw from the professional relationship, unless the client refuses to correct the error.

8. (b) The U.S. Supreme Court's decision in the Ultramares case holds that an accountant is only liable to parties for whose primary benefit the work was intended. This would include only parties in privity of contact with the accountant. The CPA would not be liable in negligence to foreseen parties not in privity of contract with the accountant.

9. (c) Negligence involves a breach of a duty of due care. A CPA would most likely be considered negligent while performing an audit when the CPA fails to warn a client of known internal control weaknesses. A CPA has no duty to detect all of a client's fraudulent activities nor to warn a client's customers of embezzlement by the client's employees. If no such duty is imposed, then negligence cannot exist. Failure to include a negligence disclaimer in a client engagement letter would also not result in a CPA being found negligent.

10. (d) A CPA is liable for common law fraud when there is (1) a misstatement of material fact, (2) scienter (which exists if the CPA acted with knowledge of the falsity or a reckless disregard for the truth and the intent to mislead), and (3) justifiable reliance by the injured party. Thus, lack of scienter would be the CPA's best defense. Contributory negligence and lack of privity are not defenses to an action for fraud. A fraud disclaimer contained in an engagement letter would not protect the CPA from liability for his/her fraudulent actions.

11. (d) Under the anti-fraud provisions of Section 10(b) of the Securities Exchange Act of 1934, a CPA may be liable for fraud if the CPA makes a material misrepresentation of fact with knowledge of its falsity or with a reckless disregard for the truth, i.e., scienter. Acting without scienter involves acting without good faith. Negligence is not an issue with fraud. A CPA should always act with independence in auditing engagements. Due diligence is a defense for fraud under the provisions of the Securities Act of 1933.

12. (b) Under Section 11 of the Securities Act of 1933 a CPA charged with fraud can use the due diligence defense. Due diligence would include following generally accepted accounting principles. There are no generally accepted fraud detection standards.

13. (c) An original public offering of stock would be governed by the provisions of the Securities Act of 1933. Under section 11 of this Act, a CPA can be liable for fraud if the registration statement contains

material misstatements. It is not necessary that the CPA have scienter or that the client relied on the registration materials.

14. (d) Since the Fifth Amendment to the U.S. Constitution does not extend to the CPA-client relationship, CPAs must turn over their working papers pursuant to a valid federal court subpoena, but need not turn over papers merely at government request. Working papers are the property of the accountant and need not be given to the client, nor may a CPA turn over working papers without a client's permission.

15. (a) The United States Supreme Court has held that the U.S. Constitution's Fifth Amendment rights regarding self-incrimination do not extend to the CPA-client relationship. A number of states, however, do recognize such a privilege pursuant to state constitutional protections. Thus, Ivor can claim the privilege in those states that recognize such a privilege. There are no other instances in which a CPA-client privilege is recognized The type of suit is irrelevant.

16. (d) Under the Uniform Partnership Act a partnership has neither unlimited duration nor an obligation for the payment of federal income tax. A partnership, unlike a corporation, dissolves every time its ownership changes, limiting its duration. For federal income tax purposes a partnership is considered a "flow-thru" in that the individual owners are obligated for the payment of federal taxes.

17. (a) All general partners in a partnership are jointly and severally liable for partnership torts. However, a general partner may be liable for the unauthorized acts of partnership employees and other partners.

18. (c) The Uniform Partnership Act provides that where a partnership agreement is silent as to the division of profits, than profits will be divided equally among the partners, regardless of their capital contributions or degree of participation in management. Liability for partnership losses is allocated according to the same ratio as distribution of profits.

19. (d) A general partner's interest in the partnership refers to that partner's right to participate in profit distributions and a return of capital upon dissolution. Thus, a general partner may transfer this interest without dissolving the partnership. The assignee receives nothing more that the assignor's interest in partnership profits and surplus. The assignee does not become a partner and thus incurs no liability for partnership debts.

20. (a) If the partnership agreement is silent as to duration, then the partnership is at-will, and either partner may terminate at any time without incurring liability. The dissolution of a partnership-at-will does not require the consent of other partners, creditors, or the courts.

21. (a) Most state enabling acts (incorporation statutes) require *both* the name of the registered agent and the number of authorized shares.

22. (c) A primary advantage of the corporate form of doing business is ownership is freely and easily transferable and does not result in a dissolution, thus permitting the business to continue indefinitely. Day to day management is the responsibility of the officers, not the directors. A corporation is subject to state regulation.

23. (c) A stockholder of a public corporation is entitled to a reasonable inspection of corporate records, for a proper purpose. A stockholder does not have the right to an annual payment of dividends or to have the corporation issue a new class of stock. A stockholder has the right to vote for corporate directors, not officers.

24. (c) The declaration of a stock dividend has no impact on the earnings and profits of the corporation for federal income tax purposes. Stock dividends are exempt securities under the Securities Act of 1933. A stock dividend, unlike a cash dividend, is not includable in the gross income of recipient taxpayers; rather it results in an adjustment to stock basis. Declaration of a stock dividend requires a vote of the board of directors, not of the stockholders.

25. (d) The Model Business Corporations Act provides that a merger requires that the stockholders of both corporations be given a copy of the merger plan as well as proper notice of a special meeting at which the merger plan will be presented. Although the merger plan must be approved by the stockholders and directors of both corporations, it is not necessary that the vote be unanimous. The articles of incorporation of the absorbing corporation may be amended, but the articles of the absorbed corporation cease to exist.

26. (b) State exemption statutes do not prevent all of a debtor's personal property from being sold to pay any creditor since property exempt by statute may be retained by the debtor. They may protect *some* of a debtor's property from being sold. Federal social security benefits are exempt from garnishment by creditors.

27. (a) Both a mechanic's lien and an artisan's lien require the lienholder to give notice of legal action before selling the debtor's property to satisfy the debt.

28. (d) A co-surety who pays more than their pro-rata share of a liability is entitled to contribution from any other co-sureties. Exoneration, subrogation and reimbursement represent rights a surety has against a debtor.

29. (d) If the principal debtor offers to satisfy the obligation (i.e., tenders performance), then the surety is released of any further liability. A principal debtor's partial release would also partially release a surety from liability. A change in the manner or time for repayment has no impact on a surety's liability.

30. (c) When a principal debtor defaults and the surety pays the entire obligation, the surety inherits from the creditor all of the creditor's rights against the debtor. This is called the right of subrogation.

31. (a) Under the Federal Insurance Contributions Act (FICA) an employer will be liable for penalties both for failure to supply taxpayer identification numbers and for failure to make timely FICA deposits.

32. (b) Taxes paid by an employer under the Federal Unemployment Tax Act (FUTA) are deductible by the employer as a business expense for federal income tax purposes. The tax rate for 1993 and 1994 is 6.2% for the first $7,000 in wages paid to each covered employee. Employers must pay the FUTA tax if they pay $1,500 or more in wages in any calendar quarter or employ more than one person at least one day a week for 20 weeks during a calendar year. FUTA taxes are paid by the employer and are not withheld from the employee.

33. (a) Worker's compensation statutes generally cover occupational diseases, even providing coverage for pre-existing conditions, if aggravated by current working conditions.

34. (b) Under worker's compensation statutes employers are held strictly liable without regard to whether or not they are at fault. The amount of damages recoverable is based on state statute, and generally payments are not payable for life. An employee's own negligence will not prevent the employee from receiving worker's compensation benefits.

35. (c) Under the Age Discrimination in Employment Act back pay is a remedy available to a covered employee, but early retirement is not.

36. (a) Sexual discrimination among employees is prohibited under both the Equal Pay Act and Title VII of the Civil Rights Act.

37. (a) Under the Fair Labor Standards Act (FLSA) hourly, weekly, and monthly pay bases may be used to pay covered, nonexempt employees who earn, on average, the minimum hourly wage.

38. (b) The Fair Labor Standards Act (FLSA) requires that covered, nonexempt employees be paid overtime for any hours in excess of forty worked in a week. In two of the weeks listed the employee worked in excess of forty hours and is entitled to overtime pay. It is irrelevant that the employee worked less than forty hours in the following weeks.

39. (a) The Employment Retirement Income Security Act (ERISA) regulates both employee vesting and plan funding of private employer pension plans.

40. (d) Neither sick pay nor vacation pay are exempt from the provisions of the National Labor Relations Act.

41. (b) UCC 2-205 states that a merchant creates a firm offer by making an offer in a signed writing. If the offer does not state the time period for which it is open, a period of 90 days will be assumed. It is not necessary for the offeree to be a merchant, nor is it necessary that the offeree give any consideration.

42. (c) UCC 2 does not eliminate the deposited acceptance (or "mail-box") rule, which states that a properly dispatched acceptance is valid upon dispatch. Both a faxed and a mailed acceptance would be valid means of acceptance, and in each case acceptance occurred upon dispatch.

43. (b) Under UCC 2 an implied warranty of title is created anytime a good is sold, regardless of whether the seller is a merchant or whether there is a writing. The implied warranty of title may be disclaimed, but where it exists provides that the seller deliver the goods free from any lien of which the buyer lacked knowledge.

44. (d) In order to prove strict liability in tort for personal injuries resulting from a defective product the injured party must show that the product was sold in a defective condition. Knowledge and due care are irrelevant in strict liability actions, and any seller in the chain of distribution may be strictly liable for consumer injuries.

45. (b)   Under the UCC Sales Article, the contract's shipping terms would be most important in determining who bears the risk of loss. The method of shipping the goods and how the goods were destroyed is irrelevant. Although title and risk of loss frequently pass together, the UCC does not require that they do so, thus a person may hold title and not have risk of loss.

46. (c)   Under the Sales Article of the UCC, in an F.O.B. place of shipment contract, risk of loss passes to the buyer when the goods are delivered to the carrier.

47. (b)   Under the Sales Article of the UCC, when a seller commits an anticipatory breach of contract the buyer can demand assurance of performance (UCC 2-609) or cancel the contract (UCC 2-610). Punitive damages are never available in breach of contract actions.

48. (b)   Under the Sales Article of the UCC, and unless otherwise agreed to, the seller's obligation to the buyer is to hold conforming goods and give the buyer necessary notice to take delivery. The UCC does not require, absent an agreement, that the goods be held for the buyer's inspection prior to delivery, that the goods be delivered to the buyer's place of business, or that all goods be delivered to a common carrier.

49. (b)   UCC 2-718 provides that a seller may retain a deposit of up to $500 when a buyer defaults even if there is no liquidated damages provision in the contract. Otherwise, an injured party may collect a reasonable amount of liquidated damages.

50. (a)   Under the UCC Sales Article, a seller has both the right to cancel the contract and the right to recover damages when the buyer materially breaches a sales contract.

51. (b)   An inter vivos (during life) conveyance terminates a joint tenancy. The grantee's (Green's) interest is a tenancy in common with the remaining joint tenants. The remaining joint tenants' interests still represent a joint tenancy. Thus Green has a 1/3 interest as a tenant in common. Green is not a joint tenant because the right of survivorship as to his share was extinguished upon the transfer from Long. The consent of other joint tenants is not necessary for an inter vivos conveyance by a joint tenant. Fall's and Pear's shares would not fall to Green upon their deaths. Rather, whichever joint tenant (Fall or Pear) survived the other became the sole owner of the remaining 2/3 share and a tenant in common with Green.

52. (d)   A sale is a method of transferring ownership of real property in what would be considered an arm's-length transaction. Inheritance, eminent domain and adverse possession would not be considered arm's-length transactions.

53. (b)   An enforceable written residential lease would have to include a description of the leased premises, but would not have to specify a due date for the payment of rent.

54. (c)   A valid deed must contain a description of the land but need not state the purchase price.

55. (b)   By recording a mortgage a creditor protects its priority against all parties having earlier (not subsequent) claims to the property. Previously filed tax liens would still have priority over the mortgage lien, thus answer A is incorrect. A creditor's rights against a debtor are already protected under the promissory note, and recording of the mortgage is not necessary.

56. (c)   Both the degree of an item's attachment to real property and the intent of the person who installed the item are factors to consider when determining whether an item of personal property is a fixture.

57. (a)   The Federal Water Pollution Control Act (Clean Water Act) regulates both the discharge of heated water by nuclear power plants and the dredging of wetlands.

58. (c)   The finder of abandoned property obtains an ownership interest in that property. The holder of a lease has only a possessory interest.

59. (d)   A common carrier has liability for even slight negligence. A common carrier would thus be liable if the goods were stolen while in the carrier's custody. The carrier would also be liable if the goods were destroyed as a result of its employees' negligence. The carrier would not, however, have any knowledge or control over how the goods were packed by the bailor or other party.

60. (a)   An insurable interest must be present at the time of loss, even if it is not present at the time of issuance. Under what type of fee the property is owned and whether the owner is an individual or a corporation are irrelevant as to whether an insurable interest exists.

61. B

The only element necessary to create a valid agency relationship is mutual consent. A writing is only necessary if the Statute of Frauds applies. Thus, if the agency is for the purchase or sale of real property or is to endure for more than one year, then a written contract is required. Neither of those situations is present here, thus the oral agreement is valid and empowered Banks to act as Lace's agent.

62. A

Clear was entitled to rely on Banks' express, implied and apparent authority to customize Lace's software since Banks had previously performed such services on Lace's behalf for Clear. Banks had no express authority to sell computers on behalf of Lace since Lace had not given Banks permission to do so.

63. B

An agent's relationship with the principal is not automatically terminated by the agent's violation of his/her express authority. The principal would have to take action to terminate the agency relationship. If a principal wants to terminate an agent's apparent authority, the principal must give actual notice to all third parties who have previously dealt with the agent. Thus Lace must notify Clear.

64. D

Banks had no actual authority to sell computers on Lace's behalf, but Banks had apparent authority to sell Lace's computers because of Bank's apparent similarity to Lace's other agents. Although a principal may ratify an agent's unauthorized acts, ratification requires that the principal accept the contract as negotiated. A principal cannot unilaterally amend the agreement.

65. A

Lace, a disclosed principal, is liable to Clear since Bank's had apparent authority to sell the computer. Banks is not contractually liable to Clear, as Banks was the apparent agent for a disclosed principal.

66. C

The rule against perpetuities limits the duration of a trust to a life in being plus 21 years. At the time the trust was created one grandchild had already been born, thus the trust could run 21 years beyond that grandchild's death. The trust thus satisfies the rule and is valid. There is nothing that prohibits a settlor from permitting principal payments to income beneficiaries in the trust instrument.

67. A

Since the trust instrument requires the distribution of trust principal upon the death of Glenn's children, the trust would terminate since there would no longer be a trust res. Although the trustees would distribute the trust principal to the grandchildren, the trust terminates due to the children's death, not the trustee's actions.

68. B

Since the trust instrument permitted the distribution of principal to the income beneficiaries, the trustees violated neither their fiduciary or any other duty by making such distributions. Although the trustees failed to comply with the instructions of the trust instrument, a breach of the fiduciary duty involves a violation of honesty, fair dealing, etc. Since the trustees did not benefit personally from their failure to distribute trust income annually, the fiduciary duty was not breached.

69. B

Stock (as opposed to cash) dividends are allocated to principal and remain as part of the trust.

70. D

The $10,000 principal payment was not an abuse of the trustees' authority since such payment was authorized by the trust instrument at the trustees' discretion. The $5,000 principal payment to a non-income beneficiary was not valid, since non-income beneficiaries are only entitled to distributions from principal upon the death of the settlor's children.

71. A

Secured creditors have the highest priority in bankruptcy distribution, thus Safe Bank will be paid first. Safe, however, is only a secured creditor for the value of the collateral. If the sale of the collateral does not satisfy the debt, Safe will become a general creditor, without a priority, for the balance.

72. B

Employee salary claims up to $4,000 per claimant will be paid before general creditor claims, but after administrative expenses, and only in full if there is sufficient money left at that level of priority to satisfy all claims.

73. B

The United States is not a secured creditor and will not be treated as such for unpaid 1994 taxes. Claims for federal and other taxes due will have last priority in a bankruptcy distribution, thus they would be paid prior to general creditor claims.

74. C

Corporate directors have an insider relationship with the corporation on whose board they sit. Preferential transfers to insiders can be avoided by the trustee if the transfer occurred up to one year prior to the filing of the petition as long as the debtor was insolvent at the time the transfer was made.

75. A

The May 1 purchase and payment was not a preferential transfer because it was a transaction in the ordinary course of business and involved a new transaction for new value. Thus there was no antecedent debt. For the above reasons it is irrelevant that the transfer occurred within 90 days of the filing of the petition, since all elements need be present.

76. A

Regulation D, Rule 506 permits public as well as non-public corporations to raise an unlimited amount of money without full registration. Transactions exempted from the full registration requirements of the 1933 Securities Act are not exempt from the reporting requirements of the Securities Exchange Act of 1934.

77. B

Shares sold under a Regulation D, Rule 506 exempt offering may be purchased by any number of investors provided there are no more than 35 non-accredited investors.

78. B

An exempt offering under Regulation D, Rule 506, has no dollar limit.

79. B

Regulation D, Rule 506, requires that the issuer exercise reasonable care to assure that purchasers of the exempt offering are buying for investment and are not underwriters. The purchaser must be notified that the securities are not registered and that resale of the securities are subject to the restrictions of Rule 144. The requirement that all investors be notified that sales of the securities are restricted to state residents for a period of nine months applies to securities exempt pursuant to an intra-state offering, not to transactions exempt under Regulation D, Rule 506.

80. D

Notification of a Regulation D, Rule 506 exempt offering must be made to the SEC within 15 days of the sale of the first security in the offering. There is no requirement that the issuer notify the SEC of the first sale of exempt offering securities on its next filed Quarterly Report (Form 10-Q).

ERRATA

Due to last minute changes, the CPA Exam schedule times are listed incorrectly in Foreword F on page F-3. The correct times are listed below:

Business Law & Professional Responsibilities	Wed. 9:00 - 12:00	3 hours
Auditing	Wed. 1:30 - 6:00	4 1/2 hours
Accounting & Reporting--Taxation, Managerial, and		
Governmental and Not-for-Profit Organizations	Thur. 8:30 - 12:00	3 1/2 hours
Financial Accounting & Reporting	Thur. 1:30 - 6:00	<u>4 1/2 hours</u>
		<u>15 1/2 hours</u>

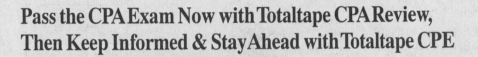

TAXATION

Guide to Limited Liability Companies

by William L. Raby, Ph.D., C.P.A.
Former National Director of Tax Services for Touche Ross & Past Chairman of the AICPA's Federal Tax Division

Get the latest edition of our already popular Guide to Limited Liability Companies program! Packed with more topic coverage than ever, this comprehensive guide to LLCs provides you with a complete overview of what you need to know about working with limited liability companies, plus shows you how to save your clients money. The limited liability company offers an attractive alternative to traditional corporate or partnership entities. Income from an LLC is taxed at a single level like a partnership, but an LLC provides limited liability to the owners like a corporation. If you're not taking advantage of tax-saving opportunities now available through LLCs, try this program RISK-FREE. Learn how to set-up an LLC and the tax consequences of converting from various business forms to a limited liability company. Dr. William Raby, well-known as the "dean" of federal taxes, and former Chairman of the AICPA's federal tax division, focuses on problem areas and pitfalls to avoid in LLCs. Plus, tax-saving tips are stressed throughout. Understand your state requirements regarding limited liability companies. Included is a state-by-state summary (including New York and California) of enacted LLC legislation containing important filing information, aspects of formation, and classification issues. Sample state forms for forming, merging, and dissolving an LLC are also included. A detailed table of contents and comprehensive index enable you to access your information quickly and easily. New on video!

Program Ordering Information: *

Audio. 6 Cassettes, Textbook & Quizzer	Item No. CPE0590 — **$159.00**	($7.95 Shipping)
Video. 2 Hr. Video, Textbook & Quizzer	Item No. CPE0597 — **$199.00**	($7.95 Shipping)
Extra Textbooks & Quizzers	Item No. CPE0591 — **$70.00**	($3.95 Shipping)
Extra Quizzers Only	Item No. CPE0596 — **$60.00**	(Free Shipping)
Software. Windows-Disks, Textbook & Quizzer	Item No. CPE0593 — **$159.00**	($7.95 Shipping)
Extra Disks & Quizzers	Item No. CPE0594 — **$60.00**	($3.95 Shipping)

Basic S Corporation Taxation

by Nathan M. Bisk, J.D., C.P.A.,
and Stephen T. Galloway, J.D.

This practical guide provides a "nuts-and-bolts" working knowledge of S corporations. We discuss the eligibility requirements for S corp status and current tax considerations. Discover when you should and *should not* change from a "C" corporation to an "S" corporation. Plus, we identify opportunities and possible problem areas. We also cover how to utilize pass-throughs for shareholder benefit, retirement plans, acquisitions & liquidations, selected Code provisions, rulings and regulations, amendments made through all recent tax acts, special planning ideas, and practice problems.

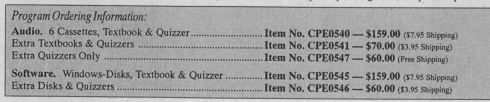

Program Ordering Information:

Audio. 6 Cassettes, Textbook & Quizzer	Item No. CPE0540 — **$159.00**	($7.95 Shipping)
Extra Textbooks & Quizzers	Item No. CPE0541 — **$70.00**	($3.95 Shipping)
Extra Quizzers Only	Item No. CPE0547 — **$60.00**	(Free Shipping)
Software. Windows-Disks, Textbook & Quizzer	Item No. CPE0545 — **$159.00**	($7.95 Shipping)
Extra Disks & Quizzers	Item No. CPE0546 — **$60.00**	($3.95 Shipping)

Overview of Federal Income Taxation

by Nathan M. Bisk, J.D., C.P.A.

Totaltape CPEasy's Overview of Federal Income Taxation program is a perfect training tool for new "staffers"—as well as a good refresher for even the most seasoned pros! Its practical instruction will provide you with a thorough understanding of the fundamentals affecting individuals, corporations, shareholders, partnerships, and estates and trusts. Emphasis centers on the taxation of individuals, and all new tax acts are fully reflected.

Program Ordering Information:

Audio. 6 Cassettes, Textbook & Quizzer	Item No. CPE0500 — **$199.00**	($7.95 Shipping)
Extra Textbooks & Quizzers	Item No. CPE0501 — **$90.00**	($3.95 Shipping)
Extra Quizzers Only	Item No. CPE0600 — **$80.00**	(Free Shipping)
Software. Disks, Textbook & Quizzer		
Windows	Item No. CPE0507 — **$199.00**	($7.95 Shipping)
DOS	Item No. CPE0504 — **$199.00**	($7.95 Shipping)
Extra Disks & Quizzers		
Windows	Item No. CPE0508 — **$80.00**	($3.95 Shipping)
DOS	Item No. CPE0505 — **$80.00**	($3.95 Shipping)

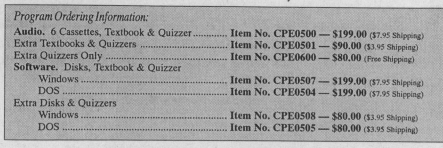

ORDER TOLL-FREE 1-800-874-7877

TAXATION

Corporate Taxation

by William L. Raby, Ph.D., C.P.A.

Totaltape CPEasy's new Corporate Taxation program features over 180 examples that show you how to save your clients tax dollars! Get comprehensive coverage of all key concepts related to the federal taxation of corporations and their shareholders. Tax planning alternatives and pitfalls to avoid are presented throughout, from formation through liquidation. PLUS, we have a new Corporate Taxation video featuring William Raby, well known as the "dean" of federal taxes and former Chairman of the AICPA's Federal Tax Division, and other leading corporate tax experts who examine the most prevalent issues affecting corporations today, and offer practical guidance to problems often encountered by practitioners.

Program Ordering Information: *

Audio. 6 Cassettes, Textbook & Quizzer .... Item No. CPE0510 — **$199.00** ($7.95 Shipping)
Video. 2 Hr. Video, Textbook & Quizzer .... Item No. CPE0512 — **$249.00** ($7.95 Shipping)
Extra Textbooks & Quizzers .... Item No. CPE0511 — **$90.00** ($3.95 Shipping)
Extra Quizzers Only .... Item No. CPE0517 — **$80.00** (Free Shipping)
Software. Windows-Disks, Textbook & Quizzer .... Item No. CPE0513 — **$199.00** ($7.95 Shipping)
Extra Disks & Quizzers .... Item No. CPE0514 — **$80.00** ($3.95 Shipping)

Real Estate Accounting & Taxation

Developed in conjunction with the Foundation for Accounting Education
by Deborah Joy Levinson, C.P.A., Kenneth Leventhal & Company,
and Allan S. Kaufman, C.P.A., Weissbarth, Altman & Michaelson

The real estate market is on the rebound and continues to strengthen despite rising interest rates. Make sure you can provide effective advice on all real estate transactions with Totaltape CPEasy's new and comprehensive Real Estate Accounting & Taxation audio/video programs. America's leading experts provide you with planning tips and strategies to minimize tax exposure, as well as insight into significant accounting & reporting concerns.

Learn about...new FASB statements, AcSec SOPs, and other GAAP news; estate planning techniques for real estate developers, owners, and investors; accounting and tax developments for co-ops and condos; real estate investment trusts, gains and transfer tax changes, newly-issued final 704(c) regulations, the impact of LLCs on investment, PAL changes, environmental clean-up costs, partnership anti-abuse rules, and other hot topics affecting real estate taxation; plus how to structure foreign investment in U.S. real estate. If you advise real estate companies or clients, this new program is a MUST for you!

Program Ordering Information:

Audio. 6 Cassettes, Textbook & Quizzer .... Item No. CPE0630 — **$259.00** ($7.95 Shipping)
Video. 6 Hr. Video, Textbook & Quizzer .... Item No. CPE0631 — **$329.00** ($7.95 Shipping)

Extra Textbooks & Quizzers .... Item No. CPE0632 — **$100.00** ($3.95 Shipping)
Extra Quizzers Only .... Item No. CPE0633 — **$90.00** (Free Shipping)

Raby Report on Tax Practice

by William L. Raby, Ph.D., C.P.A., Past Chairman of the AICPA's Federal Tax Division, and Burgess Raby, J.D.

As a tax-oriented practitioner, you need timely, reliable, clearly-focused information on what's going on in tax practice. That's where the Raby Report comes in. Written in a lively newsletter format, each month it provides you with a forum of important information most vital to your practice, like: tax practice standards set by the AICPA and the IRS; turning recent tax developments into tax benefits for your clients; the exploding number of tax malpractice cases and how to avoid one; the gap between client expectations & practice realities; the computer revolution and what it means for your research techniques, fee determination, and staff training; how to market your tax services, and much more! The Raby Report is written & presented each month by Dr. William Raby, well-known as the "dean" of federal taxes, one-time vice president of the AICPA, a past chair of its federal tax division, and the immediate past President of the Arizona State Board of Accountancy—and his son, attorney Burgess Raby, a past chair of the American Bar Association's committee on the economics of tax practice. They talk and network with the **Tax 20 Forum**, a group comprised of the "movers & shakers" in the tax profession, then share their professional insights, analyses, and planning strategies with you through the Raby Report! Plus, they literally read thousands of pages of current information that affects you, your business, and your clients, assemble 8-15 of the "hottest" topics every month...and put it right into your hands in one clear, concise report. Try your first issue RISK-FREE. Call today!

Program Ordering Information:

1 Year Subscription — 12 Monthly Written Newsletters & 6 Quizzers .... Item No. CPER010 — **$98.00** ($9.00 Shipping)
2 Year Subscription — 24 Monthly Written Newsletters & 12 Quizzers ...... Item No. CPER012 — **$176.00** ($18.00 Shipping)
3 Year Subscription — 36 Monthly Written Newsletters & 18 Quizzers ...... Item No. CPER013 — **$264.00** ($27.00 Shipping)

ORDER TOLL-FREE 1-800-874-7877

TAXATION

Employee Benefit & Retirement Planning: A Basic Guide

by Nathan M. Bisk, J.D., C.P.A.,
and Richard M. Feldheim, M.B.A., J.D., LL.M., C.P.A.

NEW

16 TAX CPE CREDIT HRS.

PREREQUISITE: None
KNOWLEDGE: Intermediate

*Coming Soon

There has been tremendous change in federal legislation and regulatory activity in the compensation area, making it more difficult to design comprehensive benefit packages and increasing the cost in taxes & penalties to employer and employee. This up-to-date 500-page guide provides you with the tools and techniques you need to put together a cost-effective benefit & compensation package that meets your needs. We cover all types of employee benefit arrangements, designed for use in both small and large companies. Learn how to install them, their advantages & disadvantages, tax & ERISA implications, available planning options, and more. This timely and accurate overview is an excellent reference source for accountants, financial planners, company managers, personnel departments, and other financial services professionals. New on video!

*Program Ordering Information:**

Audio. 6 Cassettes, Textbook & Quizzer .... Item No. CPE5040 — **$199.00** ($7.95 Shipping)
Video. 2 Hr. Video, Textbook & Quizzer .... Item No. CPE5044 — **$249.00** ($7.95 Shipping)
Extra Textbooks & Quizzers .... Item No. CPE5042 — **$100.00** ($3.95 Shipping)
Extra Quizzers Only .... Item No. CPE5043 — **$90.00** (Free Shipping)

Estate Planning: A Basic Guide

by Nathan M. Bisk, J.D., C.P.A.,
and Scott F. Barnett, J.D., LL.M., Anderson & Orcutt, P.A.

NEW

16 TAX CPE CREDIT HRS.

PREREQUISITE: None
KNOWLEDGE: Basic

This new, 650+ page practical guide will provide you with an excellent working knowledge of estate planning. Learn the 10 most common estate planning mistakes and how to avoid them—plus how the federal estate tax laws work, how to select an executor, trustee, and attorney, how to compute federal estate & gift tax, how basis is determined, and more. We also include coverage on: buy-sell agreements; charitable contributions; deferred compensation; employee stock ownership & death benefits; freezing techniques; flower bonds; family partnerships; generation-skipping transfers; profit-sharing & pension plans, IRAs & SEPS; Keogh retirement plan for the self-employed; private annuity; installment sale; interest-free and below market rate loans; life insurance; medical expense reimbursement plans; personal holding companies; incorporation; split interest purchase of property; survivor's income benefit plan; GRIT, GRAT & GRUT; uniform gifts/transfers to minors act; valuation planning; and other topics of interest to the estate planner. Includes many helpful sample filled-in forms, checklists, tables, charts, illustrations, and examples.

Program Ordering Information:

Audio. 6 Cassettes, Textbook & Quizzer .... Item No. CPE5020 — **$199.00** ($7.95 Shipping)
Video. 3 Hr. Video, Textbook & Quizzer .... Item No. CPE5021 — **$249.00** ($7.95 Shipping)
Extra Textbooks & Quizzers .... Item No. CPE5022 — **$100.00** ($3.95 Shipping)
Extra Quizzers Only .... Item No. CPE0523 — **$90.00** (Free Shipping)

Federal Estate & Gift Taxation

by Stephen T. Galloway, J.D., and Richard M. Feldheim, M.B.A., J.D., LL.M., C.P.A

12 TAX CPE CREDIT HRS.

PREREQUISITE: None
KNOWLEDGE: Intermediate

Estate planning engagements often generate from $5,000 to $25,000 in fees, and put you in contact with professionals in other fields, like insurance, providing an excellent source of referrals. Totaltape CPEasy's comprehensive Federal Estate & Gift Taxation program provides proven, practical advice on how to take advantage of this hot new growth area. We feature more than <u>250</u> examples, points of analysis, and tax tips to assist you with problems often encountered in estate planning and compliance for individuals. Two separate case studies provide practical examples of real-life situations and contain filled-in sample forms, including Forms 706 & 709. Additional coverage includes: a general overview and specific items of gross estate; special valuation rules; unified credit; miscellaneous credits against estate tax; an overview of federal gift tax; transfers subject to gift tax; allowable deductions; calculation of gift tax; generation-skipping transfer tax, and more. Even the experienced professional will find this up-to-date review of the fundamentals of estate and gift taxation convenient.

Program Ordering Information:

Audio. 6 Cassettes, Textbook & Quizzer .... Item No. CPE0550 — **$159.00** ($7.95 Shipping)
Extra Textbooks & Quizzers .... Item No. CPE0551 — **$70.00** ($3.95 Shipping)
Extra Quizzers Only .... Item No. CPE0557 — **$60.00** (Free Shipping)

Software. Windows-Disks, Textbook & Quizzer .... Item No. CPE0552 — **$159.00** ($7.95 Shipping)
Extra Disks & Quizzers .... Item No. CPE0553 — **$60.00** ($3.95 Shipping)

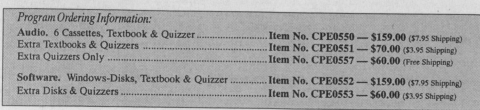

TAXATION

Form 1040: A Practical Guide

by Nathan M. Bisk, J.D., C.P.A.,Stephen T. Galloway, J.D., and George Schain, J.D.

Totaltape's Form 1040 practical reference guide features in-depth, line-by-line instructions on how to file all individual forms and schedules. We include key tax changes, helpful tax-savings tips *and* tax planning strategies, plus over 90 illustrations of important tax rules and calculations. Using real-world case studies, we show you how the forms work and how to properly apply them. We even provide you with over 100 examples to represent situations your clients could find themselves in. You get complete and comprehensive coverage on Form 1040 filing requirements; personal exemptions; gross income; compensation; depreciation; travel & entertainment; home business offices; at-risk limitations; NOLs; hobby losses; like-kind exchanges; the sale of a principal residence; related-party transactions; rental & pass-through income; passive activities; other income; adjustments to income; deductions from adjusted gross income; medical expenses; income tax computation; tax credits; AMT; tax payments; penalties; extended & amended returns; and claims for a refund. Sample charts, tables, and other reference materials are also included to greatly simplify the tax preparation process for you.

16 TAX CPE CREDIT HRS.

PREREQUISITE: None
KNOWLEDGE: Intermediate

Program Ordering Information:

Audio. 6 Cassettes, Textbook & Quizzer .... Item No. CPE1900 — **$199.00** ($7.95 Shipping)
Video. 4 Hr. Video, Textbook & Quizzer .... Item No. CPE1902 — **$249.00** ($7.95 Shipping)
Extra Textbooks & Quizzers .... Item No. CPE1901 — **$90.00** ($3.95 Shipping)
Extra Quizzers Only .... Item No. CPE1897 — **$80.00** (Free Shipping)

Software. Windows-Disks, Textbook & Quizzer .... Item No. CPE1898 — **$199.00** ($7.95 Shipping)
Extra Disks & Quizzers .... Item No. CPE1899 — **$80.00** ($3.95 Shipping)

Form 1120: A Practical Guide

by Cris VanDenBranden, C.P.A.,Machen, Powers, Disque & Boyle, and Richard M. Feldheim,M.B.A., J.D., LL.M., C.P.A.

Save time, trouble, and money on your corporate tax returns with our step-by-step guide to filing Form 1120. Packed full of sample filled-in forms and comprehensive case studies you can apply directly to your clients' situations, this year-round tool is our best Form 1120 tax source yet. Not only do we make filing easier than ever, but we also supply you with specific tax-planning *and* tax-saving strategies. Plus, we take "complex" corporate tax issues and break them down into easily understood, straightforward explanations. Fully reflects all recent tax acts.

14 TAX CPE CREDIT HRS.

PREREQUISITE: None
KNOWLEDGE: Intermediate

Program Ordering Information:

Audio. 3 Cassettes, Textbook & Quizzer .... Item No. CPE2000 — **$169.00** ($7.95 Shipping)
Extra Textbooks & Quizzers .... Item No. CPE2001 — **$80.00** ($3.95 Shipping)
Extra Quizzers Only .... Item No. CPE2006 — **$70.00** (Free Shipping)

Software. Windows-Disks, Textbook & Quizzer .... Item No. CPE2003 — **$169.00** ($7.95 Shipping)
Extra Disks & Quizzers .... Item No. CPE2004 — **$70.00** ($3.95 Shipping)

Form 1120S: A Practical Guide

by Nathan M. Bisk, J.D., C.P.A.,and Stephen T. Galloway, J.D.

Totaltape CPEasy's *Form 1120S* program provides you with the clear and concise guidance you need to prepare—and review—your S corporation returns...quickly and efficiently. Our coverage gives you step-by-step filing guidance, plus assists you in identifying opportunities and problem areas when preparing this often complex return. We also include all recent legislative, judicial, and regulatory changes, authoritative answers to tax return compliance questions, a realistic case study, and more.

14 TAX CPE CREDIT HRS.

PREREQUISITE: None
KNOWLEDGE: Intermediate

Forms 1040, 1120 & 1120S Xtra Value Package

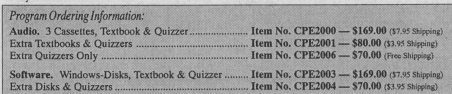

XTRA VALUE! SAVE $50

Get all the practical, step-by-step guidance of Totaltape CPEasy's Forms programs on flexible audio tape, interactive software *for Windows* or our new, quick & efficient CD-ROM! We include complete coverage of our Form 1040 individual tax prep program, our Form 1120 corporate tax prep program, and our Form 1120S S corporation tax prep program (all featured on this page). SAVE $50 off our single program prices!

44 TAX CPE CREDIT HRS.

PREREQUISITE: None
KNOWLEDGE: Intermediate

Program Ordering Information:

Audio. 15 Cassettes, Textbooks & Quizzers .... Item No. CPE0134 — **$487.00** ($14.95 Shipping)
Extra Textbooks & Quizzer .... Item No. CPE0135 — **$234.00** ($9.95 Shipping)
Extra Quizzers Only .... Item No. CPE0136 — **$204.00** (Free Shipping)

Software. Windows-Disks, Textbooks & Quizzers .... Item No. CPE0131 — **$487.00** ($14.95 Shipping)
Extra Disks & Quizzers .... Item No. CPE0132 — **$204.00** ($9.95 Shipping)

CD-ROM. Windows-CD, Textbooks & Quizzers ...... Item No. CPE0130 — **$487.00** ($14.95 Shipping)
Extra CDs & Quizzers .... Item No. CPE0133 — **$204.00** ($9.95 Shipping)

Program Ordering Information:

Audio. 6 Cassettes, Textbook & Quizzer
Item No. CPE4120 — **$169.00** ($7.95 Shipping)
Extra Textbooks & Quizzers
Item No. CPE4121 — **$80.00** ($3.95 Shipping)
Extra Quizzers Only
Item No. CPE4117 — **$70.00** (Free Shipping)

Software. Windows-Disks, Textbook & Quizzer
Item No. CPE4118 — **$169.00** ($7.95 Shipping)
Extra Disks & Quizzers
Item No. CPE4119 — **$70.00** ($3.95 Shipping)

ORDER TOLL-FREE 1-800-874-7877

TAX PLANNING—TULANE TAX INSTITUTE

Tax Planning for Individuals

by Deke G. Carbo, C.P.A., KPMG Peat Marwick and Meade Emory, J.D., Lane Powell Spears Lubersky

Get the most recent developments in the taxation of individuals. Coverage also includes: family wealth transfers; capital gains vs. ordinary income; qualified retirement plans; employee vs. independent contractor; how to avoid excess accumulation penalties; and ethical considerations.

Program Ordering Information:

Audio. 6 Cassettes, Textbook & Quizzer .... Item No. CPE3020 — **$129.00** ($7.95 Shipping)
Video. 2 Hr. Video, Textbook & Quizzer .... Item No. CPE3022 — **$199.00** ($7.95 Shipping)
Extra Textbooks & Quizzers .... Item No. CPE3021 — **$70.00** ($3.95 Shipping)
Extra Quizzers Only .... Item No. CPE3019 — **$60.00** (Free Shipping)
Software. Windows-Disks, Textbook & Quizzer .... Item No. CPE3027 — **$129.00** ($7.95 Shipping)
Extra Disks & Quizzers .... Item No. CPE3028 — **$60.00** ($3.95 Shipping)
CD-ROM. Windows, CD, Textbook & Quizzer .... Item No. CPE3062 — **$199.00** ($7.95 Shipping)
Extra CDs & Quizzers .... Item No. CPE3063 — **$70.00** ($3.95 Shipping)

12 TAX CPE CREDIT HRS. EACH

PREREQUISITES: None
KNOWLEDGE: Basic

Tax Planning for Corporations

by Glenn F. Mackles, C.P.A., Deloitte & Touche, National Tax Department,
and Robert J. Peroni, J.D., Prof. of Law,
George Washington University

Get the most recent developments in the taxation of corporations. Coverage also includes: amortization of goodwill and purchased intangibles; new design considerations for qualified plans; executive & deferred compensation; consequences of reclassification of employees as independent contractors; issues of choice of entity; and ethical considerations.

Program Ordering Information:

Audio. 6 Cassettes, Textbook & Quizzer .... Item No. CPE3030 — **$129.00** ($7.95 Shipping)
Video. 2 Hr. Video, Textbook & Quizzer .... Item No. CPE3032— **$199.00** ($7.95 Shipping)
Extra Textbooks & Quizzers .... Item No. CPE3031 — **$70.00** ($3.95 Shipping)
Extra Quizzers Only .... Item No. CPE3029 — **$60.00** (Free Shipping)
Software. Windows-Disks, Textbook & Quizzer .. Item No. CPE3037 — **$129.00** ($7.95 Shipping)
Extra Disks & Quizzers .... Item No. CPE3038 — **$60.00** ($3.95 Shipping)
CD-ROM. Windows, CD, Textbook & Quizzer ... Item No. CPE3064 — **$199.00** ($7.95 Shipping)
Extra CDs & Quizzers .... Item No. CPE3065 — **$70.00** ($3.95 Shipping)

Tax Planning for Pass-Thru Entities

by William A. Neilson, J.D., Professor of Law, Loyola Law School
and Jerald D. August, J.D., August, Comiter, Kulunas & Schepps

Get the most recent developments in S corporations. Coverage also includes: partnership developments in special allocations & service partner income; choice of business entities; amortization of goodwill and purchased intangibles; new designs for qualified plans; consequences of reclassification of employees as independent contractors; and ethical considerations.

Program Ordering Information:

Audio. 9 Cassettes, Textbook & Quizzer .... Item No. CPE3040 — **$129.00** ($7.95 Shipping)
Video. 2 Hr. Video, Textbook & Quizzer .... Item No. CPE3042 — **$199.00** ($7.95 Shipping)
Extra Textbooks & Quizzers .... Item No. CPE3041 — **$70.00** ($3.95 Shipping)
Extra Quizzers Only .... Item No. CPE3039 — **$60.00** (Free Shipping)
Software. Windows-Disks, Textbook & Quizzer Item No. CPE3047 — **$129.00** ($7.95 Shipping)
Extra Disks & Quizzers .... Item No. CPE3048 — **$60.00** ($3.95 Shipping)
CD-ROM. Windows, CD, Textbook & Quizzer Item No. CPE3066 — **$199.00** ($7.95 Shipping)
Extra CDs & Quizzers .... Item No. CPE3067 — **$70.00** ($3.95 Shipping)

Tax Planning for Estates, Gifts & Trusts

by Virginia F. Coleman, J.D., Ropes & Gray,
Alfred J. Olsen, J.D. and Susan K. Smith,
J.D., Olsen-Smith, Ltd.

Get the most recent developments in estate, gift & trust taxation. Coverage also includes: family wealth transfers; planning for the elderly client; the fiduciary's dilemma; planning to avoid excess accumulation penalties; charitable trusts; and ethical considerations.

Program Ordering Information:

Audio. 6 Cassettes, Textbook & Quizzer .... Item No. CPE3050 — **$129.00** ($7.95 Shipping)
Video. 2 Hr. Video, Textbook & Quizzer .... Item No. CPE3052 — **$199.00** ($7.95 Shipping)
Extra Textbooks & Quizzers .... Item No. CPE3051 — **$70.00** ($3.95 Shipping)
Extra Quizzers Only .... Item No. CPE3049 — **$60.00** (Free Shipping)
Software. Windows-Disks, Textbook & Quizzer .. Item No. CPE3057 — **$129.00** ($7.95 Shipping)
Extra Disks & Quizzers .... Item No. CPE3058 — **$60.00** ($3.95 Shipping)
CD-ROM. Windows, CD, Textbook & Quizzer ... Item No. CPE3068 — **$199.00** ($7.95 Shipping)
Extra CDs & Quizzers .... Item No. CPE3069 — **$70.00** ($3.95 Shipping)

ORDER TOLL-FREE 1-800-874-7877

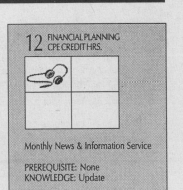

GOVERNMENTAL ACCOUNTING & AUDITING

Government Auditing Standards: 1994 Yellow Book

by Lucinda V. Upton, C.P.A., and Betty A. Pendergrass King, C.P.A.

Gain a complete understanding and working knowledge of the 1994 Government Auditing Standards revisions—and meet your mandatory governmental A&A CPE reporting requirements—with our comprehensive new Government Auditing Standards: 1994 Yellow Book program! The country's top governmental accounting experts provide you with a detailed overview and analysis of the GAO's sweeping new revisions with emphasis on the major changes, how they affect existing standards, and how they impact auditors functioning in the government and other specific environments. We feature an in-depth discussion on audits of government organizations, programs, activities, and functions, and of government assistance received by contractors, nonprofit organizations, other nongovernmental organizations, and more. A *must* program for government auditors, public accountants who conduct, or plan to conduct, government audits, and those who rely on the work of government auditors. Completely supersedes the revisions set forth in the 1988 Yellow Book on Government Auditing Standards. New on software *for Windows*.

12 A&A CPE CREDIT HRS.

PREREQUISITE: None
KNOWLEDGE: Basic

Program Ordering Information:

Audio. 3 Cassettes, Textbook & Quizzer .... **Item No. CPE2506 — $199.00** (*$7.95 Shipping*)
Extra Textbooks & Quizzers .... **Item No. CPE2507 — $90.00** (*$3.95 Shipping*)
Extra Quizzers Only .... **Item No. CPE2508 — $80.00** (*Free Shipping*)

Software. Windows-Disks, Textbook & Quizzer ...... **Item No. CPE2509 — $199.00** (*$7.95 Shipping*)

Overview of Governmental & Nonprofit Accounting

by Nathan M. Bisk, J.D., C.P.A., and Robert L. Monette, J.D., C.P.A.

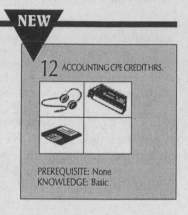

This introductory program provides the practitioner with a detailed overview of governmental and nonprofit accounting. We focus on financial reporting requirements of governmental and nonprofit organizations, and include comprehensive examples of relevant journal entries. General governmental accounting methods are discussed, key terminology is explained, and different types of fund groups are explored. Our video is designed for both CPE and CPA Review training, and provides a comprehensive overview.

12 ACCOUNTING CPE CREDIT HRS.

PREREQUISITE: None
KNOWLEDGE: Basic

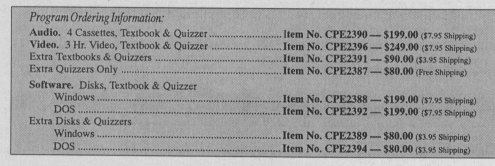

Program Ordering Information:

Audio. 4 Cassettes, Textbook & Quizzer .... Item No. CPE2390 — **$199.00** (*$7.95 Shipping*)
Video. 3 Hr. Video, Textbook & Quizzer .... Item No. CPE2396 — **$249.00** (*$7.95 Shipping*)
Extra Textbooks & Quizzers .... Item No. CPE2391 — **$90.00** (*$3.95 Shipping*)
Extra Quizzers Only .... Item No. CPE2387 — **$80.00** (*Free Shipping*)

Software. Disks, Textbook & Quizzer
    Windows .... Item No. CPE2388 — **$199.00** (*$7.95 Shipping*)
    DOS .... Item No. CPE2392 — **$199.00** (*$7.95 Shipping*)
Extra Disks & Quizzers
    Windows .... Item No. CPE2389 — **$80.00** (*$3.95 Shipping*)
    DOS .... Item No. CPE2394 — **$80.00** (*$3.95 Shipping*)

Audio Governmental Accounting Report

by the Totaltape Editorial Board, Lucinda V. Upton, C.P.A., and Betty A. Pendergrass King, C.P.A.

If you have a governmental accounting requirement to meet, this is the ideal program for you! This monthly audio news & information service not only keeps you up-to-date on GASB and Yellow Book changes, but it also provides you with the 12 hours of governmental CPE credit you need...year after year! Each 60 minute audio tape features 10-15 different governmental accounting & auditing topics, like GASB, GAO, and OMB activities, Yellow Book changes, studies on single audit issues, cost accounting standards, and more. And, we focus on practical advice and implementation issues. Each issue is also accompanied by a lively newsletter, which acts as a word-for-word transcript of your audio tape...convenient for quick reference when you need answers fast! Plus, you get a brief true/false quizzer every month, the successful completion of which qualifies you for one CPE credit per month, 12 for the year—the perfect source for meeting your 24 credit governmental CPE reporting requirement! Try your first issue today, absolutely RISK-FREE!

12 ACCOUNTING CPE CREDIT HRS.

Monthly News & Information Service

PREREQUISITE: None
KNOWLEDGE: Update

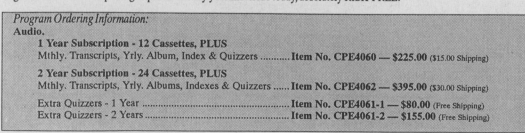

Program Ordering Information:
Audio.
    1 Year Subscription - 12 Cassettes, PLUS
    Mthly. Transcripts, Yrly. Album, Index & Quizzers .... **Item No. CPE4060 — $225.00** (*$15.00 Shipping*)

    2 Year Subscription - 24 Cassettes, PLUS
    Mthly. Transcripts, Yrly. Albums, Indexes & Quizzers ...... **Item No. CPE4062 — $395.00** (*$30.00 Shipping*)

    Extra Quizzers - 1 Year .... **Item No. CPE4061-1 — $80.00** (*Free Shipping*)
    Extra Quizzers - 2 Years .... **Item No. CPE4061-2 — $155.00** (*Free Shipping*)

ACCOUNTING & AUDITING

Corporate Financial Reporting Issues

by Paul Munter, Ph.D., C.P.A.

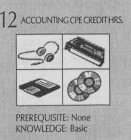

Dr. Paul Munter, the Florida Institute of CPAs' 1993 Outstanding Educator, shows you how to implement the latest changes in accounting principles, auditing standards, and more with Totaltape CPEasy's Corporate Financial Reporting program! He provides you with an analysis and professional advice on recently issued FASBs, SASs, and AcSec & EITF pronouncements—paying special attention to their impact on smaller companies and implementation issues. The program also features coverage on changes in reporting practices for not-for-profit organizations, accounting & reporting environmental clean-up costs, and legal liability for reform. Plus, Dr. Munter discusses how the auditor's responsibility for fraud detection has increased in the wake of these changes; consolidated financial reporting; a new approach to valuing impaired assets; accounting & reporting financial instruments; and the impact of an exposure draft to assign values to all stock compensation plans.

PREREQUISITE: None
KNOWLEDGE: Basic

Program Ordering Information:

Audio. 4 Cassettes, Textbook & Quizzer .... Item No. CPE1191 — $159.00 ($7.95 Shipping)
Video. 2 Hr. Video, Textbook & Quizzer .... Item No. CPE1190 — $199.00 ($7.95 Shipping)
Extra Textbooks & Quizzers .... Item No. CPE1192 — $70.00 ($3.95 Shipping)
Extra Quizzers Only .... Item No. CPE1198 — $60.00 (Free Shipping)

Software. Windows-Disks, Textbook & Quizzer .... Item No. CPE1194 — $159.00 ($7.95 Shipping)
Extra Disks & Quizzers .... Item No. CPE1196 — $60.00 ($3.95 Shipping)

CD-ROM. Windows-CD, Textbook & Quizzer ...... Item No. CPE1195 — $159.00 ($7.95 Shipping)
Extra CDs & Quizzers .... Item No. CPE1197 — $60.00 ($3.95 Shipping)

Bisk GAAP Guide

by Nathan M. Bisk, J.D., C.P.A., and Robert L. Monette, J.D., C.P.A.

Recent FASB Statements are having a major impact on financial statement presentation. But to learn only the newest pronouncements isn't enough...you must also understand how they have changed *existing* Standards. This program provides you with a current, comprehensive overview of all GAAP, and can help you avoid misapplications of accounting principles. Coverage includes current assets & liabilities; fixed assets & long-term liabilities; intangibles and R&D; stockholders' equity method; reporting the results of operations; statement of cash flows; deferred taxes; leases & pensions; business combinations; foreign operations, and more. Updated through FASB 119.

PREREQUISITE: None
KNOWLEDGE: Basic

Program Ordering Information:

Audio. 12 Cassettes, Textbook & Quizzer .... Item No. CPE0030 — $199.00 ($7.95 Shipping)
Extra Textbooks & Quizzers .... Item No. CPE0031 — $90.00 ($3.95 Shipping)
Extra Quizzers Only .... Item No. CPE0029 — $80.00 (Free Shipping)

Software. Disks, Textbook & Quizzer
    Windows .... Item No. CPE0034 — $199.00 ($7.95 Shipping)
    DOS .... Item No. CPE0033 — $199.00 ($7.95 Shipping)
Extra Disks & Quizzers
    Windows .... Item No. CPE0036 — $80.00 ($3.95 Shipping)
    DOS .... Item No. CPE0035 — $80.00 ($3.95 Shipping)

Bisk GAAS Guide

by Nathan M. Bisk, J.D., C.P.A.

This course thoroughly explains the SASs and how they change the way you should conduct an audit engagement. You'll get a clear overview of auditing standards, the code of professional conduct and standards applicable to other professional services such as compilations/reviews, tax and MAS work—plus, numerous illustrations of the wording and format required for most types of reports. We take an in-depth look at standards, ethics & related issues; internal control; audit sampling; audit evidence; programs & procedures; reports on audited financial statements; special reports; and other professional services. And we include a master status checklist and handy cross-reference index of all SASs and SSARs.

PREREQUISITE: None
KNOWLEDGE: Basic

Program Ordering Information:

Audio. 12 Cassettes, Textbook & Quizzer .... Item No. CPE0040 — $159.00 ($7.95 Shipping)
Extra Textbooks & Quizzers .... Item No. CPE0041 — $70.00 ($3.95 Shipping)
Extra Quizzers Only .... Item No. CPE0039 — $60.00 (Free Shipping)

Software. Disks, Textbook & Quizzer
    Windows .... Item No. CPE0044 — $159.00 ($7.95 Shipping)
    DOS .... Item No. CPE0043 — $159.00 ($7.95 Shipping)
Extra Disks & Quizzers
    Windows .... Item No. CPE0047 — $60.00 ($3.95 Shipping)
    DOS .... Item No. CPE0045 — $60.00 ($3.95 Shipping)

ORDER TOLL-FREE 1-800-874-7877

ACCOUNTING & AUDITING

Compilation & Review Guide

by Nathan M. Bisk, J.D., C.P.A.,
and Paul Munter, Ph.D., C.P.A.

16 A&A CPE CREDIT HRS.

PREREQUISITE: None
KNOWLEDGE: Basic

Bring Dr. Paul Munter, KPMG Peat Marwick Accounting Scholar and FICPA 1993 Outstanding Educator right into your home or office, where he'll provide you with practical answers to the most commonly asked questions about Compilation & Review engagements. Dr. Munter's unique ability to analyze and simplify even the most complex topics, ensures that you and your firm will walk away with a complete understanding of the planning, performance, and reporting requirements that are necessary to complete compilation and review engagements. You'll get a broad overview of compilations & reviews, including the planning & administration of engagements; accepting new clients; communication between predecessor and successor accountant; compilation workpapers, procedures, and reports; review reports; departures from GAAP; comparison of attestation standards with GAAS; financial forecasts & projections; financial statement form & presentation; and more.

Available in flexible video, audio, and software formats with an accompanying **650-page reference guide**, the program explores the differences inherent in various forms of unaudited financial statements, including those of nonpublic entities, personal financial statements, and more. Plus, it reflects changes required by SSARS 7, recent SASs, and the Code of Professional Conduct, and includes the "Compilation & Review Alert" to help you plan your engagements.

Program Ordering Information:

Audio. 4 Cassettes, Textbook & Quizzer .... **Item No. CPE0120 — $199.00** ($7.95 Shipping)
Video. 3 Hr. Video, Textbook & Quizzer .... **Item No. CPE0123 — $249.00** ($7.95 Shipping)
Extra Textbooks & Quizzers .... **Item No. CPE0121 — $90.00** ($3.95 Shipping)
Extra Quizzers Only .... **Item No. CPE0119 — $80.00** (Free Shipping)

Software. Windows-Disks, Textbook & Quizzer .... **Item No. CPE0127 — $199.00** ($7.95 Shipping)
Extra Disks & Quizzers .... **Item No. CPE0128 — $80.00** ($3.95 Shipping)

CD-ROM. Windows-CD, Textbook & Quizzer .... **Item No. CPE0137 — $249.00** ($7.95 Shipping)
Extra CDs & Quizzers .... **Item No. CPE0138 — $90.00** ($3.95 Shipping)

> "The flexibility of your different program formats is very helpful for the busy practitioner—I don't even have to leave my office to meet my CPE reporting requirements!"
>
> *R. Adams, CPA*
> *El Paso, TX*

Accounting & Auditing Report

by the Totaltape Editorial Board with Paul Munter, Ph.D., C.P.A., and Thomas A. Ratcliffe, Ph.D., C.P.A.

12 A&A CPE CREDIT HRS.

Monthly News & Information Service

PREREQUISITE: None
KNOWLEDGE: Update

Stop spending so much time thumbing through the journals to catch-up on the latest A&A developments! Subscribe to Totaltape CPEasy's Accounting & Auditing Report and get all the latest A&A news and information delivered right to your door each and every month...on convenient audio tape. Listen anytime, any place! Each issue features 8-10 of the hottest accounting & auditing topics, presented by Dr. Paul Munter, KPMG Peat Marwick Accounting Scholar and Accounting Professor & Department Chair at the University of Miami, and Dr. Thomas Ratcliffe, Accounting Professor and Department Chair at Troy State University. These leading experts analyze, simplify, and explain all major FASB, GASB, SEC, and AICPA pronouncements, as they happen, keeping you abreast of constantly changing developments and what they mean for you and your clients. They will save you <u>DAYS</u> of research and analysis!

We'll also send you a lively newsletter that acts as a word-for-word transcript of the audio material...convenient for quick reference when you need answers fast! Plus, you get a brief true/false quizzer every month, the successful completion of which qualifies you for 12 CPE credits a year. Try your first issue today, RISK-FREE!

Program Ordering Information:

Audio. **1 Year Subscription - 12 Cassettes, PLUS**
Mthly. Transcripts, Yrly. Album, Index & Quizzers .... **Item No. CPE0020 — $225.00** ($15.00 Shipping)

2 Year Subscription - 24 Cassettes, PLUS
Mthly. Transcripts, Yrly. Albums, Indexes & Quizzers ...... **Item No. CPE0021 — $395.00** ($30.00 Shipping)

Extra Quizzers - 1 Year .... **Item No. CPE0023-1 — $80.00** (Free Shipping)
Extra Quizzers - 2 Years .... **Item No. CPE0023-2 — $155.00** (Free Shipping)

ORDER TOLL-FREE 1-800-874-7877

ACCOUNTING & AUDITING

FASB 109: Accounting for Income Taxes

by Thomas A. Ratcliffe, Ph.D., C.P.A., and Robert L. Monette, J.D., C.P.A.

Gain an understanding of recognition and measurement issues, tax assets and the valuation allowance, disclosure requirements, and more with this comprehensive guide to Accounting for Income Taxes. In this program, we discuss major implementation issues and key benefits, and demonstrate the application of FASB 109 using real-world examples. Our FASB 109 video, designed for both CPE and CPA Review training, provides a comprehensive overview.

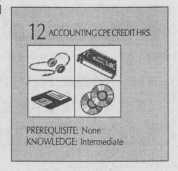

Program Ordering Information:

Audio. 6 Cassettes, Textbook & Quizzer .... Item No. CPE4220 — **$159.00** ($7.95 Shipping)
Video. 2 Hr. Video, Textbook & Quizzer .... Item No. CPE4222 — **$199.00** ($7.95 Shipping)
Extra Textbooks & Quizzers .... Item No. CPE4221 — **$70.00** ($3.95 Shipping)
Extra Quizzers Only .... Item No. CPE4219 — **$60.00** (Free Shipping)

Software. Windows-Disks, Textbook & Quizzer ..... Item No. CPE4224 — **$159.00** ($7.95 Shipping)
Extra Disks & Quizzers .... Item No. CPE4226 — **$60.00** ($3.95 Shipping)

CD-ROM. Windows-CD, Textbook & Quizzer .... Item No. CPE4225 — **$159.00** ($7.95 Shipping)
Extra CDs & Quizzers .... Item No. CPE4227 — **$60.00** ($3.95 Shipping)

12 ACCOUNTING CPE CREDIT HRS.
PREREQUISITE: None
KNOWLEDGE: Intermediate

FASB 106: Accounting for Post-Retirement Benefits & Other Pensions

by Paul Munter, Ph.D., C.P.A., and Thomas A. Ratcliffe, Ph.D., C.P.A.

Learn the required reporting of health care costs, health insurance, life insurance, and all other nonpension benefits that are provided to retired employees. Totaltape CPEasy's FASB 106 program includes comprehensive post-employment benefit plan examples, disclosure requirements, and examples of reporting settlements and curtailments. Plus, learn how to calculate the vested post-retirement benefit obligation, record amortization of the transition obligation, report immediate recognition of the transition obligation, and more.

Program Ordering Information:

Audio. 3 Cassettes, Textbook & Quizzer .... Item No. CPE4070 — **$159.00** ($7.95 Shipping)
Extra Textbooks & Quizzers .... Item No. CPE4071 — **$70.00** ($3.95 Shipping)
Extra Quizzers Only .... Item No. CPE4072 — **$60.00** (Free Shipping)

12 ACCOUNTING CPE CREDIT HRS.
PREREQUISITE: None
KNOWLEDGE: Intermediate

FASB 95: Statement of Cash Flows

by Marilyn F. Hunt, M.A., C.P.A., Professor, University of Central Florida; and Robert L. Monette, J.D., C.P.A.

Learn everything you and your clients need to know about reporting cash inflows and outflows, and assessing cash flow problems that lead to business failure. This program contains clear explanations of how cash receipts and disbursements must now be classified; how to disclose noncash investing and financing activities; and how to prepare the statement under the direct/indirect methods. Plus, we include FASBs 102 & 104 amendments. Our FASB 95 video, designed for both CPE and CPA Review training, provides a comprehensive overview.

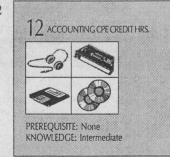

Program Ordering Information:

Audio. 6 Cassettes, Textbook & Quizzer .... Item No. CPE2030 — **$159.00** ($7.95 Shipping)
Video. 2 Hr. Video, Textbook & Quizzer .... Item No. CPE2032 — **$199.00** ($7.95 Shipping)
Extra Textbooks & Quizzers .... Item No. CPE2031 — **$70.00** ($3.95 Shipping)
Extra Quizzers Only .... Item No. CPE2029 — **$60.00** (Free Shipping)

Software. Windows-Disks, Textbook & Quizzer ..... Item No. CPE2034 — **$159.00** ($7.95 Shipping)
Extra Disks & Quizzers .... Item No. CPE2036 — **$60.00** ($3.95 Shipping)

CD-ROM. Windows-CD, Textbook & Quizzer .... Item No. CPE2035 — **$159.00** ($7.95 Shipping)
Extra CDs & Quizzers .... Item No. CPE2037 — **$60.00** ($3.95 Shipping)

12 ACCOUNTING CPE CREDIT HRS.
PREREQUISITE: None
KNOWLEDGE: Intermediate

FASB 115:
Accounting for Certain Investments in Debt & Equity Securities ▼ NEW

by Nathan M. Bisk, J.D., C.P.A., and Robert L. Monette, J.D., C.P.A.

FASB 115 supersedes FASB 12, substantially changing the accounting for, classification of, and disclosures required for investments in equity and debt securities. Totaltape CPEasy's comprehensive new audio & video programs provide you with a detailed discussion of what this pronouncement entails, its proper application, its far-reaching effects, and more. New on software *for Windows*.

Program Ordering Information:

Audio. 4 Cassettes, Textbook & Quizzer .... Item No. CPE4960 — **$129.00** ($7.95 Shipping)
Video. 1 Hr. Video, Textbook & Quizzer .... Item No. CPE4961 — **$179.00** ($7.95 Shipping)
Extra Textbooks & Quizzers .... Item No. CPE4962 — **$60.00** ($3.95 Shipping)
Extra Quizzers Only .... Item No. CPE4963 — **$50.00** (Free Shipping)
Software. Windows-Disks, Textbook & Quizzer ... Item No. CPE4964 — **$129.00** ($7.95 Shipping)
Extra Disks & Quizzers .... Item No. CPE4966 — **$50.00** ($3.95 Shipping)

8 ACCOUNTING CPE CREDIT HRS.
PREREQUISITE: None
KNOWLEDGE: Intermediate

ORDER TOLL-FREE 1-800-874-7877

Operating Systems

Get maximum performance out of your existing software—perfect for your in-house training!

Enhance your computer skills with these educational video/software/CD/textbook training programs...featuring the most current versions & specifically designed for IBM PC and compatible users. Each program comes with a 1 hour video that motivates you by guiding you through the basic, intermediate and advanced functions of your existing software program. An interactive disk accompanies each video and contains data files that you can use with your software—plus, it actually teaches you along with the video and shows you how to recreate exactly what you see on the video. A comprehensive reference text is also included that features time-saving tips, troubleshooting techniques, and more. It doubles as a handy shelf reference long after you complete the program!

Our most popular computer training programs are now available on CD-ROM, too!

Introduction to Windows

Now you can put essential Windows operating information right at your fingertips. You'll learn many tasks that are necessary to operate Windows successfully, such as step-by-step instructions on how to correctly perform the many functions involved in using: the file manager, program groups and items, the printer, fonts and hardware settings, the icons, files and directories, the clipboard, the keyboard commands, and more.

- Video with Software, Textbook & Quizzer—**Item No. CPE4440**
- CD-ROM, Textbook & Quizzer—**Item No. CPE4829**
- Extra Textbooks & Quizzers—**Item No. CPE4441**
- Extra Quizzers Only—**Item No. CPE4442**

Advanced Windows

The perfect reference guide for more experienced Windows users. Get expert advice and guidance on working with the versatile Windows Paintbrush and Write software, plus tips on Dynamic Data Exchange & OLE, so you can effortlessly integrate numbers and text between programs. Learn how to use Microsoft Mail, Scheduler+, Clipbook, and Chat. You'll also discover timely ways to customize INI files, enhance your Windows memory usage, and run Windows on a network.

- Video with Software, Textbook & Quizzer—**Item No. CPE4450**
- CD-ROM, Textbook & Quizzer—**Item No. CPE4828**
- Extra Textbooks & Quizzers—**Item No. CPE4451**
- Extra Quizzers Only—**Item No. CPE4452**

Introduction to DOS

Every computer user requires an understanding of the basic DOS features. This program teaches you how to manage both a floppy disk and a hard disk for normal day-to-day work. Featuring a compilation of the most frequently used MS-DOS commands, our introductory DOS program also includes essential information on the CONFIG.SYS, subcommands, batch files, the DOS Editor, error messages, and more.

- Video with Software, Textbook & Quizzer—**Item No. CPE4420**
- Extra Textbooks & Quizzers—**Item No. CPE4421**
- Extra Quizzers Only—**Item No. CPE4422**

Advanced DOS

This program offers DOS users a comprehensive source of information that will help them organize their work with the PC more effectively and make their hardware respond more efficiently. Designed for those individuals who have a basic familiarity with DOS, but need more information to increase their knowledge and sharpen their skills, this program presents features and functions to help DOS users make better use of managing their hard disk, using the DOS SHELL, and learning DOS' productivity features.

- Video with Software, Textbook & Quizzer—**Item No. CPE4430**
- Extra Textbooks & Quizzers—**Item No. CPE4431**
- Extra Quizzers Only—**Item No. CPE4432**

COMPUTER TRAINING PROGRAMS

Spreadsheets

Introduction to Excel for Windows

This training program covers the software's newest enhancements. Learn handy shortcuts, definitions of key terms, troubleshooting cautions—plus, how to easily create worksheets; edit and copy data; save, print and manage a workbook; create charts to add impact; simplify repetitive tasks with useful macros; and use Excel with Word and other Windows applications.

- Video with Software, Textbook & Quizzer—**Item No. CPE4530**
- CD-ROM, Textbook & Quizzer—**Item No. CPE4533**
- Extra Textbooks & Quizzers—**Item No. CPE4531**
- Extra Quizzers Only—**Item No. CPE4532**

Advanced Excel for Windows

Produce the most effective and attention-getting worksheets possible; learn how to easily link, chart, interpret, and project your numbers...and get expert tips and strategies to ensure top-notch Excel performance. Learn how to create and manipulate basic charts and charts embedded in worksheets, plus get advanced charting tricks. We show you how to use Excel's graphics, reporting features and analytical capabilities. In addition, we show you how to create and maintain a database; integrate Excel with other applications; perform advanced programming, and more.

- Video with Software, Textbook & Quizzer—**Item No. CPE4730**
- CD-ROM, Textbook & Quizzer—**Item No. CPE0690**
- Extra Textbooks & Quizzers—**Item No. CPE4731**
- Extra Quizzers Only—**Item No. CPE4732**

Introduction to Lotus for Windows

We give you the tips and techniques necessary to help you get the most from your Lotus software. We provide you with a complete understanding of 1-2-3 commands, special uses of the keyboard and mouse, methods for creating and modifying 1-2-3 worksheets, and more. You'll learn how to improve your spreadsheets and business presentations, add impact to your results with effective charts, maps and graphics, and save time and effort with tips on macros, data sharing, and efficient data analysis.

- Video with Software, Textbook & Quizzer—**Item No. CPE4500**
- Extra Textbooks & Quizzers—**Item No. CPE4501**
- Extra Quizzers Only—**Item No. CPE4502**

Advanced Lotus for Windows

This program provides you with the most extensive coverage available for the latest 1-2-3 software and shows you how to apply its newest features. Learn how to easily copy range styles to multiple locations in the worksheet with the help of Lotus' "Fast Format" feature. Discover how to open more than one worksheet file at a time from the "File Open" dialogue box; how to use and customize "SmartMaster" templates to quickly create applications for common business tasks (such as budgets and financial statements); and how to use the "Version Manager" to keep track of changing information in your worksheets.

- Video with Software, Textbook & Quizzer—**Item No. CPE4800**
- Extra Textbooks & Quizzers—**Item No. CPE4801**
- Extra Quizzers Only—**Item No. CPE0604**

Introduction to Lotus for DOS

Grasp the basics and build your spreadsheet skills with step-by-step instructions for the most common Lotus 1-2-3 DOS commands and procedures. This program features dozens of illustrated examples that demonstrate Lotus 1-2-3's "WYSIWYG" features and shows you how to create presentation quality reports and graphics, or modify existing worksheets created by others. You'll learn how to install Lotus 1-2-3 for DOS; easily enter data and formulas; use Lotus 1-2-3's built-in functions for financial, statistical, and logical analysis; and how to plan, build, and manage your own databases.

- Video with Software, Textbook & Quizzer—**Item No. CPE4480**
- Extra Textbooks & Quizzers—**Item No. CPE4481**
- Extra Quizzers Only—**Item No. CPE4482**

Advanced Lotus for DOS

Whether you're using Lotus 1-2-3 for inventory control, statistical analysis, or portfolio management, this training program is ideal for you. We cover the features and enhancements of Lotus' latest release for DOS, as well as how to accurately apply them. Learn how to speed-up your operations through the use of Lotus' new "SmartIcons" feature. Totaltape's computer video training program also show you how to apply spreadsheet publishing techniques to create effective output for presentations.

- Video with Software, Textbook & Quizzer—**Item No. CPE4490**
- Extra Textbooks & Quizzers—**Item No. CPE4491**
- Extra Quizzers Only—**Item No. CPE4492**

Introduction to Quattro Pro for Windows

Likened to an "electronic accountant's pad," Quattro Pro for Windows is a spreadsheet program that allows users to perform simple mathematical operations. This program shows you how to add, subtract, multiply, and divide—as well as figure complex equations, and then enter the data directly into a Quattro spreadsheet. In addition, we provide an overview about the computer and the keyboard layout. Discover how to move around within the spreadsheet, select commands, and more.

- Video with Software, Textbook & Quizzer—**Item No. CPE4765**
- Extra Textbooks & Quizzers—**Item No. CPE4766**
- Extra Quizzers Only—**Item No. CPE4764**

Advanced Quattro Pro for Windows

Get advanced tips and advice that will bring you to spreadsheet mastery. Discover the most effective ways to enter, edit, and format data, manage files, and use Quattro Pro functions. Perform professional data analysis using expert techniques and strategies. Learn how to manage databases and create impressive graphics and business presentations. We show you how to customize and automate Quattro Pro for Windows for maximum productivity, and provide you with advanced tricks on using macros and sharing data with other programs.

- Video with Software, Textbook & Quizzer—**Item No. CPE4767**
- Extra Textbooks & Quizzers—**Item No. CPE4768**
- Extra Quizzers Only—**Item No. CPE4769**

Introduction to Quattro Pro for DOS

Learn how to build streamlined Quattro Pro spreadsheets in short lessons you can refer to again and again as we lead you through the most important features of this popular spreadsheet package. Learn how to quickly master Quattro Pro menus, enter formulas and work with program functions, and create eye-catching charts and graphs. Plus, we show you how to develop informative databases, enhance spreadsheet printouts, link cells between different files, and much more.

- Video with Software, Textbook & Quizzer—**Item No. CPE4760**
- Extra Textbooks & Quizzers—**Item No. CPE4761**
- Extra Quizzers Only—**Item No. CPE4762**

Advanced Quattro Pro for DOS

This program provides you with the expert advice you need to use your existing Quattro Pro software to complete financial budgets and analyses for better economic forecasts. We show you how to effectively use Quattro Pro's built-in mathematical, statistical, and financial functions...and discuss ways to apply the Optimizer, Solve For, and Audit commands. You'll also discover how to develop your own macro programs and slide show presentations, how to work with Quattro Pro for DOS' new multi-page notebook technology, new SpeedBar buttons, and file translation capabilities.

- Video with Software, Textbook & Quizzer—**Item No. CPE4770**
- Extra Textbooks & Quizzers—**Item No. CPE4771**
- Extra Quizzers Only—**Item No. CPE0605**

ORDER TOLL-FREE 1-800-874-7877

Financial Accounting Report

NEW

by the Totaltape Editorial Board

12 ADVISORY SERVICES
CPE CREDIT HRS.

Monthly News & Information Service

PREREQUISITE: None
KNOWLEDGE: Update

How do you keep up with industry news and trends in a time-saving manner, and meet mandatory CPE requirements? With Totaltape's new monthly audio news & information service—Financial Accounting Report! Stay on the cutting edge of what's new, what's improved, and what's important. Each month, you'll get "in-the-trenches" perspectives on today's most relevant topics and developments from America's leading experts...consolidated into a single, fact-filled audio tape that you can review at your convenience...often during downtime commuting. You will gain a wealth of knowledge shared with you by experts from the top 60 accounting firms in the country, authorities from major universities and colleges, and industry professionals from large, medium, and small-sized companies. Get timely information and professional analysis on the topics that have a direct impact on you and your company, and learn how you can effectively deal with these changes.

Financial Accounting Report contains coverage in 5 major areas: finance, management, special topics, tax and accounting, including the hottest "need-to-know" topics like...

- Corporate Tax Strategies
- Financial Statement & Cash Flows
- Total Quality Management
- Internal Audit & Control
- FASB, SEC & Other Regulatory Updates
- Accounting Hardware, Software & Applications
- Activity-Based Costing Issues
- Reengineering
- Cash Management
- ISO 9000
- Performance Measurement
- Team Work & Other Managerial Techniques
- Business Strategies & Information Technologies
- Transfer Price Issues
- Global Trade Issues

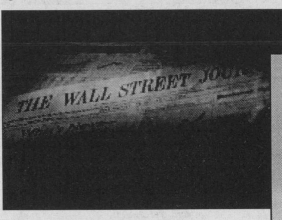

...and more. Plus, each month, your audio report is accompanied by a lively newsletter, which acts as a word-for-word transcript of your audio tape, as well as a CPE quizzer recommended for up to 12 CPE credit hours per year. Try your first issue RISK-FREE! Call today!

Program Ordering Information:

Audio. **1 Year Subscription - 12 Cassettes, PLUS**
Mthly. Transcripts, Yrly. Album, Index & Quizzers .... Item No. CPE5200 — $225.00 ($15.00 Shipping)

2 Year Subscription - 24 Cassettes, PLUS
Mthly. Transcripts, Yrly. Albums, Indexes & Quizzers .... Item No. CPE5201 — $395.00 ($30.00 Shipping)

Extra Quizzers - 1 Year .... Item No. CPE5202 — $80.00 (Free Shipping)
Extra Quizzers - 2 Years .... Item No. CPE5203 — $155.00 (Free Shipping)

Mutual Funds: BusinessWeek's Guide

NEW

by Jeffrey M. Laderman, Associate Editor, BusinessWeek, and the Totaltape Editorial Board

12 ADVISORY SERVICES
CPE CREDIT HRS.

PREREQUISITE: None
KNOWLEDGE: Basic

Mutual funds can be your best investment vehicle for achieving financial security in bad times and good. Learn everything you need to know about mutual funds to invest in them safely and successfully. Discover the questions you should ask yourself before you invest. Get step-by-step instructions on how to set up and monitor a portfolio. Find out how to balance risk against reward, and how your mutual fund investments affect your tax liability. We review and analyze types of mutual funds, including: equity, bond, money-market, and closed-end funds. The program also takes a look at the effect of a changing economy on mutual fund performance. Includes tables, charts, and complete performance data on more than 1400 mutual funds. New on video!

Program Ordering Information:

Audio. 6 Cassettes, Textbook & Quizzer .... Item No. CPE4570 — $159.00 ($7.95 Shipping)
Video. 2 Hr. Video, Textbook & Quizzer .... Item No. CPE4568 — $199.00 ($7.95 Shipping)
Extra Textbooks & Quizzers .... Item No. CPE4571 — $70.00 ($3.95 Shipping)
Extra Quizzers Only .... Item No. CPE4569 — $60.00 (Free Shipping)

BUSINESS & INDUSTRY

Financial Statement Analysis & Cash Flow Planning

by Andrew B. Titen, C.P.A., and Erich A. Helfert, D.B.A.

Cash flow is of vital concern to all businesses. And if you're a controller, this is an ideal program for you because it will take you to a new level of understanding and planning! Learn how to use financial statement analysis to analyze the financial health of your—or your client's—operation. Get proven techniques to help you identify and fix problem areas, evaluate proposals for profit potential, and improve the accuracy of your short- and long-term forecasting. Plus, we demonstrate analysis tools that can help you better manage working capital, cash, and accounts receivable. Learn how to evaluate your operating performance and corporate structure. Get capital budgeting formulas and rules for managing working capital, cash, and accounts receivable. Discover alternative methods of business financing. Learn how to measure your marketing effectiveness and the impact of recessionary or inflationary trends. Included is a comprehensive case study to demonstrate real-world situations.

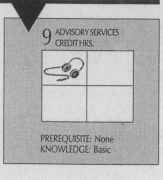

9 ADVISORY SERVICES
CREDIT HRS.

PREREQUISITE: None
KNOWLEDGE: Basic

Program Ordering Information:
Audio. 3 Cassettes, Textbook & Quizzer .... Item No. CPE4520 — $129.00 ($7.95 Shipping)
Extra Textbooks & Quizzers .... Item No. CPE4521 — $60.00 ($3.95 Shipping)
Extra Quizzers Only .... Item No. CPE4522 — $50.00 (Free Shipping)

Financial Planning: A Basic Guide

by Nathan M. Bisk, J.D., C.P.A., and David Ness, C.P.A., Raymond James & Associates

Economics have changed. Drastically lower interest rates and the failure of many financial institutions have alerted planners and clients alike to the need to do constant reviews of their investments. Totaltape CPEasy's outstanding new 550+ page guide to Financial Planning contains the very latest tools & techniques available to provide you and your clients safety of principal, consistent growth, and steady income. Written in straightforward "layman's" terms, both novices and seasoned planners will find this a refreshing review of basic investment products and concepts.

16 ADVISORY SERVICES
CPE CREDIT HRS.

PREREQUISITE: None
KNOWLEDGE: Basic

We discuss today's "hottest" financial planning areas, including asset allocation, mutual funds, "segmented" planning, risk management, and more. Plus, learn how constantly changing tax laws impact your planning decisions. We cover every major investment device currently available, and provide you with an "investment matrix" that helps you make an objective and realistic analysis of which investments are right for you—and your clients. We even provide you with a practical, step-by-step guideline that explains how to purchase financial planning tools. New on video!

Program Ordering Information:
Audio. 6 Cassettes, Textbook & Quizzer .... Item No. CPE5030 — $199.00 ($7.95 Shipping)
Video. 2 Hr. Video, Textbook & Quizzer .... Item No. CPE5034 — $249.00 ($7.95 Shipping)
Extra Textbooks & Quizzers .... Item No. CPE5032 — $100.00 ($3.95 Shipping)
Extra Quizzers Only .... Item No. CPE5033 — $90.00 (Free Shipping)

How to Manage Your Accounting Department

by Andrew B. Titen, C.P.A.

Written for managers, this program shows you how to successfully organize your department, train and supervise your staff, and evaluate, monitor, and tighten internal controls. You get practical advice on efficient cash management techniques; how to maximize working capital and minimize borrowing; effective inventory controls; and how to speed-up accounts receivable collections. Plus, we include a special section on *"budgeting and forecasting"* to help make financial decision-making easier.

12 MANAGEMENT
CPE CREDIT HRS.

PREREQUISITE: None
KNOWLEDGE: Basic

*Not accepted for Continuing Education credit in New York or New Jersey.

*Program Ordering Information:**
Audio. 6 Cassettes, Textbook & Quizzer .... Item No. CPE3100 — $159.00 ($7.95 Shipping)
Video. 2 Hr. Video, Textbook & Quizzer .... Item No. CPE3101 — $199.00 ($7.95 Shipping)
Extra Textbooks & Quizzers .... Item No. CPE3103 — $70.00 ($3.95 Shipping)
Extra Quizzers Only .... Item No. CPE3099 — $60.00 (Free Shipping)
Software. Disks, Textbook & Quizzer
Windows .... Item No. CPE3107 — $159.00 ($7.95 Shipping)
DOS .... Item No. CPE3105 — $159.00 ($7.95 Shipping)
Extra Disks & Quizzers
Windows .... Item No. CPE3108 — $60.00 ($3.95 Shipping)
DOS .... Item No. CPE3106 — $60.00 ($3.95 Shipping)

ORDER TOLL-FREE 1-800-874-7877